KU-272-584

C++ PROGRAMMING:
PROGRAM DESIGN INCLUDING DATA STRUCTURES

SIXTH EDITION

D.S. MALIK

WITHDRAWN

LIVERPOOL JMU LIBRARY

3 1111 01444 0018

CENGAGE
Learning·

Australia • Brazil • Japan • Korea • Mexico • Singapore • Spain • United Kingdom • United States

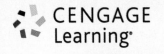

C++ Programming: From Problem Analysis to Program Design, Sixth Edition
D.S. Malik

Executive Editor: Marie Lee

Acquisitions Editor: Brandi Shailer

Senior Product Manager: Alyssa Pratt

Associate Product Manager: Stephanie Lorenz

Content Project Manager: Matthew Hutchinson

Art Director: Faith Brosnan

Print Buyer: Julio Esperas

Cover Designer: Roycroft Design/ www.roycroftdesign.com

Cover Photo: © Masterfile Royalty Free

Proofreader: Andrea Schein

Indexer: Elizabeth Cunningham

Compositor: Integra Software Services

© 2013 Cengage Learning

ALL RIGHTS RESERVED. No part of this work covered by the copyright herein may be reproduced, transmitted, stored or used in any form or by any means—graphic, electronic, or mechanical, including but not limited to photocopying, recording, scanning, digitizing, taping, Web distribution, information networks, or information storage and retrieval systems, except as permitted under Section 107 or 108 of the 1976 United States Copyright Act—without the prior written permission of the publisher.

For permission to use material from this text or product, submit all requests online at **www.cengage.com/permissions**. Further permissions questions can be e-mailed to **permissionrequest@cengage.com**.

Library of Congress Control Number: 2012931732

International Edition:

ISBN-13: 978-1-133-52635-3

Cengage Learning International Offices

Asia
www.cengageasia.com
tel: (65) 6410 1200

Australia/New Zealand
www.cengage.com.au
tel: (61) 3 9685 4111

Brazil
www.cengage.com.br
tel: (55) 11 3665 9900

India
www.cengage.co.in
tel: (91) 11 4364 1111

Latin America
www.cengage.com.mx
tel: (52) 55 1500 6000

UK/Europe/Middle East/ Africa
www.cengage.co.uk
tel: (44) 0 1264 332 424

Represented in Canada by Nelson Education, Ltd.
www.nelson.com
tel: (416) 752 9100/(800) 668 0671

Cengage Learning is a leading provider of customized learning solutions with office locations around the globe, including Singapore, the United Kingdom, Australia, Mexico, Brazil, and Japan. Locate your local office at: **www.cengage.com/global**.

For product information: **www.cengage.com/international**

Visit your local office: **www.cengage.com/global**

Visit our corporate website: **www.cengage.com**

AVAILABILITY OF RESOURCES MAY DIFFER BY REGION. Check with your local Cengage Learning representative for details.

Printed in the United States of America
1 2 3 4 5 6 7 16 17 16 15 14 13 12

TO

My Parents

Brief Contents

TABLE OF CONTENTS

PREFACE

WELCOME TO THE SIXTH EDITION OF *C++ Programming: Program Design Including Data Structures*. Designed for a two semester (CS1 and CS2) C++ course, this text will provide a breath of fresh air to you and your students. The CS1 and CS2 courses serve as the cornerstone of the Computer Science curriculum. My primary goal is to motivate and excite all introductory programming students, regardless of their level. Motivation breeds excitement for learning. Motivation and excitement are critical factors that lead to the success of the programming student. This text is a culmination and development of my classroom notes throughout more than fifty semesters of teaching successful programming to Computer Science students.

> **Warning**: This text can be expected to create a serious reduction in the demand for programming help during your office hours. Other side effects include significantly diminished student dependency on others while learning to program.

C++ Programming: Program Design Including Data Structures started as a collection of brief examples, exercises, and lengthy programming examples to supplement the books that were in use at our university. It soon turned into a collection large enough to develop into a text. *The approach taken in this book is, in fact, driven by the students' demand for clarity and readability.* The material was written and rewritten until the students felt comfortable with it. Most of the examples in this book resulted from student interaction in the classroom.

As with any profession, practice is essential. Cooking students practice their recipes. Budding violinists practice their scales. New programmers must practice solving problems and writing code. This is not a C++ cookbook. We do not simply list the C++ syntax followed by an example; we dissect the "why" behind all the concepts. The crucial question of "why?" is answered for every topic when first introduced. This technique offers a bridge to learning C++. Students must understand the "why?" in order to be motivated to learn.

Traditionally, a C++ programming neophyte needed a working knowledge of another programming language. This book assumes no prior programming experience. However, some adequate mathematics background such as college algebra is required.

Changes in the Sixth Edition

The sixth edition contains more than 250 new exercises, and more than 25 new programming exercises. Earlier editions contain two chapters on user defined functions. In this edition, without sacrificing the rigor, these chapters are combined into one chapter so that user defined functions can be learned without interruption. Since Chapters 6 and 7, of earlier editions, are combined into one chapter, sixth edition contains one less chapter than the earlier editions. The first part of Chapter 2 is rewritten and reorganized. In addition to arrays, Chapter 8 also discusses the selection sort algorithm. So in addition to learning about array and strings, the reader can also study a sequential search algorithm and a selection sort algorithm. This edition also includes various new examples, such as Examples 3-4, 3-8, 3-9, 4-8, 5-3, 5-4, 6-1, 8-4, 10-8, 11-2, 12-5, 14-14, and 19-4.

Approach

The programming language C++, which evolved from C, is no longer considered an industry-only language. Numerous colleges and universities use C++ for their first programming language course. C++ is a combination of structured programming and object-oriented programming, and this book addresses both types.

This book is intended for a two-semester course, CS1 and CS2, in Computer Science. The first 10 or 11 chapters can be covered in the first course and the remaining in the second course.

In July 1998, ANSI/ISO Standard C++ was officially approved. This book focuses on ANSI/ISO Standard C++. Even though the syntax of Standard C++ and ANSI/ISO Standard C++ is very similar, Chapter 7 discusses some of the features of ANSI/ISO Standard C++ that are not available in Standard C++.

Chapter 1 briefly reviews the history of computers and programming languages. The reader can quickly skim through this chapter and become familiar with some of the hardware components and the software parts of the computer. This chapter contains a section on processing a C++ program. This chapter also describes structured and object-oriented programming.

Chapter 2 discusses the basic elements of C++. After completing this chapter, students become familiar with the basics of C++ and are ready to write programs that are complicated enough to do some computations. Input/output is fundamental to any programming language. It is introduced early, in Chapter 3, and is covered in detail.

Chapters 4 and 5 introduce control structures to alter the sequential flow of execution. Chapters 6 study user-defined functions. It is recommended that readers with no prior programming background spend extra time on Chapters 6. Several examples are provided to help readers understand the concepts of parameter passing and the scope of an identifier.

Chapter 7 discusses the user-defined simple data type (enumeration type), the `namespace` mechanism of ANSI/ISO Standard C++, and the `string` type. The earlier versions of C did not include the enumeration type. Enumeration types have very limited use; their main purpose is to make the program readable. This book is organized such that readers can skip the section on enumeration types during the first reading without experiencing any discontinuity, and then later go through this section.

Chapter 8 discusses arrays in detail. This chapter also discusses a sequential search algorithm and a selection sort algorithm. Chapter 9 introduces records (`structs`). The introduction of `structs` in this book is similar to C `structs`. This chapter is optional; it is not a prerequisite for any of the remaining chapters.

Chapter 10 begins the study of object-oriented programming (OOP) and introduces classes. The first half of this chapter shows how classes are defined and used in a program. The second half of the chapter introduces abstract data types (ADTs). This chapter shows how classes in C++ are a natural way to implement ADTs. Chapter 11 continues with the fundamentals of object-oriented design (OOD) and OOP, and discusses inheritance and composition. It explains how classes in C++ provide a natural mechanism for OOD and how C++ supports OOP. Chapter 11 also discusses how to find the objects in a given problem.

Chapter 12 studies pointers in detail. After introducing pointers and how to use them in a program, this chapter highlights the peculiarities of classes with pointer data members and how to avoid them. Moreover, this chapter also discusses how to create and work with dynamic two-dimensional arrays. Chapter 12 also discusses abstract classes and a type of polymorphism accomplished via virtual functions.

Chapter 13 continues the study of OOD and OOP. In particular, it studies polymorphism in C++. Chapter 13 specifically discusses two types of polymorphism—overloading and templates.

Chapter 14 discusses exception handling in detail. Chapter 15 introduces and discusses recursion. This is a stand-alone chapter, so it can be studied anytime after Chapter 9.

Chapters 16 and 17 are devoted to the study of data structures. Discussed in detail are linked lists in Chapter 16 and stacks and queues in Chapter 17. The programming code developed in these chapters is generic. These chapters effectively use the fundamentals of OOD.

Chapter 18 discusses various searching and sorting algorithms. In addition to showing how these algorithms work, it also provides relevant analysis and results concerning the performance of the algorithms. The algorithm analysis allows the user to decide which algorithm to use in a particular application. This chapter also includes several sorting algorithms. The instructor can decide which algorithms to cover.

Chapter 19 provides an introduction to binary trees. Various traversal algorithms, as well as the basic properties of binary trees, are discussed and illustrated. Special binary trees, called binary search trees, are introduced. Searching, as well as item insertion and deletion from a binary search tree, are described and illustrated. Chapter 19 also discusses nonrecursive binary tree traversal algorithms. Furthermore, to enhance the flexibility of traversal algorithms, it shows how to construct and pass functions as parameters to other functions. This chapter also discusses AVL (height balanced) trees in detail. Due to text length considerations, discussion on AVL trees is provided as a separate section and is available on the Web site accompanying this book.

Graph algorithms are discussed in Chapter 20. After introducing the basic graph theory terminology, the representation of graphs in computer memory is discussed. This chapter also discusses graph traversal algorithms, the shortest path algorithm, and the minimal spanning tree algorithm. Topological sort is also discussed in this chapter and is available on the Web site accompanying this book.

C++ is equipped with a powerful library—the Standard Template Library (STL)—of data structures and algorithms that can be used effectively in a wide variety of applications. Chapter 21 describes the STL in detail. After introducing the three basic components of the STL, it shows how sequence containers are used in a program. Special containers, such as stack and queue, are also discussed. The latter half of this chapter shows how various STL algorithms can be used in a program. This chapter is fairly long; depending on the availability of time, the instructor can at least cover the sequence containers, iterators, the classes `stack` and `queue`, and certain algorithms.

Appendix A lists the reserved words in C++. Appendix B shows the precedence and associativity of the C++ operators. Appendix C lists the ASCII (American Standard Code for Information Interchange) and EBCDIC (Extended Binary Coded Decimal Interchange Code) character sets. Appendix D lists the C++ operators that can be overloaded.

Appendix E has three objectives. First, we discuss how to convert a number from decimal to binary and binary to decimal. We then discuss binary and random access files in detail. Finally, we describe the naming conventions of the header files in both ANSI/ISO Standard C++ and Standard C++. Appendix F discusses some of the most widely used library routines, and includes the names of the standard C++ header files. The programs in Appendix G show how to print the memory size for the built-in data types on your system as well as how to use a random number generator. Appendix H gives selected references for further study. Appendix I provides the answers to odd-numbered exercises in the book.

In Figure 1, dotted lines mean that the preceding chapter is used in one of the sections of the chapter and is not necessarily a prerequisite for the next chapter. For example, Chapter 8 covers arrays in detail. In Chapters 9 and 10, we show the relationship between arrays and `struct`s and arrays and classes, respectively. However, if Chapter 10 is studied before Chapter 8, then the section dealing with arrays in Chapter 10 can be skipped without any discontinuation. This particular section can be studied after studying Chapter 8.

It is recommended that the first six chapters be covered sequentially. After covering the first six chapters, if the reader is interested in learning OOD and OOP early, then Chapter 10 can be studied right after Chapter 6. Chapter 7 can be studied anytime after Chapter 6. After studying the first six chapters in sequence, some of the approaches are:

1. Study chapters in the sequence: 8, 9, 10, 11, 12, 13, 14, 15, 16, 17, 18, 19, 20, 21.
2. Study chapters in the sequence: 8, 10, 12, 13, 11, 15, 16, 17, 14, 18, 19, 20, 21
3. Study chapters in the sequence: 10, 8, 12, 13, 11, 15, 16, 17, 14, 18, 19, 20, 21.

As the chapter dependency diagram shows, Chapters 17 and 18 can be covered in any sequence. However, typically, Chapters 17 and 18 are studied in sequence. Ideally, one should study Chapters 16, 17, 18, and 19 in sequence. Chapters 20 and 21 can be studied in any sequence.

How to Use the Book

This book can be used in various ways. Figure 1 shows the dependency of the chapters.

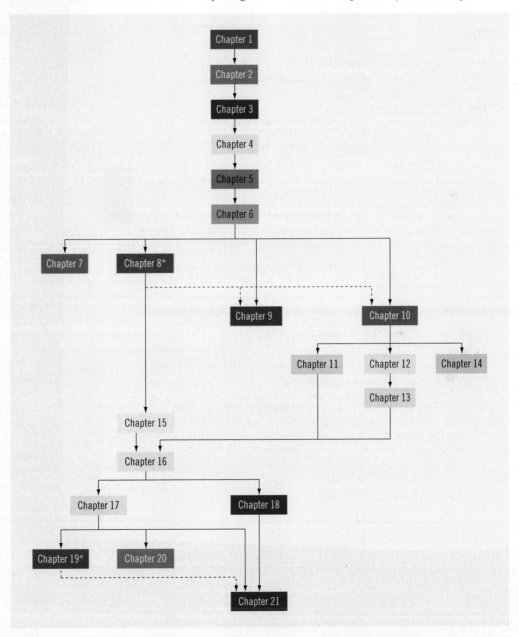

FIGURE 1 Chapter dependency diagram

FEATURES OF THE BOOK

```
noOfGuesses++;
if (guess == num)
{
    cout << "Winner!. You guessed the correct number."
         << endl;
    isGuessed = true;
}
else if (guess < num)
    cout << "Your guess is lower than the number.\n"
         << "Guess again!" << endl;
else
    cout << "Your guess is higher than the number.\n"
         << "Guess again!" << endl;
} //end while
```

Four-color interior design shows accurate C++ code and related comments.

You also need the following code to be included after the `while` loop in case the user cannot guess the correct number in five tries:

```
if (!isGuessed)
    cout << "You lose! The correct number is " << num << endl;
```

Programming Exercise 16 at the end of this chapter asks you to write a complete C++ program to implement the Number Guessing Game in which the user has, at most, five tries to guess the number.

As you can see from the preceding `while` loop, the expression in a `while` statement can be complex. The main objective of a `while` loop is to repeat certain statement(s) until certain conditions are met.

PROGRAMMING EXAMPLE: Fibonacci Number

Watch
the Video

So far, you have seen several examples of loops. Recall that in C++, `while` loops are used when a certain statement(s) must be executed repeatedly until certain conditions are met. Following is a C++ program that uses a `while` loop to find a **Fibonacci number**.

Consider the following sequence of numbers:

```
1, 1, 2, 3, 5, 8, 13, 21, 34, ....
```

This sequence is called the **Fibonacci sequence**. Given the first two numbers of the sequence (say, a_1 and a_2), the nth number a_n, $n >= 3$, of this sequence is given by:

$$a_n = a_{n-1} + a_{n-2}$$

Thus:

$$a_3 = a_2 + a_1 = 1 + 1 = 2,$$
$$a_4 = a_3 + a_2 = 2 + 1 = 3,$$

and so on.

One video is available for each chapter on the optional CourseMate that accompanies this text. Each video is designed to explain how a program works.

Chapter 2 defined a program as a sequence of statements whose objective is to accomplish some task. The programs you have examined so far were simple and straightforward. To process a program, the computer begins at the first executable statement and executes the statements in order until it comes to the end. In this chapter and Chapter 5, you will learn how to tell a computer that it does not have to follow a simple sequential order of statements; it can also make decisions and repeat certain statements over and over until certain conditions are met.

Control Structures

A computer can process a program in one of the following ways: in sequence; selectively, by making a choice, which is also called a branch; repetitively, by executing a statement over and over, using a structure called a loop; or by calling a function. Figure 4-1 illustrates the first three types of program flow. (In Chapter 6, we will show how function calls work.) The programming examples in Chapters 2 and 3 included simple sequential programs. With such a program, the computer starts at the beginning and follows the statements in order. No choices are made; there is no repetition. Control structures provide alternatives to sequential program execution and are used to alter the sequential flow of execution. The two most common control structures are selection and repetition. In *selection*, the program executes particular statements depending on some condition(s). In *repetition*, the program repeats particular statements a certain number of times based on some condition(s).

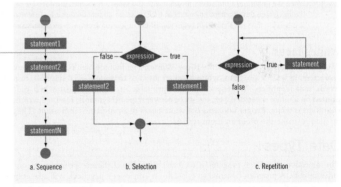

a. Sequence   b. Selection   c. Repetition

FIGURE 4-1   Flow of execution

More than 400 visual diagrams, both extensive and exhaustive, illustrate difficult concepts.

In C++, identifiers can be of any length.

EXAMPLE 2-2

The following are legal identifiers in C++:

```
first
conversion
payRate
counter1
```

Table 2-1 shows some illegal identifiers and explains why they are illegal.

TABLE 2-1 Examples of Illegal Identifiers

Illegal Identifier	Description
employee Salary	There can be no space between `employee` and `Salary`.
Hello!	The exclamation mark cannot be used in an identifier.
one + two	The symbol + cannot be used in an identifier.
2nd	An identifier cannot begin with a digit.

NOTE Compiler vendors usually begin certain identifiers with an underscore (_).
When the linker links the object program with the system resources provided by
the integrated development environment (IDE), certain errors could occur. Therefore, it
is advisable that you should not begin identifiers in your program with an underscore (_).

Whitespaces

Every C++ program contains whitespaces. Whitespaces include blanks, tabs, and newline characters. In a C++ program, whitespaces are used to separate special symbols, reserved words, and identifiers. Whitespaces are nonprintable in the sense that when they are printed on a white sheet of paper, the space between special symbols, reserved words, and identifiers is white. Proper utilization of whitespaces in a program is important. They can be used to make the program more readable.

Data Types

The objective of a C++ program is to manipulate data. Different programs manipulate different data. A program designed to calculate an employee's paycheck will add, subtract, multiply, and divide numbers, and some of the numbers might represent hours worked and pay rate. Similarly, a program designed to alphabetize a class list will manipulate names. You wouldn't use a cherry pie recipe to help you bake cookies. Similarly, you wouldn't use a

Numbered Examples illustrate the key concepts with their relevant code. The programming code in these examples is followed by a Sample Run. An explanation then follows that describes what each line in the code does.

2

Notes highlight important facts about the concepts introduced in the chapter.

Programming Examples are where everything in the chapter comes together. These examples teach problem-solving skills and include the concrete stages of input, output, problem analysis and algorithm design, class design, and a program listing. All programs are designed to be methodical, consistent, and user-friendly. Each Programming Example starts with a problem analysis that is followed by the algorithm design and/or class design, and every step of the algorithm is coded in C++. In addition to helping students learn problem-solving techniques, these detailed programs show the student how to implement concepts in an actual C++ program. We strongly recommend that students study the Programming Examples carefully in order to learn C++ effectively. Students typically learn much from completely worked-out programs. Further, programming examples considerably reduce the students' need for help outside the classroom and bolster the students' self-confidence.

PROGRAMMING EXAMPLE: Convert Length

Watch the Video

Write a program that takes as input given lengths expressed in feet and inches. The program should then convert and output the lengths in centimeters. Assume that the given lengths in feet and inches are integers.

Input   Length in feet and inches.

Output   Equivalent length in centimeters.

PROBLEM
ANALYSIS
AND
ALGORITHM
DESIGN

The lengths are given in feet and inches, and you need to find the equivalent length in centimeters. One inch is equal to 2.54 centimeters. The first thing the program needs to do is convert the length given in feet and inches to all inches. Then, you can use the conversion formula, 1 inch = 2.54 centimeters, to find the equivalent length in centimeters. To convert the length from feet and inches to inches, you multiply the number of feet by 12, as 1 foot is equal to 12 inches, and add the given inches.

For example, suppose the input is 5 feet and 7 inches. You then find the total inches as follows:

```
totalInches = (12 * feet) + inches
            = 12 * 5 + 7
            = 67
```

You can then apply the conversion formula, 1 inch = 2.54 centimeters, to find the length in centimeters.

```
centimeters = totalInches * 2.54
            = 67 * 2.54
            = 170.18
```

Based on this analysis of the problem, you can design an algorithm as follows:

1. Get the length in feet and inches.
2. Convert the length into total inches.
3. Convert total inches into centimeters.
4. Output centimeters.

Variables The input for the program is two numbers: one for feet and one for inches. Thus, you need two variables: one to store feet and the other to store inches. Because the program will first convert the given length into inches, you need another variable to store the total inches. You also need a variable to store the equivalent length in centimeters. In summary, you need the following variables:

```
int feet;              //variable to hold given feet
int inches;            //variable to hold given inches
int totalInches;       //variable to hold total inches
double centimeters;    //variable to hold length in centimeters
```

EXERCISES

1. Mark the following statements as true or false.

   a. The member variables of a class must be of the same type.
   b. The member functions of a class must be public.
   c. A class can have more than one constructor.
   d. A class can have more than one destructor.
   e. Both constructors and destructors can have parameters.

2. Find the syntax errors in the following class definition:

```
class mystery                         //Line 1
{                                     //Line 2
public:                               //Line 3
    void print() const;               //Line 4
    void setNum(double, double);      //Line 5
    int power();                      //Line 6
    double mystery();                 //Line 7
    double mystery(double, double);   //Line 8
private:                              //Line 9
    double x;                         //Line 10
    double y;                         //Line 11
};                                    //Line 12
```

3. Find the syntax errors in the following class definition:

```
class secret                          //Line 1
{                                     //Line 2
public:                               //Line 3
    bool multiply();                  //Line 4
    print() const;                    //Line 5
    secret(int = 0, int = 0);         //Line 6
private:                              //Line 7
    int one;                          //Line 8
    int two;                          //Line 9
};                                    //Line 10
```

4. Find the syntax errors in the following class definition:

```
class secret                          //Line 1
{                                     //Line 2
public:                               //Line 3
    bool compare();                   //Line 4
    void print() const;               //Line 5
    secret(int = 0, int = 0) const;   //Line 6
private:                              //Line 7
    string str;                       //Line 8
    int one;                          //Line 9
    int two;                          //Line 10
};                                    //Line 11
```

Exercises further reinforce learning and ensure that students have, in fact, mastered the material.

```
cin >> firstNum >> secondNum;
cout << endl;

//Missing statements

return 0;
}
```

33. Suppose that classStanding is a char variable, and gpa and dues are double variables. Write a switch expression that assigns the dues as following: If classStanding is 'f', the dues are $150.00; if classStanding is 's' (if gpa is at least 3.75, the dues are $75.00; otherwise, dues are 120.00); if classStanding is 'j' (if gpa is at least 3.75, the dues are $50.00; otherwise, dues are $100.00); if classStanding is 'n' (if gpa is at least 3.75, the dues are $25.00; otherwise, dues are $75.00). (Note that the code 'f' stands for first year students, the code 's' stands for second year students, the code 'j' stands for juniors, and the code 'n' stands for seniors.)

34. Suppose that billingAmount is a double variable, which denotes the amount you need to pay to the department store. if you pay the full amount, you get $10.00 or 1% of the billingAmount, whichever is smaller, as a credit on your next bill; if you pay at least 50% of the billingAmount, the penalty is 5% of the balance; if you pay at least 20% of the billingAmount and less than 50% of the billingAmount, the penalty is 10% of the balance; otherwise, the penalty is 20% of the balance. Design an algorithm that prompts the user to enter the billing amount and the desired payment. The algorithm then calculates and outputs the credit or the remaining balance. If the amount is not paid in full, the algorithm should also output the penalty amount.

PROGRAMMING EXERCISES

1. Write a program that prompts the user to input a number. The program should then output the number and a message saying whether the number is positive, negative, or zero.

2. Write a program that prompts the user to input three numbers. The program should then output the numbers in ascending order.

3. Write a program that prompts the user to input an integer between 0 and 35. If the number is less than or equal to 9, the program should output the number; otherwise, it should output A for 10, B for 11, C for 12 . . . and Z for 35. (*Hint:* Use the cast operator, static_cast<char> ( ), for numbers >= 10.)

4. The statements in the following program are in incorrect order. Rearrange the statements so that they prompt the user to input the shape type (rectangle, circle, or cylinder) and the appropriate dimension of

Programming Exercises challenge students to write C++ programs with a specified outcome.

SUPPLEMENTAL RESOURCES

CourseMate

Make the most of study time with everything you need to succeed in one place. Read your textbook, highlight and take notes, review flashcards, watch videos, and take practice quizzes online. Learn more at *www.cengage.com/coursemate*.

The *C++ Programming* CourseMate includes the following features:

- **Videos** step you through programs in each chapter, while integrated quizzes provide immediate feedback to gauge your understanding
- **Lab Manual** lets you apply material with a wealth of practical, hands-on exercises.
- **Interactive Quizzes** and **Study Games** drill key chapter concepts, while open-ended **Assignments** develop critical thinking skills.
- **Interactive eBook,** flashcards, and more!

Instructors may add CourseMate to the textbook package, or students may purchase CourseMate directly through *www.cengagebrain.com*.

Source Code

The source code, in ANSI/ISO Standard C++, is available for students to download at www.cengagebrain.com and through the CourseMate available for this text. These files are also available to instructors on the Instructor Resources CD and at *login.cengage.com*. The input files needed to run some of the programs are also included with the source code.

Instructor Resources

The following supplemental materials are available when this book is used in a classroom setting. All instructor teaching tools are available with this book on a single CD-ROM. Many are also available for download at *login.cengage.com*.

Electronic Instructor's Manual

The Instructor's Manual follows the text chapter-by-chapter and includes material to assist in planning and organizing an effective, engaging course.

The Manual includes Overviews, Chapter Objectives, Teaching Tips, Quick Quizzes, Class Discussion Topics, Additional Projects, Additional Resources, and Key Terms. A **Sample Syllabus** is also available.

ExamView®

This textbook is accompanied by ExamView, a powerful testing software package that allows instructors to create and administer printed, computer (LAN-based), and Internet exams. ExamView includes hundreds of questions that correspond to the topics covered in this text, enabling students to generate detailed study guides that include page references for further review. These computer-based and Internet testing components allow students to take exams at their computers, and save the instructor time because each exam is graded automatically. The test banks are also available in **Blackboard, WebCT, and Angel** compatible formats.

PowerPoint Presentations

This book comes with PowerPoint slides to accompany each chapter. Slides may be used to guide classroom presentation, to make available to students for chapter review, or to print as classroom handouts. Instructors can add their own slides for additional topics that they introduce to the class, as well as customize the slides with the complete **Figure Files** from the text.

Solution Files

The solution files for all programming exercises, in ANSI/ISO C++, are available at the Companion Site for the text at *login.cengage.com* and are also available on the Instructor Resources CD-ROM. The input files needed to run some of the programming exercises are also included with the solution files.

ACKNOWLEDGEMENTS

There are many people that I must thank who, one way or another, contributed to the success of this book. First, I would like to thank all the students who, during the preparation, were spontaneous in telling me if certain portions needed to be reworded for better understanding and clearer reading. Next, I would like to thank those who e-mailed numerous comments to improve upon the fifth edition. I am thankful to Professors S.C. Cheng and Randall Crist for constantly supporting this project. I am also very grateful to the reviewers who reviewed earlier versions of this book and offered many critical suggestions on how to improve it.

I owe a great deal to the following reviewers who made helpful, critical suggestions for improving this edition of the text: Gary Bricher: Lane Community College; Cliff Brozo: Monroe College; and Marie Pullan: Farmingdale State College.

Next, I express thanks to Brandi Shailer Acquisitions Editor, for recognizing the importance and uniqueness of this project. All this would not have been possible without the careful planning of Senior Product Manager Alyssa Pratt. I extend my sincere thanks to Alyssa, as well as to Content Project Manager Matthew Hutchinson. My special thanks are to Stephanie Lorenz for using her expertise in carefully editing the videos. I also thank Sreemannarayana Reddy of Integra Software Services for assisting us in keeping the project on schedule. I would like to thank Chris Scriver and Serge Palladino of Cengage Learning for patiently and carefully testing the code and discovering typos and errors.

This book is dedicated to my parents, who I thank for their blessings.

Finally, I am thankful for the support of my wife Sadhana and especially my daughter Shelly. They cheered me up whenever I was overwhelmed during the writing of this book. I welcome any comments concerning the text. Comments may be forwarded to the following e-mail address: malik@creighton.edu.

D. S. Malik

CHAPTER 1

AN OVERVIEW OF COMPUTERS AND PROGRAMMING LANGUAGES

IN THIS CHAPTER, YOU WILL:

- Learn about different types of computers
- Explore the hardware and software components of a computer system
- Learn about the language of a computer
- Learn about the evolution of programming languages
- Examine high-level programming languages
- Discover what a compiler is and what it does
- Examine a C++ program
- Explore how a C++ program is processed
- Learn what an algorithm is and explore problem-solving techniques
- Become aware of structured design and object-oriented design programming methodologies
- Become aware of Standard C++ and ANSI/ISO Standard C++

Introduction

Terms such as "the Internet," which were unfamiliar just 20 years ago are now common. Students in elementary school regularly "surf" the Internet and use computers to design their classroom projects. Many people use the Internet to look for information and to communicate with others. This is all made possible by the availability of different software, also known as computer programs. Without software, a computer is useless. Software is developed by using programming languages. The programming language C++ is especially well suited for developing software to accomplish specific tasks. Our main objective is to help you learn how to write programs in the C++ programming language. Before you begin programming, it is useful to understand some of the basic terminology and different components of a computer. We begin with an overview of the history of computers.

A Brief Overview of the History of Computers

The first device known to carry out calculations was the abacus. The abacus was invented in Asia but was used in ancient Babylon, China, and throughout Europe until the late middle ages. The abacus uses a system of sliding beads in a rack for addition and subtraction. In 1642, the French philosopher and mathematician Blaise Pascal invented the calculating device called the Pascaline. It had eight movable dials on wheels and could calculate sums up to eight figures long. Both the abacus and Pascaline could perform only addition and subtraction operations. Later in the 17th century, Gottfried von Leibniz invented a device that was able to add, subtract, multiply, and divide. In 1819, Joseph Jacquard, a French weaver, discovered that the weaving instructions for his looms could be stored on cards with holes punched in them. While the cards moved through the loom in sequence, needles passed through the holes and picked up threads of the correct color and texture. A weaver could rearrange the cards and change the pattern being woven. In essence, the cards programmed a loom to produce patterns in cloth. The weaving industry may seem to have little in common with the computer industry. However, the idea of storing information by punching holes on a card proved to be of great importance in the later development of computers.

In the early and mid-1800s, Charles Babbage, an English mathematician and physical scientist, designed two calculating machines: the difference engine and the analytical engine. The difference engine could perform complex operations such as squaring numbers automatically. Babbage built a prototype of the difference engine, but did not build the actual device. The first complete difference engine was completed in London in 2002, 153 years after it was designed. It consists of 8,000 parts, weighs five tons, and measures 11 feet long. A replica of the difference engine was completed in 2008 and is on display at the Computer History Museum in Mountain View, California (*http://www.computerhistory.org/babbage/*). Most of Babbage's work is known through the writings of his colleague Ada Augusta, Countess of Lovelace. Augusta is considered the first computer programmer.

At the end of the 19th century, U.S. Census officials needed help in accurately tabulating the census data. Herman Hollerith invented a calculating machine that ran on electricity and used punched cards to store data. Hollerith's machine was immensely successful.

1

Hollerith founded the Tabulating Machine Company, which later became the computer and technology corporation known as IBM.

The first computer-like machine was the Mark I. It was built, in 1944, jointly by IBM and Harvard University under the leadership of Howard Aiken. Punched cards were used to feed data into the machine. The Mark I was 52 feet long, weighed 50 tons, and had 750,000 parts. In 1946, the ENIAC (Electronic Numerical Integrator and Calculator) was built at the University of Pennsylvania. It contained 18,000 vacuum tubes and weighed some 30 tons.

The computers that we know today use the design rules given by John von Neumann in the late 1940s. His design included components such as an arithmetic logic unit, a control unit, memory, and input/output devices. These components are described in the next section. Von Neumann's computer design makes it possible to store the programming instructions and the data in the same memory space. In 1951, the UNIVAC (Universal Automatic Computer) was built and sold to the U.S. Census Bureau.

In 1956, the invention of transistors resulted in smaller, faster, more reliable, and more energy-efficient computers. This era also saw the emergence of the software development industry, with the introduction of FORTRAN and COBOL, two early programming languages. In the next major technological advancement, transistors were replaced by tiny integrated circuits, or "chips." Chips are smaller and cheaper than transistors and can contain thousands of circuits on a single chip. They give computers tremendous processing speed.

In 1970, the microprocessor, an entire CPU on a single chip, was invented. In 1977, Stephen Wozniak and Steven Jobs designed and built the first Apple computer in their garage. In 1981, IBM introduced its personal computer (PC). In the 1980s, clones of the IBM PC made the personal computer even more affordable. By the mid-1990s, people from many walks of life were able to afford them. Computers continue to become faster and less expensive as technology advances.

Modern-day computers are powerful, reliable, and easy to use. They can accept spoken-word instructions and imitate human reasoning through artificial intelligence. Expert systems assist doctors in making diagnoses. Mobile computing applications are growing significantly. Using hand-held devices, delivery drivers can access global positioning satellites (GPS) to verify customer locations for pickups and deliveries. Cell phones permit you to check your e-mail, make airline reservations, see how stocks are performing, and access your bank accounts.

Although there are several categories of computers, such as mainframe, midsize, and micro, all computers share some basic elements, described in the next section.

Elements of a Computer System

A computer is an electronic device capable of performing commands. The basic commands that a computer performs are input (get data), output (display result), storage, and performance of arithmetic and logical operations. There are two main components of a computer system: hardware and software. In the next few sections, we give a brief overview of these components. Let's look at hardware first.

Hardware

Major hardware components include the central processing unit (CPU); main memory (MM), also called random access memory (RAM); input/output devices; and secondary storage. Some examples of input devices are the keyboard, mouse, and secondary storage. Examples of output devices are the screen, printer, and secondary storage. Let's look at each of these components in greater detail.

Central Processing Unit and Main Memory

The **central processing unit** is the "brain" of the computer and the single most expensive piece of hardware in a computer. The more powerful the CPU, the faster the computer. Arithmetic and logical operations are carried out inside the CPU. Figure 1-1(a) shows some hardware components.

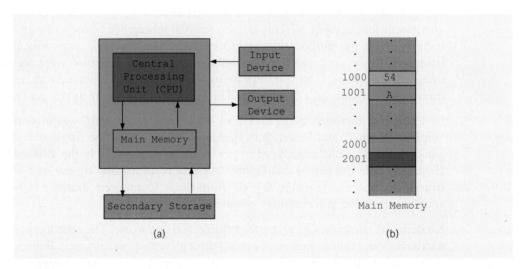

FIGURE 1-1 Hardware components of a computer and main memory

Main memory, or **random access memory**, is connected directly to the CPU. All programs must be loaded into main memory before they can be executed. Similarly, all data must be brought into main memory before a program can manipulate it. When the computer is turned off, everything in main memory is lost.

Main memory is an ordered sequence of cells, called **memory cells**. Each cell has a unique location in main memory, called the **address** of the cell. These addresses help you access the information stored in the cell. Figure 1-1(b) shows main memory with some data.

Today's computers come with main memory consisting of millions to billions of cells. Although Figure 1-1(b) shows data stored in cells, the content of a cell can be either a programming instruction or data. Moreover, this figure shows the data as numbers and letters. However, as explained later in this chapter, main memory stores everything as sequences of 0s and 1s. The memory addresses are also expressed as sequences of 0s and 1s.

SECONDARY STORAGE

Because programs and data must be stored in main memory before processing and because everything in main memory is lost when the computer is turned off, information stored in main memory must be transferred to some other device for permanent storage. The device that stores information permanently (unless the device becomes unusable or you change the information by rewriting it) is called **secondary storage**. To be able to transfer information from main memory to secondary storage, these components must be directly connected to each other. Examples of secondary storage are hard disks, flash drives, floppy disks, ZIP disks, CD-ROMs, and tapes.

Input/Output Devices

For a computer to perform a useful task, it must be able to take in data and programs and display the results of calculations. The devices that feed data and programs into computers are called **input devices**. The keyboard, mouse, and secondary storage are examples of input devices. The devices that the computer uses to display results are called **output devices**. A monitor, printer, and secondary storage are examples of output devices. Figure 1-2 shows some input and output devices.

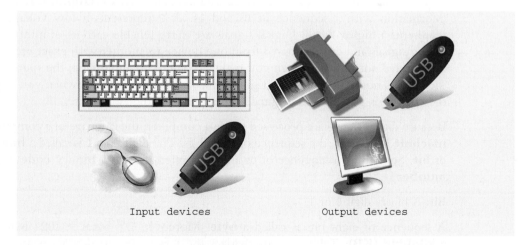

Input devices   Output devices

FIGURE 1-2   Some input and output devices

Software

Software are programs written to perform specific tasks. For example, word processors are programs that you use to write letters, papers, and even books. All software is written in programming languages. There are two types of programs: system programs and application programs.

System programs control the computer. The system program that loads first when you turn on your PC is called the operating system. Without an operating system, the computer is useless. The **operating system** monitors the overall activity of the computer and provides services. Some of these services include memory management, input/output activities, and storage management. The operating system has a special program that organizes secondary storage so that you can conveniently access information.

Application programs perform a specific task. Word processors, spreadsheets, and games are examples of application programs. The operating system is the program that runs application programs.

The Language of a Computer

When you press A on your keyboard, the computer displays A on the screen. But what is actually stored inside the computer's main memory? What is the language of the computer? How does it store whatever you type on the keyboard?

Remember that a computer is an electronic device. Electrical signals are used inside the computer to process information. There are two types of electrical signals: analog and digital. **Analog signals** are continuous wave forms used to represent such things as sound. Audio tapes, for example, store data in analog signals. **Digital signals** represent information with a sequence of 0s and 1s. A 0 represents a low voltage, and a 1 represents a high voltage. Digital signals are more reliable carriers of information than analog signals and can be copied from one device to another with exact precision. You might have noticed that when you make a copy of an audio tape, the sound quality of the copy is not as good as the original tape. On the other hand, when you copy a CD, the copy is as good as the original. Computers use digital signals.

Because digital signals are processed inside a computer, the language of a computer, called **machine language**, is a sequence of 0s and 1s. The digit 0 or 1 is called a **binary digit**, or **bit**. Sometimes a sequence of 0s and 1s is referred to as a **binary code** or a **binary number**.

Bit: A binary digit 0 or 1.

A sequence of eight bits is called a **byte**. Moreover, 2^{10} bytes = 1024 bytes is called a **kilobyte (KB)**. Table 1-1 summarizes the terms used to describe various numbers of bytes.

TABLE 1-1 Binary Units

Unit	Symbol	Bits/Bytes
Byte		8 bits
Kilobyte	KB	2^{10} bytes = 1024 bytes
Megabyte	MB	1024 KB = 2^{10} KB = 2^{20} bytes = 1,048,576 bytes
Gigabyte	GB	1024 MB = 2^{10} MB = 2^{30} bytes = 1,073,741,824 bytes
Terabyte	TB	1024 GB = 2^{10} GB = 2^{40} bytes = 1,099,511,627,776 bytes
Petabyte	PB	1024 TB = 2^{10} TB = 2^{50} bytes = 1,125,899,906,842,624 bytes
Exabyte	EB	1024 PB = 2^{10} PB = 2^{60} bytes = 1,152,921,504,606,846,976 bytes
Zettabyte	ZB	1024 EB = 2^{10} EB = 2^{70} bytes = 1,180,591,620,717,411,303,424 bytes

Every letter, number, or special symbol (such as * or {) on your keyboard is encoded as a sequence of bits, each having a unique representation. The most commonly used encoding scheme on personal computers is the *seven-bit* **American Standard Code for Information Interchange (ASCII)**. The ASCII data set consists of 128 characters numbered 0 through 127. That is, in the ASCII data set, the position of the first character is 0, the position of the second character is 1, and so on. In this scheme, A is encoded as the binary number 1000001. In fact, A is the 66th character in the ASCII character code, but its position is 65 because the position of the first character is 0. Furthermore, the binary number 1000001 is the binary representation of 65. The character 3 is encoded as 0110011. Note that in the ASCII character set, the position of the character 3 is 51, so the character 3 is the 52nd character in the ASCII set. It also follows that 0110011 is the binary representation of 51. For a complete list of the printable ASCII character set, refer to Appendix C.

NOTE The number system that we use in our daily life is called the **decimal system**, or **base 10**. Because everything inside a computer is represented as a sequence of 0s and 1s, that is, binary numbers, the number system that a computer uses is called **binary**, or **base 2**. We indicated in the preceding paragraph that the number 1000001 is the binary representation of 65. Appendix E describes how to convert a number from base 10 to base 2 and vice versa.

Inside the computer, every character is represented as a sequence of *eight* bits, that is, as a byte. Now the eight-bit binary representation of 65 is 01000001. Note that we added 0 to the left of the seven-bit representation of 65 to convert it to an eight-bit representation. Similarly, the eight-bit binary representation of 51 is 00110011.

ASCII is a seven-bit code. Therefore, to represent each ASCII character inside the computer, you must convert the seven-bit binary representation of an ASCII character to an eight-bit binary representation. This is accomplished by adding 0 to the left of the seven-bit ASCII encoding of a character. Hence, inside the computer, the character A is represented as 01000001, and the character 3 is represented as 00110011.

There are other encoding schemes, such as EBCDIC (used by IBM) and Unicode, which is a more recent development. EBCDIC consists of 256 characters; Unicode consists of 65,536 characters. To store a character belonging to Unicode, you need two bytes.

The Evolution of Programming Languages

The most basic language of a computer, the machine language, provides program instructions in bits. Even though most computers perform the same kinds of operations, the designers of the computer may have chosen different sets of binary codes to perform the operations. Therefore, the machine language of one machine is not necessarily the same as the machine language of another machine. The only consistency among computers is that in any modern computer, all data is stored and manipulated as binary codes.

Early computers were programmed in machine language. To see how instructions are written in machine language, suppose you want to use the equation:

wages = rate · hours

to calculate weekly wages. Further, suppose that the binary code 100100 stands for load, 100110 stands for multiplication, and 100010 stands for store. In machine language, you might need the following sequence of instructions to calculate weekly wages:

```
100100 010001
100110 010010
100010 010011
```

To represent the weekly wages equation in machine language, the programmer had to remember the machine language codes for various operations. Also, to manipulate data, the programmer had to remember the locations of the data in the main memory. This need to remember specific codes made programming not only very difficult, but also error prone.

Assembly languages were developed to make the programmer's job easier. In assembly language, an instruction is an easy-to-remember form called a **mnemonic**. Table 1-2 shows some examples of instructions in assembly language and their corresponding machine language code.

TABLE 1-2 Examples of Instructions in Assembly Language and Machine Language

Assembly Language	Machine Language
LOAD	100100
STOR	100010
MULT	100110
ADD	100101
SUB	100011

Using assembly language instructions, you can write the equation to calculate the weekly wages as follows:

```
LOAD   rate
MULT   hours
STOR   wages
```

As you can see, it is much easier to write instructions in assembly language. However, a computer cannot execute assembly language instructions directly. The instructions first have to be translated into machine language. A program called an **assembler** translates the assembly language instructions into machine language.

Assembler: A program that translates a program written in assembly language into an equivalent program in machine language.

Moving from machine language to assembly language made programming easier, but a programmer was still forced to think in terms of individual machine instructions. The next step toward making programming easier was to devise **high-level languages** that were closer to natural languages, such as English, French, German, and Spanish. Basic, FORTRAN, COBOL, Pascal, C, C++, C#, and Java are all high-level languages. You will learn the high-level language C++ in this book.

In C++, you write the weekly wages equation as follows:

```
wages = rate * hours;
```

The instruction written in C++ is much easier to understand and is self-explanatory to a novice user who is familiar with basic arithmetic. As in the case of assembly language, however, the computer cannot directly execute instructions written in a high-level language. To run on a computer, these C++ instructions first need to be translated into machine language. A program called a **compiler** translates instructions written in high-level languages into machine code.

Compiler: A program that translates instructions written in a high-level language into the equivalent machine language.

Processing a C++ Program

In the previous sections, we discussed machine language and high-level languages and showed a C++ program. Because a computer can understand only machine language, you are ready to review the steps required to process a program written in C++.

Consider the following C++ program:

```
#include <iostream>

using namespace std;

int main()
{
    cout << "My first C++ program." << endl;

    return 0;
}
```

At this point, you need not be too concerned with the details of this program. However, if you run (execute) this program, it will display the following line on the screen:

```
My first C++ program.
```

Recall that a computer can understand only machine language. Therefore, in order to run this program successfully, the code must first be translated into machine language. In this section, we review the steps required to execute programs written in C++.

The following steps, as shown in Figure 1-3, are necessary to process a C++ program.

1. You use a text editor to create a C++ program following the rules, or *syntax*, of the high-level language. This program is called the **source code**, or **source program**. The program must be saved in a text file that has the extension `.cpp`. For example, if you saved the preceding program in the file named `FirstCPPProgram`, then its complete name is `FirstCPPProgram.cpp`.

   Source program: A program written in a high-level language.

2. The C++ program given in the preceding section contains the statement `#include <iostream>`. In a C++ program, statements that begin with the symbol # are called preprocessor directives. These statements are processed by a program called **preprocessor**.

3. After processing preprocessor directives, the next step is to verify that the program obeys the rules of the programming language—that is, the program is syntactically correct—and translate the program into the equivalent machine language. The *compiler* checks the source program for syntax errors and, if no error is found, translates the program into the equivalent machine language. The equivalent machine language program is called an **object program**.

Object program: The machine language version of the high-level language program.

4. The programs that you write in a high-level language are developed using an integrated development environment (IDE). The IDE contains many programs that are useful in creating your program. For example, it contains the necessary code (program) to display the results of the program and several mathematical functions to make the programmer's job somewhat easier. Therefore, if certain code is already available, you can use this code rather than writing your own code. Once the program is developed and successfully compiled, you must still bring the code for the resources used from the IDE into your program to produce a final program that the computer can execute. This prewritten code (program) resides in a place called the **library**. A program called a **linker** combines the object program with the programs from libraries.

   Linker: A program that combines the object program with other programs in the library and is used in the program to create the executable code.

5. You must next load the executable program into main memory for execution. A program called a **loader** accomplishes this task.

   Loader: A program that loads an executable program into main memory.

6. The final step is to execute the program.

Figure 1-3 shows how a typical C++ program is processed.

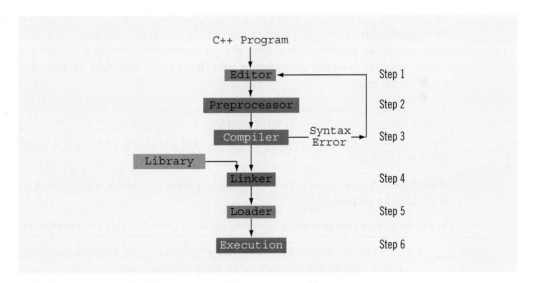

FIGURE 1-3 Processing a C++ program

As a programmer, you need to be concerned only with Step 1. That is, you must learn, understand, and master the rules of the programming language to create source programs.

As noted earlier, programs are developed using an IDE. Well-known IDEs used to create programs in the high-level language C++ include Visual C++ 2008 Express, Visual C++ 2010 Express, Visual Studio 2010 (from Microsoft), and C++ Builder (from Borland). You can also use Dev-C++ IDE from Bloodshed Software to create and test C++ programs. These IDEs contain a text editor to create the source program, a compiler to check the source program for syntax errors, a program to link the object code with the IDE resources, and a program to execute the program.

These IDEs are quite user friendly. When you compile your program, the compiler not only identifies the syntax errors, but also typically suggests how to correct them. More-over, with just a simple command, the object code is linked with the resources used from the IDE. For example, the command that does the linking on Visual C++ 2008 Express, Visual C++ 2010 Express, and Visual Studio 2010 is **Build** or **Rebuild**. (For further clarification regarding the use of these commands, check the documentation of these IDEs.) If the program is not yet compiled, each of these commands first compiles the program and then links and produces the executable code.

The Web site *http://msdn.microsoft.com/en-us/beginner/bb964629.aspx* contains a video that explains how to use Visual C++ 2008 Express to write C++ programs.

Programming with the Problem Analysis–Coding–Execution Cycle

Programming is a process of problem solving. Different people use different techniques to solve problems. Some techniques are nicely outlined and easy to follow. They not only solve the problem, but also give insight into how the solution was reached. These problem-solving techniques can be easily modified if the domain of the problem changes.

To be a good problem solver and a good programmer, you must follow good problem-solving techniques. One common problem-solving technique includes analyzing a pro-blem, outlining the problem requirements, and designing steps, called an **algorithm**, to solve the problem.

Algorithm: A step-by-step problem-solving process in which a solution is arrived at in a finite amount of time.

In a programming environment, the problem-solving process requires the following three steps:

1. Analyze the problem, outline the problem and its solution requirements, and design an algorithm to solve the problem.
2. Implement the algorithm in a programming language, such as C++, and verify that the algorithm works.
3. Maintain the program by using and modifying it if the problem domain changes.

Figure 1-4 summarizes this three-step programming process.

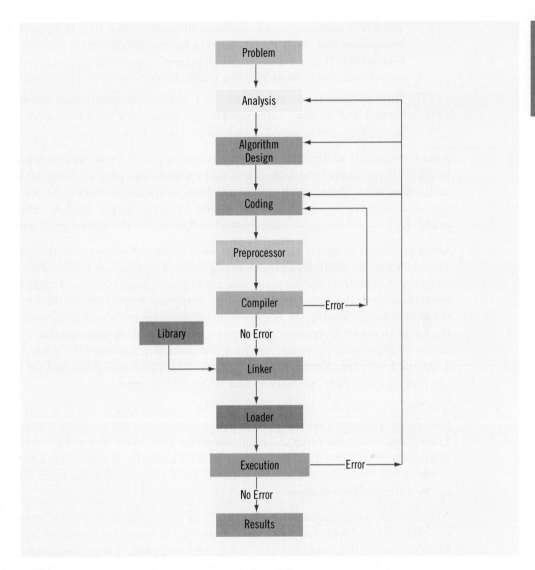

FIGURE 1-4 Problem analysis–coding–execution cycle

To develop a program to solve a problem, you start by analyzing the problem. You then design the algorithm; write the program instructions in a high-level language, or code the program; and enter the program into a computer system.

Analyzing the problem is the first and most important step. This step requires you to do the following:

1. Thoroughly understand the problem.

2. Understand the problem requirements. Requirements can include whether the program requires interaction with the user, whether it manipulates data,

whether it produces output, and what the output looks like. If the program manipulates data, the programmer must know what the data is and how it is represented. That is, you need to look at sample data. If the program produces output, you should know how the results should be generated and formatted.

3. If the problem is complex, divide the problem into subproblems and repeat Steps 1 and 2. That is, for complex problems, you need to analyze each subproblem and understand each subproblem's requirements.

After you carefully analyze the problem, the next step is to design an algorithm to solve the problem. If you broke the problem into subproblems, you need to design an algorithm for each subproblem. Once you design an algorithm, you need to check it for correctness. You can sometimes test an algorithm's correctness by using sample data. At other times, you might need to perform some mathematical analysis to test the algorithm's correctness.

Once you have designed the algorithm and verified its correctness, the next step is to convert it into an equivalent programming code. You then use a text editor to enter the programming code or the program into a computer. Next, you must make sure that the program follows the language's syntax. To verify the correctness of the syntax, you run the code through a compiler. If the compiler generates error messages, you must identify the errors in the code, remove them, and then run the code through the compiler again. When all the syntax errors are removed, the compiler generates the equivalent machine code, the linker links the machine code with the system's resources, and the loader places the program into main memory so that it can be executed.

The final step is to execute the program. The compiler guarantees only that the program follows the language's syntax. It does not guarantee that the program will run correctly. During execution, the program might terminate abnormally due to logical errors, such as division by zero. Even if the program terminates normally, it may still generate erroneous results. Under these circumstances, you may have to reexamine the code, the algorithm, or even the problem analysis.

Your overall programming experience will be successful if you spend enough time to complete the problem analysis before attempting to write the programming instructions. Usually, you do this work on paper using a pen or pencil. Taking this careful approach to programming has a number of advantages. It is much easier to discover errors in a program that is well analyzed and well designed. Furthermore, a carefully analyzed and designed program is much easier to follow and modify. Even the most experienced programmers spend a considerable amount of time analyzing a problem and designing an algorithm.

Throughout this book, you will not only learn the rules of writing programs in C++, but you will also learn problem-solving techniques. Most of the chapters contain programming examples that discuss programming problems. These programming examples teach techniques of how to analyze and solve problems, design algorithms, code the algorithms into C++, and also help you understand the concepts discussed in the chapter. To gain the full benefit of this book, we recommend that you work through these programming examples.

Next, we provide examples of various problem-analysis and algorithm-design techniques.

EXAMPLE 1-1

In this example, we design an algorithm to find the perimeter and area of a rectangle.

To find the perimeter and area of a rectangle, you need to know the rectangle's length and width.

The perimeter and area of the rectangle are then given by the following formulas:

```
perimeter = 2 · (length + width)
area = length · width
```

The algorithm to find the perimeter and area of the rectangle is:

1. Get the length of the rectangle.
2. Get the width of the rectangle.
3. Find the perimeter using the following equation:

   ```
   perimeter = 2 · (length + width)
   ```
4. Find the area using the following equation:

   ```
   area = length · width
   ```

EXAMPLE 1-2

In this example, we design an algorithm that calculates the sales tax and the price of an item sold in a particular state.

The sales tax is calculated as follows: The state's portion of the sales tax is 4%, and the city's portion of the sales tax is 1.5%. If the item is a luxury item, such as a car more than $50,000, then there is a 10% luxury tax.

To calculate the price of the item, we need to calculate the state's portion of the sales tax, the city's portion of the sales tax, and, if it is a luxury item, the luxury tax. Suppose `salePrice` denotes the selling price of the item, `stateSalesTax` denotes the state's sales tax, `citySalesTax` denotes the city's sales tax, `luxuryTax` denotes the luxury tax, `salesTax` denotes the total sales tax, and `amountDue` denotes the final price of the item.

To calculate the sales tax, we must know the selling price of the item and whether the item is a luxury item.

The `stateSalesTax` and `citySalesTax` can be calculated using the following formulas:

```
stateSalesTax = salePrice · 0.04
citySalesTax = salePrice · 0.015
```

Next, you can determine `luxuryTax` as follows:

```
if (item is a luxury item)
    luxuryTax = salePrice · 0.1
otherwise
    luxuryTax = 0
```

Next, you can determine `salesTax` as follows:

```
salesTax = stateSalesTax + citySalesTax + luxuryTax
```

Finally, you can calculate `amountDue` as follows:

```
amountDue = salePrice + salesTax
```

The algorithm to determine `salesTax` and `amountDue` is, therefore:

1. Get the selling price of the item.
2. Determine whether the item is a luxury item.
3. Find the state's portion of the sales tax using the formula:

   ```
   stateSalesTax = salePrice · 0.04
   ```

4. Find the city's portion of the sales tax using the formula:

   ```
   citySalesTax = salePrice · 0.015
   ```

5. Find the luxury tax using the following formula:

   ```
   if (item is a luxury item)
       luxuryTax = salePrice · 0.1
   otherwise
       luxuryTax = 0
   ```

6. Find `salesTax` using the formula:

   ```
   salesTax = stateSalesTax + citySalesTax + luxuryTax
   ```

7. Find `amountDue` using the formula:

   ```
   amountDue = salePrice + salesTax
   ```

Watch
the Video

EXAMPLE 1-3

In this example, we design an algorithm that calculates the monthly paycheck of a salesperson at a local department store.

Every salesperson has a base salary. The salesperson also receives a bonus at the end of each month, based on the following criteria: If the salesperson has been with the store for five years or less, the bonus is $10 for each year that he or she has worked there. If the salesperson has been with the store for more than five years, the bonus is $20 for each year that he or she has worked there. The salesperson can earn an additional bonus as follows: If the total sales made by the salesperson for the month are at least $5,000 but less than $10,000, he or she receives a 3% commission on the sale. If the total sales made by the salesperson for the month are at least $10,000, he or she receives a 6% commission on the sale.

To calculate a salesperson's monthly paycheck, you need to know the base salary, the number of years that the salesperson has been with the company, and the total sales made by the salesperson for that month. Suppose `baseSalary` denotes the base salary, `noOfServiceYears` denotes the number of years that the salesperson has been with the store, `bonus` denotes the bonus, `totalSales` denotes the total sales made by the salesperson for the month, and `additionalBonus` denotes the additional bonus.

You can determine the bonus as follows:

```
if (noOfServiceYears is less than or equal to five)
    bonus = 10 · noOfServiceYears
otherwise
    bonus = 20 · noOfServiceYears
```

Next, you can determine the additional bonus of the salesperson as follows:

```
if (totalSales is less than 5000)
    additionalBonus = 0
otherwise
    if (totalSales is greater than or equal to 5000 and
                    totalSales is less than 10000)
        additionalBonus = totalSales · (0.03)
    otherwise
        additionalBonus = totalSales · (0.06)
```

Following the above discussion, you can now design the algorithm to calculate a salesperson's monthly paycheck:

1. Get `baseSalary`.

2. Get `noOfServiceYears`.

3. Calculate bonus using the following formula:

```
if (noOfServiceYears is less than or equal to five)
    bonus = 10 · noOfServiceYears
otherwise

bonus = 20 · noOfServiceYears
```

4. Get `totalSales`.

5. Calculate `additionalBonus` using the following formula:

```
if (totalSales is less than 5000)
    additionalBonus = 0
otherwise
    if (totalSales is greater than or equal to 5000 and
            totalSales is less than 10000)
        additionalBonus = totalSales · (0.03)
    otherwise
        additionalBonus = totalSales · (0.06)
```

6.   Calculate `payCheck` using the equation:

`payCheck = baseSalary + bonus + additionalBonus`

EXAMPLE 1-4

In this example, we design an algorithm to play a number-guessing game.

The objective is to randomly generate an integer greater than or equal to 0 and less than 100. Then prompt the player (user) to guess the number. If the player guesses the number correctly, output an appropriate message. Otherwise, check whether the guessed number is less than the random number. If the guessed number is less than the random number generated, output the message, "Your guess is lower than the number. Guess again!"; otherwise, output the message, "Your guess is higher than the number. Guess again!". Then prompt the player to enter another number. The player is prompted to guess the random number until the player enters the correct number.

The first step is to generate a random number, as described above. C++ provides the means to do so, which is discussed in Chapter 5. Suppose `num` stands for the random number and `guess` stands for the number guessed by the player.

After the player enters the `guess`, you can compare the `guess` with the random number as follows:

```
if (guess is equal to num)
   Print "You guessed the correct number."
otherwise
  if guess is less than num
    Print "Your guess is lower than the number. Guess again!"
otherwise
    Print "Your guess is higher than the number. Guess again!"
```

You can now design an algorithm as follows:

1.   Generate a random number and call it `num`.

2.   *Repeat* the following steps until the player has guessed the correct number:

   a.   Prompt the player to enter `guess`.

   b.

```
   if (guess is equal to num)
       Print "You guessed the correct number."
   otherwise
     if guess is less than num
       Print "Your guess is lower than the number. Guess again!"
   otherwise
       Print "Your guess is higher than the number. Guess again!"
```

In Chapter 5, we use this algorithm to write a C++ program to play the guessing the number game.

EXAMPLE 1-5

There are 10 students in a class. Each student has taken five tests, and each test is worth 100 points. We want to design an algorithm to calculate the grade for each student, as well as the class average. The grade is assigned as follows: If the average test score is greater than or equal to 90, the grade is A; if the average test score is greater than or equal to 80 and less than 90, the grade is B; if the average test score is greater than or equal to 70 and less than 80, the grade is C; if the average test score is greater than or equal to 60 and less than 70, the grade is D; otherwise, the grade is F. Note that the data consists of students' names and their test scores.

This is a problem that can be divided into subproblems as follows: There are five tests, so you design an algorithm to find the average test score. Next, you design an algorithm to determine the grade. The two subproblems are to determine the average test score and to determine the grade.

Let us first design an algorithm to determine the average test score. To find the average test score, add the five test scores and then divide the sum by 5. Therefore, the algorithm is the following:

1. Get the five test scores.
2. Add the five test scores. Suppose **sum** stands for the sum of the test scores.
3. Suppose **average** stands for the average test score. Then

    ```
    average = sum / 5;
    ```

Next, you design an algorithm to determine the grade. Suppose **grade** stands for the grade assigned to a student. The following algorithm determines the grade:

```
if average is greater than or equal to 90
    grade = A
otherwise
  if average is greater than or equal to 80 and less than 90
      grade = B
otherwise
  if average is greater than or equal to 70 and less than 80
      grade = C
otherwise
  if average is greater than or equal to 60 and less than 70
      grade = D
otherwise
      grade = F
```

You can use the solutions to these subproblems to design the main algorithm as follows: (Suppose **totalAverage** stands for the sum of the averages of each student's test average.)

1. **totalAverage = 0;**
2. *Repeat* the following steps for each student in the class:

    a. Get student's name.
    b. Use the algorithm as discussed above to find the average test score.

    c.   Use the algorithm as discussed above to find the grade.

    d.   Update `totalAverage` by adding the current student's average test score.

3.   Determine the class average as follows:

```
classAverage = totalAverage / 10
```

A programming exercise in Chapter 8 asks you to write a C++ program to determine the average test score and grade for each student in a class.

Programming Methodologies

Two popular approaches to programming design are the structured approach and the object-oriented approach, which are outlined below.

Structured Programming

Dividing a problem into smaller subproblems is called **structured design**. Each subproblem is then analyzed, and a solution is obtained to solve the subproblem. The solutions to all of the subproblems are then combined to solve the overall problem. This process of implementing a structured design is called **structured programming**. The structured-design approach is also known as **top-down design**, **bottom-up design**, **stepwise refinement**, and **modular programming**.

Object-Oriented Programming

Object-oriented design (OOD) is a widely used programming methodology. In OOD, the first step in the problem-solving process is to identify the components called objects, which form the basis of the solution, and to determine how these objects interact with one another. For example, suppose you want to write a program that automates the video rental process for a local video store. The two main objects in this problem are the video and the customer.

After identifying the objects, the next step is to specify for each object the relevant data and possible operations to be performed on that data. For example, for a video object, the *data* might include:

- movie name
- starring actors
- producer
- production company
- number of copies in stock

Some of the *operations* on a video object might include:

- checking the name of the movie
- reducing the number of copies in stock by one after a copy is rented
- incrementing the number of copies in stock by one after a customer returns a particular video

This illustrates that each object consists of data and operations on that data. An object combines data and operations on the data into a single unit. In OOD, the final program is a collection of interacting objects. A programming language that implements OOD is called an **object-oriented programming (OOP)** language. You will learn about the many advantages of OOD in later chapters.

Because an object consists of data and operations on that data, before you can design and use objects, you need to learn how to represent data in computer memory, how to manipulate data, and how to implement operations. In Chapter 2, you will learn the basic data types of C++ and discover how to represent and manipulate data in computer memory. Chapter 3 discusses how to input data into a C++ program and output the results generated by a C++ program.

To create operations, you write algorithms and implement them in a programming language. Because a data element in a complex program usually has many operations, to separate operations from each other and to use them effectively and in a convenient manner, you use functions to implement algorithms. After a brief introduction in Chapters 2 and 3, you will learn the details of functions in Chapter 6. Certain algorithms require that a program make decisions, a process called selection. Other algorithms might require certain statements to be repeated until certain conditions are met, a process called repetition. Still other algorithms might require both selection and repetition. You will learn about selection and repetition mechanisms, called control structures, in Chapters 4 and 5. Also, in Chapter 8, using a mechanism called an array, you will learn how to manipulate data when data items are of the same type, such as items in a list of sales figures.

Finally, to work with objects, you need to know how to combine data and operations on the data into a single unit. In C++, the mechanism that allows you to combine data and operations on the data into a single unit is called a class. You will learn how classes work, how to work with classes, and how to create classes in the chapter Classes and Data Abstraction (later in this book).

As you can see, you need to learn quite a few things before working with the OOD methodology. To make this learning easier and more effective, this book purposely divides control structures into two chapters (4 and 5).

For some problems, the structured approach to program design will be very effective. Other problems will be better addressed by OOD. For example, if a problem requires manipulating sets of numbers with mathematical functions, you might use the structured design approach and outline the steps required to obtain the solution. The C++ library supplies a wealth of functions that you can use effectively to manipulate numbers. On the other hand, if you want to write a program that would make a candy machine operational, the OOD approach is more effective. C++ was designed especially to implement OOD. Furthermore, *OOD works well and is used in conjunction with structured design.*

Both the structured design and OOD approaches require that you master the basic components of a programming language to be an effective programmer. In Chapters 2 to 8, you will learn the basic components of C++, such as data types, input/output, control structures, user-defined functions, and arrays, required by either type of programming. We illustrate how these concepts work using the structured programming approach. Starting with the chapter Classes and Data Abstraction, we use the OOD approach.

ANSI/ISO Standard C++

The programming language C++ evolved from C and was designed by Bjarne Stroustrup at Bell Laboratories in the early 1980s. From the early 1980s through the early 1990s, several C++ compilers were available. Even though the fundamental features of C++ in all compilers were mostly the same, the C++ language, referred to in this book as Standard C++, was evolving in slightly different ways in different compilers. As a consequence, C++ programs were not always portable from one compiler to another.

To address this problem, in the early 1990s, a joint committee of the American National Standard Institution (ANSI) and International Standard Organization (ISO) was established to standardize the syntax of C++. In mid-1998, ANSI/ISO C++ language standards were approved. Most of today's compilers comply with these new standards. Over the last several years, the C++ committee met several times to further standardize the syntax of C++. In mid-2010, the second standard of C++ was voted on and approved. The main objective of this standard, referred to as C++0X, or tentatively as C++11, is to make the C++ code cleaner and more effective. For example, the new standard introduces the data type long long to deal with large integers, auto declaration of variables using initialization statements, enhancing the functionality of `for` loops to effectively work with arrays and containers, and new algorithms. However, not all new features of this new standard have been implemented by all the compilers currently available. In this book, we introduce the new C++ features that we know have been implemented by the well-known compilers and also comment on the ones that will be implemented in the future.

This book focuses on the syntax of C++ as approved by ANSI/ISO, referred to as ANSI/ISO Standard C++.

QUICK REVIEW

1. A computer is an electronic device capable of performing arithmetic and logical operations.
2. A computer system has two components: hardware and software.
3. The central processing unit (CPU) and the main memory are examples of hardware components.
4. All programs must be brought into main memory before they can be executed.
5. When the power is switched off, everything in main memory is lost.

6. Secondary storage provides permanent storage for information. Hard disks, flash drives, floppy disks, ZIP disks, CD-ROMs, and tapes are examples of secondary storage.

7. Input to the computer is done via an input device. Two common input devices are the keyboard and the mouse.

8. The computer sends its output to an output device, such as the computer screen.

9. Software are programs run by the computer.

10. The operating system monitors the overall activity of the computer and provides services.

11. The most basic language of a computer is a sequence of 0s and 1s called machine language. Every computer directly understands its own machine language.

12. A bit is a binary digit, 0 or 1.

13. A byte is a sequence of eight bits.

14. A sequence of 0s and 1s is referred to as a binary code or a binary number.

15. One kilobyte (KB) is $2^{10} = 1024$ bytes; one megabyte (MB) is $2^{20} = 1,048,576$ bytes; one gigabyte (GB) is $2^{30} = 1,073,741,824$ bytes; one terabyte (TB) is $2^{40} = 1,099,511,627,776$ bytes; one petabyte (PB) is $2^{50} = 1,125,899,906,842,624$ bytes; one exabyte (EB) is $2^{60} = 1,152,921,504,606,846,976$ bytes; and one zettabyte (ZB) is $2^{70} = 1,180,591,620,717,411,303,424$ bytes.

16. Assembly language uses easy-to-remember instructions called mnemonics.

17. Assemblers are programs that translate a program written in assembly language into machine language.

18. Compilers are programs that translate a program written in a high-level language into machine code, called object code.

19. A linker links the object code with other programs provided by the integrated development environment (IDE) and used in the program to produce executable code.

20. Typically, six steps are needed to execute a C++ program: edit, preprocess, compile, link, load, and execute.

21. A loader transfers executable code into main memory.

22. An algorithm is a step-by-step problem-solving process in which a solution is arrived at in a finite amount of time.

23. The problem-solving process has three steps: analyze the problem and design an algorithm, implement the algorithm in a programming language, and maintain the program.

24. Programs written using the structured design approach are easier to understand, easier to test and debug, and easier to modify.

25. In structured design, a problem is divided into smaller subproblems. Each subproblem is solved, and the solutions to all of the subproblems are then combined to solve the problem.

26. In object-oriented design (OOD), a program is a collection of interacting objects.

27. An object consists of data and operations on that data.

28. The ANSI/ISO Standard C++ syntax was approved in mid-1998.

EXERCISES

1. Mark the following statements as true or false.

   a. The first device known to carry out calculations was the Pascaline.

   b. Modern-day computers can accept spoken-word instructions but cannot imitate human reasoning.

   c. In ASCII coding, every character is coded as a sequence of 8 bits.

   d. A compiler translates a high-level program into assembly language.

   e. The arithmetic operations are performed inside the CPU, and if an error is found, it outputs the logical errors.

   f. A sequence of 0s and 1s is called a decimal code.

   g. A linker links and loads the object code from main memory into the CPU for execution.

   h. Development of a C++ program includes six steps.

   i. A program written in a high-level programming language is called a source program.

   j. ZB stands for zero byte.

   k. The first step in the problem-solving process is to analyze the problem.

   l. In object-oriented design, a program is a collection of interacting functions.

2. What are the basic commands performed by a computer?

3. Name three hardware components.

4. Why is secondary storage needed?

5. What is the function of an operating system?

6. What are the two types of programs?

7. What are the differences between machine languages and high-level languages?

8. What is a source program?

9. Why do you need a compiler?

10. What kind of errors are reported by a compiler?

11. Why do you need to translate a program written in a high-level language into machine language?

12. Why would you prefer to write a program in a high-level language rather than a machine language?

13. What is linking?

14. What are the advantages of problem analysis and algorithm design over directly writing a program in a high-level language?

15. Design an algorithm to find the weighted average of four test scores. The four test scores and their respective weights are given in the following format:

```
testScore1 weightTestScore1
...
```

For example, sample data is as follows:

```
75 0.20
95 0.35
85 0.15
65 0.30
```

16. Design an algorithm to convert the change given in quarters, dimes, nickels, and pennies into pennies.

17. Given the radius, in inches, and price of a pizza, design an algorithm to find the price of the pizza per square inch.

18. To make a profit, the prices of the items sold in a furniture store are marked up by 80%. After marking up the prices each item is put on sale at a discount of 10%. Design an algorithm to find the selling price of an item sold at the furniture store. What information do you need to find the selling price?

19. Suppose a, b, and c denote the lengths of the sides of a triangle. Then the area of the triangle can be calculated using the formula:

$$\sqrt{s(s-a)(s-b)(s-c)},$$

where $s = (1/2)(a + b + c)$. Design an algorithm that uses this formula to find the area of a triangle. What information do you need to find the area?

20. Jason typically uses the Internet to buy various items. If the total cost of the items ordered, at one time, is $200 or more, then the shipping and handling is free; otherwise, the shipping and handling is $10 per item. Design an algorithm that prompts Jason to enter the number of items ordered and the price of each item. The algorithm then outputs the total billing amount. Your algorithm must use a loop (repetition structure) to get the price of each item. (For simplicity, you may assume that Jason orders no more than five items at a time.)

21. Suppose that the cost of sending an international fax is calculated as follows: The service charge is $3.00, $.20 per page for the first 10 pages, and $0.10 for each additional page. Design an algorithm that asks the user to enter the number of pages to be faxed. The algorithm then uses the number of pages to be faxed to calculate the amount due.

22. An ATM allows a customer to withdraw a maximum of $500 per day. If a customer withdraws more than $300, the service charge is 4% of the amount over $300. If the customer does not have sufficient money in the account, the ATM informs the customer about the insufficient funds and gives the customer

the option to withdraw the money for a service charge of $25.00. If there is no money in the account or if the account balance is negative, the ATM does not allow the customer to withdraw any money. If the amount to be withdrawn is greater than $500, the ATM informs the customer about the maximum amount that can be withdrawn. Write an algorithm that allows the customer to enter the amount to be withdrawn. The algorithm then checks the total amount in the account, dispenses the money to the customer, and debits the account by the amount withdrawn and the service charges, if any.

23. You are given a list of students' names and their test scores. Design an algorithm that does the following:

   a. Calculates the average test scores.

   b. Determines and prints the names of all the students whose test scores are below the average test score.

   c. Determines the highest test score.

   d. Prints the names of all the students whose test scores are the same as the highest test score.

(You must divide this problem into subproblems as follows: The first subproblem determines the average test score. The second subproblem determines and prints the names of all the students whose test scores are below the average test score. The third subproblem determines the highest test score. The fourth subproblem prints the names of all the students whose test scores are the same as the highest test score. The main algorithm combines the solutions of the subproblems.)

CHAPTER 2

BASIC ELEMENTS OF C++

IN THIS CHAPTER, YOU WILL:

- Become familiar with the basic components of a C++ program, including functions, special symbols, and identifiers
- Explore simple data types
- Discover how to use arithmetic operators
- Examine how a program evaluates arithmetic expressions
- Learn what an assignment statement is and what it does
- Become familiar with the `string` data type
- Discover how to input data into memory using input statements
- Become familiar with the use of increment and decrement operators
- Examine ways to output results using output statements
- Learn how to use preprocessor directives and why they are necessary
- Learn how to debug syntax errors
- Explore how to properly structure a program, including using comments to document a program
- Learn how to write a C++ program

In this chapter, you will learn the basics of C++. As your objective is to learn the C++ programming language, two questions naturally arise. First, what is a computer program? Second, what is programming? A **computer program**, or a program, is a sequence of statements whose objective is to accomplish a task. **Programming** is a process of planning and creating a program. These two definitions tell the truth, but not the whole truth, about programming. It may very well take an entire book to give a good and satisfactory definition of programming. You might gain a better grasp of the nature of programming from an analogy, so let us turn to a topic about which almost everyone has some knowledge—cooking. A recipe is also a program, and everyone with some cooking experience can agree on the following:

1. It is usually easier to follow a recipe than to create one.
2. There are good recipes and there are bad recipes.
3. Some recipes are easy to follow and some are not easy to follow.
4. Some recipes produce reliable results and some do not.
5. You must have some knowledge of how to use cooking tools to follow a recipe to completion.
6. To create good new recipes, you must have a lot of knowledge and a good understanding of cooking.

These same six points are also true about programming. Let us take the cooking analogy one step further. Suppose you need to teach someone how to become a chef. How would you go about it? Would you first introduce the person to good food, hoping that a taste for good food develops? Would you have the person follow recipe after recipe in the hope that some of it rubs off? Or would you first teach the use of tools and the nature of ingredients, the foods and spices, and explain how they fit together? Just as there is disagreement about how to teach cooking, there is disagreement about how to teach programming.

Learning a programming language is like learning to become a chef or learning to play a musical instrument. All three require direct interaction with the tools. You cannot become a good chef or even a poor chef just by reading recipes. Similarly, you cannot become a player by reading books about musical instruments. The same is true of programming. You must have a fundamental knowledge of the language, and you must test your programs on the computer to make sure that each program does what it is supposed to do.

A Quick Look at a C++ Program

In this chapter, you will learn the basic elements and concepts of the C++ programming language to create C++ programs. In addition to giving examples to illustrate various concepts, we will also show C++ programs to clarify these concepts. In this section, we provide an example of a C++ program that computes the perimeter and area of a

2

rectangle. At this point you need not be too concerned with the details of this program. You only need to know the effect of an *output* statement, which is introduced in this program.

In Example 1-1 (Chapter 1), we designed an algorithm to find the perimeter and area of a rectangle. Given the length and width of a rectangle, the C++ program, in Example 2-1, computes and displays the perimeter and area.

EXAMPLE 2-1

```cpp
//************************************************************
// Given the length and width of a rectangle, this C++ program
// computes and outputs the perimeter and area of the rectangle.
//************************************************************

#include <iostream>

using namespace std;

int main()
{
    double length;
    double width;
    double area;
    double perimeter;

    cout << "Program to compute and output the perimeter and "
         << "area of a rectangle." << endl;

    length = 6.0;
    width = 4.0;
    perimeter = 2 * (length + width);
    area = length * width;

    cout << "Length = " << length << endl;
    cout << "Width =  " << width << endl;
    cout << "Perimeter = " << perimeter << endl;
    cout << "Area = " << area << endl;

    return 0;
}
```

Sample Run: (When you compile and execute this program, the following five lines are displayed on the screen.)

```
Program to compute and output the perimeter and area of a rectangle.
Length = 6
Width =  4
Perimeter = 20
Area = 24
```

These lines are displayed by the execution of the following statements:

```
cout << "Program to compute and output the perimeter and "
     << "area of a rectangle." << endl;

cout << "Length = " << length << endl;
cout << "Width =  " << width << endl;
cout << "Perimeter = " << perimeter << endl;
cout << "Area = " << area << endl;
```

Next we explain how this happens. Let us first consider the following statement:

```
cout << "Program to compute and output the perimeter and "
     << "area of a rectangle." << endl;
```

This is an example of a C++ *output* statement. It causes the computer to evaluate the *expression* after the pair of symbols << and display the result on the screen.

Usually, a C++ program contains various types of expressions such as arithmetic and strings. For example, length + width is an arithmetic expression. Anything in double quotes is a *string*. For example, "Program to compute and output the perimeter and " is a string. Similarly, "area of a rectangle." is also a string. Typically, a string evaluates to itself. Arithmetic expressions are evaluated according to rules of arithmetic operations, which you typically learn in an algebra course. Later in this chapter, we will explain how arithmetic expressions and strings are formed and evaluated.

Also note that in an output statement, endl *causes the insertion point to move to the beginning of the next line.* (Note that in endl, the last letter is lowercase el. Also, on the screen, the insertion point is where the cursor is.) Therefore, the preceding statement causes the system to display the following line on the screen.

```
Program to compute and output the area and perimeter of a rectangle.
```

Let us now consider the following statement:

```
cout << "Length = " << length << endl;
```

This output statement consists of two expressions. The first expression, (after the first <<), is "Length = " and the second expression, (after the second <<), consists of the identifier length. The expression "Length = " is a string and evaluates to itself. (Notice the space after =.) The second expression, which consists of the identifier length, evaluates to whatever the value of length is. Because the value assigned to length is 6.0, length evaluates to 6.0. Therefore, the output of the preceding statement is:

```
Length = 6
```

Note that the value of length is output as 6 not as 6.0. We will explain in the next chapter how to force the program to output the value of length as 6.0. The meaning of the remaining output statements is similar.

2

The last statement, that is,

```
return 0;
```

returns the value 0 to the operating system when the program terminates. We will elaborate on this statement later in this chapter.

Before we identify various parts of a C++ program, let's look at one more output statement. Consider the following statement:

```
cout << "7 + 8 = " << 7 + 8 << endl;
```

In this output statement, the expression `"7 + 8 = "`, which is a string, evaluates to itself. Let us consider the second expression, `7 + 8`. This expression consists of the numbers 7 and 8, and the C++ arithmetic operator +. Therefore, the result of the expression `7 + 8` is the sum of 7 and 8, which is 15. Thus, the output of the preceding statement is:

```
7 + 8 = 15
```

In the next chapter, until we explain how to properly construct a C++ program, we will be using output statements such as the preceding ones to explain various concepts. After finishing Chapter 2, you should be able to write C++ programs well enough to do some computations and show results.

Next, let us note the following about the previous C++ program. A C++ program is a collection of functions, one of which is the function `main`. Roughly speaking, a *function* is a set of statements whose objective is to accomplish something. The preceding program consists of only the function `main`; all C++ programs require a function `main`.

The first four lines of the program begins with the pair of symbols `//` (shown in green), which are comments. Comments are for the user; they typically explain the purpose of the programs, that is, the meaning of the statements. (We will elaborate on how to include comments in a program later in this chapter.) The next line of the program, that is,

```
#include <iostream>
```

allows us to use the (predefined object) `cout` to generate output and the (manipulator) `endl`. The statement

```
using namespace std;
```

allows you to use `cout` and `endl` without the prefix `std::`. It means that if you do not include this statement, then `cout` should be used as `std::cout` and `endl` should be used as `std::endl`. We will elaborate on this later in this chapter.

Next consider the following line:

```
int main()
```

This is the heading of the function main. The next line consists of a left brace. This marks the beginning of the (body) of the function main. The right brace (at the last line of the program) matches this left brace and marks the end of the body of the function main. We will explain the meaning of the other terms, such as the ones shown in blue, later in this book. Note that in C++, << is an operator, called the *stream insertion operator*.

Before ending this section, let us identify certain parts of the C++ program in Figure 2-1.

```
//*****************************************************************
// Given the length and width of a rectangle, this C++ program
// computes and outputs the perimeter and area of the rectangle.
//*****************************************************************
```
Comments

```
#include <iostream>

using namespace std;

int main()
{
    double length;
    double width;
    double area;
    double perimeter;
```
Variable declarations. A statement such as
```
    double length;
```
instructs the system to allocate memory space and name it length.

```
    cout << "Program to compute and output the perimeter and "
         << "area of a rectangle." << endl;

    length = 6.0;
```
Assignment statement. This statement instructs the system to store 6.0 in the memory space length.

```
    width = 4.0;
    perimeter = 2 * (length + width);
```

```
    area = length * width;
```
Assignment statement. This statement instructs the system to evaluate the expression length * width and store the result in the memory space area.

```
    cout << "Length = " << length << endl;
    cout << "Width = " << width << endl;
    cout << "Perimeter = " << perimeter << endl;
    cout << "Area = " << area << endl;
```
Output statements. An output statement instructs the system to display results.

```
    return 0;
}
```

FIGURE 2-1   Various parts of a C++ program

2

One of the terms that you will encounter throughout the text and that is also identified in Figure 2-1 is *variable*. Therefore, we introduce this term in this section. Recall from Chapter 1 that all data must be loaded into main memory before it can be manipulated. For example, given the length and width, the program in Figure 2-1 computes and outputs the area and perimeter of a rectangle. This means that the values of length and width must be stored in main memory. Also, recall from Chapter 1 that main memory is an ordered sequence of cells and every cell has an address. Inside the computer, the address of a memory cell is in binary. Once we store the values of length and width, and because these values might be needed in more than one place in a program, we would like to know the locations where these values are stored and how to access those memory locations. C++ makes it easy for a programmer to specify the locations because the programmer can supply an alphabetic name for each of those locations. Of course, we must follow the rules to specify the names. For example, in the program in Figure 2-1, we are telling the system to allocate four memory spaces and name them `length`, `width`, `area`, and `perimeter`, respectively. (We will explain the meaning of the word `double`, shown in blue later in this chapter.) Essentially, a *variable* is a memory location whose contents can be changed. So `length`, `width`, `area`, and `perimeter` are variables. Also during program execution, the system will allocate four memory locations large enough to store decimal numbers and those memory locations will be named `length`, `width`, `area`, and `perimeter`, respectively, see Figure 2-2.

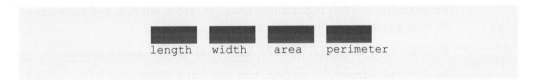

length   width   area   perimeter

FIGURE 2-2 Memory allocation

The statement `length = 6.0;` will cause the system to store `6.0` in the memory location `length`, see Figure 2-3. Examples 2-14 and 2-19 further illustrate how data is manipulated in variables.

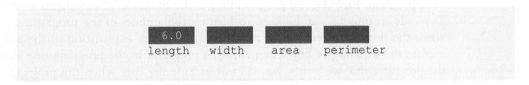

6.0
length   width   area   perimeter

FIGURE 2-3 Memory spaces after the statement `length = 6.0;` executes

As we proceed through this chapter, we will explain the meaning of the remaining parts identified in Figure 2-1.

The Basics of a C++ Program

In the previous section, we gave an example of a C++ program and also identified certain parts of the program. In general, a C++ program is a collection of one or more subprograms, called functions. Roughly speaking, a **subprogram** or a **function** is a collection of statements, and when it is activated, or executed, it accomplishes something. Some functions, called **predefined** or **standard** functions, are already written and are provided as part of the system. But to accomplish most tasks, programmers must learn to write their own functions.

Every C++ program has a function called `main`. Thus, if a C++ program has only one function, it must be the function `main`. Until Chapter 6, other than using some of the predefined functions, you will mainly deal with the function `main`. By the end of this chapter, you will have learned how to write the function `main`.

If you have never seen a program written in a programming language, the C++ program in Example 2-1 may look like a foreign language. To make meaningful sentences in a foreign language, you must learn its alphabet, words, and grammar. The same is true of a programming language. To write meaningful programs, you must learn the programming language's special symbols, words, and syntax rules. The **syntax rules** tell you which statements (instructions) are legal or valid, that is, which are accepted by the programming language and which are not. You must also learn **semantic rules**, which determine the meaning of the instructions. The programming language's rules, symbols, and special words enable you to write programs to solve problems.

Programming language: A set of rules, symbols, and special words.

In the remainder of this section, you will learn about some of the special symbols of a C++ program. Additional special symbols are introduced as other concepts are encountered in later chapters. Similarly, syntax and semantic rules are introduced and discussed throughout the book.

Comments

The program that you write should be clear not only to you, but also to the reader of your program. Part of good programming is the inclusion of comments in the program. Typically, comments can be used to identify the authors of the program, give the date when the program is written or modified, give a brief explanation of the program, and explain the meaning of key statements in a program. In the programming examples, for the programs that we write, we will not include the date when the program is written, consistent with the standard convention for writing such books.

Comments are for the reader, not for the compiler. So when a compiler compiles a program to check for the syntax errors, it completely ignores comments. Throughout this book, comments are shown in green.

The program in Example 2-1 contains the following comments:

```
//*********************************************************
// Given the length and width of a rectangle, this C++ program
// computes and outputs the perimeter and area of the rectangle.
//*********************************************************
```

There are two common types of comments in a C++ program—single-line comments and multiple-line comments.

Single-line comments begin with // and can be placed anywhere in the line. Everything encountered in that line after // is ignored by the compiler. For example, consider the following statement:

```
cout << "7 + 8 = " << 7 + 8 << endl;
```

You can put comments at the end of this line as follows:

```
cout << "7 + 8 = " << 7 + 8 << endl; //prints: 7 + 8 = 15
```

This comment could be meaningful for a beginning programmer.

Multiple-line comments are enclosed between /* and */. The compiler ignores anything that appears between /* and */. For example, the following is an example of a multiple-line comment:

```
/*
   You can include comments that can
   occupy several lines.
*/
```

In multiple-line comments, many programmers use single-line comments on every line to make the comments stand out more to the reader (as was done in the program in Example 2-1.)

Special Symbols

The smallest individual unit of a program written in any language is called a **token**. C++'s tokens are divided into special symbols, word symbols, and identifiers.

Following are some of the special symbols:

```
+      -      *      /
.      ;      ?      ,
<=     !=     ==     >=
```

The first row includes mathematical symbols for addition, subtraction, multiplication, and division. The second row consists of punctuation marks taken from English grammar. Note that the comma is also a special symbol. In C++, commas are used to separate items in a list. Semicolons are also special symbols and are used to end a C++ statement. Note that a blank, which is not shown above, is also a special symbol. You create a blank symbol by pressing the space bar (only once) on the keyboard. The third row consists of tokens made up of two characters that are regarded as a single symbol. No character can come between the two characters in the token, not even a blank.

Reserved Words (Keywords)

A second category of tokens is reserved word symbols. Some of the reserved word symbols include the following:

`int, float, double, char, const, void, return`

Reserved words are also called **keywords**. The letters that make up a reserved word are always lowercase. Like the special symbols, each is considered to be a single symbol. Furthermore, word symbols cannot be redefined within any program; that is, they cannot be used for anything other than their intended use. For a complete list of reserved words, see Appendix A.

 NOTE Throughout this book, reserved words are shown in blue.

Identifiers

A third category of tokens is identifiers. Identifiers are names of things that appear in programs, such as variables, constants, and functions. All identifiers must obey C++'s rules for identifiers.

Identifier: A C++ identifier consists of letters, digits, and the underscore character (_) and must begin with a letter or underscore.

Some identifiers are predefined; others are defined by the user. In the C++ program in Example 2-1, `cout` is a predefined identifier and `length` is a user-defined identifier. Two predefined identifiers that you will encounter frequently are `cout` and `cin`. You have already seen the effect of `cout`. Later in this chapter, you will learn how `cin`, which is used to input data, works. Unlike reserved words, predefined identifiers can be redefined, but it would not be wise to do so.

Identifiers can be made of only letters, digits, and the underscore character; no other symbols are permitted to form an identifier.

 NOTE C++ is case sensitive—uppercase and lowercase letters are considered different. Thus, the identifier NUMBER is not the same as the identifier `number`. Similarly, the identifiers X and x are different.

In C++, identifiers can be of any length.

EXAMPLE 2-2

The following are legal identifiers in C++:

```
first
conversion
payRate
counter1
```

Table 2-1 shows some illegal identifiers and explains why they are illegal.

TABLE 2-1 Examples of Illegal Identifiers

Illegal Identifier	Description
employee Salary	There can be no space between `employee` and `Salary`.
Hello!	The exclamation mark cannot be used in an identifier.
one + two	The symbol + cannot be used in an identifier.
2nd	An identifier cannot begin with a digit.

NOTE Compiler vendors usually begin certain identifiers with an underscore (_). When the linker links the object program with the system resources provided by the integrated development environment (IDE), certain errors could occur. Therefore, it is advisable that you should not begin identifiers in your program with an underscore (_).

Whitespaces

Every C++ program contains whitespaces. Whitespaces include blanks, tabs, and newline characters. In a C++ program, whitespaces are used to separate special symbols, reserved words, and identifiers. Whitespaces are nonprintable in the sense that when they are printed on a white sheet of paper, the space between special symbols, reserved words, and identifiers is white. Proper utilization of whitespaces in a program is important. They can be used to make the program more readable.

Data Types

The objective of a C++ program is to manipulate data. Different programs manipulate different data. A program designed to calculate an employee's paycheck will add, subtract, multiply, and divide numbers, and some of the numbers might represent hours worked and pay rate. Similarly, a program designed to alphabetize a class list will manipulate names. You wouldn't use a cherry pie recipe to help you bake cookies. Similarly, you wouldn't use a program designed to perform arithmetic calculations to manipulate alphabetic characters. Furthermore, you wouldn't multiply or subtract names. Reflecting these kinds of underlying differences, C++ categorizes data into different types, and only certain operations can be performed on particular types of data. Although at first it may seem confusing, by being so type conscious, C++ has built-in checks to guard against errors.

Data type: A set of values together with a set of operations.

C++ data types fall into the following three categories:

- Simple data type
- Structured data type
- Pointers

For the next few chapters, you will be concerned only with simple data types.

Simple Data Types

The simple data type is the fundamental data type in C++ because it becomes a building block for the structured data type, which you will start learning about in Chapter 8. There are three categories of simple data:

- **Integral**, which is a data type that deals with integers, or numbers without a decimal part
- **Floating-point**, which is a data type that deals with decimal numbers
- **Enumeration**, which is a user-defined data type

 NOTE The enumeration type is C++'s method for allowing programmers to create their own simple data types. This data type will be discussed in Chapter 7.

Integral data types are further classified into the following nine categories: `char`, `short`, `int`, `long`, `bool`, `unsigned char`, `unsigned short`, `unsigned int`, and `unsigned long`.

Why are there so many categories of the same data type? Every data type has a different set of values associated with it. For example, the `char` data type is used to represent integers between −128 and 127. The `int` data type is used to represent integers between −2147483648 and 2147483647, and the data type `short` is used to represent integers between −32768 and 32767.

Which data type you use depends on how big a number your program needs to deal with. In the early days of programming, computers and main memory were very expensive. Only a small amount of memory was available to execute programs and manipulate the data. As a result, programmers had to optimize the use of memory. Because writing a program and making it work is already a complicated process, not having to worry about the size of memory makes for one less thing to think about. To effectively use memory, a programmer can look at the type of data to be used by a program and thereby figure out which data type to use. (Memory constraints may still be a concern for programs written for applications such as a wristwatch.)

Newer programming languages have only five categories of simple data types: `integer`, `real`, `char`, `bool`, and the enumeration type. The integral data types that are used in this book are `int`, `bool`, and `char`.

Table 2-2 gives the range of possible values associated with these three data types and the size of memory allocated to manipulate these values.

TABLE 2-2 Values and Memory Allocation for Three Simple Data Types

Data Type	Values	Storage (in bytes)
int	−2147483648 to 2147483647	4
bool	true and false	1
char	−128 to 127	1

NOTE Use this table only as a guide. Different compilers may allow different ranges of values. Check your compiler's documentation. To find the exact size of the integral data types on a particular system, you can run a program given in Appendix G (Memory Size of a System). Furthermore, to find the maximum and minimum values of these data types, you can run another program given in Appendix F (Header File `climits`).

NOTE To deal with large integers, the new standard of C++ introduces the data type `long long`. The memory space for a `long long` data value is 64 bytes and the range of values belonging to this data type is −9223372036854775808 (-2^{63}) to 9223372036854775807 ($2^{63} - 1$).

`int` DATA TYPE

This section describes the `int` data type. This discussion also applies to other integral data types.

Integers in C++, as in mathematics, are numbers such as the following:

```
-6728, -67, 0, 78, 36782, +763
```

Note the following two rules from these examples:

1. Positive integers do not need a + sign in front of them.

2. No commas are used within an integer. Recall that in C++, commas are used to separate items in a list. So 36,782 would be interpreted as two integers: 36 and 782.

bool DATA TYPE

The data type bool has only two values: true and false. Also, true and false are called the *logical (Boolean) values*. The central purpose of this data type is to manipulate logical (Boolean) expressions. Logical (Boolean) expressions will be formally defined and discussed in detail in Chapter 4. In C++, bool, true, and false are reserved words.

char DATA TYPE

The data type char is the smallest integral data type. It is mainly used to represent single characters—that is, letters, digits, and special symbols. Thus, the char data type can represent every key on your keyboard. When using the char data type, you enclose each character represented within single quotation marks. Examples of values belonging to the char data type include the following:

```
'A', 'a', '0', '*', '+', '$', '&', ' '
```

Note that a blank space is a character and is written as ' ', with a space between the single quotation marks.

The data type char allows only one symbol to be placed between the single quotation marks. Thus, the value 'abc' is not of the type char. Furthermore, even though '!=' and similar special symbols are considered to be one symbol, they are not regarded as possible values of the data type char. All the individual symbols located on the keyboard that are printable may be considered as possible values of the char data type.

Several different character data sets are currently in use. The most common are the American Standard Code for Information Interchange (ASCII) and Extended Binary-Coded Decimal Interchange Code (EBCDIC). The ASCII character set has 128 values. The EBCDIC character set has 256 values and was created by IBM. Both character sets are described in Appendix C.

Each of the 128 values of the ASCII character set represents a different character. For example, the value 65 represents 'A', and the value 43 represents '+'. Thus, each character has a predefined ordering represented by the numeric value associated with the character. This ordering is called a **collating sequence**, in the set. The collating sequence is used when you compare characters. For example, the value representing 'B' is 66, so 'A' is smaller than 'B'. Similarly, '+' is smaller than 'A' because 43 is smaller than 65.

The 14th character in the ASCII character set is called the newline character and is represented as '\n'. (Note that the position of the newline character in the ASCII character set is 13 because the position of the first character is 0.) Even though the newline character is a combination of two characters, it is treated as one character. Similarly, the horizontal tab character is represented in C++ as `'\t'` and the null character is represented as `'\0'` (backslash followed by zero). Furthermore, the first 32 characters in the ASCII character set are nonprintable. (See Appendix C for a description of these characters.)

Floating-Point Data Types

To deal with decimal numbers, C++ provides the floating-point data type, which we discuss in this section. To facilitate the discussion, let us review a concept from a high school or college algebra course.

You may be familiar with scientific notation. For example:

```
43872918 = 4.3872918 * 10⁷      { 10 to the power of seven}
.0000265 = 2.65 * 10⁻⁵          { 10 to the power of minus five}
47.9832 = 4.79832 * 10¹         { 10 to the power of one}
```

To represent decimal numbers, C++ uses a form of scientific notation called **floating-point notation**. Table 2-3 shows how C++ might print a set of decimal numbers using one machine's interpretation of floating-point notation. In the C++ floating-point notation, the letter E stands for the exponent.

TABLE 2-3 Examples of Decimal Numbers in Scientific and C++ Floating-Point Notations

Decimal Number	Scientific Notation	C++ Floating-Point Notation
75.924	$7.5924 * 10^1$	7.592400E1
0.18	$1.8 * 10^{-1}$	1.800000E-1
0.0000453	$4.53 * 10^{-5}$	4.530000E-5
-1.482	$-1.482 * 10^0$	-1.482000E0
7800.0	$7.8 * 10^3$	7.800000E3

C++ provides three data types to manipulate decimal numbers: `float`, `double`, and `long double`. As in the case of integral data types, the data types `float`, `double`, and `long double` differ in the set of values.

> **NOTE** On most newer compilers, the data types `double` and `long double` are the same. Therefore, only the data types `float` and `double` are described here.

float: The data type **float** is used in C++ to represent any decimal number between $-3.4 * 10^{38}$ and $3.4 * 10^{38}$. The memory allocated for a value of the **float** data type is four bytes.

double: The data type **double** is used in C++ to represent any decimal number between $-1.7 * 10^{308}$ and $1.7 * 10^{308}$. The memory allocated for a value of the **double** data type is eight bytes.

The maximum and minimum values of the data types **float** and **double** are system dependent. To find these values on a particular system, you can check your compiler's documentation or, alternatively, you can run a program given in Appendix F (Header File **cfloat**).

Other than the set of values, there is one more difference between the data types **float** and **double**. The maximum number of significant digits—that is, the number of decimal places—in **float** values is six or seven. The maximum number of significant digits in values belonging to the **double** type is 15.

NOTE For values of the **double** type, for better precision, some compilers might give more than 15 significant digits. Check your compiler's documentation.

The maximum number of significant digits is called the **precision**. Sometimes **float** values are called **single precision**, and values of type **double** are called **double precision**. If you are dealing with decimal numbers, for the most part you need only the **float** type; if you need accuracy to more than six or seven decimal places, you can use the **double** type.

NOTE In C++, by default, floating-point numbers are considered type **double**. Therefore, if you use the data type **float** to manipulate floating-point numbers in a program, certain compilers might give you a warning message, such as "truncation from double to float." To avoid such warning messages, you should use the **double** data type. For illustration purposes and to avoid such warning messages in programming examples, this book mostly uses the data type **double** to manipulate floating-point numbers.

Data Types and Variables

Now that we know how to define an identifier, what a data type is, and the term variable, we can show how to declare a variable. When we declare a variable, not only do we specify the name of the variable, we also specify what type of data a variable can store. A syntax rule to declare a variable is:

```
dataType identifier;
```

For example, consider the following statements:

```
int counter;
double interestRate;
char grade;
```

In the first statement, we are telling the system to allocate a memory space large enough to store an `int` value and name that memory space `counter`. That is, `counter` is a variable that can store an `int` value. Similarly, `interestRate` is a variable that can store a value of type `double`; and `grade` is a variable that can store a value of type `char`.

Arithmetic Operators, Operator Precedence, and Expressions

One of the most important uses of a computer is its ability to calculate. You can use the standard arithmetic operators to manipulate integral and floating-point data types. There are five arithmetic operators:

Arithmetic Operators: + (**addition**), − (**subtraction** or **negation**), * (**multiplication**), / (**division**), % (**mod**, (**modulus** or **remainder**))

These operators work as follows:

- You can use the operators +, −, *, and / with both integral and floating-point data types.

  - The operators +, −, *, and / work with floating-point data types (decimal numbers), the same way you learned in a college algebra course.

  - The operators +, −, *, and / work with integral data types the same way you learned in a college algebra course.

- You use % with only the integral data type, to find the remainder in ordinary division.

- When you use / with the integral data type, it gives the quotient in ordinary division. That is, integral division truncates any fractional part; there is no rounding.

Example 2-3 shows how the operators / and % work with the integral data types.

EXAMPLE 2-3

Arithmetic Expression	Result	Description
5 / 2	2	In the division 5 / 2, the quotient is 2 and the remainder is 1. Therefore, 5 / 2 with the integral operands evaluates to the quotient, which is 2.
14 / 7	2	In the division 14 / 7, the quotient is 2.
34 % 5	4	In the division 34 / 5, the quotient is 6 and the remainder is 4. Therefore, 34 % 5 evaluates to the remainder, which is 4.
4 % 6	4	In the division 4 / 6, the quotient is 0 and the remainder is 4. Therefore, 4 % 6 evaluates to the remainder, which is 4.

In the following example, we illustrate how to use the operators / and % with integral data types.

EXAMPLE 2-4

Given length in inches, we write a program that determines and outputs the equivalent length in feet and (remaining) inches. Now there are 12 inches in a foot. Therefore, 100 inches equals 8 feet and 4 inches; similarly, 55 inches equals 4 feet and 7 inches. Note that 100 / 12 = 8 and 100 % 12 = 4; similarly, 55 / 12 = 4 and 55 % 12 = 7. From these examples, it follows that we can effectively use the operators / and % to accomplish our task. The desired program is as follows:

```cpp
// Given length in inches, this program outputs the equivalent
// length in feet and remaining inch(es).

#include <iostream>

using namespace std;

int main()
{
    int inches; //variable to store total inches

    inches = 100;  //store 100 in the variable inches

    cout << inches << " inch(es) = ";  //output the value of
                                //inches and the equal sign
    cout << inches / 12 << " feet (foot) and "; //output maximum
                                //number of feet (foot)
```

```
        cout << inches % 12 << " inch(es)" << endl; //output
                                //remaining inches
    return 0;
}
```

Sample run:

```
100 inch(es) = 8 feet (foot) and 4 inch(es)
```

Note that each time you run this program, it will output the value of 100 inches. To convert some other value of inches, you need to edit this program and store a different value in the variable inches, which is not very convenient. Later in this chapter we will illustrate how to include statements in a program that will instruct the user to enter different values. However, if you are curious to know at this point, then replace the statement

```
inches = 100;   //store 100 in the variable inches
```

with the following statements and rerun the program:

```
cout << "Enter total inches and press Enter: "; //prompt
                            //the user to enter total inches
cin >> inches;   //store the value entered by the user
                 //into the variable inches
cout << endl;
```

The modified program is available at the Web site accompanying this book and is named `Example2_4_Modified.cpp`.

Consider the following expressions, which you have been accustomed to working with since high school: –5, 8 – 7, 3 + 4, 2 + 3 * 5, 5.6 + 6.2 * 3, and x + 2 * 5 + 6 / y, where x and y are unknown numbers. These are examples of **arithmetic expressions**. The numbers appearing in the expressions are called **operands**. The numbers that are used to evaluate an operator are called the operands for that operator.

In expression –5, the symbol – specifies that the number 5 is negative. In this expression, – has only one operand. Operators that have only one operand are called **unary operators.**

In expression 8 – 7, the symbol – is used to subtract 7 from 8. In this expression, – has two operands, 8 and 7. Operators that have two operands are called **binary operators.**

Unary operator: An operator that has only one operand.

Binary operator: An operator that has two operands.

In expression 3 + 4, 3 and 4 are the operands for the operator +. In this expression, the operator + has two operands and is a binary operator. Moreover, in the expression +27, the operator + indicates that the number 27 is positive. Here, + has only one operand and so acts as a unary operator.

From the preceding discussion, it follows that – and + are both unary and binary arithmetic operators. However, as arithmetic operators, *, /, and % are binary and so must have two operands.

Order of Precedence

When more than one arithmetic operator is used in an expression, C++ uses the operator precedence rules to evaluate the expression. According to the order of precedence rules for arithmetic operators,

```
*,    /,    %
```

are at a higher level of precedence than

```
+,    -
```

Note that the operators *, /, and % have the same level of precedence. Similarly, the operators + and - have the same level of precedence.

When operators have the same level of precedence, the operations are performed from left to right. To avoid confusion, you can use parentheses to group arithmetic expressions. For example, using the order of precedence rules,

```
3 * 7 - 6 + 2 * 5 / 4 + 6
```

means the following:

```
    (((3 * 7) - 6) + ((2 * 5) / 4 )) + 6
=  ((21 - 6) + (10 / 4)) + 6     (Evaluate *)
=  ((21 - 6) + 2) + 6            (Evaluate /.   Note that this is an integer division.)
=  (15 + 2) + 6                  (Evaluate -)
=  17 + 6                        (Evaluate first +)
=  23                            (Evaluate +)
```

Note that the use of parentheses in the second example clarifies the order of precedence. You can also use parentheses to override the order of precedence rules.

Because arithmetic operators, using the precedence rules, are evaluated from left to right, unless parentheses are present, the **associativity** of the arithmetic operators is said to be from left to right.

NOTE (**Character Arithmetic**) Because the `char` data type is also an integral data type, C++ allows you to perform arithmetic operations on `char` data. However, you should use this ability carefully. There is a difference between the character `'8'` and the integer 8. The integer value of 8 is 8. The integer value of `'8'` is 56, which is the ASCII collating sequence of the character `'8'`.

When evaluating arithmetic expressions, $8 + 7 = 15$; `'8'` + `'7'` = 56 + 55, which yields 111; and `'8'` + 7 = 56 + 7, which yields 63. Furthermore, because `'8'` * `'7'` = 56 * 55 = 3080 and the ASCII character set has only 128 values, `'8'` * `'7'` is undefined in the ASCII character data set.

These examples illustrate that many things can go wrong when you are performing character arithmetic. If you must employ them, use arithmetic operations on the char data type with caution.

The following example shows how arithmetic operators work.

EXAMPLE 2-5

```
// This program illustrates how arithmetic operators work.

#include <iostream>

using namespace std;

int main()
{
    cout << "2 + 5 = " << 2 + 5 << endl;
    cout << "13 + 89 = " << 13 + 89 << endl;
    cout << "34 - 20 = " << 34 - 20 << endl;
    cout << "45 - 90 = " << 45 - 90 << endl;
    cout << "2 * 7 = " << 2 * 7 << endl;
    cout << "5 / 2 = " << 5 / 2 << endl;
    cout << "14 / 7 = " << 14 / 7 << endl;
    cout << "34 % 5 = " << 34 % 5 << endl;
    cout << "4 % 6 = " << 4 % 6 << endl << endl;

    cout << "5.0 + 3.5 = " << 5.0 + 3.5 << endl;
    cout << "3.0 + 9.4 = " << 3.0 + 9.4 << endl;
    cout << "16.3 - 5.2 = " << 16.3 - 5.2 << endl;
    cout << "4.2 * 2.5 = " << 4.2 * 2.5 << endl;
    cout << "5.0 / 2.0 = " << 5.0 / 2.0 << endl;
    cout << "34.5 / 6.0 = " << 34.5 / 6.0 << endl;
    cout << "34.5 / 6.5 = " << 34.5 / 6.5 << endl;

    return 0;
}
```

Sample Run:

```
2 + 5 = 7
13 + 89 = 102
34 - 20 = 14
45 - 90 = -45
2 * 7 = 14
5 / 2 = 2
14 / 7 = 2
34 % 5 = 4
4 % 6 = 4

5.0 + 3.5 = 8.5
3.0 + 9.4 = 12.4
16.3 - 5.2 = 11.1
4.2 * 2.5 = 10.5
5.0 / 2.0 = 2.5
34.5 / 6.0 = 5.75
34.5 / 6.5 = 5.30769
```

NOTE You should be careful when evaluating the mod operator with negative integer operands. You might not get the answer you expect. For example, −34 % 5 = −4, because in the division −34 / 5, the quotient is −6 and the remainder is −4. Similarly, 34 % −5 = 4, because in the division 34 / −5, the quotient is −6 and the remainder is 4. Also −34 % −5 = −4, because in the division −34 / −5, the quotient is 6 and the remainder is −4.

Expressions

There are three types of arithmetic expressions in C++:

- **Integral expressions**—all operands in the expression are integers. An integral expression yields an integral result.
- **Floating-point (decimal) expressions**—all operands in the expression are floating-points (decimal numbers). A floating-point expression yields a floating-point result.
- **Mixed expressions**—the expression contains both integers and decimal numbers.

Looking at some examples will help clarify these definitions.

EXAMPLE 2-6

Consider the following C++ integral expressions:

```
2 + 3 * 5
3 + x - y / 7
x + 2 * (y - z) + 18
```

In these expressions, **x**, **y**, and **z** represent variables of the integral type; that is, they can hold integer values.

EXAMPLE 2-7

Consider the following C++ floating-point expressions:

```
12.8 * 17.5 - 34.50
x * 10.5 + y - 16.2
```

Here, **x** and **y** represent variables of the floating-point type; that is, they can hold floating-point values.

Evaluating an integral or a floating-point expression is straightforward. As before, when operators have the same precedence, the expression is evaluated from left to right. You can always use parentheses to group operands and operators to avoid confusion.

Next, we discuss mixed expressions.

Mixed Expressions

An expression that has operands of different data types is called a **mixed expression**. A mixed expression contains both integers and floating-point numbers. The following expressions are examples of mixed expressions:

```
2 + 3.5
6 / 4 + 3.9
5.4 * 2 - 13.6 + 18 / 2
```

In the first expression, the operand + has one integer operand and one floating-point operand. In the second expression, both operands for the operator / are integers, the first operand of + is the result of 6 / 4, and the second operand of + is a floating-point number. The third example is an even more complicated mix of integers and floating-point numbers. The obvious question is: How does C++ evaluate mixed expressions?

Two rules apply when evaluating a mixed expression:

1. When evaluating an operator in a mixed expression:

    a. If the operator has the same types of operands (that is, either both integers or both floating-point numbers), the operator is evaluated according to the type of the operands. Integer operands thus yield an integer result; floating-point numbers yield a floating-point number.

    b. If the operator has both types of operands (that is, one is an integer and the other is a floating-point number), then during calculation, the integer is changed to a floating-point number with the decimal part of zero and the operator is evaluated. The result is a floating-point number.

2. The entire expression is evaluated according to the precedence rules; the multiplication, division, and modulus operators are evaluated before the addition and subtraction operators. Operators having the same level of precedence are evaluated from left to right. Grouping using parentheses is allowed for clarity.

From these rules, it follows that when evaluating a mixed expression, you concentrate on one operator at a time, using the rules of precedence. If the operator to be evaluated has operands of the same data type, evaluate the operator using Rule 1(a). That is, an operator with integer operands will yield an integer result, and an operator with floating-point operands will yield a floating-point result. If the operator to be evaluated has one integer operand and one floating-point operand, before evaluating this operator, convert the integer operand to a floating-point number with the decimal part of 0. The following examples show how to evaluate mixed expressions.

EXAMPLE 2-8

Mixed Expression	Evaluation	Rule Applied
3 / 2 + 5.5	= 1 + 5.5 = 6.5	3 / 2 = 1 (integer division; Rule 1(a)) (1 + 5.5 = 1.0 + 5.5 (Rule 1(b)) = 6.5)
15.6 / 2 + 5	= 7.8 + 5	15.6 / 2 = 15.6 / 2.0 (Rule 1(b)) = 7.8
	= 12.8	7.8 + 5 = 7.8 + 5.0 (Rule1(b)) = 12.8
4 + 5 / 2.0	= 4 + 2.5	5 / 2.0 = 5.0 / 2.0 (Rule1(b)) = 2.5
	= 6.5	4 + 2.5 = 4.0 + 2.5 (Rule1(b)) = 6.5
4 * 3 + 7 / 5 - 25.5	= 12+7/5 - 25.5 = 12 + 1 - 25.5 = 13 - 25.5 = -12.5	4 * 3 = 12 (Rule 1(a)) 7 / 5 = 1 (integer division; Rule 1(a)) 12 + 1 = 13 (Rule 1(a)) 13 - 25.5 = 13.0 - 25.5 (Rule 1(b)) = -12.5

The following C++ program evaluates the preceding expressions:

```
// This program illustrates how mixed expressions are evaluated.

#include <iostream>

using namespace std;

int main()
{
    cout << "3 / 2 + 5.5 = " << 3 / 2 + 5.5 << endl;
    cout << "15.6 / 2 + 5 = " << 15.6 / 2 + 5 << endl;
    cout << "4 + 5 / 2.0 = " << 4 + 5 / 2.0 << endl;
    cout << "4 * 3 + 7 / 5 - 25.5 = "
         << 4 * 3 + 7 / 5 - 25.5
         << endl;

    return 0;
}
```

Sample Run:

```
3 / 2 + 5.5 = 6.5
15.6 / 2 + 5 = 12.8
4 + 5 / 2.0 = 6.5
4 * 3 + 7 / 5 - 25.5 = -12.5
```

These examples illustrate that an integer is not converted to a floating-point number unless the operator to be evaluated has one integer and one floating-point operand.

Type Conversion (Casting)

In the previous section, you learned that when evaluating an arithmetic expression, if the operator has mixed operands, the integer value is changed to a floating-point value with the zero decimal part. When a value of one data type is automatically changed to another data type, an **implicit type coercion** is said to have occurred. As the examples in the preceding section illustrate, if you are not careful about data types, implicit type coercion can generate unexpected results.

To avoid implicit type coercion, C++ provides for explicit type conversion through the use of a cast operator. The **cast operator**, also called **type conversion** or **type casting**, takes the following form:

```
static_cast<dataTypeName>(expression)
```

First, the expression is evaluated. Its value is then converted to a value of the type specified by `dataTypeName`. In C++, `static_cast` is a reserved word.

When converting a floating-point (decimal) number to an integer using the cast operator, you simply drop the decimal part of the floating-point number. That is, the floating-point number is truncated. Example 2-9 shows how cast operators work. Be sure you understand why the last two expressions evaluate as they do.

EXAMPLE 2-9

Expression	Evaluates to
`static_cast<int>(7.9)`	7
`static_cast<int>(3.3)`	3
`static_cast<double>(25)`	25.0
`static_cast<double>(5+3)`	= `static_cast<double>(8)` = 8.0
`static_cast<double>(15) / 2`	= 15.0 / 2
	(because `static_cast<double>(15)` = 15.0)
	= 15.0 / 2.0 = 7.5
`static_cast<double>(15 / 2)`	= `static_cast<double>(7)` (because 15 / 2 = 7)
	= 7.0
`static_cast<int>(7.8 +` `static_cast<double>(15) / 2)`	= `static_cast<int>(7.8 + 7.5)`
	= `static_cast<int>(15.3)`
	= 15
`static_cast<int>(7.8 +` `static_cast<double>(15 / 2))`	= `static_cast<int>(7.8 + 7.0)`
	= `static_cast<int>(14.8)`
	= 14

The following C++ program evaluates the preceding expressions:

```cpp
// This program illustrates how explicit type conversion works.

#include <iostream>

using namespace std;

int main()
{
    cout << "static_cast<int>(7.9) = "
         << static_cast<int>(7.9)
         << endl;
    cout << "static_cast<int>(3.3) = "
         << static_cast<int>(3.3)
         << endl;
    cout << "static_cast<double>(25) = "
         << static_cast<double>(25)
         << endl;
    cout << "static_cast<double>(5 + 3) = "
         << static_cast<double>(5 + 3)
         << endl;
    cout << "static_cast<double>(15) / 2 = "
         << static_cast<double>(15) / 2
         << endl;
    cout << "static_cast<double>(15 / 2) = "
         << static_cast<double>(15 / 2)
         << endl;
    cout << "static_cast<int>(7.8 + static_cast<double>(15) / 2) = "
         << static_cast<int>(7.8 + static_cast<double>(15) / 2)
         << endl;
    cout << "static_cast<int>(7.8 + static_cast<double>(15 / 2)) = "
         << static_cast<int>(7.8 + static_cast<double>(15 / 2))
         << endl;

    return 0;
}
```

Sample Run:
```
static_cast<int>(7.9) = 7
static_cast<int>(3.3) = 3
static_cast<double>(25) = 25
static_cast<double>(5 + 3) = 8
static_cast<double>(15) / 2 = 7.5
static_cast<double>(15 / 2) = 7
static_cast<int>(7.8 + static_cast<double>(15) / 2) = 15
static_cast<int>(7.8 + static_cast<double>(15 / 2)) = 14
```

Note that the value of the expression static_cast<double>(25) is 25.0. However, it is output as 25 rather than 25.0. This is because we have not yet discussed how to output decimal numbers with 0 decimal parts to show the decimal point and the trailing zeros. Chapter 3 explains how to output decimal numbers in a desired format. Similarly, the output of other decimal numbers with zero decimal parts is without the decimal point and the 0 decimal part.

2

>
> **NOTE** In C++, the cast operator can also take the form `dataType(expression)`. This form is called C-like casting. For example, `double(5) = 5.0` and `int(17.6) = 17`. However, `static_cast` is more stable than C-like casting.

You can also use cast operators to explicitly convert `char` data values into `int` data values and `int` data values into `char` data values. To convert `char` data values into `int` data values, you use a collating sequence. For example, in the ASCII character set, `static_cast<int>('A')` is 65 and `static_cast<int>('8')` is 56. Similarly, `static_cast<char>(65)` is `'A'` and `static_cast<char>(56)` is `'8'`.

Earlier in this chapter, you learned how arithmetic expressions are formed and evaluated in C++. If you want to use the value of one expression in another expression, first you must save the value of the expression. There are many reasons to save the value of an expression. Some expressions are complex and may require a considerable amount of computer time to evaluate. By calculating the values once and saving them for further use, you not only save computer time and create a program that executes more quickly, you also avoid possible typographical errors. In C++, expressions are evaluated, and if the value is not saved, it is lost. That is, unless it is saved, the value of an expression cannot be used in later calculations. Later in this chapter, you will learn how to save the value of an expression and use it in subsequent calculations.

Before leaving the discussion of data types, let us discuss one more data type—`string`.

string Type

The data type `string` is a programmer-defined data type. It is not directly available for use in a program like the simple data types discussed earlier. To use this data type, you need to access program components from the library, which will be discussed later in this chapter. The data type `string` is a feature of ANSI/ISO Standard C++.

>
> **NOTE** Prior to the ANSI/ISO C++ language standard, the standard C++ library did not provide a `string` data type. Compiler vendors often supplied their own programmer-defined `string` type, and the syntax and semantics of string operations often varied from vendor to vendor.

A **string** is a sequence of zero or more characters. Strings in C++ are enclosed in double quotation marks. A string containing no characters is called a **null** or **empty** string. The following are examples of strings. Note that `""` is the empty string.

```
"William Jacob"
"Mickey"
""
```

Every character in a string has a relative position in the string. The position of the first character is 0, the position of the second character is 1, and so on. The length of a string is the number of characters in it.

EXAMPLE 2-10

String	Position of a Character in the String	Length of the String
"William Jacob"	Position of 'W' is 0. Position of the first 'i' is 1. Position of ' ' (the space) is 7. Position of 'J' is 8. Position of 'b' is 12.	13
"Mickey"	Position of 'M' is 0. Position of 'i' is 1. Position of 'c' is 2. Position of 'k' is 3. Position of 'e' is 4. Position of 'y' is 5.	6

When determining the length of a string, you must also count any spaces in the string. For example, the length of the following string is 22.

```
"It is a beautiful day."
```

The string type is very powerful and more complex than simple data types. It provides many operations to manipulate strings. For example, it provides operations to find the length of a string, extract part of a string, and compare strings. You will learn about this data over the next few chapters.

Variables, Assignment Statements, and Input Statements

As noted earlier, the main objective of a C++ program is to perform calculations and manipulate data. Recall that data must be loaded into main memory before it can be manipulated. In this section, you will learn how to put data into the computer's memory. Storing data in the computer's memory is a two-step process:

1. Instruct the computer to allocate memory.
2. Include statements in the program to put data into the allocated memory.

Allocating Memory with Constants and Variables

When you instruct the computer to allocate memory, you tell it not only what names to use for each memory location, but also what type of data to store in those memory locations. Knowing the location of data is essential, because data stored in one memory location might be needed at several places in the program. As you saw earlier, knowing what data type you have is crucial for performing accurate calculations. It is also critical to know whether your data needs to remain fixed throughout program execution or whether it should change.

NAMED CONSTANTS

Some data must stay the same throughout a program. For example, the pay rate is usually the same for all part-time employees. A conversion formula that converts inches into centimeters is fixed, because 1 inch is always equal to 2.54 centimeters. When stored in memory, this type of data needs to be protected from accidental changes during program execution. In C++, you can use a **named constant** to instruct a program to mark those memory locations in which data is fixed throughout program execution.

Named constant: A memory location whose content is not allowed to change during program execution.

To allocate memory, we use C++'s declaration statements. The syntax to declare a named constant is:

```
const dataType identifier = value;
```

In C++, `const` is a reserved word.

EXAMPLE 2-11

Consider the following C++ statements:

```
const double CONVERSION = 2.54;
const int NO_OF_STUDENTS = 20;
const char BLANK = ' ';
```

The first statement tells the compiler to allocate memory (eight bytes) to store a value of type `double`, call this memory space `CONVERSION`, and store the value 2.54 in it. Throughout a program that uses this statement, whenever the conversion formula is needed, the memory space `CONVERSION` can be accessed. The meaning of the other statements is similar.

Note that the identifier for a named constant is in uppercase letters. Even though there are no written rules, C++ programmers typically prefer to use uppercase letters to name a named constant. Moreover, if the name of a named constant is a combination of more than one word, called a *run-together word*, then the words are separated using an underscore. For example, in the preceding example, `NO_OF_STUDENTS` is a run-together word. (Also see the section Program Style and Form, later in this chapter, to properly structure a program.)

NOTE As noted earlier, the default type of floating-point numbers is `double`. Therefore, if you declare a named constant of type `float`, then you must specify that the value is of type `float` as follows:

```
const float CONVERSION = 2.54f;
```

Otherwise, the compiler will generate a warning message. Notice that `2.54f` says that it is a `float` value. Recall that the memory size for `float` values is four bytes; for `double` values, eight bytes. Because memory size is of little concern these days, as indicated earlier, we will mostly use the type `double` to work with floating-point values.

Using a named constant to store fixed data, rather than using the data value itself, has one major advantage. If the fixed data changes, you do not need to edit the entire program and change the old value to the new value wherever the old value is used. (For example, in the program that computes the sales tax, the sales tax rate may change.) Instead, you can make the change at just one place, recompile the program, and execute it using the new value throughout. In addition, by storing a value and referring to that memory location whenever the value is needed, you avoid typing the same value again and again and prevent accidental typos. If you misspell the name of the constant value's location, the computer will warn you through an error message, but it will not warn you if the value is mistyped.

VARIABLES

Earlier in this chapter, we introduced the term variable and how to declare it. We now review this concept and also give the general syntax to declare variables.

In some programs, data needs to be modified during program execution. For example, after each test, the average test score and the number of tests taken changes. Similarly, after each pay increase, the employee's salary changes. This type of data must be stored in those memory cells whose contents can be modified during program execution. In C++, memory cells whose contents can be modified during program execution are called variables.

Variable: A memory location whose content may change during program execution.

The syntax for declaring one variable or multiple variables is:

```
dataType identifier, identifier, . . .;
```

EXAMPLE 2-12

Consider the following statements:

```
double amountDue;
int counter;
char ch;
int x, y;
string name;
```

The first statement tells the compiler to allocate enough memory to store a value of the type **double** and call it **amountDue**. The second and third statements have similar conventions. The fourth statement tells the compiler to allocate two different memory spaces, each large enough to store a value of the type **int**; name the first memory space **x**; and name the second memory space **y**. The fifth statement tells the compiler to allocate memory space to store a string and call it **name**.

As in the case of naming named constants, there are no written rules for naming variables. However, C++ programmers typically use lowercase letters to declare variables. If a variable name is a combination of more than one word, then the first letter of each word, except the first word, is uppercase. (For example, see the variable **amountDue** in the preceding example.)

From now on, when we say "variable," we mean a variable memory location.

 NOTE In C++, you must declare all identifiers before you can use them. If you refer to an identifier without declaring it, the compiler will generate an error message (syntax error), indicating that the identifier is not declared. Therefore, to use either a named constant or a variable, you must first declare it.

Now that data types, variables, and constants have been defined and discussed, it is possible to offer a formal definition of simple data types. A data type is called **simple** if the variable or named constant of that type can store only one value at a time. For example, if **x** is an **int** variable, at a given time, only one value can be stored in **x**.

Putting Data into Variables

Now that you know how to declare variables, the next question is: How do you put data into those variables? In C++, you can place data into a variable in two ways:

1. Use C++'s assignment statement.
2. Use input (read) statements.

Assignment Statement

The assignment statement takes the following form:

```
variable = expression;
```

In an assignment statement, the value of the **expression** should match the data type of the **variable**. The expression on the right side is evaluated, and its value is assigned to the variable (and thus to a memory location) on the left side.

A variable is said to be **initialized** the first time a value is placed in the variable.

In C++, = is called the **assignment operator**.

EXAMPLE 2-13

Suppose you have the following variable declarations:

```
int num1, num2;
double sale;
char first;
string str;
```

Now consider the following assignment statements:

```
num1 = 4;
num2 = 4 * 5 - 11;
sale = 0.02 * 1000;
first = 'D';
str = "It is a sunny day.";
```

For each of these statements, the computer first evaluates the expression on the right and then stores that value in a memory location named by the identifier on the left. The first statement stores the value 4 in num1, the second statement stores 9 in num2, the third statement stores 20.00 in sale, and the fourth statement stores the character D in first. The fifth statement stores the string "It is a sunny day." in the variable str.

The following C++ program shows the effect of the preceding statements:

```
// This program illustrates how data in the variables are
// manipulated.

#include <iostream>
#include <string>

using namespace std;

int main()
{
    int num1, num2;
    double sale;
    char first;
    string str;

    num1 = 4;
    cout << "num1 = " << num1 << endl;

    num2 = 4 * 5 - 11;
    cout << "num2 = " << num2 << endl;

    sale = 0.02 * 1000;
    cout << "sale = " << sale << endl;
```

```
        first = 'D';
        cout << "first = " << first << endl;

        str = "It is a sunny day.";
        cout << "str = " << str << endl;

        return 0;
}
```

Sample Run:

```
num1 = 4
num2 = 9
sale = 20
first = D
str = It is a sunny day.
```

For the most part, the preceding program is straightforward. Let us take a look at the output statement:

```
cout << " num1 = " << num1 << endl;
```

This output statement consists of the string " num1 = ", the operator <<, and the variable num1. Here, first the value of the string " num1 = " is output, and then the value of the variable num1 is output. The meaning of the other output statements is similar.

A C++ statement such as

```
num = num + 2;
```

means "evaluate whatever is in num, add 2 to it, and assign the new value to the memory location num." The expression on the right side must be evaluated first; that value is then assigned to the memory location specified by the variable on the left side. Thus, the sequence of C++ statements:

```
num = 6;
num = num + 2;
```

and the statement:

```
num = 8;
```

both assign 8 to num. Note that if num has not been initialized, the statement num = num + 2 might give unexpected results and/or the complier might generate a warning message indicating that the variable has not been initialized.

The statement num = 5; is read as "num becomes 5" or "num gets 5" or "num is assigned the value 5." Reading the statement as "num equals 5" is incorrect, especially for statements such as num = num + 2;. Each time a new value is assigned to num, the old value is overwritten. (Recall that the equal sign in these statements is the assignment operator, not an indication of equality.)

EXAMPLE 2-14

Suppose that num1, num2, and num3 are `int` variables and the following statements are executed in sequence.

1. num1 = 18;
2. num1 = num1 + 27;
3. num2 = num1;
4. num3 = num2 / 5;
5. num3 = num3 / 4;

The following table shows the values of the variables after the execution of each statement. (A ? indicates that the value is unknown. The orange color in a box shows that the value of that variable is changed.)

	Values of the Variables			Explanation
Before Statement 1	? num1	? num2	? num3	
After Statement 1	18 num1	? num2	? num3	
After Statement 2	45 num1	? num2	? num3	num1 + 27 = 18 + 27 = 45. This value is assigned to num1, which replaces the old value of num1.
After Statement 3	45 num1	45 num2	? num3	Copy the value of num1 into num2.
After Statement 4	45 num1	45 num2	9 num3	num2 / 5 = 45 / 5 = 9. This value is assigned to num3. So num3 = 9.
After Statement 5	45 num1	45 num2	2 num3	num3 / 4 = 9 / 4 = 2. This value is assigned to num3, which replaces the old value of num3.

Thus, after the execution of the statement in Line 5, num1 = 45, num2 = 45, and num3 = 2.

Tracing values through a sequence, called a **walk-through**, is a valuable tool to learn and practice. Try it in the sequence above. You will learn more about how to walk through a sequence of C++ statements later in this chapter.

> **NOTE** Suppose that x, y, and z are `int` variables. The following is a legal statement in C++:
>
> ```
> x = y = z;
> ```
>
> In this statement, first the value of z is assigned to y, and then the new value of y is assigned to x. Because the assignment operator, =, is evaluated from right to left, the **associativity** of the **assignment operator** is said to be from right to left.

Saving and Using the Value of an Expression

Now that you know how to declare variables and put data into them, you can learn how to save the value of an expression. You can then use this value in a later expression without using the expression itself, thereby answering the question raised earlier in this chapter. To save the value of an expression and use it in a later expression, do the following:

1. Declare a variable of the appropriate data type. For example, if the result of the expression is an integer, declare an `int` variable.

2. Assign the value of the expression to the variable that was declared, using the assignment statement. This action saves the value of the expression into the variable.

3. Wherever the value of the expression is needed, use the variable holding the value. The following example further illustrates this concept.

EXAMPLE 2-15

Suppose that you have the following declaration:

```
int a, b, c, d;
int x, y;
```

Further suppose that you want to evaluate the expressions $-b + (b^2 - 4ac)$ and $-b - (b^2 - 4ac)$ and assign the values of these expressions to x and y, respectively. Because the expression $b^2 - 4ac$ appears in both expressions, you can first calculate the value of this expression and save its value in d. You can then use the value of d to evaluate the expressions, as shown by the following statements:

```
d = b * b - 4 * a * c;
x = -b + d;
y = -b - d;
```

Earlier, you learned that if a variable is used in an expression, the expression would yield a meaningful value only if the variable has first been initialized. You also learned that after declaring a variable, you can use an assignment statement to initialize it. It is possible to initialize and declare variables at the same time. Before we discuss how to use an input (read) statement, we address this important issue.

Declaring and Initializing Variables

When a variable is declared, C++ may not automatically put a meaningful value in it. In other words, C++ may not automatically initialize variables. For example, the `int` and `double` variables may not be initialized to 0, as happens in some programming languages. This does not mean, however, that there is no value in a variable after its declaration. When a variable is declared, memory is allocated for it.

Recall from Chapter 1 that main memory is an ordered sequence of cells, and each cell is capable of storing a value. Also, recall that the machine language is a sequence of 0s and 1s, or bits. Therefore, data in a memory cell is a sequence of bits. These bits are nothing but electrical signals, so when the computer is turned on, some of the bits are 1 and some are 0. The state of these bits depends on how the system functions. However, when you instruct the computer to store a particular value in a memory cell, the bits are set according to the data being stored.

During data manipulation, the computer takes the value stored in particular cells and performs a calculation. If you declare a variable and do not store a value in it, the memory cell still has a value—usually the value of the setting of the bits from their last use—and you have no way to know what this value is.

If you only declare a variable and do not instruct the computer to put data into the variable, the value of that variable is garbage. However, the computer does not warn us, regards whatever values are in memory as legitimate, and performs calculations using those values in memory. Using a variable in an expression without initializing it produces erroneous results. To avoid these pitfalls, C++ allows you to initialize variables while they are being declared. For example, consider the following C++ statements in which variables are first declared and then initialized:

```cpp
int first, second;
char ch;
double x;

first = 13;
second = 10;
ch = ' ';
x = 12.6;
```

You can declare and initialize these variables at the same time using the following C++ statements:

```cpp
int first = 13, second = 10;
char ch = ' ';
double x = 12.6;
```

The first C++ statement declares two `int` variables, `first` and `second`, and stores 13 in `first` and 10 in `second`. The meaning of the other statements is similar.

2

In reality, not all variables are initialized during declaration. It is the nature of the program or the programmer's choice that dictates which variables should be initialized during declaration. The key point is that all variables must be initialized before they are used.

Input (Read) Statement

Previously, you learned how to put data into variables using the assignment statement. In this section, you will learn how to put data into variables from the *standard input device*, using C++'s input (or read) statements.

 NOTE In most cases, the standard input device is the keyboard.

When the computer gets the data from the keyboard, the user is said to be acting interactively.

Putting data into variables from the standard input device is accomplished via the use of `cin` and the operator `>>`. The syntax of `cin` together with `>>` is:

```
cin >> variable >> variable ...;
```

This is called an **input (read)** statement. In C++, `>>` is called the **stream extraction operator**.

 NOTE In a syntax, the shading indicates the part of the definition that is optional. Furthermore, throughout this book, the syntax is enclosed in yellow boxes.

EXAMPLE 2-16

Suppose that `miles` is a variable of type `double`. Further suppose that the input is `73.65`. Consider the following statement:

```
cin >> miles;
```

This statement causes the computer to get the input, which is `73.65`, from the standard input device and stores it in the variable `miles`. That is, after this statement executes, the value of the variable `miles` is `73.65`.

Example 2-17 further explains how to input numeric data into a program.

EXAMPLE 2-17

Suppose we have the following statements:

```
int feet;
int inches;
```

Suppose the input is:

23 7

Next, consider the following statement:

```
cin >> feet >> inches;
```

This statement first stores the number 23 into the variable `feet` and then the number 7 into the variable `inches`. Notice that when these numbers are entered via the keyboard, they are separated with a blank. In fact, they can be separated with one or more blanks or lines or even the tab character.

The following C++ program shows the effect of the preceding input statements:

```cpp
// This program illustrates how input statements work.

#include <iostream>

using namespace std;

int main()
{
    int feet;
    int inches;

    cout << "Enter two integers separated by one or more spaces: ";
    cin >> feet >> inches;
    cout << endl;

    cout << "Feet = " << feet << endl;
    cout << "Inches = " << inches << endl;

    return 0;
}
```

Sample Run: In this sample run, the user input is shaded.

Enter two integers separated by one or more spaces: 23 7

Feet = 23
Inches = 7

The C++ program in Example 2-18 illustrates how to read strings and numeric data.

EXAMPLE 2-18

```cpp
// This program illustrates how to read strings and numeric data.

#include <iostream>
#include <string>

using namespace std;

int main()
{
    string firstName;                                 //Line 1
    string lastName;                                  //Line 2
    int age;                                          //Line 3
    double weight;                                    //Line 4

    cout << "Enter first name, last name, age, "
         << "and weight, separated by spaces."
         << endl;                                     //Line 5

    cin >> firstName >> lastName;                     //Line 6
    cin >> age >> weight;                             //Line 7

    cout << "Name: " << firstName << " "
         << lastName << endl;                         //Line 8

    cout << "Age: " << age << endl;                   //Line 9
    cout << "Weight: " << weight << endl;             //Line 10

    return 0;                                         //Line 11
}
```

Sample Run: In this sample run, the user input is shaded.

```
Enter first name, last name, age, and weight, separated by spaces.
Sheila Mann 23 120.5
Name: Sheila Mann
Age: 23
Weight: 120.5
```

The preceding program works as follows: The statements in Lines 1 to 4 declare the variables firstName and lastName of type string, age of type int, and weight of type double. The statement in Line 5 is an output statement and tells the user what to do. (Such output statements are called prompt lines.) As shown in the sample run, the input to the program is:

```
Sheila Mann 23 120.5
```

The statement in Line 6 first reads and stores the string Sheila into the variable firstName and then skips the space after Sheila and reads and stores the string Mann into the variable lastName. Next, the statement in Line 7 first skips the blank after Mann and reads and stores 23 into the variable age and then skips the blank after 23 and reads and stores 120.5 into the variable weight.

The statements in Lines 8, 9, and 10 produce the third, fourth, and fifth lines of the sample run.

 NOTE   During programming execution, if more than one value is entered in a line, these values must be separated by at least one blank or tab. Alternately, one value per line can be entered.

Variable Initialization

Remember, there are two ways to initialize a variable: by using the assignment statement and by using a read statement. Consider the following declaration:

```
int feet;
int inches;
```

Consider the following two sets of code:

(a)
```
feet = 35;
inches = 6;
cout << "Total inches = "
     << 12 * feet + inches;
```

(b)
```
cout << "Enter feet: ";
cin >> feet;
cout << endl;
cout << "Enter inches: ";
cin >> inches;
cout << endl;
cout << "Total inches = "
     << 12 * feet + inches;
```

In (a), feet and inches are initialized using assignment statements, and in (b), these variables are initialized using input statements. However, each time the code in (a) executes, feet and inches are initialized to the same value unless you edit the source code, change the value, recompile, and run. On the other hand, in (b), each time the program runs, you are prompted to enter values for feet and inches. Therefore, a read statement is much more versatile than an assignment statement.

Sometimes it is necessary to initialize a variable by using an assignment statement. This is especially true if the variable is used only for internal calculation and not for reading and storing data.

Recall that C++ does not automatically initialize variables when they are declared. Some variables can be initialized when they are declared, whereas others must be initialized using either an assignment statement or a read statement.

NOTE When the program is compiled, some of the newer IDEs might give warning messages if the program uses the value of a variable without first properly initializing that variable. In this case, if you ignore the warning and execute the program, the program might terminate abnormally with an error message.

 NOTE Suppose you want to store a character into a **char** variable using an input statement. During program execution, when you enter the character, you do not include the single quotes. For example, suppose that ch is a **char** variable. Consider the following input statement:

```
cin >> ch;
```

If you want to store K into ch using this statement, during program execution, you only enter K. Similarly, if you want to store a string into a **string** variable using an input statement, during program execution, you enter only the string without the double quotes.

EXAMPLE 2-19

This example further illustrates how assignment statements and input statements manipulate variables. Consider the following declarations:

```
int firstNum, secondNum;
double z;
char ch;
string name;
```

Also, suppose that the following statements execute in the order given:

```
 1.  firstNum = 4;
 2.  secondNum = 2 * firstNum + 6;
 3.  z = (firstNum + 1) / 2.0;
 4.  ch = 'A';
 5.  cin >> secondNum;
 6.  cin >> z;
 7.  firstNum = 2 * secondNum + static_cast<int>(z);
 8.  cin >> name;
 9.  secondNum = secondNum + 1;
10.  cin >> ch;
11.  firstNum = firstNum + static_cast<int>(ch);
12.  z = firstNum - z;
```

In addition, suppose the input is:

`8 16.3 Jenny D`

This line has four values, `8`, `16.3`, `Jenny`, and `D`, and each value is separated from the others by a blank.

Let's now determine the values of the declared variables after the last statement executes. To explicitly show how a particular statement changes the value of a variable, the values of the variables after each statement executes are shown. (In the following figures, a question mark [?] in a box indicates that the value in the box is unknown.)

Before statement 1 executes, all variables are uninitialized, as shown in Figure 2-4.

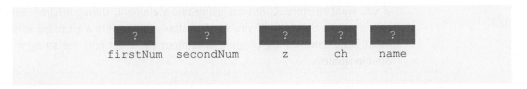

FIGURE 2-4 Variables before statement 1 executes

Next, we show the values of the variables after the execution of each statement.

After St.	Values of the Variables	Explanation
1	`4` firstNum, `?` secondNum, `?` z, `?` ch, `?` name	Store 4 into `firstNum`.
2	`4` firstNum, `14` secondNum, `?` z, `?` ch, `?` name	2 * firstNum + 6 = 2 * 4 + 6 = 14. Store 14 into `secondNum`.
3	`4` firstNum, `14` secondNum, `2.5` z, `?` ch, `?` name	(firstNum + 1) / 2.0 = (4 + 1) / 2.0 = 5 / 2.0 = 2.5. Store 2.5 into z.
4	`4` firstNum, `14` secondNum, `2.5` z, `A` ch, `?` name	Store 'A' into `ch`.
5	`4` firstNum, `8` secondNum, `2.5` z, `A` ch, `?` name	Read a number from the keyboard (which is 8) and store it into `secondNum`. This statement replaces the old value of `secondNum` with this new value.

2

After St.	Values of the Variables	Explanation
6	**16.3** `4` `firstNum` `8` `secondNum` **16.3** `z` `A` `ch` `?` `name`	Read a number from the keyboard (which is 16.3) and store this number into z. This statement replaces the old value of z with this new value.
7	**32** **32** `firstNum` `8` `secondNum` `16.3` `z` `A` `ch` `?` `name`	2 * secondNum + static_cast<int>(z) = 2 * 8 + static_cast<int> (16.3) = 16 + 16 = 32. Store 32 into firstNum. This statement replaces the old value of firstNum with this new value.
8	`32` `firstNum` `8` `secondNum` `16.3` `z` `A` `ch` **Jenny** `name`	Read the next input, Jenny, from the keyboard and store it into name.
9	`32` `firstNum` **9** `secondNum` `16.3` `z` `A` `ch` `Jenny` `name`	secondNum + 1 = 8 + 1 = 9. Store 9 into secondNum.
10	`32` `firstNum` `9` `secondNum` `16.3` `z` **D** `ch` `Jenny` `name`	Read the next input from the keyboard (which is D) and store it into ch. This statement replaces the old value of ch with the new value.
11	**100** `firstNum` `9` `secondNum` `16.3` `z` `D` `ch` `Jenny` `name`	firstNum + static_cast<int>(ch) = 32 + static_cast<int> ('D') = 32 + 68 = 100. Store 100 into firstNum.
12	`100` `firstNum` `9` `secondNum` **83.7** `z` `D` `ch` `Jenny` `name`	firstNum − z = 100 − 16.3 = 100.0 − 16.3 = 83.7. Store 83.7 into z.

NOTE When something goes wrong in a program and the results it generates are not what you expected, you should do a walk-through of the statements that assign values to your variables. Example 2-19 illustrates how to do a walk-through of your program. This is a very effective debugging technique. The Web site accompanying this book contains a C++ program that shows the effect of the 12 statements listed at the beginning of Example 2-19. The program is named Example 2_19.cpp.

NOTE If you assign the value of an expression that evaluates to a floating-point value—without using the cast operator—to a variable of type `int`, the fractional part is dropped. In this case, the compiler most likely will issue a warning message about the implicit type conversion.

Increment and Decrement Operators

Now that you know how to declare a variable and enter data into a variable, in this section, you will learn about two more operators: the **increment** and **decrement operators**. These operators are used frequently by C++ programmers and are useful programming tools.

Suppose `count` is an `int` variable. The statement:

```
count = count + 1;
```

increments the value of `count` by 1. To execute this assignment statement, the computer first evaluates the expression on the right, which is `count + 1`. It then assigns this value to the variable on the left, which is `count`.

As you will see in later chapters, such statements are frequently used to keep track of how many times certain things have happened. To expedite the execution of such statements, C++ provides the **increment operator**, `++`, which increases the value of a variable by 1, and the **decrement operator**, `--`, which decreases the value of a variable by 1. Increment and decrement operators each have two forms, pre and post. The syntax of the increment operator is:

Pre-increment: `++variable`
Post-increment: `variable++`

The syntax of the decrement operator is:

Pre-decrement: `--variable`
Post-decrement: `variable--`

Let's look at some examples. The statement:

```
++count;
```

or:

```
count++;
```

increments the value of `count` by 1. Similarly, the statement:

```
--count;
```

or:

```
count--;
```

decrements the value of `count` by 1.

Because both the increment and decrement operators are built into C++, the value of the variable is quickly incremented or decremented without having to use the form of an assignment statement.

Now, both the pre- and post-increment operators increment the value of the variable by 1. Similarly, the pre- and post-decrement operators decrement the value of the variable by 1. What is the difference between the pre and post forms of these operators? The difference becomes apparent when the variable using these operators is employed in an expression.

Suppose that x is an **int** variable. If ++x is used in an expression, first the value of x is incremented by 1, and then the new value of x is used to evaluate the expression. On the other hand, if x++ is used in an expression, first the current value of x is used in the expression, and then the value of x is incremented by 1. The following example clarifies the difference between the pre- and post-increment operators.

Suppose that x and y are **int** variables. Consider the following statements:

```
x = 5;
y = ++x;
```

The first statement assigns the value 5 to x. To evaluate the second statement, which uses the pre-increment operator, first the value of x is incremented to 6, and then this value, 6, is assigned to y. After the second statement executes, both x and y have the value 6.

Now, consider the following statements:

```
x = 5;
y = x++;
```

As before, the first statement assigns 5 to x. In the second statement, the post-increment operator is applied to x. To execute the second statement, first the value of x, which is 5, is used to evaluate the expression, and then the value of x is incremented to 6. Finally, the value of the expression, which is 5, is stored in y. After the second statement executes, the value of x is 6, and the value of y is 5.

The following example further illustrates how the pre and post forms of the increment operator work.

EXAMPLE 2-20

Suppose a and b are **int** variables and

```
a = 5;
b = 2 + (++a);
```

The first statement assigns 5 to a. To execute the second statement, first the expression 2 + (++a) is evaluated. Because the pre-increment operator is applied to a, first the value of a is incremented to 6. Then 2 is added to 6 to get 8, which is then assigned to b. Therefore, after the second statement executes, a is 6 and b is 8.

On the other hand, after the execution of the following statements:

```
a = 5;
b = 2 + (a++);
```

the value of a is 6 while the value of b is 7.

This book will most often use the increment and decrement operators with a variable in a stand-alone statement. That is, the variable using the increment or decrement operator will not be part of any expression.

Output

In the preceding sections, you have seen how to put data into the computer's memory and how to manipulate that data. We also used certain output statements to show the results on the *standard output device*. This section explains in some detail how to further use output statements to generate the desired results.

 NOTE The standard output device is usually the screen.

In C++, output on the standard output device is accomplished via the use of cout and the operator <<. The general syntax of cout together with << is:

```
cout << expression or manipulator << expression or manipulator...;
```

This is called an **output statement**. In C++, << is called the **stream insertion operator**. Generating output with cout follows two rules:

1. The expression is evaluated, and its value is printed at the current insertion point on the output device.

2. A manipulator is used to format the output. The simplest manipulator is endl (the last character is the letter el), which causes the insertion point to move to the beginning of the next line.

 NOTE On the screen, the insertion point is where the cursor is.

The next example illustrates how an output statement works. In an output statement, a string or an expression involving only one variable or a single value evaluates to itself.

NOTE   When an output statement outputs **char** values, it outputs only the character without the single quotes (unless the single quotes are part of the output statement).

For example, suppose ch is a **char** variable and ch = 'A';. The statement:

```
cout << ch;
```

or:

```
cout << 'A';
```

outputs:

A

Similarly, when an output statement outputs the value of a string, it outputs only the string without the double quotes (unless you include double quotes as part of the output).

EXAMPLE 2-21

Consider the following statements. The output is shown to the right of each statement.

	Statement	Output
1	cout << 29 / 4 << endl;	7
2	cout << "Hello there." << endl;	Hello there.
3	cout << 12 << endl;	12
4	cout << "4 + 7" << endl;	4 + 7
5	cout << 4 + 7 << endl;	11
6	cout << 'A' << endl;	A
7	cout << "4 + 7 = " << 4 + 7 << endl;	4 + 7 = 11
8	cout << 2 + 3 * 5 << endl;	17
9	cout << "Hello \nthere." << endl;	Hello
		there.

Look at the output of statement 9. Recall that in C++, the newline character is '\n'; it causes the insertion point to move to the beginning of the next line before printing there. Therefore, when \n appears in a string in an output statement, it causes the insertion point to move to the beginning of the next line on the output device. This fact explains why Hello and there. are printed on separate lines.

NOTE   In C++, \ is called the escape character and \n is called the newline escape sequence.

Recall that all variables must be properly initialized; otherwise, the value stored in them may not make much sense. Also recall that C++ does not automatically initialize variables.

If num is an **int** variable, then the output of the C++ statement:

```
cout << num << endl;
```

is meaningful provided that num has been given a value. For example, the sequence of C++ statements:

```
num = 45;
cout << num << endl;
```

will produce the output 45.

EXAMPLE 2-22

Consider the following C++ program:

```
// This program illustrates how output statements work.

#include <iostream>

using namespace std;

int main()
{
    int a, b;

    a = 65;                             //Line  1
    b = 78;                             //Line  2

    cout << 29 / 4 << endl;             //Line  3
    cout << 3.0 / 2 << endl;            //Line  4
    cout << "Hello there.\n";           //Line  5
    cout << 7 << endl;                  //Line  6
    cout << 3 + 5 << endl;              //Line  7
    cout << "3 + 5";                    //Line  8
    cout << " **";                      //Line  9
    cout << endl;                       //Line 10
    cout << 2 + 3 * 6 << endl;          //Line 11
    cout << "a" << endl;                //Line 12
    cout << a << endl;                  //Line 13
    cout << b << endl;                  //Line 14

    return 0;
}
```

In the following output, the column marked "Output of Statement at" and the line numbers are not part of the output. The line numbers are shown in this column to make it easy to see which output corresponds to which statement.

	Output of Statement at
7	Line 3
1.5	Line 4
Hello there.	Line 5
7	Line 6
8	Line 7
3 + 5 **	Lines 8 and 9
20	Line 11
a	Line 12
65	Line 13
78	Line 14

For the most part, the output is straightforward. Look at the output of the statements in Lines 7, 8, 9, and 10. The statement in Line 7 outputs the result of 3 + 5, which is 8, and moves the insertion point to the beginning of the next line. The statement in Line 8 outputs the string 3 + 5. Note that the statement in Line 8 consists only of the string 3 + 5. Therefore, after printing 3 + 5, the insertion point stays positioned after 5; it does not move to the beginning of the next line. Next the output of the statement in Line 9 outputs space and ** at the insertion point, which was positioned after 5.

The output statement in Line 10 contains only the manipulator endl, which moves the insertion point to the beginning of the next line. Therefore, when the statement in Line 11 executes, the output starts at the beginning of the line. Note that in this output, the column "Output of Statement at" does not contain Line 10. This is due to the fact that the statement in Line 10 does not produce any printable output. It simply moves the insertion point to the beginning of the next line. Next, the statement in Line 11 outputs the value of 2 + 3 * 6, which is 20. The manipulator endl then moves the insertion point to the beginning of the next line.

 NOTE   Outputting or accessing the value of a variable in an expression does not destroy or modify the contents of the variable.

Let us now take a close look at the newline character, '\n'. Consider the following C++ statements:

```
cout << "Hello there.";
cout << "My name is James.";
```

If these statements are executed in sequence, the output is:

```
Hello there.My name is James.
```

Now consider the following C++ statements:

```
cout << "Hello there.\n";
cout << "My name is James.";
```

The output of these C++ statements is:

```
Hello there.
My name is James.
```

When \n is encountered in the string, the insertion point is positioned at the beginning of the next line. Note also that \n may appear anywhere in the string. For example, the output of the statement:

```
cout << "Hello \nthere. \nMy name is James.";
```

is:

```
Hello
there.
My name is James.
```

Also, note that the output of the statement:

```
cout << '\n';
```

is the same as the output of the statement:

```
cout << "\n";
```

which is equivalent to the output of the statement:

```
cout << endl;
```

Thus, the output of the sequence of statements:

```
cout << "Hello there.\n";
cout << "My name is James.";
```

is equivalent to the output of the sequence of statements:

```
cout << "Hello there." << endl;
cout << "My name is James.";
```

EXAMPLE 2-23

Consider the following C++ statements:

```
cout << "Hello there.\nMy name is James.";
```

or:

```
cout << "Hello there.";
cout << "\nMy name is James.";
```

or:

```
cout << "Hello there.";
cout << endl << "My name is James.";
```

In each case, the output of the statements is:

```
Hello there.
My name is James.
```

2

EXAMPLE 2-24

The output of the C++ statements:

```
cout << "Count...\n....1\n.....2\n......3";
```

or:

```
cout << "Count..." << endl << "....1" << endl
     << ".....2" << endl << "......3";
```

is:

```
Count...
....1
.....2
......3
```

EXAMPLE 2-25

Suppose that you want to output the following sentence in one line as part of a message:

```
It is sunny, warm, and not a windy day. We can go golfing.
```

Obviously, you will use an output statement to produce this output. However, in the programming code, this statement may not fit in one line as part of the output statement. Of course, you can use multiple output statements as follows:

```
cout << "It is sunny, warm, and not a windy day. ";
cout << "We can go golfing." << endl;
```

Note the semicolon at the end of the first statement and the identifier cout at the beginning of the second statement. Also, note that there is no manipulator endl at the end of the first statement. Here, two output statements are used to output the sentence in one line. Equivalently, you can use the following output statement to output this sentence:

```
cout << "It is sunny, warm, and not a windy day. "
     << "We can go golfing." << endl;
```

In this statement, note that there is no semicolon at the end of the first line, and the identifier cout does not appear at the beginning of the second line. Because there is no semicolon at the end of the first line, this output statement continues at the second line. Also, note the double quotation marks at the beginning and end of the sentences on each line. The string is broken into two strings, but both strings are part of the same output statement.

If a string appearing in an output statement is long and you want to output the string in one line, you can break the string by using either of the previous two methods. However, the following statement would be incorrect:

```
cout << "It is sunny, warm, and not a windy day.
       We can go golfing." << endl;                              //illegal
```

In other words, the return (or Enter) key on your keyboard cannot be part of the string. That is, in programming code, a string *cannot* be broken into more than one line by using the return (Enter) key on your keyboard.

Recall that the newline character is \n, which causes the insertion point to move to the beginning of the next line. There are many escape sequences in C++, which allow you to control the output. Table 2-4 lists some of the commonly used escape sequences.

TABLE 2-4 Commonly Used Escape Sequences

	Escape Sequence	Description
\n	Newline	Cursor moves to the beginning of the next line
\t	Tab	Cursor moves to the next tab stop
\b	Backspace	Cursor moves one space to the left
\r	Return	Cursor moves to the beginning of the current line (not the next line)
\\	Backslash	Backslash is printed
\'	Single quotation	Single quotation mark is printed
\"	Double quotation	Double quotation mark is printed

The following example shows the effect of some of these escape sequences.

EXAMPLE 2-26

The output of the statement:

```
cout << "The newline escape sequence is \\n" << endl;
```

is:

```
The newline escape sequence is \n
```

The output of the statement:

```
cout << "The tab character is represented as \'\\t\'" << endl;
```

is:

```
The tab character is represented as '\t'
```

Note that the single quote can also be printed without using the escape sequence. Therefore, the preceding statement is equivalent to the following output statement:

```
cout << "The tab character is represented as '\\t'" << endl;
```

The output of the statement:

```
cout << "The string \"Sunny\" contains five characters." << endl;
```

is:

```
The string "Sunny" contains five characters.
```

 NOTE The Web site accompanying this text contains the C++ program that shows the effect of the statements in Example 2-26. The program is named `Example2_26.cpp`.

To use `cin` and `cout` in a program, you must include a certain header file. The next section explains what this header file is, how to include a header file in a program, and why you need header files in a program. Chapter 3 will provide a detailed explanation of `cin` and `cout`.

Preprocessor Directives

Only a small number of operations, such as arithmetic and assignment operations, are explicitly defined in C++. Many of the functions and symbols needed to run a C++ program are provided as a collection of libraries. Every library has a name and is referred to by a header file. For example, the descriptions of the functions needed to perform input/output (I/O) are contained in the header file `iostream`. Similarly, the descriptions of some very useful mathematical functions, such as power, absolute, and sine, are contained in the header file `cmath`. If you want to use I/O or math functions, you need to tell the computer where to find the necessary code. You use preprocessor directives and the names of header files to tell the computer the locations of the code provided in libraries. Preprocessor directives are processed by a program called a **preprocessor**.

Preprocessor directives are commands supplied to the preprocessor that cause the preprocessor to modify the text of a C++ program before it is compiled. All preprocessor commands begin with #. There are no semicolons at the end of preprocessor commands because they are not C++ statements. To use a header file in a C++ program, use the preprocessor directive `include`.

The general syntax to include a header file (provided by the IDE) in a C++ program is:

```
#include <headerFileName>
```

For example, the following statement includes the header file `iostream` in a C++ program:

```
#include <iostream>
```

Preprocessor directives to include header files are placed as the first line of a program so that the identifiers declared in those header files can be used throughout the program. (Recall that in C++, identifiers must be declared before they can be used.)

Certain header files are provided as part of C++. Appendix F describes some of the commonly used header files. Individual programmers can also create their own header files, which is discussed in the chapter Classes and Data Abstraction, later in this book.

Note that the preprocessor commands are processed by the preprocessor before the program goes through the compiler.

From Figure 1-3 (Chapter 1), we can conclude that a C++ system has three basic components: the program development environment, the C++ language, and the C++ library. All three components are integral parts of the C++ system. The program development environment consists of the six steps shown in Figure 1-3. As you learn the C++ language throughout the book, we will discuss components of the C++ library as we need them.

namespace and Using cin and cout in a Program

Earlier, you learned that both `cin` and `cout` are predefined identifiers. In ANSI/ISO Standard C++, these identifiers are declared in the header file `iostream`, but within a `namespace`. The name of this `namespace` is `std`. (The `namespace` mechanism will be formally defined and discussed in detail in Chapter 7. For now, you need to know only how to use `cin` and `cout` and, in fact, any other identifier from the header file `iostream`.)

There are several ways you can use an identifier declared in the namespace `std`. One way to use `cin` and `cout` is to refer to them as `std::cin` and `std::cout` throughout the program.

Another option is to include the following statement in your program:

```
using namespace std;
```

This statement should appear after the statement `#include <iostream>`. You can then refer to `cin` and `cout` without using the prefix `std::`. To simplify the use of `cin` and `cout`, this book uses the second form. That is, to use `cin` and `cout` in a program, the programs will contain the following two statements:

`#include <iostream>`

`using namespace std;`

In C++, `namespace` and `using` are reserved words.

The `namespace` mechanism is a feature of ANSI/ISO Standard C++. As you learn more C++ programming, you will become aware of other header files. For example, the header file `cmath` contains the specifications of many useful mathematical functions. Similarly, the header file `iomanip` contains the specifications of many useful functions and manipulators that help you format your output in a specific manner. However, just like the identifiers in the header file `iostream`, the identifiers in ANSI/ISO Standard C++ header files are declared within a `namespace`.

The name of the `namespace` in each of these header files is `std`. Therefore, whenever certain features of a header file in ANSI/ISO Standard C++ are discussed, this book will refer to the identifiers without the prefix `std::`. Moreover, to simplify the accessing of identifiers in programs, the statement `using namespace std;` will be included. Also, if a program uses multiple header files, only one `using` statement is needed. This `using` statement typically appears after all the header files.

Using the `string` Data Type in a Program

Recall that the `string` data type is a programmer-defined data type and is not directly available for use in a program. To use the `string` data type, you need to access its definition from the header file `string`. Therefore, to use the `string` data type in a program, you must include the following preprocessor directive:

`#include <string>`

Creating a C++ Program

In previous sections, you learned enough C++ concepts to write meaningful programs. You are now ready to create a complete C++ program.

A C++ program is a collection of functions, one of which is the function `main`. Therefore, if a C++ program consists of only one function, then it must be the function `main`. Moreover, a function is a set of instructions designed to accomplish a specific task. Until Chapter 6, you will deal mainly with the function `main`.

The statements to declare variables, the statements to manipulate data (such as assignments), and the statements to input and output data are placed within the function `main`. The statements to declare named constants are usually placed outside of the function `main`.

The syntax of the function `main` used throughout this book has the following form:

```
int main()
{
    statement_1
         .
         .
         .
    statement_n

    return 0;
}
```

In the syntax of the function `main`, each statement (`statement_1, ..., statement_n`) is usually either a declarative statement or an executable statement. The statement `return 0;` must be included in the function `main` and must be the last statement. If the statement `return 0;` is misplaced in the body of the function `main`, the results generated by the program may not be to your liking. The full meaning of the statement `return 0;` will be discussed in Chapter 6. For now, think of this statement as the end-of-program statement. In C++, `return` is a reserved word.

A C++ program might use the resources provided by the IDE, such as the necessary code to input the data, which would require your program to include certain header files. You can, therefore, divide a C++ program into two parts: preprocessor directives and the program. The preprocessor directives tell the compiler which header files to include in the program. The program contains statements that accomplish meaningful results. Taken together, the preprocessor directives and the program statements constitute the C++ **source code**. Recall that to be useful, source code must be saved in a file with the file extension `.cpp`. For example, if the source code is saved in the file `firstProgram`, then the complete name of this file is `firstProgram.cpp`. The file containing the source code is called the **source code file** or **source file**.

When the program is compiled, the compiler generates the object code, which is saved in a file with the file extension `.obj`. When the object code is linked with the system resources, the executable code is produced and saved in a file with the file extension `.exe`. Typically, the name of the file containing the object code and the name of the file containing the executable code are the same as the name of the file containing the source code. For example, if the source code is located in a file named `firstProg.cpp`, the name of the file containing the object code is `firstProg.obj`, and the name of the file containing the executable code is `firstProg.exe`.

The extensions as given in the preceding paragraph—that is, `.cpp`, `.obj`, and `.exe`—are system dependent. Moreover, some IDEs maintain programs in the form of projects. The name of the project and the name of the source file need not be the same. It is possible that the name of the executable file is the name of the project, with the extension `.exe`. To be certain, check your system or IDE documentation.

Because the programming instructions are placed in the function `main`, let us elaborate on this function.

The basic parts of the function `main` are the heading and the body. The first line of the function `main`, that is:

```
int main()
```

is called the heading of the function `main`.

The statements enclosed between the curly braces (`{` and `}`) form the body of the function `main`. The body of the function `main` contains two types of statements:

- Declaration statements
- Executable statements

Declaration statements are used to declare things, such as variables.

In C++, identifiers, such as variables, can be declared anywhere in the program, but they must be declared before they can be used.

EXAMPLE 2-27

The following statements are examples of variable declarations:

```
int a, b, c;
double x, y;
```

Executable statements perform calculations, manipulate data, create output, accept input, and so on.

Some executable statements that you have encountered so far are the assignment, input, and output statements.

EXAMPLE 2-28

The following statements are examples of executable statements:

```
a = 4;                          //assignment statement
cin >> b;                       //input statement
cout << a << " " << b << endl;  //output statement
```

In skeleton form, a C++ program looks like the following:

```
//comments, if needed

preprocessor directives to include header files

using statement

named constants, if necessary
```

```
int main()
{
    statement_1
        .
        .
        .
    statement_n

    return 0;
}
```

The C++ program in Example 2-29 shows where include statements, declaration statements, executable statements, and so on typically appear in the program.

EXAMPLE 2-29

```
//*************************************************************
// Author: D.S. Malik
//
// This program shows where the include statements, using
// statement, named constants, variable declarations, assignment
// statements, and input and output statements typically appear.
//*************************************************************

#include <iostream>                                   //Line 1

using namespace std;                                  //Line 2

const int NUMBER = 12;                                //Line 3

int main()                                            //Line 4
{                                                     //Line 5
    int firstNum;                                     //Line 6
    int secondNum;                                    //Line 7

    firstNum = 18;                                    //Line 8
    cout << "Line 9: firstNum = " << firstNum
        << endl;                                      //Line 9

    cout << "Line 10: Enter an integer: ";            //Line 10
    cin >> secondNum;                                 //Line 11
    cout << endl;                                     //Line 12

    cout << "Line 13: secondNum = " << secondNum
        << endl;                                      //Line 13

    firstNum = firstNum + NUMBER + 2 * secondNum;     //Line 14

    cout << "Line 15: The new value of "
        << "firstNum = " << firstNum << endl;         //Line 15

    return 0;                                         //Line 16
}                                                     //Line 17
```

Sample Run: In this sample run, the user input is shaded.

```
Line 9: firstNum = 18
Line 10: Enter an integer:  15

Line 13: secondNum = 15
Line 15: The new value of firstNum = 60
```

The preceding program works as follows: The statement in Line 1 includes the header file iostream so that program can perform input/output. The statement in Line 2 uses the `using namespace` statement so that identifiers declared in the header file iostream, such as cin, cout, and endl, can be used without using the prefix std::. The statement in Line 3 declares the named constant NUMBER and sets its value to 12. The statement in Line 4 contains the heading of the function main, and the left brace in Line 5 marks the beginning of the function main. The statements in Lines 6 and 7 declare the variables firstNum and secondNum.

The statement in Line 8 sets the value of firstNum to 18, and the statement in Line 9 outputs the value of firstNum. Next, the statement in Line 10 prompts the user to enter an integer. The statement in Line 11 reads and stores the integer into the variable secondNum, which is 15 in the sample run. The statement in Line 12 positions the cursor on the screen at the beginning of the next line. The statement in Line 13 outputs the value of secondNum. The statement in Line 14 evaluates the expression:

```
firstNum + NUMBER + 2 * secondNum
```

and assigns the value of this expression to the variable firstNum, which is 60 in the sample run. The statement in Line 15 outputs the new value of firstNum. The statement in Line 16 contains the `return` statement, which is the last executable statement. The right brace in Line 17 marks the end of the function main.

Debugging: Understanding and Fixing Syntax Errors

The previous sections of this chapter described the basic components of a C++ program. When you type a program, typos and unintentional syntax errors are likely to occur. Therefore, when you compile a program, the compiler will identify the syntax error. In this section, we show how to identify and fix syntax errors.

Consider the following C++ program:

```
1.  #include <iostream>
2.
3.  using namespace std;
4.
5.  int main()
```

```
6.   {
7.       int num
8.
9.       num = 18;
10.
11.      tempNum = 2 * num;
12.
13.      cout << "Num = " << num << ", tempNum = " < tempNum << endl;
14.
15.      return ;
16.  }
```

(Note that the numbers 1 to 16 on the left side are not part of the program. We have numbered the statements for easy reference.) This program contains syntax errors. When you compile this program, the compiler produces the following errors. (This program is compiled using Microsoft Visual Studio 2010.)

```
ExampleCh2_Syntax_Errors.cpp
c:\examplech2_syntax_errors.cpp(9): error C2146: syntax error : missing ';'
before identifier 'num'
c:\examplech2_syntax_errors.cpp(11): error C2065: 'tempNum' : undeclared identifier
c:\examplech2_syntax_errors.cpp(13): error C2065: 'tempNum' : undeclared identifier
c:\examplech2_syntax_errors.cpp(13): error C2563: mismatch in formal parameter list
c:\examplech2_syntax_errors.cpp(13): error C2568: '<<' : unable to resolve
function overload
        c:\program files\microsoft visual studio
10.0\vc\include\ostream(1021): could be 'std::basic_ostream<_Elem,_Traits>
&std::endl(std::basic_ostream<_Elem,_Traits> &)'
        with
        [
            _Elem=unsigned short,
            _Traits=std::char_traits<unsigned short>
        ]
        c:\program files\microsoft visual studio
10.0\vc\include\ostream(1011): or        'std::basic_ostream<_Elem,_Traits>
&std::endl(std::basic_ostream<_Elem,_Traits> &)'
        with
        [
            _Elem=wchar_t,
            _Traits=std::char_traits<wchar_t>
        ]
        c:\program files\microsoft visual studio
10.0\vc\include\ostream(1003): or        'std::basic_ostream<_Elem,_Traits>
&std::endl(std::basic_ostream<_Elem,_Traits> &)'
        with
        [
            _Elem=char,
            _Traits=std::char_traits<char>
        ]
```

```
            c:\program files\microsoft visual studio 10.0\vc\include\ostream(977):
or          'std::basic_ostream<_Elem,_Traits>
&std::endl(std::basic_ostream<_Elem,_Traits> &)'
c\examplech2_syntax_errors.cpp(15): error C2561: 'main' : function must return a
value
            c:\examplech2_syntax_errors.cpp(5) : see declaration of 'main'
```

It is best to try to correct the errors in top-down fashion because the first error may confuse the compiler and cause it to flag multiple subsequent errors when actually there was only one error on an earlier line. So, let's first consider the following error:

```
c:\examplech2_syntax_errors.cpp(9): error C2146: syntax error : missing ';'
before identifier 'num'
```

The expression `examplech2_syntax_errors.cpp(9)` indicates that there is an error in Line 9. The remaining part of this error specifies that there is a missing *;* before the identifier num. If we look at Line 7, we find that there is a missing semicolon at the end of the statement `int` num. Therefore, we must insert *;* at the end of the statement in Line 7.

Next, consider the second error:

```
c:\examplech2_syntax_errors.cpp(11): error C2065: 'tempNum' : undeclared identifier
```

This error occurs in Line 11, and it specifies that the identifier tempNum is undeclared. When we look at the code, we find that this identifier has not been declared. So we must declare tempNum as an `int` variable.

The error:

```
c:\examplech2_syntax_errors.cpp(11): error C2065: 'tempNum' : undeclared identifier
```

occurs in Line 13, and it specifies that the identifier tempNum is undeclared. As in the previous error, we must declare tempNum. Note that once we declare tempNum and recompile, this and the previous error will disappear.

The next error is:

```
c:\examplech2_syntax_errors.cpp(13): error C2563: mismatch in formal parameter list
```

This error occurs in Line 13, and it indicates that some formal parameter list is mismatched. For a beginner, this error is somewhat hard to understand. (In Chapter 13, we will explain the formal parameter list of the operator <<.) However, as you practice, you will learn how to interpret and correct syntax errors. This error becomes clear if you look at the next error, the part of which is:

```
c:\examplech2_syntax_errors.cpp(13):  error  C2568:  '<<'  :  unable  to  resolve
function overload
```

It tells us that this error has something to do with the operator <<. When we carefully look at the statement in Line 13, which is:

```
cout << "Num = " << num << ", tempNum = " < tempNum << endl;
```

we find that in the expression `< tempNum`, we have unintentionally used < in place of <<. So we must correct this error.

Let us look at the last error, which is:

```
c\examplech2_syntax_errors.cpp(15): error C2561: 'main' : function must return a value
      c:\examplech2_syntax_errors.cpp(5) : see declaration of 'main'
```

This error occurs in Line 15. However, at this point, the explanation given, especially for a beginner, is somewhat unclear. However, if you look at the statement `return ;` in Line 15 and remember the syntax of the function `main` as well as all the programs given in this book, we find that the number 0 is missing, that is, this statement must be `return 0;`.

From the errors reported by the compiler, we see that the compiler not only identifies the errors, but it also specifies the line numbers where the errors occur and the types of the errors. We can effectively use this information to fix syntax errors.

After correcting all of the syntax errors, a correct program is:

```cpp
#include <iostream>

using namespace std;

int main()
{
    int num;
    int tempNum;

    num = 18;

    tempNum = 2 * num;

    cout << "Num = " << num << ", tempNum = " << tempNum << endl;

    return 0;
}
```

The output is:

```
Num = 18, tempNum = 36
```

As you learn C++ and practice writing and executing programs, you will learn how to spot and fix syntax errors. It is possible that the list of errors reported by the compiler is longer than the program itself. This is because, as indicated above, a syntax error in one line can cause syntax errors in subsequent lines. In situations like this, correct the syntax errors in the order they are listed and compile your program, if necessary, after each correction. You will see how quickly the syntax errors list shrinks. The important thing is not to panic.

In the next section, we describe some simple rules that you can follow so that your program is properly structured.

2

Program Style and Form

In previous sections, you learned enough C++ concepts to write meaningful programs. Before beginning to write programs, however, you need to learn their proper structure, among other things. Using the proper structure for a C++ program makes it easier to understand and subsequently modify the program. There is nothing more frustrating than trying to follow and perhaps modify a program that is syntactically correct but has no structure.

In addition, every C++ program must satisfy certain rules of the language. A C++ program must contain the function main. It must also follow the syntax rules, which, like grammar rules, tell what is right and what is wrong and what is legal and what is illegal in the language. Other rules serve the purpose of giving precise meaning to the language; that is, they support the language's semantics.

The following sections are designed to help you learn how to use the C++ programming elements you have learned so far to create a functioning program. These sections cover the syntax; the use of blanks; the use of semicolons, brackets, and commas; semantics; naming identifiers; prompt lines; documentation, including comments; and form and style.

Syntax

The syntax rules of a language tell what is legal and what is not legal. Errors in syntax are detected during compilation. For example, consider the following C++ statements:

```
int x;          //Line 1
int y           //Line 2
double z;       //Line 3

y = w + x;      //Line 4
```

When these statements are compiled, a compilation error will occur at Line 2 because the semicolon is missing after the declaration of the variable y. A second compilation error will occur at Line 4 because the identifier w is used but has not been declared.

As discussed in Chapter 1, you enter a program into the computer by using a text editor. When the program is typed, errors are almost unavoidable. Therefore, when the program is compiled, you are most likely to see syntax errors. It is quite possible that a syntax error at a particular place might lead to syntax errors in several subsequent statements. It is very common for the omission of a single character to cause four or five error messages. However, when the first syntax error is removed and the program is recompiled, subsequent syntax errors caused by this syntax error may disappear. Therefore, you should correct syntax errors in the order in which the compiler lists them. As you become more familiar and experienced with C++, you will learn how to quickly spot and fix syntax errors. Also, compilers not only discover syntax errors, but also hint and sometimes tell the user where the syntax errors are and how to fix them.

Use of Blanks

In C++, you use one or more blanks to separate numbers when data is input. Blanks are also used to separate reserved words and identifiers from each other and from other symbols. Blanks must never appear within a reserved word or identifier.

Use of Semicolons, Brackets, and Commas

All C++ statements must end with a semicolon. The semicolon is also called a **statement terminator**.

Note that curly braces, { and }, are not C++ statements in and of themselves, even though they often appear on a line with no other code. You might regard brackets as delimiters, because they enclose the body of a function and set it off from other parts of the program. Brackets have other uses, which will be explained in Chapter 4.

Recall that commas are used to separate items in a list. For example, you use commas when you declare more than one variable following a data type.

Semantics

The set of rules that gives meaning to a language is called **semantics**. For example, the order-of-precedence rules for arithmetic operators are semantic rules.

If a program contains syntax errors, the compiler will warn you. What happens when a program contains semantic errors? It is quite possible to eradicate all syntax errors in a program and still not have it run. And if it runs, it may not do what you meant it to do. For example, the following two lines of code are both syntactically correct expressions, but they have different meanings:

```
2 + 3 * 5
```

and:

```
(2 + 3) * 5
```

If you substitute one of these lines of code for the other in a program, you will not get the same results—even though the numbers are the same, the semantics are different. You will learn about semantics throughout this book.

Naming Identifiers

Consider the following two sets of statements:

```
const double A = 2.54;      //conversion constant
double x;                   //variable to hold centimeters
double y;                   //variable to hold inches

x = y * a;
```

and

```
const double CENTIMETERS_PER_INCH = 2.54;
double centimeters;
double inches;

centimeters = inches * CENTIMETERS_PER_INCH;
```

The identifiers in the second set of statements, such as CENTIMETERS_PER_INCH, are usually called **self-documenting** identifiers. As you can see, self-documenting identifiers can make comments less necessary.

Consider the self-documenting identifier annualsale. This identifier is called a **run-together word**. In using self-documenting identifiers, you may inadvertently include run-together words, which may lessen the clarity of your documentation. You can make run-together words easier to understand by either capitalizing the beginning of each new word or by inserting an underscore just before a new word. For example, you could use either annualSale or annual_sale to create an identifier that is more clear.

Recall that earlier in this chapter, we specified the general rules for naming named constants and variables. For example, an identifier used to name a named constant is all uppercase. If this identifier is a run-together word, then the words are separated with the underscore character.

Prompt Lines

Part of good documentation is the use of clearly written prompts so that users will know what to do when they interact with a program. There is nothing more frustrating than sitting in front of a running program and not having the foggiest notion of whether to enter something or what to enter. **Prompt lines** are executable statements that inform the user what to do. For example, consider the following C++ statements, in which num is an **int** variable:

```
cout << "Please enter a number between 1 and 10 and "
     << "press the return key" << endl;
cin >> num;
```

When these two statements execute in the order given, first the output statement causes the following line of text to appear on the screen:

```
Please enter a number between 1 and 10 and press the return key
```

After seeing this line, users know that they must enter a number and press the return key. If the program contained only the second statement, users would have no idea that they must enter a number, and the computer would wait forever for the input. The preceding output statement is an example of a prompt line.

In a program, whenever input is needed from users, you must include the necessary prompt lines. Furthermore, these prompt lines should include as much information as possible about what input is acceptable. For example, the preceding prompt line not only tells the user to input a number, but also informs the user that the number should be between 1 and 10.

Documentation

The programs that you write should be clear not only to you, but also to anyone else. Therefore, you must properly document your programs. A well-documented program is easier to understand and modify, even a long time after you originally wrote it. You use comments to document programs. Comments should appear in a program to explain the purpose of the program, identify who wrote it, and explain the purpose of particular statements.

Form and Style

You might be thinking that C++ has too many rules. However, in practice, the rules give C++ a great degree of freedom. For example, consider the following two ways of declaring variables:

```
int feet, inch;
double x, y;
```

and

```
int feet,inches;double x,y;
```

The computer would have no difficulty understanding either of these formats, but the first form is easier to read and follow. Of course, the omission of a single comma or semicolon in either format may lead to all sorts of strange error messages.

What about blank spaces? Where are they significant and where are they meaningless? Consider the following two statements:

```
int a,b,c;
```

and

```
int    a,    b,    c;
```

Both of these declarations mean the same thing. Here, the blanks between the identifiers in the second statement are meaningless. On the other hand, consider the following statement:

```
inta,b,c;
```

This statement contains a syntax error. The lack of a blank between `int` and the identifier a changes the reserved word `int` and the identifier a into a new identifier, `inta`.

The clarity of the rules of syntax and semantics frees you to adopt formats that are pleasing to you and easier to understand.

The following example further elaborates on this.

EXAMPLE 2-30

Consider the following C++ program:

```
//An improperly formatted C++ program.

#include <iostream>
#include <string>
using namespace std;

int main()
{
int num; double height;
string name;
cout << "Enter an integer: "; cin >> num; cout << endl;
    cout<<"num: "<<num<<endl;
cout<<"Enter the first name: "; cin>>name;
    cout<<endl; cout <<"Enter the height: ";
cin>>height; cout<<endl;

cout<<"Name: "<<name<<endl;cout<<"Height: "
<<height; cout <<endl;return 0;
}
```

This program is syntactically correct; the C++ compiler would have no difficulty reading and compiling this program. However, this program is very hard to read. The program that you write should be properly indented and formatted. Note the difference when the program is reformatted:

```
//A properly formatted C++ program.

#include <iostream>
#include <string>

using namespace std;

int main()
{
    int num;
    double height;
    string name;

    cout << "Enter an integer: ";
    cin >> num;
    cout << endl;
```

```
        cout << "num: " << num << endl;

        cout << "Enter the first name: ";
        cin >> name;
        cout << endl;
        cout << "Enter the height: ";
        cin >> height;
        cout << endl;

        cout << "Name: " << name << endl;
        cout << "Height: " << height << endl;

        return 0;
}
```

As you can see, this program is easier to read. Your programs should be properly indented and formatted. To document the variables, programmers typically declare one variable per line. Also, always put a space before and after an operator. When you type your program using an IDE, typically, your program is automatically indented.

More on Assignment Statements

The assignment statements you have seen so far are called **simple assignment statements**. In certain cases, you can use special assignment statements called **compound assignment statements** to write simple assignment statements in a more concise notation.

Corresponding to the five arithmetic operators +, -, *, /, and %, C++ provides five compound operators: +=, -=, *=, /=, and %=, respectively. Consider the following simple assignment statement, in which x and y are **int** variables:

```
x = x * y;
```

Using the compound operator *=, this statement can be written as:

```
x *= y;
```

In general, using the compound operator *=, you can rewrite the simple assignment statement:

```
variable = variable * (expression);
```

as:

```
variable *= expression;
```

The other arithmetic compound operators have similar conventions. For example, using the compound operator +=, you can rewrite the simple assignment statement:

```
variable = variable + (expression);
```

as:

```
variable += expression;
```

The compound assignment statement allows you to write simple assignment statements in a concise fashion by combining an arithmetic operator with the assignment operator.

EXAMPLE 2-31

This example shows several compound assignment statements that are equivalent to simple assignment statements.

Simple Assignment Statement	Compound Assignment Statement
`i = i + 5;`	`i += 5;`
`counter = counter + 1;`	`counter += 1;`
`sum = sum + number;`	`sum += number;`
`amount = amount * (interest + 1);`	`amount *= interest + 1;`
`x = x / ( y + 5);`	`x /= y + 5;`

NOTE Any compound assignment statement can be converted into a simple assignment statement. However, a simple assignment statement may not be (easily) converted to a compound assignment statement. For example, consider the following simple assignment statement:

```
x = x * y + z - 5;
```

To write this statement as a compound assignment statement, the variable x must be a common factor in the right side, which is not the case. Therefore, you cannot immediately convert this statement into a compound assignment statement. In fact, the equivalent compound assignment statement is:

```
x *=  y + (z - 5)/x;
```

which is more complicated than the simple assignment statement. Furthermore, in the preceding compound statement, x cannot be 0. We recommend avoiding such compound expressions.

 NOTE In programming code, this book typically uses only the compound operator +=. So statements such as a = a + b; are written as a += b;.

PROGRAMMING EXAMPLE: Convert Length

Watch the Video

Write a program that takes as input given lengths expressed in feet and inches. The program should then convert and output the lengths in centimeters. Assume that the given lengths in feet and inches are integers.

Input   Length in feet and inches.

Output   Equivalent length in centimeters.

PROBLEM ANALYSIS AND ALGORITHM DESIGN

The lengths are given in feet and inches, and you need to find the equivalent length in centimeters. One inch is equal to 2.54 centimeters. The first thing the program needs to do is convert the length given in feet and inches to all inches. Then, you can use the conversion formula, 1 inch = 2.54 centimeters, to find the equivalent length in centimeters. To convert the length from feet and inches to inches, you multiply the number of feet by 12, as 1 foot is equal to 12 inches, and add the given inches.

For example, suppose the input is 5 feet and 7 inches. You then find the total inches as follows:

```
totalInches = (12 * feet) + inches
            = 12 * 5 + 7
            = 67
```

You can then apply the conversion formula, 1 inch = 2.54 centimeters, to find the length in centimeters.

```
centimeters = totalInches * 2.54
            = 67 * 2.54
            = 170.18
```

Based on this analysis of the problem, you can design an algorithm as follows:

1. Get the length in feet and inches.
2. Convert the length into total inches.
3. Convert total inches into centimeters.
4. Output centimeters.

Variables

The input for the program is two numbers: one for feet and one for inches. Thus, you need two variables: one to store feet and the other to store inches. Because the program will first convert the given length into inches, you need another variable to store the total inches. You also need a variable to store the equivalent length in centimeters. In summary, you need the following variables:

```
int feet;            //variable to hold given feet
int inches;          //variable to hold given inches
int totalInches;     //variable to hold total inches
double centimeters;  //variable to hold length in centimeters
```

2

Named
Constants

To calculate the equivalent length in centimeters, you need to multiply the total inches by 2.54. Instead of using the value 2.54 directly in the program, you will declare this value as a named constant. Similarly, to find the total inches, you need to multiply the feet by 12 and add the inches. Instead of using 12 directly in the program, you will also declare this value as a named constant. Using a named constant makes it easier to modify the program later.

```
const double CENTIMETERS_PER_INCH = 2.54;
const int INCHES_PER_FOOT = 12;
```

MAIN
ALGORITHM

In the preceding sections, we analyzed the problem and determined the formulas to do the calculations. We also determined the necessary variables and named constants. We can now expand the algorithm given in the section Problem Analysis and Algorithm Design to solve the problem given at the beginning of this programming example.

1. Prompt the user for the input. (Without a prompt line, the user will be staring at a blank screen and will not know what to do.)

2. Get the data.

3. Echo the input—that is, output what the program read as input. (Without this step, after the program has executed, you will not know what the input was.)

4. Find the length in inches.

5. Output the length in inches.

6. Convert the length to centimeters.

7. Output the length in centimeters.

Putting It
Together

Now that the problem has been analyzed and the algorithm has been designed, the next step is to translate the algorithm into C++ code. Because this is the first complete C++ program you are writing, let's review the necessary steps in sequence.

The program will begin with comments that document its purpose and functionality. As there is both input to this program (the length in feet and inches) and output (the equivalent length in centimeters), you will be using system resources for input/output. In other words, the program will use input statements to get data into the program and output statements to print the results. Because the data will be entered from the keyboard and the output will be displayed on the screen, the program must include the header file iostream. Thus, the first statement of the program, after the comments as described above, will be the preprocessor directive to include this header file.

This program requires two types of memory locations for data manipulation: named constants and variables. Typically, named constants hold special data, such as CENTIMETERS_PER_INCH. Depending on the nature of a named constant, it can be placed before the function main or within the function main. If a named constant is to be used throughout the program, then it is typically placed before the function `main`. We will comment further on where to put named constants within a program in Chapter 6, when we discuss user-defined functions in general. Until then, usually, we will place named constants before the function `main` so that they can be used throughout the program.

This program has only one function, the function `main`, which will contain all of the programming instructions in its body. In addition, the program needs variables to manipulate data, and these variables will be declared in the body of the function `main`. The reasons for declaring variables in the body of the function `main` are explained in Chapter 6. The body of the function `main` will also contain the C++ statements that implement the algorithm. Therefore, the body of the function `main` has the following form:

```
int main()
{
    declare variables

    statements

    return 0;
}
```

To write the complete length conversion program, follow these steps:

1. Begin the program with comments for documentation.
2. Include header files, if any are used in the program.
3. Declare named constants, if any.
4. Write the definition of the function `main`.

COMPLETE PROGRAM LISTING

```
//*********************************************************
// Author: D. S. Malik
//
// Program Convert Measurements: This program converts
// measurements in feet and inches into centimeters using
// the formula that 1 inch is equal to 2.54 centimeters.
//*********************************************************

    //Header file
#include <iostream>

using namespace std;

    //Named constants
const double CENTIMETERS_PER_INCH = 2.54;
const int INCHES_PER_FOOT = 12;
```

```
int main ()
{
        //Declare variables
    int feet, inches;
    int totalInches;
    double centimeter;

        //Statements: Step 1 - Step 7
    cout << "Enter two integers, one for feet and "
        << "one for inches: ";                        //Step 1
    cin >> feet >> inches;                            //Step 2
    cout << endl;
    cout << "The numbers you entered are " << feet
        << " for feet and " << inches
        << " for inches. " << endl;                   //Step 3

    totalInches = INCHES_PER_FOOT * feet + inches;    //Step 4

    cout << "The total number of inches = "
        << totalInches << endl;                       //Step 5

    centimeter = CENTIMETERS_PER_INCH * totalInches;  //Step 6

    cout << "The number of centimeters = "
        << centimeter << endl;                        //Step 7

    return 0;
}
```

Sample Run: In this sample run, the user input is shaded.

```
Enter two integers, one for feet, one for inches: 15 7

The numbers you entered are 15 for feet and 7 for inches.
The total number of inches = 187
The number of centimeters = 474.98
```

PROGRAMMING EXAMPLE: Make Change

Write a program that takes as input any change expressed in cents. It should then compute the number of half-dollars, quarters, dimes, nickels, and pennies to be returned, returning as many half-dollars as possible, then quarters, dimes, nickels, and pennies, in that order. For example, 483 cents should be returned as 9 half-dollars, 1 quarter, 1 nickel, and 3 pennies.

Input   Change in cents.

Output   Equivalent change in half-dollars, quarters, dimes, nickels, and pennies.

PROBLEM
ANALYSIS
AND
ALGORITHM
DESIGN

Suppose the given change is 646 cents. To find the number of half-dollars, you divide 646 by 50, the value of a half-dollar, and find the quotient, which is 12, and the remainder, which is 46. The quotient, 12, is the number of half-dollars, and the remainder, 46, is the remaining change.

Next, divide the remaining change by 25 to find the number of quarters. Since the remaining change is 46, division by 25 gives the quotient 1, which is the number of quarters, and a remainder of 21, which is the remaining change. This process continues for dimes and nickels. To calculate the remainder in an integer division, you use the mod operator, %.

Applying this discussion to 646 cents yields the following calculations:

1. Change = 646
2. Number of half-dollars = 646 / 50 = 12
3. Remaining change = 646 % 50 = 46
4. Number of quarters = 46 / 25 = 1
5. Remaining change = 46 % 25 = 21
6. Number of dimes = 21 / 10 = 2
7. Remaining change = 21 % 10 = 1
8. Number of nickels = 1 / 5 = 0
9. Number of pennies = remaining change = 1 % 5 = 1

This discussion translates into the following algorithm:

1. Get the change in cents.
2. Find the number of half-dollars.
3. Calculate the remaining change.
4. Find the number of quarters.
5. Calculate the remaining change.
6. Find the number of dimes.
7. Calculate the remaining change.
8. Find the number of nickels.
9. Calculate the remaining change, which is the number of pennies.

Variables From the previous discussion and algorithm, it appears that the program will need variables to hold the number of half-dollars, quarters, and so on. However, the numbers of half-dollars, quarters, and so on are not used in later calculations, so the program can simply output these values without saving each of them in a variable. The only thing that keeps changing is the change, so the program actually needs only one variable:

```
int change;
```

Named
Constants

To calculate the equivalent change, the program performs calculations using the values of a half-dollar, which is 50; a quarter, which is 25; a dime, which is 10; and a nickel, which is 5. Because these data are special and the program uses these values more than once, it makes sense to declare them as named constants. Using named constants also simplifies later modification of the program:

```
const int HALF_DOLLAR = 50;
const int QUARTER  = 25;
const int DIME = 10;
const int NICKEL = 5;
```

MAIN
ALGORITHM

1. Prompt the user for input.
2. Get input.
3. Echo the input by displaying the entered change on the screen.
4. Compute and print the number of half-dollars.
5. Calculate the remaining change.
6. Compute and print the number of quarters.
7. Calculate the remaining change.
8. Compute and print the number of dimes.
9. Calculate the remaining change.
10. Compute and print the number of nickels.
11. Calculate the remaining change.
12. Print the remaining change.

COMPLETE PROGRAM LISTING

```
//************************************************************
// Author: D. S. Malik
//
// Program Make Change: Given any amount of change expressed
// in cents, this program computes the number of half-dollars,
// quarters, dimes, nickels, and pennies to be returned,
// returning as many half-dollars as possible, then quarters,
// dimes, nickels, and pennies in that order.
//************************************************************

    //Header file
#include <iostream>

using namespace std;

    //Named constants
const int HALF_DOLLAR = 50;
const int QUARTER  = 25;
const int DIME = 10;
const int NICKEL = 5;
```

```cpp
int main()
{
        //Declare variable
     int change;

        //Statements: Step 1 - Step 12
     cout << "Enter change in cents: ";                      //Step 1
     cin >> change;                                          //Step 2
     cout << endl;

     cout << "The change you entered is " << change
          << endl;                                           //Step 3

     cout << "The number of half-dollars to be returned "
          << "is " << change / HALF_DOLLAR
          << endl;                                           //Step 4

     change = change % HALF_DOLLAR;                          //Step 5

     cout << "The number of quarters to be returned is "
          << change / QUARTER << endl;                       //Step 6

     change = change % QUARTER;                              //Step 7

     cout << "The number of dimes to be returned is "
          << change / DIME << endl;                          //Step 8

     change = change % DIME;                                 //Step 9

     cout << "The number of nickels to be returned is "
          << change / NICKEL << endl;                        //Step 10

     change = change % NICKEL;                               //Step 11

     cout << "The number of pennies to be returned is "
          << change << endl;                                 //Step 12

     return 0;
}
```

Sample Run: In this sample run, the user input is shaded.

```
Enter change in cents: 583

The change you entered is 583
The number of half-dollars to be returned is 11
The number of quarters to be returned is 1
The number of dimes to be returned is 0
The number of nickels to be returned is 1
The number of pennies to be returned is 3
```

QUICK REVIEW

1. A C++ program is a collection of functions.

2. Every C++ program has a function called `main`.

3. A single-line comment starts with the pair of symbols //anywhere in the line.

4. Multiline comments are enclosed between /* and */.

5. The compiler skips comments.

6. Reserved words cannot be used as identifiers in a program.

7. All reserved words in C++ consist of lowercase letters (see Appendix A).

8. In C++, identifiers are names of things.

9. A C++ identifier consists of letters, digits, and underscores and must begin with a letter or underscore.

10. Whitespaces include blanks, tabs, and newline characters.

11. A data type is a set of values together with a set of operations.

12. C++ data types fall into the following three categories: simple, structured, and pointers.

13. There are three categories of simple data: integral, floating-point, and enumeration.

14. Integral data types are classified into nine categories: `char`, `short`, `int`, `long`, `bool`, `unsigned char`, `unsigned short`, `unsigned int`, and `unsigned long`.

15. The values belonging to `int` data type are -2147483648 $(= -2^{31})$ to 2147483647 $(= 2^{31} - 1)$.

16. The data type `bool` has only two values: `true` and `false`.

17. The most common character sets are ASCII, which has 128 values, and EBCDIC, which has 256 values.

18. The collating sequence of a character is its preset number in the character data set.

19. C++ provides three data types to manipulate decimal numbers: `float`, `double`, and `long double`.

20. The data type `float` is used in C++ to represent any real number between $-3.4 * 10^{38}$ and $3.4 * 10^{38}$. The memory allocated for a value of the `float` data type is four bytes.

21. The data type `double` is used in C++ to represent any real number between $-1.7 * 10^{308}$ and $1.7 * 10^{308}$. The memory allocated for a value of the `double` data type is eight bytes.

22. The arithmetic operators in C++ are addition (+), subtraction (−), multiplication (*), division (/), and modulus (%).

23. The modulus operator, %, takes only integer operands.

24. Arithmetic expressions are evaluated using the precedence rules and the associativity of the arithmetic operators.

25. All operands in an integral expression, or integer expression, are integers, and all operands in a floating-point expression are decimal numbers.

26. A mixed expression is an expression that consists of both integers and decimal numbers.

27. When evaluating an operator in an expression, an integer is converted to a floating-point number, with a decimal part of 0, only if the operator has mixed operands.

28. You can use the cast operator to explicitly convert values from one data type to another.

29. A string is a sequence of zero or more characters.

30. Strings in C++ are enclosed in double quotation marks.

31. A string containing no characters is called a null or empty string.

32. Every character in a string has a relative position in the string. The position of the first character is 0, the position of the second character is 1, and so on.

33. The length of a string is the number of characters in it.

34. During program execution, the contents of a named constant cannot be changed.

35. A named constant is declared by using the reserved word `const`.

36. A named constant is initialized when it is declared.

37. All variables must be declared before they can be used.

38. C++ does not automatically initialize variables.

39. Every variable has a name, a value, a data type, and a size.

40. When a new value is assigned to a variable, the old value is lost.

41. Only an assignment statement or an input (read) statement can change the value of a variable.

42. In C++, >> is called the stream extraction operator.

43. Input from the standard input device is accomplished by using `cin` and the stream extraction operator >>.

44. When data is input in a program, the data items, such as numbers, are usually separated by blanks, lines, or tabs.

45. In C++, << is called the stream insertion operator.

46. Output of the program to the standard output device is accomplished by using `cout` and the stream insertion operator <<.

47. The manipulator `endl` positions the insertion point at the beginning of the next line on an output device.

48. Outputting or accessing the value of a variable in an expression does not destroy or modify the contents of the variable.

49. The character \ is called the escape character.

50. The sequence \n is called the newline escape sequence.

51. All preprocessor commands start with the symbol #.

52. The preprocessor commands are processed by the preprocessor before the program goes through the compiler.

53. The preprocessor command #include <iostream> instructs the preprocessor to include the header file iostream in the program.

54. To use cin and cout, the program must include the header file iostream and either include the statement using namespace std; or refer to these identifiers as std::cin and std::cout.

55. All C++ statements end with a semicolon. The semicolon in C++ is called the statement terminator.

56. A C++ system has three components: environment, language, and the standard libraries.

57. Standard libraries are not part of the C++ language. They contain functions to perform operations, such as mathematical operations.

58. A file containing a C++ program usually ends with the extension .cpp.

59. Prompt lines are executable statements that tell the user what to do.

60. Corresponding to the five arithmetic operators +, -, *, /, and %, C++ provides five compound operators: +=, -=, *=, /=, and %=, respectively.

EXERCISES

1. Mark the following statements as true or false.

   a. An identifier can be any sequence of digits and letters.

   b. In C++, there is no difference between a reserved word and a predefined identifier.

   c. A C++ identifier can start with a digit.

   d. The operands of the modulus operator must be integers.

   e. If a = 4; and b = 3;, then after the statement a = b; the value of b is still 3.

   f. In the statement cin >> y;, y can only be an **int** or a **double** variable.

   g. In an output statement, the newline character may be a part of the string.

   h. The following is a legal C++ program:
   ```
   int main()
   {
       return 0;
   }
   ```

    i. In a mixed expression, all the operands are converted to floating-point numbers.

    j. Suppose `x = 5`. After the statement `y = x++;` executes, `y` is 5 and `x` is 6.

    k. Suppose a = 5. After the statement ++a; executes, the value of a is still 5 because the value of the expression is not saved in another variable.

2. Which of the following are valid C++ identifiers?

    a. `firstCPPProject`   b. `POP_QUIZ`   c. `C++Program2`   d. `quiz7`
    e. `ProgrammingLecture2`   f. `3feetIn1Yard`
    g. `Mike'sFirstAttempt`   h. `Update Grade`   i. `4th`
    j. `New_Student`

3. Which of the following is a reserved word in C++?

    a. `Const` b. `include` c. `Char` d. `void` e. `int` f. `Return`

4. What is the difference between a keyword and a user-defined identifier?

5. Are the identifiers `firstName` and `FirstName` the same?

6. Evaluate the following expressions:

    a. `36 / 5`   b. `18 - 32 / 6 * 3`   c. `80 % 11`   d. `6 - 8 % 11`
    e. `22.0 / 5`   f. `27 - 12 / 8.0`   g. `25 - 7 % 3 + 8 / 3`
    h. `18.0 + 5.0 * 3.0 / 4.0`

7. If x = 5, y = 6, z = 4, and w = 3.5, evaluate each of the following statements, if possible. If it is not possible, state the reason.

    a. `(x + z) % y`   b. `(x + y) % w`   c. `(y + w) % x`   d. `(x + y) * w`
    e. `(x % y) % z`   f. `(y % z) % x`   g. `(x * z) % y`   h. `((x * y) * w) * z`

8. Given:

```
int num1, num2, newNum;
double x, y;
```

Which of the following assignments are valid? If an assignment is not valid, state the reason.

When not given, assume that each variable is declared.

    a. `num1 = 35;`

    b. `newNum = num1 - num2;`

    c. `num1 = 5; num2 = 2 + num1; num1 = num2 / 3;`

    d. `num1 * num2 = newNum;`

    e. `x = 12 * num1 - 15.3;`

    f. `num1 * 2 = newNum + num2;`

    g. `x / y = x * y;`

h. `num2 = num1 % 2.0;`

i. `newNum = static_cast<int> (x) % 5;`

j. `x = x + y - 5;`

k. `newNum = num1 + static_cast<int> (4.6 / 2);`

9. Do a walk-through to find the value assigned to e. Assume that all variables are properly declared.

```
a = 3;
b = 4;
c = (a % b) * 6;
d = c / b;
e = (a + b + c + d) / 4;
```

10. Which of the following variable declarations are correct? If a variable declaration is not correct, give the reason(s) and provide the correct variable declaration.

```
55 = age;                                    //Line 1
char letter = ' ';                           //Line 2
string message = 'First test is on Monday'   //Line 3
int one = 5;                                  //Line 4
int prime;                                    //Line 5
double x, y, z;                               //Line 6
```

11. Which of the following are valid C++ assignment statements? Assume that i, x, and percent are double variables.

a. `i = i + 5;`   b. `x + 2 = x;`   c. `x = 2.5 * x;`   d. `percent = 10%;`

12. Write C++ statement(s) that accomplish the following:

a. Declare int variables x and y. Initialize x to 25 and y to 18.

b. Declare and initialize an int variable temp to 10 and a char variable ch to 'A'.

c. Update the value of an int variable x by adding 5 to it.

d. Declare and initialize a double variable payRate to 12.50.

e. Copy the value of an int variable firstNum into an int variable tempNum.

f. Swap the contents of the int variables x and y. (Declare additional variables, if necessary.)

g. Suppose x and y are double variables. Output the contents of x, y, and the expression x + 12 / y - 18.

h. Declare a char variable grade and set the value of grade to 'A'.

i. Declare int variables to store four integers.

j. Copy the value of a double variable z to the nearest integer into an int variable x.

13. Write each of the following as a C++ expression:

    a. 32 times a plus b

    b. The character that represents 8

    c. The string that represents the name `Julie Nelson`.

    d. $(b^2 - 4ac) / 2a$

    e. $(a + b)/c(ef)-gh$

    f. $(-b + (b^2 - 4ac)) / 2a$

14. Suppose x, y, z, and w are `int` variables. What value is assigned to each of these variables after the last statement executes?

    ```
    x = 4;  y = 11;
    z = y - 2 * x;
    x = z + y;
    y = x + 5 * z;
    w = x - y + 2 * z;
    x = y + w - x;
    -w;
    ```

15. Suppose x, y, and z are `int` variables and w and t are `double` variables. What value is assigned to each of these variables after the last statement executes?

    ```
    x = 23;
    y = 35;
    x = x + y / 4 - 3;
    z = x % 3;
    w = 28 / 3 + 6.5 * 2;
    t = x / 4.0 + 15 % 4 - 3.5;
    ```

16. Suppose x, y, and z are `int` variables and x = 2, y = 5, and z = 6. What is the output of each of the following statements?

    a. `cout << "x = " << x << ", y = " << y << ", z = " << z << endl;`

    b. `cout << "x + y = " << x + y << endl;`

    c. `cout << "Sum of " << x << " and " << z << " is " << x + z << endl;`

    d. `cout << "z / x = " << z / x << endl;`

    e. `cout << "2 times " << x << " = " << 2 * x << endl;`

17. What is the output of the following statements? Suppose a and b are `int` variables, c is a `double` variable, and a = 13, b = 5, and c = 17.5.

    a. `cout << a + b - c << endl;`

    b. `cout << 15 / 2 + c << endl;`

    c. `cout << a / static_cast<double>(b) + 2 * c`
       `        << endl;`

    d. `cout << 14 % 3 + 6.3 + b / a << endl;`

    e. `cout << static_cast<int>(c) % 5 + a - b`
       `        << endl;`

    f. `cout << 13.5 / 2 + 4.0 * 3.5 + 18 << endl;`

2

18. Write C++ statements that accomplish the following:

   a. Output the newline character.

   b. Output the tab character.

   c. Output double quotation mark.

19. Which of the following are correct C++ statements?

   a. `cout << "Hello There!" << endl;`

   b. `cout << "Hello";`
      `<< " There!" << endl;`

   c. `cout << "Hello"`
      `<< " There!" << endl;`

   d. `cout << 'Hello There!' << endl;`

20. Give meaningful identifiers for the following variables:

   a. A variable to store the first name of a student.

   b. A variable to store the discounted price of an item.

   c. A variable to store the number of juice bottles.

   d. A variable to store the number of miles traveled.

   e. A variable to store the highest test score.

21. Write C++ statements to do the following:

   a. Declare `int` variable num1 and num2.

   b. Prompt the user to input two numbers.

   c. Input the first number in num1 and the second number in num2.

   d. Output num1, num2, and 2 times num1 minus num2. Your output must identify each number and the expression.

22. The following program has syntax errors. Correct them. On each successive line, assume that any preceding error has been corrected.

```cpp
#include <io_stream>

const int TOP_NUM = 753,409;
const PAY_RATE = 18.35

main() int
{
    int testScore, projectScore;
    double temp;
    double payCheck

    testScore = 88;
    projectScore = 22;

    cout << testScore << " " << projectScore << endl;
```

```
        temp = 82;
        newTemp = testScore + 2 * projectScore;

        first = 2 * TOP_NUM;
        TOP _NUM = TOP _NUM - 919;

        cout << first << " " TOP_NUM << endl;

        paycheck = hoursWorked * PAY_RATE

        cout << "Wages = " << paycheck << endl;

    return 0;
}
```

23. The following program has syntax mistakes. Correct them. On each successive line, assume that any preceding error has been corrected.

```
const char = STAR = '*'
const int PRIME = 71;

int main
{
    int count, sum;
    double x;

    count = 1;
    sum = count + PRIME;
    x := 25.67;
    newNum = count * ONE + 2;
    sum + count = sum;
    x = x + sum * COUNT;
    cout << " count = " << count << ", sum = " << sum
         << ", PRIME = " << Prime << endl;
}
```

24. The following program has syntax errors. Correct them. On each successive line, assume that any preceding error has been corrected.

```
#include <iostream>

using namespace std;

int main()
{
    int temp;
    string first;

    cout << "Enter first name: ;
    cin >> first
    cout << endl;

    cout << "Enter last name: ;
    cin >> last;
    cout << endl;
```

```
        cout << "Enter today's temperature: ";
        cin >> temperature;
        cout << endl;

        cout << first << " " << last << today's temperature is: ";
            << temperature << endl;

        return 0;
}
```

25. What action must be taken before a variable can be used in a program?

26. Preprocessor directives begin with which of the following symbols:

    a. *   b. #   c. $ d. !   e. None of these.

27. Write equivalent compound statements if possible.

    a. x = 2 * x   b. x = x + y - 2;   c. sum = sum + num;
    d. z = z * x + 2 * z;   e. y = y / (x + 5);

28. Write the following compound statements as equivalent simple statements.

    a. x += 5 - z;   b. y *= 2 * x + 5 - z;   c. w += 2 * z + 4;
    d. x -= z + y - t;   e. sum += num;

29. Suppose a, b, and c are **int** variables and a = 5 and b = 6. What value is assigned to each variable after each statement executes? If a variable is undefined at a particular statement, report UND (undefined).

	a	b	c
a = (b++) + 3;	___	___	___
c = 2 * a + (++b);	___	___	___
b = 2 * (++c) - (a++);	___	___	___

30. Suppose a, b, and sum are **int** variables and c is a **double** variable. What value is assigned to each variable after each statement executes? Suppose a = 3, b = 5, and c = 14.1.

	a	b	c	sum
sum = a + b + c;	___	___	___	___
c /= a;	___	___	___	___
b += c - a;	___	___	___	___
a *= 2 * b + c;	___	___	___	___

31. What is printed by the following program? Suppose the input is:

    ```
    20 15
    ```

    ```
    #include <iostream>

    using namespace std;

    const int NUM = 10;
    const double X = 20.5;
    ```

```cpp
int main()
{
    int a, b;
    double z;
    char grade;

    a = 25;

    cout << "a = " << a << endl;

    cout << "Enter two integers: ";
    cin >> a >> b;
    cout << endl;

    cout << "The numbers you entered are "
            << a << " and " << b << endl;

    z = X + 2 * a - b;
    cout << "z = " << z << endl;

    grade = 'A';
    cout << "Your grade is " << grade << endl;

    a = 2 * NUM + z;
    cout << "The value of a = " << a << endl;

    return 0;
}
```

32. What is printed by the following program? Suppose the input is:

```
Miller
34
340
```

```cpp
#include <iostream>
#include <string>

using namespace std;

const int PRIME_NUM = 11;

int main()
{
    const int SECRET = 17;

    string name;
    int id;
    int num;
    int mysteryNum;

    cout << "Enter last name: ";
    cin >> name;
    cout << endl;
```

```cpp
cout << "Enter a two digit number: ";
cin >> num;
cout << endl;

id = 100 * num + SECRET;

cout << "Enter a positive integer less than 1000: ";
cin >> num;
cout << endl;

mysteryNum = num * PRIME_NUM - 3 * SECRET;

cout << "Name: " << name << endl;
cout << "Id: " << id << endl;
cout << "Mystery number: " << mysteryNum << endl;

return 0;
}
```

33. Rewrite the following program so that it is properly formatted.

```cpp
#include <iostream>
#include <string>
using namespace std;
const double X = 13.45; const int Y=34;
const char BLANK= ' ';
int main()
{ string firstName,lastName;int num;
double salary;
cout<<"Enter first name: "; cin>> firstName; cout<<endl;
cout<<"Enter last name: "; cin
>>lastName;cout<<endl;
      cout<<"Enter a positive integer less than 70:";
cin>>num;cout<<endl; salary=num*X;
 cout<<"Name: "<<firstName<<BLANK<<lastName<<endl;cout
<<"Wages: $"<<salary<<endl; cout<<"X = "<<X<<endl;
 cout<<"X+Y = " << X+Y << endl; return 0;
}
```

34. What type of input does the following program require, and in what order does the input need to be provided?

```cpp
#include <iostream>

using namespace std;

int main()
{
    int invoiceNumber;
    double salesTaxRate;
    double productPrice;
    string productName;
```

```
cin >> productName;
cin >> salesTaxRate >> productPrice;
cin >> invoiceNumber;

return 0;
}
```

PROGRAMMING EXERCISES

1. Write a program that produces the following output:

```
**********************************
*    Programming Assignment 1    *
*     Computer Programming I     *
*          Author: ???           *
*   Due Date: Thursday, Jan. 24  *
**********************************
```

In your program, substitute ??? with your own name. If necessary, adjust the positions and the number of the stars to produce a rectangle.

2. Write a program that produces the following output:

```
CCCCCCCCC          ++                  ++
CC                 ++                  ++
CC           ++++++++++++++     ++++++++++++++
CC           ++++++++++++++     ++++++++++++++
CC                 ++                  ++
CCCCCCCCC          ++                  ++
```

3. Consider the following program segment

```
//include statement(s)
//using namespace statement

int main()
{
    //variable declaration

    //executable statements

    //return statement
}
```

a. Write C++ statements that include the header files iostream.

b. Write a C++ statement that allows you to use cin, cout, and endl without the prefix std::.

c. Write C++ statements that declare the following variables: num1, num2, num3, and average of type int.

d. Write C++ statements that store 125 into num1, 28 into num2, and -25 into num3.

e. Write a C++ statement that stores the average of num1, num2, and num3, into average.

f. Write C++ statements that output the values of num1, num2, num3, and average.

g. Compile and run your program.

4. Repeat Exercise 3 by declaring num1, num2, and num3, and average of type double. Store 75.35 into num1, -35.56 into num2, and 15.76 into num3.

5. Consider the following C++ program in which the statements are in the incorrect order. Rearrange the statements so that it prompts the user to input the radius of a circle and outputs the area and circumference of the circle.

```cpp
#include <iostream>
{
    int main()

    cout << "Enter the radius: ";
    cin >> radius;
    cout << endl;

    double radius;
    double area;

    using namespace std;

    return 0;

    cout << "Area = " << area << endl;

    area = PI * radius * radius;

    circumference = 2 * PI * radius;

    cout << "Circumference = " << circumference << endl;

    const double PI = 3.14;

    double circumference;
}
```

6. Consider the following program segment:

```
//include statement(s)
//using namespace statement

int main()
{
    //variable declaration

    //executable statements

    //return statement
}
```

a. Write C++ statements that include the header files iostream and string.

b. Write a C++ statement that allows you to use cin, cout, and endl without the prefix std::.

c. Write C++ statements that declare the following variables: name of type string and studyHours of type double.

d. Write C++ statements that prompt and input a string into name and a double value into studyHours.

e. Write a C++ statement that outputs the values of name and studyHours with the appropriate text. For example, if the value of name is "Donald" and the value of studyHours is 4.5, the output is:

```
Hello, Donald! on Saturday, you need to study 4.5 hours for the exam.
```

f. Compile and run your program.

7. Write a program that prompts the user to input a decimal number and outputs the number rounded to the nearest integer.

8. Consider the following program segment:

```
//include statement(s)
//using namespace statement

int main()
{
    //variable declaration

    //executable statements

    //return statement
}
```

a. Write C++ statements that include the header files iostream and string.

b. Write a C++ statement that allows you to use cin, cout, and endl without the prefix std::.

c. Write C++ statements that declare and initialize the following named constants: SECRET of type int initialized to 11 and RATE of type double initialized to 12.50.

d. Write C++ statements that declare the following variables: num1, num2, and newNum of type int; name of type string; and hoursWorked and wages of type double.

e. Write C++ statements that prompt the user to input two integers and store the first number in num1 and the second number in num2.

f. Write a C++ statement(s) that outputs the values of num1 and num2, indicating which is num1 and which is num2. For example, if num1 is 8 and num2 is 5, then the output is:

```
The value of num1 = 8 and the value of num2 = 5.
```

g. Write a C++ statement that multiplies the value of num1 by 2, adds the value of num2 to it, and then stores the result in newNum. Then, write a C++ statement that outputs the value of newNum.

h. Write a C++ statement that updates the value of newNum by adding the value of the named constant SECRET. Then, write a C++ statement that outputs the value of newNum with an appropriate message.

i. Write C++ statements that prompt the user to enter a person's last name and then store the last name into the variable name.

j. Write C++ statements that prompt the user to enter a decimal number between 0 and 70 and then store the number entered into hoursWorked.

k. Write a C++ statement that multiplies the value of the named constant RATE with the value of hoursWorked and then stores the result into the variable wages.

l. Write C++ statements that produce the following output:

```
Name:             //output the value of the variable name
Pay Rate: $       //output the value of the variable rate
Hours Worked:     //output the value of the variable
                  //hoursWorked
Salary: $         //output the value of the variable wages
```

For example, if the value of name is "Rainbow" and hoursWorked is 45.50, then the output is:

```
Name: Rainbow
Pay Rate: $12.50
Hours Worked: 45.50
Salary: $568.75
```

m. Write a C++ program that tests each of the C++ statements that you wrote in parts a through l. Place the statements at the appropriate place in the previous C++ program segment. Test run your program (twice) on the following input data:

    a. num1 = 13, num2 = 28; name = "Jacobson"; hoursWorked = 48.30.

    b. num1 = 32, num2 = 15; name = "Crawford"; hoursWorked = 58.45.

9. Write a program that prompts the user to enter five test scores and then prints the average test score. (Assume that the test scores are decimal numbers.)

10. Write a program that prompts the user to input five decimal numbers. The program should then add the five decimal numbers, convert the sum to the nearest integer, and print the result.

11. Write a program that does the following:

    a. Prompts the user to input five decimal numbers.

    b. Prints the five decimal numbers.

    c. Converts each decimal number to the nearest integer.

    d. Adds the five integers.

    e. Prints the sum and average of the five integers.

12. Write a program that prompts the capacity, in gallons, of an automobile fuel tank and the miles per gallon the automobile can be driven. The program outputs the number of miles the automobile can be driven without refueling.

13. Write a C++ program that prompts the user to input the elapsed time for an event in seconds. The program then outputs the elapsed time in hours, minutes, and seconds. (For example, if the elapsed time is 9630 seconds, then the output is 2:40:30.)

14. Write a C++ program that prompts the user to input the elapsed time for an event in hours, minutes, and seconds. The program then outputs the elapsed time in seconds.

15. To make a profit, a local store marks up the prices of its items by a certain percentage. Write a C++ program that reads the original price of the item sold, the percentage of the marked-up price, and the sales tax rate. The program then outputs the original price of the item, the percentage of the mark-up, the store's selling price of the item, the sales tax rate, the sales tax, and the final price of the item. (The final price of the item is the selling price plus the sales tax.)

16. (**Hard drive storage capacity**) If you buy a 40GB hard drive, then chances are that the actual storage on the hard drive is not 40GB. This is due to the fact that, typically, a manufacturer uses 1000 bytes as the value of 1K bytes,

1000K bytes as the value of 1MB, 1000MB as the value of 1GB. Therefore, a 40GB byte hard drive contains 40,000,000,000 bytes. However, in computer memory, as given in Table 1-1 (Chapter 1), 1KB is equal to 1024 bytes, and so on. So the actual storage on a 40GB hard drive is approximately 37.25GB. (You might like to read the fine print next time you buy a hard drive.) Write a program that prompts the user to enter the size of the hard drive specified by the manufacturer, on the hard drive box, and outputs the actual storage capacity of the hard drive.

17. Write a program to implement and test the algorithm that you designed for Exercise 17 of Chapter 1. (You may assume that the value of $\pi = 3.141593$. In your program, declare a named constant PI to store this value.)

18. A milk carton can hold 3.78 liters of milk. Each morning, a dairy farm ships cartons of milk to a local grocery store. The cost of producing one liter of milk is $0.38, and the profit of each carton of milk is $0.27. Write a program that does the following:

   a. Prompts the user to enter the total amount of milk produced in the morning.

   b. Outputs the number of milk cartons needed to hold milk. (Round your answer to the nearest integer.)

   c. Outputs the cost of producing milk.

   d. Outputs the profit for producing milk.

19. Redo Programming Exercise 18 so that the user can also input the cost of producing one liter of milk and the profit on each carton of milk.

20. You found an exciting summer job for five weeks. It pays, say, $15.50 per hour. Suppose that the total tax you pay on your summer job income is 14%. After paying the taxes, you spend 10% of your net income to buy new clothes and other accessories for the next school year and 1% to buy school supplies. After buying clothes and school supplies, you use 25% of the remaining money to buy savings bonds. For each dollar you spend to buy savings bonds, your parents spend $0.50 to buy additional savings bonds for you. Write a program that prompts the user to enter the pay rate for an hour and the number of hours you worked each week. The program then outputs the following:

   a. Your income before and after taxes from your summer job.

   b. The money you spend on clothes and other accessories.

   c. The money you spend on school supplies.

   d. The money you spend to buy savings bonds.

   e. The money your parents spend to buy additional savings bonds for you.

21. A permutation of three objects, *a*, *b*, and *c*, is any arrangement of these objects in a row. For example, some of the permutations of these objects are *abc*, *bca*, and *cab*. The number of permutations of three objects is six. Suppose that these three objects are strings. Write a program that prompts the user to enter three strings. The program then outputs the six permutations of those strings.

22. Write a program that prompts the user to input a number of quarters, dimes, and nickels. The program then outputs the total value of the coins in pennies.

23. Newton's law states that the force, *F*, between two bodies of masses M_1 and M_2 is given by:

$$F = k\left(\frac{M_1 M_2}{d^2}\right),$$

in which *k* is the gravitational constant and *d* is the distance between the bodies. The value of *k* is approximately 6.67×10^{-8} dyn. cm^2/g^2. Write a program that prompts the user to input the masses of the bodies and the distance between the bodies. The program then outputs the force between the bodies.

24. One metric ton is approximately 2205 pounds. Write a program that prompts the user to input the amount of rice, in pounds, in a bag. The program outputs the number of bags needed to store one metric ton of rice.

25. Cindy uses the services of a brokerage firm to buy and sell stocks. The firm charges 1.5% service charges on the total amount for each transaction, buy or sell. When Cindy sells stocks, she would like to know if she gained or lost on a particular investment. Write a program that allows Cindy to input the number of shares sold, the purchase price of each share, and the selling price of each share. The program outputs the amount invested, the total service charges, amount gained or lost, and the amount received after selling the stock.

CHAPTER 3

INPUT/OUTPUT

IN THIS CHAPTER, YOU WILL:

· Learn what a stream is and examine input and output streams

· Explore how to read data from the standard input device

· Learn how to use predefined functions in a program

· Explore how to use the input stream functions `get`, `ignore`, `putback`, and `peek`

· Become familiar with input failure

· Learn how to write data to the standard output device

· Discover how to use manipulators in a program to format output

· Learn how to perform input and output operations with the `string` data type

· Learn how to debug logic errors

· Become familiar with file input and output

In Chapter 2, you were introduced to some of C++'s input/output (I/O) instructions, which get data into a program and print the results on the screen. You used `cin` and the extraction operator `>>` to get data from the keyboard, and `cout` and the insertion operator `<<` to send output to the screen. Because I/O operations are fundamental to any programming language, in this chapter, you will learn about C++'s I/O operations in more detail. First, you will learn about statements that extract input from the standard input device and send output to the standard output device. You will then learn how to format output using manipulators. In addition, you will learn about the limitations of the I/O operations associated with the standard input/output devices and learn how to extend these operations to other devices.

I/O Streams and Standard I/O Devices

A program performs three basic operations: it gets data, it manipulates the data, and it outputs the results. In Chapter 2, you learned how to manipulate numeric data using arithmetic operations. In later chapters, you will learn how to manipulate nonnumeric data. Because writing programs for I/O is quite complex, C++ offers extensive support for I/O operations by providing substantial prewritten I/O operations, some of which you encountered in Chapter 2. In this chapter, you will learn about various I/O operations that can greatly enhance the flexibility of your programs.

In C++, I/O is a sequence of bytes, called a stream, from the source to the destination. The bytes are usually characters, unless the program requires other types of information, such as a graphic image or digital speech. Therefore, a **stream** is a sequence of characters from the source to the destination. There are two types of streams:

Input stream: A sequence of characters from an input device to the computer.

Output stream: A sequence of characters from the computer to an output device.

Recall that the standard input device is usually the keyboard, and the standard output device is usually the screen. To receive data from the keyboard and send output to the screen, every C++ program must use the header file `iostream`. This header file contains, among other things, the definitions of two data types, `istream` (input stream) and `ostream` (output stream). The header file also contains two variable declarations, one for `cin` (pronounced "see-in"), which stands for **common input**, and one for `cout` (pronounced "see-out"), which stands for **common output**.

These variable declarations are similar to the following C++ statements:

```
istream cin;
ostream cout;
```

To use `cin` and `cout`, every C++ program must use the preprocessor directive:

```
#include <iostream>
```

NOTE From Chapter 2, recall that you have been using the statement `using namespace std;` in addition to including the header file `iostream` to use `cin` and `cout`. Without the statement `using namespace std;`, you refer to these identifiers as `std::cin` and `std::cout`. In Chapter 7, you will learn about the meaning of the statement `using namespace std;` in detail.

Variables of type `istream` are called **input stream variables**; variables of type `ostream` are called **output stream variables**. A **stream variable** is either an input stream variable or an output stream variable.

Because `cin` and `cout` are already defined and have specific meanings, to avoid confusion, you should never redefine them in programs.

The variable `cin` has access to operators and functions that can be used to extract data from the standard input device. You have briefly used the extraction operator `>>` to input data from the standard input device. The next section describes in detail how the extraction operator `>>` works. In the following sections, you will learn how to use the functions `get`, `ignore`, `peek`, and `putback` to input data in a specific manner.

`cin` and the Extraction Operator `>>`

In Chapter 2, you saw how to input data from the standard input device by using `cin` and the extraction operator `>>`. Suppose `payRate` is a `double` variable. Consider the following C++ statement:

```
cin >> payRate;
```

When the computer executes this statement, it inputs the next number typed on the keyboard and stores this number in `payRate`. Therefore, if the user types `15.50`, the value stored in `payRate` is `15.50`.

The extraction operator `>>` is binary and thus takes two operands. The left-side operand must be an input stream variable, such as `cin`. Because the purpose of an input statement is to read and store values in a memory location and because only variables refer to memory locations, the right-side operand is a variable.

NOTE The extraction operator `>>` is defined only for putting data into variables of simple data types. Therefore, the right-side operand of the extraction operator `>>` is a variable of the simple data type. However, C++ allows the programmer to extend the definition of the extraction operator `>>` so that data can also be put into other types of variables by using an input statement. You will learn this mechanism in Chapter 13 later in this book.

The syntax of an input statement using `cin` and the extraction operator `>>` is:

```
cin >> variable >> variable...;
```

As you can see in the preceding syntax, a single input statement can read more than one data item by using the operator >> several times. Every occurrence of >> extracts the next data item from the input stream. For example, you can read both `payRate` and `hoursWorked` via a single input statement by using the following code:

```
cin >> payRate >> hoursWorked;
```

There is no difference between the preceding input statement and the following two input statements. Which form you use is a matter of convenience and style.

```
cin >> payRate;
cin >> hoursWorked;
```

How does the extraction operator >> work? When scanning for the next input, >> skips all whitespace characters. Recall that whitespace characters consist of blanks and certain nonprintable characters, such as tabs and the newline character. Thus, whether you separate the input data by lines or blanks, the extraction operator >> simply finds the next input data in the input stream. For example, suppose that `payRate` and `hoursWorked` are `double` variables. Consider the following input statement:

```
cin >> payRate >> hoursWorked;
```

Whether the input is:

15.50 48.30

or:

15.50   48.30

or:

15.50
48.30

the preceding input statement would store 15.50 in `payRate` and 48.30 in `hoursWorked`. Note that the first input is separated by a blank, the second input is separated by a tab, and the third input is separated by a line.

Now suppose that the input is 2. How does the extraction operator >> distinguish between the character 2 and the number 2? The right-side operand of the extraction operator >> makes this distinction. If the right-side operand is a variable of the data type `char`, the input 2 is treated as the character 2 and, in this case, the ASCII value of 2 is stored. If the right-side operand is a variable of the data type `int` or `double`, the input 2 is treated as the number 2.

Next, consider the input 25 and the statement:

```
cin >> a;
```

where a is a variable of some simple data type. If a is of the data type `char`, only the single character 2 is stored in a. If a is of the data type `int`, 25 is stored in a. If a is of the data type double, the input 25 is converted to the decimal number 25.0. Table 3-1 summarizes this discussion by showing the valid input for a variable of the simple data type.

TABLE 3-1 Valid Input for a Variable of the Simple Data Type

Data Type of a	Valid Input for a
char	One printable character except the blank
int	An integer, possibly preceded by a + or − sign
double	A decimal number, possibly preceded by a + or − sign. If the actual data input is an integer, the input is converted to a decimal number with the zero decimal part.

When reading data into a char variable, after skipping any leading whitespace characters, the extraction operator >> finds and stores only the next character; reading stops after a single character. To read data into an int or double variable, after skipping all leading whitespace characters and reading the plus or minus sign (if any), the extraction operator >> reads the digits of the number, including the decimal point for floating-point variables, and stops when it finds a whitespace character or a character other than a digit.

EXAMPLE 3-1

Suppose you have the following variable declarations:

```
int a, b;
double z;
char ch;
```

The following statements show how the extraction operator >> works.

	Statement	Input	Value Stored in Memory
1	cin >> ch;	A	ch = 'A'
2	cin >> ch;	AB	ch = 'A', 'B' is held for later input
3	cin >> a;	48	a = 48
4	cin >> a;	46.35	a = 46, .35 is held for later input
5	cin >> z;	74.35	z = 74.35
6	cin >> z;	39	z = 39.0
7	cin >> z >> a;	65.78 38	z = 65.78, a = 38

3

Statement	Input	Value Stored in Memory
8 `cin >> a >> b;`	4 60	a = 4, b = 60
9 `cin >> a >> z;`	46 32.4 68	a = 46, z = 32.4, 68 is held for later input

EXAMPLE 3-2

Suppose you have the following variable declarations:

```
int a;
double z;
char ch;
```

The following statements show how the extraction operator >> works.

Statement	Input	Value Stored in Memory
1 `cin >> a >> ch >> z;`	57 A 26.9	a = 57, ch = 'A', z = 26.9
2 `cin >> a >> ch >> z;`	57 A 26.9	a = 57, ch = 'A', z = 26.9
3 `cin >> a >> ch >> z;`	57 A 26.9	a = 57, ch = 'A', z = 26.9
4 `cin >> a >> ch >> z;`	57A26.9	a = 57, ch = 'A', z = 26.9

Note that for statements 1 through 4, the input statement is the same; however, the data is entered differently. For statement 1, data is entered on the same line separated by blanks. For statement 2, data is entered on two lines; the first two input values are separated by two blank spaces, and the third input is on the next line. For statement 3, all three input values are separated by lines, and for statement 4, all three input values are on the same line, but there is no space between them. Note that the second input is a non-numeric character. These statements work as follows.

Statements 1, 2, and 3 are easy to follow. Let us look at statement 4.

In statement 4, first the extraction operator >> extracts 57 from the input stream and stores it in a. Then, the extraction operator >> extracts the character 'A' from the input stream and stores it in ch. Next, 26.9 is extracted and stored in z.

Note that statements 1, 2, and 3 illustrate that regardless of whether the input is separated by blanks or by lines, the extraction operator >> always finds the next input.

EXAMPLE 3-3

Suppose you have the following variable declarations:

```
int a, b;
double z;
char ch, ch1, ch2;
```

The following statements show how the extraction operator >> works.

	Statement	Input	Value Stored in Memory
1	cin >> z >> ch >> a;	36.78B34	z = 36.78, ch = 'B', a = 34
2	cin >> z >> ch >> a;	36.78 B34	z = 36.78, ch = 'B', a = 34
3	cin >> a >> b >> z;	11 34	a = 11, b = 34, computer waits for the next number
4	cin >> a >> z;	78.49	a = 78, z = 0.49
5	cin >> ch >> a;	256	ch = '2', a = 56
6	cin >> a >> ch;	256	a = 256, computer waits for the input value for ch
7	cin >> ch1 >> ch2;	A B	ch1 = 'A', ch2 = 'B'

In statement 1, because the first right-side operand of >> is z, which is a **double** variable, 36.78 is extracted from the input stream, and the value 36.78 is stored in z. Next, 'B' is extracted and stored in ch. Finally, 34 is extracted and stored in a. Statement 2 works similarly.

In statement 3, 11 is stored in a, and 34 is stored in b, but the input stream does not have enough input data to fill each variable. In this case, the computer waits (and waits, and waits...) for the next input to be entered. The computer does not continue to execute until the next value is entered.

In statement 4, the first right-side operand of the extraction operator >> is a variable of the type **int**, and the input is 78.49. Now for **int** variables, after inputting the digits of the number, the reading stops at the first whitespace character or a character other than a digit. Therefore, the operator >> stores 78 into a. The next right-side operand of >> is the variable z, which is of the type **double**. Therefore, the operator >> stores the value .49 as 0.49 into z.

In statement 5, the first right-side operand of the extraction operator >> is a **char** variable, so the first nonwhitespace character, '2', is extracted from the input stream. The character '2' is stored in the variable ch. The next right-side operand of the extraction operator >> is an **int** variable, so the next input value, 56, is extracted and stored in a.

In statement 6, the first right-side operator of the extraction operator >> is an `int` variable, so the first data item, 256, is extracted from the input stream and stored in a. Now the computer waits for the next data item for the variable ch.

In statement 7, 'A' is stored into ch1. The extraction operator >> then skips the blank, and 'B' is stored in ch2.

NOTE Recall that during program execution, when entering character data such as letters, you do not enter the single quotes around the character.

What happens if the input stream has more data items than required by the program? After the program terminates, any values left in the input stream are discarded. When you enter data for processing, the data values should correspond to the data types of the variables in the input statement. Recall that when entering a number for a `double` variable, it is not necessary for the input number to have a decimal part. If the input number is an integer and has no decimal part, it is converted to a decimal value. The computer, however, does not tolerate any other kind of mismatch. For example, entering a `char` value into an `int` or `double` variable causes serious errors, called **input failure**. Input failure is discussed later in this chapter.

The extraction operator, when scanning for the next input in the input stream, skips whitespace such as blanks and the newline character. However, there are situations when these characters must also be stored and processed. For example, if you are processing text in a line-by-line fashion, you must know where in the input stream the newline character is located. Without identifying the position of the newline character, the program would not know where one line ends and another begins. The next few sections teach you how to input data into a program using the input functions, such as get, ignore, putback, and peek. These functions are associated with the data type istream and are called **istream member functions**. I/O functions, such as get, are typically called **stream member functions** or **stream functions.**

Before you can learn about the input functions get, ignore, putback, peek, and other I/O functions that are used in this chapter, you need to first understand what a function is and how it works. You will study functions in detail and learn how to write your own in Chapter 6.

Using Predefined Functions in a Program

As noted in Chapter 2, a function, also called a subprogram, is a set of instructions. When a function executes, it accomplishes something. The function main, as you saw in Chapter 2, executes automatically when you run a program. Other functions execute only when they are activated—that is, called. C++ comes with a wealth of functions, called **predefined functions**, that are already written. In this section, you will learn how to use some predefined functions that are provided as part of the C++ system. Later in this chapter, you will learn how to use stream functions to perform a specific I/O operation.

Recall from Chapter 2 that predefined functions are organized as a collection of libraries, called header files. A particular header file may contain several functions. Therefore, to use a particular function, you need to know the name of the function and a few other things, which are described shortly.

A very useful function, `pow`, called the power function, can be used to calculate x^y in a program. That is, `pow(x, y)` = x^y. For example, `pow(2.0, 3.0)` = $2.0^{3.0}$ = 8.0 and `pow(4.0, 0.5)` = $4.0^{0.5}$ = $\sqrt{4.0}$ = 2.0. The numbers `x` and `y` that you use in the function `pow` are called the **arguments** or **parameters** of the function `pow`. For example, in `pow(2.0, 3.0)`, the parameters are 2.0 and 3.0.

An expression such as `pow(2.0, 3.0)` is called a **function call**, which causes the code attached to the predefined function `pow` to execute and, in this case, computes $2.0^{3.0}$. The header file `cmath` contains the specification of the function `pow`.

To use a predefined function in a program, you need to know the name of the header file containing the specification of the function and include that header file in the program. In addition, you need to know the name of the function, the number of parameters the function takes, and the type of each parameter. You must also be aware of what the function is going to do. For example, to use the function `pow`, you must include the header file `cmath`. The function `pow` has two parameters, which are decimal numbers. The function calculates the first parameter to the power of the second parameter. (Appendix F describes some commonly used header files and predefined functions.)

The program in the following example illustrates how to use predefined functions in a program. More specifically, we use some math functions, from the header file `cmath`, and the `string` function `length`, from the header file `string`. Note that the function `length` determines the length of a `string`.

EXAMPLE 3-4

```
//How to use predefined functions.
//This program uses the math functions pow and sqrt to determine
//and output the volume of a sphere, the distance between two
//points, respectively, and the string function length to find
//the number of characters in a string.
//If the radius of the sphere is r, then the volume of the sphere
//is (4/3)*PI*r^3. If (x1,y1) and (x2,y2) are the coordinates of two
//points in the X-Y plane, then the distance between these points is
//sqrt((x2-x1)^2 + (y2-y1)^2).

#include <iostream>
#include <cmath>
#include <string>
```

```
using namespace std;

const double PI = 3.1416;

int main()
{
    double sphereRadius;                                    //Line 1
    double sphereVolume;                                   //Line 2
    double point1X, point1Y;                               //Line 3
    double point2X, point2Y;                               //Line 4
    double distance;                                       //Line 5

    string str;                                            //Line 6

    cout << "Line 7: Enter the radius of the sphere: ";    //Line 7
    cin >> sphereRadius;                                   //Line 8
    cout << endl;                                          //Line 9

    sphereVolume = (4 / 3) * PI * pow(sphereRadius, 3);    //Line 10

    cout << "Line 11: The volume of the sphere is: "
         << sphereVolume << endl << endl;                  //Line 11

    cout << "Line 12: Enter the coordinates of two "
         << "points in the X-Y plane: ";                   //Line 12
    cin >> point1X >> point1Y >> point2X >> point2Y;       //Line 13
    cout << endl;                                          //Line 14

    distance = sqrt(pow(point2X - point1X, 2)
                 + pow(point2Y - point1Y, 2));             //Line 15

    cout << "Line 16: The distance between the points "
         << "(" << point1X << ", " << point1Y << ") and "
         << "(" << point2X << ", " << point2Y << ") is: "
         << distance << endl << endl;                      //Line 16

    str = "Programming with C++";                          //Line 17

    cout << "Line 18: The number of characters, "
         << "including blanks, in \"" << str << "\" is: "
         << str.length() << endl;                          //Line 18

    return 0;                                              //Line 19
}
```

Sample Run: In this sample run, the user input is shaded.

Line 7: Enter the radius of the sphere: 3

Line 11: The volume of the sphere is: 84.8232

Line 12: Enter the coordinates of two points in the X-Y plane: 4 9 9 -5

Line 16: The distance between the points (4, 7) and (9, -5) is: 13

Line 18: The number of characters, including blanks, in "Programming with C++" is: 20

The preceding program works as follows. The statements in Lines 1 to 6 declare the variables used in the program. The statement in Line 7 prompts the user to enter the radius of the sphere, and the statement in Line 8 stores the radius in the variable `sphereRadius`. The statement in Line 10 uses the function `pow` to compute and store the volume of the sphere in the variable `sphereVolume`. The statement in Line 11 outputs the volume. The statement in Line 12 prompts the user to enter the coordinates of two points in the X-Y plane, and the statement in Line 13 stores the coordinates in the variables `point1X`, `point1Y`, `point2X`, and `point2Y`, respectively. The statement in Line 15 uses the functions `sqrt` and `pow` to determine the distance between the points. The statement in Line 16 outputs the distance between the points. The statement in Line 17 stores the string `"Programming with C++"` in `str`. The statement in Line 18 uses the string function `length` to determine and output the length of `str`. Note how the function `length` is used. Later in this chapter we will explain the meaning of expressions such as `str.length()`.

Because I/O is fundamental to any programming language and because writing instructions to perform a specific I/O operation is not a job for everyone, every programming language provides a set of useful functions to perform specific I/O operations. In the remainder of this chapter, you will learn how to use some of these functions in a program. As a programmer, you must pay close attention to how these functions are used so that you can get the most out of them. The first function you will learn about here is the function `get`.

`cin` **and the** `get` **Function**

As you have seen, the extraction operator skips all leading whitespace characters when scanning for the next input value. Consider the variable declarations:

```
char ch1, ch2;
int num;
```

and the input:

```
A 25
```

Now consider the following statement:

```
cin >> ch1 >> ch2 >> num;
```

When the computer executes this statement, `'A'` is stored in `ch1`, the blank is skipped by the extraction operator `>>`, the character `'2'` is stored in `ch2`, and 5 is stored in `num`. However, what if you intended to store `'A'` in `ch1`, the blank in `ch2`, and 25 in `num`? It is clear that you cannot use the extraction operator `>>` to input this data.

As stated earlier, sometimes you need to process the entire input, including whitespace characters, such as blanks and the newline character. For example, suppose you want to process the entered data on a line-by-line basis. Because the extraction operator >> skips the newline character and unless the program captures the newline character, the computer does not know where one line ends and the next begins.

The variable cin can access the stream function get, which is used to read character data. The get function inputs the very next character, including whitespace characters, from the input stream and stores it in the memory location indicated by its argument. The function get comes in many forms. Next, we discuss the one that is used to read a character.

The syntax of cin, together with the get function to read a character, follows:

```
cin.get(varChar);
```

In the cin.get statement, varChar is a **char** variable. varChar, which appears in parentheses following the function name, is called the **argument** or **parameter** of the function. The effect of the preceding statement would be to store the next input character in the variable varChar.

Now consider the following input again:

A 25

To store 'A' in ch1, the blank in ch2, and 25 in num, you can effectively use the get function as follows:

```
cin.get(ch1);
cin.get(ch2);
cin >> num;
```

Because this form of the get function has only one argument and reads only one character and you need to read two characters from the input stream, you need to call this function twice. Notice that you cannot use the get function to read data into the variable num because num is an **int** variable. The preceding form of the get function reads values of only the **char** data type.

The preceding set of cin.get statements is equivalent to the following statements:

```
cin >> ch1;
cin.get(ch2);
cin >> num;
```

NOTE The function get has other forms, one of which you will study in Chapter 8. For the next few chapters, you need only the form of the function get introduced here.

cin **and the** ignore **Function**

When you want to process only partial data (say, within a line), you can use the stream function ignore to discard a portion of the input. The syntax to use the function ignore is:

```
cin.ignore(intExp, chExp);
```

Here, intExp is an integer expression yielding an integer value, and chExp is a **char** expression yielding a **char** value. In fact, the value of the expression intExp specifies the maximum number of characters to be ignored in a line.

Suppose intExp yields a value of, say 100. This statement says to ignore the next 100 characters or ignore the input until it encounters the character specified by chExp, whichever comes first. To be specific, consider the following statement:

```
cin.ignore(100, '\n');
```

When this statement executes, it ignores either the next 100 characters or all characters until the newline character is found, whichever comes first. For example, if the next 120 characters do not contain the newline character, then only the first 100 characters are discarded and the next input data is the character 101. However, if the 75th character is the newline character, then the first 75 characters are discarded and the next input data is the 76th character. Similarly, the execution of the statement:

```
cin.ignore(100, 'A');
```

results in ignoring the first 100 characters or all characters until the character **'A'** is found, whichever comes first.

EXAMPLE 3-5

Consider the declaration:

```
int a, b;
```

and the input:

```
25 67 89 43 72
12 78 34
```

Now consider the following statements:

```
cin >> a;
cin.ignore(100, '\n');
cin >> b;
```

The first statement, cin >> a;, stores 25 in a. The second statement, cin.ignore(100, '\n');, discards all of the remaining numbers in the first line. The third statement, cin >> b;, stores 12 (from the next line) in b.

EXAMPLE 3-6

Consider the declaration:

```
char ch1, ch2;
```

and the input:

```
Hello there. My name is Mickey.
```

a. Consider the following statements:

```
cin >> ch1;
cin.ignore(100, '.');
cin >> ch2;
```

The first statement, cin >> ch1;, stores 'H' in ch1. The second statement, cin.ignore(100, '.');, results in discarding all characters until . (period). The third statement, cin >> ch2;, stores the character 'M' (from the same line) in ch2. (Remember that the extraction operator >> skips all leading whitespace characters. Thus, the extraction operator skips the space after . [period] and stores 'M' in ch2.)

b. Suppose that we have the following statement:

```
cin >> ch1;
cin.ignore(5, '.');
cin >> ch2;
```

The first statement, cin >> ch1;, stores 'H' in ch1. The second statement, cin.ignore(5, '.');, results in discarding the next five characters, that is, until t. The third statement, cin >> ch2;, stores the character 't' (from the same line) in ch2.

When the function ignore is used without any arguments, then it only skips the very next character. For example, the following statement will skip the very next character:

```
cin.ignore();
```

This statement is typically used to skip the newline character.

The putback **and** peek **Functions**

Suppose you are processing data that is a mixture of numbers and characters. Moreover, the numbers must be read and processed as numbers. You have also looked at many sets of sample data and cannot determine whether the next input is a character or a number. You could read the entire data set character by character and check whether a certain character is a digit. If a digit is found, you could then read the remaining digits of the number and somehow convert these characters into numbers. This programming code would be somewhat complex. Fortunately, C++ provides two very useful stream functions that can be used effectively in these types of situations.

The stream function `putback` lets you put the last character extracted from the input stream by the `get` function back into the input stream. The stream function `peek` looks into the input stream and tells you what the next character is without removing it from the input stream. By using these functions, after determining that the next input is a number, you can read it as a number. You do not have to read the digits of the number as characters and then convert these characters to that number.

The syntax to use the function `putback` is:

```
istreamVar.putback(ch);
```

Here, `istreamVar` is an input stream variable, such as `cin`, and `ch` is a **char** variable.

The `peek` function returns the next character from the input stream but does not remove the character from that stream. In other words, the function `peek` looks into the input stream and checks the identity of the next input character. Moreover, after checking the next input character in the input stream, it can store this character in a designated memory location without removing it from the input stream. That is, when you use the `peek` function, the next input character stays the same, even though you now know what it is.

The syntax to use the function `peek` is:

```
ch = istreamVar.peek();
```

Here, `istreamVar` is an input stream variable, such as `cin`, and `ch` is a **char** variable.

Notice how the function `peek` is used. First, the function `peek` is used in an assignment statement. It is not a stand-alone statement like `get`, `ignore`, and `putback`. Second, the function `peek` has empty parentheses. Until you become comfortable with using a function and learn how to write one, pay close attention to how to use a predefined function.

The following example illustrates how to use the `peek` and `putback` functions.

EXAMPLE 3-7

```cpp
//Functions peek and putback

#include <iostream>

using namespace std;

int main()
{
    char ch;

    cout << "Line 1: Enter a string: ";       //Line 1
    cin.get(ch);                              //Line 2
    cout << endl;                             //Line 3
```

```
    cout << "Line 4: After first cin.get(ch); "
        << "ch = " << ch << endl;                    //Line 4

    cin.get(ch);                                     //Line 5
    cout << "Line 6: After second cin.get(ch); "
        << "ch = " << ch << endl;                    //Line 6

    cin.putback(ch);                                 //Line 7
    cin.get(ch);                                     //Line 8
    cout << "Line 9: After putback and then "
        << "cin.get(ch); ch = " << ch << endl;       //Line 9

    ch = cin.peek();                                 //Line 10
    cout << "Line 11: After cin.peek(); ch = "
        << ch << endl;                               //Line 11

    cin.get(ch);                                     //Line 12
    cout << "Line 13: After cin.get(ch); ch = "
        << ch << endl;                               //Line 13

    return 0;
}
```

Sample Run: In this sample run, the user input is shaded.

```
Line 1: Enter a string: abcd

Line 4: After first cin.get(ch); ch = a
Line 6: After second cin.get(ch); ch = b
Line 9: After putback and then cin.get(ch); ch = b
Line 11: After cin.peek(); ch = c
Line 13: After cin.get(ch); ch = c
```

The user input, abcd, allows you to see the effect of the functions get, putback, and peek in the preceding program. The statement in Line 1 prompts the user to enter a string. In Line 2, the statement cin.get(ch); extracts the first character from the input stream and stores it in the variable ch. So after Line 2 executes, the value of ch is 'a'.

The cout statement in Line 4 outputs the value of ch. The statement cin.get(ch); in Line 5 extracts the next character from the input stream, which is 'b', and stores it in ch. At this point, the value of ch is 'b'.

The cout statement in Line 6 outputs the value of ch. The cin.putback(ch); statement in Line 7 puts the previous character extracted by the get function, which is 'b', back into the input stream. Therefore, the next character to be extracted from the input stream is 'b'.

The cin.get(ch); statement in Line 8 extracts the next character from the input stream, which is still 'b', and stores it in ch. Now the value of ch is 'b'. The cout statement in Line 9 outputs the value of ch as 'b'.

In Line 10, the statement ch = cin.peek(); checks the next character in the input stream, which is 'c', and stores it in ch. The value of ch is now 'c'. The cout statement in Line

3

11 outputs the value of ch. The `cin.get(ch);` statement in Line 12 extracts the next character from the input stream and stores it in ch. The `cout` statement in Line 13 outputs the value of ch, which is still `'c'`.

Note that the statement `ch = cin.peek();` in Line 10 did not remove the character `'c'` from the input stream; it only peeked into the input stream. The output of Lines 11 and 13 demonstrates this functionality.

The Dot Notation between I/O Stream Variables and I/O Functions: A Precaution

In the preceding sections, you learned how to manipulate an input stream to get data into a program. You also learned how to use the functions `get`, `ignore`, `peek`, and `putback`. It is important that you use these functions exactly as shown. For example, to use the `get` function, you used statements such as the following:

`cin.get(ch);`

Omitting the dot—that is, the period between the variable `cin` and the function name `get`—results in a syntax error. For example, in the statement:

`cin.get(ch);`

`cin` and `get` are two separate identifiers separated by a dot. In the statement:

`cinget(ch);`

`cinget` becomes a new identifier. If you used `cinget(ch);` in a program, the compiler would try to resolve an undeclared identifier, which would generate an error. Similarly, missing parentheses, as in `cin.getch;`, result in a syntax error. Also, remember that you must use the input functions together with an input stream variable. If you try to use any of the input functions alone—that is, without the input stream variable—the compiler might generate an error message such as "undeclared identifier." For example, the statement `get(ch);` could result in a syntax error.

As you can see, several functions are associated with an `istream` variable, each doing a specific job. Recall that the functions `get`, `ignore`, and so on are *members* of the data type `istream`. Called the **dot notation,** the dot separates the input stream variable name from the member, or function, name. In fact, in C++, the dot is an operator called the **member access operator**.

 NOTE C++ has a special name for the data types `istream` and `ostream`. The data types `istream` and `ostream` are called classes. The variables `cin` and `cout` also have special names, called objects. Therefore, `cin` is called an `istream` object, and `cout` is called an `ostream` object. In fact, stream variables are called stream objects. You will learn these concepts in Chapter 11 later in this book.

Input Failure

Many things can go wrong during program execution. A program that is syntactically correct might produce incorrect results. For example, suppose that a part-time employee's paycheck is calculated by using the following formula:

```
wages = payRate * hoursWorked;
```

If you accidentally type + in place of *, the calculated wages would be incorrect, even though the statement containing a + is syntactically correct.

What about an attempt to read invalid data? For example, what would happen if you tried to input a letter into an **int** variable? If the input data did not match the corresponding variables, the program would run into problems. For example, trying to read a letter into an **int** or **double** variable would result in an **input failure**. Consider the following statements:

```
int a, b, c;
double x;
```

If the input is:

```
W 54
```

then the statement:

```
cin >> a >> b;
```

would result in an input failure, because you are trying to input the character **'W'** into the **int** variable a. If the input were:

```
35 67.93 48
```

then the input statement:

```
cin >> a >> x > >b;
```

would result in storing 35 in a, 67.93 in x, and 48 in b.

Now consider the following read statement with the previous input (the input with three values):

```
cin >> a >> b >> c;
```

This statement stores 35 in a and 67 in b. The reading stops at . (the decimal point). Because the next variable c is of the data type **int**, the computer tries to read . into c, which is an error. The input stream then enters a state called the **fail state**.

What actually happens when the input stream enters the fail state? Once an input stream enters the fail state, all further I/O statements using that stream are ignored. Unfortunately, the program quietly continues to execute with whatever values are stored in variables and produces incorrect results. The program in Example 3-8 illustrates an input failure. This program on your system may produce different results.

EXAMPLE 3-8

```
//Input Failure program

#include <iostream>
#include <string>

using namespace std;

int main()
{
    string name;                                        //Line 1
    int age = 0;                                        //Line 2
    int weight = 0;                                     //Line 3
    double height = 0.0;                                //Line 4

    cout << "Line 5: Enter name, age, weight, and "
         << "height: ";                                 //Line 5
    cin >> name >> age >> weight >> height;             //Line 6
    cout << endl;                                       //Line 7

    cout << "Line 8: Name: " << name << endl;           //Line 8
    cout << "Line 9: Age: " << age << endl;             //Line 9
    cout << "Line 10: Weight: " << weight << endl;      //Line 10
    cout << "Line 11: Height: " << height << endl;      //Line 11

    return 0;                                           //Line 12
}
```

Sample Runs: In these sample runs, the user input is shaded.

Sample Run 1

```
Line 5: Enter name, age, weight, and height: Sam 35 q56 6.2

Line 8: Name: Sam
Line 9: Age: 35
Line 10: Weight: 0
Line 11: Height: 0
```

The statements in Lines 1, 2, 3, and 4 declare the variables `name`, `age`, `weight`, and `height`, and also initialize the variable `age`, `weight`, and `height`. The statement in Line 5 prompts the user to enter a person's name, age, weight, and height; the statement in Line 6 inputs these values into variables `name`, `age`, `weight`, and `height`, respectively.

In this sample run, the third input is `q56` and the `cin` statement tries to input this into the variable `weight`. However, the input `q56` begins with the character `'q'` and `weight` is a variable of type `int`, so `cin` enters the fail state. Note that the printed values of the variables `weight` and `height` are unchanged, as shown by the output of the statements in Lines 10 and 11.

Sample Run 2

Line 5: Enter name, age, weight, and height: `Sam 35.0 156 6.2`

Line 8: Name: Sam
Line 9: Age: 35
Line 10: Weight: 0
Line 11: Height: 0

In this **sample** run, after inputting Sam into name and 35 into age, the reading stops at the decimal point for the cin statement in Line 6. Next the cin statement tries to input the decimal point into weight, which is an int variable. So the input stream enters the fail state and the values of weight and height are unchanged, as shown by the output of the statements in Lines 10 and 11.

The clear Function

When an input stream enters the fail state, the system ignores all further I/O using that stream. You can use the stream function clear to restore the input stream to a working state.

The syntax to use the function clear is:

```
istreamVar.clear();
```

Here, istreamVar is an input stream variable, such as cin.

After using the function clear to return the input stream to a working state, you still need to clear the rest of the garbage from the input stream. This can be accomplished by using the function ignore. Example 3-9 illustrates this situation.

EXAMPLE 3-9

```
//Input failure and the clear function

#include <iostream>
#include <string>

using namespace std;

int main()
{
    string name;                                      //Line 1
    int age = 0;                                      //Line 2
    int weight = 0;                                   //Line 3
    double height = 0.0;                              //Line 4


    cout << "Line 5: Enter name, age, weight, and "
         << "height: ";                               //Line 5
```

```
cin >> name >> age >> weight >> height;           //Line 6
cout << endl;                                      //Line 7

cout << "Line 8: Name: " << name << endl;          //Line 8
cout << "Line 9: Age: " << age << endl;            //Line 9
cout << "Line 10: Weight: " << weight << endl;     //Line 10
cout << "Line 11: Height: " << height << endl;     //Line 11

cin.clear();                    //Restore input stream; Line 12

cin.ignore(200,'\n');              //Clear the buffer; Line 13

cout << "\nLine 14: Enter name, age, weight, "
     << "and height: ";                            //Line 14
cin >> name >> age >> weight >> height;            //Line 15
cout << endl;                                      //Line 16

cout << "Line 17: Name: " << name << endl;         //Line 17
cout << "Line 18: Age: " << age << endl;           //Line 18
cout << "Line 19: Weight: " << weight << endl;     //Line 19
cout << "Line 20: Height: " << height << endl;     //Line 20

return 0;                                          //Line 21
}
```

Sample Run: In this sample run, the user input is shaded.

Line 5: Enter name, age, weight, and height: Sam 35 q56 6.2

Line 8: Name: Sam
Line 9: Age: 35
Line 10: Weight: 0
Line 11: Height: 0

Line 14: Enter name, age, weight, and height: Sam 35 156 6.2

Line 17: Name: Sam
Line 18: Age: 35
Line 19: Weight: 156
Line 20: Height: 6.2

The statements in Lines 1, 2, 3, and 4 declare the variables name, age, weight, and height, and also initialize the variable age, weight, and height. The statement in Line 5 prompts the user to enter a person's name, age, weight, and height; the statement in Line 6 inputs these values into variables name, age, weight, and height, respectively.

As in Example 3-8, when the cin statement tries to input q56 into weight, it enters the fail statement. The statement in Line 12 restores the input stream by using the function clear, and the statement in Line 13 ignores the rest of the input. The statement in Line 14 again prompts the user to input a person's name, age, weight, and height; the statement in Line 15 stores these values in name, age, weight, and height, respectively. Next, the statements in Lines 17 to 20 output the values of name, age, weight, and height.

Output and Formatting Output

Other than writing efficient programs, generating the desired output is one of a programmer's highest priorities. Chapter 2 briefly introduced the process involved in generating output on the standard output device. More precisely, you learned how to use the insertion operator << and the manipulator endl to display results on the standard output device.

However, there is a lot more to output than just displaying results. Sometimes, floating-point numbers must be output in a specific way. For example, a paycheck must be printed to two decimal places, whereas the results of a scientific experiment might require the output of floating-point numbers to six, seven, or perhaps even ten decimal places. Also, you might like to align the numbers in specific columns or fill the empty space between strings and numbers with a character other than the blank. For example, in preparing the table of contents, the space between the section heading and the page number might need to be filled with dots or dashes. In this section, you will learn about various output functions and manipulators that allow you to format your output in a desired way.

Recall that the syntax of cout when used together with the insertion operator << is:

```
cout << expression or manipulator << expression or manipulator...;
```

Here, **expression** is evaluated, its value is printed, and **manipulator** is used to format the output. The simplest manipulator that you have used so far is endl, which is used to move the insertion point to the beginning of the next line.

Other output manipulators that are of interest include setprecision, fixed, showpoint, and setw. The next few sections describe these manipulators.

setprecision **Manipulator**

You use the manipulator setprecision to control the output of floating-point numbers. Usually, the default output of floating-point numbers is scientific notation. Some integrated development environments (IDEs) might use a maximum of six decimal places for the default output of floating-point numbers. However, when an employee's paycheck is printed, the desired output is a maximum of two decimal places. To print floating-point output to two decimal places, you use the setprecision manipulator to set the precision to 2.

The general syntax of the setprecision manipulator is:

```
setprecision(n)
```

where n is the number of decimal places.

You use the `setprecision` manipulator with `cout` and the insertion operator. For example, the statement:

```
cout << setprecision(2);
```

formats the output of decimal numbers to two decimal places until a similar subsequent statement changes the precision. Notice that the number of decimal places, or the precision value, is passed as an argument to `setprecision`.

To use the manipulator `setprecision`, the program must include the header file `iomanip`. Thus, the following include statement is required:

```
#include <iomanip>
```

`fixed` **Manipulator**

To further control the output of floating-point numbers, you can use other manipulators. To output floating-point numbers in a fixed decimal format, you use the manipulator `fixed`. The following statement sets the output of floating-point numbers in a fixed decimal format on the standard output device:

```
cout << fixed;
```

After the preceding statement executes, all floating-point numbers are displayed in the fixed decimal format until the manipulator `fixed` is disabled. You can disable the manipulator `fixed` by using the stream member function `unsetf`. For example, to disable the manipulator `fixed` on the standard output device, you use the following statement:

```
cout.unsetf(ios::fixed);
```

After the manipulator `fixed` is disabled, the output of the floating-point numbers returns to their default settings. The manipulator `scientific` is used to output floating-point numbers in scientific format.

NOTE   On some compilers, the statements `cin >> fixed;` and `cin >> scientific;` might not work. In this case, you can use `cin.setf(ios::fixed);` in place of `cin >> fixed;` and `cin.setf(ios::scientific);` in place of `cin >> scientific;`.

The following example shows how the manipulators `scientific` and `fixed` work without using the manipulator `setprecision`.

EXAMPLE 3-10

```
//Example: scientific and fixed

#include <iostream>

using namespace std;
```

```
int main()
{
    double hours = 35.45;
    double rate = 15.00;
    double tolerance = 0.01000;

    cout << "hours = " << hours << ", rate = " << rate
         << ", pay = " << hours * rate
         << ", tolerance = " << tolerance << endl << endl;

    cout << scientific;
    cout << "Scientific notation: " << endl;
    cout << "hours = " << hours << ", rate = " << rate
         << ", pay = " << hours * rate
         << ", tolerance = " << tolerance << endl << endl;

    cout << fixed;
    cout << "Fixed decimal notation: " << endl;
    cout << "hours = " << hours << ", rate = " << rate
         << ", pay = " << hours * rate
         << ", tolerance = " << tolerance << endl << endl;

    return 0;
}
```

Sample Run:

```
hours = 35.45, rate = 15, pay = 531.75, tolerance = 0.01

Scientific notation:
hours = 3.545000e+001, rate = 1.500000e+001, pay = 5.317500e+002, tolerance = 1
.000000e-002

Fixed decimal notation:
hours = 35.450000, rate = 15.000000, pay = 531.750000, tolerance = 0.010000
```

The sample run shows that when the value of rate and tolerance are printed without setting the scientific or fixed manipulators, the trailing zeros are not shown and, in the case of rate, the decimal point is also not shown. After setting the manipulators, the values are printed to six decimal places. In the next section, we describe the manipulator showpoint to force the system to show the decimal point and trailing zeros. We will then give an example to show how to use the manipulators setprecision, fixed, and showpoint to get the desired output.

showpoint Manipulator

Suppose that the decimal part of a decimal number is zero. In this case, when you instruct the computer to output the decimal number in a fixed decimal format, the output may not show the decimal point and the decimal part. To force the output to show the decimal point and trailing zeros, you use the manipulator `showpoint`. The following statement sets the output of decimal numbers with a decimal point and trailing zeros on the standard input device:

```
cout << showpoint;
```

Of course, the following statement sets the output of a floating-point number in a fixed decimal format with the decimal point and trailing zeros on the standard output device:

```
cout << fixed << showpoint;
```

The program in Example 3-11 illustrates how to use the manipulators `setprecision`, `fixed`, and `showpoint`.

EXAMPLE 3-11

```
//Example: setprecision, fixed, showpoint

#include <iostream>                                      //Line 1
#include <iomanip>                                       //Line 2

using namespace std;                                     //Line 3

const double PI = 3.14159265;                            //Line 4

int main()                                               //Line 5
{                                                        //Line 6
    double radius = 12.67;                               //Line 7
    double height = 12.00;                               //Line 8

    cout << fixed << showpoint;                          //Line 9

    cout << setprecision(2)
         << "Line 10: setprecision(2)" << endl;          //Line 10
    cout << "Line 11: radius = " << radius << endl;      //Line 11
    cout << "Line 12: height = " << height << endl;      //Line 12
    cout << "Line 13: volume = "
         << PI * radius * radius * height << endl;       //Line 13
    cout << "Line 14: PI = " << PI << endl << endl;      //Line 14

    cout << setprecision(3)
         << "Line 15: setprecision(3)" << endl;          //Line 15
    cout << "Line 16: radius = " << radius << endl;      //Line 16
    cout << "Line 17: height = " << height << endl;      //Line 17
    cout << "Line 18: volume = "
         << PI * radius * radius * height << endl;       //Line 18
    cout << "Line 19: PI = " << PI << endl << endl;      //Line 19

    cout << setprecision(4)
         << "Line 20: setprecision(4)" << endl;          //Line 20
    cout << "Line 21: radius = " << radius << endl;      //Line 21
    cout << "Line 22: height = " << height << endl;      //Line 22
```

```
        cout << "Line 23: volume = "
             << PI * radius * radius * height << endl;      //Line 23
        cout << "Line 24: PI = " << PI << endl << endl;     //Line 24

        cout << "Line 25: "
             << setprecision(3) << radius << ", "
             << setprecision(2) << height << ", "
             << setprecision(5) << PI << endl;              //Line 25

        return 0;                                           //Line 26
}                                                           //Line 27
```

Sample Run:

```
Line 10: setprecision(2)
Line 11: radius = 12.67
Line 12: height = 12.00
Line 13: volume = 6051.80
Line 14: PI = 3.14

Line 15: setprecision(3)
Line 16: radius = 12.670
Line 17: height = 12.000
Line 18: volume = 6051.797
Line 19: PI = 3.142

Line 20: setprecision(4)
Line 21: radius = 12.6700
Line 22: height = 12.0000
Line 23: volume = 6051.7969
Line 24: PI = 3.1416

Line 25: 12.670, 12.00, 3.14159
```

In this program, the statement in Line 2 includes the header file `iomanip`, and the statement in Line 4 declares the named constant `PI` and sets the value to eight decimal places. The statements in Lines 7 and 8 declare and initialize the variables `radius` and `height` to store the radius of the base and the height of a cylinder. The statement in Line 10 sets the output of floating-point numbers in a fixed decimal format with a decimal point and trailing zeros.

The statements in Lines 11, 12, 13, and 14 output the values of `radius`, `height`, `volume`, and `PI` to two decimal places.

The statements in Lines 16, 17, 18, and 19 output the values of `radius`, `height`, `volume`, and `PI` to three decimal places.

The statements in Lines 21, 22, 23, and 24 output the values of `radius`, `height`, `volume`, and `PI` to four decimal places.

The statement in Line 25 outputs the value of `radius` to three decimal places, the value of `height` to two decimal places, and the value of `PI` to five decimal places.

Notice how the values of `radius` are printed in Lines 11, 16, and 21. The value of `radius` printed in Line 16 contains a trailing 0. This is because the stored value of `radius` has only two decimal places; a 0 is printed at the third decimal place. In a similar manner, the value of `height` is printed in Lines 12, 17, and 22.

Also, notice how the statements in Lines 13, 18, and 23 calculate and output `volume` to two, three, and four decimal places.

Note that the value of `PI` printed in Line 24 is rounded.

The statement in Line 25 first sets the output of floating-point numbers to three decimal places and then outputs the value of `radius` to three decimal places. After printing the value of `radius`, the statement in Line 25 sets the output of floating-point numbers to two decimal places and then outputs the value of `height` to two decimal places. Next, it sets the output of floating-point numbers to five decimal places and then outputs the value of `PI` to four decimal places.

If you omit the statement in Line 9 and recompile and run the program, you will see the default output of the decimal numbers. More specifically, the value of the expression that calculates the volume might be printed in the scientific notation.

---

setw

The manipulator `setw` is used to output the value of an expression in a specific number of columns. The value of the expression can be either a string or a number. The expression `setw(n)` outputs the value of the next expression in n columns. The output is right-justified. Thus, if you specify the number of columns to be 8, for example, and the output requires only four columns, the first four columns are left blank. Furthermore, if the number of columns specified is less than the number of columns required by the output, the output automatically expands to the required number of columns; the output is not truncated. For example, if `x` is an `int` variable, the following statement outputs the value of `x` in five columns on the standard output device:

```
cout << setw(5) << x << endl;
```

To use the manipulator `setw`, the program must include the header file `iomanip`. Thus, the following `include` statement is required:

```
#include <iomanip>
```

Unlike `setprecision`, which controls the output of all floating-point numbers until it is reset, `setw` controls the output of only the next expression.

EXAMPLE 3-12

```
//Example: setw

#include <iostream>
#include <iomanip>
```

```cpp
using namespace std;

int main()
{
    int x = 19;                              //Line 1
    int a = 345;                             //Line 2
    double y = 76.384;                       //Line 3

    cout << fixed << showpoint;              //Line 4

    cout << "12345678901234567890" << endl;  //Line 5

    cout << setw(5) << x << endl;            //Line 6
    cout << setw(5) << a << setw(5) << "Hi"
         << setw(5) << x << endl << endl;    //Line 7

    cout << setprecision(2);                 //Line 8
    cout << setw(6) << a << setw(6) << y
         << setw(6) << x << endl;            //Line 9
    cout << setw(6) << x << setw(6) << a
         << setw(6) << y << endl << endl;    //Line 10

    cout << setw(5) << a << x << endl;       //Line 11
    cout << setw(2) << a << setw(4) << x << endl;  //Line 12

    return 0;
}
```

Sample Run:

```
12345678901234567890
   19
  345   Hi   19

  345 76.38      19
   19    345 76.38

  34519
345   19
```

The statements in Lines 1, 2, and 3 declare the variables x, a, and y and initialize these variables to 19, 345, and 76.384, respectively. The statement in Line 4 sets the output of floating-point numbers in a fixed decimal format with a decimal point and trailing zeros. The output of the statement in Line 5 shows the column positions when the specific values are printed; it is the first line of output.

The statement in Line 6 outputs the value of x in five columns. Because x has only two digits, only two columns are needed to output its value. Therefore, the first three columns are left blank in the second line of output. The statement in Line 7 outputs the value of a in the first five columns, the string "Hi" in the next five columns, and then the value of x in the following five columns. Because the string "Hi" contains only two characters and five columns are set to output these two characters, the first three columns are left blank. See the third line of output. The fourth line of output is blank because the manipulator endl appears twice in the statement in Line 7.

The statement in Line 8 sets the output of floating-point numbers to two decimal places. The statement in Line 9 outputs the values of a in the first six columns, y in the next six columns, and x in the following six columns, creating the fifth line of output. The output of the statement in Line 10 (which is the sixth line of output) is similar to the output of the statement in Line 9. Notice how the numbers are nicely aligned in the outputs of the statements in Lines 9 and 10. The seventh line of output is blank because the manipulator endl appears twice in the statement in Line 10.

The statement in Line 11 outputs first the value of a in five columns and then the value of x. Note that the manipulator setw in the statement in Line 11 controls only the output of a. Thus, after the value of a is printed, the value of x is printed at the current cursor position (see the eighth line of output).

In the cout statement in Line 12, only two columns are assigned to output the value of a. However, the value of a has three digits, so the output is expanded to three columns. The value of x is then printed in four columns. Because the value of x contains only two digits, only two columns are required to output the value of x. Therefore, because four columns are allocated to output the value of x, the first two columns are left blank (see the ninth line of output).

Additional Output Formatting Tools

In the previous section, you learned how to use the manipulators setprecision, fixed, and showpoint to control the output of floating-point numbers and how to use the manipulator setw to display the output in specific columns. Even though these manipulators are adequate to produce an elegant report, in some situations, you may want to do more. In this section, you will learn additional formatting tools that give you more control over your output.

setfill Manipulator

Recall that in the manipulator setw, if the number of columns specified exceeds the number of columns required by the expression, the output of the expression is right-justified and the unused columns to the left are filled with spaces. The output stream variables can use the manipulator setfill to fill the unused columns with a character other than a space.

The syntax to use the manipulator setfill is:

```
ostreamVar << setfill(ch);
```

where ostreamVar is an output stream variable and ch is a character. For example, the statement:

```
cout << setfill('#');
```

sets the fill character to '#' on the standard output device.

To use the manipulator setfill, the program must include the header file iomanip.

The program in Example 3-13 illustrates the effect of using setfill in a program.

EXAMPLE 3-13

```cpp
//Example: setfill

#include <iostream>
#include <iomanip>

using namespace std;

int main()
{
    int x = 15;                                     //Line 1
    int y = 7634;                                   //Line 2

    cout << "12345678901234567890" << endl;         //Line 3
    cout << setw(5) << x << setw(7) << y
         << setw(8) << "Warm" << endl;              //Line 4

    cout << setfill('*');                           //Line 5
    cout << setw(5) << x << setw(7) << y
         << setw(8) << "Warm" << endl;              //Line 6

    cout << setw(5) << x << setw(7) << setfill('#')
         << y << setw(8) << "Warm" << endl;         //Line 7

    cout << setw(5) << setfill('@') << x
         << setw(7) << setfill('#') << y
         << setw(8) << setfill('^') << "Warm"
         << endl;                                   //Line 8
    cout << setfill(' ');                           //Line 9
    cout << setw(5) << x << setw(7) << y
         << setw(8) << "Warm" << endl;              //Line 10

    return 0;
}
```

Sample Run:

```
12345678901234567890
   15   7634    Warm
***15***7634****Warm
***15###7634####Warm
@@@15###7634^^^^Warm
   15   7634    Warm
```

The statements in Lines 1 and 2 declare and initialize the variables x and y to 15 and 7634, respectively. The output of the statement in Line 3—the first line of output—shows the column position when the subsequent statements output the values of the variables. The statement in Line 4 outputs the value of x in five columns, the value of y in seven columns, and the string "Warm" in eight columns. In this statement, the filling character is the blank character, as shown in the second line of output.

The statement in Line 5 sets the filling character to *. The statement in Line 6 outputs the value of x in five columns, the value of y in seven columns, and the string "Warm" in eight columns. Because x is a two-digit number and five columns are assigned to output its value, the first three columns are unused by x and are, therefore, filled by the filling character *. To print the value of y, seven columns are assigned; y is a four-digit number, however, so the filling character fills the first three columns. Similarly, to print the value of the string "Warm", eight columns are assigned; the string "Warm" has only four characters, so the filling character fills the first four columns. See the third line of output.

The output of the statement in Line 7—the fourth line of output—is similar to the output of the statement in Line 6, except that the filling character for y and the string "Warm" is #. In the output of the statement in Line 8 (the fifth line of output), the filling character for x is @, the filling character for y is #, and the filling character for the string "Warm" is ^. The manipulator setfill sets these filling characters.

The statement in Line 9 sets the filling character to blank. The statement in Line 10 outputs the values of x, y, and the string "Warm" using the filling character blank, as shown in the sixth line of output.

left and right Manipulators

Recall that if the number of columns specified in the setw manipulator exceeds the number of columns required by the next expression, the default output is right-justified. Sometimes, you might want the output to be left-justified. To left-justify the output, you use the manipulator left.

The syntax to set the manipulator left is:

```
ostreamVar << left;
```

where ostreamVar is an output stream variable. For example, the following statement sets the output to be left-justified on the standard output device:

```
cout << left;
```

You can disable the manipulator left by using the stream function unsetf. The syntax to disable the manipulator left is:

```
ostreamVar.unsetf(ios::left);
```

where `ostreamVar` is an output stream variable. Disabling the manipulator `left` returns the output to the settings of the default output format. For example, the following statement disables the manipulator `left` on the standard output device:

```
cout.unsetf(ios::left);
```

The syntax to set the manipulator `right` is:

```
ostreamVar << right;
```

where `ostreamVar` is an output stream variable. For example, the following statement sets the output to be right-justified on the standard output device:

```
cout << right;
```

NOTE On some compilers, the statements `cin >> left;` and `cin >> right;` might not work. In this case, you can use `cin.setf(ios::left);` in place of `cin >> left;` and `cin.setf(ios::right);` in place of `cin >> right;`.

The program in Example 3-14 illustrates the effect of the manipulators `left` and `right`.

EXAMPLE 3-14

```cpp
//Example: left justification

#include <iostream>
#include <iomanip>

using namespace std;

int main()
{
    int x = 15;                                     //Line 1
    int y = 7634;                                   //Line 2

    cout << left;                                   //Line 3

    cout << "12345678901234567890" << endl;         //Line 4
    cout << setw(5) << x << setw(7) << y
         << setw(8) << "Warm" << endl;              //Line 5

    cout << setfill('*');                           //Line 6

    cout << setw(5) << x << setw(7) << y
         << setw(8) << "Warm" << endl;              //Line 7

    cout << setw(5) << x << setw(7) << setfill('#')
         << y << setw(8) << "Warm" << endl;         //Line 8

    cout << setw(5) << setfill('@') << x
         << setw(7) << setfill('#') << y
```

```
                    << setw(8) << setfill('^') << "Warm"
                    << endl;                                    //Line 9

            cout << right;                                      //Line 10
            cout << setfill(' ');                               //Line 11

            cout << setw(5) << x << setw(7) << y
                    << setw(8) << "Warm" << endl;               //Line 12

            return 0;
    }
```

Sample Run:

```
12345678901234567890
15    7634    Warm
15***7634***Warm****
15***7634###Warm####
15@@@7634###Warm^^^^
      15    7634    Warm
```

The output of this program is the same as the output of Example 3-13. The only difference here is that for the statements in Lines 4 through 9, the output is left-justified. You are encouraged to do a walk-through of this program.

NOTE This chapter discusses several stream functions and stream manipulators. To use stream functions such as `get`, `ignore`, `fill`, and `clear` in a program, the program must include the header file `iostream`.

There are two types of manipulators: those with parameters and those without parameters. Manipulators with parameters are called **parameterized stream manipulators**. For example, manipulators such as `setprecision`, `setw`, and `setfill` are parameterized. On the other hand, manipulators such as `endl`, `fixed`, `scientific`, `showpoint`, and `left` do not have parameters.

To use a parameterized stream manipulator in a program, you must include the header file `iomanip`. Manipulators without parameters are part of the `iostream` header file and, therefore, do not require inclusion of the header file `iomanip`.

Input/Output and the `string` Type

You can use an input stream variable, such as `cin`, and the extraction operator `>>` to read a string into a variable of the data type `string`. For example, if the input is the string `"Shelly"`, the following code stores this input into the `string` variable `name`:

```
string name;     //variable declaration
cin >> name;     //input statement
```

Recall that the extraction operator skips any leading whitespace characters and that reading stops at a whitespace character. As a consequence, you cannot use the extraction operator to read strings that contain blanks. For example, suppose that the variable `name` is defined as noted above. If the input is:

```
Alice Wonderland
```

then after the statement:

```
cin >> name;
```

executes, the value of the variable `name` is `"Alice"`.

To read a string containing blanks, you can use the function `getline`.

The syntax to use the function `getline` is:

```
getline(istreamVar, strVar);
```

where `istreamVar` is an input stream variable and `strVar` is a `string` variable. The reading is delimited by the newline character `'\n'`.

The function `getline` reads until it reaches the end of the current line. The newline character is also read but not stored in the `string` variable.

Consider the following statement:

```
string myString;
```

If the input is 29 characters:

```
bbbbHello there. How are you?
```

where b represents a blank, after the statement:

```
getline(cin, myString);
```

the value of `myString` is:

```
myString = "    Hello there. How are you?"
```

All 29 characters, including the first four blanks, are stored into `myString`.

Similarly, you can use an output stream variable, such as `cout`, and the insertion operator `<<` to output the contents of a variable of the data type `string`.

Debugging: Understanding Logic Errors and Debugging with `cout` Statements

In the debugging section of Chapter 2, we illustrated how to understand and correct syntax errors. As we have seen, syntax errors are reported by the compiler, and the compiler not only reports syntax errors, but also gives some explanation about the errors. On the other hand, logic errors are typically not caught by the compiler except for the trivial ones such as using a variable without properly initializing it. In this section, we illustrate how to spot and correct logic errors using cout statements. Suppose that we want to write a program that takes as input the temperature in Fahrenheit and outputs the equivalent temperature in Celsius. The formula to convert the temperature is: *Celsius* = 5 / 9 ∗ (*Fahrenheit* − 32). So consider the following program:

```
#include <iostream>                              //Line 1

using namespace std;                             //Line 2

int main()                                       //Line 3
{                                                //Line 4
    int fahrenheit;                              //Line 5
    int celsius;                                 //Line 6

    cout << "Enter temperature in Fahrenheit: "; //Line 7
    cin >> fahrenheit;                           //Line 8
    cout << endl;                                //Line 9

    celsius = 5 / 9 * (fahrenheit - 32);         //Line 10

    cout << fahrenheit << " degree F = "
         << celsius << " degree C. " << endl;    //Line 11

    return 0;                                    //Line 12
}                                                //Line 13
```

Sample Run 1: In this sample run, the user input is shaded.

Enter temperature in Fahrenheit: 32

32 degree F = 0 degree C.

Sample Run 2: In this sample run, the user input is shaded.

Enter temperature in Fahrenheit: 110

110 degree F = 0 degree C.

The result shown in the first calculation looks correct. However, the result in the second calculation is clearly not correct even though the same formula is used, because 110 degree F = 43 degree C. It means the value of celsius calculated in Line 10 is incorrect. Now, the value of celsius is given by the expression 5 / 9 ∗ (fahrenheit - 32). So we should look at this expression closely. To see the effect of this expression, we can separately print the values of the two expression 5 / 9 and fahrenheit - 32. This can be accomplished by temporarily inserting an output statement as shown in the following program:

```
#include <iostream>                              //Line 1

using namespace std;                             //Line 2

int main()                                       //Line 3
{                                                //Line 4
    int fahrenheit;                              //Line 5
    int celsius;                                 //Line 6
```

```
    cout << "Enter temperature in Fahrenheit: ";   //Line 7
    cin >> fahrenheit;                             //Line 8
    cout << endl;                                  //Line 9

    cout << "5 / 9 = " << 5 / 9
         << ";  fahrenheit - 32 = "
         << fahrenheit - 32 << endl;               //Line 9a

    celsius = 5 / 9 * (fahrenheit - 32);           //Line 10

    cout << fahrenheit << " degree F = "
         << celsius << " degree C. " << endl;      //Line 11

    return 0;                                      //Line 12
}                                                  //Line 13
```

Sample Run: In this sample run, the user input is shaded.

```
Enter temperature in Fahrenheit: 110

5 / 9 = 0;  fahrenheit - 32 = 78
110 degree F = 0 degree C.
```

Let us look at the sample run. We see that the value of 5 / 9 = 0 and the value of fahrenheit - 32 = 78. Because fahrenheit = 110, the value of the expression fahrenheit - 32 is correct. Now let us look at the expression 5 / 9. The value of this expression is 0. Because both of the operands, 5 and 9, of the operator / are integers, using integer division, the value of the expression is 0. That is, the value of the expression 5 / 9 = 0 is also calculated correctly. So by the precedence of the operators, the value of the expression 5 / 9 * (fahrenheit - 32) will always be 0 regardless of the value of fahrenheit. So the problem is in the integer division. We can replace the expression 5 / 9 with 5.0 / 9. In this case, the value of the expression 5.0 / 9 * (fahrenheit - 32) will be a decimal number. Because fahrenheit and celsius are int variables, we can use the cast operators to convert this value to an integer, that is, we use the following expression:

```
celsius = static_cast<int> (5.0 / 9 * (fahrenheit - 32) + 0.5);
```

(Note that in the preceding expression, we added 0.5 to round the number to the nearest integer.)

The revised program is:

```
#include <iostream>                                //Line 1

using namespace std;                               //Line 2

int main()                                         //Line 3
{                                                  //Line 4
    int fahrenheit;                                //Line 5
    int celsius;                                   //Line 6
```

```
cout << "Enter temperature in Fahrenheit: ";        //Line 7
cin >> fahrenheit;                                  //Line 8
cout << endl;                                        //Line 9

celsius = static_cast<int>
            (5.0 / 9 * (fahrenheit - 32) + 0.5);    //Line 10

cout << fahrenheit << " degree F = "
     << celsius << " degree C. " << endl;            //Line 11

return 0;                                            //Line 12
}                                                    //Line 13
```

Sample Run: In this sample run, the user input is shaded.

Enter temperature in Fahrenheit: 110

110 degree F = 43 degree C.

As we can see, using temporary cout statements, we were able to find the problem. After correcting the problem, the temporary cout statements are removed.

The temperature conversion program contained logic errors, not syntax errors. Using cout statements to print the values of expressions and/or variables to see the results of a calculation is an effective way to find and correct logic errors.

File Input/Output

The previous sections discussed in some detail how to get input from the keyboard (standard input device) and send output to the screen (standard output device). However, getting input from the keyboard and sending output to the screen have several limitations. Inputting data in a program from the keyboard is comfortable as long as the amount of input is very small. Sending output to the screen works well if the amount of data is small (no larger than the size of the screen) and you do not want to distribute the output in a printed format to others.

If the amount of input data is large, however, it is inefficient to type it at the keyboard each time you run a program. In addition to the inconvenience of typing large amounts of data, typing can generate errors, and unintentional typos cause erroneous results. You must have some way to get data into the program from other sources. By using alternative sources of data, you can prepare the data before running a program, and the program can access the data each time it runs.

Suppose you want to present the output of a program in a meeting. Distributing printed copies of the program output is a better approach than showing the output on a screen. For example, you might give a printed report to each member of a committee before an important meeting. Furthermore, output must sometimes be saved so that the output produced by one program can be used as an input to other programs.

This section discusses how to obtain data from other input devices, such as a disk (that is, secondary storage), and how to save the output to a disk. C++ allows a program to get data directly from and save output directly to secondary storage. A program can use the file I/O and read data from or write data to a file. Formally, a file is defined as follows:

File: An area in secondary storage used to hold information.

The standard I/O header file, `iostream`, contains data types and variables that are used only for input from the standard input device and output to the standard output device. In addition, C++ provides a header file called `fstream`, which is used for file I/O. Among other things, the `fstream` header file contains the definitions of two data types: `ifstream`, which means input file stream and is similar to `istream`, and `ofstream`, which means output file stream and is similar to `ostream`.

The variables `cin` and `cout` are already defined and associated with the standard input/output devices. In addition, `>>`, `get`, `ignore`, `putback`, `peek`, and so on can be used with `cin`, whereas `<<`, `setfill`, and so on can be used with `cout`. These same operators and functions are also available for file I/O, but the header file `fstream` does not declare variables to use them. You must declare variables called **file stream variables**, which include `ifstream` variables for input and `ofstream` variables for output. You then use these variables together with `>>`, `<<`, or other functions for I/O. Remember that C++ does not automatically initialize user-defined variables. Once you declare the `fstream` variables, you must associate these file variables with the input/output sources.

File I/O is a five-step process:

1. Include the header file `fstream` in the program.
2. Declare file stream variables.
3. Associate the file stream variables with the input/output sources.
4. Use the file stream variables with `>>`, `<<`, or other input/output functions.
5. Close the files.

We will now describe these five steps in detail. A skeleton program then shows how the steps might appear in a program.

Step 1 requires that the header file `fstream` be included in the program. The following statement accomplishes this task:

```
#include <fstream>
```

Step 2 requires you to declare file stream variables. Consider the following statements:

```
ifstream inData;
ofstream outData;
```

The first statement declares `inData` to be an input file stream variable. The second statement declares `outData` to be an output file stream variable.

Step 3 requires you to associate file stream variables with the input/output sources. This step is called **opening the files**. The stream member function `open` is used to open files. The syntax for opening a file is:

```
fileStreamVariable.open(sourceName);
```

Here, `fileStreamVariable` is a file stream variable, and `sourceName` is the name of the input/output file.

Suppose you include the declaration from Step 2 in a program. Further suppose that the input data is stored in a file called `prog.dat`. The following statements associate `inData` with `prog.dat` and `outData` with `prog.out`. That is, the file `prog.dat` is opened for inputting data, and the file `prog.out` is opened for outputting data.

```
inData.open("prog.dat");  //open the input file;  Line 1
outData.open("prog.out"); //open the output file; Line 2
```

NOTE IDEs such as Visual Studio .Net manage programs in the form of projects. That is, first you create a project, and then you add source files to the project. The statement in Line 1 assumes that the file `prog.dat` is in the same directory (subdirectory) as your project. However, if this is in a different directory (subdirectory), then you must specify the path where the file is located, along with the name of the file. For example, suppose that the file `prog.dat` is on a flash memory in drive H. Then the statement in Line 1 should be modified as follows:

```
inData.open("h:\\prog.dat");
```

Note that there are two \ after h:. Recall from Chapter 2 that in C++, \ is the escape character. Therefore, to produce a \ within a string, you need \\. (To be absolutely sure about specifying the source where the input file is stored, such as the drive `h:\\`, check your system's documentation.)

Similar conventions for the statement in Line 2.

NOTE Suppose that a program reads data from a file. Because different computers have drives labeled differently, for simplicity, throughout the book, we assume that the file containing the data and the program reading data from the file are in the same directory (subdirectory).

NOTE We typically use `.dat`, `.out`, or `.txt` as an extension for the input and output files and use Notepad, Wordpad, or TextPad to create and open these files. You can also use your IDE's editor, if any, to create `.txt` (text) files. (To be absolutely sure about it, check you IDE's documentation.)

Step 4 typically works as follows. You use the file stream variables with >>, <<, or other input/output functions. The syntax for using >> or << with file stream variables is exactly the same as the syntax for using `cin` and `cout`. Instead of using `cin` and `cout`, however, you use the file stream variable names that were declared. For example, the statement:

```
inData >> payRate;
```

reads the data from the file `prog.dat` and stores it in the variable `payRate`. The statement:

```
outData << "The paycheck is: $" << pay << endl;
```

stores the output—The paycheck is: $565.78—in the file prog.out. This statement assumes that the pay was calculated as 565.78.

Once the I/O is complete, Step 5 requires closing the files. Closing a file means that the file stream variables are disassociated from the storage area and are freed. Once these variables are freed, they can be reused for other file I/O. Moreover, closing an output file ensures that the entire output is sent to the file; that is, the buffer is emptied. You close files by using the stream function close. For example, assuming the program includes the declarations listed in Steps 2 and 3, the statements for closing the files are:

```
inData.close();
outData.close();
```

 NOTE   On some systems, it is not necessary to close the files. When the program terminates, the files are closed automatically. Nevertheless, it is a good practice to close the files yourself. Also, if you want to use the same file stream variable to open another file, you must close the first file opened with that file stream variable.

In skeleton form, a program that uses file I/O usually takes the following form:

```
#include <fstream>

//Add additional header files you use

using namespace std;

int main()
{
        //Declare file stream variables such as the following
    ifstream inData;
    ofstream outData;

    .
    .
    .

        //Open the files
    inData.open("prog.dat");   //open the input file
    outData.open("prog.out"); //open the output file

        //Code for data manipulation

        //Close files
    inData.close();
    outData.close();

    return 0;
}
```

Recall that Step 3 requires the file to be opened for file I/O. Opening a file associates a file stream variable declared in the program with a physical file at the source, such as a disk. In the case of an input file, the file must exist before the open statement executes. If the file does not exist, the open statement fails and the input stream enters the fail state. An output file does not have to exist before it is opened; if the output file does not exist, the computer prepares an empty file for output. If the designated output file already exists, by default, the old contents are erased when the file is opened.

NOTE To add the output at the end of an existing file, you can use the option `ios::app` as follows. Suppose that `outData` is declared as before and you want to add the output at the end of the existing file, say, `firstProg.out`. The statement to open this file is:

```
outData.open("firstProg.out", ios::app);
```

If the file `firstProg.out` does not exist, then the system creates an empty file.

NOTE Appendix E discusses binary and random access files.

PROGRAMMING EXAMPLE:
Movie Tickets Sale and Donation to Charity

Watch the Video

A movie in a local theater is in great demand. To help a local charity, the theater owner has decided to donate to the charity a portion of the gross amount generated from the movie. This example designs and implements a program that prompts the user to input the movie name, adult ticket price, child ticket price, number of adult tickets sold, number of child tickets sold, and percentage of the gross amount to be donated to the charity. The output of the program is as follows.

```
_*_*_*_*_*_*_*_*_*_*_*_*_*_*_*_*_*_*_*_*_*_*_*_*_*_*_*
Movie Name: ...................... Journey to Mars
Number of Tickets Sold: ...........      2650
Gross Amount: .................... $ 9150.00
Percentage of Gross Amount Donated:   10.00%
Amount Donated: .................. $  915.00
Net Sale: ........................ $ 8235.00
```

Note that the strings, such as "Movie Name:", in the first column are left-justified, the numbers in the right column are right-justified, and the decimal numbers are output with two decimal places.

Input   The input to the program consists of the movie name, adult ticket price, child ticket price, number of adult tickets sold, number of child tickets sold, and percentage of the gross amount to be donated to the charity.

Output   The output is as shown above.

PROBLEM
ANALYSIS
AND
ALGORITHM
DESIGN

To calculate the amount donated to the local charity and the net sale, you first need to determine the gross amount. To calculate the gross amount, you multiply the number of adult tickets sold by the price of an adult ticket, multiply the number of child tickets sold by the price of a child ticket, and then add these two numbers. That is:

```
grossAmount = adultTicketPrice * noOfAdultTicketsSold
            + childTicketPrice * noOfChildTicketsSold;
```

Next, you determine the percentage of the amount donated to the charity and then calculate the net sale amount by subtracting the amount donated from the gross amount. The formulas to calculate the amount donated and the net sale amount are given below. This analysis leads to the following algorithm:

1. Get the movie name.
2. Get the price of an adult ticket.
3. Get the price of a child ticket.
4. Get the number of adult tickets sold.
5. Get the number of child tickets sold.
6. Get the percentage of the gross amount donated to the charity.
7. Calculate the gross amount using the following formula:

```
grossAmount = adultTicketPrice * noOfAdultTicketsSold
            + childTicketPrice * noOfChildTicketsSold;
```

8. Calculate the amount donated to the charity using the following formula:

```
amountDonated = grossAmount * percentDonation / 100;
```

9. Calculate the net sale amount using the following formula:

```
netSaleAmount = grossAmount - amountDonated;
```

Variables   From the preceding discussion, it follows that you need variables to store the movie name, adult ticket price, child ticket price, number of adult tickets sold, number of child tickets sold, percentage of the gross amount donated to the charity, gross amount, amount donated, and net sale amount. Therefore, the following variables are needed:

```
string movieName;
double adultTicketPrice;
double childTicketPrice;
int noOfAdultTicketsSold;
int noOfChildTicketsSold;
double percentDonation;
```

```
double grossAmount;
double amountDonated;
double netSaleAmount;
```

Because movieName is declared as a string variable, you need to include the header file string. Therefore, the program needs, among others, the following include statement:

```
#include <string>
```

Formatting Output

In the output, the first column is left-justified and the numbers in the second column are right-justified. Therefore, when printing a value in the first column, the manipulator left is used; before printing a value in the second column, the manipulator right is used. The empty space between the first and second columns is filled with dots; the program uses the manipulator setfill to accomplish this goal. In the lines showing the gross amount, amount donated, and net sale amount, the space between the $ sign and the number is filled with blank spaces. Therefore, before printing the dollar sign, the program uses the manipulator setfill to set the filling character to blank. The following statements accomplish the desired output:

```
cout << "-*-*-*-*-*-*-*-*-*-*-*-*-*-*"
     << "-*-*-*-*-*-*-*-*-*-*-*-*-*" << endl;
cout << setfill('.') << left << setw(35) << "Movie Name: "
     << right << " " << movieName << endl;
cout << left << setw(35) << "Number of Tickets Sold: "
     << setfill(' ') << right << setw(10)
     << noOfAdultTicketsSold + noOfChildTicketsSold
     << endl;
cout << setfill('.') << left << setw(35) << "Gross Amount: "
     << setfill(' ') << right << " $"
     << setw(8) << grossAmount << endl;
cout << setfill('.') << left << setw(35)
     << "Percentage of Gross Amount Donated: "
     << setfill(' ') << right
     << setw(9) << percentDonation << '%' << endl;
cout << setfill('.') << left << setw(35) << "Amount Donated: "
     << setfill(' ') << right << " $"
     << setw(8) << amountDonated << endl;
cout << setfill('.') << left << setw(35) << "Net Sale: "
     << setfill(' ') << right << " $"
     << setw(8) << netSaleAmount << endl;
```

MAIN ALGORITHM

In the preceding sections, we analyzed the problem and determined the formulas to do the calculations. We also determined the necessary variables and named constants. We can now expand the previous algorithm to solve the problem given at the beginning of this programming example.

1. Declare the variables.

2. Set the output of the floating-point numbers to two decimal places in a fixed decimal format with a decimal point and trailing zeros. Include the header file `iomanip`.

3. Prompt the user to enter a movie name.

4. Input (read) the movie name. Because the name of a movie might contain more than one word (and, therefore, might contain blanks), the program uses the function `getline` to input the movie name.

5. Prompt the user to enter the price of an adult ticket.

6. Input (read) the price of an adult ticket.

7. Prompt the user to enter the price of a child ticket.

8. Input (read) the price of a child ticket.

9. Prompt the user to enter the number of adult tickets sold.

10. Input (read) the number of adult tickets sold.

11. Prompt the user to enter the number of child tickets sold.

12. Input (read) the number of child tickets sold.

13. Prompt the user to enter the percentage of the gross amount donated.

14. Input (read) the percentage of the gross amount donated.

15. Calculate the gross amount.

16. Calculate the amount donated.

17. Calculate the net sale amount.

18. Output the results.

COMPLETE PROGRAM LISTING

```
//************************************************************
// Author: D.S. Malik
//
// Program: Movie Tickets Sale
// This program determines the money to be donated to a
// charity. It prompts the user to input the movie name, adult
// ticket price, child ticket price, number of adult tickets
// sold, number of child tickets sold, and percentage of the
// gross amount to be donated to the charity.
//************************************************************

#include <iostream>
#include <iomanip>
#include <string>

using namespace std;
```

```cpp
int main()
{
        //Step 1
    string movieName;
    double adultTicketPrice;
    double childTicketPrice;
    int noOfAdultTicketsSold;
    int noOfChildTicketsSold;
    double percentDonation;
    double grossAmount;
    double amountDonated;
    double netSaleAmount;

    cout << fixed << showpoint << setprecision(2);   //Step 2

    cout << "Enter the movie name: ";                //Step 3
    getline(cin, movieName);                         //Step 4
    cout << endl;

    cout << "Enter the price of an adult ticket: ";  //Step 5
    cin >> adultTicketPrice;                          //Step 6
    cout << endl;

    cout << "Enter the price of a child ticket: ";   //Step 7
    cin >> childTicketPrice;                          //Step 8
    cout << endl;
    cout << "Enter the number of adult tickets "
         << "sold: ";                                 //Step 9
    cin >> noOfAdultTicketsSold;                      //Step 10
    cout << endl;

    cout << "Enter the number of child tickets "
         << "sold: ";                                 //Step 11
    cin >> noOfChildTicketsSold;                      //Step 12
    cout << endl;

    cout << "Enter the percentage of donation: ";    //Step 13
    cin >> percentDonation;                           //Step 14
    cout << endl << endl;

        //Step 15
    grossAmount = adultTicketPrice * noOfAdultTicketsSold +
                  childTicketPrice * noOfChildTicketsSold;

        //Step 16
    amountDonated = grossAmount * percentDonation / 100;

    netSaleAmount = grossAmount - amountDonated;      //Step 17

        //Step 18: Output results
    cout << "-*-*-*-*-*-*-*-*-*-*-*-*-*-*"
         << "-*-*-*-*-*-*-*-*-*-*-*-*-*-*" << endl;
```

3

```
        cout << setfill('.') << left << setw(35) << "Movie Name: "
             << right << " " << movieName << endl;
        cout << left << setw(35) << "Number of Tickets Sold: "
             << setfill(' ') << right << setw(10)
             << noOfAdultTicketsSold + noOfChildTicketsSold
             << endl;
        cout << setfill('.') << left << setw(35)
             << "Gross Amount: "
             << setfill(' ') << right << " $"
             << setw(8) << grossAmount << endl;
        cout << setfill('.') << left << setw(35)
             << "Percentage of Gross Amount Donated: "
             << setfill(' ') << right
             << setw(9) << percentDonation << '%' << endl;
        cout << setfill('.') << left << setw(35)
             << "Amount Donated: "
             << setfill(' ') << right << " $"
             << setw(8) << amountDonated << endl;
        cout << setfill('.') << left << setw(35) << "Net Sale: "
             << setfill(' ') << right << " $"
             << setw(8) << netSaleAmount << endl;

    return 0;
}
```

Sample Run: In this sample run, the user input is shaded.

```
Enter movie name: Journey to Mars

Enter the price of an adult ticket: 4.50

Enter the price of a child ticket: 3.00

Enter number of adult tickets sold: 800

Enter number of child tickets sold: 1850

Enter the percentage of donation: 10

_*_*_*_*_*_*_*_*_*_*_*_*_*_*_*_*_*_*_*_*_*_*_*_*_*_*_*_*_*_*
Movie Name: ..................... Journey to Mars
Number of Tickets Sold: ...........        2650
Gross Amount: .................... $ 9150.00
Percentage of Gross Amount Donated:     10.00%
Amount Donated: .................. $   915.00
Net Sale: ........................ $ 8235.00
```

Note that the first six lines of output get the necessary data to generate the last six lines of the output as required.

PROGRAMMING EXAMPLE: Student Grade

Write a program that reads a student name followed by five test scores. The program should output the student name, the five test scores, and the average test score. Output the average test score with two decimal places.

The data to be read is stored in a file called `test.txt`. The output should be stored in a file called `testavg.out`.

Input
A file containing the student name and the five test scores. A sample input is:

`Andrew Miller 87.50 89 65.75 37 98.50`

Output
The student name, the five test scores, and the average of the five test scores, saved to a file.

PROBLEM
ANALYSIS
AND
ALGORITHM
DESIGN

To find the average of the five test scores, you add the five test scores and divide the sum by 5. The input data is in the following form: the student name followed by the five test scores. Therefore, you must read the student name first and then read the five test scores. This problem analysis translates into the following algorithm:

1. Read the student name and the five test scores.
2. Output the student name and the five test scores.
3. Calculate the average.
4. Output the average.

You output the average test score in the fixed decimal format with two decimal places.

Variables
The program needs to read a student's first and last name and five test scores. Therefore, you need two variables to store the student name and five variables to store the five test scores.

To find the average, you must add the five test scores and then divide the sum by 5. Thus, you need a variable to store the average test score. Furthermore, because the input data is in a file, you need an `ifstream` variable to open the input file. Because the program output will be stored in a file, you need an `ofstream` variable to open the output file. The program, therefore, needs at least the following variables:

```
ifstream inFile;    //input file stream variable
ofstream outFile;   //output file stream variable

double test1, test2, test3, test4, test5; //variables to
                                  //read the five test scores
double average;     //variable to store the average test score
string firstName;   //variable to store the first name
string lastName;    //variable to store the last name
```

MAIN
ALGORITHM

In the preceding sections, we analyzed the problem and determined the formulas to perform the calculations. We also determined the necessary variables and named constants. We can now expand the previous algorithm to solve the problem given at the beginning of this programming example:

1. Declare the variables.
2. Open the input file.
3. Open the output file.
4. To output the floating-point numbers in a fixed decimal format with a decimal point and trailing zeros, set the manipulators `fixed` and `showpoint`. Also, to output the floating-point numbers with two decimal places, set the precision to two decimal places.
5. Read the student name.
6. Output the student name.
7. Read the five test scores.
8. Output the five test scores.
9. Find the average test score.
10. Output the average test score.
11. Close the input and output files.

Because this program reads data from a file and outputs data to a file, it must include the header file `fstream`. Because the program outputs the average test score to two decimal places, you need to set the precision to two decimal places. Therefore, the program uses the manipulator `setprecision`, which requires you to include the header file `iomanip`. Because `firstName` and `lastName` are `string` variables, we must include the header file `string`. The program also includes the header file `iostream` to print a message on the screen so that you will not stare at a blank screen while the program executes.

COMPLETE PROGRAM LISTING

```
//************************************************************
// Author: D.S. Malik
//
// Program to calculate the average test score.
// Given a student's name and five test scores, this program
// calculates the average test score. The student's name, the
// five test scores, and the average test score are stored in
// the file testavg.out. The data is input from the file
// test.txt.
//************************************************************

#include <iostream>
#include <fstream>
#include <iomanip>
#include <string>

using namespace std;
```

```cpp
int main()
{
        //Declare variables;  Step 1
    ifstream inFile;
    ofstream outFile;

    double test1, test2, test3, test4, test5;
    double average;

    string firstName;
    string lastName;

    inFile.open("test.txt");                            //Step 2
    outFile.open("testavg.out");                        //Step 3

    outFile << fixed << showpoint;                      //Step 4
    outFile << setprecision(2);                         //Step 4

    cout << "Processing data" << endl;

    inFile >> firstName >> lastName;                    //Step 5
    outFile << "Student name: " << firstName
            << " " << lastName << endl;                 //Step 6

    inFile >> test1 >> test2 >> test3
           >> test4 >> test5;                           //Step 7
    outFile << "Test scores: " << setw(6) << test1
            << setw(6) << test2 << setw(6) << test3
            << setw(6) << test4 << setw(6) << test5
            << endl;                                    //Step 8

    average = (test1 + test2 + test3 + test4
               + test5) / 5.0;                          //Step 9

    outFile << "Average test score: " << setw(6)
            << average << endl;                         //Step 10

    inFile.close();                                     //Step 11
    outFile.close();                                    //Step 11

    return 0;
}
```

Sample Run:

Input File (contents of the file test.txt):

Andrew Miller 87.50 89 65.75 37 98.50

Output File (contents of the file testavg.out):

```
Student name: Andrew Miller
Test scores:  87.50 89.00 65.75 37.00 98.50
Average test score:  75.55
```

NOTE   The preceding program uses five variables—test1, test2, test3, test4, and test5—to read the five test scores and then find the average test score. The Web site accompanying this book contains a modified version of this program that uses only one variable, testScore, to read the test scores and another variable, sum, to find the sum of the test scores. The program is named Ch3_AverageTestScoreVersion2.cpp.

QUICK REVIEW

1.   A stream in C++ is an infinite sequence of characters from a source to a destination.

2.   An input stream is a stream from a source to a computer.

3.   An output stream is a stream from a computer to a destination.

4.   cin, which stands for common input, is an input stream object, typically initialized to the standard input device, which is the keyboard.

5.   cout, which stands for common output, is an output stream object, typically initialized to the standard output device, which is the screen.

6.   When the binary operator >> is used with an input stream object, such as cin, it is called the stream extraction operator. The left-side operand of >> must be an input stream variable, such as cin; the right-side operand must be a variable.

7.   When the binary operator << is used with an output stream object, such as cout, it is called the stream insertion operator. The left-side operand of << must be an output stream variable, such as cout; the right-side operand of << must be an expression or a manipulator.

8.   When inputting data into a variable, the operator >> skips all leading whitespace characters.

9.   To use cin and cout, the program must include the header file iostream.

10. The function get is used to read data on a character-by-character basis and does not skip any whitespace characters.

11. The function ignore is used to skip data in a line.

12. The function putback puts the last character retrieved by the function get back into the input stream.

13. The function peek returns the next character from the input stream but does not remove the character from the input stream.

14. Attempting to read invalid data into a variable causes the input stream to enter the fail state.

15. Once an input failure has occurred, you use the function clear to restore the input stream to a working state.

16. The manipulator `setprecision` formats the output of floating-point numbers to a specified number of decimal places.

17. The manipulator `fixed` outputs floating-point numbers in the fixed decimal format.

18. The manipulator `showpoint` outputs floating-point numbers with a decimal point and trailing zeros.

19. The manipulator `setw` formats the output of an expression in a specific number of columns; the default output is right-justified.

20. If the number of columns specified in the argument of `setw` is less than the number of columns needed to print the value of the expression, the output is not truncated and the output of the expression expands to the required number of columns.

21. The manipulator `setfill` is used to fill the unused columns on an output device with a character other than a space.

22. If the number of columns specified in the `setw` manipulator exceeds the number of columns required by the next expression, the output is right-justified. To left-justify the output, you use the manipulator `left`.

23. To use the stream functions `get`, `ignore`, `putback`, `peek`, `clear`, and `unsetf` for standard I/O, the program must include the header file `iostream`.

24. To use the manipulators `setprecision`, `setw`, and `setfill`, the program must include the header file `iomanip`.

25. The header file `fstream` contains the definitions of `ifstream` and `ofstream`.

26. For file I/O, you must use the statement `#include <fstream>` to include the header file `fstream` in the program. You must also do the following: declare variables of type `ifstream` for file input and of type `ofstream` for file output and use open statements to open input and output files. You can use `<<`, `>>`, `get`, `ignore`, `peek`, `putback`, or `clear` with file stream variables.

27. To close a file as indicated by the `ifstream` variable `inFile`, you use the statement `inFile.close();`. To close a file as indicated by the `ofstream` variable `outFile`, you use the statement `outFile.close();`.

EXERCISES

1. Mark the following statements as true or false.

   a. The extraction operator `>>` skips all leading whitespace characters when searching for the next data in the input stream.

   b. In the statement `cin >> x;`, x must be a variable.

   c. The statement `cin >> x >> y;` requires the input values for x and y to appear on the same line.

d. The statement cin >> num; is equivalent to the statement num >> cin;.

e. You generate the newline character by pressing the Enter (return) key on the keyboard.

f. The function ignore is used to skip certain input in a line.

2. Suppose num1 and num2 are int variables and symbol is a char variable. Consider the following input:

47 18 * 28 $

What value (if any) is assigned to num1, num2, and symbol after each of the following statements executes? (Use the same input for each statement.)

a. cin >> num1 >> symbol >> num2;

b. cin >> symbol >> num1 >> num2;

c. cin >> num1;
   cin.get (symbol);
   cin >> num2;

d. cin >> num1 >> num2;
   cin.get (symbol);

e. cin.get (symbol);
   cin >> num1 >> num2;

3. Suppose x and y are int variables and z is a double variable. Assume the following input data:

37 86.56 32

What value (if any) is assigned to x, y, and z after each of the following statements executes? (Use the same input for each statement.)

a. cin >> x >> y >> z;

b. cin >> x >> z >> y;

c. cin >> z >> x >> y;

4. Suppose x and y are int variables and symbol is a char variable. Assume the following input data:

38 26 * 67 33
24 $ 55 # 34
& 63 85

What value (if any) is assigned to x, y, and symbol after each of the following statements executes? (Use the same input for each statement.)

a. cin >> x >> y;
   cin.ignore (100, '\n');
   cin >> symbol;

b. cin >> x;
   cin.ignore (100, '*');
   cin >> y;
   cin.get (symbol);

c. ```cpp
    cin >> y;
    cin.ignore(100, '\n');
    cin >> x >> symbol;
    ```

d.  ```cpp
    cin.get(symbol);
    cin.ignore(100, '*');
    cin >> x;
    cin.ignore(100, '\n');
    cin >> y;
    ```

e. ```cpp
    cin.ignore(100, '\n');
    cin >> x >> symbol;
    cin.ignore(100, '\n');
    cin.ignore(100, '&');
    cin >> y;
    ```

5.  Given the input:

    ```
    46 A 49
    ```

    and the C++ code:

    ```cpp
    int x = 10, y = 18;
    char z = '*';
    cin >> x >> y >> z;
    cout << x << " " << y << " " << z << endl;
    ```

    What is the output?

6. Suppose that x and y are `int` variables, z is a `double` variable, and ch is a `char` variable. Suppose the input statement is:

    ```cpp
    cin >> x >> y >> ch >> z;
    ```

    What values, if any, are stored in x, y, z, and ch if the input is:

    a. 35 62.78

    b. 86 32A 92.6

    c. 12 .45A 32

7. Which header file must be included to use the function `steprecision`?

8. Which header file must be included to use the function `pow`?

9. Which header file must be included to use the function `sqrt`?

10. What is the output of the following program?

    ```cpp
    #include <iostream>
    #include <cmath>
    #include <string>

    using namespace std;
    ```
    ```

```cpp
int main()
{
    int x, y;
    string message;
    double z;

    x = 4;
    y = 3;
    z = 2.5;

    cout << static_cast<int>(pow(x, 2.0)) << endl;
    cout << static_cast<int>(pow(z, y)) << endl;

    cout << pow(x, z) << endl;

    cout << sqrt(36.0) << endl;

    z = pow(9.0, 2.5);
    cout << z << endl;

    message = "Using C++ predefined function";

    cout << "Length of message = "
         << message.length() << endl;

    return 0;
}
```

11. To use the functions `peek` and `putback` in a program, which header file(s) must be included in the program?

12. Suppose that `num` is an `int` variable and `discard` is a `char` variable. Assume the following input data:

    #34

    What value (if any) is assigned to `num` and `discard` after each of the following statements executes? (Use the same input for each statement.)

    a. `cin.get (discard);`
       `cin >> num;`

    b. `discard = cin.peek();`
       `cin >> num;`

    c. `cin.get (discard);`
       `cin.putback (discard);`
       `cin >> discard;`
       `cin >> num;`

13. Suppose that `name` is a variable of type `string`. Write the input statement to read and store the input `Brenda Clinton` in `name`. (Assume that the input is from the standard input device.)

14. Write a C++ statement that uses the manipulator `setfill` to output a line containing 35 stars, as in the following line:

    ****

15. Suppose that age is an **int** variable and name is a **string** variable. What are the values of age and name after the following input statements execute:

```
cin >> age;
getline(cin, name);
```

if the input is:

a. 23 Lance Grant

b. 23
    Lance Grant

16. Suppose that age is an **int** variable, ch is a **char** variable, and name is a **string** variable. What are the values of age and name after the following input statements execute:

```
cin >> age;
cin.get(ch);
getline(cin, name);
```

if the input is:

a. 23 Lance Grant

b. 23
    Lance Grant

17. The following program is supposed to read two numbers from a file named `input.dat` and write the sum of the numbers to a file named `output.dat`. However, it fails to do so. Rewrite the program so that it accomplishes what it is intended to do. (Also, include statements to close the files.)

```
#include <iostream>
#include <fstream>
using namespace std;

int main()
{
    int num1, num2;
    ifstream infile;

    outfile.open("output.dat");
    infile >> num1 >> num2;
    outfile << "Sum = " << num1 + num2 << endl;
    return 0;
}
```

18. What may cause an input stream to enter the fail state? What happens when an input stream enters the fail state?

19. Which header file needs to be included in a program that uses the data types `ifstream` and `ofstream`?

20. Suppose that `infile` is an `ifstream` variable and `employee.dat` is a file that contains employees' information. Write the C++ statement that opens this file using the variable `infile`.

21. A program reads data from a file called `inputFile.dat` and, after doing some calculations, writes the results to a file called `outFile.dat`. Answer the following questions:

   a. After the program executes, what are the contents of the file `inputFile.dat`?

   b. After the program executes, what are the contents of the file `outFile.dat` if this file was empty before the program executed?

   c. After the program executes, what are the contents of the file `outFile.dat` if this file contained 100 numbers before the program executed?

   d. What would happen if the file `outFile.dat` did not exist before the program executed?

22. Suppose that `infile` is an `ifstream` variable and it is associated with the file that contains the following data: `27306 savings 7503.35`. Write the C++ statement(s) that reads and stores the first input in the `int` variable `acctNumber`, the second input in the `string` variable `accountType`, and the third input in the `double` variable `balance`.

23. Suppose that you have the following statements:

```
ofstream outfile;
double distance = 375;
double speed = 58;
double travelTime;
```

   Write C++ statements to do the following:

   a. Open the file `travel.dat` using the variable `outfile`.

   b. Write the statement to format your output to two decimal places in fixed form.

   c. Write the values of the variables `day`, `distance`, and `speed` in the file `travel.dat`.

   d. Calculate and write the `travelTime` in the file `travel.dat`.

   e. Which header files are needed to process the information in (a) to (d)?

PROGRAMMING EXERCISES

1. Consider the following incomplete C++ program:

```cpp
#include <iostream>

int main()
{
    ...
}
```

a. Write a statement that includes the header files `fstream`, `string`, and `iomanip` in this program.

b. Write statements that declare `inFile` to be an `ifstream` variable and `outFile` to be an `ofstream` variable.

c. The program will read data from the file `inData.txt` and write output to the file `outData.txt`. Write statements to open both of these files, associate `inFile` with `inData.txt`, and associate `outFile` with `outData.txt`.

d. Suppose that the file `inData.txt` contains the following data:

```
10.20 5.35
15.6
Randy Gill 31
18500 3.5
A
```

The numbers in the first line represent the length and width, respectively, of a rectangle. The number in the second line represents the radius of a circle. The third line contains the first name, last name, and the age of a person. The first number in the fourth line is the savings account balance at the beginning of the month, and the second number is the interest rate per year. (Assume that $\pi = 3.1416$.) The fifth line contains an uppercase letter between A and Y (inclusive). Write statements so that after the program executes, the contents of the file `outData.txt` are as shown below. If necessary, declare additional variables. Your statements should be general enough so that if the content of the input file changes and the program is run again (without editing and recompiling), it outputs the appropriate results.

```
Rectangle:
Length = 10.20, width = 5.35, area = 54.57, parameter = 31.10

Circle:
Radius = 15.60, area = 764.54, circumference = 98.02

Name: Randy Gill, age: 31
Beginning balance = $18500.00, interest rate = 3.50
Balance at the end of the month = $18553.96

The character that comes after A in the ASCII set is B
```

e. Write statements that close the input and output files.

f. Write a C++ program that tests the statements in parts a through e.

2. Consider the following program in which the statements are in the incorrect order. Rearrange the statements so that the program prompts the user to input the height and the radius of the base of a cylinder and outputs the volume and surface area of the cylinder. Format the output to two decimal places.

```cpp
#include <iomanip>
#include <cmath>

int main()
{ }

    double height;

    cout << "Volume of the cylinder = "
         << PI * pow(radius, 2.0)* height << endl;

    cout << "Enter the height of the cylinder: ";
    cin >> radius;
    cout << endl;

    return 0;

    double radius;

    cout << "Surface area: "
         << 2 * PI * radius * height + 2 * PI * pow(radius, 2.0)
         << endl;
    cout << fixed << showpoint << setprecision(2);

    cout << "Enter the radius of the base of the cylinder: ";
    cin >> height;
    cout << endl;

#include <iostream>
const double PI = 3.14159;

using namespace std;
```

3. Write a program that prompts the user to enter the weight of a person in kilograms and outputs the equivalent weight in pounds. Output both the weights rounded to two decimal places. (Note that 1 kilogram = 2.2 pounds.) Format your output with two decimal places.

4. During each summer, John and Jessica grow vegetables in their backyard and buy seeds and fertilizer from a local nursery. The nursery carries different types of vegetable fertilizers in various bag sizes. When buying a particular fertilizer, they want to know the price of the fertilizer per pound and the cost of fertilizing per square foot. The following program prompts

the user to enter the size of the fertilizer bag, in pounds, the cost of the bag, and the area, in square feet, that can be covered by the bag. The program should output the desired result. However, the program contains logic errors. Find and correct the logic errors so that the program works properly.

```cpp
//Logic errors.

#include <iostream>
#include <iomanip>

using namespace std;

int main()
{
    double cost;
    double area;

    double bagSize;

    cout << fixed << showpoint << setprecision(2);

    cout << "Enter the amount of fertilizer, in pounds, "
         << "in one bag: ";
    cin >> bagSize;
    cout << endl;

    cout << "Enter the cost of the " << bagSize
         << " pound fertilizer bag: ";
    cin >> cost;
    cout << endl;

    cout << "Enter the area, in square feet, that can be "
         << "fertilized by one bag: ";
    cin >> area;
    cout << endl;

    cout << "The cost of the fertilizer per pound is: $"
         << bagSize / cost << endl;
    cout << "The cost of fertilizing per square foot is: $"
         << area / cost << endl;

    return 0;
}
```

5. The manager of a football stadium wants you to write a program that calculates the total ticket sales after each game. There are four types of tickets—box, sideline, premium, and general admission. After each game, data is stored in a file in the following form:

```
ticketPrice    numberOfTicketsSold
...
```

Sample data are shown below:

```
250 5750
100 28000
 50 35750
 25 18750
```

The first line indicates that the ticket price is $250 and that 5750 tickets were sold at that price. Output the number of tickets sold and the total sale amount. Format your output with two decimal places.

6. Redo Programming Exercise 21, in Chapter 2, so that each string can store a line of text.

7. Three employees in a company are up for a special pay increase. You are given a file, say Ch3_Ex7Data.txt, with the following data:

```
Miller Andrew 65789.87 5
Green Sheila 75892.56 6
Sethi Amit 74900.50 6.1
```

Each input line consists of an employee's last name, first name, current salary, and percent pay increase. For example, in the first input line, the last name of the employee is Miller, the first name is Andrew, the current salary is 65789.87, and the pay increase is 5%. Write a program that reads data from the specified file and stores the output in the file Ch3_Ex7Output.dat. For each employee, the data must be output in the following form: firstName lastName updatedSalary. Format the output of decimal numbers to two decimal places.

8. Write a program that accepts as input the mass, in grams, and density, in grams per cubic centimeters, and outputs the volume of the object using the formula: *volume = mass / density*. Format your output to two decimal places.

9. Interest on a credit card's unpaid balance is calculated using the average daily balance. Suppose that *netBalance* is the balance shown in the bill, *payment* is the payment made, *d1* is the number of days in the billing cycle, and *d2* is the number of days payment is made before billing cycle. Then, the average daily balance is:

$$averageDailyBalance = (netBalance * d1 - payment * d2)/d1$$

If the interest rate per month is, say, 0.0152, then the interest on the unpaid balance is:

$$interest = averageDailyBalance * 0.0152$$

Write a program that accepts as input *netBalance*, *payment*, *d1*, *d2*, and interest rate per month. The program outputs the interest. Format your output to two decimal places.

10. Linda is starting a new cosmetic and clothing business and would like to make a net profit of approximately 10% after paying all the expenses, which include merchandise cost, store rent, employees' salary, and electricity cost for the store. She would like to know how much the merchandise should be marked up so that after paying all the expenses at the end of the year she gets approximately 10% net profit on the merchandise cost. Note that after marking up the price of an item she would like to put the item on 15% sale. Write a program that prompts Linda to enter the total cost of the merchandise, the salary of the employees (including her own salary), the yearly rent, and the estimated electricity cost. The program then outputs how much the merchandise should be marked up so that Linda gets the desired profit.

3

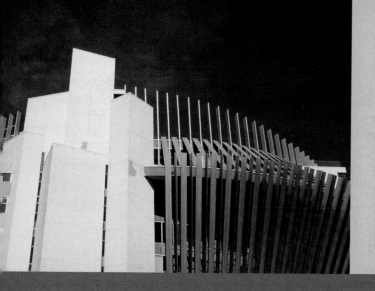

CONTROL STRUCTURES I (SELECTION)

IN THIS CHAPTER, YOU WILL:

· Learn about control structures

· Examine relational and logical operators

· Explore how to form and evaluate logical (Boolean) expressions

· Discover how to use the selection control structures `if`, `if...else`, and `switch` in a program

· Learn how to avoid bugs by avoiding partially understood concepts

· Learn to use the `assert` function to terminate a program

Chapter 2 defined a program as a sequence of statements whose objective is to accomplish some task. The programs you have examined so far were simple and straightforward. To process a program, the computer begins at the first executable statement and executes the statements in order until it comes to the end. In this chapter and Chapter 5, you will learn how to tell a computer that it does not have to follow a simple sequential order of statements; it can also make decisions and repeat certain statements over and over until certain conditions are met.

Control Structures

A computer can process a program in one of the following ways: in sequence; selectively, by making a choice, which is also called a branch; repetitively, by executing a statement over and over, using a structure called a loop; or by calling a function. Figure 4-1 illustrates the first three types of program flow. (In Chapter 6, we will show how function calls work.) The programming examples in Chapters 2 and 3 included simple sequential programs. With such a program, the computer starts at the beginning and follows the statements in order. No choices are made; there is no repetition. Control structures provide alternatives to sequential program execution and are used to alter the sequential flow of execution. The two most common control structures are selection and repetition. In *selection*, the program executes particular statements depending on some condition(s). In *repetition*, the program repeats particular statements a certain number of times based on some condition(s).

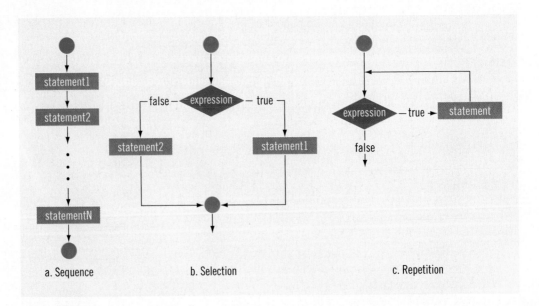

FIGURE 4-1 Flow of execution

Before you can learn about selection and repetition, you must understand the nature of conditional statements and how to use them. Consider the following three statements:

1. `if` (score is greater than or equal to 90)
   grade is A

2. `if` (hours worked are less than or equal to 40)
   wages = rate * hours
   otherwise
   wages = (rate * 40) + 1.5 * (rate * (hours − 40))

3. `if` (temperature is greater than 70 degrees and it is not raining)
   Go golfing!

These statements are examples of conditional statements. You can see that certain statements are to be executed only if certain conditions are met. A condition is met if it evaluates to `true`. For example, in statement 1:

score is greater than or equal to 90

is `true` if the value of `score` is greater than or equal to 90; it is `false` otherwise. For example, if the value of `score` is 95, the statement evaluates to `true`. Similarly, if the value of `score` is 86, the statement evaluates to `false`.

It would be useful if the computer could recognize these types of statements to be true for appropriate values. Furthermore, in certain situations, the truth or falsity of a statement could depend on more than one condition. For example, in statement 3, both `temperature is greater than 70 degrees` and `it is not raining` must be true to recommend golfing.

As you can see, for the computer to make decisions and repeat statements, it must be able to react to conditions that exist when the program executes. The next few sections discuss how to represent and evaluate conditional statements in C++.

Relational Operators

To make decisions, you must be able to express conditions and make comparisons. For example, the interest rate and service charges on a checking account might depend on the balance at the end of the month. If the balance is less than some minimum balance, not only is the interest rate lower, but there is also usually a service charge. Therefore, to determine the interest rate, you must be able to state the minimum balance and compare the account balance with the minimum balance (a condition). The premium on an insurance policy is also determined by stating conditions and making comparisons. For example, to determine an insurance premium, you must be able to check the smoking status of the policyholder. Nonsmokers (the condition) receive lower premiums than smokers. Both of these examples involve comparing items. Certain items are compared for equality against a particular condition; others are compared for inequality (greater than or less than) against a particular condition.

In C++, a condition is represented by a logical (Boolean) expression. An expression that has a value of either `true` or `false` is called **a logical (Boolean) expression**. Moreover, `true` and `false` are **logical (Boolean) values**. Suppose i and j are integers. Consider the expression:

`i > j`

If this expression is a logical expression, it will have the value `true` if the value of i is greater than the value of j; otherwise, it will have the value `false`. The symbol > is called a relational operator. A **relational operator** allows you to make comparisons in a program.

C++ includes six relational operators that allow you to state conditions and make comparisons. Table 4-1 lists the relational operators.

TABLE 4-1 Relational Operators in C++

Operator	Description
==	equal to
!=	not equal to
<	less than
<=	less than or equal to
>	greater than
>=	greater than or equal to

 NOTE In C++, the symbol ==, which consists of two equal signs, is called the equality operator. Recall that the symbol = is called the assignment operator. Remember that the equality operator, ==, determines whether two expressions are equal, whereas the assignment operator, =, assigns the value of an expression to a variable.

Each of the relational operators is a binary operator; that is, it requires two operands. Because the result of a comparison is `true` or `false`, expressions using these operators evaluate to `true` or `false`.

Relational Operators and Simple Data Types

You can use the relational operators with all three simple data types. In the following example, the expressions use both integers and real numbers:

EXAMPLE 4-1

Expression	Meaning	Value
8 < 15	8 is less than 15	true
6 != 6	6 is not equal to 6	false
2.5 > 5.8	2.5 is greater than 5.8	false
5.9 <= 7.5	5.9 is less than or equal to 7.5	true

Comparing Characters

For char values, whether an expression using relational operators evaluates to true or false depends on a machine's collating sequence. The collating sequence of some of the characters is:

ASCII Value	Char	ASCII Value	Char	ASCII Value	Char	ASCII Value	Char
32	' '	61	=	81	Q	105	i
33	!	62	>	82	R	106	j
34	"	65	A	83	S	107	k
42	*	66	B	84	T	108	l
43	+	67	C	85	U	109	m
45	-	68	D	86	V	110	n
47	/	69	E	87	W	111	o
48	0	70	F	88	X	112	p
49	1	71	G	89	Y	113	q
50	2	72	H	90	Z	114	r
51	3	73	I	97	a	115	s
52	4	74	J	98	b	116	t
53	5	75	K	99	c	117	u
54	6	76	L	100	d	118	v
55	7	77	M	101	e	119	w
56	8	78	N	102	f	120	x
57	9	79	O	103	g	121	y
60	<	80	P	104	h	122	z

The ASCII character set is described in Appendix C.

Now, because 32 < 97, and the ASCII value of ' ' is 32 and the ASCII value of 'a' is 97, it follows that ' ' < 'a' is true. Similarly, using the previous ASCII values:

'R' > 'T' is false

'+' < '*' is false

'A' <= 'a' is true

note that comparing values of different data types may produce unpredictable results. For example, the following expression compares an integer and a character:

8 < '5'

In this expression, on a particular machine, 8 would be compared with the collating sequence of '5', which is 53. That is, 8 is compared with 53, which makes this particular expression evaluate to true.

Expressions such as 4 < 6 and 'R' > 'T' are examples of **logical (Boolean) expressions**. When C++ evaluates a logical expression, it returns an integer value of 1 if the logical expression evaluates to true; it returns an integer value of 0 otherwise. In C++, any nonzero value is treated as true.

 NOTE   Chapter 2 introduced the data type bool. Recall that the data type bool has two values, true and false. In C++, true and false are reserved words. The identifier true is set to 1, and the identifier false is set to 0. For readability, whenever logical expressions are used, the identifiers true and false will be used here as the value of the logical expression.

Relational Operators and the string Type

The relational operators can be applied to variables of type string. Variables of type string are compared character by character, starting with the first character and using the ASCII collating sequence. The character-by-character comparison continues until either a mismatch is found or the last characters have been compared and are equal. The following example shows how variables of type string are compared.

EXAMPLE 4-2

Suppose that you have the following statements:

```
string str1 = "Hello";
string str2 = "Hi";
string str3 = "Air";
string str4 = "Bill";
string str5 = "Big";
```

The following expressions show how string relational expressions evaluate.

Expression	Value /Explanation
str1 < str2	true str1 = "Hello" and str2 = "Hi". The first characters of str1 and str2 are the same, but the second character 'e' of str1 is less than the second character 'i' of str2. Therefore, str1 < str2 is true.

`str1 > "Hen"`	`false` `str1 = "Hello"`. The first two characters of `str1` and `"Hen"` are the same, but the third character `'l'` of `str1` is less than the third character `'n'` of `"Hen"`. Therefore, `str1 > "Hen"` is `false`.
`str3 < "An"`	`true` `str3 = "Air"`. The first characters of `str3` and `"An"` are the same, but the second character `'i'` of `"Air"` is less than the second character `'n'` of `"An"`. Therefore, `str3 < "An"` is `true`.
`str1 == "hello"`	`false` `str1 = "Hello"`. The first character `'H'` of `str1` is less than the first character `'h'` of `"hello"` because the ASCII value of `'H'` is 72, and the ASCII value of `'h'` is 104. Therefore, `str1 == "hello"` is `false`.
`str3 <= str4`	`true` `str3 = "Air"` and `str4 = "Bill"`. The first character `'A'` of `str3` is less than the first character `'B'` of `str4`. Therefore, `str3 <= str4` is `true`.
`str2 > str4`	`true` `str2 = "Hi"` and `str4 = "Bill"`. The first character `'H'` of `str2` is greater than the first character `'B'` of `str4`. Therefore, `str2 > str4` is `true`.

If two strings of different lengths are compared and the character-by-character comparison is equal until it reaches the last character of the shorter string, the shorter string is evaluated as less than the larger string, as shown next.

Expression	Value/Explanation
`str4 >= "Billy"`	`false` `str4 = "Bill"`. It has four characters, and `"Billy"` has five characters. Therefore, `str4` is the shorter string. All four characters of `str4` are the same as the corresponding first four characters of `"Billy"`, and `"Billy"` is the larger string. Therefore, `str4 >= "Billy"` is `false`.
`str5 <= "Bigger"`	`true` `str5 = "Big"`. It has three characters, and `"Bigger"` has six characters. Therefore, `str5` is the shorter string. All three characters of `str5` are the same as the corresponding first three characters of `"Bigger"`, and `"Bigger"` is the larger string. Therefore, `str5 <= "Bigger"` is `true`.

The program `Chapter4_StringComparisons.cpp` at the Web site accompanying this book shows the results of the previous expressions.

Logical (Boolean) Operators and Logical Expressions

This section describes how to form and evaluate logical expressions that are combinations of other logical expressions. **Logical (Boolean) operators** enable you to combine logical expressions. C++ has three logical (Boolean) operators, as shown in Table 4-2.

TABLE 4-2 Logical (Boolean) Operators in C++

Operator	Description
!	not
&&	and
||	or

Logical operators take only logical values as operands and yield only logical values as results. The operator ! is unary, so it has only one operand. The operators && and || are binary operators. Tables 4-3, 4-4, and 4-5 define these operators.

Table 4-3 defines the operator ! (not). When you use the ! operator, `!true` is `false` and `!false` is `true`. Putting ! in front of a logical expression reverses the value of that logical expression.

TABLE 4-3 The ! (Not) Operator

Expression	!(Expression)
true (nonzero)	false (0)
false (0)	true (1)

EXAMPLE 4-3

Expression	Value	Explanation
!('A' > 'B')	true	Because 'A' > 'B' is false, !('A' > 'B') is true.
!(6 <= 7)	false	Because 6 <= 7 is true, !(6 <= 7) is false.

Table 4-4 defines the operator `&&` (and). From this table, it follows that `Expression1 && Expression2` is `true` if and only if both `Expression1` and `Expression2` are `true`; otherwise, `Expression1 && Expression2` evaluates to `false`.

TABLE 4-4 The `&&` (And) Operator

Expression1	Expression2	Expression1 && Expression2
true (nonzero)	true (nonzero)	true (1)
true (nonzero)	false (0)	false (0)
false (0)	true (nonzero)	false (0)
false (0)	false (0)	false (0)

EXAMPLE 4-4

Expression	Value	Explanation
(14 >= 5) && ('A' < 'B')	true	Because (14 >= 5) is true, ('A' < 'B') is true, and true && true is true, the expression evaluates to true.
(24 >= 35) && ('A' < 'B')	false	Because (24 >= 35) is false, ('A' < 'B') is true, and false && true is false, the expression evaluates to false.

Table 4-5 defines the operator `||` (or). From this table, it follows that `Expression1 || Expression2` is `true` if and only if at least one of the expressions, `Expression1` or `Expression2`, is `true`; otherwise, `Expression1 || Expression2` evaluates to `false`.

TABLE 4-5 The `||` (Or) Operator

Expression1	Expression2	Expression1 || Expression2
true (nonzero)	true (nonzero)	true (1)
true (nonzero)	false (0)	true (1)
false (0)	true (nonzero)	true (1)
false (0)	false (0)	false (0)

EXAMPLE 4-5

Expression	Value	Explanation
`(14 >= 5) || ('A' > 'B')`	`true`	Because `(14 >= 5)` is `true`, `('A' > 'B')` is `false`, and `true || false` is `true`, the expression evaluates to `true`.
`(24 >= 35) || ('A' > 'B')`	`false`	Because `(24 >= 35)` is `false`, `('A' > 'B')` is `false`, and `false || false` is `false`, the expression evaluates to `false`.
`('A' <= 'a') || (7 != 7)`	`true`	Because `('A' <= 'a')` is `true`, `(7 != 7)` is `false`, and `true || false` is `true`, the expression evaluates to `true`.

Order of Precedence

Complex logical expressions can be difficult to evaluate. Consider the following logical expression:

```
11 > 5 || 6 < 15 && 7 >= 8
```

This logical expression yields different results, depending on whether `||` or `&&` is evaluated first. If `||` is evaluated first, the expression evaluates to `false`. If `&&` is evaluated first, the expression evaluates to `true`.

An expression might contain arithmetic, relational, and logical operators, as in the expression:

```
5 + 3 <= 9 && 2 > 3
```

To work with complex logical expressions, there must be some priority scheme for evaluating operators. Table 4-6 shows the order of precedence of some C++ operators, including the arithmetic, relational, and logical operators. (See Appendix B for the precedence of all C++ operators.)

TABLE 4-6 Precedence of Operators

Operators	Precedence
`!, +, -` (unary operators)	first
`*, /, %`	second
`+, -`	third
`<, <=, >=, >`	fourth
`==, !=`	fifth
`&&`	sixth
`||`	seventh
`=` (assignment operator)	last

NOTE In C++, & and | are also operators. The meaning of these operators is different from the meaning of && and ||. Using & in place of && or | in place of ||—as might result from a typographical error—would produce very strange results.

Using the precedence rules in an expression, relational and logical operators are evaluated from left to right. Because relational and logical operators are evaluated from left to right, the **associativity** of these operators is said to be from left to right.

Example 4-6 illustrates how logical expressions consisting of variables are evaluated.

4

EXAMPLE 4-6

Suppose you have the following declarations:

```
bool found = true;
int age = 20;
double hours = 45.30;
double overTime = 15.00;
int count = 20;
char ch = 'B';
```

Consider the following expressions:

Expression	Value / Explanation
!found	false Because found is true, !found is false.
hours > 40.00	true Because hours is 45.30 and 45.30 > 40.00 is true, the expression hours > 40.00 evaluates to true.
!age	false age is 20, which is nonzero, so age is true. Therefore, !age is false.
!found && (age >= 18)	false !found is false; age > 18 is 20 > 18 is true. Therefore, !found && (age >= 18) is false && true, which evaluates to false.
!(found && (age >= 18))	false Now, found && (age >= 18) is true && true, which evaluates to true. Therefore, !(found && (age >= 18)) is !true, which evaluates to false.

Expression	**Value / Explanation**
`hours + overTime <= 75.00`	`true`
	Because `hours + overTime` is `45.30 + 15.00 =` `60.30` and `60.30 <= 75.00` is `true`, it follows that `hours + overTime <= 75.00` evaluates to `true`.
`(count >= 0) &&` `        (count <= 100)`	`true`
	Now, `count` is 20. Because `20 >= 0` is `true`, `count >= 0` is `true`. Also, `20 <= 100` is `true`, so `count <= 100` is `true`. Therefore, `(count >= 0) && (count <= 100)` is `true && true`, which evaluates to `true`.
`('A' <= ch && ch <= 'Z')`	`true`
	Here, `ch` is `'B'`. Because `'A' <= 'B'` is `true`, `'A' <= ch` evaluates to `true`. Also, because `'B' <= 'Z'` is `true`, `ch <= 'Z'` evaluates to `true`. Therefore, `('A' <= ch && ch <= 'Z')` is `true && true`, which evaluates to `true`.

The following program evaluates and outputs the values of these logical expressions. Note that if a logical expression evaluates to `true`, the corresponding output is 1; if the logical expression evaluates to `false`, the corresponding output is 0, as shown in the output at the end of the program. (Recall that if the value of a logical expression is `true`, it evaluates to 1, and if the value of the logical expression is `false`, it evaluates to 0.)

```cpp
//Chapter 4 Logical operators

#include <iostream>
#include <iomanip>

using namespace std;

int main()
{
    bool found = true;
    int age = 20;
    double hours = 45.30;
    double overTime = 15.00;
    int count = 20;
    char ch = 'B';

    cout << fixed << showpoint << setprecision(2);
    cout << "found = " << found << ", age = " << age
         << ", hours = " << hours << ", overTime = " << overTime
         << "," << endl << "count = " << count
         << ", ch = " << ch << endl << endl;

    cout << "!found evaluates to " << !found << endl;
    cout << "hours > 40.00 evaluates to " << (hours > 40.00) << endl;
    cout << "!age evaluates to " << !age << endl;
    cout << "(!found && (age >= 18)) evaluates to "
         << (!found && (age >= 18)) << endl;
```

```
        cout << "!(found && (age >= 18)) evaluates to "
             << (!(found && (age >= 18))) << endl;
        cout << "hours + overTime <= 75.00 evaluates to "
             << (hours + overTime <= 75.00) << endl;
        cout << "(count >= 0) && (count <= 100) evaluates to "
             << ((count >= 0) && (count <= 100)) << endl;
        cout << "('A' <= ch && ch <= 'Z') evaluates to "
             << ('A' <= ch && ch <= 'Z') << endl;

        return 0;
}
```

Sample Run:

```
found = 1, age = 20, hours = 45.30, overTime = 15.00,
count = 20, ch = B

!found evaluates to 0
hours > 40.00 evaluates to 1
!age evaluates to 0
(!found && (age >= 18)) evaluates to 0
!(found && (age >= 18)) evaluates to 0
hours + overTime <= 75.00 evaluates to 1
(count >= 0) && (count <= 100) evaluates to 1
('A' <= ch && ch <= 'Z') evaluates to 1
```

You can insert parentheses into an expression to clarify its meaning. You can also use parentheses to override the precedence of operators. Using the standard order of precedence, the expression:

```
11 > 5 || 6 < 15 && 7 >= 8
```

is equivalent to:

```
11 > 5 || (6 < 15 && 7 >= 8)
```

In this expression, 11 > 5 is **true**, 6 < 15 is **true**, and 7 >= 8 is **false**. Substitute these values in the expression 11 > 5 || (6 < 15 && 7 >= 8) to get **true** || (**true** && **false**) = **true** || **false** = **true**. Therefore, the expression 11 > 5 || (6 < 15 && 7 >= 8) evaluates to **true**.

In C++, logical (Boolean) expressions can be manipulated or processed in either of two ways: by using **int** variables or by using **bool** variables. The following sections describe these methods.

int **Data Type and Logical (Boolean) Expressions**

Earlier versions of C++ did not provide built-in data types that had logical (or Boolean) values **true** and **false**. Because logical expressions evaluate to either 1 or 0, the value of a logical expression was stored in a variable of the data type **int**. Therefore, you can use the **int** data type to manipulate logical (Boolean) expressions.

Recall that nonzero values are treated as `true`. Now, consider the declarations:

```
int legalAge;
int age;
```

and the assignment statement:

```
legalAge = 21;
```

If you regard `legalAge` as a logical variable, the value of `legalAge` assigned by this statement is `true`.

The assignment statement:

```
legalAge = (age >= 21);
```

assigns the value 1 to `legalAge` if the value of `age` is greater than or equal to 21. The statement assigns the value 0 if the value of `age` is less than 21.

`bool` Data Type and Logical (Boolean) Expressions

More recent versions of C++ contain a built-in data type, `bool`, that has the logical (Boolean) values `true` and `false`. Therefore, you can manipulate logical (Boolean) expressions using the `bool` data type. Recall that in C++, `bool`, `true`, and `false` are reserved words. In addition, the identifier `true` has the value 1, and the identifier `false` has the value 0. Now, consider the following declaration:

```
bool legalAge;
int age;
```

The statement:

```
legalAge = true;
```

sets the value of the variable `legalAge` to `true`. The statement:

```
legalAge = (age >= 21);
```

assigns the value `true` to `legalAge` if the value of `age` is greater than or equal to 21. This statement assigns the value `false` to `legalAge` if the value of `age` is less than 21. For example, if the value of `age` is 25, the value assigned to `legalAge` is `true`—that is, 1. Similarly, if the value of `age` is 16, the value assigned to `legalAge` is `false`—that is, 0.

 NOTE   You can use either an `int` variable or a `bool` variable to store the value of a logical expression. For the purpose of clarity, this book uses `bool` variables to store the values of logical expressions.

Selection: `if` and `if...else`

Although there are only two logical values, `true` and `false`, they turn out to be extremely useful because they permit programs to incorporate decision making that alters the processing flow. The remainder of this chapter discusses ways to incorporate decisions into a program. In C++, there are two selections, or branch control structures: `if` statements and the `switch` structure. This section discusses how `if` and `if...else` statements can be used to create one-way selection, two-way selection, and multiple selections. The `switch` structure is discussed later in this chapter.

One-Way Selection

A bank would like to send a notice to a customer if her or his checking account balance falls below the required minimum balance. That is, if the account balance is below the required minimum balance, it should send a notice to the customer; otherwise, it should do nothing. Similarly, if the policyholder of an insurance policy is a nonsmoker, the company would like to apply a 10% discount to the policy premium. Both of these examples involve one-way selection. In C++, one-way selections are incorporated using the `if` statement. The syntax of one-way selection is:

```
if (expression)
    statement
```

Note the elements of this syntax. It begins with the reserved word `if`, followed by an **expression** contained within parentheses, followed by a **statement**. Note that the parentheses around the **expression** are part of the syntax. The **expression** is sometimes called a **decision maker** because it decides whether to execute the **statement** that follows it. The **expression** is usually a logical expression. If the value of the **expression** is `true`, the **statement** executes. If the value is `false`, the **statement** does not execute and the computer goes on to the next statement in the program. The **statement** following the **expression** is sometimes called the **action statement**. Figure 4-2 shows the flow of execution of the `if` statement (one-way selection).

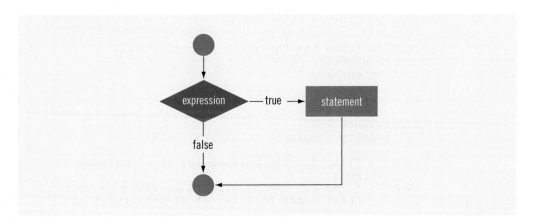

FIGURE 4-2 One-way selection

EXAMPLE 4-7

```
if (score >= 60)
    grade = 'P';
```

In this code, if the expression (score >= 60) evaluates to true, the assignment statement, grade = 'P';, executes. If the expression evaluates to false, the statements (if any) following the if structure execute. For example, if the value of score is 65, the value assigned to the variable grade is 'P'.

EXAMPLE 4-8

```
//Program to compute and output the penalty on an unpaid
//credit card balance. The program assumes that the interest
//rate on the unpaid balance is 1.5% per month.

#include <iostream>                                        //Line 1
#include <iomanip>                                         //Line 2

using namespace std;                                       //Line 3

const double INTEREST_RATE = 0.015;                        //Line 4

int main ()                                                //Line 5
{                                                          //Line 6
    double creditCardBalance;                              //Line 7
    double payment;                                        //Line 8
    double balance;                                        //Line 9
    double penalty = 0.0;                                  //Line 10

    cout << fixed << showpoint << setprecision(2);         //Line 11

    cout << "Line 12: Enter credit card balance: ";        //Line 12
    cin >> creditCardBalance;                              //Line 13
    cout << endl;                                          //Line 14

    cout << "Line 15: Enter the payment: ";                //Line 15
    cin >> payment;                                        //Line 16
    cout << endl;                                          //Line 17

    balance = creditCardBalance - payment;                 //Line 18

    if (balance > 0)                                       //Line 19
        penalty = balance * INTEREST_RATE;                 //Line 20

    cout << "Line 21: The balance is: $" << balance
         << endl;                                          //Line 21
    cout << "Line 22: The penalty to be added to your "
         << "next month bill is: $" << penalty << endl;    //Line 22

    return 0;                                              //Line 23
}                                                          //Line 24
```

Sample Run: In this sample run, the user input is shaded.

```
Line 12: Enter credit card balance: 2500.00

Line 15: Enter the payment: 275.00

Line 21: The balance is: $2225.00
Line 22: The penalty to be added to your next month bill is: $33.38
```

The statements in Lines 7 to 10 declare the variables used in the program. The statement in Line 12 prompts the user to enter the credit card billing amount. The statement in Line 13 inputs the amount into the variable `creditCardBalance`. The statement in Line 15 prompts the user to enter the payment. The statement in Line 16 inputs the payment into the variable `payment`. The statement in Line 18 computes the unpaid balance. The `if` statement in Line 19 determines if the unpaid balance is positive. If the unpaid balance is positive, the statement in Line 20 computes the penalty. The statements in Lines 21 and 22 output the results. This program assumes that the interest rate on the unpaid balance is 18% per year (that is, 1.5% per month). As you can see the interest rate on the unpaid balance can quickly add up and ruin your credit ratings as well as put you in financial trouble.

4

EXAMPLE 4-9

Consider the following statement:

```
if score >= 60      //syntax error
    grade = 'P';
```

This statement illustrates an incorrect version of an `if` statement. The parentheses around the logical expression are missing, which is a syntax error.

Putting a semicolon after the parentheses following the `expression` in an `if` statement (that is, before the `statement`) is a semantic error. If the semicolon immediately follows the closing parenthesis, the `if` statement will operate on the empty statement.

EXAMPLE 4-10

Consider the following C++ statements:

```
if (score >= 60);      //Line 1
    grade = 'P';       //Line 2
```

Because there is a semicolon at the end of the expression (see Line 1), the `if` statement in Line 1 terminates. The action of this `if` statement is null, and the statement in Line 2 is not part of the `if` statement in Line 1. Hence, the statement in Line 2 executes regardless of how the `if` statement evaluates.

Two-Way Selection

There are many programming situations in which you must choose between two alternatives. For example, if a part-time employee works overtime, the paycheck is calculated using the overtime payment formula; otherwise, the paycheck is calculated using the regular formula. This is an example of two-way selection. To choose between two alternatives—that is, to implement two-way selections—C++ provides the `if...else` statement. Two-way selection uses the following syntax:

```
if (expression)
    statement1
else
    statement2
```

Take a moment to examine this syntax. It begins with the reserved word `if`, followed by a logical expression contained within parentheses, followed by a statement, followed by the reserved word `else`, followed by a second statement. Statements 1 and 2 are any valid C++ statements. In a two-way selection, if the value of the **expression** is `true`, `statement1` executes. If the value of the **expression** is `false`, `statement2` executes. Figure 4-3 shows the flow of execution of the `if...else` statement (two-way selection).

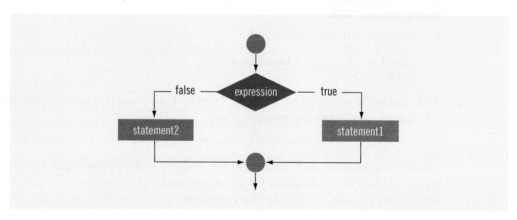

FIGURE 4-3 Two-way selection

EXAMPLE 4-11

Consider the following statements:

```
if (hours > 40.0)                          //Line 1
    wages = 40.0 * rate +
            1.5 * rate * (hours - 40.0);   //Line 2
else                                       //Line 3
    wages = hours * rate;                  //Line 4
```

If the value of the variable `hours` is greater than `40.0`, the `wages` include overtime payment. Suppose that `hours` is 50. The expression in the `if` statement, in Line 1, evaluates to `true`, so the statement in Line 2 executes. On the other hand, if `hours` is 30 or any number less than or equal to 40, the expression in the `if` statement, in Line 1, evaluates to `false`. In this case, the program skips the statement in Line 2 and executes the statement in Line 4—that is, the statement following the reserved word `else` executes.

In a two-way selection statement, putting a semicolon after the **expression** and before `statement1` creates a syntax error. If the `if` statement ends with a semicolon, `statement1` is no longer part of the `if` statement, and the `else` part of the `if...else` statement stands all by itself. There is no stand-alone `else` statement in C++. That is, it cannot be separated from the `if` statement.

4

EXAMPLE 4-12

The following statements show an example of a syntax error:

```
if (hours > 40.0);                        //Line 1
    wages = 40.0 * rate +
            1.5 * rate * (hours - 40.0);  //Line 2
else                                      //Line 3
    wages = hours * rate;                 //Line 4
```

The semicolon at the end of the `if` statement (see Line 1) ends the `if` statement, so the statement in Line 2 separates the `else` clause from the `if` statement. That is, `else` is all by itself. Because there is no stand-alone `else` statement in C++, this code generates a syntax error. As shown in Example 4-10, in a one-way selection, the semicolon at the end of an `if` statement is a logical error, whereas as shown in this example, in a two-way selection, it is a syntax error.

EXAMPLE 4-13

The following program determines an employee's weekly wages. If the hours worked exceed 40, wages include overtime payment.

```
//Program: Weekly wages

#include <iostream>
#include <iomanip>

using namespace std;

int main()
{
    double wages, rate, hours;
```

```
cout << fixed << showpoint << setprecision(2);      //Line 1
cout << "Line 2: Enter working hours and rate: "; //Line 2
cin >> hours >> rate;                               //Line 3

if (hours > 40.0)                                   //Line 4
    wages = 40.0 * rate +
            1.5 * rate * (hours - 40.0);            //Line 5
else                                                //Line 6
    wages = hours * rate;                           //Line 7

cout << endl;                                       //Line 8
cout << "Line 9: The wages are $" << wages
     << endl;                                       //Line 9

return 0;
}
```

Sample Run: In this sample run, the user input is shaded.

Line 2: Enter working hours and rate: `56.45 12.50`

Line 9: The wages are $808.44

The statement in Line 1 sets the output of the floating-point numbers in a fixed decimal format, with a decimal point, trailing zeros, and two decimal places. The statement in Line 2 prompts the user to input the number of hours worked and the pay rate. The statement in Line 3 inputs these values into the variables hours and rate, respectively. The statement in Line 4 checks whether the value of the variable hours is greater than 40.0. If hours is greater than 40.0, then the wages are calculated by the statement in Line 5, which includes overtime payment. Otherwise, the wages are calculated by the statement in Line 7. The statement in Line 9 outputs the wages.

Let us now consider another example of an **if** statement and examine some of the semantic errors that can occur.

EXAMPLE 4-14

Consider the following statements:

```
if (score >= 60)               //Line 1
    cout << "Passing" << endl;  //Line 2
    cout << "Failing" << endl;  //Line 3
```

If the expression (score >= 60) evaluates to **false**, the output statement in Line 2 does not execute. So the output would be Failing. That is, this set of statements performs the same action as an **if...else** statement. It will execute the output statement in Line 3 rather than the output statement in Line 2. For example, if the value of score is 50, these statements will output the following line:

```
Failing
```

However, if the expression (`score >= 60`) evaluates to `true`, the program will execute both of the output statements, giving a very unsatisfactory result. For example, if the value of `score` is 70, these statements will output the following lines:

```
Passing
Failing
```

The `if` statement controls the execution of only the statement in Line 2. The statement in Line 3 always executes.

The correct code to print `Passing` or `Failing`, depending on the value of `score`, is:

```
if (score >= 60)
    cout << "Passing" << endl;
else
    cout << "Failing" << endl;
```

4

Compound (Block of) Statements

The `if` and `if...else` structures control only one statement at a time. Suppose, however, that you want to execute more than one statement if the `expression` in an `if` or `if...else` statement evaluates to `true`. To permit more complex statements, C++ provides a structure called a **compound statement** or a **block of statements**. A compound statement takes the following form:

```
{
    statement_1
    statement_2
       .
       .
       .
    statement_n
}
```

That is, a compound statement consists of a sequence of statements enclosed in curly braces, `{` and `}`. In an `if` or `if ...else` structure, a compound statement functions as if it was a single statement. Thus, instead of having a simple two-way selection similar to the following code:

```
if (age >= 18)
    cout << "Eligible to vote." << endl;
else
    cout << "Not eligible to vote." << endl;
```

you could include compound statements, similar to the following code:

```
if (age >= 18)
{
    cout << "Eligible to vote." << endl;
    cout << "No longer a minor." << endl;
}
```

```
else
{
    cout << "Not eligible to vote." << endl;
    cout << "Still a minor." << endl;
}
```

The compound statement is very useful and will be used in most of the structured statements in this chapter.

Multiple Selections: Nested `if`

In the previous sections, you learned how to implement one-way and two-way selections in a program. Some problems require the implementation of more than two alternatives. For example, suppose that if the checking account balance is more than $50,000, the interest rate is 7%; if the balance is between $25,000 and $49,999.99, the interest rate is 5%; if the balance is between $1,000 and $24,999.99, the interest rate is 3%; otherwise, the interest rate is 0%. This particular problem has four alternatives—that is, multiple selection paths. You can include multiple selection paths in a program by using an `if...else` structure if the action statement itself is an `if` or `if...else` statement. When one control statement is located within another, it is said to be **nested**.

Example 4-15 illustrates how to incorporate multiple selections using a nested `if...else` structure.

EXAMPLE 4-15

Suppose that `balance` and `interestRate` are variables of type `double`. The following statements determine the `interestRate` depending on the value of the `balance`:

```
if (balance > 50000.00)                  //Line 1
    interestRate = 0.07;                 //Line 2
else                                     //Line 3
    if (balance >= 25000.00)             //Line 4
        interestRate = 0.05;             //Line 5
    else                                 //Line 6
        if (balance >= 1000.00)          //Line 7
            interestRate = 0.03;         //Line 8
        else                             //Line 9
            interestRate = 0.00;         //Line 10
```

A nested `if...else` structure demands the answer to an important question: How do you know which `else` is paired with which `if`? Recall that in C++, there is no stand-alone `else` statement. Every `else` must be paired with an `if`. The rule to pair an `else` with an `if` is as follows:

Pairing an `else` with an `if`: In a nested `if` statement, C++ associates an `else` with the most recent incomplete `if`—that is, the most recent `if` that has not been paired with an `else`.

Using this rule, in Example 4-15, the `else` in Line 3 is paired with the `if` in Line 1. The `else` in Line 6 is paired with the `if` in Line 4, and the `else` in Line 9 is paired with the `if` in Line 7.

To avoid excessive indentation, the code in Example 4-15 can be rewritten as follows:

```
if (balance > 50000.00)                    //Line 1
    interestRate = 0.07;                   //Line 2
else if (balance >= 25000.00)              //Line 3
    interestRate = 0.05;                   //Line 4
else if (balance >= 1000.00)               //Line 5
    interestRate = 0.03;                   //Line 6
else                                       //Line 7
    interestRate = 0.00;                   //Line 8
```

The following examples will help you to see the various ways in which you can use nested `if` structures to implement multiple selection.

4

EXAMPLE 4-16

Assume that `score` is a variable of type `int`. Based on the value of `score`, the following code outputs the grade:

```
if (score >= 90)
    cout << "The grade is A." << endl;
else if (score >= 80)
    cout << "The grade is B." << endl;
else if (score >= 70)
    cout << "The grade is C." << endl;
else if (score >= 60)
    cout << "The grade is D." << endl;
else
    cout << "The grade is F." << endl;
```

EXAMPLE 4-17

Assume that all variables are properly declared, and consider the following statements:

```
if (temperature >= 50)                              //Line 1
    if (temperature >= 80)                          //Line 2
        cout << "Good day for swimming." << endl;   //Line 3
    else                                            //Line 4
        cout << "Good day for golfing." << endl;    //Line 5
else                                                //Line 6
    cout << "Good day to play tennis." << endl;     //Line 7
```

In this C++ code, the `else` in Line 4 is paired with the `if` in Line 2, and the `else` in Line 6 is paired with the `if` in Line 1. Note that the `else` in Line 4 cannot be paired with the `if` in Line 1. If you pair the `else` in Line 4 with the `if` in Line 1, the `if` in Line 2 becomes the action statement part of the `if` in Line 1, leaving the `else` in Line 6 dangling. Also, the statements in Lines 2 though 5 form the statement part of the `if` in Line 1. The indentation does not determine the pairing, but should be used to communicate the pairing.

EXAMPLE 4-18

Assume that all variables are properly declared, and consider the following statements:

```cpp
if (temperature >= 70)                                    //Line 1
    if (temperature >= 80)                                //Line 2
        cout << "Good day for swimming." << endl;   //Line 3
    else                                                  //Line 4
        cout << "Good day for golfing." << endl;    //Line 5
```

In this code, the `else` in Line 4 is paired with the `if` in Line 2. Note that for the `else` in Line 4, the most recent incomplete `if` is in Line 2. In this code, the `if` in Line 1 has no `else` and is a one-way selection. Once again, the indentation does not determine the pairing, but it communicates the pairing.

EXAMPLE 4-19

Assume that all variables are properly declared, and consider the following statements:

```cpp
if (gender == 'M')                    //Line 1
    if (age < 21 )                    //Line 2
        policyRate = 0.05;            //Line 3
    else                              //Line 4
        policyRate = 0.035;          //Line 5
else if (gender == 'F')               //Line 6
    if (age < 21 )                    //Line 7
        policyRate = 0.04;           //Line 8
    else                              //Line 9
        policyRate = 0.03;           //Line 10
```

In this code, the `else` in Line 4 is paired with the `if` in Line 2. Note that for the `else` in Line 4, the most recent incomplete `if` is the `if` in Line 2. The `else` in Line 6 is paired with the `if` in Line 1. The `else` in Line 9 is paired with the `if` in Line 7. Once again, the indentation does not determine the pairing, but it communicates the pairing.

Comparing `if...else` Statements with a Series of `if` Statements

Consider the following C++ program segments, all of which accomplish the same task:

```cpp
a.  if (month == 1)                            //Line 1
        cout << "January" << endl;           //Line 2
    else if (month == 2)                       //Line 3
        cout << "February" << endl;          //Line 4
    else if (month == 3)                       //Line 5
        cout << "March" << endl;             //Line 6
    else if (month == 4)                       //Line 7
        cout << "April" << endl;             //Line 8
```

```
    else if (month == 5)                   //Line 9
        cout << "May" << endl;             //Line 10
    else if (month == 6)                   //Line 11
        cout << "June" << endl;            //Line 12
```

```
b.  if (month == 1)
        cout << "January" << endl;
    if (month == 2)
        cout << "February" << endl;
    if (month == 3)
        cout << "March" << endl;
    if (month == 4)
        cout << "April" << endl;
    if (month == 5)
        cout << "May" << endl;
    if (month == 6)
        cout << "June" << endl;
```

Program segment (a) is written as a sequence of `if...else` statements; program segment (b) is written as a series of `if` statements. Both program segments accomplish the same thing. If `month` is 3, then both program segments output `March`. If `month` is 1, then in program segment (a), the expression in the `if` statement in Line 1 evaluates to `true`. The statement (in Line 2) associated with this `if` then executes; the rest of the structure, which is the `else` of this `if` statement, is skipped; and the remaining `if` statements are not evaluated. In program segment (b), the computer has to evaluate the expression in each `if` statement because there is no `else` statement. As a consequence, program segment (b) executes more slowly than does program segment (a).

Short-Circuit Evaluation

Logical expressions in C++ are evaluated using a highly efficient algorithm. This algorithm is illustrated with the help of the following statements:

```
(x > y) || (x == 5)        //Line 1
(a == b) && (x >= 7)       //Line 2
```

In the statement in Line 1, the two operands of the operator `||` are the expressions `(x > y)` and `(x == 5)`. This expression evaluates to `true` if either the operand `(x > y)` is `true` or the operand `(x == 5)` is `true`. With short-circuit evaluation, the computer evaluates the logical expression from left to right. As soon as the value of the entire logical expression is known, the evaluation stops. For example, in statement 1, if the operand `(x > y)` evaluates to `true`, then the entire expression evaluates to `true` because `true || true` is `true` and `true || false` is `true`. Therefore, the value of the operand `(x == 5)` has no bearing on the final outcome.

Similarly, in the statement in Line 2, the two operands of the operator `&&` are `(a == b)` and `(x >= 7)`. If the operand `(a == b)` evaluates to `false`, then the entire expression evaluates to `false` because `false && true` is `false` and `false && false` is `false`.

Short-circuit evaluation (of a logical expression): A process in which the computer evaluates a logical expression from left to right and stops as soon as the value of the expression is known.

EXAMPLE 4-20

Consider the following expressions:

```
(age >= 21) || ( x == 5)        //Line 1
(grade == 'A') && (x >= 7)      //Line 2
```

For the expression in Line 1, suppose that the value of `age` is 25. Because `(25 >= 21)` is `true` and the logical operator used in the expression is `||`, the expression evaluates to `true`. Due to short-circuit evaluation, the computer does not evaluate the expression `(x == 5)`. Similarly, for the expression in Line 2, suppose that the value of `grade` is `'B'`. Because `('B' == 'A')` is `false` and the logical operator used in the expression is `&&`, the expression evaluates to `false`. The computer does not evaluate `(x >= 7)`.

Comparing Floating-Point Numbers for Equality: A Precaution

Comparison of floating-point numbers for equality may not behave as you would expect. For example, consider the following program:

```cpp
#include <iostream>
#include <iomanip>
#include <cmath>

using namespace std;

int main()
{
    double x = 1.0;
    double y = 3.0 / 7.0 + 2.0 / 7.0 + 2.0 / 7.0;

    cout << fixed << showpoint << setprecision(17);

    cout << "3.0 / 7.0 + 2.0 / 7.0 + 2.0 / 7.0 = "
         << 3.0 / 7.0 + 2.0 / 7.0 + 2.0 / 7.0 << endl;

    cout << "x = " << x << endl;
    cout << "y = " << y << endl;

    if (x == y)
        cout << "x and y are the same." << endl;
    else
        cout << "x and y are not the same." << endl;

    if (fabs(x - y) < 0.000001)
        cout << "x and y are the same within the tolerance "
             << "0.000001." << endl;
```

```
        else
            cout << " x and y are not the same within the "
                 << "tolerance 0.000001." << endl;

        return 0;
}
```

Sample Run:

```
3.0 / 7.0 + 2.0 / 7.0 + 2.0 / 7.0 = 0.99999999999999989
x = 1.00000000000000000
y = 0.99999999999999989
x and y are not the same.
x and y are the same within the tolerance 0.000001.
```

In this program, x is initialized to 1.0 and y is initialized to 3.0 / 7.0 + 2.0 / 7.0 + 2.0 / 7.0. Now, due to rounding, as shown by the output, this expression evaluates to 0.99999999999999989. Therefore, the expression (x == y) evaluates to **false**. However, if you evaluate the expression 3.0 / 7.0 + 2.0 / 7.0 + 2.0 / 7.0 by hand using a paper and a pencil, you will get 3.0 / 7.0 + 2.0 / 7.0 + 2.0 / 7.0 = (3.0 + 2.0 + 2.0) / 7.0 = 7.0 / 7.0 = 1.0. That is, the value of y should be set to 1.0.

The preceding program and its output show that you should be careful when comparing floating-point numbers for equality. One way to check whether two floating-point numbers are equal is to check whether the absolute value of their difference is less than a certain tolerance. For example, suppose the tolerance is 0.000001. Then, x and y are equal if the absolute value of (x - y) is less than 0.000001. To find the absolute value, you can use the function `fabs` of the header file `cmath`, as shown in the program. Therefore, the expression `fabs(x - y)` < 0.000001 determines whether the absolute value of (x - y) is less than 0.000001.

Associativity of Relational Operators: A Precaution

Sometimes logical expressions do not behave as you might expect, as shown by the following program, which determines if a number is between 0 and 10 (inclusive).

```
#include <iostream>

using namespace std;

int main()
{
    int num;

    cout << "Enter an integer: ";
    cin >> num;
    cout << endl;

    if (0 <= num <= 10)
        cout << num << " is within 0 and 10." << endl;
```

4

```
    else
        cout << num << " is not within 0 and 10." << endl;

    return 0;
}
```

Sample Runs: In these sample runs, the user input is shaded.

Sample Run 1:

Enter an integer: 5

5 is within 0 and 10.

Sample Run 2:

Enter an integer: 20

20 is within 0 and 10.

Sample Run 3:

Enter an integer: -10

-10 is within 0 and 10.

Clearly, Sample Run 1 is correct and Sample Runs 2 and 3 are incorrect. Because the `if` statement determines whether an integer is between 0 and 10, the problem is in the expression in the if statement. So, let us look at this expression, which is:

```
0 <= num <= 10
```

Although this statement is a legal C++ expression, you do not get the desired result. Let us evaluate this expression for certain values of num. Suppose that the value of num is 5. Then:

0 <= num <= 10	= 0 <= 5 <= 10	
	= (0 <= 5) <= 10	(Because relational operators are evaluated from left to right)
	= 1 <= 10	(Because 0 <= 5 is true, 0 <= 5 evaluates to 1)
	= 1 (true)	

Now, suppose that num = 20. Then:

0 <= num <= 10	= 0 <= 20 <= 10	
	= (0 <= 20) <= 10	(Because relational operators are evaluated from left to right)
	= 1 <= 10	(Because 0 <= 20 is true, 0 <= 20 evaluates to 1)
	= 1 (true)	

Now, you can see why the expression evaluates to `true` when num is 20. Similarly, if num is −10, the expression 0 <= num <= 10 evaluates to `true`. In fact, this expression will always evaluate to `true`, no matter what num is. This is due to the fact that the expression 0 <= num evaluates to either 0 or 1, and 0 <= 10 is `true` and 1 <= 10 is `true`. So what is wrong with the expression 0 <= num <= 10? It is missing the logical operator `&&`. A correct way to write this expression in C++ is:

```
0 <= num && num <= 10
```

You must take care when formulating logical expressions. When creating a complex logical expression, you must use the proper logical operators.

4

Avoiding Bugs by Avoiding Partially Understood Concepts and Techniques

The debugging sections in Chapters 2 and 3 illustrated how to understand and fix syntax and logic errors. In this section, we illustrate how to avoid bugs by avoiding partially understood concepts and techniques.

The programs that you have written until now should have illustrated that a small error such as omission of a semicolon at the end of a variable declaration or using a variable without properly declaring it can prevent a program from successfully compiling. Similarly, using a variable without properly initializing it can prevent a program from running correctly. Recall that the condition associated with an `if` statement must be enclosed in parentheses. Therefore, the following expression will result in a syntax error:

```
if score >= 90
```

Example 4-12 illustrates that an unintended semicolon following the condition of the following `if` statement:

```
if (hours > 40.0);
```

can prevent successful compilation or correct execution.

The approach that you take to solve a problem must use concepts and techniques correctly; otherwise, your solution will be either incorrect or deficient. If you do not understand a concept or technique completely, don't use it until your understanding is complete. The problem of using partially understood concepts and techniques can be illustrated by the following program.

Suppose that we want to write a program that analyzes students' GPA. If the GPA is greater than or equal to 3.9, the student makes the dean's honor list. If the GPA is less than 2.00, the student is sent a warning letter indicating that the GPA is below the graduation requirement. So, consider the following program:

```cpp
//GPA program with bugs.

#include <iostream>                              //Line 1

using namespace std;                             //Line 2

int main()                                       //Line 3
```

```
{                                                              //Line 4
    double gpa;                                                //Line 5

    cout << "Enter the GPA: ";                                 //Line 6
    cin >> gpa;                                                //Line 7
    cout << endl;                                              //Line 8

    if (gpa >= 2.0)                                            //Line 9
        if (gpa >= 3.9)                                        //Line 10
            cout << "Dean\'s Honor List." << endl;             //Line 11
    else                                                       //Line 12
        cout << "The GPA is below the graduation "
             << "requirement. \nSee your  "
             << "academic advisor." << endl;                   //Line 13

    return 0;                                                  //Line 14
}                                                              //Line 15
```

Sample Runs: In these sample runs, the user input is shaded.

Sample Run 1:

Enter the GPA: 3.91

Dean's Honor List.

Sample Run 2:

Enter the GPA: 3.8

The GPA is below the graduation requirement.
See your academic advisor.

Sample Run 3:

Enter the GPA: 1.95

Let us look at these sample runs. Clearly, the output in Sample Run 1 is correct. In Sample Run 2, the input is 3.8 and the output indicates that this GPA is below the graduation requirement. However, a student with a GPA of 3.8 would graduate with some type of honor. So, the output in Sample Run 2 is incorrect. In Sample Run 3, the input is 1.95, and the output does not show any warning message. Therefore, the output in Sample Run 3 is also incorrect. It means that the if...else statement in Lines 9 to 13 is incorrect. Let us look at these statements, that is:

```
if (gpa >= 2.0)                                               //Line 9
    if (gpa >= 3.9)                                           //Line 10
        cout << "Dean\'s Honor List." << endl;                //Line 11
else                                                          //Line 12
    cout << "The GPA is below the graduation "
         << "requirement. \nSee your  "
         << "academic advisor." << endl;                      //Line 13
```

Following the rule of pairing an `else` with an `if`, the `else` in Line 12 is paired with the `if` in Line 10. In other words, using the correct indentation, the code is:

```
if (gpa >= 2.0)                                          //Line 9
    if (gpa >= 3.9)                                      //Line 10
        cout << "Dean\'s Honor List." << endl;           //Line 11
    else                                                 //Line 12
        cout << "The GPA is below the graduation "
             << "requirement. \nSee your   "
             << "academic advisor." << endl;             //Line 13
```

Now, we can see that the `if` statement in Line 9 is a one-way selection. Therefore, if the input number is less than `2.0`, no action will take place, that is, no warning message will be printed. Now, suppose the input is 3.8. Then, the expression in Line 9 evaluates to `true`, so the expression in Line 10 is evaluated, which evaluates to `false`. This means the output statement in Line 13 executes, resulting in an unsatisfactory result.

In fact, the program should print the warning message only if the GPA is less than `2.0`, and it should print the message:

```
Dean's Honor List.
```

if the GPA is greater than or equal to `3.9`.

To achieve that result, the `else` in Line 12 needs to be paired with the `if` in Line 9. To pair the `else` in Line 12 with the `if` in Line 9, you need to use a compound statement, as follows:

```
if (gpa >= 2.0)                                          //Line 9
{
    if (gpa >= 3.9)                                      //Line 10
        cout << "Dean\'s Honor List." << endl; //Line 11
}
else                                                     //Line 12
    cout << "The GPA is below the graduation "
         << "requirement. \nSee your   "
         << "academic advisor." << endl;                 //Line 13
```

The correct program is as follows:

```
//Correct GPA program.

#include <iostream>                                      //Line 1

using namespace std;                                     //Line 2

int main()                                               //Line 3
{                                                        //Line 4
    double gpa;                                          //Line 5

    cout << "Enter the GPA: ";                           //Line 6
    cin >> gpa;                                          //Line 7
    cout << endl;                                        //Line 8
```

```
    if (gpa >= 2.0)                                    //Line 9
    {                                                  //Line 10
        if (gpa >= 3.9)                                //Line 11
            cout << "Dean\'s Honor List." << endl;     //Line 12
    }                                                  //Line 13
    else                                               //Line 14
        cout << "The GPA is below the graduation "
             << "requirement. \nSee your   "
             << "academic advisor." << endl;           //Line 15

    return 0;                                          //Line 16
}                                                      //Line 17
```

Sample Runs: In these sample runs, the user input is shaded.

Sample Run 1:

Enter the GPA: `3.91`

Dean's Honor List.

Sample Run 2:

Enter the GPA: `3.8`

Sample Run 3:

Enter the GPA: `1.95`

The GPA is below the graduation requirement.
See your academic advisor.

In cases such as this one, the general rule is that you cannot look inside of a block (that is, inside the braces) to pair an `else` with an `if`. The `else` in Line 14 cannot be paired with the `if` in Line 11 because the `if` statement in Line 11 is enclosed within braces, and the `else` in Line 14 cannot look inside those braces. Therefore, the `else` in Line 14 is paired with the `if` in Line 9.

In this book, the C++ programming concepts and techniques are presented in a logical order. When these concepts and techniques are learned one at a time in a logical order, they are simple enough to be understood completely. Understanding a concept or technique completely before using it will save you an enormous amount of debugging time.

Input Failure and the `if` Statement

In Chapter 3, you saw that an attempt to read invalid data causes the input stream to enter a fail state. Once an input stream enters a fail state, all subsequent input statements associated with that input stream are ignored, and the computer continues to execute the program, which produces erroneous results. You can use `if` statements to check the status of an input stream variable and, if the input stream enters the fail state, include instructions that stop program execution.

In addition to reading invalid data, other events can cause an input stream to enter the fail state. Two additional common causes of input failure are the following:

- Attempting to open an input file that does not exist
- Attempting to read beyond the end of an input file

One way to address these causes of input failure is to check the status of the input stream variable. You can check the status by using the input stream variable as the logical expression in an `if` statement. If the last input succeeded, the input stream variable evaluates to `true`; if the last input failed, it evaluates to `false`.

The statement:

```
if (cin)
    cout << "Input is OK." << endl;
```

prints:

```
Input is OK.
```

if the last input from the standard input device succeeded. Similarly, if `infile` is an `ifstream` variable, the statement:

```
if (!infile)
    cout << "Input failed." << endl;
```

prints:

```
Input failed.
```

if the last input associated with the stream variable `infile` failed.

Suppose an input stream variable tries to open a file for inputting data into a program. If the input file does not exist, you can use the value of the input stream variable, in conjunction with the `return` statement, to terminate the program.

Recall that the last statement included in the function `main` is:

```
return 0;
```

This statement returns a value of 0 to the operating system when the program terminates. A value of 0 indicates that the program terminated normally and that no error occurred during program execution. Values of type `int` other than 0 can also be returned to the operating system via the `return` statement. The return of any value other than 0, however, indicates that something went wrong during program execution.

The `return` statement can appear anywhere in the program. Whenever a `return` statement executes, it immediately exits the function in which it appears. In the case of the function `main`, the program terminates when the `return` statement executes. You can use these properties of the `return` statement to terminate the function `main` whenever the input stream fails. This technique is especially useful when a program tries to open an input file. Consider the following statements:

```
ifstream infile;

infile.open("inputdat.dat");   //open inputdat.dat

if (!infile)
{
    cout << "Cannot open the input file. "
         << "The program terminates." << endl;
    return 1;
}
```

Suppose that the file `inputdat.dat` does not exist. The operation to open this file fails, causing the input stream to enter the fail state. As a logical expression, the file stream variable `infile` then evaluates to `false`. Because `infile` evaluates to `false`, the expression `!infile` (in the `if` statement) evaluates to `true`, and the body of the `if` statement executes. The message:

```
Cannot open the input file. The program terminates.
```

is printed on the screen, and the `return` statement terminates the program by returning a value of 1 to the operating system.

Let's now use the code that responds to input failure by including these features in the Programming Example: Student Grade from Chapter 3. Recall that this program calculates the average test score based on data from an input file and then outputs the results to another file. The following programming code is the same as the code from Chapter 3, except that it includes statements to exit the program if the input file does not exist.

```
//Program to calculate the average test score.

#include <iostream>
#include <fstream>
#include <iomanip>
#include <string>
using namespace std;

int main()
{
    ifstream inFile;      //input file stream variable
    ofstream outFile;     //output file stream variable

    double test1, test2, test3, test4, test5;
    double average;

    string firstName;
    string lastName;

    inFile.open("test.txt"); //open the input file

    if (!inFile)
```

```
    {
        cout << "Cannot open the input file. "
            << "The program terminates." << endl;
        return  1;
    }

    outFile.open("testavg.out");   //open the output file

    outFile << fixed << showpoint;
    outFile << setprecision(2);

    cout << "Processing data" << endl;

    inFile >> firstName >> lastName;
    outFile << "Student name: " << firstName
            << " " << lastName << endl;

    inFile >> test1 >> test2 >> test3
           >> test4 >> test5;
    outFile << "Test scores: " << setw(4) << test1
            << setw(4) << test2 << setw(4) << test3
            << setw(4) << test4 << setw(4) << test5
            << endl;

    average = (test1 + test2 + test3 + test4 + test5) / 5.0;

    outFile << "Average test score: " << setw(6)
            << average << endl;

    inFile.close();
    outFile.close();

    return 0;
}
```

Confusion between the Equality Operator (==) and the Assignment Operator (=)

Recall that if the decision-making expression in the `if` statement evaluates to `true`, the statement part of the `if` statement executes. In addition, the **expression** is usually a logical expression. However, C++ allows you to use *any* expression that can be evaluated to either `true` or `false` as an **expression** in the `if` statement. Consider the following statement:

```
if (x = 5)
    cout << "The value is five." << endl;
```

The **expression**—that is, the decision maker—in the `if` statement is `x = 5`. The expression `x = 5` is called an assignment expression because the operator `=` appears in the expression and there is no semicolon at the end.

This expression is evaluated as follows. First, the right side of the operator `=` is evaluated, which evaluates to 5. The value 5 is then assigned to `x`. Moreover, the value 5—that is, the new value of x—also becomes the value of the expression in the if statement—that is, the value of the assignment expression. Because 5 is nonzero, the expression in the if statement evaluates to true, so the statement part of the if statement outputs: The value is five.

No matter how experienced a programmer is, almost everyone makes the mistake of using = in place of == at one time or another. One reason why these two operators are often confused is that most programming languages use = as an equality operator. Thus, experience with other programming languages can create confusion. Sometimes the error is merely typographical, another reason to be careful when typing code.

Despite the fact that an assignment expression can be used as an expression, using the assignment operator in place of the equality operator can cause serious problems in a program. For example, suppose that the discount on a car insurance policy is based on the insured's driving record. A driving record of 1 means that the driver is accident-free and receives a 25% discount on the policy. The statement:

```
if (drivingCode == 1)
    cout << "The discount on the policy is 25%." << endl;
```

outputs:

```
The discount on the policy is 25%.
```

only if the value of drivingCode is 1. However, the statement:

```
if (drivingCode = 1)
    cout << "The discount on the policy is 25%." << endl;
```

always outputs:

```
The discount on the policy is 25%.
```

because the right side of the assignment expression evaluates to 1, which is nonzero and so evaluates to true. Therefore, the expression in the if statement evaluates to true, outputting the following line of text: The discount on the policy is 25%. Also, the value 1 is assigned to the variable drivingCode. Suppose that before the if statement executes, the value of the variable drivingCode is 4. After the if statement executes, not only is the output wrong, but the new value also replaces the old driving code.

The appearance of = in place of == resembles a *silent killer*. It is not a syntax error, so the compiler does not warn you of an error. Rather, it is a logical error.

 NOTE Using = in place of == can cause serious problems, especially if it happens in a looping statement. Chapter 5 discusses looping structures.

The appearance of the equality operator in place of the assignment operator can also cause errors in a program. For example, suppose x, y, and z are int variables. The statement:

```
x = y + z;
```

assigns the value of the expression y + z to x. The statement:

```
x == y + z;
```

compares the value of the expression y + z with the value of x; the value of x remains the same, however. If somewhere else in the program you are counting on the value of x being y + z, a logic error will occur, the program output will be incorrect, and you will receive no warning of this situation from the compiler. The compiler only provides feedback about syntax errors, not logic errors. For this reason, you must use extra care when working with the equality operator and the assignment operator.

Conditional Operator (? :)

 NOTE The reader can skip this section without any discontinuation.

Certain `if...else` statements can be written in a more concise way by using C++'s conditional operator. The **conditional operator**, written as ? :, is a **ternary operator**, which means that it takes three arguments. The syntax for using the conditional operator is:

```
expression1 ? expression2 : expression3
```

This type of statement is called a **conditional expression**. The conditional expression is evaluated as follows: If `expression1` evaluates to a nonzero integer (that is, to `true`), the result of the conditional expression is `expression2`. Otherwise, the result of the conditional expression is `expression3`.

Consider the following statements:

```
if (a >= b)
    max = a;
else
    max = b;
```

You can use the conditional operator to simplify the writing of this `if...else` statement as follows:

```
max = (a >= b) ? a : b;
```

Program Style and Form (Revisited): Indentation

In the section "Program Style and Form" of Chapter 2, we specified some guidelines to write programs. Now that we have started discussing control structures, in this section, we give some general guidelines to properly indent your program.

As you write programs, typos and errors are unavoidable. If your program is properly indented, you can spot and fix errors quickly, as shown by several examples in this chapter. Typically, the IDE that you use will automatically indent your program. If for some reason your IDE does not indent your program, you can indent your program yourself.

Proper indentation can show the natural grouping of statements. You should insert a blank line between statements that are naturally separate. In this book, the statements inside braces, the statements of a selection structure, and an `if` statement within an `if` statement are all indented four spaces to the right. Throughout the book, we use four spaces to indent statements, especially to show the levels of control structures within other control structures. You can also use four spaces for indentation.

There are two commonly used styles for placing braces. In this book, we place braces on a line by themselves. Also, matching left and right braces are in the same column, that is, they are the same number of spaces away from the left side of the program. This style of placing braces easily shows the grouping of the statements and also matches left and right braces. You can also follow this style to place and indent braces.

In the second style of placing braces, the left brace need not be on a line by itself. Typically, for control structures, the left brace is placed after the last right parenthesis of the (logical) expression, and the right brace is on a line by itself. This style might save some space. However, sometimes this style might not immediately show the grouping or the block of the statements.

No matter what style of indentation you use, you should be consistent within your programs, and the indentation should show the structure of the program.

Using Pseudocode to Develop, Test, and Debug a Program

There are several ways to develop a program. One method involves using an informal mixture of C++ and ordinary language, called **pseudocode** or just **pseudo**. Sometimes pseudo provides a useful means to outline and refine a program before putting it into formal C++ code. When you are constructing programs that involve complex nested control structures, pseudo can help you quickly develop the correct structure of the program and avoid making common errors.

One useful program segment determines the larger of two integers. If x and y are integers, using pseudo, you can quickly write the following:

a.   `if (x > y) then`
           `x is larger`

b.   `if (y > x) then`
           `y is larger`

If the statement in (a) is `true`, then **x** is larger. If the statement in (b) is `true`, then **y** is larger. However, for this code to work in concert to determine the larger of two integers, the computer needs to evaluate both expressions:

`(x > y)`   **and**   `(y > x)`

even if the first statement is `true`. Evaluating both expressions is a waste of computer time.

Let's rewrite this pseudo as follows:

```
if (x > y) then
    x is larger
else
    y is larger
```

Here, only one condition needs to be evaluated. This code looks okay, so let's put it into C++.

```
#include <iostream>

using namespace std;

int main()
{
    if (x > y)
```

Wait . . . once you begin translating the pseudo into a C++ program, you should immediately notice that there is no place to store the value of **x** or **y**. The variables were not declared, which is a very common oversight, especially for new programmers. If you examine the pseudo, you will see that the program needs three variables, and you might as well make them self-documenting. Let's start the program code again:

```
#include <iostream>

using namespace std;

int main()
{
    int  num1, num2, larger;     //Line 1

    if  (num1 > num2);           //Line 2; error
        larger = num1;           //Line 3
    else                         //Line 4
        larger = num2;           //Line 5

    return  0;
}
```

Compiling this program will result in the identification of a common syntax error (in Line 2). Recall that a semicolon cannot appear after the **expression** in the `if...else` statement. However, even if you corrected this syntax error, the program still would not give satisfactory results because it tries to use identifiers that have no values. The variables have not been initialized, which is another common error. In addition, because there are no output statements, you would not be able to see the results of the program.

Because there are so many mistakes in the program, you should try a walk-through to see whether it works at all. You should always use a wide range of values in a walk-through to evaluate the program under as many different circumstances as possible. For example, does this program work if one number is zero, if one number is negative and the other number is positive, if both numbers are negative, or if both numbers are the same? Examining the program, you can see that it does not check whether the two numbers are equal. Taking all of these points into account, you can rewrite the program as follows:

```cpp
//Program: Compare Numbers
//This program compares two integers and outputs the largest.

#include <iostream>

using namespace std;

int main()
{
    int num1, num2;

    cout << "Enter any two integers: ";
    cin >> num1 >> num2;
    cout << endl;

    cout << "The two integers entered are " << num1
         << " and " << num2 << endl;

    if (num1 > num2)
        cout << "The larger number is " << num1 << endl;
    else if (num2 > num1)
        cout << "The larger number is " << num2 << endl;
    else
        cout << "Both numbers are equal." << endl;

    return 0;
}
```

Sample Run: In this sample run, the user input is shaded.

```
Enter any two integers: 78 90
The two integers entered are 78 and 90
The larger number is 90
```

One thing you can learn from the preceding program is that you must first develop a program using paper and pencil. Although a program that is first written on a piece of paper is not guaranteed to run successfully on the first try, this step is still a good starting point. On paper, it is easier to spot errors and improve the program, especially with large programs.

switch Structures

Recall that there are two selection, or branch, structures in C++. The first selection structure, which is implemented with **if** and **if...else** statements, usually requires the evaluation of a (logical) expression. The second selection structure, which does not require the evaluation of a logical expression, is called the **switch structure**. C++'s **switch** structure gives the computer the power to choose from among many alternatives.

A general syntax of the **switch** statement is:

```
switch (expression)
{
case value1:
    statements1
    break;
case value2:
    statements2
    break;
    .
    .
    .
case valuen:
    statementsn
    break;
default:
    statements
}
```

In C++, **switch**, **case**, **break**, and **default** are reserved words. In a **switch** structure, first the **expression** is evaluated. The value of the **expression** is then used to perform the actions specified in the statements that follow the reserved word **case**. Recall that in a syntax, shading indicates an optional part of the definition.

Although it need not be, the **expression** is usually an identifier. Whether it is an identifier or an expression, the value can be only integral. The **expression** is sometimes called the **selector**. Its value determines which statement is selected for execution. A particular **case** value should appear only once. One or more statements may follow a **case** label, so you do not need to use braces to turn multiple statements into a single compound statement. The **break** statement may or may not appear after each statement. Figure 4-4 shows the flow of execution of the **switch** statement.

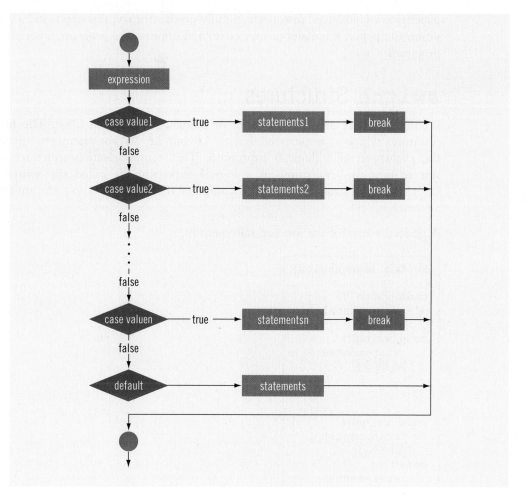

FIGURE 4-4 `switch` statement

The `switch` statement executes according to the following rules:

1. When the value of the **expression** is matched against a `case` value (also called a label), the statements execute until either a `break` statement is found or the end of the `switch` structure is reached.

2. If the value of the **expression** does not match any of the `case` values, the statements following the `default` label execute. If the `switch` structure has no `default` label and if the value of the **expression** does not match any of the `case` values, the entire `switch` statement is skipped.

3. A `break` statement causes an immediate *exit* from the `switch` structure.

EXAMPLE 4-21

Consider the following statements, in which grade is a variable of type char:

```cpp
switch (grade)
{
case 'A':
    cout << "The grade point is 4.0.";
    break;
case 'B':
    cout << "The grade point is 3.0.";
    break;
case 'C':
    cout << "The grade point is 2.0.";
    break;
case 'D':
    cout << "The grade point is 1.0.";
    break;
case 'F':
    cout << "The grade point is 0.0.";
    break;
default:
    cout << "The grade is invalid.";
}
```

In this example, the expression in the switch statement is a variable identifier. The variable grade is of type char, which is an integral type. The possible values of grade are 'A', 'B', 'C', 'D', and 'F'. Each case label specifies a different action to take, depending on the value of grade. If the value of grade is 'A', the output is:

```
The grade point is 4.0.
```

EXAMPLE 4-22

The following program illustrates the effect of the break statement. It asks the user to input a number between 0 and 10.

```cpp
//Program: Effect of break statements in a switch structure

#include <iostream>

using namespace std;

int main()
{
    int num;

    cout << "Enter an integer between 0 and 7: ";      //Line 1
    cin >> num;                                        //Line 2
    cout << endl;                                      //Line 3
```

4

```
    cout << "The number you entered is " << num
        << endl;                                      //Line 4

    switch (num)                                      //Line 5
    {
    case 0:                                           //Line 6
    case 1:                                           //Line 7
        cout << "Learning to use ";                   //Line 8
    case 2:                                           //Line 9
        cout << "C++'s ";                             //Line 10
    case 3:                                           //Line 11
        cout << "switch structure." << endl;          //Line 12
        break;                                        //Line 13
    case 4:                                           //Line 14
        break;                                        //Line 15
    case 5:                                           //Line 16
        cout << "This program shows the effect ";     //Line 17
    case 6:                                           //Line 18
    case 7:                                           //Line 19
        cout << "of the break statement." << endl;    //Line 20
        break;                                        //Line 21
    default:                                          //Line 22
        cout << "The number is out of range." << endl; //Line 23
    }

    cout << "Out of the switch structure." << endl;   //Line 24

    return 0;                                         //Line 25
}
```

Sample Runs: These outputs were obtained by executing the preceding program several times. In each of these sample runs, the user input is shaded.

Sample Run 1:

```
Enter an integer between 0 and 7: 0

The number you entered is 0
Learning to use C++'s switch structure.
Out of the switch structure.
```

Sample Run 2:

```
Enter an integer between 0 and 7: 2

The number you entered is 2
C++'s switch structure.
Out of the switch structure.
```

Sample Run 3:

```
Enter an integer between 0 and 7: 4

The number you entered is 4
Out of the switch structure.
```

Sample Run 4:

```
Enter an integer between 0 and 7: 5

The number you entered is 5
This program shows the effect of the break statement.
Out of the switch structure.
```

Sample Run 5:

```
Enter an integer between 0 and 7: 7

The number you entered is 7
of the break statement.
Out of the switch structure.
```

Sample Run 6:

```
Enter an integer between 0 and 7: 8

The number you entered is 8
The number is out of range.
Out of the switch structure.
```

A walk-through of this program, using certain values of the switch expression num, can help you understand how the break statement functions. If the value of num is 0, the value of the switch expression matches the case value 0. All statements following case 0: execute until a break statement appears.

The first break statement appears in Line 13, just before the case value of 4. Even though the value of the switch expression does not match any of the case values (that is, 1, 2, or 3), the statements following these values execute.

When the value of the switch expression matches a case value, *all* statements execute until a break is encountered, and the program skips all case labels in between. Similarly, if the value of num is 3, it matches the case value of 3, and the statements following this label execute until the break statement is encountered in Line 13. If the value of num is 4, it matches the case value of 4. In this situation, the action is empty because only the break statement, in Line 15, follows the case value of 4.

EXAMPLE 4-23

Although a switch structure's case values (labels) are limited, the switch statement expression can be as complex as necessary. For example, consider the following switch statement:

```
switch (score / 10)
{
case 0:
case 1:
case 2:
case 3:
```

```
case 4:
case 5:
    grade = 'F';
    break;
case 6:
    grade = 'D';
    break;
case 7:
    grade = 'C';
    break;
case 8:
    grade = 'B';
    break;
case 9:
case 10:
    grade = 'A';
    break;
default:
    cout << "Invalid test score." << endl;
}
```

Assume that score is an int variable with values between 0 and 100. If score is 75, score / 10 = 75 / 10 = 7, and the grade assigned is 'C'. If the value of score is between 0 and 59, the grade is 'F'. If score is between 0 and 59, then score / 10 is 0, 1, 2, 3, 4, or 5. Each of these values corresponds to the grade 'F'.

Therefore, in this switch structure, the action statements of case 0, case 1, case 2, case 3, case 4, and case 5 are all the same. Rather than write the statement grade = 'F'; followed by the break statement for each of the case values of 0, 1, 2, 3, 4, and 5, you can simplify the programming code by first specifying all of the case values (as shown in the preceding code) and then specifying the desired action statement. The case values of 9 and 10 follow similar conventions.

In addition to being a variable identifier or a complex expression, the switch expression can evaluate to a logical value. Consider the following statements:

```
switch (age >= 18)
{
case 1:
    cout << "Old enough to be drafted." << endl;
    cout << "Old enough to vote." << endl;
    break;
case 0:
    cout << "Not old enough to be drafted." << endl;
    cout << "Not old enough to vote." << endl;
}
```

If the value of age is 25, the expression age >= 18 evaluates to 1—that is, true. If the expression evaluates to 1, the statements following the case label 1 execute. If the value of age is 14, the expression age >= 18 evaluates to 0—that is, false—and the statements following the case label 0 execute.

You can use `true` and `false`, instead of 1 and 0, respectively, in the case labels, and rewrite the preceding `switch` statement as follows:

```
switch (age >= 18)
{
case true:
    cout << "Old enough to be drafted." << endl;
    cout << "Old enough to vote." << endl;
    break;
case false:
    cout << "Not old enough to be drafted." << endl;
    cout << "Not old enough to vote." << endl;
}
```

As you can see from the preceding examples, the `switch` statement is an elegant way to implement multiple selections. You will see the use of a `switch` statement in the programming example at the end of this chapter. Even though no fixed rules exist that can be applied to decide whether to use an `if...else` structure or a `switch` structure to implement multiple selections, the following considerations should be remembered. If multiple selections involve a range of values, you should use either an `if...else` structure or a `switch` structure, wherein you convert each range to a finite set of values.

For instance, in Example 4-23, the value of `grade` depends on the value of `score`. If `score` is between 0 and 59, `grade` is `'F'`. Because `score` is an `int` variable, 60 values correspond to the grade of `'F'`. If you list all 60 values as `case` values, the `switch` statement could be very long. However, dividing by 10 reduces these 60 values to only 6 values: 0, 1, 2, 3, 4, and 5.

If the range of values consists of infinitely many values and you cannot reduce them to a set containing a finite number of values, you must use the `if...else` structure. For example, if `score` happens to be a `double` variable, the number of values between 0 and 60 is infinite. However, you can use the expression `static_cast<int>(score) / 10` and still reduce this infinite number of values to just six values.

Avoiding Bugs by Avoiding Partially Understood Concepts and Techniques (Revisited)

Earlier in this chapter, we discussed how a partial understanding of a concept or technique can lead to errors in a program. In this section, we give another example to illustrate the problem of using partially understood concepts and techniques. In Example 4-23, we illustrate how to assign a grade based on a test score between 0 and 100. Next, consider the following program that assigns a grade based on a test score:

```
//Grade program with bugs.

#include <iostream>                                     //Line 1

using namespace std;                                    //Line 2
```

```
int main()                                         //Line 3
{                                                  //Line 4
    int testScore;                                 //Line 5

    cout << "Enter the test score: ";              //Line 6
    cin >> testScore;                              //Line 7
    cout << endl;                                  //Line 8

    switch (testScore / 10)                        //Line 9
    {                                              //Line 10
    case 0:                                        //Line 11
    case 1:                                        //Line 12
    case 2:                                        //Line 13
    case 3:                                        //Line 14
    case 4:                                        //Line 15
    case 5:                                        //Line 16
        cout << "The grade is F." << endl;         //Line 17
    case 6:                                        //Line 18
        cout << "The grade is D." << endl;         //Line 19
    case 7:                                        //Line 20
        cout << "The grade is C." << endl;         //LIne 21
    case 8:                                        //Line 22
        cout << "The grade is B." << endl;         //Line 23
    case 9:                                        //Line 24
    case 10:                                       //Line 25
        cout << "The grade is A." << endl;         //Line 26
    default:                                        //Line 27
        cout << "Invalid test score." << endl;     //Line 28
    }                                              //Line 29

    return 0;                                      //Line 30
}                                                  //Line 31
```

Sample Runs: In these sample runs, the user input is shaded.

Sample Run 1:

Enter the test score: 110

Invalid test score.

Sample Run 2:

Enter the test score: -70

Invalid test score.

Sample Run 3:

Enter the test score: 75

The grade is C.
The grade is B.
The grade is A.
Invalid test score.

From these sample runs, it follows that if the value of testScore is less than 0 or greater than 100, the program produces correct results, but if the value of testScore is between 0 and 100, say 75, the program produces incorrect results. Can you see why?

As in Sample Run 3, suppose that the value of testScore is 75. Then, testScore % 10 = 7, and this value matched the case label 7. So, as we indented, it should print The grade is C. However, the output is:

```
The grade is C.
The grade is B.
The grade is A.
Invalid test score.
```

But why? Clearly only at most one cout statement is associated with each case label. The problem is a result of having only a partial understanding of how the switch structure works. As we can see, the switch statement does not include any break statement. Therefore, after executing the statement(s) associated with the matching case label, execution continues with the statement(s) associated with the next case label, resulting in the printing of four unintended lines.

To output results correctly, the switch structure must include a break statement after each cout statement, except the last cout statement. We leave it as an exercise for you to modify this program so that it outputs correct results.

Once again, we can see that a partially understood concept can lead to serious errors in a program. Therefore, taking time to understand each concept and technique completely will save you hours of debugging time.

Terminating a Program with the assert Function

Certain types of errors that are very difficult to catch can occur in a program. For example, division by zero can be difficult to catch using any of the programming techniques you have examined so far. C++ includes a predefined function, assert, that is useful in stopping program execution when certain elusive errors occur. In the case of division by zero, you can use the assert function to ensure that a program terminates with an appropriate error message indicating the type of error and the program location where the error occurred.

Consider the following statements:

```
int numerator;
int denominator;
int quotient;
double hours;
double rate;
double wages;
char ch;
```

1.  ```
    quotient = numerator / denominator;
    ```
2.  ```
    if (hours > 0 && (0 < rate && rate <= 15.50))
        wages = rate * hours;
    ```
3.  ```
    if ('A' <= ch && ch <= 'Z')
    ```

In the first statement, if the `denominator` is 0, logically you should not perform the division. During execution, however, the computer would try to perform the division. If the `denominator` is 0, the program would terminate with an error message stating that an illegal operation has occurred.

The second statement is designed to compute `wages` only if `hours` is greater than 0 and `rate` is positive and less than or equal to `15.50`. The third statement is designed to execute certain statements only if `ch` is an uppercase letter.

For all of these statements (for that matter, in any situation in which certain conditions must be met), if conditions are not met, it would be useful to halt program execution with a message indicating where in the program an error occurred. You could handle these types of situations by including output and return statements in your program. However, C++ provides an effective method to halt a program if required conditions are not met through the `assert` function.

The syntax to use the `assert` function is:

```
assert(expression);
```

Here, `expression` is any logical expression. If `expression` evaluates to `true`, the next statement executes. If expression evaluates to `false`, the program terminates and indicates where in the program the error occurred.

The specification of the `assert` function is found in the header file `cassert`. Therefore, for a program to use the `assert` function, it must include the following statement:

```
#include <cassert>
```

A statement using the `assert` function is sometimes called an `assert` statement.

Returning to the preceding statements, you can rewrite statement 1 (`quotient = numerator / denominator;`) using the `assert` function. Because `quotient` should be calculated only if `denominator` is nonzero, you include an `assert` statement before the assignment statement as follows:

```
assert(denominator);
quotient = numerator / denominator;
```

Now, if `denominator` is 0, the `assert` statement halts the execution of the program with an error message similar to the following:

```
Assertion failed: denominator, file c:\temp\assert
function\assertfunction.cpp, line 20
```
```

This error message indicates that the assertion of `denominator` failed. The error message also gives the name of the file containing the source code and the line number where the assertion failed.

You can also rewrite statement 2 using an assertion statement as follows:

```
assert(hours > 0 && (0 < rate && rate <= 15.50));
if (hours > 0 && (0 < rate && rate <= 15.50))
    wages = rate * hours;
```

If the `expression` in the `assert` statement fails, the program terminates with an error message similar to the following:

```
Assertion failed: hours > 0 && (0 < rate && rate <= 15.50), file
c:\temp\assertfunction\assertfunction.cpp, line 26
```

During program development and testing, the `assert` statement is very useful for enforcing programming constraints. As you can see, the `assert` statement not only halts the program, but also identifies the expression where the assertion failed, the name of the file containing the source code, and the line number where the assertion failed.

Although `assert` statements are useful during program development, after a program has been developed and put into use, if an `assert` statement fails for some reason, an end user would have no idea what the error means. Therefore, after you have developed and tested a program, you might want to remove or disable the `assert` statements. In a very large program, it could be tedious, and perhaps impossible, to remove all of the `assert` statements that you used during development. In addition, if you plan to modify a program in the future, you might like to keep the `assert` statements. Therefore, the logical choice is to keep these statements but to disable them. You can disable `assert` statements by using the following preprocessor directive:

```
#define NDEBUG
```

This preprocessor directive `#define NDEBUG` must be placed *before* the directive `#include <cassert>`.

PROGRAMMING EXAMPLE: Cable Company Billing

Watch
the Video

This programming example demonstrates a program that calculates a customer's bill for a local cable company. There are two types of customers: residential and business. There are two rates for calculating a cable bill: one for residential customers and one for business customers. For residential customers, the following rates apply:

- Bill processing fee: $4.50
- Basic service fee: $20.50
- Premium channels: $7.50 per channel

4

For business customers, the following rates apply:

- Bill processing fee: $15.00
- Basic service fee: $75.00 for first 10 connections, $5.00 for each additional connection
- Premium channels: $50.00 per channel for any number of connections

The program should ask the user for an account number (an integer) and a customer code. Assume that R or r stands for a residential customer, and B or b stands for a business customer

Input   The customer's account number, customer code, number of premium channels to which the user subscribes, and, in the case of business customers, number of basic service connections.

Output   Customer's account number and the billing amount.

PROBLEM
ANALYSIS
AND
ALGORITHM
DESIGN

The purpose of this program is to calculate and print the billing amount. To calculate the billing amount, you need to know the customer for whom the billing amount is calculated (whether the customer is residential or business) and the number of premium channels to which the customer subscribes. In the case of a business customer, you also need to know the number of basic service connections and the number of premium channels. Other data needed to calculate the bill, such as the bill processing fees and the cost of a premium channel, are known quantities. The program should print the billing amount to two decimal places, which is standard for monetary amounts. This problem analysis translates into the following algorithm:

1. Set the precision to two decimal places.
2. Prompt the user for the account number and customer type.
3. Based on the customer type, determine the number of premium channels and basic service connections, compute the bill, and print the bill:
   a. If the customer type is R or r,
      i. Prompt the user for the number of premium channels.
      ii. Compute the bill.
      iii. Print the bill.
   b. If the customer type is B or b,
      i. Prompt the user for the number of basic service connections and number of premium channels.
      ii. Compute the bill.
      iii. Print the bill.

Variables Because the program will ask the user to input the customer account number, customer code, number of premium channels, and number of basic service connections, you need variables to store all of this information. Also, because the program will calculate the billing amount, you need a variable to store the billing amount. Thus, the program needs at least the following variables to compute and print the bill:

```
int accountNumber;     //variable to store the customer's
                       //account number
char customerType;       //variable to store the customer code
int numOfPremChannels; //variable to store the number
                       //of premium channels to which the
                       //customer subscribes
int numOfBasicServConn; //variable to store the
                       //number of basic service connections
                       //to which the customer subscribes
double amountDue;      //variable to store the billing amount
```

Named Constants As you can see, the bill processing fees, the cost of a basic service connection, and the cost of a premium channel are fixed, and these values are needed to compute the bill. Although these values are constants in the program, the cable company can change them with little warning. To simplify the process of modifying the program later, instead of using these values directly in the program, you should declare them as named constants. Based on the problem analysis, you need to declare the following named constants:

```
//Named constants - residential customers
const double RES_BILL_PROC_FEES = 4.50;
const double RES_BASIC_SERV_COST = 20.50;
const double RES_COST_PREM_CHANNEL = 7.50;

//Named constants - business customers
const double BUS_BILL_PROC_FEES = 15.00;
const double BUS_BASIC_SERV_COST = 75.00;
const double BUS_BASIC_CONN_COST = 5.00;
const double BUS_COST_PREM_CHANNEL = 50.00;
```

Formulas The program uses a number of formulas to compute the billing amount. To compute the residential bill, you need to know only the number of premium channels to which the user subscribes. The following statement calculates the billing amount for a residential customer:

```
amountDue = RES_BILL_PROC_FEES + RES_BASIC_SERV_COST
            + numOfPremChannels * RES_COST_PREM_CHANNEL;
```

To compute the business bill, you need to know the number of basic service connections and the number of premium channels to which the user subscribes. If the number of basic service connections is less than or equal to 10, the cost of the basic service connections is fixed. If the number of basic service connections exceeds 10, you must add the cost for each connection over 10. The following statement calculates the business billing amount:

```
if (numOfBasicServConn <= 10)
    amountDue = BUS_BILL_PROC_FEES + BUS_BASIC_SERV_COST
                 + numOfPremChannels * BUS_COST_PREM_CHANNEL;
else
    amountDue = BUS_BILL_PROC_FEES + BUS_BASIC_SERV_COST
             + (numOfBasicServConn - 10)
                 * BUS_BASIC_CONN_COST
         + numOfPremChannels * BUS_COST_PREM_CHANNEL;
```

MAIN ALGORITHM

Based on the preceding discussion, you can now write the main algorithm.

1. To output floating-point numbers in a fixed decimal format with a decimal point and trailing zeros, set the manipulators `fixed` and `showpoint`. Also, to output floating-point numbers with two decimal places, set the precision to two decimal places. Recall that to use these manipulators, the program must include the header file `iomanip`.

2. Prompt the user to enter the account number.

3. Get the customer account number.

4. Prompt the user to enter the customer code.

5. Get the customer code.

6. If the customer code is r or R,
   a. Prompt the user to enter the number of premium channels.
   b. Get the number of premium channels.
   c. Calculate the billing amount.
   d. Print the account number and the billing amount.

7. If the customer code is b or B,
   a. Prompt the user to enter the number of basic service connections.
   b. Get the number of basic service connections.
   c. Prompt the user to enter the number of premium channels.
   d. Get the number of premium channels.
   e. Calculate the billing amount.
   f. Print the account number and the billing amount.

8. If the customer code is something other than r, R, b, or B, output an error message.

For Steps 6 and 7, the program uses a `switch` statement to calculate the bill for the desired customer.

COMPLETE PROGRAM LISTING

```cpp
//***********************************************************
// Author: D. S. Malik
//
// Program: Cable Company Billing
// This program calculates and prints a customer's bill for
// a local cable company. The program processes two types of
// customers: residential and business.
//***********************************************************

#include <iostream>
#include <iomanip>

using namespace std;

    //Named constants - residential customers
const double RES_BILL_PROC_FEES = 4.50;
const double RES_BASIC_SERV_COST = 20.50;
const double RES_COST_PREM_CHANNEL = 7.50;

    //Named constants - business customers
const double BUS_BILL_PROC_FEES = 15.00;
const double BUS_BASIC_SERV_COST = 75.00;
const double BUS_BASIC_CONN_COST = 5.00;
const double BUS_COST_PREM_CHANNEL = 50.00;

int main()
{
        //Variable declaration
    int accountNumber;
    char customerType;
    int numOfPremChannels;
    int numOfBasicServConn;
    double amountDue;

    cout << fixed << showpoint;                          //Step 1
    cout << setprecision(2);                             //Step 1

    cout << "This program computes a cable "
         << "bill." << endl;
    cout << "Enter account number (an integer): ";       //Step 2
    cin >> accountNumber;                                //Step 3
    cout << endl;

    cout << "Enter customer type: "
         << "R or r (Residential), "
         << "B or b (Business):  ";                      //Step 4
    cin >>  customerType;                                //Step 5
    cout << endl;
```

```cpp
switch (customerType)
{
case 'r':                                       //Step 6
case 'R':
    cout << "Enter the number"
        << " of premium channels: ";            //Step 6a
    cin >> numOfPremChannels;                   //Step 6b
    cout << endl;

    amountDue = RES_BILL_PROC_FEES              //Step 6c
               + RES_BASIC_SERV_COST
               + numOfPremChannels *
                 RES_COST_PREM_CHANNEL;

    cout << "Account number: "
        << accountNumber
        << endl;                                //Step 6d
    cout << "Amount due: $"
        << amountDue
        << endl;                                //Step 6d
    break;

case 'b':                                       //Step 7
case 'B':
    cout << "Enter the number of basic "
        << "service connections: ";             //Step 7a
    cin >> numOfBasicServConn;                  //Step 7b
    cout << endl;

    cout << "Enter the number"
        << " of premium channels: ";            //Step 7c
    cin >> numOfPremChannels;                   //Step 7d
    cout << endl;

    if (numOfBasicServConn<= 10)                //Step 7e
        amountDue = BUS_BILL_PROC_FEES
                   + BUS_BASIC_SERV_COST
                   + numOfPremChannels *
                     BUS_COST_PREM_CHANNEL;

    else
        amountDue = BUS_BILL_PROC_FEES
                   + BUS_BASIC_SERV_COST
                   + (numOfBasicServConn - 10) *
                     BUS_BASIC_CONN_COST
                   + numOfPremChannels *
                     BUS_COST_PREM_CHANNEL;

    cout << "Account number: "
        << accountNumber << endl;               //Step 7f
    cout << "Amount due: $" << amountDue
        << endl;                                //Step 7f
    break;
```

```
        default:
            cout << "Invalid customer type." << endl;    //Step 8
        } //end switch

        return 0;
}
```

Sample Run: In this sample run, the user input is shaded.

```
This program computes a cable bill.
Enter account number (an integer): 12345

Enter customer type: R or r (Residential), B or b (Business): b

Enter the number of basic service connections: 16

Enter the number of premium channels: 8

Account number: 12345
Amount due: $520.00
```

QUICK REVIEW

1. Control structures alter the normal flow of control.
2. The two most common control structures are selection and repetition.
3. Selection structures incorporate decisions in a program.
4. The relational operators are == (equality), < (less than), <= (less than or equal to), > (greater than), >= (greater than or equal to), and != (not equal to).
5. Including a space between the relational operators ==, <=, >=, and != creates a syntax error.
6. Characters are compared using a machine's collating sequence.
7. Logical expressions evaluate to 1 (or a nonzero value) or 0. The logical value 1 (or any nonzero value) is treated as **true**; the logical value 0 is treated as **false**.
8. In C++, **int** variables can be used to store the value of a logical expression.
9. In C++, **bool** variables can be used to store the value of a logical expression.
10. In C++, the logical operators are ! (not), && (and), and || (or).
11. There are two selection structures in C++.
12. One-way selection takes the following form:

    ```
    if (expression)
        statement
    ```

    If expression is **true**, the statement executes; otherwise, the computer executes the statement following the if statement.

13. Two-way selection takes the following form:

```
if (expression)
    statement1
else
    statement2
```

If `expression` is `true`, then `statement1` executes; otherwise, `statement2` executes.

14. The expression in an `if` or `if...else` structure is usually a logical expression.

15. Including a semicolon before the `statement` in a one-way selection creates a semantic error. In this case, the action of the `if` statement is empty.

16. Including a semicolon before `statement1` in a two-way selection creates a syntax error.

17. There is no stand-alone `else` statement in C++. Every `else` has a related `if`.

18. An `else` is paired with the most recent `if` that has not been paired with any other `else`.

19. A sequence of statements enclosed between curly braces, { and } , is called a compound statement or block of statements. A compound statement is treated as a single statement.

20. You can use the input stream variable in an `if` statement to determine the state of the input stream.

21. Using the assignment operator in place of the equality operator creates a semantic error. This can cause serious errors in the program.

22. The `switch` structure is used to handle multiway selection.

23. The execution of a `break` statement in a `switch` statement immediately exits the `switch` structure.

24. If certain conditions are not met in a program, the program can be terminated using the `assert` function.

EXERCISES

1. Mark the following statements as true or false:

   a. The result of a logical expression cannot be assigned to an `int` variable.

   b. In a one-way selection, if a semicolon is placed after the expression in an `if` statement, the expression in the `if` statement is always `true`.

   c. Every `if` statement must have a corresponding `else`.

   d. The expression in the `if` statement:

   ```
   if (score = 30)
       grade = 'A';
   ```

   always evaluates to `true`.

e. The expression:

```
(ch >= 'A' && ch <= 'Z')
```

evaluates to `false` if either ch < 'A' or ch >= 'Z'.

f. Suppose the input is 5. The output of the code:

```
cin >> num;
if (num > 5)
    cout << num;
    num = 0;
else
    cout << "Num is zero" << endl;
is:  Num is zero
```

g. The expression in a `switch` statement should evaluate to a value of the simple data type.

h. The expression ! (x > 0) is `true` only if x is a negative number.

i. In C++, both ! and != are logical operators.

j. The order in which statements execute in a program is called the flow of control.

2. Evaluate the following expressions:

a. 5 + 6 == 3 + 7

b. 2 * 6 - 4 >= 9 - 1

c. 'U' >= 't'

d. 'A' <= 'a'

e. '#' <= '+'

f. 6.28 / 3 < 3 - 1.2

3. Suppose that x, y, and z are `int` variables, and x = 10, y = 15, and z = 20. Determine whether the following expressions evaluate to `true` or `false`:

a. ! (x > 10)

b. x <= 5 || y < 15

c. (x != 5) && (y != z)

d. x >= z || (x + y >= z)

e. (x <= y - 2) && (y >= z) || (z - 2 != 20)

4. Suppose that str1, str2, and str3 are string variables, and str1 = "English", str2 = "Computer Science", and str3 = "Programming". Evaluate the following expressions:

a. str1 >= str2

b. str1 != "english"

c. str3 < str2

d. str2 >= "Chemistry"

5. Suppose that x, y, z, and w are `int` variables, and x = 3, y = 4, z = 7, and w = 1. What is the output of the following statements?

   a. `cout << "x == y: " << (x == y) << endl;`

   b. `cout << "x != z: " << (x != z) << endl;`

   c. `cout << "y == z - 3: " << (y == z - 3) << endl;`

   d. `cout << "!(z > w): " << !(z > w) << endl;`

   e. `cout << "x + y < z: " << (x + y < z) << endl;`

6. Which of the following are relational operators?

   a. `<`   b. `<=`   c. `=`   d. `=!`   e. `<>`

7. What is the output of the following statements?

   a.
   ```
   if ('+' < '*')
       cout << "+*";
   cout << "%%" << endl;
   ```

   b.
   ```
   if (10 <= 2 * 5)
           cout << "10 ";
           cout << "2 * 5";
   cout << endl;
   ```

   c.
   ```
   if ('a' < 'A')
           cout << 'a';
           cout << 'A';
   cout << endl;
   ```

   d.
   ```
   if ("C++" >= "C--")
           cout << "C++" << endl;
   cout << "C--" << endl;
   ```

   e.
   ```
   if ("Sam" <= "Tom")
           cout << "Sam Tom" << endl;
           cout << "Tom Sam" << endl;
   ```

   f.
   ```
   if (6 == 2 * 4 - 2)
           cout << 3 * 4 / 6 - 8 << endl;
   cout << "**" << endl;
   ```

8. Which of the following are logical (Boolean) operators?

   a. `!`   b. `!=`   c. `$$`

9. What is the output of the following statements?

   a.
   ```
   if ('R' < '$' && '&' <= '#')
           cout << "$#";
           cout << "R&";
   cout << endl;
   ```

   b.
   ```
   if ('4' > '3' || 2 < -10)
           cout << "1 2 3 4" << endl;
           cout << "$$" << endl;
   ```

c.   `if ("Jack" <= "John" && "Business" >= "Accounting")`
            `cout << "Jack Accounting" << endl;`
            `cout << "John Business" << endl;`

10.   What is the output of the following code?

```
int num = 10;          //Line 1
double temp = 4.5;     //Line 2
bool found;            //Line 3

found = (num == 2 * static_cast<int>(temp) + 1);   //Line 4
cout << "The value of found is: " << found << endl; //Line 5
```

11.   How does the output in Exercise 10 change if the statement in Line 4 is replaced by the following statement?

```
found = (num == 2 * static_cast<int>(temp + 1));    //Line 4
```

12.   What is the output of the following program?

```
#include <iostream>

using namespace std;

int main()
{
    int x;
    int a = 265;

    cout << (x = 25) << endl;
    cout << (x == 90) << endl;
    cout << (x > 10) << endl;
    cout << (3 * x < a) << endl;
    cout << (10 * x == a - 15) << endl;

    return 0;
}
```

13.   Correct the following code so that it prints the correct message:

```
if (score >= 60)
    cout << "You pass." << endl;
else;
    cout << "You fail." << endl;
```

14.   Write C++ statements that output `Male` if the `gender` is `'M'`, `Female` if the `gender` is `'F'`, and `invalid gender` otherwise.

15.   If the number of items bought is less than 5, then the shipping charges are $5.00 for each item bought; if the number of items bought is at least 5, but less than 10, then the shipping charges are $2.00 for each item bought; if the number of items bought is at least 10, there are no shipping charges. Correct the following code so that it computes the correct shipping charges.

4

```
if (0 < numOfItemsBought || numOfItemsBought <> 5)
    shippingCharges = 5.00 * numOfItemsBought;
else if (5 <= numOfItemsBought && numOfItemsBought < 10);
    shippingCharges = 2.00 * numOfItemsBought;
else
    shippingCharges = 0.00;
```

16. What is the output of the following C++ code?

```
int x = 10;
int y = 20;
if (x < 20 && y > 20)
{
    x = 2 * x;
    y = y / 2;
    cout << x << " " << y << " " << x - y << endl;
}
else
{
    x = y / x;
    cout << x << " " << y << " " << x * x + y * y << endl;
}
```

17. What is the output of the following program?

```
#include <iostream>

using namespace std;

int main()
{
    int myNum = 10;
    int yourNum = 30;

    if (yourNum % myNum == 3)
    {
        yourNum = 3;
        myNum = 1;
    }
    else if (yourNum % myNum == 2)
    {
        yourNum = 2;
        myNum = 2;
    }
    else
    {
        yourNum = 1;
        myNum = 3;
    }

    cout << myNum << " " << yourNum << endl;

    return 0;
}
```

18. a. What is the output of the program in Exercise 17, if myNum = 5 and yourNum = 12?

    b. What is the output of the program in Exercise 17, if myNum = 30 and yourNum = 33?

19. Suppose that `sale` and `bonus` are `double` variables. Write an `if...else` statement that assigns a value to `bonus` as follows: If `sale` is greater than $20,000, the value assigned to `bonus` is 0.10; if `sale` is greater than $10,000 and less than or equal to $20,000, the value assigned to `bonus` is 0.05; otherwise, the value assigned to `bonus` is 0.

20. Suppose that `overSpeed` and `fine` are `double` variables. Assign the value to `fine` as follows: If 0 < `overSpeed` <= 5, the value assigned to `fine` is $20.00; if 5 < `overSpeed` <= 10, the value assigned to `fine` is $75.00; if 10 < `overSpeed` <= 15, the value assigned to `fine` is $150.00; if `overSpeed` > 15, the value assigned to `fine` is $150.00 plus $20.00 per mile over 15.

21. Suppose that `score` is an `int` variable. Consider the following `if` statements:

    ```
    if (score >= 90);
        cout << "Discount = 10%" << endl;
    ```

    a. What is the output if the value of `score` is 95? Justify your answer.

    b. What is the output if the value of `score` is 85? Justify your answer.

22. Suppose that `score` is an `int` variable. Consider the following `if` statements:

    i. ```
        if (score == 70)
            cout << "Grade is C." << endl;
        ```

    ii. ```
        if (score = 70)
            cout << "Grade is C." << endl;
        ```

    Answer the following questions:

    a. What is the output in (i) and (ii) if the value of `score` is 70? What is the value of `score` after the `if` statement executes?

    b. What is the output in (i) and (ii) if the value of `score` is 80? What is the value of `score` after the `if` statement executes?

23. Rewrite the following expressions using the conditional operator. (Assume that all variables are declared properly.)

    a. ```
       if (x >= y)
           z = x - y;
       else
           z = y - x;
       ```

    b. ```
       if (hours >= 40.0)
           wages = 40 * 7.50 + 1.5 * 7.5 * (hours - 40);
       else
           wages = hours * 7.50;
       ```

4

c.
```
if (score >= 60)
    str = "Pass";
else
    str = "Fail";
```

24. Rewrite the following expressions using an `if...else` statement. (Assume that all variables are declared properly.)

a. `(x < 5) ? y = 10 : y = 20;`

b. `(fuel >= 10) ? drive = 150 : drive = 30;`

c. `(booksBought >= 3) ? discount = 0.15 : discount = 0.0;`

25. Suppose that you have the following conditional expression. (Assume that all the variables are properly declared.)

```
(0 < backyard && backyard <= 5000) ? fertilizingCharges = 40.00
                : fertilizingCharges = 40.00 + (backyard - 5000) * 0.01;
```

a. What is the value of `fertilizingCharges` if the value of `backyard` is 3000?

b. What is the value of `fertilizingCharges` if the value of `backyard` is 5000?

c. What is the value of `fertilizingCharges` if the value of `backyard` is 6500?

26. State whether the following are valid `switch` statements. If not, explain why. Assume that n and `digit` are `int` variables.

a.
```
switch (n <= 2)
{
case 0:
    cout << "Draw." << endl;
    break;
case 1:
    cout << "Win." << endl;
    break;
case 2:
    cout << "Lose." << endl;
    break;
}
```

b.
```
switch (digit / 4)
{
case 0,
case 1:
    cout << "low." << endl;
    break;
case 1,
case 2:
    cout << "middle." << endl;
    break;
case 3:
    cout << "high." << endl;
}
```

c.
```
switch (n % 6)
{
case 1:
case 2:
case 3:
case 4:
case 5:
    cout << n;
    break;
case 0:
    cout << endl;
    break;
}
```

d.
```
switch (n % 10)
{
case 2:
case 4:
case 6:
case 8:
    cout << "Even";
    break;
case 1:
case 3:
case 5:
case 7:
    cout << "Odd";
    break;
}
```

27. Suppose that `alpha` is an `int` variable. Consider the following C++ code:

```
cin >> alpha;
switch (alpha % 6)
{
case 0:
    alpha--;
    break;
case 1: case 2:
    alpha = alpha * 2;
    break;
case 3:
    break;
case 4:
    alpha = alpha - 5;
case 5:
    alpha++;
    break;
default:
    alpha = alpha / 3;
}
```

   a.   What is the output if the input is 8?

   b.   What is the output if the input is 3?

   c.   What is the output if the input is 17?

   d.   What is the output if the input is 24?

28.   Suppose that `beta` is an `int` variable. Consider the following C++ code:

```cpp
cin >> beta;
switch (beta % 7)
{
case 0:
case 1:
    beta = beta * beta;
    break;
case 2:
    beta++;
    break;
case 3:
    beta = static_cast<int>(sqrt(beta * 1.0));
    break;
case 4:
    beta = beta + 4;
case 6:
    beta = beta--;
    break;
default:
    beta = -10;
}
```

   a.   What is the output if the input is 11?

   b.   What is the output if the input is 12?

   c.   What is the output if the input is 0?

   d.   What is the output if the input is 16?

29.   Suppose that `num` is an `int` variable. Consider the following C++ code:

```cpp
cin >> num;
if (num >= 0)
    switch (num)
    {
    case 0:
        num = static_cast<int>(pow(num, 3.0));
        break;
    case 2:
        num = ++num;
        break;
    case 4:
        num = num - 4;
        break;
    case 5:
        num = num * 4;
```

```
      case 6:
          num = num / 6;
          break;
       case 10:
          num--;
          break;
      default:
          num = -20;
      }
else
      num = num + 10;
```

a. What is the output if the input is 5?

b. What is the output if the input is 26?

c. What is the output if the input is 2?

d. What is the output if the input is −5?

30. In the following code, correct any errors that would prevent the program from compiling or running:

```
include <iostream>

main ()
{
      int num1, num2;
      bool found;

      cout << "Enter two integers: ;
      cin >> num1 >> num2;
      cout << endl;

      if (num1 >= num2)   &&   num2 > 0
          switch (num % num2)
          {
          case 1
              found = (num / num2) >= 6;
              break;
          case 2: case 3
              num1 = num2 / 2;
              brake;
          default:
              num2 = num1 * num2;
          }
      else
      {
          found = (2 * num2 < num1);
          if found
              cin >> num2
              num 1 = num2 - num1;
              temp = (num1 + num2) / 10;
```

```
            if num2
            {
                    num1 = num2;
                    num2 = temp;
            }

      cout << num1 << " " << num2 << endl;
}
```

After correcting the code, answer the following questions. (If needed, insert prompt lines to inform the user for the input.)

a. What is the output if the input is 10 8 6?

b. What is the output if the input is 4 9 11?

31. The following program contains errors. Correct them so that the program will run and output w = 21.

```
#include <iostream>

using namespace std;

const int SECRET = 5

main ()
{
    int x, y, w, z;
    z = 9;

    if z > 10
        x = 12; y = 5, w = x + y + SECRET;
    else
        x = 12; y = 4, w = x + y + SECRET;

    cout << "w = " << w << endl;
}
```

32. Write the missing statements in the following program so that it prompts the user to input two numbers. If one of the numbers is 0, the program should output a message indicating that both numbers must be nonzero. If the first number is greater than the second number, it outputs the first number divided by the second number; if the first number is less than the second number, it outputs the second number divided by the first number; otherwise, it outputs the product of the numbers.

```
#include <iostream>
using namespace std;

int main()
{
    double firstNum, secondNum;

    cout << "Enter two nonzero numbers: ";
```

```
        cin >> firstNum >> secondNum;
        cout << endl;

        //Missing statements

        return 0;
    }
```

33. Suppose that classStanding is a char variable, and gpa and dues are double variables. Write a switch expression that assigns the dues as following: If classStanding is 'f', the dues are $150.00; if classStanding is 's' (if gpa is at least 3.75, the dues are $75.00; otherwise, dues are 120.00); if classStanding is 'j' (if gpa is at least 3.75, the dues are $50.00; otherwise, dues are $100.00); if classStanding is 'n' (if gpa is at least 3.75, the dues are $25.00; otherwise, dues are $75.00). (Note that the code 'f' stands for first year students, the code 's' stands for second year students, the code 'j' stands for juniors, and the code 'n' stands for seniors.)

34. Suppose that billingAmount is a double variable, which denotes the amount you need to pay to the department store. if you pay the full amount, you get $10.00 or 1% of the billingAmount, whichever is smaller, as a credit on your next bill; if you pay at least 50% of the billingAmount, the penalty is 5% of the balance; if you pay at least 20% of the billingAmount and less than 50% of the billingAmount, the penalty is 10% of the balance; otherwise, the penalty is 20% of the balance. Design an algorithm that prompts the user to enter the billing amount and the desired payment. The algorithm then calculates and outputs the credit or the remaining balance. If the amount is not paid in full, the algorithm should also output the penalty amount.

PROGRAMMING EXERCISES

1. Write a program that prompts the user to input a number. The program should then output the number and a message saying whether the number is positive, negative, or zero.

2. Write a program that prompts the user to input three numbers. The program should then output the numbers in ascending order.

3. Write a program that prompts the user to input an integer between 0 and 35. If the number is less than or equal to 9, the program should output the number; otherwise, it should output A for 10, B for 11, C for 12 ... and Z for 35. (*Hint:* Use the cast operator, static_cast<char> ( ), for numbers >= 10.)

4. The statements in the following program are in incorrect order. Rearrange the statements so that they prompt the user to input the shape type (rectangle, circle, or cylinder) and the appropriate dimension of

the shape. The program then outputs the following information about the shape: For a rectangle, it outputs the area and perimeter; for a circle, it outputs the area and circumference; and for a cylinder, it outputs the volume and surface area. After rearranging the statements, your program should be properly indented.

```cpp
using namespace std;

#include <iostream>

int main()
{
    string shape;
    double height;

    #include <string>

    cout << "Enter the shape type: (rectangle, circle, cylinder) ";
    cin >> shape;
    cout << endl;

    if (shape == "rectangle")
    {
        cout << "Area of the circle = "
             << PI * pow(radius, 2.0) << endl;

        cout << "Circumference of the circle: "
             << 2 * PI * radius << endl;

        cout << "Enter the height of the cylinder: ";
        cin >> height;
        cout << endl;

        cout << "Enter the width of the rectangle: ";
        cin >> width;
        cout << endl;


        cout << "Perimeter of the rectangle = "
             << 2 * (length + width) << endl;
        double width;
    }

    cout << "Surface area of the cylinder: "
         << 2 * PI * radius * height + 2 * PI * pow(radius, 2.0)
         << endl;
    }
    else if (shape == "circle")
    {
        cout << "Enter the radius of the circle: ";
        cin >> radius;
        cout << endl;
```

```
        cout << "Volume of the cylinder = "
             << PI * pow(radius, 2.0)* height << endl;
        double length;
    }
    return 0;
    else if (shape == "cylinder")
    {
        double radius;

        cout << "Enter the length of the rectangle: ";
        cin >> length;
        cout << endl;

        #include <iomanip>


        cout << "Enter the radius of the base of the cylinder: ";
        cin >> radius;
        cout << endl;

        const double PI = 3.1416;
        cout << "Area of the rectangle = "
             << length * width << endl;
    else
        cout << "The program does not handle " << shape << endl;
        cout << fixed << showpoint << setprecision(2);

    #include <cmath>
}
```

5. Write a program to implement the algorithm you designed in Exercise 21 of Chapter 1.

6. In a right triangle, the square of the length of one side is equal to the sum of the squares of the lengths of the other two sides. Write a program that prompts the user to enter the lengths of three sides of a triangle and then outputs a message indicating whether the triangle is a right triangle.

7. A box of cookies can hold 24 cookies, and a container can hold 75 boxes of cookies. Write a program that prompts the user to enter the total number of cookies, the number of cookies in a box, and the number of cookie boxes in a container. The program then outputs the number of boxes and the number of containers to ship the cookies. Note that each box must contain the specified number of cookies, and each container must contain the specified number of boxes. If the last box of cookies contains less than the number of specified cookies, you can discard it and output the number of leftover cookies. Similarly, if the last container contains less than the number of specified boxes, you can discard it and output the number of leftover boxes.

8. The roots of the quadratic equation $ax^2 + bx + c = 0$, $a \neq 0$ are given by the following formula:

$$\frac{-b \pm \sqrt{b^2 - 4ac}}{2a}$$

In this formula, the term $b^2 - 4ac$ is called the **discriminant**. If $b^2 - 4ac = 0$, then the equation has a single (repeated) root. If $b^2 - 4ac > 0$, the equation has two real roots. If $b^2 - 4ac < 0$, the equation has two complex roots. Write a program that prompts the user to input the value of a (the coefficient of x^2), b (the coefficient of x), and c (the constant term) and outputs the type of roots of the equation. Furthermore, if $b^2 - 4ac \geq 0$, the program should output the roots of the quadratic equation. (*Hint:* Use the function pow from the header file cmath to calculate the square root. Chapter 3 explains how the function pow is used.)

9. Write a program that mimics a calculator. The program should take as input two integers and the operation to be performed. It should then output the numbers, the operator, and the result. (For division, if the denominator is zero, output an appropriate message.) Some sample outputs follow:

```
3 + 4 = 7
13 * 5 = 65
```

10. Redo Exercise 9 to handle floating-point numbers. (Format your output to two decimal places.)

11. Redo Programming Exercise 20 of Chapter 2, taking into account that your parents buy additional savings bonds for you as follows:

    a. If you do not spend any money to buy savings bonds, then because you had a summer job, your parents buy savings bonds for you in an amount equal to 1% of the money you save after paying taxes and buying clothes, other accessories, and school supplies.

    b. If you spend up to 25% of your net income to buy savings bonds, your parents spend $0.25 for each dollar you spend to buy savings bonds, plus money equal to 1% of the money you save after paying taxes and buying clothes, other accessories, and school supplies.

    c. If you spend more than 25% of your net income to buy savings bonds, your parents spend $0.40 for each dollar you spend to buy savings bonds, plus money equal to 2% of the money you save after paying taxes and buying clothes, other accessories, and school supplies.

12. Write a program that implements the algorithm given in Example 1-3 (Chapter 1), which determines the monthly wages of a salesperson.

13. Write a program that implements the algorithm that you designed in Exercise 34 of this chapter.

14. The number of lines that can be printed on a paper depends on the paper size, the point size of each character in a line, whether lines are double-spaced or single-spaced, the top and bottom margin, and the left and right margins of the paper. Assume that all characters are of the same point size, and all lines are either single-spaced or double-spaced. Note that 1 inch = 72 points. Moreover, assume that the lines are printed along the width of the paper. For example, if the length of the paper is 11 inches and width is 8.5 inches, then the maximum length of a line is 8.5 inches. Write a program that calculates the number of characters in a line and the number of lines that can be printed on a paper based on the following input from the user:

    a. The length and width, in inches, of the paper

    b. The top, bottom, left, and right margins

    c. The point size of a line

    d. If the lines are double-spaced, then double the point size of each character

15. Write a program that calculates and prints the bill for a cellular telephone company. The company offers two types of service: regular and premium. Its rates vary, depending on the type of service. The rates are computed as follows:

    Regular service: $10.00 plus first 50 minutes are free. Charges for over 50 minutes are $0.20 per minute.

    Premium service: $25.00 plus:

    a. For calls made from 6:00 a.m. to 6:00 p.m., the first 75 minutes are free; charges for more than 75 minutes are $0.10 per minute.

    b. For calls made from 6:00 p.m. to 6:00 a.m., the first 100 minutes are free; charges for more than 100 minutes are $0.05 per minute.

    Your program should prompt the user to enter an account number, a service code (type `char`), and the number of minutes the service was used. A service code of `r` or `R` means regular service; a service code of `p` or `P` means premium service. Treat any other character as an error. Your program should output the account number, type of service, number of minutes the telephone service was used, and the amount due from the user.

    For the premium service, the customer may be using the service during the day and the night. Therefore, to calculate the bill, you must ask the user to input the number of minutes the service was used during the day and the number of minutes the service was used during the night.

16. Write a program to implement the algorithm that you designed in Exercise 22 of Chapter 1. (Assume that the account balance is stored in the file Ch4_Ex16_Data.txt.) Your program should output account balance before and after withdrawal and service charges. Also save the account balance after withdrawal in the file Ch4_Ex16_Output.txt.

17. A new author is in the process of negotiating a contract for a new romance novel. The publisher is offering three options. In the first option, the author is paid $5,000 upon delivery of the final manuscript and $20,000 when the novel is published. In the second option, the author is paid 12.5% of the net price of the novel for each copy of the novel sold. In the third option, the author is paid 10% of the net price for the first 4000 copies sold, and 14% of the net price for the copies sold over 4000. The author has some idea about the number of copies that will be sold and would like to have an estimate of the royalties generated under each option. Write a program that prompts the author to enter the net price of each copy of the novel and the estimated number of copies that will be sold. The program then outputs the royalties under each option and the best option the author could choose. (Use appropriate named constants to store the special values such as royalties rates and fixed royalties.)

18. Samantha and Vikas are looking to buy a house in a new development. After looking at various models, the three models they like are colonial, split-entry, and single-story. The builder gave them the base price and the finished area in square feet of the three models. They want to know the model(s) with the least price per square foot. Write a program that accepts as input the base price and the finished area in square feet of the three models. The program outputs the model(s) with the least price per square foot.

19. One way to determine how healthy a person is by measuring the body fat of the person. The formulas to determine the body fat for female and male are as follows:

Body fat formula for women:

$A1 = (\text{body weight} \times 0.732) + 8.987$

$A2 = \text{wrist measurement (at fullest point)} / 3.140$

$A3 = \text{waist measurement (at navel)} \times 0.157$

$A4 = \text{hip measurement (at fullest point)} \times 0.249$

$A5 = \text{forearm measurement (at fullest point)} \times 0.434$

$B = A1 + A2 - A3 - A4 + A5$

$\text{Body fat} = \text{body weight} - B$

$\text{Body fat percentage} = \text{body fat} \times 100 / \text{body weight}$

Body fat formula for men:

A1 = (body weight × 1.082) + 94.42

A2 = wrist measurement × 4.15

B = A1 − A2

Body fat = body weight − B

Body fat percentage = body fat × 100 / body weight

Write a program to calculate the body fat of a person.

4

CONTROL STRUCTURES II (REPETITION)

IN THIS CHAPTER, YOU WILL:

· Learn about repetition (looping) control structures

· Explore how to construct and use counter-controlled, sentinel-controlled, flag-controlled, and EOF-controlled repetition structures

· Examine `break` and `continue` statements

· Discover how to form and use nested control structures

· Learn how to avoid bugs by avoiding patches

· Learn how to debug loops

In Chapter 4, you saw how decisions are incorporated in programs. In this chapter, you will learn how repetitions are incorporated in programs.

Why Is Repetition Needed?

Suppose you want to add five numbers to find their average. From what you have learned so far, you could proceed as follows (assume that all variables are properly declared):

```
cin >> num1 >> num2 >> num3 >> num4 >> num5;   //read five numbers
sum = num1 + num2 + num3 + num4 + num5;        //add the numbers
average = sum / 5;                             //find the average
```

But suppose you want to add and average 100, 1000, or more numbers. You would have to declare that many variables and list them again in `cin` statements and, perhaps, again in the output statements. This takes an exorbitant amount of space and time. Also, if you want to run this program again with different values or with a different number of values, you have to rewrite the program.

Suppose you want to add the following numbers:

5 3 7 9 4

Consider the following statements, in which `sum` and `num` are variables of type `int`:

1. `sum = 0;`
2. `cin >> num;`
3. `sum = sum + num;`

The first statement initializes `sum` to 0. Let us execute statements 2 and 3. Statement 2 stores 5 in `num`; statement 3 updates the value of `sum` by adding `num` to it. After statement 3, the value of `sum` is 5.

Let us repeat statements 2 and 3. After statement 2 (after the programming code reads the next number):

num = 3

After statement 3:

sum = sum + num = 5 + 3 = 8

At this point, `sum` contains the sum of the first two numbers. Let us again repeat statements 2 and 3 (a third time). After statement 2 (after the code reads the next number):

num = 7

After statement 3:

sum = sum + num = 8 + 7 = 15

Now, `sum` contains the sum of the first three numbers. If you repeat statements 2 and 3 two more times, `sum` will contain the sum of all five numbers.

If you want to add 10 numbers, you can repeat statements 2 and 3 ten times. And if you want to add 100 numbers, you can repeat statements 2 and 3 one hundred times. In either case, you do not have to declare any additional variables, as you did in the first code. You can use this C++ code to add any set of numbers, whereas the earlier code requires you to drastically change the code.

There are many other situations in which it is necessary to repeat a set of statements. For example, for each student in a class, the formula for determining the course grade is the same. C++ has three repetition, or looping, structures that let you repeat statements over and over until certain conditions are met. This chapter introduces all three looping (repetition) structures. The next section discusses the first repetition structure, called the while loop.

while Looping (Repetition) Structure

In the previous section, you saw that sometimes it is necessary to repeat a set of statements several times. One way to repeat a set of statements is to type the set of statements in the program over and over. For example, if you want to repeat a set of statements 100 times, you type the set of statements 100 times in the program. However, this solution of repeating a set of statements is impractical, if not impossible. Fortunately, there is a better way to repeat a set of statements. As noted earlier, C++ has three repetition, or looping, structures that allow you to repeat a set of statements until certain conditions are met. This section discusses the first looping structure, called a while **loop**.

The general form of the while statement is:

```
while (expression)
    statement
```

In C++, while is a reserved word. Of course, the statement can be either a simple or compound statement. The expression acts as a **decision maker** and is usually a logical expression. The statement is called the body of the loop. Note that the parentheses around the expression are part of the syntax. Figure 5-1 shows the flow of execution of a while loop.

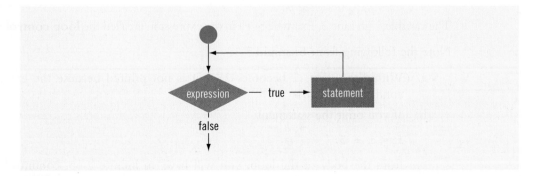

FIGURE 5-1 while loop

The expression provides an entry condition. If it initially evaluates to true, the statement executes. The loop condition—the expression—is then reevaluated. If it again evaluates to true, the statement executes again. The statement (body of the loop) continues to execute until the expression is no longer true. A loop that continues to execute endlessly is called an **infinite loop**. To avoid an infinite loop, make sure that the loop's body contains statement(s) that assure that the exit condition—the expression in the while statement—will eventually be false.

EXAMPLE 5-1

Consider the following C++ program segment: (Assume that i is an int variable.)

```
i = 0;                    //Line 1

while (i <= 20)           //Line 2
{
    cout << i << " ";     //Line 3
    i = i + 5;            //Line 4
}

cout << endl;
```

Sample Run:

```
0 5 10 15 20
```

In Line 1, the variable i is set to 0. The expression in the while statement (in Line 2), i <= 20, is evaluated. Because the expression i <= 20 evaluates to true, the body of the while loop executes next. The body of the while loop consists of the statements in Lines 3 and 4. The statement in Line 3 outputs the value of i, which is 0. The statement in Line 4 changes the value of i to 5. After executing the statements in Lines 3 and 4, the expression in the while loop (Line 2) is evaluated again. Because i is 5, the expression i <= 20 evaluates to true and the body of the while loop executes again. This process of evaluating the expression and executing the body of the while loop continues until the expression, i <= 20 (in Line 2), no longer evaluates to true.

The variable i (in Line 2, Example 5-1) in the expression is called the **loop control variable**.

Note the following from Example 5-1:

    a.   Within the loop, i becomes 25 but is not printed because the entry condition is false.

    b.   If you omit the statement:

```
i = i + 5;
```

        from the body of the loop, you will have an infinite loop, continually printing rows of zeros.

c. You must initialize the loop control variable i before you execute the loop. If the statement:

```
i = 0;
```

(in Line 1) is omitted, the loop may not execute at all. (Recall that variables in C++ are not automatically initialized.)

d. In Example 5-1, if the two statements in the body of the loop are interchanged, it may drastically alter the result. For example, consider the following statements:

```
i = 0;

while (i <= 20)
{
    i = i + 5;
    cout << i << " ";
}

cout << endl;
```

Here, the output is:

```
5 10 15 20 25
```

Typically, this would be a semantic error because you rarely want a condition to be true for i <= 20 and yet produce results for i > 20.

e. If you put a semicolon at the end of the while loop, (after the logical expression), then the action of the while loop is empty or null. For example, the action of the following while loop is empty.

```
i = 0;

while (i <= 20);
{
    i = i + 5;
    cout << i <<   " ";
}

cout << endl;
```

The statements within the braces do not form the body of the while loop.

Designing while Loops

As in Example 5-1, the body of a while executes only when the expression, in the while statement, evaluates to true. Typically, the expression checks whether a variable(s), called the **loop control variable** (**LCV**), satisfies certain conditions. For example, in Example 5-1, the expression in the while statement checks whether i <= 20. The LCV must be properly initialized before the while loop, and it should eventually make the `expression` evaluate to `false`. We do this by updating or reinitializing the LCV in the body of the `while` loop. Therefore, typically, `while` loops are written in the following form:

```
//initialize the loop control variable(s)

while (expression)   //expression tests the LCV
{
    .
    .
    .
    //update the loop control variable(s)
    .
    .
    .

}
```

For instance, in Example 5-1, the statement in Line 1 initializes the LCV `i` to 0. The expression, `i <= 20`, in Line 2, checks whether `i` is less than or equal to 20, and the statement in Line 4 updates the value of `i`.

EXAMPLE 5-2

Consider the following C++ program segment:

```
i = 20;                    //Line 1
while (i < 20)             //Line 2
{
    cout << i << " ";      //Line 3
    i = i + 5;             //Line 4
}
cout << endl;             //Line 5
```

It is easy to overlook the difference between this example and Example 5-1. In this example, in Line 1, `i` is set to 20. Because `i` is 20, the expression `i < 20` in the `while` statement (Line 2) evaluates to `false`. Because initially the loop entry condition, `i < 20`, is `false`, the body of the `while` loop never executes. Hence, no values are output, and the value of `i` remains 20.

The next few sections describe the various forms of `while` loops.

Case 1: Counter-Controlled `while` Loops

Suppose you know exactly how many times certain statements need to be executed. For example, suppose you know exactly how many pieces of data (or entries) need to be read. In such cases, the `while` loop assumes the form of a **counter-controlled `while` loop**. Suppose that a set of statements needs to be executed N times. You can set up a `counter` (initialized to 0 before the `while` statement) to track how many items have been read. Before executing the body of the `while` statement, the `counter` is compared with `N`. If `counter < N`, the body of the `while` statement executes. The body of the loop continues to execute until the value of `counter >= N`. Thus, inside the body of the `while` statement, the value of `counter` increments after it reads a new item. In this case, the `while` loop might look like the following:

```
counter = 0;          //initialize the loop control variable

while (counter < N) //test the loop control variable
{
    .
    .
    .

    counter++;        //update the loop control variable
    .
    .
    .

}
```

If `N` represents the number of data items in a file, then the value of `N` can be determined several ways. The program can prompt you to specify the number of items in the file; an input statement can read the value; or you can specify the first item in the file as the number of items in the file, so that you need not remember the number of input values (items). This is useful if someone other than the programmer enters the data. Consider Example 5-3.

EXAMPLE 5-3

Students at a local middle school volunteered to sell fresh baked cookies to raise funds to increase the number of computers for the computer lab. Each student reported the number of boxes he/she sold. We will write a program that will output the total number of boxes of cookies sold, the total revenue generated by selling the cookies, and the average number of boxes sold by each student. The data provided is in the following form:

```
studentName numOf BoxesSold
```

Consider the following program:

```
//Program: Counter-Controlled Loop
//This program computes and outputs the total number of boxes of
//cookies sold, the total revenue, and the average number of
//boxes sold by each volunteer.

#include <iostream>                                    //Line 1
#include <string>                                      //Line 2
#include <iomanip>                                     //Line 3

using namespace std;                                   //Line 4

int main()                                             //Line 5
```

```
{                                                           //Line 6
    string name;                                            //Line 7
    int numOfVolunteers;                                    //Line 8
    int numOfBoxesSold;                                     //Line 9
    int totalNumOfBoxesSold;                                //Line 10
    int counter;                                            //Line 11
    double costOfOneBox;                                    //Line 12

    cout << fixed << showpoint << setprecision(2);          //Line 13

    cout << "Line 14: Enter the number of "
         << "volunteers: ";                                 //Line 14
    cin >> numOfVolunteers;                                 //Line 15
    cout << endl;                                           //Line 16

    totalNumOfBoxesSold = 0;                                //Line 17
    counter = 0;                                            //Line 18

    while (counter < numOfVolunteers)                       //Line 19
    {                                                       //Line 20
        cout << "Line 21: Enter the volunteer's name"
             << " and the number of boxes sold: ";          //Line 21
        cin >> name >> numOfBoxesSold;                      //Line 22
        cout << endl;                                       //Line 23
        totalNumOfBoxesSold = totalNumOfBoxesSold
                              + numOfBoxesSold;             //Line 24
        counter++;                                          //Line 25
    }                                                       //Line 26

    cout << "Line 27: The total number of boxes sold: "
         << totalNumOfBoxesSold << endl;                    //Line 27

    cout << "Line 28: Enter the cost of one box: ";         //Line 28
    cin >> costOfOneBox;                                    //Line 29
    cout << endl;                                           //Line 30

    cout << "Line 31: The total money made by selling "
         << "cookies: $"
         << totalNumOfBoxesSold * costOfOneBox << endl; //Line 31

    if (counter != 0)                                       //Line 32
        cout << "Line 33: The average number of "
             << "boxes sold by each volunteer: "
             << totalNumOfBoxesSold / counter << endl;  //Line 33
    else                                                    //Line 34
        cout << "Line 35: No input." << endl;               //Line 35

    return 0;                                               //Line 36
}                                                           //Line 37
```

Sample Run: In this sample run, the user input is shaded.

```
Line 14: Enter the number of volunteers: 5

Line 21: Enter the volunteer's name and the number of boxes sold: Sara 120
```

```
Line 21: Enter the volunteer's name and the number of boxes sold: Lisa 128

Line 21: Enter the volunteer's name and the number of boxes sold: Cindy 359

Line 21: Enter the volunteer's name and the number of boxes sold: Nicole 267

Line 21: Enter the volunteer's name and the number of boxes sold: Blair 165

Line 27: The total number of boxes sold: 1039
Line 28: Enter the cost of one box: 3.50

Line 31: The total money made by selling cookies: $3636.50
Line 33: The average number of boxes sold by each volunteer: 207
```

This program works as follows. The statements in Lines 7 to 12 declare the variables used in the program. The statement in Line 14 prompts the user to enter the number of student volunteers. The statement in Line 15 inputs this number into the variables `numOfVolunteers`. The statements in Lines 17 and 18 initializes the variables `totalNumOfBoxesSold` and `counter`. (The variable `counter` is the loop control variable.)

The `while` statement in Line 19 checks the value of `counter` to determine how many students' data have been read. If `counter` is less than `numOfVolunteers`, the `while` loop proceeds for the next iteration. The statement in Line 21 prompts the user to input the student's name and the number of boxes sold by the student. The statement in Line 22 input the student's name in the variable `name` and the number of boxes sold by the student into the variable `numOfBoxesSold`. The statement in Line 24 updates the value of `totalNumOfBoxesSold` by adding the value of `numOfBoxesSold` to the previous value and the statement in Line 25 increments the value of `counter` by 1. The statement in Line 27 outputs the total number of boxes sold, the statement in Line 28 prompts the user to inputs the cost of one box of cookies, and the statement in Line 29 inputs the cost in the variable `costOfOneBox`. The statement in Line 31 outputs the total money made by selling cookies, and the statements in Lines 32 through 35 output the average number of boxes sold by each volunteer.

Note that `totalNumOfBoxesSold` is initialized to 0 in Line 17 in this program. In Line 22, after reading the number of boxes sold by a student, the program adds it to the sum of all the boxes sold before the current number of boxes sold. The first `numOfBoxesSold` read will be added to zero (because `totalNumOfBoxesSold` is initialized to 0), giving the correct sum of the first number. To find the average, divide `totalNumOfBoxesSold` by `counter`. If `counter` is 0, then dividing by zero will terminate the program and you will get an error message. Therefore, before dividing `totalNumOfBoxesSold` by counter, you must check whether or not `counter` is 0.

Notice that in this program, the statement in Line 5 initializes the LCV `counter` to 0. The expression `counter < numOfVolunteers` in Line 19 evaluates whether `counter` is less than `numOfVolunteers`. The statement in Line 25 updates the value of `counter`.

Case 2: Sentinel-Controlled `while` Loops

You do not always know how many pieces of data (or entries) need to be read, but you may know that the last entry is a special value, called a **sentinel**. In this case, you read the first item before the `while` statement. If this item does not equal the sentinel, the body of the `while` statement executes. The `while` loop continues to execute as long as the program has not read the sentinel. Such a `while` loop is called a **sentinel-controlled `while` loop**. In this case, a `while` loop might look like the following:

```
cin >> variable;              //initialize the loop control variable

while (variable != sentinel)  //test the loop control variable
{
    .
    .
    .
    cin >> variable;          //update the loop control variable
    .
    .
    .
}
```

EXAMPLE 5-4

The program in Example 5-3 computes and outputs the total number of boxes of cookies sold, the total money made, and the average number of boxes sold by each student. However, the program assumes that the programmer knows the exact number of volunteers. Now suppose that the programmer does not know the exact number of volunteers. Once again, assume that the data is in the following form: student's name followed by a space and the number of boxes sold by the student. Because we do not know the exact number of volunteers, we assume that −1 will mark the end of the data. So consider the following program:

```
//Program: Sentinel-Controlled Loop
//This program computes and outputs the total number of boxes of
//cookies sold, the total revenue, and the average number of
//boxes sold by each volunteer.

#include <iostream>                                    //Line 1
#include <string>                                      //Line 2
#include <iomanip>                                     //Line 3

using namespace std;                                   //Line 4

const string SENTINEL = "-1";                          //Line 5

int main()                                             //Line 6
{                                                      //Line 7
    string name;                                       //Line 8
    int numOfVolunteers;                               //Line 9
```

```
int numOfBoxesSold;                                    //Line 10
int totalNumOfBoxesSold;                               //Line 11
double costOfOneBox;                                   //Line 12

cout << fixed << showpoint << setprecision(2);         //Line 13

cout << "Line 14: Enter volunteers data ending "
     << "with -1: " << endl;                           //Line 14

totalNumOfBoxesSold = 0;                               //Line 15
numOfVolunteers = 0;                                   //Line 16

cin >> name;                                           //Line 17

while (name != SENTINEL)                               //Line 18
{                                                      //Line 19
    cin >> numOfBoxesSold;                             //Line 20
    totalNumOfBoxesSold = totalNumOfBoxesSold
                          + numOfBoxesSold;            //Line 21
    numOfVolunteers++;                                 //Line 22
    cin >> name;                                       //Line 23
}                                                      //Line 24

cout << endl;                                          //Line 25

cout << "Line 26: The total number of boxes sold: "
     << totalNumOfBoxesSold << endl;                   //Line 26

cout << "Line 27: Enter the cost of one box: ";        //Line 27
cin >> costOfOneBox;                                   //Line 28
cout << endl;                                          //Line 29

cout << "Line 30: The total money made by selling "
     << "cookies: $"
     << totalNumOfBoxesSold * costOfOneBox << endl;    //Line 30

if (numOfVolunteers != 0)                              //Line 31
    cout << "Line 32: The average number of "
         << "boxes sold by each volunteer: "
         << totalNumOfBoxesSold / numOfVolunteers
         << endl;                                      //Line 32
else                                                   //Line 33
    cout << "Line 34: No input." << endl;              //Line 34

return 0;                                              //Line 35
}                                                      //Line 36
```

Sample Run: In this sample run, the user input is shaded.

```
Line 14: Enter volunteers data ending with -1:
Sara 120
Lisa 128
Cindy 359
Nicole 267
Blair 165
Abby 290
Amy 190
Megan 450
Elizabeth 280
Meredith 290
Leslie 430
Chelsea 378
-1

Line 26: The total number of boxes sold: 3347
Line 27: Enter the cost of one box: 3.50

Line 30: The total money made by selling cookies: $11714.50
Line 32: The average number of boxes sold by each volunteer: 278
```

This program works as follows. The statements in Lines 8 to 12 declare the variables used in the program. The statement in Line 14 prompts the user to enter the data ending with -1. The statements in Lines 15 and 16 initialize the variables `totalNumOfBoxesSold` and `numOfVolunteers`. The statement in Line 17 reads the first name and stores it in `name`. The **while** statement in Line 18 checks whether `name` is not equal to `SENTINEL`. (The variable `name` is the loop control variable.) If `name` is not equal to `SENTINEL`, the body of the **while** loop executes. The statement in Line 20 reads and stores the number of boxes sold by the student in the variable `numOfBoxesSold` and the statement in Line 21 updates the value of `totalNumOfBoxesSold` by adding `numOfBoxesSold` to it. The statement in Line 22 increments the value of `numOfVolunteers` by 1, and the statement in Line 23 reads and stores the next name into `name`. The statements in Lines 20 through 23 repeat until the program reads the `SENTINEL`. The statement in Line 26 outputs the total number of boxes sold, the statement in Line 27 prompts the user to input the cost of one box of cookies, and the statement in Line 28 inputs the cost in the variable `costOfOneBox`. The statement in Line 30 outputs the total money made by selling cookies, and the statements in Lines 31 through 34 output the average number of boxes sold by each volunteer.

Notice that the statement in Line 17 initializes the LCV `name`. The expression `name !=` `SENTINEL` in Line 18 checks whether the value of `name` is equal to `SENTINEL`. The statement in Line 23 reinitializes the LCV `name`.

Next, consider another example of a sentinel-controlled **while** loop. In this example, the user is prompted to enter the value to be processed. If the user wants to stop the program, he or she can enter the sentinel.

EXAMPLE 5-5

Telephone Digits

The following program reads the letter codes A to Z and prints the corresponding telephone digit. This program uses a sentinel-controlled while loop. To stop the program, the user is prompted for the sentinel, which is #. This is also an example of a nested control structure, in which if...else, switch, and the while loop are nested.

```
//**********************************************************
// Program: Telephone Digits
// This is an example of a sentinel-controlled loop. This
// program converts uppercase letters to their corresponding
// telephone digits.
//**********************************************************

#include <iostream>

using namespace std;

int main()
{
    char letter;                              //Line 1

    cout << "Program to convert uppercase "
         << "letters to their corresponding "
         << "telephone digits." << endl;      //Line 2

    cout << "To stop the program enter #."
         << endl;                             //Line 3

    cout << "Enter a letter: ";               //Line 4
    cin >> letter;                            //Line 5
    cout << endl;                             //Line 6

    while (letter != '#')                     //Line 7
    {
        cout << "The letter you entered is: "
             << letter << endl;               //Line 8
        cout << "The corresponding telephone "
             << "digit is: ";                 //Line 9

        if (letter >= 'A' && letter <= 'Z')   //Line 10
            switch (letter)                   //Line 11
            {
            case 'A':
            case 'B':
            case 'C':
                cout << 2 <<endl;             //Line 12
                break;                        //Line 13
```

5

```
        case 'D':
        case 'E':
        case 'F':
            cout << 3 << endl;                  //Line 14
            break;                              //Line 15
        case 'G':
        case 'H':
        case 'I':
            cout << 4 << endl;                  //Line 16
            break;                              //Line 17
        case 'J':
        case 'K':
        case 'L':
            cout << 5 << endl;                  //Line 18
            break;                              //Line 19
        case 'M':
        case 'N':
        case 'O':
            cout << 6 << endl;                  //Line 20
            break;                              //Line 21
        case 'P':
        case 'Q':
        case 'R':
        case 'S':
            cout << 7 << endl;                  //Line 22
            break;                              //Line 23
        case 'T':
        case 'U':
        case 'V':
            cout << 8 << endl;                  //Line 24
            break;                              //Line 25
        case 'W':
        case 'X':
        case 'Y':
        case 'Z':
            cout << 9 << endl;                  //Line 26
        }
    else                                        //Line 27
        cout << "Invalid input." << endl;       //Line 28

    cout << "\nEnter another uppercase "
        << "letter to find its "
        << "corresponding telephone digit."
        << endl;                                //Line 29
    cout << "To stop the program enter #."
        << endl;                                //Line 30

    cout << "Enter a letter: ";                 //Line 31
    cin >> letter;                              //Line 32
    cout << endl;                               //Line 33
} //end while

    return 0;
}
```

Sample Run: In this sample run, the user input is shaded.

```
Program to convert uppercase letters to their corresponding telephone
digits.
To stop the program enter #.
Enter a letter: A
The letter you entered is: A
The corresponding telephone digit is: 2

Enter another uppercase letter to find its corresponding telephone digit.
To stop the program enter #.
Enter a letter: D
The letter you entered is: D
The corresponding telephone digit is: 3

Enter another uppercase letter to find its corresponding telephone digit.
To stop the program enter #.
Enter a letter: #
```

This program works as follows. The statements in Lines 2 and 3 tell the user what to do. The statement in Line 4 prompts the user to input a letter; the statement in Line 5 reads and stores that letter into the variable `letter`. The `while` loop in Line 7 checks that the letter is #. If the letter entered by the user is not #, the body of the `while` loop executes. The statement in Line 8 outputs the letter entered by the user. The `if` statement in Line 10 checks whether the letter entered by the user is uppercase. The statement part of the `if` statement is the `switch` statement (Line 11). If the letter entered by the user is uppercase, the `expression` in the `if` statement (in Line 10) evaluates to `true` and the `switch` statement executes; if the letter entered by the user is not uppercase, the `else` statement (Line 27) executes. The statements in Lines 12 through 26 determine the corresponding telephone digit.

Once the current letter is processed, the statements in Lines 29 and 30 again inform the user what to do next. The statement in Line 31 prompts the user to enter a letter; the statement in Line 32 reads and stores that letter into the variable `letter`. (Note that the statement in Line 29 is similar to the statement in Line 2 and that the statements in Lines 30 through 33 are the same as the statements in Lines 3 through 6.) After the statement in Line 33 (at the end of the `while` loop) executes, the control goes back to the top of the `while` loop and the same process begins again. When the user enters #, the program terminates.

Notice that in this program, the variable `letter` is the loop control variable. First, it is initialized in Line 5 by the input statement, and then it is updated in Line 32. The expression in Line 7 checks whether `letter` is #.

NOTE In the program in Example 5-5, you can write the statements between Lines 10 and 28 using a `switch` structure. (See Programming Exercise 3 at the end of this chapter.)

Case 3: Flag-Controlled `while` Loops

A **flag-controlled `while` loop** uses a `bool` variable to control the loop. Suppose found is a `bool` variable. The flag-controlled `while` loop takes the following form:

```
found = false;        //initialize the loop control variable

while (!found)        //test the loop control variable
{
    .
    .
    .
    if (expression)
        found = true; //update the loop control variable
    .
    .
    .
}
```

The variable `found`, which is used to control the execution of the `while` loop, is called a **flag variable**.

Example 5-6 further illustrates the use of a flag-controlled `while` loop.

EXAMPLE 5-6

Number Guessing Game

The following program randomly generates an integer greater than or equal to 0 and less than 100. The program then prompts the user to guess the number. If the user guesses the number correctly, the program outputs an appropriate message. Otherwise, the program checks whether the guessed number is less than the random number. If the guessed number is less than the random number generated by the program, the program outputs the message "Your guess is lower than the number. Guess again!"; otherwise, the program outputs the message "Your guess is higher than the number. Guess again!". The program then prompts the user to enter another number. The user is prompted to guess the random number until the user enters the correct number.

To generate a random number, you can use the function `rand` of the header file `cstdlib`. For example, the expression `rand()` returns an `int` value between 0 and 32767. Therefore, the statement:

```
cout << rand() << ", " << rand() << endl;
```

will output two numbers that appear to be random. However, each time the program is run, this statement will output the same random numbers. This is because the function `rand` uses an algorithm that produces the same sequence of random numbers each time the program is executed on the same system. To generate different random numbers each time the program is executed, you also use the function `srand` of the header file `cstdlib`. The function `srand` takes as input an `unsigned int`, which acts as the seed for the algorithm. By specifying different seed values, each time the program is executed, the function `rand` will generate a different sequence of random numbers. To specify a different seed, you can use the function `time` of the header file `ctime`, which returns the number of seconds elapsed since January 1, 1970. For example, consider the following statements:

```
srand(time(0));
num = rand() % 100;
```

The first statement sets the seed, and the second statement generates a random number greater than or equal to 0 and less than 100. Note how the function time is used. It is used with an argument, that is, parameter, which is 0.

The program uses the bool variable isGuessed to control the loop. The bool variable isGuessed is initialized to false. It is set to true when the user guesses the correct number.

```
//Flag-controlled while loop.
//Number guessing game.

#include <iostream>
#include <cstdlib>
#include <ctime>

using namespace std;

int main()
{
        //declare the variables
    int num;            //variable to store the random
                        //number
    int guess;          //variable to store the number
                        //guessed by the user
    bool isGuessed;     //boolean variable to control
                        //the loop

    srand(time(0));                                         //Line 1
    num = rand() % 100;                                     //Line 2

    isGuessed = false;                                      //Line 3

    while (!isGuessed)                                      //Line 4
    {                                                       //Line 5
        cout << "Enter an integer greater"
            << " than or equal to 0 and "
            << "less than 100: ";                           //Line 6

        cin >> guess;                                       //Line 7
        cout << endl;                                       //Line 8

        if (guess == num)                                   //Line 9
        {                                                   //Line 10
            cout << "You guessed the correct "
                << "number." << endl;                       //Line 11
            isGuessed = true;                               //Line 12
        }                                                   //Line 13
        else if (guess < num)                               //Line 14
            cout << "Your guess is lower than the "
                << "number.\n Guess again!"
                << endl;                                    //Line 15
```

5

```
        else                                    //Line 16
            cout << "Your guess is higher than "
                << "the number.\n Guess again!"
                << endl;                         //Line 17
    } //end while                                //Line 18

    return 0;
}
```

Sample Run: In this sample run, the user input is shaded.

```
Enter an integer greater than or equal to 0 and less than 100: 45

Your guess is higher than the number.
 Guess again!
Enter an integer greater than or equal to 0 and less than 100: 20

Your guess is lower than the number.
 Guess again!
Enter an integer greater than or equal to 0 and less than 100: 35

Your guess is higher than the number.
 Guess again!
Enter an integer greater than or equal to 0 and less than 100: 28

Your guess is lower than the number.
 Guess again!
Enter an integer greater than or equal to 0 and less than 100: 32

You guessed the correct number.
```

The preceding program works as follows: The statement in Line 2 creates an integer greater than or equal to 0 and less than 100 and stores this number in the variable num. The statement in Line 3 sets the bool variable isGuessed to false. The expression in the while loop at Line 4 evaluates the expression !isGuessed. If isGuessed is false, then !isGuessed is true and the body of the while loop executes; if isGuessed is true, then !isGuessed is false, so the while loop terminates.

The statement in Line 6 prompts the user to enter an integer greater than or equal to 0 and less than 100. The statement in Line 7 stores the number entered by the user in the variable guess. The expression in the if statement in Line 9 determines whether the value of guess is the same as num, that is, if the user guessed the number correctly. If the value of guess is the same as num, the statement in Line 11 outputs the message:

```
You guessed the correct number.
```

The statement in Line 12 sets the variable isGuessed to true. The control then goes back to Line 3. Because done is true, !isGuessed is false and the while loop terminates. If the expression in Line 9 evaluates to false, then the else statement in Line 14 determines whether the value of guess is less than or greater than num and outputs the appropriate message.

Case 4: EOF-Controlled `while` Loops

If the data file is frequently altered (for example, if data is frequently added or deleted), it's best not to read the data with a sentinel value. Someone might accidentally erase the sentinel value or add data past the sentinel, especially if the programmer and the data entry person are different people. Also, it can be difficult at times to select a good sentinel value. In such situations, you can use an **end-of-file (EOF)-controlled** `while` **loop**.

Until now, we have used an input stream variable, such as `cin`, and the extraction operator, `>>`, to read and store data into variables. However, the input stream variable can also return a value after reading data, as follows:

1. If the program has reached the end of the input data, the input stream variable returns the logical value `false`.

2. If the program reads any faulty data (such as a `char` value into an `int` variable), the input stream enters the fail state. Once a stream enters the fail state, any further I/O operations using that stream are considered to be null operations; that is, they have no effect. Unfortunately, the computer does not halt the program or give any error messages. It just continues executing the program, silently ignoring each additional attempt to use that stream. In this case, the input stream variable returns the value `false`.

3. In cases other than (1) and (2), the input stream variable returns the logical value `true`.

You can use the value returned by the input stream variable to determine whether the program has reached the end of the input data. Because the input stream variable returns the logical value `true` or `false`, in a `while` loop, it can be considered a logical expression.

The following is an example of an EOF-controlled `while` loop:

```
cin >> variable;        //initialize the loop control variable

while (cin)             //test the loop control variable
{
    .
    .
    .
    cin >> variable; //update the loop control variable
    .
    .
    .
}
```

Notice that here, the variable `cin` acts as the loop control variable.

`eof` Function

In addition to checking the value of an input stream variable, such as `cin`, to determine whether the end of the file has been reached, C++ provides a function that you can use with an input stream variable to determine the end-of-file status. This function is called eof. Like the I/O functions—such as get, ignore, and peek, discussed in Chapter 3—the function eof is a member of the data type istream.

The syntax to use the function eof is:

```
istreamVar.eof()
```

in which istreamVar is an input stream variable, such as cin.

Suppose you have the declaration:

```
ifstream infile;
```

Further suppose that you opened a file using the variable infile. Consider the expression:

```
infile.eof()
```

This is a logical (Boolean) expression. The value of this expression is **true** if the program has read past the end of the input file, infile; otherwise, the value of this expression is **false**.

This method of determining the end-of-file status (that is, using the function eof) works best if the input is text. The earlier method of determining the end-of-file status works best if the input consists of numeric data.

Suppose you have the declaration:

```
ifstream infile;
char ch;

infile.open("inputDat.dat");
```

The following **while** loop continues to execute as long as the program has not reached the end of the file:

```
infile.get(ch);

while (!infile.eof())
{
    cout << ch;
    infile.get(ch);
}
```

As long as the program has not reached the end of the input file, the expression:

```
infile.eof()
```

is **false** and so the expression:

```
!infile.eof()
```

in the **while** statement is **true**. When the program reads past the end of the input file, the expression:

```
infile.eof()
```

becomes `true`, so the expression:

```
!infile.eof()
```

in the `while` statement becomes `false` and the loop terminates.

 NOTE In the Windows console environment, the end-of-file marker is entered using `Ctrl+z` (hold the `Ctrl` key and press `z`). In the UNIX environment, the end-of-file marker is entered using `Ctr+d` (hold the `Ctrl` key and press `d`).

EXAMPLE 5-7

The following code uses an EOF-controlled `while` loop to find the sum of a set of numbers:

```cpp
int sum = 0;
int num;

cin >> num;

while (cin)
{
    sum = sum + num;    //Add the number to sum
    cin >> num;         //Get the next number
}

cout << "Sum = " << sum << endl;
```

EXAMPLE 5-8

Suppose we are given a file consisting of students' names and their test scores, a number between 0 and 100 (inclusive). Each line in the file consists of a student name followed by the test score. We want a program that outputs each student's name followed by the test score followed by the grade. The program also needs to output the average test score for the class. Consider the following program:

```cpp
// This program reads data from a file consisting of students'
// names and their test scores. The program outputs each student's
// name followed by the test score followed by the grade. The
// program also outputs the average test score for all the students.

#include <iostream>         //Line 1
#include <fstream>          //Line 2
#include <string>           //Line 3
#include <iomanip>          //Line 4

using namespace std;        //Line 5
```

```
int main()                                             //Line 6
{                                                      //Line 7
    //Declare variables to manipulate data
    string firstName;                                  //Line 8
    string lastName;                                   //Line 9
    double testScore;                                  //Line 10
    char grade = ' ';                                  //Line 11
    double sum = 0;                                    //Line 12
    int count = 0;                                      //Line 13

    //Declare stream variables
    ifstream inFile;                                   //Line 14
    ofstream outFile;                                  //Line 15

    //Open input file
    inFile.open("Ch5_stData.txt");                     //Line 16

    if (!inFile)                                        //Line 17
    {                                                  //Line 18
        cout << "Cannot open input file. "
             << "Program terminates!" << endl;         //Line 19
        return 1;                                      //Line 20
    }                                                  //Line 21
    //Open output file
    outFile.open("Ch5_stData.out");                    //Line 22

    outFile << fixed << showpoint << setprecision(2);  //Line 23

    inFile >> firstName >> lastName;  //read the name    Line 24
    inFile >> testScore;        //read the test score    Line 25

    while (inFile)                                     //Line 26
    {                                                  //Line 27
        sum = sum + testScore; //update sum              Line 28
        count++;                 //increment count       Line 29

        //determine the grade
        switch (static_cast<int> (testScore) / 10)     //Line 30
        {                                              //Line 31
        case 0:                                        //Line 32
        case 1:                                        //Line 33
        case 2:                                        //Line 34
        case 3:                                        //Line 35
        case 4:                                        //Line 36
        case 5:                                        //Line 37
            grade = 'F';                               //Line 38
            break;                                     //Line 39

        case 6:                                        //Line 40
            grade = 'D';                               //Line 41
            break;                                     //Line 42

        case 7:                                        //Line 43
            grade = 'C';                               //Line 44
            break;                                     //Line 45
```

```
        case 8:                                        //Line 46
            grade = 'B';                               //Line 47
            break;                                     //Line 48

        case 9:                                        //Line 49
        case 10:                                       //Line 50
            grade = 'A';                               //Line 51
            break;                                     //Line 52

        default:                                       //Line 53
            cout << "Invalid score." << endl;          //Line 54
        } //end switch                                 //Line 55

        outFile << left << setw(12) << firstName
                << setw(12) << lastName
                << right << setw(4) << testScore
                << setw(2) << grade << endl;           //Line 56

        inFile >> firstName >> lastName; //read the name Line 57
        inFile >> testScore;        //read the test score Line 58
    } //end while                                      //Line 59

    outFile << endl;                                   //Line 60

    if (count != 0)                                    //Line 61
        outFile << "Class Average: " << sum / count
                <<endl;                                //Line 62
    else                                               //Line 63
        outFile << "No data." << endl;                 //Line 64

    inFile.close();                                    //Line 65
    outFile.close();                                   //Line 66

    return 0;                                          //Line 67
}                                                      //Line 68
```

Sample Run:

Input File:

```
Steve Gill 89
Rita Johnson 91.5
Randy Brown 85.5
Seema Arora 76.5
Samir Mann 73
Samantha McCoy 88.5
```

Output File:

```
Steve       Gill        89.00 B
Rita        Johnson     91.50 A
Randy       Brown       85.50 B
Seema       Arora       76.50 C
Samir       Mann        73.00 C
Samantha    McCoy       88.50 B

Class Average: 84.00
```

The preceding program works as follows. The statements in Lines 8 to 13 declare and initialize variables needed by the program. The statement in Lines 14 and 15 declares inFile to be an ifstream variable and outFile to be an ofstream variable. The statement in Line 16 opens the input file using the variable inFile. If the input file does not exist, the statements in Lines 17 to 21 output an appropriate message and terminate the program. The statement in Line 22 opens the output file using the variable outFile. The statement in Line 23 sets the output of floating-point numbers to two decimal places in a fixed form with trailing zeros.

The statements in Lines 24 and 25 and the while loop in Line 26 read each student's first name, last name, and test score and then output the name followed by the test score followed by the grade. Specifically, the statement in Lines 24 and 57 reads the first and last name; the statement in Lines 25 and 58 reads the test score. The statement in Line 28 updates the value of sum. (After reading all the data, the value of sum stores the sum of all the test scores.) The statement in Line 29 updates the value of count. (The variable count stores the number of students in the class.) The switch statement from Lines 30 to 55 determines the grade from testScore and stores it in the variable grade. The statement in Line 56 outputs a student's first name, last name, test score, and grade.

The if...else statement in Lines 61 to 64 outputs the class average and the statements in Lines 65 and 66 close the files.

The Programming Example: Checking Account Balance, available on the Web site accompanying this book, further illustrates how to use an EOF-controlled while loop in a program.

More on Expressions in while Statements

In the examples of the previous sections, the expression in the while statement is quite simple. In other words, the while loop is controlled by a single variable. However, there are situations when the expression in the while statement may be more complex.

For example, the program in Example 5-6 uses a flag-controlled while loop to implement the Number Guessing Game. However, the program gives as many tries as the user needs to guess the number. Suppose you want to give the user no more than five tries to guess the number. If the user does not guess the number correctly within five tries, then the program outputs the random number generated by the program as well as a message that you have lost the game. In this case, you can write the while loop as follows (assume that noOfGuesses is an int variable initialized to 0):

```
while ((noOfGuesses < 5) && (!isGuessed))
{
    cout << "Enter an integer greater than or equal to 0 and "
         << "less than 100: ";
    cin >> guess;
    cout << endl;
```

```
        noOfGuesses++;
        if (guess == num)
        {
            cout << "Winner!. You guessed the correct number."
                << endl;
            isGuessed = true;
        }
        else if (guess < num)
            cout << "Your guess is lower than the number.\n"
                << "Guess again!" << endl;
        else
            cout << "Your guess is higher than the number.\n"
                << "Guess again!" << endl;
} //end while
```

You also need the following code to be included after the `while` loop in case the user cannot guess the correct number in five tries:

```
if (!isGuessed)
        cout << "You lose! The correct number is " << num << endl;
```

Programming Exercise 16 at the end of this chapter asks you to write a complete C++ program to implement the Number Guessing Game in which the user has, at most, five tries to guess the number.

As you can see from the preceding `while` loop, the expression in a `while` statement can be complex. The main objective of a `while` loop is to repeat certain statement(s) until certain conditions are met.

PROGRAMMING EXAMPLE: Fibonacci Number

**Watch
the Video**

So far, you have seen several examples of loops. Recall that in C++, `while` loops are used when a certain statement(s) must be executed repeatedly until certain conditions are met. Following is a C++ program that uses a `while` loop to find a **Fibonacci number**.

Consider the following sequence of numbers:

```
1, 1, 2, 3, 5, 8, 13, 21, 34, ....
```

This sequence is called the **Fibonacci sequence**. Given the first two numbers of the sequence (say, a_1 and a_2), the nth number a_n, $n >= 3$, of this sequence is given by:

$$a_n = a_{n-1} + a_{n-2}$$

Thus:

$$a_3 = a_2 + a_1 = 1 + 1 = 2,$$
$$a_4 = a_3 + a_2 = 2 + 1 = 3,$$

and so on.

Note that $a_2 = 1$ and $a_1 = 1$. However, given any first two numbers, using this process, you can determine the nth number, $a_n, n >= 3$, of the sequence. We will again call such a sequence a **Fibonacci sequence**. Suppose $a_2 = 6$ and $a_1 = 3$.

Then:

$$a_3 = a_2 + a_1 = 6 + 3 = 9; a_4 = a_3 + a_2 = 9 + 6 = 15$$

Next, we write a program that determines the nth Fibonacci number given the first two numbers.

Input   The first two Fibonacci numbers and the desired Fibonacci number.

Output   The nth Fibonacci number.

PROBLEM
ANALYSIS
AND
ALGORITHM
DESIGN

To find, say, the tenth Fibonacci number of a sequence, you must first find a_9 and a_8, which requires you to find a_7 and a_6, and so on. Therefore, to find a_{10}, you must first find $a_3, a_4, a_5, \ldots, a_9$. This discussion translates into the following algorithm:

1. Get the first two Fibonacci numbers.

2. Get the desired Fibonacci number. That is, get the position, n, of the Fibonacci number in the sequence.

3. Calculate the next Fibonacci number by adding the previous two elements of the Fibonacci sequence.

4. Repeat Step 3 until the nth Fibonacci number is found.

5. Output the nth Fibonacci number.

Note that the program assumes that the first number of the Fibonacci sequence is less than or equal to the second number of the Fibonacci sequence, and both numbers are nonnegative. Moreover, the program also assumes that the user enters a valid value for the position of the desired number in the Fibonacci sequence; that is, it is a positive integer. (See Programming Exercise 12 at the end of this chapter.)

Variables

Because the last two numbers must be known in order to find the current Fibonacci number, you need the following variables: two variables—say, `previous1` and `previous2` to hold the previous two numbers of the Fibonacci sequence; and one variable—say, `current`—to hold the current Fibonacci number. The number of times that Step 2 of the algorithm repeats depends on the position of the Fibonacci number you are calculating. For example, if you want to calculate the tenth Fibonacci number, you must execute Step 3 eight times. (Remember—the user gives the first two numbers of the Fibonacci sequence.) Therefore, you need a variable to store the number of times Step 3 should execute. You also need a variable to track the number of times Step 3 has executed, the loop control variable. You therefore need five variables for the data manipulation:

```
int previous1;   //variable to store the first Fibonacci number
int previous2;   //variable to store the second Fibonacci number
```

```
int current;      //variable to store the current
                  //Fibonacci number
int counter;      //loop control variable
int nthFibonacci; //variable to store the desired
                  //Fibonacci number
```

To calculate the third Fibonacci number, add the values of `previous1` and `previous2` and store the result in `current`. To calculate the fourth Fibonacci number, add the value of the second Fibonacci number (that is, `previous2`) and the value of the third Fibonacci number (that is, `current`). Thus, when the fourth Fibonacci number is calculated, you no longer need the first Fibonacci number. Instead of declaring additional variables, which could be too many, after calculating a Fibonacci number to determine the next Fibonacci number, `current` becomes `previous2` and `previous2` becomes `previous1`. Therefore, you can again use the variable `current` to store the next Fibonacci number. This process is repeated until the desired Fibonacci number is calculated. Initially, `previous1` and `previous2` are the first two elements of the sequence, supplied by the user. From the preceding discussion, it follows that you need five variables.

MAIN ALGORITHM

1. Prompt the user for the first two numbers—that is, `previous1` and `previous2`.

2. Read (input) the first two numbers into `previous1` and `previous2`.

3. Output the first two Fibonacci numbers. (Echo input.)

4. Prompt the user for the position of the desired Fibonacci number.

5. Read the position of the desired Fibonacci number into `nthFibonacci`.

6. a. `if` (nthFibonacci == 1)
      the desired Fibonacci number is the first Fibonacci number. Copy the value of `previous1` into `current`.

   b. `else if` (nthFibonacci == 2)
      the desired Fibonacci number is the second Fibonacci number. Copy the value of `previous2` into `current`.

   c. `else` calculate the desired Fibonacci number as follows:

      Because you already know the first two Fibonacci numbers of the sequence, start by determining the third Fibonacci number.

      c.1. Initialize `counter` to 3 to keep track of the calculated Fibonacci numbers.

      c.2. Calculate the next Fibonacci number, as follows:

         `current = previous2 + previous1;`

      c.3. Assign the value of `previous2` to `previous1`.

      c.4. Assign the value of `current` to `previous2`.

      c.5. Increment `counter`.

Repeat Steps c.2 through c.5 until the Fibonacci number you want is calculated.

The following `while` loop executes Steps c.2 through c.5 and determines the *n*th Fibonacci number.

```
while (counter <= nthFibonacci)
{
    current = previous2 + previous1;
    previous1 = previous2;
    previous2 = current;
    counter++;
}
```

7. Output the `nthFibonacci` number, which is current.

COMPLETE PROGRAM LISTING

```
//**********************************************************
// Authors: D.S. Malik
//
// Program: nth Fibonacci number
// Given the first two numbers of a Fibonacci sequence, this
// program determines and outputs the desired number of the
// Fibonacci sequence.
//**********************************************************

#include <iostream>

using namespace std;

int main()
{
        //Declare variables
    int previous1;
    int previous2;
    int current;
    int counter;
    int nthFibonacci;

    cout << "Enter the first two Fibonacci "
        << "numbers: ";                         //Step 1
    cin >> previous1 >> previous2;              //Step 2
    cout << endl;
    cout << "The first two Fibonacci numbers are "
        << previous1 << " and " << previous2
        << endl;                                //Step 3
    cout << "Enter the position of the desired "
        << "Fibonacci number: ";               //Step 4
    cin >> nthFibonacci;                        //Step 5
    cout << endl;

    if (nthFibonacci == 1)                      //Step 6.a
        current = previous1;
```

```
        else if (nthFibonacci == 2)              //Step 6.b
            current = previous2;
        else                                     //Step 6.c
        {
            counter = 3;                         //Step 6.c.1

                //Steps 6.c.2 - 6.c.5
            while (counter <= nthFibonacci)
            {
                current = previous2 + previous1;  //Step 6.c.2
                previous1 = previous2;            //Step 6.c.3
                previous2 = current;              //Step 6.c.4
                counter++;                        //Step 6.c.5
            } //end while
        } //end else

        cout << "The Fibonacci number at position "
            << nthFibonacci << " is " << current
            << endl;                              //Step 7

        return 0;
} //end main
```

Sample Runs: In these sample runs, the user input is shaded.

Sample Run 1:

```
Enter the first two Fibonacci numbers: 12 16

The first two Fibonacci numbers are 12 and 16
Enter the position of the desired Fibonacci number: 10

The Fibonacci number at position 10 is 796
```

Sample Run 2:

```
Enter the first two Fibonacci numbers: 1 1

The first two Fibonacci numbers are 1 and 1
Enter the position of the desired Fibonacci number: 15

The Fibonacci number at position 15 is 610
```

for Looping (Repetition) Structure

The **while** loop discussed in the previous section is general enough to implement most forms of repetitions. The C++ **for** looping structure discussed here is a specialized form of the **while** loop. Its primary purpose is to simplify the writing of counter-controlled loops. For this reason, the **for** loop is typically called a counted or indexed **for** loop.

The general form of the **for** statement is:

```
for (initial statement; loop condition; update statement)
    statement
```

The initial statement, loop condition, and update statement (called **for** loop control statements) enclosed within the parentheses control the body (statement) of the **for** statement. Figure 5-2 shows the flow of execution of a **for** loop.

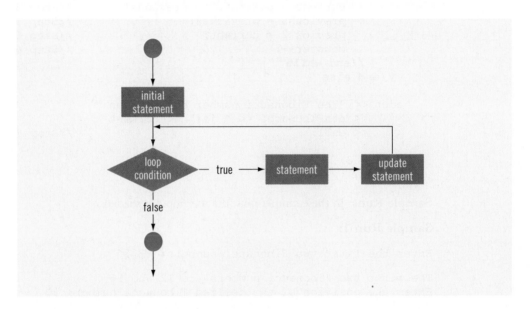

FIGURE 5-2 **for** loop

The **for** loop executes as follows:

1. The initial statement executes.
2. The loop condition is evaluated. If the loop condition evaluates to **true**:
    i.   Execute the **for** loop statement.
    ii. Execute the update statement (the third expression in the parentheses).
3. Repeat Step 2 until the loop condition evaluates to **false**.

The initial statement usually initializes a variable (called the **for loop control**, or **for indexed**, **variable**).

In C++, **for** is a reserved word.

NOTE   As the name implies, the initial statement in the **for** loop is the first statement to execute; it executes only once.

EXAMPLE 5-9

The following `for` loop prints the first 10 nonnegative integers:

```
for (i = 0; i < 10; i++)
    cout << i << " ";
cout << endl;
```

The `initial statement`, `i = 0;`, initializes the `int` variable i to 0. Next, the loop condition, i < 10, is evaluated. Because 0 < 10 is `true`, the print statement executes and outputs 0. The `update statement`, `i++`, then executes, which sets the value of i to 1. Once again, the `loop condition` is evaluated, which is still `true`, and so on. When i becomes 10, the `loop condition` evaluates to `false`, the `for` loop terminates, and the statement following the `for` loop executes.

A `for` loop can have either a simple or compound statement.

The following examples further illustrate how a `for` loop executes.

EXAMPLE 5-10

1. The following `for` loop outputs `Hello!` and a star (on separate lines) five times:

   ```
   for (i = 1; i <= 5; i++)
   {
       cout << "Hello!" << endl;
       cout << "*" << endl;
   }
   ```

2. Consider the following `for` loop:

   ```
   for (i = 1; i <= 5; i++)
       cout << "Hello!" << endl;
       cout << "*" << endl;
   ```

   This loop outputs `Hello!` five times and the star only once. Note that the `for` loop controls only the first output statement because the two output statements are not made into a compound statement. Therefore, the first output statement executes five times because the `for` loop body executes five times. After the `for` loop executes, the second output statement executes only once. The indentation, which is ignored by the compiler, is nevertheless misleading.

EXAMPLE 5-11

The following **for** loop executes five empty statements:

```
for (i = 0; i < 5; i++);      //Line 1
    cout << "*" << endl;      //Line 2
```

The semicolon at the end of the **for** statement (before the output statement, Line 1) terminates the **for** loop. The action of this **for** loop is empty, that is, null.

The preceding examples show that care is required in getting a **for** loop to perform the desired action.

The following are some comments on **for** loops:

- If the **loop condition** is initially **false**, the loop body does not execute.
- The **update expression**, when executed, changes the value of the loop control variable (initialized by the initial expression), which eventually sets the value of the **loop condition** to **false**. The **for** loop body executes indefinitely if the **loop condition** is always **true**.
- C++ allows you to use fractional values for loop control variables of the **double** type (or any real data type). Because different computers can give these loop control variables different results, you should avoid using such variables.
- A semicolon at the end of the **for** statement (just before the body of the loop) is a semantic error. In this case, the action of the **for** loop is empty.
- In the **for** statement, if the **loop condition** is omitted, it is assumed to be **true**.
- In a **for** statement, you can omit all three statements—**initial statement**, **loop condition**, and **update statement**. The following is a legal **for** loop:

  ```
  for (;;)
      cout << "Hello" << endl;
  ```

  This is an infinite **for** loop, continuously printing the word **Hello**.

Following are more examples of **for** loops.

EXAMPLE 5-12

You can count backward using a **for** loop if the **for** loop control expressions are set correctly.

For example, consider the following **for** loop:

```
for (i = 10; i >= 1; i--)
    cout << " " << i;
cout << endl;
```

The output is:

```
10 9 8 7 6 5 4 3 2 1
```

In this **for** loop, the variable i is initialized to 10. After each iteration of the loop, i is decremented by 1. The loop continues to execute as long as i >= 1.

EXAMPLE 5-13

You can increment (or decrement) the loop control variable by any fixed number. In the following **for** loop, the variable is initialized to 1; at the end of the **for** loop, i is incremented by 2. This **for** loop outputs the first 10 positive odd integers.

```
for (i = 1; i <= 20; i = i + 2)
    cout << " " << i;
cout << endl;
```

EXAMPLE 5-14

Suppose that i is an **int** variable.

1. Consider the following **for** loop:

    ```
    for (i = 10; i <= 9; i++)
        cout << i << " ";
    cout << endl;
    ```

    In this **for** loop, the initial statement sets i to 10. Because initially the loop condition (i <= 9) is **false**, nothing happens.

2. Consider the following **for** loop:

    ```
    for (i = 9; i >= 10; i--)
        cout << i << " ";
    cout << endl;
    ```

    In this **for** loop, the initial statement sets i to 9. Because initially the loop condition (i >= 10) is **false**, nothing happens.

3. Consider the following **for** loop:

    ```
    for (i = 10; i <= 10; i++)        //Line 1
        cout << i << " ";             //Line 2
    cout << endl;                     //Line 3
    ```

    In this **for** loop, the initial statement sets i to 10. The loop condition (i <= 10) evaluates to **true**, so the output statement in Line 2 executes, which outputs 10.

Next, the update statement increments the value of i by 1, so the value of i becomes 11. Now the loop condition evaluates to **false** and the **for** loop terminates. Note that the output statement in Line 2 executes only once.

4. Consider the following **for** loop:

```
for (i = 1; i <= 10; i++);    //Line 1
    cout << i << " ";          //Line 2
cout << endl;                  //Line 3
```

This **for** loop has no effect on the output statement in Line 2. The semicolon at the end of the **for** statement terminates the **for** loop; the action of the **for** loop is thus empty. The output statement is all by itself and executes only once.

5. Consider the following **for** loop:

```
for (i = 1; ; i++)
    cout << i << " ";
cout << endl;
```

In this **for** loop, because the loop condition is omitted from the **for** statement, the loop condition is always **true**. This is an infinite loop.

EXAMPLE 5-15

In this example, a **for** loop reads five numbers and finds their sum and average. Consider the following program code, in which i, newNum, sum, and average are **int** variables.

```
sum = 0;

for (i = 1; i <= 5; i++)
{
    cin >> newNum;
    sum = sum + newNum;
}

average = sum / 5;
cout << "The sum is " << sum << endl;
cout << "The average is " << average << endl;
```

In the preceding **for** loop, after reading a newNum, this value is added to the previously calculated (partial) sum of all the numbers read before the current number. The variable sum is initialized to 0 before the **for** loop. Thus, after the program reads the first number and adds it to the value of sum, the variable sum holds the correct sum of the first number.

NOTE

The syntax of the `for` loop, which is:

```
for (initial expression; logical expression; update expression)
    statement
```

is functionally equivalent to the following `while` statement:

```
initial expression
while (expression)
{
    statement
    update expression
}
```

For example, the following `for` and `while` loops are equivalent:

```
for (int i = 0; i < 10; i++)          int i = 0;
    cout << i <<  " ";                while (i < 10)
cout << endl;                         {
                                          cout << i <<  " ";
                                          i++;
                                      }
                                      cout << endl;
```

If the number of iterations of a loop is known or can be determined in advance, typically programmers use a `for` loop.

5

EXAMPLE 5-16 (FIBONACCI NUMBER PROGRAM: REVISITED)

The Programming Example: Fibonacci Number given in the previous section uses a `while` loop to determine the desired Fibonacci number. You can replace the `while` loop with an equivalent `for` loop as follows:

```
for (counter = 3; counter <= nthFibonacci; counter++)
{
    current = previous2 + previous1;
    previous1 = previous2;
    previous2 = current;
    counter++;
} //end for
```

The complete program listing of the program that uses a `for` loop to determine the desired Fibonacci number is given at the Web site accompanying this book. The program is named `Ch5_FibonacciNumberUsingAForLoop.cpp`.

In the following C++ program, we recommend that you walk through each step.

EXAMPLE 5-17

The following C++ program finds the sum of the first n positive integers.

```
//Program to determine the sum of the first n positive integers.

#include <iostream>

using namespace std;

int main()
{
    int counter;       //loop control variable
    int sum;           //variable to store the sum of numbers
    int n;             //variable to store the number of
                       //first positive integers to be added

    cout << "Line 1: Enter the number of positive "
         << "integers to be added: ";                   //Line 1
    cin >> n;                                            //Line 2
    sum = 0;                                             //Line 3
    cout << endl;                                        //Line 4

    for (counter = 1; counter <= n; counter++)          //Line 5
        sum = sum + counter;                            //Line 6

    cout << "Line 7: The sum of the first " << n
         << " positive integers is " << sum
         << endl;                                        //Line 7

    return 0;
}
```

Sample Run: In this sample run, the user input is shaded.

```
Line 1: Enter the number of positive integers to be added: 100

Line 7: The sum of the first 100 positive integers is 5050
```

The statement in Line 1 prompts the user to enter the number of positive integers to be added. The statement in Line 2 stores the number entered by the user in n, and the statement in Line 3 initializes sum to 0. The **for** loop in Line 5 executes n times. In the **for** loop, counter is initialized to 1 and is incremented by 1 after each iteration of the loop. Therefore, counter ranges from 1 to n. Each time through the loop, the value of counter is added to sum. The variable sum was initialized to 0, counter ranges from 1 to n, and the current value of counter is added to the value of sum. Therefore, after the **for** loop executes, sum contains the sum of the first n values, which in the sample run is 100 positive integers.

Recall that putting one control structure statement inside another is called **nesting**. The following programming example demonstrates a simple instance of nesting. It also nicely demonstrates counting.

PROGRAMMING EXAMPLE: Classifying Numbers

This program reads a given set of integers and then prints the number of odd and even integers. It also outputs the number of zeros.

The program reads 20 integers, but you can easily modify it to read any set of numbers. In fact, you can modify the program so that it first prompts the user to specify how many integers are to be read.

Input 20 integers—positive, negative, or zeros.

Output The number of zeros, even numbers, and odd numbers.

PROBLEM
ANALYSIS
AND
ALGORITHM
DESIGN

After reading a number, you need to check whether it is even or odd. Suppose the value is stored in number. Divide number by 2 and check the remainder. If the remainder is 0, number is even. Increment the even count and then check whether number is 0. If it is, increment the zero count. If the remainder is not 0, increment the odd count.

The program uses a `switch` statement to decide whether number is odd or even. Suppose that number is odd. Dividing by 2 gives the remainder 1 if number is positive and the remainder -1 if it is negative. If number is even, dividing by 2 gives the remainder 0 whether number is positive or negative. You can use the mod operator, %, to find the remainder. For example:

```
6 % 2 = 0; -4 % 2 = 0; -7 % 2 = -1; 15 % 2 = 1
```

Repeat the preceding process of analyzing a number for each number in the list.

This discussion translates into the following algorithm:

1. For each number in the list:

 a. Get the number.

 b. Analyze the number.

 c. Increment the appropriate count.

2. Print the results.

Variables

Because you want to count the number of zeros, even numbers, and odd numbers, you need three variables of type `int`—say, zeros, evens, and odds—to track the counts. You also need a variable—say, number—to read and store the number to be analyzed and another variable—say, counter—to count the numbers analyzed. Therefore, you need the following variables in the program:

```
int counter;    //loop control variable
int number;     //variable to store the number read
int zeros;      //variable to store the zero count
int evens;      //variable to store the even count
int odds;       //variable to store the odd count
```

Clearly, you must initialize the variables zeros, evens, and odds to zero. You can initialize these variables when you declare them.

MAIN
ALGORITHM

1. Initialize the variables.

2. Prompt the user to enter 20 numbers.

3. For each number in the list:

    a. Read the number.

    b. Output the number (echo input).

    c. If the number is even:

    ```
    {
    ```

        i. Increment the even count.

        ii. If the number is zero, increment the zero count.

    ```
    }
    otherwise
        Increment the odd count.
    ```

4. Print the results.

Before writing the C++ program, let us describe Steps 1–4 in greater detail. It will be much easier for you to then write the instructions in C++.

1. Initialize the variables. You can initialize the variables zeros, evens, and odds when you declare them.

2. Use an output statement to prompt the user to enter 20 numbers.

3. For Step 3, you can use a `for` loop to process and analyze the 20 numbers. In pseudocode, this step is written as follows:

```
for (counter = 1; counter <= 20; counter++)
{
    read the number;
    output number;

    switch (number % 2)      // check the remainder
    {
    case 0:
        increment even count;
        if (number == 0)
            increment zero count;
        break;
```

```
                    case 1:
                    case -1:
                        increment odd count;
                } //end switch
        } //end for
```

4. Print the result. Output the value of the variables zeros, evens, and odds.

COMPLETE PROGRAM LISTING

```cpp
//*********************************************************
// Author: D.S. Malik
//
// Program: Counts zeros, odds, and evens
// This program counts the number of odd and even numbers.
// The program also counts the number of zeros.
//*********************************************************

#include <iostream>
#include <iomanip>

using namespace std;

const int N = 20;

int main()
{
        //Declare variables
    int counter;      //loop control variable
    int number;       //variable to store the new number
    int zeros = 0;                                      //Step 1
    int odds = 0;                                       //Step 1
    int evens = 0;                                      //Step 1

    cout << "Please enter " << N << " integers, "
        << "positive, negative, or zeros."
        << endl;                                        //Step 2

    cout << "The numbers you entered are:" << endl;

    for (counter = 1; counter <= N; counter++)          //Step 3
    {
        cin >> number;                                  //Step 3a
        cout << number << " ";                          //Step 3b

            //Step 3c
        switch (number % 2)
```

5

```
                {
                case 0:
                    evens++;
                    if (number == 0)
                        zeros++;
                    break;
                case 1:
                case -1:
                    odds++;
                } //end switch
        } //end for loop

        cout << endl;
                        //Step 4
        cout << "There are " << evens << " evens, "
             << "which includes " << zeros << " zeros."
             << endl;
        cout << "The number of odd numbers is: " << odds
             << endl;

        return 0;
}
```

Sample Run: In this sample run, the user input is shaded.

```
Please enter 20 integers, positive, negative, or zeros.
The numbers you entered are:
  0 0 -2 -3 -5 6 7 8 0 3 0 -23 -8 0 2 9 0 12 67 54
0 0 -2 -3 -5 6 7 8 0 3 0 -23 -8 0 2 9 0 12 67 54
There are 13 evens, which includes 6 zeros.
The number of odd numbers is: 7
```

We recommend that you do a walk-through of this program using the above sample input.

do...while Looping (Repetition) Structure

This section describes the third type of looping or repetition structure, called a do...while loop. The general form of a do...while statement is as follows:

```
do
    statement
while (expression);
```

Of course, statement can be either a simple or compound statement. If it is a compound statement, enclose it between braces. Figure 5-3 shows the flow of execution of a do...while loop.

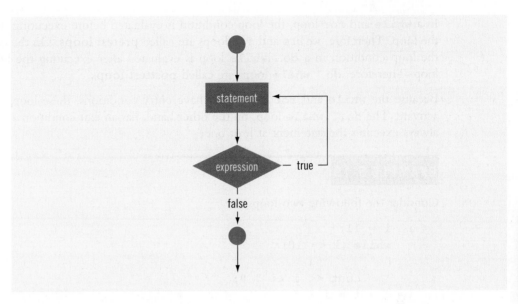

FIGURE 5-3 do...while loop

In C++, **do** is a reserved word.

The **statement** executes first, and then the **expression** is evaluated. If the **expression** evaluates to **true**, the **statement** executes again. As long as the **expression** in a do...while statement is **true**, the **statement** executes. To avoid an infinite loop, you must, once again, make sure that the loop body contains a statement that ultimately makes the **expression false** and assures that it exits properly.

EXAMPLE 5-18

```
i = 0;

do
{
    cout << i << " ";
    i = i + 5;
}
while (i <= 20);
```

The output of this code is:

```
0 5 10 15 20
```

After 20 is output, the statement:

```
i = i + 5;
```

changes the value of i to 25 and so i <= 20 becomes **false**, which halts the loop.

In a `while` and `for` loop, the loop condition is evaluated before executing the body of the loop. Therefore, `while` and `for` loops are called **pretest loops**. On the other hand, the loop condition in a `do...while` loop is evaluated after executing the body of the loop. Therefore, `do...while` loops are called **posttest loops**.

Because the `while` and `for` loops both have entry conditions, these loops may never activate. The `do...while` loop, on the other hand, has an exit condition and therefore always executes the statement at least once.

EXAMPLE 5-19

Consider the following two loops:

```
a.  i = 11;
    while (i <= 10)
    {
        cout << i << " ";
        i = i + 5;
    }
    cout << endl;

b.  i = 11;
    do
    {
        cout << i << " ";
        i = i + 5;
    }
    while (i <= 10);

    cout << endl;
```

In (a), the `while` loop produces nothing. In (b), the `do...while` loop outputs the number 11 and also changes the value of `i` to 16.

A `do...while` loop can be used for input validation. Suppose that a program prompts a user to enter a test score, which must be greater than or equal to 0 and less than or equal to 50. If the user enters a score less than 0 or greater than 50, the user should be prompted to re-enter the score. The following `do...while` loop can be used to accomplish this objective:

```
int score;

do
{
    cout << "Enter a score between 0 and 50: ";
    cin >> score;
    cout << endl;
}
while (score < 0 || score > 50);
```

EXAMPLE 5-20

Divisibility Test by 3 and 9

Suppose that m and n are integers and m is nonzero. Then m is called a **divisor** of n if $n = mt$ for some integer t; that is, when m divides n, the remainder is 0.

Let $n = a_k a_{k-1} a_{k-2} \ldots a_1 a_0$ be an integer. Let $s = a_k + a_{k-1} + a_{k-2} + \cdots + a_1 + a_0$ be the sum of the digits of n. It is known that n is divisible by 3 and 9 if s is divisible by 3 and 9. In other words, an integer is divisible by 3 and 9 if and only if the sum of its digits is divisible by 3 and 9.

For example, suppose $n = 27193257$. Then $s = 2 + 7 + 1 + 9 + 3 + 2 + 5 + 7 = 36$. Because 36 is divisible by both 3 and 9, it follows that 27193257 is divisible by both 3 and 9.

Next, we write a program that determines whether a positive integer is divisible by 3 and 9 by first finding the sum of its digits and then checking whether the sum is divisible by 3 and 9.

To find the sum of the digits of a positive integer, we need to extract each digit of the number. Consider the number 951372. Note that 951372 % 10 = 2, which is the last digit of 951372. Also note that 951372 / 10 = 95137; that is, when the number is divided by 10, it removes the last digit. Next, we repeat this process on the number 95137. Of course, we need to add the extracted digits.

Suppose that sum and num are int variables and the positive integer is stored in num. We thus have the following algorithm to find the sum of the digits:

```
sum = 0;

do
{
    sum = sum + num % 10;  //extract the last digit
                           //and add it to sum
    num = num / 10;        //remove the last digit
}
while (num > 0);
```

Using this algorithm, we can write the following program that uses a do...while loop to implement the preceding divisibility test algorithm.

```
//Program: Divisibility test by 3 and 9

#include <iostream>

using namespace std;

int main()
{
    int num, temp, sum;

    cout << "Enter a positive integer: ";
    cin >> num;
```

```cpp
    cout << endl;

    temp = num;

    sum = 0;

    do
    {
        sum = sum + num % 10;   //extract the last digit
                                //and add it to sum
        num = num / 10;         //remove the last digit
    }
    while (num > 0);

    cout << "The sum of the digits = " << sum << endl;

    if (sum % 3 == 0)
        cout << temp << " is divisible by 3" << endl;
    else
        cout << temp << " is not divisible by 3" << endl;

    if (sum % 9 == 0)
        cout << temp << " is divisible by 9" << endl;
    else
        cout << temp << " is not divisible by 9" << endl;
}
```

Sample Run: In these sample runs, the user input is shaded.

Sample Run 1:

```
Enter a positive integer: 27193257

The sum of the digits = 36
27193257 is divisible by 3
27193257 is divisible by 9
```

Sample Run 2:

```
Enter a positive integer: 609321

The sum of the digits = 21
609321 is divisible by 3
609321 is not divisible by 9
```

Sample Run 3:

```
Enter a positive integer: 161905102

The sum of the digits = 25
161905102 is not divisible by 3
161905102 is not divisible by 9
```

Choosing the Right Looping Structure

All three loops have their place in C++. If you know, or the program can determine in advance, the number of repetitions needed, the **for** loop is the correct choice. If you do not know, and the program cannot determine in advance the number of repetitions needed, and it could be 0, the **while** loop is the right choice. If you do not know, and the program cannot determine in advance the number of repetitions needed, and it is at least 1, the **do...while** loop is the right choice.

break and continue Statements

The **break** statement, when executed in a **switch** structure, provides an immediate exit from the **switch** structure. Similarly, you can use the **break** statement in **while**, **for**, and **do...while** loops. When the **break** statement executes in a repetition structure, it immediately exits from the structure. The **break** statement is typically used for two purposes:

- To exit early from a loop.
- To skip the remainder of the **switch** structure.

After the **break** statement executes, the program continues to execute with the first statement after the structure. The use of a **break** statement in a loop can eliminate the use of certain (flag) variables. The following C++ code segment helps illustrate this idea. (Assume that all variables are properly declared.)

```
sum = 0;
isNegative = false;

cin >> num;

while (cin && !isNegative)
{
    if (num < 0)     //if num is negative, terminate the loop
                     //after this iteration
    {
        cout << "Negative number found in the data." << endl;
        isNegative = true;
    }
    else
    {
        sum = sum + num;
        cin >> num;
    }
}
```

This **while** loop is supposed to find the sum of a set of positive numbers. If the data set contains a negative number, the loop terminates with an appropriate error message. This **while** loop uses the flag variable **isNegative** to accomplish the desired result. The variable **isNegative** is initialized to **false** before the **while** loop. Before adding num to sum, check whether num is negative. If num is negative, an error message appears on the screen and isNegative is set to true. In the next iteration, when the expression in the while statement is evaluated, it evaluates to false because !isNegative is false. (Note that because isNegative is true, !isNegative is false.)

The following while loop is written without using the variable isNegative:

```
sum = 0;
cin >> num;

while (cin)
{
    if (num < 0)    //if num is negative, terminate the loop
    {
        cout << "Negative number found in the data." << endl;
        break;
    }

    sum = sum + num;
    cin >> num;
}
```

In this form of the while loop, when a negative number is found, the expression in the if statement evaluates to true; after printing an appropriate message, the break statement terminates the loop. (After executing the break statement in a loop, the remaining statements in the loop are discarded.)

NOTE The break statement is an effective way to avoid extra variables to control a loop and produce an elegant code. However, break statements must be used very sparingly within a loop. An excessive use of these statements in a loop will produce spaghetti-code (loops with many exit conditions) that can be very hard to understand and manage. You should be extra careful in using break statements and ensure that the use of the break statements makes the code more readable and not less readable. If you're not sure, don't use break statements.

The continue statement is used in while, for, and do...while structures. When the continue statement is executed in a loop, it skips the remaining statements in the loop and proceeds with the next iteration of the loop. In a while and do...while structure, the expression (that is, the loop-continue test) is evaluated immediately after the continue statement. In a for structure, the update statement is executed after the continue statement, and then the loop condition (that is, the loop-continue test) executes.

If the previous program segment encounters a negative number, the while loop terminates. If you want to discard the negative number and read the next number rather than terminate the loop, replace the break statement with the continue statement, as shown in the following example:

```
sum = 0;
cin >> num;
```

```
while (cin)
{
    if (num < 0)
    {
        cout << "Negative number found in the data." << endl;
        cin >> num;
        continue;
    }

    sum = sum + num;
    cin >> num;
}
```

It was stated earlier that all three loops have their place in C++ and that one loop can often replace another. The execution of a `continue` statement, however, is where the `while` and `do...while` structures differ from the `for` structure. When the `continue` statement is executed in a `while` or a `do...while` loop, the update statement may not execute. In a `for` structure, the update statement *always* executes.

Nested Control Structures

In this section, we give examples that illustrate how to use nested loops to achieve useful results and process data.

EXAMPLE 5-21

Suppose you want to create the following pattern:

```
*
**
***
****
*****
```

Clearly, you want to print five lines of stars. In the first line, you want to print one star, in the second line, two stars, and so on. Because five lines will be printed, start with the following `for` statement:

```
for (i = 1; i <= 5; i++)
```

The value of i in the first iteration is 1, in the second iteration it is 2, and so on. You can use the value of i as the limiting condition in another `for` loop nested within this loop to control the number of stars in a line. A little more thought produces the following code:

```
for (i = 1; i <= 5; i++)            //Line 1
{                                   //Line 2
    for (j = 1; j <= i; j++)        //Line 3
        cout << "*";                //Line 4
    cout << endl;                   //Line 5
}                                   //Line 6
```

A walk-through of this code shows that the **for** loop in Line 1 starts with i = 1. When i is 1, the inner **for** loop in Line 3 outputs one star and the insertion point moves to the next line. Then i becomes 2, the inner **for** loop outputs two stars, and the output statement in Line 5 moves the insertion point to the next line, and so on. This process continues until i becomes 6 and the loop stops.

What pattern does this code produce if you replace the **for** statement in Line 1 with the following?

```
for (i = 5; i >= 1; i--)
```

EXAMPLE 5-22

Suppose you want to create the following multiplication table:

```
1   2   3   4   5   6   7   8   9  10
2   4   6   8  10  12  14  16  18  20
3   6   9  12  15  18  21  24  27  30
4   8  12  16  20  24  28  32  36  40
5  10  15  20  25  30  35  40  45  50
```

The multiplication table has five lines. Therefore, as in Example 5-21, we use a **for** statement to output these lines as follows:

```
for (i = 1; i <= 5; i++)
    //output a line of numbers
```

In the first line, we want to print the multiplication table of 1, in the second line we want to print the multiplication table of 2, and so on. Notice that the first line starts with 1 and when this line is printed, i is 1. Similarly, the second line starts with 2 and when this line is printed, the value of i is 2, and so on. If i is 1, i * 1 is 1; if i is 2, i * 2 is 2; and so on. Therefore, to print a line of numbers, we can use the value of i as the starting number and 10 as the limiting value. That is, consider the following **for** loop:

```
for (j = 1; j <= 10; j++)
    cout << setw(3) << i * j;
```

Let us take a look at this **for** loop. Suppose i is 1. Then we are printing the first line of the multiplication table. Also, j goes from 1 to 10 and so this **for** loop outputs the numbers 1 through 10, which is the first line of the multiplication table. Similarly, if i is 2, we are printing the second line of the multiplication table. Also, j goes from 1 to 10, and so this **for** loop outputs the second line of the multiplication table, and so on.

A little more thought produces the following nested loops to output the desired grid:

```
for (i = 1; i <= 5; i++)                        //Line 1
{                                               //Line 2
    for (j = 1; j <= 10; j++)                   //Line 3
        cout << setw(3) << i * j;               //Line 4
    cout << endl;                               //Line 5
}                                               //Line 6
```

EXAMPLE 5-23

Consider the following data:

```
65 78 65 89 25 98 -999
87 34 89 99 26 78 64 34 -999
23 99 98 97 26 78 100 63 87 23 -999
62 35 78 99 12 93 19 -999
```

The number -999 at the end of each line acts as a sentinel and therefore is not part of the data. Our objective is to find the sum of the numbers in each line and output the sum. Moreover, assume that this data is to be read from a file, say, Exp_5_23.txt. We assume that the input file has been opened using the input file stream variable infile.

This particular data set has four lines of input. So we can use a **for** loop or a counter-controlled **while** loop to process each line of data. Let us use a **while** loop to process these four lines. It follows that the **while** loop takes the following form:

```
counter = 0;                      //Line 1
while (counter < 4)               //Line 2
{                                 //Line 3
        //process the line        //Line 4

        //output the sum
        counter++;
}
```

Let us now concentrate on processing a line. Each line has a varying number of data items. For example, the first line has six numbers, the second line has eight numbers, and so on. Because each line ends with -999, we can use a sentinel-controlled **while** loop to find the sum of the numbers in each line. (Remember how a sentinel-controlled loop works.) Consider the following **while** loop:

```
sum = 0;                    //Line 4
infile >> num;              //Line 5
while (num != -999)         //Line 6
{                           //Line 7
    sum = sum + num;        //Line 8
    infile >> num;          //Line 9
}                           //Line 10
```

The statement in Line 4 initializes sum to 0, and the statement in Line 5 reads and stores the first number of the line into num. The Boolean expression num != -999 in Line 6 checks whether the number is -999. If num is not -999, the statements in Lines 8 and 9 execute. The statement in Line 8 updates the value of sum; the statement in Line 9 reads and stores the next number into num. The loop continues to execute as long as num is not -999.

It now follows that the nested loop to process the data is as follows. (Assume that all variables are properly declared.)

```
counter = 0;                                    //Line 1
while (counter < 4)                             //Line 2
{                                               //Line 3
    sum = 0;                                    //Line 4
    infile >> num;                              //Line 5
    while (num != -999)                         //Line 6
    {                                           //Line 7
        sum = sum + num;                        //Line 8
        infile >> num;                          //Line 9
    }                                           //Line 10

    cout << "Line " << counter + 1
         << ": Sum = " << sum << endl;          //Line 11
    counter++;                                  //Line 12
}                                               //Line 13
```

EXAMPLE 5-24

Suppose that we want to process data similar to the data in Example 5-23, but the input file is of an unspecified length. That is, each line contains the same data as the data in each line in Example 5-23, but we do not know the number of input lines.

Because we do not know the number of input lines, we must use an EOF-controlled while loop to process the data. In this case, the required code is as follows. (Assume that all variables are properly declared and the input file has been opened using the input file stream variable infile.)

```
counter = 0;                                    //Line 1
infile >> num;                                  //Line 2
while (infile)                                  //Line 3
{                                               //Line 4
    sum = 0;                                    //Line 5
    while (num != -999)                         //Line 6
    {                                           //Line 7
        sum = sum + num;                        //Line 8
        infile >> num;                          //Line 9
    }                                           //Line 10

    cout << "Line " << counter + 1
         << ": Sum = " << sum << endl;          //Line 11
    counter++;                                  //Line 12
    infile >> num;                              //Line 13
}                                               //Line 14
```

Notice that we have again used the variable counter. The only reason to do so is because we want to print the line number with the sum of each line.

EXAMPLE 5-25

Consider the following data:

```
101
John Smith
65 78 65 89 25 98 -999
102
Peter Gupta
87 34 89 99 26 78 64 34 -999
103
Buddy Friend
23 99 98 97 26 78 100 63 87 23 -999
104
Doctor Miller
62 35 78 99 12 93 19 -999
...
```

The number -999 at the end of a line acts as a sentinel and therefore is not part of the data.

Assume that this is the data of certain candidates seeking the student council's presidential seat.

For each candidate, the data is in the following form:

```
ID
Name
Votes
```

The objective is to find the total number of votes received by the candidate. We assume that the data is input from the file **Exp_5_25.txt** of unknown size. We also assume that the input file has been opened using the input file stream variable `infile`.

Because the input file is of an unspecified length, we use an EOF-controlled `while` loop. For each candidate, the first data item is the ID of type `int` on a line by itself; the second data item is the name, which may consist of more than one word; and the third line contains the votes received from the various departments.

To read the ID, we use the extraction operator >>; to read the name, we use the stream function `getline`. Notice that after reading the ID, the reading marker is after the ID and the character after the ID is the newline character. Therefore, after reading the ID, the reading marker is after the ID and before the newline character (of the line containing the ID).

The function `getline` reads until the end of the line. Therefore, if we read the name immediately after reading the ID, then what is stored in the variable name is the newline character (after the ID). It follows that to read the name, we must read and discard the newline character after the ID, which we can accomplish using the stream function `get`. Therefore, the statements to read the ID and name are as follows:

```
infile >> ID;           //read the ID
infile.get(ch);         //read the newline character after the ID
getline(infile, name);  //read the name
```

(Assume that ch is a variable of type char.) The general loop to process the data is:

```
infile >> ID;                           //Line 1
while (infile)                          //Line 2
{                                       //Line 3
    infile.get(ch);                     //Line 4
    getline(infile, name);              //Line 5

    //process the numbers in each line   //Line 6
    //output the name and total votes
    infile >> ID;      //begin processing the next line
}
```

The code to read and sum up the voting data is:

```
sum = 0;                                //Line 6
infile >> num;                          //Line 7; read the first number
while (num != -999)                     //Line 8
{                                       //Line 9
    sum = sum + num;                    //Line 10; update sum
    infile >> num;                      //Line 11; read the next number
}                                       //Line 12
```

We can now write the following nested loop to process data as follows:

```
infile >> ID;                           //Line 1
while (infile)                          //Line 2
{                                       //Line 3
    infile.get(ch);                     //Line 4
    getline(infile, name);              //Line 5
    sum = 0;                            //Line 6
    infile >> num;                      //Line 7; read the first number
    while (num != -999)                 //Line 8
    {                                   //Line 9
        sum = sum + num;                //Line 10; update sum
        infile >> num;                  //Line 11; read the next number
    }

    cout << "Name: " << name
         << ", Votes: " << sum
         << endl;                       //Line 12

    infile >> ID;      //Line 13; begin processing the next line
}
```

Avoiding Bugs by Avoiding Patches

Debugging sections in the previous chapters illustrated how to debug syntax and logical errors, and how to avoid partially understood concepts. In this section, we illustrate how to avoid a software patch to fix a code. A software patch is a piece of code written on top of an existing piece of code intended to fix a bug in the original code.

Suppose that the following data is in the file Ch5_LoopWithBugsData.txt.

```
87 78 83 94
23 89 92 70
92 78 34 56
```

The objective is to find the sum of the numbers in each line. For each line, output the numbers together with their sum. Let us consider the following program:

```cpp
#include <iostream>
#include <fstream>

using namespace std;

int main()
{
    ifstream infile;

    int i;
    int j;
    int sum;
    int num;

    infile.open("Ch5_LoopWithBugsData.txt");

    for (i = 1; i <= 4; i++)
    {
        sum = 0;

        for (j = 1; j <= 4; j++)
        {
            infile >> num;
            cout << num << " ";
            sum = sum + num;
        }

        cout << "sum = " << sum << endl;
    }

    return 0;
}
```

Sample Run:

```
87 78 83 94 sum = 342
23 89 92 70 sum = 274
92 78 34 56 sum = 260
56 56 56 56 sum = 224
```

The sample run shows that there is a bug in the program because the file contains three lines of input and the output contains four lines. Also, the number 56 in the last line repeats four times. Clearly, there is a bug in the program and we must fix the code. Some programmers, especially some beginners, address the symptom of the problem by adding a software patch. In this case, the output should contain only three lines of output.

A beginning programmer might fix the code by adding a software patch as shown in the following modified program:

```cpp
#include <iostream>
#include <fstream>

using namespace std;

int main()
{
    ifstream infile;

    int i;
    int j;
    int sum;
    int num;

    infile.open("Ch5_LoopWithBugsData.txt");

    for (i = 1; i <= 4; i++)
    {
        sum = 0;

        if (i != 4)
        {
            for (j = 1; j <= 4; j++)
            {
                infile >> num;
                cout << num << " ";
                sum = sum + num;
            }

            cout << "sum = " << sum << endl;
        }
    }

    return 0;
}
```

Sample Run:

```
87 78 83 94 sum = 342
23 89 92 70 sum = 274
92 78 34 56 sum = 260
```

Clearly, the program is working correctly now.

As we can see, the programmer merely observed the symptom and addressed the problem by adding a software patch. However, if you look at the code, not only does the program execute extra statements, it is also an example of a partially understood concept. It appears that the programmer does not have a good grasp of why the earlier program produced four lines rather than three. Adding a patch eliminated the symptom, but it is a poor programming practice. The programmer must resolve why the program produced four lines. Looking at the program closely, we can see that the four lines are produced because the outer loop executes four times. The values assigned to loop control variable i are 1, 2, 3, and 4. This is an example of the classic "off-by-one" problem. (In an "off-by-one problem," either the loop executes one too many or one too few times.) We can eliminate this problem by correctly setting the values of the loop control variable. For example, we can rewrite the loops as follows:

```
for (i = 1; i <= 3; i++)
{
    sum = 0;

    for (j = 1; j <= 4; j++)
    {
        infile >> num;
        cout << num << " ";
        sum = sum + num;
    }

    cout << "sum = " << sum << endl;
}
```

This code fixes the original problem without using a software patch. It also represents good programming practice. The complete modified program is available at the Web site accompanying this book and is named `Ch5_LoopWithBugsCorrectedProgram.cpp`.

Debugging Loops

As we have seen in the earlier debugging sections, no matter how careful a program is designed and coded, errors are likely to occur. If there are syntax errors, the compiler will identify them. However, if there are logical errors, we must carefully look at the code or even maybe at the design and try to find the errors. To increase the reliability of the program, errors must be discovered and fixed before the program is released to the users.

Once an algorithm is written, the next step is to verify that it works properly. If the algorithm is a simple sequential flow or contains a branch, it can be hand traced or you can use the debugger, if any, provided by the IDE. Typically, loops are harder to debug. The correctness of a loop can be verified by using loop invariants. A loop invariant is a set of statements that remains true each time the loop body is executed. Let p be a loop invariant and q be the (logical) expression in a loop statement. Then p && q remains true before each iteration of the loop and p && not(q) is true after the loop terminates. The full discussion of loop invariants is beyond the scope of the book. However, you can learn about loop invariants in the book: *Discrete Mathematics: Theory and Applications* (Revised Edition), D.S. Malik and M.K. Sen, Cengage Learning Asia, Singapore, 2010. Here, we give a few tips that you can use to debug a loop.

As discussed in the previous section, the most common error associated with loops is off-by-one. If a loop turns out to be an infinite loop, the error is most likely in the logical expression that controls the execution of the loop. Check the logical expression carefully and see if you have reversed an inequality, an assignment statement symbol appears in place of the equality operator, or && appears in place of ||. If the loop changes the values of variables, you can print the values of the variables before and/or after each iteration or you can use your IDE's debugger, if any, and watch the values of variables during each iteration.

The debugging sections in this book are designed to help you understand the debugging process. However, as you will realize, debugging can be a tiresome process. If your program is very bad, do not debug. Throw it away and start over.

QUICK REVIEW

1. C++ has three looping (repetition) structures: `while`, `for`, and `do...while`.

2. The syntax of the `while` statement is:

   ```
   while (expression)
       statement
   ```

3. In C++, `while` is a reserved word.

4. In the `while` statement, the parentheses around the `expression` (the decision maker) are important; they mark the beginning and end of the expression.

5. The `statement` is called the body of the loop.

6. The body of the `while` loop must contain a statement that eventually sets the expression to `false`.

7. A counter-controlled `while` loop uses a counter to control the loop.

8. In a counter-controlled `while` loop, you must initialize the counter before the loop, and the body of the loop must contain a statement that changes the value of the counter variable.

9. A sentinel is a special value that marks the end of the input data. The sentinel must be similar to, yet differ from, all the data items.

10. A sentinel-controlled `while` loop uses a sentinel to control the `while` loop. The `while` loop continues to execute until the sentinel is read.

11. An EOF-controlled `while` loop continues to execute until the program detects the end-of-file marker.

12. In the Windows console environment, the end-of-file marker is entered using `Ctrl+z` (hold the `Ctrl` key and press z). In the UNIX environment, the end-of-file marker is entered using `Ctrl+d` (hold the `Ctrl` key and press d).

13. A `for` loop simplifies the writing of a counter-controlled `while` loop.

14. In C++, `for` is a reserved word.

15. The syntax of the `for` loop is:

    ```
    for (initialize statement; loop condition; update statement)
        statement
    ```

    `statement` is called the body of the `for` loop.

16. Putting a semicolon at the end of the `for` loop (before the body of the `for` loop) is a semantic error. In this case, the action of the `for` loop is empty.

17. The syntax of the `do...while` statement is:

```
do
     statement
while (expression);
```

`statement` is called the body of the `do...while` loop.

18. Both `while` and `for` loops are called pretest loops. A `do...while` loop is called a posttest loop.

19. The `while` and `for` loops may not execute at all, but the `do...while` loop always executes at least once.

20. Executing a `break` statement in the body of a loop immediately terminates the loop.

21. Executing a `continue` statement in the body of a loop skips the loop's remaining statements and proceeds with the next iteration.

22. When a `continue` statement executes in a `while` or `do...while` loop, the expression update statement in the body of the loop may not execute.

23. After a `continue` statement executes in a `for` loop, the update statement is the next statement executed.

EXERCISES

1. Mark the following statements as true or false.

a. In a counter-controlled `while` loop, it is not necessary to initialize the loop control variable.

b. It is possible that the body of a `while` loop may not execute at all.

c. In an infinite `while` loop, the `while` expression (the decision maker) is initially false, but after the first iteration it is always true.

d. The `while` loop:

```
j = 0;
while (j <= 10)
     j++;
```

terminates if j > 10.

e. A sentinel-controlled `while` loop is an event-controlled `while` loop whose termination depends on a special value.

f. A loop is a control structure that causes certain statements to execute over and over.

g. To read data from a file of an unspecified length, an EOF-controlled loop is a good choice.

h. When a `while` loop terminates, the control first goes back to the statement just before the `while` statement, and then the control goes to the statement immediately following the `while` loop.

2. What is the output of the following C++ code?

```cpp
int i = 0;
int temp = 1;
while (i < 5)
{
    i = i + 1;
    temp = temp * i;
}
cout << "i = " << i << " and temp = " << temp << endl;
```

3. What is the output of the following C++ code?

```cpp
int count = 10;
double sum = 0;

while (count > 8)
{
    sum = sum + pow(count, 2.0);
    count--;
}
cout << sum << endl;
```

4. What is the output of the following C++ code?

```cpp
int num = 1;
while (num * num < 30)
{
    cout << num << " ";
    num = num + 1;
}
cout << endl;
```

5. When does the following `while` loop terminate?

```cpp
ch = 'D';
while ('A' <= ch && ch <= 'Z')
    ch = static_cast<char>(static_cast<int>(ch) + 1);
```

6. Suppose that the input is 10 30 16 25 76 -1. What is the output of the following code?

```cpp
int num = 0;
int sum;
int count = 0;

cin >> sum;

while (count < 3)
{
    cin >> num;
    sum = sum + num;
    count++;
}
cout << "Sum = " << sum << endl;
```

7. Suppose that the input is 25 36 18 16 −1. What is the output of the following code?

```
int num;
int sum;
cin >> sum;
num = sum;

while (num != -1)
{
    cin >> num;
    sum = sum + num;
}
cout << "Sum = " << sum << endl;
```

8. Suppose that the input is 25 36 18 16 −1. What is the output of the following code?

```
int num;
int sum;

cin >> num;
sum = num;

while (num != -1)
{
    sum = sum + num;
    cin >> num;
}
cout << "Sum = " << sum << endl;
```

9. Suppose that the input is 10 −6 12 −5 −4 0. What is the output of the following code?

```
int num;
int sum = 0;

cin >> num;

while (num != 0)
{
    if (num > 0)
        sum = sum + num;
    else
        sum = sum - num;
    cin >> num;
}
cout << "Sum = " << sum << endl;
```

10. Correct the following code so that it reads and finds the sum of 20 numbers:

```
int count = 0;
int sum = 0;

cin >> num;
while (count <= 20);
```

```
{
    cin >> num;
    count++;
    sum = sum + count;
}
```

11. Consider the following program:

```
#include <iostream>

using namespace std;

int main()
{
    int num1, num2;
    int  temp = 0;

    cout << "Enter two integers: ";
    cin >> num1 >> num2 ;
    cout << endl ;

    while (((num1 + num2) % 5) != 0)
    {
        temp = num1 + num2;
        num1 = num2;
        num2 = temp;
        cout << temp << " ";
    }
    cout << endl;

    return 0;
}
```

a. What is the output if the input is 13 16?

b. What is the output if the input is −4 6?

c. What is the output if the input is 3 5?

d. What is the output if the input is 1 3?

12. Suppose that the input is:

58   23   46   75   98   150   12   176   145 −999

What is the output of the following program?

```
#include <iostream>

using namespace std;

int main()
{
    int num;

    cin >> num;
```

```
    while (num != -999)
    {
        cout << num % 25 << "   ";
        cin >> num;
    }

    cout << endl;

    return 0;
}
```

13. The following program is designed to input two numbers and output their sum. It asks the user if he/she would like to run the program. If the answer is Y or y, it prompts the user to enter two numbers. After adding the numbers and displaying the results, it again asks the user if he/she would like to add more numbers. However, the program fails to do so. Correct the program so that it works properly.

```
#include <iostream>
#include <iomanip>

using namespace std;

int main()
{
    char response;
    double num1;
    double num2;

    cout << "This program adds two numbers." << endl;
    cout << "Would you like to run the program: (Y/y) ";
    cin >> response;
    cout << endl;

    cout << fixed << showpoint << setprecision(2);

    while (response == 'Y' && response == 'y')
    {
        cout << "Enter two numbers: ";
        cin >> num1 >> num2;
        cout << endl;

        cout << num1 << " + " << num2 << " = " << (num1 - num2)
            << endl;

        cout << "Would you like to add again: (Y/y) ";
        cin >> response;
        cout << endl;
    }

    return 0;
}
```

14. What is the output of the following program segment?

```
int count = 0;

while (count++ < 10)
    cout << "This loop can repeat statements." << endl;
```

15. What is the output of the following program segment?

```
int count = 5;

while (--count > 0)
    cout << count << " ";
cout << endl;
```

16. What is the output of the following program segment?

```
int count = 5;

while (count-- > 0)
    cout << count << " ";
cout << endl;
```

17. What is the output of the following program segment?

```
int count = 1;
while (count++ <= 5)
    cout << count * (count - 2) << " ";

cout << endl;
```

18. What type of loop, such as counter-control and sentinel-control, will you use in each of the following situations?

   a. Sum the following series: 1 + (2 / 1) + (3 / 2) + (4 / 3) + (5 / 4) + ... + (10 / 9)

   b. Sum the following numbers, except the last number: 17, 32, 62, 48, 58, −1

   c. A file contains an employee's salary. Update the employee's salary.

19. Consider the following for loop:

```
int j, s;

s = 0;
for (j = 1; j <= 10; j++)
    s = s + j * (j - 1);
```

   In this for loop, identify the loop control variable, the initialization statement, the loop condition, the update statement, and the statement that updates the value of s.

20. What is the output of the following program segment?

```
int num = 1;
int i;

for (i = 0; i < 5; i++)
```

```
{
    num = num * (5 - i);
    cout << num << " ";
}
cout << endl;
```

21. What is the output of the following program segment?

```
int num = 0;
int count;
int y = 0;

for (count = 1; count <= 5; ++count)
{
    num = 3 * (count - 1) + (y - count);
    cout << num << " ";
}
cout << count << " " << endl;
```

22. Assume that the following code is correctly inserted into a program:

```
int s = 0;
int i;

for (i = 0; i < 5; i++)
{
    s = 2 * s + i;
    cout << s << " ";
}
cout << endl;
```

    a. What is the final value of s?
       (i) 11   (ii) 4   (iii) 26   (iv) none of these

    b. If a semicolon is inserted after the right parenthesis in the **for** loop statement, what is the final value of s?
       (i) 0   (ii) 1   (iii) 2   (iv) 5   (v) none of these

    c. If the 5 is replaced with a 0 in the **for** loop control expression, what is the final value of s?
       (i) 0   (ii) 1   (iii) 2   (iv) none of these

23. State what output, if any, results from each of the following statements:

    a.
```
for (i = 1; i <= 1; i++)
    cout << "*";
cout << endl;
```

    b.
```
for (i = 2; i >= 1; i++)
    cout << "*";
cout << endl;
```

    c.
```
for (i = 1; i <= 1; i--)
    cout << "*";
cout << endl;
```

    d.
```
for (i = 12; i >= 9; i--)
    cout << "*";
cout << endl;
```

5

e.
```
for (i = 0; i <= 5; i++)
      cout << "*";
cout << endl;
```

f.
```
for (i = 1; i <= 5; i++)
{
      cout << "*";
      i = i + 1;
}
cout << endl;
```

24. Write a **for** statement to add all the multiples of 3 between 1 and 100.

25. What is the output of the following code? Is there a relationship between the variables **x** and **y**? If yes, state the relationship? What is the output?

```
int x = 19683;
int i;
int y = 0;

for (i = x; i >= 1; i = i / 3)
     y++;
cout << "x = " << x << ", y = " << y << endl;
```

26. Suppose that the input is 5 3 8. What is the output of the following code? Assume all variables are properly declared.

```
cin >> a >> b >> c;
for (j = 1; j < a; j++)
{
     d = b + c;
     b = c;
     c = d;
     cout << c << " ";
}
cout << endl;
```

27. What is the output of the following C++ program segment? Assume all variables are properly declared.

```
for (j = 0; j < 8; j++)
{
     cout << j * 25 << " - ";

     if (j != 7)
         cout << (j + 1) * 25 - 1 << endl;
     else
         cout << (j + 1) * 25 << endl;
}
```

28. Suppose that the input is 3 5 7 -6 10. What is the output of the following code?

```
int temp = 0;
int num;
int count;
```

```
cin >> temp;

for (count = 0; count <= 3; count++)
{
    cout << temp << " ";
    cin >> num;
    temp = temp + num * (count - 1);
}
cout << endl;
```

29. Which of the following apply to the **while** loop only? To the **do...while** loop only? To both?

    a. It is considered a conditional loop.

    b. The body of the loop executes at least once.

    c. The logical expression controlling the loop is evaluated before the loop is entered.

    d. The body of the loop may not execute at all.

30. The following program contains errors that prevent it from compiling and/ or running. Correct all such errors.

```
#include <iostream>

using namespace sdt;

const int SECRET = 111.25;

int main ()
{
    int num1, num2:
    double x, y;

    cout >> "Enter two integers: ""
    cin << num1 << num2;
    cout >> endl;

    for (count = 1 count > Secret; ++count)
    {
        x = (num1 + num2) / 2.0;
        y = (num1 - num2) % 2.0;
        num1 := num1 + num2;
        num2 := num2 * (count - SECRET - 1)
    }
    cout << num1 << " " << num2 << " << x % 5
         << " " << (y % 7) << end;

    return;
}
```

31. What is the difference between a pretest loop and a posttest loop?

32. How many times will each of the following loops execute? What is the output in each case?

a.
```
x = 5;   y = 50;
do
      x = x + 10;
while (x < y);
cout << x << " " << y << endl;
```

b.
```
x = 5;   y = 80;
do
      x = x * 2;
while (x < y);
cout << x << " " << y << endl;
```

c.
```
x = 5;   y = 20;
do
      x = x + 2;
while (x >= y);
cout << x << " " << y << endl;
```

d.
```
x = 5;   y = 35;
while (x < y)
      x = x + 10;
cout << x << " " << y << endl;
```

e.
```
x = 5;   y = 30;
while (x <= y)
      x = x * 2;
cout << x << " " << y << endl;
```

f.
```
x = 5;   y = 30;
while (x > y)
      x = x + 2;
cout << x << " " << y << endl;
```

33. Write an input statement validation loop that prompts the user to enter a number less than 20 or greater than 75.

34. Rewrite the following as a **for** loop:

```
int i = 0, value = 0;

while (i <= 20)
{
    if (i % 2 == 0 && i <= 10)
        value = value + i * i;
    else if (i % 2 == 0 && i > 10)
        value = value + i;
    else
        value = value - i;
    i = i + 1;
}

cout << "value = " << value << endl;
```

What is the output of this loop?

35. Write the **while** loop of Exercise 34 as a **do...while** loop.

36. The **do...while** loop in the following program is supposed to read some numbers until it reaches a sentinel (in this case, −1). It is supposed to add all of the numbers except for the sentinel. If the data looks like:

```
12    5    30    48    -1
```

the program does not add the numbers correctly. Correct the program so that it adds the numbers correctly.

```cpp
#include <iostream>

using namespace std;
int main()
{
    int total = 0,
        count = 0,
        number;
    do
    {
        cin >> number;
        total = total + number;
        count++;
    }
    while (number != -1);

    cout << "The number of data read is " << count << endl;
    cout << "The sum of the numbers entered is  " << total
         << endl;

    return 0;
}
```

37. Using the same data as in Exercise 36, the following loop also fails. Correct it.

```cpp
cin >> number;
while (number != -1)
    total =  total + number;
    cin >> number;
    cout << endl;
    cout << total << endl;
```

38. Using the same data as in Exercise 36, the following loop also fails. Correct it.

```cpp
cin >> number;
while (number != -1)
{
    cin >> number;
    total = total + number;
}
cout << endl;
cout << total << endl;
```

39. Given the following program segment:

```cpp
for (number = 1; number <= 10; number++)
    cout << setw(3) << number;
```

write a `while` loop and a `do...while` loop that have the same output.

40. Given the following program segment:

```
int limit = 4;
int first = 5;
int j;

for (j = 1; j <= limit; j++)
{
    cout << first * j << endl;
    first = first + (j - 1);
}
cout << endl;
```

write a while loop and a do...while loop that have the same output.

41. Consider the following program:

```
#include <iostream>

using namespace std;

int main()
{
    int num1, num2;
    int temp = 0;

    cout << "Enter two integers: ";
    cin >> num1 >> num2;
    cout << endl ;

    do
    {
        temp = num1 + num2 ;
        num1 = num2 ;
        num2 = temp ;
        cout << temp << " ";
    }
    while (((num1 + num2) % 5) != 0);

    cout << endl;

    return 0;
}
```

a. What is the output if the input is 13 16?

b. What is the output if the input is −4 6?

c. What is the output if the input is 3 5?

d. What is the output if the input is 13 15?

42. To learn how nested for loops work, do a walk-through of the following program segments and determine, in each case, the exact output.

a.
```
int i, j;

for (i = 1; i <= 5; i++)
{
    for (j = 1; j <= 5; j++)
        cout << setw(3) << i;
    cout << endl;
}
```

b.
```
int i, j;
for (i = 1; i <= 5; i++)
{
    for (j = (i + 1); j <= 5; j++)
        cout << setw(5) << j;
    cout << endl;
}
```

c.
```
int i, j;
for (i = 1; i <= 5; i++)
{
    for (j = 1; j <= i; j++)
        cout << setw(3) << j;
    cout << endl;
}
```

d.
```
const int M = 10;
const int N = 10;
int i, j;

for (i = 1; i <= M; i++)
{
    for (j = 1; j <= N; j++)
        cout << setw(3) << M * (i - 1) + j;
    cout << endl;
}
```

e.
```
int i, j;

for (i = 1; i <= 9; i++)
{
    for (j = 1; j <= (9 - i); j++)
        cout << " ";
    for (j = 1; j <= i; j++)
        cout << setw(1) << j;
    for (j = (i - 1); j >= 1; j--)
        cout << setw(1) << j;
    cout << endl;
}
```

43. What is the output of the following program segment?
```
int count = 1;
do
    cout << count * (count - 2) << " ";
while (count++ <= 5);

cout << endl;
```

44. What is the output of the following code?

```cpp
int num = 12;

while (num >= 0)
{
    if (num % 5 == 0)
        break;

    cout << num << " ";
    num = num - 2;
}

cout << endl;
```

45. What is the output of the following code?

```cpp
int num = 12;

while (num >= 0)
{
    if (num % 5 == 0)
    {
        num++;
        continue;
    }

    cout << num << " ";
    num = num - 2;
}
cout << endl;
```

46. What does a **break** statement do in a loop?

PROGRAMMING EXERCISES

1. Write a program that prompts the user to input an integer and then outputs both the individual digits of the number and the sum of the digits. For example, it should output the individual digits of 3456 as 3 4 5 6, output the individual digits of 8030 as 8 0 3 0, output the individual digits of 2345526 as 2 3 4 5 5 2 6, output the individual digits of 4000 as 4 0 0 0, and output the individual digits of −2345 as 2 3 4 5.

2. The value of π can be approximated by using the following series:

$$\pi = 4\left(1 - \frac{1}{3} + \frac{1}{5} - \frac{1}{7} + \cdots + \frac{1}{2n-1} + \frac{1}{2n+1}\right).$$

The following program uses this series to find the approximate value of π. However, the statements are in the incorrect order, and there is also a bug in this program. Rearrange the statements and also find and remove the bug so that this program can be used to approximate π.

```cpp
#include <iostream>
#include <iomanip>

using namespace std;

int main()
{
    double pi = 0;
    long i;
    long n;

    cin >> n;
    cout << "Enter the value of n: ";
    cout << endl;

    if (i % 2 == 0)
        pi = pi + (1 / (2 * i + 1));
    else
        pi = pi - (1 / (2 * i + 1));

    for (i = 0; i < n; i++)
    {
        pi = 0;
        pi = 4 * pi;
    }

    cout << endl << "pi = " << pi << endl;

    return 0;
}
```

5

3. Rewrite the program of Example 5-5, Telephone Digits. Replace the statements from Lines 10 to 28 so that the program uses only a **switch** structure to find the digit that corresponds to an uppercase letter.

4. The program Telephone Digits outputs only telephone digits that correspond to uppercase letters. Rewrite the program so that it processes both uppercase and lowercase letters and outputs the corresponding telephone digit. If the input is something other than an uppercase or lowercase letter, the program must output an appropriate error message.

5. To make telephone numbers easier to remember, some companies use letters to show their telephone number. For example, using letters, the telephone number 438–5626 can be shown as GET LOAN. In some cases, to make a telephone number meaningful, companies might use more than seven letters. For example, 225-5466 can be displayed as CALL HOME, which uses eight letters. Write a program that prompts the user to enter a telephone number expressed in letters and outputs the corresponding telephone number in digits. If the user enters more than seven letters, then process only the first seven letters. Also output the − (hyphen) after the third digit. Allow the user to use both uppercase and lowercase letters as well as spaces between words. Moreover, your program should process as many telephone numbers as the user wants.

6. Write a program that reads a set of integers and then finds and prints the sum of the even and odd integers.

7. Write a program that prompts the user to input a positive integer. It should then output a message indicating whether the number is a prime number. (*Note:* An even number is prime if it is 2. An odd integer is prime if it is not divisible by any odd integer less than or equal to the square root of the number.)

8. Let $n = a_k a_{k-1} a_{k-2} \ldots a_1 a_0$ be an integer and $t = a_0 - a_1 + a_2 - \cdots + (-1)^k a_k$. It is known that n is divisible by 11 if and only if t is divisible by 11. For example, suppose that $n = 8784204$. Then, $t = 4 - 0 + 2 - 4 + 8 - 7 + 8 = 11$. Because 11 is divisible by 11, it follows that 8784204 is divisible by 11. If $n = 54063297$, then $t = 7 - 9 + 2 - 3 + 6 - 0 + 4 - 5 = 2$. Because 2 is not divisible by 11, 54063297 is not divisible by 11. Write a program that prompts the user to enter a positive integer and then uses this criterion to determine whether the number is divisible by 11.

9. Write a program that uses `while` loops to perform the following steps:

   a. Prompt the user to input two integers: `firstNum` and `secondNum` (`firstNum` must be less than `secondNum`).

   b. Output all odd numbers between `firstNum` and `secondNum`.

   c. Output the sum of all even numbers between `firstNum` and `secondNum`.

   d. Output the numbers and their squares between `1` and `10`.

   e. Output the sum of the square of the odd numbers between `firstNum` and `secondNum`.

   f. Output all uppercase letters.

10. Redo Programming Exercise 9 using `for` loops.

11. Redo Programming Exercise 9 using `do...while` loops.

12. The program in the Programming Example: Fibonacci Number does not check whether the first number entered by the user is less than or equal to the second number and whether both the numbers are nonnegative. Also, the program does not check whether the user entered a valid value for the position of the desired number in the Fibonacci sequence. Rewrite that program so that it checks for these things.

13. The population of a town A is less than the population of town B. However, the population of town A is growing faster than the population of town B. Write a program that prompts the user to enter the population and growth rate of each town. The program outputs after how many years the population of town A will be greater than or equal to the population of town B and the populations of both the towns at that time. (A sample input is: Population of town $A = 5000$, growth rate of town $A = 4\%$, population of town $B = 8000$, and growth rate of town $B = 2\%$.)

14. Suppose that the first number of a sequence is x, in which x is an integer. Define $a_0 = x$; $a_{n+1} = a_n/2$ if a_n is even; $a_{n+1} = 3 \times a_n + 1$ if a_n is odd. Then, there exists an integer k such that $a_k = 1$. Write a program that prompts the user to input the value of x. The program output the integer k such that $a_k = 1$ and the numbers $a_0, a_1, a_2, \ldots, a_k$. (For example, if $x = 75$, then $k = 14$, and the numbers $a_0, a_1, a_2, \ldots, a_{14}$, respectively, are 75, 226, 113, 340, 170, 85, 256, 128, 64, 32, 16, 8, 4, 2, 1.) Test your program for the following values of x: 75, 111, 678, 732, 873, 2048, and 65535.

15. Enhance your program from Programming Exercise 14 by outputting the position of the largest number and the largest number of the sequence $a_0, a_1, a_2, \ldots, a_k$. (For example, the largest number of the sequence 75, 226, 113, 340, 170, 85, 256, 128, 64, 32, 16, 8, 4, 2, 1 is 340, and its position is 4.) Test your program for the following values of x: 75, 111, 678, 732, 873, 2048, and 65535.

16. The program in Example 5-6 implements the Number Guessing Game. However, in that program, the user is given as many tries as needed to guess the correct number. Rewrite the program so that the user has no more than five tries to guess the correct number. Your program should print an appropriate message, such as "You win!" or "You lose!".

17. Example 5-6 implements the Number Guessing Game program. If the guessed number is not correct, the program outputs a message indicating whether the guess is low or high. Modify the program as follows: Suppose that the variables num and guess are as declared in Example 5-6 and diff is an **int** variable. Let diff = the absolute value of (num − guess). If diff is 0, then guess is correct and the program outputs a message indicating that the user guessed the correct number. Suppose diff is not 0. Then the program outputs the message as follows:

   a. If diff is greater than or equal to 50, the program outputs the message indicating that the guess is very high (if guess is greater than num) or very low (if guess is less than num).

   b. If diff is greater than or equal to 30 and less than 50, the program outputs the message indicating that the guess is high (if guess is greater than num) or low (if guess is less than num).

   c. If diff is greater than or equal to 15 and less than 30, the program outputs the message indicating that the guess is moderately high (if guess is greater than num) or moderately low (if guess is less than num).

   d. If diff is greater than 0 and less than 15, the program outputs the message indicating that the guess is somewhat high (if guess is greater than num) or somewhat low (if guess is less than num).

   As in Programming Exercise 16, give the user no more than five tries to guess the number. (To find the absolute value of num − guess, use the expression abs(num − guess). The function abs is from the header file cstdlib.)

5

18. Write a program to implement the algorithm that you designed in Exercise 20 of Chapter 1. Your program should allow the user to buy as many items as the user desires.

19. The program in Example 5-4 uses a sentinel control loop to process cookies sales data. Assume that the data is provided in a file and the first line in the file specifies the cost of one box. Modify the program so that it uses an EOF-controlled loop to process the data.

20. Enhance the program that you wrote in Exercise 19 by modifying it as follows: When the students started selling cookies, they were told that the students who sell the maximum number of boxes will have 10% of the money they generate donated to their favorite charitable organization. So, in addition to the output your program generated in Exercise 19, your program should output the names of all the students selling the maximum number of boxes and the amount that will be donated to their charitable organization.

21. When you borrow money to buy a house, a car, or for some other purpose, you repay the loan by making periodic payments over a certain period of time. Of course, the lending company will charge interest on the loan. Every periodic payment consists of the interest on the loan and the payment toward the principal amount. To be specific, suppose that you borrow $1000 at the interest rate of 7.2% per year and the payments are monthly. Suppose that your monthly payment is $25. Now, the interest is 7.2% per year and the payments are monthly, so the interest rate per month is $7.2/12 = 0.6\%$. The first month's interest on $1000 is $1000 \times 0.006 = 6$. Because the payment is $25 and interest for the first month is $6, the payment toward the principal amount is $25 - 6 = 19$. This means after making the first payment, the loan amount is $1000 - 19 = 981$. For the second payment, the interest is calculated on $981. So the interest for the second month is $981 \times 0.006 = 5.886$, that is, approximately $5.89. This implies that the payment toward the principal is $25 - 5.89 = 19.11$ and the remaining balance after the second payment is $981 - 19.11 = 961.89$. This process is repeated until the loan is paid. Write a program that accepts as input the loan amount, the interest rate per year, and the monthly payment. (Enter the interest rate as a percentage. For example, if the interest rate is 7.2% per year, then enter 7.2.) The program then outputs the number of months it would take to repay the loan. (Note that if the monthly payment is less than the first month's interest, then after each payment, the loan amount will increase. In this case, the program must warn the borrower that the monthly payment is too low, and with this monthly payment, the loan amount could not be repaid.)

22. Enhance your program from Exercise 21 by first telling the user the minimum monthly payment and then prompting the user to enter the monthly payment. Your last payment might be more than the remaining loan amount and interest on it. In this case, output the loan amount before the last payment and the actual amount of the last payment. Also, output the total interest paid.

23. Write a complete program to test the code in Example 5-21.

24. Write a complete program to test the code in Example 5-22.

25. Write a complete program to test the code in Example 5-23.

26. Write a complete program to test the code in Example 5-24.

27. Write a complete program to test the code in Example 5-25.

28. (**The conical paper cup problem**) You have been given the contract for making little conical cups that come with bottled water. These cups are to be made from a circular waxed paper of 4 inches in radius by removing a sector of length x (see Figure 5-4). By closing the remaining part of the circle, a conical cup is made. Your objective is to remove the sector so that the cup is of maximum volume.

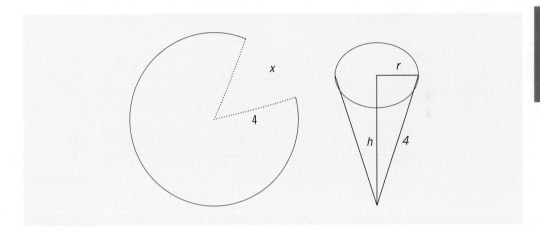

FIGURE 5-4 Conical paper cup

Write a program that prompts the user to enter the radius of the circular waxed paper. The program should then output the length of the removed sector so that the resulting cup is of maximum volume. Calculate your answer to two decimal places.

29. (**Apartment problem**) A real estate office handles, say, 50 apartment units. When the rent is, say, $600 per month, all the units are occupied. However, for each, say, $40 increase in rent, one unit becomes vacant. Moreover, each occupied unit requires an average of $27 per month for maintenance. How many units should be rented to maximize the profit?

Write a program that prompts the user to enter:

a. The rent to occupy all the units.

b. The increase in rent that results in a vacant unit.

c. Amount to maintain a rented unit.

The program then outputs the number of units to be rented to maximize the profit.

CHAPTER 6

USER-DEFINED FUNCTIONS

IN THIS CHAPTER, YOU WILL:

· Learn about standard (predefined) functions and discover how to use them in a program

· Learn about user-defined functions

· Examine value-returning functions, including actual and formal parameters

· Explore how to construct and use a value-returning, user-defined function in a program

· Learn how to construct and use void functions in a program

· Discover the difference between value and reference parameters

· Explore reference parameters and value-returning functions

· Learn about the scope of an identifier

· Examine the differences between local and global identifiers

· Discover static variables

· Learn how to debug programs using drivers and stubs

· Learn function overloading

· Explore functions with default parameters

In Chapter 2, you learned that a C++ program is a collection of functions. One such function is `main`. The programs in Chapters 1 through 5 use only the function `main`; the programming instructions are packed into one function. This technique, however, is good only for short programs. For large programs, it is not practical (although it is possible) to put the entire programming instructions into one function, as you will soon discover. You must learn to break the problem into manageable pieces. This chapter first discusses the functions previously defined and then discusses user-defined functions.

Let us imagine an automobile factory. When an automobile is manufactured, it is not made from basic raw materials; it is put together from previously manufactured parts. Some parts are made by the company itself; others, by different companies.

Functions are like building blocks. They let you divide complicated programs into manageable pieces. They have other advantages, too:

- While working on one function, you can focus on just that part of the program and construct it, debug it, and perfect it.
- Different people can work on different functions simultaneously.
- If a function is needed in more than one place in a program or in different programs, you can write it once and use it many times.
- Using functions greatly enhances the program's readability because it reduces the complexity of the function `main`.

Functions are often called **modules**. They are like miniature programs; you can put them together to form a larger program. When user-defined functions are discussed, you will see that this is the case. This ability is less apparent with predefined functions because their programming code is not available to us. However, because predefined functions are already written for us, you will learn these first so that you can use them when needed.

Predefined Functions

Before formally discussing predefined functions in C++, let us review a concept from a college algebra course. In algebra, a function can be considered a rule or correspondence between values, called the function's arguments, and the unique values of the function associated with the arguments. Thus, if $f(x) = 2x + 5$, then $f(1) = 7$, $f(2) = 9$, and $f(3) = 11$, where 1, 2, and 3 are the arguments of f, and 7, 9, and 11 are the corresponding values of the function f.

In C++, the concept of a function, either predefined or user-defined, is similar to that of a function in algebra. For example, every function has a name and, depending on the values specified by the user, it does some computation. This section discusses various predefined functions.

Some of the predefined mathematical functions are pow(x, y), sqrt(x), and floor(x).

The *power* function, pow(x, y), calculates x^y; that is, the value of pow(x, y) = x^y. For example, pow(2, 3) = 2^3 = 8.0 and pow(2.5, 3) = 2.5^3 = 15.625. Because the value of pow(x, y) is of type double, we say that the function pow is of type double or that the function pow returns a value of type double. Moreover, x and y are called the parameters (or arguments) of the function pow. Function pow has two parameters.

The *square root* function, sqrt(x), calculates the nonnegative square root of x for x >= 0.0. For example, sqrt(2.25) is 1.5. The function sqrt is of type double and has only one parameter.

The *floor* function, floor(x), calculates the largest whole number that is less than or equal to x. For example, floor(48.79) is 48.0. The function floor is of type double and has only one parameter.

In C++, predefined functions are organized into separate libraries. For example, the header file iostream contains I/O functions, and the header file cmath contains math functions. Table 6-1 lists some of the predefined functions, the name of the header file in which each function's specification can be found, the data type of the parameters, and the function type. The function type is the data type of the final value returned by the function. (For a list of additional predefined functions, see Appendix F.)

TABLE 6-1 Predefined Functions

Function	Header File	Purpose	Parameter(s) Type	Result
abs(x)	<cmath>	Returns the absolute value of its argument: abs(-7) = 7	int (double)	int (double)
ceil(x)	<cmath>	Returns the smallest whole number that is not less than x: ceil(56.34) = 57.0	double	double
cos(x)	<cmath>	Returns the cosine of angle: x: cos(0.0) = 1.0	double (radians)	double
exp(x)	<cmath>	Returns e^x, where e = 2.718: exp(1.0) = 2.71828	double	double
fabs(x)	<cmath>	Returns the absolute value of its argument: fabs(-5.67) = 5.67	double	double

TABLE 6-1 Predefined Functions (continued)

Function	Header File	Purpose	Parameter(s) Type	Result
floor(x)	<cmath>	Returns the largest whole number that is not greater than x:floor(45.67) = 45.00	double	double
islower(x)	<cctype>	Returns 1 (true) if x is a lowercase letter; otherwise, it returns 0 (false); islower('h') is 1 (true)	int	int
isupper(x)	<cctype>	Returns 1 (true) if x is an uppercase letter; otherwise, it returns 0 (false); isupper('K') is 1 (true)	int	int
pow(x, y)	<cmath>	Returns x^y; if x is negative, y must be a whole number: pow(0.16, 0.5) = 0.4	double	double
sqrt(x)	<cmath>	Returns the nonnegative square root of x; x must be nonnegative: sqrt(4.0) = 2.0	double	double
tolower(x)	<cctype>	Returns the lowercase value of x if x is uppercase; otherwise, it returns x	int	int
toupper(x)	<cctype>	Returns the uppercase value of x if x is lowercase; otherwise, it returns x	int	int

To use predefined functions in a program, you must include the header file that contains the function's specification via the include statement. For example, to use the function pow, the program must include:

```
#include <cmath>
```

Example 6-1 shows you how to use some of the predefined functions.

EXAMPLE 6-1

```cpp
// How to use predefined functions.
#include <iostream>                                      //Line 1
#include <cmath>                                         //Line 2
#include <cctype>                                        //Line 3
#include <iomanip>                                       //Line 4

using namespace std;                                     //Line 5

int main()                                               //Line 6
{                                                        //Line 7
    int num;                                             //Line 8
    double firstNum, secondNum;                          //Line 9
    char ch = 'T';                                       //Line 10

    cout << fixed << showpoint << setprecision (2)
         << endl;                                        //Line 11

    cout << "Line 12: Is " << ch
         << " a lowercase letter? "
         << islower(ch) << endl;                         //Line 12
    cout << "Line 13: Uppercase a is "
         << static_cast<char>(toupper('a')) << endl;     //Line 13

    cout << "Line 14: 4.5 to the power 6.0 = "
         << pow(4.5, 6.0) << endl;                       //Line 14

    cout << "Line 15: Enter two decimal numbers: ";      //Line 15
    cin >> firstNum >> secondNum;                        //Line 16
    cout << endl;                                        //Line 17

    cout << "Line 18: " << firstNum
         << " to the power of " << secondNum
         << " = " << pow(firstNum, secondNum) << endl;   //Line 18

    cout << "Line 19: 5.0 to the power of 4 = "
         << pow(5.0, 4) << endl;                         //Line 19

    firstNum = firstNum + pow(3.5, 7.2);                 //Line 20
    cout << "Line 21: firstNum = " << firstNum << endl;  //Line 21

    num = -32;                                           //Line 22
    cout << "Line 23: Absolute value of " << num
         << " = " << abs(num) << endl;                   //Line 23

    cout << "Line 24: Square root of 28.00 = "
         << sqrt(28.00) << endl;                         //Line 24

    return 0;                                            //Line 25
}                                                        //Line 26
```

6

Sample Run: In this sample run, the user input is shaded.

```
Line 12: Is T a lowercase letter? 0
Line 13: Uppercase a is A
Line 14: 4.5 to the power 6.0 = 8303.77
Line 15: Enter two decimal numbers: 24.7 3.8

Line 18: 24.70 to the power of 3.80 = 195996.55
Line 19: 5.0 to the power of 4 = 625.00
Line 21: firstNum = 8290.60
Line 23: Absolute value of -32 = 32
Line 24: Square root of 28.00 = 5.29
```

This program works as follows. The statements in Lines 1 to 4 include the header files that are necessary to use the functions used in the program. The statements in Lines 8 to 10 declare the variables used in the program. The statement in Line 11 sets the output of decimal numbers in fixed decimal format with two decimal places. The statement in Line 12 uses the function `islower` to determine and output whether ch is a lowercase letter. The statement in Line 13 uses the function `toupper` to output the uppercase letter that corresponds to `'a'`, which is A. Note that the function `toupper` returns an `int` value. Therefore, the value of the expression `toupper('a')` is 65, which is the ASCII value of `'A'`. To print A rather than 65, you need to apply the `cast` operator as shown in the statement in Line 13. The statement in Line 14 uses the function `pow` to output $4.5^{6.0}$. In C++ terminology, it is said that the function `pow` is called with the parameters `4.5` and `6.0`. The statements in Lines 15 to 17 prompt the user to enter two decimal numbers and store the numbers entered by the user in the variables `firstNum` and `secondNum`. In the statement in Line 18, the function `pow` is used to output $firstNum^{secondNum}$. In this case, the function `pow` is called with the parameters `firstNum` and `secondNum` and the values of `firstNum` and `secondNum` are passed to the function `pow`. The other statements have similar meanings. Once again, note that the program includes the header files `cctype` and `cmath`, because it uses the functions `islower`, `toupper`, `pow`, `abs`, and `sqrt` from these header files.

User-Defined Functions

As Example 6-1 illustrates, using functions in a program greatly enhances the program's readability because it reduces the complexity of the function `main`. Also, once you write and properly debug a function, you can use it in the program (or different programs) again and again without having to rewrite the same code repeatedly. For instance, in Example 6-1, the function `pow` is used more than once.

Because C++ does not provide every function that you will ever need and designers cannot possibly know a user's specific needs, you must learn to write your own functions.

User-defined functions in C++ are classified into two categories:

- **Value-returning functions**—functions that have a return type. These functions return a value of a specific data type using the `return` statement, which we will explain shortly.
- **Void functions**—functions that do not have a return type. These functions *do not* use a `return` statement to return a value.

We will first discuss value-returning functions. Many of the concepts discussed in regard to value-returning functions also apply to void functions.

Value-Returning Functions

The previous section introduced some predefined C++ functions such as `pow`, `abs`, `islower`, and `toupper`. These are examples of value-returning functions. To use these functions in your programs, you must know the name of the header file that contains the functions' specification. You need to include this header file in your program using the include statement and know the following items:

1. The name of the function
2. The number of **parameters**, if any
3. The data type of each parameter
4. The data type of the value computed (that is, the value returned) by the function, called the type of the function

Because the value returned by a value-returning function is unique, the natural thing for you to do is to use the value in one of three ways:

- Save the value for further calculation. For example, `x = pow(3.0, 2.5);`
- Use the value in some calculation. For example,
  `area = PI * pow(radius, 2.0);`
- Print the value. For example, `cout << abs(-5) << endl;`

This suggests that a value-returning function is used:

- In an assignment statement.
- As a parameter in a function call.
- In an output statement.

That is, a value-returning function is used (called) in an expression.

Before we look at the syntax of a user-defined, value-returning function, let us consider the things associated with such functions. In addition to the four properties described previously, one more thing is associated with functions (both value-returning and void):

5. The code required to accomplish the task

The first four properties form what is called the **heading** of the function (also called the **function header**); the fifth property is called the **body** of the function. Together, these five properties form what is called the **definition** of the function. For example, for the function abs, the heading might look like:

```
int abs(int number)
```

Similarly, the function abs might have the following definition:

```
int abs(int number)
{
    if (number < 0)
        number = -number;

    return number;
}
```

The variable declared in the heading of the function abs is called the **formal parameter** of the function abs. Thus, the formal parameter of abs is number.

The program in Example 6-1 contains several statements that use the function pow. That is, in C++ terminology, the function pow is called several times. Later in this chapter, we discuss what happens when a function is called.

Suppose that the heading of the function pow is:

```
double pow(double base, double exponent)
```

From the heading of the function pow, it follows that the formal parameters of pow are base and exponent. Consider the following statements:

```
double u = 2.5;
double v = 3.0;
double x, y;

x = pow(u, v);                                            //Line 1
y = pow(2.0, 3.2) + 5.1;                                  //Line 2
cout << u << " to the power of 7 = " <<  pow(u, 7) << endl;  //Line 3
```

In Line 1, the function pow is called with the parameters u and v. In this case, the values of u and v are passed to the function pow. In fact, the value of u is copied into base, and the value of v is copied into exponent. The variables u and v that appear in the call to the function pow in Line 1 are called the **actual parameters** of that call. In Line 2, the function pow is called with the parameters 2.0 and 3.2. In this call, the value 2.0 is copied into base, and 3.2 is copied into exponent. Moreover, in this call of the function pow, the actual parameters are 2.0 and 3.2, respectively. Similarly, in Line 3, the actual parameters of the function pow are u and 7; the value of u is copied into base, and 7.0 is copied into exponent.

We can now formally present two definitions:

Formal Parameter: A variable declared in the function heading.

Actual Parameter: A variable or expression listed in a call to a function.

For predefined functions, you only need to be concerned with the first four properties. Software companies, typically, do not give out the actual source code, which is the body of the function. Otherwise, software costs would be exorbitant.

Syntax: Value-Returning function

The syntax of a value-returning function is:

```
functionType functionName(formal parameter list)
{
    statements
}
```

in which statements are usually declaration statements and/or executable statements. In this syntax, `functionType` is the type of the value that the function returns. The `functionType` is also called the **data type** or the **return type** of the value-returning function. Moreover, statements enclosed between curly braces form the body of the function.

Syntax: Formal Parameter List

The syntax of the formal parameter list is:

```
dataType identifier, dataType identifier, ...
```

Consider the definition of the function `abs` given earlier in this chapter. Figure 6-1 identifies various parts of this function.

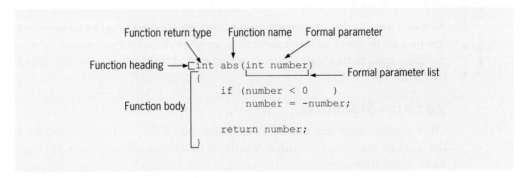

FIGURE 6-1 Various parts of the function abs

Function Call

The syntax to call a value-returning function is:

```
functionName(actual parameter list)
```

For example, in the expression x = abs(-5);, the function abs is called.

Syntax: Actual Parameter List

The syntax of the actual parameter list is:

```
expression or variable, expression or variable, ...
```

(In this syntax, `expression` can be a single constant value.) Thus, to call a value-returning function, you use its name, with the actual parameters (if any) in parentheses.

A function's formal parameter list *can* be empty. However, if the formal parameter list is empty, the parentheses are still needed. The function heading of the value-returning function thus takes, if the formal parameter list is empty, the following form:

```
functionType functionName()
```

If the formal parameter list of a value-returning function is empty, the actual parameter is also empty in a function call. In this case (that is, an empty formal parameter list), in a function call, the empty parentheses are still needed. Thus, a call to a value-returning function with an empty formal parameter list is:

```
functionName()
```

In a function call, the number of actual parameters, together with their data types, must match with the formal parameters in the order given. That is, actual and formal parameters have a one-to-one correspondence. (Later in this chapter, we discuss functions with default parameters.)

As stated previously, a value-returning function is called in an expression. The expression can be part of either an assignment statement or an output statement, or a parameter in a function call. A function call in a program causes the body of the called function to execute.

`return` Statement

Once a value-returning function computes the value, the function returns this value via the `return` statement. In other words, it passes this value outside the function via the `return` statement.

Syntax: `return` Statement

The `return` statement has the following syntax:

```
return expr;
```

in which `expr` is a variable, constant value, or expression. The `expr` is evaluated, and its value is returned. The data type of the value that `expr` computes must match the function type.

In C++, `return` is a reserved word.

When a `return` statement executes in a function, the function immediately terminates and the control goes back to the caller. Moreover, the function call statement is replaced by the value returned by the `return` statement. When a `return` statement executes in the function `main`, the program terminates.

To put the ideas in this discussion to work, let us write a function that determines the larger of two numbers. Because the function compares two numbers, it follows that this function has two parameters and that both parameters are numbers. Let us assume that the data type of these numbers is floating-point (decimal)—say, `double`. Because the larger number is of type `double`, the function's data type is also `double`. Let us name this function `larger`. The only thing you need to complete this function is the body of the function. Thus, following the syntax of a function, you can write this function as follows:

```
double larger(double x, double y)
{
    double max;

    if (x >= y)
        max = x;
    else
        max = y;

    return max;
}
```

Note that the function `larger` uses an additional variable `max` (called a **local declaration**, in which `max` is a variable local to the function `larger`). Figure 6-2 describes various parts of the function `larger`.

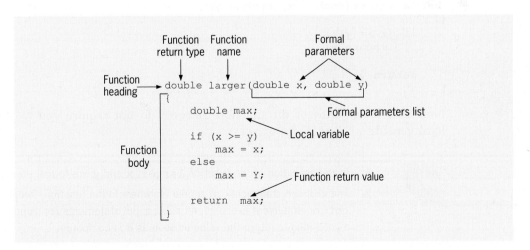

FIGURE 6-2 Various parts of the function `larger`

Suppose that num, num1, and num2 are `double` variables. Also suppose that num1 = 45.75 and num2 = 35.50. Figure 6-3 shows various calls to the function `larger`.

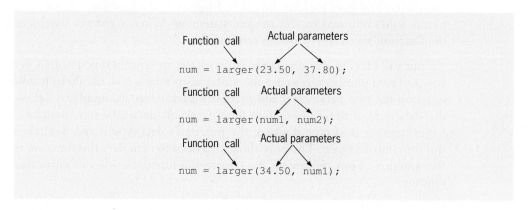

FIGURE 6-3 Function calls

You can also write the definition of the function `larger` as follows:

```
double larger(double x, double y)
{
    if (x >= y)
        return x;
    else
        return y;
}
```

Because the execution of a `return` statement in a function terminates the function, the preceding function `larger` can also be written (without the word `else`) as:

```
double larger(double x, double y)
{
    if (x >= y)
        return x;

    return y;
}
```

Note that these forms of the function `larger` do not require you to declare any local variable.

NOTE

1. In the definition of the function `larger`, x and y are formal parameters.

2. The `return` statement can appear anywhere in the function. Recall that once a `return` statement executes, all subsequent statements are skipped. Thus, it's a good idea to return the value as soon as it is computed.

EXAMPLE 6-2

Now that the function `larger` is written, the following C++ code illustrates how to use it:

```
double one = 13.00;
double two = 36.53;
double maxNum;
```

Consider the following statements:

```
cout << "The larger of 5 and 6 is " << larger(5, 6)
     << endl;                                            //Line 1

cout << "The larger of " << one << " and " << two
     << " is " << larger(one, two) << endl;              //Line 2

cout << "The larger of " << one << " and 29 is "
     << larger(one, 29) << endl;                         //Line 3

maxNum = larger(38.45, 56.78);                           //Line 4
```

- The expression `larger(5, 6)` in Line 1 is a function call, and 5 and 6 are actual parameters. When the expression `larger(5, 6)` executes, 5 is copied into `x`, and 6 is copied into `y`. Therefore, the statement in Line 1 outputs the larger of 5 and 6.

- The expression `larger(one, two)` in Line 2 is a function call. Here, `one` and `two` are actual parameters. When the expression `larger(one, two)` executes, the value of `one` is copied into `x`, and the value of `two` is copied into `y`. Therefore, the statement in Line 2 outputs the larger of `one` and `two`.

- The expression `larger(one, 29)` in Line 3 is also a function call. When the expression `larger(one, 29)` executes, the value of `one` is copied into `x`, and 29 is copied into `y`. Therefore, the statement in Line 3 outputs the larger of `one` and 29. Note that the first parameter, `one`, is a variable, while the second parameter, 29, is a constant value.

- The expression `larger(38.45, 56.78)` in Line 4 is a function call. In this call, the actual parameters are 38.45 and 56.78. In this statement, the value returned by the function `larger` is assigned to the variable `maxNum`.

6

NOTE In a function call, you specify only the actual parameter, not its data type. For example, in Example 6-2, the statements in Lines 1, 2, 3, and 4 show how to call the function `larger` with the actual parameters. However, the following statements contain incorrect calls to the function `larger` and would result in syntax errors. (Assume that all variables are properly declared.)

```
x = larger(int one, 29);            //illegal
y = larger(int one, int 29);        //illegal
cout << larger(int one, int two);   //illegal
```

Once a function is written, you can use it anywhere in the program. The function `larger` compares two numbers and returns the larger of the two. Let us now write another function that uses this function to determine the largest of three numbers. We call this function `compareThree`.

```
double compareThree(double x, double y, double z)
{
        return larger(x, larger(y, z));
}
```

In the function heading, x, y, and z are formal parameters.

Let us take a look at the expression:

```
larger(x, larger(y, z))
```

in the definition of the function `compareThree`. This expression has two calls to the function `larger`. The actual parameters to the outer call are x and `larger(y, z)`; the actual parameters to the inner call are y and z. It follows that, first, the expression `larger(y, z)` is evaluated; that is, the inner call executes first, which gives the larger of y and z. Suppose that `larger(y, z)` evaluates to, say, t. (Notice that t is either y or z.) Next, the outer call determines the larger of x and t. Finally, the `return` statement returns the largest number. It thus follows that to execute a function call, the parameters are evaluated first. For example, the actual parameter `larger(y, z)` of the outer call evaluates first.

Note that the function `larger` is much more general purpose than the function `compareThree`. Here, we are merely illustrating that once you have written a function, you can use it to write other functions. Later in this chapter, we will show how to use the function `larger` to determine the largest number from a set of numbers.

Function Prototype

Now that you have some idea of how to write and use functions in a program, the next question relates to the order in which user-defined functions should appear in a program. For example, do you place the function `larger` before or after the function `main`? Should `larger` be placed before `compareThree` or after it? Following the rule that you must declare an identifier before you can use it and knowing that the function `main` uses the identifier `larger`, logically you must place `larger` before `main`.

In reality, C++ programmers customarily place the function `main` before all other user-defined functions. However, this organization could produce a compilation error because functions are compiled in the order in which they appear in the program. For example, if the function `main` is placed before the function `larger`, the identifier `larger` is undefined when the function `main` is compiled. To work around this problem of undeclared identifiers, we place **function prototypes** before any function definition (including the definition of `main`).

Function Prototype: The function heading without the body of the function.

Syntax: Function Prototype

The general syntax of the function prototype of a value-returning function is:

```
functionType functionName(parameter list);
```

(Note that the function prototype ends with a semicolon.)

For the function `larger`, the prototype is:

```
double larger(double x, double y);   //function prototype
```

 NOTE   When writing the function prototype, you do not have to specify the variable name in the parameter list. However, you must specify the data type of each parameter.

You can rewrite the function prototype of the function `larger` as follows:

```
double larger(double, double);   //function prototype
```

6

FINAL PROGRAM

You now know enough to write the entire program, compile it, and run it. The following program uses the functions `larger`, `compareThree`, and `main` to determine the larger/largest of two or three numbers.

```cpp
//Program: Largest of three numbers

#include <iostream>

using namespace std;

double larger(double x, double y);
double compareThree(double x, double y, double z);

int main()
{
    double one, two;                                    //Line 1

    cout << "Line 2: The larger of 5 and 10 is "
         << larger(5, 10) << endl;                      //Line 2

    cout << "Line 3: Enter two numbers: ";              //Line 3
    cin >> one >> two;                                  //Line 4
    cout << endl;                                       //Line 5

    cout << "Line 6: The larger of " << one
         << " and " << two << " is "
         << larger(one, two) << endl;                   //Line 6
```

```cpp
    cout << "Line 7: The largest of 43.48, 34.00, "
         << "and 12.65 is "
         << compareThree(43.48, 34.00, 12.65)
         << endl;                                            //Line 7

    return 0;
}

double larger(double x, double y)
{
    double max;

    if (x >= y)
        max = x;
    else
        max = y;

    return max;
}

double compareThree (double x, double y, double z)
{
    return larger(x, larger(y, z));
}
```

Sample Run: In this sample run, the user input is shaded.

```
Line 2: The larger of 5 and 10 is 10
Line 3: Enter two numbers: 25.6 73.85

Line 6: The larger of 25.6 and 73.85 is 73.85
Line 7: The largest of 43.48, 34.00, and 12.65 is 43.48
```

 NOTE In the previous program, the function prototypes of the functions `larger` and `compareThree` appear before their function definitions. Therefore, the definition of the functions `larger` and `compareThree` can appear in any order.

Value-Returning Functions: Some Peculiarities

A value-returning function must return a value. Consider the following function, `secret`, that takes as a parameter an `int` value. If the value of the parameter, `x`, is greater than 5, it returns twice the value of `x`; otherwise, the value of `x` remains unchanged.

```cpp
int secret(int x)
{
    if (x > 5)              //Line 1
        return 2 * x;       //Line 2
}
```

Because this is a value-returning function of type `int`, it must return a value of type `int`. Suppose the value of `x` is 10. Then the expression `x > 5` in Line 1 evaluates to `true`. So the `return` statement in Line 2 returns the value 20. Now suppose that `x` is 3. The expression x > 5 in Line 1 now evaluates to `false`. The `if` statement therefore fails, and the `return` statement in Line 2 *does not* execute. However, there are no more statements to be executed in the body of the function. In this case, the function returns a strange value. It thus follows that if the value of x is less than or equal to 5, the function does not contain any valid `return` statements to return the value of x.

A correct definition of the function `secret` is:

```
int secret(int x)
{
    if (x > 5)              //Line 1
        return 2 * x;       //Line 2

    return x;               //Line 3
}
```

Here, if the value of x is less than or equal to 5, the `return` statement in Line 3 executes, which returns the value of x. On the other hand, if the value of x is, say 10, the `return` statement in Line 2 executes, which returns the value 20 and also terminates the function.

Recall that in a value-returning function, the `return` statement returns the value. Consider the following `return` statement:

```
return x, y;   //only the value of y will be returned
```

This is a legal `return` statement. You might think that this `return` statement is returning the values of x and y. However, this is not the case. Remember, a `return` statement returns only one value, even if the `return` statement contains more than one expression. If a `return` statement contains more than one expression, *only the value of the last expression is returned*. Therefore, in the case of the above `return` statement, the value of y is returned. The following program further illustrates this concept:

```
// This program illustrates that a value-returning function
// returns only one value, even if the return statement
// contains more than one expression. This is a legal, but not
// a recommended code.

#include <iostream>

using namespace std;

int funcRet1();
int funcRet2(int z);

int main()
{
    int num = 4;

    cout << "Line 1: The value returned by funcRet1: "
         << funcRet1() << endl;                              // Line 1
```

6

```
        cout << "Line 2: The value returned by funcRet2: "
             << funcRet2(num) << endl;                          // Line 2

        return 0;
}

int funcRet1()
{
    int x = 45;

    return 23, x;   //only the value of x is returned
}

int funcRet2(int z)
{
    int a = 2;
    int b = 3;

    return 2 * a + b, z + b; //only the value of z + b is returned
}
```

Sample Run:

```
Line 1: The value returned by funcRet1: 45
Line 2: The value returned by funcRet2: 7
```

Even though a `return` statement can contain more than one expression, a return statement in your program should contain only one expression. Having more than one expression in a `return` statement may result in redundancy, wasted code, and a confusing syntax.

More Examples of Value-Returning Functions

EXAMPLE 6-3

In this example, we write the definition of function `courseGrade`. This function takes as a parameter an `int` value specifying the score for a course and returns the grade, a value of type `char`, for the course. (We assume that the test score is a value between 0 and 100 inclusive.)

```
char courseGrade(int score)
{
    switch (score / 10)
    {
    case 0:
    case 1:
    case 2:
    case 3:
```

```
    case 4:
    case 5:
        return 'F';
    case 6:
        return 'D';
    case 7:
        return 'C';
    case 8:
        return 'B';
    case 9:
    case 10:
        return 'A';
    }
}
```

You can also write an equivalent definition of the function `courseGrade` that uses an `if...else` structure to determine the course grade.

6

EXAMPLE 6-4 (ROLLING A PAIR OF DICE)

In this example, we write a function that rolls a pair of dice until the sum of the numbers rolled is a specific number. We also want to know the number of times the dice are rolled to get the desired sum.

The smallest number on each die is 1, and the largest number is 6. So the smallest sum of the numbers rolled is 2, and the largest sum of the numbers rolled is 12. Suppose that we have the following declarations:

```
int die1;
int die2;
int sum;
int rollCount = 0;
```

We use the random number generator, discussed in Chapter 5, to randomly generate a number between 1 and 6. Then, the following statement randomly generates a number between 1 and 6 and stores that number into `die1`, which becomes the number rolled by `die1`.

```
die1 = rand() % 6 + 1;
```

Similarly, the following statement randomly generates a number between 1 and 6 and stores that number into `die2`, which becomes the number rolled by `die2`.

```
die2 = rand() % 6 + 1;
```

The sum of the numbers rolled by two dice is:

```
sum = die1 + die2;
```

Next, we determine whether sum contains the desired sum of the numbers rolled by the dice. If sum does not contain the desired sum, then we roll the dice again. This can be accomplished by the following do...while loop. (Assume that the int variable num contains the desired sum to be rolled.)

```
do
{
    die1 = rand() % 6 + 1;
    die2 = rand() % 6 + 1;
    sum = die1 + die2;
    rollCount++;
}
while (sum != num);
```

We can now write the function rollDice that takes as a parameter the desired sum of the numbers to be rolled and returns the number of times the dice are rolled to roll the desired sum.

```
int rollDice(int num)
{
    int die1;
    int die2;
    int sum;
    int rollCount = 0;

    srand(time(0));

    do
    {
        die1 = rand() % 6 + 1;
        die2 = rand() % 6 + 1;
        sum = die1 + die2;
        rollCount++;
    }
    while (sum != num);

    return rollCount;
}
```

The following program shows how to use the function rollDice in a program:

```
//Program: Roll dice

#include <iostream>
#include <cstdlib>
#include <ctime>

using namespace std;

int rollDice(int num);
```

```cpp
int main()
{
    cout << "The number of times the dice are rolled to "
         << "get the sum 10 = " << rollDice(10) << endl;
    cout << "The number of times the dice are rolled to "
         << "get the sum 6 = " << rollDice(6) << endl;

    return 0;
}

int rollDice(int num)
{
    int die1;
    int die2;
    int sum;
    int rollCount = 0;

    srand(time(0));

    do
    {
        die1 = rand() % 6 + 1;
        die2 = rand() % 6 + 1;
        sum = die1 + die2;
        rollCount++;
    }
    while (sum != num);

    return rollCount;
}
```

Sample Run:

```
The number of times the dice are rolled to get the sum 10 = 11
The number of times the dice are rolled to get the sum 6 = 7
```

We leave it as an exercise for you to modify this program so that it allows the user to enter the desired sum of the numbers to be rolled. (See Programming Exercise 7 at the end of this chapter.)

EXAMPLE 6-5 (PALINDROME)

In this example, a function, `isPalindrome`, is designed that returns `true` if a string is a palindrome and `false` otherwise. A string is a palindrome if it reads forward and backward in the same way. For example, the strings `"madamimadam"`, `"5"`, `"434"`, and `"789656987"` are all palindromes.

Suppose str is a string. To determine whether str is a palindrome, first compare the first and the last characters of str. If they are not the same, str is not a palindrome and so the function should return false. If the first and the last characters of str are the same, then we compare the second character with the second character from the end, and so on.

Note that if length = str.length(), the number of characters in str, then we need to compare str[0] with str[length - 1], str[1] with str[length - 2], and in general str[i] with str[length - 1 - i], where 0 <= i <= length / 2.

The following algorithm implements this discussion:

```
1.  int length = str.length();
2.  for (int i = 0; i < length / 2; i++)
        if (str[i] != str[length - 1 - i])
            return false;
    return true;
```

The following function implements this algorithm:

```
bool isPalindrome(string str)
{
    int length = str.length();                      //Step 1

    for (int i = 0; i < length / 2; i++)            //Step 2
        if (str[i] != str[length - 1 - i])
            return false;

    return true;
}
```

EXAMPLE 6-6 (CABLE COMPANY)

Chapter 4 contains a program to calculate the bill for a cable company. In that program, all of the programming instructions are packed in the function main. Here, we rewrite the same program using user-defined functions, further illustrating structured programming.

Because there are two types of customers, residential and business, the program contains two separate functions: one to calculate the bill for residential customers and one to calculate the bill for business customers. Both functions calculate the billing amount and then return the billing amount to the function main. The function main prints the amount due. Let us call the function that calculates the residential bill residential and the function that calculates the business bill business. The formulas to calculate the bills are the same as before.

Function residential: To compute the residential bill, you need to know the number of premium channels to which the customer subscribes. Based on the number of premium channels, you can calculate the billing amount. After calculating the billing amount, the function returns the billing amount using the `return` statement. The following four steps describe this function:

a. Prompt the user for the number of premium channels.

b. Read the number of premium channels.

c. Calculate the bill.

d. Return the amount due.

This function contains a statement to prompt the user to enter the number of premium channels (Step a) and a statement to read the number of premium channels (Step b). Other items needed to calculate the billing amount, such as the cost of basic service connection and bill processing fees, are defined as named constants (before the definition of the function `main`). Therefore, to calculate the billing amount, this function does not need to get any value from the function `main`. This function, therefore, has no parameters.

From the previous discussion, it follows that the function `residential` requires variables to store both the number of premium channels and the billing amount. This function needs only two local variables to calculate the billing amount:

```
int noOfPChannels;   //number of premium channels
double bAmount;      //billing amount
```

The definition of the function `residential` can now be written as follows:

```
double residential()
{
    int noOfPChannels;   //number of premium channels
    double bAmount;      //billing amount

    cout << "Enter the number of premium "
         << "channels used: ";
    cin >> noOfPChannels;
    cout << endl;

    bAmount= RES_BILL_PROC_FEES +
            RES_BASIC_SERV_COST +
            noOfPChannels * RES_COST_PREM_CHANNEL;

    return bAmount;
}
```

Function `business`: To compute the business bill, you need to know the number of both the basic service connections and the premium channels to which the customer subscribes. Then, based on these numbers, you can calculate the billing amount. The billing amount is then returned using the `return` statement. The following six steps describe this function:

a. Prompt the user for the number of basic service connections.

b. Read the number of basic service connections.

c. Prompt the user for the number of premium channels.

d. Read the number of premium channels.

e. Calculate the bill.

f. Return the amount due.

This function contains the statements to prompt the user to enter the number of basic service connections and premium channels (Steps a and c). The function also contains statements to input the number of basic service connections and premium channels (Steps b and d). Other items needed to calculate the billing amount, such as the cost of basic service connections and bill processing fees, are defined as named constants (before the definition of the function `main`). It follows that to calculate the billing amount this function does not need to get any values from the function `main`. Therefore, it has no parameters.

From the preceding discussion, it follows that the function `business` requires variables to store the number of basic service connections and the number of premium channels, as well as the billing amount. In fact, this function needs only three local variables to calculate the billing amount:

```
int noOfBasicServiceConnections;
int noOfPChannels; //number of premium channels
double bAmount;     //billing amount
```

The definition of the function `business` can now be written as follows:

```
double business()
{
    int noOfBasicServiceConnections;
    int noOfPChannels; //number of premium channels
    double bAmount;     //billing amount

    cout << "Enter the number of basic "
         << "service connections: ";
    cin >> noOfBasicServiceConnections;
    cout << endl;

    cout << "Enter the number of premium "
         << "channels used: ";
    cin >> noOfPChannels;
    cout << endl;

    if (noOfBasicServiceConnections <= 10)
        bAmount = BUS_BILL_PROC_FEES + BUS_BASIC_SERV_COST +
                noOfPChannels * BUS_COST_PREM_CHANNEL;
    else
        bAmount = BUS_BILL_PROC_FEES + BUS_BASIC_SERV_COST +
                (noOfBasicServiceConnections - 10) *
                BUS_BASIC_CONN_COST +
                noOfPChannels * BUS_COST_PREM_CHANNEL;

    return bAmount;
}
```

The algorithm for the main program is as follows:

1. To output floating-point numbers in a fixed decimal format with the decimal point and trailing zeros, set the manipulators `fixed` and `showpoint`.
2. To output floating-point numbers to two decimal places, set the precision to two decimal places.
3. Prompt the user for the account number.
4. Get the account number.
5. Prompt the user to enter the customer type.
6. Get the customer type.
7. a. If the customer type is R or r,

    i. Call the function `residential` to calculate the bill.

    ii. Print the bill.

  b. If the customer type is B or b,

    i. Call the function `business` to calculate the bill.

    ii. Print the bill.

  c. If the customer type is other than R, r, B, or b, it is an invalid customer type.

PROGRAM LISTING

```
//***********************************************************
// Author: D. S. Malik
//
// Program: Cable Company Billing
// This program calculates and prints a customer's bill for
// a local cable company. The program processes two types of
// customers: residential and business.
//***********************************************************

#include <iostream>
#include <iomanip>
using namespace std;

    //Named constants - residential customers
const double RES_BILL_PROC_FEES = 4.50;
const double RES_BASIC_SERV_COST = 20.50;
const double RES_COST_PREM_CHANNEL = 7.50;

    //Named constants - business customers
const double BUS_BILL_PROC_FEES = 15.00;
const double BUS_BASIC_SERV_COST = 75.00;
```

```cpp
const double BUS_BASIC_CONN_COST = 5.00;
const double BUS_COST_PREM_CHANNEL = 50.00;

double residential();   //Function prototype
double business();      //Function prototype

int main()
{
        //declare variables
    int accountNumber;
    char customerType;
    double amountDue;

    cout << fixed << showpoint;                 //Step 1
    cout << setprecision(2);                    //Step 2

    cout << "This program computes a cable bill."
         << endl;
    cout << "Enter account number: ";           //Step 3
    cin >> accountNumber;                       //Step 4
    cout << endl;

    cout << "Enter customer type: R, r "
         << "(Residential), B, b (Business): ";  //Step 5
    cin >> customerType;                        //Step 6
    cout << endl;

    switch (customerType)                       //Step 7
    {
    case 'r':                                   //Step 7a
    case 'R':
        amountDue = residential();              //Step 7a.i
        cout << "Account number = "
             << accountNumber << endl;          //Step 7a.ii
        cout << "Amount due = $"
             << amountDue << endl;              //Step 7a.ii
        break;
    case 'b':                                   //Step 7b
    case 'B':
        amountDue = business();                 //Step 7b.i
        cout << "Account number = "
             << accountNumber << endl;          //Step 7b.ii
        cout << "Amount due = $"
             << amountDue << endl;              //Step 7b.ii
        break;
    default:
        cout << "Invalid customer type."
             << endl;                           //Step 7c
    }

    return 0;
}

//Place the definitions of the functions residential and business here.
```

Sample Run: In this sample run, the user input is shaded.

```
This program computes a cable bill.
Enter account number: 21341

Enter customer type: R, r (Residential), B, b (Business): B

Enter the number of basic service connections: 25

Enter the number of premium channels used: 9

Account number = 21341
Amount due = $615.00
```

Flow of Execution

As stated earlier, a C++ program is a collection of functions. Recall that functions can appear in any order. The only thing that you have to remember is that you must declare an identifier before you can use it. The program is compiled by the compiler sequentially from beginning to end. Thus, if the function `main` appears before any other user-defined functions, it is compiled first. However, if `main` appears at the end (or middle) of the program, all functions whose definitions (not prototypes) appear before the function `main` are compiled before the function `main`, in the order they are placed.

Function prototypes appear before any function definition, so the compiler translates these first. The compiler can then correctly translate a function call. *However, when the program executes, the first statement in the function* `main` *always executes first, regardless of where in the program the function* `main` *is placed.* Other functions execute only when they are called.

A function call statement transfers control to the first statement in the body of the function. In general, after the last statement of the called function executes, control is passed back to the point immediately following the function call. A value-returning function returns a value. Therefore, after executing the value-returning function, when the control goes back to the caller, the value that the function returns replaces the function call statement. The execution continues at the point immediately following the function call.

Suppose that a program contains functions `funcA` and `funcB`, and `funcA` contains a statement that calls `funcB`. Suppose that the program calls `funcA`. When the statement that contains a call to `funcB` executes, `funcB` executes, and while `funcB` is executing, the execution of the current call of `funcA` is on hold until `funcB` is done.

6

PROGRAMMING EXAMPLE: Largest Number

In this programming example, the function `larger` is used to determine the largest number from a set of numbers. For the purpose of illustration, this program determines the largest number from a set of 10 numbers. You can easily enhance this program to accommodate any set of numbers.

Input   A set of 10 numbers.

Output   The largest of 10 numbers.

PROBLEM
ANALYSIS
AND
ALGORITHM
DESIGN

Suppose that the input data is:

15 20 7 8 28 21 43 12 35 3

Read the first number of the data set. Because this is the only number read to this point, you may assume that it is the largest number so far and call it `max`. Read the second number and call it `num`. Now compare `max` and `num` and store the larger number into `max`. Now `max` contains the larger of the first two numbers. Read the third number. Compare it with `max` and store the larger number into `max`. At this point, `max` contains the largest of the first three numbers. Read the next number, compare it with `max`, and store the larger into `max`. Repeat this process for each remaining number in the data set. Eventually, `max` will contain the largest number in the data set. This discussion translates into the following algorithm:

1. Read the first number. Because this is the only number that you have read so far, it is the largest number so far. Save it in a variable called `max`.

2. For each remaining number in the list:

   a. Read the next number. Store it in a variable called `num`.

   b. Compare `num` and `max`. If `max` < `num`, then `num` is the new largest number, so update the value of `max` by copying `num` into `max`. If `max` >= `num`, discard `num`; that is, do nothing.

3. Because `max` now contains the largest number, print it.

To find the larger of two numbers, the program uses the function `larger`.

COMPLETE PROGRAM LISTING

```cpp
//*********************************************************
// Author: D.S. Malik
//
// This program finds the largest number of a set of 10
// numbers.
//*********************************************************

#include <iostream>

using namespace std;

double larger(double x, double y);

int main()
{
    double num; //variable to hold the current number
    double max; //variable to hold the larger number
    int count;  //loop control variable

    cout << "Enter 10 numbers." << endl;
    cin >> num;                                 //Step 1
    max = num;                                  //Step 1

    for (count = 1; count < 10; count++)        //Step 2
    {
        cin >> num;                             //Step 2a
        max = larger(max, num);                 //Step 2b
    }

    cout << "The largest number is " << max
         << endl;                               //Step 3

    return 0;
} //end main

double larger(double x, double y)
{
    if (x >= y)
        return x;
    else
        return y;
}
```

Sample Run: In this sample run, the user input is shaded.

```
Enter 10 numbers.
10 56 73 42 22 67 88 26 62 11
The largest number is 88
```

Earlier in this chapter, you learned how to use value-returning functions. In this section, you will explore user-defined functions in general and, in particular, those C++ functions that do not have a data type, called **void functions**.

Void Functions

Void functions and value-returning functions have similar structures. Both have a heading and a body. Like value-returning functions, you can place user-defined void functions either before or after the function `main`. However, the program execution always begins with the first statement in the function `main`. If you place user-defined void functions after the function `main`, you should place the function prototype before the function `main`. A void function does not have a data type. Therefore, `functionType`—that is, the return type—in the heading part and the return statement in the body of the void functions are meaningless. However, in a void function, you can use the return statement without any value; it is typically used to exit the function early. Like value-returning functions, void functions may or may not have formal parameters.

Because void functions do not have a data type, they are not used (called) in an expression. A call to a void function is a stand-alone statement. Thus, to call a void function, you use the function name together with the actual parameters (if any) in a stand-alone statement. Before giving examples of void functions, next we give the syntax of a void function.

FUNCTION DEFINITION

The function definition of void functions with parameters has the following syntax:

```
void functionName(formal parameter list)
{
    statements
}
```

in which `statements` are usually declaration and/or executable statements. The formal parameter list may be empty, in which case, in the function heading, the empty parentheses are still needed.

FORMAL PARAMETER LIST

The formal parameter list has the following syntax:

```
dataType& variable, dataType& variable, ...
```

You must specify both the data type and the variable name in the formal parameter list. The symbol `&` after `dataType` has a special meaning; it is used only for certain formal parameters and is discussed later in this chapter.

FUNCTION CALL

The function call has the following syntax:

```
functionName(actual parameter list);
```

ACTUAL PARAMETER LIST

The actual parameter list has the following syntax:

```
expression or variable, expression or variable, ...
```

in which `expression` can consist of a single constant value. As with value-returning functions, in a function call, the number of actual parameters together with their data types must match the formal parameters in the order given. Actual and formal parameters have a one-to-one correspondence. (Functions with default parameters are discussed at the end of this chapter.) A function call results in the execution of the body of the called function.

Example 6-7 shows a void function with parameters.

EXAMPLE 6-7

```
void funexp(int a, double b, char c, int x)
{
    .
    .
    .
}
```

The function `funexp` has four parameters.

PARAMETER TYPES

Parameters provide a communication link between the calling function (such as `main`) and the called function. They enable functions to manipulate different data each time they are called. In general, there are two types of formal parameters: **value parameters** and **reference parameters**.

Value parameter: A formal parameter that receives a copy of the content of the corresponding actual parameter.

Reference parameter: A formal parameter that receives the location (memory address) of the corresponding actual parameter.

When you attach & after the `dataType` in the formal parameter list of a function, the variable following that `dataType` becomes a reference parameter.

Example 6-8 shows a void function with value and reference parameters.

EXAMPLE 6-8

Consider the following function definition:

```
void areaAndPerimeter(double length, double width,
                      double& area, double& perimeter)
{
    area = length * width;
    perimeter = 2 * (length + width);
}
```

The function **areaAndPerimeter** has four parameters: **length** and **width** are value parameters of type **double**; and **area** and **perimeter** are reference parameters of type **double**.

The following figure describes various parts of the function **areaAndPerimeter**.

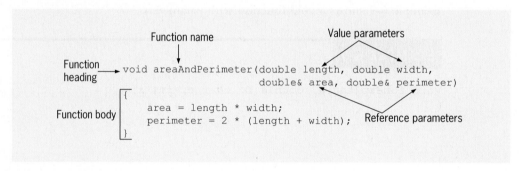

FIGURE 6-4 Various parts of the function areaAndPerimeter

EXAMPLE 6-9

Consider the following definition:

```
void averageAndGrade(int testScore, int progScore,
                     double& average, char& grade)
{
    average = (testScore + progScore) / 2.0;

    if (average >= 90.00)
        grade = 'A';
    else if (grade >= 80.00)
        grade = 'B';
```

```
        else if (grade >= 70.00)
            grade = 'C';
        else if (grade >= 60.00)
            grade = 'D';
        else
            grade = 'F';
}
```

The function `averageAndGrade` has four parameters: `testScore` and `progScore` are value parameters of type `int`, `average` is a reference parameter of type `double`, and `grade` is a reference parameter of type `char`.

EXAMPLE 6-10

6

We write a program to print a pattern (a triangle of stars) similar to the following:

```
   *
  * *
 * * *
* * * *
```

The first line has one star with some blanks before the star, the second line has two stars, some blanks before the stars, and a blank between the stars, and so on. Let's write the function `printStars` that has two parameters, a parameter to specify the number of blanks before the stars in a line and a second parameter to specify the number of stars in a line. To be specific, the definition of the function `printStars` is:

```
void printStars(int blanks, int starsInLine)
{
    int count;

    //print the number of blanks before the stars in a line
    for (count = 1; count <= blanks; count++)
        cout << ' ';

    //print the number of stars with a blanks between stars
    for (count = 1; count <= starsInLine; count++)
        cout << " *";

    cout << endl;
} //end printStars
```

The first parameter, `blanks`, determines how many blanks to print preceding the star(s); the second parameter, `starsInLine`, determines how many stars to print in a line. If the value of the parameter `blanks` is 30, for instance, then the first `for` loop in the function `printStars` executes 30 times and prints 30 blanks. Also, because you want to print a space between the stars, every iteration of the second `for` loop in the function `printStars` prints the string `" *"`—a blank followed by a star.

Next, consider the following statements:

```
int numberOfLines = 15;
int numberOfBlanks = 30;

for (counter = 1; counter <= numberOfLines; counter++)
{
    printStars(numberOfBlanks, counter);
    numberOfBlanks--;
}
```

The `for` loop calls the function `printStars`. Every iteration of this `for` loop specifies the number of blanks followed by the number of stars to print in a line, using the variables `numberOfBlanks` and `counter`. Every invocation of the function `printStars` receives one fewer blank and one more star than the previous call. For example, the first iteration of the `for` loop in the function `main` specifies 30 blanks and 1 star (which are passed as the parameters `numberOfBlanks` and `counter` to the function `printStars`). The `for` loop then decrements the number of blanks by 1 by executing the statement, `numberOfBlanks--;`. At the end of the `for` loop, the number of stars is incremented by 1 for the next iteration. This is done by executing the update statement `counter++` in the `for` statement, which increments the value of the variable `counter` by 1. In other words, the second call of the function `printStars` receives 29 blanks and 2 stars as parameters. Thus, the previous statements will print a triangle of stars consisting of 15 lines.

```
//Program: Print a triangle of stars

#include <iostream>

using namespace std;

void printStars(int blanks, int starsInLine);

int main()
{
    int noOfLines;  //variable to store the number of lines
    int counter;    //for loop control variable
    int noOfBlanks; //variable to store the number of blanks

    cout << "Enter the number of star lines (1 to 20) "
         << "to be printed: ";                              //Line 1

    cin >> noOfLines;                                        //Line 2

    while (noOfLines < 0 || noOfLines > 20)                 //Line 3
    {
        cout << "Number of star lines should be "
             << "between 1 and 20" << endl;                 //Line 4
        cout << "Enter the number of star lines "
             << "(1 to 20) to be printed: ";                //Line 5
        cin >> noOfLines;                                   //Line 6
    }
```

```
    cout << endl << endl;                               //Line 7
    noOfBlanks = 30;                                    //Line 8

    for (counter = 1; counter <= noOfLines; counter++)  //Line 9
    {
        printStars(noOfBlanks, counter);                //Line 10
        noOfBlanks--;                                   //Line 11
    }

    return 0;                                           //Line 12
}

void printStars(int blanks, int starsInLine)
{
    int count;

    for (count = 1; count <= blanks; count++)           //Line 13
        cout << ' ';                                    //Line 14
    for (count = 1; count <= starsInLine; count++)      //Line 15
        cout << " *";                                   //Line 16
    cout << endl;
}
```

Sample Run: In this sample run, the user input is shaded.

```
Enter the number of star lines (1 to 20) to be printed: 15

                          *
                         * *
                        * * *
                       * * * *
                      * * * * *
                     * * * * * *
                    * * * * * * *
                   * * * * * * * *
                  * * * * * * * * *
                 * * * * * * * * * *
                * * * * * * * * * * *
               * * * * * * * * * * * *
              * * * * * * * * * * * * *
             * * * * * * * * * * * * * *
            * * * * * * * * * * * * * * *
```

In the function main, the user is first asked to specify how many lines of stars to print (Line 1). (In this program, the user is restricted to 20 lines because a triangular grid of up to 20 lines fits nicely on the screen.) Because the program is restricted to only 20 lines, the while loop at Lines 3 through 6 ensures that the program prints only the triangular grid of stars if the number of lines is between 1 and 20.

Value Parameters

The previous section defined two types of parameters—value parameters and reference parameters. Example 6-10 showed a program that uses a function with parameters. Before considering more examples of void functions with parameters, let us make the following observation about value and reference parameters. When a function is called, the value of the actual parameter is copied into the corresponding formal parameter. If the formal parameter is a value parameter, then after copying the value of the actual parameter, there is no connection between the formal parameter and actual parameter; that is, the formal parameter has its own copy of the data. Therefore, during program execution, the formal parameter manipulates the data stored in its own memory space. The program in Example 6-11 further illustrates how a value parameter works.

EXAMPLE 6-11

The following program shows how a formal parameter of a simple data type works.

```
//Example 6-11
//Program illustrating how a value parameter works.

#include <iostream>

using namespace std;

void funcValueParam(int num);

int main()
{
    int number = 6;                                 //Line 1

    cout << "Line 2: Before calling the function "
         << "funcValueParam, number = " << number
         << endl;                                   //Line 2

    funcValueParam(number);                         //Line 3

    cout << "Line 4: After calling the function "
         << "funcValueParam, number = " << number
         << endl;                                   //Line 4

    return 0;
}

void funcValueParam(int num)
{
    cout << "Line 5: In the function funcValueParam, "
         << "before changing, num = " << num
         << endl;                                   //Line 5

    num = 15;                                       //Line 6
```

```
        cout << "Line 7: In the function funcValueParam, "
             << "after changing, num = " << num
             << endl;                                        //Line 7
}
```

Sample Run:

```
Line 2: Before calling the function funcValueParam, number = 6
Line 5: In the function funcValueParam, before changing, num = 6
Line 7: In the function funcValueParam, after changing, num = 15
Line 4: After calling the function funcValueParam, number = 6
```

This program works as follows. The execution begins at the function main. The statement in Line 1 declares and initializes the int variable number. The statement in Line 2 outputs the value of number before calling the function funcValueParam; the statement in Line 3 calls the function funcValueParam. The value of the variable number is then passed to the formal parameter num. Control now transfers to the function funcValueParam.

The statement in Line 5 outputs the value of num before changing its value. The statement in Line 6 changes the value of num to 15; the statement in Line 7 outputs the value of num. After this statement executes, the function funcValueParam exits and control goes back to the function main.

The statement in Line 4 outputs the value of number after calling the function funcValueParam. The sample run shows that the value of number (Lines 2 and 4) remains the same even though the value of its corresponding formal parameter num was changed within the function funcValueParam.

The output shows the sequence in which the statements execute.

After copying data, a value parameter has no connection with the actual parameter, so a value parameter cannot pass any result back to the calling function. When the function executes, any changes made to the formal parameters do not in any way affect the actual parameters. The actual parameters have no knowledge of what is happening to the formal parameters. Thus, value parameters cannot pass information outside of the function. Value parameters provide only a one-way link between actual parameters and formal parameters. Hence, functions with only value parameters have limitations.

Reference Variables as Parameters

The program in Example 6-11 illustrates how a value parameter works. On the other hand, suppose that a formal parameter is a reference parameter. Because a reference parameter receives the address (memory location) of the actual parameter, reference parameters can pass one or more values from a function and can change the value of the actual parameter.

Reference parameters are useful in three situations:

- When the value of the actual parameter needs to be changed
- When you want to return more than one value from a function (recall that the return statement can return only one value)
- When passing the address would save memory space and time relative to copying a large amount of data

The first two situations are illustrated throughout this book. Chapters 8 and 10 discuss the third situation, when arrays and classes are introduced.

Recall that when you attach & after the dataType in the formal parameter list of a function, the variable following that dataType becomes a reference parameter.

NOTE You can declare a reference (formal) parameter as a constant by using the keyword const. Chapters 9 and 10 discuss constant reference parameters. Until then, the reference parameters that you use will be nonconstant as defined in this chapter. From the definition of a reference parameter, it follows that a constant value or an expression cannot be passed to a nonconstant reference parameter. If a formal parameter is a nonconstant reference parameter, during a function call, its corresponding actual parameter must be a variable.

EXAMPLE 6-12

Calculate Grade

The following program takes a course score (a value between 0 and 100) and determines a student's course grade. This program has three functions: main, getScore, and printGrade, as follows:

1. main

   a. Get the course score.

   b. Print the course grade.

2. getScore

   a. Prompt the user for the input.

   b. Get the input.

   c. Print the course score.

3. printGrade

   a. Calculate the course grade.

   b. Print the course grade.

The complete program is as follows:

```cpp
//This program reads a course score and prints the
//associated course grade.

#include <iostream>
using namespace std;

void getScore(int& score);
void printGrade(int score);

int main()
{
    int courseScore;

    cout << "Line 1: Based on the course score, \n"
         << "    this program computes the "
         << "course grade." << endl;              //Line 1

    getScore(courseScore);                        //Line 2

    printGrade(courseScore);                      //Line 3

    return 0;
}

void getScore(int& score)
{
    cout << "Line 4: Enter course score: ";       //Line 4
    cin >> score;                                 //Line 5
    cout << endl << "Line 6: Course score is "
         << score << endl;                        //Line 6
}

void printGrade(int cScore)
{
    cout << "Line 7: Your grade for the course is ";  //Line 7

    if (cScore >= 90)                             //Line 8
        cout << "A." << endl;
    else if (cScore >= 80)
        cout << "B." << endl;
    else if(cScore >= 70)
        cout << "C." << endl;
    else if (cScore >= 60)
        cout << "D." << endl;
    else
        cout << "F." << endl;
}
```

6

Sample Run: In this sample run, the user input is shaded.

```
Line 1: Based on the course score,
        this program computes the course grade.
Line 4: Enter course score: 85

Line 6: Course score is 85
Line 7: Your grade for the course is B.
```

This program works as follows. The program starts to execute at Line 1, which prints the first line of the output (see the sample run). The statement in Line 2 calls the function getScore with the actual parameter courseScore (a variable declared in main). Because the formal parameter score of the function getScore is a reference parameter, the address (that is, the memory location of the variable courseScore) passes to score. Thus, both score and courseScore refer to the same memory location, which is courseScore (see Figure 6-5).

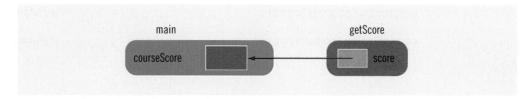

FIGURE 6-5 Variable courseScore and the parameter score

Any changes made to score immediately change the value of courseScore.

Control is then transferred to the function getScore, and the statement in Line 4 executes, printing the second line of output. This statement prompts the user to enter the course score. The statement in Line 5 reads and stores the value entered by the user (85 in the sample run) in score, which is actually courseScore (because score is a reference parameter). Thus, at this point, the value of the variables score and courseScore is 85 (see Figure 6-6).

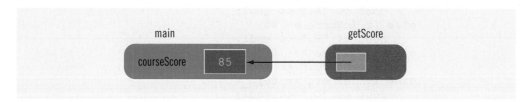

FIGURE 6-6 Variable courseScore and the parameter score after the statement in Line 5 executes

Next, the statement in Line 6 outputs the value of score as shown by the third line of the sample run. After Line 6 executes, control goes back to the function main (see Figure 6-7).

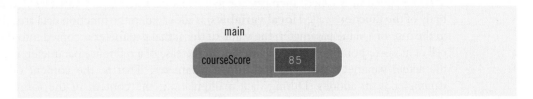

FIGURE 6-7 Variable courseScore after the statement in Line 6 is executed and control goes back to main

The statement in Line 3 executes next. It is a function call to the function printGrade with the actual parameter courseScore. Because the formal parameter cScore of the function printGrade is a value parameter, the parameter cScore receives the value of the corresponding actual parameter courseScore. Thus, the value of cScore is 85. After copying the value of courseScore into cScore, no communication exists between cScore and courseScore (see Figure 6-8).

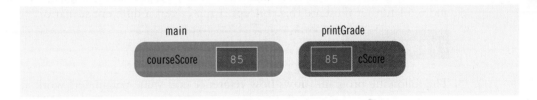

FIGURE 6-8 Variable courseScore and the parameter cScore

The program then executes the statement in Line 7, which outputs the fourth line. The if...else statement in Line 8 determines and outputs the grade for the course. Because the output statement in Line 7 does not contain the newline character or the manipulator endl, the output of the if...else statement is part of the fourth line of the output. After the if...else statement executes, control goes back to the function main. Because the next statement to execute in the function main is the last statement of the function main, the program terminates.

In this program, the function main first calls the function getScore to obtain the course score from the user. The function main then calls the function printGrade to calculate and print the grade based on this course score. The course score is retrieved by the function getScore; later, this course score is used by the function printGrade. Because the value retrieved by the getScore function is used later in the program, the function getScore must pass this value outside. Because getScore is written as a void function, the formal parameter that holds this value must be a reference parameter.

Value and Reference Parameters and Memory Allocation

When a function is called, memory for its formal parameters and variables declared in the body of the function (called **local variables**) is allocated in the function data area. Recall that in the case of a value parameter, the value of the actual parameter is copied into the memory cell of its corresponding formal parameter. In the case of a reference parameter, the address of the actual parameter passes to the formal parameter. That is, the content of the formal parameter is an address. During data manipulation, the content of the formal parameter directs the computer to manipulate the data of the memory cell indicated by its content. Thus, in the case of a reference parameter, both the actual and formal parameters refer to the same memory location. Consequently, during program execution, changes made by the formal parameter permanently change the value of the actual parameter.

 NOTE Stream variables (for example, `ifstream` and `ofstream`) should be passed by reference to a function. After opening the input/output file or after reading and/or outputting data, the state of the input and/or output stream can then be passed outside the function.

Because parameter passing is fundamental to any programming language, Examples 6-13 and 6-14 further illustrate this concept. Each covers a different scenario.

EXAMPLE 6-13

The following program shows how reference and value parameters work.

```
//Example 6-13: Reference and value parameters

#include <iostream>

using namespace std;

void funOne(int a, int& b, char v);
void funTwo(int& x, int y, char& w);

int main()
{
    int num1, num2;
    char ch;

    num1 = 10;                                          //Line 1
    num2 = 15;                                          //Line 2
    ch = 'A';                                           //Line 3

    cout << "Line 4: Inside main: num1 = " << num1
         << ", num2 = " << num2 << ", and ch = "
         << ch << endl;                                 //Line 4
```

```
    funOne(num1, num2, ch);                              //Line 5

    cout << "Line 6: After funOne: num1 = " << num1
         << ", num2 = " << num2 << ", and ch = "
         << ch << endl;                                  //Line 6

    funTwo(num2, 25, ch);                                //Line 7

    cout << "Line 8: After funTwo: num1 = " << num1
         << ", num2 = " << num2 << ", and ch = "
         << ch << endl;                                  //Line 8

    return 0;
}

void funOne(int a, int& b, char v)
{
    int one;

    one = a;                                             //Line 9
    a++;                                                 //Line 10
    b = b * 2;                                           //Line 11
    v = 'B';                                             //Line 12

    cout << "Line 13: Inside funOne: a = " << a
         << ", b = " << b << ", v = " << v
         << ", and one = " << one << endl;               //Line 13
}

void funTwo(int& x, int y, char& w)
{
    x++;                                                 //Line 14
    y = y * 2;                                           //Line 15
    w = 'G';                                             //Line 16

    cout << "Line 17: Inside funTwo: x = " << x
         << ", y = " << y << ", and w = " << w
         << endl;                                        //Line 17
}
```

Sample Run:

```
Line 4: Inside main: num1 = 10, num2 = 15, and ch = A
Line 13: Inside funOne: a = 11, b = 30, v = B, and one = 10
Line 6: After funOne: num1 = 10, num2 = 30, and ch = A
Line 17: Inside funTwo: x = 31, y = 50, and w = G
Line 8: After funTwo: num1 = 10, num2 = 31, and ch = G
```

Let us walk through this program. The values of the variables are shown before and/or after each statement executes.

LIVERPOOL JOHN MOORES UNIVERSITY
LEARNING SERVICES

Just before the statement in Line 1 executes, memory is allocated only for the variables of the function `main`; this memory is not initialized. After the statement in Line 3 executes, the variables are as shown in Figure 6-9.

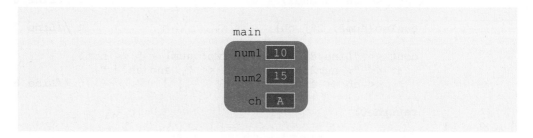

FIGURE 6-9 Values of the variables after the statement in Line 3 executes

The statement in Line 4 produces the following output:

```
Line 4: Inside main: num1 = 10, num2 = 15, and ch = A
```

The statement in Line 5 is a function call to the function `funOne`. Now function `funOne` has three parameters and one local variable. Memory for the parameters and the local variable of function `funOne` is allocated. Because the formal parameter `b` is a reference parameter, it receives the address (memory location) of the corresponding actual parameter, which is `num2`. The other two formal parameters are value parameters, so they copy the values of their corresponding actual parameters. Just before the statement in Line 9 executes, the variables are as shown in Figure 6-10.

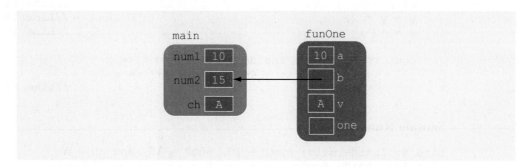

FIGURE 6-10 Values of the variables just before the statement in Line 9 executes

After the statement in Line 9, `one = a;`, executes, the variables are as shown in Figure 6-11.

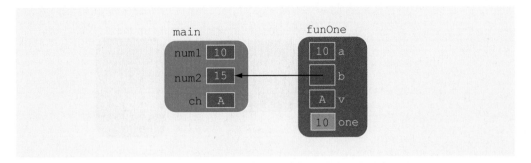

FIGURE 6-11 Values of the variables after the statement in Line 9 executes

After the statement in Line 10, `a++;`, executes, the variables are as shown in Figure 6-12.

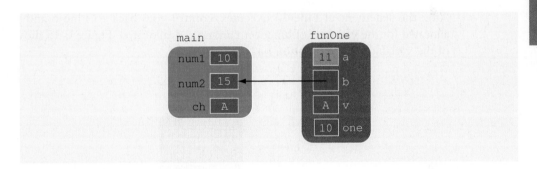

FIGURE 6-12 Values of the variables after the statement in Line 10 executes

After the statement in Line 11, `b = b * 2;`, executes, the variables are as shown in Figure 6-13. (Note that the variable `b` changed the value of `num2`.)

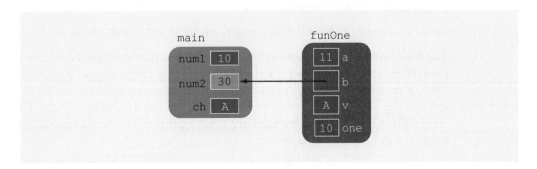

FIGURE 6-13 Values of the variables after the statement in Line 11 executes

After the statement in Line 12, v = 'B';, executes, the variables are as shown in Figure 6-14.

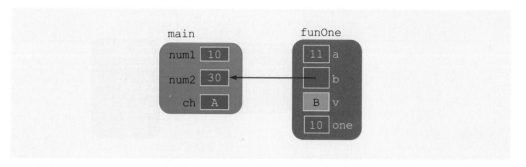

FIGURE 6-14 Values of the variables after the statement in Line 12 executes

The statement in Line 13 produces the following output:

```
Line 13: Inside funOne: a = 11, b = 30, v = B, and one = 10
```

After the statement in Line 13 executes, control goes back to Line 6 and the memory allocated for the variables of function funOne is deallocated. Figure 6-15 shows the values of the variables of the function main.

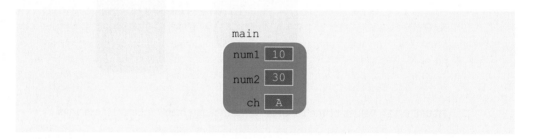

FIGURE 6-15 Values of the variables when control goes back to Line 6

Line 6 produces the following output:

```
Line 6: After funOne: num1 = 10, num2 = 30, and ch = A
```

The statement in Line 7 is a function call to the function funTwo. Now funTwo has three parameters: x, y, and w. Also, x and w are reference parameters, and y is a value parameter. Thus, x receives the address of its corresponding actual parameter, which is num2, and w receives the address of its corresponding actual parameter, which is ch. The variable y copies the value 25 into its memory cell. Figure 6-16 shows the values before the statement in Line 14 executes.

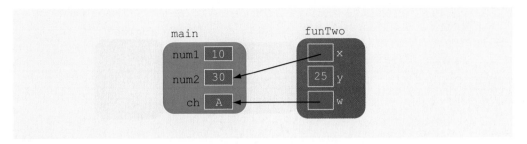

FIGURE 6-16 Values of the variables before the statement in Line 14 executes

After the statement in Line 14, **x++;**, executes, the variables are as shown in Figure 6-17. (Note that the variable **x** changed the value of num2.)

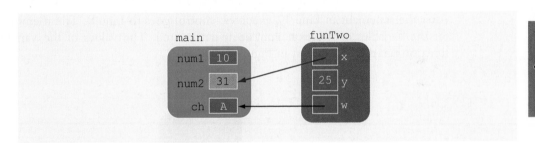

FIGURE 6-17 Values of the variables after the statement in Line 14 executes

After the statement in Line 15, **y = y * 2;**, executes, the variables are as shown in Figure 6-18.

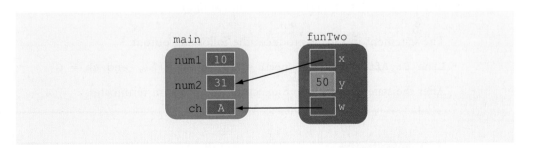

FIGURE 6-18 Values of the variables after the statement in Line 15 executes

After the statement in Line 16, **w = 'G';**, executes, the variables are as shown in Figure 6-19. (Note that the variable **w** changed the value of ch.)

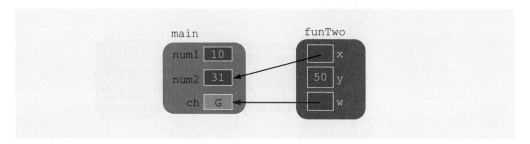

FIGURE 6-19 Values of the variables after the statement in Line 16 executes

Line 17 produces the following output:

```
Line 17: Inside funTwo: x = 31, y = 50, and w = G
```

After the statement in Line 17 executes, control goes to Line 8. The memory allocated for the variables of function `funTwo` is deallocated. The values of the variables of the function `main` are as shown in Figure 6-20.

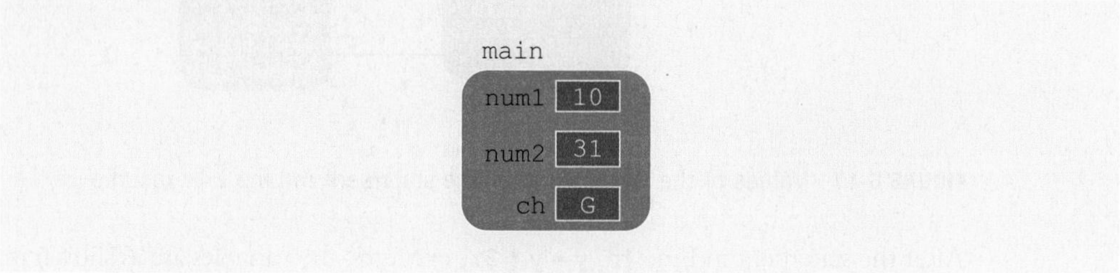

FIGURE 6-20 Values of the variables when control goes to Line 8

The statement in Line 8 produces the following output:

```
Line 8: After funTwo: num1 = 10, num2 = 31, and ch = G
```

After the statement in Line 8 executes, the program terminates.

EXAMPLE 6-14

This example also shows how reference parameters manipulate actual parameters.

```
//Example 6-14: Reference and value parameters.
//Program: Makes you think.

#include <iostream>

using namespace std;
```

```cpp
void addFirst(int& first, int& second);
void doubleFirst(int one, int two);
void squareFirst(int& ref, int val);

int main()
{
    int num = 5;

    cout << "Line 1: Inside main: num = " << num
        << endl;                                            //Line 1

    addFirst(num, num);                                     //Line 2
    cout << "Line 3: Inside main after addFirst:"
        << " num = " << num << endl;                        //Line 3

    doubleFirst(num, num);                                  //Line 4
    cout << "Line 5: Inside main after "
        << "doubleFirst: num = " << num << endl;            //Line 5

    squareFirst(num, num);                                  //Line 6
    cout << "Line 7: Inside main after "
        << "squareFirst: num = " << num << endl;            //Line 7

    return 0;
}

void addFirst(int& first, int& second)
{
    cout << "Line 8: Inside addFirst:  first = "
        << first << ", second = " << second << endl; //Line 8

    first = first + 2;                                      //Line 9

    cout << "Line 10: Inside addFirst:  first = "
        << first << ", second = " << second << endl; //Line 10

    second = second * 2;                                    //Line 11

    cout << "Line 12: Inside addFirst:  first = "
        << first << ", second = " << second << endl; //Line 12
}

void doubleFirst(int one, int two)
{
    cout << "Line 13: Inside doubleFirst:  one = "
        << one << ", two = " << two << endl;            //Line 13

    one = one * 2;                                          //Line 14

    cout << "Line 15: Inside doubleFirst:  one = "
        << one << ", two = " << two << endl;            //Line 15

    two = two + 2;                                          //Line 16
```

```
    cout << "Line 17: Inside doubleFirst:  one = "
        << one << ", two = " << two << endl;          //Line 17
}

void squareFirst(int& ref, int val)
{
    cout << "Line 18: Inside squareFirst: ref = "
        << ref << ", val = " << val << endl;          //Line 18

    ref = ref * ref;                                  //Line 19

    cout << "Line 20: Inside squareFirst: ref = "
        << ref << ", val = " << val << endl;          //Line 20

    val = val + 2;                                    //Line 21

    cout << "Line 22: Inside squareFirst: ref = "
        << ref << ", val = " << val << endl;          //Line 22
}
```

Sample Run:

```
Line 1: Inside main:  num = 5
Line 8: Inside addFirst:  first = 5, second = 5
Line 10: Inside addFirst:  first = 7, second = 7
Line 12: Inside addFirst:  first = 14, second = 14
Line 3: Inside main after addFirst:  num = 14
Line 13: Inside doubleFirst:  one = 14, two = 14
Line 15: Inside doubleFirst:  one = 28, two = 14
Line 17: Inside doubleFirst:  one = 28, two = 16
Line 5: Inside main after doubleFirst:  num = 14
Line 18: Inside squareFirst: ref = 14, val = 14
Line 20: Inside squareFirst: ref = 196, val = 14
Line 22: Inside squareFirst: ref = 196, val = 16
Line 7: Inside main after squareFirst:  num = 196
```

Both parameters of the function addFirst are reference parameters, and both parameters of the function doubleFirst are value parameters. The statement:

addFirst(num, num);

in the function main (Line 2) passes the reference of num to both formal parameters first and second of the function addFirst, because the corresponding actual parameters for both formal parameters are the same. That is, the variables first and second refer to the same memory location, which is num. Figure 6-21 illustrates this situation.

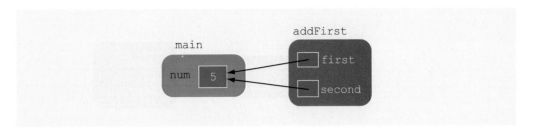

FIGURE 6-21 Parameters of the function `addFirst`

Any changes that `first` makes to its value immediately change the value of `second` and `num`. Similarly, any changes that `second` makes to its value immediately change `first` and `num`, because all three variables refer to the same memory location. (Note that `num` was initialized to 5.)

The formal parameters of the function `doubleFirst` are value parameters. So the statement:

```
doubleFirst(num, num);
```

in the function `main` (Line 4) copies the value of `num` into `one` and `two` because the corresponding actual parameters for both formal parameters are the same. Figure 6-22 illustrates this scenario.

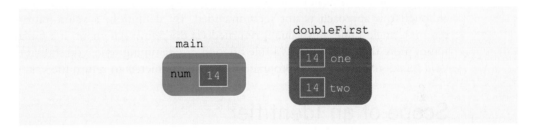

FIGURE 6-22 Parameters of the function `doubleFirst`

Because both `one` and `two` are value parameters, any changes that `one` makes to its value do not affect the values of `two` and `num`. Similarly, any changes that `two` makes to its value do not affect `one` and `num`. (Note that the value of `num` before the function `doubleFirst` executes is 14.)

The formal parameter `ref` of the function `squareFirst` is a reference parameter, and the formal parameter `val` is a value parameter. The variable `ref` receives the address of its corresponding actual parameter, which is `num`, and the variable `val` copies the value of its corresponding actual parameter, which is also `num`. Thus, both `num` and `ref` refer to the same memory location, which is `num`. Figure 6-23 illustrates this situation.

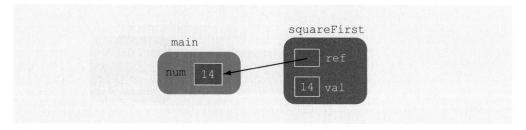

FIGURE 6-23 Parameters of the function `squareFirst`

Any changes that `ref` makes immediately change `num`. Any changes made by `val` do not affect `num`. (Note that the value of `num` before the function `squareFirst` executes is 14.)

We recommend that you walk through the program in Example 6-14. The output shows the order in which the statements execute.

Reference Parameters and Value-Returning Functions

Earlier in this chapter, in the discussion of value-returning functions, you learned how to use value parameters only. You can also use reference parameters in a value-returning function, although this approach is not recommended. By definition, a value-returning function returns a single value; this value is returned via the return statement. If a function needs to return more than one value, as a rule of good programming style, you should change it to a void function and use the appropriate reference parameters to return the values.

Scope of an Identifier

The previous sections presented several examples of programs with user-defined functions. Identifiers are declared in a function heading, within a block, or outside a block. A question naturally arises: Are you allowed to access any identifier anywhere in the program? The answer is no. You must follow certain rules to access an identifier. The **scope** of an identifier refers to where in the program an identifier is accessible (visible). Recall that an identifier is the name of something in C++, such as a variable or function name.

This section examines the scope of an identifier. First, we define the following two terms:

Local identifier: Identifiers declared within a function (or block).

Local identifiers are not accessible outside of the function (block).

Global identifier: Identifiers declared outside of every function definition.

Also, C++ does not allow the nesting of functions. That is, you cannot include the definition of one function in the body of another function.

In general, the following rules apply when an identifier is accessed:

1. Global identifiers (such as variables) are accessible by a function or a block if:

   a. The identifier is declared before the function definition (block),

   b. The function name is different than the identifier,

   c. All parameters of the function have names different than the name of the identifier, and

   d. All local identifiers (such as local variables) have names different than the name of the identifier.

2. **(Nested Block)** An identifier declared within a block is accessible:

   a. Only within the block from the point at which it is declared until the end of the block, and

   b. By those blocks that are nested within that block if the nested block does not have an identifier with the same name as that of the outside block (the block that encloses the nested block).

3. The scope of a function name is similar to the scope of an identifier declared outside any block. That is, the scope of a function name is the same as the scope of a global variable.

Before considering an example to explain these scope rules, first note the scope of the identifier declared in the `for` statement. C++ allows the programmer to declare a variable in the initialization statement of the `for` statement. For example, the following `for` statement:

```
for (int count = 1; count < 10; count++)
    cout << count << endl;
```

declares the variable `count` and initializes it to 1. The scope of the variable `count` is limited to only the body of the `for` loop.

 NOTE This scope rule for the variable declared in a `for` statement may not apply to Standard C++. In Standard C++, the scope of the variable declared in the `initialize` statement may extend from the point at which it is declared until the end of the block that immediately surrounds the `for` statement. (To be absolutely sure, check your compiler's documentation.)

The following C++ program helps illustrate the scope rules:

```
#include <iostream>

using namespace std;

const double RATE = 10.50;
int z;
double t;
```

```
void one(int x, char y);
void two(int a, int b, char x);
void three(int one, double y, int z);

int main()
{
    int num, first;
    double x, y, z;
    char name, last;
        .
        .
        .
    return 0;
}

void one(int x, char y)
{
        .
        .
        .
}

int w;

void two(int a, int b, char x)
{
    int count;
        .
        .
        .
}

void three(int one, double y, int z)
{
    char ch;
    int a;
        .
        .
        .
    //Block four
    {
        int x;
        char a;
            .
            .
    } //end Block four
        .
        .
        .
}
```

Table 6-2 summarizes the scope (visibility) of the identifiers.

TABLE 6-2 Scope (Visibility) of the Identifiers

Identifier	Visibility in `one`	Visibility in `two`	Visibility in `three`	Visibility in Block `four`	Visibility in `main`
`RATE` (before `main`)	Y	Y	Y	Y	Y
`z` (before `main`)	Y	Y	N	N	N
`t` (before `main`)	Y	Y	Y	Y	Y
`main`	Y	Y	Y	Y	Y
local variables of `main`	N	N	N	N	Y
`one` (function name)	Y	Y	N	N	Y
`x` (`one`'s formal parameter)	Y	N	N	N	N
`y` (`one`'s formal parameter)	Y	N	N	N	N
`w` (before function `two`)	N	Y	Y	Y	N
`two` (function name)	Y	Y	Y	Y	Y
`a` (`two`'s formal parameter)	N	Y	N	N	N
`b` (`two`'s formal parameter)	N	Y	N	N	N
`x` (`two`'s formal parameter)	N	Y	N	N	N
local variables of `two`	N	Y	N	N	N
`three` (function name)	Y	Y	Y	Y	Y
`one` (`three`'s formal parameter)	N	N	Y	Y	N
`y` (`three`'s formal parameter)	N	N	Y	Y	N
`z` (`three`'s formal parameter)	N	N	Y	Y	N
`ch` (`three`'s local variable)	N	N	Y	Y	N
`a` (`three`'s local variable)	N	N	Y	N	N
`x` (block `four`'s local variable)	N	N	N	Y	N
`a` (block `four`'s local variable)	N	N	N	Y	N

6

Note that function `three` cannot call function `one`, because function `three` has a formal parameter named `one`. Similarly, the block marked `four` in function `three` cannot use the `int` variable `a`, which is declared in function `three`, because block `four` has an identifier named `a`.

Before closing this section, let us note the following about global variables:

1. Chapter 2 stated that C++ does not automatically initialize variables. However, some compilers initialize global variables to their default values. For example, if a global variable is of type `int`, `char`, or `double`, it is initialized to zero.

2. In C++, `::` is called the **scope resolution operator**. By using the scope resolution operator, a global variable declared before the definition of a function (block) can be accessed by the function (or block) even if the function (or block) has an identifier with the same name as the variable. In the preceding program, by using the scope resolution operator, the function `main` can refer to the global variable `z` as `::z`. Similarly, suppose that a global variable `t` is declared before the definition of the function—say, `funExample`. Then, `funExample` can access the variable `t` using the scope resolution operator even if `funExample` has an identifier `t`. Using the scope resolution operator, `funExample` refers to the variable `t` as `::t`. Also, in the preceding program, using the scope resolution operator, function `three` can call function `one`.

3. C++ provides a way to access a global variable declared after the definition of a function. In this case, the function must not contain any identifier with the same name as the global variable. In the preceding program, the global variable `w` is declared after the definition of function `one`. The function `one` does not contain any identifier named `w`; therefore, `w` can be accessed by function `one` only if you declare `w` as an **external variable** inside one. To declare `w` as an external variable inside function `one`, the function `one` must contain the following statement:

```
extern int w;
```

In C++, `extern` is a reserved word. The word `extern` in the above statement announces that `w` is a global variable declared elsewhere. Thus, when function `one` is called, no memory for `w`, as declared inside one, is allocated. In C++, external declaration also has another use, but it is not discussed in this book.

Global Variables, Named Constants, and Side Effects

A C++ program can contain global variables and you might be tempted to make all of the variables in a program global variables so that you do not have to worry about what a function knows about which variable. Using global variables, however, has side effects. If more than one function uses the same global variable and something goes wrong, it is difficult to discover what went wrong and where. Problems caused by global variables in one area of a program might be misunderstood as problems caused in another area.

For example, consider the following program:

```cpp
//Global variable

#include <iostream>

using namespace std;

int t;

void funOne(int& a);

int main()
{
    t = 15;                                             //Line 1

    cout << "Line 2: In main: t = " << t << endl;       //Line 2

    funOne(t);                                          //Line 3

    cout << "Line 4: In main after funOne: "
         << " t = " << t << endl;                       //Line 4

    return 0;                                           //Line 5
}

void funOne(int& a)
{
    cout << "Line 6: In funOne: a = " << a
         << " and t = " << t << endl;                   //Line 6

    a = a + 12;                                         //Line 7
    cout << "Line 8: In funOne: a = " << a
         << " and t = " << t << endl;                   //Line 8

    t = t + 13;                                         //Line 9

    cout << "Line 10: In funOne: a = " << a
         << " and t = " << t << endl;                   //Line 10
}
```

This program has a variable t that is declared before the definition of any function. Because none of the functions has an identifier t, the variable t is accessible anywhere in the program. Also, the program consists of a void function with a reference parameter.

In Line 3, the function main calls the function funOne, and the actual parameter passed to funOne is t. So, a, the formal parameter of funOne, receives the address of t. Any changes that a makes to its value immediately change t. Because t can be directly accessed anywhere in the program, in Line 9, the function funOne changes the value of t by using t itself. Thus, you can manipulate the value of t by using either a reference parameter or t itself.

In the previous program, if the last value of t is incorrect, it would be difficult to determine what went wrong and in which part of the program. We strongly recommend that *you do not use global variables*; instead, use the appropriate parameters.

In the programs given in this book, we typically placed named constants before the function main, outside of every function definition. That is, the named constants we used are *global named constants*. Unlike global variables, global named constants have no side effects because their values cannot be changed during program execution. Moreover, placing a named constant in the beginning of the program can increase readability, even if it is used only in one function. If you need to later modify the program and change the value of a named constant, it will be easier to find if it is placed in the beginning of the program.

EXAMPLE 6-15 (MENU-DRIVEN PROGRAM)

The following is an example of a menu-driven program. When the program executes, it gives the user a list of choices to choose from. This program further illustrates how value and reference parameters work. It converts length from feet and inches to meters and centimeters and vice versa. The program contains three functions: showChoices, feetAndInchesToMetersAndCent, and metersAndCentTofeetAndInches. The function showChoices informs the user how to use the program. The user has the choice to run the program as long as the user wishes.

```
//Menu-driven program.

#include <iostream>

using namespace std;

const double CONVERSION = 2.54;
const int INCHES_IN_FOOT = 12;
const int CENTIMETERS_IN_METER = 100;

void showChoices();

void feetAndInchesToMetersAndCent(int f, int in,
                                  int& mt, int& ct);
void metersAndCentTofeetAndInches(int mt, int ct,
                                  int& f, int& in);

int main()
{
    int feet, inches;
    int meters, centimeters;
    int choice;
```

```cpp
    do
    {
        showChoices();
        cin >> choice;
        cout << endl;

        switch (choice)
        {
        case 1:
            cout << "Enter feet and inches: ";
            cin >> feet >> inches;
            cout << endl;
            feetAndInchesToMetersAndCent(feet, inches,
                                         meters, centimeters);
            cout << feet << " feet(foot), "
                 << inches << " inch(es) = "
                 << meters << " meter(s), "
                 << centimeters << " centimeter(s)." << endl;
            break;

        case 2:
            cout << "Enter meters and centimeters: ";
            cin >> meters >> centimeters;
            cout << endl;
            metersAndCentTofeetAndInches(meters, centimeters,
                                         feet, inches);
            cout << meters << " meter(s), "
                 << centimeters << " centimeter(s) = "
                 << feet << " feet(foot), "
                 << inches << " inch(es)."
                 << endl;
            break;

        case 99:
            break;

        default:
            cout << "Invalid input." << endl;
        }
    }
    while (choice != 99);

    return 0;
}

void showChoices()
{
    cout << "Enter--" << endl;
    cout << "1: To convert from feet and inches to meters "
         << "and centimeters." << endl;
    cout << "2: To convert from meters and centimeters to feet "
         << "and inches." << endl;
    cout << "99: To quit the program." << endl;
}
```

6

```
void feetAndInchesToMetersAndCent(int f, int in,
                                  int& mt, int& ct)
{
    int inches;

    inches = f * INCHES_IN_FOOT + in;
    ct = static_cast<int>(inches * CONVERSION);
    mt = ct / CENTIMETERS_IN_METER;
    ct = ct % CENTIMETERS_IN_METER;
}

void metersAndCentTofeetAndInches(int mt, int ct,
                                  int& f, int& in)
{
    int centimeters;

    centimeters = mt * CENTIMETERS_IN_METER + ct;
    in = static_cast<int>(centimeters / CONVERSION);
    f = in / INCHES_IN_FOOT;
    in = in % INCHES_IN_FOOT;
}
```

Sample Run: In this sample run, the user input is shaded.

```
Enter--
1: To convert from feet and inches to meters and centimeters.
2: To convert from meters and centimeters to feet and inches.
99: To quit the program.
2

Enter meters and centimeters: 4 25

4 meter(s), 25 centimeter(s) = 13 feet(foot), 11 inch(es).
Enter--
1: To convert from feet and inches to meters and centimeters.
2: To convert from meters and centimeters to feet and inches.
99: To quit the program.
1

Enter feet and inches: 15 8

15 feet(foot), 8 inch(es) = 4 meter(s), 77 centimeter(s).
Enter--
1: To convert from feet and inches to meters and centimeters.
2: To convert from meters and centimeters to feet and inches.
99: To quit the program.
99
```

The do...while loop in the function main continues to execute as long as the user has not entered 99, which allows the user to run the program as long as the user wishes. The preceding output is self-explanatory.

Static and Automatic Variables

The variables discussed so far have followed two simple rules:

1. Memory for global variables remains allocated as long as the program executes.

2. Memory for a variable declared within a block is allocated at block entry and deallocated at block exit. For example, memory for the formal parameters and local variables of a function is allocated when the function is called and deallocated when the function exits.

A variable for which memory is allocated at block entry and deallocated at block exit is called an **automatic variable**. A variable for which memory remains allocated as long as the program executes is called a **static variable**. Global variables are static variables, and by default, variables declared within a block are automatic variables. You can declare a static variable within a block by using the reserved word `static`. The syntax for declaring a static variable is:

```
static dataType identifier;
```

The statement:

```
static int x;
```

declares `x` to be a static variable of type `int`.

Static variables declared within a block are local to the block, and their scope is the same as that of any other local identifier of that block.

Most compilers initialize `static` variables to their default values. For example, `static int` variables are initialized to 0. However, it is a good practice to initialize `static` variables yourself, especially if the initial value is not the default value. In this case, `static` variables are initialized when they are declared. The statement:

```
static int x = 0;
```

declares `x` to be a static variable of type `int` and initializes `x` to 0.

6

EXAMPLE 6-16

The following program shows how static and automatic variables behave.

```cpp
//Program: Static and automatic variables

#include <iostream>

using namespace std;

void test();

int main()
{
    int count;
```

```
    for (count = 1; count <= 5; count++)
        test();

    return 0;
}

void test()
{
    static int x = 0;
    int y = 10;

    x = x + 2;
    y = y + 1;

    cout << "Inside test x = " << x << " and y = "
         << y << endl;
}
```

Sample Run:

```
Inside test x = 2 and y = 11
Inside test x = 4 and y = 11
Inside test x = 6 and y = 11
Inside test x = 8 and y = 11
Inside test x = 10 and y = 11
```

In the function test, x is a static variable initialized to 0, and y is an automatic variable initialized to 10. The function main calls the function test five times. Memory for the variable y is allocated every time the function test is called and deallocated when the function exits. Thus, every time the function test is called, it prints the same value for y. However, because x is a static variable, memory for x remains allocated as long as the program executes. The variable x is initialized once to 0. The subsequent calls of the function test use the current value of x.

Because memory for static variables remains allocated between function calls, static variables allow you to use the value of a variable from one function call to another function call. Even though you can use global variables if you want to use certain values from one function call to another, the local scope of a static variable prevents other functions from manipulating its value.

Debugging: Using Drivers and Stubs

In this and the previous chapters, you learned how to write functions to divide a problem into subproblems, solve each subproblem, and then combine the functions to form the complete program to get a solution of the problem. A program may contain a number of functions. In a complex program, usually, when a function is written, it is tested and debugged alone. You can write a separate program to test the function. The program that tests a function is called a **driver** program. For example, the program in Example 6-15 contains functions to convert the length from feet and inches to meters and centimeters and vice versa. Before writing the complete program, you could write separate driver programs to make sure that each function is working properly.

Sometimes, the results calculated by one function are needed in another function. In that case, the function that depends on another function cannot be tested alone. For example, consider the following program that determines the time to fill a swimming pool.

```cpp
#include <iostream>
#include <iomanip>

using namespace std;

const double GALLONS_IN_A_CUBIC_FOOT = 7.48;

double poolCapacity(double len, double wid, double dep);
void poolFillTime(double len, double wid, double dep,
                  double fRate, int& fTime);
void print(int fTime);

int main()
{
    double length, width, depth;
    double fillRate;
    int fillTime;

    cout << fixed << showpoint << setprecision(2);

    cout << "Enter the length, width, and the depth of the "
         << "pool (in feet): ";
    cin >> length >> width >> depth;
    cout << endl;

    cout << "Enter the rate of the water (in gallons per minute): ";
    cin >> fillRate;
    cout << endl;

    poolFillTime(length, width, depth, fillRate, fillTime);
    print(fillTime);

    return 0;
}

double poolCapacity(double len, double wid, double dep)
{
    double volume;
    double poolWaterCapacity;

    volume = len * wid * dep;
    poolWaterCapacity = volume * GALLONS_IN_A_CUBIC_FOOT;

    return poolWaterCapacity;
}
```

6

```
void poolFillTime(double len, double wid, double dep,
                  double fRate, int& fTime)
{
    double poolWaterCapacity;

    poolWaterCapacity = poolCapacity(len, wid, dep);
    fTime = static_cast<int> (poolWaterCapacity / fRate + 0.5);
}

void print(int fTime)
{
    cout << "The time to fill the pool is approximately: "
         << fTime / 60 << " hour(s) and " << fTime % 60
         << " minute(s)." << endl;
}
```

Sample Run: In this sample run, the user input is shaded.

Enter the length, width, and the depth of the pool (in feet): 30 15 10

Enter the rate of the water, (in gallons per minute): 100

The time to fill the pool is approximately: 5 hour(s) and 37 minute(s).

As you can see, the program contains the function poolCapacity to find the amount of water needed to fill the pool, the function poolFillTime to find the time to fill the pool, and some other functions. Now, to calculate the time to fill the pool, you must know the amount of the water needed and the rate at which the water is released in the pool. Because the results of the function poolCapacity are needed in the function poolFillTime, the function poolFillTime cannot be tested alone. Does this mean that we must write the functions in a specific order? Not necessarily, especially when different people are working on different parts of the program. In situations such as these, we use function stubs. A function **stub** is a function that is not fully coded. For a void function, a function stub might consist of only a function header and a set of empty braces, { } , and for a value-returning function it might contain only a return statement with a plausible return value. For example, the function stub for the function poolCapacity can be:

```
double poolCapacity(double len, double wid, double dep)
{
    return 1000.00;
}
```

This allows the function poolCapacity to be called while the program is being coded. Ultimately, the stub for function poolCapacity is replaced with a function that properly calculates the amount of water needed to fill the pool based on the values of the parameters. In the meantime, the function stub allows work to continue on other parts of the program that call the function poolCapacity.

Before we look at some programming examples, another concept about functions is worth mentioning: function overloading.

Function Overloading: An Introduction

In a C++ program, several functions can have the same name. This is called **function overloading**, or **overloading a function name**. Before we state the rules to overloading a function, let us define the following:

Two functions are said to have **different formal parameter lists** if both functions have:

- A different number of formal parameters or
- If the number of formal parameters is the same, then the data type of the formal parameters, in the order you list them, must differ in at least one position.

For example, consider the following function headings:

```
void functionOne(int x)
void functionTwo(int x, double y)
void functionThree(double y, int x)
int functionFour(char ch, int x, double y)
int functionFive(char ch, int x, string name)
```

These functions all have different formal parameter lists.

Now consider the following function headings:

```
void functionSix(int x, double y, char ch)
void functionSeven(int one, double u, char firstCh)
```

The functions `functionSix` and `functionSeven` both have three formal parameters, and the data type of the corresponding parameters is the same. Therefore, these functions have the same formal parameter list.

To overload a function name, any two definitions of the function must have different formal parameter lists.

Function overloading: Creating several functions with the same name.

The **signature** of a function consists of the function name and its formal parameter list. Two functions have different signatures if they have either different names or different formal parameter lists. (Note that the signature of a function does not include the return type of the function.)

If a function's name is overloaded, then all of the functions in the set have the same name. Therefore, all of the functions in the set have different signatures if they have different formal parameter lists. Thus, the following function headings correctly overload the function `functionXYZ`:

```
void functionXYZ()
void functionXYZ(int x, double y)
void functionXYZ(double one, int y)
void functionXYZ(int x, double y, char ch)
```

Consider the following function headings to overload the function `functionABC`:

```
void functionABC(int x, double y)
int functionABC(int x, double y)
```

Both of these function headings have the same name and same formal parameter list. Therefore, these function headings to overload the function `functionABC` are incorrect. In this case, the compiler will generate a syntax error. (Notice that the return types of these function headings are different.)

If a function is overloaded, then in a call to that function, the signature—that is, the formal parameter list of the function—determines which function to execute.

NOTE   Some authors define the signature of a function as the formal parameter list, and some consider the entire heading of the function as its signature. However, in this book, the signature of a function consists of the function's heading and its formal parameter list. If the function's names are different, then, of course, the compiler would have no problem in identifying which function is called, and it will correctly translate the code. However, if a function's name is overloaded, then, as noted, the function's formal parameter list determines which function's body executes.

Suppose you need to write a function that determines the larger of two items. Both items can be integers, floating-point numbers, characters, or strings. You could write several functions as follows:

```
int largerInt(int x, int y);
char largerChar(char first, char second);
double largerDouble(double u, double v);
string largerString(string first, string second);
```

The function `largerInt` determines the larger of two integers; the function `largerChar` determines the larger of two characters, and so on. All of these functions perform similar operations. Instead of giving different names to these functions, you can use the same name—say, `larger`—for each function; that is, you can overload the function `larger`. Thus, you can write the previous function prototypes simply as:

```
int larger(int x, int y);
char larger(char first, char second);
double larger(double u, double v);
string larger(string first, string second);
```

If the call is `larger(5, 3)`, for example, the first function is executed. If the call is `larger('A', '9')`, the second function is executed, and so on.

Function overloading is used when you have the same action for different sets of data. Of course, for function overloading to work, you must give the definition of each function.

Functions with Default Parameters

NOTE   This section is not needed until Chapter 10.

This section discusses functions with default parameters. Recall that when a function is called, the number of actual and formal parameters must be the same. C++ relaxes this condition for functions with default parameters. You specify the value of a default parameter when the function name appears for the first time, such as in the prototype. In general, the following rules apply for functions with default parameters:

- If you do not specify the value of a default parameter, the default value is used for that parameter.
- All of the default parameters must be the far-right parameters of the function.
- Suppose a function has more than one default parameter. In a function call, if a value to a default parameter is not specified, then you must omit all of the arguments to its right.
- Default values can be constants, global variables, or function calls.
- The caller has the option of specifying a value other than the default for any default parameter.
- You cannot assign a constant value as a default value to a reference parameter.

Consider the following function prototype:

```
void funcExp(int x, int y, double t, char z = 'A', int u = 67,
             char v = 'G', double w = 78.34);
```

The function `funcExp` has seven parameters. The parameters z, u, v, and w are default parameters. If no values are specified for z, u, v, and w in a call to the function `funcExp`, their default values are used.

Suppose you have the following statements:

```
int a, b;
char ch;
double d;
```

The following function calls are legal:

1. `funcExp(a, b, d);`
2. `funcExp(a, 15, 34.6, 'B', 87, ch);`
3. `funcExp(b, a, 14.56, 'D');`

In statement 1, the default values of z, u, v, and w are used. In statement 2, the default value of z is replaced by `'B'`, the default value of u is replaced by 87, the default value of v is replaced by the value of ch, and the default value of w is used. In statement 3, the default value of z is replaced by `'D'`, and the default values of u, v, and w are used.

The following function calls are illegal:

1. `funcExp(a, 15, 34.6, 46.7);`
2. `funcExp(b, 25, 48.76, 'D', 4567, 78.34);`

In statement 1, because the value of z is omitted, all other default values must be omitted. In statement 2, because the value of v is omitted, the value of w should be omitted, too.

The following are illegal function prototypes with default parameters:

1. `void funcOne(int x, double z = 23.45, char ch, int u = 45);`
2. `int funcTwo(int length = 1, int width, int height = 1);`
3. `void funcThree(int x, int& y = 16, double z = 34);`

In statement 1, because the second parameter z is a default parameter, all other parameters after z must be default parameters. In statement 2, because the first parameter is a default parameter, all parameters must be the default parameters. In statement 3, a constant value cannot be assigned to y because y is a reference parameter.

Example 6-17 further illustrates functions with default parameters.

EXAMPLE 6-17

```cpp
#include <iostream>
#include <iomanip>

using namespace std;

int volume(int l = 1, int w = 1, int h = 1);
void funcOne(int& x, double y = 12.34, char z = 'B');

int main()
{
    int a = 23;
    double b = 48.78;
    char ch = 'M';

    cout << fixed << showpoint;
    cout << setprecision(2);

    cout << "Line 1: a = " << a << ", b = "
         << b << ", ch = " << ch << endl;        //Line 1
    cout << "Line 2: Volume = " << volume()
         << endl;                                 //Line 2
    cout << "Line 3: Volume = " << volume(5, 4)
         << endl;                                 //Line 3
    cout << "Line 4: Volume = " << volume(34)
         << endl;                                 //Line 4
    cout << "Line 5: Volume = "
         << volume(6, 4, 5) << endl;              //Line 5

    funcOne(a);                                   //Line 6
    funcOne(a, 42.68);                            //Line 7
    funcOne(a, 34.65, 'Q');                       //Line 8

    cout << "Line 9: a = " << a << ", b = "
         << b << ", ch = " << ch << endl;         //Line 9

    return 0;
}
```

```
int volume(int l, int w, int h)
{
    return l * w * h;                              //Line 10
}

void funcOne(int& x, double y, char z)
{
    x = 2 * x;                                     //Line 11
    cout << "Line 12: x = " << x << ", y = "
         << y << ", z = " << z << endl;            //Line 12
}
```

Sample Run:

```
Line 1: a = 23, b = 48.78, ch = M
Line 2: Volume = 1
Line 3: Volume = 20
Line 4: Volume = 34
Line 5: Volume = 120
Line 12: x = 46, y = 12.34, z = B
Line 12: x = 92, y = 42.68, z = B
Line 12: x = 184, y = 34.65, z = Q
Line 9: a = 184, b = 48.78, ch = M
```

> **NOTE** In programs in this book, and as is recommended, the definition of the function `main` is placed before the definition of any user-defined functions. You must, therefore, specify the default value for a parameter in the function prototype and in the function prototype only, *not* in the function definition because this must occur at the first appearance of the function name.

PROGRAMMING EXAMPLE: Classify Numbers

In this example, we use functions to rewrite the program that determines the number of odds and evens from a given list of integers. This program was first written in Chapter 5.

The main algorithm remains the same:

1. Initialize the variables, zeros, odds, and evens to 0.
2. Read a number.
3. If the number is even, increment the even count, and if the number is also zero, increment the zero count; otherwise, increment the odd count.
4. Repeat Steps 2 and 3 for each number in the list.

The main parts of the program are: initialize the variables, read and classify the numbers, and then output the results. To simplify the function main and further illustrate parameter passing, the program includes:

- A function `initialize` to initialize the variables, such as `zeros`, `odds`, and `evens`.
- A function `getNumber` to get the number.
- A function `classifyNumber` to determine whether the number is odd or even (and whether it is also zero). This function also increments the appropriate count.
- A function `printResults` to print the results.

Let us now describe each of these functions.

initialize The function `initialize` initializes variables to their initial values. The variables that we need to initialize are `zeros`, `odds`, and `evens`. As before, their initial values are all zero. Clearly, this function has three parameters. Because the values of the formal parameters initializing these variables must be passed outside of the function, these formal parameters must be reference parameters. Essentially, this function is:

```
void initialize(int& zeroCount, int& oddCount, int& evenCount)
{
    zeroCount = 0;
    oddCount = 0;
    evenCount = 0;
}
```

getNumber The function `getNumber` reads a number and then passes this number to the function `main`. Because you need to pass only one number, this function has only one parameter. The formal parameter of this (void) function must be a reference parameter because the number read is passed outside of the function. Essentially, this function is:

```
void getNumber(int& num)
{
    cin >> num;
}
```

You can also write the function `getNumber` as a value-returning function. See the note at the end of this programming example.

classifyNumber The function `classifyNumber` determines whether the number is odd or even, and if the number is even, it also checks whether the number is zero. It also updates the values of some of the variables, `zeros`, `odds`, and `evens`. This function needs to know the number to be analyzed; therefore, the number must be passed as a parameter. Because this function also increments the appropriate count, the variables (that is, `zeros`, `odds`, and `evens` declared in `main`) holding the counts must be passed as parameters to this function. Thus, this function has four parameters.

Because the number will only be analyzed, you need to pass only its value. Thus, the formal parameter corresponding to this variable is a value parameter. After analyzing the number, this function increments the values of some of the variables, `zeros`, `odds`, and `evens`. Therefore, the formal parameters corresponding to these variables must be reference parameters. The algorithm to analyze the number and increment the appropriate count is the same as before. The definition of this function is:

```cpp
void classifyNumber(int num, int& zeroCount, int& oddCount,
                    int& evenCount)
{
    switch (num % 2)
    {
    case 0:
        evenCount++;
        if (num == 0)
            zeroCount++;
        break;
    case 1:
    case -1:
        oddCount++;
    } //end switch
} //end classifyNumber
```

printResults   The function printResults prints the final results. To print the results (that is, the number of zeros, odds, and evens), this function must have access to the values of the variables, zeros, odds, and evens declared in the function main. Therefore, this function has three parameters. Because this function doesn't change the values of the variables but only prints them, the formal parameters are value parameters. The definition of this function is:

```cpp
void printResults(int zeroCount, int oddCount, int evenCount)
{
    cout << "There are " << evenCount << " evens, "
         << "which includes " << zeroCount << " zeros"
         << endl;

    cout << "The number of odd numbers is: " << oddCount
         << endl;
} //end printResults
```

We now give the main algorithm and show how the function main calls these functions.

MAIN
ALGORITHM

1. Call the function initialize to initialize the variables.

2. Prompt the user to enter 20 numbers.

3. For each number in the list:

    a. Call the function getNumber to read a number.

    b. Output the number.

    c. Call the function classifyNumber to classify the number and increment the appropriate count.

4. Call the function printResults to print the final results.

6

COMPLETE PROGRAM LISTING

```cpp
//************************************************************
// Author: D.S. Malik
//
// Program: Classify Numbers
// This program reads 20 numbers and outputs the number of
// zeros, odd, and even numbers.
//************************************************************

#include <iostream>
#include <iomanip>

using namespace std;

const int N = 20;

    //Function prototypes
void initialize(int& zeroCount, int& oddCount, int& evenCount);
void getNumber(int& num);
void classifyNumber(int num, int& zeroCount, int& oddCount,
                    int& evenCount);
void printResults(int zeroCount, int oddCount, int evenCount);

int main()
{
        //Variable declaration
    int counter; //loop control variable
    int number;  //variable to store the new number
    int zeros;   //variable to store the number of zeros
    int odds;    //variable to store the number of odd integers
    int evens;   //variable to store the number of even integers

    initialize(zeros, odds, evens);                      //Step 1

    cout << "Please enter " << N << " integers."
        << endl;                                         //Step 2
    cout << "The numbers you entered are: "
        << endl;

    for (counter = 1; counter <= N; counter++)           //Step 3
    {
        getNumber(number);                               //Step 3a
        cout << number << " ";                           //Step 3b
        classifyNumber(number, zeros, odds, evens);      //Step 3c
    }  // end for loop

    cout << endl;
```

```cpp
        printResults(zeros, odds, evens);              //Step 4

        return 0;
}

void initialize(int& zeroCount, int& oddCount, int& evenCount)
{
    zeroCount = 0;
    oddCount = 0;
    evenCount = 0;
}

void getNumber(int& num)
{
    cin >> num;
}

void classifyNumber(int num, int& zeroCount, int& oddCount,
                    int& evenCount)
{
    switch (num % 2)
    {
    case 0:
        evenCount++;
        if (num == 0)
            zeroCount++;
        break;
    case 1:
    case -1:
        oddCount++;
    } //end switch
} //end classifyNumber

void printResults(int zeroCount, int oddCount, int evenCount)
{
    cout << "There are " << evenCount << " evens, "
         << "which includes " << zeroCount << " zeros"
         << endl;

    cout << "The number of odd numbers is: " << oddCount
         << endl;
} //end printResults
```

Sample Run: In this sample run, the user input is shaded.

```
Please enter 20 integers.
The numbers you entered are:
0 0 12 23 45 7 -2 -8 -3 -9 4 0 1 0 -7 23 -24 0 0 12
0 0 12 23 45 7 -2 -8 -3 -9 4 0 1 0 -7 23 -24 0 0 12
There are 12 evens, which includes 6 zeros
The number of odd numbers is: 8
```

6

NOTE In the previous program, because the data is assumed to be input from the standard input device (the keyboard) and the function `getNumber` returns only one value, you can also write the function `getNumber` as a value-returning function. If written as a value-returning function, the definition of the function `getNumber` is:

```
int getNumber()
{
    int num;

    cin >> num;

    return num;
}
```

In this case, the statement (function call):

```
getNumber(number);
```

in the function `main` should be replaced by the statement:

```
number = getNumber();
```

Of course, you also need to change the function prototype.

PROGRAMMING EXAMPLE: Data Comparison

Watch the Video

This programming example illustrates:

- How to read data from more than one file in the same program.
- How to send output to a file.
- How to generate bar graphs.
- With the help of functions and parameter passing, how to use the same program segment on different (but similar) sets of data.
- How to use structured design to solve a problem and how to perform parameter passing.

This program is broken into two parts. First, you learn how to read data from more than one file. Second, you learn how to generate bar graphs.

Two groups of students at a local university are enrolled in certain special courses during the summer semester. The courses are offered for the first time and are taught by different teachers. At the end of the semester, both groups are given the same tests for the same courses, and their scores are recorded in separate files. The data in each file is in the following form:

```
courseNo   score1, score2, ..., scoreN -999
courseNo   score1, score2, ..., scoreM -999
  .
  .
  .
```

Let us write a program that finds the average course score for each course for each group. The output is of the following form:

```
Course No    Group No    Course Average
   CSC           1            83.71
                 2            80.82

   ENG           1            82.00
                 2            78.20

    .
    .
    .
```

```
Avg for group 1: 82.04
Avg for group 2: 82.01
```

Input   Because the data for the two groups are recorded in separate files, the input data appears in two separate files.

Output   As shown above.

PROBLEM
ANALYSIS
AND
ALGORITHM
DESIGN

Reading input data from both files is straightforward. Suppose the data is stored in the file group1.txt for group 1 and file group2.txt for group 2. After processing the data for one group, we can process the data for the second group for the same course and continue until we run out of data. Processing data for each course is similar and is a two-step process:

   1. a.   Sum the scores for the course.

       b.   Count the number of students in the course.

       c.   Divide the total score by the number of students to find the course average.

   2. Output the results.

We are comparing only the averages of the corresponding courses in each group, and the data in each file is ordered according to course ID. To ensure that only the averages of the corresponding courses are compared, we compare the course IDs for each group. If the corresponding course IDs are not the same, we output an error message and terminate the program.

This discussion suggests that we should write a function, calculateAverage, to find the course average. We should also write another function, printResult, to output the data in the form given. By passing the appropriate parameters, we can use the same functions, calculateAverage and printResult, to process each course's data for both groups. (In the second part of the program, we modify the function printResult.)

6

The preceding discussion translates into the following algorithm:

1. Initialize the variables.
2. Get the course IDs for group 1 and group 2.
3. If the course IDs are different, print an error message and exit the program.
4. Calculate the course averages for group 1 and group 2.
5. Print the results in the form given above.
6. Repeat Steps 2 through 5 for each course.
7. Print the final results.

Variables (Function main) The preceding discussion suggests that the program needs the following variables for data manipulation in the function `main`:

```
string courseId1;       //course ID for group 1
string courseId2;       //course ID for group 2
int numberOfCourses;
double avg1;            //average for a course in group 1
double avg2;            //average for a course in group 2
double avgGroup1;       //average group 1
double avgGroup2;       //average group 2
ifstream group1;        //input stream variable for group 1
ifstream group2;        //input stream variable for group 2

ofstream outfile;       //output stream variable
```

Next, we discuss the functions `calculateAverage` and `printResult`. Then, we will put the function `main` together.

calculate Average This function calculates the average for a course. Because the input is stored in a file and the input file is opened in the function `main`, we must pass the `ifstream` variable associated with the input file to this function. Furthermore, after calculating the course average, this function must pass the course average to the function `main`. Therefore, this function has two parameters, and both parameters must be reference parameters.

To find the course average, we must first find the sum of all scores for the course and the number of students who took the course and then divide the sum by the number of students. Thus, we need a variable to find the sum of the scores, a variable to count the number of students, and a variable to read and store a score. Of course, we must initialize the variable to find the sum and the variable to count the number of students to zero.

Local Variables (Function calculate Average) In the previous discussion of data manipulation, we identified three variables for the function `calculateAverage`:

```
double totalScore = 0.0;
int numberOfStudents = 0;
int score;
```

The above discussion translates into the following algorithm for the function calculateAverage:

1. Declare and initialize variables.
2. Get the (next) course score, score.
3. while the score is not -999
   a. Update totalScore by adding the course score.
   b. Increment numberOfStudents by 1.
   c. Get the (next) course score, score.
4. courseAvg = totalScore / numberOfStudents;

We are now ready to write the definition of the function calculateAverage.

```
void calculateAverage(ifstream& inp, double& courseAvg)
{
    double totalScore = 0.0;
    int numberOfStudents = 0;
    int score;

    inp >> score;
    while (score != -999)
    {
        totalScore = totalScore + score;
        numberOfStudents++;
        inp >> score;
    } //end while

    courseAvg = totalScore / numberOfStudents;
} //end calculate Average
```

printResult The function printResult prints the group's course ID, group number, and course average. The output is stored in a file. So we must pass four parameters to this function: the ofstream variable associated with the output file, the group number, the course ID, and the course average for the group. The ofstream variable must be passed by reference. Because the function uses only the values of the other variables, the remaining three parameters should be value parameters. Also, from the output, it is clear that we print the course ID only before the group number.

1. In pseudocode, the algorithm is:

```
if (group number == 1)
    print course ID
else
    print a blank

print group number and course average
```

The definition of the function `printResult` follows:

```
void printResult(ofstream& outp, string courseID, int groupNo,
                 double avg)
{
    if (groupNo == 1)
        outp << "  " << courseID << "    ";
    else
        outp << "            ";

    outp << setw(8) << groupNo << setw(17) << avg << endl;
} //end printResult
```

Now that we have designed and defined the functions `calculateAverage` and `printResult`, we can describe the algorithm for the function `main`. Before outlining the algorithm, however, we note the following: It is quite possible that in both input files, the data is ordered according to the course IDs, but one file might have fewer courses than the other. We do not discover this error until after we have processed both files and discovered that one file has unprocessed data. Make sure to check for this error before printing the final answer—that is, the averages for group 1 and group 2.

MAIN
ALGORITHM:
Function `main`

1. Declare the variables (local declaration).
2. Open the input files.
3. Print a message if you are unable to open a file and terminate the program.
4. Open the output file.
5. To output floating-point numbers in a fixed decimal format with the decimal point and trailing zeros, set the manipulators `fixed` and `showpoint`. Also, to output floating-point numbers to two decimal places, set the precision to two decimal places.
6. Initialize the course average for group 1 to `0.0`.
7. Initialize the course average for group 2 to `0.0`.
8. Initialize the number of courses to `0`.
9. Print the heading.
10. Get the course ID, `courseId1`, for group 1.
11. Get the course ID, `courseId2`, for group 2.
12. For each course in group 1 and group 2,

    a. `if (courseId1 != courseId2)`
       `{`
           `cout << "Data error: Course IDs do not match.\n";`
           `return 1;`
       `}`

b. `else`
   `{`

      i. Calculate the course average for group 1 (call the function `calculateAverage` and pass the appropriate parameters).

      ii. Calculate the course average for group 2 (call the function `calculateAverage` and pass the appropriate parameters).

      iii. Print the results for group 1 (call the function `printResult` and pass the appropriate parameters).

      iv. Print the results for group 2 (call the function `printResult` and pass the appropriate parameters).

      v. Update the average for group 1.

      vi. Update the average for group 2.

      vii. Increment the number of courses.

   `}`

c. Get the course ID, `courseId1`, for group 1.

d. Get the course ID, `courseId2`, for group 2.

13. a. if not_end_of_file on group 1 and end_of_file on group 2
print "Ran out of data for group 2 before group 1"

   b. else if end_of_file on group 1 and not_end_of_file on group 2
print "Ran out of data for group 1 before group 2"

   c. else print the average of group 1 and group 2.

14. Close the input and output files.

COMPLETE PROGRAM LISTING

```
//***********************************************************
// Author: D.S. Malik
//
// Program: Comparison of Class Averages
// This program computes and compares the class averages of
// two groups of students.
//***********************************************************

#include <iostream>
#include <iomanip>
#include <fstream>
#include <string>
using namespace std;
```

```cpp
        //Function prototypes
void calculateAverage(ifstream& inp, double& courseAvg);
void printResult(ofstream& outp, string courseId,
                 int groupNo, double avg);

int main()
{
        //Step 1
    string courseId1;      //course ID for group 1
    string courseId2;      //course ID for group 2
    int numberOfCourses;
    double avg1;           //average for a course in group 1
    double avg2;           //average for a course in group 2
    double avgGroup1;      //average group 1
    double avgGroup2;      //average group 2
    ifstream group1;       //input stream variable for group 1
    ifstream group2;       //input stream variable for group 2
    ofstream outfile;      //output stream variable

    group1.open("group1.txt");                        //Step 2
    group2.open("group2.txt");                        //Step 2

    if (!group1 || !group2)                           //Step 3
    {
        cout << "Unable to open files." << endl;
        cout << "Program terminates." << endl;
        return 1;
    }

    outfile.open("student.out");                      //Step 4
    outfile << fixed << showpoint;                     //Step 5
    outfile << setprecision(2);                        //Step 5

    avgGroup1 = 0.0;                                   //Step 6
    avgGroup2 = 0.0;                                   //Step 7

    numberOfCourses = 0;                               //Step 8

    outfile << "Course No     Group No     "
            << "Course Average" << endl;               //Step 9

    group1 >> courseId1;                               //Step 10
    group2 >> courseId2;                               //Step 11
    while (group1 && group2)                           //Step 12
    {
        if (courseId1 != courseId2)                    //Step 12a
        {
            cout << "Data error: Course IDs "
                 << "do not match." << endl;
```

```
                    cout << "Program terminates." << endl;
                    return 1;
                }
                else                                    //Step 12b
                {
                    calculateAverage(group1, avg1);      //Step 12b.i
                    calculateAverage(group2, avg2);      //Step 12b.ii
                    printResult(outfile, courseId1,
                                1, avg1);                //Step 12b.iii
                    printResult(outfile, courseId2,
                                2, avg2);                //Step 12b.iv
                    avgGroup1 = avgGroup1 + avg1;         //Step 12b.v
                    avgGroup2 = avgGroup2 + avg2;         //Step 12b.vi
                    outfile << endl;
                    numberOfCourses++;                   //Step 12b.vii
                }

            group1 >> courseId1;                         //Step 12c
            group2 >> courseId2;                         //Step 12d
        } //end while

        if (group1 && !group2)                           //Step 13a
            cout << "Ran out of data for group 2 "
                 << "before group 1." << endl;
        else if (!group1 && group2)                      //Step 13b
            cout << "Ran out of data for group 1 "
                 << "before group 2." << endl;
        else                                             //Step 13c
        {
            outfile << "Avg for group 1: "
                    << avgGroup1 / numberOfCourses
                    << endl;
            outfile << "Avg for group 2: "
                    << avgGroup2 / numberOfCourses
                    << endl;
        }

        group1.close();                                  //Step 14
        group2.close();                                  //Step 14
        outfile.close();                                 //Step 14

        return 0;
    }

    void calculateAverage(ifstream& inp, double& courseAvg)
    {
        double totalScore = 0.0;
        int numberOfStudents = 0;
        int score;
```

6

```
        inp >> score;
        while (score != -999)
        {
            totalScore = totalScore + score;
            numberOfStudents++;
            inp >> score;
        } //end while

        courseAvg = totalScore / numberOfStudents;
} //end calculate Average

void printResult(ofstream& outp, string courseID, int groupNo,
                 double avg)
{
    if (groupNo == 1)
        outp << "  " << courseID << "   ";
    else
        outp << "          ";
    outp << setw(8) << groupNo << setw(17) << avg << endl;
} //end printResult
```

Sample Run:

```
Course No    Group No    Course Average
  CSC           1            83.71
                2            80.82

  ENG           1            82.00
                2            78.20

  HIS           1            77.69
                2            84.15

  MTH           1            83.57
                2            84.29

  PHY           1            83.22
                2            82.60

Avg for group 1: 82.04
Avg for group 2: 82.01
```

Input Data Group 1

```
CSC 80 100 70 80 72 90 89 100 83 70 90 73 85 90 -999
ENG 80 90 80 94 90 74 78 63 83 80 90 -999
HIS 90 70 80 70 90 50 89 83 90 68 90 60 80 -999
MTH 74 80 75 89 90 73 90 82 74 90 84 100 90 79 -999
PHY 100 83 93 80 63 78 88 89 75 -999
```

Input Data Group 2

```
CSC 90 75 90 75 80 89 100 60 80 70 80 -999
ENG 80 80 70 68 70 78 80 90 90 76 -999
HIS 100 80 80 70 90 76 88 90 90 75 90 85 80 -999
MTH 80 85 85 92 90 90 74 90 83 65 72 90 84 100 -999
PHY 90 93 73 85 68 75 67 100 87 88 -999
```

BAR
GRAPH

In the business world, company executives often like to see results in some visual form, such as bar graphs. Many currently available software packages can analyze data in several forms and then display the results in a visual form, such as bar graphs or pie charts. The second part of this program aims to display the results found earlier in the form of bar graphs, as shown below:

```
Course         Course Average
   ID    0   10   20   30   40   50   60   70   80   90   100
         |....|....|....|....|....|....|....|....|....|....|....|
  CSC    *****************************************
         #######################################
  ENG    *****************************************
         #######################################
    .
    .
    .

Group 1 -- ****
Group 2 -- ####

Avg for group 1: 82.04
Avg for group 2: 82.01
```

Each symbol (* or #) in the bar graph represents two points. If a course average is less than 2, no symbol is printed.

Because the output is in the form of a bar graph, we need to modify the function `printResult`.

Print Bars

The function `printResult` prints the course ID and the bar graph representing the average for a course. The output is stored in a file. So we must pass four parameters to this function: the `ofstream` variable associated with the output file, the group number (to print * or #), the course ID, and the course average for the department. To print the bar graph, we can use a loop to print a symbol for each two points. If the average is `78.45`, for example, we must print 39 symbols to represent this average. To find the number of symbols to print, we can use integer division as follows:

```
numberOfSymbols = static_cast<int>(average) / 2;
```

For example, `static_cast<int>(78.45) / 2 = 78 / 2 = 39`.

Following this discussion, the definition of the function `printResult` is:

6

```
void printResult(ofstream& outp, string courseID,
                 int groupNo, double avg)
{
    int noOfSymbols;
    int count;

    if (groupNo == 1)
        outp << setw(4) << courseID << "     ";
    else
        outp << "          ";

    noOfSymbols = static_cast<int>(avg)/2;

    if (groupNo == 1)
        for (count = 1; count <= noOfSymbols; count++)
            outp << '*';
    else
        for (count = 1; count <= noOfSymbols; count++)
            outp << '#';
    outp << endl;
} //end printResult
```

We also include a function `printHeading` to print the first two lines of the output. The definition of this function is:

```
void printHeading(ofstream& outp)
{
    outp << "Course          Course Average" << endl;
    outp << "  ID      0   10   20   30   40   50   60   70"
         << "   80   90   100" << endl;
    outp << "          |....|....|....|....|....|....|....|"
         << "....|....|....|" << endl;
} //end printHeading
```

Replace the function `printResult` in the preceding program, include the function `printHeading`, include the statements to output — Group 1 -- **** and Group 2 -- #### — , and rerun the program. Your program should generate a bar graph similar to the bar graph shown earlier. (The complete program listing is available on the Web site accompanying this book.)

QUICK REVIEW

1. Functions are like miniature programs and are called modules.
2. Functions enable you to divide a program into manageable tasks.
3. The C++ system provides the standard (predefined) functions.

4. To use a standard function, you must:

    i. Know the name of the header file that contains the function's specification,

    ii. Include that header file in the program, and

    iii. Know the name and type of the function and number and types of the parameters (arguments).

5. There are two types of user-defined functions: value-returning functions and void functions.

6. Variables defined in a function heading are called formal parameters.

7. Expressions, variables, or constant values used in a function call are called actual parameters.

8. In a function call, the number of actual parameters and their types must match with the formal parameters in the order given.

9. To call a function, use its name together with the actual parameter list.

10. A value-returning function returns a value. Therefore, a value-returning function is used (called) in either an expression or an output statement or as a parameter in a function call.

11. The general syntax of a user-defined function is:

```
functionType   functionName(formal parameter list)
{
     statements
}
```

12. The line `functionType functionName(formal parameter list)` is called the function heading (or function header). Statements enclosed between braces ({ and }) are called the body of the function.

13. The function heading and the body of the function are called the definition of the function.

14. If a function has no parameters, you still need the empty parentheses in both the function heading and the function call.

15. A value-returning function returns its value via the `return` statement.

16. A function can have more than one `return` statement. However, whenever a `return` statement executes in a function, the remaining statements are skipped and the function exits.

17. A `return` statement returns only one value.

18. A function prototype is the function heading without the body of the function; the function prototype ends with the semicolon.

19. A function prototype announces the function type, as well as the type and number of parameters, used in the function.

20. In a function prototype, the names of the variables in the formal parameter list are optional.

6

21. Function prototypes help the compiler correctly translate each function call.

22. In a program, function prototypes are placed before every function definition, including the definition of the function `main`.

23. When you use function prototypes, user-defined functions can appear in any order in the program.

24. When the program executes, the execution always begins with the first statement in the function `main`.

25. User-defined functions execute only when they are called.

26. A call to a function transfers control from the caller to the called function.

27. In a function call statement, you specify only the actual parameters, not their data type or the function type.

28. When a function exits, the control goes back to the caller.

29. A function that does not have a data type is called a void function.

30. A return statement without any value can be used in a void function. If a return statement is used in a void function, it is typically used to exit the function early.

31. The heading of a void function starts with the word `void`.

32. In C++, `void` is a reserved word.

33. A void function may or may not have parameters.

34. A call to a void function is a stand-alone statement.

35. To call a void function, you use the function name together with the actual parameters in a stand-alone statement.

36. There are two types of formal parameters: value parameters and reference parameters.

37. A value parameter receives a copy of its corresponding actual parameter.

38. A reference parameter receives the address (memory location) of its corresponding actual parameter.

39. The corresponding actual parameter of a value parameter is an expression, a variable, or a constant value.

40. A constant value cannot be passed to a reference parameter.

41. The corresponding actual parameter of a reference parameter must be a variable.

42. When you include `&` after the data type of a formal parameter, the formal parameter becomes a reference parameter.

43. The stream variables should be passed by reference to a function.

44. If a formal parameter needs to change the value of an actual parameter, in the function heading, you must declare this formal parameter as a reference parameter.

45. The scope of an identifier refers to those parts of the program where it is accessible.

46. Variables declared within a function (or block) are called local variables.

47. Variables declared outside of every function definition (and block) are called global variables.

48. The scope of a function name is the same as the scope of an identifier declared outside of any block.

49. See the scope rules in this chapter (section, Scope of an Identifier).

50. C++ does not allow the nesting of function definitions.

51. An automatic variable is a variable for which memory is allocated on function (or block) entry and deallocated on function (or block) exit.

52. A static variable is a variable for which memory remains allocated throughout the execution of the program.

53. By default, global variables are static variables.

54. In C++, a function can be overloaded.

55. Two functions are said to have different formal parameter lists if both functions have:

    • A different number of formal parameters, or
    • If the number of formal parameters is the same, then the data type of the formal parameters, in the order you list them, must differ in at least one position.

56. The signature of a function consists of the function name and its formal parameter list. Two functions have different signatures if they have either different names or different formal parameter lists.

57. If a function is overloaded, then in a call to that function, the signature—that is, the formal parameter list of the function—determines which function to execute.

58. C++ allows functions to have default parameters.

59. If you do not specify the value of a default parameter, the default value is used for that parameter.

60. All of the default parameters must be the far-right parameters of the function.

61. Suppose a function has more than one default parameter. In a function call, if a value to a default parameter is not specified, then you must omit all arguments to its right.

62. Default values can be constants, global variables, or function calls.

63. The calling function has the option of specifying a value other than the default for any default parameter.

64. You cannot assign a constant value as a default value to a reference parameter.

6

EXERCISES

1. Mark the following statements as true or false:

   a. To use a predefined function in a program, you need to know only the name of the function and how to use it.

   b. A value-returning function returns only one value.

   c. Parameters allow you to use different values each time the function is called.

   d. When a `return` statement executes in a user-defined function, the function immediately exits.

   e. A value-returning function returns only integer values.

   f. A function that changes the value of a reference parameter also changes the value of the actual parameter.

   g. A variable name cannot be passed to a value parameter.

   h. If a C++ function does not use parameters, parentheses around the empty parameter list are still required.

   i. In C++, the names of the corresponding formal and actual parameters must be the same.

   j. Whenever the value of a reference parameter changes, the value of the actual parameter changes.

   k. In C++, function definitions can be nested; that is, the definition of one function can be enclosed in the body of another function.

   l. Using global variables in a program is a better programming style than using local variables, because extra variables can be avoided.

   m. In a program, global constants are as dangerous as global variables.

   n. The memory for a static variable remains allocated between function calls.

2. Determine the value of each of the following expressions:

   a. `static_cast<char>(toupper('$'))`

   b. `static_cast<char>(toupper('3'))`

   c. `static_cast<char>(toupper('#'))`

   d. `static_cast<char>(toupper('d'))`

   e. `static_cast<char>(tolower('+'))`

   f. `static_cast<char>(tolower('?'))`

   g. `static_cast<char>(tolower('H'))`

   h. `static_cast<char>(tolower('%'))`

3. Determine the value of each of the following expressions:

   a. `abs(12)`   b. `fabs(23.45)`   c. `fabs(-7.8)`   d. `pow(4.8, 2)`

   e. `pow(4.0, 2.5)`   f. `sqrt(49.0)`   g. `sqrt(7.29)`

   h. `pow(6.0, 3.0) / abs(-36)`   i. `floor(36.27)`   j. `ceil(18.3)`

4. Using the functions described in Table 6-1, write each of the following as a C++ expression. (The expression in (e) denotes the absolute value of $x + 2y - 3$.)

   a. $3.75^{6.8}$ b. $\sqrt{x - 2y}$ c. $w^{t/3}$ d. $\dfrac{-b + \sqrt{b^2 - 4ac}}{2a}$ e. $|x + 2y - 3|$

5. Consider the following function definition:

```
int func(int x, double y, char u, string name)
{
      //function body
}
```

   Which of the following are correct function prototypes of the function func?

   a. `int func(x, y, u, name);`

   b. `int func(int s, double k, char ch, string name);`

   c. `int func(int, double, char, string);`

   d. `func(int, double, char, string)`

6. Consider the following program:

```
#include <iostream>
#include <cmath>

using namespace std;

int main()
{
      int num1;
      int num2;

      cout << "Enter two integers: ";
      cin >> num1 >> num2;
      cout << endl;

      if (num1 != 0 && num2 != 0)
          cout << sqrt(fabs(num1 + num2 + 0.0)) << endl;
      else if (num1 != 0)
          cout << floor(num1 + 0.0) << endl;
      else if (num2 != 0)
          cout << ceil(num2 + 0.0) << endl;
      else
          cout << 0 << endl;

      return 0;
}
```

   a. What is the output if the input is 12 4?

   b. What is the output if the input is 3 27?

   c. What is the output if the input is 25 0?

   d. What is the output if the input is 0 49?

6

7. Consider the following statements:

```
int num1, num2, num3;
double length, width, height;
double volume;
num1 = 6; num2 = 7; num3 = 4;
length = 6.2; width = 2.3; height = 3.4
```

and the function prototype:

```
double box(double, double, double);
```

Which of the following statements are valid? If they are invalid, explain why.

a. `volume = box(length, width, height);`

b. `volume = box(length, 3.8, height);`

c. `cout << box(num1, num3, num2) << endl;`

d. `cout << box(length, width, 7.0) << endl;`

e. `volume = box(length, num1, height);`

f. `cout << box(6.2, , height) << endl;`

g. `volume = box(length + width, height);`

h. `volume = box(num1, num2 + num3);`

8. Consider the following functions:

```
int find(int num)
{
    int first, second;

    first = num * num;
    second = first + num;

    if (second > 100)
        num = first / 10;
    else
        num = first / 20;

    return num + 2;
}

int discover(int one, int two)
{
    int secret = 0;

    for (int i = one; i < two; i++)
        secret = secret + i * i;

    return secret;
}
```

What is the output of each of the following program segments?

a. `cout << find(15) << endl;`

b. `cout << discover(3, 9) << endl;`

c. `cout << find(10) << " " << discover(10, find(10)) << endl;`

d. `x = 12; y = 8;`
   `cout << discover(y, x) << endl;`

9. Consider the following function prototypes:

```
int func1(int, double);
double func2(string, int, double);
char func3(int, int, double, char);
string join(string, string);
```

Answer the following questions:

a. How many parameters does the function `func1` have? What is the type of the function `func1`?

b. How many parameters does function `func2` have? What is the type of function `func2`?

c. How many parameters does function `func3` have? What is the type of function `func3`?

d. How many parameters does function `join` have? What is the type of function `join`?

e. How many actual parameters are needed to call the function `func1`? What is the type of each actual parameter, and in what order should you use these parameters in a call to the function `func1`?

f. Write a C++ statement that prints the value returned by the function `func1` with the actual parameters 3 and 8.5.

g. Write a C++ statement that prints the value returned by function `join` with the actual parameters `"John"` and `"Project Manager"`, respectively.

h. Write a C++ statement that prints the next character returned by function `func3`. (Use your own actual parameters.)

10. Why do you need to include function prototypes in a program that contains user-defined functions?

11. Write the definition of a function that takes as input a `char` value and returns `true` if the character is uppercase; otherwise, it returns `false`.

12. Consider the following function:

```
int mystery(int x, double y, char ch)
{
    if (x == 0 && ch > 'A')
        return(static_cast<int>(pow(y, 2)) + static_cast<int>(ch));
    else if (x > 0)
        return(x + static_cast<int>(sqrt(y)) - static_cast<int>(ch));
```

```
        else
            return(2 * x + static_cast<int>(y) - static_cast<int>(ch));
}
```

What is the output of the following C++ statements?

a. `cout << mystery(0, 6.5, 'K') << endl;`

b. `cout << mystery(4, 16.0, '#') << endl;`

c. `cout << 2 * mystery(-11, 13.8, '8') << endl;`

13. Consider the following function:

```
int secret(int m, int n)
{
    int temp = 0;

    for (int i = 1; i < abs(n); i++)
        temp = temp + i * m;

    return temp;
}
```

a. What is the output of the following C++ statements?

   i. `cout << secret(3, 6) << endl;`

   ii. `cout << secret(5, -4) << endl;`

b. What does the function secret do?

14. Write the definition of a function that takes as input the three numbers. The function returns **true** if the first number to the power of the second number equals the third number; otherwise, it returns **false**. (Assume that the three numbers are of type **double**.)

15. Consider the following C++ program:

```
#include <iostream>
#include <cmath>

using namespace std;

int main()
{
    int temp = 0;

    for (int counter = 1; counter <= 100; counter++)
        if (pow(floor(sqrt(counter / 1.0)), 2.0) == counter)
            temp = temp + counter;

    cout << temp << endl;

    return 0;
}
```

a. What is the output of this program?

b. What does this program do?

16. What is the output of the following program?

```cpp
#include <iostream>

using namespace std;

int mystery(int x, int y, int z);

int main()
{
    cout << mystery(7, 8, 3) << endl;
    cout << mystery(10, 5, 30) << endl;
    cout << mystery(9, 12, 11) << endl;
    cout << mystery(5, 5, 8) << endl;
    cout << mystery(10, 10, 10) << endl;

    return 0;
}

int mystery(int x, int y, int z)
{
    if (x <= y && x <= z)
        return (y + z - x);
    else if (y <= z && y <= x)
        return (z + x - y);
    else
        return (x + y - z);
}
```

17. Write the definition of a function that takes as input three decimal numbers and returns the first number multiplied by the second number to the power of the third number.

18. Consider the following C++ function:

```cpp
int mystery(int num)
{
    int y = 1;

    if (num == 0)
        return 1;
    else if (num < 0)
        return -1;
    else
        for (int count = 1; count < num; count++)
            y = y * (num - count);

    return y;
}
```

What is the output of the following statements?

a. `cout << mystery(6) << endl;`

b. `cout << mystery(0) << endl;`

    c.   `cout << mystery(-5) << endl;`

    d.   `cout << mystery(10) << endl;`

19. a.   How would you use a return statement in a void function?

    b.   Why would you want to use a return statement in a void function?

20. Identify the following items in the programming code shown below:

    a.   Function prototype, function heading, function body, and function definitions.

    b.   Function call statements, formal parameters, and actual parameters.

    c.   Value parameters and reference parameters.

    d.   Local variables and global variables.

    e.   Named constants.

```cpp
#include <iostream>                                        //Line 1

using namespace std;                                       //Line 2

const double NUM = 3.5;                                     //Line 3

int temp;                                                  //Line 4

void func(int, double&, char);                             //Line 5

int main()                                                 //Line 6
{                                                          //Line 7
    int num;                                               //Line 8
    double one;                                            //Line 9
    char ch;                                               //Line 10

    func(num, one, ch);                                    //Line 11
    cout << num << " " << one << " " << ch << endl; //Line 12
    func(16, one, '%');                                    //Line 13
    cout << num << " " << one << " " << ch << endl; //Line 14

    return 0;                                              //Line 15
}                                                          //Line 16

void func(int first, double& second, char ch)              //Line 17
{                                                          //Line 18
    int num;                                               //Line 19
    double y;                                              //Line 20
    int u;                                                 //Line 21

    num = 2 * first;                                       //Line 22
    y = second * first;                                    //Line 23
    u = static_cast<int> (ch);                             //Line 24
    second = num + y * u;                                  //Line 25
}                                                          //Line 26
```

21. a. Explain the difference between an actual and a formal parameter.

    b. Explain the difference between a value and a reference parameter.

    c. Explain the difference between a local and a global variable.

22. What is the output of the following program?

```cpp
#include <iostream>
using namespace std;

void func1();
void func2();

int main()
{
    int num;

    cout << "Enter 1 or 2: ";
    cin >> num;
    cout << endl;

    cout << "Take ";

    if (num == 1)
        func1();
    else if (num == 2)
        func2();
    else
        cout << "Invalid input. You must enter a 1 or 2" << endl;

    return 0;
}

void func1()
{
    cout << "Programming I." <<endl;
}

void func2()
{
    cout << "Programming II." << endl;
}
```

    a. What is the output if the input is 1?

    b. What is the output if the input is 2?

    c. What is the output if the input is 3?

    d. What is the output if the input is -1?

23. Write the definition of a void function that takes as input a decimal number and outputs 3 times the value of the decimal number. Format your output to two decimal places.

24. Write the definition of a void function that takes as input two decimal numbers. If the first number is nonzero, it outputs the second number divided by the first number; otherwise, it outputs a message indicating that the second number cannot be divided by the first number because the first number is 0.

25. Write the definition of a **void** function with three reference parameters of type `int`, `double`, and `string`. The function sets the values of the `int` and `double` variables to 0 and the value of the `string` variable to the empty string.

26. Write the definition of a **void** function that takes as input two parameters of type `int`, say `sum` and `testScore`. The function updates the value of `sum` by adding the value of `testScore`. The new value of `sum` is reflected in the calling environment.

27. What is the output of the following program?

```cpp
#include <iostream>
using namespace std;

void find(int a, int& b, int& c);

int main()
{
    int one, two, three;

    one = 5;
    two = 10;
    three = 15;

    find(one, two, three);
    cout << one << ", " << two << ", " << three << endl;

    find(two, one, three);
    cout << one << ", " << two << ", " << three << endl;

    find(three, two, one);
    cout << one << ", " << two << ", " << three << endl;

    find(two, three, one);
    cout << one << ", " << two << ", " << three << endl;

    return 0;
}

void find(int a, int& b, int& c)
{
    int temp;

    c = a + b;
    temp = a;
    a = b;
    b = 2 * temp;
}
```

28. What is the output of the following program?

```cpp
#include <iostream>
using namespace std;

int x;

void summer(int&, int);
void fall(int, int&);

int main()
{
    int intNum1 = 2;
    int intNum2 = 5;
    x = 6;

    summer(intNum1, intNum2);
    cout << intNum1 << " " << intNum2 << " " << x << endl;

    fall(intNum1, intNum2);
    cout << intNum1 << " " << intNum2 << " " << x << endl;
    return 0;
}

void summer(int& a, int b)
{
    int intNum1;
    intNum1 = b + 12;
    a = 2 * b + 5;
    b = intNum1 + 4;
}

void fall(int u, int& v)
{
    int intNum2;
    intNum2 = x;
    v = intNum2 * 4;
    x = u - v;
}
```

29. In the following program, number the marked statements to show the order in which they will execute (the logical order of execution). Also, what is the output if the input is 10?

```cpp
#include <iostream>

using namespace std;

int secret(int, int);

void func(int x, int& y);
```

```cpp
int main()
{
    int num1, num2;

    num1 = 6;

    cout << "Enter a positive integer: ";
    cin >> num2;
    cout << endl;
    cout << secret(num1, num2) << endl;
    num2 = num2 - num1;
    cout << num1 << " " << num2 << endl;
    func(num2, num1);
    cout << num1 << " " << num2 << endl;

    return 0;
}

int secret(int a, int b)
{
    int d;

    d = a + b;
    b = a * d;

    return b;
}

void func (int x, int& y)
{
    int val1, val2;

    val1 = x + y;
    val2 = x * y;
    y = val1 + val2;
    cout << val1 << " " << val2 << endl;
}
```

30. Consider the following program:

```cpp
#include <iostream>
#include <cmath>
#include <iomanip>

using namespace std;

void traceMe(double x, double y);

int main()
{
    double one, two;

    cout << "Enter two numbers: ";
    cin >> one >> two;
    cout << endl;
```

```
        traceMe(one, two);
        traceMe(two, one);

        return 0;
    }

void traceMe(double x, double y)
{
    double z;

    if (x != 0)
        z = sqrt(y) / x;
    else
    {
        cout << "Enter a nonzero number: ";
        cin >> x;
        cout << endl;
        z = floor(pow(y, x));
    }

    cout << fixed << showpoint << setprecision(2);
    cout << x << ", " << y << ", " << z << endl;
}
```

a. What is the output if the input is 3 625?

b. What is the output if the input is 24 1024?

c. What is the output if the input is 0 196?

31. The function traceMe in Exercise 30 outputs the values of x, y, and z. Modify the definition of this function so that rather than print these values, it sends the values back to the calling environment and the calling environment prints these values.

32. In Exercise 30, determine the scope of each identifier.

33. What is the output of the following code fragment? (*Note*: alpha and beta are int variables.)

```
alpha = 5;
beta = 10;

if (beta >= 10)
{
    int alpha = 10;
    beta = beta + alpha;
    cout << alpha << ' ' << beta << endl;
}
cout << alpha << ' ' << beta << endl;
```

34. Consider the following program. What is its exact output? Show the values of the variables after each line executes, as in Example 6-13.

```cpp
#include <iostream>

using namespace std;

void funOne(int& a);

int main()
{
    int num1, num2;

    num1 = 10;                                              //Line 1

    num2 = 20;                                              //Line 2

    cout << "Line 3: In main: num1 = " << num1
         << ", num2 = " << num2 << endl;                   //Line 3

    funOne(num1);                                          //Line 4
    cout << "Line 5: In main after funOne: num1 = "
         << num1 << ", num2 = " << num2 << endl;           //Line 5

    return 0;                                               //Line 6
}

void funOne(int& a)
{
    int x = 12;
    int z;

    z = a + x;                                             //Line 7

    cout << "Line 8: In funOne: a = " << a
         << ", x = " << x
         << ", and z = " << z << endl;                     //Line 8

    x = x + 5;                                             //Line 9

    cout << "Line 10: In funOne: a = " << a
         << ", x = " << x
         << ", and z = " << z << endl;                     //Line 10

    a = a + 8;                                             //Line 11

    cout << "Line 12: In funOne: a = " << a
         << ", x = " << x
         << ", and z = " << z << endl;                     //Line 12
}
```

35. What is the output of the following program?

```cpp
#include <iostream>
using namespace std;

void tryMe(int& v);

int main()
{
    int x = 8;

    for (int count = 1; count < 5; count++)
        tryMe(x);

    return 0;
}

void tryMe(int& v)
{
    static int num = 2;

    if (v % 2 == 0)
    {
        num++;
        v = v + 3;
    }
    else
    {
        num--;
        v = v + 5;
    }
    cout << v << ", " << num << endl;
}
```

36. What is the signature of a function?

37. Consider the following function prototype:

```cpp
void funcDefaultParam(double x = 7.3, int y = 4, char z = '*');
```

Which of the following function calls is correct?

a. `funcDefaultParam();`

b. `funcDefaultParam(2.8);`

c. `funcDefaultParam(3.2, 0, 'h');`

d. `funcDefaultParam(9.2, '*');`

e. `funcDefaultParam(7, 3);`

38. Consider the following function definition:

```
void defaultParam(int num1, int num2 = 7, double z = 2.5)
{
    int num3;

    num1 = num1 + static_cast<int>(z);
    z = num2 + num1 * z;
    num3 = num2 - num1;
    cout << "num3 = " << num3 << endl;
}
```

What is the output of the following function calls?

a. defaultParam(7);

b. defaultParam(8, 2);

c. defaultParam(0, 1, 7.5);

d. defaultParam(1, 2, 3.0);

PROGRAMMING EXERCISES

1. Write a program that uses the function isPalindrome given in Example 6-5 (Palindrome). Test your program on the following strings: "madam", "abba", "22", "67876", "444244", and "trymeuemyrt".

2. Write a value-returning function, isVowel, that returns the value true if a given character is a vowel and otherwise returns false.

3. Write a program that prompts the user to input a sequence of characters and outputs the number of vowels. (Use the function isVowel written in Programming Exercise 2.)

4. Write a program that defines the named constant PI, const double PI = 3.1419;, which stores the value of π. The program should use PI and the functions listed in Table 6-1 to accomplish the following:

a. Output the value of $\sqrt{\pi}$.

b. Prompt the user to input the value of a double variable r, which stores the radius of a sphere. The program then outputs the following:

i. The value of $4\pi r^2$, which is the surface area of the sphere.

ii. The value of $(4/3)\pi r^3$, which is the volume of the sphere.

5. The following program is designed to find the area of a rectangle, the area of a circle, or the volume of a cylinder. However, (a) the statements are in the incorrect order; (b) the function calls are incorrect; (c) the logical expression in the while loop is incorrect; and (d) the function definitions are incorrect. Rewrite the program so that it works correctly. Your program must be properly indented. (Note that the program is menu driven and allows the user to run the program as long as the user wishes.)

```cpp
#include <iostream>

using namespace std;

const double PI = 3.1419;

double rectangle(double l, double w);

#include <iomanip>

int main()
{
    double radius;
    double height;

    cout << fixed << showpoint << setprecision(2) << endl;
    cout << "This program can calculate the area of a rectangle, "
         << "the area of a circle, or volume of a cylinder." << endl;
    cout << "To run the program enter: " << endl;
    cout << "1: To find the area of rectangle." << endl;
    cout << "2: To find the area of a circle." << endl;
    cout << "3: To find the volume of a cylinder." << endl;
    cout << "-1: To terminate the program." << endl;
    cin >> choice;
    cout << endl;

    int choice;

    while (choice == -1)
    {
        {
        case 1:
            cout << "Enter the radius of the base and the "
                 << "height of the cylinder: ";
            cin >> radius >> height;
            cout << endl;

            cout << "Area = " << circle(length, height) << endl;
            break;

        case 3:
            double length, width;
            cout << "Enter the radius of the circle: ";
            cin >> radius;
            cout << endl;

            cout << "Area = " << rectangle(radius)
                 << endl;
            break;
```

6

```
        case 2:
            cout << "Enter the length and the width "
                << "of the rectangle: ";
            cin >> length >> width;
            cout << endl;

            cout << "Volume = " << cylinder(radius, height)
                << endl;
            break;
        default:
            cout << "Invalid choice!" << endl;
        }
        switch (choice)
    }

    double circle(double r)
    double cylinder(double bR, double h);

    cout << "To run the program enter: " << endl;
    cout << "2: To find the area of a circle." << endl;
    cout << "1: To find the area of rectangle." << endl;
    cout << "3: To find the volume of a cylinder." << endl;
    cout << "-1: To terminate the program." << endl;
    cin >> choice;
    cout << endl;

    return 0;
}

double rectangle(double l, double w)
{
    return l * r;
}

double circle(double r)
{
    return PI * r * w;
}

double cylinder(double bR, double h)
{
    return PI * bR * bR * l;
}
```

6. Write a function, reverseDigit, that takes an integer as a parameter and returns the number with its digits reversed. For example, the value of reverseDigit(12345) is 54321; the value of reverseDigit(5600) is 65; the value of reverseDigit(7008) is 8007; and the value of reverseDigit(-532) is -235.

7. Modify the roll dice program, Example 6-4, so that it allows the user to enter the desired sum of the numbers to be rolled. Also allow the user to call the rollDice function as many times as the user desires.

8. The following formula gives the distance between two points, (x_1, y_1) and (x_2, y_2) in the Cartesian plane:

$$\sqrt{(x_2 - x_1)^2 + (y_2 - y_1)^2}$$

Given the center and a point on the circle, you can use this formula to find the radius of the circle. Write a program that prompts the user to enter the center and a point on the circle. The program should then output the circle's radius, diameter, circumference, and area. Your program must have at least the following functions:

a. distance: This function takes as its parameters four numbers that represent two points in the plane and returns the distance between them.

b. radius: This function takes as its parameters four numbers that represent the center and a point on the circle, calls the function distance to find the radius of the circle, and returns the circle's radius.

c. circumference: This function takes as its parameter a number that represents the radius of the circle and returns the circle's circumference. (If r is the radius, the circumference is $2\pi r$.)

d. area: This function takes as its parameter a number that represents the radius of the circle and returns the circle's area. (If r is the radius, the area is πr^2.)

Assume that $\pi = 3.1416$.

9. Rewrite the program in Programming Exercise 15 of Chapter 4 (cell phone company) so that it uses the following functions to calculate the billing amount. (In this programming exercise, do not output the number of minutes during which the service is used.)

a. regularBill: This function calculates and returns the billing amount for regular service.

b. premiumBill: This function calculates and returns the billing amount for premium service.

10. Write a program that takes as input five numbers and outputs the mean (average) and standard deviation of the numbers. If the numbers are x_1, x_2, x_3, x_4, and x_5, then the mean is $x = (x_1 + x_2 + x_3 + x_4 + x_5)/5$ and the standard deviation is:

$$s = \sqrt{\frac{(x_1 - x)^2 + (x_2 - x)^2 + (x_3 - x)^2 + (x_4 - x)^2 + (x_5 - x)^2}{5}}$$

Your program must contain at least the following functions: a function that calculates and returns the mean and a function that calculates the standard deviation.

11. When you borrow money to buy a house, a car, or for some other purposes, then you typically repay it by making periodic payments. Suppose that the loan amount is L, r is the interest rate per year, m is the number of payments in a year, and the loan is for t years. Suppose that $i = (r \; / \; m)$ and r is in decimal. Then the periodic payment is:

$$R = \frac{Li}{1 - (1+i)^{-mt}},$$

You can also calculate the unpaid loan balance after making certain payments. For example, the unpaid balance after making k payments is:

$$L' = R\left[\frac{1 - (1+i)^{-(mt-k)}}{i}\right],$$

where R is the periodic payment. (Note that if the payments are monthly, then $m = 12$.)

Write a program that prompts the user to input the values of L, r, m, t, and k. The program then outputs the apropriate values. Your program must contain at least two functions, with appropriate parameters, to calculate the periodic payments and the unpaid balance after certain payments. Make the program menu driven and use a loop so that the user can repeat the program for different values.

12. During the tax season, every Friday, the J&J accounting firm provides assistance to people who prepare their own tax returns. Their charges are as follows:

   a. If a person has low income ($<=$ 25,000) and the consulting time is less than or equal to 30 minutes, there are no charges; otherwise, the service charges are 40% of the regular hourly rate for the time over 30 minutes.

   b. For others, if the consulting time is less than or equal to 20 minutes, there are no service charges; otherwise, service charges are 70% of the regular hourly rate for the time over 20 minutes.

(For example, suppose that a person has low income and spent 1 hour and 15 minutes, and the hourly rate is $70.00. Then the billing amount is $70.00 \times 0.40 \times (45 \; / \; 60) = \$21.00$.)

Write a program that prompts the user to enter the hourly rate, the total consulting time, and whether the person has low income. The program should output the billing amount. Your program must contain a function that takes as input the hourly rate, the total consulting time, and a value indicating whether the person has low income. The function should return the billing amount. Your program may prompt the user to enter the consulting time in minutes.

13. During winter when it is very cold, typically, everyone would like to know the windchill factor, especially, before going out. Meteorologists use the following formula to compute the windchill factor, W:

$$W = 35.74 + 0.6215 * T - 35.75 * V^{0.16} + 0.4275 * T * V^{0.16},$$

where V is the wind speed in miles per hour and T is the temperature in degrees Fahrenheit. Write a program that prompts the user to input the wind speed, in miles per hour, and the temperature in degrees Fahrenheit. The program then outputs the windchill factor. Your program must contain at least two functions: one to get the user input and the other to determine the windchill factor.

14. Consider the definition of the function main:

```
int main()
{
    int x, y;
    char z;
    double rate, hours;
    double amount;
        .
        .
        .
}
```

The variables x, y, z, rate, and hours referred to in items a through f below are the variables of the function main. Each of the functions described must have the appropriate parameters to access these variables. Write the following definitions:

a. Write the definition of the function initialize that initializes x and y to 0 and z to the blank character.

b. Write the definition of the function getHoursRate that prompts the user to input the hours worked and rate per hour to initialize the variables hours and rate of the function main.

c. Write the definition of the value-returning function payCheck that calculates and returns the amount to be paid to an employee based on the hours worked and rate per hour. The hours worked and rate per hour are stored in the variables hours and rate, respectively, of the function main. The formula for calculating the amount to be paid is as follows: For the first 40 hours, the rate is the given rate; for hours over 40, the rate is 1.5 times the given rate.

d. Write the definition of the function printCheck that prints the hours worked, rate per hour, and the salary.

e. Write the definition of the function funcOne that prompts the user to input a number. The function then changes the value of x by assigning the value of the expression 2 times the (old) value of x plus the value of y minus the value entered by the user.

f. Write the definition of the function nextChar that sets the value of z to the next character stored in z.

g. Write the definition of a function main that tests each of these functions.

15. Consider the following C++ code:

```cpp
#include <iostream>
#include <cmath>
#include <iomanip>

using namespace std;

void func1();
void func2(/*formal parameters*/);

int main()
{
    int num1, num2;
    double num3;

    int choice;

    cout << fixed << showpoint << setprecision(2);

    do
    {
        func1();
        cin >> choice;
        cout << endl;

        if (choice == 1)
        {
            func2(num1, num2, num3);
            cout << num1 << ", " << num2 << ", " << num3 << endl;
        }
    }
    while (choice != 99);

    return 0;
}

void func1()
{
    cout << "To run the program, enter 1." << endl;
    cout << "To exit the pogram, enter 99." << endl;
    cout << "Enter 1 or 99: ";
}

void func2(/*formal parameters*/)
{
    //Write the body of func2.
}
```

The function `func2` has three parameters of type `int`, `int`, and `double`, say a, b, and c, respectively. Write the definition of `func2` so that its action is as follows:

a. Prompt the user to input two integers and store the numbers in a and b, respectively.

b. If both of the numbers are nonzero:

    i. If a >= b, the value assigned to c is a to the power b, that is, a^b.

    ii. If a < b, the value assigned to c is b to the power a, that is, b^a.

c. If a is nonzero and b is zero, the value assigned to c is the square root of the absolute value of a.

d. If b is nonzero and a is zero, the value assigned to c is the square root of the absolute value of b.

e. Otherwise, the value assigned to c is 0.

The values of a, b, and c are passed back to the calling environment.

After completing the definition of the `func2` and writing its function prototype, test run your program.

16. The statements in the following program are not in the correct order. Rearrange the statements so that the program outputs the total time an employee spent on the job each day. The program asks the user to enter the employee's name, the arrival time (arrival hour, arrival minute, AM or PM), and departure time (departure hour, departure minute, AM or PM). The program also allows the user to run the program as long as the user wishes. After rearranging the statements, your program must be properly indented.

```cpp
#include <iostream>
#include <string>

using namespace std;

int main()
{
    string employeeName;
    int arrivalHr;

    int departureHr;
    int departureMin;
    bool departureAM;

    char response;
    char discard;
    char isAM;

    cout << "This program calculates the total time spent by an "
         << "employee on the job." << endl;
    cout << "To run the program, enter (y/Y): ";
    cin >> response;
    cout << endl;
    cin.get(discard);
```

6

```cpp
    while (response == 'y' || response == 'Y')
    {
        cout << "Enter employee's name: ";
        getline(cin, employeeName);
        cout << endl;


        if (isAM == 'y' || isAM == 'Y')
            arrivalAM = true;
        else
            arrivalAM = false;

        cout << "Enter departure hour: ";
        cin >> departureHr;
        cout << endl;
        cout << "Enter departure minute: ";
        cin >> departureMin;
        cout << endl;
        cout << "Enter (y/Y) if departure is before 12:00PM: ";
        cin >> isAM;
        cout << endl;

        if (isAM == 'y' || isAM == 'Y')
            departureAM = true;
        else
            departureAM = false;

        cout << employeeName << endl;
        timeOnJob(arrivalHr, arrivalMin, arrivalAM,
                  departureHr, departureMin, departureAM);

        cout << "Enter arrival hour: ";
        cin >> arrivalHr;
        cout << endl;
        cout << "Enter arrival minute: ";
        cin >> arrivalMin;
        cout << endl;
        cout << "Enter (y/Y) if arrival is before 12:00PM: ";
        cin >> isAM;
        cout << endl;

        int arrivalMin;
        bool arrivalAM;
        cout << "Run program again (y/Y): ";
        cin >> response;
        cout << endl;
        cin.get(discard);
    }

    return 0;
}
```

```
        void timeOnJob(int arvHr, int arvMin, bool arvIsAM,
                    int depHr, int depMin, bool depIsAM)
    {
        int arvTimeInMin;
        int depTimeInMin;
        int timeOnJobInMin;

        else if (arvIsAM == true && depIsAM == false)
        {
            arvTimeInMin = arvHr * 60 + arvMin;
            depTimeInMin = depHr * 60 + depMin;

            timeOnJobInMin = (720 - arvTimeInMin) + depTimeInMin;
            cout << "Time spent of job: "
                << timeOnJobInMin / 60 << " hour(s) and "
                << timeOnJobInMin % 60 << " minutes." << endl;
        }

        else
        if (arvTimeInMin <= depTimeInMin)
        {
            timeOnJobInMin = depTimeInMin - arvTimeInMin;
            cout << "Time spent of job: "
                << timeOnJobInMin / 60 << " hour(s) and "
                << timeOnJobInMin % 60 << " minutes." << endl;
        }
        else
          cout << "Invalid input." << endl;
        if ((arvIsAM == true && depIsAM == true)
            || (arvIsAM == false && depIsAM == false))
        {
            cout << "Invalid input." << endl;
        }


        void timeOnJob(int arvHr, int arvMin, bool arvIsAM,
                    int depHr, int depMin, bool depIsAM);
    }
```

17. The function printGrade in Example 6-12 is written as a void function to compute and output the course grade. The course score is passed as a parameter to the function printGrade. Rewrite the function printGrade as a value-returning function so that it computes and returns the course grade. (The course grade must be output in the function main.) Also, change the name of the function to calculateGrade.

18. In this exercise, you are to modify the Classify Numbers programming example in this chapter. As written, the program inputs the data from the standard input device (keyboard) and outputs the results on the standard

output device (screen). The program can process only 20 numbers. Rewrite the program to incorporate the following requirements:

a. Data to the program is input from a file of an unspecified length; that is, the program does not know in advance how many numbers are in the file.

b. Save the output of the program in a file.

c. Modify the function `getNumber` so that it reads a number from the input file (opened in the function `main`), outputs the number to the output file (opened in the function `main`), and sends the number read to the function `main`. Print only 10 numbers per line.

d. Have the program find the sum and average of the numbers.

e. Modify the function `printResult` so that it outputs the final results to the output file (opened in the function `main`). Other than outputting the appropriate counts, this new definition of the function `printResult` should also output the sum and average of the numbers.

19. Write a program that prints the day number of the year, given the date in the form month-day-year. For example, if the input is 1-1-2006, the day number is 1; if the input is 12-25-2006, the day number is 359. The program should check for a leap year. A year is a leap year if it is divisible by 4, but not divisible by 100. For example, 1992 and 2008 are divisible by 4, but not by 100. A year that is divisible by 100 is a leap year if it is also divisible by 400. For example, 1600 and 2000 are divisible by 400. However, 1800 is not a leap year because 1800 is not divisible by 400.

20. Write a progam that reads a string and outputs the number of times each lowercase vowel appears in it. Your program must contain a function with one of its parameters as a `string` variable and return the number of times each lowercase vowel appears in it. Also write a program to test your function. (Note that if `str` is a variable of type `string`, then `str.at(i)` returns the character at the ith position. The position of the first character is 0. Also, `str.length()` returns the length of the `str`, that is, the number of characters in `str`.)

21. Redo Programming Exercise 20 as follows. Write a progam that reads a string and outputs the number of times each lowercase vowel appears in it. Your program must contain a function with one of its parameters as a **char** variable, and if the character is a vowel, it increments that vowel's count.

22. Write a function that takes as a parameter an integer (as a **long** value) and returns the number of odd, even, and zero digits. Also write a program to test your function.

23. The cost to become a member of a fitness center is as follows: (a) the senior citizens discount is 30%; (b) if the membership is bought and paid for 12 or more months, the discount is 15%; and (c) if more than five personal training sessions are bought and paid for, the discount on each session is 20%. Write a menu-driven program that determines the cost of a new membership.

Your program must contain a function that displays the general information about the fitness center and its charges, a function to get all of the necessary information to determine the membership cost, and a function to determine the membership cost. Use appropriate parameters to pass information in and out of a function. (Do not use any global variables.)

24. Write a program that outputs inflation rates for two successive years and whether the inflation is increasing or decreasing. Ask the user to input the current price of an item and its price one year and two years ago. To calculate the inflation rate for a year, subtract the price of the item for that year from the price of the item one year ago and then divide the result by the price a year ago. Your program must contain at least the following functions: a function to get the input, a function to calculate the results, and a function to output the results. Use appropriate parameters to pass the information in and out of the function. Do not use any global variables.

25. Write a program to convert the time from 24-hour notation to 12-hour notation and vice versa. Your program must be menu driven, giving the user the choice of converting the time between the two notations. Furthermore, your program must contain at least the following functions: a function to convert the time from 24-hour notation to 12-hour notation, a function to convert the time from 12-hour notation to 24-hour notation, a function to display the choices, function(s) to get the input, and function(s) to display the results. (For 12-hour time notation, your program must display AM or PM.)

26. Jason opened a coffee shop at the beach and sells coffee in three sizes: small (9oz), medium (12oz), and large (15oz). The cost of one small cup is $1.75, one medium cup is $1.90, and one large cup is $2.00. Write a menu-driven program that will make the coffee shop operational. Your program should allow the user to do the following:

    a. Buy coffee in any size and in any number of cups.

    b. At any time show the total number of cups of each size sold.

    c. At any time show the total amount of coffee sold.

    d. At any time show the total money made.

    Your program should consist of at least the following functions: a function to show the user how to use the program, a function to sell coffee, a function to show the number of cups of each size sold, a function to show the total amount of coffee sold, and a function to show the total money made. Your program should not use any global variables and special values such as coffee cup sizes and cost of a coffee cup must be declared as named constants.

27. (**The box problem**) You have been given a flat cardboard of area, say, 70 square inches to make an open box by cutting a square from each corner and folding the sides (see Figure 6-24). Your objective is to determine the dimensions, that is, the length and width, and the side of the square to be cut from the corners so that the resulting box is of maximum length.

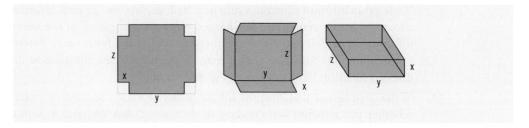

FIGURE 6-24 Cardboard box

Write a program that prompts the user to enter the area of the flat cardboard. The program then outputs the length and width of the cardboard and the length of the side of the square to be cut from the corner so that the resulting box is of maximum volume. Calculate your answer to three decimal places. Your program must contain a function that takes as input the length and width of the cardboard and returns the side of the square that should be cut to maximize the volume. The function also returns the maximum volume.

28. **(The power station problem)** A power station is on one side of a river that is one-half mile wide, and a factory is eight miles downstream on the other side of the river (see Figure 6-25). It costs $7 per foot to run power lines over land and $9 per foot to run them under water. Your objective is to determine the most economical path to lay the power line. That is, determine how long the power line should run under water and how long it should run over land to achieve the minimum total cost of laying the power line.

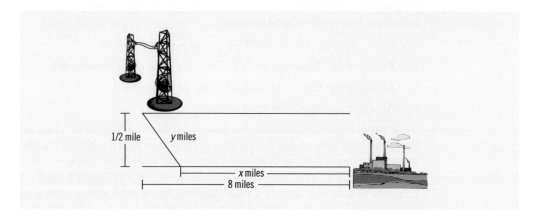

FIGURE 6-25 Power station, river, and factory

Write a program that prompts the user to enter:

a. The width of the river

b. The distance of the factory downstream on the other side of the river

c. The cost of laying the power line under water

d. The cost of laying the power line over land

The program then outputs the length of the power line that should run under water and the length that should run over land so the cost of constructing the power line is at the minimum. The program should also output the total cost of constructing the power line.

29. **(Pipe problem, requires trigonometry)** A pipe is to be carried around the right-angled corner of two intersecting corridors. Suppose that the widths of the two intersecting corridors are 5 feet and 8 feet (see Figure 6-26). Your objective is to find the length of the longest pipe, rounded to the nearest foot, that can be carried level around the right-angled corner.

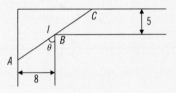

FIGURE 6-26 Pipe problem

Write a program that prompts the user to input the widths of both of the hallways. The program then outputs the length of the longest pipe, rounded to the nearest foot, that can be carried level around the right-angled corner. (Note that the length of the pipe is given by $l = AB + BC = 8 \, / \sin \theta + 5 \, / \cos \theta$, where $0 < \theta < \pi/2$.)

User-Defined Simple Data Types, Namespaces, and the string Type

IN THIS CHAPTER, YOU WILL:

- Learn how to create and manipulate your own simple data type called the enumeration type
- Become familiar with the `typedef` statement
- Learn about the `namespace` mechanism
- Explore the `string` data type and learn how to use the various `string` functions to manipulate strings

In Chapter 2, you learned that C++'s simple data type is divided into three categories: integral, floating-point, and `enum`. In subsequent chapters, you worked mainly with integral and floating-point data types. In this chapter, you will learn about the `enum` type. Moreover, the statement `using namespace std;` (discussed in Chapter 2) is used in every C++ program that uses ANSI/ISO Standard C++ style header files. The second half of this chapter examines the purpose of this statement. In fact, you will learn what the `namespace` mechanism is. You will also learn about the `string` type and many useful functions that you can use to effectively manipulate strings.

Enumeration Type

 NOTE   This section may be skipped without any loss of continuity.

Chapter 2 defined a data type as a set of values together with a set of operations on them. For example, the `int` data type consists of integers from –2,147,483,648 to 2,147,483,647 and the set of operations on these numbers—namely, the arithmetic operations (+, –, *, /, and %). Because the main objective of a program is to manipulate data, the concept of a data type becomes fundamental to any programming language. By providing data types, you specify what values are legal and tell the user what kinds of operations are allowed on those values. The system thus provides you with built-in checks against errors.

The data types that you have worked with until now were mostly `int`, `bool`, `char`, and `double`. Even though these data types are sufficient to solve just about any problem, situations occur when these data types are not adequate to solve a particular problem. C++ provides a mechanism for users to create their own data types, which greatly enhances the flexibility of the programming language.

In this section, you will learn how to create your own simple data types, known as the enumeration types. In ensuing chapters, you will learn more advanced techniques to create complex data types.

To define an **enumeration type**, you need the following items:

- A name for the data type
- A set of values for the data type
- A set of operations on the values

C++ lets you define a new simple data type wherein you specify its name and values, but not the operations. Preventing users from creating their own operations helps to avoid potential system failures.

The values that you specify for the data type must be identifiers.

The syntax for enumeration type is:

```
enum typeName {value1, value2, ...};
```

in which value1, value2, ... are identifiers called **enumerators**. In C++, enum is a reserved word.

By listing all of the values between the braces, you also specify an ordering between the values. That is, value1 < value2 < value3 <.... Thus, the enumeration type is an ordered set of values. Moreover, the default value assigned to these enumerators starts at 0. That is, the default value assigned to value1 is 0, the default value assigned to value2 is 1, and so on. (You can assign different values—other than the default values—for the enumerators when you define the enumeration type.) Also notice that the enumerators value1, value2, ... are *not* variables.

EXAMPLE 7-1

The statement:

```
enum colors {BROWN, BLUE, RED, GREEN, YELLOW};
```

defines a new data type called colors, and the values belonging to this data type are BROWN, BLUE, RED, GREEN, and YELLOW.

EXAMPLE 7-2

The statement:

```
enum standing {FRESHMAN, SOPHOMORE, JUNIOR, SENIOR};
```

defines standing to be an enumeration type. The values belonging to standing are FRESHMAN, SOPHOMORE, JUNIOR, and SENIOR.

EXAMPLE 7-3

Consider the following statements:

```
enum grades {'A', 'B', 'C', 'D', 'F'}; //illegal enumeration type
enum places {1ST, 2ND, 3RD, 4TH};   //illegal enumeration type
```

These are illegal enumeration types because none of the values is an identifier. The following, however, are legal enumeration types:

```
enum grades {A, B, C, D, F};
enum places {FIRST, SECOND, THIRD, FOURTH};
```

If a value has already been used in one enumeration type, it cannot be used by any other enumeration type in the same block. The same rules apply to enumeration types declared outside of any blocks. Example 7-4 illustrates this concept.

EXAMPLE 7-4

Consider the following statements:

```
enum mathStudent {JOHN, BILL, CINDY, LISA, RON};
enum compStudent {SUSAN, CATHY, JOHN, WILLIAM}; //illegal
```

Suppose that these statements are in the same program in the same block. The second enumeration type, compStudent, is not allowed because the value JOHN was used in the previous enumeration type mathStudent.

Declaring Variables

Once a data type is defined, you can declare variables of that type. The syntax for declaring variables of an **enum** type is the same as before:

```
dataType identifier, identifier,...;
```

The statement:

```
enum sports {BASKETBALL, FOOTBALL, HOCKEY, BASEBALL, SOCCER,
             VOLLEYBALL};
```

defines an enumeration type called **sports**. The statement:

```
sports popularSport, mySport;
```

declares **popularSport** and **mySport** to be variables of type **sports**.

Assignment

Once a variable is declared, you can store values in it. Assuming the previous declaration, the statement:

```
popularSport = FOOTBALL;
```

stores FOOTBALL in popularSport. The statement:

```
mySport = popularSport;
```

copies the value of popularSport into mySport.

Operations on Enumeration Types

No arithmetic operations are allowed on the enumeration type. So the following statements are illegal:

```
mySport = popularSport + 2;            //illegal
popularSport = FOOTBALL + SOCCER;      //illegal
popularSport = popularSport * 2;       //illegal
```

Also, the increment and decrement operations are not allowed on enumeration types. So the following statements are illegal:

```
popularSport++; //illegal
popularSport--; //illegal
```

Suppose you want to increment the value of popularSport by 1. You can use the cast operator as follows:

```
popularSport = static_cast<sports>(popularSport + 1);
```

When the type name is used, the compiler assumes that the user understands what he or she is doing. Thus, the preceding statement is compiled, and during execution, it advances the value of popularSport to the next value in the list. Consider the following statements:

```
popularSport = FOOTBALL;
popularSport = static_cast<sports>(popularSport + 1);
```

After the second statement, the value of popularSport is HOCKEY. Similarly, the statements:

```
popularSport = FOOTBALL;
popularSport = static_cast<sports>(popularSport - 1);
```

result in storing BASKETBALL in popularSport.

Relational Operators

Because an enumeration is an ordered set of values, the relational operators can be used with the enumeration type. Once again, suppose you have the enumeration type sports and the variables popularSport and mySport as defined earlier. Then:

```
FOOTBALL <= SOCCER is true
HOCKEY > BASKETBALL is true
BASEBALL < FOOTBALL is false
```

7

Suppose that:

```
popularSport = SOCCER;
mySport = VOLLEYBALL;
```

Then:

```
popularSport < mySport is true
```

ENUMERATION TYPES AND LOOPS

Recall that the enumeration type is an integral type and that, using the cast operator (that is, type name), you can increment, decrement, and compare the values of the enumeration type. Therefore, you can use these enumeration types in loops. Suppose `mySport` is a variable as declared earlier. Consider the following `for` loop:

```
for (mySport = BASKETBALL; mySport <= SOCCER;
                     mySport = static_cast<sports>(mySport + 1))
    .
    .
    .
```

This `for` loop has five iterations.

Using enumeration types in loops increases the readability of the program.

Input/Output of Enumeration Types

Because input and output are defined only for built-in data types such as `int`, `char`, `double`, and so on, the enumeration type can be neither input nor output (directly). However, you can input and output enumeration indirectly. Example 7-5 illustrates this concept.

EXAMPLE 7-5

Suppose you have the following statements:

```
enum courses {ALGEBRA, BASIC, PASCAL, CPP, PHILOSOPHY, ANALYSIS,
              CHEMISTRY, HISTORY};
courses registered;
```

The first statement defines an enumeration type, `courses`; the second declares a variable `registered` of type `courses`. You can read (that is, input) the enumeration type with the help of the `char` data type. Note that you can distinguish between some of the values in the enumeration type `courses` just by reading the first character and others by reading the first two characters. For example, you can distinguish between `ALGEBRA` and `BASIC` just by reading the first character; you can distinguish between `ALGEBRA` and `ANALYSIS` by reading the first two characters. To read these values from, say, the keyboard, you read two characters and then use a selection structure to assign the value to the variable `registered`. Thus, you need to declare two variables of type `char`.

```
char ch1, ch2;
cin >> ch1 >> ch2; //Read two characters
```

The following `switch` statement assigns the appropriate value to the variable `registered`:

```
switch (ch1)
{
case 'a':
case 'A':
    if (ch2 == 'l' || ch2 == 'L')
        registered = ALGEBRA;
    else
        registered = ANALYSIS;
    break;
case 'b':
case 'B':
    registered = BASIC;
    break;
case 'c':
case 'C':
    if (ch2 == 'h' || ch2 == 'H')
        registered = CHEMISTRY;
    else
        registered = CPP;
    break;
case 'h':
case 'H':
    registered = HISTORY;
    break;
case 'p':
case 'P':
    if (ch2 == 'a' || ch2 == 'A')
        registered = PASCAL;
    else
        registered = PHILOSOPHY;
    break;
default:
    cout << "Illegal input." << endl;
}
```

You can also use the `string` type to input value in the variable `registered`. For example, the following code accomplishes this:

```
string course;
cin >> course;
if (course == "algebra")
    registered = ALGEBRA;
else if (course == "analysis")
    registered = ANALYSIS;
else if (course == "basic")
    registered = BASIC;
else if (course == "chemistry")
    registered = CHEMISTRY;
else if (course == "cpp")
    registered = CPP;
```

7

```
else if (course == "history")
    registered = HISTORY;
else if (course == "pascal")
    registered = PASCAL;
else if (course == "Philosophy")
    registered = PHILOSOPHY;
else
    cout << "Illegal input." << endl;
```

Similarly, you can output the enumeration type indirectly:

```
switch (registered)
{
case ALGEBRA:
    cout << "Algebra";
    break;
case ANALYSIS:
    cout << "Analysis";
    break;
case BASIC:
    cout << "Basic";
    break;
case CHEMISTRY:
    cout << "Chemistry";
    break;
case CPP:
    cout << "CPP";
    break;
case HISTORY:
    cout << "History";
    break;
case PASCAL:
    cout << "Pascal";
    break;
case PHILOSOPHY:
    cout << "Philosophy";
}
```

> **NOTE** If you try to output the value of an enumerator directly, the computer will output the value assigned to the enumerator. For example, suppose that `registered = ALGEBRA;`. The following statement will output the value 0 because the (default) value assigned to ALGEBRA is 0:
>
> ```
> cout << registered << endl;
> ```
>
> Similarly, the following statement will output 4:
>
> ```
> cout << PHILOSOPHY << endl;
> ```

Functions and Enumeration Types

You can pass the enumeration type as a parameter to functions just like any other simple data type—that is, by either value or reference. Also, just like any other simple data type, a function can return a value of the enumeration type. Using this facility, you can use functions to input and output enumeration types.

The following function inputs data from the keyboard and returns a value of the enumeration type. Assume that the enumeration type `courses` is defined as before:

```cpp
courses readCourses()
{
    courses registered;
    char ch1, ch2;

    cout << "Enter the first two letters of the course: "
         << endl;
    cin >> ch1 >> ch2;

    switch (ch1)
    {
    case 'a':
    case 'A':
        if (ch2 == 'l' || ch2 == 'L')
            registered = ALGEBRA;
        else
            registered = ANALYSIS;
        break;
    case 'b':
    case 'B':
        registered = BASIC;
        break;
    case 'c':
    case 'C':
        if (ch2 == 'h' || ch2 == 'H')
            registered = CHEMISTRY;
        else
            registered = CPP;
        break;
    case 'h':
    case 'H':
        registered = HISTORY;
        break;
    case 'p':
    case 'P':
        if (ch2 == 'a' || ch2 == 'A')
            registered = PASCAL;
        else
            registered = PHILOSOPHY;
        break;
```

7

```
        default:
            cout << "Illegal input." << endl;
        }
        return registered;
}   //end readCourses
```

As shown previously, you can also use the `string` type in the function `readCourses` to input a value in a variable of type `courses`. We leave the details as an exercise.

The following function outputs an enumeration type value:

```
void printEnum(courses registered)
{
    switch (registered)
    {
    case ALGEBRA:
        cout << "Algebra";
        break;
    case ANALYSIS:
        cout << "Analysis";
        break;
    case BASIC:
        cout << "Basic";
        break;
    case CHEMISTRY:
        cout << "Chemistry";
        break;
    case CPP:
        cout << "CPP";
        break;
    case HISTORY:
        cout << "History";
        break;
    case PASCAL:
        cout << "Pascal";
        break;
    case PHILOSOPHY:
        cout << "Philosophy";
    }//end switch
}//end printEnum
```

Declaring Variables When Defining the Enumeration Type

In previous sections, you first defined an enumeration type and then declared variables of that type. C++ allows you to combine these two steps into one. That is, you can declare variables of an enumeration type when you define an enumeration type. For example, the statement:

```
enum grades {A, B, C, D, F} courseGrade;
```

defines an enumeration type, `grades`, and declares a variable `courseGrade` of type `grades`.

Similarly, the statement:

```
enum coins {PENNY, NICKEL, DIME, HALFDOLLAR, DOLLAR} change, usCoins;
```

defines an enumeration type, `coins`, and declares two variables, `change` and `usCoins`, of type `coins`.

Anonymous Data Types

A data type wherein you directly specify values in the variable declaration with no type name is called an **anonymous type**. The following statement creates an anonymous type:

```
enum {BASKETBALL, FOOTBALL, BASEBALL, HOCKEY} mySport;
```

This statement specifies the values and declares a variable `mySport`, but no name is given to the data type.

Creating an anonymous type, however, has drawbacks. First, because there is no name for the type, you cannot pass an anonymous type as a parameter to a function, and a function cannot return an anonymous type value. Second, values used in one anonymous type can be used in another anonymous type, but variables of those types are treated differently. Consider the following statements:

```
enum {ENGLISH, FRENCH, SPANISH, GERMAN, RUSSIAN} languages;
enum {ENGLISH, FRENCH, SPANISH, GERMAN, RUSSIAN} foreignLanguages;
```

Even though the variables `languages` and `foreignLanguages` have the same values, the compiler treats them as variables of different types. The following statement is, therefore, illegal:

```
languages = foreignLanguages; //illegal
```

Even though these facilities are available, use them with care. To avoid confusion, first define an enumeration type and then declare the variables.

We now describe the `typedef` statement in C++.

typedef Statement

In C++, you can create synonyms or aliases to a previously defined data type by using the `typedef` statement. The general syntax of the `typedef` statement is:

```
typedef existingTypeName newTypeName;
```

In C++, `typedef` is a reserved word. Note that the `typedef` statement does not create any new data type; it only creates an alias to an existing data type.

EXAMPLE 7-6

The statement:

```
typedef int integer;
```

creates an alias, `integer`, for the data type `int`. Similarly, the statement:

```
typedef double real;
```

creates an alias, `real`, for the data type `double`. The statement:

```
typedef double decimal;
```

creates an alias, `decimal`, for the data type `double`.

Using the `typedef` statement, you can create your own Boolean data type, as shown in Example 7-7.

EXAMPLE 7-7

From Chapter 4, recall that logical (Boolean) expressions in C++ evaluate to 1 or 0, which are, in fact, `int` values. As a logical value, 1 represents `true` and 0 represents `false`. Consider the following statements:

```
typedef int Boolean;            //Line 1
const Boolean TRUE = 1;         //Line 2
const Boolean FALSE = 0;        //Line 3
Boolean flag;                   //Line 4
```

The statement in Line 1 creates an alias, `Boolean`, for the data type `int`. The statements in Lines 2 and 3 declare the named constants `TRUE` and `FALSE` and initialize them to 1 and 0, respectively. The statement in Line 4 declares `flag` to be a variable of type `Boolean`. Because `flag` is a variable of type `Boolean`, the following statement is legal:

```
flag = TRUE;
```

PROGRAMMING EXAMPLE: The Game of Rock, Paper, and Scissors

Watch the Video

Children often play the game of rock, paper, and scissors. This game has two players, each of whom chooses one of the three objects: rock, paper, or scissors. If player 1 chooses rock and player 2 chooses paper, player 2 wins the game because paper covers the rock. The game is played according to the following rules:

- If both players choose the same object, this play is a tie.
- If one player chooses rock and the other chooses scissors, the player choosing the rock wins this play because the rock breaks the scissors.
- If one player chooses rock and the other chooses paper, the player choosing the paper wins this play because the paper covers the rock.
- If one player chooses scissors and the other chooses paper, the player choosing the scissors wins this play because the scissors cut the paper.

Write an interactive program that allows two people to play this game.

Input   This program has two types of input:

- The users' responses when asked to play the game.
- The players' choices.

Output   The players' choices and the winner of each play. After the game is over, the total number of plays and the number of times that each player won should be output as well.

PROBLEM ANALYSIS AND ALGORITHM DESIGN

Two players play this game. Players enter their choices via the keyboard. Each player enters R or r for Rock, P or p for Paper, or S or s for Scissors. While the first player enters a choice, the second player looks elsewhere. Once both entries are in, if the entries are valid, the program outputs the players' choices and declares the winner of the play. The game continues until one of the players decides to quit the game. After the game ends, the program outputs the total number of plays and the number of times that each player won. This discussion translates into the following algorithm:

1. Provide a brief explanation of the game and how it is played.
2. Ask the users if they want to play the game.
3. Get plays for both players.
4. If the plays are valid, output the plays and the winner.
5. Update the total game count and winner count.
6. Repeat Steps 2 through 5 while the users agree to play the game.
7. Output the number of plays and times that each player won.

We will use the enumeration type to describe the objects.

```
enum objectType {ROCK, PAPER, SCISSORS};
```

7

Variables
(Function `main`**)** It is clear that you need the following variables in the function `main`:

```
int gameCount;  //variable to store the number of
                //games played
int winCount1;  //variable to store the number of games
                //won by player 1
int winCount2;  //variable to store the number of games
                //won by player 2
int gamewinner;
char response;  //variable to get the user's response to
                //play the game
char selection1;
char selection2;
objectType play1;   //player1's selection
objectType play2;   //player2's selection
```

This program is divided into the following functions, which the ensuing sections describe in detail.

- **displayRules:** This function displays some brief information about the game and its rules.

- **validSelection:** This function checks whether a player's selection is valid. The only valid selections are R, r, P, p, S, and s.

- **retrievePlay:** Because enumeration types cannot be read directly, this function converts the entered choice (R, r, P, p, S, or s) and returns the appropriate object type.

- **gameResult:** This function outputs the players' choices and the winner of the game.

- **convertEnum:** This function is called by the function `gameResult` to output the enumeration type values.

- **winningObject:** This function determines and returns the winning object.

- **displayResults:** After the game is over, this function displays the final results.

Function
`displayRules` This function has no parameters. It consists only of output statements to explain the game and rules of play. Essentially, this function's definition is:

```
void displayRules()
{
    cout << "  Welcome to the game of Rock, Paper, "
         << "and Scissors." << endl;
    cout << "  This is a game for two players. For each "
         << "game, each" << endl;
```

```
        cout << " player selects one of the objects Rock, "
             << "Paper, or Scissors." << endl;
        cout << " The rules for winning the game are: " << endl;
        cout << "1. If both players select the same object, it "
             << "is a tie." << endl;
        cout << "2. Rock breaks Scissors: So player who selects "
             << "Rock wins." << endl;
        cout << "3. Paper covers Rock: So player who selects "
             << "Paper wins." << endl;
        cout << "4. Scissors cuts Paper: So player who selects "
             << "Scissors wins." << endl << endl;
        cout << "Enter R or r to select Rock, P or p to select "
             << "Paper, and S or s to select Scissors." << endl;
    }
```

Function validSelection This function checks whether a player's selection is valid.

```
if selection is 'R' or 'r' or 'S' or 's' or 'P' or 'p', then
   it is a valid selection;
otherwise the selection is invalid.
```

Let's use a `switch` statement to check for the valid selection. The definition of this function is:

```
bool validSelection(char selection)
{
    switch (selection)
    {
    case 'R':
    case 'r':
    case 'P':
    case 'p':
    case 'S':
    case 's':
        return true;
    default:
        return false;
    }
}
```

Function retrievePlay Because the enumeration type cannot be read directly, this function converts the entered choice (R, r, P, p, S, or s) and returns the appropriate object type. This function thus has one parameter, of type `char`. It is a value-returning function, and it returns a value of type `objectType`. In pseudocode, the algorithm of this function is:

```
if selection is 'R' or 'r'
   return ROCK;

if selection is 'P' or 'p'
   return PAPER;

if selection is 'S' or 's'
   return  SCISSORS;
```

7

The definition of the function `retrievePlay` is:

```
objectType retrievePlay(char selection)
{
    objectType object;

    switch (selection)
    {
    case 'R':
    case 'r':
        object = ROCK;
        break;
    case 'P':
    case 'p':
        object = PAPER;
        break;
    case 'S':
    case 's':
        object = SCISSORS;
    }

    return object;
}
```

Function gameResult This function decides whether a game is a tie or which player is the winner. It outputs the players' selections and the winner of the game. Clearly, this function has three parameters: player 1's choice, player 2's choice, and a parameter to return the winner. In pseudocode, this function is:

a. `if` player1 and player2 have the same selection, then this is a tie game.
b. `else`
```
    {
        1. Determine the winning object. (Call function winningObject)
        2. Output each player's choice.
        3. Determine the winning player.
        4. Return the winning player via a reference parameter to the
           function main so that the function main can update the
           winning player's win count.
    }
```

The definition of this function is:

```
void gameResult(objectType play1, objectType play2,
                int& winner)
{
    objectType winnerObject;

    if (play1 == play2)
    {
        winner = 0;
        cout << "Both players selected ";
```

```
            convertEnum(play1);
            cout << ". This game is a tie." << endl;
        }
    else
        {

            winnerObject = winningObject(play1, play2);

                //Output each player's choice
            cout << "Player 1 selected ";
            convertEnum(play1);
            cout << " and player 2 selected ";
            convertEnum(play2);
            cout << ". ";

                //Decide the winner
            if (play1 == winnerObject)
                winner = 1;
            else if (play2 == winnerObject)
                winner = 2;

                //Output the winner
            cout << "Player " << winner << " wins this game."
                << endl;
        }
    }
```

Function convertEnum Because enumeration types cannot be output directly, let's write the function convertEnum to output objects of the enum type objectType. This function has one parameter, of type objectType. It outputs the string that corresponds to the objectType. In pseudocode, this function is:

```
if object is ROCK
    output "Rock"

if object is PAPER
    output "Paper"

if object is SCISSORS
    output "Scissors"
```

The definition of the function convertEnum is:

```
void convertEnum(objectType object)
{
    switch (object)
    {
    case ROCK:
        cout << "Rock";
        break;
    case PAPER:
        cout << "Paper";
        break;
```

7

```
case SCISSORS:
    cout << "Scissors";
}
}
```

Function winningObject

To decide the winner of the game, you look at the players' selections and then at the rules of the game. For example, if one player chooses ROCK and another chooses PAPER, the player who chose PAPER wins. In other words, the winning object is PAPER. The function winningObject, given two objects, decides and returns the winning object. Clearly, this function has two parameters of type objectType, and the value returned by this function is also of type objectType. The definition of this function is:

```
objectType winningObject(objectType play1, objectType play2)
{
    if ((play1 == ROCK && play2 == SCISSORS)
            || (play2 == ROCK && play1 == SCISSORS))
        return ROCK;
    else if ((play1 == ROCK && play2 == PAPER)
                || (play2 == ROCK && play1 == PAPER))
        return PAPER;
    else
        return SCISSORS;
}
```

Function displayResults

After the game is over, this function outputs the final results—that is, the total number of plays and the number of plays won by each player. The total number of plays is stored in the variable gameCount, the number of plays won by player 1 is stored in the variable winCount1, and the number of plays won by player 2 is stored in the variable winCount2. This function has three parameters corresponding to these three variables. Essentially, the definition of this function is:

```
void displayResults(int gCount, int wCount1, int wCount2)
{
    cout << "The total number of plays: " << gCount
        << endl;
    cout << "The number of plays won by player 1: "
        << wCount1 << endl;
    cout << "The number of plays won by player 2: "
        << wCount2 << endl;
}
```

We are now ready to write the algorithm for the function main.

MAIN ALGORITHM

1. Declare the variables.

2. Initialize the variables.

3. Display the rules.

4. Prompt the users to play the game.

5. Get the users' responses to play the game.

6. `while` (response is yes)

    {

    a. Prompt player 1 to make a selection.

    b. Get the play for player 1.

    c. Prompt player 2 to make a selection.

    d. Get the play for player 2.

    e. If both plays are legal:

        {

        i. Increment the total game count.

        ii. Declare the winner of the game.

        iii. Increment the winner's game win count by 1.

        }

    f. Prompt the users to determine whether they want to play again.

    g. Get the players' responses.

    }

7. Output the game results.

PROGRAM LISTING

```
//***********************************************************
// Author: D.S. Malik
//
// Program: Rock, Paper, and Scissors
// This program plays the game of rock, paper, and scissors.
//***********************************************************

#include <iostream>

using namespace std;

enum objectType {ROCK, PAPER, SCISSORS};

    //Function prototypes
void displayRules();
objectType retrievePlay(char selection);
bool validSelection(char selection);
void convertEnum(objectType object);
objectType winningObject(objectType play1, objectType play2);
void gameResult(objectType play1, objectType play2, int& winner);
void displayResults(int gCount, int wCount1, int wCount2);
```

7

```cpp
int main()
{
        //Step 1
    int gameCount; //variable to store the number of
                   //games played
    int winCount1; //variable to store the number of games
                   //won by player 1
    int winCount2; //variable to store the number of games
                   //won by player 2
    int gamewinner;
    char response;  //variable to get the user's response to
                    //play the game
    char selection1;
    char selection2;
    objectType play1;   //player1's selection
    objectType play2;   //player2's selection

        //Initialize variables; Step 2
    gameCount = 0;
    winCount1 = 0;
    winCount2 = 0;

    displayRules();                                     //Step 3

    cout << "Enter Y/y to play the game: ";             //Step 4
    cin >> response;                                    //Step 5
    cout << endl;
    while (response == 'Y' ||  response == 'y')         //Step 6
    {
        cout << "Player 1 enter your choice: ";         //Step 6a
        cin >> selection1;                              //Step 6b
        cout << endl;

        cout << "Player 2 enter your choice: ";         //Step 6c
        cin >> selection2;                              //Step 6d
        cout << endl;

            //Step 6e
        if (validSelection(selection1)
              && validSelection(selection2))
        {
            play1 = retrievePlay(selection1);
            play2 = retrievePlay(selection2);
            gameCount++;                                //Step 6e.i
            gameResult(play1, play2, gamewinner); //Step 6e.ii

            if (gamewinner == 1)                        //Step 6e.iii
                winCount1++;
            else if (gamewinner == 2)
                winCount2++;
        }//end if
```

```
            cout << "Enter Y/y to play the game: ";    //Step 6f
            cin >> response;                            //Step 6g
            cout << endl;
      }//end while

      displayResults(gameCount, winCount1,
                     winCount2);                        //Step 7

      return 0;
}//end main

//Place the definitions of the functions displayRules,
//validSelection, retrievePlay, convertEnum, winningObject,
//gameResult, and displayResults as described previously here.
```

Namespaces

In July 1998, ANSI/ISO Standard C++ was officially approved. Most recent compilers are also compatible with ANSI/ISO Standard C++. (To be absolutely sure, check your compiler's documentation.) The two standards, Standard C++ and ANSI/ISO Standard C++, are virtually the same. The ANSI/ISO Standard C++ language has some features that are not available in Standard C++, which the remainder of this chapter addresses. In subsequent chapters, unless specified otherwise, the C++ syntax applies to both standards. First, we discuss the **namespace** mechanism of the ANSI/ISO Standard C++, which was introduced in Chapter 2.

When a header file, such as **iostream**, is included in a program, the global identifiers in the header file also become the global identifiers in the program. Therefore, if a global identifier in a program has the same name as one of the global identifiers in the header file, the compiler generates a syntax error (such as "identifier redefined"). The same problem can occur if a program uses third-party libraries. To overcome this problem, third-party vendors begin their global identifiers with a special symbol. In Chapter 2, you learned that because compiler vendors begin their global identifier names with an underscore (_), to avoid linking errors, you should not begin identifier names in your program with an underscore (_).

ANSI/ISO Standard C++ tries to solve this problem of overlapping global identifier names with the **namespace** mechanism.

The general syntax of the statement **namespace** is:

```
namespace namespace_name
{
    members
}
```

where **members** is usually named constants, variable declarations, functions, or another **namespace**. Note that **namespace_name** is a C++ identifier.

In C++, namespace is a reserved word.

EXAMPLE 7-8

The statement:

```
namespace globalType
{
    const int N = 10;
    const double RATE = 7.50;
    int count = 0;
    void printResult();
}
```

defines globalType to be a namespace with four members: named constants N and RATE, the variable count, and the function printResult.

The scope of a namespace member is local to the namespace. You can usually access a namespace member outside the namespace in one of two ways, as described below.

The general syntax for accessing a namespace member is:

```
namespace_name::identifier
```

Recall that in C++, :: is called the scope resolution operator.

To access the member RATE of the namespace globalType, the following statement is required:

```
globalType::RATE
```

To access the member printResult (which is a function), the following statement is required:

```
globalType::printResult();
```

Thus, to access a member of a namespace, you use the namespace_name, followed by the scope resolution operator, followed by the member name.

To simplify the accessing of a namespace member, ANSI/ISO Standard C++ provides the use of the statement using. The syntax to use the statement using is as follows:

a. To simplify the accessing of all namespace members:

```
using namespace namespace_name;
```

b. To simplify the accessing of a specific namespace member:

```
using namespace_name::identifier;
```

For example, the using statement:

```
using namespace globalType;
```

simplifies the accessing of all members of the namespace globalType. The statement:

```
using globalType::RATE;
```

simplifies the accessing of the member RATE of the namespace globalType.

In C++, using is a reserved word.

You typically put the using statement after the namespace declaration. For the namespace globalType, for example, you usually write the code as follows:

```
namespace globalType
{
    const int N = 10;
    const double RATE = 7.50;
    int count = 0;
    void printResult();
}
using namespace globalType;
```

After the using statement, to access a namespace member, you do not have to put the namespace_name and the scope resolution operator before the namespace member. However, if a namespace member and a global identifier in a program have the same name, to access this namespace member in the program, the namespace_name and the scope resolution operator must precede the namespace member. Similarly, if a namespace member and an identifier in a block have the same name, to access this namespace member in the block, the namespace_name and the scope resolution operator must precede the namespace member.

Examples 7-9 through 7-12 help clarify the use of the namespace mechanism.

EXAMPLE 7-9

Consider the following C++ code:

```
#include <iostream>

using namespace std;
    .
    .
    .
int main()
{
        .
        .
        .
}
    .
    .
    .
```

In this example, you can refer to the global identifiers of the header file `iostream`, such as `cin`, `cout`, and `endl`, without using the prefix `std::` before the identifier name. The obvious restriction is that the block (or function) that refers to the global identifier (of the header file `iostream`) must not contain any identifier with the same name as this global identifier.

EXAMPLE 7-10

Consider the following C++ code:

```
#include <cmath>

int main()
{
    double x = 15.3;
    double y;

    y = std::pow(x, 2);
    .
    .
    .
}
```

This example accesses the function **pow** of the header file **cmath**.

EXAMPLE 7-11

Consider the following C++ code:

```
#include <iostream>
    .
    .
    .
int main()
{
    using namespace std;
    .
    .
    .
}
    .
    .
    .
```

In this example, the function **main** can refer to the global identifiers of the header file `iostream` without using the prefix `std::` before the identifier name. The **using** statement appears inside the function `main`. Therefore, other functions (if any) should use the prefix `std::` before the name of the global identifier of the header file `iostream` unless the function has a similar `using` statement.

EXAMPLE 7-12

Consider the following C++ code:

```
#include <iostream>

using namespace std;         //Line 1

int t;                       //Line 2
double u;                    //Line 3

namespace expN
{
    int x;                   //Line 4
    char t;                  //Line 5
    double u;                //Line 6
    void printResult();      //Line 7
}

using namespace expN;

int main()
{
    int one;                 //Line 8
    double t;                //Line 9
    double three;            //Line 10

        .
        .
        .

}

void expN::printResult() //Definition of the function printResult
{
        .
        .
        .

}
```

In this C++ program:

1. To refer to the variable `t` in Line 2 in `main`, use the *scope resolution operator*, which is `::` (that is, refer to `t` as `::t`), because the function `main` has a variable named `t` (declared in Line 9). For example, to copy the value of `x` into `t`, you can use the statement `::t = x;`.

2. To refer to the member t (declared in Line 5) of the namespace expN in main, use the prefix expN:: with t (that is, refer to t as expN::t) because there is a global variable named t (declared in Line 2) and a variable named t in main.

3. To refer to the member u (declared in Line 6) of the namespace expN in main, use the prefix expN:: with u (that is, refer to u as expN::u) because there is a global variable named u (declared in Line 3).

4. You can reference the member x (declared in Line 4) of the namespace expN in main as either x or expN::x because there is no global identifier named x and the function main does not contain any identifier named x.

5. The definition of a function that is a member of a namespace, such as printResult, is usually written outside the namespace as in the preceding program. To write the definition of the function printResult, the name of the function in the function heading can be either printResult or expN::printResult (because no other global identifier is named printResult).

NOTE The identifiers in the system-provided header files, such as iostream, cmath, and iomanip, are defined in the namespace std. For this reason, to simplify the accessing of identifiers from these header files, we have been using the following statement in the programs that we write:

```
using namespace std;
```

---

string Type

In Chapter 2, you were introduced to the data type string. Recall that prior to the ANSI/ISO C++ language standard, the Standard C++ library did not provide a string data type. Compiler vendors often supplied their own programmer-defined string type, and the syntax and semantics of string operations often varied from vendor to vendor.

The data type string is a programmer-defined type and is not part of the C++ language; the C++ standard library supplies it. Before using the data type string, the program must include the header file string, as follows:

```
#include <string>
```

Recall that in C++, a string is a sequence of zero or more characters, and strings are enclosed in double quotation marks.

The statement:

```
string name = "William Jacob";
```

declares `name` to be a `string` variable and initializes `name` to `"William Jacob"`. The position of the first character, `W`, in `name` is 0; the position of the second character, `i`, is 1; and so on. That is, the position of the first character in a `string` variable starts with 0, not 1.

The variable `name` can store (just about) any size string.

Chapter 3 discussed I/O operations on the `string` type; Chapter 4 explained relational operations on the `string` type. We recommend that you revisit Chapters 3 and 4 and review the I/O and relational operations on the `string` type.

Other operators, such as the binary operator + (to allow the string concatenation operation) and the array index (subscript) operator [ ], have also been defined for the data type `string`. Let's see how these operators work on the `string` data type.

Suppose you have the following declarations:

```
string str1, str2, str3;
```

The statement:

```
str1 = "Hello There";
```

stores the string `"Hello There"` in `str1`. The statement:

```
str2 = str1;
```

copies the value of `str1` into `str2`.

If `str1 = "Sunny"`, the statement:

```
str2 = str1 + " Day";
```

stores the string `"Sunny Day"` into `str2`.

Suppose `str1 = "Hello"` and `str2 = "There"`. The statement:

```
str3 = str1 + " " + str2;
```

stores `"Hello There"` into `str3`. This statement is equivalent to the statement:

```
str3 = str1 + ' ' + str2;
```

Also, the statement:

```
str1 = str1 + " Mickey";
```

updates the value of `str1` by appending the string `" Mickey"` to its old value. Therefore, the new value of `str1` is `"Hello Mickey"`.

7

> **NOTE**
> For the operator + to work with the `string` data type, one of the operands of + must be a `string` variable. For example, the following statements will not work:
>
> ```
> str1 = "Hello " + "there!"; //illegal
> str2 = "Sunny Day" + '!';    //illegal
> ```

If `str1` = "Hello there", the statement:

`str1[6] = 'T';`

replaces the character t with the character T. Recall that the position of the first character in a `string` variable is 0. Therefore, because t is the seventh character in `str1`, its position is 6.

In C++, `[ ]` is called the **array subscript operator**.

As illustrated previously, using the array subscript operator together with the position of the character, you can access an individual character within a string.

EXAMPLE 7-13

The following program shows the effect of the preceding statements.

```
//Example string operations

#include <iostream>
#include <string>

using namespace std;

int main()
{
    string name = "William Jacob";              //Line 1
    string str1, str2, str3, str4;              //Line 2

    cout << "Line 3: Name = " << name << endl;  //Line 3

    str1 = "Hello There";                       //Line 4
    cout << "Line 5: str1 = " << str1 << endl;  //Line 5

    str2 = str1;                                //Line 6
    cout << "Line 7: str2 = " << str2 << endl;  //Line 7

    str1 = "Sunny";                             //Line 8
    str2 = str1 + " Day";                       //Line 9
    cout << "Line 10: str2 = " << str2 << endl; //Line 10

    str1 = "Hello";                             //Line 11
    str2 = "There";                             //Line 12
    str3 = str1 + " " + str2;                   //Line 13
    cout << "Line 14: str3 = " << str3 << endl; //Line 14
```

```
    str3 = str1 + ' ' + str2;                       //Line 15
    cout << "Line 16: str3 = " << str3 << endl;     //Line 16

    str1 = str1 + " Mickey";                         //Line 17
    cout << "Line 18: str1 = " << str1 << endl;     //Line 18

    str1 = "Hello there";                            //Line 19
    cout << "Line 20: str1[6] = " << str1[6]
         << endl;                                    //Line 20

    str1[6] = 'T';                                   //Line 21
    cout << "Line 22: str1 = " << str1 << endl;     //Line 22

        //String input operations
    cout << "Line 23: Enter a string with "
         << "no blanks: ";                           //Line 23
    cin >> str1;                                     //Line 24

    char ch;                                         //Line 25
    cin.get(ch);            //Read the newline character; Line 26
    cout << endl;                                    //Line 27

    cout << "Line 28: The string you entered = "
         << str1 << endl;                            //Line 28

    cout << "Line 29: Enter a sentence: ";          //Line 29
    getline(cin, str2);                              //Line 30
    cout << endl;                                    //Line 31

    cout << "Line 32: The sentence is: " << str2
         << endl;                                    //Line 32

    return 0;
}
```

Sample Run: In the following sample run, the user input is shaded.

```
Line 3: Name = William Jacob
Line 5: str1 = Hello There
Line 7: str2 = Hello There
Line 10: str2 = Sunny Day
Line 14: str3 = Hello There
Line 16: str3 = Hello There
Line 18: str1 = Hello Mickey
Line 20: str1[6] = t
Line 22: str1 = Hello There
Line 23: Enter a string with no blanks: Programming

Line 28: The string you entered = Programming
Line 29: Enter a sentence: Testing string operations

Line 32: The sentence is: Testing string operations
```

The preceding output is self-explanatory, and its unraveling is left as an exercise for you.

Additional `string` Operations

The data type `string` has a data type, `string::size_type`, and a named constant, `string::npos`, defined as follows:

string::size_type	An unsigned integer (data) type
string::npos	The maximum value of the (data) type `string::size_type`, a number such as `4294967295` on many machines

The data type `string` contains several other functions for string manipulation. The following table describes some these functions. In this table, we assume that `strVar` is a `string` variable and `str` is a string variable, a string constant, or a character array. (Arrays are disussed in Chapter 8.)

TABLE 7-1 Some `string` functions

Expression	Effect
strVar.**at**(index)	Returns the element at the position specified by index.
strVar[index]	Returns the element at the position specified by index.
strVar.**append**(n, ch)	Appends n copies of ch to strVar, in which ch is a char variable or a char constant.
strVar.**append**(str)	Appends str to strVar.
strVar.**clear**()	Deletes all the characters in strVar.
strVar.**compare**(str)	Returns 1 if strVar > str; returns 0 if strVar == str; returns –1 if strVar < str.
strVar.**empty**()	Returns true if strVar is empty; otherwise, it returns false.
strVar.**erase**()	Deletes all the characters in strVar.
strVar.**erase**(pos, n)	Deletes n characters from strVar starting at position pos.

TABLE 7-1 Some string functions (continued)

Expression	Effect
strVar.**find**(str)	Returns the index of the first occurrence of str in strVar. If str is not found, the special value string::npos is returned.
strVar.**find**(str, pos)	Returns the index of the first occurrence at or after pos where str is found in strVar.
strVar.**find_first_of** (str, pos)	Returns the index of the first occurrence of any character of strVar in str. The search starts at pos.
strVar.**find_first_not_of** (str, pos)	Returns the index of the first occurrence of any character of str not in strVar. The search starts at pos.
strVar.**insert**(pos, n, ch);	Inserts n occurrences of the character ch at index pos into strVar; pos and n are of type string::size_type; ch is a character.
strVar.**insert**(pos, str);	Inserts all the characters of str at index pos into strVar.
strVar.**length**()	Returns a value of type string::size_type giving the number of characters strVar.
strVar.**replace**(pos, n, str);	Starting at index pos, replaces the next n characters of strVar with all the characters of str. If n > length of strVar, then all the characters until the end of strVar are replaced.
strVar.**substr**(pos, len)	Returns a string that is a substring of strVar starting at pos. The length of the substring is at most len characters. If len is too large, it means "to the end" of the string in strVar.
strVar.**size**()	Returns a value of type string::size_type giving the number of characters strVar.
strVar.**swap**(str1);	Swaps the contents of strVar and str1. str1 is a string variable.

7

Next, we show how some of these functions work.

EXAMPLE 7-14 (clear, empty, erase, length, AND size FUNCTIONS)

Consider the following statements:

```
string firstName = "Elizabeth";
string name = firstName + " Jones";
string str1 = "It is sunny.";
string str2 = "";
string str3 = "computer science";
string str4 = "C++ programming.";
string str5 = firstName + " is taking " + str4;

string::size_type len;
```

Next, we show the effect of clear, empty, erase, length, and size functions.

Statement	Effect
str3.clear();	str3 = "";
str1.empty();	Returns false;
str2.empty();	Returns true;
str4.erase(11, 4);	str4 = "C++ program.";
cout << firstName.length() << endl;	Outputs 9
cout << name.length() << endl;	Outputs 15
cout << str1.length() << endl;	Outputs 12
cout << str5.size() << endl;	Outputs 36
len = name.length();	The value of len is 15

The following program illustrates the use of the length function.

```
//Example: clear, empty, erase, length, and size functions

#include <iostream>
#include <string>

using namespace std;

int main()
{
    string firstName = "Elizabeth";              //Line 1
    string name = firstName + " Jones";          //Line 2
    string str1 = "It is sunny.";                //Line 3
    string str2 = "";                            //Line 4
    string str3 = "computer science";            //Line 5
    string str4 = "C++ programming.";            //Line 6
    string str5 = firstName + " is taking " + str4;  //Line 7
```

```
    string::size_type len;                                  //Line 8

    cout << "Line 9: str3: " << str3 << endl;               //Line 9
    str3.clear();                                           //Line 10
    cout << "Line 11: After clear, str3: " << str3
         << endl;                                           //Line 11

    cout << "Line 12: str1.empty(): " << str1.empty()
         << endl;                                           //Line 12
    cout << "Line 13: str2.empty(): " << str2.empty()
         << endl;                                           //Line 13

    cout << "Line 14: str4: " << str4 << endl;              //Line 14
    str4.erase(11, 4);                                      //Line 15
    cout << "Line 16: After erase(11, 4), str4: "
         << str4 << endl;                                   //Line 16

    cout << "Line 17: Length of \"" << firstName << "\" = "
         << static_cast<unsigned int> (firstName.length())
         << endl;                                           //Line 17
    cout << "Line 18: Length of \"" << name << "\" = "
         << static_cast<unsigned int> (name.length())
         << endl;                                           //Line 18
    cout << "Line 19: Length of \"" << str1 << "\" = "
         << static_cast<unsigned int> (str1.length())
         << endl;                                           //Line 19
    cout << "Line 20: Size of \"" << str5 << "\" = "
         << static_cast<unsigned int> (str5.size())
         << endl;                                           //Line 20

    len = name.length();                                    //Line 21
    cout << "Line 22: len = "
         << static_cast<unsigned int> (len) << endl;        //Line 22

    return 0;                                               //Line 23
}
```

Sample Run:

```
Line 9: str3: computer science
Line 11: After clear, str3:
Line 12: str1.empty(): 0
Line 13: str2.empty(): 1
Line 14: str4: C++ programming.
Line 16: After erase(11, 4), str4: C++ program.
Line 17: Length of "Elizabeth" = 9
Line 18: Length of "Elizabeth Jones" = 15
Line 19: Length of "It is sunny." = 12
Line 20: Size of "Elizabeth is taking C++ programming." = 36
Line 22: len = 15
```

The output of this program is self-explanatory. The details are left as an exercise for you. Notice that this program uses the static cast operator to output the value returned by the function length. This is because the function length returns a value of the type string::size_type. Without the cast operator, some compilers might give the following warning message:

```
conversion from 'size_t' to 'unsigned int', possible loss of data
```

EXAMPLE 7-15 (find FUNCTION)

Suppose str1 and str2 are of type string. The following are valid calls to the function find:

```
str1.find(str2)
str1.find("the")
str1.find('a')
str1.find(str2 + "xyz")
str1.find(str2 + 'b')
```

Consider the following statements:

```
string sentence = "Outside it is cloudy and warm.";
string str = "cloudy";

string::size_type position;
```

Next, we show the effect of the find function.

Statement	Effect
cout << sentence.find("is") << endl;	Outputs 11
cout << sentence.find('s') << endl;	Outputs 3
cout << sentence.find(str) << endl;	Outputs 14
cout << sentence.find("the") << endl;	Outputs the value of string::npos
cout << sentence.find('i', 6) << endl;	Outputs 8
position = sentence.find("warm");	Assigns 25 to position

Note that the search is case sensitive. Therefore, the position of o (lowercase o) in the string sentence is 16.

The following program evaluates the previous statements.

```
//Example: find function

#include <iostream>
#include <string>

using namespace std;
```

```cpp
int main()
{
    string sentence = "Outside it is cloudy and warm."; //Line 1
    string str = "cloudy";                               //Line 2

    string::size_type position;                          //Line 3

    cout << "Line 4: sentence = \"" << sentence
         << "\"" << endl;                                //Line 4

    cout << "Line 5: The position of \"is\" in sentence = "
         << static_cast<unsigned int> (sentence.find("is"))
         << endl;                                        //Line 5

    cout << "Line 6: The position of 's' in sentence = "
         << static_cast<unsigned int> (sentence.find('s'))
         << endl;                                        //Line 6

    cout << "Line 7: The position of \"" << str
         << "\" in sentence = "
         << static_cast<unsigned int> (sentence.find(str))
         << endl;                                        //Line 7

    cout << "Line 8: The position of \"the\" in sentence = "
         << static_cast<unsigned int> (sentence.find("the"))
         << endl;                                        //Line 8

    cout << "Line 9: The first occurrence of \'i\' in "
         << "sentence \n           after position 6 = "
         << static_cast<unsigned int> (sentence.find('i', 6))
         << endl;                                        //Line 9

    position = sentence.find("warm");                    //Line 10
    cout << "Line 11: " << "Position = "
         << position << endl;                            //Line 11

    return 0;                                            //Line 12
}
```

Sample Run:

```
Line 4: sentence = "Outside it is cloudy and warm."
Line 5: The position of "is" in sentence = 11
Line 6: The position of 's' in sentence = 3
Line 7: The position of "cloudy" in sentence = 14
Line 8: The position of "the" in sentence = 4294967295
Line 9: The first occurrence of 'i' in sentence
         after position 6 = 8
Line 11: Position = 25
```

The output of this program is self-explanatory. The details are left as an exercise for you. Notice that this program uses the static cast operator to output the value returned by the function `find`. This is because the function `find` returns a value of the type `string::size_type`. Without the cast operator, some compilers might give the following warning message:

```
conversion from 'size_t' to 'unsigned int', possible loss of data
```

EXAMPLE 7-16 (insert AND replace FUNCTIONS)

Suppose that you have the following statements:

```
string firstString = "Cloudy and warm.";
string secondString ="Hello there";
string thirdString = "Henry is taking programming I.";
string str1 = " very ";
string str2 = "Lisa";
```

Next, we show the effect of `insert` and `replace` functions.

Statement	Effect
`firstString.insert(10, str1);`	`firstString = "Cloudy and very warm."`
`secondString.insert(11, 5, '!');`	`secondString = "Hello there!!!!!"`
`thirdString.replace(0, 5, str2);`	`thirdString = "Lisa is taking programming I."`

The following program evaluates the previous statements.

```
//Example: insert and replace functions

#include <iostream>
#include <string>

using namespace std;

int main()
{
    string firstString = "Cloudy and warm.";                    //Line 1
    string secondString = "Hello there";                        //Line 2
    string thirdString = "Henry is taking programming I."; //Line 3
```

```
string str1 = " very ";                                        //Line 4
string str2 = "Lisa";                                          //Line 5

cout << "Line 6: firstString = " << firstString
     << endl;                                                  //Line 6
firstString.insert(10, str1);                                  //Line 7
cout << "Line 8: After insert; firstString = "
     << firstString << endl;                                   //Line 8

cout << "Line 9: secondString = " << secondString
     << endl;                                                  //Line 9
secondString.insert(11, 5, '!');                               //Line 10
cout << "Line 11: After insert; secondString = "
     << secondString << endl;                                  //Line 11

cout << "Line 12: thirdString = " << thirdString
     << endl;                                                  //Line 12
thirdString.replace(0, 5, str2);                               //Line 13
cout << "Line 14: After replace, thirdString = "
     << thirdString << endl;                                   //Line 14

return 0;                                                      //Line 15
}
```

Sample Run:

```
Line 6: firstString = Cloudy and warm.
Line 8: After insert; firstString = Cloudy and very  warm.
Line 9: secondString = Hello there
Line 11: After insert; secondString = Hello there!!!!!
Line 12: thirdString = Henry is taking programming I.
Line 14: After replace, thirdString = Lisa is taking programming I.
```

The output of this program is self-explanatory. The details are left as an exercise for you.

EXAMPLE 7-17 (substr FUNCTION)

Consider the following statements:

```
string sentence;
string str;

sentence = "It is cloudy and warm.";
```

Next, we show the effect of the `substr` function.

Statement	Effect
`cout << sentence.substr(0, 5) << endl;`	Outputs: `It is`
`cout << sentence.substr(6, 6) << endl;`	Outputs: `cloudy`
`cout << sentence.substr(6, 16) << endl;`	Outputs: `cloudy and warm.`
`cout << sentence.substr(17, 10) << endl;`	Outputs: `warm.`
`cout << sentence.substr(3, 6) << endl;`	Outputs: `is clo`
`str = sentence.substr(0, 8);`	`str = "It is cl"`
`str = sentence.substr(2, 10);`	`str = " is cloudy"`

The following program illustrates how to use the `string` function `substr`.

```cpp
//Example: substr function

#include <iostream>
#include <string>

using namespace std;

int main()
{
    string sentence;                                        //Line 1
    string str;                                             //Line 2

    sentence = "It is cloudy and warm.";                    //Line 3

    cout << "Line 4: substr(0, 5) in \""
         << sentence << "\" = \""
         << sentence.substr(0, 5) << "\"" << endl;          //Line 4

    cout << "Line 5: substr(6, 6) in \""
         << sentence << "\" = \""
         << sentence.substr(6, 6) << "\"" << endl;          //Line 5

    cout << "Line 6: substr(6, 16) in \""
         << sentence << "\" = " << endl
         << "           \"" << sentence.substr(6, 16)
         << "\"" << endl;                                   //Line 6

    cout << "Line 7: substr(17, 10) in \""
         << sentence << "\" = \""
         << sentence.substr(17, 10) << "\"" << endl; //Line 7

    cout << "Line 8: substr(3, 6) in \""
         << sentence << "\" = \""
         << sentence.substr(3, 6) << "\"" << endl;          //Line 8
```

```
    str = sentence.substr(0, 8);                    //Line 9
    cout << "Line 10: " << "str = \"" << str
        << "\"" << endl;                             //Line 10

    str = sentence.substr(2, 10);                    //Line 11
    cout << "Line 12: " << "str = \"" << str
        << "\"" << endl;                             //Line 12

    return 0;
}
```

Sample Run:

```
Line 4: substr(0, 5) in "It is cloudy and warm." = "It is"
Line 5: substr(6, 6) in "It is cloudy and warm." = "cloudy"
Line 6: substr(6, 16) in "It is cloudy and warm." =
        "cloudy and warm."
Line 7: substr(17, 10) in "It is cloudy and warm." = "warm."
Line 8: substr(3, 6) in "It is cloudy and warm." = "is clo"
Line 10: str = "It is cl"
Line 12: str = " is cloudy"
```

The output of this program is self-explanatory. The details are left as an exercise for you.

7

EXAMPLE 7-18 (swap FUNCTION)

The **swap** function is used to swap—that is, interchange—the contents of two string variables.

Suppose you have the following statements:

```
string str1 = "Warm";
string str2 = "Cold";
```

After the following statement executes, the value of **str1** is **"Cold"** and the value of **str2** is **"Warm"**.

```
str1.swap(str2);
```

NOTE   Additional **string** functions are described in Appendix F (Header File **string**).

PROGRAMMING EXAMPLE: Pig Latin Strings

In this programming example, we write a program that prompts the user to input a string and then outputs the string in the pig Latin form. The rules for converting a string into pig Latin form are as follows:

1. If the string begins with a vowel, add the string **"-way"** at the end of the string. For example, the pig Latin form of the string **"eye"** is **"eye-way"**.

2. If the string does not begin with a vowel, first add **"-"** at the end of the string. Then rotate the string one character at a time; that is, move the first character of the string to the end of the string until the first character of the string becomes a vowel. Then add the string **"ay"** at the end. For example, the pig Latin form of the string **"There"** is **"ere-Thay"**.

3. Strings such as **"by"** contain no vowels. In cases like this, the letter y can be considered a vowel. So, for this program, the vowels are a, e, i, o, u, y, A, E, I, O, U, and Y. Therefore, the pig Latin form of **"by"** is **"y-bay"**.

4. Strings such as **"1234"** contain no vowels. The pig Latin form of the string **"1234"** is **"1234-way"**. That is, the pig Latin form of a string that has no vowels in it is the string followed by the string **"-way"**.

Input   Input to the program is a string.

Output   Output of the program is the string in the pig Latin form.

PROBLEM
ANALYSIS
AND
ALGORITHM
DESIGN

Suppose that `str` denotes a string. To convert `str` into pig Latin, check the first character, `str[0]`, of `str`. If `str[0]` is a vowel, add **"-way"** at the end of `str`—that is, `str = str + "-way"`.

Suppose that the first character of `str`, `str[0]`, is not a vowel. First, add **"-"** at the end of the string. Then, remove the first character of `str` from `str` and put it at the end of `str`. Now, the second character of `str` becomes the first character of `str`. This process of checking the first character of `str` and moving it to the end of `str` if the first character of `str` is not a vowel is repeated until either the first character of `str` is a vowel or all the characters of `str` are processed, in which case `str` does not contain any vowels.

In this program, we write a function `isVowel` to determine whether a character is a vowel, a function `rotate` to move the first character of `str` to the end of `str`, and a function `pigLatinString` to find the pig Latin form of `str`. The previous discussion translates into the following algorithm:

1. Get `str`.
2. Find the pig Latin form of `str` by using the function `pigLatinString`.
3. Output the pig Latin form of `str`.

Before writing the main algorithm, each of these functions is described in detail.

Function isVowel This function takes a character as a parameter and returns `true` if the character is a vowel and `false` otherwise. The definition of the function `isVowel` is:

```
bool isVowel(char ch)
{
    switch (ch)
    {
    case 'A':
    case 'E':
    case 'I':
    case 'O':
    case 'U':
    case 'Y':
    case 'a':
    case 'e':
    case 'i':
    case 'o':
    case 'u':
    case 'y':
        return true;
    default:
        return false;
    }
}
```

Function rotate This function takes a string as a parameter, removes the first character of the string, and places it at the end of the string. This is done by extracting the substring, starting at position 1 (which is the second character) until the end of the string, and then adding the first character of the string. The new string is returned as the value of this function. Essentially, the definition of the function `rotate` is:

```
string rotate(string pStr)
{
    string::size_type len = pStr.length();

    string rStr;

    rStr = pStr.substr(1, len - 1) + pStr[0];

    return rStr;
}
```

Function pigLatinString This function takes a string, pStr, as a parameter and returns the pig Latin form of pStr. Suppose pStr denotes the string to be converted to its pig Latin form. There are three possible cases: pStr[0] is a vowel, pStr contains a vowel and the first character of pStr is not a vowel, or pStr contains no vowels. Suppose that pStr[0] is not a vowel. Move the first character of pStr to the end of pStr. This process is repeated until either the first character of pStr has become a vowel or all the characters of pStr are checked, in which case pStr does not contain any vowels. This discussion translates into the following algorithm:

1. If pStr[0] is a vowel, add **"-way"** at the end of pStr.
2. Suppose pStr[0] is not a vowel.
3. Move the first character of pStr to the end of pStr. The second character of pStr becomes the first character of pStr. Now pStr may or may not contain a vowel. We use a `bool` variable, foundVowel, which is set to `true` if pStr contains a vowel and `false` otherwise.

    a. Suppose that len denotes the length of pStr.
    b. Initialize foundVowel to `false`.
    c. If pStr[0] is not a vowel, move pStr[0] to the end of pStr by calling the function rotate.
    d. Repeat Step b until either the first character of pStr becomes a vowel or all the characters of pStr have been checked.
4. Convert pStr into the pig Latin form.
5. Return pStr.

The definition of the function pigLatinString is:

```
string pigLatinString(string pStr)
{
    string::size_type len;

    bool foundVowel;

    string::size_type counter;

    if (isVowel(pStr[0]))                              //Step 1
        pStr = pStr + "-way";
    else                                               //Step 2
    {
        pStr = pStr + '-';
        pStr = rotate(pStr);                           //Step 3

        len = pStr.length();                           //Step 3.a
        foundVowel = false;                            //Step 3.b
```

```cpp
        for (counter = 1; counter < len - 1;
                          counter++)            //Step 3.d
            if (isVowel(pStr[0]))
            {
                foundVowel = true;
                break;
            }
            else                                //Step 3.c
                pStr = rotate(pStr);

        if (!foundVowel)                         //Step 4
            pStr = pStr.substr(1, len) + "-way";
        else
            pStr = pStr + "ay";
    }

    return pStr;                                 //Step 5
}
```

MAIN
ALGORITHM

1. Get the string.
2. Call the function pigLatinString to find the pig Latin form of the string.
3. Output the pig Latin form of the string.

PROGRAM LISTING

```cpp
//************************************************************
// Author: D.S. Malik
//
// Program: Pig Latin Strings
// This program reads a string and outputs the pig Latin form
// of the string.
//************************************************************

#include <iostream>
#include <string>

using namespace std;

bool isVowel(char ch);
string rotate(string pStr);
string pigLatinString(string pStr);

int main()
{
    string str;

    cout << "Enter a string: ";
    cin >> str;
```

```
    cout << endl;

    cout << "The pig Latin form of " << str << " is: "
         << pigLatinString(str) << endl;

    return 0;
}
```

```
//Place the definitions of the functions isVowel, rotate, and
//pigLatinString and as described previously here.
```

Sample Runs: In these sample runs, the user input is shaded.

Sample Run 1:

```
Enter a string: eye

The pig Latin form of eye is: eye-way
```

Sample Run 2:

```
Enter a string: There

The pig Latin form of There is: ere-Thay
```

Sample Run 3:

```
Enter a string: why

The pig Latin form of why is: y-whay
```

Sample Run 4:

```
Enter a string: 123456

The pig Latin form of 123456 is: 123456-way
```

QUICK REVIEW

1. An enumeration type is a set of ordered values.
2. C++'s reserved word **enum** is used to create an enumeration type.
3. The syntax of **enum** is:

   ```
   enum typeName {value1, value2,...};
   ```

   in which `value1, value2,...` are identifiers, and `value1 < value2 < ...`.
4. No arithmetic operations are allowed on the enumeration type.

5. Relational operators can be used with `enum` values.

6. Enumeration type values cannot be input or output directly.

7. Enumeration types can be passed as parameters to functions either by value or by reference.

8. A function can return a value of the enumeration type.

9. An anonymous type is one in which a variable's values are specified without any type name.

10. C++'s reserved word `typedef` is used to create synonyms or aliases to previously defined data types.

11. Anonymous types cannot be passed as parameters to functions.

12. The `namespace` mechanism is a feature of ANSI/ISO Standard C++.

13. A `namespace` member is usually a named constant, variable, function, or another `namespace`.

14. The scope of a `namespace` member is local to the `namespace`.

15. One way to access a `namespace` member outside the `namespace` is to precede the `namespace` member name with the `namespace` name and scope resolution operator.

16. In C++, `namespace` is a reserved word.

17. To use the `namespace` mechanism, the program must include the ANSI/ISO Standard C++ header files—that is, the header files without the extension h.

18. The `using` statement simplifies the accessing of `namespace` members.

19. In C++, `using` is a reserved word.

20. The keyword `namespace` must appear in the `using` statement.

21. When accessing a `namespace` member without the `using` statement, the `namespace` name and the scope resolution operator must precede the name of the `namespace` member.

22. To use an identifier declared in the standard header files without the `namespace` name, after including all the necessary header files, the following statement must appear in the program:

    `using namespace std;`

23. A string is a sequence of zero or more characters.

24. Strings in C++ are enclosed in double quotation marks.

25. To use the type `string`, the program must include the header file `string`. The other header files used in the program should be ANSI/ISO Standard C++ style header files.

26. The assignment operator can be used with the `string` type.

27. The operator + can be used to concatenate two values of the type `string`. For the operator + to work with the `string` data type, one of the operands of + must be a `string` variable.

28. Relational operators, discussed in Chapter 4, can be applied to the `string` type.

29. In a string, the position of the first character is 0, the position of the second character is 1, and so on.

30. The length of a string is the number of characters in the string.

31. In C++, `[ ]` is called the array subscript operator.

32. To access an individual character within a string, use the array subscript operator together with the position of the character.

33. The `string` type contains functions such as `at`, `append`, `clear`, `compare`, `erase`, `find`, `find_first_of`, `find_first_not_of`, `insert`, `length`, `replace`, `size`, `substr`, and `swap` to manipulate strings. These functions are describe in Table 7-1.

EXERCISES

1. Mark the following statements as true or false.

   a. The following is a valid C++ enumeration type:

   ```
   enum romanNumerals {I, V, X, L, C, D, M};
   ```

   b. Given the declaration:

   ```
   enum cars {FORD, GM, TOYOTA, HONDA};
   cars domesticCars = FORD;
   ```

   the statement:

   ```
   domesticCars = domesticCars + 1;
   ```

   sets the value of `domesticCars` to `GM`.

   c. A function can return a value of an enumeration type.

   d. You can input the value of an enumeration type directly from a standard input device.

   e. The only arithmetic operations allowed on the enumeration type are increment and decrement.

   f. The values in the domain of an enumeration type are called enumerators.

   g. The following are legal C++ statements in the same block of a C++ program:

   ```
   enum mathStudent {BILL, JOHN, LISA, RON, CINDY, SHELLY};
   enum historyStudent {AMANDA, BOB, JACK, TOM, SUSAN};
   ```

   h. The following statement creates an anonymous type:

   ```
   enum {A, B, C, D, F} studentGrade;
   ```

   i. You can use the `namespace` mechanism with header files with the extension h.

j. Suppose `str = "ABCD";`. After the statement `str[1] = 'a';`, the value of `str` is `"aBCD"`.

k. Suppose `str = "abcd"`. After the statement:

```
str = str + "ABCD";
```

the value of `str` is `"ABCD"`.

2. Write C++ statements that do the following:

a. Define an `enum` type, `courseType`, with the values ALGEBRA, BEGINNING_SPANISH, ASTRONOMY, GENERAL_CHEMISTRY, PHYSICS, and LOGIC.

b. Declare a variable `newClass` of the type `courseType`.

c. Assign ASTRONOMY to the variable `newClass`.

d. Advance `newClass` to the next value in the list.

e. Output the value of the variable `newClass`.

f. Input value in the variable `newClass`.

3. Given:

```
enum currencyType {DOLLAR, POUND, FRANK, LIRA, MARK};
currencyType currency;
```

which of the following statements are valid?

a. `currency = DOLLAR;`

b. `cin >> currency;`

c. `currency = static_cast<currencyType>(currency + 1);`

d. `for (currency = DOLLAR; currency <= MARK; currency++)`
   `    cout << "*";`

4. Consider the following declaration:

```
enum seasonType {FALL, WINTER, SPRING, SUMMER, RAINY};
seasonType   season;
```

Answer the following questions:

a. What is the value of `static_cast<int>(SPRING)`?

b. What is the value, if any, of the following expression?
   `static_cast<seasonType>(static_cast<int>(RAINY) - 1)`

c. What is the value, if any, of the following expression?
   `static_cast<seasonType>(static_cast<int>(WINTER) + 2)`

d. What is the value, if any, of the expression: `WINTER <= SUMMER`

e. What is the output, if any, of the following code?

```
for (season = FALL; season < SUMMER; season++)
   cout << "$";
cout << endl;
```

7

5. Suppose that the **enum** `courseType` is as defined in Exercise 2. Write a C++ function that can be used to input a value in a variable of type `courseType`.

6. Suppose that the **enum** `courseType` is as defined in Exercise 2. Write a C++ function that can be used to ouput the value of a variable of type `courseType`.

7. What are some of the drawbacks of an anonymous type?

8. Define an enumeration type `triangleType` with values EQUILATERAL, RIGHT, ISOSCELES, and SCALENE. Also declare the variable `triangle` of type `triangleType` while defining this type.

9. What is wrong with the following program?

```
#include <iostream>          //Line 1

namespace std;               //Line 2

int main()                   //Line 3
{                            //Line 4
    cout << "*$*" << endl;   //Line 5

    return 0;                //Line 6
}                            //Line 7
```

10. What is wrong with the following program?

```
#include <iostream.h>                            //Line 1

int main()                                       //Line 2
{                                                //Line 3
    int num = 5;                                 //Line 4
    std::cout << "num = " << num << endl;        //Line 5
    return 0;                                     //Line 6
}                                                //Line 7
```

11. What is wrong with the following program?

```
#include <iostream>             //Line 1

using namespace sdt;            //Line 2

int main()                      //Line 3
{                               //Line 4
    int x;                      //Line 5

    std::cin >> x;              //Line 6
    cout << "x = " << x << endl; //Line 7

    return 0;                   //Line 8
}                               //Line 9
```

12. What is wrong with the following program?

```
#include <iostream>                                //Line 1

namespace mySpace                                  //Line 2
{                                                  //Line 3
    const double RATE = 15.35;                     //Line 4
    int a;                                         //Line 5
}                                                  //Line 6

using namespace std;                               //Line 7

int main()                                         //Line 8
{                                                  //Line 9
    int b;                                         //Line 10

    cin >> b;                                      //Line 11
    a = b;                                         //Line 12
    cout << RATE << " " << a + 2 << " " << b
        << endl;                                   //Line 13

    return 0;                                      //Line 14
}                                                  //Line 15
```

13. What is wrong with the following program?

```
#include <iostream>                                //Line 1

namespace aaa                                      //Line 2
{
    const int X = 0;                               //Line 3
    double y;                                      //Line 4
}

using namespace std;                               //Line 5

int main()                                         //Line 6
{
    y = 34.50;                                     //Line 7
    cout << "X = " << X << ", y = " << y
        << endl;                                   //Line 8
    return 0;                                      //Line 9
}
```

14. What is wrong with the following program?

```
#include <iostream>                                //Line 1
#include <cmath>                                   //Line 2

using std;                                         //Line 3

int main()                                         //Line 4
{                                                  //Line 5
    std::cout << pow(3, 4.0) << endl;              //Line 6
    return 0;                                      //Line 7
}                                                  //Line 8
```

15. Consider the following C++ code:

```
string str1;
string str2;
char ch;
int index;

cin >> str1;
cin >> str2;
cin >> index;

ch = str1[index];
str1[index] = str2[index];
str2[index] = ch;

cout << str1 << " " << str2 << endl;
```

Answer the following questions:

a. What is the output if the input is `Hello There 2`?

b. What is the output if the input is `Diamond Gold 0`?

c. What is the output if the input is `C++ Java 1`?

16. Suppose that you have the following statements:

```
string str1, str2;

cin >> str1 >> str2;

if (str1 == str2)
    cout << str1 + '!' << endl;
else if (str1 > str2)
    cout << str1 + " > " + str2 << endl;
else
    cout << str1 + " < " + str2 << endl;
```

Answer the following questions:

a. What is the output if the input is `Programming Project`?

b. What is the output if the input is `Summer Trip`?

c. What is the output if the input is `Winter Cold`?

17. What is the output of the following program?

```
#include <iostream>
#include <string>

using namespace std;

int main()
{
    string str1 = "Trip to Hawaii";
    string str2 = "Summer or Fall";
    string newStr;

    newStr = str2 + ' ' + str1;
```

```
        cout << newStr << endl;
        cout << str1 + " in " +  str2 << endl;
        cout << newStr.length() << endl;
        cout << str1.find('H') << endl;
        cout << str2.find("or") << endl;
        cout << newStr.substr(10, 19) << endl;
        cout << newStr.replace(23, 6, "******") << endl;

        string str = "C++ Programming";
        cout << str << endl;
        cout << str.length() << endl;

        str[0] = 'J';
        str[2] = '$';

        cout << str << endl;

        return 0;
    }
```

18. Consider the following statement:

    ```
    string str = "Now is the time for the party!";
    ```

    What is the output of the following statements? (Assume that all parts are independent of each other.)

    a. `cout << str.size() << endl;`

    b. `cout << str.substr(7, 8) << endl;`

    c. ```
        string::size_type ind = str.find('f');
        string s = str.substr(ind + 4, 9);
        cout << s << endl;
        ```

    d.  `cout << str.insert(11, "best ") << endl;`

    e.  ```
        str.erase(16, 14);
        str.insert(16, "to study for the exam? ");
        cout << str << endl;
        ```

PROGRAMMING EXERCISES

1. a. Define an enumeration type, `triangleType`, that has the values `scalene`, `isosceles`, `equilateral`, and `noTriangle`.

    b. Write a function, `triangleShape`, that takes as parameters three numbers, each of which represents the length of a side of the triangle. The function should return the shape of the triangle. (*Note:* In a triangle, the sum of the lengths of any two sides is greater than the length of the third side.)

    c. Write a program that prompts the user to input the length of the sides of a triangle and outputs the shape of the triangle.

7

2. Redo Programming Exercise 15 of Chapter 4 (cell phone company) so that all of the named constants are defined in a **namespace**.

3. The Programming Example: Pig Latin Strings converts a string into the pig Latin form, but it processes only one word. Rewrite the program so that it can be used to process a text of an unspecified length. If a word ends with a punctuation mark, in the pig Latin form, put the punctuation at the end of the string. For example, the pig Latin form of `Hello!` is `ello-Hay!`. Assume that the text contains the following punctuation marks: `,` (comma), `.` (period), `?` (question mark), `;` (semicolon), and `:` (colon). (Your program may store the output in a file.)

4. Write a program that prompts the user to input a string. The program then uses the function **substr** to remove all the vowels from the string. For example, if `str = "There"`, then after removing all the vowels, `str = "Thr"`. After removing all the vowels, output the string. Your program must contain a function to remove all the vowels and a function to determine whether a character is a vowel.

5. Write a program that can be used to calculate the federal tax. The tax is calculated as follows: For single people, the standard exemption is $4,000; for married people, the standard exemption is $7,000. A person can also put up to 6% of his or her gross income in a pension plan. The tax rates are as follows: If the taxable income is:

   - Between $0 and $15,000, the tax rate is 15%.
   - Between $15,001 and $40,000, the tax is $2,250 plus 25% of the taxable income over $15,000.
   - Over $40,000, the tax is $8,460 plus 35% of the taxable income over $40,000.

   Prompt the user to enter the following information:

   - Marital status
   - If the marital status is "married," ask for the number of children under the age of 14
   - Gross salary (If the marital status is "married" and both spouses have income, enter the combined salary.)
   - Percentage of gross income contributed to a pension fund

   Your program must consist of at least the following functions:

   a. Function **getData**: This function asks the user to enter the relevant data.

   b. Function **taxAmount**: This function computes and returns the tax owed.

   To calculate the taxable income, subtract the sum of the standard exemption, the amount contributed to a pension plan, and the personal exemption, which is $1,500 per person. (Note that if a married couple has two children under the age of 14, then the personal exemption is $1,500 ★ 4 = $6,000.)

6. Write a program that uses a random number generator to generate a two digit positive integer and allows the user to perform one or more of the following operations:

   a. Double the number.

   b. Reverse the digits of the number.

   c. Raise the number to the power of 2, 3, or 4.

   d. Sum the digits of the number.

   e. If the number is a two digit number, then raise the first digit to the power of the second digit.

   f. If the number is a three digit number and the last digit is less than or equal to 4, then raise the first two digits to the power of the last digit.

   After performing an operation if the number is less than 10, add 10 to the number. Also, after each operation determine if the number is prime.

   Each successive operation should be performed on the number generated by the last operation. Your program should not contain any global variables and each of these operations must be implemented by a separate function. Also, your program should be menu driven.

7. (**Fraction calculator**) Write a program that lets the user perform arithmetic operations on fractions. Fractions are of the form a/b, in which a and b are integers and $b \neq 0$. Your program must be menu driven, allowing the user to select the operation (+, -, *, or /) and input the numerator and denominator of each fraction. Furthermore, your program must consist of at least the following functions:

   a. Function `menu`: This function informs the user about the program's purpose, explains how to enter data, and allows the user to select the operation.

   b. Function `addFractions`: This function takes as input four integers representing the numerators and denominators of two fractions, adds the fractions, and returns the numerator and denominator of the result. (Notice that this function has a total of six parameters.)

   c. Function `subtractFractions`: This function takes as input four integers representing the numerators and denominators of two fractions, subtracts the fractions, and returns the numerator and denominator of the result. (Notice that this function has a total of six parameters.)

   d. Function `multiplyFractions`: This function takes as input four integers representing the numerators and denominators of two fractions, multiplies the fractions, and returns the numerators and denominators of the result. (Notice that this function has a total of six parameters.)

e. Function `divideFractions`: This function takes as input four integers representing the numerators and denominators of two fractions, divides the fractions, and returns the numerator and denominator of the result. (Notice that this function has a total of six parameters.)

Some sample outputs are:

```
3 / 4 + 2 / 5 = 23 / 20
2 / 3 * 3 / 5 = 6 / 15
```

Your answer need not be in the lowest terms.

8. Write a program that reads in a line consisting of a student's name, Social Security number, user ID, and password. The program outputs the string in which all the digits of the Social Security number, and all the characters in the password are replaced by **x**. (The Social Security number is in the form 000-00-0000, and the user ID and the password do not contain any spaces.) Your program should not use the operator [ ] to access a string element. Use the appropriate functions described in Table 7-1.

9. You are given a file consisting of students' names in the following form: `lastName, firstName middleName`. (Note that a student may not have a middle name.) Write a program that converts each name to the following form: `firstName middleName lastName`. Your program must read each student's entire name in a variable and must consist of a function that takes as input a string, consists of a student's name, and returns the string consisting of the altered name. Use the string function `find` to find the index of `,`; the function `length` to find the length of the string; and the function `substr` to extract the `firstName`, `middleName`, and `lastName`.

CHAPTER

8

ARRAYS AND STRINGS

IN THIS CHAPTER, YOU WILL:

- · Learn about arrays
- · Explore how to declare and manipulate data into arrays
- · Learn about "array index out of bounds"
- · Become familiar with the restrictions on array processing
- · Discover how to pass an array as a parameter to a function
- · Learn how to search an array
- · Learn how to sort an array
- · Learn about C-strings
- · Examine the use of string functions to process C-strings
- · Discover how to input data into—and output data from—a C-string
- · Learn about parallel arrays
- · Discover how to manipulate data in a two-dimensional array
- · Learn about multidimensional arrays

In previous chapters, you worked with simple data types. In Chapter 2, you learned that C++ data types fall into three categories. One of these categories is the structured data type. This chapter and the next few chapters focus on structured data types.

Recall that a data type is called **simple** if variables of that type can store only one value at a time. In contrast, in a **structured data type**, each data item is a collection of other data items. Simple data types are building blocks of structured data types. The first structured data type that we will discuss is an array. In Chapters 9 and 10, we will discuss other structured data types.

Before formally defining an array, let us consider the following problem. We want to write a C++ program that reads five numbers, finds their sum, and prints the numbers in reverse order.

In Chapter 5, you learned how to read numbers, print them, and find the sum and average. Suppose that you are given five test scores and you are asked to write a program that finds the average test score and output all the test scores that are less than the average test score. (For simplicity, we are considering only five test scores. After introducing arrays, we will show how to effectively process more than five test scores.)

```cpp
//Program to find the average test score and output the average
//test score and all the test scores that are less than
//the average test score.

#include <iostream>
#include <iomanip>

using namespace std;

int main()
{
    int test0, test1, test2, test3, test4;
    double average;

    cout << fixed << showpoint << setprecision(2);

    cout << "Enter five test scores: ";
    cin >> test0 >> test1 >> test2 >> test3 >> test4;
    cout << endl;

    average = (test0 + test1 + test2 + test3 + test4) / 5.0;

    cout << "The average test score = " << average << endl;

    if (test0 < average)
        cout << test0 << " is less than the average test score." << endl;

    if (test1 < average)
        cout << test1 << " is less than the average test score." << endl;

    if (test2 < average)
        cout << test2 << " is less than the average test score." << endl;

    if (test3 < average)
        cout << test3 << " is less than the average test score." << endl;
```

```
      if (test4 < average)
          cout << test4 << " is less than the average test score." << endl;

      return 0;
}
```

Sample Run: In this sample run, the user input is shaded.

```
Enter five test scores: 85 62 94 56 71

The average test score = 73.60
62 is less than the average test score.
56 is less than the average test score.
71 is less than the average test score.
```

This program works fine. However, if you need to read and process 100 (or more) test scores, you would have to declare 100 variables and write many cin, cout, and if statements. Thus, for large amounts of data, this type of program is not desirable.

Note the following in the previous program:

1. Five variables must be declared because test scores less than the average test scores need to be printed.

2. All test scores are of type int—that is, of the same data type.

3. The way in which these variables are declared indicates that the variables to store these numbers all have the same name—except the last character, which is a number.

4. All the if statements are similar, except the name of the variables to store the test scores.

Statement 1 tells you that you have to declare five variables. Statements 3 and 4 tell you that it would be convenient if you could somehow put the last character, which is a number, into a counter variable and use one for loop to count from 0 to 4 for reading and another for loop to process the if statements. Finally, because all variables are of the same type, you should be able to specify how many variables must be declared—and their data type—with a simpler statement than the one we used earlier.

The data structure that lets you do all of these things in C++ is called an array.

Arrays

An **array** is a collection of a fixed number of components all of the same data type. A **one-dimensional array** is an array in which the components are arranged in a list form. This section discusses only one-dimensional arrays. Arrays of two dimensions or more are discussed later in this chapter.

The general form for declaring a one-dimensional array is:

```
dataType arrayName[intExp];
```

in which intExp is any constant expression that evaluates to a positive integer. Also, intExp specifies the number of components in the array.

EXAMPLE 8-1

The statement:

```
int num[5];
```

declares an array num of five components. Each component is of type int. The components are num[0], num[1], num[2], num[3], and num[4]. Figure 8-1 illustrates the array num.

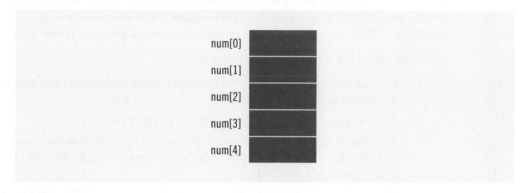

FIGURE 8-1 Array num

NOTE To save space, we also draw an array, as shown in Figure 8-2(a) or 8-2(b).

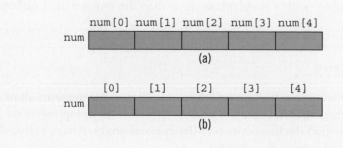

FIGURE 8-2 Array num

Accessing Array Components

The general form (syntax) used for accessing an array component is:

```
arrayName[indexExp]
```

in which `indexExp`, called the **index**, is any expression whose value is a nonnegative integer. The index value specifies the position of the component in the array.

In C++, `[]` is an operator called the **array subscripting operator**. Moreover, in C++, the array index starts at 0.

Consider the following statement:

```
int list[10];
```

This statement declares an array `list` of 10 components. The components are `list[0]`, `list[1]`, ..., `list[9]`. In other words, we have declared 10 variables (see Figure 8-3).

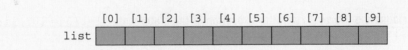

FIGURE 8-3 Array `list`

The assignment statement:

```
list[5] = 34;
```

stores 34 in `list[5]`, which is the sixth component of the array `list` (see Figure 8-4).

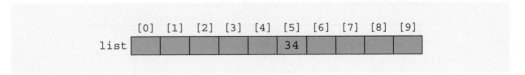

FIGURE 8-4 Array `list` after execution of the statement `list[5]= 34;`

Suppose `i` is an `int` variable. Then, the assignment statement:

```
list[3] = 63;
```

is equivalent to the assignment statements:

```
i = 3;
list[i] = 63;
```

If i is 4, then the assignment statement:

```
list[2 * i - 3] = 58;
```

stores 58 in list[5] because 2 * i - 3 evaluates to 5. The index expression is evaluated first, giving the position of the component in the array.

Next, consider the following statements:

```
list[3] = 10;
list[6] = 35;
list[5] = list[3] + list[6];
```

The first statement stores 10 in list[3], the second statement stores 35 in list[6], and the third statement adds the contents of list[3] and list[6] and stores the result in list[5] (see Figure 8-5).

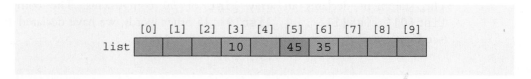

FIGURE 8-5 Array list after execution of the statements list[3]= 10;, list[6]= 35;, and list[5] = list[3] + list[6];

EXAMPLE 8-2

You can also declare arrays as follows:

```
const int ARRAY_SIZE = 10;
int list[ARRAY_SIZE];
```

That is, you can first declare a named constant and then use the value of the named constant to declare an array and specify its size.

NOTE When you declare an array, its size must be known. For example, you cannot do the following:

```
int arraySize;                              //Line 1

cout << "Enter the size of the array: "; //Line 2
cin >> arraySize;                           //Line 3
cout << endl;                               //Line 4

int list[arraySize];                        //Line 5; not allowed
```

The statement in Line 2 asks the user to enter the size of the array when the program executes. The statement in Line 3 inputs the size of the array into `arraySize`. When the compiler compiles Line 1, the value of the variable `arraySize` is unknown. Thus, when the compiler compiles Line 5, the size of the array is unknown and the compiler will not know how much memory space to allocate for the array. In Chapter 12, you will learn how to specify the size of an array during program execution and then declare an array of that size using pointers. Arrays that are created by using pointers during program execution are called **dynamic arrays**. For now, whenever you declare an array, its size must be known.

Processing One-Dimensional Arrays

Some of the basic operations performed on a one-dimensional array are initializing, inputting data, outputting data stored in an array, and finding the largest and/or smallest element. Moreover, if the data is numeric, some other basic operations are finding the sum and average of the elements of the array. Each of these operations requires the ability to step through the elements of the array. This is easily accomplished using a loop. For example, suppose that we have the following statements:

```
int list[100];     //list is an array of size 100
int i;
```

The following `for` loop steps through each element of the array `list`, starting at the first element of `list`:

```
for (i = 0; i < 100; i++)     //Line 1
    //process list[i]         //Line 2
```

If processing the list requires inputting data into `list`, the statement in Line 2 takes the form of an input statement, such as the `cin` statement. For example, the following statements read 100 numbers from the keyboard and store the numbers in `list`:

```
for (i = 0; i < 100; i++)     //Line 1
    cin >> list[i];           //Line 2
```

Similarly, if processing `list` requires outputting the data, then the statement in Line 2 takes the form of an output statement. Example 8-3 further illustrates how to process one-dimensional arrays.

8

EXAMPLE 8-3

This example shows how loops are used to process arrays. The following declaration is used throughout this example:

```
double sales[10];
int index;
double largestSale, sum, average;
```

The first statement declares an array `sales` of 10 components, with each component being of type `double`. The meaning of the other statements is clear.

a. **Initializing an array:** The following loop initializes every component of the array `sales` to `0.0`.

```
for (index = 0; index < 10; index++)
    sales[index] = 0.0;
```

b. **Reading data into an array:** The following loop inputs the data into the array `sales`. For simplicity, we assume that the data is entered from the keyboard.

```
for (index = 0; index < 10; index++)
    cin >> sales[index];
```

c. **Printing an array:** The following loop outputs the array `sales`. For simplicity, we assume that the output goes to the screen.

```
for (index = 0; index < 10; index++)
    cout << sales[index] << " ";
```

d. **Finding the sum and average of an array:** Because the array `sales`, as its name implies, represents certain sales data, it is natural to find the total sale and average sale amounts. The following C++ code finds the sum of the elements of the array `sales` and the average sale amount:

```
sum = 0;
for (index = 0; index < 10; index++)
    sum = sum + sales[index];

average = sum / 10;
```

e. **Largest element in the array:** We now discuss the algorithm to find the first occurrence of the largest element in an array—that is, the first array component with the largest value. However, in general, the user is more interested in determining the location of the largest element in the array. Of course, if you know the location (that is, the index of the largest element in the array), you can easily determine the value of the largest element in the array. So let us describe the algorithm to determine the index of the first occurrence of the largest element in an array—in particular, the index of the largest sale amount in the array `sales`. We will use the index of the first occurrence of the largest element in the array to find the largest sale.

We assume that `maxIndex` will contain the index of the first occurrence of the largest element in the array `sales`. The general algorithm is straightforward. Initially, we assume that the first element in the list is the largest element, so `maxIndex` is initialized to 0. We then compare the element pointed to by `maxIndex` with every subsequent element in the list. Whenever we find an element in the array larger than the element pointed to by `maxIndex`, we update `maxIndex` so that it points to the new larger element. The algorithm is as follows:

```
maxIndex = 0;
for (index = 1; index < 10; index++)
    if (sales[maxIndex] < sales[index])
        maxIndex = index;
largestSale = sales[maxIndex];
```

Let us demonstrate how this algorithm works with an example. Suppose the array `sales` is as given in Figure 8-6.

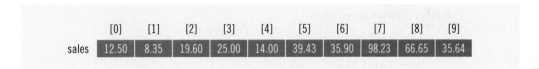

	[0]	[1]	[2]	[3]	[4]	[5]	[6]	[7]	[8]	[9]
sales	12.50	8.35	19.60	25.00	14.00	39.43	35.90	98.23	66.65	35.64

FIGURE 8-6 Array `sales`

Here, we determine the largest element in the array `sales`. Before the **for** loop begins, `maxIndex` is initialized to 0, and the **for** loop initializes `index` to 1. In the following, we show the values of `maxIndex`, `index`, and certain array elements during each iteration of the **for** loop.

index	maxIndex	sales [maxIndex]	sales [index]	sales[maxIndex] < sales[index]
1	0	12.50	8.35	12.50 < 8.35 is **false**
2	0	12.50	19.60	12.50 < 19.60 is **true**; maxIndex = 2
3	2	19.60	25.00	19.60 < 25.00 is **true**; maxIndex = 3
4	3	25.00	14.00	25.00 < 14.00 is **false**
5	3	25.00	39.43	25.00 < 39.43 is **true**; maxIndex = 5
6	5	39.43	35.90	39.43 < 35.90 is **false**
7	5	39.43	98.23	39.43 < 98.23 is **true**; maxIndex = 7
8	7	98.23	66.65	98.23 < 66.65 is **false**
9	7	98.23	35.64	98.23 < 35.64 is **false**

After the **for** loop executes, `maxIndex` = 7, giving the index of the largest element in the array `sales`. Thus, `largestSale = sales[maxIndex]` = 98.23.

8

NOTE You can write an algorithm to find the smallest element in the array that is similar to the algorithm for finding the largest element in an array. (See Programming Exercise 2 at the end of this chapter.)

Now that we know how to declare and process arrays, let us rewrite the program that we discussed in the beginning of this chapter. Recall that this program reads five test scores, finds the average test score, and outputs all the test scores that are less than the average test score.

EXAMPLE 8-4

```cpp
//Program to find the average test score and output the average
//test score and all the test scores that are less than the
//average test score.

#include <iostream>
#include <iomanip>

using namespace std;

int main()
{
    int test[ 5] ;
    int sum = 0;
    double average;
    int index;

    cout << fixed << showpoint << setprecision(2);

    cout << "Enter five test scores: ";

    for (index = 0; index < 5; index++)
    {
        cin >> test[index];
        sum = sum + test[index];
    }

    cout << endl;

    average = sum / 5.0;

    cout << "The average test score = " << average << endl;

    for (index = 0; index < 5; index++)
        if (test[index] < average)
            cout << test[index]
                 << " is less than the average test score." << endl;
    return 0;
}
```

Sample Run: In this sample run, the user input is shaded.

```
Enter five test scores: 85 62 94 56 71

The average test score = 73.60
62 is less than the average test score.
56 is less than the average test score.
71 is less than the average test score.
```

NOTE

C++0X introduces the **range-based** `for` statement to work with arrays. For example, consider the following statements:

```
int list[10];

for (int &x : list)
    cout << x << endl;
```

The variable **x** ranges over the elements of `list`. However, at the time of the writing of this book, the compilers that we used have not implemented it. Once it is implemented, it should simplify the processing of list elements. In fact, C++0X also introduces auto declaration of elements, which allows a programmer to declare and initialize a variable without specifying its type. For example, the following statement declares the variable num and stores 15 in it.

```
auto num = 15;
```

Because the initializer, which is 15, is an `int` value, the type of num will be `int`. However, at the time of the writing of this book, the compilers that we used have not implemented it. Once these new features are implemented, we can use the auto declaration in the range-based `for` statement without knowing the type of an array.

8

Array Index Out of Bounds

Consider the following declaration:

```
double num[10];
int i;
```

The component num[i] is valid, that is, i is a valid index if i = 0, 1, 2, 3, 4, 5, 6, 7, 8, or 9.

The index—say, index—of an array is **in bounds** if index >= 0 and index <= ARRAY_SIZE − 1. If either index < 0 or index > ARRAY_SIZE − 1, then we say that the index is **out of bounds**.

Unfortunately, in C++, there is no guard against out-of-bound indices. Thus, C++ does not check whether the index value is within range—that is, between 0 and ARRAY_SIZE − 1. If the index goes out of bounds and the program tries to access the component specified by the index, then whatever memory location is indicated by the index that location is accessed. This situation can result in altering or accessing the data of a memory location that you never intended to modify or access. Consequently, several strange things can happen if the index goes out of bounds during execution. It is solely the programmer's responsibility to make sure that the index is within bounds.

A loop such as the following can set the index out of bounds:

```cpp
for (i = 0; i <= 10; i++)
    list[i] = 0;
```

Here, we assume that `list` is an array of 10 components. When i becomes 10, the loop test condition i <= 10 evaluates to `true` and the body of the loop executes, which results in storing 0 in `list[10]`. Logically, `list[10]` does not exist.

 NOTE On some new compilers, if an array index goes out of bounds in a progam, it is possible that the program terminates with an error message. For example, see the programs `Example_ArrayIndexOutOfBoundsA.cpp` and `Example_ArrayIndexOutOfBoundsB.cpp` at the Web site accompanying this book.

Array Initialization During Declaration

Like any other simple variable, an array can be initialized while it is being declared. For example, the following C++ statement declares an array, `sales`, of five components and initializes these components.

```cpp
double sales[5] = {12.25, 32.50, 16.90, 23, 45.68};
```

The values are placed between curly braces and separated by commas—here, `sales[0] = 12.25`, `sales[1] = 32.50`, `sales[2] = 16.90`, `sales[3] = 23.00`, and `sales[4] = 45.68`.

When initializing arrays as they are declared, it is not necessary to specify the size of the array. The size is determined by the number of initial values in the braces. However, you must include the brackets following the array name. The previous statement is, therefore, equivalent to:

```cpp
double sales[] = {12.25, 32.50, 16.90, 23, 45.68};
```

Although it is not necessary to specify the size of the array if it is initialized during declaration, it is a good practice to do so.

Partial Initialization of Arrays During Declaration

When you declare and initialize an array simultaneously, you do not need to initialize all components of the array. This procedure is called **partial initialization of an array during declaration**. However, if you partially initialize an array during declaration, you must exercise some caution. The following examples help to explain what happens when you declare and partially initialize an array.

The statement:

```cpp
int list[10] = {0};
```

declares `list` to be an array of 10 components and initializes all of the components to 0. The statement:

```cpp
int list[10] = {8, 5, 12};
```

declares `list` to be an array of 10 components and initializes `list[0]` to 8, `list[1]` to 5, `list[2]` to 12, and all other components to 0. Thus, if all of the values are not specified in the initialization statement, the array components for which the values are not specified are initialized to 0. Note that, here, the size of the array in the declaration statement does matter. For example, the statement:

```
int list[] = {5, 6, 3};
```

declares `list` to be an array of three components and initializes `list[0]` to 5, `list[1]` to 6, and `list[2]` to 3. In contrast, the statement:

```
int list[25] = {4, 7};
```

declares `list` to be an array of 25 components. The first two components are initialized to 4 and 7, respectively, and all other components are initialized to 0.

When you partially initialize an array, then all of the elements that follow the last uninitialized elements must be uninitialized. Therefore, the following statement will result in a syntax error:

```
int list[10] = {2, 5, 6, , 8}; //illegal
```

In this initialization, because the fourth element is uninitialized, all elements that follow the fourth element must be left unintialized.

Some Restrictions on Array Processing

8

Consider the following statements:

```
int myList[5] = {0, 4, 8, 12, 16};   //Line 1
int yourList[5];   //Line 2
```

The statement in Line 1 declares and initializes the array `myList`, and the statement in Line 2 declares the array `yourList`. Note that these arrays are of the same type and have the same number of components. Suppose that you want to copy the elements of `myList` into the corresponding elements of `yourList`. The following statement is illegal:

```
yourList = myList;   //illegal
```

In fact, this statement will generate a syntax error. C++ does not allow aggregate operations on an array. An **aggregate operation** on an array is any operation that manipulates the entire array as a single unit.

To copy one array into another array, you must copy it component-wise—that is, one component at a time. This can be done using a loop, such as the following:

```
for (int index = 0; index < 5; index ++)
    yourList[index] = myList[index];
```

Next, suppose that you want to read data into the array `yourList`. The following statement is illegal and, in fact, would generate a syntax error:

```
cin >> yourList; //illegal
```

To read data into `yourList`, you must read one component at a time, using a loop such as the following:

```
for (int index = 0; index < 5; index ++)
    cin >> yourList[index];
```

Similarly, determining whether two arrays have the same elements and printing the contents of an array must be done component-wise. Note that the following statements are illegal in the sense that they do not generate a syntax error; however, they do not give the desired results.

```
cout << yourList;

if (myList <= yourList)
    .
    .
    .
```

We will comment on these statements in the section Base Address of an Array and Array in Computer Memory later in this chapter.

Arrays as Parameters to Functions

Now that you have seen how to work with arrays, a question naturally arises: How are arrays passed as parameters to functions?

By reference only: In C++, arrays are passed by reference only.

Because arrays are passed by reference only, you *do not* use the symbol & when declaring an array as a formal parameter.

When declaring a one-dimensional array as a formal parameter, the size of the array is usually omitted. If you specify the size of a one-dimensional array when it is declared as a formal parameter, the size is ignored by the compiler.

EXAMPLE 8-5

Consider the following function:

```
void funcArrayAsParam(int listOne[], double listTwo[])
{
    .
    .
    .
}
```

The function `funcArrayAsParam` has two formal parameters: (1) `listOne`, a one-dimensional array of type `int` (that is, the component type is `int`) and (2) `listTwo`, a one-dimensional array of type `double`. In this declaration, the size of both arrays is unspecified.

Sometimes, the number of elements in the array might be less than the size of the array. For example, the number of elements in an array storing student data might increase or decrease as students drop or add courses. In such situations, we want to process only the components of the array that hold actual data. To write a function to process such arrays, in addition to declaring an array as a formal parameter, we declare another formal parameter specifying the number of elements in the array, as in the following function:

```
void initialize(int list[], int listSize)
{
    int count;

    for (count = 0; count < listSize; count++)
        list[count] = 0;
}
```

The first parameter of the function `initialize` is an `int` array of any size. When the function `initialize` is called, the size of the actual array is passed as the second parameter of the function `initialize`.

Constant Arrays as Formal Parameters

Recall that when a formal parameter is a reference parameter, then whenever the formal parameter changes, the actual parameter changes as well. However, even though an array is always passed by reference, you can still prevent the function from changing the actual parameter. You do so by using the reserved word `const` in the declaration of the formal parameter. Consider the following function:

```
void example(int x[], const int y[], int sizeX, int sizeY)
{
    .
    .
    .
}
```

Here, the function `example` can modify the array `x`, but not the array `y`. Any attempt to change `y` results in a compile-time error. It is a good programming practice to declare an array to be constant as a formal parameter if you do not want the function to modify the array.

EXAMPLE 8-6

This example shows how to write functions for array processing and declare an array as a formal parameter.

```
    //Function to initialize an int array to 0.
    //The array to be initialized and its size are passed
    //as parameters. The parameter listSize specifies the
    //number of elements to be initialized.
void initializeArray(int list[], int listSize)
```

8

```
{
    int index;

    for (index = 0; index < listSize; index++)
        list[index] = 0;
}

    //Function to read and store the data into an int array.
    //The array to store the data and its size are passed as
    //parameters. The parameter listSize specifies the number
    //of elements to be read.
void fillArray(int list[], int listSize)
{
    int index;

    for (index = 0; index < listSize; index++)
        cin >> list[index];
}

    //Function to print the elements of an int array.
    //The array to be printed and the number of elements
    //are passed as parameters. The parameter listSize
    //specifies the number of elements to be printed.
void printArray(const int list[], int listSize)
{
    int index;

    for (index = 0; index < listSize; index++)
        cout << list[index] << " ";
}
    //Function to find and return the sum of the
    //elements of an int array. The parameter listSize
    //specifies the number of elements to be added.
int sumArray(const int list[], int listSize)
{
    int index;
    int sum = 0;

    for (index = 0; index < listSize; index++)
        sum = sum + list[index];

    return sum;
}

    //Function to find and return the index of the first
    //largest element in an int array. The parameter listSize
    //specifies the number of elements in the array.
int indexLargestElement(const int list[], int listSize)
{
    int index;
    int maxIndex = 0; //assume the first element is the largest
```

```
    for (index = 1; index < listSize; index++)
        if (list[maxIndex] < list[index])
            maxIndex = index;

    return maxIndex;
}
    //Function to copy some or all of the elements of one array
    //into another array. Starting at the position specified
    //by src, the  elements of list1 are copied into list2
    //starting at the position specified by tar. The parameter
    //numOfElements specifies the number of elements of list1 to
    //be copied into list2. Starting at the position specified
    //by tar, the list2 must have enough components to copy the
    //elements of list1. The following call copies all of the
    //elements of list1 into the corresponding positions in
    //list2:  copyArray(list1, 0, list2, 0, numOfElements);
void copyArray(int list1[], int src, int list2[],
               int tar, int numOfElements)
{
    for (int index = src; index < src + numOfElements; index++)
    {
        list2[index] = list1[tar];
        tar++;
    }
}
```

Example 8-7 will illustrate how to use some of these functions in a program.

Base Address of an Array and Array in Computer Memory

The **base address** of an array is the address (that is, the memory location) of the first array component. For example, if list is a one-dimensional array, then the base address of list is the address of the component list[0].

Consider the following statements:

```
int myList[5];          //Line 1
```

This statement declares myList to be an array of five components of type int. The components are myList[0], myList[1], myList[2], myList[3], and myList[4]. The computer allocates five memory spaces, each large enough to store an int value, for these components. Moreover, the five memory spaces are contiguous.

The base address of the array myList is the address of the component myList[0]. Suppose that the base address of the array myList is 1000. Then, the address of the component myList[0] is 1000. Typically, the memory allocated for an int variable is four bytes. Recall from Chapter 1 that main memory is an ordered sequence of cells, and each cell has a unique address. Typically, each cell is one byte. Therefore, to store a value into myList[0], starting at the address 1000, the next four bytes are allocated for myList[0]. It follows that the starting address of myList[1] is 1004, the starting address of myList[2] is 1008, and so on (see Figure 8-7).

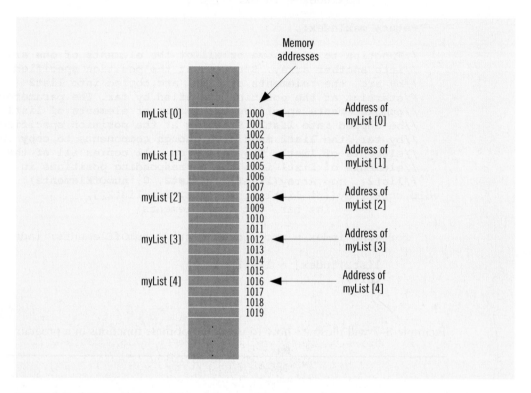

FIGURE 8-7 Array myList and the addresses of its components

Now myList is the name of an array. There is also a memory space associated with the identifier myList, and the base address of the array is stored in that memory space. Consider the following statement:

```
cout << myList << endl;          //Line 2
```

Earlier, we said that this statement will not give the desired result. That is, this statement will not output the values of the *components* of myList. In fact, the statement outputs the value of myList, which is the base address of the array. This is why the statement will not generate a syntax error.

Suppose that you also have the following statement:

```
int yourList[5];
```

Then, in the statement:

```
if (myList <= yourList)          //Line 3
 .
 .
 .
```

the expression `myList <= yourList` evaluates to **true** if the base address of the array `myList` is less than the base address of the array `yourList`; and evaluates to **false** otherwise. It *does not* determine whether the elements of `myList` are less than or equal to the corresponding elements of `yourList`.

NOTE The Web site accompanying this book contains the program `BaseAddressOfAnArray.cpp`, which clarifies statements such as those in Lines 2 and 3.

You might be wondering why the base address of an array is so important. The reason is that when you declare an array, the only things about the array that the computer remembers are the name of the array, its base address, the data type of each component, and (possibly) the number of components. Using the base address of the array and the index of an array component, the computer determines the address of a particular component. For example, suppose you want to access the value of `myList[3]`. Now, the base address of `myList` is 1000. Each component of `myList` is of type `int`, so it uses four bytes to store a value, and the index is 3. To access the value of `myList[3]`, the computer calculates the address 1000 + 4 * 3 = 1000 + 12 = 1012. That is, this is the starting address of `myList[3]`. So, starting at 1012, the computer accesses the next four bytes.

When you pass an array as a parameter, the base address of the actual array is passed to the formal parameter. For example, suppose that you have the following function:

```
void arrayAsParameter(int list[], int size)
{
     .
     .
     .

    list[2] = 28;          //Line 4

     .
     .
     .
}
```

Also, suppose that you have the following call to this function:

```
arrayAsParameter(myList, 5);   //Line 5
```

In this statement, the base address of `myList` is passed to the formal parameter `list`. Therefore, the base address of `list` is 1000. The definition of the function contains the statement `list[2] = 28;`. This statement stores 28 into `list[2]`. To access `list[2]`, the computer calculates the address as follows: 1000 + 4 * 2 = 1008. So, starting at the address 1008, the computer accesses the next four bytes and stores 28. Note that, in fact, 1008 is the address of myList[2] (see Figure 8-7). It follows that during the execution of the statement in Line 5, the statement in Line 4 stores the value 28 into myList[2]. It also follows that during the execution of the function call statement in Line 5, list[index] and myList[index] refer to the same memory space, where 0 <= index and index < 5.

NOTE If C++ allowed arrays to be passed by value, the computer would have to allocate memory for the components of the formal parameter and copy the contents of the actual array into the corresponding formal parameter when the function is called. If the array size was large, this process would waste memory as well as the computer time needed for copying the data. That is why in C++ arrays are always passed by reference.

Functions Cannot Return a Value of the Type Array

C++ does not allow functions to return a value of the type array. Note that the functions sumArray and indexLargestElement described earlier return values of type int.

EXAMPLE 8-7

The following program illustrates how arrays are passed as actual parameters in a function call. (Note that this program uses the functions written in Example 8-6).

```cpp
//Arrays as parameters to functions

#include <iostream>

using namespace std;

const int ARRAY_SIZE = 10;

void initializeArray(int x[],int sizeX);
void fillArray(int x[],int sizeX);
void printArray(const int x[],int sizeX);
int sumArray(const int x[],int sizeX);
int indexLargestElement(const int x[],int sizeX);
void copyArray(int list1[], int src, int list2[],
               int tar, int numOfElements);
int main()
{
    int listA[ARRAY_SIZE] = {0};   //Declare the array listA
                                   //of 10 components and
                                   //initialize each component
                                   //to 0.
    int listB[ARRAY_SIZE];         //Declare the array listB
                                   //of 10 components.
```

```cpp
cout << "Line 1: listA elements: ";              //Line 1

    //Output the elements of listA using
    //the function printArray
printArray(listA, ARRAY_SIZE);                   //Line 2
cout << endl;                                    //Line 3

    //Initialize listB using the function
    //initializeArray
initializeArray(listB, ARRAY_SIZE);              //Line 4

cout << "Line 5: listB elements: ";              //Line 5

    //Output the elements of listB
printArray(listB, ARRAY_SIZE);                   //Line 6
cout << endl << endl;                            //Line 7

cout << "Line 8: Enter " << ARRAY_SIZE
     << " integers: ";                           //Line 8

    //Input data into listA using the
    //function fillArray
fillArray(listA, ARRAY_SIZE);                    //Line 9
cout << endl;                                    //Line 10

cout << "Line 11: After filling listA, "
     << "the elements are:" << endl;             //Line 11

    //Output the elements of listA
printArray(listA, ARRAY_SIZE);                   //Line 12
cout << endl << endl;                            //Line 13

    //Find and output the sum of the elements
    //of listA
cout << "Line 14: The sum of the elements of "
     << "listA is: "
     << sumArray(listA, ARRAY_SIZE) << endl
     << endl;                                    //Line 14

    //Find and output the position of the largest
    //element in listA
cout << "Line 15: The position of the largest "
     << "element in listA is: "
     << indexLargestElement(listA, ARRAY_SIZE)
     << endl;                                    //Line 15

    //Find and output the largest element
    //in listA
cout << "Line 16: The largest element in "
     << "listA is: "
     << listA[indexLargestElement(listA, ARRAY_SIZE)]
     << endl << endl;                            //Line 16
```

8

```
        //Copy the elements of listA into listB using the
        //function copyArray
    copyArray(listA, 0, listB, 0, ARRAY_SIZE);          //Line 17

    cout << "Line 18: After copying the elements "
         << "of listA into listB," << endl
         << "           listB elements are: ";          //Line 18

        //Output the elements of listB
    printArray(listB, ARRAY_SIZE);                      //Line 19
    cout << endl;                                       //Line 20

    return 0;
}

//Place the definitions of the functions initializeArray,
//fillArray, and so on here. Example 8-6 gives the definitions
//of these functions.
```

Sample Run: In this sample run, the user input is shaded.

```
Line 1: listA elements: 0 0 0 0 0 0 0 0 0 0
Line 5: ListB elements: 0 0 0 0 0 0 0 0 0 0

Line 8: Enter 10 integers: 33 77 25 63 56 48 98 39 5 12

Line 11: After filling listA, the elements are:
33 77 25 63 56 48 98 39 5 12

Line 14: The sum of the elements of listA is: 456

Line 15: The position of the largest element in listA is: 6
Line 16: The largest element in listA is: 98

Line 18: After copying the elements of listA into listB,
         listB elements are: 33 77 25 63 56 48 98 39 5 12
```

The output of this program is straightforward. First, we declare the array listA of 10 components and initialize each component of listA to 0. Then, we declare the array listB of 10 components. The statement in Line 2 calls the function printArray and outputs the values stored in listA. The statement in Line 9 calls the function fillArray to input the data into listA. The statement in Line 14 calls the function sumArray and outputs the sum of all of the elements of listA. Similarly, the statement in Line 16 outputs the value of the largest element in listA.

Integral Data Type and Array Indices

 NOTE The sections "Enumeration Type" and "typedef Statement" from Chapter 7 are required to understand this section.

Other than integers, C++ allows any integral type to be used as an array index. This feature can greatly enhance a program's readability. Consider the following statements:

```
enum paintType {GREEN, RED, BLUE, BROWN, WHITE, ORANGE, YELLOW};
double paintSale[7];
paintType paint;
```

The following loop initializes each component of the array paintSale to 0:

```
for (paint = GREEN; paint <= YELLOW;
                    paint = static_cast<paintType>(paint + 1))
    paintSale[paint] = 0.0;
```

The following statement updates the sale amount of RED paint:

```
paintSale[RED] = paintSale[RED] + 75.69;
```

As you can see, the above code is much easier to follow than the code that used integers for the index. For this reason, you should use the enumeration type for the array index or other integral data types wherever possible. Note that when using the enumeration type for array indices, use the default values of the identifiers in the enumeration type. That is, the value of the first identifier must be 0, and so on. (Recall from Chapter 7 that the default values of identifiers in an enumeration type start at 0; however, the identifiers can be set to other values.)

Other Ways to Declare Arrays

Suppose that a class has 20 students and you need to keep track of their scores. Because the number of students can change from semester to semester, instead of specifying the size of the array while declaring it, you can declare the array as follows:

```
const int NO_OF_STUDENTS = 20;
int testScores[NO_OF_STUDENTS];
```

Other forms used to declare arrays are:

```
const int SIZE = 50;            //Line 1
typedef double list[SIZE];      //Line 2

list yourList;                  //Line 3
list myList;                    //Line 4
```

The statement in Line 2 defines a data type list, which is an array of 50 components of type double. The statements in Lines 3 and 4 declare two variables, yourList and myList. Both are arrays of 50 components of type double. Of course, these statements are equivalent to:

```
double yourList[50];
double myList[50];
```

Searching an Array for a Specific Item

Searching a list for a given item is one of the most common operations performed on a list. The search algorithm we describe is called the **sequential search** or **linear search**. As the name implies, you search the array sequentially, starting from the first array element. You compare `searchItem` with the elements in the array (the list) and continue the search until either you find the item or no more data is left in the `list` to compare with `searchItem`.

Consider the list of seven elements shown in Figure 8-8.

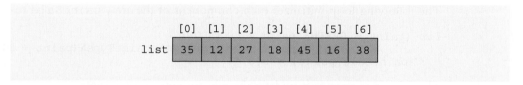

FIGURE 8-8 List of seven elements

Suppose that you want to determine whether 27 is in the list. A sequential search works as follows: First, you compare 27 with `list[0]`, that is, compare 27 with 35. Because `list[0]` ≠ 27, you then compare 27 with `list[1]`, that is, with 12, the second item in the list. Because `list[1]` ≠ 27, you compare 27 with the next element in the list, that is, compare 27 with `list[2]`. Because `list[2]` = 27, the search stops. This search is successful.

Let us now search for 10. As before, the search starts at the first element in the list, that is, at `list[0]`. Proceeding as before, we see that, this time, the search item, which is 10, is compared with every item in the list. Eventually, no more data is left in the list to compare with the search item. This is an unsuccessful search.

It now follows that, as soon as you find an element in the list that is equal to the search item, you must stop the search and report success. (In this case, you usually also report the location in the list where the search item was found.) Otherwise, after the search item is unsuccessfully compared with every element in the list, you must stop the search and report failure.

Suppose that the name of the array containing the list elements is `list`. The previous discussion translates into the following algorithm for the sequential search:

```
found is set to false
loc = 0;

while (loc < listLength and not found)
    if (list[loc] is equal to searchItem)
        found is set to true
    else
        increment loc

if (found)
    return loc;
else
    return -1;
```

The following function performs a sequential search on a list. To be specific, and for illustration purposes, we assume that the list elements are of type int.

```cpp
int seqSearch(const int list[], int listLength, int searchItem)
{
    int loc;
    bool found = false;

    loc = 0;

    while (loc < listLength && !found)
        if (list[loc] == searchItem)
            found = true;
        else
            loc++;

    if (found)
        return loc;
    else
        return -1;

}
```

If the function seqSearch returns a value greater than or equal to 0, it is a successful search; otherwise, it is an unsuccessful search.

As you can see from this code, you start the search by comparing searchItem with the first element in the list. If searchItem is equal to the first element in the list, you exit the loop; otherwise, loc is incremented by 1 to point to the next element in the list. You then compare searchItem with the next element in the list, and so on.

8

EXAMPLE 8-8

```cpp
// This program illustrates how to use a sequential search in a
// program.

#include <iostream>                                         //Line 1

using namespace std;                                        //Line 2

const int ARRAY_SIZE = 10;                                  //Line 3

int seqSearch(const int list[], int listLength,
              int searchItem);                              //Line 4

int main()                                                  //Line 5
{                                                           //Line 6
    int intList[ARRAY_SIZE];                                //Line 7
    int number;                                             //Line 8

    cout << "Line 9: Enter " << ARRAY_SIZE
         << " integers." << endl;                           //Line 9
```

```
    for (int index  = 0; index < ARRAY_SIZE; index++)    //Line 10
        cin >> intList[index];                           //Line 11

    cout << endl;                                         //Line 12

    cout << "Line 13: Enter the number to be "
         << "searched: ";                                //Line 13
    cin >> number;                                       //Line 14
    cout << endl;                                         //Line 15

    int pos = seqSearch(intList, ARRAY_SIZE, number);    //Line 16

    if (pos!= -1)                                        //Line 17
        cout <<"Line 18: " << number
             << " is found at position " << pos
             << endl;                                    //Line 18
    else                                                 //Line 19
        cout << "Line 20: " << number
             << " is not in the list." << endl;          //Line 20

    return 0;                                            //Line 21
}                                                        //Line 22

//Place the definition of the function seqSearch
//given previously here.
```

Sample Run 1: In this sample run, the user input is shaded.

```
Line 9: Enter 10 integers.
2 56 34 25 73 46 89 10 5 16

Line 13: Enter the number to be searched: 25

Line 18: 25 is found at position 3
```

Sample Run 2:

```
Line 9: Enter 10 integers.
2 56 34 25 73 46 89 10 5 16

Line 13: Enter the number to be searched: 38

Line 20: 38 is not in the list.
```

Selection Sort

The previous section discussed a searching algorithm. In this section, we discuss how to sort an array using the algorithm, called **selection sort**. Additional searching and sorting algorithms are discussed in Chapter 16.

As the name implies, in the **selection sort** algorithm, we rearrange the list by selecting an element in the list and moving it to its proper position. This algorithm finds the location of the smallest element in the unsorted portion of the list and moves it to the top of the unsorted portion of the list. The first time, we locate the smallest item in the entire list. The second time, we locate the smallest item in the list starting from the second element in the list, and so on.

Suppose you have the list shown in Figure 8-9.

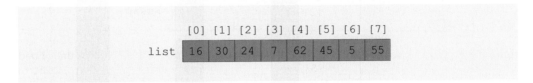

FIGURE 8-9 List of eight elements

Figure 8-10 shows the elements of `list` in the first iteration.

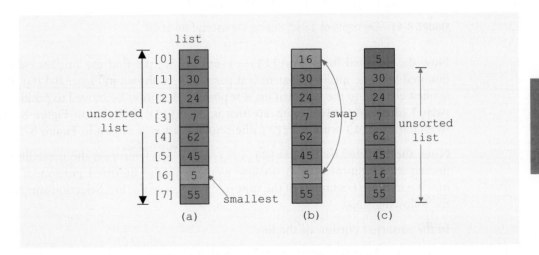

FIGURE 8-10 Elements of `list` during the first iteration

Initially, the entire list is unsorted. So, we find the smallest item in the list. The smallest item is at position 6, as shown in Figure 8-10(a). Because this is the smallest item, it must be moved to position 0. So, we swap 16 (that is, `list[0]`) with 5 (that is, `list[6]`), as shown in Figure 8-10(b). After swapping these elements, the resulting list is as shown in Figure 8-10(c).

Figure 8-11 shows the elements of `list` during the second iteration.

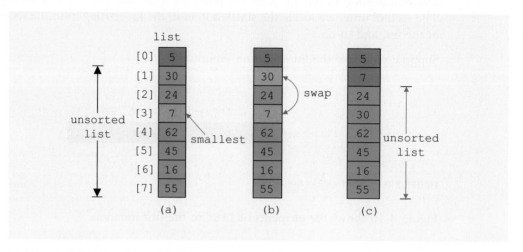

FIGURE 8-11 Elements of `list` during the second iteration

Now the unsorted list is `list[1]...list[7]`. So, we find the smallest element in the unsorted list. The smallest element is at position 3, as shown in Figure 8-11(a). Because the smallest element in the unsorted list is at position 3, it must be moved to position 1. So, we swap 7 (that is, `list[3]`) with 30 (that is, `list[1]`), as shown in Figure 8-11(b). After swapping `list[1]` with `list[3]`, the resulting list is as shown in Figure 8-11(c).

Now, the unsorted list is `list[2]...list[7]`. So, we repeat the preceding process of finding the (position of the) smallest element in the unsorted portion of the list and moving it to the beginning of the unsorted portion of the list. Selection sort thus involves the following steps.

In the unsorted portion of the list:

    a.   Find the location of the smallest element.

    b.   Move the smallest element to the beginning of the unsorted list.

Initially, the entire list (that is, `list[0]...list[length - 1]`) is the unsorted list. After executing Steps a and b once, the unsorted list is `list[1]... list[length - 1]`. After executing Steps a and b a second time, the unsorted list is `list[2]...list[length - 1]`, and so on. In this way, we can keep track of the unsorted portion of the list and repeat Steps a and b with the help of a **for** loop, as shown in the following pseudocode:

```
for (index = 0; index < length - 1; index++)
{
    a. Find the location, smallestIndex, of the smallest element in
       list[index]...list[length - 1].
    b. Swap the smallest element with list[index]. That is, swap
       list[smallestIndex] with list[index].
}
```

The first time through the loop, we locate the smallest element in `list[0]`...`list[length - 1]` and swap the smallest element with `list[0]`. The second time through the loop, we locate the smallest element in `list[1]`...`list[length - 1]` and swap the smallest element with `list[1]`, and so on.

Step a is similar to the algorithm for finding the index of the largest item in the list, as discussed earlier in this chapter. (Also see Programming Exercise 2 at the end of this chapter.) Here, we find the index of the smallest item in the list. The general form of Step a is:

```
smallestIndex = index;   //assume first element is the smallest

for (location = index + 1; location < length; location++)
     if (list[location] < list[smallestIndex])
          smallestIndex = location;   //current element in the list
                                      //is smaller than the smallest so
                                      //far, so update smallestIndex
```

Step b swaps the contents of `list[smallestIndex]` with `list[index]`. The following statements accomplish this task:

```
temp = list[smallestIndex];
list[smallestIndex] = list[index];
list[index] = temp;
```

It follows that to swap the values, three item assignments are needed. The following function, `selectionSort`, implements the selection sort algorithm:

```
void selectionSort(int list[], int length)
{
    int index;
    int smallestIndex;
    int location;
    int temp;

    for (index = 0; index < length - 1; index++)
    {
            //Step a
        smallestIndex = index;

        for (location = index + 1; location < length; location++)
            if (list[location] < list[smallestIndex])
                smallestIndex = location;

            //Step b
        temp = list[smallestIndex];
        list[smallestIndex] = list[index];
        list[index] = temp;
    }
}
```

8

The program in Example 8-9 illustrates how to use the selection sort algorithm in a program.

EXAMPLE 8-9

```
//Selection sort

#include <iostream>

using namespace std;

void selectionSort(int list[],  int length);

int main()
{
    int list[]= {2, 56, 34, 25, 73, 46, 89, 10, 5, 16};   //Line 1
    int i;                                                 //Line 2

    selectionSort(list, 10);                               //Line 3

    cout << "After sorting, the list elements are:"
         << endl;                                          //Line 4
    for (i = 0; i < 10; i++)                               //Line 5
        cout << list[i] << " ";                            //Line 6

    cout << endl;                                          //Line 7

    return 0;                                              //Line 8
}

//Place the definition of the function selectionSort given
//previously here.
```

Sample Run:

```
After sorting, the list elements are:
2 5 10 16 25 34 46 56 73 89
```

The statement in Line 1 declares and initializes list to be an array of 10 components of type int. The statement in Line 3 uses the function selectionSort to sort list. Notice that both list and its length (the number of elements in it, which is 10) are passed as parameters to the function selectionSort. The for loop in Lines 5 and 6 outputs the elements of list.

To illustrate the selection sort algorithm in this program, we declared and initialized the array list. However, you can also prompt the user to input the data during program execution.

For a list of length n, selection sort makes exactly $\frac{n(n-1)}{2}$ key comparisons and $3(n-1)$ item assignments. Therefore, if $n = 1000$, then to sort the list, selection sort makes about 500,000 key comparisons and about 3000 item assignments. The next section presents the insertion sort algorithm that reduces the number of comparisons.

C-Strings (Character Arrays)

Until now, we have avoided discussing character arrays for a simple reason: Character arrays are of special interest, and you process them differently than you process other arrays. C++ provides many (predefined) functions that you can use with character arrays.

Character array: An array whose components are of type `char`.

Recall that the most widely used character sets are ASCII and EBCDIC. The first character in the ASCII character set is the null character, which is nonprintable. Also, recall that in C++, the null character is represented as `'\0'`, a backslash followed by a zero.

The statement:

```
ch = '\0';
```

stores the null character in `ch`, wherein `ch` is a `char` variable.

As you will see, the null character plays an important role in processing character arrays. Because the collating sequence of the null character is 0, the null character is less than any other character in the `char` data set.

The most commonly used term for character arrays is C-strings. However, there is a subtle difference between character arrays and C-strings. Recall that a string is a sequence of zero or more characters, and strings are enclosed in double quotation marks. In C++, C-strings are null terminated; that is, the last character in a C-string is always the null character. A character array might not contain the null character, but the last character in a C-string is always the null character. As you will see, the null character should not appear anywhere in the C-string except the last position. Also, C-strings are stored in (one-dimensional) character arrays.

The following are examples of C-strings:

```
"John L. Johnson"
"Hello there."
```

From the definition of C-strings, it is clear that there is a difference between `'A'` and `"A"`. The first one is character A; the second is C-string A. Because C-strings are null terminated, `"A"` represents two characters: `'A'` and `'\0'`. Similarly, the C-string `"Hello"` represents six characters: `'H'`, `'e'`, `'l'`, `'l'`, `'o'`, and `'\0'`. To store `'A'`, we need only one memory cell of type `char`; to store `"A"`, we need two memory cells of type char—one for 'A' and one for '\0'. Similarly, to store the C-string "Hello" in computer memory, we need six memory cells of type char.

Consider the following statement:

```
char name[16];
```

This statement declares an array name of 16 components of type char. Because C-strings are null terminated and name has 16 components, the largest string that can be stored in name is of length 15. If you store a C-string of length 10 in name, the first 11 components of name are used and the last 5 are left unused.

The statement:

```
char name[16] = {'J', 'o', 'h', 'n', '\0'};
```

declares an array name containing 16 components of type char and stores the C-string "John" in it. During char array variable declaration, C++ allows the C-string notation to be used in the initialization statement. The above statement is, therefore, equivalent to:

```
char name[16] = "John";          //Line A
```

Recall that the size of an array can be omitted if the array is initialized during the declaration.

The statement:

```
char name[] = "John";          //Line B
```

declares a C-string variable name of a length large enough—in this case, 5—and stores "John" in it. There is a difference between the last two statements: Both statements store "John" in name, but the size of name in the statement in Line A is 16, and the size of name in the statement in Line B is 5.

Most rules that apply to other arrays also apply to character arrays. Consider the following statement:

```
char studentName[26];
```

Suppose you want to store "Lisa L. Johnson" in studentName. Because aggregate operations, such as assignment and comparison, are not allowed on arrays, the following statement is not legal:

```
studentName = "Lisa L. Johnson"; //illegal
```

C++ provides a set of functions that can be used for C-string manipulation. The header file cstring describes these functions. We often use three of these functions: strcpy (string copy, to copy a C-string into a C-string variable—that is, assignment); strcmp (string comparison, to compare C-strings); and `strlen` (string length, to find the length of a C-string). Table 8-1 summarizes these functions.

TABLE 8-1 `strcpy`, `strcmp`, and `strlen` Functions

Function	Effect
`strcpy(s1, s2)`	Copies the string s2 into the string variable s1 The length of s1 should be at least as large as s2
`strcmp(s1, s2)`	Returns a value < 0 if s1 is less than s2 Returns 0 if s1 and s2 are the same Returns a value > 0 if s1 is greater than s2
`strlen(s)`	Returns the length of the string s, excluding the null character

To use these functions, the program must include the header file `cstring` via the `include` statement. That is, the following statement must be included in the program:

`#include <cstring>`

String Comparison

In C++, C-strings are compared character by character using the system's collating sequence. Let us assume that you use the ASCII character set.

1. The C-string `"Air"` is less than the C-string `"Boat"` because the first character of `"Air"` is less than the first character of `"Boat"`.

2. The C-string `"Air"` is less than the C-string `"An"` because the first characters of both strings are the same, but the second character `'i'` of `"Air"` is less than the second character `'n'` of `"An"`.

3. The C-string `"Bill"` is less than the C-string `"Billy"` because the first four characters of `"Bill"` and `"Billy"` are the same, but the fifth character of `"Bill"`, which is `'\0'` (the null character), is less than the fifth character of `"Billy"`, which is `'y'`. (Recall that C-strings in C++ are null terminated.)

4. The C-string `"Hello"` is less than `"hello"` because the first character `'H'` of the C-string `"Hello"` is less than the first character `'h'` of the C-string `"hello"`.

8

As you can see, the function strcmp compares its first C-string argument with its second C-string argument character by character.

EXAMPLE 8-10

Suppose you have the following statements:

```
char studentName[21];
char myname[16];
char yourname[16];
```

The following statements show how string functions work:

Statement	Effect
strcpy(myname, "John Robinson");	myname = "John Robinson"
strlen("John Robinson");	Returns 13, the length of the string "John Robinson"
int len; len = strlen("Sunny Day");	Stores 9 into len
strcpy(yourname, "Lisa Miller"); strcpy(studentName, yourname);	yourname = "Lisa Miller" studentName = "Lisa Miller"
strcmp("Bill", "Lisa");	Returns a value < 0

strcpy(yourname, "Kathy Brown");
strcpy(myname, "Mark G. Clark");
strcmp(myname, yourname);
	yourname = "Kathy Brown"
	myname = "Mark G. Clark"
	Returns a value > 0

NOTE In this chapter, we defined a C-string to be a sequence of zero or more characters. C-strings are enclosed in double quotation marks. We also said that C-strings are null terminated, so the C-string "Hello" has six characters even though only five are enclosed in double quotation marks. Therefore, to store the C-string "Hello" in computer memory, you must use a character array of size 6. The length of a C-string is the number of actual characters enclosed in double quotation marks; for example, the length of the C-string "Hello" is 5. Thus, in a logical sense, a C-string is a sequence of zero or more characters, but in the physical sense (that is, to store the C-string in computer memory), a C-string has at least one character. Because the length of the C-string is the actual number of characters enclosed in double quotation marks, we defined a C-string to be a sequence of zero or more characters. However, you must remember that the null character stored in computer memory at the end of the C-string plays a key role when we compare C-strings, especially C-strings such as "Bill" and "Billy".

Reading and Writing Strings

As mentioned earlier, most rules that apply to arrays apply to C-strings as well. Aggregate operations, such as assignment and comparison, are not allowed on arrays. Even the input/output of arrays is done component-wise. However, the one place where C++ allows aggregate operations on arrays is the input and output of C-strings (that is, character arrays).

We will use the following declaration for our discussion:

```
char name[31];
```

String Input

Because aggregate operations are allowed for C-string input, the statement:

```
cin >> name;
```

stores the next input C-string into `name`. The length of the input C-string must be less than or equal to 30. If the length of the input string is 4, the computer stores the four characters that are input and the null character `'\0'`. If the length of the input C-string is more than 30, then because there is no check on the array index bounds, the computer continues storing the string in whatever memory cells follow `name`. This process can cause serious problems, because data in the adjacent memory cells will be corrupted.

 NOTE When you input a C-string using an input device, such as the keyboard, you do not include the double quotes around it unless the double quotes are part of the string. For example, the C-string `"Hello"` is entered as `Hello`.

Recall that the extraction operator, `>>`, skips all leading whitespace characters and stops reading data into the current variable as soon as it finds the first whitespace character or invalid data. As a result, C-strings that contain blanks cannot be read using the extraction operator, `>>`. For example, if a first name and last name are separated by blanks, they cannot be read into `name`.

How do you input C-strings with blanks into a character array? Once again, the function `get` comes to our rescue. Recall that the function `get` is used to read character data. Until now, the form of the function `get` that you have used (Chapter 3) read only a single character. However, the function `get` can also be used to read strings. To read C-strings, you use the form of the function `get` that has two parameters. The first parameter is a C-string variable; the second parameter specifies how many characters to read into the string variable.

To read C-strings, the general form (syntax) of the `get` function, together with an input stream variable such as `cin`, is:

```
cin.get(str, m + 1);
```

This statement stores the next m characters, or all characters until the newline character `'\n'` is found, into `str`. The newline character is not stored in `str`. If the input C-string has fewer than m characters, then the reading stops at the newline character.

Consider the following statements:

```
char str[31];
cin.get(str, 31);
```

If the input is:

```
William T. Johnson
```

then `"William T. Johnson"` is stored in `str`. Suppose that the input is:

```
Hello there. My name is Mickey Blair.
```

Then, because `str` can store, at most, 30 characters, the C-string `"Hello there. My name is Mickey"` is stored in `str`.

Now, suppose that we have the statements:

```
char str1[26];
char str2[26];
char discard;
```

and the two lines of input:

```
Summer is warm.
Winter will be cold.
```

Further, suppose that we want to store the first C-string in `str1` and the second C-string in `str2`. Both `str1` and `str2` can store C-strings that are up to 25 characters in length. Because the number of characters in the first line is 15, the reading stops at `'\n'`. You must read and discard the newline character at the end of the first line to store the second line into `str2`. The following sequence of statements stores the first line into `str1` and the second line into `str2`:

```
cin.get(str1, 26);
cin.get(discard);
cin.get(str2, 26);
```

To read and store a line of input, including whitespace characters, you can also use the stream function `getline`. Suppose that you have the following declaration:

```
char textLine[100];
```

The following statement will read and store the next 99 characters, or until the newline character, into `textLine`. The null character will be automatically appended as the last character of `textLine`.

```
cin.getline(textLine, 100);
```

String Output

The output of C-strings is another place where aggregate operations on arrays are allowed. You can output C-strings by using an output stream variable, such as `cout`, together with the insertion operator, `<<`. For example, the statement:

```
cout << name;
```

outputs the contents of `name` on the screen. The insertion operator, `<<`, continues to write the contents of `name` until it finds the null character. Thus, if the length of `name` is 4, the above statement outputs only four characters. If `name` does not contain the null character, then you will see strange output because the insertion operator continues to output data from memory adjacent to `name` until `'\0'` is found.

Specifying Input/Output Files at Execution Time

In Chapter 3, you learned how to read data from a file. In subsequent chapters, the name of the input file was included in the `open` statement. By doing so, the program always received data from the same input file. In real-world applications, the data may actually be collected at several locations and stored in separate files. Also, for comparison purposes, someone might want to process each file separately and then store the output in separate files. To accomplish this task efficiently, the user would prefer to specify the name of the input and/or output file at execution time rather than in the programming code. C++ allows the user to do so.

Consider the following statements:

```
ifstream infile;
ofstream outfile;

char fileName[51];      //assume that the file name is at most
                        //50 characters long
```

The following statements prompt and allow the user to specify the input and output files at execution time:

```
cout << "Enter the input file name: ";
cin >> fileName;

infile.open(fileName);   //open the input file
 .
 .
 .
cout << "Enter the output file name: ";
cin >> fileName;

outfile.open(fileName);  //open the output file
```

The Programming Example: Code Detection, given later in this chapter, further illustrates how to specify the names of input and output files during program execution.

string **Type and Input/Output Files**

In Chapter 7, we discussed the data type `string`. We now want to point out that values (that is, strings) of type `string` are not null terminated. Variables of type `string` can also be used to read and store the names of input/output files. However, the argument to the function `open` must be a null-terminated string—that is, a C-string. Therefore, if we use a variable of type `string` to read the name of an input/output file and then use this variable to open a file, the value of the variable must (first) be converted to a C-string (that is, a null-terminated string). The header file `string` contains the function `c_str`, which converts a value of type `string` to a null-terminated character array (that is, C-string). The syntax to use the function `c_str` is:

```
strVar.c_str()
```

in which `strVar` is a variable of type `string`.

8

The following statements illustrate how to use variables of type `string` to read the names of the input/output files during program execution and open those files:

```
ifstream infile;
string fileName;

cout << "Enter the input file name: ";
cin >> fileName;

infile.open(fileName.c_str());    //open the input file
```

Of course, you must also include the header file `string` in the program. The output file has similar conventions.

Parallel Arrays

Two (or more) arrays are called **parallel** if their corresponding components hold related information.

Suppose you need to keep track of students' course grades, together with their ID numbers, so that their grades can be posted at the end of the semester. Further, suppose that there is a maximum of 50 students in a class and their IDs are 5 digits long. Because there may be 50 students, you need 50 variables to store the students' IDs and 50 variables to store their grades. You can declare two arrays: `studentId` of type `int` and `courseGrade` of type `char`. Each array has 50 components. Furthermore, `studentId[0]` and `courseGrade[0]` will store the ID and course grade of the first student, `studentId[1]` and `courseGrade[1]` will store the ID and course grade of the second student, and so on.

The statements:

```
int studentId[50];
char courseGrade[50];
```

declare these two arrays.

Suppose you need to input data into these arrays, and the data is provided in a file in the following form:

```
studentId courseGrade
```

For example, a sample data set is:

```
23456 A
86723 B
22356 C
92733 B
11892 D
  .
  .
  .
```

Suppose that the input file is opened using the `ifstream` variable `infile`. Because the size of each array is 50, a maximum of 50 elements can be stored into each array. Moreover, it is possible that there may be fewer than 50 students in the class. Therefore, while reading the data, we also count the number of students and ensure that the array indices do not go out of bounds. The following loop reads the data into the parallel arrays `studentId` and `courseGrade`:

```
int noOfStudents = 0;

infile >> studentId[noOfStudents] >> courseGrade[noOfStudents];

while (infile && noOfStudents < 50)
{
    noOfStudents++;
    infile >> studentId[noOfStudents]
           >> courseGrade[noOfStudents];
}
```

Note that, in general, when swapping values in one array, the corresponding values in parallel arrays must also be swapped.

Two- and Multidimensional Arrays

The remainder of this chapter discusses two-dimensional arrays and ways to work with multidimensional arrays.

In the previous section, you learned how to use one-dimensional arrays to manipulate data. If the data is provided in a list form, you can use one-dimensional arrays. However, sometimes data is provided in a table form. For example, suppose that you want to track the number of cars in a particular color that are in stock at a local dealership. The dealership sells six types of cars in five different colors. Figure 8-12 shows sample data.

inStock	[RED]	[BROWN]	[BLACK]	[WHITE]	[GRAY]
[GM]	10	7	12	10	4
[FORD]	18	11	15	17	10
[TOYOTA]	12	10	9	5	12
[BMW]	16	6	13	8	3
[NISSAN]	10	7	12	6	4
[VOLVO]	9	4	7	12	11

FIGURE 8-12 Table `inStock`

You can see that the data is in a table format. The table has 30 entries, and every entry is an integer. Because the table entries are all of the same type, you can declare a one-dimensional array of 30 components of type `int`. The first five components of the one-dimensional array can store the data of the first row of the table, the next five components of the one-dimensional array can store the data of the second row of the table, and so on. In other words, you can simulate the data given in a table format in a one-dimensional array.

If you do so, the algorithms to manipulate the data in the one-dimensional array will be somewhat complicated, because you must know where one row ends and another begins. You must also correctly compute the index of a particular element. C++ simplifies the processing of manipulating data in a table form with the use of two-dimensional arrays. This section first discusses how to declare two-dimensional arrays and then looks at ways to manipulate data in a two-dimensional array.

Two-dimensional array: A collection of a fixed number of components arranged in rows and columns (that is, in two dimensions), wherein all components are of the same type.

The syntax for declaring a two-dimensional array is:

```
dataType   arrayName[intExp1][intExp2];
```

wherein `intExp1` and `intExp2` are constant expressions yielding positive integer values. The two expressions, `intExp1` and `intExp2`, specify the number of rows and the number of columns, respectively, in the array.

The statement:

`double sales[10][5];`

declares a two-dimensional array `sales` of 10 rows and 5 columns, in which every component is of type `double`. As in the case of a one-dimensional array, the rows are numbered 0...9 and the columns are numbered 0...4 (see Figure 8-13).

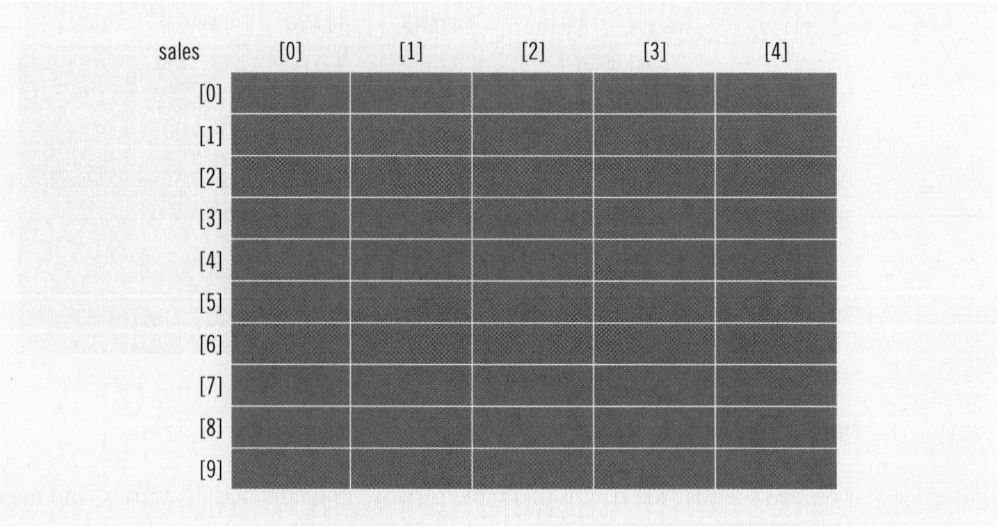

FIGURE 8-13 Two-dimensional array `sales`

Accessing Array Components

To access the components of a two-dimensional array, you need a pair of indices: one for the row position and one for the column position.

The syntax to access a component of a two-dimensional array is:

```
arrayName[indexExp1][indexExp2]
```

wherein `indexExp1` and `indexExp2` are expressions yielding nonnegative integer values. `indexExp1` specifies the row position; `indexExp2` specifies the column position.

The statement:

```
sales[5][3] = 25.75;
```

stores 25.75 into row number 5 and column number 3 (that is, the sixth row and the fourth column) of the array `sales` (see Figure 8-14).

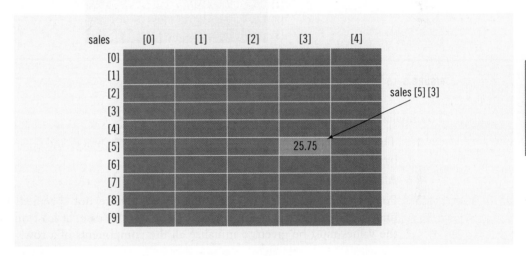

FIGURE 8-14 `sales[5][3]`

Suppose that:

```
int i = 5;
int j = 3;
```

Then, the previous statement:

```
sales[5][3] = 25.75;
```

is equivalent to:

```
sales[i][j] = 25.75;
```

So the indices can also be variables.

Two-Dimensional Array Initialization During Declaration

Like one-dimensional arrays, two-dimensional arrays can be initialized when they are declared. The following example helps illustrate this concept. Consider the following statement:

```
int board[4][3] = {{2, 3, 1},
                    {15, 25, 13},
                    {20, 4, 7},
                    {11, 18, 14}};
```

This statement declares `board` to be a two-dimensional array of `four` rows and `three` columns. The components of the first row are 2, 3, and 1; the components of the second row are 15, 25, and 13; the components of the third row are 20, 4, and 7; and the components of the fourth row are 11, 18, and 14, respectively. Figure 8-15 shows the array `board`.

board	[0]	[1]	[2]
[0]	2	3	1
[1]	15	25	13
[2]	20	4	7
[3]	11	18	14

FIGURE 8-15 Two-dimensional array `board`

To initialize a two-dimensional array when it is declared:

1. The elements of each row are enclosed within curly braces and separated by commas.

2. All rows are enclosed within curly braces.

3. For number arrays, if all components of a row are not specified, the unspecified components are initialized to 0. In this case, at least one of the values must be given to initialize all the components of a row.

Two-Dimensional Arrays and Enumeration Types

 NOTE The section "Enumeration Type" in Chapter 7 is required to understand this section.

You can also use the enumeration type for array indices. Consider the following statements:

```
const int NUMBER_OF_ROWS = 6;
const int NUMBER_OF_COLUMNS = 5;
enum carType {GM, FORD, TOYOTA, BMW, NISSAN, VOLVO};
enum colorType {RED, BROWN, BLACK, WHITE, GRAY};

int inStock[NUMBER_OF_ROWS][NUMBER_OF_COLUMNS];
```

These statements define the `carType` and `colorType` enumeration types and define `inStock` as a two-dimensional array of `six` rows and `five` columns. Suppose that each row in `inStock` corresponds to a car type, and each column in `inStock` corresponds to a color type. That is, the first row corresponds to the car type `GM`, the second row corresponds to the car type `FORD`, and so on. Similarly, the first column corresponds to the color type `RED`, the second column corresponds to the color type `BROWN`, and so on. Suppose further that each entry in `inStock` represents the number of cars of a particular type and color (see Figure 8-16).

inStock	[RED]	[BROWN]	[BLACK]	[WHITE]	[GRAY]
[GM]					
[FORD]					
[TOYOTA]					
[BMW]					
[NISSAN]					
[VOLVO]					

FIGURE 8-16 Two-dimensional array `inStock`

The statement:

`inStock[1][3] = 15;`

is equivalent to the following statement (see Figure 8-17):

`inStock[FORD][WHITE] = 15;`

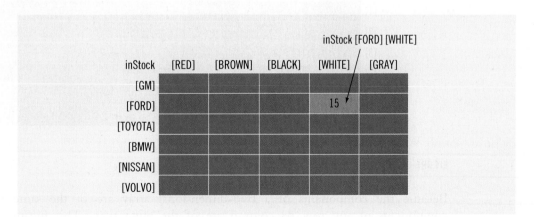

inStock [FORD] [WHITE]

inStock	[RED]	[BROWN]	[BLACK]	[WHITE]	[GRAY]
[GM]					
[FORD]				15	
[TOYOTA]					
[BMW]					
[NISSAN]					
[VOLVO]					

FIGURE 8-17 `inStock[FORD][WHITE]`

The second statement easily conveys the message—that is, set the number of WHITE FORD cars to 15. This example illustrates that enumeration types can be used effectively to make the program readable and easy to manage.

PROCESSING TWO-DIMENSIONAL ARRAYS

A two-dimensional array can be processed in three ways:

1. Process the entire array.
2. Process a particular row of the array, called **row processing**.
3. Process a particular column of the array, called **column processing**.

Initializing and printing the array are examples of processing the entire two-dimensional array. Finding the largest element in a row (column) or finding the sum of a row (column) are examples of row (column) processing. We will use the following declaration for our discussion:

```
const int NUMBER_OF_ROWS = 7;    //This can be set to any number.
const int NUMBER_OF_COLUMNS = 6; //This can be set to any number.

int matrix[NUMBER_OF_ROWS][NUMBER_OF_COLUMNS];
int row;
int col;
int sum;
int largest;
int temp;
```

Figure 8-18 shows the array matrix.

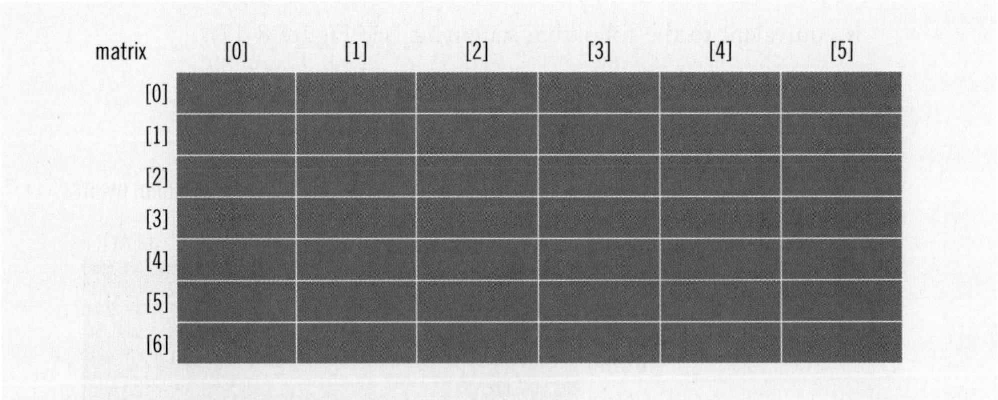

FIGURE 8-18 Two-dimensional array matrix

Because the components of a two-dimensional array are of the same type, the components of any row or column are of the same type. This means that each row and each column of a two-dimensional array is a one-dimensional array. There-fore, when processing a particular row or column of a two-dimensional array, we use algorithms similar to those that process one-dimensional arrays. We further explain this concept with the help of the two-dimensional array `matrix`, as declared previously.

Suppose that we want to process row number 5 of `matrix` (that is, the sixth row of `matrix`). The components of row number 5 of `matrix` are:

```
matrix[5][0], matrix[5][1], matrix[5][2], matrix[5][3], matrix[5][4],
matrix[5][5]
```

We see that in these components, the first index (the row position) is fixed at 5. The second index (the column position) ranges from 0 to 5. Therefore, we can use the following `for` loop to process row number 5:

```
for (col = 0; col < NUMBER_OF_COLUMNS; col++)
    process matrix[5][col]
```

Clearly, this `for` loop is equivalent to the following `for` loop:

```
row = 5;
for (col = 0; col < NUMBER_OF_COLUMNS; col++)
    process matrix[row][col]
```

Similarly, suppose that we want to process column number 2 of `matrix`, that is, the third column of `matrix`. The components of this column are:

```
matrix[0][2], matrix[1][2], matrix[2][2], matrix[3][2], matrix[4][2],
matrix[5][2], matrix[6][2]
```

Here, the second index (that is, the column position) is fixed at 2. The first index (that is, the row position) ranges from 0 to 6. In this case, we can use the following `for` loop to process column 2 of `matrix`:

```
for (row = 0; row < NUMBER_OF_ROWS; row++)
    process matrix[row][2]
```

Clearly, this `for` loop is equivalent to the following `for` loop:

```
col = 2;
for (row = 0; row < NUMBER_OF_ROWS; row++)
    process matrix[row][col]
```

Next, we discuss specific processing algorithms.

Initialization

Suppose that you want to initialize row number 4, that is, the fifth row, to 0. As explained earlier, the following `for` loop does this:

```
row = 4;
for (col = 0; col < NUMBER_OF_COLUMNS; col++)
    matrix[row][col] = 0;
```

If you want to initialize the entire `matrix` to 0, you can also put the first index, that is, the row position, in a loop. By using the following nested `for` loops, we can initialize each component of `matrix` to 0:

8

```
for (row = 0; row < NUMBER_OF_ROWS; row++)
    for (col = 0; col < NUMBER_OF_COLUMNS; col++)
        matrix[row][col] = 0;
```

Print

By using a nested **for** loop, you can output the components of **matrix**. The following nested **for** loops print the components of **matrix**, one row per line:

```
for (row = 0; row < NUMBER_OF_ROWS; row++)
{
    for (col = 0; col < NUMBER_OF_COLUMNS; col++)
        cout << setw(5) << matrix[row][col] << " ";

    cout << endl;
}
```

Input

The following **for** loop inputs the data into row number 4, that is, the fifth row of **matrix**:

```
row = 4;

for (col = 0; col < NUMBER_OF_COLUMNS; col++)
    cin >> matrix[row][col];
```

As before, by putting the row number in a loop, you can input data into each component of **matrix**. The following **for** loop inputs data into each component of **matrix**:

```
for (row = 0; row < NUMBER_OF_ROWS; row++)
    for (col = 0; col < NUMBER_OF_COLUMNS; col++)
        cin >> matrix[row][col];
```

Sum by Row

The following **for** loop finds the sum of row number 4 of **matrix**; that is, it adds the components of row number 4:

```
sum = 0;
row = 4;
for (col = 0; col < NUMBER_OF_COLUMNS; col++)
    sum = sum + matrix[row][col];
```

Once again, by putting the row number in a loop, we can find the sum of each row separately. The following is the C++ code to find the sum of each individual row:

```
    //Sum of each individual row
for (row = 0; row < NUMBER_OF_ROWS; row++)
{
    sum = 0;
    for (col = 0; col < NUMBER_OF_COLUMNS; col++)
        sum = sum + matrix[row][col];

    cout << "Sum of row " << row + 1 << " = " << sum << endl;
}
```

Sum by Column

As in the case of sum by row, the following nested `for` loop finds the sum of each individual column:

```
    //Sum of each individual column
for (col = 0; col < NUMBER_OF_COLUMNS; col++)
{
    sum = 0;
    for (row = 0; row < NUMBER_OF_ROWS; row++)
        sum = sum + matrix[row][col];

    cout << "Sum of column " << col + 1 << " = " << sum
        << endl;
}
```

Largest Element in Each Row and Each Column

As stated earlier, two other operations on a two-dimensional array are finding the largest element in each row and each column and finding the sum of both diagonals. Next, we give the C++ code to perform these operations.

The following `for` loop determines the largest element in row number 4:

```
row = 4;
largest = matrix[row][0]; //Assume that the first element of
                          //the row is the largest.
for (col = 1; col < NUMBER_OF_COLUMNS; col++)
    if (largest < matrix[row][col])
        largest = matrix[row][col];
```

The following C++ code determines the largest element in each row and each column:

```
    //Largest element in each row
for (row = 0; row < NUMBER_OF_ROWS; row++)
{
    largest = matrix[row][0]; //Assume that the first element
                              //of the row is the largest.
    for (col = 1; col < NUMBER_OF_COLUMNS; col++)
        if (largest < matrix[row][col])
            largest = matrix[row][col];

    cout << "The largest element in row " << row + 1 << " = "
        << largest << endl;
}

    //Largest element in each column
for (col = 0; col < NUMBER_OF_COLUMNS; col++)
{
    largest = matrix[0][col]; //Assume that the first element
                              //of the column is the largest.
    for (row = 1; row < NUMBER_OF_ROWS; row++)
        if (largest < matrix[row][col])
            largest = matrix[row][col];

    cout << "The largest element in column " << col + 1
        << " = " << largest << endl;
}
```

8

Passing Two-Dimensional Arrays as Parameters to Functions

Two-dimensional arrays can be passed as parameters to a function, and they are passed by reference. The base address (that is, the address of the first component of the actual parameter) is passed to the formal parameter. If `matrix` is the name of a two-dimensional array, then `matrix[0][0]` is the first component of `matrix`.

When storing a two-dimensional array in the computer's memory, C++ uses the **row order form**. That is, the first row is stored first, followed by the second row, followed by the third row, and so on.

In the case of a one-dimensional array, when declaring it as a formal parameter, we usually omit the size of the array. Because C++ stores two-dimensional arrays in row order form, to compute the address of a component correctly, the compiler must know where one row ends and the next row begins. Thus, when declaring a two-dimensional array as a formal parameter, you can omit the size of the first dimension, but not the second; that is, you must specify the number of columns.

Suppose we have the following declaration:

```
const int NUMBER_OF_ROWS = 6;
const int NUMBER_OF_COLUMNS = 5;
```

Consider the following definition of the function `printMatrix`:

```
void printMatrix(int matrix[][NUMBER_OF_COLUMNS],
                 int noOfRows)
{
    int row, col;

    for (row = 0; row < noOfRows; row++)
    {
        for (col = 0; col < NUMBER_OF_COLUMNS; col++)
            cout << setw(5) << matrix[row][col] << " ";

        cout << endl;
    }
}
```

This function takes as a parameter a two-dimensional array of an unspecified number of rows and **five** columns, and outputs the content of the two-dimensional array. During the function call, the number of columns of the actual parameter must match the number of columns of the formal parameter.

Similarly, the following function outputs the sum of the elements of each row of a two-dimensional array whose elements are of type `int`:

```
void sumRows(int matrix[][NUMBER_OF_COLUMNS], int noOfRows)
{
    int row, col;
    int sum;

        //Sum of each individual row
    for (row = 0; row < noOfRows; row++)
```

```
{
    sum = 0;

    for (col = 0; col < NUMBER_OF_COLUMNS; col++)
        sum = sum + matrix[row][col];

    cout << "Sum of row " << (row + 1) << " = " << sum
         << endl;
    }
}
```

The following function determines the largest element in each row:

```
void largestInRows(int matrix[][NUMBER_OF_COLUMNS],
                   int noOfRows)
{
    int row, col;
    int largest;

        //Largest element in each row
    for (row = 0; row < noOfRows; row++)
    {
        largest = matrix[row][0]; //Assume that the first element
                                  //of the row is the largest.
        for (col = 1; col < NUMBER_OF_COLUMNS; col++)
            if (largest < matrix[row][col])
                largest = matrix[row][col];

        cout << "The largest element of row " << (row + 1)
             << " = " << largest << endl;
    }
}
```

Likewise, you can write a function to find the sum of the elements of each column, read the data into a two-dimensional array, find the largest and/or smallest element in each row or column, and so on.

Example 8-11 shows how the functions printMatrix, sumRows, and largestInRows are used in a program.

EXAMPLE 8-11

The following program illustrates how two-dimensional arrays are passed as parameters to functions.

```
// Two-dimensional arrays as parameters to functions.

#include <iostream>
#include <iomanip>

using namespace std;

const int NUMBER_OF_ROWS = 6;
const int NUMBER_OF_COLUMNS = 5;
```

8

```
void printMatrix(int matrix[][NUMBER_OF_COLUMNS],
                 int NUMBER_OF_ROWS);
void sumRows(int matrix[][NUMBER_OF_COLUMNS],
             int NUMBER_OF_ROWS);
void largestInRows(int matrix[][NUMBER_OF_COLUMNS],
                   int NUMBER_OF_ROWS);

int main()
{
    int board[NUMBER_OF_ROWS][NUMBER_OF_COLUMNS]
                    = {{23, 5, 6, 15, 18},
                       {4, 16, 24, 67, 10},
                       {12, 54, 23, 76, 11},
                       {1, 12, 34, 22, 8},
                       {81, 54, 32, 67, 33},
                       {12, 34, 76, 78, 9}};      //Line 1

    printMatrix(board, NUMBER_OF_ROWS);           //Line 2
    cout << endl;                                 //Line 3
    sumRows(board, NUMBER_OF_ROWS);               //Line 4
    cout << endl;                                 //Line 5
    largestInRows(board, NUMBER_OF_ROWS);         //Line 6

    return 0;
}

//Place the definitions of the functions printMatrix,
//sumRows, and largestInRows as described previously here.
```

Sample Run:

```
23     5     6    15    18
 4    16    24    67    10
12    54    23    76    11
 1    12    34    22     8
81    54    32    67    33
12    34    76    78     9

Sum of row 1 = 67
Sum of row 2 = 121
Sum of row 3 = 176
Sum of row 4 = 77
Sum of row 5 = 267
Sum of row 6 = 209

The largest element in row 1 = 23
The largest element in row 2 = 67
The largest element in row 3 = 76
The largest element in row 4 = 34
The largest element in row 5 = 81
The largest element in row 6 = 78
```

In this program, the statement in Line 1 declares and initializes board to be a two-dimensional array of six rows and five columns. The statement in Line 2 uses the function `printMatrix` to output the elements of `board` (see the first six lines of the Sample Run). The statement in Line 4 uses the function `sumRows` to calculate and print the sum of each row. The statement in Line 6 uses the function `largestInRows` to find and print the largest element in each row.

Arrays of Strings

Suppose that you need to perform an operation, such as alphabetizing a list of names. Because every name is a string, a convenient way to store the list of names is to use an array. Strings in C++ can be manipulated using either the data type `string` or character arrays (C-strings). Also, on some compilers, the data type `string` may not be available in Standard C++ (that is, non-ANSI/ISO Standard C++). This section illustrates both ways to manipulate a list of strings.

Arrays of Strings and the `string` Type

Processing a list of strings using the data type `string` is straightforward. Suppose that the list consists of a maximum of 100 names. You can declare an array of 100 components of type `string` as follows:

```
string list[100];
```

Basic operations, such as assignment, comparison, and input/output, can be performed on values of the `string` type. Therefore, the data in `list` can be processed just like any one-dimensional array discussed in the first part of this chapter.

8

Arrays of Strings and C-Strings (Character Arrays)

Suppose that the largest string (for example, name) in your list is 15 characters long and your list has 100 strings. You can declare a two-dimensional array of characters of 100 rows and 16 columns as follows (see Figure 8-19):

```
char list[100][16];
```

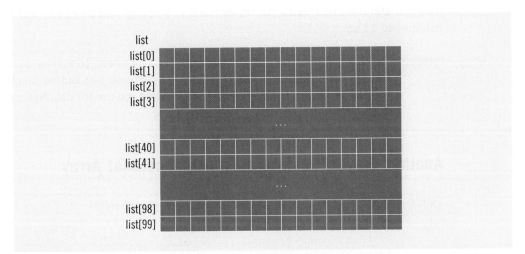

FIGURE 8-19 Array `list` of strings

Now `list[j]` for each j, 0 <= j <= 99, is a string of at most 15 characters in length. The following statement stores `"Snow White"` in `list[1]` (see Figure 8-20):

```
strcpy(list[1], "Snow White");
```

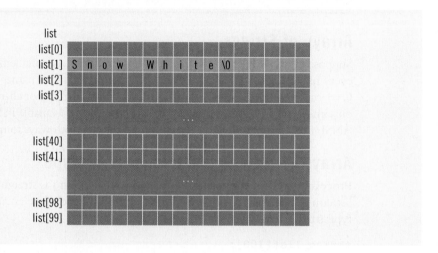

FIGURE 8-20 Array `list`, showing `list[1]`

Suppose that you want to read and store data in `list` and that there is one entry per line. The following `for` loop accomplishes this task:

```
for (j = 0; j < 100; j++)
    cin.get(list[j], 16);
```

The following `for` loop outputs the string in each row:

```
for (j = 0; j < 100; j++)
    cout << list[j] << endl;
```

You can also use other string functions (such as `strcmp` and `strlen`) and `for` loops to manipulate `list`.

 NOTE The data type `string` has operations such as assignment, concatenation, and relational operations defined for it. If you use Standard C++ header files and the data type `string` is available on your compiler, we recommend that you use the data type `string` to manipulate lists of strings.

Another Way to Declare a Two-Dimensional Array

 NOTE This section may be skipped without any loss of continuity.

If you know the size of the tables with which the program will be working, then you can use `typedef` to first define a two-dimensional array data type and then declare variables of that type.

For example, consider the following:

```
const int NUMBER_OF_ROWS = 20;
const int NUMBER_OF_COLUMNS = 10;

typedef int tableType[NUMBER_OF_ROWS][NUMBER_OF_COLUMNS];
```

The previous statement defines a two-dimensional array data type `tableType`. Now we can declare variables of this type. So:

```
tableType matrix;
```

declares a two-dimensional array `matrix` of 20 rows and 10 columns.

You can also use this data type when declaring formal parameters, as shown in the following code:

```
void initialize(tableType table)
{
    int row;
    int col;

    for (row = 0; row < NUMBER_OF_ROWS; row++)
        for (col = 0; col < NUMBER_OF_COLUMNS; col++)
            table[row][col] = 0;
}
```

This function takes as an argument any variable of type `tableType`, which is a two-dimensional array, and initializes the array to 0.

By first defining a data type, you do not need to keep checking the exact number of columns when you declare a two-dimensional array as a variable or formal parameter, or when you pass an array as a parameter during a function call.

Multidimensional Arrays

In this chapter, we defined an array as a collection of a fixed number of elements (called components) of the same type. A one-dimensional array is an array in which the elements are arranged in a list form; in a two-dimensional array, the elements are arranged in a table form. We can also define three-dimensional or larger arrays. In C++, there is no limit on the dimension of arrays. Following is the general definition of an array.

n-dimensional array: A collection of a fixed number of elements (called components) arranged in n dimensions ($n >= 1$).

The general syntax for declaring an *n*-dimensional array is:

```
dataType arrayName[intExp1][intExp2] ... [intExpn];
```

where `intExp1`, `intExp2`, . . . , and `intExpn` are constant expressions yielding positive integer values.

The syntax to access a component of an *n*-dimensional array is:

```
arrayName[indexExp1][indexExp2] ... [indexExpn]
```

where `indexExp1`, `indexExp2`, . . ., and `indexExpn` are expressions yielding non negative integer values. `indexExpi` gives the position of the array component in the `ith` dimension.

For example, the statement:

```
double carDealers[10][5][7];
```

declares `carDealers` to be a three-dimensional array. The size of the first dimension is 10, the size of the second dimension is 5, and the size of the third dimension is 7. The first dimension ranges from 0 to 9, the second dimension ranges from 0 to 4, and the third dimension ranges from 0 to 6. The base address of the array `carDealers` is the address of the first array component—that is, the address of `carDealers[0][0][0]`. The total number of components in the array `carDealers` is 10 * 5 * 7 = 350.

The statement:

```
carDealers[5][3][2] = 15564.75;
```

sets the value of the component `carDealers[5][3][2]` to `15564.75`.

You can use loops to process multidimensional arrays. For example, the nested **for** loops:

```
for (i = 0; i < 10; i++)
    for (j = 0; j < 5; j++)
        for (k = 0; k < 7; k++)
            carDealers[i][j][k] = 0.0;
```

initialize the entire array to `0.0`.

When declaring a multidimensional array as a formal parameter in a function, you can omit the size of the first dimension but not the other dimensions. As parameters, multi-dimensional arrays are passed by reference only, and a function cannot return a value of the array type. There is no check to determine whether the array indices are within bounds.

PROGRAMMING EXAMPLE: Code Detection

When a message is transmitted in secret code over a transmission channel, it is usually sent as a sequence of bits, that is, 0s and 1s. Due to noise in the transmission channel, the transmitted message may become corrupted. That is, the message received at the destination is not the same as the message transmitted; some of the bits may have been changed. There are several techniques to check the validity of the transmitted message at the destination. One technique is to transmit the same message twice. At the destination, both copies of the message are compared bit by bit. If the corresponding bits are the same, the message received is error-free.

Let's write a program to check whether the message received at the destination is error-free. For simplicity, assume that the secret code representing the message is a sequence of digits (0 to 9) and the maximum length of the message is 250 digits. Also, the first number in the message is the length of the message. For example, if the secret code is:

7 9 2 7 8 3 5 6

then the actual message is 7 digits long, and it is transmitted twice.

The above message is transmitted as:

7 9 2 7 8 3 5 6 7 9 2 7 8 3 5 6

Input A file containing the secret code and its copy

Output The secret code, its copy, and a message—if the received code is error-free—in the following form:

Code Digit	Code Digit Copy
9	9
2	2
7	7
8	8
3	3
5	5
6	6

Message transmitted OK.

PROBLEM ANALYSIS AND ALGORITHM DESIGN

Because we have to compare the corresponding digits of the secret code and its copy, we first read the secret code and store it in an array. Then we read the first digit of the copy and compare it with the first digit of the secret code, and so on. If any of the corresponding digits are not the same, we indicate this fact by printing a message next to the digits. Because the maximum length of the message is 250, we use an array of 250 components. The first number in the secret code, and in the copy of the secret code, indicates the length of the code. This discussion translates into the following algorithm:

1. Open the input and output files.
2. If the input file does not exist, exit the program.
3. Read the length of the secret code.
4. If the length of the secret code is greater than 250, terminate the program because the maximum length of the code in this program is 250.
5. Read and store the secret code into an array.
6. Read the length of the copy.
7. If the length of the secret code and its copy are the same, compare the codes. Otherwise, print an error message.

To simplify the function main, let us write a function, readCode, to read the secret code and another function, compareCode, to compare the codes.

readCode This function first reads the length of the secret code. If the length of the secret code is greater than 250, a bool variable lenCodeOk, which is a reference parameter, is set to false and the function terminates. The value of lenCodeOk is passed to the calling function to indicate whether the secret code was read successfully. If the length of the code is less than 250, the readCode function reads and stores the secret code into an array. Because the input is stored into a file and the file was opened in the function main, the input stream variable corresponding to the input file must be passed as a parameter to this function. Furthermore, after reading the length of the secret code and the code itself, the readCode function must pass these values to the function main. Therefore, this function has four parameters: an input file stream variable, an array to store the secret code, the length of the code, and the bool parameter lenCodeOk. The definition of the function readCode is as follows:

```
void readCode(ifstream& infile, int list[], int& length,
              bool& lenCodeOk)
{
    int count;

    lenCodeOk = true;

    infile >> length;   //get the length of the secret code

    if (length > MAX_CODE_SIZE)
    {
        lenCodeOk = false;
        return;
    }

        //Get the secret code.
    for (count = 0; count < length; count++)
        infile >> list[count];
}
```

compareCode This function compares the secret code with its copy. Therefore, it must have access to the array containing the secret code and the length of the secret code. The copy of the secret code and its length are stored in the input file. Thus, the input stream variable corresponding to the input file must be passed as a parameter to this function. Also, the compareCode function compares the secret code with the copy and prints an appropriate message. Because the output will be stored in a file, the output stream variable corresponding to the output file must also be passed as a parameter to this function. Therefore, the function has four parameters: an input file stream variable, an output file stream variable, the array containing the secret code, and the length of the secret code. This discussion translates into the following algorithm for the function compareCode:

    a.   Declare the variables.

    b.   Set a bool variable codeOk to true.

    c.   Read the length of the copy of the secret code.

    d.   If the length of the secret code and its copy are not the same, output an appropriate error message and terminate the function.

    e.   For each digit in the input file:

        e.1.   Read the next digit of the copy of the secret code.

        e.2.   Output the corresponding digits from the secret code and its copy.

        e.3.   If the corresponding digits are not the same, output an error message and set the bool variable codeOk to false.

    f.   If the bool variable codeOk is true

        Output a message indicating that the secret code was transmitted correctly.

    else

        Output an error message.

Following this algorithm, the definition of the function compareCode is:

```
void compareCode(ifstream& infile, ofstream& outfile,
                 const int list[], int length)
{
        //Step a
    int length2;
    int digit;
    bool codeOk;
    int count;

    codeOk = true;                              //Step b

    infile >> length2;                          //Step c
```

8

```
    if (length != length2)                              //Step d
    {
        cout << "The original code and its copy "
             << "are not of the same length."
             << endl;
        return;
    }

    outfile << "Code Digit     Code Digit Copy"
            << endl;

    for (count = 0; count < length; count++)            //Step e
    {
        infile >> digit;                                //Step e.1
        outfile << setw(5) << list[count]
                << setw(17) << digit;                   //Step e.2

        if (digit != list[count])                       //Step e.3
        {
            outfile << "  code digits are not the same"
                    << endl;
            codeOk = false;
        }
        else
            outfile << endl;
    }

    if (codeOk)                                          //Step f
        outfile << "Message transmitted OK."
                << endl;
    else
        outfile << "Error in transmission. "
                << "Retransmit!!" << endl;
}
```

The following is the algorithm for the function main:

Main Algorithm

1. Declare the variables.
2. Open the files.
3. Call the function readCode to read the secret code.
4. if (length of the secret code <= 250)

   Call the function compareCode to compare the codes.

   else

   Output an appropriate error message.

COMPLETE PROGRAM LISTING

```cpp
//**************************************************************
// Author: D.S. Malik
//
// Program: Check Code
// This program determines whether a code is transmitted
// correctly.
//**************************************************************

#include <iostream>
#include <fstream>
#include <iomanip>

using namespace std;

const int MAX_CODE_SIZE = 250;

void readCode(ifstream& infile, int list[],
              int& length, bool& lenCodeOk);
void compareCode(ifstream& infile, ofstream& outfile,
                 const int list[], int length);

int main()
{
        //Step 1
    int codeArray[MAX_CODE_SIZE]; //array to store the secret
                                  //code
    int codeLength;               //variable to store the
                                  //length of the secret code
    bool lengthCodeOk;   //variable to indicate if the length
                         //of the secret code is less than or
                         //equal to 250

    ifstream incode;     //input file stream variable
    ofstream outcode;    //output file stream variable

    char inputFile[51]; //variable to store the name of the
                        //input file
    char outputFile[51];    //variable to store the name of
                            //the output file

    cout << "Enter the input file name: ";
    cin >> inputFile;
    cout << endl;

        //Step 2
    incode.open(inputFile);
    if (!incode)
    {
        cout << "Cannot open the input file." << endl;
        return 1;
    }
```

8

```
        cout << "Enter the output file name: ";
        cin >> outputFile;
        cout << endl;

        outcode.open(outputFile);

        readCode(incode, codeArray, codeLength,
                 lengthCodeOk);                               //Step 3

        if (lengthCodeOk)                                     //Step 4
            compareCode(incode, outcode, codeArray,
                        codeLength);
        else
            cout << "Length of the secret code "
                 << "must be <= " << MAX_CODE_SIZE
                 << endl;                                     //Step 5

        incode.close();
        outcode.close();

        return 0;
}

//Place the definitions of the functions readCode and
//compareCode, as described previously, here.
```

Sample Run: In this sample run, the user input is shaded.

```
Enter the input file name:  Ch8_SecretCodeData.txt

Enter the output file name:  Ch8_SecretCodeOut.txt
```

Input File Data: (Ch8_SecretCodeData.txt)

```
7 9 2 7 8 3 5 6 7 9 2 7 8 3 5 6
```

Output File Data: (Ch8_SecretCodeOut.txt)

```
Code Digit     Code Digit Copy
    9               9
    2               2
    7               7
    8               8
    3               3
    5               5
    6               6
Message transmitted OK.
```

PROGRAMMING EXAMPLE: Text Processing

Watch the Video

(Line and letter count) Let us now write a program that reads a given text, outputs the text as is, and also prints the number of lines and the number of times each letter appears in the text. An uppercase letter and a lowercase letter are treated as being the same; that is, they are tallied together.

Because there are 26 letters, we use an array of 26 components to perform the letter count. We also need a variable to store the line count.

The text is stored in a file, which we will call `textin.txt`. The output will be stored in a file, which we will call `textout.out`.

Input A file containing the text to be processed.

Output A file containing the text, number of lines, and the number of times a letter appears in the text.

PROBLEM ANALYSIS AND ALGORITHM DESIGN

Based on the desired output, it is clear that we must output the text as is. That is, if the text contains any whitespace characters, they must be output as well. Furthermore, we must count the number of lines in the text. Therefore, we must know where the line ends, which means that we must trap the newline character. This requirement suggests that we cannot use the extraction operator to process the input file. Because we also need to perform the letter count, we use the `get` function to read the text.

Let us first describe the variables that are necessary to develop the program. This will simplify the discussion that follows.

Variables We need to store the line count and the letter count. Therefore, we need a variable to store the line count and 26 variables to perform the letter count. We will use an array of 26 components to perform the letter count. We also need a variable to read and store each character in turn, because the input file is to be read character by character. Because data is to be read from an input file and output is to be saved in a file, we need an input stream variable to open the input file and an output stream variable to open the output file. These statements indicate that the function `main` needs (at least) the following variables:

```
int lineCount;          //variable to store the line count
int letterCount[26];    //array to store the letter count
char ch;                //variable to store a character
ifstream infile;        //input file stream variable
ofstream outfile;       //output file stream variable
```

In this declaration, `letterCount[0]` stores the A count, `letterCount[1]` stores the B count, and so on. Clearly, the variable `lineCount` and the array `letterCount` must be initialized to 0.

The algorithm for the program is:

1. Declare the variables.
2. Open the input and output files.
3. Initialize the variables.
4. While there is more data in the input file:
   4.1. For each character in a line:
      4.1.1. Read and write the character.
      4.1.2. Increment the appropriate letter count.
   4.2. Increment the line count.
5. Output the line count and letter counts.
6. Close the files.

To simplify the function `main`, we divide it into four functions:

- Function `initialize`
- Function `copyText`
- Function `characterCount`
- Function `writeTotal`

The following sections describe each of these functions in detail. Then, with the help of these functions, we describe the algorithm for the function `main`.

initialize This function initializes the variable `lineCount` and the array `letterCount` to 0. It, therefore, has two parameters: one corresponding to the variable `lineCount` and one corresponding to the array `letterCount`. Clearly, the parameter corresponding to `lineCount` must be a reference parameter. The definition of this function is:

```
void initialize(int& lc, int list[])
{
    int j;
    lc = 0;

    for (j = 0; j < 26; j++)
        list[j] = 0;
} //end initialize
```

copyText This function reads a line and outputs the line. After reading a character, it calls the function `characterCount` to update the letter count. Clearly, this function has four parameters: an input file stream variable, an output file stream variable, a `char` variable, and the array to update the letter count.

Note that the `copyText` function does not perform the letter count, but we still pass the array `letterCount` to it. We take this step because this function calls the function `characterCount`, which needs the array `letterCount` to update the appropriate letter count. Therefore, we must pass the array `letterCount` to the `copyText` function so that it can pass the array to the function `characterCount`.

```
void copyText(ifstream& intext, ofstream& outtext, char& ch,
              int list[])
{
    while (ch != '\n')          //process the entire line
    {
        outtext << ch;          //output the character
        characterCount(ch, list);   //call the function
                                //character count
        intext.get(ch);         //read the next character
    }
    outtext << ch;              //output the newline character
} //end copyText
```

characterCount This function increments the letter count. To increment the appropriate letter count, it must know what the letter is. Therefore, the `characterCount` function has two parameters: a `char` variable and the array to update the letter count. In pseudocode, this function is:

    a.   Convert the letter to uppercase.

    b.   Find the index of the array corresponding to this letter.

    c.   If the index is valid, increment the appropriate count. At this step, we must ensure that the character is a letter. We are counting only letters, so other characters—such as commas, hyphens, and periods—are ignored.

Following this algorithm, the definition of this function is:

```
void characterCount(char ch, int list[])
{
    int index;

    ch = toupper(ch);                           //Step a

    index = static_cast<int>(ch)
            - static_cast<int>('A');            //Step b

    if (0 <= index && index < 26)               //Step c
        list[index]++;
} //end characterCount
```

writeTotal This function outputs the line count and the letter count. It has three parameters: the output file stream variable, the line count, and the array to output the letter count. The definition of this function is:

```
void writeTotal(ofstream& outtext, int lc, int list[])
{
    int index;

    outtext << endl << endl;
    outtext << "The number of lines = " << lc << endl;

    for (index = 0; index < 26; index++)
        outtext << static_cast<char>(index
                                + static_cast<int>('A'))
                << " count = " << list[index] << endl;
} //end writeTotal
```

We now describe the algorithm for the function main.

MAIN
ALGORITHM

1. Declare the variables.
2. Open the input file.
3. If the input file does not exist, exit the program.
4. Open the output file.
5. Initialize the variables, such as lineCount and the array letterCount.
6. Read the first character.
7. While (not end of input file):

   7.1. Process the next line; call the function copyText.

   7.2. Increment the line count. (Increment the variable lineCount.)

   7.3. Read the next character.

8. Output the line count and letter counts. Call the function writeTotal.
9. Close the files.

COMPLETE PROGRAM LISTING

```
//************************************************************
// Author: D.S. Malik
//
// Program: Line and Letter Count
// This programs reads a text, outputs the text as is, and also
// prints the number of lines and the number of times each
// letter appears in the text. An uppercase letter and a
// lowercase letter are treated as being the same; that is,
// they are tallied together.
//************************************************************
```

```cpp
#include <iostream>
#include <fstream>
#include <cctype>

using namespace std;

void initialize(int& lc, int list[]);
void copyText(ifstream& intext, ofstream& outtext, char& ch,
              int list[]);
void characterCount(char ch, int list[]);
void writeTotal(ofstream& outtext, int lc, int list[]);

int main()
{
        //Step 1; Declare variables
    int lineCount;
    int letterCount[26];
    char ch;
    ifstream infile;
    ofstream outfile;

    infile.open("textin.txt");                          //Step 2

    if (!infile)                                        //Step 3
    {
        cout << "Cannot open the input file."
             << endl;
        return 1;
    }

    outfile.open("textout.out");                        //Step 4

    initialize(lineCount, letterCount);                 //Step 5

    infile.get(ch);                                     //Step 6

    while (infile)                                      //Step 7
    {
        copyText(infile, outfile, ch, letterCount);     //Step 7.1
        lineCount++;                                    //Step 7.2
        infile.get(ch);                                 //Step 7.3
    }

    writeTotal(outfile, lineCount, letterCount);        //Step 8

    infile.close();                                     //Step 9
    outfile.close();                                    //Step 9

    return 0;
}
```

8

```cpp
void initialize(int& lc, int list[])
{
    int j;
    lc = 0;

    for (j = 0; j < 26; j++)
        list[j] = 0;
} //end initialize

void copyText(ifstream& intext, ofstream& outtext, char& ch,
              int list[])
{
    while (ch != '\n')          //process the entire line

    {
        outtext << ch;          //output the character

        characterCount(ch, list);    //call the function
                                     //character count
        intext.get(ch);         //read the next character
    }

    outtext << ch;              //output the newline character
} //end copyText

void characterCount(char ch, int list[])
{
    int index;

    ch = toupper(ch);                               //Step a

    index = static_cast<int>(ch)
            - static_cast<int>('A');                //Step b

    if (0 <= index & index < 26)                    //Step c
        list[index]++;
} //end characterCount

void writeTotal(ofstream& outtext, int lc, int list[])
{
    int index;

    outtext << endl << endl;
    outtext << "The number of lines = " << lc << endl;

    for (index = 0; index < 26; index++)
        outtext << static_cast<char>(index
                                     + static_cast<int>('A'))
                << " count = " << list[index] << endl;
} //end writeTotal
```

Sample Run (textout.out):

Today we live in an era where information is processed almost at the
speed of light. Through computers, the technological revolution is
drastically changing the way we live and communicate with one
another. Terms such as "the Internet," which were unfamiliar just
a few years ago, are very common today. With the help of computers you
can send letters to, and receive letters from, loved ones within
seconds. You no longer need to send a résumé by mail to apply for a
job; in many cases you can simply submit your job application via
the Internet. You can watch how stocks perform in real time, and
instantly buy and sell them. Students regularly "surf" the Internet
and use computers to design their classroom projects. They also use
powerful word-processing software to complete their term papers.
Many people maintain and balance their checkbooks on computers.

```
The number of lines = 15
A count = 53
B count = 7
C count = 30
D count = 19
E count = 81
F count = 11
G count = 10
H count = 29
I count = 41
J count = 4
K count = 3
L count = 31
M count = 26
N count = 50
O count = 59
P count = 21
Q count = 0
R count = 45
S count = 48
T count = 62
U count = 24
V count = 7
W count = 15
X count = 0
Y count = 20
Z count = 0
```

8

QUICK REVIEW

1. A data type is simple if variables of that type can hold only one value at a time.

2. In a structured data type, each data item is a collection of other data items.

3. An array is a structured data type with a fixed number of components. Every component is of the same type, and components are accessed using their relative positions in the array.

4. Elements of a one-dimensional array are arranged in the form of a list.

5. There is no check on whether an array index is out of bounds.

6. In C++, an array index starts with 0.

7. An array index can be any expression that evaluates to a nonnegative integer. The value of the index must always be less than the size of the array.

8. There are no aggregate operations on arrays, except for the input/output of character arrays (C-strings).

9. Arrays can be initialized during their declaration. If there are fewer initial values than the array size, the remaining elements are initialized to 0.

10. The base address of an array is the address of the first array component. For example, if `list` is a one-dimensional array, the base address of `list` is the address of `list[0]`.

11. When declaring a one-dimensional array as a formal parameter, you usually omit the array size. If you specify the size of a one-dimensional array in the formal parameter declaration, the compiler will ignore the size.

12. In a function call statement, when passing an array as an actual parameter, you use only its name.

13. As parameters to functions, arrays are passed by reference only.

14. Because as parameters, arrays are passed by reference only, when declaring an array as a formal parameter, you do not use the symbol & after the data type.

15. A function cannot return a value of type array.

16. Although as parameters, arrays are passed by reference, when declaring an array as a formal parameter, using the reserved word `const` before the data type prevents the function from modifying the array.

17. Individual array components can be passed as parameters to functions.

18. The sequential search algorithm searches a list for a given item, starting with the first element in the list. It continues to compare the search item with the other elements in the list until either the item is found or the list has no more elements left to be compared with the search item.

19. Selection sort sorts the list by finding the smallest (or equivalently largest) element in the list and moving it to the beginning (or end) of the list.

20. For a list of length n, selection sort makes exactly $\dfrac{n(n-1)}{2}$ key comparisons and $3(n-1)$ item assignments.

21. In C++, a string is any sequence of characters enclosed between double quotation marks.

22. In C++, C-strings are null terminated.

23. In C++, the null character is represented as `'\0'`.

24. In the ASCII character set, the collating sequence of the null character is 0.

25. C-strings are stored in character arrays.

26. Character arrays can be initialized during declaration using string notation.

27. Input and output of C-strings is the only place where C++ allows aggregate operations.

28. The header file `cstring` contains the specifications of the functions that can be used for C-string manipulation.

29. Commonly used C-string manipulation functions include `strcpy` (string copy), `strcmp` (string comparison), and `strlen` (string length).

30. C-strings are compared character by character.

31. Because C-strings are stored in arrays, individual characters in the C-string can be accessed using the array component access notation.

32. Parallel arrays are used to hold related information.

33. In a two-dimensional array, the elements are arranged in a table form.

34. To access an element of a two-dimensional array, you need a pair of indices: one for the row position and one for the column position.

35. In a two-dimensional array, the rows are numbered 0 to ROW_SIZE − 1 and the columns are numbered 0 to COLUMN_SIZE − 1.

36. If `matrix` is a two-dimensional array, then the base address of `matrix` is the address of the array component `matrix[0][0]`.

37. In row processing, a two-dimensional array is processed one row at a time.

38. In column processing, a two-dimensional array is processed one column at a time.

39. When declaring a two-dimensional array as a formal parameter, you can omit the size of the first dimension but not the second.

40. When a two-dimensional array is passed as an actual parameter, the number of columns of the actual and formal arrays must match.

41. C++ stores, in computer memory, two-dimensional arrays in a row order form.

EXERCISES

1. Mark the following statements as true or false.

   a. A `double` type is an example of a simple data type.

   b. A one-dimensional array is an example of a structured data type.

   c. Arrays can be passed as parameters to a function either by value or by reference.

   d. A function can return a value of type array.

   e. The size of an array is determined at compile time.

f. The only aggregate operations allowable on `int` arrays are the increment and decrement operations.

g. Given the declaration:

```
int list[10];
```

the statement:

```
list[5] = list[3] + list[2];
```

updates the content of the fifth component of the array `list`.

h. If an array index goes out of bounds, the program always terminates in an error.

i. In C++, some aggregate operations are allowed for strings.

j. The declaration:

```
char name[16] = "John K. Miller";
```

declares `name` to be an array of 15 characters because the string `"John K. Miller"` has only 14 characters.

k. The declaration:

```
char str = "Sunny Day";
```

declares `str` to be a string of an unspecified length.

l. As parameters, two-dimensional arrays are passed either by value or by reference.

2. Consider the following declaration:

```
double passwords[100];
```

In this declaration, identify the following:

a. The array name.

b. The array size.

c. The data type of each array component.

d. The range of values for the index of the array.

3. Identify error(s), if any, in the following array declarations. If a statement is incorrect, provide the correct statement.

a. `double weights[100];`

b. `int age[0..80];`

c. `string students[101];`

d. `int100 list[];`

e. `double[50] salaries;`

f. `const double LENGTH = 30.00;`
   `double list[LENGTH];`

g. `const int SIZE = 100;`
   `int list[SIZE - 1];`

4. Determine whether the following array declarations are valid. If a declaration is invalid, explain why.

   a. `string employees[82];`

   b. `int myArray[50;`

   c. `int SIZE;`
      `double list[SIZE];`

   d. `int X = 50;`
      `double list[X - 60];`

   e. `int ids[-30];`

   f. `names string[10];`

5. What would be a valid range for the index of an array of size 64?

6. Write C++ statements to do the following:

   a. Declare an array `beta` of 20 components of type `double`.

   b. Initialize each component of the array `beta` to 0.

   c. Output the value of the fifth component of the array `beta`.

   d. Set the value of the ninth component of the array `beta` to `70.50`.

   e. Set the value of the twelth component of `beta` to four times the value of the eighth component of `beta` minus 15.

   f. Use a `for` loop to output the value of a component of `beta` if its index is a multiple of 3.

   g. Output the value of the last component of `beta`.

   h. Output the value of `beta` so that ten components per line are printed.

7. What is the output of the following program segment?

```
double temp[5];

for (int i = 0; i < 5; i++)
    temp[i] = pow(i, 2.0) + 2;

for (int i = 0; i < 5; i++)
    cout << temp[i] << " ";
cout << endl;

temp[0] = pow(temp[1], 3);
temp[1] = temp[4] - temp[2];
temp[2] = temp[0] - 5;

for (int i = 0; i < 5; i++)
    cout << temp[i] << " ";
cout << endl;
```

8

8. What is stored in `list` after the following C++ code executes?

```cpp
int list[10];

for (int i = 0; i < 5; i++)
{
    list[i] = i * i - 5;
    if (i % 3 == 0)
        list[i] = list[i] + i;
    else
        list[i] = list[i] - i;
}
```

9. What is stored in `list` after the following C++ code executes?

```cpp
int list[10];

list[0] = 2;
list[1] = 3;
for (int i = 2; i < 10; i++)
{
    list[i] = list[i - 1] +  list[i - 2];
    if (i > 7)
        list[i] = 2 * list[i] - list[i - 2];
}
```

10. What is stored in `myList` after the following C++ code executes?

```cpp
double myList[5];

myList[0] = 3.0;
myList[1] = 4.0;

for (int i = 2; i < 5; i++)
{
    myList[i] = myList[i - 1] *  myList[i - 2];
    if (i > 3)
        myList[i] = myList[i] / 4;
}
```

11. Correct the following code so that it correctly sets the value of each element of `myList` to the index of the element.

```cpp
int myList[10];

for (int i = 1; i <= 10; i--)
    myList[i] = [i];
```

12. Correct the following code so that it correctly initializes and outputs the elements of the array `myList`.

```cpp
int myList[10];

for (int i = 1; i <= 10; i++)
    cin >> myList;
```

```
for (int i = 1; i <= 10; i++)
    cout << myList[i] << " ";
cout << endl;
```

13. What is array index out of bounds? Does C++ check for array indices within bounds?

14. Suppose that `scores` is an array of 10 components of type `double`, and:

    ```
    scores = {2.5, 3.9, 4.8, 6.2, 6.2, 7.4, 7.9, 8.5, 8.5, 9.9}
    ```

    The following is supposed to ensure that the elements of `scores` are in nondecreasing order. However, there are errors in the code. Find and correct the errors.

    ```
    for (int i = 1; i <= 10; i++)
        if (scores[i] >= scores[i + 1])
            cout << i << " and " << (i + 1)
                 << " elements of scores are out of order." << endl;
    ```

15. Write C++ statements to define and initialize the following arrays.

    a. Array `heights` of 10 components of type `double`. Initialize this array to the following values: 5.2, 6.3, 5.8, 4.9, 5.2, 5.7, 6.7, 7.1, 5.10, 6.0.

    b. Array `weights` of 7 components of type `int`. Initialize this array to the following values: 120, 125, 137, 140, 150, 180, 210.

    c. Array `specialSymbols` of type `char`. Initialize this array to the following values: `'$'`, `'#'`, `'%'`, `'@'`, `'&'`, `'! '`, `'^'`.

    d. Array `seasons` of 4 components of type `string`. Initialize this array to the following values: `"fall"`, `"winter"`, `"spring"`, `"summer"`.

16. Determine whether the following array declarations are valid. If a declaration is valid, determine the size of the array.

    a. `int list[] = {18, 13, 14, 16};`

    b. `int x[10] = {1, 7, 5, 3, 2, 8};`

    c. `double y[4] = {2.0, 5.0, 8.0, 11.0, 14.0};`

    d. `double lengths[] = {8.2, 3.9, 6.4, 5.7, 7.3};`

    e. `int list[7] = {12, 13, , 14, 16, , 8};`

    f. `string names[8] = {"John","Lisa", "Chris", "Katie"};`

17. Suppose that you have the following declaration:

    ```
    int list[7] = {6, 10, 14, 18, 22};
    ```

    If this declaration is valid, what is stored in each components of `list`.

18. Consider the following declaration:

    ```
    int list[] = {3, 8, 10, 13, 6, 11};
    ```

    a. Write a C++ code that will output the value stored in each component of `list`.

    b. Write a C++ code that will set the values of the first five components of `list` as follows: The value of the ith component is the value of the ith component minus three times the value of the $(i+1)$th component.

19. What is the output of the following C++ code?

```cpp
#include <iostream>

using namespace std;

int main()
{
    int beta[7] = {3, 5};

    for (int i = 2; i < 7; i++)
    {
        beta[i] = 3 * i + 2;
        beta[i - 1] = beta[i - 1] + beta[i];
        beta[i - 2] = beta[i - 2] + beta [i - 1];
    }

    for (int i = 0; i < 7; i++)
        cout << beta[i] << " ";
    cout << endl;

    return 0;
}
```

20. What is the output of the following C++ code?

```cpp
#include <iostream>

using namespace std;

int main()
{
    int list1[5];
    int list2[15];

    for (int i = 0; i < 5; i++)
        list1[i] = i * i - 2;

    cout << "list1: ";
    for (int i = 0; i < 5; i++)
        cout << list1[i] << " ";
    cout << endl;

    for (int i = 0; i < 5; i++)
    {
        list2[i] = list1[i] * i;
        list2[i + 5] = list1[4 - i] + i;
        list2[i + 10] = list2[9 - i] + list2[i];
    }

    cout << "list2: ";
    for (int i = 0; i < 7; i++)
        cout << list2[i] << " ";
    cout << endl;

    return 0;
}
```

21. Consider the following function heading:

```
void tryMe(int x[], int size);
```

and the declarations:

```
int list[100];
int score[50];
double gpas[50];
```

Which of the following function calls is valid?

   a.   `tryMe(list, 100);`

   b.   `tryMe(list, 75);`

   c.   `tryMe(score, 100);`

   d.   `tryMe(score, 49);`

   e.   `tryMe(gpas, 50);`

22. Suppose that you have the following function definition:

```
void sum(int x, int y, int& z)
{
    z = x + y;
}
```

Consider the following declarations:

```
int list1[10], list2[10], list3[10];
int a, b, c;
```

Which of the following function calls is valid?

   a.   `sum(a, b, c);`

   b.   `sum(list1[0], list2[0], a);`

   c.   `sum(list1, list2, c);`

   d.   `for (int i = 1; i <= 10; i++)`
           `sum(list1[i], list2[i], list3[i]);`

23. What is the output of the following C++ code?

```
double salary[5] = {25000, 36500, 85000, 62500, 97000};
double raise = 0.03;

cout << fixed << showpoint << setprecision(2);

for (int i = 0; i < 5; i++)
    cout << (i + 1) << " " << salary[i] << " "
         << salary[i] * raise << endl;
```

24. A car dealer has 10 salespersons. Each salesperson keeps track of the number of cars sold each month and reports it to the management at the end of the month. The management keeps the data in a file and assigns a number, 1 to 10, to each salesperson. The following statement declares an array, `cars`, of

10 components of type `int` to store the number of cars sold by each salesperson:

```
int cars[10];
```

Write the code to store the number of cars sold by each salesperson in the array `cars`, output the total numbers of cars sold at the end of each month, and output the salesperson number selling the maximum number of cars. (Assume that data is in the file `cars.dat`, and that this file has been opened using the `ifstream` variable `inFile`.)

25. What is the output of the following program?

```
#include <iostream>

using namespace std;

int main()
{
    int count;
    int alpha[5];

    alpha[0] = 5;
    for (count = 1; count < 5; count++)
    {
        alpha[count] = 5 * count + 10;
        alpha[count - 1] = alpha[count] - 4;
    }

    cout << "List elements: ";
    for (count = 0; count < 5; count++)
        cout << alpha[count] << " ";
    cout << endl;

    return 0;
}
```

26. What is the output of the following program?

```
#include <iostream>

using namespace std;

int main()
{
    int j;
    int one[5];
    int two[10];

    for (j = 0; j < 5; j++)
        one[j] = 5 * j + 3;

    cout << "One contains: ";
    for (j = 0; j < 5; j++)
        cout << one[j] << " ";
```

```
        cout << endl;
        for (j = 0; j < 5; j++)
        {
            two[j] = 2 * one[j] - 1;
            two[j + 5] = one[4 - j] + two[j];
        }

        cout << "Two contains: ";
        for (j = 0; j < 10; j++)
            cout << two[j] << " ";
        cout << endl;

        return 0;
    }
```

27. What is the output of the following C++ code?

```
    const double PI = 3.14159;
    double cylinderRadii[5] = {3.5, 7.2, 10.5, 9.8, 6.5};
    double cylinderHeights[5] = {10.7, 6.5, 12.0, 10.5, 8.0};
    double cylinderVolumes[5];

    cout << fixed << showpoint << setprecision(2);

    for (int i = 0; i < 5; i++)
        cylinderVolumes[i] = 2 * PI * cylinderRadii[i]
                             * cylinderHeights[i];

    for (int i = 0; i < 5; i++)
        cout << (i + 1) << " " << cylinderRadii[i] << " "
             << cylinderHeights[i] << " " << cylinderVolumes[i] << endl;
```

28. When an array is passed as an actual parameter to a function, what is actually being passed?

29. In C++, as an actual parameter, can an array be passed by value?

30. Sort the following list using the selection sort algorithm as discussed in this chapter. Show the list after each iteration of the outer `for` loop.

    6, 45, 10, 25, 58, 2, 50, 30, 86

31. Sort the following list using the selection sort algorithm as discussed in this chapter. Show the list after each iteration of the outer `for` loop.

    36, 55, 17, 35, 63, 85, 12, 48, 3, 66

32. Given the declaration:

    `char string15[16];`

    Mark the following statements as valid or invalid. If a statement is invalid, explain why.

    a. `strcpy(string15, "Hello there");`

    b. `strlen(string15);`

    c. `string15 = "Jacksonville";`

8

    d.   `cin >> string15;`

    e.   `cout << string15;`

    f.   `if (string15 >= "Nice day")`
           `cout << string15;`

    g.   `string15[6] = 't';`

33. Given the declaration:

```
char str1[15];
char str2[15] = "Good day";
```

Mark the following statements as valid or invalid. If a statement is invalid, explain why.

    a.   `str1 = str2;`

    b.   `if (str1 == str2)`
           `cout << " Both strings are of the same length." << endl;`

    c.   `if (strlen(str1) >= strlen(str2))`
           `str1 = str2;`

    d.   `if (strcmp(str1, str2) < 0)`
           `cout << "str1 is less that str2." << endl;`

34. Given the declaration:

```
char name[8] = "Shelly";
```

Mark the following statements as "Yes" if they output `Shelly`. Otherwise, mark the statement as "No" and explain why it does not output `Shelly`.

    a.   `cout << name;`

    b.   `for (int j = 0; j < 6; j++)`
           `cout << name[j];`

    c.   `int j = 0;`
       `while (name[j] != '\0')`
           `cout << name[j++];`

    d.   `int j = 0;`
       `while (j < 8)`
           `cout << name[j++];`

35. Given the declaration:

```
char str1[21];
char str2[21];
```

    a.   Write a C++ statement that stores `"Sunny Day"` in `str1`.

    b.   Write a C++ statement that stores the length of `str1` into the `int` variable `length`.

    c.   Write a C++ statement that copies the value of `name` into `str2`.

    d.   Write C++ code that outputs `str1` if `str1` is less than or equal to `str2`, and otherwise outputs `str2`.

36. Assume the following declarations:

```
char name[21];
char yourName[21];
char studentName[31];
```

Mark the following statements as valid or invalid. If a statement is invalid, explain why.

a. `cin >> name;`

b. `cout << studentName;`

c. `yourName[0] = '\0';`

d. `yourName = studentName;`

e. `if (yourName == name)`
      `studentName = name;`

f. `int x = strcmp(yourName, studentName);`

g. `strcpy(studentName, name);`

h. `for (int j = 0; j < 21; j++)`
      `cout << name[j];`

37. Define a two-dimensional array named `temp` of three rows and four columns of type `int` such that the first row is initialized to 6, 8, 12, 9; the second row is initialized to 17, 5, 10, 6; and the third row is initialized to 14, 13, 16, 20.

38. Suppose that array `temp` is as defined in Exercise 37. Write C++ statements to accomplish the following:

a. Output the contents of the first row and first column element of `temp`.

b. Output the contents of the first row and last column element of `temp`.

c. Output the contents of the last row and first column element of `temp`.

d. Output the contents of the last row and last column element of `temp`.

39. Consider the following declarations:

```
const int CAR_TYPES = 5;
const int COLOR_TYPES = 6;

double sales[CAR_TYPES][COLOR_TYPES];
```

a. How many components does the array `sales` have?

b. What is the number of rows in the array `sales`?

c. What is the number of columns in the array `sales`?

d. To sum the sales by `CAR_TYPES`, what kind of processing is required?

e. To sum the sales by `COLOR_TYPES`, what kind of processing is required?

40. Write C++ statements that do the following:

a. Declare an array `alpha` of 10 rows and 20 columns of type `int`.

b. Initialize the array `alpha` to 0.

c. Store 1 in the first row and 2 in the remaining rows.

8

    d.   Store 5 in the first column, and make sure that the value in each subsequent column is twice the value in the previous column.

    e.   Print the array `alpha` one row per line.

    f.   Print the array `alpha` one column per line.

41.   Consider the following declaration:

```
int beta[3][3];
```

What is stored in `beta` after each of the following statements executes?

    a.
```
for (i = 0; i < 3; i++)
    for (j = 0; j < 3; j++)
        beta[i][j] = 0;
```

    b.
```
for (i = 0; i < 3; i++)
    for (j = 0; j < 3; j++)
        beta[i][j] = i + j;
```

    c.
```
for (i = 0; i < 3; i++)
    for (j = 0; j < 3; j++)
        beta[i][j] = i * j;
```

    d.
```
for (i = 0; i < 3; i++)
    for (j = 0; j < 3; j++)
        beta[i][j] =  2 * (i + j) % 4;
```

42.   Suppose that you have the following declarations:

```
int times[30][7];
int speed[15][7];
int trees[100][7];
int students[50][7];
```

    a.   Write the definition of the function `print` that can be used to output the contents of these arrays.

    b.   Write the C++ statements that calls the function `print` to output the contents of the arrays `times`, `speed`, `trees`, and `students`.

PROGRAMMING EXERCISES

1.   Write a C++ program that declares an array `alpha` of 50 components of type `double`. Initialize the array so that the first 25 components are equal to the square of the index variable, and the last 25 components are equal to three times the index variable. Output the array so that 10 elements per line are printed.

2.   Write a C++ function, `smallestIndex`, that takes as parameters an `int` array and its size and returns the index of the first occurrence of the smallest element in the array. Also, write a program to test your function.

3.   Write a C++ function, `lastLargestIndex`, that takes as parameters an `int` array and its size and returns the index of the last occurrence of the largest element in the array. Also, write a program to test your function.

4. Write a program that reads a file consisting of students' test scores in the range 0–200. It should then determine the number of students having scores in each of the following ranges: 0–24, 25–49, 50–74, 75–99, 100–124, 125–149, 150–174, and 175–200. Output the score ranges and the number of students. (Run your program with the following input data: 76, 89, 150, 135, 200, 76, 12, 100, 150, 28, 178, 189, 167, 200, 175, 150, 87, 99, 129, 149, 176, 200, 87, 35, 157, 189.)

5. Write a program that prompts the user to input a string and outputs the string in uppercase letters. (Use a character array to store the string.)

6. The history teacher at your school needs help in grading a True/False test. The students' IDs and test answers are stored in a file. The first entry in the file contains answers to the test in the form:

TFFTFFTTTTFFTFTFTFTT

Every other entry in the file is the student ID, followed by a blank, followed by the student's responses. For example, the entry:

ABC54301 TFTFTFTT TFTFTFFTTFT

indicates that the student ID is ABC54301 and the answer to question 1 is True, the answer to question 2 is False, and so on. This student did not answer question 9. The exam has 20 questions, and the class has more than 150 students. Each correct answer is awarded two points, each wrong answer gets one point deducted, and no answer gets zero points. Write a program that processes the test data. The output should be the student's ID, followed by the answers, followed by the test score, followed by the test grade. Assume the following grade scale: 90%–100%, A; 80%–89.99%, B; 70%–79.99%, C; 60%–69.99%, D; and 0%–59.99%, F.

7. Write a program that allows the user to enter the last names of five candidates in a local election and the number of votes received by each candidate. The program should then output each candidate's name, the number of votes received, and the percentage of the total votes received by the candidate. Your program should also output the winner of the election. A sample output is:

Candidate	Votes Received	% of Total Votes
Johnson	5000	25.91
Miller	4000	20.73
Duffy	6000	31.09
Robinson	2500	12.95
Ashtony	1800	9.33
Total	19300	

The Winner of the Election is Duffy.

8. Consider the following function `main`:

```cpp
int main()
{
    int inStock[10][4];
    int alpha[20];
    int beta[20];
    int gamma[4] = {11, 13, 15, 17};
    int delta[10] = {3, 5, 2, 6, 10, 9, 7, 11, 1, 8};

        .
        .
        .
}
```

a. Write the definition of the function `setZero` that initializes any one-dimensional array of type `int` to 0.

b. Write the definition of the function `inputArray` that prompts the user to input 20 numbers and stores the numbers into `alpha`.

c. Write the definition of the function `doubleArray` that initializes the elements of `beta` to two times the corresponding elements in `alpha`. Make sure that you prevent the function from modifying the elements of `alpha`.

d. Write the definition of the function `copyGamma` that sets the elements of the first row of `inStock` to `gamma` and the remaining rows of `inStock` to three times the previous row of `inStock`. Make sure that you prevent the function from modifying the elements of `gamma`.

e. Write the definition of the function `copyAlphaBeta` that stores `alpha` into the first five rows of `inStock` and `beta` into the last five rows of `inStock`. Make sure that you prevent the function from modifying the elements of `alpha` and `beta`.

f. Write the definition of the function `printArray` that prints any one-dimensional array of type `int`. Print 15 elements per line.

g. Write the definition of the function `setInStock` that prompts the user to input the elements for the first column of `inStock`. The function should then set the elements in the remaining columns to two times the corresponding element in the previous column, minus the corresponding element in `delta`.

h. Write C++ statements that call each of the functions in parts a through g.

i. Write a C++ program that tests the function `main` and the functions discussed in parts a through g. (Add additional functions, such as printing a two-dimensional array, as needed.)

9. Write a program that uses a two-dimensional array to store the highest and lowest temperatures for each month of the year. The program should output the average high, average low, and the highest and lowest temperatures for the year. Your program must consist of the following functions:

a. Function `getData`: This function reads and stores data in the two-dimensional array.

b. Function `averageHigh`: This function calculates and returns the average high temperature for the year.

c. Function `averageLow`: This function calculates and returns the average low temperature for the year.

d. Function `indexHighTemp`: This function returns the index of the highest high temperature in the array.

e. Function `indexLowTemp`: This function returns the index of the lowest low temperature in the array.

(These functions must all have the appropriate parameters.)

10. Programming Exercise 10 in Chapter 6 asks you find the mean and standard deviation of five numbers. Extend this programming exercise to find the mean and standard deviation of up to 100 numbers. Suppose that the mean (average) of n numbers $x_1, x_2, \ldots, x_n$ is x. Then, the standard deviation of these numbers is:

$$s = \sqrt{\frac{(x_1 - x)^2 + (x_2 - x)^2 + \cdots + (x_i - x)^2 + \cdots + (x_n - x)^2}{n}}$$

11. (**Adding Large Integers**) In C++, the largest `int` value is `2147483647`. So, an integer larger than this cannot be stored and processed as an integer. Similarly, if the sum or product of two positive integers is greater than `2147483647`, the result will be incorrect. One way to store and manipulate large integers is to store each individual digit of the number in an array. Write a program that inputs two positive integers of, at most, 20 digits and outputs the sum of the numbers. If the sum of the numbers has more than 20 digits, output the sum with an appropriate message. Your program must, at least, contain a function to read and store a number into an array and another function to output the sum of the numbers. (*Hint*: Read numbers as strings and store the digits of the number in the reverse order.)

12. Jason, Samantha, Ravi, Sheila, and Ankit are preparing for an upcoming marathon. Each day of the week, they run a certain number of miles and write them into a notebook. At the end of the week, they would like to know the number of miles run each day, the total miles for the week, and average miles run each day. Write a program to help them analyze their data. Your program must contain parallel arrays: an array to store the names of the runners and a two-dimensional array of five rows and seven columns to store the number of miles run by each runner each day. Furthermore, your program must contain at least the following functions: a function to read and store the runners' names and the numbers of miles run each day; a function to find the total miles run by each runner and the average number

of miles run each day; and a function to output the results. (You may assume that the input data is stored in a file and each line of data is in the following form: `runnerName milesDay1 milesDay2 milesDay3 milesDay4 milesDay5 milesDay6 milesDay7`.)

13. Write a program to calculate students' average test scores and their grades. You may assume the following input data:

```
Johnson 85 83 77 91 76
Aniston 80 90 95 93 48
Cooper 78 81 11 90 73
Gupta 92 83 30 69 87
Blair 23 45 96 38 59
Clark 60 85 45 39 67
Kennedy 77 31 52 74 83
Bronson 93 94 89 77 97
Sunny 79 85 28 93 82
Smith 85 72 49 75 63
```

Use three arrays: a one-dimensional array to store the students' names, a (parallel) two-dimensional array to store the test scores, and a parallel one-dimensional array to store grades. Your program must contain at least the following functions: a function to read and store data into two arrays, a function to calculate the average test score and grade, and a function to output the results. Have your program also output the class average.

14. A company hired 10 temporary workers who are paid hourly and you are given a data file that contains the last name of the employees, the number of hours each employee worked in a week, and the hourly pay rate of each employee. You are asked to write a program that computes each employee's weekly pay and the average salary of all the workers. The program then outputs the weekly pay of each employee, the average weekly pay, and the names of all the employees whose pay is greater than or equal to the average pay. If the number of hours worked in a week is more than 40 hours, then the pay rate for the hours over 40 is 1.5 times the regular hourly rate. Use two parallel arrays: a one-dimensional array to store the names of all the employees, and a two-dimensional array of 10 rows and 3 columns to store the number of hours an employee worked in a week, the hourly pay rate, and the weekly pay. Your program must contain at least the following functions—a function to read the data from the file into the arrays, a function to determine the weekly pay, a function to output the names of all the employees whose pay is greater than or equal to the average weekly pay, and a function to output each employee's data.

15. Children often play a memory game in which a deck of cards containing matching pairs is used. The cards are shuffled and placed face down on a table. The players then take turns and select two cards at a time. If both cards match, they are left face up; otherwise, the cards are placed face down at the same positions. Once the players see the selected pair of cards and if

the cards do not match, then they can memorize the cards and use their memory to select the next pair of cards. The game continues until all the cards are face up. Write a program to play the memory game. Use a two-dimensional array of 4 rows and 4 columns to use a deck of 16 cards with 8 matching pairs and you can use numbers 1 to 8 to mark the cards. (If you use a 6 by 6 array, then you will need 18 matching pairs, and so on.) Use random number generators to randomly store the pairs in the array. Use appropriate functions in your program, and the main program should be merely a call to functions.

16. **(Airplane Seating Assignment)** Write a program that can be used to assign seats for a commercial airplane. The airplane has 13 rows, with six seats in each row. Rows 1 and 2 are first class, rows 3 through 7 are business class, and rows 8 through 13 are economy class. Your program must prompt the user to enter the following information:

a. Ticket type (first class, business class, or economy class)

b. Desired seat

Output the seating plan in the following form:

	A	B	C	D	E	F
Row 1	*	*	X	*	X	X
Row 2	*	X	*	X	*	X
Row 3	*	*	X	X	*	X
Row 4	X	*	X	*	X	X
Row 5	*	X	*	X	*	*
Row 6	*	X	*	*	*	X
Row 7	X	*	*	*	X	X
Row 8	*	X	*	X	X	*
Row 9	X	*	X	X	*	X
Row 10	*	X	*	X	X	X
Row 11	*	*	X	*	X	*
Row 12	*	*	X	X	*	X
Row 13	*	*	*	*	X	*

Here, * indicates that the seat is available; X indicates that the seat is occupied. Make this a menu-driven program; show the user's choices and allow the user to make the appropriate choices.

RECORDS (structs)

IN THIS CHAPTER, YOU WILL:

· Learn about records (structs)

· Examine various operations on a struct

· Explore ways to manipulate data using a struct

· Learn about the relationship between a struct and functions

· Discover how arrays are used in a struct

· Learn how to create an array of struct items

In Chapter 8, you learned how to group values of the same type by using arrays. You also learned how to process data stored in an array and how to perform list operations, such as searching and sorting.

 NOTE This chapter may be skipped without experiencing any discontinuation.

In this chapter, you will learn how to group related values that are of different types. C++ provides another structured data type, called a struct (some languages use the term "record"), to group related items of different types. An array is a homogeneous data structure; a struct is typically a heterogeneous data structure. The treatment of a struct in this chapter is similar to the treatment of a struct in C. A struct in this chapter, therefore, is a C-like struct. Chapter 10 introduces and discusses another structured data type, called a class.

Records (structs)

Suppose that you want to write a program to process student data. A student record consists of, among other things, the student's name, student ID, GPA, courses taken, and course grades. Thus, various components are associated with a student. However, these components are all of different types. For example, the student's name is a string, and the GPA is a floating-point number. Because these components are of different types, you cannot use an array to group all of the items associated with a student. C++ provides a structured data type called struct to group items of different types. Grouping components that are related but of different types offers several advantages. For example, a single variable can pass all the components as parameters to a function.

struct: A collection of a fixed number of components in which the components are accessed by name. The components may be of different types.

The components of a struct are called the members of the struct. The general syntax of a struct in C++ is:

```
struct structName
{
    dataType1 identifier1;
    dataType2 identifier2;
        .
        .
        .
    dataTypen identifiern;
};
```

In C++, struct is a reserved word. The members of a struct, even though they are enclosed in braces (that is, they form a block), are not considered to form a compound statement. Thus, a semicolon (after the right brace) is essential to end the `struct` statement. A semicolon at the end of the `struct` definition is, therefore, a part of the syntax.

The statement:

```
struct houseType
{
    string style;
    int numOfBedrooms;
    int numOfBathrooms;
    int numOfCarsGarage;
    int yearBuilt;
    int finishedSquareFootage;
    double price;
    double tax;
};
```

defines a `struct` houseType with 8 members. The member style is of type `string`, the members numOfBedrooms, numOfBathrooms, numOfCarsGarage, yearBuilt, and finishedSquareFootage are of type `int`, and the members `price` and `tax` are of type `double`.

Like any type definition, a `struct` is a definition, not a declaration. That is, it defines only a data type; no memory is allocated.

Once a data type is defined, you can declare variables of that type.

For example, the following statement defines `newHouse` to be a `struct` variable of type houseType:

```
    //variable declaration
houseType newHouse;
```

The memory allocated is large enough to store style, numOfBedrooms, numOfBathrooms, numOfCarsGarage, yearBuilt, finishedSquareFootage, price, and tax (see Figure 9-1).

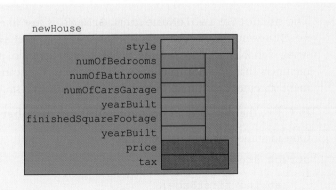

FIGURE 9-1 `struct` newHouse

NOTE You can also declare `struct` variables when you define the `struct`. For example, consider the following statements:

```
struct houseType
{
    string style;
    int numOfBedrooms;
    int numOfBathrooms;
    int numOfCarsGarage;
    int yearBuilt;
    int finishedSquareFootage;
    double price;
    double tax;
} tempHouse;
```

These statements define the `struct` houseType and also declare `tempHouse` to be a variable of type houseType.

Typically, in a program, a `struct` is defined before the definitions of all the functions in the program, so that the `struct` can be used throughout the program. Therefore, if you define a `struct` and also simultaneously declare a `struct` variable (as in the preceding statements), then that `struct` variable becomes a global variable and thus can be accessed anywhere in the program. Keeping in mind the side effects of global variables, you should first only define a `struct` and then declare the `struct` variables.

Accessing `struct` Members

In arrays, you access a component by using the array name together with the relative position (index) of the component. The array name and index are separated using square brackets. To access a structure member (component), you use the `struct` variable name together with the member name; these names are separated by a dot (period). The syntax for accessing a `struct` member is:

```
structVariableName.memberName
```

The `structVariableName.memberName` is just like any other variable. For example, `newStudent.courseGrade` is a variable of type `char`, `newStudent.firstName` is a string variable, and so on. As a result, you can do just about anything with `struct` members that you normally do with variables. You can, for example, use them in assignment statements or input/output (where permitted) statements.

In C++, the dot (.) is an operator called the **member access operator**.

Consider the following statements:

```
struct studentType
{
    string firstName;
    string lastName;
    char courseGrade;
```

```
    int testScore;
    int programmingScore;
    double GPA;
};

    //variables
studentType newStudent;
studentType student;
```

Suppose you want to initialize the member GPA of newStudent to 0.0. The following statement accomplishes this task:

```
newStudent.GPA = 0.0;
```

Similarly, the statements:

```
newStudent.firstName = "John";
newStudent.lastName = "Brown";
```

store "John" in the member firstName and "Brown" in the member lastName of newStudent.

After the preceding three assignment statements execute, newStudent is as shown in Figure 9-2.

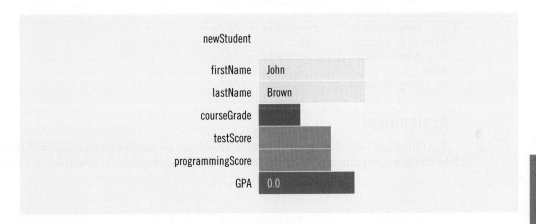

FIGURE 9-2 **struct** newStudent

The statement:

```
cin >> newStudent.firstName;
```

reads the next string from the standard input device and stores it in:

```
newStudent.firstName
```

The statement:

```
cin >> newStudent.testScore >> newStudent.programmingScore;
```

reads two integer values from the keyboard and stores them in `newStudent.testScore` and `newStudent.programmingScore`, respectively.

Suppose that `score` is a variable of type `int`. The statement:

```
score = (newStudent.testScore + newStudent.programmingScore) / 2;
```

assigns the average of `newStudent.testScore` and `newStudent.programmingScore` to `score`.

The following statement determines the course grade and stores it in `newStudent.courseGrade`:

```
if (score >= 90)
    newStudent.courseGrade = 'A';
else if (score >= 80)
    newStudent.courseGrade = 'B';
else if (score >= 70)
    newStudent.courseGrade = 'C';
else if (score >= 60)
    newStudent.courseGrade = 'D';
else
    newStudent.courseGrade = 'F';
```

Assignment

We can assign the value of one **struct** variable to another **struct** variable of the same type by using an assignment statement. Suppose that `newStudent` is as shown in Figure 9-3.

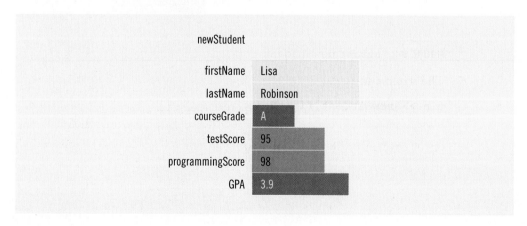

FIGURE 9-3 **struct** newStudent

The statement:

```
student = newStudent;
```

copies the contents of `newStudent` into `student`. After this assignment statement executes, the values of `student` are as shown in Figure 9-4.

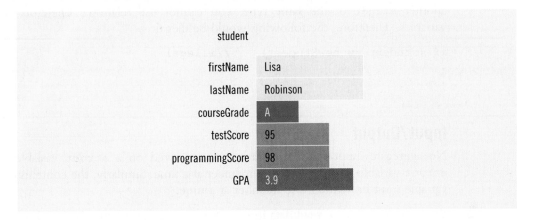

FIGURE 9-4 `student` after `student = newStudent`

In fact, the assignment statement:

```
student = newStudent;
```

is equivalent to the following statements:

```
student.firstName = newStudent.firstName;
student.lastName = newStudent.lastName;
student.courseGrade = newStudent.courseGrade;
student.testScore = newStudent.testScore;
student.programmingScore = newStudent.programmingScore;
student.GPA = newStudent.GPA;
```

Comparison (Relational Operators)

To compare `struct` variables, you compare them member-wise. As with an array, no aggregate relational operations are performed on a `struct`. For example, suppose that `newStudent` and `student` are declared as shown earlier. Furthermore, suppose that you want to see whether `student` and `newStudent` refer to the same student. Now `newStudent` and `student` refer to the same student if they have the same first name and the same last name. To compare the values of `student` and `newStudent`, you must compare them member-wise, as follows:

```
if (student.firstName == newStudent.firstName &&
    student.lastName == newStudent.lastName)
    .
    .
    .
```

Although you can use an assignment statement to copy the contents of one `struct` into another `struct` of the same type, you cannot use relational operators on `struct` variables. Therefore, the following would be illegal:

```
if (student == newStudent)     //illegal
    .
    .
    .
```

Input/Output

No aggregate input/output operations are allowed on a `struct` variable. Data in a `struct` variable must be read one member at a time. Similarly, the contents of a `struct` variable must be written one member at a time.

We have seen how to read data into a `struct` variable. Let us now see how to output a `struct` variable. The statement:

```
cout << newStudent.firstName << " " << newStudent.lastName
     << " " << newStudent.courseGrade
     << " " << newStudent.testScore
     << " " << newStudent.programmingScore
     << " " << newStudent.GPA << endl;
```

outputs the contents of the `struct` variable `newStudent`.

struct Variables and Functions

Recall that arrays are passed by reference only, and a function cannot return a value of type `array`. However:

- A `struct` variable can be passed as a parameter either by value or by reference, and
- A function can return a value of type `struct`.

The following function reads and stores a student's first name, last name, test score, programming score, and GPA. It also determines the student's course grade and stores it in the member `courseGrade`.

```
void readIn(studentType& student)
{
    int score;

    cin >> student.firstName >> student.lastName;
    cin >> student.testScore >> student.programmingScore;
    cin >> student.GPA;

    score = (newStudent.testScore + newStudent.programmingScore) / 2;
```

```
if (score >= 90)
    student.courseGrade = 'A';
else if (score >= 80)
    student.courseGrade = 'B';
else if (score >= 70)
    student.courseGrade = 'C';
else if (score >= 60)
    student.courseGrade = 'D';
else
    student.courseGrade = 'F';
}
```

The statement:

```
readIn(newStudent);
```

calls the function `readIn`. The function `readIn` stores the appropriate information in the variable `newStudent`.

Similarly, we can write a function that will print the contents of a **struct** variable. For example, the following function outputs the contents of a **struct** variable of type studentType on the screen:

```
void printStudent(studentType student)
{
    cout << student.firstName << " " << student.lastName
         << " " << student.courseGrade
         << " " << student.testScore
         << " " << student.programmingScore
         << " " << student.GPA << endl;
}
```

Arrays versus structs

The previous discussion showed us that a **struct** and an array have similarities as well as differences. Table 9-1 summarizes this discussion.

TABLE 9-1 Arrays vs. structs

Aggregate Operation	Array	struct
Arithmetic	No	No
Assignment	No	Yes
Input/output	No (except strings)	No
Comparison	No	No
Parameter passing	By reference only	By value or by reference
Function returning a value	No	Yes

9

Arrays in structs

A list is a set of elements of the same type. Thus, a list has two things associated with it: the values (that is, elements) and the length. Because the values and the length are both related to a list, we can define a struct containing both items.

```
const int ARRAY_SIZE = 1000;

struct listType
{
    int listElem[ARRAY_SIZE];    //array containing the list
    int listLength;              //length of the list
};
```

The following statement declares intList to be a struct variable of type listType (see Figure 9-5):

```
listType intList;
```

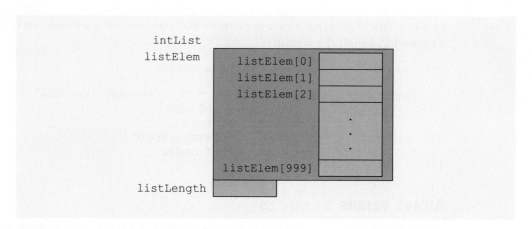

FIGURE 9-5 struct variable intList

The variable intList has two members: listElem, an array of 1000 components of type int, and listLength, of type int. Moreover, intList.listElem accesses the member listElem, and intList.listLength accesses the member listLength.

Consider the following statements:

```
intList.listLength = 0;        //Line 1
intList.listElem[0] = 12;      //Line 2
intList.listLength++;          //Line 3
intList.listElem[1] = 37;      //Line 4
intList.listLength++;          //Line 5
```

The statement in Line 1 sets the value of the member listLength to 0. The statement in Line 2 stores 12 in the first component of the array listElem. The statement in Line 3 increments the value of listLength by 1. The meaning of the other statements is similar. After these statements execute, intList is as shown in Figure 9-6.

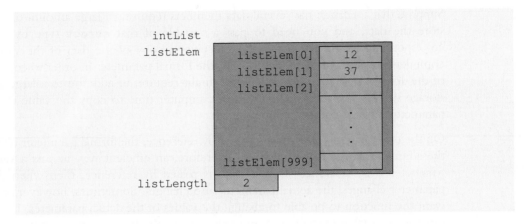

FIGURE 9-6 intList after the statements in Lines 1 through 5 execute

Next, we write the sequential search algorithm to determine whether a given item is in the list. If searchItem is found in the list, then the function returns its location in the list; otherwise, the function returns −1.

```
int seqSearch(const listType& list, int searchItem)
{
    int loc;

    bool found = false;

    for (loc = 0; loc < list.listLength; loc++)
        if (list.listElem[loc] == searchItem)
        {
            found = true;
            break;
        }

    if (found)
        return loc;
    else
        return -1;
}
```

In this function, because listLength is a member of list, we access this by list.listLength. Similarly, we can access an element of list via list.listElem[loc].

Notice that the formal parameter list of the function seqSearch is declared as a constant reference parameter. This means that list receives the address of the corresponding actual parameter, but list cannot modify the actual parameter.

Recall that when a variable is passed by value, the formal parameter copies the value of the actual parameter. Therefore, if the formal parameter modifies the data, the modification has no effect on the data of the actual parameter.

9

Suppose that a **struct** has several data members requiring a large amount of memory to store the data, and you need to pass a variable of that **struct** type by value. The corresponding formal parameter then receives a copy of the data of the variable. The compiler must then allocate memory for the formal parameter in order to copy the value of the actual parameter. This operation might require, in addition to a large amount of storage space, a considerable amount of computer time to copy the value of the actual parameter into the formal parameter.

On the other hand, if a variable is passed by reference, the formal parameter receives only the address of the actual parameter. Therefore, an efficient way to pass a variable as a parameter is by reference. If a variable is passed by reference, then when the formal parameter changes, the actual parameter also changes. Sometimes, however, you do not want the function to be able to change the values of the actual parameter. In C++, you can pass a variable by reference and still prevent the function from changing its value. This is done by using the keyword **const** in the formal parameter declaration, as shown in the definition of the function seqSearch.

Likewise, we can also rewrite the sorting, binary search, and other list-processing functions.

structs in Arrays

Suppose a company has 50 full-time employees. We need to print their monthly paychecks and keep track of how much money has been paid to each employee in the year-to-date. First, let's define an employee's record:

```
struct employeeType
{
    string firstName;
    string lastName;
    int    personID;
    string deptID;
    double yearlySalary;
    double monthlySalary;
    double yearToDatePaid;
    double monthlyBonus;
};
```

Each employee has the following members (components): first name, last name, personal ID, department ID, yearly salary, monthly salary, year-to-date paid, and monthly bonus.

Because we have 50 employees and the data type of each employee is the same, we can use an array of 50 components to process the employees' data.

```
employeeType employees[50];
```

This statement declares the array employees of 50 components of type employeeType (see Figure 9-7). Every element of employees is a **struct**. For example, Figure 9-7 also shows employees[2].

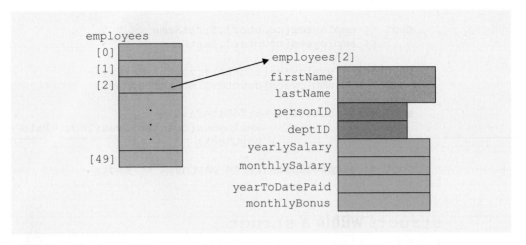

FIGURE 9-7 Array of employees

Suppose we also have the following declaration:

```
int   counter;
```

Further, suppose that every employee's initial data—first name, last name, personal ID, department ID, and yearly salary—are provided in a file. For our discussion, we assume that each employee's data is stored in a file, say, `employee.dat`. The following C++ code loads the data into the employees' array. We assume that, initially, `yearToDatePaid` is 0 and that the monthly bonus is determined each month based on performance.

```
ifstream infile; //input stream variable
                 //assume that the file employee.dat has been opened
for (counter = 0; counter < 50; counter++)
{
    infile >> employees[counter].firstName
           >> employees[counter].lastName
           >> employees[counter].personID
           >> employees[counter].deptID
           >> employees[counter].yearlySalary;
    employees[counter].monthlySalary =
                employees[counter].yearlySalary / 12;
    employees[counter].yearToDatePaid = 0.0;
    employees[counter].monthlyBonus = 0.0;
}
```

Suppose that for a given month, the monthly bonuses are already stored in each employee's record, and we need to calculate the monthly paycheck and update the `yearToDatePaid` amount. The following loop computes and prints the employee's paycheck for the month:

```
double payCheck; //variable to calculate the paycheck

for (counter = 0; counter < 50; counter++)
```

9

```
{
    cout << employees[counter].firstName << " "
         << employees[counter].lastName << " ";

    payCheck = employees[counter].monthlySalary +
               employees[counter].monthlyBonus;

    employees[counter].yearToDatePaid =
                        employees[counter].yearToDatePaid +
                        payCheck;

    cout << setprecision(2) << payCheck << endl;
}
```

structs within a struct

You have seen how the struct and array data structures can be combined to organize information. You also saw examples wherein a member of a struct is an array, and the array type is a struct. In this section, you will learn about situations for which it is beneficial to organize data in a struct by using another struct.

Let us consider the following employee record:

```
struct  employeeType
{
    string firstname;
    string middlename;
    string lastname;
    string empID;
    string address1;
    string address2;
    string city;
    string state;
    string zip;
    int hiremonth;
    int hireday;
    int hireyear;
    int quitmonth;
    int quitday;
    int quityear;
    string phone;
    string cellphone;
    string fax;
    string pager;
    string email;
    string deptID;
    double salary;
};
```

As you can see, a lot of information is packed into one struct. This struct has 22 members. Some members of this struct will be accessed more frequently than others, and some members are more closely related than others. Moreover, some members will have the same underlying structure. For example, the hire date and the quit date are of the date type int. Let us reorganize this struct as follows:

```
struct nameType
{
    string first;
    string middle;
    string last;
};

struct addressType
{
    string address1;
    string address2;
    string city;
    string state;
    string zip;
};

struct dateType
{
    int month;
    int day;
    int year;
};

struct contactType
{
    string phone;
    string cellphone;
    string fax;
    string pager;
    string email;
};
```

We have separated the employee's name, address, and contact type into subcategories. Furthermore, we have defined a struct dateType. Let us rebuild the employee's record as follows:

```
struct employeeType
{
    nameType name;
    string empID;
    addressType address;
    dateType hireDate;
    dateType quitDate;
    contactType contact;
    string deptID;
    double salary;
};
```

The information in this employee's struct is easier to manage than the previous one. Some of this struct can be reused to build another struct. For example, suppose that you want to define a customer's record. Every customer has a first name, last name, and middle name, as well as an address and a way to be contacted. You can, therefore, quickly put together a customer's record by using the structs nameType, addressType, contactType, and the members specific to the customer.

Next, let us declare a variable of type employeeType and discuss how to access its members.

Consider the following statement:

```
employeeType newEmployee;
```

This statement declares newEmployee to be a struct variable of type employeeType (see Figure 9-8).

FIGURE 9-8 struct variable newEmployee

The statement:

```
newEmployee.salary = 45678.00;
```

sets the salary of newEmployee to 45678.00. The statements:

```
newEmployee.name.first = "Mary";
newEmployee.name.middle = "Beth";
newEmployee.name.last = "Simmons";
```

set the first, middle, and last name of newEmployee to "Mary", "Beth", and "Simmons", respectively. Note that newEmployee has a member called name. We access this member via newEmployee.name. Note also that newEmployee.name is a struct and has three members. We apply the member access criteria to access the member first of the struct newEmployee.name. So, newEmployee.name.first is the member where we store the first name.

The statement:

```
cin >> newEmployee.name.first;
```

reads and stores a string into newEmployee.name.first. The statement:

```
newEmployee.salary = newEmployee.salary * 1.05;
```

updates the salary of newEmployee.

The following statement declares employees to be an array of 100 components, wherein each component is of type employeeType:

```
employeeType employees[100];
```

The for loop:

```
for (int j = 0; j < 100; j++)
    cin >> employees[j].name.first >> employees[j].name.middle
        >> employees[j].name.last;
```

reads and stores the names of 100 employees in the array employees. Because employees is an array, to access a component, we use the index. For example, employees[50] is the 51st component of the array employees (recall that an array index starts with 0). Because employees[50] is a struct, we apply the member access criteria to select a particular member.

9

PROGRAMMING EXAMPLE: Sales Data Analysis

A company has six salespeople. Every month, they go on road trips to sell the company's product. At the end of each month, the total sales for each salesperson, together with that salesperson's ID and the month, is recorded in a file. At the end of each year, the manager of the company wants to see this report in this following tabular format:

```
----------- Annual Sales Report -----------

   ID        QT1          QT2          QT3          QT4          Total

  12345     1892.00         0.00       494.00       322.00       2708.00
  32214      343.00       892.00      9023.00         0.00      10258.00
  23422     1395.00      1901.00         0.00         0.00       3296.00
  57373      893.00       892.00      8834.00         0.00      10619.00
  35864     2882.00      1221.00         0.00      1223.00       5326.00
  54654      893.00         0.00       392.00      3420.00       4705.00
  Total     8298.00      4906.00     18743.00      4965.00

Max Sale by SalesPerson: ID = 57373, Amount = $10619.00
Max Sale by Quarter: Quarter = 3, Amount = $18743.00
```

In this report, QT1 stands for quarter 1 (months 1 to 3), QT2 for quarter 2 (months 4 to 6), QT3 for quarter 3 (months 7 to 9), and QT4 for quarter 4 (months 10 to 12).

The salespeople's IDs are stored in one file; the sales data is stored in another file. The sales data is in the following form:

```
salesPersonID   month   saleAmount
.
.
.
```

Furthermore, the sales data is in no particular order; it is not ordered by ID.

A sample sales data is:

```
12345 1 893
32214 1 343
23422 3 903
57373 2 893
.
.
.
```

Let us write a program that produces the output in the specified format.

Input   One file containing each salesperson's ID and a second file containing the sales data.

Output   A file containing the annual sales report in the above format.

Based on the problem's requirements, it is clear that the main components for each salesperson are the salesperson's ID, quarterly sales amount, and total annual sales amount. Because the components are of different types, we can group them with the help of a `struct`, defined as follows:

```
struct salesPersonRec
{
    string ID;        //salesperson's ID
    double saleByQuarter[4];     //array to store the total
                                 //sales for each quarter
    double totalSale;    //salesperson's yearly sales amount
};
```

Because there are six salespeople, we use an array of six components, wherein each component is of type `salesPersonRec`, defined as follows:

```
salesPersonRec salesPersonList[NO_OF_SALES_PERSON];
```

wherein the value of `NO_OF_SALES_PERSON` is 6.

Because the program requires us to find the company's total sales for each quarter, we need an array of four components to store the data. Note that this data will be used to determine the quarter in which the maximum sales were made. Therefore, the program also needs the following array:

```
double totalSaleByQuarter[4];
```

Recall that in C++, the array index starts with 0. Therefore, `totalSaleByQuarter[0]` stores data for quarter 1, `totalSaleByQuarter[1]` stores data for quarter 2, and so on.

We will refer to these variables throughout the discussion.

The array `salesPersonList` is as shown in Figure 9-9.

9

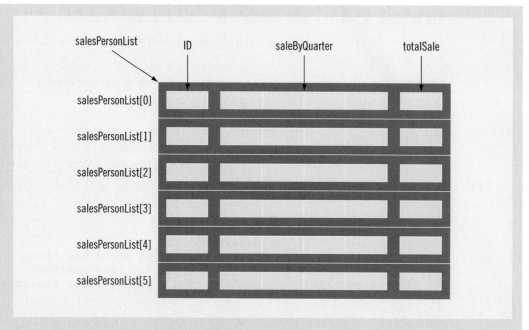

FIGURE 9-9 Array salesPersonList

The first step of the program is to read the salespeople's IDs into the array salesPersonList and initialize the quarterly sales and total sales for each salesperson to 0. After this step, the array salesPersonList is as shown in Figure 9-10.

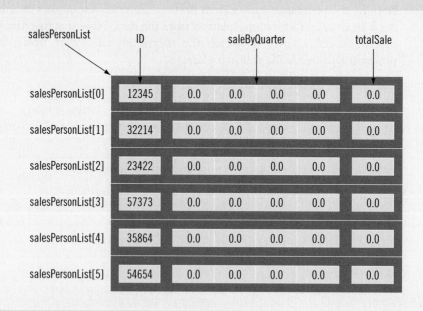

FIGURE 9-10 Array salesPersonList after initialization

The next step is to process the sales data. Processing the sales data is quite straightforward. For each entry in the file containing the sales data:

1. Read the salesperson's ID, month, and sale amount for the month.
2. Search the array salesPersonList to locate the component corresponding to this salesperson.
3. Determine the quarter corresponding to the month.
4. Update the sales for the quarter by adding the sale amount for the month.

Once the sales data file is processed:

1. Calculate the total sales by salesperson.
2. Calculate the total sales by quarter.
3. Print the report.

This discussion translates into the following algorithm:

1. Initialize the array salesPersonList.
2. Process the sales data.
3. Calculate the total sales by quarter.
4. Calculate the total sales by salesperson.
5. Print the report.
6. Calculate and print the maximum sales by salesperson.
7. Calculate and print the maximum sales by quarter.

To reduce the complexity of the main program, let us write a separate function for each of these seven steps.

Function initialize This function reads the salesperson's ID from the input file and stores the salesperson's ID in the array salesPersonList. It also initializes the quarterly sales amount and the total sales amount for each salesperson to 0. The definition of this function is:

```
void initialize(ifstream& indata, salesPersonRec list[],
                int listSize)
{
    int index;
    int quarter;

    for (index = 0; index < listSize; index++)
    {
        indata >> list[index].ID; //get salesperson's ID

        for (quarter = 0; quarter < 4; quarter++)
            list[index].saleByQuarter[quarter] = 0.0;

        list[index].totalSale = 0.0;
    }
} //end initialize
```

9

Function This function reads the sales data from the input file and stores the appropriate
getData information in the array `salesPersonList`. The algorithm for this function is:

1. Read the salesperson's ID, month, and sales amount for the month.
2. Search the array `salesPersonList` to locate the component corresponding to the salesperson. (Because the salespeople's IDs are not sorted, we will use a sequential search to search the array.)
3. Determine the quarter corresponding to the month.
4. Update the sales for the quarter by adding the sales amount for the month.

Suppose that the entry read is:

57373 2 350

Here, the salesperson's ID is 57373, the month is 2, and the sale amount is 350.
Suppose that the array `salesPersonList` is as shown in Figure 9-11.

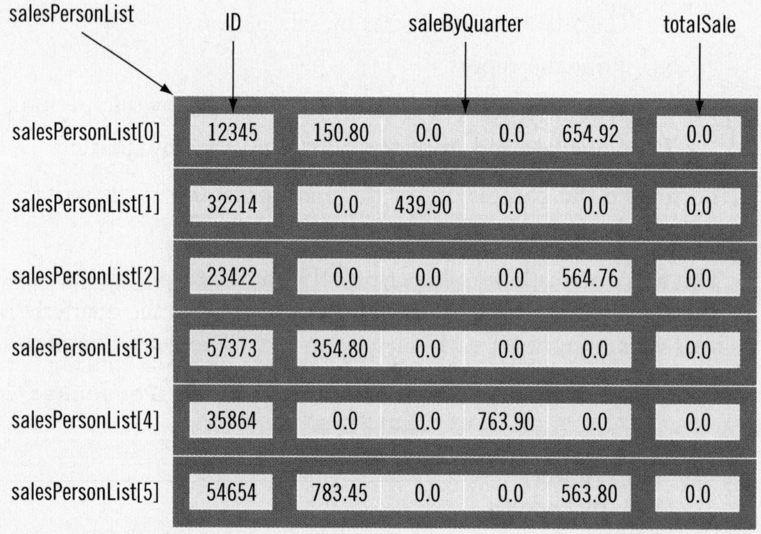

salesPersonList	ID	saleByQuarter				totalSale
salesPersonList[0]	12345	150.80	0.0	0.0	654.92	0.0
salesPersonList[1]	32214	0.0	439.90	0.0	0.0	0.0
salesPersonList[2]	23422	0.0	0.0	0.0	564.76	0.0
salesPersonList[3]	57373	354.80	0.0	0.0	0.0	0.0
salesPersonList[4]	35864	0.0	0.0	763.90	0.0	0.0
salesPersonList[5]	54654	783.45	0.0	0.0	563.80	0.0

FIGURE 9-11 Array `salesPersonList`

Now, ID 57373 corresponds to the array component `salesPersonList[3]`, and
month 2 corresponds to quarter 1. Therefore, you add 350 to 354.80 to get the
new amount, 704.80. After processing this entry, the array `salesPersonList` is
as shown in Figure 9-12.

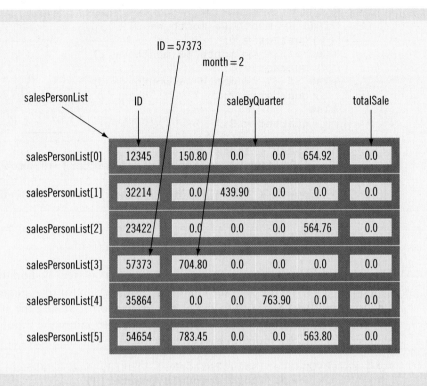

FIGURE 9-12 Array `salesPersonList` after processing entry `57373 2 350`

The definition of the function `getData` is:

```
void getData(ifstream& infile, salesPersonRec list[],
             int listSize)
{
    int index;
    int quarter;
    string sID;
    int month;
    double amount;

    infile >> sID;        //get salesperson's ID

    while (infile)
    {
        infile >> month >> amount;  //get the sale month and
                                    //the sale amount

        for (index = 0; index < listSize; index++)
            if (sID == list[index].ID)
                break;
```

```
        if (1 <= month && month <= 3)
            quarter = 0;
        else if (4 <= month && month <= 6)
            quarter = 1;
        else if (7 <= month && month <= 9)
            quarter = 2;
        else
            quarter = 3;

        if (index < listSize)
            list[index].saleByQuarter[quarter] += amount;
        else
            cout << "Invalid salesperson's ID." << endl;

        infile >> sID;
    } //end while
} //end getData
```

Function saleByQuarter This function finds the company's total sales for each quarter. To find the total sales for each quarter, we add the sales amount of each salesperson for that quarter. Clearly, this function must have access to the array `salesPersonList` and the array `totalSaleByQuarter`. This function also needs to know the number of rows in each array. Thus, this function has three parameters. The definition of this function is:

```
void saleByQuarter(salesPersonRec list[], int listSize,
                    double totalByQuarter[])
{
    int quarter;
    int index;

    for (quarter = 0; quarter < 4; quarter++)
        totalByQuarter[quarter] = 0.0;

    for (quarter = 0; quarter < 4; quarter++)
        for (index = 0; index < listSize; index++)
            totalByQuarter[quarter] +=
                        list[index].saleByQuarter[quarter];
} //end saleByQuarter
```

Function totalSaleBy Person This function finds each salesperson's yearly sales amount. To find an employee's yearly sales amount, we add that employee's sales amount for the four quarters. Clearly, this function must have access to the array `salesPersonList`. This function also needs to know the size of the array. Thus, this function has two parameters.

The definition of this function is:

```
void totalSaleByPerson(salesPersonRec list[], int listSize)
{
    int index;
    int quarter;
```

```
        for (index = 0; index < listSize; index++)
            for (quarter = 0; quarter < 4; quarter++)
                list[index].totalSale +=
                            list[index].saleByQuarter[quarter];
    } //end totalSaleByPerson
```

Function printReport This function prints the annual report in the specified format. The algorithm in pseudocode is:

1. Print the heading—that is, the first three lines of output.

2. Print the data for each salesperson.

3. Print the last line of the table.

Note that the next two functions will produce the final two lines of output.

Clearly, the printReport function must have access to the array salesPersonList and the array totalSaleByQuarter. Also, because the output will be stored in a file, this function must have access to the ofstream variable associated with the output file. Thus, this function has four parameters: a parameter corresponding to the array salesPersonList, a parameter corresponding to the array totalSaleByQuarter, a parameter specifying the size of the array, and a parameter corresponding to the ofstream variable. The definition of this function is:

```
void printReport(ofstream& outfile, salesPersonRec list[],
                  int listSize, double saleByQuarter[])
{
    int index;
    int quarter;

    outfile << "----------- Annual Sales Report ---------"
            << "----" << endl;
    outfile << endl;
    outfile << "  ID          QT1          QT2         QT3          "
            << "QT4         Total" << endl;
    outfile << "_____"
            << "_____" << endl;

    for (index = 0; index < listSize; index++)
    {
        outfile << list[index].ID << "    ";

        for (quarter = 0; quarter < 4; quarter++)
            outfile << setw(10)
                    << list[index].saleByQuarter[quarter];

        outfile << setw(10) << list[index].totalSale << endl;
    }

    outfile << "Total    ";
```

```
        for (quarter = 0; quarter < 4; quarter++)
            outfile << setw(10)<< saleByQuarter[quarter];

        outfile << endl << endl;
} //end printReport
```

Function maxSaleBy Person This function prints the name of the salesperson who produces the maximum sales amount. To identify this salesperson, we look at the sales total for each salesperson and find the largest sales amount. Because each employee's sales total is maintained in the array `salesPersonList`, this function must have access to the array `salesPersonList`. Also, because the output will be stored in a file, this function must have access to the `ofstream` variable associated with the output file. Therefore, this function has three parameters: a parameter corresponding to the array `salesPersonList`, a parameter specifying the size of this array, and a parameter corresponding to the output file.

The algorithm to find the largest sales amount is similar to the algorithm to find the largest element in an array (discussed in Chapter 8). The definition of this function is:

```
void maxSaleByPerson(ofstream& outData, salesPersonRec list[],
                     int listSize)
{
    int maxIndex = 0;
    int index;

    for (index = 1; index <listSize; index++)
        if (list[maxIndex].totalSale <list[index].totalSale)
            maxIndex = index;

    outData << "Max Sale by SalesPerson: ID = "
            << list[maxIndex].ID
            << ", Amount = $" << list[maxIndex].totalSale
            << endl;
} //end maxSaleByPerson
```

Function maxSaleBy Quarter This function prints the quarter in which the maximum sales were made. To identify this quarter, we look at the total sales for each quarter and find the largest sales amount. Because the sales total for each quarter is in the array `totalSaleByQuarter`, this function must have access to the array `totalSaleByQuarter`. Also, because the output will be stored in a file, this function must have access to the `ofstream` variable associated with the output file. Therefore, this function has two parameters: a parameter corresponding to the array `totalSaleByQuarter` and a parameter corresponding to the output file.

The algorithm to find the largest sales amount is the same as the algorithm to find the largest element in an array (discussed in Chapter 8). The definition of this function is:

```
void maxSaleByQuarter(ofstream& outData,
                      double saleByQuarter[])
```

```
{
    int quarter;
    int maxIndex = 0;

    for (quarter = 0; quarter < 4; quarter++)
        if (saleByQuarter[maxIndex] < saleByQuarter[quarter])
            maxIndex = quarter;

    outData << "Max Sale by Quarter: Quarter = "
            << maxIndex + 1
            << ", Amount = $" << saleByQuarter[maxIndex]
            << endl;
} //end maxSaleByQuarter
```

To make the program more flexible, we will prompt the user to specify the input and output files during its execution.

We are now ready to write the algorithm for the function `main`.

Main
Algorithm

1. Declare the variables.
2. Prompt the user to enter the name of the file containing the salesperson's ID data.
3. Read the name of the input file.
4. Open the input file.
5. If the input file does not exist, exit the program.
6. Initialize the array `salesPersonList`. Call the function `initialize`.
7. Close the input file containing the salesperson's ID data and clear the input stream.
8. Prompt the user to enter the name of the file containing the sales data.
9. Read the name of the input file.
10. Open the input file.
11. If the input file does not exist, exit the program.
12. Prompt the user to enter the name of the output file.
13. Read the name of the output file.
14. Open the output file.
15. To output floating-point numbers in a fixed decimal format with the decimal point and trailing zeroes, set the manipulators `fixed` and `showpoint`. Also, to output floating-point numbers to two decimal places, set the precision to two decimal places.

9

16. Process the sales data. Call the function getData.
17. Calculate the total sales by quarter. Call the function saleByQuarter.
18. Calculate the total sales for each salesperson. Call the function totalSaleByPerson.
19. Print the report in a tabular format. Call the function printReport.
20. Find and print the salesperson who produces the maximum sales for the year. Call the function maxSaleByPerson.
21. Find and print the quarter that produces the maximum sales for the year. Call the function maxSaleByQuarter.
22. Close the files.

PROGRAM LISTING

```
//************************************************************
// Author: D.S. Malik
//
// Program: Sales Data Analysis
// This program processes sales data for a company. For each
// salesperson, it outputs the ID, the total sales by each
// quarter, and the total sales for the year. It also outputs
// the salesperson's ID generating the maximum sale for the
// year and the sales amount. The quarter generating the
// maximum sale and the sales amount is also output.
//************************************************************

#include <iostream>
#include <fstream>
#include <iomanip>
#include <string>

using namespace std;

const int NO_OF_SALES_PERSON = 6;

struct salesPersonRec
{
    string ID;          //salesperson's ID
    double saleByQuarter[4];  //array to store the total
                              //sales for each quarter
    double totalSale;   //salesperson's yearly sales amount
};

void initialize(ifstream& indata, salesPersonRec list[],
                int listSize);
```

```
void getData(ifstream& infile, salesPersonRec list[],
             int listSize);
void saleByQuarter(salesPersonRec list[], int listSize,
                   double totalByQuarter[]);
void totalSaleByPerson(salesPersonRec list[], int  listSize);
void printReport(ofstream& outfile, salesPersonRec list[],
                 int listSize, double saleByQuarter[]);
void maxSaleByPerson(ofstream& outData, salesPersonRec list[],
                     int listSize);
void maxSaleByQuarter(ofstream& outData, double saleByQuarter[]);

int main()
{
        //Step 1
    ifstream infile;    //input file stream variable
    ofstream outfile;   //output file stream variable

    string inputFile;   //variable to hold the input file name
    string outputFile;  //variable to hold the output file name

    double totalSaleByQuarter[4];    //array to hold the
                                     //sale by quarter

    salesPersonRec salesPersonList[NO_OF_SALES_PERSON]; //array
                              //to hold the salesperson's data

    cout << "Enter the salesPerson ID file name: "; //Step 2
    cin >> inputFile;                               //Step 3
    cout << endl;

    infile.open(inputFile.c_str());                 //Step 4

    if (!infile)                                    //Step 5
    {
        cout << "Cannot open the input file."
             << endl;
        return 1;
    }

    initialize(infile, salesPersonList,
            NO_OF_SALES_PERSON);                    //Step 6

    infile.close();                                 //Step 7
    infile.clear();                                 //Step 7

    cout << "Enter the sales data file name: ";     //Step 8
    cin >> inputFile;                               //Step 9
    cout << endl;

    infile.open(inputFile.c_str());                 //Step 10
```

9

```
        if (!infile)                                 //Step 11
        {
            cout << "Cannot open the input file."
                << endl;
            return 1;
        }

        cout << "Enter the output file name: ";        //Step 12
        cin >> outputFile;                             //Step 13
        cout << endl;

        outfile.open(outputFile.c_str());              //Step 14
        outfile << fixed << showpoint
                << setprecision(2);                    //Step 15

        getData(infile, salesPersonList,
                NO_OF_SALES_PERSON);                   //Step 16
        saleByQuarter(salesPersonList,
                    NO_OF_SALES_PERSON,
                    totalSaleByQuarter);               //Step 17
        totalSaleByPerson(salesPersonList,
                    NO_OF_SALES_PERSON);               //Step 18

        printReport(outfile, salesPersonList,
                    NO_OF_SALES_PERSON,
                    totalSaleByQuarter);               //Step 19
        maxSaleByPerson(outfile, salesPersonList,
                    NO_OF_SALES_PERSON);               //Step 20
        maxSaleByQuarter(outfile, totalSaleByQuarter); //Step 21

        infile.close();                                //Step 22
        outfile.close();                               //Step 22

        return  0;
}

//Place the definitions of the functions initialize,
//getData, saleByQuarter, totalSaleByPerson,
//printReport, maxSaleByPerson, and maxSaleByQuarter here.
```

Sample Run: In this sample run, the user input is shaded.

```
Enter the salesPerson ID file name: Ch9_SalesManID.txt

Enter the sales data file name: Ch9_SalesData.txt

Enter the output file name: Ch9_SalesDataAnalysis.txt
```

Input File: Salespeople's IDs

```
12345
32214
23422
57373
35864
54654
```

Input File: Salespeople's Data

```
12345 1 893
32214 1 343
23422 3 903
57373 2 893
35864 5 329
54654 9 392
12345 2 999
32214 4 892
23422 4 895
23422 2 492
57373 6 892
35864 10 1223
54654 11 3420
12345 12 322
35864  5 892
54654  3 893
12345 8 494
32214 8 9023
23422 6 223
23422 4 783
57373 8 8834
35864 3 2882
```

Sample Run:

```
------------ Annual Sales Report ------------
```

ID	QT1	QT2	QT3	QT4	Total
12345	1892.00	0.00	494.00	322.00	2708.00
32214	343.00	892.00	9023.00	0.00	10258.00
23422	1395.00	1901.00	0.00	0.00	3296.00
57373	893.00	892.00	8834.00	0.00	10619.00
35864	2882.00	1221.00	0.00	1223.00	5326.00
54654	893.00	0.00	392.00	3420.00	4705.00
Total	8298.00	4906.00	18743.00	4965.00	

```
Max Sale by SalesPerson: ID = 57373, Amount = $10619.00
Max Sale by Quarter: Quarter = 3, Amount = $18743.00
```

QUICK REVIEW

1. A `struct` is a collection of a fixed number of components.

2. Components of a `struct` can be of different types.

3. The syntax to define a `struct` is:

```
struct structName
{
    dataType1 identifier1;
    dataType2 identifier2;
        .
        .
        .
    dataTypen identifiern;
};
```

4. In C++, `struct` is a reserved word.

5. In C++, `struct` is a definition; no memory is allocated. Memory is allocated for the `struct` variables only when you declare them.

6. Components of a `struct` are called members of the `struct`.

7. Components of a `struct` are accessed by name.

8. In C++, the dot (.) operator is called the member access operator.

9. Members of a `struct` are accessed by using the dot (.) operator. For example, if `employeeType` is a `struct`, `employee` is a variable of type `employeeType`, and `name` is a member of `employee`, then the expression `employee.name` accesses the member `name`. That is, `employee.name` is a variable and can be manipulated like other variables.

10. The only built-in operations on a `struct` are the assignment and member access operations.

11. Neither arithmetic nor relational operations are allowed on `struct`(s).

12. As a parameter to a function, a `struct` can be passed either by value or by reference.

13. A function can return a value of type `struct`.

14. A `struct` can be a member of another `struct`.

EXERCISES

1. Mark the following statements as true or false.

   a. All members of a `struct` must be of different types.

   b. A function cannot return a value of type `struct`.

   c. A member of a `struct` can be another `struct`.

   d. The only allowable operations on a `struct` are assignment and member selection.

e. An array can be a member of a `struct`.

f. In C++, some aggregate operations are allowed on a `struct`.

g. Because a `struct` has a finite number of components, relational operations are allowed on a `struct`.

2. Define a `struct`, `carType`, to store the following data about a car: Manufacturer (`string`), model (`string`), model type (`string`), color (`string`), number of doors (`int`), miles per gallon in city (`int`), miles per gallon on highway (`int`), year when the car was built (`int`), and the price (`double`).

3. Assume the definition of Exercise 2. Declare a `carType` variable and write C++ statements to store the following information: Manufacturer—GMT, model—Cyclone, type—sedan, color—blue, number of doors—4, miles per gallon in city—28, miles per gallon on highway—32, year when the car was built—2006, and the price—25000.00.

4. Define a `struct`, `fruitType`, to store the following data about a fruit: Fruit name (`string`), color (`string`), fat (`int`), sugar (`int`), and carbohydrate (`int`).

5. Assume the definition of Exercise 4. Declare a variable of type `fruitType` to store the following data: Fruit name—banana, color—yellow, fat—1, sugar—15, carbohydrate—22.

6. Consider the following statements:

```
struct nameType          struct courseType          struct studentType
{                        {                          {
    string first;            string name;               nameType name;
    string last;             int callNum;               double gpa;
};                           int credits;               courseType course;
                             char grade;            };
                         };
```

```
studentType student;
studentType classList[100];
courseType course;
nameType name;
```

Mark the following statements as valid or invalid. If a statement is invalid, explain why.

a. `student.course.callNum = "CSC230";`

b. `cin >> student.name;`

c. `classList[0] = name;`

d. `classList[1].gpa = 3.45;`

e. `name = classList[15].name;`

f. `student.name = name;`

g. `cout << classList[10] << endl;`

h. `for (int j = 0; j < 100; j++)`
   `classList[j].name = name;`

9

    i.   `classList.course.credits = 3;`

    j.   `course = studentType.course;`

7.   Assume the declarations of Exercise 6. Write C++ statements to store the following information in `student`:

```
name: Linda Brown
gpa:   3.78
course name: Calculus
course call number: 23827
course credits: 4
course grade: A
```

8.   Assume the declarations of Exercise 6. Write C++ statements that do the following:

    a.   Store the following information in `course`:

```
name: Programming I
callNum:   13452
credits: 3
grade: ""
```

    b.   In the array `classList`, initialize each `gpa` to `0.0`.

    c.   Copy the information of the thirty-first component of the array `classList` into `student`.

    d.   Update the `gpa` of the tenth student in the array `classList` by adding `0.75` to its previous value.

9.   Consider the following statements (`nameType` is as defined in Exercise 6):

```
struct employeeType
{
    nameType name;
    int performanceRating;
    int pID;
    string dept;
    double salary;
};
employeeType employees[100];
employeeType newEmployee;
```

Mark the following statements as valid or invalid. If a statement is invalid, explain why.

    a.   `newEmployee.name = "John Smith";`

    b.   `cout << newEmployee.name;`

    c.   `employees[35] = newEmployee;`

    d.   `if (employees[45].pID == 555334444)`
           `employees[45].performanceRating = 1;`

    e.   `employees.salary = 0;`

10. Assume the declarations of Exercises 6 and 9. Write C++ statements that do the following:

    a. Store the following information in newEmployee:

```
name: Mickey Doe
pID:  111111111
performanceRating: 2
dept: ACCT
salary: 34567.78
```

    b. In the array employees, initialize each performanceRating to 0.

    c. Copy the information of the 20th component of the array employees into newEmployee.

    d. Update the salary of the 50th employee in the array employees by adding 5735.87 to its previous value.

11. Assume that you have the following definition of a struct:

```
struct partsType
{    string partName;
     int partNum;
     double price;
     int quantitiesInStock;
};
```

Declare an array, inventory, of 100 components of type partsType.

12. Assume the definition of Exercise 11.

    a. Write a C++ code to initialize each component of inventory as follows: partName to null string, partNum to -1, price to 0.0, and quantitiesInStock to 0.

    b. Write a C++ code that uses a loop to output the data stored in inventory. Assume that the variable length indicates the number of elements in inventory.

13. Assume the definition and declaration of Exercise 11. Write the definition of a void function that can be used to input data in a variable of type partsType. Also write a C++ code that uses your function to input data in inventory.

14. Suppose that you have the following definitions:

```
struct timeType                 struct tourType
{                               {
    int hr;                         string cityName;
    double min;                     int distance;
    int sec;                        timeType travelTime;
};                              };
```

    a. Declare the variable destination of type tourType.

    b. Write C++ statements to store the following data in destination: cityName—Chicago, distance—550 miles, travelTime—9 hours and 30 minutes.

9

c. Write the definition of a function to output the data stored in a variable of type tourType.

d. Write the definition of a value-returning function that inputs data into a variable of type tourType.

e. Write the definition of a void function with a reference parameter of type tourType to input data in a variable of type tourType.

PROGRAMMING EXERCISES

1. Assume the definition of Exercise 4, which defines the struct fruitType. Write a program that declares a variable of type fruitType, prompts the user to input data about a fruit, and outputs the fruit data.

2. Write a program that reads students' names followed by their test scores. The program should output each student's name followed by the test scores and the relevant grade. It should also find and print the highest test score and the name of the students having the highest test score.

   Student data should be stored in a struct variable of type studentType, which has four components: studentFName and studentLName of type string, testScore of type int (testScore is between 0 and 100), and grade of type char. Suppose that the class has 20 students. Use an array of 20 components of type studentType.

   Your program must contain at least the following functions:

   a. A function to read the students' data into the array.

   b. A function to assign the relevant grade to each student.

   c. A function to find the highest test score.

   d. A function to print the names of the students having the highest test score.

   Your program must output each student's name in this form: last name followed by a comma, followed by a space, followed by the first name; the name must be left justified. Moreover, other than declaring the variables and opening the input and output files, the function main should only be a collection of function calls.

3. Define a struct, menuItemType, with two components: menuItem of type string and menuPrice of type double.

4. Write a program to help a local restaurant automate its breakfast billing system. The program should do the following:

   a. Show the customer the different breakfast items offered by the restaurant.

   b. Allow the customer to select more than one item from the menu.

c. Calculate and print the bill.

Assume that the restaurant offers the following breakfast items (the price of each item is shown to the right of the item):

Plain Egg	$1.45
Bacon and Egg	$2.45
Muffin	$0.99
French Toast	$1.99
Fruit Basket	$2.49
Cereal	$0.69
Coffee	$0.50
Tea	$0.75

Use an array, menuList, of the **struct** menuItemType, as defined in Programming Exercise 3. Your program must contain at least the following functions:

- Function getData: This function loads the data into the array menuList.

- Function showMenu: This function shows the different items offered by the restaurant and tells the user how to select the items.

- Function printCheck: This function calculates and prints the check. (Note that the billing amount should include a 5% tax.)

  A sample output is:

```
Welcome to Johnny's Restaurant
Bacon and Egg    $2.45
Muffin           $0.99
Coffee           $0.50
Tax              $0.20
Amount Due       $4.14
```

Format your output with two decimal places. The name of each item in the output must be left justified. You may assume that the user selects only one item of a particular type.

5. Redo Exercise 4 so that the customer can select multiple items of a particular type. A sample output in this case is:

```
Welcome to Johnny's Restaurant
1 Bacon and Egg    $2.45
2 Muffin           $1.98
1 Coffee           $0.50
   Tax             $0.25
   Amount Due      $5.18
```

6. Write a program whose main function is merely a collection of variable declarations and function calls. This program reads a text and outputs the letters, together with their counts, as explained below in the function

9

printResult. (There can be no global variables! All information must be passed in and out of the functions. Use a structure to store the information.) Your program must consist of at least the following functions:

- Function openFile: Opens the input and output files. You must pass the file streams as parameters (by reference, of course). If the file does not exist, the program should print an appropriate message and exit. The program must ask the user for the names of the input and output files.

- Function count: Counts every occurrence of capital letters A-Z and small letters a-z in the text file opened in the function openFile. This information must go into an array of structures. The array must be passed as a parameter, and the file identifier must also be passed as a parameter.

- Function printResult: Prints the number of capital letters and small letters, as well as the percentage of capital letters for every letter A-Z and the percentage of small letters for every letter a-z. The percentages should look like this: "25%". This information must come from an array of structures, and this array must be passed as a parameter.

7. Write a program that declares a **struct** to store the data of a football player (player's name, player's position, number of touchdowns, number of catches, number of passing yards, number of receiving yards, and the number of rushing yards). Declare an array of 10 components to store the data of 10 football players. Your program must contain a function to input data and a function to output data. Add functions to search the array to find the index of a specific player, and update the data of a player. (You may assume that input data is stored in a file.) Before the program terminates, give the user the option to save data in a file. Your program should be menu driven, giving the user various choices.

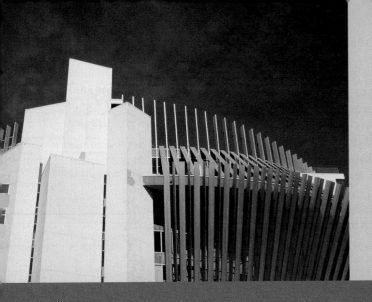

CLASSES AND DATA ABSTRACTION

IN THIS CHAPTER, YOU WILL:

- Learn about classes
- Learn about `private`, `protected`, and `public` members of a class
- Explore how classes are implemented
- Examine constructors and destructors
- Learn about the abstract data type (ADT)
- Explore how classes are used to implement ADTs
- Learn about information hiding
- Explore how information hiding is implemented in C++
- Learn about the `static` members of a class

In Chapter 9, you learned how to group data items that are of different types by using a `struct`. The definition of a `struct` given in Chapter 9 is similar to the definition of a C-`struct`. However, the members of a C++ `struct` can be data items as well as functions. C++ provides another structured data type, called a **class**, which is specifically designed to group data and functions. This chapter first introduces classes and explains how to use them and then discusses the similarities and differences between a `struct` and a `class`.

 NOTE   Chapter 9 is not a prerequisite for this chapter. In fact, a `struct` and a `class` have similar capabilities, as discussed in the section "A `struct` versus a `class`" in this chapter.

Classes

Chapter 1 introduced the problem-solving methodology called **object-oriented design (OOD)**. In OOD, the first step is to identify the components, called **objects**. An object combines data and the operations on that data in a single unit. In C++, the mechanism that allows you to combine data and the operations on that data in a single unit is called a class. Now that you know how to store and manipulate data in computer memory and how to construct your own functions, you are ready to learn how objects are constructed. This and subsequent chapters develop and implement programs using OOD. This chapter first explains how to define a class and use it in a program.

A **class** is a collection of a fixed number of components. The components of a class are called the **members** of the class.

The general syntax for defining a class is:

```
class classIdentifier
{
    classMembersList
};
```

in which `classMembersList` consists of variable declarations and/or functions. That is, a member of a class can be either a variable (to store data) or a function.

- If a member of a class is a variable, you declare it just like any other variable. Also, in the definition of the class, you cannot initialize a variable when you declare it.

- If a member of a class is a function, you typically use the function prototype to declare that member.

- If a member of a class is a function, it can (directly) access any member of the class—member variables and member functions. That is, when you write the definition of a member function, you can directly access any member variable of the class without passing it as a parameter. The only obvious condition is that you must declare an identifier before you can use it.

In C++, `class` is a reserved word, and it defines only a data type; no memory is allocated. It announces the declaration of a class. Moreover, note the semicolon (;) after the right brace. The semicolon is part of the syntax. A missing semicolon, therefore, will result in a syntax error.

The members of a `class` are classified into three categories: `private`, `public`, and `protected`. This chapter mainly discusses the first two types, `private` and `public`.

In C++, `private`, `protected`, and `public` are reserved words and are called member access specifiers.

Following are some facts about `public` and `private` members of a class:

- By default, all members of a class are `private`.
- If a member of a class is `private`, you cannot access it outside of the class. (Example 10-1 illustrates this concept.)
- A `public` member is accessible outside of the `class`. (Example 10-1 illustrates this concept.)
- To make a member of a class `public`, you use the member access specifier `public` with a colon, :.

Suppose that we want to define a class to implement the time of day in a program. Because a clock gives the time of day, let us call this `class clockType`. Furthermore, to represent time in computer memory, we use three `int` variables: one to represent the hours, one to represent the minutes, and one to represent the seconds.

Suppose these three variables are:

```
int hr;
int min;
int sec;
```

We also want to perform the following operations on the time:

1. Set the time.
2. Retrieve the time.
3. Print the time.
4. Increment the time by one second.
5. Increment the time by one minute.
6. Increment the time by one hour.
7. Compare the two times for equality.

To implement these seven operations, we will write seven functions—`setTime`, `getTime`, `printTime`, `incrementSeconds`, `incrementMinutes`, `incrementHours`, and `equalTime`.

From this discussion, it is clear that the `class clockType` has 10 members: three member variables and seven member functions.

Some members of the `class clockType` will be `private`; others will be `public`. Deciding which member to make `public` and which to make `private` depends on the nature of the member. The general rule is that any member that needs to be accessed outside of the class is declared `public`; any member that should not be accessed directly by the user should be declared `private`. For example, the user should be able to set the time and print the time. Therefore, the members that set the time and print the time should be declared `public`.

Similarly, the members to increment the time and compare the time for equality should be declared `public`. On the other hand, to prevent the *direct* manipulation of the member variables `hr`, `min`, and `sec`, we will declare them `private`. Furthermore, note that if the user has direct access to the member variables, member functions such as `setTime` are not needed. The second part of this chapter (beginning with the section "Information Hiding") explains why some members need to be `public` and others should be `private`.

The following statements define the `class clockType`:

```
class clockType
{
public:
    void setTime(int, int, int);
    void getTime(int&, int&, int&) const;
    void printTime() const;
    void incrementSeconds();
    void incrementMinutes();
    void incrementHours();
    bool equalTime(const clockType&) const;

private:
    int hr;
    int min;
    int sec;
};
```

In this definition:

- The `class clockType` has seven member functions: `setTime`, `getTime`, `printTime`, `incrementSeconds`, `incrementMinutes`, `incrementHours`, and `equalTime`. It has three member variables: `hr`, `min`, and `sec`.

- The three member variables—`hr`, `min`, and `sec`—are `private` to the class and cannot be accessed outside of the class. (Example 10-1 illustrates this concept.)

- The seven member functions—`setTime`, `getTime`, `printTime`, `incrementSeconds`, `incrementMinutes`, `incrementHours`, and `equalTime`—can directly access the member variables (`hr`, `min`, and `sec`). In other words, when we write the definitions of these functions, we do not pass these member variables as parameters to the member functions.

- In the function `equalTime`, the formal parameter is a constant reference parameter. That is, in a call to the function `equalTime`, the formal parameter receives the address of the actual parameter, but the formal parameter cannot modify the value of the actual parameter. You could have declared the formal parameter as a value parameter, but that would require the formal parameter to copy the value of the actual parameter, which could result in poor performance. (See the section "Reference Parameters and Class Objects (Variables)" in this chapter for an explanation.)

- The word `const` at the end of the member functions `getTime`, `printTime`, and `equalTime` specifies that these functions cannot modify the member variables of a variable of type `clockType`.

 NOTE The `private` and `public` members can appear in any order. If you want, you can declare the `private` members first and then declare the `public` ones. The section "Order of `public` and `private` Members of a Class" in this chapter discusses this issue.

 NOTE In the definition of the `class clockType`, all member variables are `private` and all member functions are `public`. However, a member function can also be `private`. For example, if a member function is used only to implement other member functions of the class and the user does not need to access this function, you make it `private`. Similarly, a member variable of a class can also be `public`.

Note that we have not yet written the definitions of the member functions of the class. You will learn how to write them shortly.

The function `setTime` sets the three member variables—hr, min, and sec—to a given value. The given values are passed as parameters to the function `setTime`. The function `printTime` prints the time, that is, the values of hr, min, and sec. The function `incrementSeconds` increments the time by one second, the function `incrementMinutes` increments the time by one minute, the function `incrementHours` increments the time by one hour, and the function `equalTime` compares two times for equality.

Note that the function `equalTime` has only one parameter, although you need two things to make a comparison. We will explain this point with the help of an example in the section "Implementation of Member Functions," later in this chapter.

Unified Modeling Language Class Diagrams

A class and its members can be described graphically using a notation known as the **Unified Modeling Language** (UML) notation. For example, Figure 10-1 shows the UML class diagram of the **class** clockType.

```
                        clockType

-hr: int
-min: int
-sec: int

+setTime(int, int, int): void
+getTime(int&, int&, int&) const: void
+printTime() const: void
+incrementSeconds(): int
+incrementMinutes(): int
+incrementHours(): int
+equalTime(const clockType&) const: bool
```

FIGURE 10-1   UML class diagram of the **class** clockType

The top box contains the name of the class. The middle box contains the member variables and their data types. The last box contains the member function name, parameter list, and the return type of the function. A + (plus) sign in front of a member name indicates that this member is a **public** member; a – (minus) sign indicates that this is a **private** member. The symbol # before the member name indicates that the member is a **protected** member.

Variable (Object) Declaration

Once a class is defined, you can declare variables of that type. In C++ terminology, a class variable is called a **class object** or **class instance**. To help you become familiar with this terminology, from now on we will use the term class object, or simply **object**, for a class variable.

The syntax for declaring a class object is the same as that for declaring any other variable. The following statements declare two objects of type clockType:

```
clockType myClock;
clockType yourClock;
```

Each object has 10 members: seven member functions and three member variables. Each object has separate memory allocated for hr, min, and sec.

In actuality, memory is allocated only for the member variables of each class object. The C++ compiler generates only one physical copy of a member function of a class, and each class object executes the same copy of the member function. Therefore, whenever we draw the figure of a class object, we will show only the member variables. As an example, Figure 10-2 shows the objects myClock and yourClock with values in their member variables.

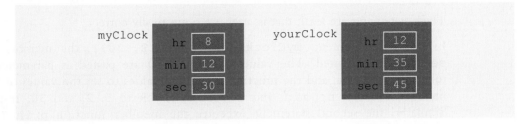

FIGURE 10-2 Objects myClock and yourClock

Accessing Class Members

Once an object of a class is declared, it can access the members of the class. The general syntax for an object to access a member of a class is:

```
classObjectName.memberName
```

The class members that a class object can access depend on where the object is declared.

- If the object is declared in the definition of a member function of the class, then the object can access both the **public** and **private** members. (We will elaborate on this when we write the definition of the member function equalTime of the **class** clockType in the section "Implementation of Member Functions," later in this chapter.)
- If the object is declared elsewhere (for example, in a user's program), then the object can access *only* the **public** members of the class.

Recall that in C++, the dot, **.** (period), is an operator called the **member access operator**.

Example 10-1 illustrates how to access the members of a class.

EXAMPLE 10-1

Suppose we have the following declaration (say, in a user's program):

```
clockType myClock;
clockType yourClock;
```

Consider the following statements:

```
myClock.setTime(5, 2, 30);
myClock.printTime();
yourClock.setTime(x, y, z);    //assume x, y, and z are
                               //variables of type int
```

```
if (myClock.equalTime(yourClock))
    .
    .
    .
```

These statements are legal; that is, they are syntactically correct.

In the first statement, `myClock.setTime(5, 2, 30);`, the member function `setTime` is executed. The values 5, 2, and 30 are passed as parameters to the function `setTime`, and the function uses these values to set the values of the three member variables `hr`, `min`, and `sec` of `myClock` to 5, 2, and 30, respectively. Similarly, the second statement executes the member function `printTime` and outputs the contents of the three member variables of `myClock`. In the third statement, the values of the variables `x`, `y`, and `z` are used to set the values of the three member variables of `yourClock`.

In the fourth statement, the member function `equalTime` executes and compares the three member variables of `myClock` to the corresponding member variables of `yourClock`. Because in this statement `equalTime` is a member of the object `myClock`, it has direct access to the three member variables of `myClock`. So it needs one more object, which in this case is `yourClock`, to compare. This explains why the function `equalTime` has only one parameter.

The objects `myClock` and `yourClock` can access only `public` members of the class. Thus, the following statements are illegal because `hr` and `min` are declared as `private` members of the `class` `clockType` and, therefore, cannot be accessed by the objects `myClock` and `yourClock`:

```
myClock.hr = 10;                //illegal
myClock.min = yourClock.min;    //illegal
```

Built-in Operations on Classes

Most of C++'s built-in operations do not apply to classes. You cannot use arithmetic operators to perform arithmetic operations on class objects (unless they are overloaded; see Chapter 13). For example, you cannot use the operator + to add two class objects of, say, type `clockType`. Also, you cannot use relational operators to compare two class objects for equality (unless they are overloaded; see Chapter 13).

The two built-in operations that are valid for class objects are member access (.) and assignment (=). You have seen how to access an individual member of a class by using the name of the class object, then a dot, and then the member name. (For example, if `myClock` is a `clockType` object, in the statement `myClock.incrementSeconds();`, `myClock` accesses the member `incrementSeconds`.)

We now show how an assignment statement works with the help of an example.

Assignment Operator and Classes

Suppose that myClock and yourClock are clockType objects, as defined previously. Furthermore, suppose that the values of myClock and yourClock are as shown in Figure 10-3(a).

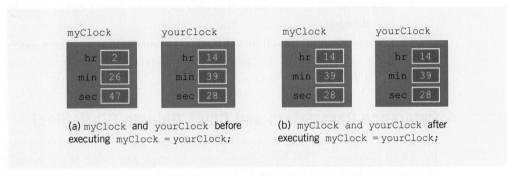

(a) myClock and yourClock before executing myClock = yourClock;

(b) myClock and yourClock after executing myClock = yourClock;

FIGURE 10-3 myClock and yourClock before and after executing the statement myClock = yourClock;

The statement:

```
myClock = yourClock;            //Line 1
```

copies the value of yourClock into myClock. That is,

- the value of yourClock.hr is copied into myClock.hr,
- the value of yourClock.min is copied into myClock.min, and
- the value of yourClock.sec is copied into myClock.sec.

In other words, the values of the three member variables of yourClock are copied into the corresponding member variables of myClock. Therefore, an assignment statement performs a member-wise copy. After the statement in Line 1 executes, the values of myClock and yourClock are as shown in Figure 10-3(b).

Class Scope

A class object can be either automatic (that is, created each time the control reaches its declaration and destroyed when the control exits the surrounding block) or static (that is, created once, when the control reaches its declaration, and destroyed when the program terminates). Also, you can declare an array of class objects. A class object has the same scope as other variables. A member of a class has the same scope as a member of a struct. That is, a member of a class is local to the class. You access a class member outside of the class by using the class object name and the member access operator (.).

Functions and Classes

The following rules describe the relationship between functions and classes:

- Class objects can be passed as parameters to functions and returned as function values.
- As parameters to functions, class objects can be passed either by value or by reference.
- If a class object is passed by value, the contents of the member variables of the actual parameter are copied into the corresponding member variables of the formal parameter.

Reference Parameters and Class Objects (Variables)

Recall that when a variable is passed by value, the formal parameter copies the value of the actual parameter. That is, memory space to copy the value of the actual parameter is allocated for the formal parameter. As a parameter, a class object can be passed by value.

Suppose that a class has several member variables requiring a large amount of memory to store data, and you need to pass a variable by value. The corresponding formal parameter then receives a copy of the data of the variable. That is, the compiler must allocate memory for the formal parameter, so as to copy the value of the member variables of the actual parameter. This operation might require, in addition to a large amount of storage space, a considerable amount of computer time to copy the value of the actual parameter into the formal parameter.

On the other hand, if a variable is passed by reference, the formal parameter receives only the address of the actual parameter. Therefore, an efficient way to pass a variable as a parameter is by reference. If a variable is passed by reference, then when the formal parameter changes, the actual parameter also changes. Sometimes, however, you do not want the function to be able to change the values of the member variables. In C++, you can pass a variable by reference and still prevent the function from changing its value by using the keyword const in the formal parameter declaration. As an example, consider the following function definition:

```
void testTime(const clockType& otherClock)
{
    clockType dClock;
    .
    .
    .
}
```

The function testTime contains a reference parameter, otherClock. The parameter otherClock is declared using the keyword const. Thus, in a call to the function testTime, the formal parameter otherClock receives the address of the actual parameter, but otherClock cannot modify the contents of the actual parameter. For example, after the following statement executes, the value of myClock will not be altered:

```
testTime(myClock);
```

Generally, if you want to declare a class object as a value parameter, you declare it as a reference parameter using the keyword `const`, as described previously.

Recall that if a formal parameter is a value parameter, within the function definition, you can change the value of the formal parameter. That is, you can use an assignment statement to change the value of the formal parameter (which, of course, would have no effect on the actual parameter). However, if a formal parameter is a constant reference parameter, you cannot use an assignment statement to change its value within the function, nor can you use any other function to change its value. Therefore, within the definition of the function `testTime`, you cannot alter the value of `otherClock`. For example, the following would be illegal in the definition of the function `testTime`:

```
otherClock.setTime(5, 34, 56); //illegal
otherClock = dClock;           //illegal
```

Implementation of Member Functions

When we defined the `class clockType`, we included only the function prototype for the member functions. For these functions to work properly, we must write the related algorithms. One way to implement these functions is to provide the function definition rather than the function prototype in the class itself. Unfortunately, the class definition would then be very long and difficult to comprehend. Another reason for providing function prototypes instead of function definitions relates to information hiding; that is, we want to hide the details of the operations on the data. We will discuss this issue later in this chapter, in the section "Information Hiding."

Next, let us write the definitions of the member functions of the `class clockType`. That is, we will write the definitions of the functions `setTime`, `getTime`, `printTime`, `incrementSeconds`, `equalTime`, and so on. Because the identifiers `setTime`, `printTime`, and so forth are local to the class, we cannot reference them (directly) outside of the class. In order to reference these identifiers, we use the **scope resolution operator**, `::` (double colon). In the function definition's heading, the name of the function is the name of the class, followed by the scope resolution operator, followed by the function name. For example, the definition of the function `setTime` is as follows:

```
void clockType::setTime(int hours, int minutes, int seconds)
{
    if (0 <= hours && hours < 24)
        hr = hours;
    else
        hr = 0;

    if (0 <= minutes && minutes < 60)
        min = minutes;
    else
        min = 0;
```

1
0

```
    if (0 <= seconds && seconds < 60)
        sec = seconds;
    else
        sec = 0;
}
```

Note that the definition of the function setTime checks for the valid values of hours, minutes, and seconds. If these values are out of range, the member variables hr, min, and sec are initialized to 0. Let us now explain how the member function setTime works when accessed by an object of type clockType.

The member function setTime is a **void** function and has three parameters. Therefore:

- A call to this function is a stand-alone statement.
- We must use three parameters in a call to this function.

Furthermore, recall that because setTime is a member of the **class** clockType, it can directly access the member variables hr, min, and sec, as shown in the definition of setTime.

Suppose that myClock is an object of type clockType (as declared previously). The object myClock has three member variables, as shown in Figure 10-4(a).

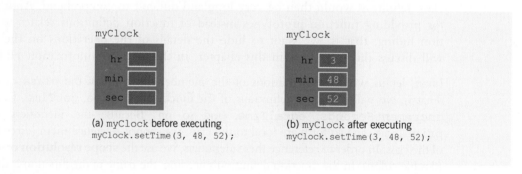

FIGURE 10-4   myClock before and after executing the statement myClock.setTime(3, 48, 52);

Consider the following statement:

```
myClock.setTime(3, 48, 52);
```

In the statement myClock.setTime(3, 48, 52);, setTime is accessed by the object myClock. Therefore, the three variables—hr, min, and sec—referred to in the body of the function setTime are the three member variables of myClock. Thus, the values 3, 48, and 52, which are passed as parameters in the preceding statement, are assigned to the three member variables of myClock by the function setTime (see the body of the function setTime). After the previous statement executes, the object myClock is as shown in Figure 10-4(b).

Next, let us give the definitions of the other member functions of the **class** clockType.
The definitions of these functions are simple and easy to follow:

```cpp
void clockType::getTime(int& hours, int& minutes,
                        int& seconds) const
{
    hours = hr;
    minutes = min;
    seconds = sec;
}

void clockType::printTime() const
{
    if (hr < 10)
        cout << "0";
    cout << hr << ":";

    if (min < 10)
        cout << "0";
    cout << min << ":";

    if (sec < 10)
        cout << "0";
    cout << sec;
}

void clockType::incrementHours()
{
    hr++;
    if (hr > 23)
        hr = 0;
}

void clockType::incrementMinutes()
{
    min++;
    if (min > 59)
    {
        min = 0;
        incrementHours(); //increment hours
    }
}

void clockType::incrementSeconds()
{
    sec++;

    if (sec > 59)
    {
        sec = 0;
        incrementMinutes(); //increment minutes
    }
}
```

From the definitions of the functions `incrementMinutes` and `incrementSeconds`, it is clear that a member function of a class can call other member functions of the class.

The function `equalTime` has the following definition:

```
bool clockType::equalTime(const clockType& otherClock) const
{
    return (hr == otherClock.hr
            && min == otherClock.min
            && sec == otherClock.sec);
}
```

Let us see how the member function `equalTime` works.

Suppose that `myClock` and `yourClock` are objects of type `clockType`, as declared previously. Further suppose that we have `myClock` and `yourClock`, as shown in Figure 10-5.

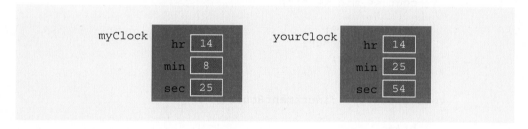

FIGURE 10-5 Objects `myClock` and `yourClock`

Consider the following statement:

```
if (myClock.equalTime(yourClock))
    .
    .
    .
```

In the expression:

```
myClock.equalTime(yourClock)
```

the object `myClock` accesses the member function `equalTime`. Because `otherClock` is a reference parameter, the address of the actual parameter `yourClock` is passed to the formal parameter `otherClock`, as shown in Figure 10-6.

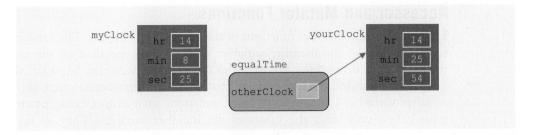

FIGURE 10-6 Object `myClock` and parameter `otherClock`

The member variables `hr`, `min`, and `sec` of `otherClock` have the values 14, 25, and 54, respectively. In other words, when the body of the function `equalTime` executes, the value of `otherClock.hr` is 14, the value of `otherClock.min` is 25, and the value of `otherClock.sec` is 54. The function `equalTime` is a member of `myClock`. When the function `equalTime` executes, the variables `hr`, `min`, and `sec` in the body of the function `equalTime` are the member variables of the object `myClock`. Therefore, the member `hr` of `myClock` is compared with `otherClock.hr`, the member `min` of `myClock` is compared with `otherClock.min`, and the member `sec` of `myClock` is compared with `otherClock.sec`.

Once again, from the definition of the function `equalTime`, it is clear why it has only one parameter.

Let us again take a look at the definition of the function `equalTime`. Notice that within the definition of this function, the object `otherClock` accesses the member variables `hr`, `min`, and `sec`. However, these member variables are **private**. So is there any violation? The answer is no. The function `equalTime` is a member of the **class** `clockType`, and `hr`, `min`, and `sec` are the member variables. Moreover, `otherClock` is an object of type `clockType`. Therefore, the object `otherClock` can access its **private** member variables within the definition of the function `equalTime`.

The same is true for any member function of a class. In general, when you write the definition of a member function, say, `dummyFunction`, of a **class**, say, `dummyClass`, and the function uses an object, `dummyObject` of the **class** `dummyClass`, then within the definition of `dummyFunction`, the object `dummyObject` can access its **private** member variables (in fact, any **private** member of the class).

Once a class is properly defined and implemented, it can be used in a program. A program or software that uses and manipulates the objects of a class is called a **client** of that class.

When you declare objects of the **class** `clockType`, every object has its own copy of the member variables `hr`, `min`, and `sec`. In object-oriented terminology, variables such as `hr`, `min`, and `sec` are called **instance variables** of the class because every object has its own instance of the data.

Accessor and Mutator Functions

Let us look at the member functions of the `class clockType`. The function `setTime` sets the values of the member variables to the values specified by the user. In other words, it alters or modifies the values of the member variables. Similarly, the functions `incrementSeconds`, `incrementMinutes`, and `incrementHours` also modify the member variables. On the other hand, functions such as `getTime`, `printTime`, and `equalTime` only *access* the values of the member variables. They *do not* modify the member variables. We can, therefore, categorize the member functions of the `class clockType` into two categories: member functions that modify the member variables and member functions that only access, and do not modify, the member variables.

This is typically true for any class. That is, every class has member functions that only access and do not modify the member variables, called accessor functions, and member functions that modify the member variables, called mutator functions.

Accessor function: A member function of a class that only accesses (that is, does not modify) the value(s) of the member variable(s).

Mutator function: A member function of a class that modifies the value(s) of the member variable(s).

Because an accessor function only accesses the values of the member variables, as a safeguard, we typically include the reserved word `const` at the end of the headings of these functions. Moreover, a constant member function of a class cannot modify the member variables of that class. For example, see the headings of the member functions `getTime`, `printTime`, and `equalTime` of the `class clockType`.

A member function of a class is called a **constant function** if its heading contains the reserved word `const` at the end. For example, the member functions `getTime`, `printTime`, and `equalTime` of the `class clockType` are constant functions. A constant member function of a class cannot modify the member variables of that class, so these are accessor functions. One thing that should be remembered about constant member functions is that a constant member function of a class can *only* call other constant member functions of that class. Therefore, you should be careful when you make a member function constant.

Example 10-2 shows how to use the `class clockType` in a program. Note that we have combined the definition of the class, the definition of the member functions, and the main function to create a complete program. Later in this chapter, you will learn how to separate the definition of the `class clockType`, the definitions of the member functions, and the main program, using three files.

EXAMPLE 10-2

```
//The program listing of the program that defines
//and uses the class clockType
```

```cpp
#include <iostream>
using namespace std;

class clockType
{
public:
    void setTime(int, int, int);
    void getTime(int&, int&, int&) const;
    void printTime() const;
    void incrementSeconds();
    void incrementMinutes();
    void incrementHours();
    bool equalTime(const clockType&) const;

private:
    int hr;
    int min;
    int sec;
};

int main()
{
    clockType myClock;
    clockType yourClock;

    int hours;
    int minutes;
    int seconds;

        //Set the time of myClock
    myClock.setTime(5, 4, 30);                              //Line 1

    cout << "Line 2: myClock: ";                            //Line 2
    myClock.printTime();   //print the time of myClock      Line 3
    cout << endl;                                           //Line 4

    cout << "Line 5: yourClock: ";                          //Line 5
    yourClock.printTime(); //print the time of yourClock Line 6
    cout << endl;                                           //Line 7

        //Set the time of yourClock
    yourClock.setTime(5, 45, 16);                           //Line 8

    cout << "Line 9: After setting, yourClock: ";           //Line 9
    yourClock.printTime(); //print the time of yourClock Line 10
    cout << endl;                                           //Line 11

        //Compare myClock and yourClock
    if (myClock.equalTime(yourClock))                       //Line 12
        cout << "Line 13: Both times are equal."
             << endl;                                       //Line 13
```

10

```
        else                                                   //Line 14
            cout << "Line 15: The two times are not equal."
                << endl;                                        //Line 15

        cout << "Line 16: Enter the hours, minutes, and "
            << "seconds: ";                                     //Line 16
        cin >> hours >> minutes >> seconds;                     //Line 17
        cout << endl;                                           //Line 18

            //Set the time of myClock using the value of the
            //variables hours, minutes, and seconds
        myClock.setTime(hours, minutes, seconds);              //Line 19

        cout << "Line 20: New myClock: ";                       //Line 20
        myClock.printTime();    //print the time of myClock    Line 21
        cout << endl;                                           //Line 22

            //Increment the time of myClock by one second
        myClock.incrementSeconds();                            //Line 23

        cout << "Line 24: After incrementing myClock by "
            << "one second, myClock: ";                         //Line 24
        myClock.printTime();    //print the time of myClock    Line 25
        cout << endl;                                           //Line 26

            //Retrieve the hours, minutes, and seconds of the
            //object myClock
        myClock.getTime(hours, minutes, seconds);              //Line 27

            //Output the value of hours, minutes, and seconds
        cout << "Line 28: hours = " << hours
            << ", minutes = " << minutes
            << ", seconds = " << seconds << endl;              //Line 28

    return  0;
}//end main

void clockType::setTime(int hours, int minutes, int seconds)
{
    if (0 <= hours && hours < 24)
        hr = hours;
    else
        hr = 0;

    if (0 <= minutes && minutes < 60)
        min = minutes;
    else
        min = 0;

    if (0 <= seconds && seconds < 60)
        sec = seconds;
    else
        sec = 0;
}
```

```
//Place the definitions of the remaining functions, getTime,
//incrementHours, incrementMinutes, incrementSeconds, printTime,
//and  equalTime, of the class clockType, as described
//previously here.
```

Sample Run: In this sample run, the user input is shaded.

```
Line 2: myClock: 05:04:30
Line 5: yourClock: 0-858993460:0-858993460:0-858993460
Line 9: After setting, yourClock: 05:45:16
Line 15: The two times are not equal.
Line 16: Enter the hours, minutes, and seconds: 5 23 59

Line 20: New myClock: 05:23:59
Line 24: After incrementing myClock by one second, myClock: 05:24:00
Line 28: hours = 5, minutes = 24, seconds = 0
```

The value of yourClock, as printed in the second line of the output (Line 5), is machine dependent you might get different values.

Order of public and private Members of a Class

C++ has no fixed order in which you declare public and private members; you can declare them in any order. The only thing you need to remember is that, by default, all members of a class are private. You must use the member access specifier public to make a member available for public access. If you decide to declare the private members after the public members (as is done in the case of clockType), you must use the member access specifier private to begin the declaration of the private members.

We can declare the class clockType in one of three ways, as shown in Examples 10-3 through 10-5.

1 0

EXAMPLE 10-3

This declaration is the same as before. For the sake of completeness, we include the class definition:

```
class clockType
{
public:
    void setTime(int, int, int);
    void getTime(int&, int&, int&) const;
    void printTime() const;
    void incrementSeconds();
    void incrementMinutes();
    void incrementHours();
    bool equalTime(const clockType&) const;
```

```
private:
    int hr;
    int min;
    int sec;
};
```

EXAMPLE 10-4

```
class clockType
{
private:
    int hr;
    int min;
    int sec;

public:
    void setTime(int, int, int);
    void getTime(int&, int&, int&) const;
    void printTime() const;
    void incrementSeconds();
    void incrementMinutes();
    void incrementHours();
    bool equalTime(const clockType&) const;
};
```

EXAMPLE 10-5

```
class clockType
{
    int hr;
    int min;
    int sec;

public:
    void setTime(int, int, int);
    void getTime(int&, int&, int&) const;
    void printTime() const;
    void incrementSeconds();
    void incrementMinutes();
    void incrementHours();
    bool equalTime(const clockType&) const;
};
```

In Example 10-5, because the identifiers hr, min, and sec do not follow any member access specifier, they are private.

It is a common practice to list all of the public members first and then the private members. This way, you can focus your attention on the public members.

Constructors

In the program in Example 10-2, when we printed the value of yourClock without calling the function setTime, the output was some strange numbers (see the output of Line 5 in the sample run). This is due to the fact that C++ does not automatically initialize the variables. Because the private members of a class cannot be accessed outside of the class (in our case, the member variables), if the user forgets to initialize these variables by calling the function setTime, the program will produce erroneous results.

To guarantee that the member variables of a class are initialized, you use constructors. There are two types of constructors: with parameters and without parameters. The constructor without parameters is called the **default constructor**.

Constructors have the following properties:

- The name of a constructor is the same as the name of the class.
- A constructor, even though it is a function, has no type. That is, it is neither a value-returning function nor a void function.
- A class can have more than one constructor. However, all constructors of a class have the same name.
- If a class has more than one constructor, the constructors must have different formal parameter lists. That is, either they have a different number of formal parameters or, if the number of formal parameters is the same, then the data type of the formal parameters, in the order you list, must differ in at least one position.
- Constructors execute automatically when a class object enters its scope. Because they have no types, they cannot be called like other functions.
- Which constructor executes depends on the types of values passed to the class object when the class object is declared.

Let us extend the definition of the class clockType by including two constructors:

```
class clockType
{
public:
    void setTime(int, int, int);
    void getTime(int&, int&, int&) const;
    void printTime() const;
    void incrementSeconds();
```

10

```
    void incrementMinutes();
    void incrementHours();
    bool equalTime(const clockType&) const;
    clockType(int, int, int);  //constructor with parameters
    clockType();  //default constructor

private:
    int hr;
    int min;
    int sec;
};
```

This definition of the **class** clockType includes two constructors: one with three parameters and one without any parameters. Let us now write the definitions of these constructors:

```
clockType::clockType(int hours, int minutes, int seconds)
{
    if (0 <= hours && hours < 24)
        hr = hours;
    else
        hr = 0;

    if (0 <= minutes && minutes < 60)
        min = minutes;
    else
        min = 0;

    if (0 <= seconds && seconds < 60)
        sec = seconds;
    else
        sec = 0;
}

clockType::clockType()  //default constructor
{
    hr = 0;
    min = 0;
    sec = 0;
}
```

From the definitions of these constructors, it follows that the default constructor sets the three member variables—hr, min, and sec—to 0. Also, the constructor with parameters sets the member variables to whatever values are assigned to the formal parameters. Moreover, we can write the definition of the constructor with parameters by calling the function setTime, as follows:

```
clockType::clockType(int hours, int minutes, int seconds)
{
    setTime(hours, minutes, seconds);
}
```

Invoking a Constructor

Recall that when a class object is declared, a constructor is automatically executed. Because a class might have more than one constructor, including the default constructor, next we discuss how to invoke a specific constructor.

Invoking the Default Constructor

Suppose that a class contains the default constructor. The syntax to invoke the default constructor is:

```
className classObjectName;
```

For example, the statement:

```
clockType yourClock;
```

declares `yourClock` to be an object of type `clockType`. In this case, the default constructor executes, and the member variables of `yourClock` are initialized to 0.

 NOTE If you declare an object and want the default constructor to be executed, the empty parentheses after the object name are not required in the object declaration statement. In fact, if you accidentally include the empty parentheses, the compiler generates a syntax error message. For example, the following statement to declare the object `yourClock` is illegal:

```
clockType yourClock();   //illegal object declaration
```

Invoking a Constructor with Parameters

Suppose a class contains constructors with parameters. The syntax to invoke a constructor with a parameter is:

```
className classObjectName(argument1, argument2, ...);
```

in which `argument1`, `argument2`, and so on are either a variable or an expression.

Note the following:

- The number of arguments and their type should match the formal parameters (in the order given) of one of the constructors.
- If the type of the arguments does not match the formal parameters of any constructor (in the order given), C++ uses type conversion and looks for the best match. For example, an integer value might be converted to a floating-point value with a zero decimal part. Any ambiguity will result in a compile-time error.

Consider the statement:

```
clockType myClock(5, 12, 40);
```

10

This statement declares an object myClock of type clockType. Here, we are passing three values of type int, which matches the type of the formal parameters of the constructor with a parameter. Therefore, the constructor with parameters of the class clockType executes, and the three member variables of the object myClock are set to 5, 12, and 40.

Example 10-6 further illustrates how constructors are executed.

EXAMPLE 10-6

Consider the following class definition:

```
class inventory
{
public:
    inventory();                            //Line 1
    inventory(string);                      //Line 2
    inventory(string, int, double);         //Line 3
    inventory(string, int, double, int);    //Line 4

    //Add additional functions

private:
    string name;
    int itemNum;
    double price;
    int unitsInStock;
};
```

This class has four constructors and four member variables. Suppose that the definitions of the constructors are as follows:

```
inventory::inventory() //default constructor
{
    name = "";
    itemNum = -1;
    price = 0.0;
    unitsInStock = 0;
}

inventory::inventory(string n)
{
    name = n;
    itemNum = -1;
    price = 0.0;
    unitsInStock = 0;
}

inventory::inventory(string n, int iNum, double cost)
{
    name = n;
    itemNum = iNum;
    price = cost;
    unitsInStock = 0;
}
```

```
inventory::inventory(string n, int iNum, double cost, int inStock)
{
    name = n;
    itemNum = iNum;
    price = cost;
    unitsInStock = inStock;
}
```

Consider the following declarations:

```
inventory item1;
inventory item2("Dryer");
inventory item3("Washer", 2345, 278.95);
inventory item4("Toaster", 8231, 34.49, 200);
```

For `item1`, the default constructor in Line 1 executes because no value is passed to this variable. For `item2`, the constructor in Line 2 executes because only one parameter, which is of type `string`, is passed, and it matches with the constructor in Line 2. For `item3`, the constructor in Line 3 executes because three parameters are passed to `item3`, and they match with the constructor in Line 3. Similarly, for `item4`, the constructor in Line 4 executes (see Figure 10-7).

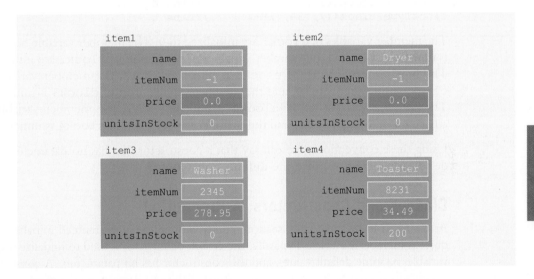

FIGURE 10-7 Effect of constructors on objects

NOTE   If the values passed to a class object do not match the parameters of any constructor and if no type conversion is possible, a compile-time error will be generated.

Constructors and Default Parameters

A constructor can also have default parameters. In such cases, the rules for declaring formal parameters are the same as those for declaring default formal parameters in a function. Moreover, actual parameters to a constructor with default parameters are passed according to the rules for functions with default parameters. (Chapter 6 discusses functions with default parameters.) Using the rules for defining default parameters, in the definition of the **class** clockType, you can replace both constructors using the following statement. (Recall that in the function prototype, the name of a formal parameter is optional.)

```
clockType clockType(int = 0, int = 0, int = 0);    //Line 1
```

In the implementation file, the definition of this constructor is the same as the definition of the constructor with parameters.

If you replace the constructors of the **class** clockType with the constructor in Line 1 (the constructor with the default parameters), then you can declare clockType objects with zero, one, two, or three arguments, as follows:

```
clockType clock1;               //Line 2
clockType clock2(5);            //Line 3
clockType clock3(12, 30);       //Line 4
clockType clock4(7, 34, 18);    //Line 5
```

The member variables of clock1 are initialized to 0. The member variable hr of clock2 is initialized to 5, and the member variables min and sec of clock2 are initialized to 0. The member variable hr of clock3 is initialized to 12, the member variable min of clock3 is initialized to 30, and the member variable sec of clock3 is initialized to 0. The member variable hr of clock4 is initialized to 7, the member variable min of clock4 is initialized to 34, and the member variable sec of clock4 is initialized to 18.

Using these conventions, we can say that a constructor that has no parameters, or has all default parameters, is called the **default constructor**.

Classes and Constructors: A Precaution

As discussed in the preceding section, constructors provide guaranteed initialization of the object's member variables. Typically, the default constructor is used to initialize the member variables to some default values, and this constructor has no parameters. A constructor with parameters is used to initialize the member variables to some specific values.

We have seen that if a class has no constructor(s), then the object created is uninitialized because C++ does not automatically initialize variables when they are declared. In reality, if a class has no constructor(s), then C++ automatically provides the default constructor. However, this default constructor does not do anything. The object declared is still uninitialized.

The important things to remember about classes and constructors are the following:

- If a class has no constructor(s), C++ *automatically provides* the default constructor. However, the object declared is still uninitialized.

- On the other hand, suppose a class, say, dummyClass, includes constructor(s) with parameter(s) and does not include the default constructor. In this case, C++ *does not* provide the default constructor for the class dummyClass. Therefore, when an object of the class dummyClass is declared, we must include the appropriate arguments in its declaration.

The following code further explains this. Consider the definition of the following class:

```
class dummyClass
{
public:
    void print() const;

    dummyClass(int dX, int dY);

private:
    int x;
    int y;
};
```

The class dummyClass *does not* have the default constructor. It has a constructor with parameters. Given this definition of the class dummyClass, the following object declaration is legal:

```
dummyClass myObject(10, 25);   //object declaration is legal
```

However, because the class dummyClass does not contain the default constructor, the following declaration is incorrect and would generate a syntax error:

```
dummyClass dummyObject;   //incorrect object declaration
```

Therefore, to avoid such pitfalls, if a class has constructor(s), the class should also include the default constructor.

Arrays of Class Objects (Variables) and Constructors

If a class has constructors and you declare an array of that class's objects, the class should have the default constructor. The default constructor is typically used to initialize each (array) class object.

For example, if you declare an array of 100 class objects, then it is impractical (if not impossible) to specify different constructors for each component. (We will further clarify this at the end of this section.)

Suppose that you have 100 employees who are paid on an hourly basis, and you need to keep track of their arrival and departure times. You can declare two arrays—arrivalTimeEmp and departureTimeEmp—of 100 components each, wherein each component is an object of type clockType.

Consider the following statement:

```
clockType arrivalTimeEmp[100];                    //Line 1
```

The statement in Line 1 creates the array of objects arrivalTimeEmp[0], arrivalTimeEmp[1], ..., arrivalTimeEmp[99], as shown in Figure 10-8.

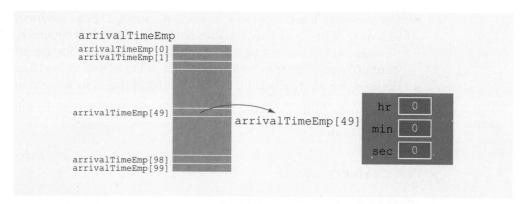

FIGURE 10-8 Array `arrivalTimeEmp`

You can now use the functions of the **class** `clockType` to manipulate the time for each employee. For example, the following statement sets the arrival time, that is, `hr`, `min`, and `sec`, of the 50th employee to 8, 5, and 10, respectively (see Figure 10-9).

```
arrivalTimeEmp[49].setTime(8, 5, 10);          //Line 2
```

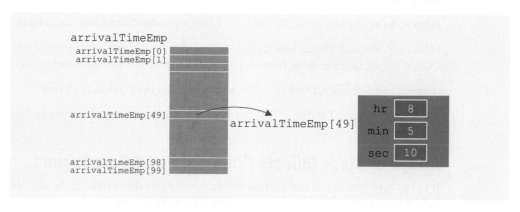

FIGURE 10-9 Array `arrivalTimeEmp` after setting the time of employee 49

To output the arrival time of each employee, you can use a loop, such as the following:

```
for (int j = 0; j < 100; j++)                  //Line 3
{
    cout << "Employee " << (j + 1)
        << " arrival time: ";
    arrivalTimeEmp[j].printTime();             //Line 4
    cout << endl;
}
```

The statement in Line 4 outputs the arrival time of an employee in the form `hr:min:sec`.

To keep track of the departure time of each employee, you can use the array departureTimeEmp.

Similarly, you can use arrays to manage a list of names or other objects.

 NOTE

Before leaving our discussion of arrays of class objects, we would like to point out the following: The beginning of this section stated that if you declare an array of class objects and the class has constructor(s), then the class should have the default constructor. The compiler uses the default constructor to initialize the array of objects. If the array size is large, then it is impractical to specify a different constructor with parameters for each object. For a small-sized array, we can manage to specify a different constructor with parameters.

For example, the following statement declares clocks to be an array of two components. The member variables of the first component are initialized to 8, 35, and 42, respectively. The member variables of the second component are initialized to 6, 52, and 39, respectively.

```
clockType clocks[2] = {clockType(8, 35, 42), clockType(6, 52, 39)};
```

In fact, the expression clockType(8, 35, 42) creates an anonymous object of the class clockType; initializes its member variables to 8, 35, and 42, respectively; and then uses a member-wise copy to initialize the object clock[0].

Consider the following statement, which creates the object myClock and initializes its member variables to 10, 45, and 38, respectively. This is how we have been creating and initializing objects. In fact, the statement:

```
clockType myClock(10, 45, 38);
```

is equivalent to the statement:

```
clockType myClock = clockType(10, 45, 38);
```

However, the first statement is more efficient. It does not first require that an anonymous object be created and then member-wise copied in order to initialize myClock.

The main point that we are stressing here, and that we discussed in the preceding section, is the following: To avoid any pitfalls, if a class has constructor(s), it should also have the default constructor.

Destructors

Like constructors, destructors are also functions. Moreover, like constructors, a destructor does not have a type. That is, it is neither a value-returning function nor a void function. However, a class can have only one destructor, and the destructor has no parameters. The name of a destructor is the *tilde* character (~), followed by the name of the class. For example, the name of the destructor for the class clockType is:

```
~clockType();
```

The destructor automatically executes when the class object goes out of scope. The use of destructors is discussed in subsequent chapters.

Data Abstraction, Classes, and Abstract Data Types

For the car that we drive, most of us want to know how to start the car and drive it. Most people are not concerned with the complexity of how the engine works. By separating the design details of a car's engine from its use, the manufacturer helps the driver focus on how to drive the car. Our daily life has other similar examples. For the most part, we are concerned only with how to use certain items, rather than with how they work.

Separating the design details (that is, how the car's engine works) from its use is called **abstraction**. In other words, abstraction focuses on what the engine does and not on how it works. Thus, abstraction is the process of separating the logical properties from the implementation details. Driving the car is a logical property; the construction of the engine constitutes the implementation details. We have an abstract view of what the engine does but are not interested in the engine's actual implementation.

Abstraction can also be applied to data. Earlier sections of this chapter defined a data type clockType. The data type clockType has three member variables and the following basic operations:

1. Set the time.
2. Return the time.
3. Print the time.
4. Increment the time by one second.
5. Increment the time by one minute.
6. Increment the time by one hour.
7. Compare two times to see whether they are equal.

The actual implementation of the operations, that is, the definitions of the member functions of the class clockType, was postponed.

Data abstraction is defined as a process of separating the logical properties of the data from its implementation. The definition of clockType and its basic operations are the logical properties; the storing of clockType objects in the computer and the algorithms to perform these operations are the implementation details of clockType.

Abstract data type (ADT): A data type that separates the logical properties from the implementation details.

Like any other data type, an ADT has three things associated with it: the name of the ADT, called the **type name**; the set of values belonging to the ADT, called the **domain**; and the set of **operations** on the data. Following these conventions, we can define the clockType ADT as follows:

```
dataTypeName
    clockType
domain
    Each clockType value is a time of day in the form of hours,
    minutes, and seconds.
operations
    Set the time.
    Return the time.
    Print the time.
    Increment the time by one second.
    Increment the time by one minute.
    Increment the time by one hour.
    Compare the two times to see whether they are equal.
```

EXAMPLE 10-7

A list is defined as a set of values of the same type. Because all values in a list are of the same type, a convenient way to represent and process a list is to use an array. You can define a list as an ADT as follows:

```
dataTypeName
    listType
domain
    Every listType value is an array of, say, 1000 numbers
operations
    Check to see whether the list is empty.
    Check to see whether the list is full.
    Search the list for a given item.
    Delete an item from the list.
    Insert an item in the list.
    Sort the list.
    Destroy the list.
    Print the list.
```

The next obvious question is how to implement an ADT in a program. To implement an ADT, you must represent the data and write algorithms to perform the operations.

The previous section used classes to group data and functions together. Furthermore, our definition of a class consisted only of the specifications of the operations; functions to implement the operations were written separately. Thus, we see that classes are a convenient way to implement an ADT. In fact, in C++, classes were specifically designed to handle ADTs.

Next, we define the `class listType` to implement a list as an ADT. Typically in a list, not only do we store the elements, but we also keep track of the number of elements in the list. Therefore, our `class listType` has two member variables: one to store the elements and another to keep track of the number of elements in the list. The following `class`, `listType`, defines the list as an ADT.

```
class listType
{
public:
    bool isEmptyList() const;
    bool isFullList() const;
    int search(int searchItem) const;
    void insert(int newElement);
    void remove(int removeElement);
    void destroyList();
    void printList() const;
    listType(); //constructor

private:
    int list[1000];
    int length;
};
```

Figure 10-10 shows the UML class diagram of the `class listType`.

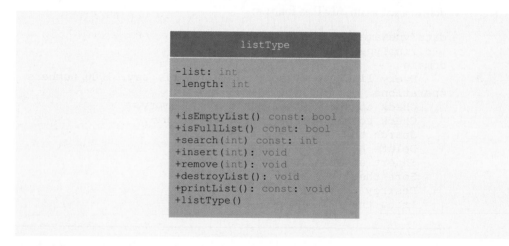

FIGURE 10-10   UML class diagram of the `class` listType

A struct Versus a class

Chapter 9 defined a `struct` as a fixed collection of components, wherein the components can be of different types. This definition of components in a `struct` included only member variables. However, a C++ `struct` is very similar to a C++ `class`. As with a class, members of a struct can also be functions, including constructors and a destructor. The only difference between a struct and a class is that, by default, all members of a struct are public, and all members of a class are private. You can use the member access specifier private in a struct to make a member private.

In C, the definition of a struct is similar to the definition of a struct in C++, as given in Chapter 9. Because C++ evolved from C, the standard C-structs are perfectly acceptable in C++. However, the definition of a struct in C++ was expanded to include member functions and constructors and destructors. In the future, because a class is a syntactically separate entity, specially designed to handle an ADT, the definition of a class may evolve in a completely different way than the definition of a C-like struct.

Both C++ classes and structs have the same capabilities. However, most programmers restrict their use of structures to adhere to their C-like structure form and thus do not use them to include member functions. In other words, if all of the member variables of a class are public and the class has no member functions, you typically use a struct to group these members. This is, in fact, how it is done in this book.

Information Hiding

The previous section defined the class clockType to implement the time in a program. We then wrote a program that used the class clockType. In fact, we combined the class clockType with the function definitions to implement the operations and the function main so as to complete the program. That is, the specification and implementation details of the class clockType were directly incorporated into the program.

Is it a good practice to include the specification and implementation details of a class in the program? Definitely not. There are several reasons for not doing so. Suppose the definition of the class and the definitions of the member functions are directly included in the user's program. The user then has direct access to the definition of the class and the definitions of the member functions. Therefore, the user can modify the operations in any way the user pleases. The user can also modify the member variables of an object in any way the user pleases. Thus, in this sense, the private member variables of an object are no longer private to the object.

If several programmers use the same object in a project and if they have direct access to the internal parts of the object, there is no guarantee that every programmer will use the same object in exactly the same way. Thus, we must hide the implementation details. The user should know only what the object does, not how it does it. Hiding the implementation details frees the user from having to fit this extra piece of code in the program. Also, by hiding the details, we can ensure that an object will be used in exactly the same way throughout the project. Furthermore, once an object has been written, debugged, and tested properly, it becomes (and remains) error-free.

This section discusses how to hide the implementation details of an object. For illustration purposes, we will use the **class** clockType.

To implement clockType in a program, the user must declare objects of type clockType and know which operations are allowed and what the operations do. So, the user must have access to the specification details. Because the user is not concerned with the implementation details, we must put those details in a separate file called an **implementation file**. Also, because the specification details can be too long, we must free the user from having to include them directly in the program. However, the user must be able to look at the specification details so that he or she can correctly call the functions, and so forth. We must, therefore, put the specification details in a separate file. The file that contains the specification details is called the **header file** (or **interface file**).

The implementation file contains the definitions of the functions to implement the operations of an object. This file contains, among other things (such as the preprocessor directives), the C++ statements. Because a C++ program can have only one function, main, the implementation file does not contain the function main. Only the user program contains the function main. Because the implementation file does not contain the function main, we cannot produce the executable code from this file. In fact, we produce what is called the object code from the implementation file. The user then links the object code produced by the implementation file with the object code of the program that uses the class to create the final executable code.

Finally, the header file has an extension h, whereas the implementation file has an extension cpp. Suppose that the specification details of the **class** clockType are in a file called clockType. The complete name of this file should then be clockType.h. If the implementation details of the **class** clockType are in a file—say, clockTypeImp—the name of this file must be clockTypeImp.cpp.

The file clockTypeImp.cpp contains only the definitions of the functions, not the definition of the class. Thus, to resolve the problem of an undeclared identifier (such as the function names and variable names), we include the header file clockType.h in the file clockTypeImp.cpp with the help of the include statement. The following include statement is required by any program that uses the **class** clockType, as well as by the implementation file that defines the operations for the **class** clockType:

```
#include "clockType.h"
```

Note that the header file clockType.h is enclosed in double quotation marks, not angular brackets. The header file clockType.h is called the user-defined header file. Typically, all user-defined header files are enclosed in double quotation marks, whereas the system-provided header files (such as iostream) are enclosed between angular brackets.

The implementation contains the definitions of the functions, and these definitions are hidden from the user because the user is typically provided *only* the object code.

However, the user of the class should be aware of what a particular function does and how to use it. Therefore, in the specification file with the function prototypes, we include comments that briefly describe the function and specify any preconditions and/or postconditions.

Precondition: A statement specifying the condition(s) that must be true before the function is called.

Postcondition: A statement specifying what is true after the function call is completed.

Following are the specification and implementation files for the **class** clockType:

```
//clockType.h, the specification file for the class clockType

class clockType
{
public:
    void  setTime(int  hours, int  minutes, int seconds);
      //Function to set the time.
      //The time is set according to the parameters.
      //Postcondition: hr = hours; min = minutes;
      //                sec = seconds;
      //                The function checks whether the
      //                values of hours, minutes, and seconds
      //                are valid. If a value is invalid, the
      //                default value 0 is assigned.

    void getTime(int& hours, int& minutes, int& seconds) const;
      //Function to return the time.
      //Postcondition: hours = hr; minutes = min;
      //                seconds = sec;

    void printTime() const;
      //Function to print the time.
      //Postcondition: The time is printed in the form
      //                hh:mm:ss.

    void incrementSeconds();
      //Function to increment the time by one second.
      //Postcondition: The time is incremented by one second.
      //                If the before-increment time is
      //                23:59:59, the time is reset to 00:00:00.

    void incrementMinutes();
      //Function to increment the time by one minute.
      //Postcondition: The time is incremented by one minute.
      //                If the before-increment time is
      //                23:59:53, the time is reset to 00:00:53.

    void incrementHours();
      //Function to increment the time by one hour.
      //Postcondition: The time is incremented by one hour.
```

```
//                     If the before-increment time is
//                     23:45:53, the time is reset to 00:45:53.

bool equalTime(const clockType& otherClock) const;
    //Function to compare the two times.
    //Postcondition: Returns true if this time is equal to
    //               otherClock; otherwise, returns false.

clockType(int hours, int minutes, int seconds);
    //Constructor with parameters.
    //The time is set according to the parameters.
    //Postcondition: hr = hours; min = minutes;
    //               sec = seconds;
    //               The constructor checks whether the
    //               values of hours, minutes, and seconds
    //               are valid. If a value is invalid, the
    //               default value 0 is assigned.

clockType();
    //Default constructor
    //The time is set to 00:00:00.
    //Postcondition: hr = 0; min = 0; sec = 0;

private:
    int hr;  //variable to store the hours
    int min; //variable to store the minutes
    int sec; //variable to store the seconds
};

//clockTypeImp.cpp, the implementation file

#include <iostream>
#include "clockType.h"

using namespace std;
    .
    .
    .

//Place the definitions of the member functions of the class
//clockType here.
    .
    .
    .
```

Next, we describe the user file containing the program that uses the class clockType.

```
//The user program that uses the class clockType

#include <iostream>
#include "clockType.h"
```

```
using namespace  std;
    .
    .
    .
//Place the definitions of the function main and the other
//user-defined functions here
    .
    .
    .
```

 NOTE To save space, we have not provided the complete details of the implementation file and the file that contains the user program. However, you can find these files and the specification (header) file at the Web site accompanying this book.

Executable Code

The previous section discussed how to hide the implementation details of a class. To use an object in a program, during execution, the program must be able to access the implementation details of the object (that is, the algorithms to implement the operations on the object). This section discusses how a client's program obtains access to the implementation details of an object. For illustration purposes, we will use the `class` `clockType`.

As explained previously, to use the `class` `clockType`, the program must include the header file `clockType.h` via the `include` statement. For example, the following program segment includes the header file `clockType.h`:

```
//Program test.cpp

#include "clockType.h"
    .
    .
    .
int main()
{
    .
    .
    .
}
```

The program `test.cpp` must include only the header file, not the implementation file. To create the executable code to run the program `test.cpp`, the following steps are required:

1. We separately compile the file `clockTypeImp.cpp` and create the object code file `clockTypeImp.obj`. The object code file contains the machine language code, but the code is not in an executable form.

Suppose that the command cc invokes the C++ compiler or linker, or both, on the computer's system command line. The command:

```
cc -c clockTypeImp.cpp
```

creates the object code file clockTypeImp.obj.

2. To create the executable code for the source code file test.cpp, we compile the source code file test.cpp, create the object code file test.obj, and then link the files test.obj and clockTypeImp.obj to create the executable file test.exe. The following command on the system command line creates the executable file test.exe:

```
cc test.cpp clockTypeImp.obj
```

NOTE

1. To create the object code file for any source code file, we use the command line option -c on the system command line. For example, to create the object code file for the source code file, called exercise.cpp, we use the following command on the system command line:

```
cc -c exercise.cpp
```

2. To link more than one object code file with a source code file, we list all of the object code files on the system command line. For example, to link A.obj and B.obj with the source code file test.cpp, we use the command:

```
cc test.cpp A.obj B.obj
```

3. If a source code file is modified, it must be recompiled.

4. If modifications in one source file affect other files, the other files must be recompiled and relinked.

5. The user must have access to the header file and the object code file. Access to the header file is needed to see what the objects do and how to use them. Access to the object code file is needed so that the user can link the program with the object code to produce an executable code. The user does not need access to the source code file containing the implementation details.

As stated in Chapter 1, IDEs Visual C++ 2008 Express, Visual C++ 2010 Express, Visual Studio 2010, and C++ Builder put the editor, compiler, and linker all into one package. With one command, the program is compiled and linked with the other necessary files. These systems also manage multiple-file programs in the form of a project. Thus, a project consists of several files, called the project files. These systems usually have a command, called **build**, **rebuild**, or **make**. (Check your system's documentation.) When the build, rebuild, or make command is applied to a project, the system automatically compiles and links all of the files required to create the executable code.

When one or more files in the project change, you can use these commands to recompile and relink the files.

More Examples of Classes

In this section, we give various examples of classes and how to use them in a program.

EXAMPLE 10-8

The following statements define the **class circleType** to implement the basic properties of a circle:

```
class circleType
{
public:
    void setRadius(double r);
        //Function to set the radius.
        //Postcondition: if (r >= 0) radius = r;
        //               otherwise radius = 0;

    double getRadius();
        //Function to return the radius.
        //Postcondition: The value of radius is returned.

    double area();
        //Function to return the area of a circle.
        //Postcondition: Area is calculated and returned.

    double circumference();
        //Function to return the circumference of a circle.
        //Postcondition: Circumference is calculated and returned.

    circleType(double r = 0);
        //Constructor with a default parameter.
        //Radius is set according to the parameter.
        //The default value of the radius is 0.0;
        //Postcondition: radius = r;

private:
    double radius;
};
```

The definitions of the member functions are as follows:

```
void circleType::setRadius(double r)
{
    if (r >= 0)
        radius = r;
    else
        radius = 0;
}
```

```cpp
double circleType::getRadius()
{
    return radius;
}

double circleType::area()
{
    return 3.1416 * radius * radius;
}

double circleType::circumference()
{
    return 2 * 3.1416 * radius;
}

circleType::circleType(double r)
{
    setRadius(r);
}
```

The following illustrates how to use the **class** circleType in a program:

```cpp
//The user program that uses the class circleType

#include <iostream>
#include <iomanip>
#include "circleType.h"

using namespace std;

int main()                                              //Line 1
{                                                       //Line 2
    circleType circle1(8);                              //Line 3
    circleType circle2;                                 //Line 4

    double radius;                                      //Line 5

    cout << fixed << showpoint << setprecision(2);      //Line 6

    cout << "Line 7: circle1 - "
         << "radius: " << circle1.getRadius()
         << ", area: " << circle1.area()
         << ", circumference: " << circle1.circumference()
         << endl;                                       //Line 7

    cout << "Line 8: circle2 - "
         << "radius: " << circle2.getRadius()
         << ", area: " << circle2.area()
         << ", circumference: " << circle2.circumference()
         << endl << endl;                               //Line 8

    cout << "Line 9: Enter the radius of a circle: ";   //Line 9
    cin >> radius;                                      //Line 10
    cout << endl;                                       //Line 11
```

```
        circle2.setRadius(radius);                            //Line 12

        cout << "Line 13: After setting the radius." << endl;  //Line 13
        cout << "Line 14: circle2 - "
             << "radius: " << circle2.getRadius()
             << ", area: " << circle2.area()
             << ", circumference: " << circle2.circumference()
             << endl;                                         //Line 14

        return 0;                                            //Line 15
}  //end main                                                //Line 16
```

Sample Run: In this sample run, the user input is shaded.

```
Line 7: circle1 - radius: 8.00, area: 201.06, circumference: 50.27
Line 8: circle2 - radius: 0.00, area: 0.00, circumference: 0.00

Line 9: Enter the radius of a circle: 5.5

Line 13: After setting the radius.
Line 14: circle2 - radius: 5.50, area: 95.03, circumference: 34.56
```

The preceding program works as follows. The statements in Lines 3 and 4 create the objects circle1 and circle2. The radius of circle1 is set to 8; and the radius of circle2 is set to 0 by using the default value by the constructor. The statements in Lines 7 and 8 output the data of circle1 and circle2. The statements in Lines 9 and 10 prompt the user to enter the radius of a circle and store the radius in the variable radius. The statement in Line 12 uses the member function setRadius and the value of radius to set the radius of circle2. The statement in Line 14 ouputs the (new) data of circle2.

EXAMPLE 10-9

In Example 6-4, in Chapter 6, the function rollDice rolls a pair of dice until the sum of the numbers rolled is a given number and returns the number of times the dice are rolled to get the desired sum. In fact, we can design a class that implements the basic properties of a die. Consider the definition of the following class die.

```
class die
{
public:
    die();
        //Default constructor
        //Sets the default number rolled by a die to 1

    int roll();
        //Function to roll a die.
        //This function uses a random number generator to randomly
        //generate a number between 1 and 6, and stores the number
        //in the instance variable num and returns the number.
```

```
    int getNum() const;
        //Function to return the number on the top face of the die.
        //Returns the value of the instance variable num.

private
    int num;
};
```

The definitions of the member functions are given next.

```
die::die()
{
    num = 1;
    srand(time(0));
}

int die::roll()
{
    num = rand() % 6 + 1;

    return num;
}

int die::getNum() const
{
    return num;
}
```

The following program shows how to use the **class die** in a program:

```
//The user program that uses the class die

#include <iostream>
#include "die.h"

using namespace std;

int main()                                                      //Line 1
{                                                               //Line 2
    die die1;                                                   //Line 3
    die die2;

    cout << "Line 4: die1: " << die1.getNum() << endl;  //Line 4

    cout << "Line 5: die2: " << die2.getNum() << endl;  //Line 5

    cout << "Line 6: After rolling die1: "
         << die1.roll() << endl;                                //Line 6

    cout << "Line 7: After rolling die2: "
         << die2.roll() << endl;                                //Line 7
    cout << "Line 8: The sum of the numbers rolled"
         << " by the dice is: "
         << die1.getNum() + die2.getNum() << endl;             //Line 8
```

```
        cout << "Line 9: After again rolling, the sum of "
             << "the numbers rolled is: "
             << die1.roll() + die2.roll() << endl;            //Line 9

        return 0;                                             //Line 10
} //end main                                                  //Line 11
```

Sample Run:

```
Line 4: die1: 1
Line 5: die2: 1
Line 6: After rolling die1: 3
Line 7: After rolling die2: 4
Line 8: The sum of the numbers rolled by the dice is: 7
Line 9: After again rolling, the sum of the numbers rolled is: 5
```

The preceding program works as follows. The statements in Lines 2 and 3 create the objects die1 and die2, and, using the default constructor, set both the dice to 1. The statements in Lines 4 and 5 output the number of both the dice. The statement in Line 6 rolls die1 and outputs the number rolled. Similarly, the statement in Line 7 rolls die2 and outputs the number rolled. The statement in Line 8 outputs the sum of the numbers rolled by die1 and die2. The statement in Line 9 again rolls both the dice and outputs the sum of the numbers rolled.

Example 10-10 further illustrates how classes are designed and implemented. The **class** personType that is designed in Example 10-10 is very useful; we will use this class in subsequent chapters.

EXAMPLE 10-10

The most common attributes of a person are the person's first and last name. The typical operations on a person's name are to set the name and print the name. The following statements define a class with these properties.

```
#include <string>

using namespace std;

class personType
{
public:
    void print() const;
      //Function to output the first name and last name
      //in the form firstName lastName.

    void setName(string first, string last);
      //Function to set firstName and lastName according
      //to the parameters.
      //Postcondition: firstName = first; lastName = last;
```

```
    string getFirstName() const;
      //Function to return the first name.
      //Postcondition: The value of firstName is returned.

    string getLastName() const;
      //Function to return the last name.
      //Postcondition: The value of lastName is returned.

    personType(string first = "", string last = "");
      //Constructor
      //Sets firstName and lastName according to the parameters.
      //The default values of the parameters are null strings.
      //Postcondition: firstName = first; lastName = last;

private:
    string firstName; //variable to store the first name
    string lastName;  //variable to store the last name
};
```

Figure 10-11 shows the UML class diagram of the **class** personType.

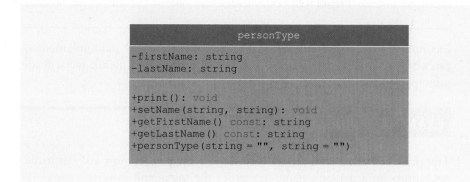

FIGURE 10-11   UML class diagram of the **class** personType

We now give the definitions of the member functions of the **class** personType.

```
void personType::print() const
{
    cout << firstName << " " << lastName;
}

void personType::setName(string first, string last)
{
    firstName = first;
    lastName = last;
}
```

```
string personType::getFirstName() const
{
    return firstName;
}

string personType::getLastName() const
{
    return lastName;
}

    //constructor
personType::personType(string first, string last)
{
    firstName = first;
    lastName = last;
}
```

Static Members of a Class

 NOTE This section may be skipped without any loss of continuation.

In Chapter 6, we described two types of variables: automatic and `static`. Recall that if a local variable of a function is `static`, it exists between function calls. Similar to `static` variables, a class can have `static` members, functions, or variables. Let us note the following about the `static` members of a class:

- If a function of a class is `static`, in the class definition it is declared using the keyword `static` in its heading.
- If a member variable of a class is `static`, it is declared using the keyword `static`, as discussed in Chapter 6 and also illustrated in Example 10-11.
- A `public static` member, function, or variable of a class can be accessed using the class name and the scope resolution operator.

Example 10-11 clarifies the effect of the keyword `static`.

EXAMPLE 10-11

Consider the following definition of the `class` illustrate:

```
class illustrate
{
public:
    static int count;    //public static variable
```

```
    void print() const;
      //Function to output x, y, and count.

    void setX(int a);
      //Function to set x.
      //Postcondition: x = a;

    static void incrementY();
      //static function
      //Function to increment y by 1.
      //Postcondition: y = y + 1

    illustrate(int a = 0);
      //constructor
      //Postcondition: x = a;
      //                     If no value is specified for a, x = 0;

private:
    int x;
    static int y;   //private static variable
};
```

Suppose that the static member variables and the definitions of the member functions of the class illustrate are as follows. (These statements are all placed in the implementation file. Also, notice that all static member variables are initialized, as shown below.)

```
int illustrate::count = 0;
int illustrate::y = 0;

void illustrate::print() const
{
    cout << "x = " << x << ", y = " << y
         << ", count = " << count << endl;
}

void illustrate::setX(int a)
{
    x = a;
}

void illustrate::incrementY()
{
    y++;
}

illustrate::illustrate(int a)
{
    x = a;
}
```

Because the function `incrementY` is `static` and `public`, the following statement is legal:

```
illustrate::incrementY();
```

Similarly, because the member variable `count` is `static` and `public`, the following statement is legal:

```
illustrate::count++;
```

Next, we elaborate on `static` member variables a bit more. Suppose that you have a `class`, say, `myClass`, with member variables (`static` as well as non-`static`). When you create objects of type `myClass`, only non-`static` member variables of the `class` `myClass` become the member variables of each object. For each `static` member variable of a `class`, C++ allocates only one memory space. All `myClass` objects refer to the same memory space. In fact, `static` member variables of a `class` *exist* even when no object of that `class` type exists. You can access the `public` `static` member variables outside of the `class`, as explained earlier in this section.

Next, we explain how memory space is allocated for `static` and non-`static` member variables of a class.

Suppose that you have the `class` `illustrate`, as given in Example 10-10. Memory space then exists for the `static` member variables `y` and `count`.

Consider the following statements:

```
illustrate illusObject1(3);    //Line 1
illustrate illusObject2(5);    //Line 2
```

The statements in Lines 1 and 2 declare `illusObject1` and `illusObject2` to be `illustrate` type objects (see Figure 10-12).

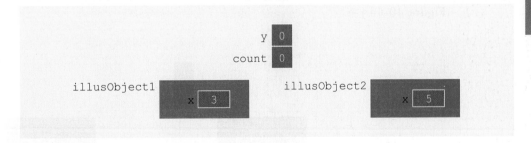

FIGURE 10-12 `illusObject1` and `illusObject2`

Now, consider the following statements:

```
illustrate::incrementY();
illustrate::count++;
```

After these statements execute, the objects and static members are as shown in Figure 10-13.

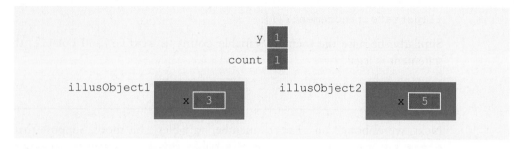

FIGURE 10-13 `illusObject1` and `illusObject2` after the statements `illustrate::incrementY();` and `illustrate::count++;` execute

The output of the statement:

`illusObject1.print();`

is:

`x = 3, y = 1, count = 1`

Similarly, the output of the statement:

`illusObject2.print();`

is:

`x = 5, y = 1, count = 1`

Now consider the statement:

`illustrate::count++;`

After this statement executes, the objects and static members are as shown in Figure 10-14.

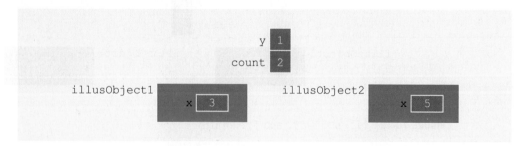

FIGURE 10-14 `illusObject1` and `illusObject2` after the statement `illustrate::count++;` executes

The output of the statements:

```
illusObject1.print();
illusObject2.print();
```

is:

```
x = 3, y = 1, count = 2
x = 5, y = 1, count = 2
```

The program in Example 10-12 further illustrates how `static` members of a class work.

EXAMPLE 10-12

```
#include <iostream>

#include "illustrate.h"

using namespace std;

int main()
{
    illustrate illusObject1(3);                       //Line 1
    illustrate illusObject2(5);                       //Line 2

    illustrate::incrementY();                         //Line 3
    illustrate::count++;                              //Line 4
    illusObject1.print();                             //Line 5
    illusObject2.print();                             //Line 6
    cout << "Line 7: ***Increment y using "
         << "illusObject1***" << endl;                //Line 7

    illusObject1.incrementY();                        //Line 8
    illusObject1.setX(8);                             //Line 9
    illusObject1.print();                             //Line 10
    illusObject2.print();                             //Line 11

    cout << "Line 12: ***Increment y using "
         << "illusObject2***" << endl;                //Line 12

    illusObject2.incrementY();                        //Line 13
    illusObject2.setX(23);                            //Line 14
    illusObject1.print();                             //Line 15
    illusObject2.print();                             //Line 16

    return 0;
}
```

1
0

Sample Run:

```
x = 3, y = 1, count = 1
x = 5, y = 1, count = 1
Line 7: ***Increment y using illusObject1***
x = 8, y = 2, count = 1
x = 5, y = 2, count = 1
Line 12: ***Increment y using illusObject2***
x = 8, y = 3, count = 1
x = 23, y = 3, count = 1
```

The preceding program works as follows. The `static` member variables y and count are initialized to 0. The statement in Line 1 declares `illusObject1` to be an object of the `class` `illustrate` and initializes its member variable x to 3. The statement in Line 2 declares `illusObject2` to be an object of the `class` `illustrate` and initializes its member variable x to 5.

The statement in Line 3 uses the name of the `class` `illustrate` and the function `incrementY` to increment y. Now, count is a `public` `static` member of the `class` `illustrate`. So the statement in Line 4 uses the name of the `class` `illustrate` to directly access count and increments it by 1. The statements in Lines 5 and 6 output the data stored in the objects `illusObject1` and `illusObject2`. Notice that the value of y for both objects is the same. Similarly, the value of count for both objects is the same.

The statement in Line 7 is an output statement. The statement in Line 8 uses the object `illusObject1` and the function `incrementY` to increment y. The statement in Line 9 sets the value of the member variable x of `illusObject1` to 8. Lines 10 and 11 output the data stored in the objects `illusObject1` and `illusObject2`. Notice that the value of y for both objects is the same. Similarly, the value of count for both objects is the same. Moreover, notice that the statement in Line 9 changes only the value of the member variable x of `illusObject1` because x is *not* a `static` member of the `class` `illustrate`.

The statement in Line 13 uses the object `illusObject2` and the function `incrementY` to increment y. The statement in Line 14 sets the value of the member variable x of `illusObject2` to 23. Lines 15 and 16 output the data stored in the objects `illusObject1` and `illusObject2`. Notice that the value of y for both objects is the same. Similarly, the value of count for both objects is the same. Moreover, notice that the statement in Line 14 changes only the value of the member variable x of `illusObject2`, because x is *not* a `static` member of the `class` `illustrate`.

NOTE   Here are some additional comments on `static` members of a class. As you have seen in this section, a `static` member function of a class does not need any object to be invoked. It can be called using the name of the class and the scope resolution operator, as illustrated. There-fore, a `static` member function cannot use anything that depends on a calling object. In other words, in the definition of a `static` member function, you cannot use a non-`static` member variable or a non-`static` function unless there is an object declared locally that accesses the non-`static` member variable or the non-`static` member function.

Let us again consider the `class  illustrate`, as defined in Example 10-11. This class contains both `static` and non-`static` member variables. When we declare objects of this class, each object has its own copy of the member variable `x`, which is non-`static`, and all objects share the member variables `y` and `count`, which are `static`. Earlier in this chapter, we defined the terminology instance variables of a class using the `class clockType`. However, at that point, we did not discuss `static` member variables of a class. A class can have `static` as well as non-`static` member variables. We can, therefore, make the general statement that non-`static` member variables of a class are called the instance variables of the class.

PROGRAMMING EXAMPLE: Juice Machine

**Watch
the Video**

A common place to buy juice is from a machine. A new juice machine has been purchased for the gym, but it is not working properly. The machine sells the following types of juices: orange, apple, mango, and strawberry–banana. You have been asked to write a program for this juice machine so that it can be put into operation.

The program should do the following:

1. Show the customer the different products sold by the juice machine.
2. Let the customer make the selection.
3. Show the customer the cost of the item selected.
4. Accept money from the customer.
5. Release the item.

Input   The item selection and the cost of the item.

Output   The selected item.

PROBLEM
ANALYSIS
AND
ALGORITHM
DESIGN

A juice machine has two main components: a built-in cash register and several dispensers to hold and release the products.

1
0

Cash Register   Let us first discuss the properties of a cash register. The register has some cash on hand, it accepts the amount from the customer, and if the amount deposited is more than the cost of the item, then—if possible—it returns the change. For simplicity, we assume that the user deposits the money greater than or equal to the cost of the product. The cash register should also be able to show to the juice machine's owner the amount of money in the register at any given time. The following class defines the properties of a cash register:

```
class cashRegister
{
public:
    int getCurrentBalance() const;
    //Function to show the current amount in the cash
    //register.
    //Postcondition: The value of cashOnHand is returned.

    void acceptAmount(int amountIn);
    //Function to receive the amount deposited by
    //the customer and update the amount in the register.
    //Postcondition: cashOnHand = cashOnHand + amountIn;

    cashRegister(int cashIn = 500);
    //Constructor
    //Sets the cash in the register to a specific amount.
    //Postcondition: cashOnHand = cashIn;
    //               If no value is specified when the
    //               object is declared, the default value
    //               assigned to cashOnHand is 500.

private:
    int cashOnHand;   //variable to store the cash
                      //in the register
};
```

Figure 10-15 shows the UML class diagram of the `class` `cashRegister`.

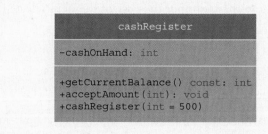

FIGURE 10-15 UML class diagram of the `class` `cashRegister`

Next, we give the definitions of the functions to implement the operations of the class cashRegister. The definitions of these functions are very simple and easy to follow.

The function getCurrentBalance shows the current amount in the cash register. It returns the value of the private member variable cashOnHand. So its definition is:

```cpp
int cashRegister::getCurrentBalance() const
{
    return cashOnHand;
}
```

The function acceptAmount accepts the amount of money deposited by the customer. It updates the cash in the register by adding the amount deposited by the customer to the previous amount in the cash register. Essentially, the definition of this function is:

```cpp
void cashRegister::acceptAmount(int amountIn)
{
    cashOnHand = cashOnHand + amountIn;
}
```

In the definition of the class cashRegister, the constructor is declared with a default value. Therefore, if the user does not specify any value when the object is declared, the default value is used to initialize the member variable cashOnHand. Recall that because we have specified the default value for the constructor's parameter in the definition of the class, in the heading of the definition of the constructor, we do not specify the default value. The definition of the constructor is as follows:

```cpp
cashRegister::cashRegister(int cashIn)
{
    if (cashIn >= 0)
        cashOnHand = cashIn;
    else
        cashOnHand = 500;
}
```

Note that the definition of the constructor checks for valid values of the parameter cashIn. If the value of cashIn is less than 0, the value assigned to the member variable cashOnHand is 500.

Dispenser The dispenser releases the selected item if it is not empty. It should show the number of items in the dispenser and the cost of the item. The following class defines the properties of a dispenser. Let us call this class dispenserType:

```cpp
class dispenserType
{
public:
    int getNoOfItems() const;
    //Function to show the number of items in the machine.
    //Postcondition: The value of numberOfItems is returned.
```

```
    int getCost() const;
        //Function to show the cost of the item.
        //Postcondition: The value of cost is returned.

    void makeSale();
        //Function to reduce the number of items by 1.
        //Postcondition: numberOfItems--;

    dispenserType(int setNoOfItems = 50, int setCost = 50);
        //Constructor
        //Sets the cost and number of items in the dispenser
        //to the values specified by the user.
        //Postcondition: numberOfItems = setNoOfItems;
        //                cost = setCost;
        //                If no value is specified for a
        //                parameter, then its default value is
        //                assigned to the corresponding member
        //                variable.

private:
    int numberOfItems;    //variable to store the number of
                          //items in the dispenser
    int cost;  //variable to store the cost of an item
};
```

Figure 10-16 shows the UML class diagram of the `class dispenserType`.

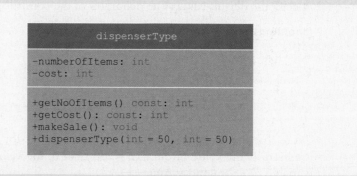

FIGURE 10-16 UML class diagram of the `class dispenserType`

Because the juice machine sells four types of items, we shall declare four objects of type `dispenserType`. For example, the statement:

`dispenserType apple(100, 65);`

declares `apple` to be an object of type `dispenserType`, sets the number of apple juice bottles in the dispenser to 100, and sets the cost of each apple juice bottle to 65 cents (see Figure 10-17).

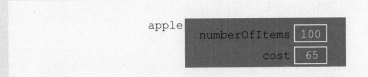

FIGURE 10-17 Object `apple`

Next, we discuss the definitions of the functions to implement the operations of the `class dispenserType`.

The function `getNoOfItems` returns the number of items of a particular product. Because the number of items currently in the dispenser is stored in the `private` member variable `numberOfItems`, the function returns the value of `numberOfItems`. The definition of this function is:

```
int dispenserType::getNoOfItems() const
{
    return numberOfItems;
}
```

The function `getCost` returns the cost of a product. Because the cost of a product is stored in the `private` member variable `cost`, the function returns the value of `cost`. The definition of this function is:

```
int dispenserType::getCost() const
{
    return cost;
}
```

When a product is sold, the number of items in that dispenser is reduced by 1. There-fore, the function `makeSale` reduces the number of items in the dispenser by 1. That is, it decrements the value of the `private` member variable `numberOfItems` by 1. The definition of this function is:

```
void dispenserType::makeSale()
{
    numberOfItems--;
}
```

The definition of the constructor checks for valid values of the parameters. If these values are less than 0, the default values are assigned to the member variables. The definition of the constructor is:

```
    //constructor
dispenserType::dispenserType(int setNoOfItems, int setCost)
{
    if (setNoOfItems >= 0)
        numberOfItems = setNoOfItems;
    else
        numberOfItems = 50;
```

```
        if (setCost >= 0)
            cost = setCost;
        else
            cost = 50;
    }
```

MAIN PROGRAM

When the program executes, it must do the following:

1. Show the different products sold by the juice machine.
2. Show how to select a particular product.
3. Show how to terminate the program.

Furthermore, these instructions must be displayed after processing each selection (except exiting the program) so that the user need not remember what to do if he or she wants to buy two or more items. Once the user has made the appropriate selection, the juice machine must act accordingly. If the user has opted to buy a product and that product is available, the juice machine should show the cost of the product and ask the user to deposit the money. If the amount deposited is at least the cost of the item, the juice machine should sell the item and display an appropriate message.

This discussion translates into the following algorithm:

1. Show the selection to the customer.
2. Get the selection.
3. If the selection is valid and the dispenser corresponding to the selection is not empty, sell the product.

We divide this program into three functions: showSelection, sellProduct, and main.

showSelection

This function displays the information necessary to help the user select and buy a product. This definition of the function showSelection is:

```
void showSelection()
{
    cout << "*** Welcome to Shelly's Juice Shop ***" << endl;
    cout << "To select an item, enter " << endl;
    cout << "1 for orange juice" << endl;
    cout << "2 for apple juice" << endl;
    cout << "3 for mango juice" << endl;
    cout << "4 for strawberry banana juice" << endl;
    cout << "9 to exit" << endl;
}//end showSelection
```

sellProduct

This function attempts to sell the product selected by the customer. Therefore, it must have access to the dispenser holding the product. The first thing that this function does is check whether the dispenser holding the product is empty. If the dispenser is empty, the function informs the customer that this product is sold out. If the dispenser is not empty, it tells the user to deposit the necessary amount to buy the product.

If the user does not deposit enough money to buy the product, sellProduct tells the user how much additional money must be deposited. If the user fails to deposit enough money in two tries to buy the product, the function simply returns the money. (Programming Exercise 11, at the end of this chapter, asks you to revise the definition of the function sellProduct so that it keeps asking the user to enter the additional amount as long as the user has not entered enough money to buy the product.) If the amount deposited by the user is sufficient, it accepts the money and sells the product. Selling the product means to decrement the number of items in the dispenser by 1 and to update the money in the cash register by adding the cost of the product. (Because this program does not return the extra money deposited by the customer, the cash register is updated by adding the money entered by the user.)

From this discussion, it is clear that the function sellProduct must have access to the dispenser holding the product (to decrement the number of items in the dispenser by 1 and to show the cost of the item) as well as the cash register (to update the cash). Therefore, this function has two parameters: one corresponding to the dispenser and the other corresponding to the cash register. Furthermore, both parameters must be referenced.

In pseudocode, the algorithm for this function is:

1. If the dispenser is not empty,

    a. Show and prompt the customer to enter the cost of the item.

    b. Get the amount entered by the customer.

    c. If the amount entered by the customer is less than the cost of the product,

        i. Show and prompt the customer to enter the additional amount.

        ii. Calculate the total amount entered by the customer.

    d. If the amount entered by the customer is at least the cost of the product,

        i. Update the amount in the cash register.

        ii. Sell the product—that is, decrement the number of items in the dispenser by 1.

        iii. Display an appropriate message.

    e. If the amount entered by the user is less than the cost of the item, return the amount.

2. If the dispenser is empty, tell the user that this product is sold out.

This definition of the function sellProduct is:

```
void sellProduct(dispenserType& product,
                 cashRegister& pCounter)
```

```
{
    int amount;  //variable to hold the amount entered
    int amount2; //variable to hold the extra amount needed

    if (product.getNoOfItems() > 0) //if the dispenser is not
                                    //empty
    {
        cout << "Please deposit " << product.getCost()
            << " cents" << endl;
        cin >> amount;

        if (amount < product.getCost())
        {
            cout << "Please deposit another "
                << product.getCost()- amount
                << " cents" << endl;
            cin >> amount2;
            amount = amount + amount2;
        }

        if (amount >= product.getCost())
        {
            pCounter.acceptAmount(amount);
            product.makeSale();
            cout << "Collect your item at the bottom and "
                << "enjoy." << endl;
        }
        else
            cout << "The amount is not enough. "
                << "Collect what you deposited." << endl;

        cout << "*-*-*-*-*-*-*-*-*-*-*-*-*-*-*-*-*-*-*-*-*"
            << endl << endl;
    }
    else
        cout << "Sorry, this item is sold out." << endl;
}//end sellProduct
```

Now that we have described the functions `showSelection` and `sellProduct`, the function `main` is described next.

main The algorithm for the function `main` is as follows:

1. Create the cash register—that is, declare an object of type `cashRegister`.

2. Create four dispensers—that is, declare four objects of type `dispenserType` and initialize these objects. For example, the statement:

   `dispenserType orange(100, 50);`

   creates a dispenser object, `orange`, to hold the juice. The number of items in the dispenser is 100, and the cost of an item is 50 cents.

3. Declare additional variables as necessary.

4. Show the selection; call the function `showSelection`.

5. Get the selection.

6. While not done (a selection of 9 exits the program),

   a. Sell the product; call the function `sellProduct`.

   b. Show the selection; call the function `showSelection`.

   c. Get the selection.

The definition of the function `main` is as follows:

```cpp
int main()
{
    cashRegister counter;
    dispenserType orange(100, 50);
    dispenserType apple(100, 65);
    dispenserType mango(75, 80);
    dispenserType strawberry banana(100, 85);

    int choice;   //variable to hold the selection

    showSelection();
    cin >> choice;

    while (choice != 9)
    {
        switch (choice)
        {
        case 1:
            sellProduct(orange, counter);
            break;
        case 2:
            sellProduct(apple, counter);
            break;
        case 3:
            sellProduct(mango, counter);
            break;
        case 4:
            sellProduct(strawberry banana, counter);
            break;
        default :
            cout << "Invalid selection." << endl;
        }//end switch

        showSelection();
        cin >> choice;
    }//end while

    return 0;

}//end main
```

COMPLETE PROGRAM LISTING

In the previous sections, we designed the classes to implement cash registers and dispensers to implement a juice machine. In this section, for the sake of completeness, we give complete definitions of the classes, the implementation file, and the user program to implement a juice machine.

```
//**********************************************************
// Author: D.S. Malik
//
// class cashRegister
// This class specifies the members to implement a cash
// register.
//**********************************************************

class cashRegister
{
public:
    int getCurrentBalance() const;
        //Function to show the current amount in the cash
        //register.
        //Postcondition: The value of cashOnHand is returned.

    void acceptAmount(int amountIn);
        //Function to receive the amount deposited by
        //the customer and update the amount in the register.
        //Postcondition: cashOnHand = cashOnHand + amountIn;

    cashRegister(int cashIn = 500);
        //Constructor
        //Sets the cash in the register to a specific amount.
        //Postcondition: cashOnHand = cashIn;
        //               If no value is specified when the
        //               object is declared, the default value
        //               assigned to cashOnHand is 500.

private:
    int cashOnHand;      //variable to store the cash
                         //in the register
};

//**********************************************************
// Author: D.S. Malik
//
// class dispenserType
// This class specifies the members to implement a dispenser.
//**********************************************************

class dispenserType
{
public:
    int getNoOfItems() const;
        //Function to show the number of items in the machine.
        //Postcondition: The value of numberOfItems is returned.
```

```cpp
    int getCost() const;
        //Function to show the cost of the item.
        //Postcondition: The value of cost is returned.

    void makeSale();
        //Function to reduce the number of items by 1.
        //Postcondition: numberOfItems--;

    dispenserType(int setNoOfItems = 50, int setCost = 50);
        //Constructor
        //Sets the cost and number of items in the dispenser
        //to the values specified by the user.
        //Postcondition: numberOfItems = setNoOfItems;
        //               cost = setCost;
        //               If no value is specified for a
        //               parameter, then its default value is
        //               assigned to the corresponding member
        //               variable.

private:
    int numberOfItems;      //variable to store the number of
                            //items in the dispenser
    int cost;  //variable to store the cost of an item
};


//***********************************************************
// Author: D.S. Malik
//
// Implementation file juiceMachineImp.cpp
// This file contains the definitions of the functions to
// implement the operations of the classes cashRegister and
// dispenserType.
//***********************************************************

#include <iostream>
#include "juiceMachine.h"

using namespace std;

int cashRegister::getCurrentBalance() const
{
    return cashOnHand;
}

void cashRegister::acceptAmount(int amountIn)
{
    cashOnHand = cashOnHand + amountIn;
}

cashRegister::cashRegister(int cashIn)
{
    if (cashIn >= 0)
        cashOnHand = cashIn;
    else
        cashOnHand = 500;
}
```

```cpp
int dispenserType::getNoOfItems() const
{
    return numberOfItems;
}

int dispenserType::getCost() const
{
    return cost;
}

void dispenserType::makeSale()
{
    numberOfItems--;
}

dispenserType::dispenserType(int setNoOfItems, int setCost)
{
    if (setNoOfItems >= 0)
        numberOfItems = setNoOfItems;
    else
        numberOfItems = 50;

    if (setCost >= 0)
        cost = setCost;
    else
        cost = 50;
}
```

Main Program

```cpp
//****************************************************
// Author: D.S. Malik
//
// This program uses the classes cashRegister and
// dispenserType to implement a juice machine.
//****************************************************

#include <iostream>
#include "juiceMachine.h"

using namespace std;

void showSelection();
void sellProduct(dispenserType& product,
                 cashRegister& pCounter);

int main()
{
    cashRegister counter;
    dispenserType orange(100, 50);
    dispenserType apple(100, 65);
    dispenserType mango(75, 80);
    dispenserType strawberry banana(100, 85);

    int choice;  //variable to hold the selection

    showSelection();
    cin >> choice;
```

```cpp
    while (choice != 9)
    {
        switch (choice)
        {
        case 1:
            sellProduct(orange, counter);
            break;
        case 2:
            sellProduct(apple, counter);
            break;
        case 3:
            sellProduct(mango, counter);
            break;
        case 4:
            sellProduct(strawberry banana, counter);
            break;
        default:
            cout << "Invalid selection." << endl;
        }//end switch
        showSelection();
        cin >> choice;
    }//end while

    return 0;
}//end main

void showSelection()
{
    cout << "*** Welcome to Shelly's Juice Shop ***" << endl;
    cout << "To select an item, enter " << endl;
    cout << "1 for orange juice" << endl;
    cout << "2 for apple juice" << endl;
    cout << "3 for mango juice" << endl;
    cout << "4 for strawberry banana" << endl;
    cout << "9 to exit" << endl;
}//end showSelection

void sellProduct(dispenserType& product,
                 cashRegister& pCounter)
{
    int amount;  //variable to hold the amount entered
    int amount2; //variable to hold the extra amount needed

    if (product.getNoOfItems() > 0) //if the dispenser is not
                                    //empty
    {
        cout << "Please deposit " << product.getCost()
             << " cents" << endl;
        cin >> amount;

        if (amount < product.getCost())
        {
            cout << "Please deposit another "
                 << product.getCost()- amount
                 << " cents" << endl;
            cin >> amount2;
            amount = amount + amount2;
        }
```

```
        if (amount >= product.getCost())
        {
            pCounter.acceptAmount(amount);
            product.makeSale();
            cout << "Collect your item at the bottom and "
                 << "enjoy." << endl;
        }
        else
            cout << "The amount is not enough. "
                 << "Collect what you deposited." << endl;

        cout << "*-*-*-*-*-*-*-*-*-*-*-*-*-*-*-*-*-*-*-*"
             << endl << endl;
    }
    else
        cout << "Sorry, this item is sold out." << endl;
}//end sellProduct
```

Sample Run: In this sample run, the user input is shaded.

```
*** Welcome to Shelly's Juice Shop ***
To select an item, enter
1 for orange juice
2 for apple juice
3 for mango juice
4 for strawberry banana
9 to exit
1
Please deposit 50 cents
50
Collect your item at the bottom and enjoy.
*-*-*-*-*-*-*-*-*-*-*-*-*-*-*-*-*-*-*-*

*** Welcome to Shelly's Juice Shop ***
To select an item, enter
1 for orange
2 for apple
3 for mango
4 for strawberry banana
9 to exit
9
```

NOTE We placed the definitions of the `classes` `cashRegister` and `dispenserType` in the same header file `juiceMachine.h`. However, you can also place the definitions of these classes in separate header files and include those header files in the files that use these classes, such as the implementation file of these classes and the file that contains the main program. Similarly, you can also create separate implementation files for these classes. The Web site accompanying this book contains these header and implementation files.

QUICK REVIEW

1. A `class` is a collection of a fixed number of components.

2. Components of a `class` are called the members of the `class`.

3. Members of a `class` are accessed by name.

4. In C++, `class` is a reserved word.

5. Members of a `class` are classified into one of three categories: `private`, `protected`, and `public`.

6. The `private` members of a `class` are not accessible outside of the `class`.

7. The `public` members of a `class` are accessible outside of the `class`.

8. By default, all members of a `class` are `private`.

9. The `public` members are declared using the member access specifier `public` and the colon, :.

10. The `private` members are declared using the member access specifier `private` and the colon, :.

11. A member of a `class` can be a function or a variable.

12. If any member of a `class` is a function, you usually use the function prototype to declare it.

13. If any member of a `class` is a variable, it is declared like any other variable.

14. In the definition of a `class`, you cannot initialize a variable when you declare it.

15. In the Unified Modeling Language (UML) diagram of a `class`, the top box contains the name of the `class`. The middle box contains the member variables and their data types. The last box contains the member function name, parameter list, and the return type of the function. A + (plus) sign in front of a member indicates that this member is a `public` member. A – (minus) sign preceding a member indicates that this is a `private` member. The symbol # before the member name indicates that the member is a `protected` member.

16. In C++, a `class` is a definition. No memory is allocated for the `class` itself; memory is allocated for the `class` variables when you declare them.

17. In C++, `class` variables are called `class` objects or `class` instances or, simply, objects.

18. A `class` member is accessed using the `class` variable name, followed by the dot operator (`.`), followed by the member name.

19. The only built-in operations on classes are the assignment and member selection.

20. As parameters to functions, classes can be passed either by value or by reference.

21. A function can return a value of type `class`.

22. Any program (or software) that uses a `class` is called a client of the `class`.

1
0

23. A member function of a `class` that only accesses (that is, does not modify) the value(s) of the member variable(s) is called an accessor function.

24. A member function of a `class` that modifies the value(s) of the member variable(s) is called a mutator function.

25. A member function of a `class` is called a constant function if its heading contains the reserved word `const` at the end. Moreover, a constant member function of a `class` cannot modify the member variables of the `class`.

26. A constant member function of a `class` can only call the other constant member functions of the `class`.

27. Constructors guarantee that the member variables are initialized when an object is declared.

28. The name of a constructor is the same as the name of the `class`.

29. A `class` can have more than one constructor.

30. A constructor without parameters is called the default constructor.

31. Constructors automatically execute when a `class` object enters its scope.

32. Destructors automatically execute when a `class` object goes out of scope.

33. A `class` can have only one destructor, and the destructor has no parameters.

34. The name of a destructor is the tilde (~), followed by the `class` name (no spaces in between).

35. Constructors and destructors are functions without any type; that is, they are neither value-returning nor void. As a result, they cannot be called like other functions.

36. A data type that separates the logical properties from the implementation details is called an abstract data type (ADT).

37. Classes were specifically designed in C++ to handle ADTs.

38. To implement an ADT, you must represent the data and write related algorithms to implement the operations.

39. A precondition is a statement specifying the condition(s) that must be true before the function is called.

40. A postcondition is a statement specifying what is true after the function call is completed.

41. A `public` `static` member, function or variable, of a `class` can be accessed using the `class` name and the scope resolution operator.

42. For each `static` variable of a `class`, C++ allocates only one memory space. All objects of the `class` refer to the same memory space.

43. `static` member variables of a `class` exist even when no object of the `class` type exists.

44. Non-`static` member variables of a `class` are called the instance variables of the `class`.

EXERCISES

1. Mark the following statements as true or false.

   a. The member variables of a class must be of the same type.

   b. The member functions of a class must be public.

   c. A class can have more than one constructor.

   d. A class can have more than one destructor.

   e. Both constructors and destructors can have parameters.

2. Find the syntax errors in the following class definition:

```
class mystery                           //Line 1
{                                       //Line 2
public:                                 //Line 3
    void print() const;                 //Line 4
    void setNum(double, double);        //Line 5
    int power();                        //Line 6
    double mystery();                   //Line 7
    double mystery(double, double);     //Line 8
private:                                //Line 9
    double x;                           //Line 10
    double y;                           //Line 11
};                                      //Line 12
```

3. Find the syntax errors in the following class definition:

```
class secret                            //Line 1
{                                       //Line 2
public:                                 //Line 3
    bool multiply();                    //Line 4
    print() const;                      //Line 5
    secret(int = 0, int = 0);           //Line 6
private:                                //Line 7
    int one;                            //Line 8
    int two;                            //Line 9
};                                      //Line 10
```

4. Find the syntax errors in the following class definition:

```
class secret                            //Line 1
{                                       //Line 2
public:                                 //Line 3
    bool compare();                     //Line 4
    void print() const;                 //Line 5
    secret(int = 0, int = 0) const;     //Line 6
private:                                //Line 7
    string str;                         //Line 8
    int one;                            //Line 9
    int two;                            //Line 10
};                                      //Line 11
```

5. Find the syntax errors in the following `class` definition:

```
class discover                              //Line 1
{                                           //Line 2
public;                                     //Line 3
    void set(string, int, int);             //Line 4
    void print() const;                     //Line 5
    discover();                             //Line 6
    discover(string, int, int);             //Line 7
    bool discover(string, int, int);        //Line 8
private:                                     //Line 9
    string type;                            //Line 10
    int l;                                  //Line 11
    int w;                                  //Line 12
  }                                         //Line 13
```

6. Consider the following declarations:

```
class bagType
{
public:
    void set(string, double, double, double, double);
    void print() const;
    string getStyle() const;
    double getPrice() const;
    void get(double, double, double, double);
    bagType();
    bagType(string, double, double, double, double);
private:
    string style;
    double l;
    double w;
    double h;
    double price;
};

bagType newBag;   //variable declaration
```

a. How many members does `class bagType` have?

b. How many `private` members does `class bagType` have?

c. How many constructors does `class bagType` have?

d. How many constant functions does `class bagType` have?

e. Which constructor is used to initialize the object `newBag`?

7. Assume the definition of `class bagType` as given in Exercise 6. Answer the following questions:

a. Write the definition of the member function `set` so that `private` members are set according to the parameters.

b. Write the definition of the member function `print` that prints the values of the data members.

c. Write the definition of the default constructor of the `class bagType` so that the `private` member variables are initialized to `""`, `0.0`, `0.0`, `0.0`, `0.0`, respectively.

d. Write a C++ statement that prints the value of the object `newBag`.

e. Write a C++ statement that declares the object `tempBag` of type `bagType`, and initializes the member variables of `tempBag` to `"backPack"`, `15`, `8`, `20`, and `49.99`, respectively.

8. Consider the definition of the following `class`:

```
class employee                                //Line 1
{                                             //Line 2
public:                                       //Line 3
    employee();                               //Line 4
    employee(string, int, double);           //Line 5
    employee(int, double);                    //Line 6
    employee(string);                         //Line 7

    void setData(string, int, double);       //Line 8
    void print() const;                       //Line 9
    void updatePay(double x);                 //Line 10
    int getNumOfServiceYears() const;         //Line 11
    double getPay() const;                    //Line 12

private:                                       //Line 13
    string name;                              //Line 14
    int numOfServiceYears;                    //Line 15
    double pay;                               //Line 16
};                                            //Line 17
```

a. Give the line number containing the constructor that is executed in each of the following declarations:

   i. `employee tempEmployee;`

   ii. `employee newEmployee("Harry Miller", 0, 25000);`

   iii. `employee oldEmployee("Bill Dunbar", 15, 55000);`

b. Write the definition of the constructor in Line 4 so that the instance variables are initialized to `""`, `0`, and `0.0`, respectively.

c. Write the definition of the constructor in Line 5 so that the instance variables are initialized according to the parameters.

d. Write the definition of the constructor in Line 6 so that the instance variable `name` is initialized to the empty string and the remaining instance variables are initialized according to the parameters.

9. Consider the definition of the `class employee` as given in Exercise 8. Which function members are accessors and which are mutators?

10. Consider the definition of the `class employee` as given in Exercise 8. Answer the following questions:

1
0

a. Write the definition of the function `setData` so that the instance variables are set according to the parameters.

b. Write the definition of the function `print` to output the values of the instance variables.

c. Write the definition of the function `updatePay` to update the value of the instance variable `pay` by adding the value of the parameter.

d. Write the definition of the function `getNumOfServiceYears` to return the value of the instance variable `numOfServiceYears`.

e. Write the definition of the function `getPay` to return the value of the instance variable `pay`.

f. Write a program to test the `class employee`.

11. Consider the following statements:

```
class temporary
{
public:
    void set(string, double, double);
    void print();
    double manipulate();
    void get(string&, double&, double&);
    void setDescription(string);
    void setFirst(double);
    void setSecond(double);
    string getDescription() const;
    double getFirst() const;
    double getSecond() const;

    temporary(string = "", double = 0.0, double = 0.0);

private:
    string description;
    double first;
    double second;
};
```

a. How many members does `class temporary` have?

b. How many `private` members does `class temporary` have?

c. How many constructors does `class temporary` have? Can this constructor be used to initialize an object without specifying any parameters? If yes, then illustrate with an example; otherwise, explain why it cannot be used to initialize an object witout specifying any parameters.

12. Assume the definition of `class temporary` as given in Exercise 11. Answer the following questions:

a. Write the definition of the member function `set` so that the instance variables are set according to the parameters.

b. Write the definition of the member function `manipulate` that returns a decimal number as follows: If the value of `description` is `"rectangle"`, it returns `first * second`; if the value of `description` is `"circle"`, it returns the area of the circle with radius `first`; if the value of `description` is `"sphere"`, it returns the volume of the sphere with radius `first`; if the value of `description` is `"cylinder"`, it returns the volume of the `cylinder` with radius `first` and height `second`; otherwise, it returns the value `-1`.

c. Write the definition of the function `print` to print the values of the instance variables and the values returned by the function `manipulate`. For example, if `description = "rectangle"`, `first = 8.5`, and `second = 5`, it should print:

```
rectangle: length = 8.50, width = 5.00, area = 42.50
```

d. Write the definition of the constructor so that it initializes the instance variables using the function `set`.

e. Write the definition of the remaining functions to set or retrieve the values of the instance variables. Note that the function `get` returns the values of all instance variables.

13. Assume the definition of **class** `temporary` as given in Exercise 11. What is the effect of the following statements?

```
temporary object1;                           //Line 1
temporary object2("rectangle", 3.0, 5.0);    //Line 2
temporary object3("circle", 6.5, 0.0);       //Line 3
temporary object4("cylinder", 6.0, 3.5);     //Line 4
```

14. Assume the definition of **class** `temporary` as given in Exercise 11 and the definitions of the member functions and the constructor as specified in Exercise 12. What is the output of the following statements?

```
temporary object1;
temporary object2("rectangle", 8.5, 5);
temporary object3("circle", 6, 0);
temporary object4("cylinder", 6, 3.5);

cout << fixed << showpoint << setprecision(2);

object1.print();
object2.print();
object3.print();
object4.print();

object1.set("sphere", 4.5, 0);
object1.print();
```

15. What are the built-in operations on classes?

16. What is the main difference between a **struct** and a **class**?

10

17. Consider the definition of the following `class`:

```
class testClass
{
public:
    int sum();
        //Returns the sum of the private member variables
    void print() const;
        //Prints the values of the private member variables
    testClass();
        //Default constructor
        //Initializes the private member variables to 0
    testClass(int a, int b);
        //Constructors with parameters
        //initializes the private member variables to the values
        //specified by the parameters
        //Postcondition: x = a; y = b;
private:
    int x;
    int y;
};
```

a. Write the definitions of the member functions as described in the definition of the class `testClass`.

b. Write a test program to test the various operations of the class `testClass`.

18. Given the definition of the `class` `clockType` with constructors (as described in this chapter), what is the output of the following C++ code?

```
clockType clock1;
clockType clock2(23, 13, 75);

clock1.printTime();
cout << endl;
clock2.printTime();
cout << endl;

clock1.setTime(6, 59, 39);
clock1.printTime();
cout << endl;

clock1.incrementMinutes();
clock1.printTime();
cout << endl;

clock1.setTime(0, 13, 0);

if (clock1.equalTime(clock2))
        cout << "clock1 time is the same as clock2 time."
            << endl;
else
        cout << "The two times are different." << endl;
```

19. Assume the definition of the **class** `personType` as given in this chapter.

   a. Write a C++ statement that declares `student` to be a `personType` object, and initialize its first name to `"Buddy"` and last name to `"Arora"`.

   b. Write a C++ statement that outputs the data stored in the object `student`.

   c. Write a C++ statement that changes the first name of `student` to `"Susan"` and the last name to `"Gilbert"`.

20. Explain why you would need both **public** and **private** members in a **class**.

21. What is a constructor? Why would you include a constructor in a **class**?

22. Which of the following characters appears before a destructor's name?

   a. # b. ! c. ~ d. $

23. What is a destructor and what is its purpose?

24. Write the definition of a **class** that has the following properties:

   a. The name of the **class** is `secretType`.

   b. The **class** `secretType` has four member variables: `name` of type `string`, `age` and `weight` of type `int`, and `height` of type `double`.

   c. The **class** `secretType` has the following member functions. (Make each accessor function constant.)

   `print`—outputs the data stored in the member variables with the appropriate titles

   `setName`—function to set the name

   `setAge`—function to set the age

   `setWeight`—function to set the weight

   `setHeight`—function to set the height

   `getName`—value-returning function to return the name

   `getAge`—value-returning function to return the age

   `getWeight`—value-returning function to return the weight

   `getHeight`—value-returning function to return the height

   `constructor`—with default parameters: The default value of `name` is the empty string `" "`, and the default values of `age`, `weight`, and `height` are 0.

   d. Write the definition of the member functions of the **class** `secretType`, as described in Part c.

25. Consider the following definition of the class myClass:

```cpp
class myClass
{
public:
    void setX(int a);
    //Function to set the value of x.
    //Postcondition: x = a;
    void printX() const;
    //Function to output x.
    static void printCount();
    //Function to output count.
    static void incrementCount();
    //Function to increment count.
    //Postcondition: count++;
    myClass(int a = 0);
    //constructor with default parameters
    //Postcondition x = a;
    //If no value is specified for a, x = 0;

private:
    int x;
    static int count;
};
```

a. Write a C++ statement that initializes the member variable count to 0.

b. Write a C++ statement that increments the value of count by 1.

c. Write a C++ statement that outputs the value of count.

d. Write the definitions of the functions of the class myClass as described in its definition.

e. Write a C++ statement that declares myObject1 to be a myClass object and initializes its member variable x to 5.

f. Write a C++ statement that declares myObject2 to be a myClass object and initializes its member variable x to 7.

g. Which of the following statements are valid? (Assume that myObject1 and myObject2 are as declared in Parts e and f.)

```cpp
myObject1.printCount();      //Line 1
myObject1.printX();          //Line 2
myClass.printCount();        //Line 3
myClass.printX();            //Line 4
myClass::count++;            //Line 5
```

h. Assume that myObject1 and myObject2 are as declared in Parts e and f. What is the output of the following C++ code?

```cpp
myObject1.printX();
cout << endl;
myObject1.incrementCount();
myClass::incrementCount();
```

```
myObject1.printCount();
cout << endl;
myObject2.printCount();
cout << endl;
myObject2.printX();
cout << endl;
myObject1.setX(14);
myObject1.incrementCount();
myObject1.printX();
cout << endl;
myObject1.printCount();
cout << endl;
myObject2.printCount();
cout << endl;
```

26. In Example 10-9, we designed the **class** die. Using this **class**, declare an array named **rolls**, of 100 components of type die. Write C++ statements to roll each die of the array **rolls**, find and output the heighest number rolled and the number of times this number was rolled, and find and output the number that is rolled the maximum number of times together with its count. Also write a program to test your statements.

PROGRAMMING EXERCISES

1. Chapter 9 defined the **struct** houseType to implement the basic properties of a house. Define the **class** houseType with the same components as the **struct** houseType, and add member functions to manipulate the data members. (Note that the data members of the **class** houseType must be **private**.) Write a program to illustrate how to use the **class** houseType.

2. Write a program to illustrate how to use the **class** temporary, designed in Exercises 11 and 12 of this chapter. Your program should not use the statements given in Exercises 13 and 14. Also, your program must contain statements that would ask the user to enter data of an object and use the member function set to initialize the object.

3. Write a program that converts a number entered in Roman numerals to a decimal. Your program should consist of a **class**, say, romanType. An object of type romanType should do the following:

   a. Store the number as a Roman numeral.

   b. Convert and store the number into decimal form.

   c. Print the number as a Roman numeral or decimal number as requested by the user.

The decimal values of the Roman numerals are:

M	1000
D	500
C	100
L	50
X	10
V	5
I	1

d. Test your program using the following Roman numerals: MCXIV, CCCLIX, MDCLXVI.

4. Design and implement a `class` `dayType` that implements the day of the week in a program. The `class` `dayType` should store the day, such as `Sun` for Sunday. The program should be able to perform the following operations on an object of type `dayType`:

   a. Set the day.

   b. Print the day.

   c. Return the day.

   d. Return the next day.

   e. Return the previous day.

   f. Calculate and return the day by adding certain days to the current day. For example, if the current day is Monday and we add 4 days, the day to be returned is Friday. Similarly, if today is Tuesday and we add 13 days, the day to be returned is Monday.

   g. Add the appropriate constructors.

5. Write the definitions of the functions to implement the operations for the `class` `dayType` as defined in Programming Exercise 4. Also, write a program to test various operations on this `class`.

6. This chapter defines the `class` `clockType` to implement time in a program. Add functions to this `class` so that a program that uses this `class` can set only the hours, minutes, or seconds and retrieve only the hours, minutes, or seconds. Also write a program to test your `class`.

7. Example 10-10 defined a `class` `personType` to store the name of a person. The member functions that we included merely print the name and set the name of a person. Redefine the `class` `personType` so that, in addition to what the existing `class` does, you can:

   a. Set the first name only.

   b. Set the last name only.

   c. Store and set the middle name.

d. Check whether a given first name is the same as the first name of this person.

e. Check whether a given last name is the same as the last name of this person.

  Write the definitions of the member functions to implement the operations for this `class`. Also, write a program to test various operations on this `class`.

8. a. Some of the characteristics of a book are the title, author(s), publisher, ISBN, price, and year of publication. Design a `class` bookType that defines the book as an ADT.

   i. Each object of the `class` bookType can hold the following information about a book: title, up to four authors, publisher, ISBN, price, and number of copies in stock. To keep track of the number of authors, add another member variable.

   ii. Include the member functions to perform the various operations on objects of type bookType. For example, the usual operations that can be performed on the title are to show the title, set the title, and check whether a title is the same as the actual title of the book. Similarly, the typical operations that can be performed on the number of copies in stock are to show the number of copies in stock, set the number of copies in stock, update the number of copies in stock, and return the number of copies in stock. Add similar operations for the publisher, ISBN, book price, and authors. Add the appropriate constructors and a destructor (if one is needed).

  b. Write the definitions of the member functions of the `class` bookType.

  c. Write a program that uses the `class` bookType and tests various operations on the objects of the `class` bookType. Declare an array of 100 components of type bookType. Some of the operations that you should perform are to search for a book by its title, search by ISBN, and update the number of copies of a book.

9. In this exercise, you will design a `class` memberType.

  a. Each object of memberType can hold the name of a person, member ID, number of books bought, and amount spent.

  b. Include the member functions to perform the various operations on the objects of memberType—for example, modify, set, and show a person's name. Similarly, update, modify, and show the number of books bought and the amount spent.

  c. Add the appropriate constructors.

  d. Write the definitions of the member functions of memberType.

  e. Write a program to test various operations of your `class` memberType.

10. Using the classes designed in Programming Exercises 8 and 9, write a program to simulate a bookstore. The bookstore has two types of customers: those who are members of the bookstore and those who buy books from the bookstore only occasionally. Each member has to pay a $10 yearly membership fee and receives a 5% discount on each book purchased.

For each member, the bookstore keeps track of the number of books purchased and the total amount spent. For every eleventh book that a member buys, the bookstore takes the average of the total amount of the last 10 books purchased, applies this amount as a discount, and then resets the total amount spent to 0.

Write a program that can process up to 1000 book titles and 500 members. Your program should contain a menu that gives the user different choices to effectively run the program; in other words, your program should be user driven.

11. The method sellProduct of the Juice Machine programming example gives the user only two chances to enter enough money to buy the product. Rewrite the definition of the method sellProduct so that it keeps prompting the user to enter more money as long as the user has not entered enough money to buy the product. Also, write a program to test your method.

12. Write the definition of a class, swimmingPool, to implement the properties of a swimming pool. Your class should have the instance variables to store the length (in feet), width (in feet), depth (in feet), the rate (in gallons per minute) at which the water is filling the pool, and the rate (in gallons per minute) at which the water is draining from the pool. Add appropriate constructors to initialize the instance variables. Also add member functions to do the following: determine the amount of water needed to fill an empty or partially filled pool; determine the time needed to completely or partially fill or empty the pool; add or drain water for a specific amount of time.

13. (Tic-Tac-Toe) Write a program that allows two players to play the tic-tac-toe game. Your program must contain the class ticTacToe to implement a ticTacToe object. Include a 3-by-3 two-dimensional array, as a private member variable, to create the board. If needed, include additional member variables. Some of the operations on a ticTacToe object are printing the current board, getting a move, checking if a move is valid, and determining the winner after each move. Add additional operations as needed.

14. The equation of a line in standard form is $ax + by = c$, wherein both a and b cannot be zero, and a, b, and c are real numbers. If $b \neq 0$, then $-a/b$ is the slope of the line. If $a = 0$, then it is a horizontal line, and if $b = 0$, then it is a vertical line. The slope of a vertical line is undefined. Two lines are parallel if they have the same slope or both are vertical lines. Two lines are perpendicular if either one of the lines is horizontal and the other is vertical or the product of their slopes is -1. Design the class lineType to store a line. To store a line, you need to store the values of a (coefficient of x), b (coefficient of y), and c. Your class must contain the following operations:

a. If a line is nonvertical, then determine its slope.

b. Determine if two lines are equal. (Two lines $a_1x + b_1y = c_1$ and $a_2x + b_2y = c_2$ are equal if either $a_1 = a_2$, $b_1 = b_2$, and $c_1 = c_2$ or $a_1 = ka_2$, $b_1 = kb_2$, and $c_1 = kc_2$ for some real number k.)

c. Determine if two lines are parallel.

d. Determine if two lines are perpendicular.

e. If two lines are not parallel, then find the point of intersection.

Add appropriate constructors to initialize variables of lineType. Also write a program to test your class.

15. Typically, everyone saves money periodically for retirement, buying a house, or for some other purposes. If you are saving money for retirement, then the money you put in a retirement fund is tax sheltered and your employer also makes some contribution into your retirement fund. In this exercise, for simplicity, we assume that the money is put into an account that pays a fixed interest rate, and money is deposited into the account at the end of the specified period. Suppose that a person deposits R dollars m times a year into an account that pays $r\%$ interest compounded m times a year for t years. Then the total accumulated at the end of t years is given by $R\left[\frac{(1+r/m)^{mt}-1}{r/m}\right]$. For example, suppose that you deposit $500 at the end of each month into an account that pays 4.8% interest per year compounded monthly for 25 years. Then the total money accumulated into the account is $500[(1 + 0.048/12)^{300} - 1]/(0.048/12) = \$289,022.42$.

On the other hand, suppose that you want to accumulate S dollars in t years and would like to know how much money, m times a year, you should deposit into an account that pays $r\%$ interest compounded m times a year. The periodic payment is given by the formula $\frac{s(r/m)}{(1+r/m)^{mt}-1}$.

Design a class that uses the above formulas to determine the total accumulated into an account and the periodic deposits to accumulate a specifc amount. Your class should have instance variables to store the periodic deposit, the value of m, the interest rate, and the number of years the money will be saved. Add appropriate constructors to initialize instance variables, functions to set the values of the instance variables, functions to retrieve the values of the instance variables, and functions to do the necessary calculations and output results.

16. Define the class bankAccount to implement the basic properties of a bank account. An object of this class should store the following data: Account holder's name (string), account number (int), account type (string, checking/saving), balance (double), and interest rate (double). (Store interest rate as a decimal number.) Add appropriate member functions to manipulate an object. Use a static member in the class to automatically assign account numbers. Also declare an array of 10 components of type bankAccount to process up to 10 customers and write a program to illustrate how to use your class.

INHERITANCE AND COMPOSITION

IN THIS CHAPTER, YOU WILL:

· Learn about inheritance

· Learn about derived and base classes

· Explore how to redefine the member functions of a base class

· Examine how the constructors of base and derived classes work

· Learn how to construct the header file of a derived class

· Explore three types of inheritance: `public`, `protected`, and `private`

· Learn about composition (aggregation)

· Become familiar with the three basic principles of object-oriented design

Chapter 10 introduced classes, abstract data types (ADT), and ways to implement ADT in C++. By using classes, you can combine data and operations in a single unit. An object, therefore, becomes a self-contained entity. Operations can directly access the data, but the internal state of an object cannot be manipulated directly.

In addition to implementing ADT, classes have other features. For instance, classes can create new classes from existing classes. This important feature encourages code reuse. In C++, you can relate two or more classes in more than one way. Two common ways to relate classes in a meaningful way are:

- **Inheritance** ("is-a" relationship)
- **Composition (aggregation)** ("has-a" relationship)

Inheritance

Suppose that you want to design a **class**, **partTimeEmployee**, to implement and process the characteristics of a part-time employee. The main features associated with a part-time employee are the name, pay rate, and number of hours worked. In Example 10-10 (in Chapter 10), we designed a class to implement a person's name. Every part-time employee is a person. Therefore, rather than design the **class partTimeEmployee** from scratch, we want to be able to extend the definition of the **class personType** (from Example 10-10) by adding additional members (data and/or functions).

Of course, we do not want to make the necessary changes directly to the **class personType**—that is, edit the **class personType** and add and/or delete members. In fact, we want to create the **class partTimeEmployee** without making any physical changes to the **class personType** by adding only the members that are necessary. For example, because the **class personType** already has members to store the first name and last name, we will not include any such members in the **class partTimeEmployee**. In fact, these member variables will be inherited from the **class personType**. (We will design such a **class** in Example 11-3.)

In Chapter 10, we extensively studied and designed the **class clockType** to implement the time of day in a program. The **class clockType** has three member variables to store the hours, minutes, and seconds. Certain applications, in addition to the hours, minutes, and seconds, might also require us to store the time zone. In this case, we would like to extend the definition of the **class clockType** and create a **class**, **extClockType**, to accommodate this new information. That is, we want to derive the **class extClockType** by adding a member variable—say, **timeZone**—and the necessary member functions to manipulate the time (see Programming Exercise 1 at the end of this chapter). In C++, the mechanism that allows us to accomplish this task is the principle of inheritance. Inheritance is an "is-a" relationship; for instance, "every employee is a person."

Inheritance lets us create new classes from existing classes. The new classes that we create from the existing classes are called the **derived classes**; the existing classes are called the

base classes. The derived classes inherit the properties of the base classes. So rather than create completely new classes from scratch, we can take advantage of inheritance and reduce software complexity.

Each derived class, in turn, becomes a base class for a future derived class. Inheritance can be either single inheritance or multiple inheritance. In **single inheritance**, the derived class is derived from a single base class; in **multiple inheritance**, the derived class is derived from more than one base class. This chapter concentrates on single inheritance.

Inheritance can be viewed as a treelike, or hierarchical, structure wherein a base class is shown with its derived classes. Consider the tree diagram shown in Figure 11-1.

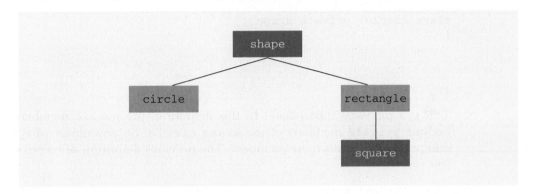

FIGURE 11-1 Inheritance hierarchy

In this diagram, `shape` is the base class. The `classes` `circle` and `rectangle` are derived from `shape`, and the `class` `square` is derived from `rectangle`. Every `circle` and every `rectangle` is a `shape`. Every `square` is a `rectangle`.

The general syntax of a derived class is:

```
class className: memberAccessSpecifier baseClassName
{
    member list
};
```

in which `memberAccessSpecifier` is `public`, `protected`, or `private`. When no `memberAccessSpecifier` is specified, it is assumed to be a `private` inheritance. (We will discuss `protected` inheritance later in this chapter.)

EXAMPLE 11-1

Suppose that we have defined a class called shape. The following statements specify that the class circle is derived from shape, and it is a public inheritance.

```
class circle: public shape
{
        .
        .
        .
};
```

On the other hand, consider the following definition of the class circle:

```
class circle: private shape
{
        .
        .
        .
};
```

This is a private inheritance. In this definition, the public members of shape become private members of the class circle. So any object of type circle cannot directly access these members. The previous definition of circle is equivalent to:

```
class circle: shape
{
        .
        .
        .
};
```

That is, if we do not use either the memberAccessSpecifier public or private, the public members of a base class are inherited as private members.

The following facts about the base and the derived classes should be kept in mind.

1. The private members of a base class are private to the base class; hence, the members of the derived class cannot directly access them. In other words, when you write the definitions of the member functions of the derived class, you cannot directly access the private members of the base class.

2. The public members of a base class can be inherited either as public members or as private members by the derived class. That is, the public members of the base class can become either public or private members of the derived class.

3. The derived class can include additional members—data and/or functions.

4.   The derived class can redefine the `public` member functions of the base class. That is, in the derived class, you can have a member function with the same name, number, and types of parameters as a function in the base class. However, this redefinition applies only to the objects of the derived class, not to the objects of the base class.

5.   All member variables of the base class are also member variables of the derived class. Similarly, the member functions of the base class (unless redefined) are also member functions of the derived class. (Remember Rule 1 when accessing a member of the base class in the derived class.)

The next sections describe two important issues related to inheritance. The first issue is the redefinition of the member functions of the base class in the derived class. While discussing this issue, we will also address how to access the `private` (data) members of the base class in the derived class. The second key inheritance issue is related to the constructor. The constructor of a derived class cannot *directly* access the `private` member variables of the base class. Thus, we need to ensure that the `private` member variables that are inherited from the base class are initialized when a constructor of the derived class executes.

Redefining (Overriding) Member Functions of the Base Class

Suppose that a `class derivedClass` is derived from the `class baseClass`. Further assume that both `derivedClass` and `baseClass` have some member variables. It then follows that the member variables of the `class derivedClass` are its own member variables, together with the member variables of `baseClass`. Suppose that `baseClass` contains a function, `print`, that prints the values of the member variables of `baseClass`. Now `derivedClass` contains member variables in addition to the member variables inherited from `baseClass`. Suppose that you want to include a function that prints the values of the member variables of `derivedClass`. You can give any name to this function. However, in the `class derivedClass`, you can also name this function as `print` (the same name used by `baseClass`). This is called redefining (or overriding) the member function of the base class. Next, we illustrate how to redefine the member functions of a base class with the help of an example.

NOTE   To redefine a `public` member function of a base class in the derived class, the corresponding function in the derived class must have the same name, number, and types of parameters. In other words, the name of the function being redefined in the derived class must have the same name and the same set of parameters. If the corresponding functions in the base class and the derived class have the same name but different sets of parameters, then this is function overloading in the derived class, which is also allowed.

Consider the definition of the following class:

```
class rectangleType
{
public:
    void setDimension(double l, double w);
      //Function to set the length and width of the rectangle.
      //Postcondition: length = l; width = w;

    double getLength() const;
      //Function to return the length of the rectangle.
      //Postcondition: The value of length is returned.

    double getWidth() const;
      //Function to return the width of the rectangle.
      //Postcondition: The value of width is returned.

    double area() const;
      //Function to return the area of the rectangle.
      //Postcondition: The area of the rectangle is
      //               calculated and returned.

    double perimeter() const;
      //Function to return the perimeter of the rectangle.
      //Postcondition: The perimeter of the rectangle is
      //               calculated and returned.

    void print() const;
      //Function to output the length and width of
      //the rectangle.

    rectangleType();
      //Default constructor
      //Postcondition: length = 0; width = 0;

    rectangleType(double l, double w);
      //Constructor with parameters
      //Postcondition: length = l; width = w;

private:
    double length;
    double width;
};
```

Figure 11-2 shows the UML class diagram of the class rectangleType.

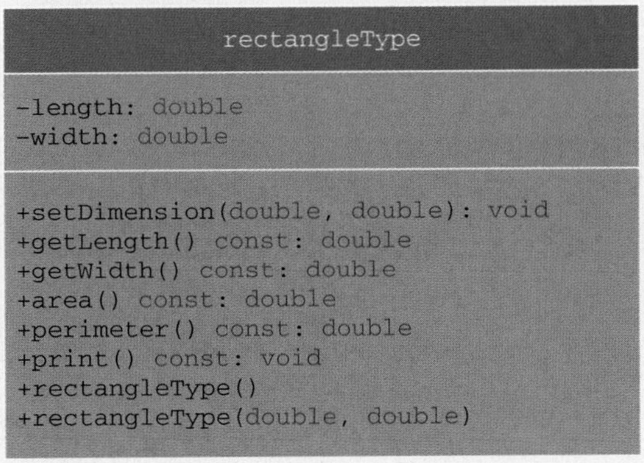

FIGURE 11-2 UML class diagram of the **class** rectangleType

The **class** rectangleType has 10 members.

Suppose that the definitions of the member functions of the **class** rectangleType are as follows:

```
void rectangleType::setDimension(double l, double w)
{
    if (l >= 0)
        length = l;
    else
        length = 0;

    if (w >= 0)
        width = w;
    else
        width = 0;
}

double rectangleType::getLength() const
{
    return length;
}

double rectangleType::getWidth() const
{
    return width;
}

double rectangleType::area() const
{
    return length * width;
}
```

```
double rectangleType::perimeter() const
{
    return 2 * (length + width);
}

void rectangleType::print() const
{
    cout << "Length = " << length
         << "; Width = " << width;
}

rectangleType::rectangleType(double l, double w)
{
    setDimension(l, w);
}

rectangleType::rectangleType()
{
    length = 0;
    width = 0;
}
```

Now consider the definition of the following class boxType, derived from the class rectangleType:

```
class boxType: public rectangleType
{
public:
    void setDimension(double l, double w, double h);
    //Function to set the length, width, and height
    //of the box.
    //Postcondition: length = l; width = w; height = h;

    double getHeight() const;
    //Function to return the height of the box.
    //Postcondition: The value of height is returned.

    double area() const;
    //Function to return the surface area of the box.
    //Postcondition: The surface area of the box is
    //                 calculated and returned.

    double volume() const;
    //Function to return the volume of the box.
    //Postcondition: The volume of the box is
    //                 calculated and returned.

    void print() const;
    //Function to output the length, width, and height of a box.

    boxType();
    //Default constructor
    //Postcondition: length = 0; width = 0; height = 0;
```

```
boxType(double l, double w, double h);
    //Constructor with parameters
    //Postcondition: length = l; width = w; height = h;

private:
    double height;
};
```

Figure 11-3 shows the UML class diagram of the **class** boxType and the inheritance hierarchy.

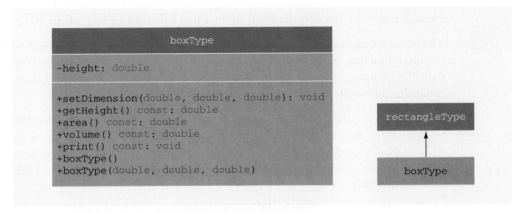

FIGURE 11-3 UML class diagram of the **class** boxType and the inheritance hierarchy

From the definition of the **class** boxType, it is clear that the **class** boxType is derived from the **class** rectangleType, and it is a **public** inheritance. Therefore, all **public** members of the **class** rectangleType are **public** members of the **class** boxType. The **class** boxType also overrides (redefines) the functions print and area.

In general, while writing the definitions of the member functions of a derived class to specify a call to a **public** member function of the base class, we do the following:

- If the derived class overrides a **public** member function of the base class, then to specify a call to that **public** member function of the base class, you use the name of the base class, followed by the scope resolution operator, ::, followed by the function name with the appropriate parameter list.

- If the derived class does not override a **public** member function of the base class, you may specify a call to that **public** member function by using the name of the function and the appropriate parameter list. (See the following note for member functions of the base class that are overloaded in the derived class.)

1
1

> **NOTE** If a derived class *overloads* a `public` member function of the base class, then while writing the definition of a member function of the derived class, to specify a call to that (overloaded) member function of the base class, you might need (depending on the compiler) to use the name of the base class, followed by the scope resolution operator, `::`, followed by the function name with the appropriate parameter list. For example, the `class boxType` overloads the member function `setDimension` of the `class rectangleType`. (See the definition of the function `setDimension` [of the `class boxType`], given later in this section.)

Next, let us write the definition of the member function `print` of the `class boxType`.

The `class boxType` has three member variables: `length`, `width`, and `height`. The member function `print` of the `class boxType` prints the values of these member variables. To write the definition of the function `print` of the `class boxType`, keep in mind the following:

- The member variables `length` and `width` are `private` members of the `class rectangleType`, so they cannot be directly accessed in the `class boxType`. Therefore, when writing the definition of the function `print` of the `class boxType`, we cannot access `length` and `width` directly.

- The member variables `length` and `width` of the `class rectangleType` are accessible in the `class boxType` through the `public` member functions of the `class rectangleType`. Therefore, when writing the definition of the member function `print` of the `class boxType`, we first call the member function `print` of the `class rectangleType` to print the values of `length` and `width`. After printing the values of `length` and `width`, we output the values of `height`.

To call the member function `print` of `rectangleType` in the definition of the member function `print` of `boxType`, we must use the following statement:

```
rectangleType::print();
```

This statement ensures that we call the member function `print` of the base `class rectangleType`, not of the `class boxType`.

The definition of the member function `print` of the `class boxType` is:

```
void boxType::print() const
{
    rectangleType::print();
    cout << "; Height = " << height;
}
```

Let us write the definitions of the remaining member functions of the `class boxType`.

The definition of the function setDimension is:

```
void boxType::setDimension(double l, double w, double h)
{
    rectangleType::setDimension(l, w);

    if (h >= 0)
        height = h;
    else
        height = 0;
}
```

Notice that in the preceding definition of the function setDimension, a call to the member function setDimension of the class rectangleType is preceded by the name of the class and the scope resolution operator, even though the class boxType overloads—not overrides—the function setDimension.

The definition of the function getHeight is:

```
double boxType::getHeight() const
{
    return height;
}
```

The member function area of the class boxType determines the surface area of a box. To determine the surface area of a box, we need to access the length and width of the box, which are declared as private members of the class rectangleType. Therefore, we use the member functions getLength and getWidth of the class rectangleType to retrieve the length and width, respectively. Because the class boxType does not contain any member functions that have the names getLength or getWidth, we call these member functions of the class rectangleType without using the name of the base class.

```
double boxType::area() const
{
    return  2 * (getLength() * getWidth()
            + getLength() * height
            + getWidth() * height);
}
```

The member function volume of the class boxType determines the volume of a box. To determine the volume of a box, you multiply the length, width, and height of the box or multiply the area of the base of the box by its height. Let us write the definition of the member function volume by using the second alternative. To do this, you can use the member function area of the class rectangleType to determine the area of the base. Because the class boxType overrides the member function area, to specify a call to the member function area of the class rectangleType, we use the name of the base class and the scope resolution operator, as shown in the following definition:

```
double boxType::volume() const
{
    return rectangleType::area() * height;
}
```

In the next section, we discuss how to specify a call to the constructor of the base class when writing the definition of a constructor of the derived class.

Constructors of Derived and Base Classes

A derived class can have its own `private` member variables, so a derived class can explicitly include its own constructors. A constructor typically serves to initialize the member variables. When we declare a derived class object, this object inherits the members of the base class, but the derived class object cannot directly access the `private` (data) members of the base class. The same is true for the member functions of a derived class. That is, the member functions of a derived class cannot directly access the `private` members of the base class.

As a consequence, the constructors of a derived class can (directly) initialize only the (`public` data) members inherited from the base class of the derived class. Thus, when a derived class object is declared, it must also automatically execute one of the constructors of the base class. Because constructors cannot be called like other functions, the execution of a derived class's constructor must trigger the execution of one of the base class's constructors. This is, in fact, what happens. Furthermore, a call to the base class's constructor is specified in the *heading of the definition* of a derived class constructor.

In the preceding section, we defined the `class rectangleType` and derived the `class boxType` from it. Moreover, we illustrated how to override a member function of the `class rectangleType`. Let us now discuss how to write the definitions of the constructors of the `class boxType`.

The `class rectangleType` has two constructors and two member variables. The `class boxType` has three member variables: `length`, `width`, and `height`. The member variables `length` and `width` are inherited from the `class rectangleType`.

First, let us write the definition of the default constructor of the `class boxType`. Recall that, if a class contains the default constructor and no values are specified when the object is declared, the default constructor executes and initializes the object. Because the `class rectangleType` contains the default constructor, when writing the definition of the default constructor of the `class boxType`, we do not specify any constructor of the base class.

```
boxType::boxType()
{
    height = 0.0;
}
```

Next, we discuss how to write the definitions of constructors with parameters. To trigger the execution of a constructor (with parameters) of the base class, you specify the name of a constructor of the base class with the parameters in the heading of the definition of the constructor of the derived class.

Consider the following definition of the constructor with parameters of the **class boxType**:

```
boxType::boxType(double l, double w, double h)
        : rectangleType(l, w)
{
    if (h >= 0)
        height = h;
    else
        height = 0;
}
```

In this definition, we specify the constructor of `rectangleType` with two parameters. When this constructor of `boxType` executes, it triggers the execution of the constructor with two parameters of type `double` of the **class rectangleType**.

Consider the following statements:

```
rectangleType myRectangle(5.0, 3.0);   //Line 1
boxType myBox(6.0, 5.0, 4.0);          //Line 2
```

The statement in Line 1 creates the `rectangleType` object `myRectangle`. Thus, the object `myRectangle` has two member variables: `length` and `width`. The statement in Line 2 creates the `boxType` object `myBox`. Thus, the object `myBox` has three member variables: `length`, `width`, and `height` (see Figure 11-4).

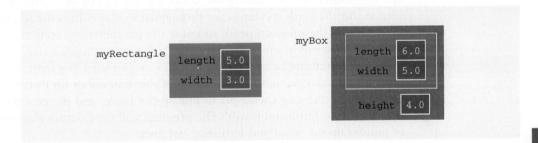

FIGURE 11-4 Objects `myRectangle` and `myBox`

Consider the following statements:

```
myRectangle.print();    //Line 3
cout << endl;           //Line 4
myBox.print();          //Line 5
cout << endl;           //Line 6
```

In the statement in Line 3, the member function `print` of the **class rectangleType** is executed. In the statement in Line 5, the function `print` associated with the **class boxType** is executed. Recall that, if a derived class overrides a member function of the base class, the redefinition applies only to the objects of the derived class. Thus, the output of the statement in Line 3 is:

```
Length = 5.0; Width = 3.0
```

The output of the statement in Line 5 is:

```
Length = 6.0; Width = 5.0; Height = 4.0
```

When the object myBox enters its scope, the constructors of the classes rectangleType and boxType execute. Note that the constructors of a base class are *not* inherited in a derived class. A call to a constructor of a base class is specified in the definition of a constructor of the derived class. When a derived class constructor executes, first a constructor of the base class executes to initialize the data members inherited from the base class, and then the constructor of the derived class executes to initialize the data members declared by the derived class. So first, the constructor of the class rectangleType executes to initialize the instance variables length and width, and then the constructor of the class boxType executes to initialize the instance variable height.

The program in Example 11-2 shows how the objects of a base class and a derived class behave.

EXAMPLE 11-2

In this example, we write a program to solve the following problems:

1. Jim's lawn care store specializes in putting up fences around small farms and home lawns and fertilizing the farms and lawns. For simplicity, we assume that the yards and farms are rectangular in shape. In order to put up the fence, the program needs to know the perimeter and to fertilize, the program needs to know the area. We will write a program that uses the class rectangle to store the dimensions of a yard or a farm. The program will also prompt the user to input the dimensions (in feet) of a yard or farm, the cost (per foot) to put up the fence, and the cost (per square foot) to fertilize the area. The program will then output the cost of putting up the fence and fertilizing the area.

2. Linda's gift store specializes in wrapping small packages. For simplicity, we assume that a package is in the shape of a box with a specific length, width, and height. We will write a program that uses the class boxType to store the dimensions of a package. The program will ask the user to input the dimensions of the package and the cost (per square foot) to wrap the package. The program will then output the cost of wrapping the package. (The program assumes that the minimum cost of wrapping a package is $1.00.)

Consider the following C++ program:

```cpp
#include <iostream>        //Line 1
#include <iomanip>         //Line 2
#include "rectangleType.h" //Line 3
#include "boxType.h"       //Line 4
```

```
using namespace std;                                            //Line 5

int main()                                                      //Line 6
{                                                               //Line 7
    rectangleType yard;                                         //Line 8
    double fenceCostPerFoot;                                    //Line 9
    double fertilizerCostPerSquareFoot;                         //Line 10
    double length, width;                                       //Line 11
    double billingAmount;                                       //Line 12

    cout << fixed << showpoint << setprecision(2);              //Line 13

    cout << "Line 14: Enter the length and width of the "
         << "yard (in feet): ";                                 //Line 14
    cin >> length >> width;                                     //Line 15
    cout << endl;                                               //Line 16

    yard.setDimension(length, width);                           //Line 17

    cout << "Line 18: Enter the cost of fence "
         << "(per foot): $";                                    //Line 18
    cin >> fenceCostPerFoot;                                    //Line 19
    cout << endl;                                               //Line 20

    cout << "Line 21: Enter the cost of fertilizer "
         << "(per square foot): $";                             //Line 21
    cin >> fertilizerCostPerSquareFoot;                         //Line 22
    cout << endl;                                               //Line 23

    billingAmount = yard.perimeter() * fenceCostPerFoot
              + yard.area() * fertilizerCostPerSquareFoot;      //Line 24

    cout << "Line 25: Amount due: $" << billingAmount
         << endl;                                               //Line 25

    boxType package;                                            //Line 26
    double height;                                              //Line 27
    double wrappingCostPerSquareFeet;                           //Line 28

    cout << "Line 29: Enter the length, width, and height "
         << "of the package (in feet): ";                       //Line 29
    cin >> length >> width >> height;                           //Line 30
    cout << endl;                                               //Line 31

    package.setDimension(length, width, height);               //Line 32

    cout << "Line 33: Enter the cost (25 to 50 cents) of "
         << "wrapping per square foot: ";                       //Line 33
    cin >> wrappingCostPerSquareFeet;                           //Line 34
    cout << endl;                                               //Line 35

    billingAmount = wrappingCostPerSquareFeet
                * package.area() / 100;                         //Line 36

    if (billingAmount < 1.00)                                   //Line 37
        billingAmount = 1.00;                                   //Line 38
```

11

```
        cout << "Line 39: Amount due: $" << billingAmount
                << endl;                                         //Line 39

        return 0;                                               //Line 40
}                                                                //Line 41
```

Sample Run: In this sample run, the user input is shaded.

Line 14: Enter the length and width of the yard (in feet): 70 50

Line 18: Enter the cost of fence (per foot): $10.00

Line 21: Enter the cost of fertilizer (per square foot): $0.25

Line 25: Amount due: $3275.00

Line 29: Enter the length, width, and height of the package (in feet): 3 2 0.25

Line 33: Enter the cost (25 to 50 cents) of wrapping per square foot: 25

Line 39: Amount due: $3.63

The preceding program works as follows: The statements in Lines 8 to 12 and 26 to 28 declare the variables and objects used in the program. (Note that the statement in Line 8 creates the object yard, and the statement in Line 26 creates the object package.) The statement in Line 14 prompts the user to input the length and width of the yard and the statement in Line 15 inputs these values in the variables length and width, respectively. The statement in Line 17 uses the function setDimension to initialize the instance variables of the object yard. The statements in Lines 18 to 23 prompt the user to input the cost of putting up the fence and fertilizing the yard, and they store the values in the variables fenceCostPerFoot and fertilizerCostPerSquareFoot. The statement in Line 24 calculates the billing amount. Note that this statement uses the functions perimeter and area of the class rectangleType to compute the length of the fence and the area of the yard. Then the statement in Line 25 outputs the billing amount.

The statement in Line 29 prompts the user to input the length, width, and height of the package and the statement in Line 30 inputs these values in the variables length, width, and height, respectively. The statement in Line 32 uses the function setDimension to initialize the instance variables of the object package. The statement in Line 33 prompts the user to input the cost (per square foot) of wrapping the package and the statement in Line 34 stores the cost in the variable wrappingCostPerSquareFeet. The statement in Line 36 calculates the billing amount. Note that this statement uses the function area of the class boxType to compute the surface area of the package. The statement in Line 37 checks if the value of the billing amount is less than $1.00, and the statement in Line 38 sets the value of the billing amount to 1.00. Then the statement in Line 39 outputs the billing amount.

Note that in this program the length of the yard is 70 feet and the width is 50 feet. So the perimeter of the yard is 2 * (70 + 50) = 240 feet, and the area of the yard is 70 * 50 = 3500 square feet. The total cost of putting up the fence and fertilizing the yard = $(240 * 10 + 3500 * 0.25) = $(2400 + 875) = $3275.00.

Next, the length, width, and height of the package are 3 feet, 2 feet, and 0.25 feet. So the surface area of the package = 2 * (3 * 2 + 3 * 0.25 + 2 * 0.25) = 14.50 square feet. Therefore, the cost of wrapping the package is $14.50 * 25 / 100 = $3.625 = $3.63 (rounded to two decimal places).

Now both the classes rectangleType and boxType have the functions setDimension and area. It follows that the program correctly calls the function setDimension of each class to initialize the objects yard and package. Similarly, in the case of yard, the function area of the class rectangleType is called to calculate the area of the yard, and in the case of package, the function area of the class boxType is called to calculate the surface area of the package.

From the output of this program, it follows that the redefinition of the functions setDimension and area in the class boxType applies only to an object of the type boxType.

NOTE The Web site accompanying this book contains a program in the folder Ch11_InheritanceAndConstructors that further illustrates how to use the classes rectangleType and boxType in a program.

NOTE (Constructors with default parameters and the inheritance hierarchy) Recall that a class can have a constructor with default parameters. Therefore, a derived class can also have a constructor with default parameters. For example, suppose that the definition of the class rectangleType is as shown below. (To save space, these definitions have no documentation.)

```
class rectangleType
{
public:
    void setDimension(double l, double w);
    double getLength() const;
    double getWidth() const;
    double area() const;
    double perimeter() const;
    void print() const;
    rectangleType(double l = 0, double w = 0);
        //Constructor with default parameters

private:
    double length;
    double width;
};
```

Suppose the definition of the constructor is:

```
rectangleType::rectangleType(double l, double w)
{
    setDimension(l, w);
}
```

Now suppose that the definition of the `class boxType` is:

```
class boxType: public rectangleType
{
public:
    void setDimension(double l, double w, double h);
    double getHeight() const;
    double area() const;
    double volume() const;
    void print() const;
    boxType(double l = 0, double w = 0, double h = 0);
        //Constructor with default parameters

private:
    double height;
};
```

You can write the definition of the constructor of the `class boxType` as follows:

```
boxType::boxType(double l, double w, double h)
        : rectangleType(l, w)
{
    if (h >= 0)
        height = h;
    else
        height = 0;
}
```

Notice that this definition also takes care of the default constructor of the `class boxType`.

NOTE   Suppose that a base `class`, baseClass, has *private* member variables and constructors. Further suppose that the `class` derivedClass is derived from baseClass, and derivedClass has no member variables. Therefore, the member variables of derivedClass are the ones inherited from baseClass. A constructor cannot be called like other functions, and the member variables of baseClass cannot be directly accessed by the member functions of derivedClass. To guarantee the initialization of the inherited member variables of an object of type derivedClass, even though derivedClass has no member variables, it must have the appropriate constructors. A constructor (with parameters) of derivedClass merely issues a call to a constructor (with parameters) of baseClass. Therefore, when you write the definition of the constructor (with parameters) of derivedClass, the heading of the definition of the constructor contains a call to an appropriate constructor (with parameters) of baseClass, and the body of the constructor is empty—that is, it contains only the opening and closing braces.

EXAMPLE 11-3

Suppose that you want to define a class to group the attributes of an employee. There are both full-time and part-time employees. Part-time employees are paid based on the number of hours worked and an hourly rate. Suppose that you want to define a class to keep track of a part-time employee's information, such as name, pay rate, and hours worked. You can then print the employee's name together with his or her wages. Because every employee is a person and Example 10-10 (Chapter 10) defined the class personType to store the first name and the last name together with the necessary operations on name, we can define a class partTimeEmployee based on the class personType. You can also redefine the print function to print the appropriate information.

```
class partTimeEmployee: public personType
{
public:
    void print() const;
      //Function to output the first name, last name, and
      //the wages.
      //Postcondition: Outputs
      //           firstName lastName wages are $$$$.$$

    double calculatePay() const;
      //Function to calculate and return the wages.
      //Postcondition: Pay is calculated and returned

    void setNameRateHours(string first, string last,
                          double rate, double hours);
      //Function to set the first name, last name, payRate,
      //and hoursWorked according to the parameters.
      //Postcondition: firstName = first; lastName = last;
      //                 payRate = rate; hoursWorked = hours

    partTimeEmployee(string first = "", string last = "",
                     double rate = 0, double hours = 0);
      //Constructor with parameters
      //Sets the first name, last name, payRate, and hoursWorked
      //according to the parameters. If no value is specified,
      //the default values are assumed.
      //Postcondition: firstName = first; lastName = last;
      //                 payRate = rate; hoursWorked = hours

private:
    double payRate;      //variable to store the pay rate
    double hoursWorked; //variable to store the hours worked
};
```

Figure 11-5 shows the UML class diagram of the class partTimeEmployee and the inheritance hierarchy.

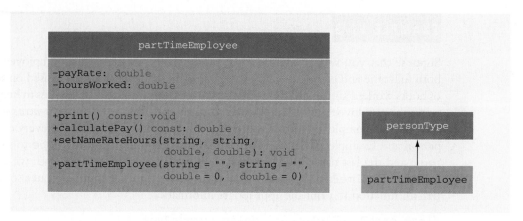

FIGURE 11-5 UML class diagram of the `class` partTimeEmployee and inheritance hierarchy

The definitions of the member functions of the `class` partTimeEmployee are as follows:

```
void partTimeEmployee::print() const
{
    personType::print();   //print the name of the employee
    cout << "'s wages are: $" << calculatePay() << endl;
}

double partTimeEmployee::calculatePay() const
{
    return (payRate * hoursWorked);
}

void partTimeEmployee::setNameRateHours(string first,
                       string last, double rate, double hours)
{
    personType::setName(first, last);
    payRate = rate;
    hoursWorked = hours;
}

    //Constructor
partTimeEmployee::partTimeEmployee(string first, string last,
                                   double rate, double hours)
    : personType(first, last)
{
    if (rate >= 0)
        payRate = rate;
    else
        payRate = 0;

    if (hours >= 0)
        hoursWorked = hours;
    else
        hoursWorked = 0;
}
```

Destructors in a Derived Class

Recall from Chapter 10 that a class can have a destructor. As we will see in the next chapter, destructors are typically used to deallocate dynamic memory allocated by the objects of a class. (A memory space that is allocated during execution time is called a dynamic memory space. The next chapter explains how to create and work with dynamic memory.) Suppose that a base class and its derived class have destructors. When a derived class object goes out of scope, it automatically invokes its destructor. When the destructor of the derived class executes, it automatically invokes the destructor of the base class. So when writing the definition of the destructor of the derived class, an explicit call to the destructor of the base class is not needed. Furthermore, when the destructor of the derived class executes first, it executes its own code and then calls the destructor of the base class. For example, suppose that `class three` is derived from `class two`, `class two` is derived from `class one`, and these classes have destructors. When an object of `class three` goes out of scope, first the destructor of `class three` executes, then the destructor of `class two` executes, and finally, the destructor of `class one` executes. That is, the destructors execute in the reverse order.

HEADER FILE OF A DERIVED CLASS

The previous section explained how to derive new classes from previously defined classes. To define new classes, you create new header files. The base classes are already defined, and header files contain their definitions. Thus, to create new classes based on the previously defined classes, the header files of the new classes contain commands that tell the computer where to look for the definitions of the base classes.

Suppose that the definition of the `class personType` is placed in the header file `personType.h`. To create the definition of the `class partTimeEmployee`, the header file—say, `partTimeEmployee.h`—must contain the preprocessor directive:

```
#include "personType.h"
```

before the definition of the `class partTimeEmployee`. To be specific, the header file `partTimeEmployee.h` is as shown below.

```
//Header file partTimeEmployee

#include "personType.h"

class partTimeEmployee: public personType
{
public:
    void print() const;
        //Function to output the first name, last name, and
        //the wages.
        //Postcondition: Outputs
        //          firstName lastName wages are $$$$.$$
```

```
    double calculatePay() const;
      //Function to calculate and return the wages.
      //Postcondition: Pay is calculated and returned

    void setNameRateHours(string first, string last,
                          double rate, double hours);
      //Function to set the first name, last name, payRate,
      //and hoursWorked according to the parameters.
      //Postcondition: firstName = first; lastName = last;
      //               payRate = rate; hoursWorked = hours

    partTimeEmployee(string first = "", string last = "",
                     double rate = 0, double hours = 0);
      //Constructor with parameters
      //Sets the first name, last name, payRate, and hoursWorked
      //according to the parameters. If no value is specified,
      //the default values are assumed.
      //Postcondition: firstName = first; lastName = last;
      //               payRate = rate; hoursWorked = hours

private:
    double payRate;      //variable to store the pay rate
    double hoursWorked; //variable to store the hours worked
};
```

The definitions of the member functions can be placed in a separate file. Recall that to include a system-provided header file, such as `iostream`, in a user program, you enclose the header file between angular brackets; to include a user-defined header file in a program, you enclose the header file between double quotation marks.

Multiple Inclusions of a Header File

The previous section discussed how to create the header file of a derived class. To include a header file in a program, you use the preprocessor command. Recall that before a program is compiled, the preprocessor first processes the program. Consider the following header file:

```
//Header file test.h

const int ONE = 1;
const int TWO = 2;
```

Suppose that the header file `testA.h` includes the file `test.h` in order to use the identifiers `ONE` and `TWO`. To be specific, suppose that the header file `testA.h` looks like:

```
//Header file testA.h

#include "test.h"
  .
  .
  .
```

Now, consider the following program code:

```
//Program headerTest.cpp

#include "test.h"
#include "testA.h"
    .
    .
    .
```

When the program `headerTest.cpp` is compiled, it is first processed by the preprocessor. The preprocessor includes first the header file `test.h` and then the header file `testA.h`. When the header file `testA.h` is included, because it contains the preprocessor directive `#include "test.h"`, the header file `test.h` is included twice in the program. The second inclusion of the header file `test.h` results in compile-time errors, such as the identifier ONE already being declared. This problem occurs because the first inclusion of the header file `test.h` has already defined the variables ONE and TWO. To avoid multiple inclusion of a file in a program, we use certain preprocessor commands in the header file. Let us first rewrite the header file `test.h` using these preprocessor commands and then explain the meaning of these commands.

```
//Header file test.h

#ifndef H_test
#define H_test
const int ONE = 1;
const int TWO = 2;
#endif
```

    a.   `#ifndef H_test` means "if not defined H_test"

    b.   `#define H_test` means "define H_test"

    c.   `#endif` means "end if"

Here, `H_test` is a preprocessor identifier.

The effect of these commands is as follows: If the identifier `H_test` is not defined, we must define the identifier `H_test` and let the remaining statements between `#define` and `#endif` pass through the compiler. If the header file `test.h` is included the second time in the program, the statement `#ifndef` fails and all of the statements until `#endif` are skipped. In fact, all header files are written using similar preprocessor commands.

C++ Stream Classes

Chapter 3 described in detail how to perform input/output (I/O) using standard I/O devices and file I/O. In particular, you used the object `cin`, the extraction operator `>>`, and functions such as `get` and `ignore` to read data from the standard input device. You also used the object `cout` and the insertion operator `<<` to send output to the standard output device. To use `cin` and `cout`, the programs included the header file `iostream`, which includes the definitions of the classes istream and ostream. Moreover, for file I/O, the programs included the header file fstream, and they used objects of type ifstream for file input and objects of type ofstream for file output. This section briefly describes how stream classes are related and implemented in C++.

In C++, stream classes are implemented using the inheritance mechanism, as shown in Figure 11-6.

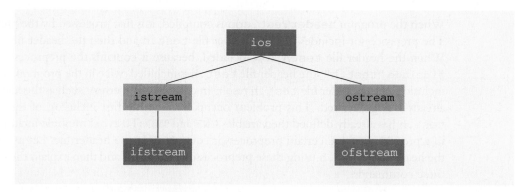

FIGURE 11-6 C++ stream classes hierarchy

Figure 11-6 shows the stream classes that we have encountered in previous chapters. From this figure, it follows that the **class ios** is the base class for all stream classes. Classes istream and ostream are directly derived from the **class ios**. The **class ifstream** is derived from the **class istream**, and the **class ofstream** is derived from the **class ostream**. Moreover, using the mechanism of multiple inheritance, the **class iostream** (not to be confused with the *header* file iostream—these are separate things) and the **class fstream** are derived from the **class iostream**. (The classes iostream and fstream are not discussed in this book.)

The **class ios** contains formatting flags and member functions to access and/or modify the setting of these flags. To identify the I/O status, the **class ios** contains an integer status word. This integer status word provides a continuous update reporting the status of the stream.

The **classes istream** and **ostream** are responsible for providing the operations for the data transfer between memory and devices. The **class istream** defines the extraction operator, >>, and functions such as get and ignore. The **class ostream** defines the insertion operator, <<, which is used by the object cout.

The **class ifstream** is derived from the **class istream** to provide the file input operations. Similarly, the **class ofstream** is derived from the **class ostream** to provide the file output operations. Objects of type ifstream are used for file input; objects of type ofstream are used for file output. The header file fstream contains the definitions of the **classes ifstream** and **ofstream**.

Protected Members of a Class

The `private` members of a class are `private` to the class and cannot be directly accessed outside of the class. Only member functions of that class can access the `private` members. As discussed previously, the derived class cannot directly access the `private` members of a base class. However, it is sometimes necessary (say, for efficiency and/or to simplify the code) for a derived class to directly access a `private` member of a base class. If you make a `private` member become `public`, then anyone can access that member. Recall that the members of a class are classified into three categories: `public`, `private`, and `protected`. So, for a base class to give access to a member to its derived class and still prevent its direct access outside of the class, you must declare that member under the `memberAccessSpecifier` `protected`. Thus, the accessibility of a `protected` member of a class is in between `public` and `private`. A derived class can directly access the `protected` members of a base class.

To summarize, if a member of a base class needs to be accessed by a derived class, that member is declared under the `memberAccessSpecifier` `protected`.

Inheritance as `public`, `protected`, or `private`

Suppose `class` B is derived from `class` A. Then, B cannot directly access the `private` members of A. That is, the `private` members of A are hidden in B. What about the `public` and `protected` members of A? This section gives the rules that generally apply when accessing the members of a base class.

Consider the following statement:

```
class B: memberAccessSpecifier A
{
    .
    .
    .
};
```

In this statement, `memberAccessSpecifier` is either `public`, `protected`, or `private`.

1. If `memberAccessSpecifier` is `public`—that is, the inheritance is `public`—then:

    a. The `public` members of A are `public` members of B. They can be directly accessed in `class` B.

    b. The `protected` members of A are `protected` members of B. They can be directly accessed by the member functions (and `friend` functions) of B.

    c. The `private` members of A are hidden in B. They cannot be directly accessed in B. They can be accessed by the member functions (and `friend` functions) of B through the `public` or `protected` members of A.

2. If memberAccessSpecifier is protected—that is, the inheritance is protected—then:

   a. The public members of A are protected members of B. They can be accessed by the member functions (and friend functions) of B.

   b. The protected members of A are protected members of B. They can be accessed by the member functions (and friend functions) of B.

   c. The private members of A are hidden in B. They cannot be directly accessed in B. They can be accessed by the member functions (and friend functions) of B through the public or protected members of A.

3. If memberAccessSpecifier is private—that is, the inheritance is private—then:

   a. The public members of A are private members of B. They can be accessed by the member functions (and friend functions) of B.

   b. The protected members of A are private members of B. They can be accessed by the member functions (and friend functions) of B.

   c. The private members of A are hidden in B. They cannot be directly accessed in B. They can be accessed by the member functions (and friend functions) of B through the public or protected members of A.

NOTE   Chapter 13 describes the friend functions.

Example 11-4 illustrates how the member functions of a derived class can directly access a protected member of the base class.

EXAMPLE 11-4

(Accessing protected Members in the Derived Class)

Consider the following definition of the class bClass:

```
class bClass
{
public:
    void setData(double);
    void setData(char, double);
    void print() const;
```

```
bClass(char ch = '*', double u = 0.0);

protected:
    char bCh;

private:
    double bX;
};
```

The definition of the `class bClass` contains a `protected` member variable bCh of type `char` and a `private` member variable bX of type `double`. It also contains an overloaded member function setData. One version is used to set both member variables; the other version is used to set only the `private` member variable. The class also has a constructor with default parameters. Suppose that the definitions of the member functions and the constructor are as follows:

```
void bClass::setData(double u)
{
    bX = u;
}
void bClass::setData(char ch, double u)
{
    bCh = ch;
    bX = u;
}

void bClass::print() const
{
    cout << "Base class: bCh = " << bCh << ", bX = " << bX
         << endl;
}

bClass::bClass(char ch, double u)
{
    bCh = ch;
    bX = u;
}
```

Next, we derive a `class dClass` from the `class bClass` using `public` inheritance as follows:

```
class dClass: public bClass
{
public:
    void setData(char, double, int);
    void print() const;

    dClass(char ch = '*', double u = 0.0, int x = 0);

private:
    int dA;
};
```

The `class dClass` contains a `private` member variable `dA` of type `int`. It also contains a constructor, a member function `setData` with three parameters, and the function `print`.

Let us now write the definition of the function `setData`. Because `bCh` is a `protected` member variable of the `class bClass`, it can be directly accessed in the definition of the function `setData`. However, because `bX` is a `private` member variable of the `class bClass`, the function `setData` cannot directly access it. Thus, the function `setData` must set `bX` by using the function `setData` of the `class bClass`. The definition of the function `setData` of the `class dClass` can be written as follows:

```
void dClass::setData(char ch, double v, int a)
{
    bClass::setData(v);

    bCh = ch; //initialize bCh using the assignment statement
    dA = a;
}
```

Note that the definition of the function `setData` calls the function `bClass::setData`, with one parameter to set the member variable `bX`, and then directly sets the value of `bCh`. Next, let us write the definition of the function `print` (of the `class dClass`).

Notice that in the definition of the `class bClass`, the member function `print` is not overloaded as in the member function `setData`. It prints the values of both member variables, `bCh` and `bX`. The member variable `bX` is a `private` member variable, so it cannot be directly accessed in the `class dClass`. Even though `bCh` is a `protected` member variable and it can be directly accessed in the `class dClass`, we must print its value using the function `print` of the `class bClass`, because this function outputs the values of both `bCh` and `dX`. For this reason, we first call the function `print` (of the `class bClass`) and then output only the value of `dA`. The definition of the function `print` is:

```
void dClass::print() const
{
    bClass::print();

    cout << "Derived class dA = " << dA << endl;
}
```

The definition of the constructor is:

```
dClass::dClass(char ch, double u, int x)
    : bClass(ch, u)
{
    dA = x;
}
```

The following program illustrates how the objects of `bClass` and `dClass` work. We assume that the definition of the `class bClass` is in the header file `protectMembClass.h`, and the definition of the `class dClass` is in the header file `protectMembInDerivedCl.h`.

```
//Accessing protected members of a base class in the derived
//class.

#include <iostream>
#include "protectMembClass.h"
#include "protectMembInDerivedCl.h"

using namespace std;

int main()
{
    bClass bObject;                                            //Line 1
    dClass dObject;                                            //Line 2

    bObject.print();                                           //Line 3
    cout << endl;                                              //Line 4

    cout << "*** Derived class object ***" << endl; //Line 5

    dObject.setData('&', 2.5, 7);                              //Line 6

    dObject.print();                                           //Line 7

    return 0;
}
```

Sample Run:

```
Base class: bCh = *, bX = 0

*** Derived class object ***
Base class: bCh = &, bX = 2.5
Derived class dA = 7
```

When you write the definitions of the member functions of the class dClass, the protected member variable bCh can be accessed directly. However, dClass objects cannot directly access bCh. That is, the following statement is illegal (it is, in fact, a syntax error):

```
dObject.bCh = '&';      //illegal
```

Composition (Aggregation)

Composition (aggregation) is another way to relate two classes. In **composition (aggregation)**, one or more members of a class are objects of another class type. Composition is a "has-a" relation; for example, "every person has a date of birth."

Example 10-10 in Chapter 10 defined a class called personType. The class personType stores a person's first and last name. Suppose we want to keep track of additional information for a person, such as a personal ID (e.g., a Social Security number) and a date of birth. Because every person has a personal ID and a date of birth, we can define a new class, called `personalInfo`, in which one of the members is an object of type `personType`. We can declare additional members to store the personal ID and date of birth for the **class** `personalInfo`.

First, we define another **class**, `dateType`, to store only a person's date of birth. Then, we construct the **class** `personalInfo` from the **classes** `personType` and `dateType`. This way, we can demonstrate how to define a new class using two classes.

To define the **class** `dateType`, we need three member variables—to store the month, day number, and year. Some of the operations that need to be performed on a date are to set the date and to print the date. The following statements define the `class dateType`:

```
class dateType
{
public:
    void setDate(int month, int day, int year);
    //Function to set the date.
    //The member variables dMonth, dDay, and dYear are set
    //according to the parameters.
    //Postcondition: dMonth = month; dDay = day;
    //               dYear = year

    int getDay() const;
    //Function to return the day.
    //Postcondition: The value of dDay is returned.

    int getMonth() const;
    //Function to return the month.
    //Postcondition: The value of dMonth is returned.

    int getYear() const;
    //Function to return the year.
    //Postcondition: The value of dYear is returned.

    void printDate() const;
    //Function to output the date in the form mm-dd-yyyy.

    dateType(int month = 1, int day = 1, int year = 1900);
    //Constructor to set the date
    //The member variables dMonth, dDay, and dYear are set
    //according to the parameters.
    //Postcondition: dMonth = month; dDay = day; dYear = year;
    //               If no values are specified, the default
    //               values are used to initialize the member
    //               variables.
```

```
private:
    int dMonth; //variable to store the month
    int dDay;   //variable to store the day
    int dYear;  //variable to store the year
};
```

Figure 11-7 shows the UML class diagram of the **class** dateType.

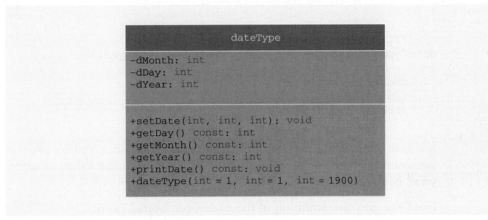

FIGURE 11-7 UML class diagram of the **class** dateType

The definitions of the member functions of the **class** dateType are as follows:

```
void dateType::setDate(int month, int day, int year)
{
    dMonth = month;
    dDay = day;
    dYear = year;
}
```

The definition of the function setDate, before storing the date into the member variables, does not check whether the date is valid. That is, it does not confirm whether month is between 1 and 12, year is greater than 0, and day is valid (for example, for January, day should be between 1 and 31). In Programming Exercise 2 at the end of this chapter, you are asked to rewrite the definition of the function setDate so that the date is validated before storing it in the member variables. The definitions of the remaining member functions are as follows:

```
int dateType::getDay() const
{
    return dDay;
}

int dateType::getMonth() const
{
    return dMonth;
}
```

```
int dateType::getYear() const
{
    return dYear;
}

void dateType::printDate() const
{
    cout << dMonth << "-" << dDay << "-" << dYear;
}

    //Constructor with parameters
dateType::dateType(int month, int day, int year)
{
    dMonth = month;
    dDay = day;
    dYear = year;
}
```

Just as in the case of setDate, in Programming Exercise 2, you are asked to rewrite the definition of the constructor so that it checks for the valid values of month, day, and year before storing the date into the member variables.

Next, we give the definition of the class personalInfo:

```
class personalInfo
{
public:
    void setpersonalInfo(string first, string last, int month,
                         int day, int year, int ID);
      //Function to set the personal information.
      //The member variables are set according to the
      //parameters.
      //Postcondition: firstName = first; lastName = last;
      //               dMonth = month; dDay = day;
      //               dYear = year; personID = ID;

    void printpersonalInfo () const;
      //Function to print the personal information.

    personalInfo(string first = "", string last = "",
                int month = 1, int day = 1, int year = 1900,
                int ID = 0);
      //Constructor
      //The member variables are set according to the
      //parameters.
      //Postcondition: firstName = first; lastName = last;
      //               dMonth = month; dDay = day;
      //               dYear = year; personID = ID;
      //               If no values are specified, the default
      //               values are used to initialize the member
      //               variables.
```

```
private:
    personType name;
    dateType bDay;
    int personID;
};
```

Figure 11-8 shows the UML class diagram of the **class** `personalInfo` and composition (aggregation).

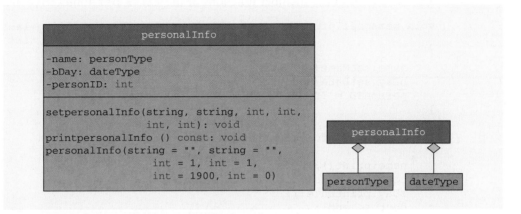

FIGURE 11-8 UML class diagram of the **class** `personalInfo` and composition (aggregation)

Before we give the definition of the member functions of the **class** `personalInfo`, let us discuss how the constructors of the objects `bDay` and `name` are invoked.

Recall that a class constructor is automatically executed when a class object enters its scope. Suppose that we have the following statement:

`personalInfo student;`

When the object `student` enters its scope, the objects `bDay` and `name`, which are members of `student`, also enter their scopes. As a result, one of their constructors is executed. We, therefore, need to know how to pass arguments to the constructors of the member objects (that is, `bDay` and `name`), which occurs when we give the definitions of the constructors of the class. Recall that constructors do not have a type and so cannot be called like other functions. The arguments to the constructor of a member object (such as `bDay`) are specified in the heading part of the definition of the constructor of the class. Furthermore, member objects of a class are constructed (that is, initialized) in the order they are declared (not in the order they are listed in the constructor's member initialization list) and before the containing class objects are constructed. Thus, in our case, the object `name` is initialized first, then `bDay`, and finally, `student`.

The following statements illustrate how to pass arguments to the constructors of the member objects `name` and `bDay`:

```
personalInfo::personalInfo(string first, string last, int month,
                           int day, int year, int ID)
        : name(first, last), bDay(month, day, year)
{
    .
    .
    .
}
```

The definitions of the member functions of the **class** personalInfo are as follows:

```
void personalInfo::setpersonalInfo(string first, string last,
                        int month, int day, int year, int ID)
{
    name.setName(first,last);
    bDay.setDate(month,day,year);
    personID = ID;
}

void personalInfo::printpersonalInfo() const
{
    name.print();
    cout << "'s date of birth is ";
    bDay.printDate();
    cout << endl;
    cout << "and personal ID is " << personID;
}

personalInfo::personalInfo(string first, string last, int month,
                           int day, int year, int ID)
        : name(first, last), bDay(month, day, year)
{
    personID = ID;

}
```

NOTE In the case of inheritance, use the class name to invoke the base class's constructor. In the case of composition, use the member object name to invoke its own constructor.

Object-Oriented Design (OOD) and Object-Oriented Programming (OOP)

The first 11 chapters of this book used the top-down approach to programming, also called structured programming, to write programs. Problems were broken down into modules, and each module solved a particular part of the problem. Data requirements were identified, and functions were written to manipulate the data. The functions and the data were kept separate, and the functions acted on the data in a passive way. Structured programming, therefore, has certain limitations. In structured programming, functions are dependent on the data, and functions are designed specifically to solve a particular problem. It is quite difficult, if not impossible, to reuse a function written for one program in another program. For some of these reasons, structured programming is not very efficient for large software development.

Chapter 10 began with the introduction of classes. We learned how classes are defined and used. Later in that chapter, we concentrated on the data requirements of a problem and the logical operations on that data. With the help of classes, we combined the data—and the operations on that data—in a single unit. That is, the data and operations were encapsulated in a single unit. Also, with the help of classes, we were able to separate the data and the algorithms to manipulate that data. However, the functions to implement the operations on the data had direct access to the data. This chapter explains how to create new classes from existing classes through inheritance (and also using composition). Furthermore, an object has the capability to hide the information details. These are some of the features of object-oriented design (OOD).

The three basic principles of OOD are as follows:

- **Encapsulation**—The ability to combine data and operations on that data in a single unit.
- **Inheritance**—The ability to create new objects (classes) from existing objects (classes).
- **Polymorphism**—The ability to use the same expression to denote different operations.

In OOD, an object is a fundamental entity; in structured programming, a function is a fundamental entity. In OOD, we debug classes; in structured programming, we debug functions. In OOD, a program is a collection of interacting objects; in structured programming, a program is a collection of interacting functions. Also, OOD encourages code reuse. Once a class becomes error-free, it can be reused in many programs because it is a self-contained entity. Object-oriented programming (OOP) implements OOD.

To create objects, we must know how to represent the data and write functions to manipulate that data. Thus, we must know everything that we have learned in Chapters 2 through 8. The first eight chapters are essential for any type of programming, whether structured or object-oriented.

C++ supports OOP through the use of classes. We have already examined the first two features of OOP, encapsulation and inheritance, in this chapter and Chapter 10. Chapter 13 discusses the third feature of OOD: polymorphism. A polymorphic function or operator has many forms.

In C++, a function name and the operators can be overloaded. An example of function overloading occurs when the function is called, and the operator is evaluated according to the arguments used. For instance, if both operands are integers, the division operator yields an integer result; otherwise, the division operator yields a decimal result. Suppose a class has constructors. If no arguments are passed to an object when it is declared, the default constructor is executed; otherwise, one of the constructors with parameters is executed. However, all constructors have the same name.

C++ also provides parametric polymorphism. In parametric polymorphism, the (data) type is left unspecified and then later instantiated. Templates (discussed in Chapter 13) provide parametric polymorphism. Also, C++ provides virtual functions as a means to implement polymorphism in an inheritance hierarchy, which allows the run-time selection of appropriate member functions. (Chapter 12 discusses virtual functions.)

There are several OOP languages in existence today, including Ada, Modula-2, Object Pascal, Turbo Pascal, Eiffel, C++, Java, and Smalltalk. The earliest OOP language was Simula, developed in 1967. The OOP terminology is influenced by the vocabulary of Smalltalk, the OOP language largely developed at a Xerox research center during the 1970s. An OOP language uses many "fancy" words, such as methods, message passing, and so forth.

OOP is a natural and intuitive way to view the programming process. When we view an object, we immediately think of what it can do. For example, when we think about a car, we also think about the operations on the car, such as starting the car and driving the car. When programmers think about a list, they also think about the operations on the list, such as searching, sorting, and inserting. OOP allows ADT to be created and used. In C++, we implement ADT through the use of classes.

Objects are created when class variables are declared. Objects interact with each other via function calls. Every object has an internal state and an external state. The `private` members form the internal state; the `public` members form the external state. Only the object can manipulate its internal state.

Identifying Classes, Objects, and Operations

In this book's first 9 chapters, in the problem analysis phase, we analyzed the problem, identified the data, and outlined the algorithm. To reduce the complexity of the function `main`, we wrote functions to manipulate the data. In Chapter 10, we used the OOD technique and first identified the objects that made up the overall problem. The objects were designed and implemented independently of the main program. The hardest part in OOD is to identify the classes and objects. In this section, we describe a common and simple technique to identify classes and objects.

We begin with a description of the problem and then identify all of the nouns and verbs. We choose our classes from the list of nouns, and we choose our operations from the list of verbs.

For example, suppose that we want to write a program that calculates and prints the volume and surface area of a cylinder. We can state this problem as follows:

Write a **program** to *input* the **dimensions** of a **cylinder** and *calculate* and *print* the **surface area** and **volume**.

In this statement, the nouns are bold, and the verbs are italic. From the list of nouns— **program, dimensions, cylinder, surface area**, and **volume**—we can easily visualize

cylinder to be a class—say, `cylinderType`—from which we can create many cylinder objects of various dimensions. The nouns **dimensions**, **surface area**, and **volume** are characteristics of a **cylinder** and thus can hardly be considered classes.

After we identify a class, the next step is to determine three pieces of information:

- Operations that an object of that class type can perform
- Operations that can be performed on an object of that class type
- Information that an object of that class type must maintain

From the list of verbs identified in the problem description, we choose a list of possible operations that an object of that class can perform, or has performed, on itself. For example, from the list of verbs for the cylinder problem description—*write*, *input*, *calculate*, and *print*—the possible operations for a cylinder object are *input*, *calculate*, and *print*.

For the **class** `cylinderType`, the dimensions represent the data. The `center` of the base, `radius` of the base, and `height` of the cylinder are the characteristics of the dimensions. You can input data to the object either by a constructor or by a mutator function.

The verb *calculate* applies to determining the volume and the surface area. From this, you can deduce the operations: `cylinderVolume` and `cylinderSurfaceArea`. Similarly, the verb *print* applies to the display of the volume and the surface area on an output device. In Programming Exercise 3 at the end of this chapter, you are asked to design a class to implement the characteristics of a cylinder.

Identifying classes via the nouns and verbs from the descriptions of the problem is not the only technique possible. There are several other OOD techniques in the literature. However, this technique is sufficient for the programming exercises in this book.

PROGRAMMING EXAMPLE: Grade Report

Watch the Video

This programming example further illustrates the concepts of inheritance and composition.

The mid-semester point at your local university is approaching. The registrar's office wants to prepare the grade reports as soon as the students' grades are recorded. However, some of the students enrolled have not yet paid their tuition.

1. If a student has paid the tuition, the grades are shown on the grade report together with the grade point average (GPA).

2. If a student has not paid the tuition, the grades are not printed. For these students, the grade report contains a message indicating that the grades have been held for nonpayment of the tuition. The grade report also shows the billing amount.

The registrar's office and the business office want your help in writing a program that can analyze the students' data and print the appropriate grade reports. The data is stored in a file in the following form:

```
15000 345
studentName studentID isTuitionPaid numberOfCourses
courseName courseNumber creditHours grade
courseName courseNumber creditHours grade
  .
  .
  .
studentName studentID isTuitionPaid numberOfCourses
courseName courseNumber creditHours grade
courseName courseNumber creditHours grade
  .
  .
  .
```

The first line indicates the number of students enrolled and the tuition rate per credit hour. The students' data is given thereafter.

A sample input file is as follows:

```
3 345
Lisa Miller 890238 Y 4
Mathematics MTH345 4 A
Physics PHY357 3 B
ComputerSci CSC478 3 B
History HIS356 3 A
  .
  .
  .
```

The first line indicates that the input file contains three students' data, and the tuition rate is $345 per credit hour. Next, the course data for student Lisa Miller is given: Lisa Miller's ID is 890238, she has paid the tuition, and she is taking four courses. The course number for the mathematics class she is taking is MTH345, the course has four credit hours, her mid-semester grade is A, and so on.

The desired output for each student is in the following form:

```
Student Name: Lisa Miller
Student ID: 890238
Number of courses enrolled: 4
```

Course No	Course Name	Credits	Grade
CSC478	ComputerSci	3	B
HIS356	History	3	A
MTH345	Mathematics	4	A
PHY357	Physics	3	B

```
Total number of credits: 13
Mid-Semester GPA: 3.54
```

It is clear from this output that the courses must be ordered according to the course number. To calculate the GPA, we assume that the grade A is equivalent to four points, B is equivalent to three points, C is equivalent to two points, D is equivalent to one point, and F is equivalent to zero points.

Input   A file containing the data in the form given previously. For easy reference, let us assume that the name of the input file is stData.txt.

Output   A file containing the output in the form given previously.

PROBLEM
ANALYSIS
AND
ALGORITHM
DESIGN

We must first identify the main components of the program. The university has students, and every student takes courses. Thus, the two main components are the student and the course.

Let us first describe the course component.

Course

The main characteristics of a course are the course name, course number, and number of credit hours.

Some of the basic operations that need to be performed on an object of the course type are:

1. Set the course information.
2. Print the course information.
3. Show the credit hours.
4. Show the course number.

The following class defines the course as an ADT:

```cpp
class courseType
{
public:
    void setCourseInfo(string cName, string cNo, int credits);
    //Function to set the course information.
    //The course information is set according to the
    //parameters.
    //Postcondition: courseName = cName; courseNo = cNo;
    //                courseCredits = credits;

    void print(ostream& outF);
    //Function to print the course information.
    //This function sends the course information to the
    //output device specified by the parameter outF. If the
    //actual parameter to this function is the object cout,
    //then the output is shown on the standard output device.
    //If the actual parameter is an ofstream variable, say,
    //outFile, then the output goes to the file specified by
    //outFile.

    int getCredits();
    //Function to return the credit hours.
    //Postcondition: The value of courseCredits is returned.
```

1
1

```
    string getCourseNumber();
       //Function to return the course number.
       //Postcondition: The value of courseNo is returned.

    string getCourseName();
       //Function to return the course name.
       //Postcondition: The value of courseName is returned.

    courseType(string cName = "", string cNo = "",
              int credits = 0);
       //Constructor
       //The object is initialized according to the parameters.
       //Postcondition: courseName = cName; courseNo = cNo;
       //                courseCredits = credits;

private:
    string courseName;   //variable to store the course name
    string courseNo;     //variable to store the course number
    int courseCredits;   //variable to store the credit hours
};
```

Figure 11-9 shows the UML class diagram of the class courseType.

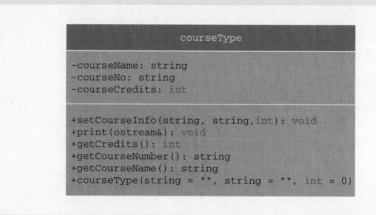

FIGURE 11-9 UML class diagram of the class courseType

Next, we discuss the definitions of the functions to implement the operations of the class courseType. These definitions are quite straightforward and easy to follow.

The function setCourseInfo sets the values of the private member variables according to the values of the parameters. Its definition is:

```
void courseType::setCourseInfo(string cName, string cNo,
                               int credits)
{
    courseName = cName;
    courseNo = cNo;
    courseCredits = credits;
} //end setCourseInfo
```

The function print prints the course information. The parameter outF specifies the output device. Also, we print the course name and course number left-justified rather than right-justified (the default). Thus, we need to set the left manipulator. Before printing the credit hours, the manipulator is set to be right-justified. The following steps describe this function:

1. Set the left manipulator.

2. Print the course number.

3. Print the course name.

4. Set the right manipulator.

5. Print the credit hours.

The definition of the function print is:

```
void courseType::print(ostream& outF)
{
    outF << left;                                        //Step 1
    outF << setw(8) << courseNo << "   ";                //Step 2
    outF << setw(15) << courseName;                      //Step 3
    outF << right;                                       //Step 4
    outF << setw(3) << courseCredits << "   ";           //Step 5
} //end print
```

The constructor is declared with the default values. If no values are specified when a courseType object is declared, the constructor uses the default to initialize the object. Using the default values, the object's member variables are initialized as follows: courseNo to blank, courseName to blank, and courseCredits to 0. Otherwise, the values specified in the object declaration are used to initialize the object. Its definition is:

```
courseType::courseType(string cName, string cNo, int credits)
{
    courseName = cName;
    courseNo =   cNo;
    courseCredits = credits;
} //end default constructor
```

The definitions of the remaining functions are as follows:

```
int courseType::getCredits()
{
    return courseCredits;
} //end getCredits

string courseType::getCourseNumber()
{
    return courseNo;
}//end getCourseNumber

string courseType::getCourseName()
{
    return courseName;
} //end getCourseName
```

Next, we discuss the student component.

 NOTE Notice that in the definition of the `class` `courseType`, the member functions, such as `print` and `getCredits`, are accessor functions. This class also has other accessor functions. As noted in Chapter 10, we typically define the accessor functions with the keyword `const` at the end of their headings. We leave it as an exercise for you to redefine this class so that the accessor functions are declared as constant functions. (See Programming Exercise 12 at the end of this chapter.)

Student The main characteristics of a student are the student name, student ID, number of courses in which enrolled, courses in which enrolled, and grade for each course. Because every student has to pay tuition, we also include a member to indicate whether the student has paid the tuition.

Every student is a person, and every student takes courses. We have already designed a `class` `personType` to process a person's first and last name. We have also designed a class to process the information for a course. Thus, we see that we can derive the `class` `studentType` to keep track of a student's information from the `class` `personType`, and one member of this class is of type `courseType`. We can add more members as needed.

The basic operations to be performed on an object of type `studentType` are as follows:

1. Set the student information.
2. Print the student information.
3. Calculate the number of credit hours taken.

4. Calculate the GPA.

5. Calculate the billing amount.

6. Because the grade report will print the courses in ascending order, sort the courses according to the course number.

The following class defines studentType as an ADT. We assume that a student takes no more than six courses per semester.

```cpp
class studentType: public personType
{
public:
    void setInfo(string fname, string lName, int ID,
                 int nOfCourses, bool isTPaid,
                 courseType courses[], char courseGrades[]);
    //Function to set the student's information.
    //Postcondition: The member variables are set
    //               according to the parameters.

    void print(ostream& outF, double tuitionRate);
    //Function to print the student's grade report.
    //If the member variable isTuitionPaid is true, the grades
    //are shown; otherwise, three stars are printed. If the
    //actual parameter corresponding to outF is the object
    //cout, then the output is shown on the standard output
    //device. If the actual parameter corresponding to outF
    //is an ofstream object, say outFile, then the output
    //goes to the file specified by outFile.

    studentType();
    //Default constructor
    //The member variables are initialized.

    int getHoursEnrolled();
    //Function to return the credit hours a student is
    //enrolled in.
    //Postcondition: The number of credit hours is
    //               calculated and returned.

    double getGpa();
    //Function to return the grade point average.
    //Postcondition: The gpa is calculated and returned.

    double billingAmount(double tuitionRate);
    //Function to return the tuition fees.
    //Postcondition: The billing amount is calculated
    //and returned.
```

11

```
private:
    void sortCourses();
    //Function to sort the courses.
    //Postcondition: The array coursesEnrolled is sorted.
    //                For each course, its grade is stored in
    //                the array coursesGrade. Therefore, when
    //                the array coursesEnrolled is sorted, the
    //                corresponding entries in the array
    //                coursesGrade are adjusted.

    int sId;                 //variable to store the student ID
    int numberOfCourses;     //variable to store the number
                             //of courses
    bool isTuitionPaid;      //variable to indicate whether the
                             //tuition is paid
    courseType coursesEnrolled[6]; //array to store the courses
    char coursesGrade[6];     //array to store the course grades
};
```

Figure 11-10 shows the UML class diagram of the **class** studentType together with the inheritance and composition (aggregation) relation.

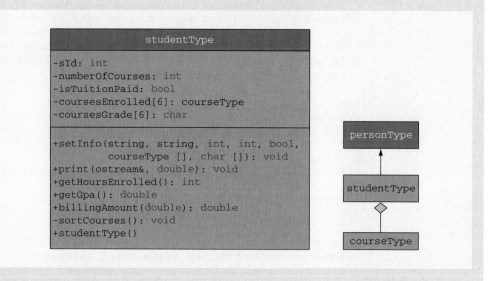

FIGURE 11-10 UML class diagram of the **class** studentType together with inheritance and composition (aggregation) relation

Before writing the definitions of the member functions of the **class** studentType, we make the following note.

NOTE Notice that in the definition of the `class` `studentType`, the member functions, such as `print` and `getGpa`, are accessor functions. This class also has other accessor functions. As noted in Chapter 10, we typically define the accessor functions with the keyword `const` at the end of their headings. We leave it as an exercise for you to redefine this class so that the accessor functions are declared as constant functions. (See Programming Exercise 12 at the end of this chapter.)

Note that the member function `sortCourses` to sort the array `coursesEnrolled` is a `private` member of the `class` `studentType`. This is due to the fact that this function is needed for internal data manipulation, and the user of the class does not need to access this member.

Next, we discuss the definitions of the functions to implement the operations of the `class` `studentType`.

The function `setInfo` first initializes the `private` member variables according to the incoming parameters. This function then calls the function `sortCourses` to sort the array `coursesEnrolled` by course number. The `class` `studentType` is derived from the `class` `personType`, and the variables to store the first and last name are `private` member variables of that class. Therefore, we call the member function `setName` of the `class` `personType` and pass the appropriate variables to set the first and last names. The definition of the function `setInfo` is as follows:

```
void studentType::setInfo(string fName, string lName, int ID,
                          int nOfCourses, bool isTPaid,
                          courseType courses[], char cGrades[])
{
    int i;

    setName(fName, lName);          //set the name

    sId = ID;                       //set the student ID
    isTuitionPaid = isTPaid;        //set isTuitionPaid
    numberOfCourses = nOfCourses;   //set the number of courses

        //set the course information
    for (i = 0; i < numberOfCourses; i++)
    {
        coursesEnrolled[i] = courses[i];
        coursesGrade[i] = cGrades[i];
    }

    sortCourses();     //sort the array coursesEnrolled
} //end setInfo
```

The default constructor initializes the `private` member variables to the default values. Note that because the `private` member variable `coursesEnrolled` is of type `courseType` and is an array, the default constructor of the `class` `courseType` executes automatically, and the entire array is initialized.

```
studentType::studentType()
{
    numberOfCourses = 0;
    sId = 0;
    isTuitionPaid = false;

    for (int i = 0; i < 6; i++)
        coursesGrade[i] = '*';
} //end default constructor
```

The function `print` prints the grade report. The parameter `outF` specifies the output device. If the student has paid his or her tuition, the grades and the GPA are shown. Otherwise, three stars are printed in place of each grade, the GPA is not shown, a message indicates that the grades are being held for nonpayment of the tuition, and the amount due is shown. This function has the following steps:

1. Output the student's name.
2. Output the student's ID.
3. Output the number of courses in which the student is enrolled.
4. Output the heading:
   `Course No  Course Name   Credits    Grade`
5. Print each course's information.

   For each course, print:

   a. `Course No, Course Name, Credits`
   b. `if isTuitionPaid is true`

      Output the grade

      `else`

      Output three stars.
6. Print the total credit hours.
7. To output the GPA and billing amount in a fixed decimal format with the decimal point and trailing zeros, set the necessary flag. Also, set the precision to two decimal places.
8. `if isTuitionPaid is true`

   Output the GPA

   `else`

   Output the billing amount and a message about withholding the grades.

The definition of the function print is as follows:

```cpp
void studentType::print(ostream& outF, double tuitionRate)
{
    int i;

    outF << "Student Name: " << getFirstName()
         << " " << getLastName() << endl;          //Step 1

    outF << "Student ID: " << sId << endl;          //Step 2

    outF << "Number of courses enrolled: "
         << numberOfCourses << endl;                //Step 3
    outF << endl;

    outF << left;
    outF << "Course No" << setw(15) << "  Course Name"
         << setw(8) << "Credits"
         << setw(6) << "Grade" << endl;             //Step 4

    outF << right;
    for (i = 0; i < numberOfCourses; i++)           //Step 5
    {
        coursesEnrolled[i].print(outF);             //Step 5a

        if (isTuitionPaid)                          //Step 5b
            outF <<setw(4) << coursesGrade[i] << endl;
        else
            outF << setw(4) << "***" << endl;
    }
    outF << endl;

    outF << "Total number of credit hours: "
         << getHoursEnrolled() << endl;             //Step 6

    outF << fixed << showpoint << setprecision(2);  //Step 7

    if (isTuitionPaid)                              //Step 8
        outF << "Mid-Semester GPA: " << getGpa()
             << endl;
    else
    {
        outF << "*** Grades are being held for not paying "
             << "the tuition. ***" << endl;
        outF << "Amount Due: $" << billingAmount(tuitionRate)
             << endl;
    }

    outF << "-*-*-*-*-*-*-*-*-*-*-*-*-*-*-*-*-*-*-*-*"
         << "-*-*-*-*-" << endl << endl;
} //end print
```

NOTE Let us take a look at the formal parameter of the function `print`. The formal parameter `outF` is an object of the `class ostream`. We can use this function to send the output to the standard output device, the screen, or to a file. As indicated in the definition of the class, if the actual parameter is, say, `cout`, then the output is displayed on the screen. If the actual parameter is, say, `outfile`, an object of the `class ofstream`, then the output is sent to the device indicated by `outfile`. As mentioned in the section, "C++ Stream Classes," the `class ofstream` is derived from the `class ostream`. Therefore, the `class ostream` is the base class. In C++, if a formal reference parameter is of the type `ostream`, it can refer to an object of the `class ofstream`.

In general, C++ allows a formal reference parameter of the base class type to refer to an object of the derived class. Of course, for user-defined classes, some other things need to be taken into account for this mechanism to work properly, which we will discuss in Chapter 12 (in the section "Inheritance, Pointers, and Virtual Functions").

The function `getHoursEnrolled` calculates and returns the total credit hours that a student is taking. These credit hours are needed to calculate both the GPA and the billing amount. The total credit hours are calculated by adding the credit hours of each course in which the student is enrolled. Because the credit hours for a course are in the `private` member variable of an object of type `courseType`, we use the member function `getCredits` of the `class courseType` to retrieve the credit hours. The definition of this function is:

```
int studentType::getHoursEnrolled()
{
    int totalCredits = 0;
    int i;

    for (i = 0; i < numberOfCourses; i++)
        totalCredits += coursesEnrolled[i].getCredits();

    return totalCredits;
} //end getHoursEnrolled
```

If a student has not paid the tuition, the function `billingAmount` calculates and returns the amount due, based on the number of credit hours enrolled. The definition of this function is:

```
double studentType::billingAmount(double tuitionRate)
{
    return tuitionRate * getHoursEnrolled();
} //end billingAmount
```

We now discuss the function getGpa. This function calculates a student's GPA. To find the GPA, we find the equivalent points for each grade, add the points, and then divide the sum by the total credit hours the student is taking. The definition of this function is:

```cpp
double studentType::getGpa()
{
    int i;
    double sum = 0.0;

    for (i = 0; i < numberOfCourses; i++)
    {
        switch (coursesGrade[i])
        {
        case 'A':
            sum += coursesEnrolled[i].getCredits() * 4;
            break;
        case 'B':
            sum += coursesEnrolled[i].getCredits() * 3;
            break;
        case 'C':
            sum += coursesEnrolled[i].getCredits() * 2;
            break;
        case 'D':
            sum += coursesEnrolled[i].getCredits() * 1;
            break;
        case 'F':
            break;
        default:
            cout << "Invalid Course Grade." << endl;
        }
    }

    return sum / getHoursEnrolled();
} //end getGpa
```

The function sortCourses sorts the array coursesEnrolled by course number. To sort the array, we use a selection sort algorithm. Because we will compare the course numbers, which are strings and **private** member variables of the **class** courseType, we first retrieve and store the course numbers in local variables.

```cpp
void studentType::sortCourses()
{
    int i, j;
    int minIndex;
    courseType temp;      //variable to swap the data
    char tempGrade;       //variable to swap the grades
    string course1;
    string course2;
```

```
for (i = 0; i < numberOfCourses - 1; i++)
{
    minIndex = i;

    for (j = i + 1; j < numberOfCourses; j++)
    {
            //get the course numbers
        course1 =
            coursesEnrolled[minIndex].getCourseNumber();
        course2 = coursesEnrolled[j].getCourseNumber();

        if (course1 > course2)
            minIndex = j;
    }//end for

    temp = coursesEnrolled[minIndex];
    coursesEnrolled[minIndex] = coursesEnrolled[i];
    coursesEnrolled[i] = temp;

    tempGrade = coursesGrade[minIndex];
    coursesGrade[minIndex] = coursesGrade[i];
    coursesGrade[i] = tempGrade;
} //end for
} //end sortCourses
```

MAIN PROGRAM

Now that we have designed the classes `courseType` and `studentType`, we will use these classes to complete the program.

We will restrict our program to process a maximum of 10 students. Note that this program can easily be enhanced to process any number of students.

Because the `print` function of the class does the necessary computations to print the final grade report, the main program has very little work to do. In fact, all that is left for the main program is to declare the objects to hold the students' data, load the data into these objects, and then print the grade reports. Because the input is in a file and the output will be sent to a file, we declare stream variables to access the input and output files. Essentially, the main algorithm for the program is:

1. Declare the variables.
2. Open the input file.
3. If the input file does not exist, exit the program.
4. Open the output file.
5. Get the number of students registered and the tuition rate.
6. Load the students' data.
7. Print the grade reports.

VARIABLES

This program processes a maximum of 10 students. Therefore, we must declare an array of 10 components of type `studentType` to hold the students' data. We also need to store the number of students registered and the tuition rate. Because the data will be read from a file and because the output is sent to a file, we need two stream variables to access the input and output files. Thus, we need the following variables:

```
studentType studentList[MAX_NO_OF_STUDENTS]; //array to store
                                             //the students' data

int noOfStudents;      //variable to store the number of students
double tuitionRate;    //variable to store the tuition rate

ifstream infile;       //input stream variable
ofstream outfile;      //output stream variable
```

Function
getStudentData

This function has three parameters: a parameter to access the input file, a parameter to access the array `studentList`, and a parameter to know the number of students registered. In pseudocode, the definition of this function is as follows:

For each student in the university,

1. Get the first name, last name, student ID, and `isPaid`.

2. `if isPaid` is 'Y'
       set `isTuitionPaid` to `true`
   `else`
       set `isTuitionPaid` to `false`

3. Get the number of courses the student is taking.

4. For each course:
   Get the course name, course number, credit hours, and grade.
   Load the course information into a `courseType` object.

5. Load the data into a `studentType` object.

We need to declare several local variables to read and store the data. The definition of the function `getStudentData` is:

```
void getStudentData(ifstream& infile,
                    studentType studentList[],
                    int numberOfStudents)
{
        //local variables
    string fName;      //variable to store the first name
    string lName;      //variable to store the last name
    int ID;            //variable to store the student ID
    int noOfCourses;   //variable to store the number of courses
    char isPaid;       //variable to store Y/N, that is,
                       //is tuition paid
    bool isTuitionPaid; //variable to store true/false
```

```
    string cName;    //variable to store the course name
    string cNo;      //variable to store the course number
    int credits;     //variable to store the course credit hours

    int count;        //loop control variable
    int i;            //loop control variable

    courseType courses[6]; //array of objects to store the
                           //course information
    char cGrades[6];       //array to hold the course grades

    for (count = 0; count < numberOfStudents; count++)
    {
        infile >> fName >> lName >> ID >> isPaid;   //Step 1

        if (isPaid == 'Y')                          //Step 2
            isTuitionPaid = true;
        else
            isTuitionPaid = false;

        infile >> noOfCourses;                      //Step 3

        for (i = 0; i < noOfCourses; i++)           //Step 4
        {
            infile >> cName >> cNo >> credits
                    >> cGrades[i];                  //Step 4.a
            courses[i].setCourseInfo(cName, cNo,
                                     credits);      //Step 4.b
        }
        studentList[count].setInfo(fName, lName, ID,
                                   noOfCourses,
                                   isTuitionPaid,
                                   courses, cGrades); //Step 5
    }//end for
} //end getStudentData
```

Function printGradeReports   This function prints the grade reports. For each student, it calls the function print of the class studentType to print the grade report. The definition of the function printGradeReports is:

```
void printGradeReports(ofstream& outfile,
                       studentType studentList[],
                       int numberOfStudents,
                       double tuitionRate)
{
    int count;
    for (count = 0; count < numberOfStudents; count++)
        studentList[count].print(outfile, tuitionRate);
} //end printGradeReports
```

PROGRAMMING LISTING

```
//**********************************************************
// Author: D.S. Malik
//
// class courseType
// This class specifies the members to implement a course's
// information.
//**********************************************************

#ifndef H_courseType
#define H_courseType

#include <fstream>
#include <string>

using namespace std;

//The definition of the class courseType goes here.
    .
    .
    .
#endif


//**********************************************************
// Author: D.S. Malik
//
// Implementation file courseTypeImp.cpp
// This file contains the definitions of the functions to
// implement the operations of the class courseType.
//**********************************************************

#include <iostream>
#include <fstream>
#include <string>
#include <iomanip>
#include "courseType.h"

using namespace std;

//The definitions of the member functions of the class
//courseType go here.
    .
    .
    .
```

```
//**********************************************************
// Author: D.S. Malik
//
// class personType
// This class specifies the members to implement a person's
// first name and last name.
//**********************************************************

#ifndef H_personType
#define H_personType

#include <string>

using namespace std;

//The definition of the class personType goes here.
    .
    .
    .
#endif


//**********************************************************
// Author: D.S. Malik
//
// Implementation file personTypeImp.cpp
// This file contains the definitions of the functions to
// implement the operations of the class personType.
//**********************************************************

#include <iostream>
#include <string>
#include "personType.h"

using namespace std;

//The definitions of the member functions of the class
//personType go here.
    .
    .
    .


//**********************************************************
// Author: D.S. Malik
//
// class studentType
// This class specifies the members to implement a student's
// information.
//**********************************************************
```

```
#ifndef H_studentType
#define H_studentType

#include <fstream>
#include <string>
#include "personType.h"
#include "courseType.h"

using namespace std;

//The definition of the class studentType goes here.
    .
    .
    .

#endif


//***********************************************************
// Author: D.S. Malik
//
// Implementation file studentTypeImp.cpp
// This file contains the definitions of the functions to
// implement the operations of the class studentType.
//***********************************************************

#include <iostream>
#include <iomanip>
#include <fstream>
#include <string>
#include "personType.h"
#include "courseType.h"
#include "studentType.h"

using namespace std;

//The definitions of the member functions of the class
//studentType go here.
    .
    .
    .

//***********************************************************
// Author: D.S. Malik
//
// This program reads students' data from a file and outputs
// the grades. If student has not paid the tuition, the
// grades are not shown, and an appropriate message is
// output. The output is stored in a file.
//***********************************************************
```

11

```
#include <iostream>
#include <fstream>
#include <string>
#include "studentType.h"

using namespace std;

const int MAX_NO_OF_STUDENTS = 10;

void getStudentData(ifstream& infile,
                    studentType studentList[],
                    int numberOfStudents);

void printGradeReports(ofstream& outfile,
                       studentType studentList[],
                       int numberOfStudents,
                       double tuitionRate);

int main()
{
    studentType studentList[MAX_NO_OF_STUDENTS];

    int noOfStudents;
    double tuitionRate;
    ifstream infile;
    ofstream outfile;

    infile.open("stData.txt");

    if (!infile)
    {
        cout << "The input file does not exist. "
             << "Program terminates." << endl;
        return 1;
    }

    outfile.open("sDataOut.txt");

    infile >> noOfStudents; //get the number of students
    infile >> tuitionRate;  //get the tuition rate

    getStudentData(infile, studentList, noOfStudents);
    printGradeReports(outfile, studentList,
                      noOfStudents, tuitionRate);

    return 0;
}

//Place the definitions of the functions getStudentData and
//printGradeReports here.
```

Sample Run:

```
Student Name: Lisa Miller
Student ID: 890238
Number of courses enrolled: 4

Course No  Course Name  Credits Grade
CSC478     ComputerSci     3       B
HIS356     History         3       A
MTH345     Mathematics     4       A
PHY357     Physics         3       B

Total number of credit hours: 13
Mid-Semester GPA: 3.54
-*-*-*-*-*-*-*-*-*-*-*-*-*-*-*-*-*-*-*-*-*-*-*-*-

Student Name: Bill Wilton
Student ID: 798324
Number of courses enrolled: 5

Course No  Course Name  Credits Grade
BIO234     Biology         4      ***
CHM256     Chemistry       4      ***
ENG378     English         3      ***
MTH346     Mathematics     3      ***
PHL534     Philosophy      3      ***

Total number of credit hours: 17
*** Grades are being held for not paying the tuition. ***
Amount Due: $5865.00
-*-*-*-*-*-*-*-*-*-*-*-*-*-*-*-*-*-*-*-*-*-*-*-*-

Student Name: Dandy Goat
Student ID: 746333
Number of courses enrolled: 6

Course No  Course Name  Credits Grade
BUS128     Business        3       C
CHM348     Chemistry       4       B
CSC201     ComputerSci     3       B
ENG328     English         3       B
HIS101     History         3       A
MTH137     Mathematics     3       A

Total number of credit hours: 19
Mid-Semester GPA: 3.16
-*-*-*-*-*-*-*-*-*-*-*-*-*-*-*-*-*-*-*-*-*-*-*-*-
```

11

Input File:

```
3 345
Lisa Miller 890238 Y 4
Mathematics MTH345 4 A
Physics PHY357 3 B
ComputerSci CSC478 3 B
History HIS356 3 A

Bill Wilton 798324 N 5
English ENG378 3 B
Philosophy PHL534 3 A
Chemistry CHM256 4 C
Biology BIO234 4 A
Mathematics MTH346 3 C

Dandy Goat 746333 Y 6
History HIS101 3 A
English ENG328 3 B
Mathematics MTH137 3 A
Chemistry CHM348 4 B
ComputerSci CSC201 3 B
Business BUS128 3 C
```

QUICK REVIEW

1. Inheritance and composition (aggregation) are meaningful ways to relate two or more classes.

2. Inheritance is an "is–a" relation.

3. Composition (aggregation) is a "has–a" relation.

4. In a single inheritance, the derived class is derived from only one existing class called the base class.

5. In a multiple inheritance, a derived class is derived from more than one base class.

6. The `private` members of a base class are `private` to the base class. The derived class cannot directly access them.

7. The `public` members of a base class can be inherited either as `public` or `private` by the derived class.

8. A derived class can redefine the member functions of a base class, but this redefinition applies only to the objects of the derived class.

9. A call to a base class's constructor (with parameters) is specified in the heading of the definition of the derived class's constructor.

10. If in the heading of the definition of a derived class's constructor, no call to a constructor (with parameters) of a base class is specified, then during the derived class's object declaration and initialization, the default constructor (if any) of the base class executes.

11. When initializing the object of a derived class, the constructor of the base class is executed first.

12. Review the inheritance rules given in this chapter.

13. In composition (aggregation), a member of a class is an object of another class.

14. In composition (aggregation), a call to the constructor of the member objects is specified in the heading of the definition of the class's constructor.

15. The three basic principles of OOD are encapsulation, inheritance, and polymorphism.

16. An easy way to identify classes, objects, and operations is to describe the problem in English and then identify all of the nouns and verbs. Choose your classes (objects) from the list of nouns and operations from the list of verbs.

EXERCISES

1. Mark the following statements as true or false.

   a. The constructor of a derived class can specify a call to the constructor of the base class in the heading of the function definition.

   b. The constructor of a derived class can specify a call to the constructor of the base class using the name of the class.

   c. Suppose that `x` and `y` are classes, one of the member variables of `x` is an object of type `y`, and both classes have constructors. The constructor of `x` specifies a call to the constructor of `y` by using the object name of type `y`.

2. Draw a class hierarchy in which several classes are derived from a single base class.

3. Suppose that a `class employeeType` is derived from the `class personType` (see Example 10-10, in Chapter 10). Give examples of members—data and functions—that can be added to the `class employeeType`. Also write the definition of the `class employeeType` that you derived from the `class personType`.

4. Consider the `class circleType` as defined in Example 10-8 (Chapter 10). Suppose that the `class sphereType` is derived from the `class circleType`.

   a. Name some of the functions and/or data members that can be added to the `class sphereType`.

   b. Write the definition of the `class sphereType`.

   c. Write the definitions of the member functions of the `class sphereType`.

5. Consider the following statements:

```
class molecules: atom
{
    ...
};
```

a. In this declaration, which class is the base class and which class is the derived class?

b. What is the type of this inheritance?

6. Consider the following statements:

```
class pigeon: public bird
{
    ...
};
```

a. In this declaration, which class is the base class and which class is the derived class?

b. What is the type of this inheritance?

7. Consider the following class definition:

```
class circle                          class cylinder: public circle
{                                     {
public:                               public:
    void print() const;                   void print() const;
    void setRadius(double);               void setHeight(double);
    void setCenter(double, double);       double getHeight();
    void getCenter(double&, double&);     double volume();
    double getRadius();                   double area();
    double area();                        cylinder();
    circle();                             cylinder(double, double,
    circle(double, double, double);              double, double);
private:                              private:
    double xCoordinate;                   double height;
    double yCoordinate;               };
    double radius;
};
```

Suppose that you have the declaration:

```
cylinder newCylinder;
```

Determine the private members of the object newCylinder.

8. Suppose that you have the declarations of Exercise 7. Write the definitions of the member functions of the classes circle and cylinder. Identify the member functions of the class cylinder that overrides the member functions of the class circle.

9. Consider the following class definition:

```
class temp
{
public:
    void print() const;
    void setDescription(string);
    void setX(double);
    string getDescription();
    double getX();
    temp();
    temp(string, double);

private:
    string description;
    double x;
};
```

What is wrong with the following class definition?

```
class derivedFromTemp public temp
{
public:
    void print();
    void setZ(double);
    double getZ();
    double power();
      //returns x to the power of z.

private:
    double z;
}
```

10. Assume the definition of the **class** temp as given in Exercise 9. Consider the following class definition:

```
class derivedFromTemp: public temp;
{
public:
    void print();
      //outputs the values of all the instance variables.
    void setZ(double);
      //sets the value of z according to the parameter.
    double getZ();
      //returns the value of z.
    double power() const;
      //returns x to the power of z.

    derivedFromTemp();
      //sets the values of instance variables to "",
      //0.0, and 0.0, respectively.
```

```
derivedFromTemp(string, double, double);
    //sets the values of instance variables according
    //to the parameters.
private:
    double z;
}
```

a. Identify and correct errors, if any, in the definition of the `class` derivedFromTemp. Also give a correct definition of this class.

b. After correcting errors, if any, in the definition of the `class` derivedFromTemp, write the definition of the member functions of the `class` derivedFromTemp.

11. Consider the following statements:

```
class base                          class derived: public base
{                                   {
public:                                 public:
    void print() const;                     .
    void set(int, int);                     .
    void get(int&, int&);                   .
    base();
    base(int, int);
                                        private:
private:                                    int c;
    int a;
    int b;                          };
};
```

a. Suppose that `class` derived overrides the function print of the `class` base. What is the heading of the function print in the `class` derived?

b. Suppose that the class overloads the functions set and get of the `class` base. What are the headings of these functions in the `class` derived?

12. Explain the difference between overriding and overloading a member function of a base class in a derived class.

13. Suppose that `class` three is derived from `class` two and `class` two is derived from `class` one and that each class has instance variables. Suppose that an object of `class` three enters its scope, so the constructors of these classes will execute. Determine the order in which the constructors of these classes will execute.

14. Consider the following class definitions:

```
class smart                          class superSmart: public smart
{                                    {
public:                              public:
   void print() const;                 void print() const;
   void set(int, int);                 void set(int, int, int);
   int sum();                          int manipulate();
   smart();                            superSmart();
   smart(int, int);                    superSmart(int, int, int);
private:                             private:
   int x;                              int z;
   int y;                           };
   int secret();
};
```

a. Which **private** members, if any, of smart are **public** members of superSmart?

b. Which members, functions, and/or data of the **class** smart are directly accessible in **class** superSmart?

15. Assume the definitions of the **class**es smart and superSmart as given in Exercise 14. Suppose that the following statements are in a user program (client code):

```
smart smartObject;
superSmart superSmartObject;
```

Mark the following statements as valid or invalid. If a statement is invalid, explain why.

a.
```
int smart::sum()
{
    return x + y + z;
}
```

b.
```
smartObject.secret();
superSmartObject.z = 0;
```

c.
```
void superSmart::set(int a, int b, int c)
{
    smart::set(a, b);
    z = c;
}
```

d. Assume that the following statement is in a user program:

```
smart.print();
```

e. Assume that the following statement is in a user program:

```
cout << superSmart.sum() << superSmart.z << endl;
```

16. Assume the declaration of Exercise 14.

   a. Write the definition of the default constructor of smart so that the instance variables of smart are initialized to 0.

   b. Write the definition of the default constructor of superSmart so that the instance variables of superSmart are initialized to 0.

   c. Write the definition of the member function set of smart so that the instance variables are initialized according to the parameters.

   d. Write the definition of the member function sum of the **class** smart so that it returns the sum of the instance variables.

   e. Write the definition of the member function manipulate of the **class** superSmart so that it returns the $(x + y)^z$, that is, return x plus y to the power of z.

17. Explain how in a **private** inheritance, the members of the base class are inherited by a derived class.

18. Explain how in a **protected** inheritance, the members of the base class are inherited by a derived class.

19. Explain how in a **public** inheritance, the members of the base class are inherited by a derived class.

20. Explain the difference between the **private** and **protected** members of a class.

21. Explain the difference between the **protected** and **public** members of a class.

22. Consider the following class definition:

```
class first
{
public:
    void setX();
    void print const();
protected:
    int y;
    void setY(int a);
private:
    int x;
};
```

Suppose that **class** second is derived from **class** first using the statement:

```
class second: private first
```

Determine which members of **class** first are **private**, **protected**, and **public** in **class** second.

23. Assume the declaration of Exercise 22. Suppose that class third is derived from class first using the statement:

    class third: protected first

    Determine which members of class first are private, protected, and public in class third.

24. Assume the declaration of Exercise 22. Suppose that class fourth is derived from class first using the statement:

    class fourth: public first

    Determine which members of class first are private, protected, and public in class fourth.

25. Assume the declaration of Exercise 22. Suppose that class fifth is derived from class first using the statement:

    class fifth: first

    Determine which members of class first are private, protected, and public in class fifth.

26. What is wrong with the following code?

```
class classA
{
protected:
    void setX(int a);              //Line 1
        //Postcondition: x = a;    //Line 2

private:                           //Line 3
    int x;                         //Line 4
};
    .
    .
    .
int main()
{
    classA aObject;                //Line 5

    aObject.setX(4);               //Line 6
    return 0;                      //Line 7
}
```

27. Consider the following code:

```cpp
class one
{
public:
    void print() const;
        //Output the values of x and y
protected:
    void setData(int u, int v);
        //Postcondition: x = u; y = v;
private:
    int x;
    int y;
};

class two: public one
{
public:
    void setData(int a, int b, int c);
        //Postcondition: x = a; y = b; z = c;
    void print() const;
        //Output the values of x, y, and z
private:
    int z;
};
```

a. Write the definition of the function setData of class two.

b. Write the definition of the function print of class two.

28. What is the output of the following C++ program?

```cpp
#include <iostream>
#include <string>

using namespace std;

class baseClass
{
public:
    void print() const;

    baseClass(string s = " ", int a = 0);
        //Postcondition: str = s; x = a;

protected:
    int x;

private:
    string str;
};
```

```cpp
class derivedClass: public baseClass
{
public:
    void print() const;

    derivedClass(string s = "", int a = 0, int b = 0);
      //Postcondition: str = s; x = a; y = b;

private:
    int y;
};

int main()
{
    baseClass baseObject("This is the base class", 2);
    derivedClass derivedObject("DDDDDD", 3, 7);

    baseObject.print();
    derivedObject.print();

    return 0;
}
void baseClass::print() const
{
    cout << x << " " << str << endl;
}

baseClass::baseClass(string s, int a)
{
    str = s;
    x = a;
}

void derivedClass::print() const
{
    cout << "Derived class: " << y << endl;
    baseClass::print();
}

derivedClass::derivedClass(string s, int a, int b)
            :baseClass("Hello Base", a + b)
{
    y = b;
}
```

PROGRAMMING EXERCISES

1. In Chapter 10, the **class** **clockType** was designed to implement the time of day in a program. Certain applications, in addition to hours, minutes, and seconds, might require you to store the time zone. Derive the **class** **extClockType** from the **class** **clockType** by adding a member variable to store the time zone. Add the necessary member functions and constructors to make the class functional. Also, write the definitions of the member functions and the constructors. Finally, write a test program to test your class.

2. In this chapter, the **class** **dateType** was designed to implement the date in a program, but the member function **setDate** and the constructor do not check whether the date is valid before storing the date in the member variables. Rewrite the definitions of the function **setDate** and the constructor so that the values for the month, day, and year are checked before storing the date into the member variables. Add a member function, **isLeapYear**, to check whether a year is a leap year. Moreover, write a test program to test your class.

3. Chapter 10 defined the **class** **circleType** to implement the basic properties of a circle. (Add the function **print** to this class to output the radius, area, and circumference of a circle.) Now every cylinder has a base and height, where the base is a circle. Design a **class** **cylinderType** that can capture the properties of a cylinder and perform the usual operations on the cylinder. Derive this class from the **class** **circleType** designed in Chapter 10. Some of the operations that can be performed on a cylinder are as follows: calculate and print the volume, calculate and print the surface area, set the height, set the radius of the base, and set the center of the base. Also, write a program to test various operations on a cylinder.

4. Amanda and Tyler opened a business that specializes in shipping liquids, such as milk, juice, and water, in cylinderical containers. The shipping charges depend on the amount of the liquid in the container. (For simplicity, you may assume that the container is filled to the top.) They also provide the option to paint the outside of the container for a reasonable amount. Write a program that does the following:

    a. Prompts the user to input the dimensions (in feet) of the container (radius of the base and the height).

    b. Prompts the user to input the shipping cost per liter.

    c. Prompts the user to input the paint cost per square foot. (Assume that the entire container including the top and bottom needs to be painted.)

    d. Separately outputs the shipping cost and the cost of painting.

    Your program must use the **class** **cylinderType** (designed in Programming Exercise 3) to store the radius of the base and the height of the container. (Note that 1 cubic feet = 28.32 liters or 1 liter = 0.353146667 cubic feet.)

5. Using classes, design an online address book to keep track of the names, addresses, phone numbers, and dates of birth of family members, close friends, and certain business associates. Your program should be able to handle a maximum of 500 entries.

   a. Define a **class addressType** that can store a street address, city, state, and ZIP code. Use the appropriate functions to print and store the address. Also, use constructors to automatically initialize the member variables.

   b. Define a **class extPersonType** using the **class personType** (as defined in Example 10-10, Chapter 10), the **class dateType** (as designed in this chapter's Programming Exercise 2), and the **class addressType**. Add a member variable to this class to classify the person as a family member, friend, or business associate. Also, add a member variable to store the phone number. Add (or override) the functions to print and store the appropriate information. Use constructors to automatically initialize the member variables.

   c. Define the **class addressBookType** using the previously defined classes. An object of the type **addressBookType** should be able to process a maximum of 500 entries.

   The program should perform the following operations:

   i. Load the data into the address book from a disk.

   ii. Sort the address book by last name.

   iii. Search for a person by last name.

   iv. Print the address, phone number, and date of birth (if it exists) of a given person.

   v. Print the names of the people whose birthdays are in a given month.

   vi. Print the names of all the people between two last names.

   vii. Depending on the user's request, print the names of all family members, friends, or business associates.

6. In Programming Exercise 2, the **class dateType** was designed and implemented to keep track of a date, but it has very limited operations. Redefine the **class dateType** so that it can perform the following operations on a date, in addition to the operations already defined:

   a. Set the month.

   b. Set the day.

   c. Set the year.

   d. Return the month.

   e. Return the day.

   f. Return the year.

g. Test whether the year is a leap year.

h. Return the number of days in the month. For example, if the date is 3-12-2015, the number of days to be returned is 31 because there are 31 days in March.

i. Return the number of days passed in the year. For example, if the date is 3-18-2015, the number of days passed in the year is 77. Note that the number of days returned also includes the current day.

j. Return the number of days remaining in the year. For example, if the date is 3-18-2015, the number of days remaining in the year is 288.

k. Calculate the new date by adding a fixed number of days to the date. For example, if the date is 3-18-2015 and the days to be added are 25, the new date is 4-12-2015.

7. Write the definitions of the functions to implement the operations defined for the **class dateType** in Programming Exercise 6.

8. The **class dateType** defined in Programming Exercise 6 prints the date in numerical form. Some applications might require the date to be printed in another form, such as March 24, 2015. Derive the **class extDateType** so that the date can be printed in either form.

Add a member variable to the **class extDateType** so that the month can also be stored in string form. Add a member function to output the month in the string format, followed by the year—for example, in the form March 2015.

Write the definitions of the functions to implement the operations for the **class extDateType**.

9. Using the **classes extDateType** (Programming Exercise 8) and **dayType** (Chapter 10, Programming Exercise 4), design the **class calendarType** so that, given the month and the year, we can print the calendar for that month. To print a monthly calendar, you must know the first day of the month and the number of days in that month. Thus, you must store the first day of the month, which is of the form **dayType**, and the month and the year of the calendar. Clearly, the month and the year can be stored in an object of the form **extDateType** by setting the day component of the date to 1 and the month and year as specified by the user. Thus, the **class calendarType** has two member variables: an object of the type **dayType** and an object of the type **extDateType**.

Design the **class calendarType** so that the program can print a calendar for any month starting January 1, 1500. Note that the day for January 1 of the year 1500 is a Monday. To calculate the first day of a month, you can add the appropriate days to Monday of January 1, 1500.

For the **class** **calendarType**, include the following operations:

a. Determine the first day of the month for which the calendar will be printed. Call this operation **firstDayOfMonth**.

b. Set the month.

c. Set the year.

d. Return the month.

e. Return the year.

f. Print the calendar for the particular month.

g. Add the appropriate constructors to initialize the member variables.

10. a. Write the definitions of the member functions of the **class** **calendarType** (designed in Programming Exercise 9) to implement the operations of the **class** **calendarType**.

b. Write a test program to print the calendar for either a particular month or a particular year. For example, the calendar for September 2015 is:

```
                  September 2015
    Sun    Mon    Tue    Wed    Thu    Fri    Sat
                    1      2      3      4      5
     6      7      8      9     10     11     12
    13     14     15     16     17     18     19
    20     21     22     23     24     25     26
    27     28     29     30
```

11. In this exercise, you will design various classes and write a program to computerize the billing system of a hospital.

a. Design the **class** **doctorType**, inherited from the **class** **personType**, defined in Chapter 10, with an additional data member to store a doctor's speciality. Add appropriate constructors and member functions to initialize, access, and manipulate the data members.

b. Design the **class** **billType** with data members to store a patient's ID and a patient's hospital charges, such as pharmacy charges for medicine, doctor's fee, and room charges. Add appropriate constructors and member functions to initialize, access, and manipulate the data members.

c. Design the **class** **patientType**, inherited from the **class** **personType**, defined in Chapter 10, with additional data members to store a patient's ID, age, date of birth, attending physician's name, the date when the patient was admitted in the hospital, and the date when the patient was discharged from the hospital. (Use the **class** **dateType** to store the date of birth, admit date, discharge date, and the **class** **doctorType** to store the attending physician's name.) Add appropriate constructors and member functions to initialize, access, and manipulate the data members.

Write a program to test your classes.

12. In the Programming Example Grade Report, in the definitions of the classes `courseType` and `studentType`, the accessor functions are not made constants; that is, they are not defined with the reserved word `const` at the end of their headings. Redefine these classes so that all of the accessor functions are constant functions. Accordingly, modify the definitions of the accessor functions and rerun the program.

13. a. Define the `class bankAccount` to store a bank customer's account number and balance. Suppose that account number is of type `int`, and balance is of type `double`. Your class should, at least, provide the following operations: set the account number, retrieve the account number, retrieve the balance, deposit and withdraw money, and print account information. Add appropriate constructors.

b. Every bank offers a checking account. Derive the `class checkingAccount` from the `class bankAccount` (designed in part (a)). This class inherits members to store the account number and the balance from the base class. A customer with a checking account typically receives interest, maintains a minimum balance, and pays service charges if the balance falls below the minimum balance. Add member variables to store this additional information. In addition to the operations inherited from the base class, this class should provide the following operations: set interest rate, retrieve interest rate, set minimum balance, retrieve minimum balance, set service charges, retrieve service charges, post interest, verify if the balance is less than the minimum balance, write a check, withdraw (override the method of the base class), and print account information. Add appropriate constructors.

c. Every bank offers a savings account. Derive the `class savingsAccount` from the `class bankAccount` (designed in part (a)). This class inherits members to store the account number and the balance from the base class. A customer with a savings account typically receives interest, makes deposits, and withdraws money. In addition to the operations inherited from the base class, this class should provide the following operations: set interest rate, retrieve interest rate, post interest, withdraw (override the method of the base class), and print account information. Add appropriate constructors.

d. Write a program to test your classes designed in parts (b) and (c).

POINTERS, CLASSES, VIRTUAL FUNCTIONS, ABSTRACT CLASSES, AND LISTS

IN THIS CHAPTER, YOU WILL:

- Learn about the pointer data type and pointer variables
- Explore how to declare and manipulate pointer variables
- Learn about the address of operator and the dereferencing operator
- Discover dynamic variables
- Explore how to use the `new` and `delete` operators to manipulate dynamic variables
- Learn about pointer arithmetic
- Discover dynamic arrays
- Become aware of the shallow and deep copies of data
- Discover the peculiarities of classes with pointer member variables
- Learn about virtual functions
- Examine the relationship between the address of operator and classes
- Become aware of abstract classes

In Chapter 2, you learned that C++'s data types are classified into three categories: simple, structured, and pointers. Until now, you have studied only the first two data types. This chapter discusses the third data type called the pointer data type. You will first learn how to declare pointer variables (or pointers, for short) and manipulate the data to which they point. Later, you will use these concepts when you study dynamic arrays and linked lists. Linked lists are discussed in Chapter 16.

Pointer Data Type and Pointer Variables

Chapter 2 defined a data type as a set of values together with a set of operations. Recall that the set of values is called the domain of the data type. In addition to these two properties, until now, all of the data types you have encountered have one more thing associated with them: the name of the data type. For example, there is a data type called `int`. The set of values belonging to this data type includes integers that range between −2147483648 and 2147483647, and the operations allowed on these values are the arithmetic operators described in Chapter 2. To manipulate numeric integer data in the range −2147483648 to 2147483647, you can declare variables using the word `int`. The name of the data type allows you to declare a variable. Next, we will describe the pointer data type.

The values belonging to pointer data types are the memory addresses of your computer. As in many other languages, there is no name associated with the pointer data type in C++. Because the domain—that is, the set of values of a pointer data type—is the addresses (memory locations), a pointer variable is a variable whose content is an address, that is, a memory location.

Pointer variable: A variable whose content is an address (that is, a memory address).

Declaring Pointer Variables

As remarked previously, there is no name associated with pointer data types. Moreover, pointer variables store memory addresses. So the obvious question is: If no name is associated with a pointer data type, how do you declare pointer variables?

The value of a pointer variable is an address. That is, the value refers to another memory space. The data is typically stored in this memory space. Therefore, when you declare a pointer variable, you also specify the data type of the value to be stored in the memory location pointed to by the pointer variable.

In C++, you declare a pointer variable by using the asterisk symbol (*) between the data type and the variable name. The general syntax to declare a pointer variable is:

```
dataType *identifier;
```

As an example, consider the following statements:

```
int *p;
char *ch;
```

In these statements, both `p` and `ch` are pointer variables. The content of `p` (when properly assigned) points to a memory location of type `int`, and the content of `ch` points to a memory location of type `char`. Usually, `p` is called a pointer variable of type `int`, and `ch` is called a pointer variable of type `char`.

Before discussing how pointers work, let us make the following observations. The statement:

```
int *p;
```

is equivalent to the statement:

```
int*  p;
```

which is equivalent to the statement:

```
int * p;
```

Thus, the character `*` can appear anywhere between the data type name and the variable name.

Now, consider the following statement:

```
int* p, q;
```

In this statement, only `p` is the pointer variable, not `q`. Here, `q` is an `int` variable. To avoid confusion, we prefer to attach the character `*` to the variable name. So the preceding statement is written as:

```
int *p, q;
```

Of course, the statement:

```
int *p, *q;
```

declares both `p` and `q` to be pointer variables of type `int`.

Now that you know how to declare pointers, next we will discuss how to make a pointer point to a memory space and how to manipulate the data stored in these memory locations.

Because the value of a pointer is a memory address, a pointer can store the address of a memory space of the designated type. For example, if `p` is a pointer of type `int`, `p` can store the address of any memory space of type `int`. C++ provides two operators—the address of operator (`&`) and the dereferencing operator (`*`)—to work with pointers. The next two sections describe these operators.

Address of Operator (&)

In C++, the ampersand, `&`, called the **address of operator**, is a unary operator that returns the address of its operand. For example, given the statements:

```
int x;
int *p;
```

the statement:

```
p = &x;
```

assigns the address of x to p. That is, x and the value of p refer to the same memory location.

Dereferencing Operator (*)

Every chapter until now has used the asterisk character, *, as the binary multiplication operator. C++ also uses * as a unary operator. When used as a unary operator, *, commonly referred to as the **dereferencing operator** or **indirection operator**, refers to the object to which its operand (that is, the pointer) points. For example, given the statements:

```
int x = 25;
int *p;
p = &x;    //store the address of x in p
```

the statement:

```
cout << *p << endl;
```

prints the value stored in the memory space pointed to by p, which is the value of x. Also, the statement:

```
*p = 55;
```

stores 55 in the memory location pointed to by p—that is, in x.

EXAMPLE 12-1

Let us consider the following statements:

```
int *p;
int num;
```

In these statements, p is a pointer variable of type int, and num is a variable of type int. Let us assume that memory location 1200 is allocated for p, and memory location 1800 is allocated for num (see Figure 12-1).

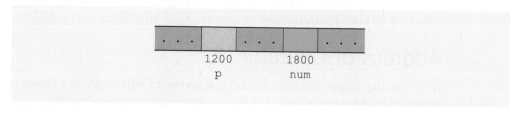

FIGURE 12-1 Variables p and num

Consider the following statements:

```
1. num = 78;
2. p = &num;
3. *p = 24;
```

The following shows the values of the variables after the execution of each statement.

After Statement	Values of the Variables	Explanation
1	1200 → p, 1800 → num = 78	The statement num = 78; stores 78 into num.
2	1200 → p = 1800, 1800 → num = 78	The statement p = # stores the address of num, which is 1800, into p.
3	1200 → p = 1800, 1800 → num = 24	The statement *p = 24; stores 24 into the memory location to which p points. Because the value of p is 1800, statement 3 stores 24 into memory location 1800. Note that the value of num is also changed.

Let us summarize the preceding discussion.

1. A declaration such as int *p; allocates memory for p only, not for *p. Later, you will learn how to allocate memory for *p.

2. The content of p points only to a memory location of type int.

3. &p, p, and *p all have different meanings.

4. &p means the address of p—that is, 1200 (in Figure 12-1).

5. p means the content of p, which is 1800, after the statement p = # executes.

6. *p means the content of the memory location to which p points. Note that after the statement p = # executes, the value of *p is 78; after the statement *p = 24; executes, the value of *p is 24.

EXAMPLE 12-2

Consider the following statements:

```
int *p;
int x;
```

Suppose that we have the memory allocation for p and x as shown in Figure 12-2.

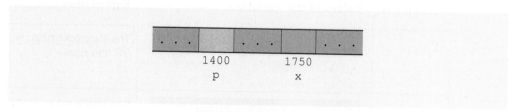

FIGURE 12-2 Variables p and x

The values of &p, p, *p, &x, and x are as follows:

&p | 1400   p | ? (unknown)   *p | Does not exist (undefined)   &x | 1750   x | ? (unknown)

Suppose that the following statements are executed in the order given:

```
x = 50;
p = &x;
*p = 38;
```

The values of &p, p, *p, &x, and x are shown after each of these statements executes.

After the statement x = 50; executes, the values of &p, p, *p, &x, and x are as follows:

&p | 1400   p | ? (unknown)   *p | Does not exist (undefined)   &x | 1750   x | 50

After the statement p = &x; executes, the values of &p, p, *p, &x, and x are as follows:

&p | 1400   p | 1750   *p | 50   &x | 1750   x | 50

After the statement *p = 38; executes, the values of &p, p, *p, &x, and x are as follows. (Because *p and x refer to the same memory space, the value of x is also changed to 38.)

&p | 1400   p | 1750   *p | 38   &x | 1750   x | 38

Let us note the following:

1. p is a pointer variable.
2. The content of p points only to a memory location of type int.
3. Memory location x exists and is of type int. Therefore, the assignment statement:

    p = &x;

    is legal. After this assignment statement executes, *p is valid and meaningful.

The program in Example 12-3 further illustrates how a pointer variable works.

EXAMPLE 12-3

The following program illustrates how pointer variables work:

```cpp
//Chapter 12: Example 12-3

#include <iostream>                                         //Line 1
#include <iomanip>                                          //Line 2

using namespace std;                                        //Line 3

const double PI = 3.1416;                                   //Line 4

int main()                                                  //Line 5
{                                                           //Line 6
    double radius;                                          //Line 7
    double *radiusPtr;                                      //Line 8

    cout << fixed << showpoint << setprecision(2);          //Line 9

    radius = 2.5;                                           //Line 10
    radiusPtr = &radius;                                    //Line 11

    cout << "Line 12: Radius = " << radius
         << ", area = " << PI * radius * radius << endl;    //Line 12

    cout << "Line 13: Radius = " << *radiusPtr
         << ", area = "
         << PI * (*radiusPtr) * (*radiusPtr) << endl;       //Line 13

    cout << "Line 14: Enter the radius: ";                  //Line 14
    cin >> *radiusPtr;                                      //Line 15
    cout << endl;                                           //Line 16
```

```
    cout << "Line 17: Radius = " << radius << ", area = "
         << PI * radius * radius << endl;                      //Line 17
    cout << "Line 18: Radius = " << *radiusPtr
         << ", area = "
         << PI * (*radiusPtr) * (*radiusPtr) << endl
         << endl;                                              //Line 18

    cout << "Line 19: Address of radiusPtr: "
         << &radiusPtr << endl;                                //Line 19
    cout << "Line 20: Value stored in radiusPtr: "
         << radiusPtr << endl;                                 //Line 20
    cout << "Line 21: Address of radius: "
         << &radius << endl;                                   //Line 21
    cout << "Line 22: Value stored in radius: "
         << radius << endl;                                    //Line 22

    return 0;                                                  //Line 23
}                                                              //Line 24
```

Sample Run: In this sample run, the user input is shaded.

```
Line 12: Radius = 2.50, area = 19.64
Line 13: Radius = 2.50, area = 19.64
Line 14: Enter the radius: 4.90

Line 17: Radius = 4.90, area = 75.43
Line 18: Radius = 4.90, area = 75.43

Line 19: Address of radiusPtr: 0012FF50
Line 20: Value stored in radiusPtr: 0012FF5C
Line 21: Address of radius: 0012FF5C
Line 22: Value stored in radius: 4.90
```

The preceding program works as follows. The statement in Line 7 declares radius to be a variable of type **double** and the statement in Line 8 declares radiusPtr to be a pointer variable of type **double**. The statement in Line 10 stores 2.5 in radius and the statement in Line 11 stores the address of radius in radiusPtr. The statement in Line 12 outputs the radius and area of the circle using the value stored in the memory location radius. The statement in Line 13 outputs the radius and area of the circle using the value stored in the memory location to which radiusPtr is pointing. Note that the output of the statements in Lines 12 and 13 is the same because radiusPtr points to radius. Next, the statement in Line 14 prompts the user to input the radius and the statement in Line 15 stores the radius in the memory location to which radiusPtr is pointing. Next, similar to the statements in Lines 12 and 13, the statements in Lines 17 and 18 output the radius and area using the variables radius and radiusPtr. The statements in Lines 19 to 22, output the address of radiusPtr, the value stored in radiusPtr, the address of radius, and the value stored in radius.

From the output of the statements in Lines 20 and 21, it follows that `radiusPtr` stores the address of the variable `radius`. (Note that the address of `radiusPtr`, the value of `radiusPtr`, and the address of `radius` as shown by the output of Lines 19, 20, and 21, respectively, are machine dependent. When you run this program on your machine, you are likely to get different values. Furthermore, the pointer values, that is, the addresses, are printed in hexadecimal by default.)

Classes, Structs, and Pointer Variables

In the previous section, you learned how to declare and manipulate pointers of simple data types, such as `int` and `char`. You can also declare pointers to other data types, such as classes. You will now learn how to declare and manipulate pointers to classes and structs. (Recall that both classes and structs have the same capabilities. The only difference between classes and structs is that, by default, all members of a class are `private`, and, by default, all members of a struct are `public`. Therefore, the following discussion applies to both.)

Consider the following declaration of a `struct`:

```
struct studentType
{
    char name[26];
    double gpa;
    int sID;
    char grade;
};

studentType  student;
studentType *studentPtr;
```

In the preceding declaration, `student` is an object of type `studentType`, and `studentPtr` is a pointer variable of type `studentType`. The following statement stores the address of `student` in `studentPtr`:

```
studentPtr = &student;
```

The following statement stores 3.9 in the component `gpa` of the object `student`:

```
(*studentPtr).gpa = 3.9;
```

The expression `(*studentPtr).gpa` is a mixture of pointer dereferencing and the class component selection. In C++, the dot operator, `.`, has a higher precedence than the dereferencing operator.

Let us elaborate on this a bit. In the expression `(*studentPtr).gpa`, the operator `*` evaluates first, so the expression `*studentPtr` evaluates first. Because `studentPtr` is a pointer variable of type `studentType`, `*studentPtr` refers to a memory space of type `studentType`, which is a `struct`. Therefore, `(*studentPtr).gpa` refers to the component gpa of that `struct`.

Consider the expression `*studentPtr.gpa`. Let us see how this expression gets evaluated. Because `.` (dot) has a higher precedence than `*`, the expression `studentPtr.gpa` evaluates first. The expression `studentPtr.gpa` would result in a syntax error, as `studentPtr` is *not* a `struct` variable, so it has no such component as gpa.

As you can see, in the expression `(*studentPtr).gpa`, the parentheses are important. However, typos can be problematic. Therefore, to simplify the accessing of `class` or `struct` components via a pointer, C++ provides another operator called the **member access operator arrow**, `->`. The operator `->` consists of two consecutive symbols: a hyphen and the "greater than" sign.

The syntax for accessing a `class` (`struct`) member using the operator `->` is:

```
pointerVariableName->classMemberName
```

Thus, the statement:

```
(*studentPtr).gpa = 3.9;
```

is equivalent to the statement:

```
studentPtr->gpa = 3.9;
```

Accessing `class` (`struct`) components via pointers using the operator `->` thus eliminates the use of both parentheses and the dereferencing operator. Because typos are unavoidable and missing parentheses can result in either an abnormal program termination or erroneous results, when accessing `class` (`struct`) components via pointers, this book uses the arrow notation.

Example 12-4 illustrates how pointers work with class member functions.

EXAMPLE 12-4

Consider the following class:

```
class classExample
{
public:
    void setX(int a);
        //Function to set the value of x
        //Postcondition: x = a;
    void print() const;
        //Function to output the value of x

private:
    int x;
};
```

The definition of the member function is as follows:

```
void classExample::setX(int a)
{
    x = a;
}

void classExample::print() const
{
    cout << "x = " << x << endl;
}
```

Consider the following function main:

```
int main()
{
    classExample *cExpPtr;          //Line 1
    classExample cExpObject;        //Line 2

    cExpPtr = &cExpObject;          //Line 3

    cExpPtr->setX(5);               //Line 4
    cExpPtr->print();               //Line 5

    return 0;
}
```

Sample Run:

```
x = 5
```

In the function main, the statement in Line 1 declares cExpPtr to be a pointer of type classExample, and the statement in Line 2 declares cExpObject to be an object of type classExample. The statement in Line 3 stores the address of cExpObject into cExpPtr (see Figure 12-3).

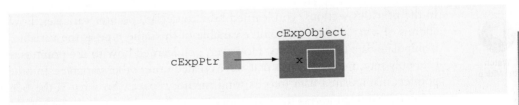

FIGURE 12-3 cExpObject and cExpPtr after the statement cExpPtr = &cExpObject; executes

In the statement in Line 4, the pointer cExpPtr accesses the member function setX to set the value of the member variable x (see Figure 12-4).

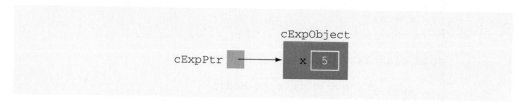

FIGURE 12-4 cExpObject and cExpPtr after the statement cExpPtr->setX(5); executes

In the statement in Line 5, the pointer cExpPtr accesses the member function print to print the value of x, as shown above.

Initializing Pointer Variables

Because C++ does not automatically initialize variables, pointer variables must be initialized if you do not want them to point to anything. Pointer variables are initialized using the constant value 0, called the **null pointer**. Thus, the statement p = 0; stores the null pointer in p, that is, p points to nothing. Some programmers use the named constant NULL to initialize pointer variables. The following two statements are equivalent:

```
p = NULL;
p = 0;
```

The number 0 is the only number that can be directly assigned to a pointer variable.

Dynamic Variables

Watch the Video

In the previous sections, you learned how to declare pointer variables, how to store the address of a variable into a pointer variable of the same type as the variable, and how to manipulate data using pointers. However, you learned how to use pointers to manipulate data only into memory spaces that were created using other variables. In other words, the pointers manipulated data into existing memory spaces. So what is the benefit of using pointers? You can access these memory spaces by working with the variables that were used to create them. In this section, you will learn about the power behind pointers. In particular, you will learn how to allocate and deallocate memory during program execution using pointers.

Variables that are created during program execution are called **dynamic variables**. With the help of pointers, C++ creates dynamic variables. C++ provides two operators, `new` and `delete`, to create and destroy dynamic variables, respectively. When a program requires a new variable, the operator `new` is used. When a program no longer needs a dynamic variable, the operator `delete` is used.

In C++, `new` and `delete` are reserved words.

Operator `new`

The operator `new` has two forms: one to allocate a single variable and another to allocate an array of variables. The syntax to use the operator `new` is:

```
new dataType;            //to allocate a single variable
new dataType[intExp];    //to allocate an array of variables
```

in which `intExp` is any expression evaluating to a positive integer.

The operator `new` allocates memory (a variable) of the designated type and returns a pointer to it—that is, the address of this allocated memory. Moreover, the allocated memory is uninitialized.

Consider the following declaration:

```
int *p;
char *q;
int x;
```

The statement:

```
p = &x;
```

stores the address of `x` in `p`. However, no new memory is allocated. On the other hand, consider the following statement:

```
p = new int;
```

This statement creates a variable during program execution somewhere in memory and stores the address of the allocated memory in `p`. The allocated memory is accessed via pointer dereferencing—namely, `*p`. Similarly, the statement:

```
q = new char[16];
```

creates an array of 16 components of type `char` and stores the base address of the array in `q`.

1
2

Because a dynamic variable is unnamed, it cannot be accessed directly. It is accessed indirectly by the pointer returned by new. The following statements illustrate this concept:

```
int *p;            //p is a pointer of type int
char *name;        //name is a pointer of type char
string *str;       //str is a pointer of type string

p = new int;       //allocates memory of type int
                   //and stores the address of the
                   //allocated memory in p
*p = 28;           //stores 28 in the allocated memory

name = new char[5];   //allocates memory for an array of
                      //five components of type char and
                      //stores the base address of the array
                      //in name
strcpy(name, "John");  //stores John in name

str = new string;  //allocates memory of type string
                   //and stores the address of the
                   //allocated memory in str
*str = "Sunny Day";    //stores the string "Sunny Day" in
                       //the memory pointed to by str
```

 NOTE Recall that the operator new allocates memory space of a specific type and returns the address of the allocated memory space. However, if the operator new is unable to allocate the required memory space (for example, there is not enough memory space), then it throws a bad_alloc exception, and if this exception is not handled, it terminates the program with an error message. Exceptions are covered in detail in Chapter 14. This chapter also discusses bad_alloc exception.

Operator delete

Suppose you have the following declaration:

```
int *p;
```

This statement declares p to be a pointer variable of type int. Next, consider the following statements:

```
p = new int;    //Line 1
*p = 54;        //Line 2
p = new int;    //Line 3
*p = 73;        //Line 4
```

Figure 12-5 shows the effect of these statements.

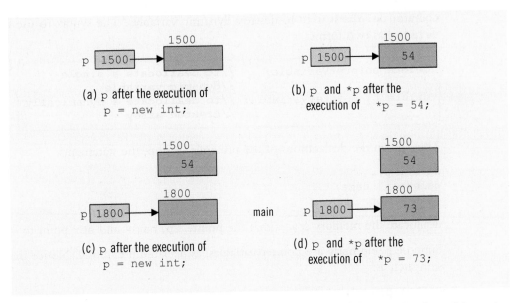

(a) p after the execution of
    p = new int;

(b) p and *p after the
    execution of   *p = 54;

(c) p after the execution of
    p = new int;

(d) p and *p after the
    execution of   *p = 73;

FIGURE 12-5   p after the memory space it points to following the execution of various statements

(The number 1500 on top of the box indicates the address of the memory space.) The statement in Line 1 allocates memory space of type int and stores the address of the allocated memory space into p. Suppose that the address of allocated memory space is 1500. Then, the value of p after the execution of this statement is 1500 (see Figure 12-5(a)). The statement in Line 2 stores 54 into the memory space that p points to, which is 1500 (see Figure 12-5(b)).

Next, the statement in Line 3 executes, which allocates a memory space of type int and stores the address of the allocated memory space into p. Suppose the address of this allocated memory space is 1800. It follows that the value of p is now 1800 (see Figure 12-5(c)). The statement in Line 4 stores 73 into the memory space that p points to, which is 1800. In other words, after the execution of the statement in Line 4, the value stored into memory space at location 1800 is 73 (see Figure 12-5(d)).

Now the obvious question is what happened to the memory space 1500 that p was pointing to after execution of the statement in Line 1. After execution of the statement in Line 3, p points to the new memory space at location 1800. The previous memory space at location 1500 is now inaccessible. In addition, the memory space 1500 remains as marked allocated. In other words, it cannot be reallocated. This is called **memory leak**. That is, there is an unused memory space that cannot be allocated.

Imagine what would happen if you executed statements, such as Line 3, a few thousand or a few million times. There would be a good amount of memory leak. The program might then run out of memory spaces for data manipulation and eventually result in an abnormal termination of the program.

The question at hand is how to *avoid* memory leak. When a dynamic variable is no longer needed, it can be destroyed; that is, its memory can be deallocated. The C++

operator `delete` is used to destroy dynamic variables. The syntax to use the operator `delete` has two forms:

```
delete pointerVariable;      //to deallocate a single
                             //dynamic variable
delete [] pointerVariable;   //to deallocate a dynamically
                             //created array
```

Thus, given the declarations of the previous section, the statements:

```
delete p;
delete [] name;
delete str;
```

deallocate the memory spaces that the pointers p, `name`, and `str` point to.

Suppose p and `name` are pointer variables, as declared previously. Notice that an expression such as:

```
delete p;
```

or:

```
delete [] name;
```

only marks the memory spaces that these pointer variables point to as deallocated. Depending on a particular system, after these statements execute, these pointer variables may still contain the addresses of the deallocated memory spaces. In this case, we say that these pointers are **dangling**. Therefore, if later you access the memory spaces via these pointers without properly initializing them, depending on a particular system, either the program will access a wrong memory space, which may result in corrupting data, or the program will terminate with an error message. One way to avoid this pitfall is to set these pointers to NULL after the `delete` operation. Also note that for the operator `delete` to work properly, the pointer must point to a valid memory space.

In Example 12-3, we used the pointer variable `radiusPtr` to access the memory location of the variable `radius`. However, in that example, the `radiusPtr` pointed to an existing memory, which was not created during program execution. In the following example, we illustrate how to use the new and `delete` operators to allocate and deallocate dynamic memory.

EXAMPLE 12-5

The following program illustrates how to use the operators new and `delete`.

```
//This program illustrates how to use the operators new and delete.

#include <iostream>                                          //Line 1
#include <iomanip>                                           //Line 2
```

```cpp
using namespace std;                                        //Line 3
const double PI = 3.1416;                                   //Line 4

int main()                                                  //Line 5
{                                                           //Line 6
    double *radiusPtr;                                      //Line 7

    cout << fixed << showpoint << setprecision(2);          //Line 8

    radiusPtr = new double;                                 //Line 9

    cout << "Line 10: Enter the radius: ";                  //Line 10
    cin >> *radiusPtr;                                      //Line 11
    cout << endl;                                           //Line 12

    cout << "Line 13: Radius = " << *radiusPtr
         << ", area = " << PI * (*radiusPtr) * (*radiusPtr)
         << endl << endl;                                   //Line 13

    cout << "Line 14: Address of radiusPtr: "
         << &radiusPtr << endl;                             //Line 14
    cout << "Line 15: Value stored in radiusPtr: "
         << radiusPtr << endl;                              //Line 15
    cout << "Line 16: Value stored in the memory "
         << "location to which \n          radiusPtr "
         << "is pointing: " << *radiusPtr << endl;          //Line 16

    delete radiusPtr;                                       //Line 17

    cout << "Line 18: After using the delete operator, "
         << "the value stored in the location\n         "
         << "to which radiusPtr is pointing: "
         << *radiusPtr << endl;                             //Line 18

    double *lengthPtr = new double;                         //Line 19
    radiusPtr = new double;                                 //Line 20

    *radiusPtr = 5.38;                                      //Line 21

    cout << "Line 22: Address of radiusPtr: "
         << &radiusPtr << endl;                             //Line 22
    cout << "Line 23: Value stored in radiusPtr: "
         << radiusPtr << endl;                              //Line 23
    cout << "Line 24: Value stored in the memory "
         << "location to which radiusPtr is pointing: "
         << *radiusPtr << endl;                             //Line 24
    cout << "Line 25: Value stored in lengthPtr: "
         << lengthPtr << endl;                              //Line 25

    return 0;                                               //Line 26
}                                                           //Line 27
```

Sample Run: In this sample run, the user input is shaded.

```
Line 10: Enter the radius: 2.5

Line 13: Radius = 2.50, area = 19.64

Line 14: Address of radiusPtr: 0012FF60
Line 15: Value stored in radiusPtr: 003450A8
Line 16: Value stored in the memory location to which
         radiusPtr is pointing: 2.50
Line 18: After using the delete operator, the value stored in the location
         to which radiusPtr is pointing: -1456815990147462900000000000000000
00000000000000000000000000000000000000000000000000000000000000000000000000000000
000000000000000000000000000000000000000.00
Line 22: Address of radiusPtr: 0012FF60
Line 23: Value stored in radiusPtr: 00345550
Line 24: Value stored in the memory location to which radiusPtr is pointing:
5.38
Line 25: Value stored in lengthPtr: 003450A8
```

For the most part, the preceding program is the same as the program in Example 12-3. However, let us note the following: the statement in Line 9 allocates memory of type `double` and stores the address of the allocated memory in `radiusPtr`. The output of the statement in Line 15 shows that the address of the allocated memory is `003450A8`. Next the statement in Line 17 deallocates the memory space to which `radiusPtr` is pointing. The statement in Line 18 outputs the value stored in the memory location to which `radiusPtr` is pointing. As shown by the output of this statement, the value stored is a strange number. This is because after the `delete` operation in Line 17, `radiusPtr` does not point to a valid memory location. Next, the statement in Line 19 declares the pointer variable `lengthPtr`, allocates memory space of type `double`, and stores the address of the allocated memory space in `lengthPtr`. The statement in Line 20 allocates (another) memory space of type `double` and stores the address of the allocated memory space in `radiusPtr`, and the statement in Line 21 stores `5.38` in the allocated memory space. The statements in Lines 22 to 25 output the addresses as shown by the output. (Note that the addresses and the value printed by the statement in Line 18 are machine dependent. When you run this program on your machine, you are likely to get different values.)

Operations on Pointer Variables

The operations that are allowed on pointer variables are the assignment and relational operations and some limited arithmetic operations. The value of one pointer variable can be assigned to another pointer variable of the same type. Two pointer variables of the same type can be compared for equality, and so on. Integer values can be added and subtracted from a pointer variable. The value of one pointer variable can be subtracted from another pointer variable.

For example, suppose that we have the following statements:

```
int *p, *q;
```

The statement:

```
p = q;
```

copies the value of q into p. After this statement executes, both p and q point to the same memory location. Any changes made to *p automatically change the value of *q, and vice versa.

The expression:

```
p == q
```

evaluates to **true** if p and q have the same value—that is, if they point to the same memory location. Similarly, the expression:

```
p != q
```

evaluates to **true** if p and q point to different memory locations.

The arithmetic operations that are allowed differ from the arithmetic operations on numbers. First, let us use the following statements to explain the increment and decrement operations on pointer variables:

```
int *p;
double *q;
char *chPtr;
studentType *stdPtr;   //studentType is as defined before
```

Recall that the size of the memory allocated for an **int** variable is 4 bytes, a **double** variable is 8 bytes, and a **char** variable is 1 byte. The memory allocated for a variable of type studentType is then 40 bytes.

The statement:

```
p++;   or   p = p + 1;
```

increments the value of p by 4 bytes because p is a pointer of type **int**. Similarly, the statements:

```
q++;
chPtr++;
```

increment the value of q by 8 bytes and the value of chPtr by 1 byte, respectively. The statement:

```
stdPtr++;
```

increments the value of stdPtr by 40 bytes.

The increment operator increments the value of a pointer variable by the size of the memory to which it is pointing. Similarly, the decrement operator decrements the value of a pointer variable by the size of the memory to which it is pointing.

Moreover, the statement:

```
p = p + 2;
```

increments the value of p by 8 bytes.

Thus, when an integer is added to a pointer variable, the value of the pointer variable is incremented by the integer times the size of the memory to which the pointer is pointing. Similarly, when an integer is subtracted from a pointer variable, the value of the pointer variable is decremented by the integer times the size of the memory to which the pointer is pointing.

 NOTE Pointer arithmetic can be very dangerous. Using pointer arithmetic, the program can accidentally access the memory locations of other variables and change their content without warning, leaving the programmer trying to find out what went wrong. If a pointer variable tries to access either the memory spaces of other variables or an illegal memory space, some systems might terminate the program with an appropriate error message. Always exercise extra care when doing pointer arithmetic.

Dynamic Arrays

In Chapter 8, you learned how to declare and process arrays. The arrays discussed in Chapter 8 are called static arrays because their size was fixed at compile time. One of the limitations of a static array is that every time you execute the program, the size of the array is fixed, so it might not be possible to use the same array to process different data sets of the same type. One way to handle this limitation is to declare an array that is large enough to process a variety of data sets. However, if the array is very big and the data set is small, such a declaration would result in memory waste. On the other hand, it would be helpful if, during program execution, you could prompt the user to enter the size of the array and then create an array of the appropriate size. This approach is especially helpful if you cannot even guess the array size. In this section, you will learn how to create arrays during program execution and process such arrays.

An array created during the execution of a program is called a **dynamic array**. To create a dynamic array, we use the second form of the `new` operator.

The statement:

```
int *p;
```

declares p to be a pointer variable of type `int`. The statement:

```
p = new int[10];
```

allocates 10 contiguous memory locations, each of type `int`, and stores the address of the first memory location into p. In other words, the operator `new` creates an array of 10 components of type `int`, it returns the base address of the array, and the assignment operator stores the base address of the array into p. Thus, the statement:

```
*p = 25;
```

stores 25 into the first memory location, and the statements:

```
p++;        //p points to the next array component
*p = 35;
```

store 35 into the second memory location. Thus, by using the increment and decrement operations, you can access the components of the array. Of course, after performing a few increment operations, it is possible to lose track of the first array component. C++ allows us to use array notation to access these memory locations. For example, the statements:

```
p[0] = 25;
p[1] = 35;
```

store 25 and 35 into the first and second array components, respectively. That is, p[0] refers to the first array component, p[1] refers to the second array component, and so on. In general, p[i] refers to the (i + 1)th array component. After the preceding statements execute, p still points to the first array component. Moreover, the following for loop initializes each array component to 0:

```
for (j = 0; j < 10; j++)
    p[j] = 0;
```

in which j is an int variable.

When the array notation is used to process the array pointed to by p, p stays fixed at the first memory location. Moreover, p is a dynamic array created during program execution.

NOTE The statement:

```
int list[5];
```

declares list to be an array of five components. Recall from Chapter 8 that list itself is a variable, and the value stored in list is the base address of the array—that is, the address of the first array component. Suppose the address of the first array component is 1000. Figure 12-6 shows list and the array list.

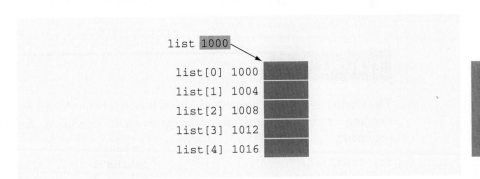

FIGURE 12-6 list and array list

Because the value of list, which is 1000, is a memory address, list is a pointer variable. However, the value stored in list, which is 1000, *cannot be altered during program execution.* That is, the value of `list` is *constant.* Therefore, the increment and decrement operations cannot be applied to `list`. In fact, any attempt to use the increment or decrement operations on `list` results in a compile-time error.

Notice that here we are *only* saying that the value of `list` cannot be changed. However, the data into the array list can be manipulated as before. For example, the statement `list[0] = 25;` stores 25 into the first array component. Similarly, the statement `list[3] = 78;` stores 78 into the fourth component of `list` (see Figure 12-7).

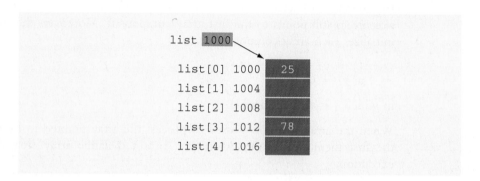

FIGURE 12-7   Array `list` after the execution of the statements `list[0] = 25;` and `list[3] = 78;`

If `p` is a pointer variable of type `int`, then the statement:

`p = list;`

copies the value of `list`, which is `1000`, the base address of the array, into `p`. We are allowed to perform increment and decrement operations on `p`.

An *array name* is a *constant pointer.*

EXAMPLE 12-6

The following program segment illustrates how to obtain a user's response to get the array size and create a dynamic array during program execution. Consider the following statements:

```
int *intList;                          //Line 1
int arraySize;                         //Line 2

cout << "Enter array size: ";          //Line 3
cin >> arraySize;                      //Line 4
cout << endl;                          //Line 5

intList = new int[arraySize];          //Line 6
```

The statement in Line 1 declares intList to be a pointer of type int, and the statement in Line 2 declares arraySize to be an int variable. The statement in Line 3 prompts the user to enter the size of the array, and the statement in Line 4 inputs the array size into the variable arraySize. The statement in Line 6 creates an array of the size specified by arraySize, and the base address of the array is stored in intList. From this point on, you can treat intList just like any other array. For example, you can use the array notation to process the elements of intList and pass intList as a parameter to the function.

Functions and Pointers

A pointer variable can be passed as a parameter to a function either by value or by reference. To declare a pointer as a value parameter in a function heading, you use the same mechanism as you use to declare a variable. To make a formal parameter be a reference parameter, you use & when you declare the formal parameter in the function heading. Therefore, to declare a formal parameter as a reference pointer parameter, between the data type name and the identifier name, you must include * to make the identifier a pointer and & to make it a reference parameter. The obvious question is: In what order should & and * appear between the data type name and the identifier to declare a pointer as a reference parameter? In C++, to make a pointer a reference parameter in a function heading, * appears before the & between the data type name and the identifier. The following example illustrates this concept:

```
void pointerParameters(int* &p, double *q)
{
    .
    .
    .
}
```

In the function pointerParameters, both p and q are pointers. The parameter p is a reference parameter; the parameter q is a value parameter. Furthermore, the function pointerParameters can change the value of *q, but not the value of q. However, the function pointerParameters can change the value of both p and *p.

Pointers and Function Return Values

In C++, the return type of a function can be a pointer. For example, the return type of the function:

```
int* testExp(...)
{
    .
    .
    .
}
```

is a pointer type int.

1
2

Dynamic Two-Dimensional Arrays

The beginning of this section discussed how to create dynamic one-dimensional arrays. You can also create dynamic multidimensional arrays. In this section, we discuss how to create dynamic two-dimensional arrays. Dynamic multidimensional arrays are created similarly.

There are various ways you can create dynamic dimensional arrays. One way is as follows. Consider the statement:

```
int *board[4];
```

This statement declares board to be an array of four pointers wherein each pointer is of type int. Because board[0], board[1], board[2], and board[3] are pointers, you can now use these pointers to create the rows of board. Suppose that each row of board has six columns. Then, the following for loop creates the rows of board.

```
for (int row = 0; row < 4; row++)
    board[row] = new int[6];
```

Note that the expression new int[6] creates an array of six components of type int and returns the base address of the array. The assignment statement then stores the returned address into board[row]. It follows that after the execution of the previous for loop, board is a two-dimensional array of four rows and six columns.

In the previous for loop, if you replace the number 6 with the number 10, then the loop will create a two-dimensional array of four rows and 10 columns. In other words, the number of columns of board can be specified during execution. However, the way board is declared, the number of rows is fixed. So in reality, board is not a true dynamic two-dimensional array.

Next, consider the following statement:

```
int **board;
```

This statement declares board to be a pointer to a pointer. In other words, board and *board are pointers. Now board can store the address of a pointer or an array of pointers of type int, and *board can store the address of an int memory space or an array of int values.

Suppose that you want board to be an array of 10 rows and 15 columns. To accomplish this, first we create an array of 10 pointers of type int and assign the address of that array to board. The following statement accomplishes this:

```
board = new int* [10];
```

Next, we create the columns of board. The following for loop accomplishes this:

```
for (int row = 0; row < 10; row++)
    board[row] = new int[15];
```

To access the components of board, you can use the array subscripting notation discussed in Chapter 8.

Note that the number of rows and the number of columns of board can be specified during program execution. The following program further explains how to create two-dimensional arrays.

EXAMPLE 12-7

```cpp
// Dynamic two-dimensional arrays

#include <iostream>
#include <iomanip>

using namespace std;

void fill(int **p, int rowSize, int columnSize);
void print(int **p, int rowSize, int columnSize);

int main()
{
    int **board;                              //Line 1

    int rows;                                 //Line 2
    int columns;                              //Line 3

    cout << "Line 4: Enter the number of rows "
         <<"and columns: ";                   //Line 4
    cin >> rows >> columns;                    //Line 5
    cout << endl;                             //Line 6

        //Create the rows of board
    board = new int* [rows];                  //Line 7

        //Create the columns of board
    for (int row = 0; row < rows; row++)      //Line 8
        board[row] = new int[columns];        //Line 9

        //Insert elements into board
    fill(board, rows, columns);               //Line 10

    cout << "Line 11: Board:" << endl;        //Line 11

        //Output the elements of board
    print(board, rows, columns);              //Line 12

    return 0;
}
```

```
void fill(int **p, int rowSize, int columnSize)
{
    for (int row = 0; row < rowSize; row++)
    {
        cout << "Enter " << columnSize << " number(s) for row "
            << "number " << row << ": ";
        for (int col = 0; col < columnSize; col++)
            cin >> p[row][col];
        cout << endl;
    }
}

void print(int **p, int rowSize, int columnSize)
{
    for (int row = 0; row < rowSize; row++)
    {
        for (int col = 0; col < columnSize; col++)
            cout << setw(5) << p[row][col];
        cout << endl;
    }
}
```

Sample Run: In this sample run, the user input is shaded.

```
Line 4: Enter the number of rows and columns: 3 4

Enter 4 number(s) for row number 0: 1 2 3 4

Enter 4 number(s) for row number 1: 5 6 7 8

Enter 4 number(s) for row number 2: 9 10 11 12

Line 11: Board:
    1    2    3    4
    5    6    7    8
    9   10   11   12
```

The preceding program contains the functions fill and print. The function fill prompts the user to enter the elements of a two-dimensional array of type int. The function print outputs the elements of a two-dimensional array of type int.

For the most part, the preceding output is self-explanatory. Let us look at the statements in the function main. The statement in Line 1 declares board to be a pointer to a pointer of type int. The statements in Lines 2 and 3 declare int variables rows and columns. The statement in Line 4 prompts the user to input the number of rows and number of columns. The statement in Line 5 stores the number of rows in the variable rows and the number of columns in the variable columns. The statement in Line 7 creates the rows of board, and the for loop in Lines 8 and 9 creates the columns of board. The statement in Line 10 uses the function fill to fill the array board, and the statement in Line 12 uses the function print to output the elements of board.

Shallow versus Deep Copy and Pointers

In an earlier section, we discussed pointer arithmetic and explained that if we are not careful, one pointer might access the data of another (completely unrelated) pointer. This event might result in unsuspected or erroneous results. Here, we discuss another peculiarity of pointers. To facilitate the discussion, we will use diagrams to show pointers and their related memory.

Consider the following statements:

```
int *first;
int *second;

first = new int[10];
```

The first two statements declare `first` and `second` pointer variables of type `int`. The third statement creates an array of 10 components, and the base address of the array is stored into `first` (see Figure 12-8). (Note that `first` together with the arrow indicates that first points to the allocated memory.)

FIGURE 12-8 Pointer `first` and the array to which it points

Suppose that some meaningful data is stored in the array pointed to by `first`. To be specific, suppose that this array is as shown in Figure 12-9.

FIGURE 12-9 Pointer `first` and its array

Next, consider the following statement:

```
second = first;          //Line A
```

This statement copies the value of `first` into `second`. After this statement executes, both `first` and `second` point to the same array, as shown in Figure 12-10.

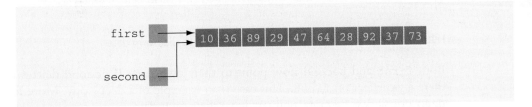

FIGURE 12-10 `first` and `second` after the statement `second = first;` executes

Let us next execute the following statement:

```
delete [] second;
```

After this statement executes, the array pointed to by second is deleted. This action results in Figure 12-11.

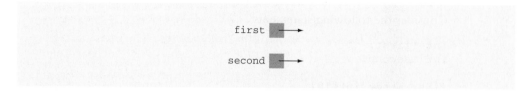

FIGURE 12-11   first and second after the statement delete [] second; executes

Because first and second point to the same array, after the statement:

```
delete [] second;
```

executes, first becomes invalid, that is, first (as well as second) are now dangling pointers. Therefore, if the program later tries to access the memory pointed to by first, either the program will access the wrong memory or it will terminate in an error. This case is an example of a shallow copy. More formally, in a **shallow copy**, two or more pointers of the same type point to the same memory; that is, they point to the same data.

On the other hand, suppose that instead of the earlier statement, second = first; (in Line A), we have the following statements:

```
second = new int[10];

for (int j = 0; j < 10; j++)
    second[j] = first[j];
```

The first statement creates an array of 10 components of type int, and the base address of the array is stored in second. The second statement copies the array pointed to by first into the array pointed to by second (see Figure 12-12).

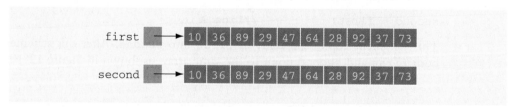

FIGURE 12-12   first and second both pointing to their own data

Both first and second now point to their own data. If second deletes its memory, there is no effect on first. This case is an example of a deep copy. More formally, in a **deep copy**, two or more pointers have their own data.

From the preceding discussion, it follows that you must know when to use a shallow copy and when to use a deep copy.

Classes and Pointers: Some Peculiarities

In the previous section, we discussed how to use the arrow notation to access class members via the pointer if a pointer variable is of a class type. Because a class can have pointer member variables, this section discusses some peculiarities of such classes. To facilitate the discussion, we will use the following class:

```
class ptrMemberVarType
{
public:
    .
    .
    .
private:
    int x;
    int lenP;
    int *p;
};
```

Also, consider the following statements (see Figure 12-13):

```
ptrMemberVarType objectOne;
ptrMemberVarType objectTwo;
```

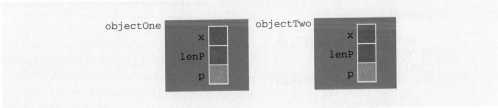

FIGURE 12-13 Objects objectOne and objectTwo

Destructor

The object objectOne has a pointer member variable p. Suppose that during program execution, the pointer p creates a dynamic array. When objectOne goes out of scope, all of the member variables of objectOne are destroyed. However, p created a dynamic array, and dynamic memory must be deallocated using the operator **delete**. Thus, if the pointer p does not use the **delete** operator to deallocate the dynamic array, the memory space of the dynamic array would stay marked as allocated, even though it cannot be accessed. How do we ensure that when p is destroyed, the dynamic memory created by p is also destroyed? Suppose that objectOne is as shown in Figure 12-14.

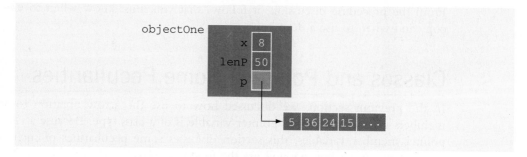

FIGURE 12-14 Object `objectOne` and its data

Recall that if a class has a destructor, the destructor automatically executes whenever a class object goes out of scope (see Chapter 10). Therefore, we can put the necessary code in the destructor to ensure that when `objectOne` goes out of scope, the memory created by the pointer p is deallocated. For example, the definition of the destructor for the **class** `ptrMemberVarType` is:

```
ptrMemberVarType::~ptrMemberVarType()
{
    delete [] p;
}
```

Of course, you must include the destructor as a member of the class in its definition. Let us extend the definition of the **class** `ptrMemberVarType` by including the destructor. Moreover, the remainder of this section assumes that the definition of the destructor is as given previously—that is, the destructor deallocates the memory space pointed to by p.

```
class ptrMemberVarType
{
public:
    ~ptrMemberVarType();
        .
        .
        .

private:
    int x;
    int lenP;
    int *p;
};
```

NOTE For the destructor to work properly, the pointer p must have a valid value. If p is not properly initialized (that is, if the value of p is garbage) and the destructor executes, either the program terminates with an error message or the destructor deallocates an unrelated memory space. For this reason, you should exercise extra caution while working with pointers.

Assignment Operator

This section describes the limitations of the built-in assignment operators for classes with pointer member variables. Suppose that `objectOne` and `objectTwo` are as shown in Figure 12-15.

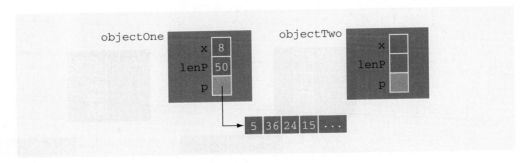

FIGURE 12-15 Objects `objectOne` and `objectTwo`

Recall that one of the built-in operations on classes is the assignment operator. For example, the statement:

```
objectTwo = objectOne;
```

copies the member variables of `objectOne` into `objectTwo`. That is, the value of `objectOne.x` is copied into `objectTwo.x`, and the value of `objectOne.p` is copied into `objectTwo.p`. Because p is a pointer, this member-wise copying of the data would lead to a shallow copying of the data. That is, both `objectTwo.p` and `objectOne.p` would point to the same memory space, as shown in Figure 12-16.

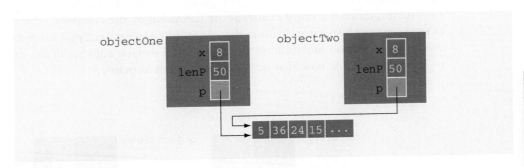

FIGURE 12-16 Objects `objectOne` and `objectTwo` after the statement `objectTwo = objectOne;` executes

Now, if `objectTwo.p` deallocates the memory space to which it points, `objectOne.p` would become invalid. This situation could very well happen if the **class** `ptrMemberVarType` has a destructor that deallocates the memory space pointed to by p when an object of type `ptrMemberVarType` goes out of scope. It suggests that there must be a way to avoid this pitfall. To avoid this shallow copying of data for classes with a pointer member variable, C++ allows the programmer to extend the definition of the assignment operator. This process is called overloading the assignment operator. Chapter 13 explains how to accomplish this task by using operator overloading. Once the assignment operator is properly overloaded, both objectOne and objectTwo have their own data, as shown in Figure 12-17.

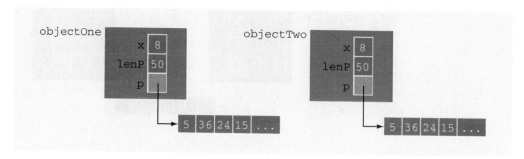

FIGURE 12-17 Objects objectOne and objectTwo

Copy Constructor

When declaring a class object, you can initialize it by using the value of an existing object of the same type. For example, consider the following statement:

```
ptrMemberVarType objectThree(objectOne);
```

The object objectThree is being declared and is also being initialized by using the value of objectOne. That is, the values of the member variables of objectOne are copied into the corresponding member variables of objectThree. This initialization is called the default member-wise initialization. The default member-wise initialization is due to the constructor, called the **copy constructor** (provided by the compiler). Just as in the case of the assignment operator, because the **class** ptrMemberVarType has pointer member variables, this default initialization would lead to a shallow copying of the data, as shown in Figure 12-18. (Assume that objectOne is given as before.)

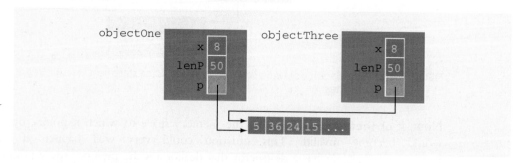

FIGURE 12-18 Objects objectOne and objectThree

Before describing how to overcome this deficiency, let us describe one more situation that could also lead to a shallow copying of the data. The solution to both these problems is the same.

Recall that as parameters to a function, class objects can be passed either by reference or by value. Remember that the **class** ptrMemberVarType has the destructor, which deallocates the memory space pointed to by p. Suppose that objectOne is as shown in Figure 12-19.

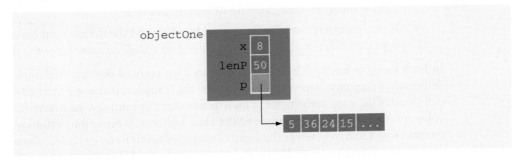

FIGURE 12-19 Object objectOne

Let us consider the following function prototype:

void destroyList(ptrMemberVarType paramObject);

The function destroyList has a formal value parameter, paramObject. Now consider the following statement:

destroyList(objectOne);

In this statement, objectOne is passed as a parameter to the function destroyList. Because paramObject is a value parameter, the copy constructor copies the member variables of objectOne into the corresponding member variables of paramObject. Just as in the previous case, paramObject.p and objectOne.p would point to the same memory space, as shown in Figure 12-20.

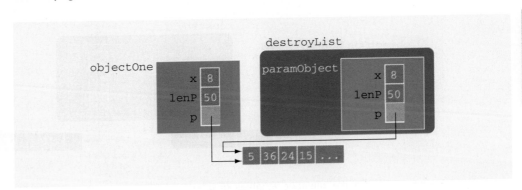

FIGURE 12-20 Pointer member variables of objects objectOne and paramObject pointing to the same array

Because objectOne is passed by value, the member variables of paramObject should have their own copy of the data. In particular, paramObject.p should have its own memory space. How do we ensure that this is, in fact, the case?

If a class has pointer member variables:

- During object declaration, the initialization of one object using the value of another object would lead to a shallow copying of the data if the default member-wise copying of data is allowed.

- If, as a parameter, an object is passed by value and the default member-wise copying of data is allowed, it would lead to a shallow copying of the data.

In both cases, to force each object to have its own copy of the data, we must override the definition of the copy constructor provided by the compiler; that is, we must provide our own definition of the copy constructor. This is usually done by putting a statement that includes the copy constructor in the definition of the class and then writing the definition of the copy constructor. Then, whenever the copy constructor needs to be executed, the system would execute the definition provided by us, not the one provided by the compiler. Therefore, for the class ptrMemberVarType, we can overcome this shallow copying problem by including the copy constructor in the class ptrMemberVarType. Example 12-8 illustrates this.

The copy constructor automatically executes in three situations (the first two are described previously).

- When an object is declared and initialized by using the value of another object
- When, as a parameter, an object is passed by value
- When the return value of a function is an object

Therefore, once the copy constructor is properly defined for the class ptrMemberVarType, both objectOne.p and objectThree.p will have their own copies of the data. Similarly, objectOne.p and paramObject.p will have their own copies of the data, as shown in Figure 12-21.

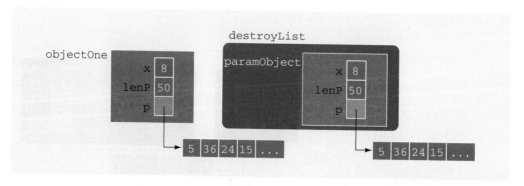

FIGURE 12-21 Pointer member variables of objects objectOne and paramObject with their own data

When the function destroyList exits, the formal parameter paramObject goes out of scope, and the destructor for the object paramObject deallocates the memory space pointed to by paramObject.p. However, this deallocation has no effect on objectOne.

The general syntax to include the copy constructor in the definition of a class is:

```
className(const className& otherObject);
```

Notice that the formal parameter of the copy constructor is a constant reference parameter.

Example 12-8 illustrates how to include the copy constructor in a class and how it works.

EXAMPLE 12-8

Consider the following class:

```
class ptrMemberVarType
{
public:
    void print() const;
        //Function to output the data stored in the array p.

    void insertAt(int index, int num);
        //Function to insert num into the array p at the
        //position specified by index.
        //If index is out of bounds, the program is terminated.
        //If index is within bounds, but greater than the index
        //of the last item in the list, num is added at the end
        //of the list.

    ptrMemberVarType(int size = 10);
        //Constructor
        //Creates an array of the size specified by the
        //parameter size; the default array size is 10.

    ~ptrMemberVarType();
        //Destructor
        //deallocates the memory space occupied by the array p.

    ptrMemberVarType(const ptrMemberVarType& otherObject);
        //Copy constructor

private:
    int maxSize; //variable to store the maximum size of p
    int length;  //variable to store the number elements in p
    int *p;      //pointer to an int array
};
```

Suppose that the definitions of the members of the class ptrMemberVarType are as follows:

1
2

```cpp
void ptrMemberVarType::print() const
{
    for (int i = 0; i < length; i++)
        cout << p[i] << " ";
}

void ptrMemberVarType::insertAt(int index, int num)
{
        //if index is out of bounds, terminate the program
    assert(index >= 0 && index < maxSize);

    if (index < length)
        p[index] = num;
    else
    {
        p[length] = num;
        length++;
    }
}

ptrMemberVarType::ptrMemberVarType(int size)
{
    if (size <= 0)
    {
        cout << "The array size must be positive." << endl;
        cout << "Creating an array of the size 10." << endl;

        maxSize = 10;
    }
    else
        maxSize = size;

    length = 0;

    p = new int[maxSize];

}

ptrMemberVarType::~ptrMemberVarType()
{
    delete [] p;
}

        //copy constructor
ptrMemberVarType::ptrMemberVarType
                (const ptrMemberVarType& otherObject)
{
    maxSize = otherObject.maxSize;
    length = otherObject.length;
```

```
    p = new int[maxSize];

    for (int i = 0; i < length; i++)
        p[i] = otherObject.p[i];
}
```

Consider the following function main. (We assume that the definition of the `class ptrMemberVarType` is in the header file `ptrMemberVarType.h`.)

```
#include <iostream>
#include "ptrMemberVarType.h"

using namespace std;

void testCopyConst(ptrMemberVarType temp);

int main()
{
    ptrMemberVarType listOne;                              //Line 1

    int num;                                               //Line 2
    int index;                                             //Line 3

    cout << "Line 4: Enter 5 integers." << endl;           //Line 4

    for (index = 0; index < 5; index++)                    //Line 5
    {
        cin >> num;                                        //Line 6
        listOne.insertAt(index, num);                      //Line 7
    }

    cout << "Line 8: listOne: ";                           //Line 8
    listOne.print();                                       //Line 9
    cout << endl;                                          //Line 10

        //Declare listTwo and initialize it using listOne
    ptrMemberVarType listTwo(listOne);                     //Line 11

    cout << "Line 12: listTwo: ";                          //Line 12
    listTwo.print();                                       //Line 13
    cout << endl;                                          //Line 14

    listTwo.insertAt(5, 34);                               //Line 15
    listTwo.insertAt(2, -76);                              //Line 16

    cout << "Line 17: After modifying listTwo: ";          //Line 17
    listTwo.print();                                       //Line 18
    cout << endl;                                          //Line 19

    cout << "Line 20: After modifying listTwo, "
         << "listOne: ";                                   //Line 20
    listOne.print();                                       //Line 21
    cout << endl;                                          //Line 22
```

1
2

```
    cout << "Line 23: Calling the function testCopyConst"
         << endl;                                          //Line 23

        //Call function testCopyConst
    testCopyConst(listOne);                                //Line 24

    cout << "Line 25: After a call to the function "
         << "testCopyConst, " << endl
         << "            listOne is: ";                     //Line 25

    listOne.print();                                       //Line 26
    cout << endl;                                          //Line 27

    return 0;                                              //Line 28
}

void testCopyConst(ptrMemberVarType temp)
{
    cout << "Line 29: *** Inside the function "
         << "testCopyConst ***" << endl;                   //Line 29

    cout << "Line 30: Object temp data: ";                 //Line 30
    temp.print();                                          //Line 31
    cout << endl;                                          //Line 32

    temp.insertAt(3, -100);                                //Line 33
    cout << "Line 34: After changing temp: ";              //Line 34
    temp.print();                                          //Line 35
    cout << endl;                                          //Line 36

    cout << "Line 37: *** Exiting the function "
         << "testCopyConst ***" << endl;                   //Line 37
}
```

Sample Run: In this sample run, the user input is shaded.

```
Line 4: Enter 5 integers.
14 8 34 2 58
Line 8: listOne: 14 8 34 2 58
Line 12: listTwo: 14 8 34 2 58
Line 17: After modifying listTwo: 14 8 -76 2 58 34
Line 20: After modifying listTwo, listOne: 14 8 34 2 58
Line 23: Calling the function testCopyConst
Line 29: *** Inside the function testCopyConst ***
Line 30: Object temp data: 14 8 34 2 58
Line 34: After changing temp: 14 8 34 -100 58
Line 37: *** Exiting the function testCopyConst ***
Line 25: After a call to the function testCopyConst,
        listOne is: 14 8 34 2 58
```

In the preceding program, the statement in Line 1 declares listOne to be an object of type
ptrMemberVarType. The member variable p of listOne is an array of size 10, which is

the default array size. The **for** loop in Line 5 reads and stores five integers in listOne.p. The statement in Line 9 outputs the numbers stored in listOne, that is, the five numbers stored in p. (See the output of the line marked Line 8 in the sample run.)

The statement in Line 11 declares listTwo to be an object of type ptrMemberVarType and also initializes listTwo using the values of listOne. The statement in Line 13 outputs the numbers stored in listTwo. (See the output of the line marked Line 12 in the sample run.)

The statements in Lines 15 and 16 modify listTwo, and the statement in Line 18 outputs the modified data of listTwo. (See the output of the line marked Line 17 in the sample run.) The statement in Line 21 outputs the data stored in listOne. Notice that the data stored in listOne is unchanged, even though listTwo modified its data. It follows that the copy constructor used to initialize listTwo using listOne (at Line 11) provides listTwo its own copy of the data.

The statements in Lines 23 through 28 show that when listOne is passed as a parameter by value to the function testCopyConst (see Line 24), the corresponding formal parameter temp has its own copy of data. Notice that the function testCopyConst modifies the object temp; however, the object listOne remains unchanged. See the outputs of the lines marked Line 23 (before the function testCopyConst is called) and Line 25 (after the function testCopyConst terminates) in the sample run. Also notice that when the function testCopyConst terminates, the destructor of the **class** ptrMemberVarType deallocates the memory space occupied by temp.p, which has no effect on listOne.p.

For classes with pointer member variables, three things are normally done:

1. Include the destructor in the class.
2. Overload the assignment operator for the class.
3. Include the copy constructor.

Chapter 13 discusses overloading the assignment operator. Until then, whenever we discuss classes with pointer member variables, out of the three items in the previous list, we will implement only the destructor and the copy constructor.

Inheritance, Pointers, and Virtual Functions

Recall that as a parameter, a class object can be passed either by value or by reference. Earlier chapters also said that the types of the actual and formal parameters must match. However, in the case of classes, C++ *allows the user to pass an object of a derived class to a formal parameter of the base class type.*

First, let us discuss the case in which the formal parameter is either a reference parameter or a pointer. To be specific, let us consider the following classes:

```
class petType
{
public:
```

```
    void print();
    petType(string n = "");

private:
    string name;
};

class dogType: public petType
{
public:
    void print();
    dogType(string n = "", string b = "");

private:
    string breed;
};
```

The class petType has three members. The class dogType is derived from the class petType and has three members of its own. Both classes have a member function print. Suppose that the definitions of the member functions of both classes are as follows:

```
void petType::print()
{
    cout << "Name: " << name;
}

petType::petType(string n)
{
    name = n;
}

void dogType::print()
{
    petType::print();
    cout << ", Breed: " << breed << endl;
}
```

Consider the following function in a user program (client code):

```
void callPrint(petType& p)
{
    p.print();
}
```

The function callPrint has a formal reference parameter p of type petType. You can call the function callPrint by using an object of either type petType or type dogType as a parameter. Moreover, the body of the function callPrint calls the member function print. Consider the following function main:

```
int main()
{
    petType pet("Lucky");                          //Line 1
    dogType dog("Tommy", "German Shepherd");       //Line 2

    pet.print();                                   //Line 3
    cout << endl;                                  //Line 4
    dog.print();                                   //Line 5
```

```
    cout << "*** Calling the function callPrint ***"        //Line 6
        << endl;                                             //Line 7
    callPrint(pet);                                          //Line 8
    cout << endl;                                            //Line 9
    callPrint(dog);                                          //Line 10
    cout << endl;

    return 0;
}
```

Sample Run:

```
Name: Lucky
Name: Tommy, Breed: German Shepherd
*** Calling the function callPrint ***
Name: Lucky
Name: Tommy
```

The statements in Lines 1 through 6 are quite straightforward. Let us look at the statements in Lines 7 and 9. The statement in Line 7 calls the function `callPrint` and passes the object `pet` as the parameter; it generates the fourth line of the output. The statement in Line 9 also calls the function `callPrint` but passes the object `dog` as the parameter; it generates the fifth line of the output. The output generated by the statements in Lines 7 and 9 shows only the value of `name`, even though each time a different class object was passed as a parameter. Because in Line 9, object `dog` is passed as a parameter to the function `callPrint`, one would expect that the output generated by the statement in Line 9 should be the same as the second line of the output. What actually occurred is that for both statements (Lines 7 and 9), the member function `print` of the class `petType` was executed. This is due to the fact that the binding of the member function `print` in the body of the function `callPrint` occurred at compile time. Because the formal parameter `p` of the function `callPrint` is of type `petType`, for the statement `p.print();`, the compiler associates the function `print` of the class `petType`. More specifically, in **compile-time** binding, the necessary code to call a specific function is generated by the compiler. (Compile-time binding is also known as **static binding** or **early binding**.)

For the statement in Line 9, the actual parameter is of type `dogType`. Thus, when the body of the function `callPrint` executes, logically the `print` function of object `dog` should execute, which is not the case. So, during program execution, how does C++ correct this problem of making the call to the appropriate function? C++ corrects this problem by providing the mechanism of **virtual functions**. The binding of virtual functions occurs at program execution time, not at compile time. This kind of binding is called **run-time binding** or **late binding**. More formally, in run-time binding, the compiler does not generate the code to call a specific function. Instead, it generates enough information to enable the run-time system to generate the specific code for the appropriate function call. Run-time binding is also known as **dynamic binding**.

In C++, virtual functions are declared using the reserved word `virtual`. Let us redefine the previous classes using this feature.

```
class petType
{
public:
    virtual void print();          //virtual function
    petType(string n = "");

private:
    string name;
};

class dogType: public petType
{
public:
    void print();
    dogType(string n = "", string b = "");

private:
    string breed;
};
```

Note that we need to declare a `virtual` function only in the base `class`.

The definition of the member function `print` is the same as before. If we execute the previous program with these modifications, the output is as follows:

Sample Run:

```
Name: Lucky
Name: Tommy, Breed: German Shepherd
*** Calling the function callPrint ***
Name: Lucky
Name: Tommy, Breed: German Shepherd
```

This output shows that for the statement in Line 9, the `print` function of `dogType` is executed (see the last two lines of the output).

The previous discussion also applies when a formal parameter is a pointer to a class, and a pointer of the derived class is passed as an actual parameter. To illustrate this feature, suppose we have the preceding classes. (We assume that the definition of the `class` `petType` is in the header file `petType.h`, and the definition of the `class` `dogType` is in the header file `dogType.h`.) Consider the following program:

```
#include <iostream>
#include "petType.h"
#include "dogType.h"

using namespace std;

void callPrint(petType *p);

int main()
{
    petType *q;                                         //Line 1
    dogType *r;                                         //Line 2

    q = new petType("Lucky");                           //Line 3
    r = new dogType("Tommy", "German Shepherd"); //Line 4
```

```
    q->print();                                                //Line 5
    cout << endl;                                              //Line 6
    r->print();                                                //Line 7

    cout << "*** Calling the function callPrint ***"
                                                               //Line 8
         << endl;                                              //Line 9
    callPrint(q);                                              //Line 10
    cout << endl;
    callPrint(r);                                              //Line 11

    return 0;
}

void callPrint(petType *p)
{
    p->print();
}
```

Sample Run:

```
Name: Lucky
Name: Tommy, Breed: German Shepherd
*** Calling the function callPrint ***
Name: Lucky
Name: Tommy, Breed: German Shepherd
```

The preceding examples show that if a formal parameter, say p of a class type, is either a reference parameter or a pointer and p uses a virtual function of the base class, we can effectively pass a derived class object as an actual parameter to p.

However, if p is a *value parameter*, then this mechanism of passing a derived class object as an actual parameter to p does not work, even if p uses a virtual function. Recall that, if a formal parameter is a value parameter, the value of the actual parameter is copied into the formal parameter. Therefore, if a formal parameter is of a `class` type, the member variables of the actual object are copied into the corresponding member variables of the formal parameter.

Suppose that we have the above classes—that is, `petType` and `dogType`. Consider the following function definition:

```
void callPrint(petType p)    //p is a value parameter
{
    p.print();
}
```

Further suppose that we have the following declaration:

```
dogType dog;
```

The object dog has two member variables, name and breed. The member variable name is inherited from the base class. Consider the following function call:

```
callPrint(dog);
```

In this statement, because the formal parameter p is a value parameter, the member variables of dog are copied into the member variables of p. However, because p is an object of type petType, it has only one member variable. Consequently, only the member variable name of dog will be copied into the member variable name of p. Also, the statement:

```
p.print();
```

in the body of the function will result in executing the member function print of the class petType.

The output of the following program further illustrates this concept. (As before, we assume that the definition of the class petType is in the header file petType.h, and the definition of the class dogType is in the header file dogType.h.)

```
//Chapter 12: Virtual Functions and Value Parameters

#include <iostream>
#include "petType.h"
#include "dogType.h"

using namespace std;

void callPrint(petType p);

int main()
{
    petType pet("Lucky");                        //Line 1
    dogType dog("Tommy", "German Shepherd");     //Line 2

    pet.print();                                 //Line 3
    cout << endl;                                //Line 4
    dog.print();                                 //Line 5

    cout << "*** Calling the function callPrint ***"
         << endl;                                //Line 6
    callPrint(pet);                              //Line 7
    cout << endl;                                //Line 8
    callPrint(dog);                              //Line 9
    cout << endl;                                //Line 10

    return 0;
}


void callPrint(petType p)   //p is a value parameter
{
    p.print();
}
```

Sample Run:

```
Name: Lucky
Name: Tommy, Breed: German Shepherd
*** Calling the function callPrint ***
Name: Lucky
Name: Tommy
```

Look closely at the output of the statements in Lines 7 and 9 (the last two lines of output). In Line 9, because the formal parameter p is a value parameter, the member variables of dog are copied into the corresponding member variables of p. However, because p is an object of type petType, it has only one member variable. Consequently, only the member variable name of dog is copied into the member variable name of p. Moreover, the statement p.print(); in the function callPrint executes the function print of the class petType, not of the class dogType. Therefore, the last line of the output shows only the value of name (the member variable of dog).

 NOTE   An object of the base class type cannot be passed to a formal parameter of the derived class type.

Before closing this section, we discuss another issue related to virtual functions.

Suppose that the definition of the class petType is as before, and the definition of the class dogType is modified slightly as follows:

```
class dogType: public petType
{
public:
    void print();
    void setBreed(string b = "");
    dogType(string n = "", string b = "");

private:
    string breed;
};
```

Consider the following statements:

```
petType pet("Lucky");
dogType dog("Tommy", "German Shepherd");

pet = dog;
```

C++ allows this type of assignment, that is, the values of a derived class object can be copied into a base class object. (Note that the reverse statement, that is, dog = pet; is not allowed.) Now, because the object pet has only one data member (name) and the object dog has two data members (name and breed), only the value of the data member name of dog is copied into the data member name of pet. This is called the **slicing problem**. The following statement will result in a compile-time error.

```
pet.setBreed("Siberian Husky");
```

C++ offers a way to treat a dogType object as a petType object without losing the additional properties of the class dogType by using pointers.

For example, suppose that you have the following statements:

```
petType *pet;
dogType *dog;

dog = new dogType("Tommy", "German Shepherd");
dog->setBreed("Siberian Husky ");

pet = dog;
```

In this case, the output of the statements `pet->print();`

is: `Name: Tommy, Breed: Siberian Husky`

Classes and Virtual Destructors

One thing recommended for classes with pointer member variables is that these classes should have the destructor. The destructor executes automatically when the class object goes out of scope. Thus, if the object creates dynamic memory space, the destructor can be designed to deallocate that memory space. If a derived class object is passed to a formal parameter of the base class type, the destructor of the base class executes regardless of whether the derived class object is passed by reference or by value. Logically, however, the destructor of the derived class should be executed when the derived class object goes out of scope.

To correct this problem, the destructor of the base class must be virtual. The **virtual destructor** of a base class automatically makes the destructor of a derived class virtual. When a derived class object is passed to a formal parameter of the base class type, then when the object goes out of scope, the destructor of the derived class executes. After executing the destructor of the derived class, the destructor of the base class executes. Therefore, when the derived class object is destroyed, the base class part (that is, the members inherited from the base class) of the derived class object is also destroyed.

If a base class contains virtual functions, make the destructor of the base class virtual.

Abstract Classes and Pure Virtual Functions

The preceding sections discussed virtual functions. Other than enforcing run-time binding of functions, virtual functions also have another use, which is discussed in this section. Chapter 11 discussed the second principle of OOD—inheritance. Through inheritance we can derive new classes without designing them from scratch. The derived classes, in addition to inheriting the existing members of the base class, can add their own members and also redefine or override public and protected member functions of the base class. The base class can contain functions that you would want each derived class to implement. There are many scenarios for which a class is desired to be served as a base class for a number of derived classes; however, the base class may contain certain functions that may not have meaningful definitions in the base class.

Let us consider the `class` shape given in Chapter 11. As noted in that chapter, from the `class` shape, you can derive other `classes`, such as rectangle, circle, ellipse, and so on. Some of the things common to every shape are its center, using the center to move a shape to a different location, and drawing the shape. We can include these in the `class` shape. For example, you could have the definition of the `class` shape similar to the following:

```
class shape
{
public:
    virtual void draw();
      //Function to draw the shape.

    virtual void move(double x, double y);
      //Function to move the shape at the position
      //(x, y).

        .
        .
        .

};
```

Because the definitions of the functions `draw` and `move` are specific to a particular shape, each derived class can provide an appropriate definition of these functions. Note that we have made the functions `draw` and `move` `virtual` to enforce run-time binding of these functions.

This definition of the `class` shape requires you to write the definitions of the functions `draw` and `move`. However, at this point, there is no shape to draw or move. Therefore, these function bodies have no code. One way to handle this is to make the body of these functions empty. This solution would work, but it has another drawback. Once we write the definitions of the functions of the `class` shape, then we could create an object of this class. Because there is no shape to work with, we would like to prevent the user from creating objects of the `class` shape. It follows that we would like to do the following two things—to not include the definitions of the functions `draw` and `move` and to prevent the user from creating objects of the `class` shape.

Because we do not want to include the definitions of the functions `draw` and `move` of the `class` shape, we must convert these functions to **pure virtual functions**. In this case, the prototypes of these functions are:

```
virtual void draw() = 0;
virtual void move(double x, double y) = 0;
```

Note the expression = 0 before the semicolon. Once you make these functions pure `virtual` functions in the `class` shape, you no longer need to provide the definitions of these functions for the `class` shape.

Once a class contains one or more pure virtual functions, then that class is called an **abstract class**. Thus, the abstract definition of the `class` shape is similar to the following:

```
class shape
{
public:
    virtual void draw() = 0;
      //Function to draw the shape. Note that this is a
      //pure virtual function.
    virtual void move(double x, double y) = 0;
      //Function to move the shape at the position
      //(x, y). Note that this is a pure virtual
      //function.
    .
    .
    .

};
```

Because an abstract class is *not* a complete class, as it (or its implementation file) does not contain the definitions of certain functions, you cannot create objects of that class.

Now suppose that we derive the class rectangle from the class shape. To make rectangle a nonabstract class so that we can create objects of this class, the class (or its implementation file) must provide the definitions of the pure virtual functions of its base class, which is the class shape.

Note that in addition to the pure virtual functions, an abstract class can contain instance variables, constructors, and functions that are not pure virtual. However, the abstract class must provide the definitions of the constructor and functions that are not pure virtual. The following example further illustrates how abstract classes work.

EXAMPLE 12-9

In Chapter 11, we defined the class partTimeEmployee, which was derived from the class personType, to illustrate inheritance. We also noted that there are two types of employees: full-time and part-time. The base salary of a full-time employee is usually fixed for a year. In addition, a full-time employee may receive a bonus. On the other hand, the salary of a part-time employee is usually calculated according to the pay rate per hour and the number of hours worked. In this example, we first define the class employeeType, derived from the class personType, to store an employee's name and ID. We include functions to set the ID and retrieve the ID. We also include pure virtual functions print and calculatePay to print an employee's data, which includes the employee's ID, name, and wages.

From the class employeeType, we derive the classes fullTimeEmployee and partTimeEmployee and provide the definitions of the pure virtual functions of the class employeeType.

The definition of the `class employeeType` is:

```cpp
#include "personType.h"

class employeeType: public personType
{
public:
    virtual void print() const = 0;
        //Function to output employee's data.
    virtual double calculatePay() const = 0;
        //Function to calculate and return the wages.
        //Postcondition: Pay is calculated and returned

    void setId(long id);
        //Function to set the salary.
        //Postcondition: personId = id;

    long getId() const;
        //Function to retrieve the id.
        //Postcondition: returns personId

    employeeType(string first = "", string last = "",
                 long id = 0);
        //Constructor with parameters
        //Sets the first name, last name, payRate, and
        //hoursWorked according to the parameters. If
        //no value is specified, the default values are
        //assumed.
        //Postcondition: firstName = first;
        //               lastName = last; personId = id;

private:
    long personId;        //stores the id
};
```

The definitions of the constructor and functions of the `class employeeType` that are not pure `virtual` are:

```cpp
void employeeType::setId(long id)
{
    personId = id;
}

long employeeType::getId() const
{
    return personId;
}

employeeType::employeeType(string first, string last, long id)
            : personType(first, last)
{
    personId = id;
}
```

The definition of the **class** `fullTimeEmployee` is:

```cpp
#include "employeeType.h"

class fullTimeEmployee: public employeeType
{
public:
    void set(string first, string last, long id,
             double salary, double bonus);
      //Function to set the first name, last name,
      //id, and salary according to the parameters.
      //Postcondition: firstName = first; lastName = last;
      //               personId = id; empSalary = salary;
      //               empBonus = bonus;

    void setSalary(double salary);
      //Function to set the salary.
      //Postcondition: empSalary = salary;

    double getSalary();
      //Function to retrieve the salary.
      //Postcondition: returns empSalary

    void setBonus(double bonus);
      //Function to set the bonus.
      //Postcondition: empBonus = bonus;

    double getBonus();
      //Function to retrieve the bonus.
      //Postcondition: returns empBonus;

    void print() const;
      //Function to output the first name, last name,
      //and the wages.
      //Postcondition: Outputs
      //        Id:
      //        Name: firstName lastName
      //        Wages: $$$$.$$

    double calculatePay() const;
      //Function to calculate and return the wages.
      //Postcondition: Pay is calculated and returned

    fullTimeEmployee(string first = "", string last = "",
                     long id = 0, double salary = 0,
                     double bonus = 0);
      //Constructor with default parameters.
      //Sets the first name, last name, id, salary, and
      //bonus according to the parameters. If
      //no value is specified, the default values are
      //assumed.
      //Postcondition: firstName = first; lastName = last;
      //               personId = id; empSalary = salary;
      //               empBonus = bonus;
```

```
private:
    double empSalary;
    double empBonus;
};
```

The definitions of the constructor and functions of the class fullTimeEmployee are:

```
void fullTimeEmployee::set(string first, string last,
                            long id,
                            double salary, double bonus)
{
    setName(first, last);
    setId(id);
    empSalary = salary;
    empBonus = bonus;
}

void fullTimeEmployee::setSalary(double salary)
{
    empSalary = salary;
}

double fullTimeEmployee::getSalary()
{
    return empSalary;
}

void fullTimeEmployee::setBonus(double bonus)
{
    empBonus = bonus;
}

double fullTimeEmployee::getBonus()
{
    return empBonus;
}

void fullTimeEmployee::print() const
{
    cout << "Id: " << getId() << endl;
    cout << "Name: ";
    personType::print();
    cout << endl;
    cout << "Wages: $" << calculatePay() << endl;
}

double fullTimeEmployee::calculatePay() const
{
    return empSalary + empBonus;
}
```

1
2

```
fullTimeEmployee::fullTimeEmployee(string first, string last,
                                   long id, double salary,
                                   double bonus)
               : employeeType(first, last, id)
{
    empSalary = salary;
    empBonus = bonus;
}
```

The definition of the class partTimeEmployee is:

```
#include "employeeType.h"

class partTimeEmployee: public employeeType
{
public:
    void set(string first, string last, long id, double rate,
            double hours);
      //Function to set the first name, last name, id,
      //payRate, and hoursWorked according to the
      //parameters.
      //Postcondition: firstName = first; lastName = last;
      //                personId = id;
      //                payRate = rate; hoursWorked = hours

    double calculatePay() const;
      //Function to calculate and return the wages.
      //Postcondition: Pay is calculated and returned.

    void setPayRate(double rate);
      //Function to set the salary.
      //Postcondition: payRate = rate;

    double getPayRate();
      //Function to retrieve the salary.
      //Postcondition: returns payRate;

    void setHoursWorked(double hours);
      //Function to set the bonus.
      //Postcondition: hoursWorked = hours

    double getHoursWorked();
      //Function to retrieve the bonus.
      //Postcondition: returns empBonus;

    void print() const;
      //Function to output the id, first name, last name,
      //and the wages.
      //Postcondition: Outputs
      //        Id:
      //        Name: firstName lastName
      //        Wages: $$$$.$$
```

```
    partTimeEmployee(string first = "", string last = "",
                     long id = 0,
                     double rate = 0, double hours = 0);
    //Constructor with parameters
    //Sets the first name, last name, payRate, and
    //hoursWorked according to the parameters. If
    //no value is specified, the default values are
    //assumed.
    //Postcondition: firstName = first; lastName = last;
    //               personId = id, payRate = rate;
    //               hoursWorked = hours;

private:
    double payRate;      //stores the pay rate
    double hoursWorked;  //stores the hours worked
};
```

The definitions of the constructor and functions of the class partTimeEmployee are:

```
void partTimeEmployee::set(string first, string last, long id,
                           double rate, double hours)
{
    setName(first, last);
    setId(id);
    payRate = rate;
    hoursWorked = hours;
}

void partTimeEmployee::setPayRate(double rate)
{
    payRate = rate;
}

double partTimeEmployee::getPayRate()
{
    return payRate;
}

void partTimeEmployee::setHoursWorked(double hours)
{
    hoursWorked = hours;
}

double partTimeEmployee::getHoursWorked()
{
    return hoursWorked;
}

void partTimeEmployee::print() const
{
    cout << "Id: " << getId() << endl;
    cout << "Name: ";
```

1
2

```
        personType::print();
        cout << endl;
        cout << "Wages: $" << calculatePay() << endl;
}

double partTimeEmployee::calculatePay() const
{
    return (payRate * hoursWorked);
}

    //constructor
partTimeEmployee::partTimeEmployee(string first, string last,
                                   long id,
                                   double rate, double hours)
                : employeeType(first, last, id)
{
    payRate = rate;
    hoursWorked = hours;
}
```

The following function main tests these classes:

```
#include <iostream>
#include "partTimeEmployee.h"
#include "fullTimeEmployee.h"

int main()
{
    fullTimeEmployee newEmp("John", "Smith", 75, 56000, 5700);
    partTimeEmployee tempEmp("Bill", "Nielson", 275, 15.50, 57);

    newEmp.print();
    cout << endl;
    tempEmp.print();

    return 0;
}
```

Sample Run:

```
Id: 75
Name: John Smith
Wages: $61700

Id: 275
Name: Bill Nielson
Wages: $883.5
```

The preceding output is self-explanatory. We leave the details as an exercise.

Array-Based Lists

A previous section of this chapter discussed how to use pointers to create dynamic arrays. Chapter 8 briefly explained how loops can be used to process elements stored in an array. Moreover, the previous sections of this chapter discussed abstract classes. Using these features, this section discusses how to use arrays to manipulate lists. Let us first make the following definition.

List: A collection of elements of the same type.

The **length** of a list is the number of elements in the list. Some of the operations performed on a list are as follows:

1. Create the list. The list is initialized to an empty state.
2. Determine whether the list is empty.
3. Determine whether the list is full.
4. Find the size of the list.
5. Destroy, or clear, the list.
6. Determine whether an item is the same as a given list element.
7. Insert an item in the list at the specified location.
8. Remove an item from the list at the specified location.
9. Replace an item at the specified location with another item.
10. Retrieve an item from the list at the specified location.
11. Search the list for a given item.

The list we create can be sorted or unsorted. However, the algorithms to implement certain operations are the same whether the list is sorted or unsorted. For example, a list, sorted or unsorted, is empty if the length of the list is empty. However, the search algorithms for sorted and unsorted lists are typically different. Therefore, next we create the abstract class that implements some of these operations. We will separately describe the classes to create sorted and unsorted lists. However, we must first decide how to store the list in the computer's memory.

Because all the elements of a list are of the same type, an effective, convenient, and a common way to process a list is to store it in an array. Initially, the size of the array holding the list elements is usually larger than the number of elements in the list so that, at a later stage, the list can grow to a specific size. Thus, we must know how full the array is, that is, we must keep track of the number of list elements stored in the array. Now, C++ allows the programmer to create dynamic arrays. Therefore, we will leave it for the user to specify the size of the array. The size of the array can be specified when a list object is declared. It follows that, in order to maintain and process the list in an array, we need the following three variables:

1
2

1. The array, `list`, holding the list elements.

2. A variable, `length`, to store the length of the list (that is, the number of list elements currently in the array).

3. A variable, `maxSize`, to store the size of the array (that is, the maximum number of elements that can be stored in the array).

Now that you know the operations to be performed on a list and ways to store the list into computer memory, we can define the class implementing the list as an ADT (abstract data type). For illustration purposes, we assume that the elements of the list are of type `int`. We will remove this restriction when we discuss class templates in Chapter 13; there, we will develop a generic class that can be used to process a variety of lists.

The following class defines array-based `int` lists as an ADT:

Now that you know the operations to be performed on a list and how to store the list into the computer's memory, next we define the abstract `class arrayListType` implementing the list as an ADT (abstract data type).

```
class arrayListType
{
public:
    bool isEmpty() const;
      //Function to determine whether the list is empty
      //Postcondition: Returns true if the list is empty;
      //               otherwise, returns false.

    bool isFull() const;
      //Function to determine whether the list is full
      //Postcondition: Returns true if the list is full;
      //               otherwise, returns false.

    int listSize() const;
      //Function to determine the number of elements in
      //the list.
      //Postcondition: Returns the value of length.

    int maxListSize() const;
      //Function to determine the maximum size of the list
      //Postcondition: Returns the value of maxSize.

    void print() const;
      //Function to output the elements of the list
      //Postcondition: Elements of the list are output on the
      //               standard output device.

    bool isItemAtEqual(int location, int item) const;
      //Function to determine whether item is the same as
      //the item in the list at the position specified
      //by location.
      //Postcondition: Returns true if the list[location]
      //               is the same as item; otherwise,
      //               returns false.
      //               If location is out of range, an
      //               appropriate message is displayed.
```

```cpp
virtual void insertAt(int location, int insertItem) = 0;
    //Function to insert insertItem in the list at the
    //position specified by location.
    //Note that this is an abstract function.
    //Postcondition: Starting at location, the elements of
    //               the list are shifted down,
    //               list[location] = insertItem; length++;
    //               If the list is full or location is out of
    //               range, an appropriate message is displayed.

virtual void insertEnd(int insertItem) = 0;
    //Function to insert insertItem at the end of
    //the list. Note that this is an abstract function.
    //Postcondition: list[length] = insertItem; and length++;
    //               If the list is full, an appropriate
    //               message is displayed.

void removeAt(int location);
    //Function to remove the item from the list at the
    //position specified by location
    //Postcondition: The list element at list[location] is
    //               removed and length is decremented by 1.
    //               If location is out of range, an
    //               appropriate message is displayed.

void retrieveAt(int location, int& retItem) const;
    //Function to retrieve the element from the list at the
    //position specified by location
    //Postcondition: retItem = list[location]
    //               If location is out of range, an
    //               appropriate message is displayed.

virtual void replaceAt(int location, int repItem) = 0;
    //Function to replace repItem the element in the list
    //at the position specified by location.
    //Note that this is an abstract function.
    //Postcondition: list[location] = repItem
    //               If location is out of range, an
    //               appropriate message is displayed.

void clearList();
    //Function to remove all the elements from the list
    //After this operation, the size of the list is zero.
    //Postcondition: length = 0;

virtual int seqSearch(int searchItem) const = 0;
    //Function to search the list for searchItem.
    //Note that this is an abstract function.
    //Postcondition: If the item is found, returns the
    //               location in the array where the item is
    //               found; otherwise, returns -1.

virtual void remove(int removeItem) = 0;
    //Function to remove removeItem from the list.
    //Note that this is an abstract function.
    //Postcondition: If removeItem is found in the list,
    //               it is removed from the list and length
    //               is decremented by one.
```

12

```
arrayListType(int size = 100);
  //Constructor
  //Creates an array of the size specified by the
  //parameter size. The default array size is 100.
  //Postcondition: The list points to the array, length = 0,
  //                and maxSize = size;

arrayListType (const arrayListType& otherList);
  //Copy constructor

virtual ~arrayListType();
  //Destructor
  //Deallocate the memory occupied by the array.

protected:
    int *list;      //array to hold the list elements
    int length;     //variable to store the length of the list
    int maxSize;    //variable to store the maximum
                    //size of the list

};
```

Figure 12-22 shows the UML class diagram of the **class** arrayListType. Note that in the UML class diagram, the name of an abstract class and abstract function is shown in italics.

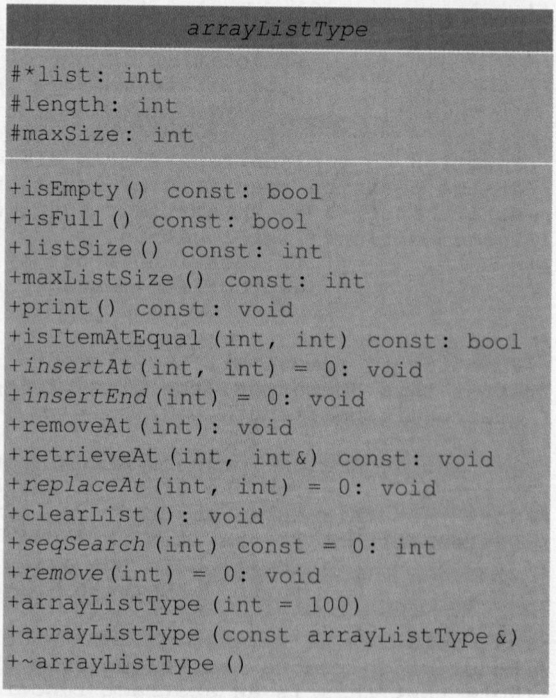

```
              arrayListType

#*list: int
#length: int
#maxSize: int

+isEmpty() const: bool
+isFull() const: bool
+listSize() const: int
+maxListSize() const: int
+print() const: void
+isItemAtEqual (int, int) const: bool
+insertAt (int, int) = 0: void
+insertEnd (int) = 0: void
+removeAt (int): void
+retrieveAt (int, int&) const: void
+replaceAt (int, int) = 0: void
+clearList (): void
+seqSearch (int) const = 0: int
+remove (int) = 0: void
+arrayListType (int = 100)
+arrayListType (const arrayListType &)
+~arrayListType ()
```

FIGURE 12-22 UML diagram of the **class** arrayListType

Notice that the member variables of the `class arrayListType` are declared as `protected`. Moreover notice that the functions `insertAt`, `insertEnd`, `replaceAt`, `seqSearch`, `insert`, and `remove` are declared as abstract. This is because, as noted earlier, typically we deal with two types of lists—lists whose elements are arranged according to some criteria, such as sorted list, and lists whose elements are in no particular order, unsorted lists. The algorithms to implement the operations, search, insert, and remove slightly differs for sorted and unsorted lists. Therefore, by using the principle of inheritance, from the `class arrayListType`, we in fact, will derive two `class`es: `orderedArrayListType` and `unorderedArrayListType`.

Objects of the `class unorderedArrayListType` would arrange list elements in no particular order, that is, these lists are unsorted. On the other hand, objects of the `class orderedArrayListType` would arrange elements according to some comparison criteria, usually, greater than or equal to. That is, these lists will be in ascending order. Moreover, after inserting an element into or removing an element from an ordered list, the resulting list will be ordered. We will, therefore, separately describe the algorithm to implement the operations search, insert, and remove for unsorted and sorted lists. Because each of the classes `orderedArrayListType` and `unorderedArrayListType` will provide separate definitions of the functions `insertAt`, `insertEnd`, `replaceAt`, `seqSearch`, `insert`, and `remove`, and because these functions would access the instance variable, to provide direct access to the instance variables, the instance variables are declared as protected.

Next, we write the definitions of the nonabstract functions.

The list is empty if `length` is `0`; it is full if `length` is equal to `maxSize`. Therefore, the definitions of the functions `isEmpty` and `isFull` are

```
bool arrayListType::isEmpty() const
{
    return (length == 0);
} //end isEmpty

bool arrayListType::isFull() const
{
    return (length == maxSize);
} //end isFull
```

The member variable length of the `class arrayListType` stores the number of elements currently in the list. Similarly, because the size of the array holding the list elements is stored in the member variable `maxSize`, `maxSize` specifies the maximum size of the list. Therefore, the definitions of the functions `listSize` and `maxListSize` are

```
int arrayListType::listSize() const
{
    return length;
} //end listSize

int arrayListType::maxListSize() const
{
    return maxSize;
} //end maxListSize
```

The member function `print` outputs the elements of the list. We assume that the output is sent to the standard output device:

```
void arrayListType::print() const
{
    for (int i = 0; i < length; i++)
        cout << list[i] << " ";
    cout << endl;
} //end print
```

The definition of the function `isItemAtEqual` is straightforward. If element at the position `location` is the same as `item`, it returns `true`. If either `location` is out of range or `item` is not in the list, it returns `false`. The definition of this function is:

```
bool arrayListType::isItemAtEqual(int location, int item)  const
{
    if (location < 0 || location >= length)
    {
        cout << "The location of the item to be removed "
             << "is out of range." << endl;

        return false;
    }
    else
        return (list[location] == item);
} //end isItemAtEqual
```

The function `removeAt` removes an item from a specific location in the list. The location of the item to be removed is passed as a parameter to this function. After removing the item from the list, the length of the list is reduced by 1. If the item to be removed is somewhere in the middle of the list, after removing the item we must move certain elements up one array slot because we cannot leave holes in the portion of the array containing the list. Figure 12-23 illustrates this concept.

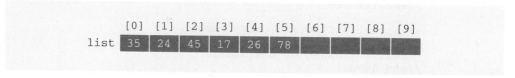

FIGURE 12-23 Array `list`

The number of elements currently in the list is 6, so `length` is 6. Thus, after removing an element, the length of the list is 5. Suppose that the item to be removed is at, say location 3. Clearly, we must move `list[4]` into `list[3]` and `list[5]` into `list[4]`, in this order.

The definition of the function `removeAt` is

```
void arrayListType::removeAt(int location)
{
    if (location < 0 || location >= length)
        cout << "The location of the item to be removed "
             << "is out of range." << endl;
```

```
    else
    {
        for (int i = location; i < length - 1; i++)
            list[i] = list[i+1];
        length--;
    }
} //end removeAt
```

The definition of the function `retrieveAt` is straightforward. The index of the item to be retrieved, and the location where to retrieve the item, are passed as parameters to this function. The definition of this function is:

```
void arrayListType::retrieveAt(int location, int& retItem) const
{
    if (location < 0 || location >= length)
        cout << "The location of the item to be retrieved is "
             << "out of range" << endl;
    else
        retItem = list[location];
} //end retrieveAt
```

The function `clearList` removes the elements from the list, leaving it empty. Because the member variable `length` indicates the number of elements in the list, the elements are removed by simply setting `length` to 0. Therefore, the definition of this function is

```
void arrayListType::clearList()
{
    length = 0;
} //end clearList
```

We now discuss the definition of the constructors and destructor. The constructor creates an array of the size specified by the user, and initializes the `length` of the list to 0 and the `maxSize` to the size of the array specified by the user. The size of the array is passed as a parameter to the constructor. The default array size is 100. The destructor deallocates the memory occupied by the array holding the list elements. The definitions of the constructor and the destructor are as follows:

```
arrayListType::arrayListType(int size)
{
    if (size <= 0)
    {
        cout << "The array size must be positive. Creating "
             << "an array of the size 100." << endl;

        maxSize = 100;
    }
    else
        maxSize = size;

    length = 0;

    list = new int[maxSize];
} //end constructor

arrayListType::~arrayListType()
{
    delete [] list;
} //end destructor
```

Next we describe the copy constructor. Recall that the copy constructor is called when an object is passed as a (value) parameter to a function, and when an object is declared and initialized using the value of another object of the same type. It copies the values of the member variables of the actual object into the corresponding member variables of the formal parameter and the object being created. Its definition is

```
arrayListType::arrayListType(const arrayListType& otherList)
{
    maxSize = otherList.maxSize;
    length = otherList.length;

    list = new int[maxSize]; //create the array

    for (int j = 0; j < length; j++)   //copy otherList
        list[j] = otherList.list[j];
}//end copy constructor
```

Unordered Lists

As described in the preceding section, we derive the **class** unorderedArrayListType from the abstract **class** arrayListType and implement the operations insertAt, insertEnd, replaceAt, seqSearch, insert, and remove.

The definition of the **class** unorderedArrayListType is: (To save space, we list the member functions without documentation. The descriptions of these functions are the same as the descriptions of the functions of the **class** arrayListType.)

```
class unorderedArrayListType: public arrayListType
{
public:
    void insertAt(int location, int insertItem);
    void insertEnd(int insertItem);
    void replaceAt(int location, int repItem);
    int seqSearch(int searchItem) const;
    void remove(int removeItem);

    unorderedArrayListType(int size = 100);
      //Constructor.
};
```

We leave the UML class diagram and its inheritance hierarchy of the **class** unorderedArrayListType as an exercise for you.

The function insertAt inserts an item at a specific location in the list. The item to be inserted and the insert location in the array are passed as parameters to this function. In order to insert the item somewhere in the middle of the list, we must first make room for the new item. That is, we need to move certain elements down one array slot. Consider the list in Figure 12-24.

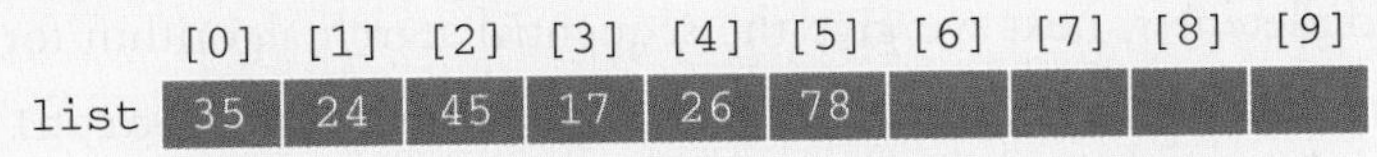

FIGURE 12-24 Array list

The number of elements currently in the list is 6, so length is 6. Thus, after inserting a new element, the length of the list is 7. If the item is to be inserted at, say location 6, we can easily accomplish this by copying the item in list[6]. On the other hand, if the item is to be inserted at, say location 3, we first need to move elements list[3], list[4], and list[5] one array slot left to make room for the new item. Thus, we must first copy list[5] into list[6], list[4] into list[5], and list[3] into list[4], in this order. Then we can copy the new item into list[3].

Of course, special cases such as trying to insert in a full list must be handled separately. Some of these cases can be accomplished by other member functions.

The definition of the function insertAt is as follows:

```
void unorderedArrayListType::insertAt(int location,
                                      int insertItem)
{
    if (location < 0 || location >= maxSize)
        cout << "The position of the item to be inserted "
             << "is out of range." << endl;
    else if (length >= maxSize)  //list is full
        cout << "Cannot insert in a full list" << endl;
    else
    {
        for (int i = length; i > location; i--)
            list[i] = list[i - 1];  //move the elements down

        list[location] = insertItem; //insert the item at
                                     //the specified position

        length++;  //increment the length
    }
} //end insertAt
```

The function insertEnd can be implemented by using the function insertAt. However, the function insertEnd does not require the shifting of elements. Therefore, we give its definition directly.

```
void unorderedArrayListType::insertEnd(int insertItem)
{
    if (length >= maxSize)  //the list is full
        cout << "Cannot insert in a full list." << endl;
    else
    {
        list[length] = insertItem; //insert the item at the end
        length++; //increment the length
    }
} //end insertEnd
```

Chapter 8 describes a **sequential** or **linear** search. For easy reference and the sake of completeness, next we give the sequential search algorithm for array-based lists:

```
int unorderedArrayListType::seqSearch(int searchItem) const
{
    int loc;
    bool found = false;

    loc = 0;

    while (loc < length && !found)
        if (list[loc] == searchItem)
            found = true;
        else
            loc++;

    if (found)
        return loc;
    else
        return -1;
} //end seqSearch
```

The function `remove` deletes an item from the list. The item to be deleted is passed as a parameter to this function. In order to delete the item, the function calls the member function `seqSearch` to determine whether or not the item to be deleted is in the list. If the item to be deleted is found in the list, the item is removed from the list and the length of the list is decremented by 1. If the item to be removed is found in the list, the function `seqSearch` returns the `index` of the item in the list to be deleted. We can now use the `index` returned by the function `seqSearch`, and use the function `removeAt` to remove the item from the list. Therefore, the definition of the function `remove` is:

```
void unorderedArrayListType::remove(int removeItem)
{
    int loc;

    if (length == 0)
        cout << "Cannot delete from an empty list." << endl;
    else
    {
        loc = seqSearch(removeItem);

        if (loc != -1)
            removeAt(loc);
        else
            cout << "The item to be deleted is not in the list."
                << endl;
    }
} //end remove
```

The definition of the function `replaceAt` is:

```
void unorderedArrayListType::replaceAt(int location, int repItem)
{
    if (location < 0 || location >= length)
        cout << "The location of the item to be "
            << "replaced is out of range." << endl;
```

```
    else
        list[location] = repItem;
} //end replaceAt
```

The definition of the constructor is:

```
unorderedArrayListType::unorderedArrayListType(int size)
                        : arrayListType(size)
{
} //end constructor
```

The following program tests the various operations on an unordered list.

EXAMPLE 12-10

```
#include <iostream>
#include "unorderedArrayListType.h"

using namespace std;

int main()
{
    unorderedArrayListType intList(25);               //Line 1

    int number;                                       //Line 2

    cout << "List 3: Enter 8 integers: ";             //Line 3

    for (int count = 0; count < 8; count++)           //Line 4
    {
        cin >> number;                                //Line 5
        intList.insertEnd(number);                    //Line 6
    }
    cout << endl;                                     //Line 7
    cout << "Line 8: intList: ";                      //Line 8
    intList.print();                                  //Line 9
    cout << endl;                                     //Line 10

    cout << "Line 11: Enter the number to be "
         << "deleted: ";                              //Line 11
                                                      //Line 12
    cin >> number;                                    //Line 13
    cout << endl;

    intList.remove(number);                           //Line 14

    cout << "Line 15: After removing " << number
         << " intList: ";                             //Line 15
    intList.print();                                  //Line 16
    cout << endl;                                     //Line 17

    cout << "Line 18: Enter the search item: ";       //Line 18

    cin >> number;                                    //Line 19
    cout << endl;                                     //Line 20

    if (intList.seqSearch(number) != -1)              //Line 21
        cout << "Line 22: " << number
             << " found in intList." << endl;         //Line 22
```

```
    else                                        //Line 23
        cout << "Line 24: " << number
            << " is not in intList." << endl;   //Line 24

    return 0;
}
```

Sample Run: In this sample run, the user input is shaded.

```
List 3: Enter 8 integers: 23 89 54 32 56 11 88 39
Line 8: intList: 23 89 54 32 56 11 88 39
Line 11: Enter the number to be deleted: 23
Line 15: After removing 23 intList: 89 54 32 56 11 88 39
Line 18: Enter the search item: 11
Line 22: 11 found in intList.
```

The preceding program is self-explanatory. We leave the details as an exercise.

 NOTE   The Web site accompanying this book contains the program
testProgUnorderedList_II.cpp, which illustrates how the copy constructor
on an unorderedArrayListType object works.

 NOTE   **(Unordered Set)** Recall that a list is a collection of elements of the same type. However, in
a list an element may repeat. That is, the elements of the list need not be distinct. On
the other hand, a **set** is also a collection of elements of the same type. However, the
elements of a set are distinct. It follows that a set is a list with distinct elements. In this
section we designed the **class** unorderedArrayListType to process unordered
lists. Note that the functions insertAt and insertEnd do not check whether the item
to be inserted is already in the list. Similarly, the function replaceAt, does not check if
the item to be replaced is already in the list. Just as you can design a class to manipulate
lists, you can also design a class to manipulate sets. Programming Exercise 12, at the end
of this chapter asks you to design the **class** unorderedSetType, derived from the
class unorderedArrayListType, to manipulate sets.

Ordered Lists

As described earlier we derive two classes from the abstract **class** arrayListType,
which are: unorderedArrayListType and orderedArrayListType. Elements of an
unorderedArrayListType object are in no particular order. However, elements of an
object orderedArrayListType are in ascending order. The preceding section described
the operation of the **class** unorderedArrayListType. This section describes the
class orderedArrayListType.

The **class** orderedArrayListType also contains the function insert to insert an item
at the proper place in the list. The following class defines ordered array-based **int** lists as

an ADT. (To save space, we list the member function without any documentation, which is left as an exercise for you.)

```cpp
class orderedArrayListType: public arrayListType
{
public:
    void insertAt(int location, int insertItem);
    void insertEnd(int insertItem);
    void replaceAt(int location, int repItem);
    int seqSearch(int searchItem) const;
    void insert(int insertItem);
    void remove(int removeItem);

    orderedArrayListType(int size = 100);
        //Constructor
};
```

We leave the UML class diagram and its inheritance hierarchy of the class orderedArrayListType as an exercise for you.

We give only the definition of the function insert and leave others as an exercise for you.

The function insert inserts a new item at the proper place in the list and the length of the list is increased by 1. The definition of this function is:

```cpp
void orderedArrayListType::insert(int insertItem)
{
    if (length == 0)                 //list is empty
        list[length++] = insertItem;   //insert insertItem
                                        //and increment length
    else if (length == maxSize)
        cout << "Cannot insert in a full list." << endl;
    else
    {
        //Find the location in the list where to insert
        //insertItem.
        int loc;

        bool found = false;

        for (loc = 0; loc < length; loc++)
        {
            if (list[loc] >= insertItem)
            {
                found = true;
                break;
            }
        }

        for (int i = length; i > loc; i--)
            list[i] = list[i - 1];   //move the elements down

        list[loc] = insertItem;   //insert insertItem
        length++;     //increment the length
    }
} //end insert
```

NOTE (**Ordered Set**) An ordered set is a collection of distinct elements of the same type. Programming Exercise 13, at the end of this chapter asks you to design the `class orderedSetType`, derived from the `class orderedArrayListType`, to manipulate ordered sets.

Address of Operator and Classes

This chapter has used the address of operator, `&`, to store the address of a variable into a pointer variable. The address of operator is also used to create aliases to an object. Consider the following statements:

```
int x;
int &y = x;
```

The first statement declares x to be an `int` variable, and the second statement declares y to be an alias of x. That is, both x and y refer to the same memory location. Thus, y is like a constant pointer variable. The statement:

```
y = 25;
```

sets the value of y and, hence, the value of x to 25. Similarly, the statement:

```
x = 2 * x + 30;
```

updates the value of x and, hence, the value of y.

The address of operator can also be used to return the address of a `private` member variable of a class. However, if you are not careful, this operation can result in serious errors in the program. The following example helps illustrate this idea.

Consider the following class definition:

```
//header file testadd.h

#ifndef H_testAdd
#define H_testAdd

class testAddress
{
public:
    void setX(int);
    void printX() const;
    int& addressOfX();      //this function returns the address
                            //of the x
private:
    int x;
};

#endif
```

The definitions of the functions to implement the member functions are as follows:

```
//Implementation file testAdd.cpp

#include <iostream>
#include "testAdd.h"

using namespace std;

void testAddress::setX(int inX)
{
    x = inX;
}
void testAddress::printX() const
{
    cout << x;
}

int& testAddress::addressOfX()
{
    return x;
}
```

Because the return type of the function `addressOfX`, which is `int&`, is an address of an `int` memory location, the effect of the statement:

```
return x;
```

is that the address of x is returned.

Next, let us write a simple program that uses the **class** `testAddress` and illustrates what can go wrong. Later, we will show how to fix the problem.

```
//Test program.
#include <iostream>
#include "testAdd.h"

using namespace std;

int main()
{
    testAddress a;
    int &y = a.addressOfX();

    a.setX(50);
    cout << "x in class testAddress = ";
    a.printX();
    cout << endl;

    y = 25;
    cout << "After y = 25, x in class testAddress = ";
    a.printX();
    cout << endl;

    return 0;
}
```

Sample Run:

```
x in class testAddress = 50
After y = 25, x in class testAddress = 25
```

In the preceding program, after the statement:

```
int &y = a.addressOfX();
```

executes, y becomes an alias of the `private` member variable x of the object a. Thus, the statement:

```
y = 25;
```

changes the value of x.

Chapter 10 said that `private` member variables are not accessible outside of the class. However, by returning their addresses, the programmer can manipulate them. One way to resolve this problem is to never provide the user of the class with the addresses of the `private` member variables. Sometimes, however, it is necessary to return the address of a `private` member variable, as we will see in the next chapter. How can we prevent the program from directly manipulating the `private` member variables? To fix this problem, we use the word `const` before the return type of the function. This way, we can still return the addresses of the `private` member variables, but at the same time prevent the programmer from directly manipulating the `private` member variables. Let us rewrite the `class testAddress` using this feature:

```
#ifndef H_testAdd
#define H_testAdd

class testAddress
{
public:
    void setX(int);
    void printX() const;
    const int& addressOfX(); //this function returns the
                             //address of the private data
                             //member
private:
    int x;
};

#endif
```

The definition of the function `addressOfX` in the implementation file is:

```
const int& testAddress::addressOfX()
{
    return x;
}
```

The same program will now generate a compile-time error.

QUICK REVIEW

1. Pointer variables contain the addresses of other variables as their values.

2. In C++, no name is associated with the pointer data type.

3. A pointer variable is declared using an asterisk, *, between the data type and the variable. For example, the statements:

```
int *p;
char *ch;
```

declare p and ch to be pointer variables. The value of p points to a memory space of type int, and the value of ch points to a memory space of type char. Usually, p is called a pointer variable of type int, and ch is called a pointer variable of type char.

4. In C++, & is called the address of operator.

5. The address of operator returns the address of its operand. For example, if p is a pointer variable of type int and num is an int variable, the statement:

```
p = &num;
```

sets the value of p to the address of num.

6. When used as a unary operator, * is called the dereferencing operator.

7. The memory location indicated by the value of a pointer variable is accessed by using the dereferencing operator, *. For example, if p is a pointer variable of type int, the statement:

```
*p = 25;
```

sets the value of the memory location indicated by the value of p to 25.

8. You can use the member access operator arrow, ->, to access the component of an object pointed to by a pointer.

9. Pointer variables are initialized using either 0 (the integer zero), NULL, or the address of a variable of the same type.

10. The only number that can be directly assigned to a pointer variable is 0.

11. The only arithmetic operations allowed on pointer variables are increment (++), decrement (--), addition of an integer to a pointer variable, subtraction of an integer from a pointer variable, and subtraction of a pointer from another pointer.

12. Pointer arithmetic is different than ordinary arithmetic. When an integer is added to a pointer, the value added to the value of the pointer variable is the integer times the size of the object to which the pointer is pointing. Similarly, when an integer is subtracted from a pointer, the value subtracted from the value of the pointer variable is the integer times the size of the object to which the pointer is pointing.

13. Pointer variables can be compared using relational operators. (It makes sense to compare pointers of the same type.)

1
2

14. The value of one pointer variable can be assigned to another pointer variable of the same type.

15. A variable created during program execution is called a dynamic variable.

16. The operator `new` is used to create a dynamic variable.

17. The operator `delete` is used to deallocate the memory occupied by a dynamic variable.

18. In C++, both `new` and `delete` are reserved words.

19. The operator `new` has two forms: one to create a single dynamic variable and another to create an array of dynamic variables.

20. If p is a pointer of type `int`, the statement:

    ```
    p = new int;
    ```

    allocates storage of type `int` somewhere in memory and stores the address of the allocated storage in p.

21. The operator `delete` has two forms: one to deallocate the memory occupied by a single dynamic variable and another to deallocate the memory occupied by an array of dynamic variables.

22. If p is a pointer of type `int`, the statement:

    ```
    delete p;
    ```

    deallocates the memory pointed to by p.

23. The array name is a constant pointer. It always points to the same memory location, which is the location of the first array component.

24. To create a dynamic array, the form of the `new` operator that creates an array of dynamic variables is used. For example, if p is a pointer of type `int`, the statement:

    ```
    p = new int[10];
    ```

    creates an array of 10 components of type `int`. The base address of the array is stored in p. We call p a dynamic array.

25. Array notation can be used to access the components of a dynamic array. For example, suppose p is a dynamic array of 10 components. Then, p[0] refers to the first array component, p[1] refers to the second array component, and so on. In particular, p[i] refers to the (i + 1)th component of the array.

26. An array created during program execution is called a dynamic array.

27. If p is a dynamic array, then the statement:

    ```
    delete [] p;
    ```

    deallocates the memory occupied by p—that is, the components of p.

28. C++ allows a program to create dynamic multidimensional arrays.

29. In the statement `int **board;`, the variable `board` is a pointer to a pointer.

30. In a shallow copy, two or more pointers of the same type point to the same memory space; that is, they point to the same data.

31. In a deep copy, two or more pointers of the same type have their own copies of the data.

32. If a class has a destructor, the destructor is automatically executed whenever a class object goes out of scope.

33. If a class has pointer member variables, the built-in assignment operators provide a shallow copy of the data.

34. A copy constructor executes when an object is declared and initialized by using the value of another object and when an object is passed by value as a parameter.

35. C++ allows a user to pass an object of a derived class to a formal parameter of the base class type.

36. The binding of virtual functions occurs at execution time, not at compile time, and is called dynamic, or run-time, binding.

37. In C++, virtual functions are declared using the reserved word `virtual`.

38. A class is called an abstract class if it contains one or more pure virtual functions.

39. Because an abstract class is *not* a complete class—as it (or its implementation file) does not contain the definitions of certain functions—you cannot create objects of that class.

40. In addition to the pure virtual functions, an abstract class can contain instance variables, constructors, and functions that are not pure virtual. However, the abstract class must provide the definitions of constructors and functions that are not pure virtual.

41. A list is a collection of elements of the same type.

42. The commonly performed operations on a list are create the list, determine whether the list is empty, determine whether the list is full, find the size of the list, destroy or clear the list, determine whether an item is the same as a given list element, insert an item in the list at the specified location, remove an item from the list at the specified location, replace an item at the specified location with another item, retrieve an item from the list from the specified location, and search the list for a given item.

43. The address of operator can be used to return the address of a `private` member variable of a class.

EXERCISES

1. Mark the following statements as true or false.

   a. In C++, pointer is a reserved word.

   b. In C++, pointer variables are declared using the word pointer.

   c. The statement `delete p;` deallocates the variable pointer p.

   d. The statement `delete p;` deallocates the dynamic variable that is pointed to by p.

e. Given the declaration:

```
int list[10];
int *p;
```

the statement:

```
p = list;
```

is valid in C++.

f. Given the declaration:

```
int *p;
```

the statement:

```
p = new int[50];
```

dynamically allocates an array of 50 components of type `int`, and p contains the base address of the array.

g. The address of operator returns the address and value of its operand.

h. If p is a pointer variable, then the statement p = p * 2; is valid in C++.

2. Given the following declaration:

```
int num;
int *ptr1;
int *ptr2;
double *ptr3;
```

Mark the following statements as valid or invalid. If a statement is invalid, explain why.

a. `ptr1 = ptr2;`

b. `num = ptr1;`

c. `ptr3 = ptr1;`

d. `*prt3 = *ptr2;`

e. `*ptr1 = *ptr2;`

f. `num = *ptr2;`

g. `ptr1 = &ptr2;`

h. `ptr1 = &num;`

i. `num = &ptr1;`

3. Explain how the operator * is used to work with pointers.

4. Consider the following statement:

```
int* p, q;
```

This statement could lead to what type of misinterpretation?

5. Suppose that you have the declaration int *numPtr;. What is the difference between the expressions: *numPtr and &numPtr?

6. What is the output of the following C++ code?

```
int x;
int y;
int *p = &x;
int *q = &y;
x = 35;
y = 46;
p = q;
*p = 27;
cout << x << "    " << y << endl;
cout << *p << "    " << *q << endl;
```

7. Given the following statements:

```
int num;
int *numPtr;
```

Write C++ statements that use the variable numPtr to increment the value of the variable num.

8. What is the output of the following C++ code?

```
string *str;
string fName, lName;
str = &fName;
*str = "Miller";
str = &lName;
*str = "Tommy";
cout << fName << " " << lName << endl;
```

9. What is the output of the following C++ code?

```
int num1;
int num2;
int *p = &num1;
p = &num2;
*p = 25;
num1 = num2 + 6;
p = &num1;
num2 = 73;
*p = 47;
cout << *p << " " << num1 << " " << num2 << endl;
```

10. What is the output of the following C++ code?

```
int *length;
int *width;
length = new int;
*length = 5;
width = length;
length = new int;
*length = 2 * (*width);
cout << *length << " " << *width << " " << (*length) * (*width)
     << endl;
```

11. What is the output of the following C++ code?

```cpp
int *first = new int;
int *second;
*first = 85;
second = first;
*second = *second + *first;
first = new int;
*first = *second - 100;
cout << *first << " " << *second << endl;
```

12. What is the output of the following C++ code?

```cpp
int *p = new int;
int *q = new int;
*p = 26;
*q = 10;
cout << 2 * (*p) << " " << (*q + 3) << endl;
p = q;
*p = 42;
cout << *p << " " << *q << endl;
q = new int;
*p = 25;
*q = 18;
cout << *p << " " << *q << endl;
```

13. What is the output of the following C++ code? (Assume that decimal numbers are output with two decimal places.)

```cpp
double *test1 = new double;
double *test2 = new double;
double *average;
average = test1;
*test1 = 45.00;
*test2 = 90.00;
test1 = test2;
test2 = new double;
*test2 = 86.00;
*average = ((*test1) + (*test2)) / 2;
cout << *test1 << " " << *test2 << " " << *average << endl;
```

14. What is wrong with the following C++ code?

```cpp
double *deposit;          //Line 1
double *intRate;          //Line 2
double interest;          //Line 3

deposit = new double;     //Line 4
*deposit = 25000;         //Line 5

interest = (*deposit) * (*intRate); //Line 6

cout << interest << endl;  //Line 7
```

15. What is wrong with the following C++ code?

```
double *firstPtr = new double;      //Line 1
double *nextPtr = new double;       //Line 2

*firstPtr = 62;                     //Line 3
nextPtr = firstPtr;                 //Line 4
delete firstPtr;                    //Line 5
delete nextPtr;                     //Line 6
firstPtr = new double;              //Line 7
*firstPtr = 28;                     //Line 8

cout << *firstPtr << " " << *nextPtr << endl;   //Line 9
```

16. What is the output of the following C++ code?

```
int *p;
int *q = new int;
p = q;
*q = 75;
delete p;
p = new int;
*p = 62;
q = new int;
q = p;
*q = 26;
cout << *p << " " << *q << endl;
```

17. What is stored in `list` after the following code executes?

```
int list[7] = {10, 8, 15, 14, 16, 24, 36};
int *ptr = list;

*ptr = *ptr + 2;
ptr = ptr + 2;
*ptr = (*ptr) - *(ptr - 1);
ptr++;
*ptr = 2 * (*ptr) - 3;
```

18. What is the output of the following C++ code?

```
int num;
int *listPtr;
int *temp;
listPtr = new int[5];
num = 8;
temp = listPtr;

for (int j = 0; j < 5; j++)
{
    *listPtr = num;
    num = num + 2;
    listPtr++;
}

listPtr = temp;
```

```
for (int k = 0; k < 5; k++)
{
    *temp = *temp + 3;
    temp++;
}

for (int k = 0; k < 5; k++)
{
    cout << *listPtr << " ";
    listPtr ++;
}
cout << endl;
```

19. Suppose that `numPtr` is a pointer of type `int` and `gpaPtr` is a pointer of type `double`. Further suppose that `numPtr = 1050` and `gpaPtr = 2000`. Also suppose that the size of the memory allocated for an `int` value is 4 bytes and the size of the memory allocated for a `double` value is 8 bytes. What are the values of `numPtr` and `gpaPtr` after the statements `numPtr = numPtr + 2`; and `gpaPtr = gpaPtr + 3`; execute?

20. What does the operator `new` do?

21. What does the operator `delete` do?

22. What is the output of the following C++ code?

```
int *tempList;
int num = 3;

tempList = new int[7];
tempList[6] = 4;
for (int j = 5; j >= 0; j--)
    tempList[j] = tempList[j + 1] + j * num;
for (int j = 0; j < 7; j++)
    cout << tempList [j] << " ";
cout << endl;
```

23. Consider the following statement:

```
int *num;
```

a. Write the C++ statement that dynamically creates an array of 10 components of type `int` and num contains the base address of the array.

b. Write a C++ code that inputs data into the array num from the standard input device.

c. Write a C++ statement that deallocates the memory space of array to which num points.

24. Consider the following C++ code:

```
int *p;
p = new int[10];
for (int j = 0; j < 10; j++)
    p[i] = 2 * j - 2;
```

Write the C++ statement that deallocates the memory space occupied by the array to which p points.

25. Explain the difference between a shallow copy and a deep copy of data.

26. What is wrong with the following C++ code?

```cpp
int *p;                          //Line 1
int *q;                          //Line 2

p = new int[5];                  //Line 3
*p = 2;                          //Line 4

for (int i = 1; i < 5; i++)      //Line 5
    p[i] = p[i - 1] + i;         //Line 6

q = p;                           //Line 7

delete [] p;                     //Line 8

for (int j = 0; j < 5; j++)      //Line 9
    cout << q[j] << " ";         //Line 10

cout << endl;                    //Line 11
```

27. What is the output of the following C++ code?

```cpp
int *myList = new int[5];
int *yourList = new int[10];

myList[0] = 3;

for (int i = 1; i < 5; i++)
    myList[i] = myList[i - 1] + i;

for (int i = 0; i < 5; i++)
{
    yourList[i] = myList[i] + 4;
    yourList[i + 5] = myList[4 - i] - 3;
}

cout << "myList: ";
for (int i = 0; i < 5; i++)
    cout << myList[i] << " ";
cout << endl;

cout << "yourList: ";
for (int i = 0; i < 10; i++)
    cout << yourList[i] << " ";

cout << endl;
```

1
2

28. a. Write a statement that declares `sales` to be a pointer to a pointer of type `double`.

    b. Write a C++ code that dynamically creates a two-dimensional array of five rows and seven columns and `sales` contains the base address of that array.

    c. Write a C++ code that inputs data from the standard input device into the array `sales`.

    d. Write a C++ code that deallocates the memory space occupied by the two-dimensional array to which `sales` points.

29. What is the purpose of a copy constructor?

30. Name two situations in which a copy constructor executes.

31. Name three things that you should do for classes with pointer member variables.

32. Suppose that you have the following `classes`, `classA` and `classB`:

```cpp
class classA
{
public:
    virtual void print() const;
    void doubleNum();
    classA(int a = 0);

private:
    int x;
};

void classA::print() const
{
    cout << "ClassA x: " << x << endl;
}

void classA::doubleNum()
{
    x = 2 * x;
}

classA::classA(int a)
{
    x = a;
}

class classB: public classA
{
public:
    void print() const;
    void doubleNum();
    classB(int a = 0, int b = 0);

private:
    int y;
};
```

```cpp
void classB::print() const
{
    classA::print();
    cout << "ClassB y: " << y << endl;
}

void classB::doubleNum()
{
    classA::doubleNum();

    y = 2 * y;
}

classB::classB(int a, int b)
        : classA(a)
{
    y = b;
}
```

What is the output of the following function main?

```cpp
int main()
{
    classA *ptrA;
    classA objectA(2);

    classB objectB(3, 5);

    ptrA = &objectA;
    ptrA->doubleNum();
    ptrA->print();
    cout << endl;

    ptrA = &objectB;

    ptrA->doubleNum();
    ptrA->print();
    cout << endl;

    return 0;
}
```

33. What is the output of the function main of Exercise 32, if the definition of classA is replaced by the following definition?

```cpp
class classA
{
public:
    virtual void print() const;
    virtual void doubleNum();
    classA(int a = 0);

private:
    int x;
};
```

34. What is the difference between compile-time binding and run-time binding?

35. Is it legal to have an abstract class with all member functions pure virtual?

36. Consider the following definition of the `class` studentType:

```
public studentType: public personType
{
public:
    void print();
    void calculateGPA();
    void setID(long id);
    void setCourses(const string c[], int noOfC);
    void setGrades(const char cG[], int noOfC);

    void getID();
    void getCourses(string c[], int noOfC);
    void getGrades(char cG[], int noOfC);
    void studentType(string fName = "", string lastName = "",
                     long id, string c[] = NULL,
                     char cG[] = NULL, int noOfC = 0);

private:
    long studentId;
    string courses[6];
    char coursesGrade[6]
    int noOfCourses;
}
```

Rewrite the definition of the `class` studentType so that the functions print and calculateGPA are pure `virtual` functions.

37. Suppose that the definitions of the `classes` employeeType, fullTimeEmployee, and partTimeEmployee are as given in Example 12-9 of this chapter. Which of the following statements is legal?

   a. `employeeType tempEmp;`

   b. `fullTimeEmployee newEmp();`

   c. `partTimeEmployee pEmp("Molly", "Burton", 101, 0.0, 0);`

38. What is the effect of the following statements?

   a. `unorderedArrayListType intList1(50);`

   b. `unorderedArrayListType intList2(1000);`

   c. `unorderedArrayListType intList3(-10);`

PROGRAMMING EXERCISES

1. Redo Programming Exercise 5 of Chapter 8 using dynamic arrays.

2. Redo Programming Exercise 6 of Chapter 8 using dynamic arrays.

3. Redo Programming Exercise 7 of Chapter 8 using dynamic arrays. You must ask the user for the number of candidates and then create the appropriate arrays to hold the data.

4. Programming Exercise 11 in Chapter 8 explains how to add large integers using arrays. However, in that exercise, the program could add only integers of, at most, 20 digits. This chapter explains how to work with dynamic integers. Design a `class` named `largeIntegers` such that an object of this class can store an integer of any number of digits. Add operations to add, subtract, multiply, and compare integers stored in two objects. Also add constructors to properly initialize objects and functions to set, retrieve, and print the values of objects.

5. Banks offer various types of accounts, such as savings, checking, certificate of deposits, and money market, to attract customers as well as meet their specific needs. Two of the most commonly used accounts are savings and checking. Each of these accounts has various options. For example, you may have a savings account that requires no minimum balance but has a lower interest rate. Similarly, you may have a checking account that limits the number of checks you may write. Another type of account that is used to save money for the long term is certificate of deposit (CD).

    In this programming exercise, you use abstract classes and pure virtual functions to design classes to manipulate various types of accounts. For simplicity, assume that the bank offers three types of accounts: savings, checking, and certificate of deposit, as described next.

    Savings accounts: Suppose that the bank offers two types of savings accounts: one that has no minimum balance and a lower interest rate and another that requires a minimum balance and has a higher interest rate.

    Checking accounts: Suppose that the bank offers three types of checking accounts: one with a monthly service charge, limited check writing, no minimum balance, and no interest; another with no monthly service charge, a minimum balance requirement, unlimited check writing and lower interest; and a third with no monthly service charge, a higher minimum requirement, a higher interest rate, and unlimited check writing.

    Certificate of deposit (CD): In an account of this type, money is left for some time, and these accounts draw higher interest rates than savings or checking accounts. Suppose that you purchase a CD for six months. Then we say that the CD will mature in six months. The penalty for early withdrawal is stiff.

1
2

Figure 12-25 shows the inheritance hierarchy of these bank accounts.

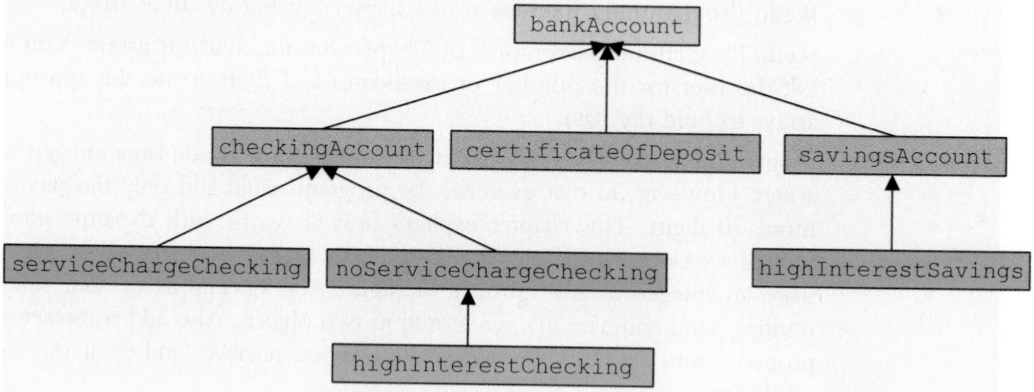

FIGURE 12-25   Inheritance hierarchy of banking accounts

Note that the `classes` bankAccount and checkingAccount are abstract. That is, we cannot instantiate objects of these classes. The other classes in Figure 12-25 are not abstract.

bankAccount: Every bank account has an account number, the name of the owner, and a balance. Therefore, instance variables such as `name`, `accountNumber`, and `balance` should be declared in the abstract `class` bankAccount. Some operations common to all types of accounts are retrieve account owner's name, account number, and account balance; make deposits; withdraw money; and create monthly statement. So include functions to implement these operations. Some of these functions will be pure virtual.

checkingAccount: A checking account is a bank account. Therefore, it inherits all the properties of a bank account. Because one of the objectives of a checking account is to be able to write checks, include the pure virtual function `writeCheck` to write a check.

serviceChargeChecking: A service charge checking account is a checking account. Therefore, it inherits all the properties of a checking account. For simplicity, assume that this type of account does not pay any interest, allows the account holder to write a limited number of checks each month, and does not require any minimum balance. Include appropriate named constants, instance variables, and functions in this class.

noServiceChargeChecking: A checking account with no monthly service charge is a checking account. Therefore, it inherits all the properties of a checking account. Furthermore, this type of account pays interest, allows the account holder to write checks, and requires a minimum balance.

highInterestChecking: A checking account with high interest is a checking account with no monthly service charge. Therefore, it inherits all the properties of a no service charge checking account. Furthermore, this type of account pays higher interest and requires a higher minimum balance than the no service charge checking account.

savingsAccount: A savings account is a bank account. Therefore, it inherits all the properties of a bank account. Furthermore, a savings account also pays interest.

highInterestSavings: A high-interest savings account is a savings account. Therefore, it inherits all the properties of a savings account. It also requires a minimum balance.

certificateOfDeposit: A certificate of deposit account is a bank account. Therefore, it inherits all the properties of a bank account. In addition, it has instance variables to store the number of CD maturity months, interest rate, and the current CD month.

Write the definitions of the classes described in this programming exercise and a program to test your classes.

6. The function `retrieveAt` of the `class arrayListType` is written as a `void` function. Rewrite this function so that it is written as a value returning function, returning the required item. If location of the item to be returned is out of range, use the assert function to terminate the program. Also, write a program to test your function. Use the `class unorderedArrayListType` to test your function.

7. The function `removeAt` of the `class arrayListType` removes an element from the list by shifting the elements of the list. However, if the element to be removed is at the beginning of the list and the list is fairly large it could take a lot of computer time. Because the list elements are in no particular order, you could simply remove the element by swapping the last element of the list with the item to be removed and reducing the length of the list. Rewrite the definition of the function `removeAt` using this technique. Use the `class unorderedArrayListType` to test your function.

8. The function `remove` of the `class arrayListType` removes only the first occurrence of an element. Add the function `removeAll` as an abstract function to the `class arrayListType`, which would remove all occurrences of a given element. Also, write the definition of the function `removeAll` in the `class unorderedArrayListType` and write a program to test this function.

9. Add the function `min` as an abstract function to the `class arrayListType` to return the smallest element of the list. Also, write the definition of the function `min` in the `class unorderedArrayListType` and write a program to test this function.

1
2

10. Add the function max as an abstract function to the class arrayListType to return the largest element of the list. Also, write the definition of the function max in the class unorderedArrayListType and write a program to test this function.

11. Write the definitions of the functions of the class orderedArrayListType that are not given in this chapter. Also, write a program to test various operations of this class.

12. **(Unordered Sets)** As explained in this chapter, a set is a collection of distinct elements of the same type. Design the class unorderedSetType, derived from the class unorderedArrayListType, to manipulate sets. Note that you need to redefine only the functions insertAt, insertEnd, and replaceAt. If the item to be inserted is already in the list, the functions insertAt and insertEnd output an appropriate message. Similarly, if the item to be replaced is already in the list, the function replaceAt outputs an appropriate message. Also, write a program to test your class.

13. **(Ordered Sets)** Programming Exercise 12 asks you to define the class unorderedSetType to manipulate sets. The elements of an unorderedSetType object are distinct, but in no particular order. Design the class orderedSetType, derived from the class orderedArrayListType, to manipulate ordered sets. The elements of an orderedSetType object are distinct and in ascending order. Note that you need to redefine only the functions insert and replaceAt. If the item to be inserted is already in the list, the function insert outputs an appropriate message. Similarly, if the item to be replaced is already in the list, the function replaceAt outputs an appropriate message. Also, write a program to test your class.

OVERLOADING AND TEMPLATES

IN THIS CHAPTER, YOU WILL:

- Learn about overloading
- Become aware of the restrictions on operator overloading
- Examine the pointer `this`
- Learn about `friend` functions
- Explore the members and nonmembers of a class
- Discover how to overload various operators
- Learn about templates
- Explore how to construct function templates and class templates

In Chapter 10, you learned how classes in C++ are used to combine data and operations on that data in a single entity. The ability to combine data and operations on the data is called encapsulation. It is the first principle of object-oriented design (OOD). Chapter 10 defined the abstract data type (ADT) and described how classes in C++ implement ADT. Chapter 11 discussed how new classes can be derived from existing classes through the mechanism of inheritance. Inheritance, the second principle of OOD, encourages code reuse.

This chapter covers **operator overloading** and **templates**. Templates enable the programmer to write generic code for related functions and classes. We will also simplify function overloading (introduced in Chapter 6) through the use of templates, called **function templates**.

Why Operator Overloading Is Needed

Chapter 10 defined and implemented the `class` clockType. It also showed how you can use the `class` clockType to represent the time of day in a program. Let us review some of the characteristics of the `class` clockType.

Consider the following statements:

```
clockType myClock(8, 23, 34);
clockType yourClock(4, 5, 30);
```

The first statement declares myClock to be an object of type clockType and initializes the member variables hr, min, and sec of myClock to 8, 23, and 34, respectively. The second statement declares yourClock to be an object of type clockType and initializes the member variables hr, min, and sec of yourClock to 4, 5, and 30, respectively.

Now consider the following statements:

```
myClock.printTime();

myClock.incrementSeconds();

if (myClock.equalTime(yourClock))
    .
    .
    .
```

The first statement prints the value of myClock in the form hr:min:sec. The second statement increments the value of myClock by one second. The third statement checks whether the value of myClock is the same as the value of yourClock.

These statements do their job. However, if we can use the insertion operator << to output the value of myClock, the increment operator ++ to increment the value of myClock by one second, and relational operators for comparison, we can enhance the flexibility of the **class clockType** considerably. More specifically, we prefer to use the following statements instead of the previous statements:

```
cout << myClock;

myClock++;

if (myClock == yourClock)
    .
    .
    .
```

Recall that the only built-in operations on classes are the assignment operator and the member selection operator. Therefore, other operators cannot be directly applied to class objects. However, C++ allows the programmer to extend the definitions of most of the operators so that operators—such as relational operators, arithmetic operators, the insertion operator for data output, and the extraction operator for data input—can be applied to classes. In C++ terminology, this is called **operator overloading**.

Operator Overloading

Recall how the arithmetic operator / works. If both operands of / are integers, the result is an integer; otherwise, the result is a floating-point number. Similarly, the stream insertion operator, <<, and the stream extraction operator, >>, are overloaded. The operator >> is used as both a stream extraction operator and a right shift operator. The operator << is used as both a stream insertion operator and a left shift operator. These are examples of operator overloading. (Note that the operators << and >> have also been overloaded for various data types, such as **int**, **double**, and **string**.)

Other examples of overloaded operators are + and −. The results of + and − are different for integer arithmetic, floating-point arithmetic, and pointer arithmetic.

C++ allows the user to overload most of the operators so that the operators can work effectively in a specific application. It does not allow the user to create new operators. Most of the existing operators can be overloaded to manipulate class objects.

In order to overload operators, you must write functions (that is, the header and body). The name of the function that overloads an operator is the reserved word **operator** followed by the operator to be overloaded. For example, the name of the function to overload the operator >= is:

```
operator>=
```

Operator function: The function that overloads an operator.

1
3

Syntax for Operator Functions

The result of an operation is a value. Therefore, the operator function is a value-returning function.

The syntax of the heading for an operator function is:

> `returnType operator operatorSymbol(formal parameter list)`

In C++, `operator` is a reserved word.

Recall that the only built-in operations on classes are assignment (=) and member selection. To use other operators on class objects, they must be explicitly overloaded. Operator overloading provides the same concise expressions for user-defined data types as it does for built-in data types.

To overload an operator for a class:

1. Include the statement to declare the function to overload the operator (that is, the operator function) prototype in the definition of the class.
2. Write the definition of the operator function.

Certain rules must be followed when you include an operator function in a class definition. These rules are described in the section, "Operator Functions as Member Functions and Nonmember Functions" later in this chapter.

Overloading an Operator: Some Restrictions

When overloading an operator, keep the following in mind:

1. You cannot change the precedence of an operator.
2. The associativity cannot be changed. (For example, the associativity of the arithmetic operator addition is from left to right, and it cannot be changed.)
3. Default parameters cannot be used with an overloaded operator.
4. You cannot change the number of parameters an operator takes.
5. You cannot create new operators. Only existing operators can be overloaded.
6. The operators that cannot be overloaded are:

   .   .*   ::   ?:   sizeof

7. The meaning of how an operator works with built-in types, such as `int`, remains the same.
8. Operators can be overloaded either for objects of the user-defined types, or for a combination of objects of the user-defined type and objects of the built-in type.

Pointer `this`

A member function of a class can (directly) access the member variables of that class for a given object. Sometimes, it is necessary for a member function to refer to the object as a whole, rather than the object's individual member variables. How do you refer to the object as a whole (that is, as a single unit) in the definition of the member function, especially when the object is not passed as a parameter? Every object of a class maintains a (hidden) pointer to itself, and the name of this pointer is `this`. In C++, `this` is a reserved word. The pointer `this` (in a member function) is available for you to use. When an object invokes a member function, the member function references the pointer `this` of the object. For example, suppose that `test` is a class and has a member function called `one`. Further suppose that the definition of `one` looks like the following:

```
test test::one()
{
    .
    .
    .
    return *this;
}
```

If `x` and `y` are objects of type `test`, then the statement:

```
y = x.one();
```

copies the value of object `x` into object `y`. That is, the member variables of `x` are copied into the corresponding member variables of `y`. When object `x` invokes function `one`, the pointer `this` in the definition of member function `one` refers to object `x`, so `this` means the address of `x` and `*this` means the value of `x`.

The following example illustrates how the pointer `this` works.

EXAMPLE 13-1

In Chapter 11, we defined the **class** `rectangleType`. We will add a function to this class to illustrate how the pointer `this` works. We do not give the complete definition of this class. We only show the function that uses the pointer `this` to return the whole object. The complete definition can be found at the Web site accompanying this book.

```
class rectangleType
{
public:
    //The functions setDimension, getLength, getWidth, area,
    //perimeter, print, and the constructors are the same as before.

    rectangleType doubleDimensions();
      //Postcondition: length = 2 * length;
      //               width = 2 * width;
```

1
3

```
private:
    double length;
    double width;
};
```

Suppose that the definition of the member function `doubleDimensions` is:

```
rectangleType rectangleType::doubleDimensions()
{
    length = 2 * length;
    width = 2 * width;

    return *this;
}
```

The function `doubleDimensions` doubles both the length and width of the object and using the pointer `this` returns the value of the entire object.

Consider the following function `main`:

```
//Chapter 13: this pointer illustration

#include <iostream>                                  //Line 1
#include <iomanip>                                   //Line 2
#include "rectangleType.h"                           //Line 3

using namespace std;                                 //Line 4

int main()                                           //Line 5
{                                                    //Line 6
    rectangleType oldYard(20.00, 10.00);             //Line 7
    rectangleType newYard;                           //Line 8

    cout << fixed << showpoint << setprecision(2);   //Line 9

    cout << "Line 10: Area of oldYard = "
         << oldYard.area() << endl;                  //Line 10

    newYard = oldYard.doubleDimensions();            //Line 11

    cout << "Line 12: Area of newYard = "
         << newYard.area() << endl;                  //Line 12

    return 0;                                        //Line 13
}                                                    //Line 14
```

Sample Run

```
Line 10: Area of oldYard = 200.00
Line 12: Area of newYard = 800.00
```

For the most part, the output is self-explanatory. The statement in Line 7 creates the object `oldYard` and sets the length and width to `20.00` and `10.00`, respectively. The statement in Line 8 creates the object `newYard` and using the default constructor sets the length and width to 0.00, and 0.00, respectively. The statement in Line 10 outputs the area of oldYard. The statement in Line 11 doubles the dimensions of oldYard and then the object oldYard, with new length and width, is returned by the pointer this. The assignment operator then copies the value of oldYard into newYard. The statement in Line 12 outputs the area of newYard.

The following example shows another way of how the pointer this works.

EXAMPLE 13-2

Consider the following class:

```
class rectangleType
{
public:
    void setDimension(double l, double w);
    double getLength() const;
    double getWidth() const;
    double area() const;
    double perimeter() const;
    void print() const;

    rectangleType& setLength(double l);
      //Function to set the length.
      //Postcondition: length = l
      //      After setting the length, a reference to the object,
      //      that is, the address of the object, is returned.
    rectangleType& setWidth(double w);
      //Function to set the width.
      //Postcondition: width = w
      //      After setting the width a reference to the object,
      //      that is, the address of the object, is returned.

    rectangleType(double l = 0.0, double w = 0.0);

private:
    double length;
    double width;
};
```

Note that the definition of the class rectangleType is the same as given in Chapter 11, except that here, in the definition of the class rectangleType, we have added the functions setLength and setWidth to individually set a rectangle's length and width, and then return the entire object. We have also replaced the constructors with the constructor with default parameters.

The definitions of the functions print, setDimension, getLength, getWidth, area, and perimeter are the same as before. The definition of the constructor with default parameters is the same as the definition of the constructor with parameters. The definitions of the functions setLength and setWidth are as follows:

```
rectangleType& rectangleType::setLength(double l)
{
    length = l;
    return *this;
}

rectangleType& rectangleType::setWidth(double w)
{
    width = w;
    return *this;
}
```

The following program shows how to use the **class** rectangleType. (We assume that the definition of the **class** rectangleType is in the file rectangleType.h.)

```
//Test Program: class rectangleType

#include <iostream>                              //Line 1
#include <iomanip>                               //Line 2
#include "rectangleType.h"                       //Line 3

using namespace std;                             //Line 4

int main()                                       //Line 5
{                                                //Line 6
    rectangleType myRectangle;                   //Line 7
    rectangleType yourRectangle;                 //Line 8

    cout << fixed << showpoint << setprecision(2);   //Line 9

    myRectangle.setLength(15.25).setWidth(12.00);    //Line 10

    cout << "Line 11 -- myRectangle: ";          //Line 11
    myRectangle.print();                         //Line 12
    cout << endl;                                //Line 13

    yourRectangle.setLength(18.50);              //Line 14

    cout << "Line 15 -- yourRectangle: ";        //Line 15
    yourRectangle.print();                       //Line 16
    cout << endl;                                //Line 17

    yourRectangle.setWidth(7.50);                //Line 18

    cout << "Line 19 -- yourRectangle: ";        //Line 19
    yourRectangle.print();                       //Line 20
    cout << endl;                                //Line 21

    return 0;                                    //Line 22
}                                                //Line 23
```

Sample Run

```
Line 11: myRectangle: Length = 15.25; Width = 12.00
Line 15: yourRectangle: Length = 18.50; Width = 0.00
Line 19: yourRectangle: Length = 18.50; Width = 7.50
```

The statements in Lines 7 and 8 declare and initialize the objects `myRectangle` and `yourRectangle`, to default values. Consider the statement in Line 10, which is:

```
myRectangle.setLength(15.25).setWidth(12.00);
```

First the expression:

```
myRectangle.setLength(15.25)
```

is executed because the associativity of the dot operator is from left to right. This expression sets the length of `myRectangle` to `15.25` and returns a reference of the object, which is `myRectangle`. Thus, the next expression executed is:

```
myRectangle.setWidth(12.00)
```

which sets the width of `myRectangle` to `12.00`. The statement in Line 12 outputs the value of `myRectangle`.

The statement in Line 14 sets the length of the object `yourRectangle` to `18.50`, and ignores the value returned. The statement in Line 16 outputs the value of `yourRectangle`. Notice the output in Line 15. The value printed for width is `0.00`, which was stored when the object was declared in Line 8. Next, the statement in Line 18 sets the width of `yourRectangle`, and the statement in Line 20 outputs the value of `yourRectangle`.

Friend Functions of Classes

A **friend function** of a class is a nonmember function of the class but has access to all of the members (`public` or non-`public`) of the class. To make a function be a friend to a class, the reserved word **friend** precedes the function prototype (in the class definition). The word **friend** appears only in the function prototype in the class definition, not in the definition of the **friend** function.

Consider the following statements:

```
class classIllusFriend
{
    friend void two(/*parameters*/);
         .
         .
         .
};
```

In the definition of the **class classIllusFriend**, `two` is declared as a **friend** of the **class classIllusFriend**. That is, it is a nonmember function of the **class classIllusFriend**. When you write the definition of the function `two`, any object of type `classIllusFriend`—which is either a local variable of `two` or a formal parameter of `two`—can access its `private` members within the definition of the function `two`. (Example 13-3 illustrates this concept.) Moreover, because a `friend` function is not a member of a class, its declaration can be placed within the `private`, `protected`, or `public` part of the class. However, they are typically placed before any member function declaration.

DEFINITION OF A `friend` FUNCTION

When writing the definition of a `friend` function, the name of the class and the scope resolution operator do not precede the name of the `friend` function in the function heading. Also, recall that the word `friend` does not appear in the heading of the `friend` function's definition. Thus, the definition of the function `two` in the previous `class classIllusFriend` is:

```
void two(/*parameters*/)
{
    .
    .
    .
}
```

Of course, we will place the definition of the `friend` function in the implementation file.

The next section illustrates the difference between a member function and a nonmember function (`friend` function) when we overload some of the operators for a specific class.

The following example shows how a `friend` function accesses the `private` members of a class.

EXAMPLE 13-3

In this example, we use the `class rectangleType` to illustrate how a `friend` function works. In the following definition we do not document the functions. The complete definition of this class is available at the Web site accompanying this book.

```
class rectangleType
{
    friend void rectangleFriend(rectangleType recObject);
public:
    void setDimension(double l, double w);
    double getLength() const;
    double getWidth() const;
    double area() const;
    double perimeter() const;
    void print() const;

    rectangleType();
    rectangleType(double l, double w);
```

```
private:
    double length;
    double width;
};
```

In the definition of the **class** rectangleType, rectangleFriend is declared as a **friend** function. Suppose that the definition of the function rectangleFriend is:

```
void rectangleFriend(rectangleType recFriendObject)
{
    cout << "recFriendObject area: " << recFriendObject.area()
         << endl;

    recFriendObject.length = recFriendObject.length + 5;
    recFriendObject.width = recFriendObject.width + 5;

    cout << "After increasing length and width by 5 units "
         << "each, \n         recFriendObject area: "
         << recFriendObject.area() << endl;
}
```

The function rectangleFriend contains a (value) formal parameter recFriendObject of type rectangleType. (Note that because rectangleType is a value parameter, it will copy the value of its actual parameter.) The first statement outputs the area of the object recFriendObject. The next two statements increase the length and width of recFriendObject by 5 units. The next statement outputs the area of the the object recFriendObject using the new length and width. Note that the recFriendObject accesses its **private** member variables length and width and increase their values by 5 units. If rectangleFriend is not declared as a **friend** function of the **class** rectangleType, then this statement would result in a syntax error because an object cannot directly access its **private** members.

The definition of the remaining functions and constructors of the **class** rectangleType is as given in Chapter 11.

Now consider the definition of the following function main:

```
//Friend Function Illustration

#include <iostream>                                //Line 1
#include <iomanip>                                 //Line 2
#include "rectangleType.h"                         //Line 3

using namespace std;                               //Line 4

int main()                                         //Line 5
{                                                  //Line 6
    rectangleType myYard(25, 18);                  //Line 7

    cout << fixed << showpoint << setprecision(2); //Line 8

    cout << "myYard area: " << myYard.area()
         << endl;                                  //Line 9
```

13

```
    cout << "Passing object myYard to the friend "
        << "function rectangleFriend." << endl;    //Line 10

    rectangleFriend(myYard);                       //Line 11

    return 0;                                       //Line 12
}                                                   //Line 13
```

Sample Run

```
myYard area: 450.00
Passing object myYard to the friend function rectangleFriend.
recFriendObject area: 450.00
After increasing length and width by 5 units each,
    recFriendObject area: 690.00
```

For the most part, the output is self-explanatory. The statement in Line 9 outputs the area of `myYard`. The statement in Line 11 calls the function `rectangleFriend` (a **friend** function of the **class** `rectangleType`) and passes the object `myYard` as an actual parameter. Notice that the function `rectangleFriend` generates the last three lines of the output.

Later in this chapter, you will learn that for a class, stream insertion and extraction operators can be overloaded only as **friend** functions.

Operator Functions as Member Functions and Nonmember Functions

The beginning of this chapter stated that certain rules must be followed when you include an operator function in the definition of a class. This section describes these rules.

Most operator functions can be either member functions or nonmember functions—that is, **friend** functions of a class. To make an operator function be a member or nonmember function of a class, keep the following in mind:

1. The function that overloads any of the operators (), [], ->, or = for a class must be declared as a member of the class.

2. Suppose that an operator op is overloaded for a class—say, opOverClass. (Here, op stands for an operator that can be overloaded, such as + or >>.)

   a. If the far left operand of op is an object of a different type (that is, not of type opOverClass), the function that overloads the operator op for opOverClass must be a nonmember—that is, a friend of the **class** opOverClass.

   b. If the operator function that overloads the operator op for the **class** opOverClass is a member of the **class** opOverClass, then when applying op on objects of type opOverClass, the far left operand of op must be of type opOverClass.

You must follow these rules when including an operator function in a class definition.

You will see later in this chapter that functions that overload the insertion operator, <<, and the extraction operator, >>, for a class must be nonmembers—that is, `friend` functions of the class.

Except for certain operators noted previously, operators can be overloaded either as member functions or as nonmember functions. The following discussion shows the difference between these two types of functions.

To facilitate our discussion of operator overloading, we will use the `class rectangleType`, given next. (Although Chapter 11 defines this class, Chapter 11 is not a prerequisite for this chapter. For easy reference, we reproduce the definition of this class and the definitions of the member functions.)

```
class rectangleType
{
public:
    void setDimension(double l, double w);
        //Function to set the length and width of the rectangle.
        //Postcondition: length = l; width = w;

    double getLength() const;
        //Function to return the length of the rectangle.
        //Postcondition: The value of length is returned.

    double getWidth() const;
        //Function to return the width of the rectangle.
        //Postcondition: The value of width is returned.

    double area() const;
        //Function to return the area of the rectangle.
        //Postcondition: The area of the rectangle is
        //               calculated and returned.

    double perimeter() const;
        //Function to return the perimeter of the rectangle.
        //Postcondition: The perimeter of the rectangle is
        //               calculated and returned.

    void print() const;
        //Function to output the length and width of
        //the rectangle.

    rectangleType();
        //Default constructor
        //Postcondition: length = 0; width = 0;

    rectangleType(double l, double w);
        //Constructor with parameters
        //Postcondition: length = l; width = w;
```

```
private:
    double length;
    double width;
};
```

The definitions of the member functions of the `class` `rectangleType` are as follows:

```
void rectangleType::setDimension(double l, double w)
{
    if (l >= 0)
        length = l;
    else
        length = 0;

    if (w >= 0)
        width = w;
    else
        width = 0;
}
```

```
double rectangleType::getLength() const
{
    return length;
}
```

```
double rectangleType::getWidth()const
{
    return width;
}
```

```
double rectangleType::area() const
{
    return length * width;
}
```

```
double rectangleType::perimeter() const
{
    return 2 * (length + width);
}
```

```
void rectangleType::print() const
{
    cout << "Length = "  << length
         << "; Width = " << width;
}
```

```
rectangleType::rectangleType(double l, double w)
{
    setDimension(l, w);
}
```

```
rectangleType::rectangleType()
{
    length = 0;
    width = 0;
}
```

The `class` `rectangleType` has two `private` member variables: `length` and `width`, both of type `double`. We will add operator functions to the `class` `rectangleType` as we overload the operators.

Also, suppose that you have the following statements:

```
rectangleType myRectangle;
rectangleType yourRectangle;
rectangleType tempRect;
```

That is, `myRectangle`, `yourRectangle`, and `tempRect` are objects of type `rectangleType`.

C++ consists of both binary and unary operators. It also has a ternary operator, which *cannot* be overloaded. The next few sections discuss how to overload various binary and unary operators.

Overloading Binary Operators

Suppose that # represents a binary operator (arithmetic, such as +; or relational, such as ==) that is to be overloaded for the `class` `rectangleType`. This operator can be overloaded as either a member function of the class or as a `friend` function. We will describe both ways to overload this operator.

OVERLOADING THE BINARY OPERATORS AS MEMBER FUNCTIONS

Suppose that # is overloaded as a member function of the `class` `rectangleType`. The name of the function to overload # for the `class` `rectangleType` is:

`operator#`

Because `myRectangle` and `yourRectangle` are objects of type `rectangleType`, you can perform the operation:

`myRectangle # yourRectangle`

The compiler translates this expression into the following expression:

`myRectangle.operator#(yourRectangle)`

This expression clearly shows that the function `operator#` has only one parameter, which is `yourRectangle`.

Because `operator#` is a member of the `class` `rectangleType` and `myRectangle` is an object of type `rectangleType`, in the previous statement, `operator#` has direct access to the `private` members of the object `myRectangle`. Thus, the first parameter of `operator#` is the object that is invoking the function `operator#`, and the second parameter is passed as a parameter to this function.

13

GENERAL SYNTAX TO OVERLOAD THE BINARY (ARITHMETIC OR RELATIONAL) OPERATORS AS MEMBER FUNCTIONS

This section describes the general form of the functions to overload the binary operators as member functions of a class.

Function Prototype (to be included in the definition of the class):

```
returnType operator#(const className&) const;
```

in which # stands for the binary operator, arithmetic or relational, to be overloaded; `returnType` is the type of value returned by the function; and `className` is the name of the class for which the operator is being overloaded.

Function Definition:

```
returnType className::operator#
                    (const className& otherObject) const
{
    //algorithm to perform the operation

    return value;
}
```

> **NOTE** The return type of the functions that overload relational operators is `bool`.

EXAMPLE 13-4

Let us overload +, *, ==, and != for the `class rectangleType`. These operators are overloaded as member functions.

```
class rectangleType
{
public:
    void setDimension(double l, double w);
    double getLength() const;
    double getWidth() const;
    double area() const;
    double perimeter() const;
    void print() const;

    rectangleType operator+(const rectangleType&) const;
        //Overload the operator +
    rectangleType operator*(const rectangleType&) const;
        //Overload the operator *
```

```
    bool operator==(const rectangleType&) const;
      //Overload the operator ==
    bool operator!=(const rectangleType&) const;
      //Overload the operator !=

    rectangleType();
    rectangleType(double l, double w);

private:
    double length;
    double width;
};
```

The definition of the function `operator+` is as follows:

```
rectangleType rectangleType::operator+
                        (const rectangleType& rectangle) const
{
    rectangleType tempRect;

    tempRect.length = length + rectangle.length;
    tempRect.width = width + rectangle.width;

    return tempRect;
}
```

Notice that `operator+` adds the corresponding lengths and widths of the two rectangles. The definition of the function `operator*` is as follows:

```
rectangleType rectangleType::operator*
                        (const rectangleType& rectangle) const
{
    rectangleType tempRect;

    tempRect.length = length * rectangle.length;
    tempRect.width = width * rectangle.width;

    return tempRect;
}
```

Notice that `operator*` multiplies the corresponding lengths and widths of the two rectangles.

Two rectangles are equal if their lengths and widths are equal. Therefore, the definition of the function to overload the operator `==` is:

```
bool rectangleType::operator==
                    (const rectangleType& rectangle) const
{
    return (length == rectangle.length &&
            width == rectangle.width);
}
```

Two rectangles are not equal if either their lengths are not equal or their widths are not equal. Therefore, the definition of the function to overload the operator `!=` is:

```
bool rectangleType::operator!=
                         (const rectangleType& rectangle) const
{
    return (length != rectangle.length ||
            width != rectangle.width);
}
```

(Note that after writing the definition of the function to overload the operator ==, you can use it to write the definition of the function to overload the operator !=. We leave the details as an exercise.)

Consider the following program. (We assume that the definition of the class rectangleType is in the header file rectangleType.h.)

```
//This program shows how to use the class rectangleType.

#include <iostream>
#include "rectangleType.h"

using namespace std;

int main()
{
    rectangleType rectangle1(23, 45);            //Line 1
    rectangleType rectangle2(12, 10);            //Line 2
    rectangleType rectangle3;                    //Line 3
    rectangleType rectangle4;                    //Line 4

    cout << "Line 5: rectangle1: ";              //Line 5
    rectangle1.print();                          //Line 6
    cout << endl;                                //Line 7

    cout << "Line 8: rectangle2: ";              //Line 8
    rectangle2.print();                          //Line 9
    cout << endl;                                //Line 10

    rectangle3 = rectangle1 + rectangle2;        //Line 11

    cout << "Line 12: rectangle3: ";             //Line 12
    rectangle3.print();                          //Line 13
    cout << endl;                                //Line 14

    rectangle4 = rectangle1 * rectangle2;        //Line 15

    cout << "Line 16: rectangle4: ";             //Line 16
    rectangle4.print();                          //Line 17
    cout << endl;                                //Line 18

    if (rectangle1 == rectangle2)                //Line 19
        cout << "Line 20: rectangle1 and "
             << "rectangle2 are equal." << endl; //Line 20
    else                                         //Line 21
        cout << "Line 22: rectangle1 and "
             << "rectangle2 are not equal."
             << endl;                            //Line 22
```

```
        if (rectangle1 != rectangle3)                          //Line 23
            cout << "Line 24: rectangle1 and "
                 << "rectangle3 are not equal."                 //Line 24
                 << endl;                                       //Line 25
        else
            cout << "Line 25: rectangle1 and "
                 << "rectangle3 are equal." << endl;            //Line 26

        return 0;
}
```

Sample Run:

```
Line 5: rectangle1: Length = 23; Width = 45
Line 8: rectangle2: Length = 12; Width = 10
Line 12: rectangle3: Length = 35; Width = 55
Line 16: rectangle4: Length = 276; Width = 450
Line 22: rectangle1 and rectangle2 are not equal.
Line 24: rectangle1 and rectangle3 are not equal.
```

For the most part, the preceding output is self-explanatory. However, let us look at the statements in Lines 11, 15, 19, and 23. The statement in Line 11 uses the operator + to add the lengths and widths of rectangle1 and rectangle2 and stores the result in rectangle3. (That is, after the execution of this statement, the length of rectangle3 is the sum of the lengths of rectangle1 and rectangle2, and the width of rectangle3 is the sum of the widths of rectangle1 and rectangle2. The statement in Line 13 outputs the length and width of rectangle3.) Similarly, the statement in Line 15 uses the operator * to multiply the lengths and widths of rectangle1 and rectangle2 and stores the result in rectangle4. (The statement in Line 17 outputs the length and width of rectangle4.) The statement in Line 19 uses the relational operator == to determine whether the dimensions of rectangle1 and rectangle2 are the same. Similarly, the statement in Line 23 uses the relational operator != to determine whether the dimensions of rectangle1 and rectangle3 are the same.

OVERLOADING THE BINARY OPERATORS (ARITHMETIC OR RELATIONAL) AS NONMEMBER FUNCTIONS

Suppose that # represents the binary operator (arithmetic or relational) that is to be overloaded as a *nonmember* function of the **class** rectangleType.

Further suppose that the following operation is to be performed:

myRectangle # yourRectangle

In this case, the expression is compiled as:

operator#(myRectangle, yourRectangle)

Here, we see that the function operator# has two parameters. This expression also clearly shows that the function operator# is neither a member of the object myRectangle nor a member of the object `yourRectangle`. Both of the objects, `myRectangle` and `yourRectangle`, are passed as parameters to the function `operator#`.

To include the operator function `operator#` as a nonmember function of the class in the definition of the class, the reserved word `friend` must appear before the function heading. Also, the function `operator#` must have two parameters.

GENERAL SYNTAX TO OVERLOAD THE BINARY (ARITHMETIC OR RELATIONAL) OPERATORS AS NONMEMBER FUNCTIONS

This section describes the general form of the functions to overload the binary operators as nonmember functions of a class.

Function Prototype (to be included in the definition of the class):

```
friend returnType operator#(const className&,
                            const className&);
```

in which **#** stands for the binary operator to be overloaded, `returnType` is the type of value returned by the function, and `className` is the name of the class for which the operator is being overloaded.

Function Definition:

```
returnType operator#(const className& firstObject,
                     const className& secondObject)
{
     //algorithm to perform the operation

   return value;
}
```

EXAMPLE 13-5

This example illustrates how to overload the operators + and == as nonmember functions of the `class rectangleType`.

To include the operator function `operator+` as a nonmember function of the `class rectangleType`, its prototype in the definition of `rectangleType` is:

```
friend rectangleType operator+(const rectangleType&,
                               const rectangleType&);
```

The definition of the function `operator+` is as follows:

```
rectangleType operator+(const rectangleType& firstRect,
                        const rectangleType& secondRect)
```

```
{
    rectangleType tempRect;

    tempRect.length = firstRect.length + secondRect.length;
    tempRect.width = firstRect.width + secondRect.width;

    return tempRect;
}
```

In the preceding definition, the corresponding member variables of firstRect and secondRect are added, and the result is stored in tempRect. Recall that the private members of a class are local to the class and, therefore, cannot be accessed outside of the class. If we follow this rule, then because operator+ is not a member of the class rectangleType, its definition expressions such as firstRect.length must be illegal because length is a private member of firstRect. However, because operator+ is declared as a friend function of the class rectangleType, an object of type rectangleType can access its private members in the definition of operator+. Also, note that in the function heading, the name of the class—that is, rectangleType—and the scope resolution operator *are not included* before the name of the function operator+, because the function operator+ is not a member of the class.

To include the operator function operator== as a nonmember function of the class rectangleType, its prototype in the definition of rectangleType is:

```
friend bool operator==(const rectangleType& ,
                       const rectangleType&);
```

The definition of the function operator== is as follows:

```
bool operator==(const rectangleType& firstRect,
                const rectangleType& secondRect)
{
    return (firstRect.length == secondRect.length &&
            firstRect.width == secondRect.width);
}
```

You can write a program similar to the one in Example 13-4 to test the overloading of the operators + and == as nonmembers.

Overloading the Stream Insertion (<<) and Extraction (>>) Operators

The operator function that overloads the insertion operator, <<, or the extraction operator, >>, for a class must be a nonmember function of that class for the following reason.

Consider the expression:

```
cout << myRectangle;
```

In this expression, the far left operand of << (that is, cout) is an ostream object, not an object of type rectangleType. Because the far left operand of << is not an object of type `rectangleType`, the operator function that overloads the insertion operator for `rectangleType` must be a *nonmember* function of the **class** `rectangleType`.

Similarly, the operator function that overloads the stream extraction operator for `rectangleType` must be a nonmember function of the **class** `rectangleType`.

OVERLOADING THE STREAM INSERTION OPERATOR (<<)

The general syntax to overload the stream insertion operator, <<, for a class is described next.

Function Prototype (to be included in the definition of the class):

```
friend ostream& operator<<(ostream&, const className&);
```

Function Definition:

```
ostream& operator<<(ostream& osObject, const className& cObject)
{
    //local declaration, if any
    //Output the members of cObject.
    //osObject << . . .

    //Return the stream object.
    return osObject;
}
```

In this function definition:

- Both parameters are reference parameters.
- The first parameter—that is, `osObject`— is a reference to an `ostream` object.
- The second parameter is usually a **const** reference to a particular class, because (recall from Chapter 10) the most effective way to pass an object as a parameter to a class is by reference. In this case, the formal parameter does not need to copy the member variables of the actual parameter. The word **const** appears before the class name because we want to print only the member variables of the object. That is, the function should not modify the member variables of the object.
- The function return type is a reference to an `ostream` object.

The return type of the function to overload the operator << must be a reference to an `ostream` object for the following reasons.

Suppose that the operator << is overloaded for the **class** `rectangleType`. The statement:

```
cout << myRectangle;
```

is equivalent to the statement:

```
operator<<(cout, myRectangle);
```

This is a perfectly legal statement because both of the actual parameters are objects, not the value of the objects. The first parameter, cout, is of type ostream; the second parameter, myRectangle, is of type rectangleType.

Now consider the following statement:

```
cout << myRectangle << yourRectangle;
```

This statement is equivalent to the statement:

```
operator<<(operator<<(cout, myRectangle), yourRectangle); //Line A
```

because the associativity of the operator << is from left to right.

To execute the previous statement, you must first execute the expression:

```
cout << myRectangle
```

that is, the expression:

```
operator<<(cout, myRectangle)
```

After executing this expression, which outputs the value of myRectangle, whatever is returned by the function operator << will become the left-side parameter of the operator << (that is, the first parameter of the function operator<<) in order to output the value of object yourRectangle (see the statement in Line A). Because the left-side parameter of the operator << must be an object of the ostream type, the expression:

```
cout << myRectangle
```

must return the object cout (not its value) in order to output the value of yourRectangle.

Therefore, the return type of the function operator<< must be a reference to an object of the ostream type.

OVERLOADING THE STREAM EXTRACTION OPERATOR (>>)

The general syntax to overload the stream extraction operator, >>, for a class is described next.

Function Prototype (to be included in the definition of the class):

```
friend istream& operator>>(istream&, className&);
```

Function Definition:

```
istream& operator>>(istream& isObject, className& cObject)
{
        //local declaration, if any
        //Read the data into cObject.
        //isObject >> . . .

        //Return the stream object.
    return isObject;
}
```

In this function definition:

- Both parameters are reference parameters.
- The first parameter—that is, isObject—is a reference to an istream object.
- The second parameter is usually a reference to a particular class. The data read will be stored in the object.
- The function return type is a reference to an istream object.

For the same reasons as explained previously (when we overloaded the insertion operator <<), the return type of the function operator>> must be a reference to an istream object. We can then successfully execute statements of the following type:

```
cin >> myRectangle >> yourRectangle;
```

Example 13-6 shows how the stream insertion and extraction operators are overloaded for the class rectangleType.

EXAMPLE 13-6

The definition of the class rectangleType and the definitions of the operator functions are:

```
#include <iostream>

using namespace std;

class rectangleType
{
    //Overload the stream insertion and extraction operators
    friend ostream& operator<< (ostream&, const rectangleType &);
    friend istream& operator>> (istream&, rectangleType &);

public:
    void setDimension(double l, double w);
    double getLength() const;
    double getWidth() const;
    double area() const;
    double perimeter() const;
    void print() const;

    rectangleType operator+(const rectangleType&) const;
      //Overload the operator +
    rectangleType operator*(const rectangleType&) const;
      //Overload the operator *

    bool operator==(const rectangleType&) const;
      //Overload the operator ==
    bool operator!=(const rectangleType&) const;
      //Overload the operator !=
```

```
    rectangleType();
    rectangleType(double l, double w);

private:
    double length;
    double width;
};
```

Notice that we have removed the member function `print` because we are overloading the stream insertion operator <<.

```
//The definitions of the functions operator+, operator*,
//operator==, and operator!= are the same as in Example 13-5.

ostream& operator<< (ostream& osObject,
                     const rectangleType& rectangle)
{
    osObject << "Length = "  << rectangle.length
             << "; Width = " << rectangle.width;

    return osObject;
}

istream& operator>> (istream& isObject,
                     rectangleType& rectangle)
{
    isObject >> rectangle.length >> rectangle.width;

    return isObject;
}
```

Consider the following program. (We assume that the definition of the `class` `rectangleType` is in the header file `rectangleType.h`.)

```
//This program shows how to use the modified class rectangleType.

#include <iostream>

#include "rectangleType.h"

using namespace std;

int main()
{
    rectangleType myRectangle(23, 45);          //Line 1
    rectangleType yourRectangle;                //Line 2

    cout << "Line 3: myRectangle: " << myRectangle
         << endl;                               //Line 3

    cout << "Line 4: Enter the length and width "
         <<"of a rectangle: ";                  //Line 4
    cin >> yourRectangle;                       //Line 5
    cout << endl;                               //Line 6
```

```
        cout << "Line 7: yourRectangle: "
             << yourRectangle << endl;                        //Line 7

        cout << "Line 8: myRectangle + yourRectangle: "
             << myRectangle + yourRectangle << endl;          //Line 8
        cout << "Line 9: myRectangle * yourRectangle: "
             << myRectangle * yourRectangle << endl;          //Line 9

    return 0;
}
```

Sample Run: In this sample run, the user input is shaded.

```
Line 3: myRectangle: Length = 23; Width = 45
Line 4: Enter the length and width of a rectangle: 32 15

Line 7: yourRectangle: Length = 32; Width = 15
Line 8: myRectangle + yourRectangle: Length = 55; Width = 60
Line 9: myRectangle * yourRectangle: Length = 736; Width = 675
```

The statements in Lines 1 and 2 declare and initialize myRectangle and yourRectangle to be objects of type rectangleType. The statement in Line 3 outputs the value of myRectangle using cout and the insertion operator. The statement in Line 5 inputs the data into yourRectangle using cin and the extraction operator. The statement in Line 7 outputs the value of yourRectangle using cout and the insertion operator. The cout statement in Line 8 adds the lengths and widths of myRectangle and yourRectangle and outputs the result. Similarly, the cout statement in Line 9 multiplies the lengths and widths of myRectangle and yourRectangle and outputs the result. The output shows that both the stream insertion and stream extraction operators were overloaded successfully.

Overloading the Assignment Operator (=)

One of the built-in operations on classes is the assignment operation. The assignment operator causes a member-wise copy of the member variables of the class. For example, the statement:

```
myRectangle = yourRectangle;
```

is equivalent to the statements:

```
myRectangle.length = yourRectangle.length;
myRectangle.width = yourRectangle.width;
```

From Chapter 12, recall that the built-in assignment operator works well for classes that do not have pointer member variables, but not for classes with pointer member variables. Therefore, to avoid the shallow copy of data for classes with pointer member variables, we must explicitly overload the assignment operator.

Recall that to overload the assignment operator = for a class, the operator function operator= must be a member of that class.

GENERAL SYNTAX TO OVERLOAD THE ASSIGNMENT OPERATOR = FOR A CLASS

The general syntax to overload the assignment operator = for a class is described next.

Function Prototype (to be included in the definition of the class):

```
const className& operator=(const className&);
```

Function Definition:

```
const className& className::operator=
                          (const className& rightObject)
{
      //local declaration, if any

    if (this != &rightObject)  //avoid self-assignment
    {
         //algorithm to copy rightObject into this object
    }

      //Return the object assigned.
    return *this;
}
```

In the definition of the function `operator=`:

- There is only one formal parameter.
- The formal parameter is usually a `const` reference to a particular class.
- The function return type is a `const` reference to a particular class.

We now explain why the return type of the function `operator=` should be a reference of the class type.

Suppose that the assignment operator = is overloaded for the `class rectangleType`. The statement:

```
myRectangle = yourRectangle;
```

is equivalent to the statement:

```
myRectangle.operator=(yourRectangle);
```

That is, the object `yourRectangle` becomes the actual parameter to the function:

```
operator=
```

Now consider the statement:

```
myRectangle = yourRectangle = tempRect;
```

Because the associativity of the operator = is from right to left, this statement is equivalent to the statement:

```
myRectangle.operator=(yourRectangle.operator=(tempRect)); //Line A
```

Clearly, we must first execute the expression:

```
yourRectangle.operator=(tempRect)
```

that is, the expression:

```
yourRectangle = tempRect
```

The value returned by the expression:

```
yourRectangle.operator=(tempRect)
```

will become the parameter to the function `operator=` in order to assign a value to the object `myRectangle` (see the statement in Line A). Because the formal parameter of the function `operator=` is a reference parameter, the expression:

```
yourRectangle.operator=(tempRect)
```

must return a reference to the object, rather than its value. That is, it must return a reference to the object `yourRectangle`, not the value of `yourRectangle`. For this reason, the return type of the function to overload the assignment operator = for a class must be a reference to the class type.

Now consider the statement:

```
myRectangle = myRectangle;                    //Line B
```

Here, we are trying to copy the value of `myRectangle` into `myRectangle`; that is, this statement is a self-assignment. One reason why we must prevent such assignments is because they waste computer time. First, however, we explain how the body of the assignment operator prevents such assignments.

As noted above, the body of the function `operator=` does prevent assignments, such as the one given in Line B. Let us see how.

Consider the `if` statement in the body of the operator function `operator=`:

```
if (this != &rightObject)   //avoid self-assignment
{
    //algorithm to copy rightObject into this object
}
```

The statement:

```
myRectangle = myRectangle;
```

is compiled into the statement:

```
myRectangle.operator=(myRectangle);
```

Because the function `operator=` is invoked by the object `myRectangle`, the pointer `this` in the body of the function `operator=` refers to the object `myRectangle`. Furthermore, because `myRectangle` is also a parameter of the function `operator=`, the formal parameter `rightObject` also refers to the object `myRectangle`. Therefore, in the expression:

`this != &rightObject`

`this` and `&rightObject` both mean the address of `myRectangle`. Thus, the expression will evaluate to **false** and, therefore, the body of the **if** statement will be skipped.

 NOTE

This note illustrates another reason why the body of the operator function must prevent self-assignments. Let us consider the following class:

```
class arrayClass
{
public:
    const arrayClass& operator= (const& arrayClass);
        .
        .
        .
private:
    int *list;
    int length;
    int maxSize;
};
```

The **class arrayClass** has a pointer member variable, `list`, which is used to create an array to store integers. Suppose that the definition of the function to overload the assignment operator for the **class arrayClass** is written without the **if** statement, as follows:

```
const arrayClass & arrayClass::operator=
                    (const arrayClass& otherList)
{
    delete [] list;                          //Line 1
    maxSize = otherList.maxSize;             //Line 2
    length = otherList.length;               //Line 3

    list = new int[maxSize];                 //Line 4

    for (int i = 0; i < length; i++)         //Line 5
        list[i] = otherList.list[i];         //Line 6

    return *this;                            //Line 7
}
```

Suppose that we have the following declaration in a user program:

`arrayClass myList;`

Consider the following statement:

`myList = myList;`

This is a self-assignment. When this statement executes in the body of the function `operator=`:

1. `list` means `myList.list`, `maxSize` means `myList.maxSize`, and `length` means `myList.length`.
2. `otherList` is the same as `myList`.

The statement in Line 1 destroys `list`, that is, `myList.list`, so the array holding the numbers no longer exists. That is, it is not valid. The problem is in Line 6. Here, the expression `list[i] = otherList.list[i]` is equivalent to the statement `myList.list[i] = myList.list[i]`. Because `myList.list[i]` has no valid data (it was destroyed in Line 1), the statement in Line 6 produces garbage.

It follows that the definition of the function `operator=` must prevent self-assignments. The correct definition of `operator=` for the `class arrayClass` is:

```
const arrayClass& arrayClass::operator=
                      (const arrayClass& otherList)
{
    if (this != & otherList)                      //Line 1
    {
        delete [] list;                           //Line 2
        maxSize = otherList.maxSize;              //Line 3
        length = otherList.length;               //Line 4

        list = new int[maxSize];                  //Line 5

        for (int i = 0; i < length; i++)          //Line 6
            list[i] = otherList.list[i];          //Line 7
    }

    return * this;                                //Line 8
}
```

The following example illustrates how to overload the assignment operator.

EXAMPLE 13-7

Consider the following class:

```
class cAssignmentOprOverload
{
public:
    const cAssignmentOprOverload&
            operator=(const cAssignmentOprOverload& otherList);
        //Overload assignment operator
```

```
    void print() const;
      //Function to print the list

    void insertEnd(int item);
      //Function to insert an item at the end of the list
      //Postcondition: if the list is not full,
      //                      length++; list[length] = item;
      //                if the list is full,
      //                      output an appropriate message

    void destroyList();
      //Function to destroy the list
      //Postcondition: length = 0; maxSize = 0; list = NULL;

    cAssignmentOprOverload(int size = 0);
      //Constructor
      //Postcondition: length = 0; maxSize = size;
      //                      list is an array of size maxSize

private:
    int maxSize;
    int length;
    int *list;
};
```

The definitions of the member functions of the **class** cAssignmentOprOverload are:

```
void cAssignmentOprOverload::print() const
{
    if (length == 0)
        cout << "The list is empty." << endl;
    else
    {
        for (int i = 0; i < length; i++)
            cout << list[i] << " ";
        cout << endl;
    }
}

void cAssignmentOprOverload::insertEnd(int item)
{
    if (length == maxSize)
        cout << "List is full" << endl;
    else
        list[length++] = item;
}

void cAssignmentOprOverload::destroyList()
{
    delete [] list;
    list = NULL;
    length = 0;
    maxSize = 0;
}
```

1
3

```
cAssignmentOprOverload::cAssignmentOprOverload(int size)
{
    maxSize = size;
    length = 0;

    if (maxSize == 0)
        list = NULL;
    else
        list = new int[maxSize];
}

const cAssignmentOprOverload& cAssignmentOprOverload::operator=
                    (const cAssignmentOprOverload& otherList)
{
    if (this != &otherList)   //avoid self-assignment; Line 1
    {
        delete [] list;                               //Line 2
        maxSize = otherList.maxSize;                  //Line 3
        length = otherList.length;                    //Line 4

        list = new int[maxSize];                      //Line 5

        for (int i = 0; i < length; i++)              //Line 6
            list[i] = otherList.list[i];              //Line 7
    }

    return *this;                                     //Line 8
}
```

The function to overload the assignment operator works as follows. The statement in Line 1 checks whether an object is copying itself. The statement in Line 2 destroys list. The statements in Lines 3 and 4 copy the values of the member variables maxSize and length of otherList into the member variables maxSize and length of list, respectively. The statement in Line 5 creates the array to store the numbers. The for loop in Line 6 copies otherList into list. The statement in Line 8 returns the address of this object, because the return type of the function operator= is a reference type.

The following program tests the class cAssignmentOprOverload:

```
#include <iostream>

#include "classAssignmentOverload.h"

using namespace std;
int main()
{
    cAssignmentOprOverload intList1(10);          //Line 9
    cAssignmentOprOverload intList2;              //Line 10
    cAssignmentOprOverload intList3;              //Line 11
```

```
    int i;                                              //Line 12
    int number;                                         //Line 13

    cout << "Line 14: Enter 5 integers: ";              //Line 14

    for (i = 0; i < 5; i++)                             //Line 15
    {
        cin >> number;                                  //Line 16
        intList1.insertEnd(number);                     //Line 17
    }

    cout << endl;                                       //Line 18
    cout << "Line 19: intList1: ";                      //Line 19
    intList1.print();                                   //Line 20

    intList3 = intList2 = intList1;                     //Line 21

    cout << "Line 22: intList2: ";                      //Line 22
    intList2.print();                                   //Line 23

    intList2.destroyList();                             //Line 24

    cout << endl;                                       //Line 25
    cout << "Line 26: intList2: ";                      //Line 26
    intList2.print();                                   //Line 27

    cout << "Line 28: After destroying intList2, "
         << "intList1: ";                               //Line 28
    intList1.print();                                   //Line 29

    cout << "Line 30: After destroying intList2, "
         << "intList3: ";                               //Line 30
    intList3.print();                                   //Line 31
    cout << endl;                                       //Line 32

    return 0;
}
```

Sample Run: In this sample run, the user input is shaded.

```
Line 14: Enter 5 integers: 8 5 3 7 2

Line 19: intList1: 8 5 3 7 2
Line 22: intList2: 8 5 3 7 2

Line 26: intList2: The list is empty.
Line 28: After destroying intList2, intList1: 8 5 3 7 2
Line 30: After destroying intList2, intList3: 8 5 3 7 2
```

The statement in Line 9 creates intList1 of size 10; the statements in Lines 10 and 11 create intList2 and intList3 of (default) size 50. The statements in Lines 15 through 17 input the data into intList1, and the statement in Line 20 outputs intList1. The statement in Line 21 copies `intList1` into `intList2` and then copies `intList2` into `intList3`. The statement in Line 23 outputs `intList2` (see Line 22 in the sample run, which contains the output of Lines 22 and 23). The statement in Line 24 destroys `intList2`. The statement in Line 27 outputs `intList2`, which is empty. (See Line 26 in the sample run, which contains the output of Lines 26 and 27.) After destroying `intList2`, the program outputs the contents of `intList1` and `intList3` (see Lines 28 and 30 in the sample run). The sample run clearly shows that the destruction of `intList2` affects neither `intList1` nor `intList3`, because `intList1` and `intList3` each have their own data.

Overloading Unary Operators

The process of overloading unary operators is similar to the process of overloading binary operators. The only difference is that in the case of binary operators, the operator has two operands. In the case of unary operators, the operator has only one parameter. Therefore, to overload a unary operator for a class:

1. If the operator function is a member of the class, it has no parameters.

2. If the operator function is a nonmember—that is, a `friend` function of the class—it has one parameter.

Next, we describe how to overload the increment and decrement operators.

OVERLOADING THE INCREMENT (++) AND DECREMENT (−−) OPERATORS

The increment operator has two forms: pre-increment (++u) and post-increment (u++), in which u is a variable, say, of type `int`. In the case of pre-increment, ++u, the value of the variable, u, is incremented by 1 before the value of u is used in an expression. In the case of post-increment, the value of u is used in the expression before it is incremented by 1.

Overloading the Pre-Increment Operator. Overloading the pre-increment operator is quite straightforward. In the function definition, first we increment the value of the object, and then we use the pointer `this` to return the object's value.

For example, suppose that we overload the pre-increment operator for the `class rectangleType` to increment the length and width of a rectangle by 1. Also, suppose that the operator function `operator++` is a member of the `class rectangleType`. The operator function `operator++` then has no parameters. Because the operator function `operator++` has no parameters, we use the pointer `this` to return the incremented value of the object:

```
rectangleType rectangleType::operator++()
{
       //increment the length and width
    ++length;
    ++width;
```

```
    return *this; //return the incremented value of the object
}
```

Because `myRectangle` is an object of type `rectangleType`, the statement:

```
++myRectangle;
```

increments the values of the length and width of `myRectangle` by 1. Moreover, the pointer `this` associated with `myRectangle` returns the incremented value of `myRectangle`, which is ignored.

Now, `yourRectangle` is also an object of type `rectangleType`, so the statement:

```
yourRectangle = ++myRectangle;
```

increments the length and width of `myRectangle` by 1, and the pointer `this` associated with `myRectangle` returns the incremented value of `myRectangle`, which is copied into `yourRectangle`.

GENERAL SYNTAX TO OVERLOAD THE PRE-INCREMENT OPERATOR ++ AS A MEMBER FUNCTION

The general syntax to overload the pre-increment operator ++ as a member function is described next.

Function Prototype (to be included in the definition of the class):

```
className operator++();
```

Function Definition:

```
className className::operator++()
{
    //increment the value of the object by 1
    return *this;
}
```

The operator function to overload the pre-increment operator can also be a nonmember of the `class rectangleType`, which we describe next.

Because the operator function `operator++` is a nonmember function of the `class rectangleType`, it has one parameter, which is an object of type `rectangleType`. (As before, we assume that the increment operator increments the length and width of a rectangle by 1.)

```
rectangleType operator++(rectangleType& rectangle)
{
    //increment the length and width of the rectangle
    (rectangle.length)++;
    (rectangle.width)++;
    return rectangle; //return the incremented
                      //value of the object
}
```

13

GENERAL SYNTAX TO OVERLOAD THE PRE-INCREMENT OPERATOR ++ AS A NONMEMBER FUNCTION

The general syntax to overload the pre-increment operator ++ as a nonmember function is described next.

Function Prototype (to be included in the definition of the class):

```
friend className operator++(className&);
```

Function Definition:

```
className operator++(className& incObj)
{
      //increment incObj by 1
   return incObj;
}
```

OVERLOADING THE POST-INCREMENT OPERATOR

We now discuss how to overload the post-increment operator. As in the case of the pre-increment operator, we first describe the overloading of this operator as a member of a class.

Let us overload the post-increment operator for the **class** rectangleType. In both cases, pre- and post-increment, the name of the operator function is the same—operator++. To distinguish between pre- and post-increment operator overloading, we use a dummy parameter (of type int) in the function heading of the operator function. Thus, the function prototype for the post-increment operator of the **class** rectangleType is:

```
rectangleType operator++(int);
```

The statement:

```
myRectangle++;
```

is compiled by the compiler in the statement:

```
myRectangle.operator++(0);
```

and so the function operator++ with a parameter executes. The parameter 0 is used merely to distinguish between the pre- and post-increment operator functions.

The post-increment operator first uses the value of the object in the expression and then increments the value of the object. So the steps required to implement this function are:

1. Save the value of the object—in, say, temp.
2. Increment the value of the object.
3. Return the value that was saved in temp.

The function definition of the post-increment operator for the **class** rectangleType is:

```
rectangleType rectangleType::operator++(int u)
```

```
{
    rectangleType temp = *this;   //use this pointer to copy
                                  //the value of the object

        //increment the length and width
    length++;
    width++;

    return temp;   //return the old value of the object
}
```

GENERAL SYNTAX TO OVERLOAD THE POST-INCREMENT OPERATOR ++ AS A MEMBER FUNCTION

The general syntax to overload the post-increment operator ++ as a member function is described next.

Function Prototype (to be included in the definition of the class):

```
className operator++(int);
```

Function Definition:

```
className className::operator++(int u)
{
    className temp = *this;     //use this pointer to copy
                                //the value of the object
        //increment the object

    return temp;   //return the old value of the object
}
```

The post-increment operator can also be overloaded as a nonmember function of the class. In this situation, the operator function operator++ has two parameters. The definition of the function to overload the post-increment operator for the class rectangleType as a nonmember is:

```
rectangleType operator++(rectangleType& rectangle, int u)
{
    rectangleType temp = rectangle; //copy rectangle into temp

        //increment the length and width of rectangle
    (rectangle.length)++;
    (rectangle.width)++;

    return temp;   //return the old value of the object
}
```

GENERAL SYNTAX TO OVERLOAD THE POST-INCREMENT OPERATOR ++ AS A NONMEMBER FUNCTION

The general syntax to overload the post-increment operator ++ as a nonmember function is described next.

Function Prototype (to be included in the definition of the class):

```
friend className operator++(className&, int);
```

Function Definition:

```
className operator++(className& incObj, int u)
{
    className temp = incObj; //copy incObj into temp

      //increment incObj

    return temp;    //return the old value of the object
}
```

The decrement operators can be overloaded in a similar way, the details of which are left as an exercise for you.

Let us now write the definition of the `class rectangleType` and show how the operator functions appear in the class definition. Because certain operators can be overloaded as either member or nonmember functions, we give two equivalent definitions of the `class rectangleType`. In the first definition, the increment, decrement, arithmetic, and relational operators are overloaded as member functions. In the second definition, the increment, decrement, arithmetic, and relational operators are overloaded as nonmember functions.

The definition of the `class rectangleType` is as follows:

```
//Definition of the class rectangleType
//The increment, decrement, arithmetic, and relational
//operator functions are members of the class.

#include <iostream>

using namespace std;

class rectangleType
{
      //Overload the stream insertion and extraction operators
    friend ostream& operator<<(ostream&, const rectangleType &);
    friend istream& operator>>(istream&, rectangleType &);

public:
    void setDimension(double l, double w);
    double getLength() const;
    double getWidth() const;
    double area() const;
    double perimeter() const;

      //Overload the arithmetic operators
    rectangleType operator+(const rectangleType &) const;
    rectangleType operator-(const rectangleType &) const;
```

```
    rectangleType operator*(const rectangleType&) const;
    rectangleType operator/(const rectangleType&) const;

       //Overload the increment and decrement operators
    rectangleType operator++();            //pre-increment
    rectangleType operator++(int);         //post-increment
    rectangleType operator--();            //pre-decrement
    rectangleType operator--(int);         //post-decrement

       //Overload the relational operators
    bool operator==(const rectangleType&) const;
    bool operator!=(const rectangleType&) const;
    bool operator<=(const rectangleType&) const;
    bool operator<(const rectangleType&) const;
    bool operator>=(const rectangleType&) const;
    bool operator>(const rectangleType&) const;

       //Constructors
    rectangleType();
    rectangleType(double l, double w);

private:
    double length;
    double width;
};
```

Following is the definition of the class rectangleType, in which the increment, decrement, arithmetic, and relational operators are overloaded as nonmembers.

```
//Definition of the class rectangleType
//The increment, decrement, arithmetic, and relational
//operator functions are nonmembers of the class.

#include <iostream>

using namespace std;

class rectangleType
{
       //Overload the stream insertion and extraction operators
    friend ostream& operator<<(ostream&, const rectangleType&);
    friend istream& operator>>(istream&, rectangleType&);

       //Overload the arithmetic operators
    friend rectangleType operator+(const rectangleType&,
                                   const rectangleType&);
    friend rectangleType operator-(const rectangleType&,
                                   const rectangleType&);
    friend rectangleType operator*(const rectangleType&,
                                   const rectangleType&);
    friend rectangleType operator/(const rectangleType&,
                                   const rectangleType&);
```

```
    //Overload the increment and decrement operators
friend rectangleType operator++(rectangleType&);
    //pre-increment
friend rectangleType operator++(rectangleType&, int);
    //post-increment
friend rectangleType operator--(rectangleType&);
    //pre-decrement
friend rectangleType operator--(rectangleType&, int);
    //post-decrement

    //Overload the relational operators
friend bool operator==(const rectangleType&,
                       const rectangleType&);
friend bool operator!=(const rectangleType&,
                       const rectangleType&);
friend bool operator<=(const rectangleType&,
                       const rectangleType&);
friend bool operator<(const rectangleType&,
                      const rectangleType&);
friend bool operator>=(const rectangleType&,
                       const rectangleType&);
friend bool operator>(const rectangleType&,
                      const rectangleType&);

public:
    void setDimension(double l, double w);
    double getLength() const;
    double getWidth() const;
    double area() const;
    double perimeter() const;

    //Constructors
    rectangleType();
    rectangleType(double l, double w);

private:
    double length;
    double width;
};
```

The definitions of the functions to overload the operators for the **class** rectangleType are left as an exercise for you. (See Programming Exercises 1 and 2 at the end of this chapter.)

Operator Overloading: Member versus Nonmember

The preceding sections discussed and illustrated how to overload operators. Certain operators must be overloaded as member functions of the class, and some must be overloaded as nonmember (**friend**) functions. What about the operators that can be overloaded as either member functions or nonmember functions? For example, the binary arithmetic operator + can be overloaded as a member function or a nonmember function. If you overload + as a member function, then the operator + has direct access to the member variables of one of the objects, and you need to pass only one object as a parameter. On the other hand, if you overload + as a nonmember function, then you must pass both objects as parameters. When both objects are passed as parameters, the code may become somewhat clearer. So it is a matter of preference whether you overload + as a member or as a nonmember function. In the remainder of this chapter, if we overload an operator as a member function, we will leave it as an exercise for you to overload it as a nonmember function.

Classes and Pointer Member Variables (Revisited)

Chapter 12 described the peculiarities of classes with pointer member variables. Now that we have discussed how to overload various operators, let us review the peculiarities of classes with pointer member variables, for the sake of completeness, and how to avoid them.

Recall that the only built-in operations on classes are assignment and member selection. The assignment operator provides a member-wise copy of the data. That is, the member variables of an object are copied into the corresponding member variables of another object of the same type. We have seen that this member-wise copy does not work well for classes with pointer member variables. Other problems that may arise with classes with pointer member variables relate to deallocating dynamic memory when an object goes out of scope and passing a class object as a parameter by value. To resolve these problems, classes with pointer member variables must:

1. Explicitly overload the assignment operator
2. Include the copy constructor
3. Include the destructor

Operator Overloading: One Final Word

Next, we will look at three examples that illustrate operator overloading. Before delving into these examples, you must remember the following: Suppose that an operator op is overloaded for a **class**—say, `rectangleType`. Whenever we use the operator op on objects of type `rectangleType`, the body of the function that overloads the operator op for the **class** `rectangleType` executes. Therefore, whatever code you put in the body of the function executes.

Watch the Video

PROGRAMMING EXAMPLE: clockType

Chapter 10 defined a **class** clockType to implement the time of day in a program. We implemented the operations to print the time, increment the time, and compare the two times for equality using functions. This example redefines the **class** clockType. It also overloads the stream insertion and extraction operators for easy input and output, relational operators for comparisons, and the increment operator to increment the time by one second. The program that uses the **class** clockType requires the user to input the time in the form `hr:min:sec`.

The definition of the **class** `clockType` is as follows:

```
//Header file newClock.h

#ifndef H_newClock
#define H_newClock

#include <iostream>

using namespace std;

class clockType
{
    friend ostream& operator<<(ostream&, const clockType&);
    friend istream& operator>>(istream&, clockType&);

public:
    void setTime(int hours, int minutes, int seconds);
      //Function to set the member variables hr, min, and sec.
      //Postcondition: hr = hours; min = minutes; sec = seconds;

    void getTime(int& hours, int& minutes, int& seconds) const;
      //Function to return the time.
      //Postcondition: hours = hr; minutes = min; seconds = sec;

    clockType operator++();
      //Overload the pre-increment operator.
      //Postcondition: The time is incremented by one second.

    bool operator==(const clockType& otherClock) const;
      //Overload the equality operator.
      //Postcondition: Returns true if the time of this clock
      //               is equal to the time of otherClock,
      //               otherwise it returns false.

    bool operator!=(const clockType& otherClock) const;
      //Overload the not equal operator.
      //Postcondition: Returns true if the time of this clock
      //               is not equal to the time of otherClock,
      //               otherwise it returns false.

    bool operator<=(const clockType& otherClock) const;
      //Overload the less than or equal to operator.
      //Postcondition: Returns true if the time of this clock
      //               is less than or equal to the time of
      //               otherClock, otherwise it returns false.

    bool operator<(const clockType& otherClock) const;
      //Overload the less than operator.
      //Postcondition: Returns true if the time of this clock
      //               is less than the time of otherClock,
      //               otherwise it returns false.
```

```
bool operator>=(const clockType& otherClock) const;
    //Overload the greater than or equal to operator.
    //Postcondition: Returns true if the time of this clock
    //               is greater than or equal to the time of
    //               otherClock, otherwise it returns false.

bool operator>(const clockType& otherClock) const;
    //Overload the greater than operator.
    //Postcondition: Returns true if the time of this clock
    //               is greater than the time of otherClock,
    //               otherwise it returns false.

clockType(int hours = 0, int minutes = 0, int seconds = 0);
    //Constructor to initialize the object with the values
    //specified by the user. If no values are specified,
    //the default values are assumed.
    //Postcondition: hr = hours; min = minutes;
    //               sec = seconds;


private:
    int hr;  //variable to store the hours
    int min; //variable to store the minutes
    int sec; //variable to store the seconds
};

#endif
```

Figure 13-1 shows a UML class diagram of the **class** clockType.

```
                    clockType

-hr: int
-min: int
-sec: int

+operator<<(ostream&, const clockType&): ostream&
+operator>>(istream&, clockType&): istream&
+setTime(int, int, int): void
+getTime(int&, int&, int&) const: void
+operator++(): clockType
+operator==(const clockType&) const: bool
+operator!=(const clockType&) const: bool
+operator<=(const clockType&) const: bool
+operator<(const clockType&) const: bool
+operator>=(const clockType&) const: bool
+operator>(const clockType&) const: bool
+clockType(int = 0, int = 0, int = 0)
```

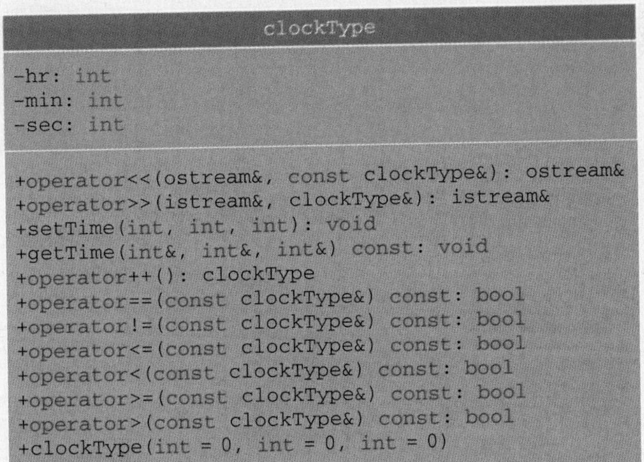

FIGURE 13-1 UML class diagram of the **class** clockType

Let us now write the definitions of the functions to implement the operations of the class clockType. Notice that the class clockType overloads only the pre-increment operator. For consistency, however, the class should also overload the post-increment operator. This step is left as an exercise for you. (See Programming Exercise 5 at the end of this chapter.)

First, we write the definition of the function operator++. The algorithm to increment the time by one second is as follows:

    a.   Increment the seconds by 1.

    b.   If seconds > 59,

        b.1.   Set the seconds to 0.

        b.2.   Increment the minutes by 1.

        b.3.   If minutes > 59

            b.3.1.   Set the minutes to 0.

            b.3.2.   Increment the hours by 1.

            b.3.3.   If hours > 23,

                b.3.3.1.   Set the hours to 0.

    c.   Return the incremented value of the object.

The definition of the function operator++ is:

```
//Overload the pre-increment operator.
clockType clockType::operator++()
{
    sec++;                          //Step a

    if (sec > 59)                   //Step b
    {
        sec = 0;                    //Step b.1
        min++;                      //Step b.2

        if (min > 59)               //Step b.3
        {
            min = 0;                //Step b.3.1
            hr++;                   //Step b.3.2

            if (hr > 23)            //Step b.3.3
                hr = 0;             //Step b.3.3.1
        }
    }

    return *this;                   //Step c
}
```

The definition of the function operator== is quite simple. The two times are the same if they have the same hours, minutes, and seconds. Therefore, the definition of the function operator== is:

```cpp
//Overload the equality operator.
bool clockType::operator==(const clockType& otherClock) const
{
    return (hr == otherClock.hr && min == otherClock.min
            && sec == otherClock.sec);
}
```

The definition of the function `operator<=` is given next. The first time is less than or equal to the second time if:

1. The hours of the first time are less than the hours of the second time, or

2. The hours of the first time and the second time are the same, but the minutes of the first time are less than the minutes of the second time, or

3. The hours and minutes of the first time and the second time are the same, but the seconds of the first time are less than or equal to the seconds of the second time.

The definition of the function `operator<=` is:

```cpp
//Overload the less than or equal to operator.
bool clockType::operator<=(const clockType& otherClock) const
{
    return ((hr < otherClock.hr) ||
            (hr == otherClock.hr && min < otherClock.min) ||
            (hr == otherClock.hr && min == otherClock.min &&
             sec <= otherClock.sec));
}
```

In a similar manner, we can write the definitions of the other relational operator functions as follows:

```cpp
//Overload the not equal operator.
bool clockType::operator!=(const clockType& otherClock) const
{
    return (hr != otherClock.hr || min != otherClock.min
            || sec != otherClock.sec);
}


//Overload the less than operator.
bool clockType::operator<(const clockType& otherClock) const
{
    return ((hr < otherClock.hr) ||
            (hr == otherClock.hr && min < otherClock.min) ||
            (hr == otherClock.hr && min == otherClock.min &&
             sec < otherClock.sec));
}


//Overload the greater than or equal to operator.
bool clockType::operator>=(const clockType& otherClock) const
```

```
{
    return ((hr > otherClock.hr) ||
            (hr == otherClock.hr && min > otherClock.min) ||
            (hr == otherClock.hr && min == otherClock.min &&
             sec >= otherClock.sec));
}

    //Overload the greater than operator.
bool clockType::operator>(const clockType& otherClock) const
{
    return ((hr > otherClock.hr) ||
            (hr == otherClock.hr && min > otherClock.min) ||
            (hr == otherClock.hr && min == otherClock.min &&
             sec > otherClock.sec));
}
```

(Note that after writing the definition of the function to overload the operator ==, you can use the operator == to write the definition of the function to overload the operator !=. Similarly, you can use the operators == and < to write the definition of the function to overload the operator <=, and so on. We leave the details as an exercise.)

The definitions of the functions setTime and getTime are the same as given in Chapter 10. They are included here for the sake of completeness. Moreover, we have modified the definition of the constructor so that it uses the function setTime to set the time. The definitions are as follows:

```
void clockType::setTime(int hours, int minutes, int seconds)
{
    if (0 <= hours && hours < 24)
        hr = hours;
    else
        hr = 0;

    if (0 <= minutes && minutes < 60)
        min = minutes;
    else
        min = 0;

    if (0 <= seconds && seconds < 60)
        sec = seconds;
    else
        sec = 0;
}

void clockType::getTime(int& hours, int& minutes,
                        int& seconds) const
{
    hours = hr;
    minutes = min;
    seconds = sec;
}
```

```
//Constructor
clockType::clockType(int hours, int minutes, int seconds)
{
    setTime(hours, minutes, seconds);
}
```

We now discuss the definition of the function `operator<<`. The time must be output in the form:

hh:mm:ss

The algorithm to output the time in this format is the same as the body of the `printTime` function of `clockType` given in Chapter 10. Here, after printing the time in the previous format, we must return the `ostream` object. Therefore, the definition of the function `operator<<` is:

```
//Overload the stream insertion operator.
ostream& operator<<(ostream& osObject, const clockType& timeOut)
{
    if (timeOut.hr < 10)
        osObject << '0';
    osObject << timeOut.hr << ':';

    if (timeOut.min < 10)
        osObject << '0';
    osObject << timeOut.min << ':';

    if (timeOut.sec < 10)
        osObject << '0';
    osObject << timeOut.sec;

    return osObject;   //return the ostream object
}
```

Let us now discuss the definition of the function `operator>>`. The input to the program is of the form:

hh:mm:ss

That is, the input is the hours followed by a colon, followed by the minutes, followed by a colon, followed by the seconds. Clearly, the algorithm to input the time is:

a. Get the input, which is a number, and store it in the member variable `hr`. Also check if the input is valid.

b. Get the next input, which is a colon, and discard it.

c. Get the next input, which is a number, and store it in the member variable `min`. Also check if the input is valid.

d. Get the next input, which is a colon, and discard it.

e. Get the next input, which is a number, and store it in the member variable `sec`. Also check if the input is valid.

f. Return the `istream` object.

1
3

Clearly, we need a local variable of type `char` to read the colon.

The definition of the function `operator>>` is:

```
    //overload the stream extraction operator
istream& operator>> (istream& is, clockType& timeIn)
{
    char ch;

    is >> timeIn.hr;                                    //Step a

    if (timeIn.hr < 0 || timeIn.hr >= 24)       //Step a
        timeIn.hr = 0;

    is.get(ch);              //Read and discard :. Step b

    is >> timeIn.min;                                   //Step c

    if (timeIn.min < 0 || timeIn.min >= 60)     //Step c
        timeIn.min = 0;

    is.get(ch);              //Read and discard :. Step d

    is >> timeIn.sec;                                   //Step e

    if (timeIn.sec < 0 || timeIn.sec >= 60)     //Step e
        timeIn.sec = 0;

    return is;                                          //Step f
}
```

The following test program uses the `class clockType`:

```
//********************************************************
// Author: D.S. Malik
//
// This program shows how to use the class clockType.
//********************************************************

#include <iostream>
#include "newClock.h"

using namespace std;

int main()
{
    clockType myClock(5, 6, 23);                        //Line 1
    clockType yourClock;                                //Line 2

    cout << "Line 3: myClock = " << myClock
         << endl;                                       //Line 3
```

```cpp
    cout << "Line 4: yourClock = " << yourClock
         << endl;                                           //Line 4

    cout << "Line 5: Enter the time in the form "           //Line 5
         << "hr:min:sec ";                                  //Line 6
    cin >> myClock;                                         //Line 7
    cout << endl;

    cout << "Line 8: The new time of myClock = "
         << myClock << endl;                                //Line 8

    ++myClock;                                              //Line 9

    cout << "Line 10: After incrementing the time, "
         << "myClock = " << myClock << endl;                //Line 10

    yourClock.setTime(13, 35, 38);                         //Line 11

    cout << "Line 12: After setting the time, "
         << "yourClock = " << yourClock << endl;            //Line 12

    if (myClock == yourClock)                              //Line 13
        cout << "Line 14: The times of myClock and "       //Line 14
             << "yourClock are equal." << endl;            //Line 15
    else
        cout << "Line 16: The times of myClock and "
             << "yourClock are not equal." << endl;        //Line 16

    if (myClock <= yourClock)                              //Line 17
        cout << "Line 18: The time of myClock is "
             << "less than or equal to " << endl
             << "the time of yourClock." << endl;          //Line 18
                                                           //Line 19
    else
        cout << "Line 20: The time of myClock is "
             << "greater than the time of "
             << "yourClock." << endl;                      //Line 20

    return 0;
}
```

Sample Run: In this sample run, the user input is shaded.

```
Line 3: myClock = 05:06:23
Line 4: yourClock = 00:00:00
Line 5: Enter the time in the form hr:min:sec 4:50:59

Line 8: The new time of myClock = 04:50:59
Line 10: After incrementing the time, myClock = 04:51:00
Line 12: After setting the time, yourClock = 13:35:38
Line 16: The times of myClock and yourClock are not equal.
Line 18: The time of myClock is less than or equal to
the time of yourClock.
```

PROGRAMMING EXAMPLE: Complex Numbers

A number of the form $a + ib$, in which $i^2 = -1$ and a and b are real numbers, is called a **complex number**. We call a the real part and b the imaginary part of $a + ib$. Complex numbers can also be represented as ordered pairs (a, b). The addition and multiplication of complex numbers are defined by the following rules:

$$(a + ib) + (c + id) = (a + c) + i(b + d)$$

$$(a + ib) \star (c + id) = (ac - bd) + i(ad + bc)$$

Using the ordered pair notation, these rules are written as:

$$(a, b) + (c, d) = ((a + c), (b + d))$$

$$(a, b) \star (c, d) = ((ac - bd), (ad + bc))$$

C++ has no built-in data type that allows us to manipulate complex numbers. In this example, we will construct a data type, `complexType`, that can be used to process complex numbers. We will overload the stream insertion and stream extraction operators for easy input and output. We will also overload the operators + and $\star$ to perform addition and multiplication of complex numbers. If x and y are complex numbers, we can evaluate expressions such as $x + y$ and $x \star y$.

```
//Specification file complexType.h

#ifndef H_complexNumber
#define H_complexNumber

#include <iostream>
using namespace std;

class complexType
{
        //Overload the stream insertion and extraction operators
    friend ostream& operator<<(ostream&, const complexType&);
    friend istream& operator>>(istream&, complexType&);

public:
    void setComplex(const double& real, const double& imag);
    //Function to set the complex numbers according to
    //the parameters.
    //Postcondition: realPart = real; imaginaryPart = imag;

    void getComplex(double& real, double& imag) const;
    //Function to retrieve the complex number.
    //Postcondition: real = realPart; imag = imaginaryPart;
```

```
    complexType(double real = 0, double imag = 0);
      //Constructor
      //Initializes the complex number according to
      //the parameters.
      //Postcondition: realPart = real; imaginaryPart = imag;

    complexType operator+
                    (const complexType& otherComplex) const;
      //Overload the operator +

    complexType operator*
                    (const complexType& otherComplex) const;
      //Overload the operator *

    bool operator== (const complexType& otherComplex) const;
      //Overload the operator ==
private:
    double realPart;        //variable to store the real part
    double imaginaryPart;   //variable to store the
                            //imaginary part

};

#endif
```

Figure 13-2 shows a UML class diagram of the class complexType.

```
                      complexType

-realPart: double
-imaginaryPart: double

+operator<<(ostream&, const complexType&): ostream&
+operator>>(istream&, complexType&): istream&
+setComplex(const double&, const double&): void
+getComplex(double&  double&) const: void
+operator+(const complexType&) const: complexType
+operator*(const complexType&) const: complexType
+operator==(const complexType&) const: bool
+complexType(double = 0, double = 0)
```

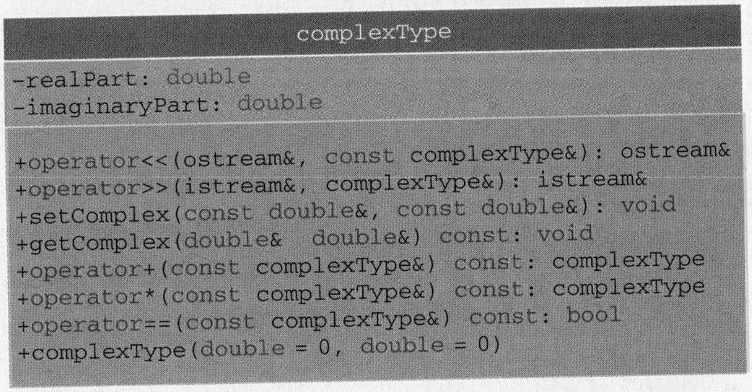

FIGURE 13-2   UML class diagram of the class complexType

Next, we write the definitions of the functions to implement various operations of the class complexType.

The definitions of most of these functions are straightforward. We will discuss only the definitions of the functions to overload the stream insertion operator, <<, and the stream extraction operator, >>.

To output a complex number in the form:

```
(a, b)
```

in which a is the real part and b is the imaginary part, clearly the algorithm is:

    a.   Output the left parenthesis, (.

    b.   Output the real part.

    c.   Output the comma and a space.

    d.   Output the imaginary part.

    e.   Output the right parenthesis,).

Therefore, the definition of the function operator<< is:

```
ostream& operator<<(ostream& osObject,
                    const complexType& complex)
{
    osObject << "(";                          //Step a
    osObject << complex.realPart;             //Step b
    osObject << ", ";                         //Step c
    osObject << complex.imaginaryPart;        //Step d
    osObject << ")";                          //Step e

    return osObject;        //return the ostream object
}
```

Next, we discuss the definition of the function to overload the stream extraction operator, >>.

The input is of the form:

```
(3, 5)
```

In this input, the real part of the complex number is 3, and the imaginary part is 5. Clearly, the algorithm to read this complex number is:

    a.   Read and discard the left parenthesis.

    b.   Read and store the real part.

    c.   Read and discard the comma.

    d.   Read and store the imaginary part.

    e.   Read and discard the right parenthesis.

Following these steps, the definition of the function operator>> is:

```
istream& operator>>(istream& isObject, complexType& complex)
{
    char ch;

    isObject >> ch;                           //Step a
    isObject >> complex.realPart;             //Step b
```

```
    isObject >> ch;                      //Step c
    isObject >> complex.imaginaryPart;   //Step d
    isObject >> ch;                      //Step e

    return isObject;        //return the istream object
}
```

The definitions of the other functions are as follows:

```
bool complexType::operator==
                    (const complexType& otherComplex) const
{
    return (realPart == otherComplex.realPart &&
            imaginaryPart == otherComplex.imaginaryPart);
}


    //Constructor
complexType::complexType(double real, double imag)
{
    realPart = real;
    imaginaryPart = imag;
}

    //Function to set the complex number after the object
    //has been declared.
void complexType::setComplex(const double& real,
                             const double& imag)

{
    realPart = real;
    imaginaryPart = imag;
}

void complexType::getComplex(double& real, double& imag) const
{
    real = realPart;
    imag = imaginaryPart;
}

    //overload the operator +
complexType complexType::operator+
                    (const complexType& otherComplex) const
{
    complexType temp;

    temp.realPart = realPart + otherComplex.realPart;
    temp.imaginaryPart = imaginaryPart
                         + otherComplex.imaginaryPart;

    return temp;
}
```

```cpp
    //overload the operator *
complexType complexType::operator*
                        (const complexType& otherComplex) const
{
    complexType temp;
    temp.realPart = (realPart * otherComplex.realPart) -
                (imaginaryPart * otherComplex.imaginaryPart);
    temp.imaginaryPart = (realPart * otherComplex.imaginaryPart)
                + (imaginaryPart * otherComplex.realPart);
    return temp;
}
```

The following program illustrates the use of the class complexType:

```cpp
//************************************************************
// Author: D.S. Malik
//
// This program shows how to use the class complexType.
//************************************************************

#include <iostream>
#include "complexType.h"

using namespace std;

int main()
{
    complexType num1(23, 34);                       //Line 1
    complexType num2;                               //Line 2
    complexType num3;                               //Line 3

    cout << "Line 4: Num1 = " << num1 << endl;      //Line 4
    cout << "Line 5: Num2 = " << num2 << endl;      //Line 5

    cout << "Line 6: Enter the complex number "
        << "in the form (a, b) ";                   //Line 6
    cin >> num2;                                    //Line 7
    cout << endl;                                   //Line 8

    cout << "Line 9: New value of num2 = "
        << num2 << endl;                            //Line 9

    num3 = num1 + num2;                             //Line 10

    cout << "Line 11: Num3 = " << num3 << endl;     //Line 11

    cout << "Line 12: " << num1 << " + " << num2
        << " = " << num1 + num2 << endl;            //Line 12

    cout << "Line 13: " << num1 << " * " << num2
        << " = " << num1 * num2 << endl;            //Line 13

    return 0;
}
```

Sample Run: In this sample run, the user input is shaded.

```
Line 4: Num1 = (23, 34)
Line 5: Num2 = (0, 0)
Line 6: Enter the complex number in the form (a, b) (3, 4)
Line 9: New value of num2 = (3, 4)
Line 11: Num3 = (26, 38)
Line 12: (23, 34) + (3, 4) = (26, 38)
Line 13: (23, 34) * (3, 4) = (-67, 194)
```

You can extend this data type to perform subtraction and division on complex numbers.

Next, we will define a class, called `newString`, and overload the assignment and relational operators. That is, when we declare a variable of type `newString`, we will be able to use the assignment operator to copy one string into another and relational operators to compare the two strings.

Before discussing the `class newString`, however, we will examine the overloading of the operator [ ]. Recall that we have used the operator [ ] to access the components of an array. To access individual characters in a string of type `newString`, we have to overload the operator [ ] for the `class newString`.

Overloading the Array Index (Subscript) Operator ([ ])

Recall that the function to overload the operator [ ] for a class must be a member of the class. Furthermore, because an array can be declared as constant or nonconstant, we need to overload the operator [ ] to handle both cases.

The syntax to declare the operator function `operator[]` as a member of a class for nonconstant arrays is:

```
Type& operator[](int index);
```

The syntax to declare the operator function `operator[]` as a member of a class for constant arrays is:

```
const Type& operator[](int index) const;
```

in which `Type` is the data type of the array elements.

Suppose that `classTest` is a class that has an array member variable. The definition of `classTest` to overload the operator [ ] is:

```
class classTest
{
public:
```

```
Type& operator[](int index);
    //Overload the operator for nonconstant arrays
const Type& operator[](int index) const;
    //Overload the operator for constant arrays
    .
    .
    .

private:
    Type *list; //pointer to the array
    int arraySize;
};
```

in which Type is the data type of the array elements.

The definitions of the functions to overload the operator [] for classTest are:

```
    //Overload the operator [] for nonconstant arrays
Type& classTest::operator[](int index)
{
    assert(0 <= index && index < arraySize);
    return list[index];    //return a pointer of the
                           //array component
}

    //Overload the operator [] for constant arrays
const Type& classTest::operator[](int index) const
{
    assert(0 <= index && index < arraySize);
    return list[index];    //return a pointer of the
                           //array component
}
```

 NOTE The preceding function definitions use the assert statement. (For an explanation of the assert statement, see Chapter 4 or the Appendix.)

Consider the following statements:

```
classTest list1;
classTest list2;
const classTest list3;
```

In the case of the statement:

```
list1[2] = list2[3];
```

the body of the operator function operator[] for nonconstant arrays is executed. In the case of the statement:

```
list1[2] = list3[5];
```

first, the body of the operator function operator[] for constant arrays is executed because list3 is a constant array. Next, the body of the operator function operator[] for nonconstant arrays is executed to complete the execution of the assignment statement.

PROGRAMMING EXAMPLE: newString

Chapter 8 discussed C-strings. Recall that:

1. A C-string is a sequence of one or more characters.
2. C-strings are enclosed in double quotation marks.
3. C-strings are null terminated.
4. C-strings are stored in character arrays.

The only aggregate operations allowed on C-strings are input and output. To use other operations, the programmer needs to include the header file cstring, which contains the specifications of many functions for string manipulation.

Initially, C++ did not provide any built-in data types to handle C-strings. More recent versions of C++, however, provide a string class to handle C-strings and operations on C-strings.

Our objective in this example is to define our own class for C-string manipulation and, at the same time, to further illustrate operator overloading. More specifically, we overload the assignment operator, the relational operators, and the stream insertion and extraction operators for easy input and output. Let us call this class newString. First, we give the definition of the class newString:

```
//Header file myString.h

#ifndef H_myString
#define H_myString

#include <iostream>

using namespace std;

class newString
{
    //Overload the stream insertion and extraction operators.
    friend ostream& operator << (ostream&, const newString&);
    friend istream& operator >> (istream&, newString&);

public:
    const newString& operator=(const newString&);
    //overload the assignment operator
    newString(const char *);
    //constructor; conversion from the char string
    newString();
    //Default constructor to initialize the string to null
    newString(const newString&);
    //Copy constructor
```

1

3

```
     ~newString();
        //Destructor
     char &operator[] (int);
     const char &operator[](int) const;

        //overload the relational operators
     bool operator==(const newString&) const;
     bool operator!=(const newString&) const;
     bool operator<=(const newString&) const;
     bool operator<(const newString&) const;
     bool operator>=(const newString&) const;
     bool operator>(const newString&) const;

private:
     char *strPtr;     //pointer to the char array
                       //that holds the string
       int strLength;   //variable to store the length
                       //of the string
};

#endif
```

The `class` `newString` has two `private` member variables: one to store the C-string and one to store the length of the C-string.

Next, we give the definitions of the functions to implement the `newString` operations. The implementation file includes the header file `cassert` because we are using the function `assert`. (For an explanation of the function `assert`, see Chapter 4 or the header file `cassert` in the Appendix.)

```
//Implementation file myStringImp.cpp
#include <iostream>
#include <iomanip>
#include <cstring>
#include <cassert>
#include "myString.h"

using namespace std;

    //Constructor: conversion from the char string to newString
newString::newString(const char *str)
{
    strLength = strlen(str);
    strPtr = new char[strLength + 1]; //allocate memory to
                                      //store the char string
    strcpy(strPtr, str);  //copy string into strPtr
}
```

```cpp
    //Default constructor to store the null string
newString::newString()
{
    strLength = 0;
    strPtr = new char[1];
    strcpy(strPtr, "");
}

newString::newString(const newString& rightStr)  //copy constructor
{
    strLength = rightStr.strLength;
    strPtr = new char[strLength + 1];
    strcpy(strPtr, rightStr.strPtr);
}

newString::~newString()  //destructor
{
    delete [] strPtr;
}

    //overload the assignment operator
const newString& newString::operator=(const newString& rightStr)
{
    if (this != &rightStr) //avoid self-copy
    {
        delete [] strPtr;
        strLength = rightStr.strLength;
        strPtr = new char[strLength + 1];
        strcpy(strPtr, rightStr.strPtr);
    }

    return *this;
}

char& newString::operator[] (int index)
{
    assert(0 <= index && index < strLength);
    return strPtr[index];
}

const char& newString::operator[](int index) const
{
    assert(0 <= index && index < strLength);
    return strPtr[index];
}

    //Overload the relational operators.
bool newString::operator==(const newString& rightStr) const
{
    return (strcmp(strPtr, rightStr.strPtr) == 0);
}
```

```cpp
bool newString::operator<(const newString& rightStr) const
{
    return (strcmp(strPtr, rightStr.strPtr) < 0);
}

bool newString::operator<=(const newString& rightStr) const
{
    return (strcmp(strPtr, rightStr.strPtr) <= 0);
}

bool newString::operator>(const newString& rightStr) const
{
    return (strcmp(strPtr, rightStr.strPtr) > 0);
}

bool newString::operator>=(const newString& rightStr) const
{
    return (strcmp(strPtr, rightStr.strPtr) >= 0);
}

bool newString::operator!=(const newString& rightStr) const
{
    return (strcmp(strPtr, rightStr.strPtr) != 0);
}

  //Overload the stream insertion operator <<
ostream& operator << (ostream& osObject, const newString& str)
{
    osObject << str.strPtr;

    return osObject;
}

  //Overload the stream extraction operator >>
istream& operator >> (istream& isObject, newString& str)
{
    char temp[81];

    isObject >> setw(81) >> temp;
    str = temp;
    return isObject;
}
```

Consider the statement:

```cpp
isObject >> setw(81) >> temp;
```

in the definition of the function `operator>>`. Because `temp` is declared to be an array of size 81, the largest string that can be stored into `temp` is of length 80. The manipulator `setw` in this statement (that is, in the input statement) ensures that no more than 80 characters are read into `temp`.

Most of these functions are quite straightforward. Let us explain the functions that overload the conversion constructor, the assignment operator, and the copy constructor.

The **conversion constructor** is a single-parameter function that converts its argument to an object of the constructor's class. In our case, the conversion constructor converts a string to an object of the `newString` type.

Note that the assignment operator is explicitly overloaded only for objects of the `newString` type. However, the overloaded assignment operator also works if we want to store a C-string into a `newString` object. Consider the declaration:

```
newString str;
```

and the statement:

```
str = "Hello there";
```

The compiler translates this statement into:

```
str.operator=("Hello there");
```

1. First, the compiler automatically invokes the conversion constructor to create an object of the `newString` type to temporarily store the string `"Hello there"`.

2. Second, the compiler invokes the overloaded assignment operator to assign the temporary `newString` object to the object `str`.

Hence, it is not necessary to explicitly overload the assignment operator to store a C-string into an object of type `newString`.

Next, we write a C++ program that tests some of the operations of the `class` newString.

```
//*********************************************************
// Author: D.S. Malik
//
// This program shows how to use the class newString.
//*********************************************************

#include <iostream>
#include "myString.h"

using namespace std;

int main()
{
    newString str1 = "Sunny";        //initialize str1 using
                                     //the assignment operator
    const newString str2("Warm");    //initialize str2 using the
                                     //conversion constructor
```

```
           newString str3;  //initialize str3 to the empty string
           newString str4;  //initialize str4 to the empty string

           cout << "Line 1: " << str1 << "    " << str2
                << "  ***" << str3 << "###." << endl;        //Line 1

           if (str1 <= str2)           //compare str1 and str2; Line 2
               cout << "Line 3: " << str1 << " is less "
                    << "than or equal to" << str2 << endl; //Line 3
           else                                            //Line 4
               cout << "Line 5: " << str2 << " is less "
                    << "than " << str1 << endl;            //Line 5

           cout << "Line 6: Enter a string with a length "
                << "of at least 7: ";                      //Line 6
           cin >> str1;          //input str1;              Line 7
           cout << endl;                                   //Line 8

           cout << "Line 9: The new value of "
                << "str1 = " << str1 << endl;              //Line 9

           str4 = str3 = "Birth Day";                      //Line 10

           cout << "Line 11: str3 = " << str3
                << ", str4 = " << str4 << endl;            //Line 11

           str3 = str1;                                    //Line 12
           cout << "Line 13: The new value of str3 = "
                << str3 << endl;                           //Line 13

           str1 = "Bright Sky";                            //Line 14

           str3[1] = str1[5];                              //Line 15
           cout << "Line 16: After replacing the second "
                << "character of str3 = " << str3 << endl; //Line 16

           str3[2] = str2[0];                              //Line 17
           cout << "Line 18: After replacing the third "
                << "character of str3 = " << str3 << endl; //Line 18

           str3[5] = 'g';                                  //Line 19
           cout << "Line 20: After replacing the sixth "
                << "character of str3 = " << str3 << endl; //Line 20

           return 0;
       }
```

Sample Run: In this sample run, the user input is shaded.

```
Line 1: Sunny    Warm  ***###.
Line 3: Sunny is less than or equal to Warm
```

```
Line  6: Enter a string with a length of at least 7: 123456789
Line  9: The new value of str1 = 123456789
Line 11: str3 = Birth Day, str4 = Birth Day
Line 13: The new value of str3 = 123456789
Line 16: After replacing the second character of str3 = 1t3456789
Line 18: After replacing the third character of str3 = 1tW456789
Line 20: After replacing the sixth character of str3 = 1tW45g789
```

The preceding program works as follows. The statement in Line 1 outputs the values of `str1`, `str2`, and `str3`. Notice that the value of `str3` is to be printed between ******* and **###**. Because `str3` is empty, nothing is printed between ******* and **###**; see Line 1 in the sample run. The statements in Lines 2 through 5 compare `str1` and `str2` and output the result. The statement in Line 7 inputs a string with a length of at least 7 into `str1`, and the statement in Line 9 outputs the new value of `str1`. Note that in the statement (see Line 10):

```
str4 = str3 = "Birth Day";
```

Because the associativity of the assignment operator is from right to left, first the statement `str3 = "Birth Day";` executes, and then the statement `str4 = str3;` executes. The statement in Line 11 outputs the values of `str3` and `str4`. The statements in Lines 15, 17, and 19 use the array subscripting operator `[ ]` to individually manipulate the characters of `str3`. The meanings of the remaining statements are straightforward.

Function Overloading

The previous section discussed operator overloading. Operator overloading provides the programmer with the same concise notation for user-defined data types as the operator has for built-in types. The types of parameters used with an operator determine the action to take. Similar to operator overloading, C++ allows the programmer to overload a function name. Chapter 6 introduced function overloading. For easy reference in the following discussion, let us review this concept.

Recall that a class can have more than one constructor, but all constructors of a class have the same name, which is the name of the class. This is an example of overloading a function. Further recall that overloading a function refers to having several functions with the same name but different parameter lists. The parameter list determines which function will execute.

For function overloading to work, we must give the definition of each function. The next section teaches you how to overload functions with a single code segment and leave the job of generating code for separate functions for the compiler.

1
3

Templates

Templates are a very powerful feature of C++. They allow you to write a single code segment for a set of related functions, called a **function template**, and for a set of related classes, called a **class template**. The syntax we use for templates is:

```
template <class Type>
declaration;
```

in which `Type` is the name of a data type, built-in or user-defined, and `declaration` is either a function declaration or a class declaration. In C++, `template` is a reserved word. The word `class` in the heading refers to any user-defined type or built-in type. `Type` is referred to as a formal parameter to the template. (Note that in the first line, `template <class Type>`, the keyword `class` can be replaced with the keyword `typename`.)

Similar to variables being parameters to functions, types (that is, data types) are parameters to templates.

Function Templates

In Chapter 6, when we introduced function overloading, the function `larger` was overloaded to find the larger of two integers, characters, floating-point numbers, or strings. To implement the function `larger`, we need to write four function definitions for the data type: one for `int`, one for `char`, one for `double`, and one for `string`. However, the body of each function is similar. C++ simplifies the process of overloading functions by providing function templates.

The syntax of the function template is:

```
template <class Type>
function definition;
```

in which `Type` is referred to as a formal parameter of the template. It is used to specify the type of parameters to the function and the return type of the function and to declare variables within the function.

The statements:

```
template <class Type>
Type larger(Type x, Type y)
{
    if (x >= y)
        return x;
    else
        return y;
}
```

define a function template `larger`, which returns the larger of two items. In the function heading, the type of the formal parameters `x` and `y` is `Type`, which will be specified by the type of the actual parameters when the function is called. The statement:

```
cout << larger(5, 6) << endl;
```

is a call to the function template `larger`. Because 5 and 6 are of type `int`, the data type `int` is substituted for `Type`, and the compiler generates the appropriate code.

Note that the function template `larger` will work only for those data types for which the operator `>=` has been defined.

If we omit the body of the function in the function template definition, the function template, as usual, is the prototype.

The following example illustrates the use of function templates.

EXAMPLE 13-8

The following program uses the function template `larger` to determine the larger of the two items.

```
// Template larger

#include <iostream>
#include "myString.h"

using namespace std;

template <class Type>
Type larger(Type x, Type y);

int main()
{
    cout << "Line 1: Larger of 5 and 6 = "
         << larger(5, 6) << endl;                       //Line 1
    cout << "Line 2: Larger of A and B = "
         << larger('A', 'B') << endl;                   //Line 2
    cout << "Line 3: Larger of 5.6 and 3.2 = "
         << larger(5.6, 3.2) << endl;                   //Line 3

    newString str1 = "Hello";                           //Line 4
    newString str2 = "Happy";                           //Line 5

    cout << "Line 6: Larger of " << str1 << " and "
         << str2 << " = " << larger(str1, str2)
         << endl;                                       //Line 6

    return 0;
}

template <class Type>
Type larger(Type x, Type y)
{
    if (x >= y)
```

```
            return x;
    else
            return y;
}
```

Sample Run:

```
Line 1: Larger of 5 and 6 = 6
Line 2: Larger of A and B = B
Line 3: Larger of 5.6 and 3.2 = 5.6
Line 6: Larger of Hello and Happy = Hello
```

Class Templates

Like function templates, class templates are used to write a single code segment for a set of related classes. For example, in Chapter 10, we defined a list as an ADT; our list element type was `int`. If the list element type changes from `int` to, say, `char`, `double`, or `string`, we need to write separate classes for each element type. For the most part, the operations on the list and the algorithms to implement those operations remain the same. Using class templates, we can create a generic `class listType`, and the compiler can generate the appropriate source code for a specific implementation.

The syntax we use for a class template is:

```
template <class Type>
class declaration
```

Class templates are called **parameterized types** because, based on the parameter type, a specific class is generated.

The following statements define `listType` to be a class template:

```
template <class elemType>
class listType
{
public:
    bool isEmpty() const;
      //Function to determine whether the list is empty.
      //Postcondition: Returns true if the list is empty,
      //               otherwise it returns false.

    bool isFull() const;
      //Function to determine whether the list is full.
      //Postcondition: Returns true if the list is full,
      //               otherwise it returns false.

    bool search(const elemType& searchItem) const;
      //Function to search the list for searchItem.
      //Postcondition: Returns true if searchItem
      //               is found in the list, and
      //               false otherwise.
```

```
    void insert(const elemType& newElement);
      //Function to insert newElement in the list.
      //Precondition: Prior to insertion, the list must
      //                 not be full.
      //Postcondition: The list is the old list plus
      //                 newElement.

    void remove(const elemType& removeElement);
      //Function to remove removeElement from the list.
      //Postcondition: If removeElement is found in the list,
      //                 it is deleted from the list, and the
      //                 list is the old list minus removeElement.
      //                 If the list is empty, output the message
      //                 "Cannot delete from the empty list."

    void destroyList();
      //Function to destroy the list.
      //Postcondition: length = 0;

     void printList();
      //Function to output the elements of the list.

     listType();
      //Default constructor
      //Sets the length of the list to 0.
      //Postcondition: length = 0;

protected:
    elemType list[100];     //array to hold the list elements
    int length;             //variable to store the number of
                            //elements in the list
};
```

This definition of the class template `listType` is a generic definition and includes only the basic operations on a list. To derive a specific list from this list and to add or rewrite the operations, we declare the array containing the list elements and the length of the list as `protected`.

Next, we describe a specific list. Suppose that you want to create a list to process integer data. The statement:

```
listType<int> intList;                    //Line 1
```

declares `intList` to be an object of `listType`. The `protected` member `list` is an array of 100 components, with each component being of type `int`. Similarly, the statement:

```
listType<newString> stringList;           //Line 2
```

declares `stringList` to be an object of `listType`. The `protected` member `list` is an array of 100 components, with each component being of type `newString`.

In the statements in Lines 1 and 2, `listType<int>` and `listType<newString>` are referred to as *template instantiations* or *instantiations of the class template* `listType<elemType>`, in which `elemType` is the class parameter in the template header. A template instantiation can be created with either a built-in or user-defined type.

The function members of a class template are considered function templates. Thus, when giving the definitions of the function members of a class template, we must follow the definition of the function template. For example, the definition of the member `insert` of the **class** `listType` is:

```
template <class elemType>
void listType<elemType>::insert(elemType newElement)
{
    .
    .
    .
}
```

In the heading of the member function's definition, the name of the class is specified with the parameter `elemType`.

The statement in Line 1 declares `intList` to be a list of 100 components. When the compiler generates the code for `intList`, it replaces the word `elemType` with `int` in the definition of the **class** `listType`. The template parameter in the definitions of the member functions (for example, `elemType` in the definition of `insert`) of the **class** `listType` is also replaced by `int`.

HEADER FILE AND IMPLEMENTATION FILE OF A CLASS TEMPLATE

Until now, we have placed the definition of the class (in the header file) and the definitions of the member functions (in the implementation file) in separate files. The object code was generated from the implementation file and linked with the user code. However, this mechanism of separating the class definition and the definitions of the member functions does not work with class templates. Passing parameters to a function has an effect at run time, whereas passing a parameter to a class template has an effect at compile time. Because the actual parameter to a class is specified in the user code and because the compiler cannot instantiate a function template without the actual parameter to the template, we can no longer compile the implementation file independently of the user code.

This problem has several possible solutions. We could put the class definition and the definitions of the function templates directly in the client code, or we could put the class definition and the definitions of the function templates together in the same header file. Another alternative is to put the class definition and the definitions of the functions in separate files (as usual), but include a directive to the implementation file at the end of the header file. In either case, the function definitions and the client code are compiled together. For illustrative purposes, we will put the class definition and the function definitions in the same header file.

Array-Based Lists (Revisited)

In Chapter 12, we designed the `classes` `arrayListType`, `unorderedArrayListType`, and `orderedArrayListType` to process lists in an array. However, these classes, as designed in Chapter 12, process only those lists whose elements are of type `int`. Now that we have discussed how to use class templates to create a generic code, in this section, we redesign these classes so that they can be used to process any type of list. Moreover, in this chapter, we discussed how to overload the assignment operator. Therefore, in addition to the operations discussed in Chapter 12, we also overload the assignment operator for the `class` `arrayListType` because it has a pointer member variable.

The following class template defines the abstract `class` `arrayListType` as an ADT. (To save space, we only list the functions. The documentation of these functions is similar to ones given in Chapter 12. The source code file at the Web site accompanying this book contains the documentation of these functions.)

```cpp
template <class elemType>
class arrayListType
{
public:
    const arrayListType<elemType>&
                 operator=(const arrayListType<elemType>&);
        //Overloads the assignment operator

    bool isEmpty() const;
    bool isFull() const;
    int listSize() const;
    int maxListSize() const;
    void print() const;
    bool isItemAtEqual(int location, const elemType& item) const;
    virtual void insertAt(int location, const elemType& insertItem) = 0;
    virtual void insertEnd(const elemType& insertItem) = 0;
    void removeAt(int location);
    void retrieveAt(int location, elemType& retItem) const;
    virtual void replaceAt(int location, const elemType& repItem) = 0;
    void clearList();
    virtual int seqSearch(const elemType& searchItem) const = 0;
    virtual void remove(const elemType& removeItem) = 0;
    arrayListType(int size = 100);
    arrayListType (const arrayListType<elemType>& otherList);
    virtual ~arrayListType();

protected:
    elemType *list; //array to hold the list elements
    int length;     //variable to store the length of the list
    int maxSize;    //variable to store the maximum
                    //size of the list
};
```

The definitions of the functions to implement the operations of the **class** `arrayListType` are similar to the ones given in Chapter 12. Here the functions to implement these operations are function templates. For example, the definitions of the functions `print`, `isItemAtEqual`, `removeAt`, `retrieveAt`, the constructor, and the destructor are:

```cpp
template <class elemType>
void arrayListType<elemType>::print() const
{
    for (int i = 0; i < length; i++)
        cout << list[i] << " ";
    cout << endl;
}

template <class elemType>
bool arrayListType<elemType>::isItemAtEqual(int location,
                                const elemType& item)  const
{
    if (location < 0 || location >= length)
    {
        cout << "The location of the item to be removed "
             << "is out of range." << endl;

        return false;
    }
    else
        return (list[location] == item);
} //end isItemAtEqual

template <class elemType>
void arrayListType<elemType>::removeAt(int location)
{
    if (location < 0 || location >= length)
        cout << "The location of the item to be removed "
             << "is out of range." << endl;
    else
    {
        for (int i = location; i < length - 1; i++)
            list[i] = list[i + 1];

        length--;
    }
} //end removeAt

template <class elemType>
void arrayListType<elemType>::retrieveAt(int location,
                                elemType& retItem) const
{
    if (location < 0 || location >= length)
        cout << "The location of the item to be retrieved is "
             << "out of range" << endl;
```

```
        else
            retItem = list[location];
}  //end retrieveAt

template <class elemType>
arrayListType<elemType>::arrayListType(int size)
{
    if (size <= 0)
    {
        cout << "The array size must be positive. Creating "
             << "an array of the size 100. " << endl;

        maxSize = 100;
    }
    else
        maxSize = size;

    length = 0;

    list = new elemType[maxSize];
}

template <class elemType>
arrayListType<elemType>::~arrayListType()
{
    delete [] list;
}
```

Next, because we are overloading the assignment for the class `arrayListType`, we give the definition of the function template to overload the assignment operator.

```
template <class elemType>
const arrayListType<elemType>& arrayListType<elemType>::
            operator=(const arrayListType<elemType>& otherList)
{
    if (this != &otherList)      //avoid self-assignment
    {
        delete [] list;
        maxSize = otherList.maxSize;
        length = otherList.length;

        list = new elemType[maxSize];

        for (int i = 0; i < length; i++)
            list[i] = otherList.list[i];
    }
    return *this;
}
```

We leave it as an exercise for you to provide the definitions of the remaining function templates for the **class** arrayListType. (See Programming Exercise 20 at the end of this chapter.)

Recall that the **class** arrayListType is an abstract class. So its objects cannot be instantiated. Next we describe the nonabstract **class** unorderedArrayListType derived from the **class** arrayListType.

```
template <class elemType>
class unorderedArrayListType: public arrayListType <elemType>
{
public:
    void insertAt(int location, const elemType& insertItem);
    void insertEnd(const elemType& insertItem);
    void replaceAt(int location, const elemType& repItem);
    int seqSearch(const elemType& searchItem) const;
    void remove(const elemType& removeItem);

    unorderedArrayListType(int size = 100);
        //Constructor
};
```

As in the case of the **class** arrayListType, the definitions of the member functions of the **class** unorderedArrayListType is similar to ones given in Chapter 12. For example, the definitions of the functions insertEnd, seqSearch, replaceAt, and remove, and constructor are as follows:

```
template <class elemType>
void unorderedArrayListType<elemType>::insertEnd
                                    (const elemType& insertItem)
{
    if (length >= maxSize)   //the list is full
        cout << "Cannot insert in a full list." << endl;
    else
    {
        list[length] = insertItem; //insert the item at the end
        length++; //increment the length
    }
} //end insertEnd

template <class elemType>
int unorderedArrayListType<elemType>::seqSearch
                            (const elemType& searchItem) const
{
    int loc;
    bool found = false;

    for (loc = 0; loc < length; loc++)
        if (list[loc] == searchItem)
        {
            found = true;
            break;
        }
```

```
            if (found)
                return loc;
            else
                return -1;
    } //end seqSearch

    template <class elemType>
    void unorderedArrayListType<elemType>::remove
                                        (const elemType& removeItem)
    {
        int loc;

        if (length == 0)
            cout << "Cannot delete from an empty list." << endl;
        else
        {
            loc = seqSearch(removeItem);

            if (loc != -1)
                removeAt(loc);
            else
                cout << "The item to be deleted is not in the list."
                    << endl;
        }
    } //end remove

    template <class elemType>
    void unorderedArrayListType<elemType>::replaceAt(int location,
                                        const elemType& repItem)
    {
        if (location < 0 || location >= length)
            cout << "The location of the item to be "
                << "replaced is out of range." << endl;
        else
            list[location] = repItem;
    } //end replaceAt

    template <class elemType>
    unorderedArrayListType<elemType>::
                        unorderedArrayListType(int size)
                        : arrayListType<elemType>(size)
    {
    }
```

We leave it as an exercise for you to provide the definitions of the remaining function templates for the **class** unorderedArrayListType. (See Programming Exercise 20 at the end of this chapter.)

The following example illustrates how to use the **class** unorderedArrayListType to process a list of strings.

EXAMPLE 13-9

The following program tests the various operations on an array-based list.

```cpp
#include <iostream>
#include <string>
#include "unorderedArrayListType.h"

using namespace std;

int main()
{
    unorderedArrayListType<string> stringList(25);   //Line 1

    string str;                                       //Line 2

    cout << "List 3: Enter 5 strings: ";              //Line 3

    for (int count = 0; count < 5; count++)           //Line 4
    {
        cin >> str;                                   //Line 5
        stringList.insertEnd(str);                    //Line 6
    }

    cout << endl;                                     //Line 7
    cout << "Line 8: stringList: ";                   //Line 8
    stringList.print();                               //Line 9
    cout << endl;                                     //Line 10

    cout << "Line 11: Enter the string to be "
         << "deleted: ";                              //Line 11
    cin >> str;                                       //Line 12
    cout << endl;                                     //Line 13

    stringList.remove(str);                           //Line 14
    cout << "Line 15: After removing " << str
         << " stringList: ";                          //Line 15
    stringList.print();                               //Line 16
    cout << endl;                                     //Line 17

    cout << "Line 18: Enter the search item: ";       //Line 18

    cin >> str;                                       //Line 19
    cout << endl;                                     //Line 20

    if (stringList.seqSearch(str) != -1)              //Line 21
        cout << "Line 22: " << str
             << " found in stringList." << endl;      //Line 22
    else                                              //Line 23
        cout << "Line 24: " << str
             << " is not in stringList." << endl;     //Line 24

    return 0;
}
```

Sample Run: In this sample run, the user input is shaded.

```
List 3: Enter 5 strings: hello sunny warm winter summer
Line 8: stringList: hello sunny warm winter summer
Line 11: Enter the string to be deleted: hello
Line 15: After removing hello stringList: sunny warm winter summer
Line 18: Enter the search item: winter
Line 22: winter found in stringList.
```

The preceding program works as follows. The statement in Line 1 declares `stringList` to be an object of the type `unorderedArrayListType`. The member variable `list` of `stringList` is an array of 25 components and the component type is `string`. The statement in Line 2 declares the `string` variable `str`. The statement in Line 3 prompts the user to enter 5 strings. The statement in Line 5 gets the next string from the input stream. The statement in Line 6 uses the member function `insertEnd` of `stringList` to store the string into `stringList`. The statement in Line 9 uses the member function `print` of `stringList` to output the elements of `stringList`. The statement in Line 11 prompts the user to enter the string to be deleted from `stringList`, and the statement in Line 12 gets the string to be deleted from the input stream. The statement in Line 14 uses the member function `remove` of `stringList` to remove the string from `string-List`. The statement in Line 16 outputs the modified `stringList`.

The statements in Lines 18 through 24 tests the function `seqSearch`.

 NOTE The Web site accompanying this book contains additional programs illustrating how to use the `class template` `unorderedArrayListType` to create lists of `double` elements and `clockType` objects.

Just as we can derive the `class template` `unorderedArrayListType`, from the abstact `class template` `arrayListType`, to manipulate unordered lists, we can also derive the `class template` `orderedArrayListType` to manipulate ordered lists. (See Programming Exercise 21 at the end of this chapter.)

QUICK REVIEW

1. An operator that has different meanings with different data types is said to be overloaded.
2. In C++, `>>` is used as a stream extraction operator and as a right shift operator. Similarly, `<<` is used as a stream insertion operator and as a left shift operator. Both are examples of operator overloading.
3. Any function that overloads an operator is called an operator function.
4. The syntax of the heading of the operator function is:

   `returnType operator operatorSymbol(parameters)`

5. In C++, `operator` is a reserved word.

6. Operator functions are value-returning functions.

7. Except for the assignment operator and the member selection operator, to use an operator on class objects, that operator must be overloaded. The assignment operator performs a default member-wise copy.

8. For classes with pointer member variables, the assignment operator must be explicitly overloaded.

9. Operator overloading provides the same concise notation for user-defined data types as is available for built-in data types.

10. When an operator is overloaded, its precedence cannot be changed, its associativity cannot be changed, default parameters cannot be used with an overloaded operator, the number of parameters that the operator takes cannot be changed, and the meaning of how an operator works with built-in data types remains the same.

11. It is not possible to create new operators. Only existing operators can be overloaded.

12. Most C++ operators can be overloaded.

13. The operators that cannot be overloaded are `.`, `.*`, `::`, `?:`, and `sizeof`.

14. The pointer `this` refers to the object as a whole.

15. The operator functions that overload the operators `()`, `[]`, `->`, or `=` for a class must be members of that class.

16. A `friend` function is a nonmember of a class.

17. The heading of the prototype of a `friend` function is preceded by the word `friend`.

18. In C++, `friend` is a reserved word.

19. If an operator function is a member of a class, the far left operand of the operator must be a class object (or a reference to a class object) of that operator's class.

20. The binary operator function as a member of a class has only one parameter; as a nonmember of a class, it has two parameters.

21. The operator functions that overload the stream insertion operator, `<<`, and the stream extraction operator, `>>`, for a class must be `friend` functions of that class.

22. To overload the pre-increment (`++`) operator for a class if the operator function is a member of that class, it must have no parameters. Similarly, to overload the pre-decrement (`--`) operator for a class if the operator function is a member of that class, it must have no parameters.

23. To overload the post-increment (`++`) operator for a class if the operator function is a member of that class, it must have one parameter, of type `int`. The user does not specify any value for the parameter. The dummy parameter in the function heading helps the compiler generate the correct code. The post-decrement operator has similar conventions.

24. A conversion constructor is a single-parameter function.

25. A conversion constructor converts its argument to an object of the constructor's class. The compiler implicitly calls such constructors.

26. Classes with pointer member variables must overload the assignment operator and include both the copy constructor and the destructor.

27. In C++, a function name can be overloaded.

28. In C++, `template` is a reserved word.

29. Using templates, you can write a single code segment for a set of related functions—called the function template.

30. Using templates, you can write a single code segment for a set of related classes—called the class template.

31. The syntax of a template is:

```
template <class Type>
declaration;
```

in which `Type` is a user-defined identifier, which is used to pass types (that is, data types) as parameters, and `declaration` is either a function or a class. The word `class` in the heading refers to any user-defined data type or built-in data type.

32. Class templates are called parameterized types.

33. In a class template, the parameter `Type` specifies how a generic class template is to be customized to form a specific template class.

34. The parameter `Type` is mentioned in every class header and member function definition.

35. Suppose `cType` is a class template, and `func` is a member function of `cType`. The heading of the function definition of `func` is:

```
template <class Type>
funcType cType<Type>::func(parameters)
```

in which `funcType` is the type of the function, such as `void`.

36. Suppose `cType` is a class template, which can take `int` as a parameter. The statement:

```
cType<int> x;
```

declares `x` to be an object of type `cType`, and the type passed to the `class` `cType` is `int`.

EXERCISES

1. Mark the following statements as true or false.

   a. In C++, all operators can be overloaded for user-defined data types.

   b. In C++, operators cannot be redefined for built-in types.

   c. The function that overloads an operator is called the operator function.

   d. C++ allows users to create their own operators.

e. The precedence of an operator cannot be changed, but its associativity can be changed.

f. Every instance of an overloaded function has the same number of parameters.

g. It is not necessary to overload relational operators for classes that have only `int` member variables.

h. The member function of a `class` template is a function template.

i. When writing the definition of a `friend` function, the keyword `friend` must appear in the function heading.

j. Templates provide the capability for software reuse.

k. The function heading of the operator function to overload the pre-increment operator (++) and the post-increment operator (++) is the same because both operators have the same symbols.

2. What is a `friend` function?

3. What is the difference between a `friend` function of a class and a member function of a class?

4. Consider the definition of the `class` `dateType` given in Chapter 11.

    a. Write the statement that includes a `friend` function named **before** in the `class` `dateType` that takes as parameters two objects of type `dateType` and returns `true` if the date represented by the first object comes before the date represented by the second object; otherwise, the function returns `false`.

    b. Write the definition of the function you defined in part a.

5. Suppose that the operator `<<` is to be overloaded for a user-defined `class` `mystery`. Why must `<<` be overloaded as a `friend` function?

6. Suppose that the binary operator `+` is overloaded as a member function for a `class` `strange`. How many parameters does the function `operator+` have?

7. When should a class overload the assignment operator and define the copy constructor?

8. Consider the following declaration:

```
class strange
{
    .
    .
    .
};
```

    a. Write a statement that shows the declaration in the `class` `strange` to overload the operator `>>`.

    b. Write a statement that shows the declaration in the `class` `strange` to overload the operator `=`.

    c. Write a statement that shows the declaration in the `class` `strange` to overload the binary operator `+` as a member function.

d. Write a statement that shows the declaration in the **class strange** to overload the operator **==** as a member function.

e. Write a statement that shows the declaration in the **class strange** to overload the post-increment operator **++** as a member function.

9. Assume the declaration of Exercise 8.

a. Write a statement that shows the declaration in the **class strange** to overload the binary operator **+** as a **friend** function.

b. Write a statement that shows the declaration in the **class strange** to overload the operator **==** as a **friend** function.

c. Write a statement that shows the declaration in the **class strange** to overload the post-increment operator **++** as a **friend** function.

10. Find the error(s) in the following code:

```
class secret                          //Line 1
{                                      //Line 2
public:                                //Line 3
    secret operator>=(secret);        //Line 4
    secret();                          //Line 5
    secret(int, int);                  //Line 6
private:                               //Line 7
    int a;                             //Line 8
    int b;                             //Line 9
};                                     //Line 10
```

11. Find the error(s) in the following code:

```
class temp                                        //Line 1
{                                                  //Line 2
public:                                            //Line 3
    int operator* (const temp& obj);              //Line 4
        //Returns the object containing the
        //product of the corresponding members
        //of this object and obj.
    temp();                                        //Line 5
    temp(int, int);                                //Line 6
private:                                           //Line 7
    int a;                                         //Line 8
    int b;                                         //Line 9
};                                                 //Line 10
```

12. Find the error(s) in the following code:

```
class discover                                    //Line 1
{                                                  //Line 2
public:                                            //Line 3
    discover operator+(const discover& a,
                       const discover& b);         //Line 4
        //Returns the object containing the
        //sum of the corresponding members
        //of the objects a and b.

    discover();                                    //Line 5
    discover(int, int);                            //Line 6
```

1
3

```
private:                                          //Line 7
    int first;                                    //Line 8
    int second;                                   //Line 9
};                                                //Line 10
```

13. Find the error(s) in the following code:

```
class mystery                                     //Line 1
{                                                 //Line 2
    friend mystery operator<(const mystery& a,
                         const mystery& b);    //Line 3
      //Return true if object a is less than
      //object b; otherwise it returns false
      .
      .
      .
private:                                           //Line 4
    double r;                                      //Line 5
};                                                 //Line 6
```

14. Find the error(s) in the following code:

```
class mystery                                         //Line 1
{                                                     //Line 2
    friend mystery operator+(const mystery& a,
                      const mystery& b) const;   //Line 3
      //Return true if object a is less than
      //object b; otherwise it returns false
      .
      .
      .
private:                                               //Line 4
    double r;                                          //Line 5
};                                                     //Line 6
```

15. Find the error(s) in the following code:

```
class discover                                      //Line 1
{                                                   //Line 2
    friend double operator+(const discover&,
                     const discover&);          //Line 3
public:                                             //Line 4
    discover();                                     //Line 5
    discover(double, double);                       //Line 6
private:                                            //Line 7
    double first;                                   //Line 8
    double second;                                  //Line 9
};                                                  //Line 10

double discover::operator+(const discover& a,
                     const discover& b)         //Line 11
{                                                   //Line 12
    discover temp;
    temp.first = a.first + b.first;                 //Line 13
    temp.second = a.second + b.second;              //Line 14
    return temp;                                    //Line 15
}                                                   //Line 16
```

16. a. In a class, why do you include the function that overloads the stream insertion operator, <<, as a `friend` function?

    b. In a class, why do you include the function that overloads the stream extraction operator, >>, as a `friend` function?

17. What is returned by the function that overloads the operator >> for a class?

18. What is returned by the function that overloads the operator << for a class?

19. What is the purpose of a dummy parameter in a function that overloads the post-increment or post-decrement operator for a class?

20. What type of value should be returned by a function that overloads a relational operator?

21. How many parameters are required to overload the pre-increment operator for a class as a member function?

22. How many parameters are required to overload the pre-increment operator for a class as a `friend` function?

23. How many parameters are required to overload the post-increment operator for a class as a member function?

24. How many parameters are required to overload the post-increment operator for a class as a `friend` function?

25. Let $a + ib$ be a complex number. The conjugate of $a + ib$ is $a - ib$, and the absolute value of $a + ib$ is $\sqrt{a^2 + b^2}$. Extend the definition of the `class complexType` of the Programming Example: Complex Numbers by overloading the operators ~ and ! as member functions so that ~ returns the conjugate of a complex number and ! returns the absolute value. Also, write the definitions of these operator functions.

26. Redo Exercise 25 so that the operators ~ and ! are overloaded as non-member functions.

27. Find the error(s) in the following code:

```
template <class type>        //Line 1
class strange                //Line 2
{
    .
    .
    .
};

strange<int> s1;             //Line 3
strange<type> s2;            //Line 4
```

28. Consider the following declaration:

```
template <class type>
class strange
{
    .
    .
    .
```

```
private:
    type a;
    type b;
};
```

a. Write a statement that declares sObj to be an object of type strange such that the private member variables a and b are of type int.

b. Write a statement that shows the declaration in the class strange to overload the operator == as a member function.

c. Assume that two objects of type strange are equal if their corresponding member variables are equal. Write the definition of the function operator== for the class strange, which is overloaded as a member function.

29. Consider the definition of the following function template:

```
template <class Type>
Type surprise(Type x, Type y)
{
    return x + y;
}
```

What is the output of the following statements?

a. `cout << surprise(5, 7) << endl;`

b.
```
string str1 = "Sunny";
string str2 = " Day";
cout << surprise(str1, str2) << endl;
```

30. Consider the definition of the following function template:

```
template <class type>
type funcExp(type list[], int size)
{
    type x = list[0];
    type y = list[size - 1];

    for (int j = 1; j < size - 1; j++)
    {
        if (x < list[j])
            x = list[j];
        if (y > list[size - 1 - j])
            y = list[size - 1 - j];
    }

    return y + x;
}
```

Further suppose that you have the following declarations:

```
double sales[7] = {280.50, 320.00, 56.00, 78.90, 300.00,
                   100.00, 250.00};
string names[] = {"Mike", "Lisa", "Nancy", "Robinson",
                  "Miller", "Sam"};
```

What is the output of the following statements?

   a.   `cout << funcExp(sales, 7) << endl;`

   b.   `cout << funcExp(names, 6) << endl;`

31. Write the definition of the function template that swaps the contents of two variables.

32. a. Overload the operator + for the **class** newString to perform string concatenation. For example, if s1 is "Hello " and s2 is "there", the statement:

     `s3 = s1 + s2;`

     should assign "Hello there" to s3, in which s1, s2, and s3 are newString objects.

    b. Overload the operator += for the **class** newString to perform the following string concatenation. Suppose that s1 is "Hello " and s2 is "there". Then, the statement:

     `s1 += s2;`

     should assign "Hello there" to s1, in which s1 and s2 are newString objects.

PROGRAMMING EXERCISES

1. This chapter uses the **class** rectangleType to illustate how to overload the operators +, *, ==, !=, >>, and <<. In this exercise, first redefine the **class** rectangleType by declaring the instance variables as **protected** and then overload additional operators as defined in parts a to c.

   a. Overload the pre- and post-increment and decrement operators to increment and decrement, respectively, the length and width of a rectangle by one unit. (Note that after decrementing the length and width, they must be postive.)

   b. Overload the binary operator – to subtract the dimensions of one rectangle from the corresponding dimensions of another rectangle. If the resulting dimensions are not positive, output an appropriate message and do not perform the operation.

   c. The operators == and != are overloaded by considering the lengths and widths of rectangles. Redefine the functions to overload the relational operator by considering the areas of rectangles as follows: Two rectangles are the same, if they have the same area; otherwise, the rectangles are not the same. Similary, rectangle yard1 is greater than rectangle yard2 if the area of yard1 is greater than the area of yard2. Overload the remaining relational operators using similar definitions.

13

d. Write the definitions of the functions to overload the operators defined in parts a to c.

e. Write a test program that tests various operations on the class rectangleType.

2. a. Redo Programming Exercise 1 by overloading the operators as nonmembers of the class rectangleType.

b. Write a test program that tests various operations on the class rectangleType.

3. a. Chapter 11 defined the class boxType by extending the definition of the class rectangleType. In this exercise, derive the class boxType from the class rectangleType, defined in Exercise 1, add the functions to overload the operators +, -, *, ==, !=, <=, <, >=, >, and pre- and post-increment and decrement operators as members of the class boxType. Also overload the operators << and >>. Overload the relational operators by considering the volume of the boxes. For example, two boxes are the same if they have the same volume.

b. Write the definitions of the functions of the class boxType as defined in part a.

c. Write a test program that tests various operations on the class rectangleType.

4. a. Redo Programming Exercise 3 by overloading the operators as nonmembers of the class boxType.

b. Write a test program that tests various operations on the class boxType.

5. a. Extend the definition of the class clockType by overloading the post-increment operator function as a member of the class clockType.

b. Write the definition of the function to overload the post-increment operator for the class clockType as defined in part a.

6. a. The increment and relational operators in the class clockType are overloaded as member functions. Rewrite the definition of the class clockType so that these operators are overloaded as nonmember functions. Also, overload the post-increment operator for the class clockType as a nonmember.

b. Write the definitions of the member functions of the class clockType as designed in part a.

c. Write a test program that tests various operations on the class as designed in parts a and b.

7. a. Extend the definition of the class complexType so that it performs the subtraction and division operations. Overload the operators subtraction and division for this class as member functions.

If (a, b) and (c, d) are complex numbers:

$(a, b) - (c, d) = (a - c, b - d)$.

If (c, d) is nonzero:

$(a, b) / (c, d) = ((ac + bd) / (c^2 + d^2), (-ad + bc) / (c^2 + d^2))$.

b. Write the definitions of the functions to overload the operators - and / as defined in part a.

c. Write a test program that tests various operations on the **class** **complexType**. Format your answer with two decimal places.

8. a. Rewrite the definition of the **class complexType** so that the arithmetic and relational operators are overloaded as nonmember functions.

b. Write the definitions of the member functions of the **class complexType** as designed in part a.

c. Write a test program that tests various operations on the **class** **complexType** as designed in parts a and b. Format your answer with two decimal places.

9. a. Extend the definition of the **class newString** as follows:

i. Overload the operators + and += to perform the string concatenation operations.

ii. Add the function **length** to return the length of the string.

b. Write the definition of the function to implement the operations defined in part a.

c. Write a test program to test various operations on the **newString** objects.

10. Rational fractions are of the form a / b, in which a and b are integers and $b \neq 0$. In this exercise, by "fractions" we mean rational fractions. Suppose a / b and c / d are fractions. Arithmetic operations on fractions are defined by the following rules:

$a/b + c/d = (ad + bc)/bd$

$a/b - c/d = (ad - bc)/bd$

$a/b \times c/d = ac/bd$

$(a/b)/(c/d) = ad/bc$, in which $c/d \neq 0$.

Fractions are compared as follows: a / b *op* c / d if ad *op* bc, in which *op* is any of the relational operations. For example, $a / b < c / d$ if $ad < bc$.

Design a **class**—say, **fractionType**—that performs the arithmetic and relational operations on fractions. Overload the arithmetic and relational operators so that the appropriate symbols can be used to perform the operation. Also, overload the stream insertion and stream extraction operators for easy input and output.

Write a C++ program that, using the **class** fractionType, performs operations on fractions.

Among other things, test the following: Suppose x, y, and z are objects of type fractionType. If the input is 2/3, the statement:

```
cin >> x;
```

should store 2/3 in x. The statement:

```
cout << x + y << endl;
```

should output the value of x + y in fraction form. The statement:

```
z = x + y;
```

should store the sum of x and y in z in fraction form. Your answer need not be in the lowest terms.

11. Recall that in C++, there is no check on an array index out of bounds. However, during program execution, an array index out of bounds can cause serious problems. Also, in C++, the array index starts at 0.

Design and implement the **class** myArray that solves the array index out of bounds problem and also allows the user to begin the array index starting at any integer, positive or negative. Every object of type myArray is an array of type **int**. During execution, when accessing an array component, if the index is out of bounds, the program must terminate with an appropriate error message. Consider the following statements:

```
myArray<int> list(5);              //Line 1
myArray<int> myList(2, 13);        //Line 2
myArray<int> yourList(-5, 9);      //Line 3
```

The statement in Line 1 declares list to be an array of 5 components, the component type is **int**, and the components are: list[0], list[1], ..., list[4]; the statement in Line 2 declares myList to be an array of 11 components, the component type is **int**, and the components are: myList[2], myList[3], ..., myList[12]; the statement in Line 3 declares yourList to be an array of 14 components, the component type is **int**, and the components are: yourList[-5], yourList[-4], ..., yourList[0], ..., yourList[8]. Write a program to test the **class** myArray.

12. Programming Exercise 11 processes only **int** arrays. Redesign the **class** myArray using class templates so that the **class** can be used in any application that requires arrays to process data.

13. Design a class to perform various matrix operations. A matrix is a set of numbers arranged in rows and columns. Therefore, every element of a matrix has a row position and a column position. If A is a matrix of **five** rows and **six** columns, we say that the matrix A is of the size 5×6 and sometimes denote it as $A_{5 \times 6}$. Clearly, a convenient place to store a matrix is in a two-dimensional array. Two matrices can be added and subtracted if they have the same size. Suppose $A = [a_{ij}]$ and $B = [b_{ij}]$ are two matrices of the size $m \times n$, in which a_{ij} denotes the element of A in the ith row and the jth column, and so on. The sum and difference of A and B are given by:

$$A + B = [a_{ij} + b_{ij}]$$

$$A - B = [a_{ij} - b_{ij}]$$

The multiplication of A and B ($A * B$) is defined only if the number of columns of A is the same as the number of rows of B. If A is of the size $m \times n$ and B is of the size $n \times t$, then $A * B = [c_{ik}]$ is of the size $m \times t$ and the element c_{ik} is given by the formula:

$$c_{ik} = a_{i1}b_{1k} + a_{i2}b_{2k} + \cdots + a_{in}b_{nk}$$

Design and implement a **class matrixType** that can store a matrix of any size. Overload the operators +, -, and * to perform the addition, subtraction, and multiplication operations, respectively, and overload the operator << to output a matrix. Also, write a test program to test various operations on the matrices.

14. a. In Programming Exercise 3 in Chapter 10, we defined a **class romanType** to implement Roman numbers in a program. In that exercise, we also implemented a function, **romanToDecimal**, to convert a Roman number into its equivalent decimal number.

   Modify the definition of the **class romanType** so that the member variables are declared as **protected**. Use the **class newString**, as designed in Programming Exercise 9, to manipulate strings. Furthermore, overload the stream insertion and stream extraction operators for easy input and output. The stream insertion operator outputs the Roman number in the Roman format.

   Also, include a member function, **decimalToRoman**, that converts the decimal number (the decimal number must be a positive integer) to an equivalent Roman number format. Write the definition of the member function **decimalToRoman**.

   For simplicity, we assume that only the letter I can appear in front of another letter and that it appears only in front of the letters V and X. For example, 4 is represented as **IV**, 9 is represented as **IX**, 39 is represented as **XXXIX**, and 49 is represented as **XXXXIX**. Also, 40 will be represented as **XXXX**, 190 will be represented as **CLXXXX**, and so on.

b. Derive a **class** extRomanType from the **class** romanType to do the following: In the **class** extRomanType, overload the arithmetic operators +, −, *, and / so that arithmetic operations can be performed on Roman numbers. Also, overload the pre- and post-increment and decrement operators as member functions of the **class** extRomanType.

To add (subtract, multiply, or divide) Roman numbers, add (subtract, multiply, or divide, respectively) their decimal representations and then convert the result to the Roman number format. For subtraction, if the first number is smaller than the second number, output a message saying that, "Because the first number is smaller than the second, the numbers cannot be subtracted". Similarly, for division, the numerator must be larger than the denominator. Use similar conventions for the increment and decrement operators.

c. Write the definitions of the functions to overload the operators described in part b.

d. Write a program to test your class.

15. In Example 13-9, the class template listType is designed to implement a list in a program. For illustration purposes, that example included only the sorting operation. Extend the definition of the class template to include the remove and search operations. Write the definitions of the member functions to implement the class template listType. Also, write a test program to test various operations on a list.

16. Consider the **class** dateType given in Chapter 11. In this class, add the functions to overload the increment and decrement operators to increase the date by a day and decrease the date by a day, respectively; relational operators to compare two dates; and stream operators for easy input and output. (Assume that the date is input and output in the form MM−DD−YYYY.) Also write a program to test your class.

17. Programming Exercise 14, Chapter 10, describes how to design the **class** lineType to implement a line. Redo this programming exercise so that the **class** lineType:

a. Overloads the stream insertion operator, <<, for easy output.

b. Overloads the stream extraction operator, >>, for easy intput. (The line $ax + by = c$ is input as (a, b, c).)

c. Overloads the assignment operator to copy a line into another line.

d. Overloads the unary operator +, as a member function, so that it returns **true** if a line is vertical; **false** otherwise.

e. Overloads the unary operator −, as a member function, so that it returns **true** if a line is horizontal; **false** otherwise.

f. Overloads the operator ==, as a member function, so that it returns **true** if two lines are equal; **false** otherwise.

g. Overloads the operator ||, as a member function, so that it returns true if two lines are parallel; false otherwise.

h. Overloads the operator &&, as a member function, so that it returns true if two lines are perpendicular; false otherwise.

Write a program to test your class.

18. Consider the classes cashRegister and dispenserType given in the Programming Example "Juice Machine" in Chapter 10.

a. In the class cashRegister, add the functions to overload the binary operators + and − to add and subtract an amount in a cash register; the relational operators to compare the amount in two cash registers; and the stream insertion operator for easy output.

b. The class dispenserType, in the Programming Example "Juice Machine" in Chapter 10, is designed to implement a dispenser to hold and release products. In this class, add the functions to overload the increment and decrement operators to increment and decrement the number of items by one, respectively, and the stream insertion operator for easy output.

c. Write a program to test the classes designed in parts a and b.

19. (**Stock Market**) Write a program to help a local stock trading company automate its systems. The company invests only in the stock market. At the end of each trading day, the company would like to generate and post the listing of its stocks so that investors can see how their holdings performed that day. We assume that the company invests in, say, 10 different stocks. The desired output is to produce two listings, one sorted by stock symbol and another sorted by percent gain from highest to lowest.

The input data is provided in a file in the following format:

```
symbol openingPrice closingPrice todayHigh todayLow
prevClose volume
```

For example, the sample data is:

```
MSMT 112.50 115.75 116.50 111.75 113.50 6723823
CBA 67.50 75.50 78.75 67.50 65.75 378233
 .
 .
 .
```

The first line indicates that the stock symbol is MSMT, today's opening price was 112.50, the closing price was 115.75, today's high price was 116.50, today's low price was 111.75, yesterday's closing price was 113.50, and the number of shares currently being held is 6723823.

The listing sorted by stock symbols must be of the following form:

```
*********  First Investor's Heaven  **********
*********      Financial Report         **********
Stock              Today                    Previous  Percent
Symbol  Open    Close   High     Low        Close     Gain       Volume
------  -----   -----   -----    -----      --------  -------    ------
   ABC  123.45  130.95  132.00   125.00     120.50     8.67%      10000
  AOLK   80.00   75.00   82.00    74.00      83.00    -9.64%       5000
  CSCO  100.00  102.00  105.00    98.00     101.00     0.99%      25000
   IBD   68.00   71.00   72.00    67.00      75.00    -5.33%      15000
  MSET  120.00  140.00  145.00   140.00     115.00    21.74%      30920
Closing Assets: $9628300.00
-*-*-*-*-*-*-*-*-*-*-*-*-*-*-*-*-*-*-*-*-*-*-*
```

Develop this programming exercise in two steps. In the first step (part a), design and implement a stock object. In the second step (part b), design and implement an object to maintain a list of stocks.

a. (Stock Object) Design and implement the stock object. Call the class that captures the various characteristics of a stock object `stockType`.

The main components of a stock are the stock symbol, stock price, and number of shares. Moreover, we need to output the opening price, closing price, high price, low price, previous price, and the percent gain/loss for the day. These are also all the characteristics of a stock. Therefore, the stock object should store all this information.

Perform the following operations on each stock object:

i. Set the stock information.

ii. Print the stock information.

iii. Show the different prices.

iv. Calculate and print the percent gain/loss.

v. Show the number of shares.

   a.1. The natural ordering of the stock list is by stock symbol. Overload the relational operators to compare two stock objects by their symbols.

   a.2. Overload the insertion operator, <<, for easy output.

   a.3. Because the data is stored in a file, overload the stream extraction operator, >>, for easy input.

For example, suppose `infile` is an `ifstream` object and the input file was opened using the object `infile`. Further suppose that `myStock` is a stock object. Then, the statement:

```
infile >> myStock;
```

reads the data from the input file and stores it in the object `myStock`. (Note that this statement reads and stores the data in the relevant components of `myStock`.)

b.   Now that you have designed and implemented the `class stockType` to implement a stock object in a program, it is time to create a list of stock objects.

Let us call the class to implement a list of stock objects `stockListType`.

The `class stockListType` must be derived from the `class listType`, which you designed and implemented in the previous exercise. However, the `class stockListType` is a very specific class, designed to create a list of stock objects. Therefore, the `class stockListType` is no longer a template.

Add and/or overwrite the operations of the `class listType` to implement the necessary operations on a stock list.

The following statement derives the `class stockListType` from the `class listType`.

```
class stockListType: public listType<stockType>
{
    member list
};
```

The member variables to hold the list elements, the length of the list, and the `max listSize` were declared as `protected` in the `class listType`. Therefore, these members can be directly accessed in the `class stockListType`.

Because the company also requires you to produce the list ordered by the percent gain/loss, you need to sort the stock list by this component. However, you are not to physically sort the list by the component percent gain/loss. Instead, you will provide a logical ordering with respect to this component.

To do so, add a member variable, an array, to hold the indices of the stock list ordered by the component percent gain/loss. Call this array `sortIndicesGainLoss`. When printing the list ordered by the component percent gain/loss, use the array `sortIndicesGainLoss` to print the list. The elements of the array `sortIndicesGainLoss` will tell which component of the stock list to print next.

c.   Write a program that uses these two classes to automate the company's analysis of stock data.

20.   Write the definitions of the member functions of the `class`es `arrayListType` and `unorderedArrayListType`, which are not given in this chapter. Also, write a program to test your function.

21. Write the definition of the **class template** orderedArrayListType, derived from the **class** arrayListType, to implement an ordered list. As in Chapter 12, add the function insert in this class. Provide the definitions of the nonabstract functions. Also, write a program to test your class.

22. (Unordered Sets) Redo Programming Exercise 12 of Chapter 12 using templates.

23. (Ordered Sets) Redo Programming Exercise 13 of Chapter 12 using templates.

EXCEPTION HANDLING

IN THIS CHAPTER, YOU WILL:

- · Learn what an exception is

- · Learn how to handle exceptions within a program

- · See how a `try`/`catch` block is used to handle exceptions

- · Become familiar with C++ exception classes

- · Learn how to create your own exception classes

- · Discover how to throw and rethrow an exception

- · Explore stack unwinding

An exception is an occurrence of an undesirable situation that can be detected during program execution. For example, division by zero is an exception. Similarly, trying to open an input file that does not exist is an exception, as is an array index that goes out of bounds.

Until now, we have dealt with certain exceptions by using either an `if` statement or the `assert` function. For instance, in Examples 5-3 and 5-4, before dividing `sum` by `counter` or `count`, we checked whether `counter` or `count` was nonzero. Similarly, in the Programming Example `newString` (Chapter 13), we used the `assert` function to determine whether the array index is within bounds.

On the other hand, there were places where we simply ignored the exception. For instance, while determining a substring in a string (Chapter 7), we never checked whether the starting position of the substring was within range. Also, we did not handle the array index out-of-bounds exception. However, in all of these cases, if exceptions occurred during program execution, either we included code to terminate the program or the program terminated with an appropriate error message. For instance, if we opened an input file in the function `main` and the input file did not exist, we terminated the function `main`, so the program was terminated.

There are situations when an exception occurs, but you don't want the program to simply ignore the exception and terminate. For example, a program that monitors stock performance should not automatically sell if the account balance goes below a certain level. It should inform the stockholder and request an appropriate action. Similarly, a program that monitors a patient's heartbeat cannot be terminated if the blood pressure goes very high. A program that monitors a satellite in space cannot be terminated if there is a temporary power failure in some section of the satellite.

The code to handle exceptions depends on the type of application you develop. One common way to provide exception-handling code is to add exception-handling code at the point where an error can occur. This technique allows the programmer reading the code to see the exception-handling code together with the actual code and to determine whether the error-checking code is properly implemented. The disadvantage of this approach is that the program can become cluttered with exception-handling code, which can make understanding and maintaining the program difficult. This can distract the programmer from ensuring that the program functions correctly.

Handling Exceptions within a Program

In Chapter 3, we noted that if you try to input invalid data into a variable, the input stream enters the fail state, so an exception occurs. This occurs, for example, if you try to input a letter into an `int` variable. Chapter 3 also showed how to clear and restore the input stream. Chapter 4 introduced the `assert` function and explained how to use it to avoid certain unforeseeable errors, such as division by zero. Even though the function `assert` can check whether an expression meets the required condition(s), if the conditions are not met, it terminates the program. As indicated in the previous section, situations occur in which, if something goes wrong, the program should not be simply terminated.

This section discusses how to handle exceptions. However, first we offer some examples that show what can happen if an exception is not handled. We also review some of the ways to handle exceptions.

The program in Example 14-1 shows what happens when division by zero occurs and the problem is not addressed.

EXAMPLE 14-1

```cpp
// Division by zero.

#include <iostream>

using namespace std;

int main()
{
    int dividend, divisor, quotient;           //Line 1

    cout << "Line 2: Enter the dividend: ";    //Line 2
    cin >> dividend;                           //Line 3
    cout << endl;                              //Line 4

    cout << "Line 5: Enter the divisor: ";     //Line 5
    cin >> divisor;                            //Line 6
    cout << endl;                              //Line 7

    quotient = dividend / divisor;             //Line 8
    cout << "Line 9: Quotient = " << quotient
         << endl;                              //Line 9

    return 0;                                  //Line 10
}
```

Sample Run 1:

Line 2: Enter the dividend: 12

Line 5: Enter the divisor: 5

Line 9: Quotient = 2

Sample Run 2:

Line 2: Enter the dividend: 24

Line 5: Enter the divisor: 0

CPP_Proj1.exe has encountered a problem and needs to close. We are sorry for the inconvenience.

In Sample Run 1, the value of divisor is nonzero, so no exception occurs. The program calculates and outputs the quotient and terminates normally.

In Sample Run 2, the value entered for `divisor` is 0. The statement in Line 8 divides `dividend` by the divisor. However, the program does not check whether `divisor` is 0 before dividing `dividend` by `divisor`. So the program crashes with the message shown. Notice that the error message is platform independent, that is, IDE dependent. Some IDEs might not give this error message and might simply hang.

Next, consider Example 14-2. This is the same program as in Example 14-1, except that in Line 8, the program checks whether `divisor` is zero.

EXAMPLE 14-2

```cpp
// Checking division by zero.

#include <iostream>

using namespace std;

int main()
{
    int dividend, divisor, quotient;                    //Line 1

    cout << "Line 2: Enter the dividend: ";             //Line 2
    cin >> dividend;                                    //Line 3
    cout << endl;                                       //Line 4

    cout << "Line 5: Enter the divisor: ";              //Line 5
    cin >> divisor;                                     //Line 6
    cout << endl;                                       //Line 7

    if (divisor != 0)                                   //Line 8
    {
        quotient = dividend / divisor;                  //Line 9
        cout << "Line 10: Quotient = " << quotient
            << endl;                                    //Line 10
    }
    else                                                //Line 11
        cout << "Line 12: Cannot divide by zero."
            << endl;                                    //Line 12

    return 0;                                           //Line 13
}
```

Sample Run 1:

```
Line 2: Enter the dividend: 12

Line 5: Enter the divisor: 5

Line 10: Quotient = 2
```

Sample Run 2:

```
Line 2: Enter the dividend: 24

Line 5: Enter the divisor: 0

Line 12: Cannot divide by zero.
```

In Sample Run 1, the value of `divisor` is nonzero, so no exception occurs. The program calculates and outputs the quotient and terminates normally.

In Sample Run 2, the value entered for `divisor` is 0. In Line 8, the program checks whether `divisor` is 0. Because `divisor` is 0, the expression in the `if` statement fails, so the `else` part executes, which outputs the third line of the sample run.

The program in Example 14-3 uses the function `assert` to determine whether the divisor is zero. If the divisor is zero, the function `assert` terminates the program with an error message.

EXAMPLE 14-3

```cpp
// Division by zero and the assert function.

#include <iostream>
#include <cassert>

using namespace std;

int main()
{
    int dividend, divisor, quotient;               //Line 1

    cout << "Line 2: Enter the dividend: ";        //Line 2
    cin >> dividend;                               //Line 3
    cout << endl;                                  //Line 4

    cout << "Line 5: Enter the divisor: ";         //Line 5
    cin >> divisor;                                //Line 6
    cout << endl;                                  //Line 7

    assert(divisor != 0);                          //Line 8
    quotient = dividend / divisor;                 //Line 9

    cout << "Line 10: Quotient = " << quotient
         << endl;                                  //Line 10

    return 0;                                       //Line 11
}
```

Sample Run 1:

```
Line 2: Enter the dividend: 26

Line 5: Enter the divisor: 7

Line 10: Quotient = 3
```

1
4

Sample Run 2:

Line 2: Enter the dividend: 24

Line 5: Enter the divisor: 0

Assertion failed: divisor != 0, file c:\chapter 14 source code\ch14_exp3.cpp, line 20

In Sample Run 1, the value of `divisor` is nonzero, so no exception occurs. The program calculates and outputs the quotient and terminates normally.

In Sample Run 2, the value entered for `divisor` is 0. In Line 8, the function `assert` checks whether `divisor` is nonzero. Because `divisor` is 0, the expression in the `assert` statement evaluates to `false`, and the function `assert` terminates the program with the error message shown in the third line of the output.

C++ Mechanisms of Exception Handling

Examples 14-1 through 14-3 show what happens when an exception occurs in a program and is not processed. This section describes how to include the necessary code to handle exceptions within a program.

try/catch Block

The statements that may generate an exception are placed in a `try` block. The `try` block also contains statements that should not be executed if an exception occurs. The `try` block is followed by one or more `catch` blocks. A `catch` block specifies the type of exception it can catch and contains an exception handler.

The general syntax of the `try/catch` block is:

```
try
{
    //statements
}
catch (dataType1 identifier)
{
    //exception-handling code
}
    .
    .
    .
catch (dataTypen identifier)
{
    //exception-handling code
}
    .
    .
    .
catch (...)
{
    //exception-handling code
}
```

Suppose there is a statement that can generate an exception, for example, division by 0. Usually, before executing such a statement, we check whether certain conditions are met. For example, before performing the division, we check whether the divisor is nonzero. If the conditions are not met, we typically generate an exception, which in C++ terminology is called throwing an exception. This is typically done using the `throw` statement, which we will explain shortly. We will show what is typically thrown to generate an exception.

Let us now note the following about `try`/`catch` blocks.

- If no exception is thrown in a `try` block, all `catch` blocks associated with that `try` block are ignored and program execution resumes after the last `catch` block.

- If an exception is thrown in a `try` block, the remaining statements in that `try` block are ignored. The program searches the `catch` blocks in the order they appear after the `try` block and looks for an appropriate exception handler. If the type of thrown exception matches the parameter type in one of the `catch` blocks, the code of that `catch` block executes, and the remaining `catch` blocks after this `catch` block are ignored.

- The last `catch` block that has an ellipses (three dots) is designed to catch any type of exception.

Consider the following `catch` block:

```
catch (int x)
{
    //exception-handling code
}
```

In this `catch` block:

- The identifier **x** acts as a parameter. In fact, it is called a `catch` block parameter.
- The data type `int` specifies that this `catch` block can catch an exception of type `int`.
- A `catch` block can have *at most* one `catch` block parameter.

Essentially, the `catch` block parameter becomes a placeholder for the value thrown. In this case, **x** becomes a placeholder for any thrown value that is of type `int`. In other words, if the thrown value is caught by this `catch` block, then the thrown value is stored in the `catch` block parameter. This way, if the exception-handling code wants to do something with that value, it can be accessed via the `catch` block parameter.

Suppose in a `catch` block heading only the data type is specified, that is, there is no `catch` block parameter. The thrown value then *may not* be accessible in the `catch` block exception-handling code.

THROWING AN EXCEPTION

In order for an exception to occur in a `try` block and be caught by a `catch` block, the exception must be thrown in the `try` block. The general syntax to `throw` an exception is:

```
throw expression;
```

in which **expression** is a constant value, variable, or object. The object being thrown can be either a specific object or an anonymous object. It follows that in C++, an *exception is a value*.

In C++, `throw` is a reserved word.

Example 14-4 illustrates how to use a `throw` statement.

EXAMPLE 14-4

Suppose we have the following declaration:

```
int num = 5;
string str = "Something is wrong!!!";
```

throw **expression**	**Effect**
`throw 4;`	The constant value 4 is thrown.
`throw x;`	The value of the variable x is thrown.
`throw str;`	The object str is thrown.
`throw string("Exception found!");`	An anonymous string object with the string "Exception found!" is thrown.

ORDER OF `catch` BLOCKS

A `catch` block can catch either all exceptions of a specific type or all types of exceptions. The heading of a `catch` block specifies the type of exception it handles. As noted previously, the `catch` block that has an ellipses (three dots) is designed to catch any type of exception. Therefore, if we put this `catch` block first, then this `catch` block can catch all types of exceptions.

Suppose that an exception occurs in a `try` block and is caught by a `catch` block. The remaining `catch` blocks associated with that `try` block are then ignored. Therefore, you should be careful about the order in which you list `catch` blocks following a `try` block. For example, consider the following sequence of `try/catch` blocks:

```
try                     //Line 1
{
    //statements
}
catch (...)             //Line 2
{
    //statements
}
catch (int x)           //Line 3
{
    //statements
}
```

Suppose that an exception is thrown in the `try` block. Because the `catch` block in Line 2 can catch exceptions of all types, the `catch` block in Line 3 cannot be reached. For this sequence of `try`/`catch` blocks, some compilers might, in fact, give a syntax error (check your compiler's documentation).

In a sequence of `try`/`catch` blocks, if the `catch` block with an ellipses (in the heading) is needed, then it should be the last `catch` block of that sequence.

USING `try`/`catch` BLOCKS IN A PROGRAM

Next, we provide examples that illustrate how a `try`/`catch` block might appear in a program.

A common error that might occur when performing numeric calculations is division by zero with integer values. If, during program execution, division by zero occurs with integer values and is not addressed by the program, the program might terminate with an error message or might simply hang. Example 14-5 shows how to handle division by zero exceptions.

EXAMPLE 14-5

This example illustrates how to catch and handle division by zero exceptions. It also shows how a `try`/`catch` block might appear in a program.

```
// Handling division by zero exception.

#include <iostream>

using namespace std;

int main()
{
    int dividend, divisor, quotient;              //Line 1

    try                                           //Line 2
    {
        cout << "Line 3: Enter the dividend: ";   //Line 3
        cin >> dividend;                          //Line 4
        cout << endl;                             //Line 5

        cout << "Line 6: Enter the divisor: ";    //Line 6
        cin >> divisor;                           //Line 7
        cout << endl;                             //Line 8

        if (divisor == 0)                         //Line 9
            throw 0;                              //Line 10

        quotient = dividend / divisor;            //Line 11

        cout << "Line 12: Quotient = " << quotient
             << endl;                             //Line 12
    }
    catch (int)                                   //Line 13
```

1
4

```
    {
        cout << "Line 14: Division by 0." << endl;    //Line 14
    }

    return 0;                                          //Line 15
}
```

Sample Run 1: In this sample run, the user input is shaded.

```
Line 3: Enter the dividend: 17

Line 6: Enter the divisor: 8

Line 12: Quotient = 2
```

Sample Run 2: In this sample run, the user input is shaded.

```
Line 3: Enter the dividend: 34

Line 6: Enter the divisor: 0

Line 14: Division by 0.
```

This program works as follows. The statement in Line 1 declares the `int` variables `dividend`, `divisor`, and `quotient`. The `try` block starts at Line 2. The statement in Line 3 prompts the user to enter the value for the dividend; the statement in Line 4 stores this number in the variable `dividend`. The statement in Line 6 prompts the user to enter the value for the divisor, and the statement in Line 7 stores this number in the variable `divisor`. The statement in Line 9 checks whether the value of `divisor` is 0. If the value of `divisor` is 0, the statement in Line 10 throws the constant value 0. The statement in Line 11 calculates the quotient and stores it in `quotient`. The statement in Line 12 outputs the value of `quotient`.

The `catch` block starts in Line 13 and catches an exception of type `int`.

In Sample Run 1, the program does not throw any exception.

In Sample Run 2, the entered value of `divisor` is 0. Therefore, the statement in Line 10 throws 0, which is caught by the `catch` block starting in Line 13. The statement in Line 14 outputs the appropriate message.

The program in Example 14-6 is the same as the program in Example 14-5, except that the `throw` statement throws the value of the variable `divisor`.

EXAMPLE 14-6

```
// Handling division by zero exception.

#include <iostream>

using namespace std;
```

```
int main()
{
    int dividend, divisor, quotient;                    //Line 1

    try                                                 //Line 2
    {
        cout << "Line 3: Enter the dividend: ";         //Line 3
        cin >> dividend;                                //Line 4
        cout << endl;                                   //Line 5

        cout << "Line 6: Enter the divisor: ";          //Line 6
        cin >> divisor;                                 //Line 7
        cout << endl;                                   //Line 8

        if (divisor == 0)                               //Line 9
            throw divisor;                              //Line 10

        quotient = dividend / divisor;                  //Line 11

        cout << "Line 12: Quotient = " << quotient
             << endl;                                   //Line 12
    }
    catch (int x)                                       //Line 13
    {
        cout << "Line 14: Division by " << x
             << endl;                                   //Line 14
    }

    return 0;                                           //Line 15
}
```

Sample Run 1: In this sample run, the user input is shaded.

```
Line 3: Enter the dividend: 14

Line 6: Enter the divisor: 5

Line 12: Quotient = 2
```

Sample Run 2: In this sample run, the user input is shaded.

```
Line 3: Enter the dividend: 23

Line 6: Enter the divisor: 0

Line 14: Division by 0
```

This program works the same way as the program in Example 14-5.

The program in Example 14-7 illustrates how to handle division by zero, division by a negative integer, and input failure exceptions. It also shows how to throw and catch an object. This program is similar to the programs in Examples 14-5 and 14-6.

EXAMPLE 14-7

```cpp
// Handle division by zero, division by a negative integer,
// and input failure exceptions.

#include <iostream>
#include <string>

using namespace std;

int main()
{
    int dividend, divisor = 1, quotient;               //Line 1

    string inpStr
        = "The input stream is in the fail state.";    //Line 2

    try                                                //Line 3
    {
        cout << "Line 4: Enter the dividend: ";        //Line 4
        cin >> dividend;                               //Line 5
        cout << endl;                                  //Line 6

        cout << "Line 7: Enter the divisor: ";         //Line 7
        cin >> divisor;                                //Line 8
        cout << endl;                                  //Line 9

        if (divisor == 0)                              //Line 10
            throw divisor;                             //Line 11
        else if (divisor < 0)                          //Line 12
            throw string("Negative divisor.");         //Line 13
        else if (!cin)                                 //Line 14
            throw inpStr;                              //Line 15

        quotient = dividend / divisor;                 //Line 16

        cout << "Line 17: Quotient = " << quotient
            << endl;                                   //Line 17
    }
    catch (int x)                                      //Line 18
    {
        cout << "Line 19: Division by " << x
            << endl;                                   //Line 19
    }
    catch (string s)                                   //Line 20
    {
        cout << "Line 21: " << s << endl;              //Line 21
    }

    return 0;                                          //Line 22
}
```

Sample Run 1: In this sample run, the user input is shaded.

```
Line 4: Enter the dividend: 23

Line 7: Enter the divisor: 6

Line 17: Quotient = 3
```

Sample Run 2: In this sample run, the user input is shaded.

```
Line 4: Enter the dividend: 34

Line 7: Enter the divisor: -6

Line 21: Negative divisor.
```

Sample Run 3: In this sample run, the user input is shaded.

```
Line 4: Enter the dividend: 34

Line 7: Enter the divisor: g

Line 21: The input stream is in the fail state.
```

In this program, the statements in Lines 1 and 2 declare the variables used in the program. Notice that the `string` object `inpStr` is also initialized.

The statements in Lines 4 through 9 input the data into the variables `dividend` and `divisor`. The statement in Line 10 checks whether `divisor` is 0, the statement in Line 12 checks whether `divisor` is negative, and the statement in Line 14 checks whether the standard input stream is in the fail state.

The statement in Line 11 throws the variable `divisor`, the statement in Line 13 throws an anonymous string object with the string `"Negative divisor."`, and the statement in Line 15 throws the object `inpStr`.

The `catch` block in Line 18 catches an exception of type `int`, and the `catch` block in Line 20 catches an exception of type `string`. If the exception is thrown by the statement in Line 11, it is caught and processed by the `catch` block in Line 18. If the exception is thrown by the statements in Lines 13 or 15, it is caught and processed by the `catch` block in Line 20.

In Sample Run 1, the program does not encounter any problems. In Sample Run 2, division by a negative number occurs. In Sample Run 3, the standard input stream enters the fail state.

Using C++ Exception Classes

C++ provides support to handle exceptions via a hierarchy of classes. The `class` `exception` is the base of the classes designed to handle exceptions. Among others, this class contains the function `what`. The function `what` returns a string containing an appropriate message. All derived classes of the `class` exception override the function `what` to issue their own error messages.

Two classes are immediately derived from the `class` exception: `logic_error` and `runtime_error`. Both of these classes are defined in the header file `stdexcept`.

To deal with logical errors in a program, such as a string subscript out of range or an invalid argument to a function call, several classes are derived from the `class` `logic_error`. For example, the `class` `invalid_argument` is designed to deal with illegal arguments used in a function call. The `class` `out_of_range` deals with the string subscript out of range error. If a length greater than the maximum allowed for a string object is used, the `class` `length_error` deals with this error. For example, recall that every string object has a maximum length (see Chapter 7). If a length larger then the maximum length allowed for a string is used, then the `length_error` exception is generated. If the operator `new` cannot allocate memory space, this operator throws a `bad_alloc` exception.

The `class` `runtime_error` is designed to deal with errors that can be detected only during program execution. For example, to deal with arithmetic overflow and underflow exceptions, the `classes` `overflow_error` and `underflow_error` are derived from the `class` `runtime_error`.

Examples 14-8 and 14-9 illustrate how C++'s exception classes are used to handle exceptions in a program.

The program in Example 14-8 shows how to handle the exceptions `out_of_range` and `length_error`. Notice that in this program, these exceptions are thrown by the string functions `substr` and the string concatenation operator +. Because the exceptions are thrown by these functions, we do not include any `throw` statement in the `try` block.

EXAMPLE 14-8

```
// Handling out_of_range and length_error exceptions.

#include <iostream>
#include <string>

using namespace std;

int main()
{
    string sentence;                                    //Line 1
    string str1, str2, str3;                            //Line 2

    try                                                 //Line 3
    {
        sentence = "Testing string exceptions!";        //Line 4
        cout << "Line 5: sentence = " << sentence
             << endl;                                   //Line 5
```

```
        cout << "Line 6: sentence.length() = "
             << static_cast<int>(sentence.length())
             << endl;                                //Line 6

        str1 = sentence.substr(8, 20);              //Line 7
        cout << "Line 8: str1 = " << str1
             << endl;                                //Line 8

        str2 = sentence.substr(28, 10);             //Line 9
        cout << "Line 10: str2 = " << str2
             << endl;                                //Line 10

        str3 = "Exception handling. " + sentence;   //Line 11
        cout << "Line 12: str3 = " << str3
             << endl;                                //Line 12

    }
    catch (out_of_range re)                          //Line 13
    {
        cout << "Line 14: In the out_of_range "
             << "catch block: " << re.what()
             << endl;                                //Line 14
    }
    catch (length_error le)                          //Line 15
    {
        cout << "Line 16: In the length_error "
             << "catch block: " << le.what()
             << endl;                                //Line 16
    }

    return 0;                                        //Line 17
}
```

Sample Run:

```
Line 5: sentence = Testing string exceptions!
Line 6: sentence.length() = 26
Line 8: str1 = string exceptions!
Line 14: In the out_of_range catch block: invalid string position
```

In this program, the statement in Line 7 uses the function substr to determine a substring in the string object sentence. The length of the string sentence is 26. Because the starting position of the substring is 8, which is less than 26, no exception is thrown. However, in the statement in Line 9, the starting position of the substring is 28, which is greater than 26 (the length of sentence). Therefore, the function substr throws an out_of_range exception, which is caught and processed by the catch block in Line 13. Notice that in the statement in Line 14, the object re uses the function what to return the error message, invalid string position.

The program in Example 14-9 illustrates how to handle the exception bad_alloc thrown by the operator new.

1
4

EXAMPLE 14-9

```cpp
// Handling bad_alloc exception thrown by the operator new.

#include <iostream>

using namespace std;

int main()
{
    int *list[100];                              //Line 1

    try                                          //Line 2
    {
        for (int i = 0; i < 100; i++)            //Line 3
        {
            list[i] = new int[50000000];         //Line 4
            cout << "Line 4: Created list[" << i
                 << "] of 50000000 components."
                 << endl;                        //Line 5
        }
    }
    catch (bad_alloc be)                         //Line 6
    {
        cout << "Line 7: In the bad_alloc catch "
             << "block: " << be.what() << "."
             << endl;                            //Line 7
    }

    return 0;                                    //Line 8
}
```

Sample Run:

```
Line 4: Created list[0] of 50000000 components.
Line 4: Created list[1] of 50000000 components.
Line 4: Created list[2] of 50000000 components.
Line 4: Created list[3] of 50000000 components.
Line 4: Created list[4] of 50000000 components.
Line 4: Created list[5] of 50000000 components.
Line 4: Created list[6] of 50000000 components.
Line 4: Created list[7] of 50000000 components.
Line 7: In the bad_alloc catch block: bad allocation.
```

The preceding program works as follows. The statement in Line 1 declares list to be an array of 100 pointers. The body of the for loop in Line 3 is designed to execute 100 times. For each iteration of the for loop, the statement in Line 4 uses the operator new to allocate an array of 50000000 components of type int. As shown in the sample run, the operator new is able to create eight arrays of 50000000 components each. In the ninth iteration, the operator new is unable to create the array and throws a bad_alloc exception. This exception is caught and processed by the `catch` block in Line 6. Notice that the expression `be.what()` returns the string `bad allocation`. (Moreover, the string returned by `be.what()` is IDE dependent. Some IDEs might return the string `bad_alloc`.) After the statement in Line 7 executes, control exits the `try/catch` block, and the statement in Line 8 terminates the program.

Creating Your Own Exception Classes

Watch the Video

Whenever you create your own classes or write programs, exceptions are likely to occur. As you have seen, C++ provides numerous exception classes to deal with these situations. However, it does not provide all of the exception classes you will ever need. Therefore, C++ enables programmers to create their own exception classes to handle both the exceptions not covered by C++'s exception classes and their own exceptions. This section describes how to create your own exception classes.

C++ uses the same mechanism to process the exceptions that you define as it uses for built-in exceptions. However, you must throw your own exceptions using the `throw` statement.

In C++, any class can be considered an exception class. Therefore, an exception class is simply a class. It need not be inherited from the `class` `exception`. What makes a class an exception is how you use it.

The exception class that you define can be very simple in the sense that it does not contain any members. For example, the following code can be considered an exception class:

```
class dummyExceptionClass
{
};
```

The program in Example 14-10 uses a user-defined class (with no members) to throw an exception.

EXAMPLE 14-10

```
// Using a user-defined exception class.

#include <iostream>

using namespace std;

class divByZero
{};

int main()
{
    int dividend, divisor, quotient;            //Line 1
```

1
4

```
    try                                                //Line 2
    {
        cout << "Line 3: Enter the dividend: ";        //Line 3
        cin >> dividend;                               //Line 4
        cout << endl;                                  //Line 5

        cout << "Line 6: Enter the divisor: ";         //Line 6
        cin >> divisor;                                //Line 7
        cout << endl;                                  //Line 8

        if (divisor == 0)                              //Line 9
            throw divByZero();                         //Line 10

        quotient = dividend / divisor;                 //Line 11
        cout << "Line 12: Quotient = " << quotient
             << endl;                                  //Line 12
    }
    catch (divByZero)                                  //Line 13
    {
        cout << "Line 14: Division by zero!"
             << endl;                                  //Line 14
    }

    return 0;                                          //Line 15
}
```

Sample Run 1: In this sample run, the user input is shaded.

```
Line 3: Enter the dividend: 34

Line 6: Enter the divisor: 5

Line 12: Quotient = 6
```

Sample Run 2: In this sample run, the user input is shaded.

```
Line 3: Enter the dividend: 56

Line 6: Enter the divisor: 0

Line 14: Division by zero!
```

The preceding program works as follows. If the user enters 0 for the divisor, the statement in Line 10 throws an anonymous object of the `class divByZero`. The `class divByZero` has no members, so we cannot really do anything with the thrown object. Therefore, in the `catch` block in Line 13, we specify only the data type name without the parameter name. The statement in Line 14 outputs the appropriate error message.

Let us again consider the statement `throw divByZero();` in Line 10. Notice that in this statement, `divByZero` is the name of the class, the expression `divByZero()` creates an anonymous object of this class, and the `throw` statement throws the object.

The exception `class` `divByZero` designed and used in Example 14-10 has no members. Next, we illustrate how to create exception classes with members.

If you want to include members in your exception class, you typically include constructors and the function `what`. Consider the following definition of the `class` `divisionByZero`.

```
// User-defined exception class.

#include <iostream>
#include <string>

using namespace std;

class divisionByZero                          //Line 1
{                                             //Line 2
public:                                       //Line 3
    divisionByZero()                          //Line 4
    {
        message = "Division by zero";         //Line 5
    }                                         //Line 6

    divisionByZero(string str)                //Line 7
    {                                         //Line 8
        message = str;                        //Line 9
    }                                         //Line 10

    string what()                             //Line 11
    {                                         //Line 12
        return message;                       //Line 13
    }                                         //Line 14

private:                                      //Line 15
    string message;                           //Line 16
};                                            //Line 17
```

The definition of the `class` `divisionByZero` contains two constructors: the default constructor and the constructor with parameters. The default constructor stores the string `"Division by zero"` in an object. The constructor with parameters allows users to create their own error messages. The function `what` is used to return the string stored in the object.

 NOTE   In the definition of the `class` `divisionByZero`, the constructors can also be written as:

```
divisionByZero() : message("Division by zero"){}
divisionByZero(string str) : message(str){}
```

The program in Example 14-11 uses the preceding class to throw an exception.

1
4

EXAMPLE 14-11

```
// Using user-defined exception class divisionByZero with
// default error message.

#include <iostream>
#include "divisionByZero.h"

using namespace std;

int main()
{
    int dividend, divisor, quotient;                        //Line 1

    try                                                     //Line 2
    {
        cout << "Line 3: Enter the dividend: ";             //Line 3
        cin >> dividend;                                    //Line 4
        cout << endl;                                       //Line 5

        cout << "Line 6: Enter the divisor: ";              //Line 6
        cin >> divisor;                                     //Line 7
        cout << endl;                                       //Line 8

        if (divisor == 0)                                   //Line 9
            throw divisionByZero();                         //Line 10

        quotient = dividend / divisor;                      //Line 11
        cout << "Line 12: Quotient = " << quotient
             << endl;                                       //Line 12
    }
    catch (divisionByZero divByZeroObj)                     //Line 13
    {
        cout << "Line 14: In the divisionByZero "
             << "catch block: "
             << divByZeroObj.what() << endl;                //Line 14
    }

    return 0;                                               //Line 15
}
```

Sample Run 1: In this sample run, the user input is shaded.

```
Line 3: Enter the dividend: 34

Line 6: Enter the divisor: 5

Line 12: Quotient = 6
```

Sample Run 2: In this sample run, the user input is shaded.

Line 3: Enter the dividend: 56

Line 6: Enter the divisor: 0

Line 14: In the divisionByZero catch block: Division by zero

In this program, the statement in Line 10 throws an object (exception) of the `class` `divisionByZero` if the user enters 0 for the `divisor`. This thrown exception is caught and processed by the `catch` block in Line 13. The parameter `divByZeroObj` in the `catch` block catches the value of the thrown object and then uses the function `what` to return the string stored in the object. The statement in Line 14 outputs the appropriate error message.

The program in Example 14-12 is similar to the program in Example 14-11. Here, the thrown object is still an anonymous object, but the error message is specified by the user (see the statement in Line 10).

EXAMPLE 14-12

```cpp
// Using user-defined exception class divisionByZero with a
// specific error message.

#include <iostream>
#include "divisionByZero.h"

using namespace std;

int main()
{
    int dividend, divisor, quotient;            //Line 1

    try                                          //Line 2
    {
        cout << "Line 3: Enter the dividend: "; //Line 3
        cin >> dividend;                         //Line 4
        cout << endl;                            //Line 5

        cout << "Line 6: Enter the divisor: ";   //Line 6
        cin >> divisor;                          //Line 7
        cout << endl;                            //Line 8

        if (divisor == 0)                                       //Line 9
            throw divisionByZero("Found division by zero"); //Line 10

        quotient = dividend / divisor;           //Line 11
        cout << "Line 12: Quotient = " << quotient
             << endl;                            //Line 12
    }
```

14

```
    catch(divisionByZero divByZeroObj)                          //Line 13
    {
        cout << "Line 14: In the divisionByZero "
            << "catch block: "
            << divByZeroObj.what() << endl;                     //Line 14
    }

    return 0;                                                   //Line 15
}
```

Sample Run 1: In this sample run, the user input is shaded.

Line 3: Enter the dividend: 34

Line 6: Enter the divisor: 5

Line 12: Quotient = 6

Sample Run 2: In this sample run, the user input is shaded.

Line 3: Enter the dividend: 56

Line 6: Enter the divisor: 0

Line 14: In the divisionByZero catch block: Found division by zero

This program works the same way as the program in Example 14-11. The details are left as an exercise for you.

In the programs in Examples 14-11 and 14-12, the data manipulation is done in the function main. Therefore, the exception is thrown, caught, and processed in the function main. The program in Example 14-13 uses the user-defined function doDivision to manipulate the data. Therefore, the exception is thrown, caught, and processed in the function doDivision.

EXAMPLE 14-13

```
// Handling an exception thrown by a function.

#include <iostream>
#include "divisionByZero.h"

using namespace std;

void doDivision();

int main()
{
    doDivision();                                               //Line 1

    return 0;                                                   //Line 2
}
```

```
void doDivision()
{
    int dividend, divisor, quotient;                    //Line 3

    try
    {
        cout << "Line 4: Enter the dividend: ";         //Line 4
        cin >> dividend;                                //Line 5
        cout << endl;                                   //Line 6

        cout << "Line 7: Enter the divisor: ";          //Line 7
        cin >> divisor;                                 //Line 8
        cout << endl;                                   //Line 9

        if (divisor == 0)                               //Line 10
            throw divisionByZero();                     //Line 11

        quotient = dividend / divisor;                  //Line 12
        cout << "Line 13: Quotient = " << quotient
            << endl;                                    //Line 13
    }
    catch (divisionByZero divByZeroObj)                 //Line 14
    {
        cout << "Line 15: In the function "
            << "doDivision: "
            << divByZeroObj.what() << endl;             //Line 15
    }
}
```

Sample Run 1: In this sample run, the user input is shaded.

```
Line 4: Enter the dividend: 34

Line 7: Enter the divisor: 5

Line 13: Quotient = 6
```

Sample Run 2: In this sample run, the user input is shaded.

```
Line 4: Enter the dividend: 56

Line 7: Enter the divisor: 0

Line 15: In the function doDivision: Division by zero
```

EXAMPLE 14-14

Example 10-8 defined the **class** circleType to implement the basic properties of a circle. If a circleType object tries to set the radius to a negative number, then the function setRadius of this class sets the radius to 0. In this example, first we define the **class** negativeNumber to handle negative number exceptions and then use this class to throw an exception if a circleType object tries to set the radius to a negative number. So consider the following class:

1
4

```cpp
// User-defined exception class.

#include <iostream>
#include <string>

using namespace std;

class negativeNumber
{
public:
    negativeNumber()
    {
        message = "Number cannot be negative";
    }

    negativeNumber(string str)
    {
        message = str + " cannot be negative";
    }

    string what()
    {
        return message;
    }

private:
    string message;
};
```

Note that the definition of the `class negativeNumber` is similar to the definition of the `class divisionByZero`.

The definition of the `class circleType` is the same as in Example 10-8, except for the definition of function `setRadius`. The modified definition of this function is:

```cpp
void circleType::setRadius(double r)
{
    if (r < 0)
        throw negativeNumber("Radius");

    radius = r;
}
```

If the value of the parameter `r` is a negative number, the function `setRadius` throws a `negativeNumber` object. In this case, the value of the instance variable `message` of the object thrown is `"Radius cannot be negative"`. The user program will handle the exception, if any, thrown by this function.

Consider the following program:

```cpp
//The user program that uses the class circleType

#include <iostream>
#include <iomanip>
#include "circleType.h"
#include "negativeNumber.h"
```

```
using namespace std;

int main()                                                        //Line 1
{                                                                 //Line 2
    circleType circle;                                            //Line 3

    double radius;                                                //Line 4

    cout << fixed << showpoint << setprecision(2);                //Line 5

    try                                                           //Line 6
    {                                                             //Line 7
        cout << "Line 8: Enter the radius of a circle: ";         //Line 8
        cin >> radius;                                            //Line 9
        cout << endl;                                             //Line 10

        circle.setRadius(radius);                                 //Line 11

        cout << "Line 12: circle - "
             << "radius: " << circle.getRadius()
             << ", area: " << circle.area()
             << ", circumference: "
             << circle.circumference() << endl;                   //Line 12
    }                                                             //Line 13
    catch (negativeNumber obj)                                    //Line 14
    {                                                             //Line 15
        cout << "Line 16: " << obj.what() << endl;                //Line 16
    }                                                             //Line 17

    return 0;                                                     //Line 18
}//end main                                                       //Line 19
```

Sample Run 1: In this sample run, the user input is shaded.

Line 8: Enter the radius of a circle: 4.75

Line 12: circle - radius: 4.75, area: 70.88, circumference: 29.85

Sample Run 2: In this sample run, the user input is shaded.

Line 8: Enter the radius of a circle: -2.65

Line 16: Radius cannot be negative

The preceding program works as follows. The statement in Line 3 creates the `circleType` object `circle` and using the default constructor sets the radius to `0.0`. The statement in Line 4 declares the `double` variable `radius`. The `try/catch` block between Lines 7 and 17 contains the code to prompt the user to enter the radius of the circle and, depending on the value entered by the user, generates the output. For example, if the user enters a nonnegative radius, the statement in Line 11 sets the radius of the circle and the statement in Line 12 outputs the radius, area, and the perimeter of the circle. If the user enters a negative number, the statement in Line 11 throws an exception, which is a `negativeNumber` object, and the `catch` block processes the exception. In Sample Run 1, the user enters `4.75`, a nonnegative number, and the program outputs the radius, area, and the perimeter of the circle. In Sample Run 2, the user enters `-2.65`, which is a negative number, and the statement in Line 16 outputs that the radius cannot be negative.

Rethrowing and Throwing an Exception

When an exception occurs in a `try` block, control immediately passes to one of the `catch` blocks. Typically, a `catch` block either handles the exception or partially processes the exception and then rethrows the same exception, or it rethrows another exception in order for the calling environment to handle the exception. The `catch` block in Examples 14-4 through 14-14 handles the exception. The mechanism of rethrowing or throwing an exception is quite useful in cases in which a `catch` block catches the exception but cannot handle the exception, or if the `catch` block decides that the exception should be handled by the calling block or environment. This allows the programmer to provide the exception-handling code all in one place.

To rethrow or throw an exception, we use the `throw` statement. The general syntax to rethrow an exception caught by a `catch` block is:

```
throw;
```

(in this case, the same exception is rethrown) or:

```
throw expression;
```

in which `expression` is a constant value, variable, or object. The object being thrown can be either a specific object or an anonymous object.

A function specifies the exceptions it throws (to be handled somewhere) in its heading using the `throw` clause. For example, the following function specifies that it throws exceptions of type `int`, `string`, and `divisionByZero`, in which `divisionByZero` is the class, as defined previously.

```
void expThrowExcep(int x) throw (int, string, divisionByZero)
{
    .
    .
    .
    //include the appropriate throw statements
    .
    .
    .
}
```

The program in Example 14-15 further explains how a function specifies the exception it throws.

EXAMPLE 14-15

```
// Handling an exception, in the main function, thrown by another
// function. The function throws the same exception object.

#include <iostream>
#include "divisionByZero.h"
```

```cpp
using namespace std;

void doDivision() throw (divisionByZero);

int main()                                                        //Line 1
{
    try                                                           //Line 2
    {
        doDivision();
    }
    catch (divisionByZero divByZeroObj)                           //Line 3
    {
        cout << "Line 4: In main: "
             << divByZeroObj.what() << endl;                      //Line 4

        return 0;                                                 //Line 5
    }
}

void doDivision() throw (divisionByZero)
{
    int dividend, divisor, quotient;                              //Line 6

    try                                                           //Line 7
    {
        cout << "Line 8: Enter the dividend: ";                   //Line 8
        cin >> dividend;                                          //Line 9
        cout << endl;                                             //Line 10

        cout << "Line 11: Enter the divisor: ";                   //Line 11
        cin >> divisor;                                           //Line 12
        cout << endl;                                             //Line 13

        if (divisor == 0)                                         //Line 14
            throw divisionByZero("Found division by 0!");         //Line 15

        quotient = dividend / divisor;                            //Line 16
        cout << "Line 17: Quotient = " << quotient
             << endl;                                             //Line 17
    }
    catch (divisionByZero)                                        //Line 18
    {
        throw;                                                    //Line 19
    }
}
```

Sample Run 1: In this sample run, the user input is shaded.

```
Line 8: Enter the dividend: 34

Line 11: Enter the divisor: 5

Line 17: Quotient = 6
```

14

Sample Run 2: In this sample run, the user input is shaded.

```
Line 8: Enter the dividend: 56
```

```
Line 11: Enter the divisor: 0
```

```
Line 4: In main: Found division by 0!
```

In this program, if the value of `divisor` is 0, the statement in Line 15 throws an exception of type `divisionByZero`, which is an anonymous object of this class, with the message string:

```
"Found division by 0!"
```

The statement in Line 19, in the `catch` block, throws the same exception value, which in this case is an object.

In Sample Run 1, no exception is thrown.

Let us see what happens in Sample Run 2. The function `main` calls the function `doDivision` in the `try` block. In the function `doDivision`, the value of `divisor` is 0, so the statement in Line 15 throws an exception. The exception is caught by the `catch` block in Line 18. The statement in Line 19 rethrows the same exception. In other words, the `catch` block catches and rethrows the same exception. Therefore, the function call statement in Line 2 results in throwing an exception. This exception is caught and processed by the `catch` block in Line 3.

EXAMPLE 14-16

```cpp
// Handling exception, in the main function, thrown by another
// function. The function throws a different exception object.

#include <iostream>
#include "divisionByZero.h"

using namespace std;

void doDivision() throw (divisionByZero);

int main()
{
    try                                             //Line 1
    {
        doDivision();                               //Line 2
    }
    catch (divisionByZero divByZeroObj)             //Line 3
    {
        cout << "Line 4: In main: "
             << divByZeroObj.what() << endl;        //Line 4
    }

    return 0;                                        //Line 5
}
```

```
void doDivision() throw (divisionByZero)
{
    int dividend, divisor, quotient;                    //Line 6

    try                                                 //Line 7
    {
        cout << "Line 8: Enter the dividend: ";         //Line 8
        cin >> dividend;                                //Line 9
        cout << endl;                                   //Line 10

        cout << "Line 11: Enter the divisor: ";         //Line 11
        cin >> divisor;                                 //Line 12
        cout << endl;                                   //Line 13

        if (divisor == 0)                               //Line 14
            throw divisionByZero();                     //Line 15

        quotient = dividend / divisor;                  //Line 16
        cout << "Line 17: Quotient = " << quotient
                << endl;                                //Line 17
    }
    catch (divisionByZero)                              //Line 18
    {
        throw
            divisionByZero("Division by zero found!");  //Line 19
    }
}
```

Sample Run 1: In this sample run, the user input is shaded.

```
Line 8: Enter the dividend: 34

Line 11: Enter the divisor: 5

Line 17: Quotient = 6
```

Sample Run 2: In this sample run, the user input is shaded.

```
Line 8: Enter the dividend: 56

Line 11: Enter the divisor: 0

Line 4: In main: Division by zero found!
```

This program works the same way as the program in Example 14-15. The only difference is that here, the `catch` block in Line 18 rethrows a different exception value, that is, object.

The programs in Examples 14-15 and 14-16 illustrate how a function can rethrow the same exception or throw another exception for the calling function to handle. This mechanism is quite useful because it allows a program to handle all of the exceptions in one location, rather than spread the exception-handling code throughout the program.

Exception-Handling Techniques

When an exception occurs in a program, the programmer usually has three choices: terminate the program, include code in the program to recover from the exception, or log the error and continue. The following sections discuss each of these situations.

Terminate the Program

In some cases, it is best to let the program terminate when an exception occurs. Suppose you have written a program that inputs data from a file. If the input file does not exist when the program executes, then there is no point in continuing with the program. In this case, the program can output an appropriate error message and terminate.

Fix the Error and Continue

In other cases, you will want to handle the exception and let the program continue. Suppose that you have a program that takes as input an integer. If a user inputs a letter in place of a number, the input stream will enter the fail state. This is a situation in which you can include the necessary code to keep prompting the user to input a number until the entry is valid. The program in Example 14-17 illustrates this situation.

EXAMPLE 14-17

```cpp
// Handle exceptions by fixing the errors. The program continues to
// prompt the user until a valid input is entered.

#include <iostream>
#include <string>

using namespace std;

int main()
{
    int number;                                    //Line 1
    bool done = false;                             //Line 2

    string str =
        "The input stream is in the fail state.";  //Line 3

    do                                             //Line 4
    {                                              //Line 5
        try                                        //Line 6
        {                                          //Line 7
            cout << "Line 8: Enter an integer: ";  //Line 8
            cin >> number;                         //Line 9
```

```
        cout << endl;                          //Line 10

        if (!cin)                              //Line 11
            throw str;                         //Line 12

        done = true;                           //Line 13
        cout << "Line 14: Number = " << number
            << endl;                           //Line 14
                                               //Line 15
    }                                          //Line 16
    catch (string messageStr)                  //Line 17
    {
        cout << "Line 18: " << messageStr
            << endl;                           //Line 18
        cout << "Line 19: Restoring the "
            << "input stream." << endl;        //Line 19
        cin.clear();                           //Line 20
        cin.ignore(100, '\n');                 //Line 21
    }                                          //Line 22

}
while (!done);                                 //Line 23

return 0;                                       //Line 24
}
```

Sample Run: In this sample run, the user input is shaded.

```
Line 8: Enter an integer: r5

Line 18: The input stream is in the fail state.
Line 19: Restoring the input stream.
Line 8: Enter an integer: d45

Line 18: The input stream is in the fail state.
Line 19: Restoring the input stream.
Line 8: Enter an integer: hw3

Line 18: The input stream is in the fail state.
Line 19: Restoring the input stream.
Line 8: Enter an integer: 48

Line 14: Number = 48
```

This program prompts the user to enter an integer. If the input is invalid, the standard input stream enters the fail state. In the `try` block, the statement in Line 12 throws an exception, which is a string object. Control passes to the `catch` block, and the exception is caught and processed. The statement in Line 20 restores the input stream to its good state, and the statement in Line 21 clears the rest of the input from the line. The `do...while` loop continues to prompt the user until the user inputs a valid number.

14

Log the Error and Continue

The program that terminates when an exception occurs usually assumes that this termination is reasonably safe. However, if your program is designed to run a nuclear reactor or continuously monitor a satellite, it cannot be terminated if an exception occurs. These programs should report the exception, but the program must continue to run.

For example, consider a program that analyzes an airline's ticketing transactions. Because numerous ticketing transactions occur each day, a program is run at the end of each day to validate that day's transactions. This type of program would take an enormous amount of time to process the transactions and use exceptions to identify any erroneous entries. Instead, when an exception occurs, the program should write the exception into a file and continue to analyze the transactions.

Stack Unwinding

The examples given in this chapter show how to catch and process an exception. In particular, you learned how to catch and process an exception in the same block, as well as process the caught exception in the calling environment.

When an exception is thrown in, say, a function, the function can do the following:

- Do nothing.
- Partially process the exception and throw the same exception or a new exception.
- Throw a new exception.

In each of these cases, the function-call stack is unwound so that the exception can be caught in the next `try/catch` block. When the function call stack is unwound, the function in which the exception was not caught and/or rethrown terminates, and the memory for its local variables is destroyed. The stack unwinding continues until either a `try/catch` handles the exception or the program does not handle the exception. If the program does not handle the exception, then the function `terminate` is called to terminate the program.

Examples 14-18 and 14-19 illustrate how the exceptions are propagated. For this, let us define the following exception class:

```
// User-defined myException class.

#include <string>

using namespace std;
```

```
class myException
{
public:
    myException()
    {
        message = "Something is wrong!";
    }

    myException(string str)
    {
        message = str;
    }

    string what()
    {
        return message;
    }

private:
    string message;
};
```

NOTE

In the definition of the **class** myException, the constructors can also be written as follows:

```
myException() : message("Something is wrong!"){}
myException(string str) : message(str){}
```

The program in Example 14-18 illustrates how exceptions thrown in a function get processed in the calling environment.

EXAMPLE 14-18

```
// Processing exceptions thrown by a function in the calling
// environment.

#include <iostream>
#include "myException.h"

using namespace std;

void functionA() throw (myException);
void functionB() throw (myException);
void functionC() throw (myException);

int main()
{
    try
    {
        functionA();
    }
```

1
4

```
    catch (myException me)
    {
        cout << me.what() << " Caught in main." << endl;
    }

    return 0;
}

void functionA() throw (myException)
{
    functionB();
}

void functionB()  throw (myException)
{
    functionC();
}

void functionC() throw (myException)
{
    throw myException("Exception generated in function C.");
}
```

Sample Run:

```
Exception generated in function C. Caught in main.
```

In this program, the function main calls functionA, functionA calls functionB, and functionB calls functionC. The function functionC creates and throws an exception of type myException. The functions functionA and functionB do not process the exception thrown by functionC.

The function main calls functionA in the try block and catches the exception thrown by functionC. The parameter me in the catch block heading catches the value of the exception and then uses the function what to return the string stored in that object. The output statement in the catch block outputs the appropriate message.

The program in Example 14-19 is similar to the program in Example 14-18. Here, the exception is caught and processed by the immediate calling environment.

EXAMPLE 14-19

```
// Processing exceptions, thrown by a function, in the
// immediate calling environment.

#include <iostream>
#include "myException.h"
```

```cpp
using namespace std;

void functionA();
void functionB();
void functionC() throw (myException);

int main()
{
    try
    {
        functionA();
    }
    catch (myException e)
    {
        cout << e.what() << " Caught in main." << endl;
    }

    return 0;
}

void functionA()
{
    functionB();
}

void functionB()
{
    try
    {
        functionC();
    }
    catch (myException me)
    {
        cout << me.what() << " Caught in functionB." << endl;
    }
}

void functionC() throw (myException)
{
    throw myException("Exception generated in functionC.");
}
```

Sample Run:

```
Exception generated in functionC. Caught in functionB.
```

In this program, the exception is caught and processed by functionB. Even though the function main contains the try/catch block, the try block does not throw any exceptions because the exception thrown by functionC is caught and processed by functionB.

14

QUICK REVIEW

1. An exception is an occurrence of an undesirable situation that can be detected during program execution.

2. Some typical ways of dealing with exceptions are to use an `if` statement or the `assert` function.

3. The function `assert` can check whether an expression meets the required condition(s). If the conditions are not met, it terminates the program.

4. The `try/catch` block is used to handle exceptions within a program.

5. Statements that may generate an exception are placed in a `try` block. The `try` block also contains statements that should not be executed if an exception occurs.

6. The `try` block is followed by one or more `catch` blocks.

7. A `catch` block specifies the type of exception it can catch and contains an exception handler.

8. If the heading of a `catch` block contains...(ellipses) in place of parameters, then this `catch` block can catch exceptions of all types.

9. If no exceptions are thrown in a `try` block, all `catch` blocks associated with that `try` block are ignored and program execution resumes after the last `catch` block.

10. If an exception is thrown in a `try` block, the remaining statements in the `try` block are ignored. The program searches the `catch` blocks, in the order they appear after the `try` block, and looks for an appropriate exception handler. If the type of the thrown exception matches the parameter type in one of the `catch` blocks, then the code in that `catch` block executes and the remaining `catch` blocks after this `catch` block are ignored.

11. The data type of the `catch` block parameter specifies the type of exception that the `catch` block can catch.

12. A `catch` block can have, at most, one `catch` block parameter.

13. If only the data type is specified in a `catch` block heading, that is, if there is no `catch` block parameter, then the thrown value may not be accessible in the `catch` block exception-handling code.

14. In order for an exception to occur in a `try` block and be caught by a `catch` block, the exception must be thrown in the `try` block.

15. The general syntax to `throw` an exception is:

    `throw expression;`

    in which `expression` is a constant value, variable, or object. The object being thrown can be either a specific object or an anonymous object.

16. C++ provides support to handle exceptions via a hierarchy of classes.

17. The **class** exception is the base class of the exception classes provided by C++.

18. The function **what** returns the string containing the exception object thrown by C++'s built-in exception classes.

19. The **class** exception is contained in the header file **exception**.

20. The two classes that are immediately derived from the **class** exception are **logic_error** and **runtime_error**. Both of these classes are defined in the header file **stdexcept**.

21. The **class invalid_argument** is designed to deal with illegal arguments used in a function call.

22. The **class out_of_range** deals with the string subscript **out_of_range** error.

23. If a length greater than the maximum allowed for a string object is used, the **class length_error** deals with the error that occurs when a length greater than the maximum size allowed for the object being manipulated is used.

24. If the operator **new** cannot allocate memory space, this operator throws a **bad_alloc** exception.

25. The **class runtime_error** is designed to deal with errors that can be detected only during program execution. For example, to deal with arithmetic overflow and underflow exceptions, the classes **overflow_error** and **underflow_error** are derived from the **class runtime_error**.

26. A **catch** block typically handles the exception or partially processes the exception and then either rethrows the same exception or rethrows another exception in order for the calling environment to handle the exception.

27. C++ enables programmers to create their own exception classes to handle both the exceptions not covered by C++'s exception classes and their own exceptions.

28. C++ uses the same mechanism to process the exceptions you define as it uses for built-in exceptions. However, you must throw your own exceptions using the **throw** statement.

29. In C++, any class can be considered an exception class. It need not be inherited from the **class** exception. What makes a class an exception is how it is used.

30. The general syntax to rethrow an exception caught by a **catch** block is:

    `throw;`

    (in this case, the same exception is rethrown) or:

    `throw expression;`

    in which **expression** is a constant value, variable, or object. The object being thrown can be either a specific object or an anonymous object.

1
4

31. A function specifies the exceptions it throws in its heading using the `throw` clause.

32. When an exception is thrown in a function, the function can do the following: do nothing; partially process the exception and throw the same exception or a new exception; or throw a new exception. In each of these cases, the function-call stack is unwound so that the exception can be caught in the next `try/catch` block. The stack unwinding continues until a `try/catch` handles the exception or the program does not handle the exception.

33. If the program does not handle the exception, then the function `terminate` is called to terminate the program.

EXERCISES

1. Mark the following statements as true or false.

    a. The order in which `catch` blocks are listed is not important.

    b. An exception can be caught either in the function where it occurred or in any of the functions that led to the invocation of this method.

    c. One way to handle an exception is to print an error message and exit the program.

    d. All exceptions need to be reported to avoid compilation errors.

2. What is the difference between a `try` block and a `catch` block?

3. What will happen if an exception is thrown but not caught?

4. What happens if no exception is thrown in a `try` block?

5. What happens if an exception is thrown in a `try` block?

6. What is wrong with the following C++ code? Also, provide the correct code.

```
double balance = 25000;
double intRate;

catch (double x)
{
    cout << "Negative interest rate: " << x << endl;
}
try
{
    cout << "Enter the interest rate: ";
    cin >> intRate;
    cout << endl;

    if (intRate < 0.0)
        throw intRate;

    cout << "Interest: $" << balance * intRate / 100 << endl;
}
```

LIVERPOOL JOHN MOORES UNIVERSITY
LEARNING SERVICES

7. What is wrong with the following C++ code? Also, provide the correct code.

```cpp
double radius;

try
{
    cout << "Enter the radius: ";
    cin >> radius;
    cout << endl;

    if (radius < 0.0)
        throw radius;

    cout << "Area: " << 3.1416 * radius * radius << endl;
}
cout << "Entering the catch block." << endl;
catch (double x)
{
    cout << "Negative radius: " << x << endl;
}
```

8. Consider the following C++ code:

```cpp
double balance;

try
{
    cout << "Enter the balance: ";
    cin >> balance;
    cout << endl;

    if (balance < 1000.00)
        throw balance;

    cout << "Leaving the try block." << endl;
}
catch (double x)
{
    cout << "Current balance: " << x << endl
         << "Balance must be greater than 1000.00" << endl;
}
```

   a. In this code, identify the `try` block.

   b. In this code, identify the `catch` block.

   c. In this code, identify the `catch` block parameter and its type.

   d. In this code, identify the `throw` statement.

9. Assume the code given in Exercise 8.

   a. What is the output if the input is 1200?

   b. What is the output if the input is 975?

   c. What is the output if the input is –2000?

1
4

10. Consider the following C++ code:

```
int lowerLimit;
  .
  .
  .
try
{
    cout << "Entering the try block." << endl;

    if (lowerLimit < 100)
        throw exception("Lower limit violation.");

    cout << "Exiting the try block." << endl;
}
catch (exception eObj)
{
    cout << "Exception: " << eObj.what() << endl;
}
cout << "After the catch block" << endl;
```

What is the output if:

a. The value of lowerLimit is 50?

b. The value of lowerLimit is 150?

11. Consider the following C++ code:

```
int lowerLimit;
int divisor;
int result;

try
{
    cout << "Entering the try block." << endl;

    if (divisor == 0)
        throw 0;
    if (lowerLimit < 100)
        throw string("Lower limit violation.");

    result = lowerLimit / divisor;
    cout << "Exiting the try block." << endl;
}
catch (int x)
{
    cout << "Exception: " << x << endl;
    result = 120;
}
catch (string str)
{
    cout << "Exception: " << str << endl;
}

cout << "After the catch block" << endl;
```

What is the output if:

a. The value of lowerLimit is 50, and the value of divisor is 10?

b. The value of lowerLimit is 50, and the value of divisor is 0?

c. The value of lowerLimit is 150, and the value of divisor is 10?

d. The value of lowerLimit is 150, and the value of divisor is 0?

12. If you define your own exception class, what is typically included in that class?

13. What type of statement is used to rethrow an exception?

14. Define an exception class called tornadoException. The class should have two constructors, including the default constructor. If the exception is thrown with the default constructor, the method what should return "Tornado: Take cover immediately!". The other constructor has a single parameter, say, m, of the int type. If the exception is thrown with this constructor, the method what should return "Tornado: m miles away; and approaching!"

15. Write a C++ program to test the class tornadoException specified in Exercise 14.

16. Suppose the exception class myException is defined as follows:

```cpp
class myException
{
public:
    myException()
    {
        message = "myException thrown!";
        cout << "Immediate attention required!"
            << endl;
    }

    myException(string msg)
    {
        message = msg;
        cout << "Attention required!" << endl;
    }

    string what()
    {
        return message;
    }

private:
    string message;
}
```

Suppose that in a user program, the catch block has the following form:

```cpp
catch (myException mE)
{
    cout << mE.what() << endl;
}
```

What output will be produced if the exception is thrown with the default constructor? Also, what output will be produced if the exception is thrown with the constructor with parameters with the following actual parameter?

`"May Day, May Day"`

17. If a function throws an exception, how does it specify that exception?

18. Name three exception-handling techniques.

PROGRAMMING EXERCISES

1. Write a program that prompts the user to enter a length in feet and inches and outputs the equivalent length in centimeters. If the user enters a negative number or a nondigit number, throw and handle an appropriate exception and prompt the user to enter another set of numbers.

2. Redo Programming Exercise 9 of Chapter 4 so that your program handles exceptions such as division by zero and invalid input.

3. Redo Programming Exercise 7 of Chapter 7 so that your program handles exceptions such as division by zero and invalid input.

4. Write a program that prompts the user to enter time in 12-hour notation. The program then outputs the time in 24-hour notation. Your program must contain three exception classes: `invalidHr`, `invalidMin`, and `invalidSec`. If the user enters an invalid value for hours, then the program should throw and catch an `invalidHr` object. Similar conventions for the invalid values of minutes and seconds.

5. Write a program that prompts the user to enter a person's date of birth in numeric form such as 8-27-1980. The program then outputs the date of birth in the form: August 27, 1980. Your program must contain at least two exception classes: `invalidDay` and `invalidMonth`. If the user enters an invalid value for day, then the program should throw and catch an `invalidDay` object. Similar conventions for the invalid values of month and year. (Note that your program must handle a leap year.)

RECURSION

In previous chapters, to devise solutions to problems, we used the most common technique called iteration. For certain problems, however, using the iterative technique to obtain the solution is quite complicated. This chapter introduces another problem-solving technique called recursion and provides several examples demonstrating how recursion works.

Recursive Definitions

The process of solving a problem by reducing it to smaller versions of itself is called **recursion**. Recursion is a very powerful way to solve certain problems for which the solution would otherwise be very complicated. Let us consider a problem that is familiar to most everyone.

In mathematics, the factorial of a nonnegative integer is defined as follows:

$$0! = 1 \qquad\qquad\qquad (15\text{-}1)$$

$$n! = n \times (n - 1)! \quad \text{if} \quad n > 0 \qquad (15\text{-}2)$$

In this definition, 0! is defined to be 1, and if n is an integer greater than 0, first we find $(n - 1)!$ and then multiply it by n. To find $(n - 1)!$, we apply the definition again. If $(n - 1) > 0$, then we use Equation 15-2; otherwise, we use Equation 15-1. Thus, for an integer n greater than 0, $n!$ is obtained by first finding $(n - 1)!$ (that is, $n!$ is reduced to a smaller version of itself) and then multiplying $(n - 1)!$ by n.

Let us apply this definition to find 3!. Here, $n = 3$. Because $n > 0$, we use Equation 15-2 to obtain:

$$3! = 3 \times 2!$$

Next, we find 2! Here, $n = 2$. Because $n > 0$, we use Equation 15-2 to obtain:

$$2! = 2 \times 1!$$

Now, to find 1!, we again use Equation 15-2 because $n = 1 > 0$. Thus:

$$1! = 1 \times 0!$$

Finally, we use Equation 15-1 to find 0!, which is 1. Substituting 0! into 1! gives 1! = 1. This gives 2! = 2 × 1! = 2 × 1 = 2, which, in turn, gives 3! = 3 × 2! = 3 × 2 = 6.

The solution in Equation 15-1 is direct—that is, the right side of the equation contains no factorial notation. The solution in Equation 15-2 is given in terms of a smaller version of itself. The definition of the factorial given in Equations 15-1 and 15-2 is called a **recursive definition**. Equation 15-1 is called the **base case** (that is, the case for which the solution is obtained directly); Equation 15-2 is called the **general case**.

Recursive definition: A definition in which something is defined in terms of a smaller version of itself.

From the previous example (factorial), it is clear that:

1. Every recursive definition must have one (or more) base cases.
2. The general case must eventually be reduced to a base case.
3. The base case stops the recursion.

The concept of recursion in computer science works similarly. Here, we talk about recursive algorithms and recursive functions. An algorithm that finds the solution to a given problem by reducing the problem to smaller versions of itself is called a **recursive algorithm**. The recursive algorithm must have one or more base cases, and the general solution must eventually be reduced to a base case.

A function that calls itself is called a **recursive function**. That is, the body of the recursive function contains a statement that causes the same function to execute again before completing the current call. Recursive algorithms are implemented using recursive functions.

Next, let us write the recursive function that implements the factorial function:

```
int fact(int num)
{
    if (num == 0)
        return 1;
    else
        return num * fact(num - 1);
}
```

Figure 15-1 traces the execution of the following statement:

```
cout << fact(3) << endl;
```

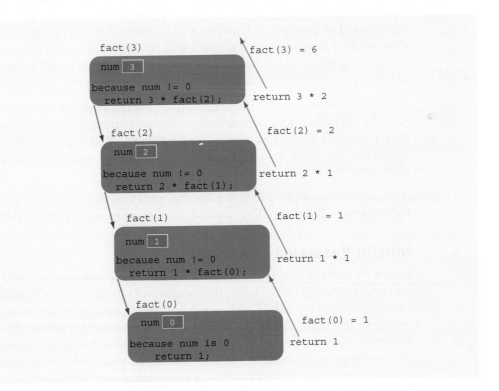

FIGURE 15-1 Execution of `fact(3)`

The output of the previous `cout` statement is:

6

In Figure 15-1, the down arrow represents the successive calls to the function `fact`, and the upward arrows represent the values returned to the caller, that is, the calling function.

Let us note the following from the preceding example, involving the factorial function.

- Logically, you can think of a recursive function as having an unlimited number of copies of itself.

- Every call to a recursive function—that is, every recursive call—has its own code and its own set of parameters and local variables.

- After completing a particular recursive call, control goes back to the calling environment, which is the previous call. The current (recursive) call must execute completely before control goes back to the previous call. The execution in the previous call begins from the point immediately following the recursive call.

Direct and Indirect Recursion

A function is called **directly recursive** if it calls itself. A function that calls another function and eventually results in the original function call is said to be **indirectly recursive**. For example, if function A calls function B and function B calls function A, then function A is indirectly recursive. Indirect recursion can be several layers deep. For example, suppose that function A calls function B, function B calls function C, function C calls function D, and function D calls function A. Function A is then indirectly recursive.

Indirect recursion requires the same careful analysis as direct recursion. The base cases must be identified, and appropriate solutions to them must be provided. However, tracing through indirect recursion can be tedious. You must, therefore, exercise extra care when designing indirect recursive functions. For simplicity, the problems in this book involve only direct recursion.

A recursive function in which the last statement executed is the recursive call is called a **tail recursive function**. The function `fact` is an example of a tail recursive function.

Infinite Recursion

Figure 15-1 shows that the sequence of recursive calls eventually reached a call that made no further recursive calls. That is, the sequence of recursive calls eventually reached a base case. On the other hand, if every recursive call results in another recursive call, then the recursive function (algorithm) is said to have infinite recursion. In theory, infinite recursion executes forever. Every call to a recursive function requires the system to allocate memory for the local variables and formal parameters. The system also saves this information so that after completing a call, control can be transferred back to the right caller. Therefore, because computer memory is finite, if you execute an infinite recursive function on a computer, the function executes until the system runs out of memory and results in an abnormal termination of the program.

Recursive functions (algorithms) must be carefully designed and analyzed. You must make sure that every recursive call eventually reduces to a base case. This chapter provides several examples that illustrate how to design and implement recursive algorithms.

To design a recursive function, you must do the following:

a.   Understand the problem requirements.

b.   Determine the limiting conditions. For example, for a list, the limiting condition is the number of elements in the list.

c.   Identify the base cases and provide a direct solution to each base case.

d.   Identify the general cases and provide a solution to each general case in terms of smaller versions of itself.

Problem Solving Using Recursion

Examples 15-1 through 15-3 illustrate how recursive algorithms are developed and implemented in C++ using recursive functions.

EXAMPLE 15-1: LARGEST ELEMENT IN AN ARRAY

In Chapter 8, we used a loop to find the largest element in an array. In this example, we use a recursive algorithm to find the largest element in an array. Consider the list given in Figure 15-2.

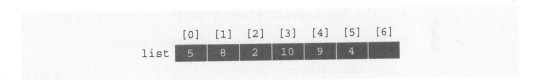

FIGURE 15-2   list with six elements

The largest element in the list in Figure 15-2 is 10.

Suppose list is the name of the array containing the list elements. Also, suppose that list[a]...list[b] stands for the array elements list[a], list[a + 1], ..., and list[b]. For example, list[0]...list[5] represents the array elements list[0], list[1], list[2], list[3], list[4], and list[5]. Similarly, list[1]...list[5] represents the array elements list[1], list[2], list[3], list[4], and list[5]. To write a recursive algorithm to find the largest element in list, let us think in terms of recursion.

If list is of length 1, then list has only one element, which is the largest element. Suppose the length of list is greater than 1. To find the largest element in list[a]... list[b], we first find the largest element in list[a + 1]...list[b] and then compare this largest element with list[a]. That is, the largest element in list[a]...list[b] is given by:

maximum(list[a], largest(list[a + 1]...list[b]))

Let us apply this formula to find the largest element in the list shown in Figure 15-2. This list has six elements, given by list[0]...list[5]. Now, the largest element in list is:

maximum(list[0], largest(list[1]...list[5]))

That is, the largest element in list is the maximum of list[0] and the largest element in list[1]...list[5]. To find the largest element in list[1]...list[5], we use the same formula again because the length of this list is greater than 1. The largest element in list[1]...list[5] is then:

maximum(list[1], largest(list[2]...list[5]))

and so on. We see that every time we use the preceding formula to find the largest element in a sublist, the length of the sublist in the next call is reduced by one. Eventually, the sublist is of length 1, in which case the sublist contains only one element, which is the largest element in the sublist. From this point onward, we backtrack through the recursive calls. This discussion translates into the following recursive algorithm, which is presented in pseudocode.

Base Case: The size of the list is 1
       The only element in the list is the largest element

General Case: The size of the list is greater than 1
       To find the largest element in list[a]...list[b]

   a. Find the largest element in list[a + 1]...list[b]
      and call it max
   b. Compare the elements list[a] and max
      if (list[a] >= max)
          the largest element in list[a]...list[b] is list[a]
      otherwise
          the largest element in list[a]...list[b] is max

This algorithm translates into the following C++ function to find the largest element in an array:

```cpp
int largest(const int list[], int lowerIndex, int upperIndex)
{
    int max;

    if (lowerIndex == upperIndex) //size of the sublist is one
        return list[lowerIndex];
    else
    {
        max = largest(list, lowerIndex + 1, upperIndex);

        if (list[lowerIndex] >= max)
            return list[lowerIndex];
```

```
        else
            return max;
    }
}
```

Consider the `list` given in Figure 15-3.

```
              [0]  [1]  [2]  [3]
        list   5   10   12    8
```

FIGURE 15-3 `list` with four elements

Let us trace the execution of the following statement:

`cout << largest(list, 0, 3) << endl;`

Here, `upperIndex` = 3 and the list have four elements. Figure 15-4 traces the execution of `largest(list, 0, 3)`.

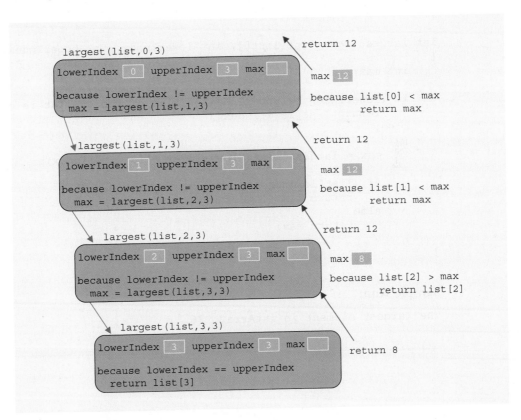

FIGURE 15-4 Execution of `largest(list, 0, 3)`

The value returned by the expression largest(list, 0, 3) is 12, which is the largest element in list.

The following C++ program uses the function largest to determine the largest element in a list.

```
//Largest Element in an Array

#include <iostream>

using namespace std;

int largest(const int list[], int lowerIndex, int upperIndex);

int main()
{
    int intArray[10] = {23, 43, 35, 38, 67, 12, 76, 10, 34, 8};

    cout << "The largest element in intArray: "
         << largest(intArray, 0, 9);
    cout << endl;

    return 0;
}

int largest(const int list[], int lowerIndex, int upperIndex)
{
    int max;

    if (lowerIndex == upperIndex) //size of the sublist is one
        return list[lowerIndex];
    else
    {
        max = largest(list, lowerIndex + 1, upperIndex);

        if (list[lowerIndex] >= max)
            return list[lowerIndex];
        else
            return max;
    }
}
```

Sample Run:

```
The largest element in intArray: 76
```

EXAMPLE 15-2: FIBONACCI NUMBER

In Chapter 5, we designed a program to determine the desired Fibonacci number. In this example, we write a recursive function, rFibNum, to determine the desired Fibonacci number. The function rFibNum takes as parameters three numbers representing the first two numbers of the Fibonacci sequence and a number n, the desired nth Fibonacci number. The function rFibNum returns the nth Fibonacci number in the sequence.

Recall that the third Fibonacci number is the sum of the first two Fibonacci numbers. The fourth Fibonacci number in a sequence is the sum of the second and third Fibonacci numbers. Therefore, to calculate the fourth Fibonacci number, we add the second Fibonacci number and the third Fibonacci number (which is itself the sum of the first two Fibonacci numbers). The following recursive algorithm calculates the nth Fibonacci number, in which a denotes the first Fibonacci number, b the second Fibonacci number, and n the nth Fibonacci number.

$$rFibNum(a,b,n) = \begin{cases} a & \text{if } n = 1 \\ b & \text{if } n = 2 \quad (15\text{-}3) \\ rFibNum(a,b,n-1) + rFibNum(a,b,n-2) & \text{if } n > 2. \end{cases}$$

Suppose that we want to determine:

rFibNum(2, 5, 4)

Here, $a = 2$, $b = 5$, and $n = 4$. That is, we want to determine the fourth Fibonacci number of the sequence whose first number is 2 and whose second number is 5. Because n is 4 > 2:

1. rFibNum(2, 5, 4) = rFibNum(2, 5, 3) + rFibNum(2, 5, 2)

    Next, we determine rFibNum(2, 5, 3) and rFibNum(2, 5, 2). Let us first determine rFibNum(2, 5, 3). Here, $a = 2$, $b = 5$, and n is 3. Because n is 3:

    1.a. rFibNum(2, 5, 3) = rFibNum(2, 5, 2) + rFibNum(2, 5, 1)

        This statement requires us to determine rFibNum(2, 5, 2) and rFibNum(2, 5, 1). In rFibNum(2, 5, 2), $a = 2$, $b = 5$, and $n = 2$. Therefore, from the definition given in Equation 15-3, it follows that:

        1.a.1. rFibNum(2, 5, 2) = 5

            To find rFibNum(2, 5, 1), note that $a = 2$, $b = 5$, and $n = 1$. Therefore, by the definition given in Equation 15-3:

1.a.2. rFibNum(2, 5, 1) = 2

We substitute the values of rFibNum(2, 5, 2) and rFibNum(2, 5, 1) into (1.a) to get:

rFibNum(2, 5, 3) = 5 + 2 = 7

Next, we determine rFibNum(2, 5, 2). As in (1.a.1), rFibNum(2, 5, 2) = 5. We can substitute the values of rFibNum(2, 5, 3) and rFibNum(2, 5, 2) into (1) to get:

rFibNum(2, 5, 4) = 7 + 5 = 12

The following recursive function implements this algorithm:

```
int rFibNum(int a, int b, int n)
{
    if (n == 1)
        return a;
    else if (n == 2)
        return b;
    else
        return rFibNum(a, b, n - 1) + rFibNum(a, b, n - 2);
}
```

Let us trace the execution of the following statement:

```
cout << rFibNum(2, 3, 5) << endl;
```

In this statement, the first number is 2, the second number is 3, and we want to determine the fifth Fibonacci number of the sequence. Figure 15-5 traces the execution of the expression rFibNum(2,3,5). The value returned is 13, which is the fifth Fibonacci number of the sequence whose first number is 2 and second number is 3.

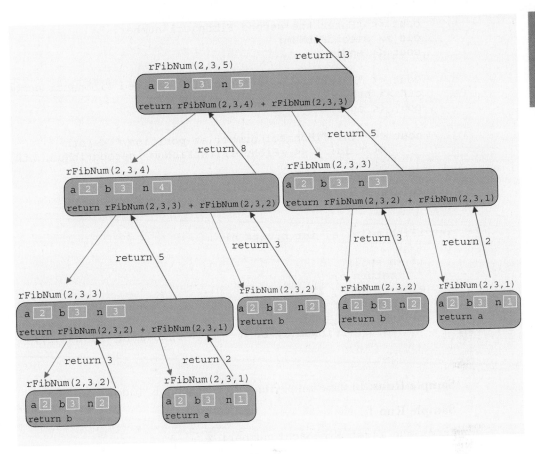

FIGURE 15-5 Execution of rFibNum(2, 3, 5)

The following C++ program uses the function rFibNum:

```
//Chapter 15: Fibonacci Number

#include <iostream>

using namespace std;

int rFibNum(int a, int b, int n);

int main()
{
    int firstFibNum;
    int secondFibNum;
    int nth;

    cout << "Enter the first Fibonacci number: ";
    cin >> firstFibNum;
    cout << endl;
```

```
        cout << "Enter the second Fibonacci number: ";
        cin >> secondFibNum;
        cout << endl;

        cout << "Enter the position of the desired Fibonacci number: ";
        cin >> nth;
        cout << endl;

        cout << "The Fibonacci number at position " << nth
             << " is: " << rFibNum(firstFibNum, secondFibNum, nth)
             << endl;

        return 0;
}

int rFibNum(int a, int b, int n)
{
    if (n == 1)
        return a;
    else if (n == 2)
        return b;
    else
        return rFibNum(a, b, n - 1) + rFibNum(a, b, n - 2);
}
```

Sample Runs: In these sample runs, the user input is shaded.

Sample Run 1

```
Enter the first Fibonacci number: 2

Enter the second Fibonacci number: 5

Enter the position of the desired Fibonacci number: 6

The Fibonacci number at position 6 is: 31
```

Sample Run 2

```
Enter the first Fibonacci number: 12

Enter the second Fibonacci number: 18

Enter the position of the desired Fibonacci number: 15

The Fibonacci number at position 15 is: 9582
```

EXAMPLE 15-3: TOWER OF HANOI

In the nineteenth century, a game called the Tower of Hanoi became popular in Europe. This game represents work that is under way in the temple of Brahma. At the creation of the universe, priests in the temple of Brahma were supposedly given three diamond needles, with one needle containing 64 golden disks. Each golden disk is slightly smaller than the disk below it. The priests' task is to move all 64 disks from the first needle to the third needle. The rules for moving the disks are as follows:

1. Only one disk can be moved at a time.
2. The removed disk must be placed on one of the needles.
3. A larger disk cannot be placed on top of a smaller disk.

The priests were told that once they had moved all of the disks from the first needle to the third needle, the universe would come to an end.

Our objective is to write a program that prints the sequence of moves needed to transfer the disks from the first needle to the third needle. Figure 15-6 shows the Tower of Hanoi problem with three disks.

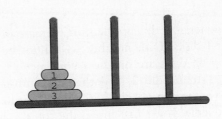

FIGURE 15-6 Tower of Hanoi problem with three disks

As before, we think in terms of recursion. Let us first consider the case in which the first needle contains only one disk. In this case, the disk can be moved directly from needle 1 to needle 3. So let us consider the case in which the first needle contains only two disks. In this case, first we move the first disk from needle 1 to needle 2, and then we move the second disk from needle 1 to needle 3. Finally, we move the first disk from needle 2 to needle 3. Next, we consider the case in which the first needle contains three disks and then generalize this to the case of 64 disks (in fact, to an arbitrary number of disks).

Suppose that needle 1 contains three disks. To move disk number 3 to needle 3, the top two disks must first be moved to needle 2. Disk number 3 can then be moved from needle 1 to needle 3. To move the top two disks from needle 2 to needle 3, we use the same strategy as before. This time, we use needle 1 as the intermediate needle. Figure 15-7 shows a solution to the Tower of Hanoi problem with three disks.

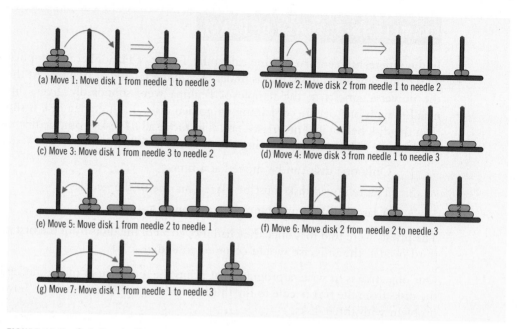

(a) Move 1: Move disk 1 from needle 1 to needle 3

(b) Move 2: Move disk 2 from needle 1 to needle 2

(c) Move 3: Move disk 1 from needle 3 to needle 2

(d) Move 4: Move disk 3 from needle 1 to needle 3

(e) Move 5: Move disk 1 from needle 2 to needle 1

(f) Move 6: Move disk 2 from needle 2 to needle 3

(g) Move 7: Move disk 1 from needle 1 to needle 3

FIGURE 15-7 Solution to Tower of Hanoi problem with three disks

Let us now generalize this problem to the case of 64 disks. To begin, the first needle contains all 64 disks. Disk number 64 cannot be moved from needle 1 to needle 3 unless the top 63 disks are on the second needle. So first, we move the top 63 disks from needle 1 to needle 2, and then we move disk number 64 from needle 1 to needle 3. Now the top 63 disks are all on needle 2. To move disk number 63 from needle 2 to needle 3, we first move the top 62 disks from needle 2 to needle 1, and then we move disk number 63 from needle 2 to needle 3. To move the remaining 62 disks, we use a similar procedure. This discussion translates into the following recursive algorithm given in pseudocode. Suppose that needle 1 contains n disks, in which $n \geq 1$.

1. Move the top $n - 1$ disks from needle 1 to needle 2, using needle 3 as the intermediate needle.
2. Move disk number n from needle 1 to needle 3.
3. Move the top $n - 1$ disks from needle 2 to needle 3, using needle 1 as the intermediate needle.

This recursive algorithm translates into the following C++ function:

```
void moveDisks(int count, int needle1, int needle3, int needle2)
{
    if (count > 0)
    {
        moveDisks(count - 1, needle1, needle2, needle3);

        cout << "Move disk " << count << " from " << needle1
             << " to " << needle3 << "." << endl;

        moveDisks(count - 1, needle2, needle3, needle1);
    }
}
```

Tower of Hanoi: Analysis

Let us determine how long it would take to move all 64 disks from needle 1 to needle 3. If needle 1 contains three disks, then the number of moves required to move all three disks from needle 1 to needle 3 is $2^3 - 1 = 7$. Similarly, if needle 1 contains 64 disks, then the number of moves required to move all 64 disks from needle 1 to needle 3 is $2^{64} - 1$. Because $2^{10} = 1024 \approx 1000 = 10^3$, we have:

$$2^{64} = 2^4 \times 2^{60} \approx 2^4 \times 10^{18} = 1.6 \times 10^{19}$$

The number of seconds in one year is approximately 3.2×10^7. Suppose the priests move one disk per second and they do not rest. Now:

$$1.6 \times 10^{19} = 5 \times 3.2 \times 10^{18} = 5 \times (3.2 \times 10^7) \times 10^{11} = (3.2 \times 10^7) \times (5 \times 10^{11})$$

The time required to move all 64 disks from needle 1 to needle 3 is roughly 5×10^{11} years. It is estimated that our universe is about 15 billion years old (1.5×10^{10}). Also, $5 \times 10^{11} = 50 \times 10^{10} \approx 33 \times (1.5 \times 10^{10})$. This calculation shows that our universe would last about 33 times as long as it already has.

Assume that a computer can generate 1 billion (10^9) moves per second. Then the number of moves that the computer can generate in one year is:

$$(3.2 \times 10^7) \times 10^9 = 3.2 \times 10^{16}$$

So the computer time required to generate 2^{64} moves is:

$$2^{64} \approx 1.6 \times 10^{19} = 1.6 \times 10^{16} \times 10^3 = (3.2 \times 10^{16}) \times 500$$

Thus, it would take about 500 years for the computer to generate 2^{64} moves at the rate of 1 billion moves per second.

Recursion or Iteration?

In Chapter 5, we designed a program to determine a desired Fibonacci number. That program used a loop to perform the calculation. In other words, the programs in Chapter 5 used an iterative control structure to repeat a set of statements. More formally, **iterative**

control structures use a looping structure, such as `while`, `for`, or `do...while`, to repeat a set of statements. In Example 15-2, we designed a recursive function to calculate a Fibonacci number. From the examples here, it follows that in recursion, a set of statements is repeated by having the function call itself. Moreover, a selection control structure is used to control the repeated calls in recursion.

Similarly, in Chapter 8, we used an iterative control structure (a `for` loop) to determine the largest element in a list. In this chapter, we use recursion to determine the largest element in a list. In addition, this chapter began by designing a recursive function to find the factorial of a nonnegative integer. Using an iterative control structure, we can also write an algorithm to find the factorial of a nonnegative integer. The only reason to give a recursive solution to a factorial problem is to illustrate how recursion works.

We thus see that there are usually two ways to solve a particular problem—iteration and recursion. The obvious question is which method is better—iteration or recursion? There is no simple answer. In addition to the nature of the problem, the other key factor in determining the best solution method is efficiency.

Example 6-13 (Chapter 6), while tracing the execution of the problem, showed us that whenever a function is called, memory space for its formal parameters and (automatic) local variables is allocated. When the function terminates, that memory space is then deallocated.

This chapter, while tracing the execution of recursive functions, also shows us that every (recursive) call has its own set of parameters and (automatic) local variables. That is, every (recursive) call requires the system to allocate memory space for its formal parameters and (automatic) local variables and then deallocate the memory space when the function exits. Thus, there is overhead associated with executing a (recursive) function both in terms of memory space and computer time. Therefore, a recursive function executes more slowly than its iterative counterpart. On slower computers, especially those with limited memory space, the (slow) execution of a recursive function would be visible.

Today's computers, however, are fast and have inexpensive memory. Therefore, the execution of a recursion function is not noticeable. Keeping the power of today's computers in mind, the choice between the two alternatives—iteration or recursion—depends on the nature of the problem. Of course, for problems such as mission control systems, efficiency is absolutely critical and, therefore, the efficiency factor would dictate the solution method.

As a general rule, if you think that an iterative solution is more obvious and easier to understand than a recursive solution, use the iterative solution, which would be more efficient. On the other hand, problems exist for which the recursive solution is more obvious or easier to construct, such as the Tower of Hanoi problem. (In fact, it turns out that it is difficult to construct an iterative solution for the Tower of Hanoi problem.) Keeping the power of recursion in mind, if the definition of a problem is inherently recursive, then you should consider a recursive solution.

PROGRAMMING EXAMPLE: Converting a Number from Binary to Decimal

Watch the Video

In Chapter 1, we explained that the language of a computer, called machine language, is a sequence of 0s and 1s. When you press the key A on the keyboard, 01000001 is stored in the computer. Also, you know that the collating sequence of A in the ASCII character set is 65. In fact, the binary representation of A is 01000001, and the decimal representation of A is 65.

The numbering system we use is called the decimal system, or base 10 system. The numbering system that the computer uses is called the binary system, or base 2 system. In this and the next programming example, we discuss how to convert a number from base 2 to base 10 and from base 10 to base 2.

Binary to Decimal

To convert a number from base 2 to base 10, we first find the weight of each bit in the binary number. The weight of each bit in the binary number is assigned from right to left. The weight of the rightmost bit is 0. The weight of the bit immediately to the left of the rightmost bit is 1, the weight of the bit immediately to the left of it is 2, and so on. Consider the binary number 1001101. The weight of each bit is as follows:

```
Weight  6  5  4  3  2  1  0
        1  0  0  1  1  0  1
```

We use the weight of each bit to find the equivalent decimal number. For each bit, we multiply the bit by 2 to the power of its weight and then we add all of the numbers. For the above binary number, the equivalent decimal number is:

$$1 \times 2^6 + 0 \times 2^5 + 0 \times 2^4 + 1 \times 2^3 + 1 \times 2^2 + 0 \times 2^1 + 1 \times 2^0$$
$$= 64 + 0 + 0 + 8 + 4 + 0 + 1$$
$$= 77$$

To write a program that converts a binary number into the equivalent decimal number, we note two things: (1) the weight of each bit in the binary number must be known, and (2) the weight is assigned from right to left. Because we do not know in advance how many bits are in the binary number, we must process the bits from right to left. After processing a bit, we can add 1 to its weight, giving the weight of the bit immediately to the left of it. Also, each bit must be extracted from the binary number and multiplied by 2 to the power of its weight. To extract a bit, we can use the mod operator. Consider the following recursive algorithm, which is given in pseudocode.

```
if (binaryNumber > 0)
{
    bit = binaryNumber % 10;          //extract the rightmost bit
    decimal = decimal + bit * power(2, weight);
    binaryNumber = binaryNumber / 10; //remove the rightmost
                                       //bit
    weight++;
    convert the binaryNumber into decimal
}
```

This algorithm assumes that the memory locations `decimal` and `weight` have been initialized to 0 before using the algorithm. This algorithm translates to the following C++ recursive function:

```
void binToDec(int binaryNumber, int& decimal, int& weight)
{
    int bit;

    if (binaryNumber > 0)
    {
        bit = binaryNumber % 10;
        decimal = decimal
                    + bit * static_cast<int>(pow(2.0, weight));
        binaryNumber = binaryNumber / 10;
        weight++;
        binToDec(binaryNumber, decimal, weight);
    }
}
```

In this function, both `decimal` and `weight` are reference parameters. The actual parameters corresponding to these parameters are initialized to 0. After extracting the rightmost bit, this function updates the decimal number and the weight of the next bit. Suppose `decimalNumber` and `bitWeight` are `int` variables. Consider the following statements:

```
decimalNumber = 0;
bitWeight = 0;
binToDec(1101, decimalNumber, bitWeight);
```

Figure 15-8 traces the execution of the last statement, that is, `binToDec(1101, decimalNumber, bitWeight);`. It shows the content of the variables `decimalNumber` and `bitWeight` next to each function call.

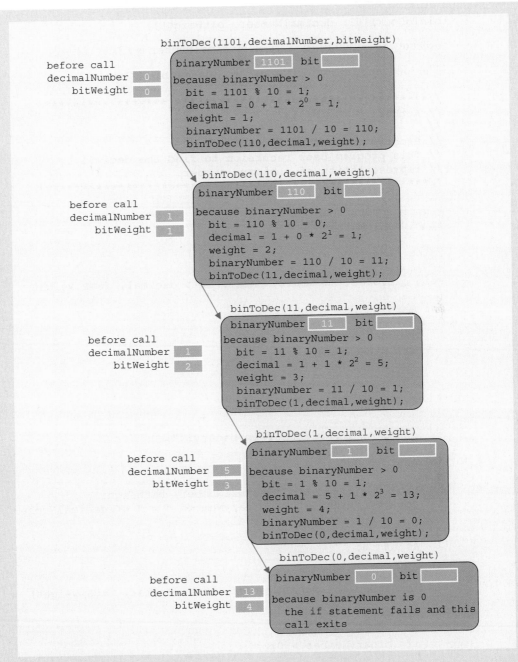

FIGURE 15-8 Execution of binToDec(1101, decimalNumber, bitWeight);

In Figure 15-8, each down arrow represents the successive function call. Because the last statement of the function binToDec is a function call, after this statement executes, nothing happens. After the statement:

```
binToDec(1101, decimalNumber, bitWeight);
```

executes, the value of the variable decimalNumber is 13.

The following C++ program tests the function binToDec:

```cpp
//********************************************************
// Author: D. S. Malik
//
// Program: Binary to decimal
// This program uses recursion to find the decimal
// representation of a binary number.
//********************************************************

#include <iostream>
#include <cmath>

using namespace std;

void binToDec(int binaryNumber, int& decimal, int& weight);

int main()
{
    int decimalNumber;
    int bitWeight;
    int binaryNum;

    decimalNumber = 0;
    bitWeight = 0;

    cout << "Enter number in binary: ";
    cin >> binaryNum;
    cout << endl;

    binToDec(binaryNum, decimalNumber, bitWeight);
    cout << "Binary " << binaryNum << " = " << decimalNumber
         << " decimal" << endl;

    return 0;
}

void binToDec(int binaryNumber, int& decimal, int& weight)
{
    int bit;

    if (binaryNumber > 0)
    {
        bit = binaryNumber % 10;
        decimal = decimal
                    + bit * static_cast<int>(pow(2.0, weight));
        binaryNumber = binaryNumber / 10;
```

```
            weight++;
            binToDec(binaryNumber, decimal, weight);
        }
    }
```

Sample Run: In this sample run, the user input is shaded.

```
Enter a number in binary: 11010110

Binary 11010110 = 214 decimal
```

PROGRAMMING EXAMPLE: Converting a Number from Decimal to Binary

The previous programming example discussed and designed a program to convert a number from a binary representation to a decimal format—that is, from base 2 to base 10. This programming example discusses and designs a program that uses recursion to convert a nonnegative integer in decimal format—that is, base 10—into the equivalent binary number—that is, base 2. First, we define some terms.

Let x be an integer. We call the remainder of x after division by 2 the **rightmost bit** of x.

Thus, the rightmost bit of 33 is 1 because 33 % 2 is 1, and the rightmost bit of 28 is 0 because 28 % 2 is 0.

We first illustrate the algorithm to convert an integer in base 10 to the equivalent number in binary format, with the help of an example.

Suppose we want to find the binary representation of 35. First, we divide 35 by 2. The quotient is 17, and the remainder—that is, the rightmost bit of 35—is 1. Next, we divide 17 by 2. The quotient is 8, and the remainder—that is, the rightmost bit of 17—is 1. Next, we divide 8 by 2. The quotient is 4, and the remainder—that is, the rightmost bit of 8—is 0. We continue this process until the quotient becomes 0.

The rightmost bit of 35 cannot be printed until we have printed the rightmost bit of 17. The rightmost bit of 17 cannot be printed until we have printed the rightmost bit of 8, and so on. Thus, the binary representation of 35 is the binary representation of 17 (that is, the quotient of 35 after division by 2), followed by the rightmost bit of 35.

Thus, to convert an integer *num* in base 10 into the equivalent binary number, we first convert the quotient *num* / 2 into an equivalent binary number and then append the rightmost bit of *num* to the binary representation of *num* / 2.

This discussion translates into the following recursive algorithm, in which binary(num) denotes the binary representation of num.

1. binary(num) = num if num = 0.
2. binary(num) = binary(num / 2) followed by num % 2 if num > 0.

The following recursive function implements this algorithm:

```cpp
void decToBin(int num, int base)
{
    if (num > 0)
    {
        decToBin(num / base, base);
        cout << num % base;
    }
}
```

Figure 15-9 traces the execution of the following statement:

```cpp
decToBin(13, 2);
```

in which num is 13 and base is 2.

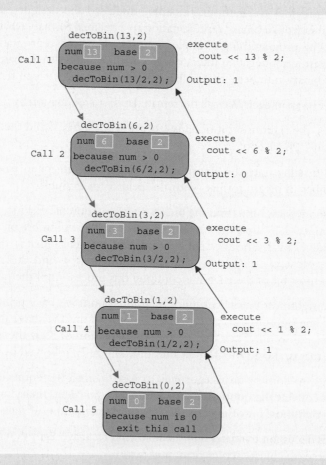

FIGURE 15-9 Execution of decToBin(13, 2)

Because the `if` statement in call 5 fails, this call does not print anything. The first output is produced by call 4, which prints 1; the second output is produced by call 3, which prints 1; the third output is produced by call 2, which prints 0; and the fourth output is produced by call 1, which prints 1. Thus, the output of the statement:

```
decToBin(13, 2);
```

is:

```
1101
```

The following C++ program tests the function decToBin.

```cpp
//********************************************************
// Author: D. S. Malik
//
// Program: Decimal to binary
// This program uses recursion to find the binary
// representation of a nonnegative integer.
//********************************************************

#include <iostream>

using namespace std;

void decToBin(int num, int base);

int main()
{
    int decimalNum;
    int base;

    base = 2;

    cout << "Enter number in decimal: ";
    cin >> decimalNum;
    cout << endl;

    cout << "Decimal " << decimalNum << " = ";
    decToBin(decimalNum, base);
    cout << " binary" << endl;

    return 0;
}

void decToBin(int num, int base)
{
    if (num > 0)
    {
        decToBin(num / base, base);
        cout << num % base;
    }
}
```

Sample Run: In this sample run, the user input is shaded.

```
Enter a number in decimal: 57

Decimal 57 = 111001 binary
```

QUICK REVIEW

1. The process of solving a problem by reducing it to smaller versions of itself is called recursion.
2. A recursive definition defines a problem in terms of smaller versions of itself.
3. Every recursive definition has one or more base cases.
4. A recursive algorithm solves a problem by reducing it to smaller versions of itself.
5. Every recursive algorithm has one or more base cases.
6. The solution to the problem in a base case is obtained directly.
7. A function is called recursive if it calls itself.
8. Recursive algorithms are implemented using recursive functions.
9. Every recursive function must have one or more base cases.
10. The general solution breaks the problem into smaller versions of itself.
11. The general case must eventually be reduced to a base case.
12. The base case stops the recursion.
13. While tracing a recursive function:
    - Logically, you can think of a recursive function as having an unlimited number of copies of itself.
    - Every call to a recursive function—that is, every recursive call—has its own code and its own set of parameters and local variables.
    - After completing a particular recursive call, control goes back to the calling environment, which is the previous call. The current (recursive) call must execute completely before control goes back to the previous call. The execution in the previous call begins from the point immediately following the recursive call.
14. A function is called directly recursive if it calls itself.
15. A function that calls another function and eventually results in the original function call is said to be indirectly recursive.
16. A recursive function in which the last statement executed is the recursive call is called a tail recursive function.
17. To design a recursive function, you must do the following:
    a. Understand the problem requirements.
    b. Determine the limiting conditions. For example, for a list, the limiting condition is the number of elements in the list.

12. Consider the following function:

```
int test(int x, int y)
{
    if (x <= y)
        return y - x;
    else
        return test(x - 1, y + 1);
}
```

What is the output of the following statements?

a. cout << test(3, 100) << endl;

b. cout << test(15, 7) << endl;

13. Consider the following function:

```
int func(int x)
{
    if (x == 0)
        return 2;
    else if (x == 1)
        return 3;
    else
        return (func(x - 1) + func(x - 2));
}
```

What is the output of the following statements?

a. cout << func(0) << endl;

b. cout << func(1) << endl;

c. cout << func(2) << endl;

d. cout << func(5) << endl;

14. Suppose that intArray is an array of integers, and length specifies the number of elements in intArray. Also, suppose that low and high are two integers such that 0 <= low < length, 0 <= high < length, and low < high. That is, low and high are two indices in intArray. Write a recursive definition that reverses the elements in intArray between low and high.

15. Write a recursive algorithm to multiply two positive integers m and n using repeated addition. Specify the base case and the recursive case.

16. Consider the following problem: How many ways can a committee of four people be selected from a group of 10 people? There are many other similar problems in which you are asked to find the number of ways to select a set of items from a given set of items. The general problem can be stated as follows: Find the number of ways r different things can be chosen from a set of n items, in which r and n are nonnegative integers and $r \leq n$. Suppose $C(n, r)$ denotes the number of ways r different things can be chosen from a set of n items. Then, $C(n, r)$ is given by the following formula:

$$C(n,r) = \frac{n!}{r!(n-r)!}$$

in which the exclamation point denotes the factorial function. Moreover, $C(n, 0) = C(n, n) = 1$. It is also known that $C(n, r) = C(n-1, r-1) + C(n-1, r)$.

a. Write a recursive algorithm to determine $C(n, r)$. Identify the base case(s) and the general case(s).

b. Using your recursive algorithm, determine $C(5, 3)$ and $C(9, 4)$.

PROGRAMMING EXERCISES

1. Write a recursive function that takes as a parameter a nonnegative integer and generates the following pattern of stars. If the nonnegative integer is 4, then the pattern generated is:

```
****
***
**
*
*
**
***
****
```

Also, write a program that prompts the user to enter the number of lines in the pattern and uses the recursive function to generate the pattern. For example, specifying 4 as the number of lines generates the above pattern.

2. Write a recursive function to generate the following pattern of stars:

```
      *
    *   *
   *  *  *
  *  *  *  *
   *  *  *
    *   *
      *
```

Also, write a program that prompts the user to enter the number of lines in the pattern and uses the recursive function to generate the pattern. For example, specifying 4 as the number of lines generates the above pattern.

3. Write a recursive function, vowels, that returns the number of vowels in a string. Also, write a program to test your function.

4. Write a recursive function named sumSquares that returns the sum of the squares of the numbers from 0 to num, in which num is a nonnegative int variable. Do not use global variables; use the appropriate parameters. Also write a program to test your function.

5. Write a recursive function that finds and returns the sum of the elements of an int array. Also, write a program to test your function.

6. A palindrome is a string that reads the same both forward and backward. For example, the string "madam" is a palindrome. Write a program that uses

a recursive function to check whether a string is a palindrome. Your program must contain a value-returning recursive function that returns `true` if the string is a palindrome and `false` otherwise. Do not use any global variables; use the appropriate parameters.

7. Write a recursive function that returns both the smallest and the largest element in an `int` array. Also, write a program to test your function.

8. Write a recursive function that returns `true` if the digits of a positive integer are in increasing order; otherwise, the function returns `false`. Also, write a program to test your function.

9. Write a recursive function, `reverseDigits`, that takes an integer as a parameter and returns the number with the digits reversed. Also, write a program to test your function.

10. Write a recursive function, `power`, that takes as parameters two integers x and y such that x is nonzero and returns x^y. You can use the following recursive definition to calculate x^y. If $y \geq 0$:

$$power(x, y) = \begin{cases} 1 & \text{if } y = 0 \\ x & \text{if } y = 1 \\ x \times power(x, y - 1) & \text{if } y > 1. \end{cases}$$

If $y < 0$:

$$power(x, y) = \frac{1}{power(x, -y)}.$$

Also, write a program to test your function.

11. (**Greatest Common Divisor**) Given two integers x and y, the following recursive definition determines the greatest common divisor of x and y, written gcd(x,y):

$$gcd(x, y) = \begin{cases} x & \text{if } y = 0 \\ gcd(y, x\%y) & \text{if } y \neq 0 \end{cases}$$

Note: In this definition, % is the mod operator.

Write a recursive function, `gcd`, that takes as parameters two integers and returns the greatest common divisor of the numbers. Also, write a program to test your function.

12. (**Ackermann's Function**) The Ackermann's function is defined as follows:

$$A(m, n) = \begin{cases} n + 1, & \text{if } m = 0 \\ A(m - 1, 1), & \text{if } n = 0 \\ A(m - 1, A(m, n - 1)), & \text{otherwise,} \end{cases}$$

in which m and n are nonnegative integers. Write a recursive function to implement Ackermann's function. Also write a program to test your function. What happens when you call the function with $m = 4$ and $n = 3$?

13. Write a recursive function to implement the recursive algorithm of Exercise 14 (reversing the elements of an array between two indices). Also, write a program to test your function.

14. Write a recursive function to implement the recursive algorithm of Exercise 15 (multiplying two positive integers using repeated addition). Also, write a program to test your function.

15. Write a recursive function to implement the recursive algorithm of Exercise 16 (determining the number of ways to select a set of things from a given set of things). Also, write a program to test your function.

16. **(Recursive Sequential Search)** The sequential search algorithm given in Chapter 8 is nonrecursive. Write and implement a recursive version of the sequential search algorithm.

17. In the Programming Example, Converting a Number from Decimal to Binary, given in this chapter, you learned how to convert a decimal number into the equivalent binary number. Two more number systems, octal (base 8) and hexadecimal (base 16), are of interest to computer scientists. In fact, in C++, you can instruct the computer to store a number in octal or hexadecimal. (Appendix C describes these number systems.)

The digits in the octal number system are 0, 1, 2, 3, 4, 5, 6, and 7. The digits in the hexadecimal number system are 0, 1, 2, 3, 4, 5, 6, 7, 8, 9, A, B, C, D, E, and F. So A in hexadecimal is 10 in decimal, B in hexadecimal is 11 in decimal, and so on.

The algorithm to convert a positive decimal number into an equivalent number in octal (or hexadecimal) is the same as discussed for binary numbers. Here, we divide the decimal number by 8 (for octal) and by 16 (for hexadecimal). Suppose a_b represents the number a to the base b. For example, 75_{10} means 75 to the base 10 (that is decimal), and 83_{16} means 83 to the base 16 (that is, hexadecimal). Then $753_{10} = 1361_8$ and $753_{10} = 2F1_{16}$.

Write a program that uses a recursive function to convert a number in decimal to base 8 or base 16.

18. The function `sqrt` from the header file `cmath` can be used to find the square root of a nonnegative real number. Using Newton's method, you can also write an algorithm to find the square root of a nonnegative real number within a given tolerance as follows: Suppose x is a nonnegative real number, a is the approximate square root of x, and *epsilon* is the tolerance. Start with $a = x$.

   a. If $|a^2 - x| \leq epsilon$, then a is the square root of x within the tolerance; otherwise:

   b. Replace a with $(a^2 + x) / (2a)$ and repeat Step a in which $|a^2 - x|$ denotes the absolute value of $a^2 - x$.

   Write a recursive function to implement this algorithm to find the square root of a nonnegative real number. Also, write a program to test your function.

LINKED LISTS

IN THIS CHAPTER, YOU WILL:

·   Learn about linked lists

·   Become aware of the basic properties of linked lists

·   Explore the insertion and deletion operations on linked lists

·   Discover how to build and manipulate a linked list

·   Learn how to construct a doubly linked list

You have already seen how data is organized and processed sequentially using an array called a *sequential list*. You have performed several operations on sequential lists, such as sorting, inserting, deleting, and searching. You also found that if data is not sorted, then searching for an item in the list can be very time consuming especially with large lists. Once the data is sorted, you can use a binary search and improve the search algorithm. However, in this case, insertion and deletion become time consuming especially with large lists, because these operations require data movement. Also, because the array size must be fixed during execution, new items can be added only if there is room. Thus, there are limitations on when you organize data in an array.

This chapter helps you to overcome some of these problems. Chapter 12 showed how memory (variables) can be dynamically allocated and deallocated using pointers. This chapter uses pointers to organize and process data in lists called **linked lists**. Recall that when data is stored in an array, memory for the components of the array is contiguous—that is, the blocks are allocated one after the other. However, as we will see, the components (called nodes) of a linked list need not be contiguous.

Linked Lists

A linked list is a collection of components called **nodes.** Every node (except the last node) contains the address of the next node. Thus, every node in a linked list has two components: one to store the relevant information (that is, data) and one to store the address, called the **link**, of the next node in the list. The address of the first node in the list is stored in a separate location called the **head** or **first**. Figure 16-1 is a pictorial representation of a node.

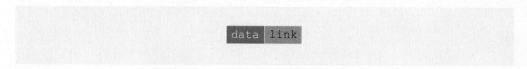

FIGURE 16-1   Structure of a node

Linked list: A list of items, called **nodes**, in which the order of the nodes is determined by the address, called the **link**, stored in each node.

The list in Figure 16-2 is an example of a linked list.

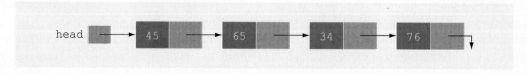

FIGURE 16-2   Linked list

The arrow in each node indicates that the address of the node to which it is pointing is stored in that node. The down arrow in the last node indicates that this link field is NULL.

For a better understanding of this notation, suppose that the first node is at memory location 1200, and the second node is at memory location 1575. We thus have Figure 16-3.

FIGURE 16-3 Linked list and values of the links

The value of the head is 1200, the data part of the first node is 45, and the link component of the first node contains 1575, the address of the second node. If no confusion arises, then we will use the arrow notation whenever we draw the figure of a linked list.

For simplicity and for the ease of understanding and clarity, Figures 16-3 through 16-6 use decimal integers as the values of memory addresses. However, in computer memory, the memory addresses are in binary.

Because each node of a linked list has two components, we need to declare each node as a `class` or `struct`. The data type of each node depends on the specific application—that is, what kind of data is being processed. However, the link component of each node is a pointer. The data type of this pointer variable is the node type itself. For the previous linked list, the definition of the node is as follows. (Suppose that the data type is `int`.)

```
struct nodeType
{
    int info;
    nodeType *link;
};
```

The variable declaration is:

```
nodeType *head;
```

Linked Lists: Some Properties

To help you better understand the concept of a linked list and a node, some important properties of linked lists are described next.

Consider the linked list in Figure 16-4.

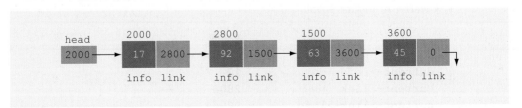

FIGURE 16-4 Linked list with four nodes

This linked list has four nodes. The address of the first node is stored in the pointer head. Each node has two components: info, to store the info, and link, to store the address of the next node. For simplicity, we assume that info is of type int.

Suppose that the first node is at location 2000, the second node is at location 2800, the third node is at location 1500, and the fourth node is at location 3600. Therefore, the value of head is 2000, the value of the component link of the first node is 2800, the value of the component link of the second node is 1500, and so on. Also, the value 0 in the component link of the last node means that this value is NULL, which we indicate by drawing a down arrow. The number at the top of each node is the address of that node. The following table shows the values of head and some other nodes in the list shown in Figure 16-4.

	Value	Explanation
head	2000	
head->info	17	Because head is 2000 and the info of the node at location 2000 is 17
head->link	2800	
head->link->info	92	Because head->link is 2800 and the info of the node at location 2800 is 92

Suppose that current is a pointer of the same type as the pointer head. Then, the statement:

current = head;

copies the value of head into current (see Figure 16-5).

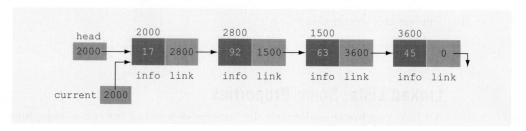

FIGURE 16-5 Linked list after the statement current = head; executes

Clearly, in Figure 16-5:

	Value
current	2000
current->info	17
current->link	2800
current->link->info	92

Now consider the statement:

```
current = current->link;
```

This statement copies the value of current->link, which is 2800, into current. Therefore, after this statement executes, current points to the second node in the list. (When working with linked lists, we typically use these types of statements to advance a pointer to the next node in the list.) See Figure 16-6.

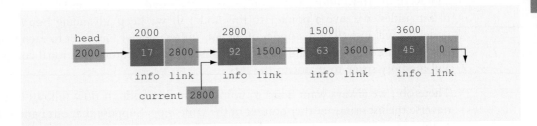

FIGURE 16-6 List after the statement current = current->link; executes

In Figure 16-6:

	Value
current	2800
current->info	92
current->link	1500
current->link->info	63

Finally, note that in Figure 16-6:

	Value
head->link->link	1500
head->link->link->info	63
head->link->link->link	3600
head->link->link->link->info	45
current->link->link	3600
current->link->link->info	45
current->link->link->link	0 (that is, NULL)
current->link->link->link->info	Does not exist

From now on, when working with linked lists, we will use only the arrow notation.

TRAVERSING A LINKED LIST

The basic operations of a linked list are as follows: search the list to determine whether a particular item is in the list, insert an item in the list, and delete an item from the list.

These operations require the list to be traversed. That is, given a pointer to the first node of the list, we must step through the nodes of the list.

Suppose that the pointer head points to the first node in the list, and the link of the last node is NULL. We cannot use the pointer head to traverse the list because if we use head to traverse the list, we would lose the nodes of the list. This problem occurs because the links are in only one direction. The pointer head contains the address of the first node, the first node contains the address of the second node, the second node contains the address of the third node, and so on. If we move head to the second node, the first node is lost (unless we save a pointer to this node). If we keep advancing head to the next node, we will lose all of the nodes of the list (unless we save a pointer to each node before advancing head, which is impractical because it would require additional computer time and memory space to maintain the list).

Therefore, we always want head to point to the first node. It now follows that we must traverse the list using another pointer of the same type. Suppose that current is a pointer of the same type as head. The following code traverses the list:

```
current = head;

while (current != NULL)
{
    //Process the current node
    current = current->link;
}
```

For example, suppose that head points to a linked list of numbers. The following code outputs the data stored in each node:

```
current = head;

while (current != NULL)
{
    cout << current->info << " ";
    current = current->link;
}
```

ITEM INSERTION AND DELETION

This section discusses how to insert an item into, and delete an item from, a linked list. Consider the following definition of a node. (For simplicity, we assume that the info type is int. The next section, which discusses linked lists as an abstract data type (ADT) using templates, uses the generic definition of a node.)

```
struct nodeType
{
    int info;
    nodeType *link;
};
```

We will use the following variable declaration:

```
nodeType *head, *p, *q, *newNode;
```

INSERTION

Consider the linked list shown in Figure 16-7.

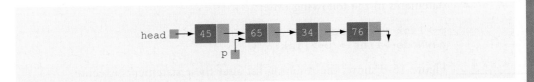

FIGURE 16-7 Linked list before item insertion

Suppose that p points to the node with `info` 65, and a new node with `info` 50 is to be created and inserted after p. Consider the following statements:

```
newNode = new nodeType;    //create newNode
newNode->info = 50;        //store 50 in the new node
newNode->link = p->link;
p->link = newNode;
```

Table 16-1 shows the effect of these statements.

TABLE 16-1 Inserting a Node in a Linked List

Statement	Effect
`newNode = new nodeType;`	head → 45 → 65 → 34 → 76 p newNode →
`newNode->info = 50;`	head → 45 → 65 → 34 → 76 p newNode → 50
`newNode->link = p->link;`	head → 45 → 65 → 34 → 76 p newNode → 50
`p->link = newNode;`	head → 45 → 65 → 34 → 76 p newNode → 50

Note that the sequence of statements to insert the node is very important because to insert newNode in the list, we use only one pointer, p, to adjust the links of the node of the linked list. Suppose that we reverse the sequence of the statements and execute the statements in the following order:

```
p->link = newNode;
newNode->link = p->link;
```

Figure 16-8 shows the resulting list after these statements execute.

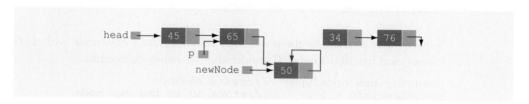

FIGURE 16-8 List after the execution of the statement p->link = newNode; followed by the execution of the statement newNode->link = p->link;

From Figure 16-8, it is clear that newNode points back to itself and the remainder of the list is lost.

Using two pointers, we can simplify the insertion code somewhat. Suppose q points to the node with info 34 (see Figure 16-9).

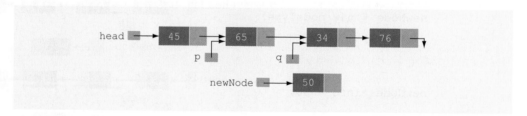

FIGURE 16-9 List with pointers p and q

The following statements insert newNode between p and q:

```
newNode->link = q;
p->link = newNode;
```

The order in which these statements execute does not matter. To illustrate this, suppose that we execute the statements in the following order:

```
p->link = newNode;
newNode->link = q;
```

Table 16-2 shows the effect of these statements.

TABLE 16-2 Inserting a Node in a Linked List Using Two Pointers

Statement	Effect
p->link = newNode;	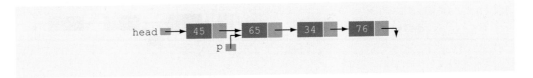
newNode->link = q;	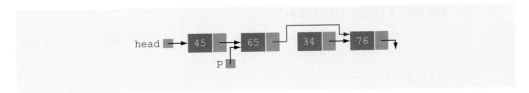

Deletion

Consider the linked list shown in Figure 16-10.

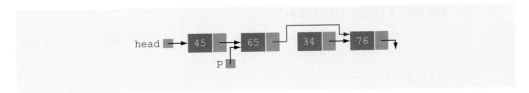

FIGURE 16-10 Node to be deleted is with info 34

Suppose that the node with info 34 is to be deleted from the list. The following statement removes the node from the list.

```
p->link = p->link->link;
```

Figure 16-11 shows the resulting list after the preceding statement executes.

FIGURE 16-11 List after the statement newNode->link = q; executes

From Figure 16-11, it is clear that the node with info 34 is removed from the list. However, the memory is still occupied by this node, and this memory is inaccessible; that is, this node is dangling. To deallocate the memory, we need a pointer to this node. The following statements delete the node from the list and deallocate the memory occupied by this node.

```
q = p->link;
p->link = q->link;
delete q;
```

Table 16-3 shows the effect of these statements.

TABLE 16-3 Deleting a Node from a Linked List

Statement	Effect
`q = p->link;`	
`p->link = q->link;`	
`delete q;`	

Building a Linked List

Now that we know how to insert a node in a linked list, let us see how to build a linked list. First, we consider a linked list in general. If the data we read is unsorted, the linked list will be unsorted. Such a list can be built in two ways: forward and backward. In the forward manner, a new node is always inserted at the end of the linked list. In the backward manner, a new node is always inserted at the beginning of the list. We will consider both cases.

BUILDING A LINKED LIST FORWARD

Suppose that the nodes are in the usual `info-link` form, and `info` is of type `int`. Let us assume that we process the following data:

2 15 8 24 34

We need three pointers to build the list: one to point to the first node in the list, which cannot be moved; one to point to the last node in the list; and one to create the new node. Consider the following variable declaration:

```
nodeType *first, *last, *newNode;
int num;
```

Suppose that `first` points to the first node in the list. Initially, the list is empty, so both `first` and `last` are NULL. Thus, we must have the statements:

```
first = NULL;
last = NULL;
```

to initialize `first` and `last` to NULL.

Next, consider the following statements:

```
1  cin >> num;              //read and store a number in num
2  newNode = new nodeType;  //allocate memory of type nodeType
                            //and store the address of the
                            //allocated memory in newNode
3  newNode->info = num;     //copy the value of num into the
                            //info field of newNode
4  newNode->link = NULL;    //initialize the link field of
                            //newNode to NULL
5  if (first == NULL)       //if first is NULL, the list is empty;
                            //make first and last point to newNode
   {
5a    first = newNode;
5b    last = newNode;
   }
6  else                     //list is not empty
   {
6a    last->link = newNode; //insert newNode at the end of the list
6b    last = newNode;       //set last so that it points to the
                            //actual last node in the list
   }
```

Let us now execute these statements. Initially, both `first` and `last` are NULL. Therefore, we have the list as shown in Figure 16-12.

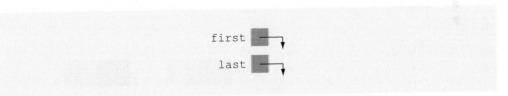

FIGURE 16-12 Empty list

After statement 1 executes, num is 2. Statement 2 creates a node and stores the address of that node in newNode. Statement 3 stores 2 in the `info` field of newNode, and statement 4 stores NULL in the link field of newNode (see Figure 16-13).

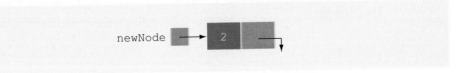

FIGURE 16-13 newNode with `info` 2

Because `first` is NULL, we execute statements 5a and 5b. Figure 16-14 shows the resulting list.

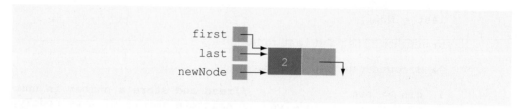

FIGURE 16-14 List after inserting `newNode` in it

We now repeat statements 1 through 6b. After statement 1 executes, num is 15. Statement 2 creates a node and stores the address of this node in `newNode`. Statement 3 stores 15 in the `info` field of `newNode`, and statement 4 stores NULL in the link field of `newNode` (see Figure 16-15).

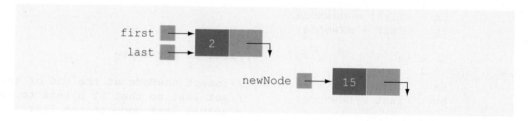

FIGURE 16-15 List and `newNode` with `info` 15

Because `first` is not NULL, we execute statements 6a and 6b. Figure 16-16 shows the resulting list.

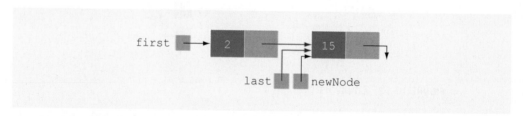

FIGURE 16-16 List after inserting `newNode` at the end

We now repeat statements 1 through 6b three more times. Figure 16-17 shows the resulting list.

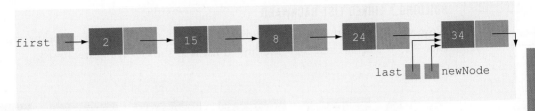

FIGURE 16-17 List after inserting 8, 24, and 34

To build the linked list, we can put the previous statements in a loop and execute the loop until certain conditions are met. We can, in fact, write a C++ function to build a linked list.

Suppose that we read a list of integers ending with -999. The following function, `buildListForward`, builds a linked list (in a forward manner) and returns the pointer of the built list:

```cpp
nodeType* buildListForward()
{
    nodeType *first, *newNode, *last;
    int num;

    cout << "Enter a list of integers ending with -999."
         << endl;
    cin >> num;
    first = NULL;

    while (num != -999)
    {
        newNode = new nodeType;
        newNode->info = num;
        newNode->link = NULL;

        if (first == NULL)
        {
            first = newNode;
            last = newNode;
        }
        else
        {
            last->link = newNode;
            last = newNode;
        }
        cin >> num;
    } //end while

    return first;
} //end buildListForward
```

BUILDING A LINKED LIST BACKWARD

Now we consider the case of building a linked list backward. For the previously given data—2, 15, 8, 24, and 34—the linked list is as shown in Figure 16-18.

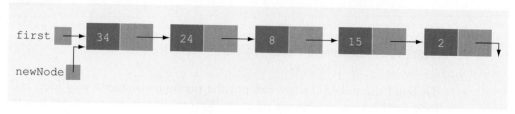

FIGURE 16-18 List after building it backward

Because the new node is always inserted at the beginning of the list, we do not need to know the end of the list, so the pointer `last` is not needed. Also, after inserting the new node at the beginning, the new node becomes the first node in the list. Thus, we need to update the value of the pointer `first` to correctly point to the first node in the list. We see, then, that we need only two pointers to build the linked list: one to point to the list and one to create the new node. Because initially the list is empty, the pointer `first` must be initialized to NULL. In pseudocode, the algorithm is:

1. Initialize `first` to NULL.

2. For each item in the list:

    a. Create the new node, `newNode`.

    b. Store the item in `newNode`.

    c. Insert `newNode` before `first`.

    d. Update the value of the pointer `first`.

The following C++ function builds the linked list backward and returns the pointer of the built list:

```
nodeType* buildListBackward()
{
    nodeType *first, *newNode;
    int num;

    cout << "Enter a list of integers ending with -999."
         << endl;
    cin >> num;
    first = NULL;

    while (num != -999)
    {
        newNode = new nodeType;    //create a node
        newNode->info = num;       //store the data in newNode
        newNode->link = first;     //put newNode at the beginning
```

```
                first = newNode;          //of the list
                                          //update the head pointer of
                                          //the list, that is, first
                cin >> num;               //read the next number
        }

    return first;
} //end buildListBackward
```

Linked List as an ADT

The previous sections taught you the basic properties of linked lists and how to construct and manipulate them. Because a linked list is a very important data structure, rather than discuss specific lists such as a list of integers or a list of strings, this section discusses linked lists as an abstract data type (ADT). Using templates, this section gives a generic definition of linked lists, which is then used in the next section and later in this book. The programming example at the end of this chapter also uses this generic definition of linked lists.

The basic operations on linked lists are:

1. Initialize the list.
2. Determine whether the list is empty.
3. Print the list.
4. Find the length of the list.
5. Destroy the list.
6. Retrieve the info contained in the first node.
7. Retrieve the info contained in the last node.
8. Search the list for a given item.
9. Insert an item in the list.
10. Delete an item from the list.
11. Make a copy of the linked list.

In general, there are two types of linked lists—sorted lists, whose elements are arranged according to some criteria, and unsorted lists, whose elements are in no particular order. The algorithms to implement the operations search, insert, and remove slightly differ for sorted and unsorted lists. Therefore, we will define the class linkedListType to implement the basic operations on a linked list as an abstract class. Using the principle of inheritance, we, in fact, will derive two classes—unorderedLinkedList and orderedLinkedList—from the class linkedListType.

Objects of the class unorderedLinkedList would arrange list elements in no particular order, that is, these lists may not be sorted. On the other hand, objects of the class orderedLinkedList would arrange elements according to some comparison criteria, usually less than or equal to. That is, these lists will be in ascending order. Moreover, after inserting an element into or removing an element from an ordered list, the resulting list will be ordered.

If a linked list is unordered, we can insert a new item at either the end or the beginning. Furthermore, you can build such a list in either a forward manner or a backward manner. The function `buildListForward` inserts the new item at the end, whereas the function `buildListBackward` inserts the new item at the beginning. To accommodate both operations, we will write two functions: `insertFirst` to insert the new item at the beginning of the list and `insertLast` to insert the new item at the end of the list. Also, to make the algorithms more efficient, we will use two pointers in the list: `first`, which points to the first node in the list, and `last`, which points to the last node in the list.

Structure of Linked List Nodes

Recall that each node of a linked list must store the data as well as the address for the next node in the list (except the last node of the list). Therefore, the node has two member variables. To simplify operations such as insert and delete, we define the class to implement the node of a linked list as a `struct`. The definition of the `struct` `nodeType` is:

```
//Definition of the node

template <class Type>
struct nodeType
{
    Type info;
    nodeType<Type> *link;
};
```

NOTE   The class to implement the node of a linked list is declared as a `struct`. Programming Exercise 9, at the end of this chapter, asks you to redefine the class to implement the nodes of a linked list so that the member variables of the `class` `nodeType` are `private`.

Member Variables of the `class` `linkedListType`

To maintain a linked list, we use two pointers: `first` and `last`. The pointer `first` points to the first node in the list, and `last` points to the last node in the list. We also keep a count of the number of nodes in the list. Therefore, the `class` `linkedListType` has three member variables, as follows:

```
protected:
    int count;     //variable to store the number of
                   //elements in the list
    nodeType<Type> *first; //pointer to the first node
                           //of the list
    nodeType<Type> *last;  //pointer to the last node
                           //of the list
```

Linked List Iterators

One of the basic operations performed on a list is to process each node of the list. This requires the list to be traversed, starting at the first node. Moreover, a specific application requires each node to be processed in a very specific way. A common technique to accomplish this is to provide an iterator. So what is an iterator? An **iterator** is an object that produces each element of a container, such as a linked list, one element at a time. The two most common operations on iterators are ++ (the increment operator) and * (the dereferenceing operator). The increment operator advances the iterator to the next node in the list, and the dereferencing operator returns the info of the current node.

Note that an iterator is an object. So we need to define a class, which we will call linkedListIterator, to create iterators to objects of the class linkedListType. The iterator class would have one member variable pointing to (the current) node.

```
template <class Type>
class linkedListIterator
{
public:
    linkedListIterator();
      //Default constructor.
      //Postcondition: current = NULL;

    linkedListIterator(nodeType<Type> *ptr);
      //Constructor with a parameter.
      //Postcondition: current = ptr;

    Type operator*();
      //Function to overload the dereferencing operator *.
      //Postcondition: Returns the info contained in the node.

    linkedListIterator<Type> operator++();
      //Overload the pre-increment operator.
      //Postcondition: The iterator is advanced to the next
      //               node.

    bool operator==(const linkedListIterator<Type>& right) const;
      //Overload the equality operator.
      //Postcondition: Returns true if this iterator is equal to
      //               the iterator specified by right,
      //               otherwise it returns false.

    bool operator!=(const linkedListIterator<Type>& right) const;
      //Overload the not equal to operator.
      //Postcondition: Returns true if this iterator is not equal
      //               to the iterator specified by right,
      //               otherwise it returns false.

private:
    nodeType<Type> *current; //pointer to point to the current
                             //node in the linked list
};
```

Figure 16-19 shows the UML class diagram of the `class linkedListIterator`.

```
                    linkedListIterator<Type>

-*current: nodeType<Type>

+linkedListIterator()
+linkedListIterator(nodeType<Type>)
+operator*(): Type
+operator++(): linkedListIterator<Type>
+operator==(const linkedListIterator<Type>&) const: bool
+operator!=(const linkedListIterator<Type>&) const: bool
```

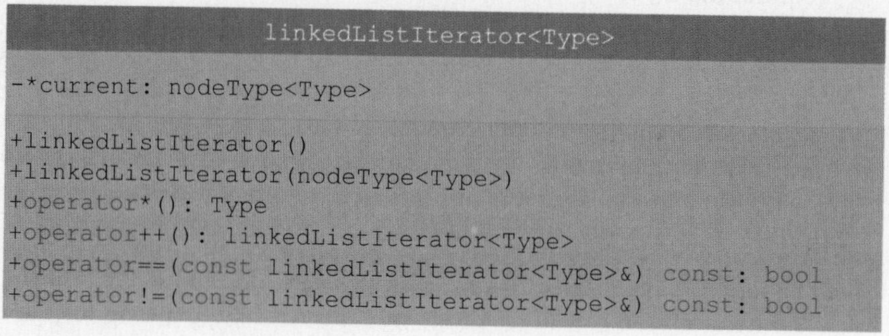

FIGURE 16-19 UML class diagram of the `class` linkedListIterator

The definitions of the functions of the `class linkedListIterator` are:

```cpp
template <class Type>
linkedListIterator<Type>::linkedListIterator()
{
    current = NULL;
}

template <class Type>
linkedListIterator<Type>::
                  linkedListIterator(nodeType<Type> *ptr)
{
    current = ptr;
}

template <class Type>
Type linkedListIterator<Type>::operator*()
{
    return current->info;
}

template <class Type>
linkedListIterator<Type> linkedListIterator<Type>::operator++()
{
    current = current->link;

    return *this;
}

template <class Type>
bool linkedListIterator<Type>::operator==
                (const linkedListIterator<Type>& right) const
{
    return (current == right.current);
}
```

```
template <class Type>
bool linkedListIterator<Type>::operator!=
                    (const linkedListIterator<Type>& right) const
{
    return (current != right.current);
}
```

Now that we have defined the classes to implement the node of a linked list and an iterator to a linked list, next we describe the `class linkedListType` to implement the basic properties of a linked list.

The following abstract class defines the basic properties of a linked list as an ADT:

```
template <class Type>
class linkedListType
{
public:
    const linkedListType<Type>& operator=
                        (const linkedListType<Type>&);
        //Overload the assignment operator.

    void initializeList();
        //Initialize the list to an empty state.
        //Postcondition: first = NULL, last = NULL, count = 0;

    bool isEmptyList() const;
        //Function to determine whether the list is empty.
        //Postcondition: Returns true if the list is empty,
        //               otherwise it returns false.

    void print() const;
        //Function to output the data contained in each node.
        //Postcondition: none

    int length() const;
        //Function to return the number of nodes in the list.
        //Postcondition: The value of count is returned.

    void destroyList();
        //Function to delete all the nodes from the list.
        //Postcondition: first = NULL, last = NULL, count = 0;

    Type front() const;
        //Function to return the first element of the list.
        //Precondition: The list must exist and must not be
        //              empty.
        //Postcondition: If the list is empty, the program
        //               terminates; otherwise, the first
        //               element of the list is returned.

    Type back() const;
        //Function to return the last element of the list.
        //Precondition: The list must exist and must not be
        //              empty.
        //Postcondition: If the list is empty, the program
        //               terminates; otherwise, the last
        //               element of the list is returned.
```

```
virtual bool search(const Type& searchItem) const = 0;
    //Function to determine whether searchItem is in the list.
    //Postcondition: Returns true if searchItem is in the
    //               list, otherwise the value false is
    //               returned.

virtual void insertFirst(const Type& newItem) = 0;
    //Function to insert newItem at the beginning of the list.
    //Postcondition: first points to the new list, newItem is
    //               inserted at the beginning of the list,
    //               last points to the last node in the list,
    //               and count is incremented by 1.

virtual void insertLast(const Type& newItem) = 0;
    //Function to insert newItem at the end of the list.
    //Postcondition: first points to the new list, newItem
    //               is inserted at the end of the list,
    //               last points to the last node in the list,
    //               and count is incremented by 1.

virtual void deleteNode(const Type& deleteItem) = 0;
    //Function to delete deleteItem from the list.
    //Postcondition: If found, the node containing
    //               deleteItem is deleted from the list.
    //               first points to the first node, last
    //               points to the last node of the updated
    //               list, and count is decremented by 1.

linkedListIterator<Type> begin();
    //Function to return an iterator at the begining of the
    //linked list.
    //Postcondition: Returns an iterator such that current is
    //               set to first.

linkedListIterator<Type> end();
    //Function to return an iterator one element past the
    //last element of the linked list.
    //Postcondition: Returns an iterator such that current is
    //               set to NULL.

linkedListType();
    //default constructor
    //Initializes the list to an empty state.
    //Postcondition: first = NULL, last = NULL, count = 0;

linkedListType(const linkedListType<Type>& otherList);
    //copy constructor

~linkedListType();
    //destructor
    //Deletes all the nodes from the list.
    //Postcondition: The list object is destroyed.

protected:
    int count;    //variable to store the number of
                  //elements in the list
```

```
nodeType<Type> *first; //pointer to the first node of the list
nodeType<Type> *last;  //pointer to the last node of the list

private:
    void copyList(const linkedListType<Type>& otherList);
    //Function to make a copy of otherList.
    //Postcondition: A copy of otherList is created and
    //                      assigned to this list.
};
```

Figure 16-20 shows the UML class diagram of the class linkedListType.

```
                    linkedListType<Type>
────────────────────────────────────────────────────
#count: int
#*first: nodeType<Type>
#*last: nodeType<Type>
────────────────────────────────────────────────────
+operator=(const linkedListType<Type>&):
                        const linkedListType<Type>&
+initializeList(): void
+isEmptyList() const: bool
+print() const: void
+length() const: int
+destroyList(): void
+front() const: Type
+back() const: Type
+search(const Type&) const = 0: bool
+insertFirst(const Type&) = 0: void
+insertLast(const Type&) = 0: void
+deleteNode(const Type&) = 0: void
+begin(): linkedListIterator<Type>
+end(): linkedListIterator<Type>
+linkedListType()
+linkedListType(const linkedListType<Type>&)
+~linkedListType()
-copyList(const linkedListType<Type>&): void
```

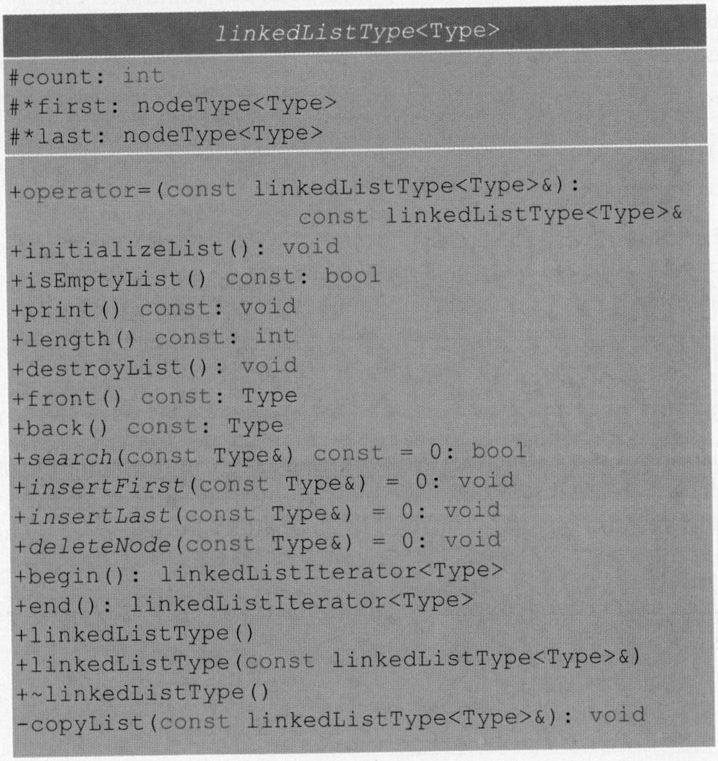

FIGURE 16-20 UML class diagram of the class linkedListType

Note that typically, in the UML diagram, the name of an abstract class and abstract function is shown in italics.

The instance variables first and last, as defined earlier, of the class linkedListType are protected, not private, because as noted previously, we will derive the classes unorderedLinkedList and orderedLinkedList from the class linkedListType. Because each of the classes unorderedLinkedList and `orderedLinkedList` will provide separate definitions of the functions `search`, `insertFirst`, `insertLast`, and `deleteNode` and because these functions would access the instance variable, to provide direct access to the instance variables, the instance variables are declared as `protected`.

The definition of the `class linkedListType` includes a member function to overload the assignment operator. For classes that include pointer data members, the assignment operator must be explicitly overloaded (see Chapters 12 and 13). For the same reason, the definition of the class also includes a copy constructor.

Notice that the definition of the `class linkedListType` contains the member function `copyList`, which is declared as a `private` member. This is due to the fact that this function is used only to implement the copy constructor and overload the assignment operator.

Next, we write the definitions of the nonabstract functions of the `class LinkedListClass`.

The list is empty if `first` is `NULL`. Therefore, the definition of the function `isEmptyList` to implement this operation is as follows:

```
template <class Type>
bool linkedListType<Type>::isEmptyList() const
{
    return (first == NULL);
}
```

DEFAULT CONSTRUCTOR

The default constructor, `linkedListType`, is quite straightforward. It simply initializes the list to an empty state. Recall that when an object of the `linkedListType` type is declared and no value is passed, the default constructor is executed automatically.

```
template <class Type>
linkedListType<Type>::linkedListType() //default constructor
{
    first = NULL;
    last = NULL;
    count = 0;
}
```

DESTROY THE LIST

The function `destroyList` deallocates the memory occupied by each node. We traverse the list starting from the first node and deallocate the memory by calling the operator `delete`. We need a temporary pointer to deallocate the memory. Once the entire list is destroyed, we must set the pointers `first` and `last` to `NULL` and count to 0.

```
template <class Type>
void linkedListType<Type>::destroyList()
{
    nodeType<Type> *temp;      //pointer to deallocate the memory
                               //occupied by the node
```

```
    while (first != NULL)    //while there are nodes in the list
    {
        temp = first;          //set temp to the current node
        first = first->link; //advance first to the next node
        delete temp;    //deallocate the memory occupied by temp
    }

    last = NULL; //initialize last to NULL; first has already
                 //been set to NULL by the while loop
    count = 0;
}
```

INITIALIZE THE LIST

The function `initializeList` initializes the list to an empty state. Note that the default constructor or the copy constructor has already initialized the list when the list object was declared. This operation, in fact, reinitializes the list to an empty state, so it must delete the nodes (if any) from the list. This task can be accomplished by using the `destroyList` operation, which also resets the pointers `first` and `last` to NULL and sets count to 0.

```
template <class Type>
void linkedListType<Type>::initializeList()
{
    destroyList(); //if the list has any nodes, delete them
}
```

Print the List

The member function `print` prints the data contained in each node. To do so, we must traverse the list, starting at the first node. Because the pointer `first` always points to the first node in the list, we need another pointer to traverse the list. (If we use `first` to traverse the list, the entire list will be lost.)

```
template <class Type>
void linkedListType<Type>::print() const
{
    nodeType<Type> *current; //pointer to traverse the list

    current = first;     //set current so that it points to
                         //the first node
    while (current != NULL) //while more data to print
    {
        cout << current->info << " ";
        current = current->link;
    }
}//end print
```

Length of a List

The length of a linked list (that is, how many nodes are in the list) is stored in the variable count. Therefore, this function returns the value of this variable:

```
template <class Type>
int linkedListType<Type>::length() const
{
    return count;
}
```

Retrieve the Data of the First Node

The function front returns the info contained in the first node, and its definition is straightforward:

```
template <class Type>
Type linkedListType<Type>::front() const
{
    assert(first != NULL);

    return first->info; //return the info of the first node
}//end front
```

Notice that if the list is empty, the assert statement terminates the program. Therefore, before calling this function, check to see whether the list is nonempty.

Retrieve the Data of the Last Node

The function back returns the info contained in the last node, and its definition is straightforward:

```
template <class Type>
Type linkedListType<Type>::back() const
{
    assert(last != NULL);

    return last->info; //return the info of the last node
}//end back
```

Notice that if the list is empty, the assert statement terminates the program. Therefore, before calling this function, check to see whether the list is nonempty.

Begin and End

The function begin returns an iterator to the first node in the linked list, and the function end returns an iterator to one past the last node in the linked list. Their definitions are:

```
template <class Type>
linkedListIterator<Type> linkedListType<Type>::begin()
{
    linkedListIterator<Type> temp(first);

    return temp;
}
```

```
template <class Type>
linkedListIterator<Type> linkedListType<Type>::end()
{
    linkedListIterator<Type> temp(NULL);

    return temp;
}
```

Copy the List

The function copyList makes an identical copy of a linked list. Therefore, we traverse the list to be copied, starting at the first node. Corresponding to each node in the original list, we:

    a.   Create a node, and call it newNode.

    b.   Copy the info of the node (in the original list) into newNode.

    c.   Insert newNode at the end of the list being created.

The definition of the function copyList is:

```
template <class Type>
void linkedListType<Type>::copyList
                    (const linkedListType<Type>& otherList)
{
    nodeType<Type> *newNode; //pointer to create a node
    nodeType<Type> *current; //pointer to traverse the list

    if (first != NULL) //if the list is nonempty, make it empty
        destroyList();

    if (otherList.first == NULL) //otherList is empty
    {
        first = NULL;
        last = NULL;
        count = 0;
    }
    else
    {
        current = otherList.first; //current points to the
                                   //list to be copied
        count = otherList.count;

            //copy the first node
        first = new nodeType<Type>;  //create the node
        first->info = current->info; //copy the info
        first->link = NULL;          //set the link field of
                                     //the node to NULL
        last = first;                //make last point to the
                                     //first node
        current = current->link;     //make current point to
                                     //the next node
```

```
            //copy the remaining list
        while (current != NULL)
        {
            newNode = new nodeType<Type>;   //create a node
            newNode->info = current->info; //copy the info
            newNode->link = NULL;          //set the link of
                                           //newNode to NULL
            last->link = newNode;   //attach newNode after last
            last = newNode;         //make last point to
                                    //the actual last node

            current = current->link;   //make current point
                                       //to the next node

        }//end while
    }//end else
}//end copyList
```

Destructor

The destructor deallocates the memory occupied by the nodes of a list when the class object goes out of scope. Because memory is allocated dynamically, resetting the pointers first and last does not deallocate the memory occupied by the nodes in the list. We must traverse the list, starting at the first node, and delete each node in the list. The list can be destroyed by calling the function destroyList. Therefore, the definition of the destructor is:

```
template <class Type>
linkedListType<Type>::~linkedListType() //destructor
{
    destroyList();
}
```

Copy Constructor

Because the class linkedListType contains pointer data members, the definition of this class contains the copy constructor. Recall that if a formal parameter is a value parameter, the copy constructor provides the formal parameter with its own copy of the data. The copy constructor also executes when an object is declared and initialized using another object. (For more information, see Chapter 12.)

The copy constructor makes an identical copy of the linked list. This can be done by calling the function copyList. Because the function copyList checks whether the original is empty by checking the value of first, we must first initialize the pointer first to NULL before calling the function copyList.

The definition of the copy constructor is:

```
template <class Type>
linkedListType<Type>::linkedListType
                    (const linkedListType<Type>& otherList)
{
    first = NULL;
    copyList(otherList);
}//end copy constructor
```

Overloading the Assignment Operator

The definition of the function to overload the assignment operator for the `class` `linkedListType` is similar to the definition of the copy constructor. We give its definition for the sake of completeness.

```cpp
        //overload the assignment operator
template <class Type>
const linkedListType<Type>& linkedListType<Type>::operator=
                        (const linkedListType<Type>& otherList)
{
    if (this != &otherList) //avoid self-copy
    {
        copyList(otherList);
    }//end else

    return *this;
}
```

Unordered Linked Lists

As described in the preceding section, we derive the `class` `unorderedLinkedList` from the abstract `class` `linkedListType` and implement the operations `search`, `insertFirst`, `insertLast`, and `deleteNode`.

The following class defines an unordered linked list as an ADT:

```cpp
template <class Type>
class unorderedLinkedList: public linkedListType<Type>
{
public:
    bool search(const Type& searchItem) const;
        //Function to determine whether searchItem is in the list.
        //Postcondition: Returns true if searchItem is in the
        //               list, otherwise the value false is
        //               returned.

    void insertFirst(const Type& newItem);
        //Function to insert newItem at the beginning of the list.
        //Postcondition: first points to the new list, newItem is
        //               inserted at the beginning of the list,
        //               last points to the last node in the
        //               list, and count is incremented by 1.

    void insertLast(const Type& newItem);
        //Function to insert newItem at the end of the list.
        //Postcondition: first points to the new list, newItem
        //               is inserted at the end of the list,
        //               last points to the last node in the
        //               list, and count is incremented by 1.

    void deleteNode(const Type& deleteItem);
        //Function to delete deleteItem from the list.
        //Postcondition: If found, the node containing
```

```
    //              deleteItem is deleted from the list.
    //              first points to the first node, last
    //              points to the last node of the updated
    //              list, and count is decremented by 1.
};
```

Figure 16-21 shows a UML class diagram of the **class** unorderedLinkedList and the inheritance hierarchy.

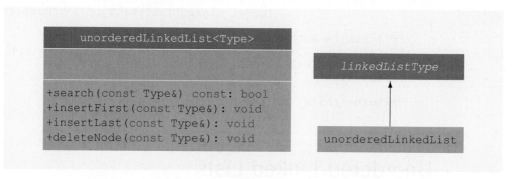

FIGURE 16-21   UML class diagram of the **class** unorderedLinkedList and inheritance hierarchy

Next, we give the definitions of the member functions of the **class** unorderedLinkedList.

Search the List

The member function search searches the list for a given item. If the item is found, it returns **true**; otherwise, it returns **false**. Because a linked list is not a random–access data structure, we must sequentially search the list, starting from the first node.

This function has the following steps:

1. Compare the search item with the current node in the list. If the info of the current node is the same as the search item, stop the search; otherwise, make the next node the current node.

2. Repeat Step 1 until either the item is found or no more data is left in the list to compare with the search item.

```
template <class Type>
bool unorderedLinkedList<Type>::
                   search(const Type& searchItem) const
{
    nodeType<Type> *current; //pointer to traverse the list
    bool found = false;
    current = first; //set current to point to the first
                     //node in the list
```

```
          while (current != NULL && !found)      //search the list
              if (current->info == searchItem) //searchItem is found
                  found = true;
              else
                  current = current->link; //make current point to
                                             //the next node

      return found;
}//end search
```

> **NOTE** The function search can also be written as:
>
> ```
> template <class Type>
> bool unorderedLinkedList<Type>::search(const Type& searchItem)
>     const
> {
>     nodeType<Type> *current; //pointer to traverse the list
>
>     current = first; //set current to point to the first
>                      //node in the list
>
>     while (current != NULL)                    //search the list
>         if (current->info == searchItem)  //searchItem is found
>             return true;
>         else
>             current = current->link; //make current point to
>                                        //the next node
>
>     return false; //searchItem is not in the list, return false
> }//end search
> ```

Insert the First Node

The function insertFirst inserts the new item at the beginning of the list—that is, before the node pointed to by first. The steps needed to implement this function are as follows:

1. Create a new node.
2. Store the new item in the new node.
3. Insert the node before first.
4. Increment count by 1.

```
template <class Type>
void unorderedLinkedList<Type>::insertFirst(const Type& newItem)
{
    nodeType<Type> *newNode; //pointer to create the new node
    newNode = new nodeType<Type>; //create the new node
    newNode->info = newItem;    //store the new item in the node
```

```
    newNode->link = first;       //insert newNode before first
    first = newNode;             //make first point to the
                                 //actual first node
    count++;                     //increment count

    if (last == NULL)    //if the list was empty, newNode is also
                         //the last node in the list
        last = newNode;
}//end insertFirst
```

Insert the Last Node

The definition of the member function `insertLast` is similar to the definition of the member function `insertFirst`. Here, we insert the new node after `last`. Essentially, the function `insertLast` is:

```
template <class Type>
void unorderedLinkedList<Type>::insertLast(const Type& newItem)
{
    nodeType<Type> *newNode; //pointer to create the new node

    newNode = new nodeType<Type>; //create the new node
    newNode->info = newItem;    //store the new item in the node
    newNode->link = NULL;    //set the link field of newNode
                             //to NULL

    if (first == NULL)   //if the list is empty, newNode is
                         //both the first and last node
    {
        first = newNode;
        last = newNode;
        count++;              //increment count
    }
    else    //the list is not empty, insert newNode after last
    {
        last->link = newNode; //insert newNode after last
        last = newNode; //make last point to the actual
                        //last node in the list
        count++;              //increment count
    }
}//end insertLast
```

DELETE A NODE

Next, we discuss the implementation of the member function `deleteNode`, which deletes a node from the list with a given `info`. We need to consider several cases:

Case 1: The list is empty.

Case 2: The first node is the node with the given `info`. In this case, we need to adjust the pointer `first`.

Case 3: The node with the given `info` is somewhere in the list. If the node to be deleted is the last node, then we must adjust the pointer `last`.

Case 4: The list does not contain the node with the given `info`.

If `list` is empty, we can simply print a message indicating that the list is empty. If `list` is not empty, we search the list for the node with the given `info` and, if such a node is found, we delete this node. After deleting the node, `count` is decremented by 1. In pseudocode, the algorithm is:

```
if list is empty
    Output(cannot delete from an empty list);
else
{
    if the first node is the node with the given info
        adjust the head pointer, that is, first, and deallocate
        the memory;
    else
    {
        search the list for the node with the given info
        if such a node is found, delete it and adjust the
        values of last (if necessary) and count.
    }
}
```

Case 1: The list is empty.

If the list is empty, output an error message as shown in the pseudocode.

Case 2: The list is not empty. The node to be deleted is the first node.

This case has two scenarios: `list` has only one node, and `list` has more than one node. Consider the list with one node, as shown in Figure 16-22.

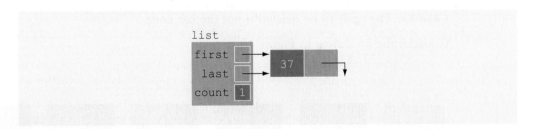

FIGURE 16-22 `list` with one node

Suppose that we want to delete 37. After deletion, the list becomes empty. Therefore, after deletion, both `first` and `last` are set to `NULL`, and `count` is set to 0.

Now consider the list of more than one node, as shown in Figure 16-23.

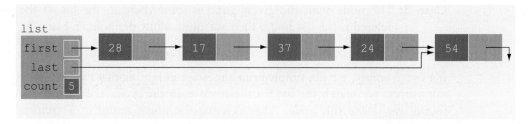

FIGURE 16-23 `list` with more than one node

Suppose that the node to be deleted is 28. After deleting this node, the second node becomes the first node. Therefore, after deleting this node, the value of the pointer `first` changes; that is, after deletion, `first` contains the address of the node with `info` 17, and `count` is decremented by 1. Figure 16-24 shows the list after deleting 28.

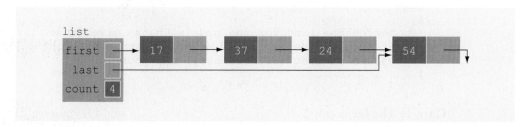

FIGURE 16-24 `list` after deleting node with `info` 28

Case 3: The node to be deleted is not the first node but is somewhere in the list.

This case has two subcases: (a) the node to be deleted is not the last node, and (b) the node to be deleted is the last node. Let us illustrate both cases.

Case 3a: The node to be deleted is not the last node.

Consider the list shown in Figure 16-25.

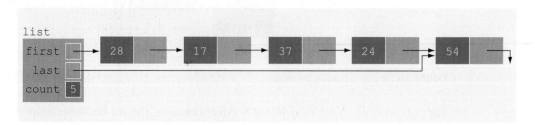

FIGURE 16-25 `list` before deleting 37

Suppose that the node to be deleted is 37. After deleting this node, the resulting list is as shown in Figure 16-26. (Notice that the deletion of 37 does not require us to change the values of `first` and `last`. The link field of the previous node—that is, 17—changes. After deletion, the node with `info` 17 contains the address of the node with 24.)

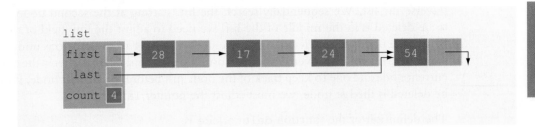

FIGURE 16-26 `list` after deleting 37

Case 3b: The node to be deleted is the last node.

Consider the list shown in Figure 16-27. Suppose that the node to be deleted is 54.

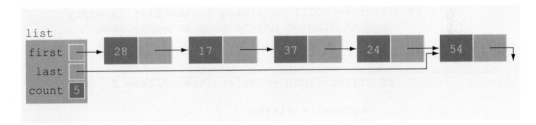

FIGURE 16-27 `list` before deleting 54

After deleting 54, the node with `info` 24 becomes the last node. Therefore, the deletion of 54 requires us to change the value of the pointer `last`. After deleting 54, `last` contains the address of the node with `info` 24. Also, `count` is decremented by 1. Figure 16-28 shows the resulting list.

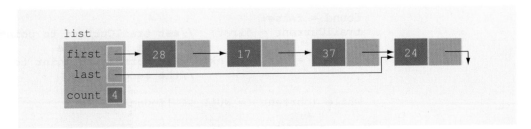

FIGURE 16-28 `list` after deleting 54

Case 4: The node to be deleted is not in the list. In this case, the list requires no adjustment. We simply output an error message, indicating that the item to be deleted is not in the list.

From Cases 2, 3, and 4, it follows that the deletion of a node requires us to traverse the list. Because a linked list is not a random-access data structure, we must sequentially search the list. We handle Case 1 separately, because it does not require us to traverse the list. We sequentially search the list, starting at the second node. If the node to be deleted is in the middle of the list, we need to adjust the link field of the node just before the node to be deleted. Thus, we need a pointer to the previous node. When we search the list for the given `info`, we use two pointers: one to check the `info` of the current node and one to keep track of the node just before the current node. If the node to be deleted is the last node, we must adjust the pointer `last`.

The definition of the function `deleteNode` is:

```cpp
template <class Type>
void unorderedLinkedList<Type>::deleteNode(const Type& deleteItem)
{
    nodeType<Type> *current; //pointer to traverse the list
    nodeType<Type> *trailCurrent; //pointer just before current
    bool found;

    if (first == NULL)      //Case 1; the list is empty
        cout << "Cannot delete from an empty list."
             << endl;
    else
    {
        if (first->info == deleteItem) //Case 2
        {
            current = first;
            first = first->link;
            count--;

            if (first == NULL)     //the list has only one node
                last = NULL;

            delete current;
        }
        else //search the list for the node with the given info
        {
            found = false;
            trailCurrent = first;  //set trailCurrent to point
                                   //to the first node
            current = first->link; //set current to point to
                                   //the second node

            while (current != NULL && !found)
            {
                if (current->info != deleteItem)
                {
                    trailCurrent = current;
                    current = current-> link;
                }
                else
                    found = true;
            }//end while
```

```
                    if (found) //Case 3; if found, delete the node
                    {
                        trailCurrent->link = current->link;
                        count--;

                        if (last == current)     //node to be deleted
                                                 //was the last node
                            last = trailCurrent; //update the value
                                                 //of last
                            delete current;   //delete the node from the list
                    }
                    else
                        cout << "The item to be deleted is not in "
                             << "the list." << endl;
                }//end else
            }//end else
        }//end deleteNode
```

Header File of the Unordered Linked List

For the sake of completeness, we will show how to create the header file that defines the class unorderedListType and the operations on such lists. (We assume that the definition of the class linkedListType and the definitions of the functions to implement the operations are in the header file linkedlist.h.)

```
#ifndef H_UnorderedLinkedList
#define H_UnorderedLinkedList

#include "linkedList.h"

using namespace std;

template <class Type>
class unorderedLinkedList: public linkedListType<Type>
{
public:
    bool search(const Type& searchItem) const;
        //Function to determine whether searchItem is in the list.
        //Postcondition: Returns true if searchItem is in the
        //               list, otherwise the value false is
        //               returned.

    void insertFirst(const Type& newItem);
        //Function to insert newItem at the beginning of the list.
        //Postcondition: first points to the new list, newItem is
        //               inserted at the beginning of the list,
        //               last points to the last node in the
        //               list, and count is incremented by 1.

    void insertLast(const Type& newItem);
        //Function to insert newItem at the end of the list.
        //Postcondition: first points to the new list, newItem
        //               is inserted at the end of the list,
        //               last points to the last node in the
        //               list, and count is incremented by 1.
```

```
    void deleteNode(const Type& deleteItem);
      //Function to delete deleteItem from the list.
      //Postcondition: If found, the node containing
      //               deleteItem is deleted from the list.
      //               first points to the first node, last
      //               points to the last node of the updated
      //               list, and count is decremented by 1.
};

//Place the definitions of the functions search,
//insertFirst, insertLast, and deleteNode here.
      .
      .
      .
#endif
```

 NOTE   The Web site accompanying this book contains several programs illustrating how to use the `class` unorderedLinkedList.

Ordered Linked Lists

The preceding section described the operations on an unordered linked list. This section deals with ordered linked lists. As noted earlier, we derive the `class` orderedLinkedList from the `class` linkedListType and provide the definitions of the abstract functions insertFirst, insertLast, search, and deleteNode to take advantage of the fact that the elements of an ordered linked list are arranged using some ordering criteria. For simplicity, we assume that elements of an ordered linked list are arranged in ascending order.

Because the elements of an ordered linked list are in order, we include the function insert to insert an element in an ordered list at the proper place.

The following class defines an ordered linked list as an ADT:

```
template <class Type>
class orderedLinkedList: public linkedListType<Type>
{
public:
    bool search(const Type& searchItem) const;
      //Function to determine whether searchItem is in the list.
      //Postcondition: Returns true if searchItem is in the list,
      //               otherwise the value false is returned.

    void insert(const Type& newItem);
      //Function to insert newItem in the list.
      //Postcondition: first points to the new list, newItem
      //               is inserted at the proper place in the
      //               list, and count is incremented by 1.

    void insertFirst(const Type& newItem);
      //Function to insert newItem at the beginning of the list.
      //Postcondition: first points to the new list, newItem is
```

```
//                              inserted at the proper place in the list,
//                              last points to the last node in the
//                              list, and count is incremented by 1.

    void insertLast(const Type& newItem);
        //Function to insert newItem at the end of the list.
        //Postcondition: first points to the new list, newItem is
        //                inserted at the proper place in the list,
        //                last points to the last node in the
        //                list, and count is incremented by 1.

    void deleteNode(const Type& deleteItem);
        //Function to delete deleteItem from the list.
        //Postcondition: If found, the node containing
        //                deleteItem is deleted from the list;
        //                first points to the first node of the
        //                new list, and count is decremented by 1.
        //                If deleteItem is not in the list, an
        //                appropriate message is printed.
};
```

Figure 16-29 shows a UML class diagram of the **class** orderedLinkedList and the inheritance hierarchy.

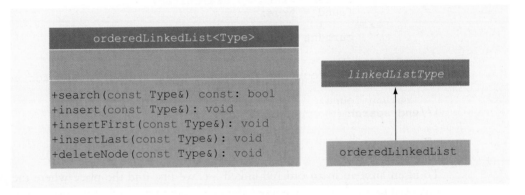

FIGURE 16-29 UML class diagram of the **class** orderedLinkedList and the inheritance hierarchy

Next, we give the definitions of the member functions of the **class** orderedLinkedList.

Search the List

First, we discuss the search operation. The algorithm to implement the search operation is similar to the search algorithm for general lists discussed earlier. Here, because the list is sorted, we can improve the search algorithm somewhat. As before, we start the search at the first node in the list. We stop the search as soon as we find a node in the list with info greater than or equal to the search item or when we have searched the entire list.

The following steps describe this algorithm:

1. Compare the search item with the current node in the list. If the `info` of the current node is greater than or equal to the search item, stop the search; otherwise, make the next node the current node.

2. Repeat Step 1 until either an item in the list that is greater than or equal to the search item is found or no more data is left in the list to compare with the search item.

Note that the loop does not explicitly check whether the search item is equal to an item in the list. Thus, after the loop executes, we must check whether the search item is equal to the item in the list.

```
template <class Type>
bool orderedLinkedList<Type>::
                        search(const Type& searchItem) const
{
    bool found = false;
    nodeType<Type> *current; //pointer to traverse the list

    current = first;  //start the search at the first node

    while (current != NULL && !found)
        if (current->info >= searchItem)
            found = true;
        else
            current = current->link;

    if (found)
        found = (current->info == searchItem); //test for equality

    return found;
}//end search
```

Insert a Node

To insert an item in an ordered linked list, we first find the place where the new item is supposed to go, and then we insert the item in the list. To find the place for the new item, as before, we search the list. Here, we use two pointers, current and trailCurrent, to search the list. The pointer current points to the node whose info is being compared with the item to be inserted, and trailCurrent points to the node just before current. Because the list is in order, the search algorithm is the same as before. The following cases arise:

Case 1: The list is initially empty. The node containing the new item is the only node and thus the first node in the list.

Case 2: The new item is smaller than the smallest item in the list. The new item goes at the beginning of the list. In this case, we need to adjust the list's head pointer— that is, first. Also, count is incremented by 1.

Case 3: The item is to be inserted somewhere in the list.

3a: The new item is larger than all of the items in the list. In this case, the new item is inserted at the end of the list. Thus, the value of current is NULL, and the new item is inserted after trailCurrent. Also, count is incremented by 1.

3b: The new item is to be inserted somewhere in the middle of the list. In this case, the new item is inserted between trailCurrent and current. Also, count is incremented by 1.

The following statements can accomplish both Cases 3a and 3b. Assume newNode points to the new node.

```
trailCurrent->link = newNode;
newNode->link = current;
```

Let us next illustrate these cases.

Case 1: The list is empty.

Consider the list shown in Figure 16–30(a).

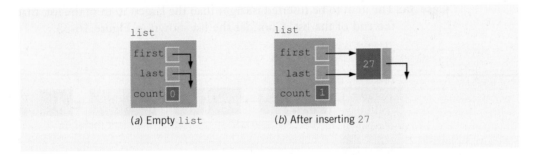

(a) Empty list   (b) After inserting 27

FIGURE 16-30 list

Suppose that we want to insert 27 in the list. To accomplish this task, we create a node, copy 27 into the node, set the link of the node to NULL, and make first point to the node. Figure 16-30(b) shows the resulting list. Notice that, after inserting 27, the values of both first and count change.

Case 2: The list is not empty, and the item to be inserted is smaller than the smallest item in the list. Consider the list shown in Figure 16-31.

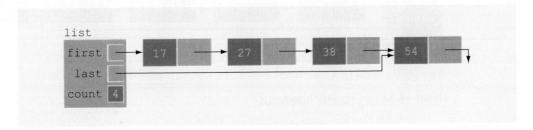

FIGURE 16-31 Nonempty list before inserting 10

Suppose that 10 is to be inserted. After inserting 10 in the list, the node with info 10 becomes the first node of list. This requires us to change the value of first. Also, count is incremented by 1. Figure 16-32 shows the resulting list.

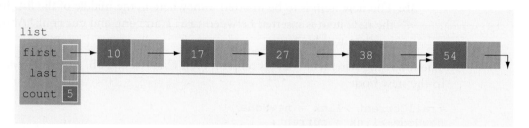

FIGURE 16-32 list after inserting 10

Case 3: The list is not empty, and the item to be inserted is larger than the first item in the list. As indicated previously, this case has two scenarios.

Case 3a: The item to be inserted is larger than the largest item in the list; that is, it goes at the end of the list. Consider the list shown in Figure 16-33.

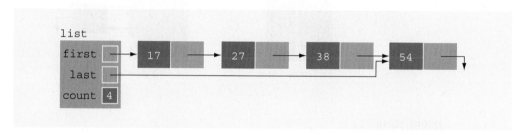

FIGURE 16-33 list before inserting 65

Suppose that we want to insert 65 in the list. After inserting 65, the resulting list is as shown in Figure 16-34.

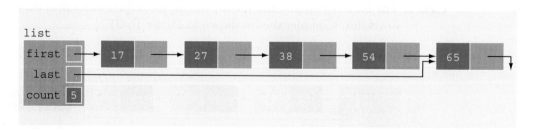

FIGURE 16-34 list after inserting 65

Case 3b: The item to be inserted goes somewhere in the middle of the list. Consider the list shown in Figure 16-35.

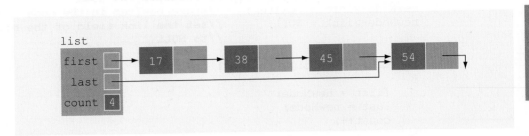

FIGURE 16-35 `list` before inserting 27

Suppose that we want to insert 27 in this list. Clearly, 27 goes between 17 and 38, which would require the link of the node with `info` 17 to be changed. After inserting 27, the resulting list is as shown in Figure 16-36.

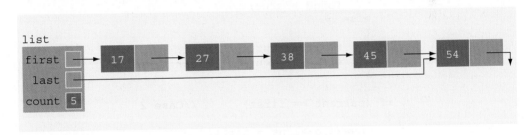

FIGURE 16-36 `list` after inserting 27

From Case 3, it follows that we must first traverse the list to find the place where the new item is to be inserted. It also follows that we should traverse the list with two pointers—say, `current` and `trailCurrent`. The pointer `current` is used to traverse the list and compare the `info` of the node in the list with the item to be inserted. The pointer `trailCurrent` points to the node just before `current`. For example, in Case 3b, when the search stops, `trailCurrent` points to node 17 and `current` points to node 38. The item is inserted after `trailCurrent`. In Case 3a, after searching the list to find the place for 65, `trailCurrent` points to node 54 and `current` is NULL.

Essentially, the function `insert` is as follows:

```
template <class Type>
void orderedLinkedList<Type>::insert(const Type& newItem)
{
    nodeType<Type> *current; //pointer to traverse the list
    nodeType<Type> *trailCurrent; //pointer just before current
    nodeType<Type> *newNode;  //pointer to create a node
```

```
    bool found;

    newNode = new nodeType<Type>; //create the node
    newNode->info = newItem;    //store newItem in the node
    newNode->link = NULL;       //set the link field of the node
                                //to NULL

    if (first == NULL)  //Case 1
    {
        first = newNode;
        last = newNode;
        count++;
    }
    else
    {
        current = first;
        found = false;

        while (current != NULL && !found) //search the list
            if (current->info >= newItem)
                found = true;
            else
            {
                trailCurrent = current;
                current = current->link;
            }

        if (current == first)       //Case 2
        {
            newNode->link = first;
            first = newNode;
            count++;
        }
        else                        //Case 3
        {
            trailCurrent->link = newNode;
            newNode->link = current;

            if (current == NULL)
                last = newNode;

            count++;
        }
    }//end else
}//end insert
```

Insert First and Insert Last

The function insertFirst inserts the new item at the beginning of the list. However, because the resulting list must be sorted, the new item must be inserted at the proper place. Similarly, the function insertLast must insert the new item at the proper place.

Therefore, we use the function `insertNode` to insert the new item at its proper place. The definitions of these functions are:

```
template <class Type>
void orderedLinkedList<Type>::insertFirst(const Type& newItem)
{
    insert(newItem);
}//end insertFirst

template <class Type>
void orderedLinkedList<Type>::insertLast(const Type& newItem)
{
    insert(newItem);
}//end insertLast
```

Note that in reality, the functions `insertFirst` and `insertLast` do not apply to ordered linked lists because the new item must be inserted at the proper place in the list. However, you must provide its definition as these functions are declared as abstract in the parent class.

Delete a Node

To delete a given item from an ordered linked list, first we search the list to see whether the item to be deleted is in the list. The function to implement this operation is the same as the delete operation on general linked lists. Here, because the list is sorted, we can somewhat improve the algorithm for ordered linked lists.

As in the case of `insertNode`, we search the list with two pointers, `current` and `trailCurrent`. Similar to the operation `insertNode`, several cases arise:

Case 1: The list is initially empty. We have an error. We cannot delete from an empty list.

Case 2: The item to be deleted is contained in the first node of the list. We must adjust the head pointer of the list—that is, `first`.

Case 3: The item to be deleted is somewhere in the list. In this case, `current` points to the node containing the item to be deleted, and `trailCurrent` points to the node just before the node pointed to by `current`.

Case 4: The list is not empty, but the item to be deleted is not in the list.

After deleting a node, `count` is decremented by 1. The definition of the function `deleteNode` is:

```
template <class Type>
void orderedLinkedList<Type>::deleteNode(const Type& deleteItem)
{
    nodeType<Type> *current; //pointer to traverse the list
    nodeType<Type> *trailCurrent; //pointer just before current
    bool found;
```

```
    if (first == NULL) //Case 1
        cout << "Cannot delete from an empty list." << endl;
    else
    {
        current = first;
        found = false;

        while (current != NULL && !found)  //search the list
            if (current->info >= deleteItem)
                found = true;
            else
            {
                trailCurrent = current;
                current = current->link;
            }

        if (current == NULL)    //Case 4
            cout << "The item to be deleted is not in the "
                 << "list." << endl;
        else
            if (current->info == deleteItem) //the item to be
                                        //deleted is in the list
            {
                if (first == current)          //Case 2
                {
                    first = first->link;

                    if (first == NULL)
                        last = NULL;

                    delete current;
                }
                else                           //Case 3
                {
                    trailCurrent->link = current->link;

                    if (current == last)
                        last = trailCurrent;

                    delete current;
                }
                count--;
            }
            else                               //Case 4
                cout << "The item to be deleted is not in the "
                     << "list." << endl;
    }
}//end deleteNode
```

Header File of the Ordered Linked List

For the sake of completeness, we will show how to create the header file that defines the class orderedListType, as well as the operations on such lists. (We assume that the definition of the `class` `linkedListType` and the definitions of the functions to implement the operations are in the header file `linkedlist.h`.)

```cpp
#ifndef H_orderedListType
#define H_orderedListType

#include "linkedList.h"

using namespace std;

template <class Type>
class orderedLinkedList: public linkedListType<Type>
{
public:
    bool search(const Type& searchItem) const;
      //Function to determine whether searchItem is in the list.
      //Postcondition: Returns true if searchItem is in the list,
      //               otherwise the value false is returned.

    void insert(const Type& newItem);
      //Function to insert newItem in the list.
      //Postcondition: first points to the new list, newItem
      //               is inserted at the proper place in the
      //               list, and count is incremented by 1.

    void insertFirst(const Type& newItem);
      //Function to insert newItem at the beginning of the list.
      //Postcondition: first points to the new list, newItem is
      //               inserted at the proper place in the list,
      //               last points to the last node in the
      //               list, and count is incremented by 1.

    void insertLast(const Type& newItem);
      //Function to insert newItem at the end of the list.
      //Postcondition: first points to the new list, newItem is
      //               inserted at the proper place in the list,
      //               last points to the last node in the
      //               list, and count is incremented by 1.

    void deleteNode(const Type& deleteItem);
      //Function to delete deleteItem from the list.
      //Postcondition: If found, the node containing
      //               deleteItem is deleted from the list;
      //               first points to the first node of the
      //               new list, and count is decremented by 1.
      //               If deleteItem is not in the list, an
      //               appropriate message is printed.
};

//Place the definitions of the functions search, insert,
//insertFirst, insertLast, and deleteNode here.
   .
   .
   .
#endif
```

The following program tests various operations on an ordered linked list:

```
//Program to test the various operations on an ordered linked list

#include <iostream>
#include "orderedLinkedList.h"

using namespace std;

int main()
{
    orderedLinkedList<int> list1, list2;        //Line 1
    int num;                                     //Line 2

    cout << "Line 3: Enter numbers ending "
         << "with -999." << endl;                //Line 3
    cin >> num;                                  //Line 4
    while (num != -999)                          //Line 5
    {
        list1.insert(num);                       //Line 6
        cin >> num;                              //Line 7
    }

    cout << endl;                                //Line 8

    cout << "Line 9: list1: ";                   //Line 9
    list1.print();                               //Line 10
    cout << endl;                                //Line 11

    list2 = list1; //test the assignment operator Line 12

    cout << "Line 13: list2: ";                  //Line 13
    list2.print();                               //Line 14
    cout << endl;                                //Line 15

    cout << "Line 16: Enter the number to be "
         << "deleted: ";                         //Line 16
    cin >> num;                                  //Line 17
    cout << endl;                                //Line 18

    list2.deleteNode(num);                       //Line 19

    cout << "Line 20: After deleting "
         << num << ", list2: " << endl;          //Line 20
    list2.print();                               //Line 21
    cout<<endl;                                   //Line 22

    return 0;
}
```

Sample Run: In this sample run, the user input is shaded.

```
Line 3: Enter numbers ending with -999.
23 65 34 72 12 82 36 55 29 -999

Line 9: list1: 12 23 29 34 36 55 65 72 82
Line 13: list2: 12 23 29 34 36 55 65 72 82
Line 16: Enter the number to be deleted: 34

Line 20: After deleting 34, list2:
12 23 29 36 55 65 72 82
```

The preceding output is self-explanatory. The details are left as an exercise for you.

NOTE   Notice that the function `insert` does not check whether the item to be inserted is already in the list, that is, it does not check for duplicates. Programming Exercise 8 at the end of this chapter asks you to revise the definition of the function `insert` so that before inserting the item, it checks whether it is already in the list. If the item to be inserted is already in the list, the function outputs an appropriate error message. In other words, duplicates are not allowed.

Print a Linked List in Reverse Order (Recursion Revisited)

The nodes of an ordered list (as constructed previously) are in ascending order. Certain applications, however, might require the data to be printed in descending order, which means that we must print the list backward. We now discuss the function `reversePrint`. Given a pointer to a list, this function prints the elements of the list in reverse order.

Consider the linked list shown in Figure 16-37.

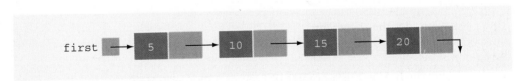

FIGURE 16-37 Linked list

For the list in Figure 16-37, the output should be in the following form:

```
20 15 10 5
```

Because the links are in only one direction, we cannot traverse the list backward starting from the last node. Let us see how we can effectively use recursion to print the list in reverse order.

Let us think in terms of recursion. We cannot print the info of the first node until we have printed the remainder of the list (that is, the tail of the first node). Similarly, we cannot print the info of the second node until we have printed the tail of the second node, and so on. Every time we consider the tail of a node, we reduce the size of the list by 1. Eventually, the size of the list will be reduced to zero, in which case the recursion will stop. Let us first write the algorithm in pseudocode. (Suppose that current is a pointer to a linked list.)

```
if (current != NULL)
{
    reversePrint(current->link);    //print the tail
    cout << current->info << endl; //print the node
}
```

Here, we do not see the base case; it is hidden. The list is printed only if the pointer to the list is not NULL. Also, in the body of the if statement, the recursive call is on the tail of the list. Because eventually the tail of the list will be empty, the if statement in the next call will fail, and the recursion will stop. Also, note that statements (for example, printing the info of the node) appear after the recursive call; thus, when the transfer comes back to the calling function, we must execute the remaining statements. Recall that the function exits only after the last statement executes. (By the "last statement," we do not mean the physical last statement, but rather the logical last statement.)

Let us write the previous function in C++ and then apply it to a list.

```
template <class Type>
void linkedListType<Type>::reversePrint
                         (nodeType<Type> *current) const
{
    if (current != NULL)
    {
        reversePrint(current->link);    //print the tail
        cout << current->info << " "; //print the node
    }
}
```

Consider the statement:

```
reversePrint(first);
```

in which first is a pointer of type nodeType<Type>.

Let us trace the execution of this statement, which is a function call, for the list shown in Figure 16-37. Because the formal parameter is a value parameter, the value of the actual parameter is passed to the formal parameter. (See Figure 16-38.)

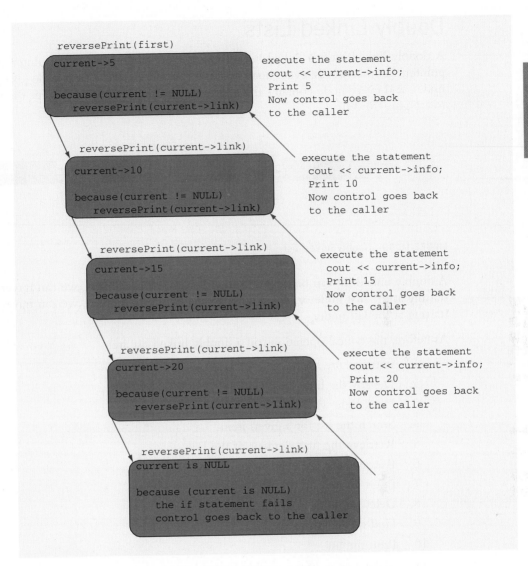

FIGURE 16-38 Execution of the statement reversePrint(first);

printListReverse

Now that we have written the function reversePrint, we can write the definition of the function printListReverse. Its definition is:

```cpp
template <class Type>
void linkedListType<Type>::printListReverse() const
{
    reversePrint(first);
    cout << endl;
}
```

Doubly Linked Lists

A doubly linked list is a linked list in which every node has a next pointer and a back pointer. In other words, every node contains the address of the next node (except the last node), and every node contains the address of the previous node (except the first node) (see Figure 16-39).

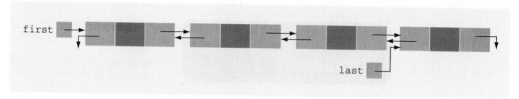

FIGURE 16-39   Doubly linked list

A doubly linked list can be traversed in either direction. That is, we can traverse the list starting at the first node or, if a pointer to the last node is given, we can traverse the list starting at the last node.

As before, the typical operations on a doubly linked list are:

1. Initialize the list.
2. Destroy the list.
3. Determine whether the list is empty.
4. Search the list for a given item.
5. Retrieve the first element of the list.
6. Retrieve the last element of the list.
7. Insert an item in the list.
8. Delete an item from the list.
9. Find the length of the list.
10. Print the list.
11. Make a copy of the doubly linked list.

Next, we describe these operations for an ordered doubly linked list. The following class defines a doubly linked list as an ADT:

```cpp
    //Definition of the node
template <class Type>
struct nodeType
{
    Type info;
    nodeType<Type> *next;
    nodeType<Type> *back;
};
```

```
template <class Type>
class doublyLinkedList
{
public:
    const doublyLinkedList<Type>& operator=
                          (const doublyLinkedList<Type> &);
      //Overload the assignment operator.

    void initializeList();
      //Function to initialize the list to an empty state.
      //Postcondition: first = NULL; last = NULL; count = 0;

    bool isEmptyList() const;
      //Function to determine whether the list is empty.
      //Postcondition: Returns true if the list is empty,
      //               otherwise returns false.

    void destroy();
      //Function to delete all the nodes from the list.
      //Postcondition: first = NULL; last = NULL; count = 0;

    void print() const;
      //Function to output the info contained in each node.

    void reversePrint() const;
      //Function to output the info contained in each node
      //in reverse order.

    int length() const;
      //Function to return the number of nodes in the list.
      //Postcondition: The value of count is returned.

    Type front() const;
      //Function to return the first element of the list.
      //Precondition: The list must exist and must not be empty.
      //Postcondition: If the list is empty, the program
      //               terminates; otherwise, the first
      //               element of the list is returned.

    Type back() const;
      //Function to return the last element of the list.
      //Precondition: The list must exist and must not be empty.
      //Postcondition: If the list is empty, the program
      //               terminates; otherwise, the last
      //               element of the list is returned.

    bool search(const Type& searchItem) const;
      //Function to determine whether searchItem is in the list.
      //Postcondition: Returns true if searchItem is found in
      //               the list, otherwise returns false.
```

1
6

```
    void insert(const Type& insertItem);
      //Function to insert insertItem in the list.
      //Precondition: If the list is nonempty, it must be in
      //               order.
      //Postcondition: insertItem is inserted at the proper place
      //               in the list, first points to the first
      //               node, last points to the last node of the
      //               new list, and count is incremented by 1.

    void deleteNode(const Type& deleteItem);
      //Function to delete deleteItem from the list.
      //Postcondition: If found, the node containing deleteItem
      //               is deleted from the list; first points
      //               to the first node of the new list, last
      //               points to the last node of the new list,
      //               and count is decremented by 1; otherwise
      //               an appropriate message is printed.

    doublyLinkedList();
      //default constructor
      //Initializes the list to an empty state.
      //Postcondition: first = NULL; last = NULL; count = 0;

    doublyLinkedList(const doublyLinkedList<Type>& otherList);
      //copy constructor
    ~doublyLinkedList();
      //destructor
      //Postcondition: The list object is destroyed.

protected:
    int count;
    nodeType<Type> *first; //pointer to the first node
    nodeType<Type> *last;  //pointer to the last node

private:
    void copyList(const doublyLinkedList<Type>& otherList);
      //Function to make a copy of otherList.
      //Postcondition: A copy of otherList is created and
      //               assigned to this list.
};
```

We leave the UML class diagram of the class doublyLinkedList as an exercise for you.

The functions to implement the operations of a doubly linked list are similar to the ones discussed earlier. Here, because every node has two pointers, back and next, some of the operations require the adjustment of two pointers in each node. For the insert and delete operations, because we can traverse the list in either direction, we use only one pointer to traverse the list. Let us call this pointer current. We can set the value of trailCurrent by using both the current pointer and the back pointer of the node pointed to by current. We give the definition of each function here, with four exceptions. Definitions of the functions copyList, the copy constructor, overloading the assignment operator, and the destructor are left as exercises for you. (See Programming Exercise 11 at the end of this chapter.) Moreover, the function copyList is used only to implement the copy constructor and overload the assignment operator.

Default Constructor

The default constructor initializes the doubly linked list to an empty state. It sets first and last to NULL and count to 0.

```
template <class Type>
doublyLinkedList<Type>::doublyLinkedList()
{
    first= NULL;
    last = NULL;
    count = 0;
}
```

isEmptyList

This operation returns true if the list is empty; otherwise, it returns false. The list is empty if the pointer first is NULL.

```
template <class Type>
bool doublyLinkedList<Type>::isEmptyList() const
{
    return (first == NULL);
}
```

Destroy the List

This operation deletes all of the nodes in the list, leaving the list in an empty state. We traverse the list starting at the first node and then delete each node. Furthermore, count is set to 0.

```
template <class Type>
void doublyLinkedList<Type>::destroy()
{
    nodeType<Type> *temp; //pointer to delete the node

    while (first != NULL)
    {
        temp = first;
        first = first->next;
        delete temp;
    }

    last = NULL;
    count = 0;
}
```

Initialize the List

This operation reinitializes the doubly linked list to an empty state. This task can be done by using the operation `destroy`. The definition of the function `initializeList` is:

```
template <class Type>
void doublyLinkedList<Type>::initializeList()
{
    destroy();
}
```

Length of the List

The length of a linked list (that is, how many nodes are in the list) is stored in the variable `count`. Therefore, this function returns the value of this variable.

```
template <class Type>
int doublyLinkedList<Type>::length() const
{
    return count;
}
```

Print the List

The function `print` outputs the `info` contained in each node. We traverse the list, starting from the first node.

```
template <class Type>
void doublyLinkedList<Type>::print() const
{
    nodeType<Type> *current; //pointer to traverse the list

    current = first;  //set current to point to the first node

    while (current != NULL)
    {
        cout << current->info << "   ";  //output info
        current = current->next;
    }//end while
}//end print
```

Reverse Print the List

This function outputs the `info` contained in each node in reverse order. We traverse the list in reverse order, starting from the last node. Its definition is:

```
template <class Type>
void doublyLinkedList<Type>::reversePrint() const
{
    nodeType<Type> *current; //pointer to traverse
                             //the list
```

```
        current = last;   //set current to point to the
                          //last node

    while (current != NULL)
    {
        cout << current->info << "   ";
        current = current->back;
    }//end while
}//end reversePrint
```

Search the List

The function `search` returns `true` if `searchItem` is found in the list; otherwise, it returns `false`. The search algorithm is exactly the same as the search algorithm for an ordered linked list.

```
template <class Type>
bool doublyLinkedList<Type>::
                        search(const Type& searchItem) const
{
    bool found = false;
    nodeType<Type> *current; //pointer to traverse the list

    current = first;

    while (current != NULL && !found)
        if (current->info >= searchItem)
            found = true;
        else
            current = current->next;

    if (found)
        found = (current->info == searchItem); //test for
                                                //equality

    return found;
}//end search
```

First and Last Elements

The function `front` returns the first element of the list, and the function `back` returns the last element of the list. If the list is empty, both functions terminate the program. Their definitions are:

```
template <class Type>
Type doublyLinkedList<Type>::front() const
{
    assert(first != NULL);

    return first->info;
}
```

```
template <class Type>
Type doublyLinkedList<Type>::back() const
{
    assert(last != NULL);

    return last->info;
}
```

INSERT A NODE

Because we are inserting an item in a doubly linked list, the insertion of a node in the list requires the adjustment of two pointers in certain nodes. As before, we find the place where the new item is supposed to be inserted, create the node, store the new item, and adjust the link fields of the new node and other particular nodes in the list. There are four cases:

Case 1: Insertion in an empty list

Case 2: Insertion at the beginning of a nonempty list

Case 3: Insertion at the end of a nonempty list

Case 4: Insertion somewhere in a nonempty list

Both Cases 1 and 2 require us to change the value of the pointer `first`. Cases 3 and 4 are similar. After inserting an item, `count` is incremented by 1. Next, we show Case 4.

Consider the doubly linked list shown in Figure 16-40.

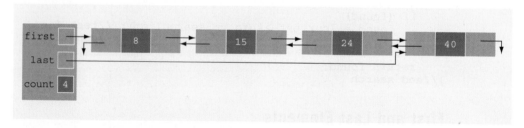

FIGURE 16-40 Doubly linked list before inserting 20

Suppose that 20 is to be inserted in the list. After inserting 20, the resulting list is as shown in Figure 16-41.

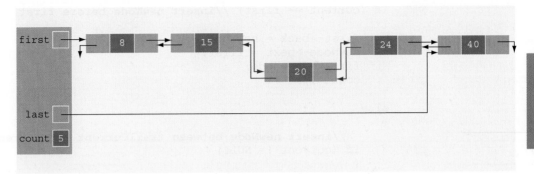

FIGURE 16-41 Doubly linked list after inserting 20

From Figure 16-41, it follows that the next pointer of node 15, the back pointer of node 24, and both the next and back pointers of node 20 need to be adjusted.

The definition of the function insert is:

```
template <class Type>
void doublyLinkedList<Type>::insert(const Type& insertItem)
{
    nodeType<Type> *current;       //pointer to traverse the list
    nodeType<Type> *trailCurrent;  //pointer just before current
    nodeType<Type> *newNode;       //pointer to create a node
    bool found;

    newNode = new nodeType<Type>; //create the node
    newNode->info = insertItem;   //store the new item in the node
    newNode->next = NULL;
    newNode->back = NULL;

    if (first == NULL) //if the list is empty, newNode is
                       //the only node
    {
        first = newNode;
        last = newNode;
        count++;
    }
    else
    {
        found = false;
        current = first;

        while (current != NULL && !found) //search the list
            if (current->info >= insertItem)
                found = true;
            else
            {
                trailCurrent = current;
                current = current->next;
            }
```

16

```
        if (current == first) //insert newNode before first
        {
            first->back = newNode;
            newNode->next = first;
            first = newNode;
            count++;
        }
        else
        {
            //insert newNode between trailCurrent and current
            if (current != NULL)
            {
                trailCurrent->next = newNode;
                newNode->back = trailCurrent;
                newNode->next = current;
                current->back = newNode;
            }
            else
            {
                trailCurrent->next = newNode;
                newNode->back = trailCurrent;
                last = newNode;
            }

            count++;
        }//end else
    }//end else
}//end insert
```

DELETE A NODE

This operation deletes a given item (if found) from the doubly linked list. As before, we first search the list to see whether the item to be deleted is in the list. The search algorithm is the same as before. Similar to the insertNode operation, this operation (if the item to be deleted is in the list) requires the adjustment of two pointers in certain nodes. The delete operation has several cases:

Case 1: The list is empty.

Case 2: The item to be deleted is in the first node of the list, which would require us to change the value of the pointer first.

Case 3: The item to be deleted is somewhere in the list.

Case 4: The item to be deleted is not in the list.

After deleting a node, count is decremented by 1. Let us demonstrate Case 3. Consider the list shown in Figure 16-42.

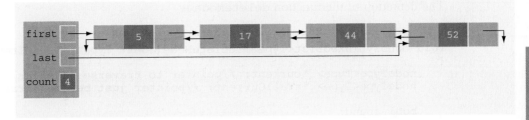

FIGURE 16-42 Doubly linked list before deleting 17

Suppose that the item to be deleted is 17. First, we search the list with two pointers and find the node with `info` 17 and then adjust the link field of the affected nodes (see Figure 16-43).

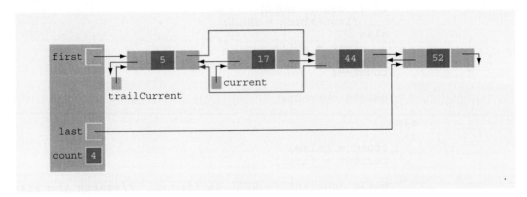

FIGURE 16-43 List after adjusting the links of the nodes before and after the node with `info` 17

Next, we delete the node pointed to by `current` (see Figure 16-44).

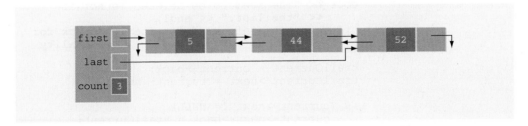

FIGURE 16-44 List after deleting the node with `info` 17

The definition of the function `deleteNode` is:

```cpp
template <class Type>
void doublyLinkedList<Type>::deleteNode(const Type& deleteItem)
{
    nodeType<Type> *current; //pointer to traverse the list
    nodeType<Type> *trailCurrent; //pointer just before current

    bool found;

    if (first == NULL)
        cout << "Cannot delete from an empty list." << endl;
    else if (first->info == deleteItem) //node to be deleted is
                                        //the first node
    {
        current = first;
        first = first->next;

        if (first != NULL)
            first->back = NULL;
        else
            last = NULL;

        count--;

        delete current;
    }
    else
    {
        found = false;
        current = first;

        while (current != NULL && !found)  //search the list
            if (current->info >= deleteItem)
                found = true;
            else
                current = current->next;

        if (current == NULL)
            cout << "The item to be deleted is not in "
                 << "the list." << endl;
        else if (current->info == deleteItem) //check for
                                              //equality
        {
            trailCurrent = current->back;
            trailCurrent->next = current->next;

            if (current->next != NULL)
                current->next->back = trailCurrent;

            if (current == last)
                last = trailCurrent;

            count--;
            delete current;
        }
```

```
        else
            cout << "The item to be deleted is not in list."
                << endl;
    }//end else
}//end deleteNode
```

Circular Linked Lists

A linked list in which the last node points to the first node is called a **circular linked list**. Figure 16-45 show various circular linked lists.

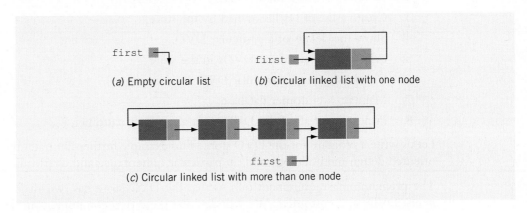

(a) Empty circular list   (b) Circular linked list with one node

(c) Circular linked list with more than one node

FIGURE 16-45 Circular linked lists

In a circular linked list with more than one node, as in Figure 16-45(c), it is convenient to make the pointer `first` point to the last node of the list. Then, by using `first`, you can access both the first and the last nodes of the list. For example, `first` points to the last node, and `first->link` points to the first node.

As before, the usual operations on a circular list are:

1. Initialize the list (to an empty state).
2. Determine if the list is empty.
3. Destroy the list.
4. Print the list.
5. Find the length of the list.
6. Search the list for a given item.
7. Insert an item in the list.
8. Delete an item from the list.
9. Copy the list.

We leave it as an exercise for you to design a class to implement a sorted circular linked list. (See Programming Exercise 13 at the end of this chapter.)

PROGRAMMING EXAMPLE: DVD Store

Watch the Video

For a family or an individual, a favorite place to go on weekends or holidays is to a DVD store to rent movies. A new DVD store in your neighborhood is about to open. However, it does not have a program to keep track of its DVDs and customers. The store managers want someone to write a program for their system so that the DVD store can function. The program should be able to perform the following operations:

1. Rent a DVD; that is, check out a DVD.
2. Return, or check in, a DVD.
3. Create a list of DVDs owned by the store.
4. Show the details of a particular DVD.
5. Print a list of all of the DVDs in the store.
6. Check whether a particular DVD is in the store.
7. Maintain a customer database.
8. Print a list of all of the DVDs rented by each customer.

Let us write a program for the DVD store. This example further illustrates the object-oriented design methodology and, in particular, inheritance and overloading.

The programming requirement tells us that the DVD store has two major components: DVDs and customers. We will describe these two components in detail. We also need to maintain the following lists:

- A list of all of the DVDs in the store
- A list of all of the store's customers
- Lists of the DVDs currently rented by the customers

We will develop the program in two parts. In Part 1, we design, implement, and test the DVD component. In Part 2, we design and implement the customer component, which is then added to the DVD component developed in Part 1. That is, after completing Parts 1 and 2, we can perform all of the operations listed previously.

PART 1: DVD COMPONENT

DVD Object

This is the first stage, wherein we discuss the DVD component. The common things associated with a DVD are:

- Name of the movie
- Names of the stars
- Name of the producer
- Name of the director

- Name of the production company
- Number of copies in the store

From this list, we see that some of the operations to be performed on a DVD object are:

1. Set the DVD information—that is, the title, stars, production company, and so on.
2. Show the details of a particular DVD.
3. Check the number of copies in the store.
4. Check out (that is, rent) the DVD. In other words, if the number of copies is greater than zero, decrement the number of copies by one.
5. Check in (that is, return) the DVD. To check in a DVD, first we must check whether the store owns such a DVD and, if it does, increment the number of copies by one.
6. Check whether a particular DVD is available—that is, check whether the number of copies currently in the store is greater than zero.

The deletion of a DVD from the DVD list requires that the list be searched for the DVD to be deleted. Thus, we need to check the title of a DVD to find out which DVD is to be deleted from the list. For simplicity, we assume that two DVDs are the same if they have the same title.

The following class defines the DVD object as an ADT.

```
//**********************************************************
// Author: D.S. Malik
//
// class dvdType
// This class specifies the members to implement a DVD.
//**********************************************************

#include <iostream>
#include <string>

using namespace std;

class dvdType
{
    friend ostream& operator<< (ostream&, const dvdType&);

public:
    void setDVDInfo(string title, string star1,
                    string star2, string producer,
                    string director, string productionCo,
                    int setInStock);
    //Function to set the details of a DVD.
    //The member variables are set according to the
    //parameters.
```

```
    //Postcondition: dvdTitle = title; movieStar1 = star1;
    //      movieStar2 = star2; movieProducer = producer;
    //      movieDirector = director;
    //      movieProductionCo = productionCo;
    //      copiesInStock = setInStock;

int getNoOfCopiesInStock() const;
    //Function to check the number of copies in stock.
    //Postcondition: The value of copiesInStock is returned.

void checkOut();
    //Function to rent a DVD.
    //Postcondition: The number of copies in stock is
    //               decremented by one.

void checkIn();
    //Function to check in a DVD.
    //Postcondition: The number of copies in stock is
    //               incremented by one.

void printTitle() const;
    //Function to print the title of a movie.

void printInfo() const;
    //Function to print the details of a DVD.
    //Postcondition: The title of the movie, stars,
    //               director, and so on are displayed
    //               on the screen.

bool checkTitle(string title);
    //Function to check whether the title is the same as the
    //title of the DVD.
    //Postcondition: Returns the value true if the title
    //               is the same as the title of the DVD;
    //               false otherwise.

void updateInStock(int num);
    //Function to increment the number of copies in stock by
    //adding the value of the parameter num.
    //Postcondition: copiesInStock = copiesInStock + num;

void setCopiesInStock(int num);
    //Function to set the number of copies in stock.
    //Postcondition: copiesInStock = num;

string getTitle() const;
    //Function to return the title of the DVD.
    //Postcondition: The title of the DVD is returned.

dvdType(string title = "", string star1 = "",
        string star2 = "", string producer = "",
```

```
                        string director = "", string productionCo = "",
                        int setInStock = 0);
    //constructor
    //The member variables are set according to the
    //incoming parameters. If no values are specified, the
    //default values are assigned.
    //Postcondition: dvdTitle = title; movieStar1 = star1;
    //               movieStar2 = star2;
    //               movieProducer = producer;
    //               movieDirector = director;
    //               movieProductionCo = productionCo;
    //               copiesInStock = setInStock;

    //Overload the relational operators.
    bool operator==(const dvdType&) const;
    bool operator!=(const dvdType&) const;

private:
    string dvdTitle;      //variable to store the name
                          //of the movie
    string movieStar1;    //variable to store the name
                          //of the star
    string movieStar2;    //variable to store the name
                          //of the star
    string movieProducer; //variable to store the name
                          //of the producer
    string movieDirector; //variable to store the name
                          //of the director
    string movieProductionCo; //variable to store the name
                              //of the production company
    int copiesInStock;    //variable to store the number of
                          //copies in stock
};
```

We leave the UML diagram of the class dvdType as an exercise for you.

For easy output, we will overload the output stream insertion operator, <<, for the class dvdType.

Next, we will write the definitions of each function in the class dvdType. The definitions of these functions, as given below, are quite straightforward and easy to follow.

```
void dvdType::setDVDInfo(string title, string star1,
                         string star2, string producer,
                         string director,
                         string productionCo,
                         int setInStock)
{
    dvdTitle = title;
    movieStar1 = star1;
```

```cpp
    movieStar2 = star2;
    movieProducer = producer;
    movieDirector = director;
    movieProductionCo = productionCo;
    copiesInStock = setInStock;
}

void dvdType::checkOut()
{
    if (getNoOfCopiesInStock() > 0)
        copiesInStock--;
    else
        cout << "Currently out of stock" << endl;
}

void dvdType::checkIn()
{
    copiesInStock++;
}

int dvdType::getNoOfCopiesInStock() const
{
    return copiesInStock;
}

void dvdType::printTitle() const
{
    cout << "DVD Title: " << dvdTitle << endl;
}

void dvdType::printInfo() const
{
    cout << "DVD Title: " << dvdTitle << endl;
    cout << "Stars: " << movieStar1 << " and "
         << movieStar2 << endl;
    cout << "Producer: " << movieProducer << endl;
    cout << "Director: " << movieDirector << endl;
    cout << "Production Company: " << movieProductionCo
         << endl;
    cout << "Copies in stock: " << copiesInStock
         << endl;
}

bool dvdType::checkTitle(string title)
{
    return(dvdTitle == title);
}

void dvdType::updateInStock(int num)
{
    copiesInStock += num;
}
```

```cpp
void dvdType::setCopiesInStock(int num)
{
    copiesInStock = num;
}

string dvdType::getTitle() const
{
    return dvdTitle;
}

dvdType::dvdType(string title, string star1,
                string star2, string producer,
                string director,
                string productionCo, int setInStock)
{
    setDVDInfo(title, star1, star2, producer, director,
               productionCo, setInStock);
}

bool dvdType::operator==(const dvdType& other) const
{
    return (dvdTitle == other.dvdTitle);
}

bool dvdType::operator!=(const dvdType& other) const
{
    return (dvdTitle != other.dvdTitle);
}

ostream& operator<< (ostream& osObject, const dvdType& dvd)
{
    osObject << endl;
    osObject << "DVD Title: " << dvd.dvdTitle << endl;
    osObject << "Stars: " << dvd.movieStar1 << " and "
             << dvd.movieStar2 << endl;
    osObject << "Producer: " << dvd.movieProducer << endl;
    osObject << "Director: " << dvd.movieDirector << endl;
    osObject << "Production Company: "
             << dvd.movieProductionCo << endl;
    osObject << "Copies in stock: " << dvd.copiesInStock
             << endl;
    osObject << "_____"
             << endl;

    return osObject;
}
```

DVD List   This program requires us to maintain a list of all of the DVDs in the store. We also should be able to add a new DVD to our list. In general, we would not know how many DVDs are in the store, and adding or deleting a DVD from the store would change the number of DVDs in the store. Therefore, we will use a linked list to create a list of DVDs (see Figure 16-46).

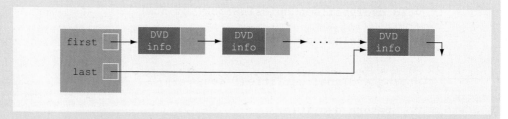

FIGURE 16-46 dvdList

Earlier in this chapter, we defined the **class** unorderedLinkedList to create a linked list of objects. We also defined the basic operations such as insertion and deletion of a DVD in the list. However, some operations are very specific to the DVD list, such as check out a DVD, check in a DVD, set the number of copies of a DVD, and so on. These operations are not available in the **class** unorderedLinkedList. We will, therefore, derive a **class** dvdListType from the **class** unorderedLinkedList and add these operations.

The definition of the **class** dvdListType is:

```
//*************************************************************
// Author: D.S. Malik
//
// class dvdListType
// This class specifies the members to implement a list of
// DVDs.
//*************************************************************

#include <string>
#include "unorderedLinkedList.h"
#include "dvdType.h"

using namespace std;

class dvdListType:public unorderedLinkedList<dvdType>
{
public:
    bool dvdSearch(string title) const;
      //Function to search the list to see whether a
      //particular title, specified by the parameter title,
      //is in the store.
      //Postcondition: Returns true if the title is found,
      //               and false otherwise.

    bool isDVDAvailable(string title) const;
      //Function to determine whether a copy of a particular
      //DVD is in the store.
      //Postcondition: Returns true if at least one copy of the
      //               DVD specified by title is in the store,
      //               and false otherwise.
```

```
    void dvdCheckOut(string title);
      //Function to check out a DVD, that is, rent a DVD.
      //Postcondition: copiesInStock is decremented by one.

    void dvdCheckIn(string title);
      //Function to check in a DVD returned by a customer.
      //Postcondition: copiesInStock is incremented by one.

    bool dvdCheckTitle(string title) const;
      //Function to determine whether a particular DVD is in
      //the store.
      //Postcondition: Returns true if the DVD's title is
      //               the same as title, and false otherwise.

    void dvdUpdateInStock(string title, int num);
      //Function to update the number of copies of a DVD
      //by adding the value of the parameter num. The
      //parameter title specifies the name of the DVD for
      //which the number of copies is to be updated.
      //Postcondition: copiesInStock = copiesInStock + num;

    void dvdSetCopiesInStock(string title, int num);
      //Function to reset the number of copies of a DVD.
      //The parameter title specifies the name of the DVD
      //for which the number of copies is to be reset, and the
      //parameter num specifies the number of copies.
      //Postcondition: copiesInStock = num;

    void dvdPrintTitle() const;
      //Function to print the titles of all the DVD in
      //the store.

private:
    void searchDVDList(string title, bool& found,
                       nodeType<dvdType>* &current) const;
      //This function searches the DVD list for a
      //particular DVD, specified by the parameter title.
      //Postcondition: If the DVD is found, the parameter
      //               found is set to true, otherwise it is set
      //               to false. The parameter current points
      //               to the node containing the DVD.
};
```

Note that the class dvdListType is derived from the class
unorderedLinkedList via a public inheritance. Furthermore,
unorderedLinkedList is a class template, and we have passed the class
dvdType as a parameter to this class. That is, the class dvdListType is not a

template. Because we are now dealing with a very specific data type, the `class` `dvdListType` is no longer required to be a template. Thus, the `info` type of each node in the linked list is now `dvdType`. Through the member functions of the `class` `dvdType`, certain members—such as `dvdTitle` and `copiesInStock` of an object of type `dvdType`—can now be accessed.

The definitions of the functions to implement the operations of the `class` `dvdListType` are given next.

The primary operations on the DVD list are to check in a DVD and to check out a DVD. Both operations require the list to be searched and the location of the DVD being checked in or checked out to be found in the DVD list. Other operations, such as determining whether a particular DVD is in the store, updating the number of copies of a DVD, and so on, also require the list to be searched. To simplify the search process, we will write a function that searches the DVD list for a particular DVD. If the DVD is found, it sets a parameter found to `true` and returns a pointer to the DVD so that check-in, check-out, and other operations on the DVD object can be performed. Note that the function `searchDVDList` is a `private` data member of the `class` `dvdListType` because it is used only for internal manipulation. First, we describe the search procedure.

Consider the node of the DVD list shown in Figure 16-47.

FIGURE 16-47 Node of a DVD list

The component `info` is of type `dvdType` and contains the necessary information about a DVD. In fact, the component `info` of the node has seven members: `dvdTitle`, `movieStar1`, `movieStar2`, `movieProducer`, `movieDirector`, `movieProductionCo`, and `copiesInStock`. (See the definition of the `class` `dvdType`.) Therefore, the node of a DVD list has the form shown in Figure 16-48.

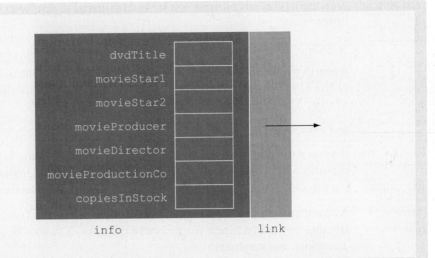

FIGURE 16-48 DVD list node showing components of `info`

These member variables are all **private** and cannot be accessed directly. The member functions of the **class** `dvdType` will help us in checking and/or setting the value of a particular component.

Suppose a pointer—say, `current`—points to a node in the DVD list (see Figure 16-49).

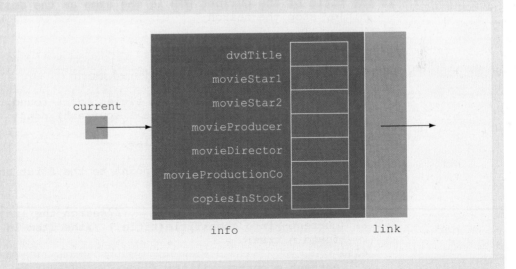

FIGURE 16-49 Pointer `current` and DVD list node

Now:

```
current->info
```

refers to the info part of the node. Suppose that we want to know whether the title of the DVD stored in this node is the same as the title specified by the variable title. The expression:

```
current->info.checkTitle(title)
```

is true if the title of the DVD stored in this node is the same as the title specified by the parameter title, and false otherwise. (Note that the member function checkTitle is a value-returning function. See its declaration in the class dvdType.)

As another example, suppose that we want to set copiesInStock of this node to 10. Because copiesInStock is a private member, it cannot be accessed directly. Therefore, the statement:

```
current->info.copiesInStock = 10;   //illegal
```

is incorrect and will generate a compile-time error. We have to use the member function setCopiesInStock as follows:

```
current->info.setCopiesInStock(10);
```

Now that we know how to access a member variable of a DVD stored in a node, let us describe the algorithm to search the DVD list.

```
while (not found)
    if the title of the current DVD is the same as the desired
        title, stop the search
    else
        check the next node
```

The following function definition performs the desired search:

```
void dvdListType::searchDVDList(string title, bool& found,
                    nodeType<dvdType>* &current) const
{
    found = false;    //set found to false

    current = first; //set current to point to the first node
                     //in the list

    while (current != NULL && !found)     //search the list
        if (current->info.checkTitle(title)) //the item is found
            found = true;
        else
            current = current->link; //advance current to
                                     //the next node
}//end searchDVDList
```

If the search is successful, the parameter found is set to true and the parameter current points to the node containing the DVD info. If it is unsuccessful, found is set to false and current will be NULL.

The definitions of the other functions of the class dvdListType follow:

```cpp
bool dvdListType::isDVDAvailable(string title) const
{
    bool found;
    nodeType<dvdType> *location;

    searchDVDList(title, found, location);

    if (found)
        found = (location->info.getNoOfCopiesInStock() > 0);
    else
        found = false;

    return found;
}

void dvdListType::dvdCheckIn(string title)
{
    bool found = false;
    nodeType<dvdType> *location;

    searchDVDList(title, found, location); //search the list

    if (found)
        location->info.checkIn();
    else
        cout << "The store does not carry " << title
             << endl;
}

void dvdListType::dvdCheckOut(string title)
{
    bool found = false;
    nodeType<dvdType> *location;

    searchDVDList(title, found, location); //search the list

    if (found)
        location->info.checkOut();
    else
        cout << "The store does not carry " << title
             << endl;
}
```

```cpp
bool dvdListType::dvdCheckTitle(string title) const
{
    bool found = false;
    nodeType<dvdType> *location;

    searchDVDList(title, found, location); //search the list

    return found;
}

void dvdListType::dvdUpdateInStock(string title, int num)
{
    bool found = false;
    nodeType<dvdType> *location;

    searchDVDList(title, found, location); //search the list

    if (found)
        location->info.updateInStock(num);
    else
        cout << "The store does not carry " << title
             << endl;
}

void dvdListType::dvdSetCopiesInStock(string title, int num)
{
    bool found = false;
    nodeType<dvdType> *location;

    searchDVDList(title, found, location);

    if (found)
        location->info.setCopiesInStock(num);
    else
        cout << "The store does not carry " << title
             << endl;
}

bool dvdListType::dvdSearch(string title) const
{
    bool found = false;
    nodeType<dvdType> *location;

    searchDVDList(title, found, location);

    return found;
}
```

```cpp
void dvdListType::dvdPrintTitle() const
{
    nodeType<dvdType>* current;

    current = first;
    while (current != NULL)
    {
        current->info.printTitle();
        current = current->link;
    }
}
```

PART 2: CUSTOMER COMPONENT

Customer Object The customer object stores information about a customer, such as the first name, last name, account number, and a list of DVDs rented by the customer.

Every customer is a person. We have already designed the `class` `personType` in Example 10-10 (Chapter 10) and described the necessary operations on the name of a person. Therefore, we can derive the `class` `customerType` from the `class` `personType` and add the additional members that we need. First, however, we must redefine the `class` `personType` to take advantage of the new features of object-oriented design that you have learned, such as operator overloading, and then derive the `class` `customerType`.

Recall that the basic operations on an object of type `personType` are:

1. Print the name.
2. Set the name.
3. Show the first name.
4. Show the last name.

Similarly, the basic operations on an object of type `customerType` are:

1. Print the name, account number, and the list of rented DVDs.
2. Set the name and the account number.
3. Rent a DVD; that is, add the rented DVD to the list.
4. Return a DVD; that is, delete the rented DVD from the list.
5. Show the account number.

The details of implementing the customer component are left as an exercise for you. (See Programming Exercise 14 at the end of this chapter.)

Main Program We will now write the main program to test the DVD object. We assume that the necessary data for the DVDs are stored in a file. We will open the file and create the list of DVDs owned by the DVD store. The data in the input file is in the following form:

```
DVD title (that is, the name of the movie)
movie star1
movie star2
movie producer
movie director
movie production co.
number of copies
     .
     .
     .
```

We will write a function, createDVDList, to read the data from the input file and create the list of DVDs. We will also write a function, displayMenu, to show the different choices—such as check in a movie or check out a movie—that the user can make. The algorithm of the function main is:

1. Open the input file.
   If the input file does not exist, exit the program.
2. Create the list of DVDs (createDVDList).
3. Show the menu (displayMenu).
4. While not done
   Perform various operations.

Opening the input file is straightforward. Let us describe Steps 2 and 3, which are accomplished by writing two separate functions: createDVDList and displayMenu.

createDVDList This function reads the data from the input file and creates a linked list of DVDs. Because the data will be read from a file and the input file was opened in the function main, we pass the input file pointer to this function. We also pass the DVD list pointer, declared in the function main, to this function. Both parameters are reference parameters. Next, we read the data for each DVD and then insert the DVD in the list. The general algorithm is:

a. Read the data and store it in a DVD object.
b. Insert the DVD in the list.
c. Repeat steps a and b for each DVD's data in the file.

displayMenu This function informs the user what to do. It contains the following output statements:

Select one of the following:

1. To check whether the store carries a particular DVD
2. To check out a DVD

3. To check in a DVD

4. To check whether a particular DVD is in stock

5. To print only the titles of all the DVDs

6. To print a list of all the DVDs

9. To exit

In pseudocode, Step 4 (of the main program) is:

```
a. get choice
b.
   while (choice != 9)
   {
       switch (choice)
       {
       case 1:
           a. get the movie name
           b. search the DVD list
           c. if found, report success
              else report "failure"
           break;
       case 2:
           a. get the movie name
           b. search the DVD list
           c. if found, check out the DVD
              else report "failure"
           break;
       case 3:
           a. get the movie name
           b. search the DVD list
           c. if found, check in DVD
              else report "failure"
           break;
       case 4:
           a. get the movie name
           b. search the DVD list
           c. if found
                   if number of copies > 0
                       report "success"
                   else
                       report "currently out of stock"
              else report "failure"
           break;
       case 5:
           print the titles of the DVDs
           break;
       case 6:
           print all the DVDs in the store
           break;
       default: invalid selection
       } //end switch
```

```
            displayMenu();
            get choice;
    }//end while
```

PROGRAM
LISTING

```
    /***************************************************************
    // Author: D.S. Malik
    //
    // This program uses the classes dvdType and dvdListType to
    // create a list of DVDs for a DVD store. It also performs
    // basic operations such as check in and check out DVDs.
    //***************************************************************

    #include <iostream>
    #include <fstream>
    #include <string>
    #include "dvdType.h"
    #include "dvdListType.h"

    using namespace std;

    void createDVDList(ifstream& infile,
                        dvdListType& dvdList);
    void displayMenu();

    int main()
    {
        dvdListType dvdList;
        int choice;
        char ch;
        string title;

        ifstream infile;

            //open the input file
        infile.open("dvdDat.txt");
        if (!infile)
        {
            cout << "The input file does not exist. "
                 << "The program terminates!!!" << endl;
            return 1;
        }

            //create the DVD list
        createDVDList(infile, dvdList);
        infile.close();

            //show the menu
        displayMenu();
        cout << "Enter your choice: ";
        cin >> choice;     //get the request
        cin.get(ch);
        cout << endl;
```

```cpp
        //process the requests
while (choice != 9)
{
    switch (choice)
    {
    case 1:
        cout << "Enter the title: ";
        getline(cin, title);
        cout << endl;

        if (dvdList.dvdSearch(title))
            cout << "The store carries " << title
                << endl;
        else
            cout << "The store does not carry "
                << title << endl;
        break;

    case 2:
        cout << "Enter the title: ";
        getline(cin, title);
        cout << endl;

        if (dvdList.dvdSearch(title))
        {
            if (dvdList.isDVDAvailable(title))
            {
                dvdList.dvdCheckOut(title);
                cout << "Enjoy your movie: "
                    << title << endl;
            }
            else
                cout << "Currently " << title
                    << " is out of stock." << endl;
        }
        else
            cout << "The store does not carry "
                << title << endl;
        break;

    case 3:
        cout << "Enter the title: ";
        getline(cin, title);
        cout << endl;

        if (dvdList.dvdSearch(title))
        {
            dvdList.dvdCheckIn(title);
            cout << "Thanks for returning "
                << title << endl;
        }
```

```cpp
        else
            cout << "The store does not carry "
                 << title << endl;
        break;

    case 4:
        cout << "Enter the title: ";
        getline(cin, title);
        cout << endl;

        if (dvdList.dvdSearch(title))
        {
            if (dvdList.isDVDAvailable(title))
                cout << title << " is currently in "
                     << "stock." << endl;
            else
                cout << title << " is currently out "
                     << "of stock." << endl;
        }
        else
            cout << "The store does not carry "
                 << title << endl;
        break;

    case 5:
        dvdList.dvdPrintTitle();
        break;

    case 6:
        dvdList.print();
        break;

    default:
        cout << "Invalid selection." << endl;
    }//end switch

    displayMenu();      //display menu

    cout << "Enter your choice: ";
    cin >> choice;      //get the next request
    cin.get(ch);
    cout << endl;
    }//end while

    return 0;
}
```

```cpp
void createDVDList(ifstream& infile,
                   dvdListType& dvdList)
{
    string title;
    string star1;
    string star2;
    string producer;
    string director;
    string productionCo;

    char ch;
    int inStock;

    dvdType newDVD;

    getline(infile, title);

    while (infile)
    {
        getline(infile, star1);
        getline(infile, star2);
        getline(infile, producer);
        getline(infile, director);
        getline(infile, productionCo);
        infile >> inStock;
        infile.get(ch);
        newDVD.setDVDInfo(title, star1, star2, producer,
                          director, productionCo, inStock);
        dvdList.insertFirst(newDVD);

        getline(infile, title);
    }//end while
}//end createDVDList

void displayMenu()
{
    cout << "Select one of the following:" << endl;
    cout << "1: To check whether the store carries a "
         << "particular DVD." << endl;
    cout << "2: To check out a DVD." << endl;
    cout << "3: To check in a DVD." << endl;
    cout << "4: To check whether a particular DVD is "
         << "in stock." << endl;
    cout << "5: To print only the titles of all the DVDs."
         << endl;
    cout << "6: To print a list of all the DVDs." << endl;
    cout << "9: To exit" << endl;
}//end displayMenu
```

1
6

QUICK REVIEW

1. A linked list is a list of items, called nodes, in which the order of the nodes is determined by the address, called a link, stored in each node.

2. The pointer to a linked list—that is, the pointer to the first node in the list—is stored in a separate location called the head or first.

3. A linked list is a dynamic data structure.

4. The length of a linked list is the number of nodes in the list.

5. Item insertion and deletion from a linked list do not require data movement; only the pointers are adjusted.

6. A (single) linked list is traversed in only one direction.

7. The search on a linked list is sequential.

8. The first (or head) pointer of a linked list is always fixed, pointing to the first node in the list.

9. To traverse a linked list, the program must use a pointer different than the head pointer of the list, initialized to the first node in the list.

10. In a doubly linked list, every node has two links: one points to the next node and one points to the previous node.

11. A doubly linked list can be traversed in either direction.

12. In a doubly linked list, item insertion and deletion require the adjustment of two pointers in a node.

13. A linked list in which the last node points to the first node is called a circular linked list.

EXERCISES

1. Mark the following statements as true or false.

   a. In a linked list, the order of the elements is determined by the order in which the nodes were created to store the elements.

   b. In a linked list, memory allocated for the nodes is sequential.

   c. A single linked list can be traversed in either direction.

   d. In a linked list, nodes are always inserted either at the beginning or the end because a linked link is not a random-access data structure.

2. Describe the two typical components of a single linked list node.

3. What is stored in the link field of the last node of a nonempty single linked list?

4. Suppose that `first` is a pointer to a linked list. What is stored in `first`?

5. Suppose that the fourth node of a linked list is to be deleted, and p points to the fourth node? Why do you need a pointer to the third node of the linked list?

Consider the linked list shown in Figure 16-50. Assume that the nodes are in the usual `info-link` form. Use this list to answer Exercises 6 through 14. If necessary, declare additional variables. (Assume that `list`, `current`, `temp`, `trail`, and `last` are pointers of type `nodeType`.)

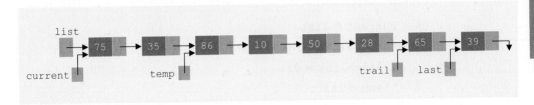

FIGURE 16-50 Linked list for exercises 6 through 14

6. What is the output, if any, of each of the following C++ statements?

    a. `cout << current->info;`

    b. `current = current->link;`
        `cout << current->info;`

    c. `cout << temp->link->link->info;`

    d. `trail->link = NULL;`
        `cout << trail->info;`

    e. `cout << last->link->info;`

7. What is the value of each of the following relational expressions?

    a. `current->link == temp`

    b. `temp->link->link->info == 50`

    c. `trail->link->link == 0`

    d. `last->link == NULL`

    e. `list == current`

8. What are the effects, if any, of each of the following C++ statements?

    a. `trail->link = NULL;`
        `delete last;`

    b. `temp->link = trail;`

    c. `list->info = 19;`

    d. `current = current->link;`
        `current->link = temp->link;`

9. Write C++ statements to do the following:

    a. Set the `info` of the second node to 52.

    b. Make `current` point to the node with `info` 10.

    c. Make `trail` point to the node before `temp`.

d. Make `temp` point to an empty list.

e. Set the value of the node before `trail` to 36.

f. Write a `while` loop to make `current` point to the node with `info 10`.

10. Mark each of the following statements as valid or invalid. If a statement is invalid, explain why.

a. `current = list;`

b. `temp->link->link = NULL;`

c. `trail->link = 0;`

d. `*temp = last;`

e. `list = 75;`

f. `temp->link->info = 75;`

g. `current->info = trail->link;`

h. `*list = *last;`

i. `current = last;`

j. `cout << trail->link->link->info;`

11. Write C++ statements to do the following:

a. Write a C++ code so that `current` traverses the entire list.

b. Create the node with `info 68` and insert between `trail` and `last`.

c. Delete the last node of the list and also deallocate the memory occupied by this node. After deleting the node, make `last` point to the last node of the list and the link of the last node must be `NULL`.

d. Delete the node with `info 10`. Also, deallocate the memory occupied by this node.

12. What is the output of the following C++ code?

a.
```
while (current != NULL)
    cout << current->info << " ";
    current = current->link;
cout << endl;
```

b.
```
while (current != last)
    current = current->link;
    cout << current->info << " ";
cout << endl;
```

13. If the following C++ code is valid, show the output. If it is invalid, explain why.

```
temp = current;                  //Line 1
current = current->link;         //Line 2
current->link = last;            //Line 3
trail = current->link;           //Line 4
trail = trail->link;             //Line 5
cout << current->info << " "
        << trail->info << endl;  //Line 6
```

14. If the following C++ code is valid, show the output. If it is invalid, explain why.

```
current = temp->link;
trail = list;
temp = list->link;
trail = temp;
temp->link = current->link;
current = trail->link;
cout << trail->info << " " << current->info << endl;
```

15. Show what is produced by the following C++ code. Assume the node is in the usual info-link form with the info of the type int. (list, trail, and current are pointers of type nodeType.)

```
list = new nodeType;
list->info = 28;
trail = new nodeType;
trail->info = 33;
trail->link = list;
list->link = NULL;
current = new nodeType;
current->info = 62;
trail->link = current;
current->link = list;
list = trail;
current = list->link;
trail = current->link;
cout << list->info << " " << current->info << " "
     << trail->info << endl;
```

16. Show what is produced by the following C++ code. Assume the node is in the usual info-link form with the info of the type int. (list, trail, and current are pointers of type nodeType.)

```
current = new nodeType;
current->info = 72;
current->link = NULL;
trail = current;
current = new nodeType;
current->info = 46;
current->link = trail;
list = current;
current = new nodeType;
current->info = 52;
list->link = current;
current->link = trail;
trail = current;
current = new nodeType;
current->info = 91;
current->link = trail->link;
trail->link = current;
current = list;
while (current!= NULL)
```

```
{
        cout << current->info << " ";
        current = current->link;
}
cout << endl;
```

17. Assume that the node of a linked list is in the usual `info-link` form with the `info` of type `int`. The following data, as described in parts (a) to (d), is to be inserted into an initially linked list: `72, 43, 8, 12`. Suppose that `head` is a pointer of type `nodeType`. After the linked list is created, `head` should point to the first node of the list. Declare additional variables as you need them. Write the C++ code to create the linked list. After the linked list is created, write a code to print the list. What is the output of your code?

    a. Insert 72 into an empty linked list.

    b. Insert 43 before 72.

    c. Insert 8 at the end of the list.

    d. Insert 12 after 43.

18. Assume that the node of a linked list is in the usual `info-link` form with the `info` of type `int`. (`list` and `ptr` are pointers of type `nodeType`.) The following code creates a linked list:

```
ptr = new nodeType;
ptr->info = 16;
list = new nodeType;
list->info = 25;
list->link = ptr;
ptr = new nodeType;
ptr->info = 12;
ptr->link = NULL;
list->link->link = ptr;
```

    Use the linked list created by this code to answer the following questions. (These questions are independent of each other.) Declare additional pointers if you need them.

    a. Which pointer points to the first node of the linked list?

    b. Determine the order of the nodes of the linked list.

    c. Write a C++ code that creates and inserts a node with `info 45` after the node with `info 16`.

    d. Write a C++ code that creates and inserts a node with `info 58` before the node with `info 25`. Does this require you to the change the value of the pointer that was pointing to the first node of the linked list?

    e. Write a C++ code that deletes the node with `info 25`. Does this require you to the change the value of the pointer that was pointing to the first node of the linked list?

19. Consider the following C++ statements. (The `class` unorderedLinkedList is as defined in this chapter.)

```
unorderedLinkedList<int> list;

list.insertFirst(38);
list.insertFirst(42);
list.insertLast(55);
list.insertFirst(60);
list.insertLast(18);
list.insertLast(35);
list.insertFirst(66);
list.deleteNode(60);
list.insertFirst(93);
list.deleteNode(42);
list.deleteNode(12);
list.print();
cout << endl;
```

What is the output of this program segment?

20. Suppose the input is:

```
45 35 12 83 40 23 11 98 64 120 16 -999
```

What is the output of the following C++ code? (The `class` unorderedLinkedList is as defined in this chapter.)

```
unorderedLinkedList<int> list;
unorderedLinkedList<int> copyList;
int num;

cin >> num;
while (num != -999)
{
    if (num % 4 == 0 || num % 3 == 0)
        list.insertFirst(num);
    else
        list.insertLast(num);
    cin >> num;
}

cout << "list = ";
list.print();
cout << endl;

copyList = list;

copyList.deleteNode(33);
copyList.deleteNode(58);

cout << "copyList = ";
copyList.print();
cout << endl;
```

21. Draw the UML diagram of the `class` `doublyLinkedList` as discussed in this chapter.

22. Draw the UML diagram of the `class` `dvdType` of the DVD Store programming example.

23. Draw the UML diagram of the `class` `dvdListType` of the DVD Store programming example.

PROGRAMMING EXERCISES

1. (**Online Address Book revisited**) Programming Exercise 5 in Chapter 11 could handle a maximum of only 500 entries. Using linked lists, redo the program to handle as many entries as required. Add the following operations to your program:

    a. Add or delete a new entry to the address book.

    b. Allow the user to save the data in the address book.

2. Extend the `class` `linkedListType` by adding the following operations:

    a. Find and delete the node with the smallest `info` in the list. (Delete only the first occurrence and traverse the list only once.)

    b. Find and delete all occurrences of a given `info` from the list. (Traverse the list only once.)

    Add these as abstract functions in the `class` `linkedListType` and provide the definitions of these functions in the `class` `unorderedLinkedList`. Also, write a program to test these functions.

3. Extend the `class` `linkedListType` by adding the following operations:

    a. Write a function that returns the `info` of the kth element of the linked list. If no such element exists, terminate the program.

    b. Write a function that deletes the kth element of the linked list. If no such element exists, terminate the program.

    Provide the definitions of these functions in the `class` `linkedListType`. Also, write a program to test these functions. (Use either the `class` `unorderedLinkedList` or the `class` `orderedLinkedList` to test your function.)

4. (**Printing a single linked list backward**) Include the functions `reversePrint` and `recursiveReversePrint`, as discussed in this chapter, in the `class` `linkedListType`. Also, write a program function to print a (single) linked list backward. (Use either the `class` `unorderedLinkedList` or the `class` `orderedLinkedList` to test your function.)

5. (**Dividing a linked list into two sublists of almost equal sizes**)

a. Add the operation divideMid to the class linkedListType as follows:

```
void divideMid(linkedListType<Type> &sublist);
  //This operation divides the given list into two sublists
  //of (almost) equal sizes.
  //Postcondition: first points to the first node and last
  //               points to the last node of the first
  //               sublist.
  //               sublist.first points to the first node
  //               and sublist.last points to the last node
  //               of the second sublist.
```

Consider the following statements:

```
unorderedLinkedList<int> myList;
unorderedLinkedList<int> subList;
```

Suppose myList points to the list with elements 34 65 27 89 12 (in this order). The statement:

```
myList.divideMid(subList);
```

divides myList into two sublists: myList points to the list with the elements 34 65 27, and subList points to the sublist with the elements 89 12.

b. Write the definition of the function template to implement the operation divideMid. Also, write a program to test your function.

6. **(Splitting a linked list, at a given node, into two sublists)**

a. Add the following operation to the class linkedListType:

```
void divideAt(linkedListType<Type> &secondList,
              const Type& item);
  //Divide the list at the node with the info item into two
  //sublists.
  //Postcondition: first and last point to the first and
  //               last nodes of the first sublist.
  //               secondList.first and secondList.last
  //               point to the first and last nodes of the
  //               second sublist.
```

Consider the following statements:

```
unorderedLinkedList<int> myList;
unorderedLinkedList<int> otherList;
```

Suppose myList points to the list with the elements 34 65 18 39 27 89 12 (in this order). The statement:

```
myList.divideAt(otherList, 18);
```

divides myList into two sublists: myList points to the list with the elements 34 65, and otherList points to the sublist with the elements 18 39 27 89 12.

b. Write the definition of the function template to implement the operation divideAt. Also, write a program to test your function.

7. a. Add the following operation to the **class** orderedLinkedList:

```
void mergeLists(orderedLinkedList<Type> &list1,
               orderedLinkedList<Type> &list2);
  //This function creates a new list by merging the
  //elements of list1 and list2.
  //Postcondition: first points to the merged list
  //                list1 and list2 are empty
```

Consider the following statements:

```
orderedLinkedList<int> newList;
orderedLinkedList<int> list1;
orderedLinkedList<int> list2;
```

Suppose list1 points to the list with the elements 2 6 7, and list2 points to the list with the elements 3 5 8. The statement:

```
newList.mergeLists(list1, list2);
```

creates a new linked list with the elements in the order 2 3 5 6 7 8, and the object newList points to this list. Also, after the preceding statement executes, list1 and list2 are empty.

b. Write the definition of the function template mergeLists to implement the operation mergeLists.

8. The function insert of the **class** orderedLinkedList does not check if the item to be inserted is already in the list; that is, it does not check for duplicates. Rewrite the definition of the function insert so that before inserting the item, it checks whether the item to be inserted is already in the list. If the item to be inserted is already in the list, the function outputs an appropriate error message. Also, write a program to test your function.

9. In this chapter, the class to implement the nodes of a linked list is defined as a struct. The following rewrites the definition of the struct nodeType so that it is declared as a class and the member variables are private:

```
template <class Type>
class nodeType
{
```

```
public:
    const nodeType<Type>& operator=(const nodeType<Type>&);
      //Overload the assignment operator.

    void setInfo(const Type& elem);
      //Function to set the info of the node.
      //Postcondition: info = elem;

    Type getInfo() const;
      //Function to return the info of the node.
      //Postcondition: The value of info is returned.

    void setLink(nodeType<Type> *ptr);
      //Function to set the link of the node.
      //Postcondition: link = ptr;

    nodeType<Type>* getLink() const;
      //Function to return the link of the node.
      //Postcondition: The value of link is returned.

    nodeType();
      //Default constructor
      //Postcondition: link = NULL;

    nodeType(const Type& elem, nodeType<Type> *ptr);
      //Constructor with parameters
      //Sets info to point to the object elem points to, and
      //link is set to point to the object ptr points to.
      //Postcondition: info = elem; link = ptr

    nodeType(const nodeType<Type> &otherNode);
      //Copy constructor
    ~nodeType();
      //Destructor

private:
    Type info;
    nodeType<Type> *link;
};
```

Write the definitions of the member functions of the class nodeType. Also, write a program to test your class.

10. Programming Exercise 9 asks you to redefine the class to implement the nodes of a linked list so that the instance variables are private. Therefore, the class linkedListType and its derived classes unorderedLinkedList and orderedLinkedList can no longer directly access the instance variables of the class nodeType. Rewrite the definitions of these classes so that they use

the member functions of the `class` `nodeType` to access the `info` and `link` fields of a node. Also, write programs to test various operations of the classes `unorderedLinkedList` and `orderedLinkedList`.

11. Write the definitions of the function `copyList`, the copy constructor, and the function to overload the assignment operator for the `class` `doublyLinkedList`.

12. Write a program to test various operations of the `class` `doublyLinkedList`.

13. **(Circular linked lists)** This chapter defined and identified various operations on a circular linked list.

   a. Write the definitions of the `class` `circularLinkedList` and its member functions. (You may assume that the elements of the circular linked list are in ascending order.)

   b. Write a program to test various operations of the class defined in (a).

14. **(DVD Store programming example)**

   a. Complete the design and implementation of the `class` `customerType` defined in the DVD Store programming example.

   b. Design and implement the `class` `customerListType` to create and maintain a list of customers for the DVD store.

15. **(DVD Store programming example)** Complete the design and implementation of the DVD store program. In other words, write a program that uses the classes designed in the DVD Store programming example and in Programming Exercise 14 to make a DVD store operational.

16. Extend the `class` `linkedListType` by adding the following function:
    ```
    void rotate();
    //Function to remove the first node of a linked list and put it
    //at the end of the linked list.
    ```

    Also write a program to test your function. Use the `class` `unorderedLinkedList` to create a linked list.

17. Write a program that prompts the user to input a string and then outputs the string in the pig Latin form. The rules for converting a string into pig Latin form are described in Programming Example: Pig Latin Strings of Chapter 7. Your program must store the characters of a string into a linked list and use the function `rotate`, as described in Programming Exercise 16, to rotate the string.

STACKS AND QUEUES

IN THIS CHAPTER, YOU WILL:

· Learn about stacks

· Examine various stack operations

· Learn how to implement a stack as an array

· Learn how to implement a stack as a linked list

· Discover stack applications

· Learn how to use a stack to remove recursion

· Learn about queues

· Examine various queue operations

· Learn how to implement a queue as an array

· Learn how to implement a queue as a linked list

· Discover queue applications

This chapter discusses two very useful data structures: stacks and queues. Both stacks and queues have numerous applications in computer science.

Stacks

Suppose that you have a program with several functions. To be specific, suppose that you have functions A, B, C, and D in your program. Now suppose that function A calls function B, function B calls function C, and function C calls function D. When function D terminates, control goes back to function C; when function C terminates, control goes back to function B; and when function B terminates, control goes back to function A. During program execution, how do you think the computer keeps track of the function calls? What about recursive functions? How does the computer keep track of the recursive calls? In Chapter 16, we designed a recursive function to print a linked list backward. What if you want to write a nonrecursive algorithm to print a linked list backward?

This section discusses the data structure called the **stack**, which the computer uses to implement function calls. You can also use stacks to convert recursive algorithms into nonrecursive algorithms, especially recursive algorithms that are not tail recursive. Stacks have numerous applications in computer science. After developing the tools necessary to implement a stack, we will examine some applications of stacks.

A stack is a list of homogeneous elements in which the addition and deletion of elements occur only at one end, called the **top** of the stack. For example, in a cafeteria, the second tray in a stack of trays can be removed only if the first tray has been removed. For another example, to get to your favorite computer science book, which is underneath your math and history books, you must first remove the math and history books. After removing these books, the computer science book becomes the top book—that is, the top element of the stack. Figure 17-1 shows some examples of stacks.

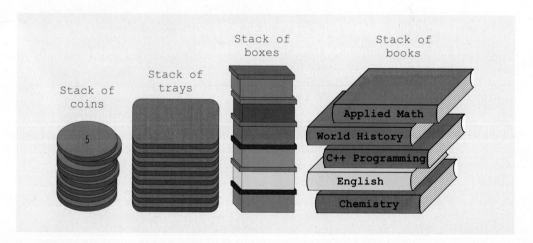

FIGURE 17-1 Various types of stacks

The elements at the bottom of the stack have been in the stack the longest. The top element of the stack is the last element added to the stack. Because the elements are added and removed from one end (that is, the top), it follows that the item that is added last will be removed first. For this reason, a stack is also called a **Last In First Out (LIFO)** data structure.

Stack: A data structure in which the elements are added and removed from one end only; a Last In First Out (LIFO) data structure.

Now that you know what a stack is, let us see what kinds of operations can be performed on a stack. Because new items can be added to the stack, we can perform the add operation, called **push**, to add an element onto the stack. Similarly, because the top item can be retrieved and/or removed from the stack, we can perform the operation **top** to retrieve the top element of the stack and the operation **pop** to remove the top element from the stack.

The push, top, and pop operations work as follows: Suppose there are boxes lying on the floor that need to be stacked on a table. Initially, all of the boxes are on the floor, and the stack is empty (see Figure 17-2).

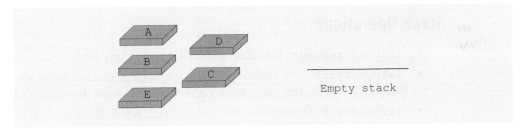

FIGURE 17-2 Empty stack

First, we push box **A** onto the stack. After the push operation, the stack is as shown in Figure 17-3(a).

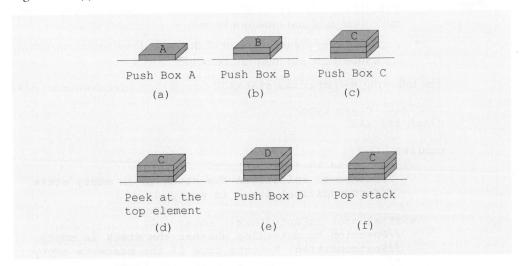

FIGURE 17-3 Stack operations

We then push box B onto the stack. After this push operation, the stack is as shown in Figure 17-3(b). Next, we push box C onto the stack. After this push operation, the stack is as shown in Figure 17-3(c). Next, we look, that is, peek, at the top element of the stack. After this operation, the stack is unchanged and shown in Figure 17-3(d). We then push box D onto the stack. After this push operation, the stack is as shown in Figure 17-3(e). Next, we pop the stack. After the pop operation, the stack is as shown in Figure 17-3(f).

An element can be removed from the stack only if there is something in the stack, and an element can be added to the stack only if there is room. The two operations that immediately follow from push, top, and pop are **isFullStack** (checks whether the stack is full) and **isEmptyStack** (checks whether the stack is empty). Because a stack keeps changing as we add and remove elements, the stack must be empty before we first start using it. Thus, we need another operation, called **initializeStack**, which initializes the stack to an empty state. Therefore, to successfully implement a stack, we need at least these six operations, which are described in the next section. We might also need other operations on a stack, depending on the specific implementation.

Stack Operations

- **initializeStack**: Initializes the stack to an empty state.
- **isEmptyStack**: Determines whether the stack is empty. If the stack is empty, it returns the value `true`; otherwise, it returns the value `false`.
- **isFullStack**: Determines whether the stack is full. If the stack is full, it returns the value `true`; otherwise, it returns the value `false`.
- **push**: Adds a new element to the top of the stack. The input to this operation consists of the stack and the new element. Prior to this operation, the stack must exist and must not be full.
- **top**: Returns the top element of the stack. Prior to this operation, the stack must exist and must not be full.
- **pop**: Removes the top element of the stack. Prior to this operation, the stack must exist and must not be empty.

The following abstract `class stackADT` defines these operations as an ADT:

```
template <class Type>
class stackADT
{
public:
    virtual void initializeStack() = 0;
        //Method to initialize the stack to an empty state.
        //Postcondition: Stack is empty.

    virtual bool isEmptyStack() const = 0;
        //Function to determine whether the stack is empty.
        //Postcondition: Returns true if the stack is empty,
        //                otherwise returns false.
```

```
    virtual bool isFullStack() const = 0;
      //Function to determine whether the stack is full.
      //Postcondition: Returns true if the stack is full,
      //                 otherwise returns false.

    virtual void push(const Type& newItem) = 0;
      //Function to add newItem to the stack.
      //Precondition: The stack exists and is not full.
      //Postcondition: The stack is changed and newItem
      //                 is added to the top of the stack.

    virtual Type top() const = 0;
      //Function to return the top element of the stack.
      //Precondition: The stack exists and is not empty.
      //Postcondition: If the stack is empty, the program
      //                 terminates; otherwise, the top element
      //                 of the stack is returned.

    virtual void pop() = 0;
      //Function to remove the top element of the stack.
      //Precondition: The stack exists and is not empty.
      //Postcondition: The stack is changed and the top
      //                 element is removed from the stack.
};
```

Figure 17-4 shows the UML class diagram of the **class** stackADT.

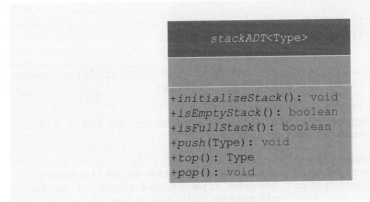

FIGURE 17-4 UML class diagram of the **class** stackADT

We now consider the implementation of our abstract stack data structure. Because all of the elements of a stack are of the same type, a stack can be implemented as either an array or a linked structure. Both implementations are useful and are discussed in this chapter.

Implementation of Stacks as Arrays

Because all of the elements of a stack are of the same type, you can use an array to implement a stack. The first element of the stack can be put in the first array slot, the second element of the stack in the second array slot, and so on. The top of the stack is the index of the last element added to the stack.

In this implementation of a stack, stack elements are stored in an array, and an array is a random access data structure; that is, you can directly access any element of the array. However, by definition, a stack is a data structure in which the elements are accessed (popped or pushed) at only one end—that is, a Last In First Out data structure. Thus, a stack element is accessed only through the top, not through the bottom or middle. This feature of a stack is extremely important and must be recognized in the beginning.

To keep track of the top position of the array, we can simply declare another variable called `stackTop`.

The following `class`, `stackType`, implements the functions of the abstract `class` `stackADT`. By using a pointer, we can dynamically allocate arrays, so we will leave it for the user to specify the size of the array (that is, the stack size). We assume that the default stack size is 100. Because the `class` `stackType` has a pointer member variable (the pointer to the array to store the stack elements), we must overload the assignment operator and include the copy constructor and destructor. Moreover, we give a generic definition of the stack. Depending on the specific application, we can pass the stack element type when we declare a stack object.

```
template <class Type>
class stackType: public stackADT<Type>
{
public:
    const stackType<Type>& operator=(const stackType<Type>&);
      //Overload the assignment operator.

    void initializeStack();
      //Function to initialize the stack to an empty state.
      //Postcondition: stackTop = 0;

    bool isEmptyStack() const;
      //Function to determine whether the stack is empty.
      //Postcondition: Returns true if the stack is empty,
      //               otherwise returns false.

    bool isFullStack() const;
      //Function to determine whether the stack is full.
      //Postcondition: Returns true if the stack is full,
      //               otherwise returns false.

    void push(const Type& newItem);
      //Function to add newItem to the stack.
      //Precondition: The stack exists and is not full.
      //Postcondition: The stack is changed and newItem
      //               is added to the top of the stack.
```

```
Type top() const;
    //Function to return the top element of the stack.
    //Precondition: The stack exists and is not empty.
    //Postcondition: If the stack is empty, the program
    //               terminates; otherwise, the top element
    //               of the stack is returned.

void pop();
    //Function to remove the top element of the stack.
    //Precondition: The stack exists and is not empty.
    //Postcondition: The stack is changed and the top
    //               element is removed from the stack.


stackType(int stackSize = 100);
    //Constructor
    //Create an array of the size stackSize to hold
    //the stack elements. The default stack size is 100.
    //Postcondition: The variable list contains the base
    //               address of the array, stackTop = 0, and
    //               maxStackSize = stackSize.

stackType(const stackType<Type>& otherStack);
    //Copy constructor

~stackType();
    //Destructor
    //Remove all the elements from the stack.
    //Postcondition: The array (list) holding the stack
    //               elements is deleted.

private:
    int maxStackSize;  //variable to store the maximum stack size
    int stackTop;      //variable to point to the top of the stack
    Type *list;        //pointer to the array that holds the
                       //stack elements

    void copyStack(const stackType<Type>& otherStack);
        //Function to make a copy of otherStack.
        //Postcondition: A copy of otherStack is created and
        //               assigned to this stack.
};
```

Figure 17-5 shows the UML class diagram of the class stackType.

stackType<Type>
-maxStackSize: int -stackTop: int -*list: Type
+operator=(const stackType<Type>&):   const stackType<Type>& +initializeStack(): void +isEmptyStack() const: bool +isFullStack() const: bool +push(const Type&): void +top() const: Type +pop(): void -copyStack(const stackType<Type>&): void +stackType(int = 100) +stackType(const stackType<Type>&) +~stackType()

FIGURE 17-5 UML class diagram of the **class** stackType

NOTE

Because C++ arrays begin with the index 0, we need to distinguish between the value of stackTop and the array position indicated by stackTop. If stackTop is 0, the stack is empty; if stackTop is nonzero, then the stack is nonempty and the top element of the stack is given by stackTop - 1.

Notice that the function copyStack is included as a **private** member. This is because we want to use this function only to implement the copy constructor and overload the assignment operator. To copy a stack into another stack, the program can use the assignment operator.

Figure 17-6 shows this data structure, wherein stack is an object of type stackType. Note that stackTop can range from 0 to maxStackSize. If stackTop is nonzero, then stackTop - 1 is the index of the stackTop element of the stack. Suppose that max-StackSize = 100.

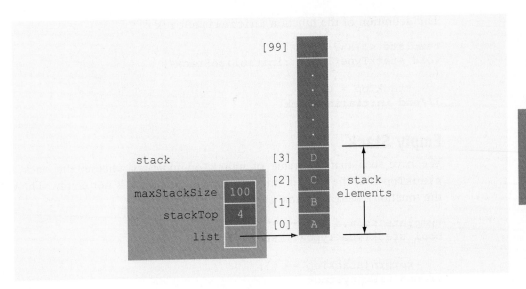

FIGURE 17-6 Example of a stack

Note that the pointer `list` contains the base address of the array (holding the stack elements)—that is, the address of the first array component. Next, we discuss how to implement the member functions of the **class** stackType.

Initialize Stack

Let us consider the `initializeStack` operation. Because the value of `stackTop` indicates whether the stack is empty, we can simply set `stackTop` to 0 to initialize the stack (see Figure 17-7).

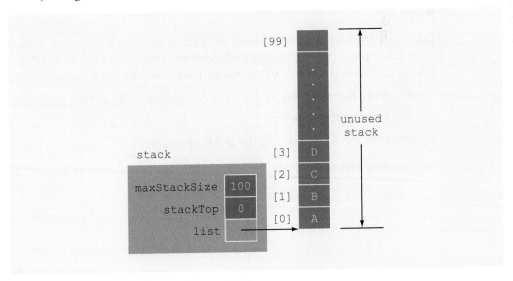

FIGURE 17-7 Empty stack

The definition of the function `initializeStack` is:

```
template <class Type>
void stackType<Type>::initializeStack()
{
    stackTop = 0;
}//end initializeStack
```

Empty Stack

We have seen that the value of `stackTop` indicates whether the stack is empty. If `stackTop` is 0, the stack is empty; otherwise, the stack is not empty. The definition of the function `isEmptyStack` is:

```
template <class Type>
bool stackType<Type>::isEmptyStack() const
{
    return(stackTop == 0);
}//end isEmptyStack
```

Full Stack

Next, we consider the operation `isFullStack`. It follows that the stack is full if `stackTop` is equal to `maxStackSize`. The definition of the function `isFullStack` is:

```
template <class Type>
bool stackType<Type>::isFullStack() const
{
    return (stackTop == maxStackSize);
} //end isFullStack
```

Push

Adding, or pushing, an element onto the stack is a two-step process. Recall that the value of `stackTop` indicates the number of elements in the stack, and `stackTop - 1` gives the position of the top element of the stack. Therefore, the `push` operation is as follows:

1. Store the `newItem` in the array component indicated by `stackTop`.
2. Increment `stackTop`.

Figures 17-8 and 17-9 illustrate the `push` operation.

Suppose that before the `push` operation, the stack is as shown in Figure 17-8.

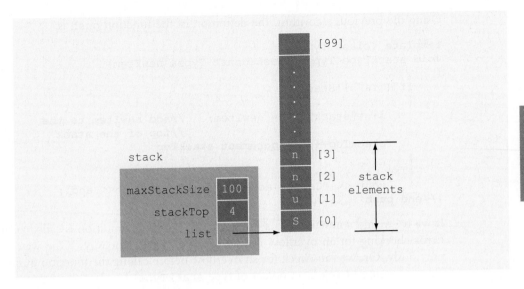

FIGURE 17-8 Stack before pushing y

Assume `newItem` is `'y'`. After the push operation, the stack is as shown in Figure 17-9.

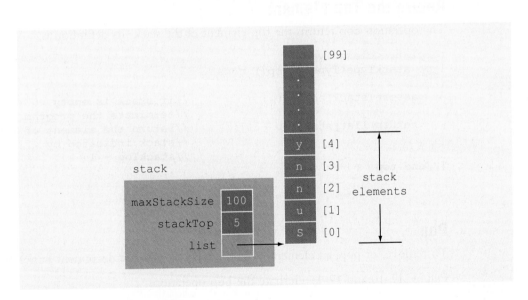

FIGURE 17-9 Stack after pushing y

Using the previous algorithm, the definition of the function push is:

```
template <class Type>
void stackType<Type>::push(const Type& newItem)
{
    if (!isFullStack())
    {
        list[stackTop] = newItem;    //add newItem to the
                                     //top of the stack
        stackTop++; //increment stackTop
    }
    else
        cout << "Cannot add to a full stack." << endl;
}//end push
```

If we try to add a new item to a full stack, the resulting condition is called an **overflow**. Error checking for an overflow can be handled in different ways. One way is as shown previously. Or, we can check for an overflow before calling the function push, as shown next (assuming stack is an object of type stackType).

```
if (!stack.isFullStack())
    stack.push(newItem);
```

Return the Top Element

The operation top returns the top element of the stack. Its definition is:

```
template <class Type>
Type stackType<Type>::top() const
{
    assert(stackTop != 0);            //if stack is empty,
                                      //terminate the program
    return list[stackTop - 1];        //return the element of the
                                      //stack indicated by
                                      //stackTop - 1

}//end top
```

Pop

To remove, or pop, an element from the stack, we simply decrement stackTop by 1. Figures 17-10 and 17-11 illustrate the pop operation.

Suppose that before the pop operation, the stack is as shown in Figure 17-10.

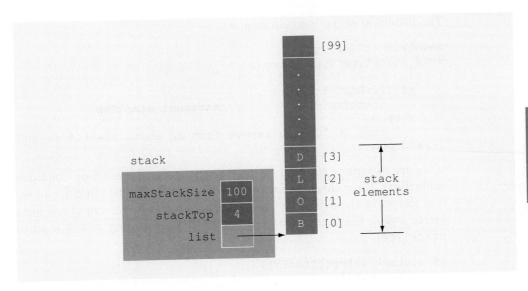

FIGURE 17-10 Stack before popping D

After the pop operation, the stack is as shown in Figure 17-11.

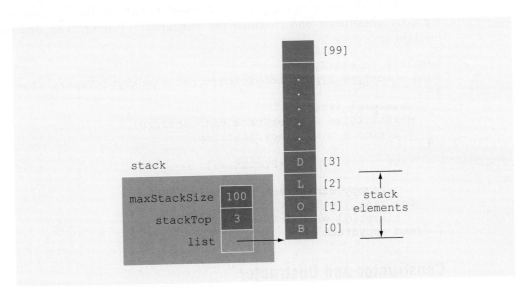

FIGURE 17-11 Stack after popping D

The definition of the function pop is:

```
template <class Type>
void stackType<Type>::pop()
{
    if (!isEmptyStack())
        stackTop--;                //decrement stackTop
    else
        cout << "Cannot remove from an empty stack." << endl;
}//end pop
```

If we try to remove an item from an empty stack, the resulting condition is called an **underflow**. Error checking for an underflow can be handled in different ways. One way is as shown in the definition of the function pop. Or, we can check for an underflow before calling the function pop, as shown next (assuming stack is an object of type stackType).

```
if (!stack.isEmptyStack())
    stack.pop();
```

Copy Stack

The function copyStack makes a copy of a stack. The stack to be copied is passed as a parameter to the function copyStack. We will, in fact, use this function to implement the copy constructor and overload the assignment operator. The definition of this function is:

```
template <class Type>
void stackType<Type>::copyStack(const stackType<Type>& otherStack)
{
    delete [] list;
    maxStackSize = otherStack.maxStackSize;
    stackTop = otherStack.stackTop;

    list = new Type[maxStackSize];

        //copy otherStack into this stack
    for (int j = 0; j < stackTop; j++)
        list[j] = otherStack.list[j];
} //end copyStack
```

Constructor and Destructor

The functions to implement the constructor and the destructor are straightforward. The constructor with parameters sets the stack size to the size specified by the user, sets stackTop to 0, and creates an appropriate array in which to store the stack elements. If the user does not specify the size of the array in which to store the stack elements, the constructor uses the default value, which is 100, to create an array of size 100. The destructor simply deallocates the memory occupied by the array (that is, the stack) and sets stackTop to 0. The definitions of the constructor and destructor are:

```
template <class Type>
stackType<Type>::stackType(int stackSize)
{
    if (stackSize <= 0)
    {
        cout << "Size of the array to hold the stack must "
             << "be positive." << endl;
        cout << "Creating an array of size 100." << endl;

        maxStackSize = 100;
    }
    else
        maxStackSize = stackSize;     //set the stack size to
                                      //the value specified by
                                      //the parameter stackSize

    stackTop = 0;                     //set stackTop to 0
    list = new Type[maxStackSize];    //create the array to
                                      //hold the stack elements
}//end constructor

template <class Type>
stackType<Type>::~stackType() //destructor
{
    delete [] list; //deallocate the memory occupied
                    //by the array
}//end destructor
```

Copy Constructor

The copy constructor is called when a stack object is passed as a (value) parameter to a function. It copies the values of the member variables of the actual parameter into the corresponding member variables of the formal parameter. Its definition is:

```
template <class Type>
stackType<Type>::stackType(const stackType<Type>& otherStack)
{
    list = NULL;

    copyStack(otherStack);
}//end copy constructor
```

Overloading the Assignment Operator (=)

Recall that for classes with pointer member variables, the assignment operator must be explicitly overloaded. The definition of the function to overload the assignment operator for the class stackType is:

```
template <class Type>
const stackType<Type>& stackType<Type>::operator=
                        (const stackType<Type>& otherStack)
```

```
{
    if (this != &otherStack) //avoid self-copy
        copyStack(otherStack);

    return *this;
} //end operator=
```

Stack Header File

Now that you know how to implement the stack operations, you can put the definitions of the class and the functions to implement the stack operations together to create the stack header file. For the sake of completeness, we next describe the header file. (To save space, only the definition of the class is shown; no documentation is provided.) Suppose that the name of the header file containing the definition of the **class** stackType is myStack.h. We will refer to this header file in any program that uses a stack.

```
//Header file: myStack.h

#ifndef H_StackType
#define H_StackType

#include <iostream>
#include <cassert>

#include "stackADT.h"

using namespace std;

template <class Type>
class stackType: public stackADT<Type>
{
public:
    const stackType<Type>& operator=(const stackType<Type>&);

    void initializeStack();

    bool isEmptyStack() const;

    bool isFullStack() const;

    void push(const Type& newItem);

    Type top() const;

    void pop();

    stackType(int stackSize = 100);

    stackType(const stackType<Type>& otherStack);

    ~stackType();
```

```
private:
    int maxStackSize; //variable to store the maximum stack size
    int stackTop;     //variable to point to the top of the stack
    Type *list;       //pointer to the array that holds the
                      //stack elements

    void copyStack(const stackType<Type>& otherStack);
};

template <class Type>
void stackType<Type>::initializeStack()
{
    stackTop = 0;
}//end initializeStack

template <class Type>
bool stackType<Type>::isEmptyStack() const
{
    return (stackTop == 0);
}//end isEmptyStack

template <class Type>
bool stackType<Type>::isFullStack() const
{
    return (stackTop == maxStackSize);
} //end isFullStack

template <class Type>
void stackType<Type>::push(const Type& newItem)
{
    if (!isFullStack())
    {
        list[stackTop] = newItem;   //add newItem to the
                                    //top of the stack
        stackTop++; //increment stackTop
    }
    else
        cout << "Cannot add to a full stack." << endl;
}//end push

template <class Type>
Type stackType<Type>::top() const
{
    assert(stackTop != 0);          //if stack is empty,
                                    //terminate the program
    return list[stackTop - 1];      //return the element of the
                                    //stack indicated by
                                    //stackTop - 1
}//end top

template <class Type>
void stackType<Type>::pop()
{
    if (!isEmptyStack())
        stackTop--;                 //decrement stackTop
    else
        cout << "Cannot remove from an empty stack." << endl;
}//end pop
```

```cpp
template <class Type>
stackType<Type>::stackType(int stackSize)
{
    if (stackSize <= 0)
    {
        cout << "Size of the array to hold the stack must "
             << "be positive." << endl;
        cout << "Creating an array of size 100." << endl;

        maxStackSize = 100;
    }
    else
        maxStackSize = stackSize;       //set the stack size to
                                        //the value specified by
                                        //the parameter stackSize

    stackTop = 0;                       //set stackTop to 0
    list = new Type[maxStackSize];      //create the array to
                                        //hold the stack elements
}//end constructor

template <class Type>
stackType<Type>::~stackType() //destructor
{
    delete [] list; //deallocate the memory occupied
                    //by the array
}//end destructor

template <class Type>
void stackType<Type>::copyStack(const stackType<Type>& otherStack)
{
    delete [] list;
    maxStackSize = otherStack.maxStackSize;
    stackTop = otherStack.stackTop;

    list = new Type[maxStackSize];

        //copy otherStack into this stack
    for (int j = 0; j < stackTop; j++)
        list[j] = otherStack.list[j];
} //end copyStack


template <class Type>
stackType<Type>::stackType(const stackType<Type>& otherStack)
{
    list = NULL;

    copyStack(otherStack);
}//end copy constructor

template <class Type>
const stackType<Type>& stackType<Type>::operator=
                            (const stackType<Type>& otherStack)
{
    if (this != &otherStack) //avoid self-copy
        copyStack(otherStack);
```

```
        return *this;
} //end operator=

#endif
```

EXAMPLE 17-1

Before we give a programming example, let us first write a simple program that uses the `class stackType` and tests some of the stack operations. Among others, we will test the assignment operator and the copy constructor. The program and its output are as follows:

```
//Program to test the various operations of a stack

#include <iostream>
#include "myStack.h"

using namespace std;

void testCopyConstructor(stackType<int> otherStack);

int main()
{
    stackType<int> stack(50);
    stackType<int> copyStack(50);
    stackType<int> dummyStack(100);

    stack.initializeStack();
    stack.push(23);
    stack.push(45);
    stack.push(38);
    copyStack = stack;   //copy stack into copyStack

    cout << "The elements of copyStack: ";

    while (!copyStack.isEmptyStack())   //print copyStack
    {
        cout << copyStack.top() << " ";
        copyStack.pop();
    }
    cout << endl;

    copyStack = stack;
    testCopyConstructor(stack);   //test the copy constructor

    if (!stack.isEmptyStack())
        cout << "The original stack is not empty." << endl
            << "The top element of the original stack: "
            << copyStack.top() << endl;

    dummyStack = stack;   //copy stack into dummyStack
    cout << "The elements of dummyStack: ";
```

```
        while (!dummyStack.isEmptyStack())   //print dummyStack
        {
            cout << dummyStack.top() << " ";
            dummyStack.pop();
        }
        cout << endl;

        return 0;
}

void testCopyConstructor(stackType<int> otherStack)
{
        if (!otherStack.isEmptyStack())
            cout << "otherStack is not empty." << endl
                 << "The top element of otherStack: "
                 << otherStack.top() << endl;
}
```

Sample Run:

```
The elements of copyStack: 38 45 23
otherStack is not empty.
The top element of otherStack: 38
The original stack is not empty.
The top element of the original stack: 38
The elements of dummyStack: 38 45 23
```

It is recommended that you do a walk-through of this program.

PROGRAMMING EXAMPLE: Highest GPA

Watch the Video

In this example, we write a C++ program that reads a data file consisting of each student's GPA followed by the student's name. The program then prints the highest GPA and the names of all of the students who received that GPA. The program scans the input file only once. Moreover, we assume that there is a maximum of 100 students in the class.

Input   The program reads an input file consisting of each student's GPA, followed by the student's name. Sample data is:

```
3.4 Randy
3.2 Kathy
2.5 Colt
3.4 Tom
3.8 Ron
3.8 Mickey
3.6 Peter
```

Output   The highest GPA and all of the names associated with the highest GPA. For example, for the above data, the highest GPA is 3.8, and the students with that GPA are Ron and Mickey.

PROBLEM
ANALYSIS
AND
ALGORITHM
DESIGN

We read the first GPA and the name of the student. Because this data is the first item read, it is the highest GPA so far. Next, we read the second GPA and the name of the student. We then compare this (second) GPA with the highest GPA so far. Three cases arise:

1. The new GPA is greater than the highest GPA so far. In this case, we:

    a. Update the value of the highest GPA so far.

    b. Initialize the stack—that is, remove the names of the students from the stack.

    c. Save the name of the student having the highest GPA so far in the stack.

2. The new GPA is equal to the highest GPA so far. In this case, we add the name of the new student to the stack.

3. The new GPA is smaller than the highest GPA so far. In this case, we discard the name of the student having this grade.

We then read the next GPA and the name of the student and repeat Steps 1 through 3. We continue this process until we reach the end of the input file.

From this discussion, it is clear that we need the following variables:

```
double GPA;          //variable to hold the current GPA
double highestGPA;   //variable to hold the highest GPA
string name;         //variable to hold the name of the student
stackType<string> stack(100); //object to implement the stack
```

The preceding discussion translates into the following algorithm:

1. Declare the variables and initialize stack.

2. Open the input file.

3. If the input file does not exist, exit the program.

4. Set the output of the floating-point numbers to a fixed decimal format with a decimal point and trailing zeroes. Also, set the precision to two decimal places.

5. Read the GPA and the student name.

6. `highestGPA = GPA;`

7. `while` (not end of file)

   {

   7.1. `if` (GPA > highestGPA)

      {

      7.1.1. `clearstack(stack);`

      7.1.2. `push(stack, student name);`

      7.1.3. `highestGPA = GPA;`
      }

   7.2. `else`
         `if` (GPA is equal to highestGPA)
            `push(stack, student name);`

   7.3. Read GPA and student name;
   }

8. Output the highest GPA.

9. Output the names of the students having the highest GPA.

PROGRAM LISTING

```
//************************************************************
// Author: D.S. Malik
//
// This program uses the class myStack to determine the
// highest GPA from a list of students with their GPA.
// The program also outputs the names of the students
// who received the highest GPA.
//************************************************************

#include <iostream>
#include <iomanip>
#include <fstream>
#include <string>

#include "myStack.h"

using namespace std;

int main()
{
        //Step 1
    double GPA;
    double highestGPA;
    string name;

    stackType<string> stack(100);

    ifstream infile;
```

```cpp
infile.open("HighestGPAData.txt");              //Step 2

if (!infile)                                    //Step 3
{
    cout << "The input file does not "
         << "exist. Program terminates!"
         << endl;
    return 1;
}

cout << fixed << showpoint;                      //Step 4
cout << setprecision(2);                         //Step 4

infile >> GPA >> name;                           //Step 5

highestGPA = GPA;                                //Step 6

while (infile)                                   //Step 7
{
    if (GPA > highestGPA)                        //Step 7.1
    {
        stack.initializeStack();                 //Step 7.1.1

        if (!stack.isFullStack())                //Step 7.1.2
            stack.push(name);

        highestGPA = GPA;                        //Step 7.1.3
    }
    else if (GPA == highestGPA)                  //Step 7.2
        if (!stack.isFullStack())
            stack.push(name);
        else
        {
            cout << "Stack overflows. "
                 << "Program terminates!"
                 << endl;
            return 1;  //exit program
        }
    infile >> GPA >> name;                       //Step 7.3
}

cout << "Highest GPA = " << highestGPA
     << endl;                                    //Step 8
cout << "The students holding the "
     << "highest GPA are:" << endl;

while (!stack.isEmptyStack())                    //Step 9
{
    cout << stack.top() << endl;
    stack.pop();
}
```

17

```
        cout << endl;

        return 0;
}
```

Sample Run:

Input File (HighestGPAData.txt)

```
3.4 Randy
3.2 Kathy
2.5 Colt
3.4 Tom
3.8 Ron
3.8 Mickey
3.6 Peter
3.5 Donald
3.8 Cindy
3.7 Dome
3.9 Andy
3.8 Fox
3.9 Minnie
2.7 Gilda
3.9 Vinay
3.4 Danny
```

Output

```
Highest GPA = 3.90
The students holding the highest GPA are:
Vinay
Minnie
Andy
```

Note that the names of the students with the highest GPA are output in the reverse order, relative to the order they appear in the input, due to the fact that the top element of the stack is the last element added to the stack.

Linked Implementation of Stacks

Because an array size is fixed, in the array (linear) representation of a stack, only a fixed number of elements can be pushed onto the stack. If in a program the number of elements to be pushed exceeds the size of the array, the program may terminate in an error. We must overcome these problems.

We have seen that by using pointer variables, we can dynamically allocate and deallocate memory, and by using linked lists, we can dynamically organize data (such as an ordered list). Next, we will use these concepts to implement a stack dynamically.

Recall that in the linear representation of a stack, the value of `stackTop` indicates the number of elements in the stack, and the value of `stackTop - 1` points to the top item in the stack. With the help of `stackTop`, we can do several things: find the top element, check whether the stack is empty, and so on.

Similar to the linear representation, in a linked representation, `stackTop` is used to locate the top element in the stack. However, there is a slight difference. In the former case, `stackTop` gives the index of the array. In the latter case, `stackTop` gives the address (memory location) of the top element of the stack.

The following class implements the functions of the abstract `class stackADT`:

```
//Definition of the node
template <class Type>
struct nodeType
{
    Type info;
    nodeType<Type> *link;
};

template <class Type>
class linkedStackType: public stackADT<Type>
{
public:
    const linkedStackType<Type>& operator=
                        (const linkedStackType<Type>&);
      //Overload the assignment operator.

    bool isEmptyStack() const;
      //Function to determine whether the stack is empty.
      //Postcondition: Returns true if the stack is empty;
      //               otherwise returns false.

    bool isFullStack() const;
      //Function to determine whether the stack is full.
      //Postcondition: Returns false.

    void initializeStack();
      //Function to initialize the stack to an empty state.
      //Postcondition: The stack elements are removed;
      //               stackTop = NULL;

    void push(const Type& newItem);
      //Function to add newItem to the stack.
      //Precondition: The stack exists and is not full.
      //Postcondition: The stack is changed and newItem
      //               is added to the top of the stack.
```

```
    Type top() const;
      //Function to return the top element of the stack.
      //Precondition: The stack exists and is not empty.
      //Postcondition: If the stack is empty, the program
      //                terminates; otherwise, the top
      //                element of the stack is returned.
    void pop();
      //Function to remove the top element of the stack.
      //Precondition: The stack exists and is not empty.
      //Postcondition: The stack is changed and the top
      //                element is removed from the stack.

    linkedStackType();
      //Default constructor
      //Postcondition: stackTop = NULL;

    linkedStackType(const linkedStackType<Type>& otherStack);
      //Copy constructor

    ~linkedStackType();
      //Destructor
      //Postcondition: All the elements of the stack are
      //                removed from the stack.

private:
    nodeType<Type> *stackTop; //pointer to the stack

    void copyStack(const linkedStackType<Type>& otherStack);
      //Function to make a copy of otherStack.
      //Postcondition: A copy of otherStack is created and
      //                assigned to this stack.
};
```

 NOTE   In this linked implementation of stacks, the memory to store the stack elements is allocated dynamically. Logically, the stack is never full. The stack is full only if we run out of memory space. Therefore, in reality, the function isFullStack does not apply to linked implementation of stacks. However, the **class** linkedStackType must provide the definition of the function isFullStack, because it is defined in the parent abstract **class** stackADT.

We leave the UML class diagram of the **class** linkedStackType as an exercise for you. (See Exercise 28 at the end of this chapter.)

EXAMPLE 17-2

Suppose that stack is an object of type linkedStackType. Figure 17-12(a) shows an empty stack, and Figure 17-12(b) shows a nonempty stack.

LIVERPOOL JOHN MOORES UNIVERSITY
LEARNING SERVICES

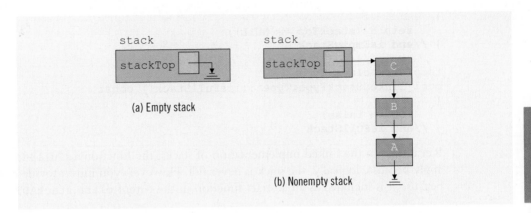

FIGURE 17-12   Empty and nonempty linked stack

In Figure 17-12(b), the top element of the stack is C; that is, the last element pushed onto the stack is C.

Next, we discuss the definitions of the functions to implement the operations of a linked stack.

Default Constructor

The first operation that we consider is the default constructor. The default constructor initializes the stack to an empty state when a stack object is declared. Thus, this function sets stackTop to NULL. The definition of this function is:

```
template <class Type>
linkedStackType<Type>::linkedStackType()
{
    stackTop = NULL;
}
```

Empty Stack and Full Stack

The operations isEmptyStack and isFullStack are quite straightforward. The stack is empty if stackTop is NULL. Also, because the memory for a stack element is allocated and deallocated dynamically, the stack is never full. (The stack is full only if we run out of memory.) Thus, the function isFullStack always returns the value **false**. The definitions of the functions to implement these operations are:

```
template <class Type>
bool linkedStackType<Type>::isEmptyStack() const
```

```
{
    return (stackTop == NULL);
} //end isEmptyStack

template <class Type>
bool linkedStackType<Type>:: isFullStack() const
{
    return false;
} //end isFullStack
```

Recall that in the linked implementation of stacks, the function isFullStack does not apply because, logically, the stack is never full. However, you must provide its definition because it is included as an abstract function in the parent class stackADT.

Initialize Stack

The operation initializeStack reinitializes the stack to an empty state. Because the stack may contain some elements and we are using a linked implementation of a stack, we must deallocate the memory occupied by the stack elements and set stackTop to NULL. The definition of this function is:

```
template <class Type>
void linkedStackType<Type>:: initializeStack()
{
    nodeType<Type> *temp; //pointer to delete the node

    while (stackTop != NULL)   //while there are elements in
                               //the stack
    {
        temp = stackTop;       //set temp to point to the
                               //current node
        stackTop = stackTop->link;   //advance stackTop to the
                                     //next node
        delete temp;           //deallocate memory occupied by temp
    }
} //end initializeStack
```

Next, we consider the push, top, and pop operations. From Figure 17-12(b), it is clear that the newElement will be added (in the case of push) at the beginning of the linked list pointed to by stackTop. In the case of pop, the node pointed to by stackTop will be removed. In both cases, the value of the pointer stackTop is updated. The operation top returns the info of the node that stackTop is pointing to.

Push

Consider the stack shown in Figure 17-13.

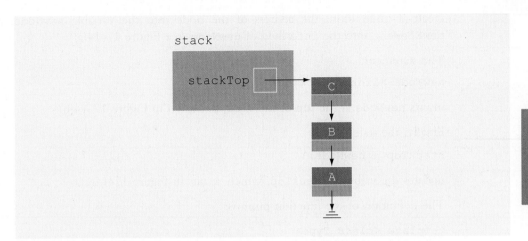

FIGURE 17-13 Stack before the push operation

Figure 17-14 shows the steps of the push operation. (Assume that the new element to be pushed is `'D'`.)

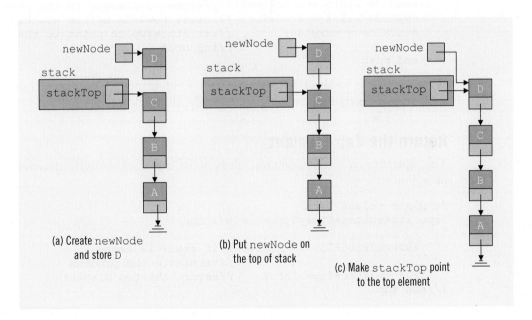

(a) Create newNode
and store D

(b) Put newNode on
the top of stack

(c) Make stackTop point
to the top element

FIGURE 17-14 Push operation

The statements:

```
newNode = new nodeType<Type>; //create the new node
newNode->info = newElement;
```

create a node, store the address of the node into the variable `newNode`, and store `newElement` into the `info` field of `newNode` (see Figure 17-14(a)).

The statement:

```
newNode->link = stackTop;
```

inserts `newNode` at the top of the stack, as shown in Figure 17-14(b).

Finally, the statement:

```
stackTop = newNode;
```

updates the value of `stackTop`, which results in Figure 17-14(c).

The definition of the function `push` is:

```
template <class Type>
void linkedStackType<Type>::push(const Type& newElement)
{
    nodeType<Type> *newNode;   //pointer to create the new node

    newNode = new nodeType<Type>; //create the node

    newNode->info = newElement; //store newElement in the node
    newNode->link = stackTop; //insert newNode before stackTop
    stackTop = newNode;        //set stackTop to point to the
                               //top node
} //end push
```

We do not need to check whether the stack is full before we push an element onto the stack because in this implementation, logically, the stack is never full.

Return the Top Element

The operation to return the top element of the stack is quite straightforward. Its definition is:

```
template <class Type>
Type linkedStackType<Type>::top() const
{
    assert(stackTop != NULL); //if stack is empty,
                              //terminate the program
    return stackTop->info;    //return the top element
}//end top
```

Pop

Now we consider the `pop` operation, which removes the top element of the stack. Consider the stack shown in Figure 17-15.

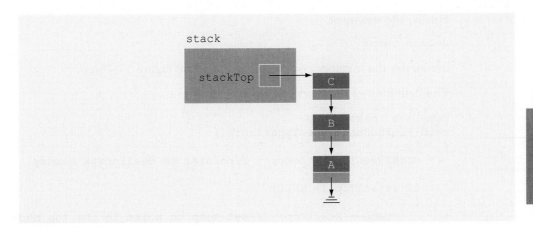

FIGURE 17-15 Stack before the pop operation

Figure 17-16 shows the pop operation.

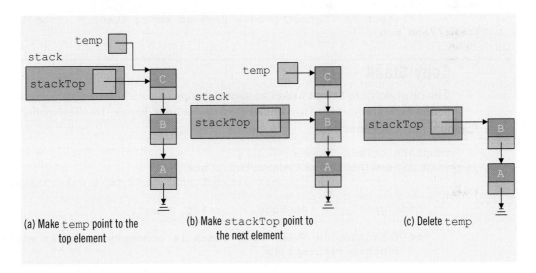

(a) Make temp point to the top element

(b) Make stackTop point to the next element

(c) Delete temp

FIGURE 17-16 Pop operation

The statement:

```
temp = stackTop;
```

makes temp point to the top of the stack (see Figure 17-16(a)). Next, the statement:

```
stackTop = stackTop->link;
```

makes the second element of the stack become the top element of the stack (see Figure 17-16(b)).

Finally, the statement:

```
delete temp;
```

deallocates the memory pointed to by `temp` (see Figure 17-16(c)).

The definition of the function `pop` is:

```
template <class Type>
void linkedStackType<Type>::pop()
{
    nodeType<Type> *temp;    //pointer to deallocate memory

    if (stackTop != NULL)
    {
        temp = stackTop;   //set temp to point to the top node

        stackTop = stackTop->link;   //advance stackTop to the
                                     //next node
        delete temp;      //delete the top node
    }
    else
        cout << "Cannot remove from an empty stack." << endl;
}//end pop
```

Copy Stack

The function `copyStack` makes an identical copy of a stack. Its definition is similar to the definition of `copyList` for linked lists, given in Chapter 16. The definition of the function `copyStack` is:

```
template <class Type>
void linkedStackType<Type>::copyStack
                    (const linkedStackType<Type>& otherStack)
{
    nodeType<Type> *newNode, *current, *last;

    if (stackTop != NULL) //if stack is nonempty, make it empty
        initializeStack();

    if (otherStack.stackTop == NULL)
        stackTop = NULL;
    else
    {
        current = otherStack.stackTop;  //set current to point
                                        //to the stack to be copied

            //copy the stackTop element of the stack
        stackTop = new nodeType<Type>;   //create the node

        stackTop->info = current->info; //copy the info
```

```
        stackTop->link = NULL;   //set the link field of the
                                 //node to NULL
        last = stackTop;         //set last to point to the node
        current = current->link;   //set current to point to
                                   //the next node

            //copy the remaining stack
        while (current != NULL)
        {
            newNode = new nodeType<Type>;

            newNode->info = current->info;
            newNode->link = NULL;
            last->link = newNode;
            last = newNode;
            current = current->link;
        }//end while
    }//end else
} //end copyStack
```

Constructors and Destructors

We have already discussed the default constructor. To complete the implementation of the stack operations, next we give the definitions of the functions to implement the copy constructor and the destructor and to overload the assignment operator. (These functions are similar to those discussed for linked lists in Chapter 16.)

```
    //copy constructor
template <class Type>
linkedStackType<Type>::linkedStackType(
                    const linkedStackType<Type>& otherStack)
{
    stackTop = NULL;
    copyStack(otherStack);
}//end copy constructor

    //destructor
template <class Type>
linkedStackType<Type>::~linkedStackType()
{
    initializeStack();
}//end destructor
```

Overloading the Assignment Operator (=)

The definition of the function to overload the assignment operator for the class linkedStackType is:

```
template <class Type>
const linkedStackType<Type>& linkedStackType<Type>::operator=
                    (const linkedStackType<Type>& otherStack)
```

```
{
    if (this != &otherStack) //avoid self-copy
        copyStack(otherStack);

    return *this;
}//end operator=
```

The definition of a stack and the functions to implement the stack operations discussed previously are generic. Also, as in the case of an array representation of a stack, in the linked representation of a stack, we must put the definition of the stack and the functions to implement the stack operations together in a (header) file. A client's program can include this header file via the `include` statement.

Example 17-3 illustrates how a `linkedStack` object is used in a program.

EXAMPLE 17-3

We assume that the definition of the `class linkedStackType` and the functions to implement the stack operations are included in the header file `"linkedStack.h"`.

```
//This program tests various operations of a linked stack

#include <iostream>
#include "linkedStack.h"

using namespace std;

void testCopy(linkedStackType<int> OStack);

int main()
{
    linkedStackType<int> stack;
    linkedStackType<int> otherStack;
    linkedStackType<int> newStack;

        //Add elements into stack
    stack.push(34);
    stack.push(43);
    stack.push(27);

        //Use the assignment operator to copy the elements
        //of stack into newStack
    newStack = stack;

    cout << "After the assignment operator, newStack: "
        << endl;

        //Output the elements of newStack
    while (!newStack.isEmptyStack())
    {
        cout << newStack.top() << endl;
        newStack.pop();
    }
```

```
        //Use the assignment operator to copy the elements
        //of stack into otherStack
    otherStack = stack;

    cout << "Testing the copy constructor." << endl;

    testCopy(otherStack);

    cout << "After the copy constructor, otherStack: " << endl;

    while (!otherStack.isEmptyStack())
    {
        cout << otherStack.top() << endl;
        otherStack.pop();
    }

    return 0;
}

    //Function to test the copy constructor
void testCopy(linkedStackType<int> OStack)
{
    cout << "Stack in the function testCopy:" << endl;

    while (!OStack.isEmptyStack())
    {
        cout << OStack.top() << endl;
        OStack.pop();
    }
}
```

Sample Run:

```
After the assignment operator, newStack:
27
43
34
Testing the copy constructor.
Stack in the function testCopy:
27
43
34
After the copy constructor, otherStack:
27
43
34
```

Stack as Derived from the `class` unorderedLinkedList

If we compare the push function of the stack with the insertFirst function discussed for general lists in Chapter 16, we see that the algorithms to implement these operations are similar. A comparison of other functions—such as initializeStack and initializeList, isEmptyList and isEmptyStack, and so on—suggests that the `class` linkedStackType can be derived from the `class` linkedListType. Moreover, the functions pop and isFullStack can be implemented as in the previous section. Note that the `class` linkedListType is an abstract and does not implement all of the operations. However, the `class` unorderedLinkedListType is derived from the `class` linkedListType and provides the definitions of the abstract functions of the `class` linkedListType. Therefore, we can derive the `class` linkedStackType from the `class` unorderedLinkedListType.

Next, we define the `class` linkedStackType that is derived from the `class` unorderedLinkedList. The definitions of the functions to implement the stack operations are also given.

```
#include <iostream>
#include "unorderedLinkedList.h"

using namespace std;

template <class Type>
class linkedStackType: public unorderedLinkedList<Type>
{
public:
    void initializeStack();
    bool isEmptyStack() const;
    bool isFullStack() const;
    void push(const Type& newItem);
    Type top() const;
    void pop();
};

template <class Type>
void linkedStackType<Type>::initializeStack()
{
    unorderedLinkedList<Type>::initializeList();
}

template <class Type>
bool linkedStackType<Type>::isEmptyStack() const
{
    return unorderedLinkedList<Type>::isEmptyList();
}
template <class Type>
bool linkedStackType<Type>::isFullStack() const
{
    return false;
}
```

```
template <class Type>
void linkedStackType<Type>::push(const Type& newElement)
{
    unorderedLinkedList<Type>::insertFirst(newElement);
}

template <class Type>
Type linkedStackType<Type>::top() const
{
    return unorderedLinkedList<Type>::front();
}

template <class Type>
void linkedStackType<Type>::pop()
{
    nodeType<Type> *temp;

    temp = first;
    first = first->link;
    delete temp;
}
```

Application of Stacks: Postfix Expressions Calculator

The usual notation for writing arithmetic expressions (the notation we learned in elementary school) is called **infix** notation, in which the operator is written between the operands. For example, in the expression $a + b$, the operator $+$ is between the operands a and b. In infix notation, the operators have precedence. That is, we must evaluate expressions from left to right, and multiplication and division have higher precedence than do addition and subtraction. If we want to evaluate the expression in a different order, we must include parentheses. For example, in the expression $a + b \star c$, we first evaluate $\star$ using the operands b and c, and then we evaluate $+$ using the operand a and the result of $b \star c$.

In the early 1920s, the Polish mathematician Jan Lukasiewicz discovered that if operators were written before the operands (**prefix** or **Polish** notation; for example, $+ a b$), the parentheses could be omitted. In the late 1950s, the Australian philosopher and early computer scientist Charles L. Hamblin proposed a scheme in which the operators *follow* the operands (postfix operators), resulting in the **Reverse Polish** notation. This has the advantage that the operators appear in the order required for computation.

For example, the expression:

$a + b \star c$

in a postfix expression is:

$a\ b\ c \star +$

The following example shows various infix expressions and their equivalent postfix expressions.

EXAMPLE 17-4

Infix Expression	Equivalent Postfix Expression
$a + b$	$a\ b +$
$a + b * c$	$a\ b\ c * +$
$a * b + c$	$a\ b * c +$
$(a + b) * c$	$a\ b + c *$
$(a - b) * (c + d)$	$a\ b - c\ d + *$
$(a + b) * (c - d\,/\,e) + f$	$a\ b + c\ d\ e\,/\, - * f +$

Shortly after Lukasiewicz's discovery, it was realized that postfix notation had important applications in computer science. In fact, many compilers now first translate arithmetic expressions into some form of postfix notation and then translate this postfix expression into machine code. Postfix expressions can be evaluated using the following algorithm:

Scan the expression from left to right. When an operator is found, back up to get the required number of operands, perform the operation, and continue.

Consider the following postfix expression:

6 3 + 2 * =

Let us evaluate this expression using a stack and the previous algorithm. Figure 17-17 shows how this expression gets evaluated.

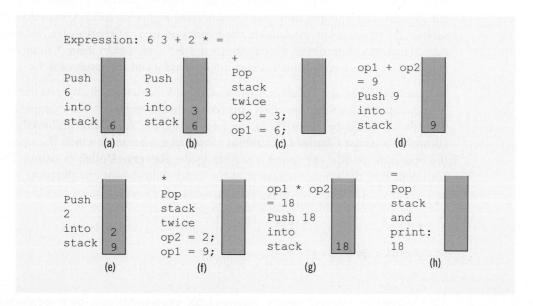

FIGURE 17-17 Evaluating the postfix expression: 6 3 + 2 * =

Read the first symbol, 6, which is a number. Push the number onto the stack (see Figure 17-17(a)). Read the next symbol, 3, which is a number. Push the number onto the stack (see Figure 17-17(b)). Read the next symbol, +, which is an operator. Because an operator requires two operands to be evaluated, pop the stack twice (see Figure 17-17(c)). Perform the operation and put the result back onto the stack (see Figure 17-17(d)).

Read the next symbol, 2, which is a number. Push the number onto the stack (see Figure 17-17(e)). Read the next symbol, *, which is an operator. Because an operator requires two operands to be evaluated, pop the stack twice (see Figure 17-17(f)). Perform the operation, and put the result back onto the stack (see Figure 17-17(g)).

Scan the next symbol, =, which is the equal sign, indicating the end of the expression. Therefore, print the result. The result of the expression is in the stack, so pop and print (see Figure 17-17(h)).

The value of the expression 6 3 + 2 * = 18.

From this discussion, it is clear that when we read a symbol other than a number, the following cases arise:

1. The symbol we read is one of the following: +, -, *, /, or =.

    a. If the symbol is +, -, *, or /, the symbol is an operator, so we must evaluate it. Because an operator requires two operands, the stack must have at least two elements; otherwise, the expression has an error.

    b. If the symbol is = (an equal sign), the expression ends and we must print the answer. At this step, the stack must contain exactly one element; otherwise, the expression has an error.

2. The symbol we read is something other than +, -, *, /, or =. In this case, the expression contains an illegal operator.

It is also clear that when an operand (number) is encountered in an expression, it is pushed onto the stack because the operator comes after the operands.

Consider the following expressions:

    a. 7 6 + 3 ; 6 - =
    b. 14 + 2 3 * =
    c. 14 2 3 + =

Expression (a) has an illegal operator, expression (b) does not have enough operands for +, and expression (c) has too many operands. In the case of expression (c), when we encounter the equal sign (=), the stack will have two elements, and this error cannot be discovered until we are ready to print the value of the expression.

To make the input easier to read, we assume that the postfix expressions are in the following form:

#6 #3 + #2 * =

The symbol # precedes each number in the expression. If the symbol scanned is #, then the next input is a number (that is, an operand). If the symbol scanned is not #, then it is either an operator (may be illegal) or an equal sign (indicating the end of the expression). Furthermore, we assume that each expression contains only the +, -, *, and / operators.

This program outputs the entire postfix expression together with the answer. If the expression has an error, the expression is discarded. In this case, the program outputs the expression together with an appropriate error message. Because an expression may contain an error, we must clear the stack before processing the next expression. Also, the stack must be initialized; that is, the stack must be empty.

Main Algorithm

Following the previous discussion, the main algorithm in pseudocode is:

```
Read the first character
while not the end of input data
{
    a. initialize the stack
    b. process the expression
    c. output result
    d. get the next expression
}
```

To simplify the complexity of the function main, we write four functions: evaluateExpression, evaluateOpr, discardExp, and printResult. The function evaluateExpression, if possible, evaluates the expression and leaves the result in the stack. If the postfix expression is error free, the function printResult outputs the result. The function evaluateOpr evaluates an operator, and the function discardExp discards the current expression if there is any error in the expression.

Function evaluateExpression

The function evaluateExpression evaluates each postfix expression. Each expression ends with the symbol =. The general algorithm is:

```
while (ch is not = '=') //process each expression
                        //= marks the end of an expression
{
    switch (ch)
    {
    case '#':
        read a number
        output the number;
        push the number onto the stack;
        break;
    default:
        assume that ch is an operation
        evaluate the operation;
    } //end switch
```

```
     if no error was found, then
     {
         read next ch;
         output ch;
     }
     else
         Discard the expression
} //end while
```

From this algorithm, it follows that this method has five parameters—one to access the input file, one to access the output file, one to access the stack, one to pass a character of the expression, and one to indicate whether there is an error in the expression. The definition of this function is:

```
void evaluateExpression(ifstream& inpF, ofstream& outF,
                        stackType<double>& stack,
                        char& ch, bool& isExpOk)
{
    double num;

    while (ch != '=')
    {
        switch (ch)
        {
        case '#':
            inpF >> num;
            outF << num << " ";
            if (!stack.isFullStack())
                stack.push(num);
            else
            {
                cout << "Stack overflow. "
                     << "Program terminates!" << endl;
                exit(0);   //terminate the program
            }

            break;
        default:
            evaluateOpr(outF, stack, ch, isExpOk);
        }//end switch

        if (isExpOk) //if no error
        {
            inpF >> ch;
            outF << ch;

            if (ch != '#')
                outF << " ";
        }
        else
            discardExp(inpF, outF, ch);
    } //end while (!= '=')
}
```

Note that the function `exit` terminates the program.

Function `evaluateOpr`

This function (if possible) evaluates an expression. Two operands are needed to evaluate an operation, and operands are saved in the stack. Therefore, the stack must contain at least two numbers. If the stack contains fewer than two numbers, then the expression has an error. In this case, the entire expression is discarded, and an appropriate message is printed. This function also checks for any illegal operations. In pseudocode, this function is:

```
if stack is empty
{
    error in the expression
    set expressionOk to false
}
else
{
    retrieve the top element of stack into op2
    pop stack
    if stack is empty
    {
        error in the expression
        set expressionOk to false
    }
    else
    {
        retrieve the top element of stack into op1
        pop stack

            //If the operation is legal, perform the
            //operation and push the result onto the stack.
        switch (ch)
        {
        case '+':
            //Perform the operation and push the result
            //onto the stack.
            stack.push(op1 + op2);
            break;
        case '-':
            //Perform the operation and push the result
            //onto the stack.
            stack.push(op1 - op2);
            break;
        case '*':
            //Perform the operation and push the
            //result onto the stack.
            stack.push(op1 * op2);
            break;
        case '/':
            //If (op2 != 0), perform the operation and
            //push the result onto the stack.
            stack.push(op1 / op2);
```

```
                //Otherwise, report the error.
                //Set expressionOk to false.
            break;
        otherwise operation is illegal
            {
                output an appropriate message;
                set expressionOk to false
            }
        } //end switch
}
```

Following this pseudocode, the definition of the function evaluateOpr is:

```
void evaluateOpr(ofstream& out, stackType<double>& stack,
                 char& ch, bool& isExpOk)
{
    double op1, op2;

    if (stack.isEmptyStack())
    {
        out << " (Not enough operands)";
        isExpOk = false;
    }
    else
    {
        op2 = stack.top();
        stack.pop();

        if (stack.isEmptyStack())
        {
            out << " (Not enough operands)";
            isExpOk = false;
        }
        else
        {
            op1 = stack.top();
            stack.pop();

            switch (ch)
            {
            case '+':
                stack.push(op1 + op2);
                break;
            case '-':
                stack.push(op1 - op2);
                break;
            case '*':
                stack.push(op1 * op2);
                break;
            case '/':
                if (op2 != 0)
                    stack.push(op1 / op2);
```

```
            else
            {
                out << " (Division by 0)";
                isExpOk = false;
            }
            break;
        default:
            out << " (Illegal operator)";
            isExpOk = false;
        }//end switch
    } //end else
} //end else
} //end evaluateOpr
```

Function discardExp

This function is called whenever an error is discovered in the expression. It reads and writes the input data only until the input is `'='`, the end of the expression. The definition of this function is:

```
void discardExp(ifstream& in, ofstream& out, char& ch)
{
    while (ch != '=')
    {
        in.get(ch);
        out << ch;
    }
} //end discardExp
```

Function printResult

If the postfix expression contains no errors, the function `printResult` prints the result; otherwise, it outputs an appropriate message. The result of the expression is in the stack, and the output is sent to a file. Therefore, this function must have access to the stack and the output file. Suppose that no errors were encountered by the method `evaluateExpression`. If the stack has only one element, then the expression is error free and the top element of the stack is printed. If either the stack is empty or it has more than one element, then there is an error in the postfix expression. In this case, this method outputs an appropriate error message. The definition of this method is:

```
void printResult(ofstream& outF, stackType<double>& stack,
                 bool isExpOk)
{
    double result;

    if (isExpOk) //if no error, print the result
```

```
    {
        if (!stack.isEmptyStack())
        {
            result = stack.top();
            stack.pop();

            if (stack.isEmptyStack())
                outF << result << endl;
            else
                outF << " (Error: Too many operands)" << endl;
        } //end if
        else
            outF << " (Error in the expression)" << endl;
    }
    else
        outF << " (Error in the expression)" << endl;

    outF << "_____"
         << endl << endl;
} //end printResult
```

PROGRAM LISTING

```
//************************************************************
// Author: D.S. Malik
//
// Program: Postfix Calculator
// This program evaluates postfix expressions.
//************************************************************

#include <iostream>
#include <iomanip>
#include <fstream>
#include "mystack.h"

using namespace std;

void evaluateExpression(ifstream& inpF, ofstream& outF,
                        stackType<double>& stack,
                        char& ch, bool& isExpOk);
void evaluateOpr(ofstream& out, stackType<double>& stack,
                 char& ch, bool& isExpOk);
void discardExp(ifstream& in, ofstream& out, char& ch);
void printResult(ofstream& outF, stackType<double>& stack,
                 bool isExpOk);

int main()
{
    bool expressionOk;
    char ch;
```

1168 | Chapter 17: Stacks and Queues

```cpp
    stackType<double> stack(100);
    ifstream infile;
    ofstream outfile;

    infile.open("RpnData.txt");

    if (!infile)
    {
        cout << "Cannot open the input file. "
             << "Program terminates!" << endl;
        return 1;
    }

    outfile.open("RpnOutput.txt");

    outfile << fixed << showpoint;
    outfile << setprecision(2);

    infile >> ch;
    while (infile)
    {
        stack.initializeStack();
        expressionOk = true;
        outfile << ch;

        evaluateExpression(infile, outfile, stack, ch,
                           expressionOk);
        printResult(outfile, stack, expressionOk);
        infile >> ch; //begin processing the next expression
    } //end while

    infile.close();
    outfile.close();

    return 0;

} //end main
//Place the definitions of the function evaluateExpression,
//evaluateOpr, discardExp, and printResult as described
//previously here.
```

Sample Run:

Input File

```
#35 #27 + #3 * =
#26 #28 + #32 #2 ; - #5 / =
#23 #30 #15 * / =
#2 #3 #4 + =
#20 #29 #9 * ; =
#25 #23 - + =
#34 #24 #12 #7 / * + #23 - =
```

Output

```
#35.00 #27.00 + #3.00 * = 186.00
```

```
#26.00 #28.00 + #32.00 #2.00 ; (Illegal operator) - #5 / = (Error in the expression)
```

```
#23.00 #30.00 #15.00 * / = 0.05
```

```
#2.00 #3.00 #4.00 + = (Error: Too many operands)
```

```
#20.00 #29.00 #9.00 * ; (Illegal operator) = (Error in the expression)
```

```
#25.00 #23.00 - + (Not enough operands) = (Error in the expression)
```

```
#34.00 #24.00 #12.00 #7.00 / * + #23.00 - = 52.14
```

Removing Recursion: Nonrecursive Algorithm to Print a Linked List Backward

In Chapter 16, we used recursion to print a linked list backward. In this section, you will learn how a stack can be used to design a nonrecursive algorithm to print a linked list backward.

Consider the linked list shown in Figure 17-18.

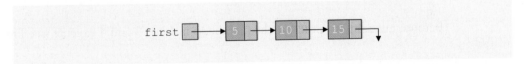

FIGURE 17-18 Linked list

To print the list backward, first we need to get to the last node of the list, which we can do by traversing the linked list starting at the first node. However, once we are at the last node, how do we get back to the previous node, especially given that links go in only one direction? You can again traverse the linked list with the appropriate loop termination condition, but this approach might waste a considerable amount of computer time, especially if the list is very large. Moreover, if we do this for every node in the list, the program might execute very slowly. Next, we show how to use a stack effectively to print the list backward.

After printing the info of a particular node, we need to move to the node immediately behind this node. For example, after printing 15, we need to move to the node with info 10. Thus, while initially traversing the list to move to the last node, we must save a pointer to each node. For example, for the list in Figure 17-18, we must save a pointer to each of the nodes with info 5 and 10. After printing 15, we go back to the node with info 10; after printing 10, we go back to the node with info 5. From this, it follows that we must save pointers to each node in a stack, so as to implement the Last In First Out principle.

Because the number of nodes in a linked list is usually not known, we will use the linked implementation of a stack. Suppose that stack is an object of type linkedListType, and current is a pointer of the same type as the pointer first. Consider the following statements:

```
current = first;                    //Line 1

while (current != NULL)             //Line 2
{
    stack.push(current);           //Line 3
    current = current->link;       //Line 4
}
```

After the statement in Line 1 executes, current points to the first node (see Figure 17-19).

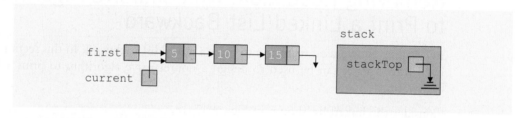

FIGURE 17-19 List after the statement current = first; executes

Because current is not NULL, the statements in Lines 3 and 4 execute (see Figure 17-20).

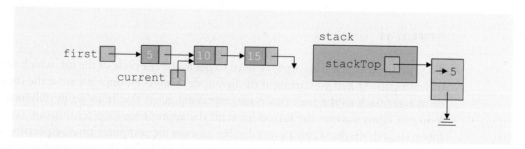

FIGURE 17-20 List and stack after the statements stack.push(current); and current = current->link; execute

After the statement in Line 4 executes, the loop condition in Line 2 is reevaluated. Because `current` is not `NULL`, the loop condition evaluates to **true**, so the statements in Lines 3 and 4 execute (see Figure 17-21).

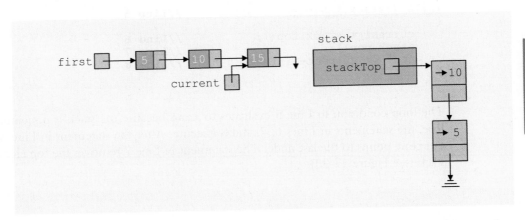

FIGURE 17-21 List and stack after the statements `stack.push(current);` and `current = current->link;` execute

After the statement in Line 4 executes, the loop condition, in Line 2, is evaluated again. Because `current` is not `NULL`, the loop condition evaluates to **true**, so the statements in Lines 3 and 4 execute (see Figure 17-22).

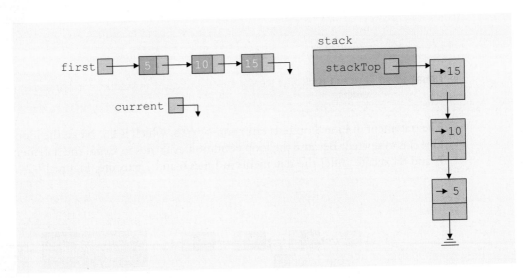

FIGURE 17-22 List and stack after the statements `stack.push(current);` and `current = current->link;` execute

After the statement in Line 4 executes, the loop condition in Line 2 is evaluated again. Because `current` is `NULL`, the loop condition evaluates to **false**, and the **while** loop in

Line 2 terminates. From Figure 17-22, it follows that a pointer to each node in the linked list is saved in the stack. The top element of the stack contains a pointer to the last node in the list, and so on. Let us now execute the following statements:

```
while (!stack.isEmptyStack())          //Line 5
{
    current = stack.top();             //Line 6
    stack.pop();                       //Line 7
    cout << current->info << " ";      //Line 8
}
```

The loop condition in Line 5 evaluates to **true** because the stack is nonempty. Therefore, the statements in Lines 6, 7, and 8 execute. After the statement in Line 6 executes, `current` points to the last node. The statement in Line 7 removes the top element of the stack (see Figure 17-23).

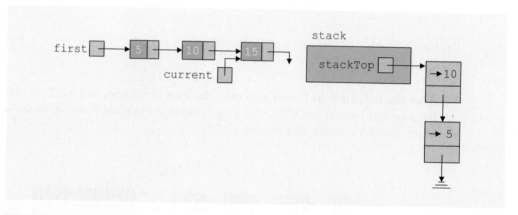

FIGURE 17-23   List and stack after the statements `current = stack.top();` and `stack.pop();` execute

The statement in Line 8 outputs `current->info`, which is 15. Next, the loop condition in Line 5 is evaluated. Because the loop condition evaluates to **true**, the statements in Lines 6, 7, and 8 execute. After the statements in Lines 6 and 7 execute, Figure 17-24 results.

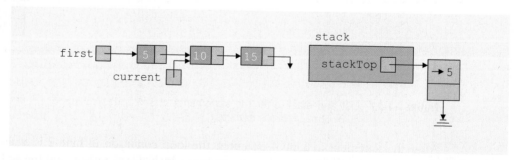

FIGURE 17-24   List and stack after the statements `current = stack.top();` and `stack.pop();` execute

The statement in Line 8 outputs `current->info`, which is 10. Next, the loop condition in Line 5 is evaluated. Because the loop condition evaluates to `true`, the statements in Lines 6, 7, and 8 execute. After the statements in Lines 6 and 7 execute, Figure 17-25 results.

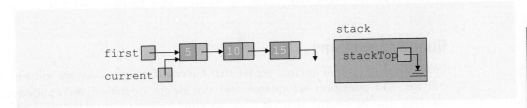

FIGURE 17-25 List and stack after the statements `current = stack.top();` and `stack.pop();` execute

The statement in Line 8 outputs `current->info`, which is 5. Next, the loop condition in Line 5 is evaluated. Because the loop condition evaluates to `false`, the `while` loop terminates. The `while` loop in Line 5 produces the following output:

```
15 10 5
```

Queues

This section discusses another important data structure called a **queue**. The notion of a queue in computer science is the same as the notion of the queues to which you are accustomed in everyday life. There are queues of customers in a bank or in a grocery store and queues of cars waiting to pass through a tollbooth. Similarly, because a computer can send a print request faster than a printer can print, a queue of documents is often waiting to be printed at a printer. The general rule to process elements in a queue is that the customer at the front of the queue is served next, and when a new customer arrives, he or she stands at the end of the queue. That is, a queue is a First In First Out data structure.

Queues have numerous applications in computer science. Whenever a system is modeled on the First In First Out principle, queues are used. At the end of this section, we will discuss one of the most widely used applications of queues, computer simulation. First, however, we need to develop the tools necessary to implement a queue. The next few sections discuss how to design classes to implement queues as an ADT.

A queue is a set of elements of the same type in which the elements are added at one end, called the **back** or **rear**, and deleted from the other end, called the **front**. For example, consider a line of customers in a bank, wherein the customers are waiting to withdraw/deposit money or to conduct some other business. Each new customer gets in the line at the rear. Whenever a teller is ready for a new customer, the customer at the front of the line is served.

The rear of the queue is accessed whenever a new element is added to the queue, and the front of the queue is accessed whenever an element is deleted from the queue. As in a stack, the middle elements of the queue are inaccessible, even if the queue elements are stored in an array.

Queue: A data structure in which the elements are added at one end, called the rear, and deleted from the other end, called the front; a First In First Out (FIFO) data structure.

Queue Operations

From the definition of queues, we see that the two key operations are add and delete. We call the add operation **addQueue** and the delete operation **deleteQueue**. Because elements can be neither deleted from an empty queue nor added to a full queue, we need two more operations to successfully implement the **addQueue** and **deleteQueue** operations: **isEmptyQueue** (checks whether the queue is empty) and **isFullQueue** (checks whether a queue is full).

We also need an operation, **initializeQueue**, to initialize the queue to an empty state. Moreover, to retrieve the first and last elements of the queue, we include the operations **front** and **back**, as described in the following list. Some of the queue operations are:

- **initializeQueue**: Initializes the queue to an empty state.
- **isEmptyQueue**: Determines whether the queue is empty. If the queue is empty, it returns the value **true**; otherwise, it returns the value **false**.
- **isFullQueue**: Determines whether the queue is full. If the queue is full, it returns the value **true**; otherwise, it returns the value **false**.
- **front**: Returns the front, that is, the first element of the queue. Input to this operation consists of the queue. Prior to this operation, the queue must exist and must not be empty.
- **back**: Returns the last element of the queue. Input to this operation consists of the queue. Prior to this operation, the queue must exist and must not be empty.
- **addQueue**: Adds a new element to the rear of the queue. Input to this operation consists of the queue and the new element. Prior to this operation, the queue must exist and must not be full.
- **deleteQueue**: Removes the front element from the queue. Input to this operation consists of the queue. Prior to this operation, the queue must exist and must not be empty.

As in the case of a stack, a queue can be stored in an array or in a linked structure. We will consider both implementations. Because elements are added at one end and removed from the other end, we need two pointers to keep track of the front and rear of the queue, called **queueFront** and **queueRear**.

The following abstract `class` `queueADT` defines these operations as an ADT:

```
template <class Type>
class queueADT
{
public:
    virtual bool isEmptyQueue() const = 0;
        //Function to determine whether the queue is empty.
        //Postcondition: Returns true if the queue is empty,
        //               otherwise returns false.

    virtual bool isFullQueue() const = 0;
        //Function to determine whether the queue is full.
        //Postcondition: Returns true if the queue is full,
        //               otherwise returns false.

    virtual void initializeQueue() = 0;
        //Function to initialize the queue to an empty state.
        //Postcondition: The queue is empty.
    virtual Type front() const = 0;
        //Function to return the first element of the queue.
        //Precondition: The queue exists and is not empty.
        //Postcondition: If the queue is empty, the program
        //               terminates; otherwise, the first
        //               element of the queue is returned.

    virtual Type back() const = 0;
        //Function to return the last element of the queue.
        //Precondition: The queue exists and is not empty.
        //Postcondition: If the queue is empty, the program
        //               terminates; otherwise, the last
        //               element of the queue is returned.

    virtual void addQueue(const Type& queueElement) = 0;
        //Function to add queueElement to the queue.
        //Precondition: The queue exists and is not full.
        //Postcondition: The queue is changed and queueElement
        //               is added to the queue.

    virtual void deleteQueue() = 0;
        //Function to remove the first element of the queue.
        //Precondition: The queue exists and is not empty.
        //Postcondition: The queue is changed and the first
        //               element is removed from the queue.
};
```

We leave it as an exercise for you to draw the UML class diagram of the `class` queueADT.

Implementation of Queues as Arrays

Before giving the definition of the class to implement a queue as an ADT, we need to decide how many member variables are needed to implement the queue. Of course, we need an array to store the queue elements, the variables queueFront and queueRear to keep track of the first and last elements of the queue and the variable maxQueueSize to specify the maximum size of the queue. Thus, we need at least four member variables.

Before writing the algorithms to implement the queue operations, we need to decide how to use queueFront and queueRear to access the queue elements. How do queueFront and queueRear indicate that the queue is empty or full? Suppose that queueFront gives the index of the first element of the queue, and queueRear gives the index of the last element of the queue. To add an element to the queue, first we advance queueRear to the next array position, and then we add the element to the position that queueRear is pointing to. To delete an element from the queue, first we retrieve the element that queueFront is pointing to, and then we advance queueFront to the next element of the queue. Thus, queueFront changes after each deleteQueue operation, and queueRear changes after each addQueue operation.

Let's see what happens when queueFront changes after a deleteQueue operation and queueRear changes after an addQueue operation. Assume that the array to hold the queue elements is of size 100.

Initially, the queue is empty. After the operation:

addQueue(Queue, 'A');

the array is as shown in Figure 17-26.

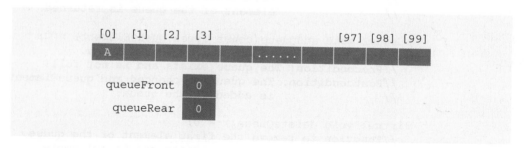

FIGURE 17-26 Queue after the first addQueue operation

After two more addQueue operations:

addQueue(Queue, 'B');
addQueue(Queue, 'C');

the array is as shown in Figure 17-27.

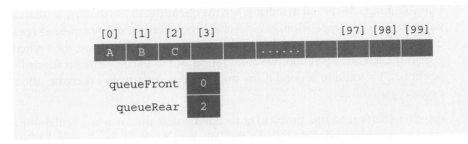

FIGURE 17-27 Queue after two more addQueue operations

Now consider the deleteQueue operation:

deleteQueue();

After this operation, the array containing the queue is as shown in Figure 17-28.

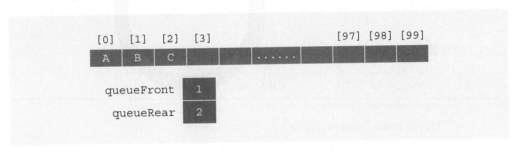

FIGURE 17-28 Queue after the deleteQueue operation

Will this queue design work? Suppose A stands for adding (that is, addQueue) an element to the queue, and D stands for deleting (that is, deleteQueue) an element from the queue. Consider the following sequence of operations:

AAADADADADADADADA...

This sequence of operations would eventually set the index queueRear to point to the last array position, giving the impression that the queue is full. However, the queue has only two or three elements, and the front of the array is empty (see Figure 17-29).

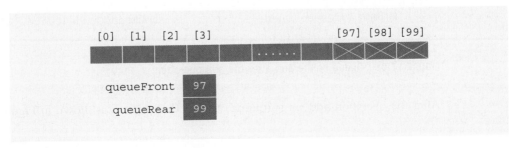

FIGURE 17-29 Queue after the sequence of operations AAADADADADADA...

One solution to this problem is that when the queue overflows to the rear (that is, queueRear points to the last array position), we can check the value of the index queueFront. If the value of queueFront indicates that there is room in the front of the array, then when queueRear gets to the last array position, we can slide all of the queue elements toward the first array position. This solution is good if the queue size is very small; otherwise, the program may execute more slowly.

Another solution to this problem is to assume that the array is circular—that is, the first array position immediately follows the last array position (see Figure 17–30).

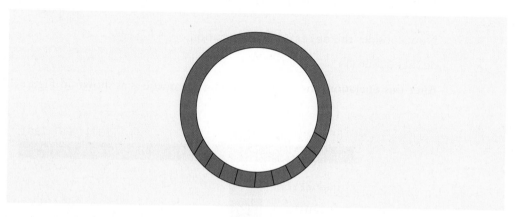

FIGURE 17-30 *Circular queue*

We will consider the array containing the queue to be circular, although we will draw the figures of the array holding the queue elements as before.

Suppose that we have the queue as shown in Figure 17-31(a).

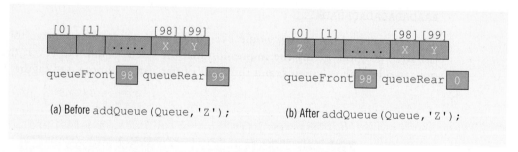

(a) Before addQueue(Queue, 'Z');

(b) After addQueue(Queue, 'Z');

FIGURE 17-31 Queue before and after the add operation

After the operation addQueue(Queue, 'Z');, the queue is as shown in Figure 17-31(b).

Because the array containing the queue is circular, we can use the following statement to advance `queueRear` (`queueFront`) to the next array position:

```
queueRear = (queueRear + 1) % maxQueueSize;
```

If `queueRear < maxQueueSize - 1`, then `queueRear + 1 <= maxQueueSize - 1`, so `(queueRear + 1) % maxQueueSize = queueRear + 1`. If `queueRear == maxQueueSize - 1` (that is, `queueRear` points to the last array position), `queueRear + 1 == maxQueueSize`, so `(queueRear + 1) % maxQueueSize = 0`. In this case, `queueRear` will be set to 0, which is the first array position.

This queue design seems to work well. Before we write the algorithms to implement the queue operations, consider the following two cases.

Case 1: Suppose that after certain operations, the array containing the queue is as shown in Figure 17-32(a).

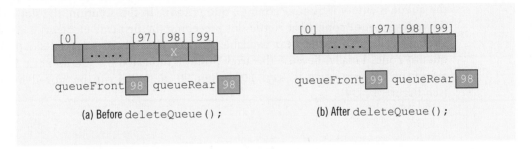

FIGURE 17-32 Queue before and after the delete operation

After the operation `deleteQueue();`, the resulting array is as shown in Figure 17-32(b).

Case 2: Let us now consider the queue shown in Figure 17-33(a).

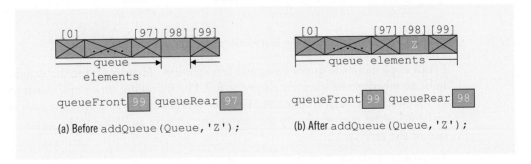

FIGURE 17-33 Queue before and after the add operation

After the operation `addQueue(Queue, 'Z');`, the resulting array is as shown in Figure 17-33(b).

The arrays in Figures 17–32(b) and 17–33(b) have identical values for `queueFront` and `queueRear`. However, the resulting array in Figure 17–32(b) represents an empty queue, whereas the resulting array in Figure 17–33(b) represents a full queue. This latest queue design has brought up another problem of distinguishing between an empty and a full queue.

This problem has several solutions. One solution is to keep a count. In addition to the member variables `queueFront` and `queueRear`, we need another variable, `count`, to implement the queue. The value of `count` is incremented whenever a new element is added to the queue, and it is decremented whenever an element is removed from the queue. In this case, the function `initializeQueue` initializes `count` to 0. This solution is very useful if the user of the queue frequently needs to know the number of elements in the queue.

Another solution is to let `queueFront` indicate the index of the array position *preceding* the first element of the queue, rather than the index of the (actual) first element itself. In this case, assuming `queueRear` still indicates the index of the last element in the queue, the queue is empty if `queueFront == queueRear`. In this solution, the slot indicated by the index `queueFront` (that is, the slot preceding the first true element) is reserved. The queue will be full if the next available space is the special reserved slot indicated by `queueFront`. Finally, because the array position indicated by `queueFront` is to be kept empty, if the array size is, say, 100, then 99 elements can be stored in the queue (see Figure 17–34).

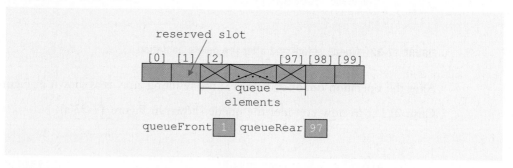

FIGURE 17-34 Array to store the queue elements with a reserved slot

Let us implement the queue using the first solution. That is, we use the variable `count` to indicate whether the queue is empty or full. The following class implements the functions of the abstract **class** `queueADT`. Because arrays can be allocated dynamically, we will leave it for the user to specify the size of the array to implement the queue. The default size of the array is 100.

```
template <class Type>
class queueType: public queueADT<Type>
{
public:
    const queueType<Type>& operator=(const queueType<Type>&);
        //Overload the assignment operator.
```

```cpp
    bool isEmptyQueue() const;
      //Function to determine whether the queue is empty.
      //Postcondition: Returns true if the queue is empty,
      //               otherwise returns false.

    bool isFullQueue() const;
      //Function to determine whether the queue is full.
      //Postcondition: Returns true if the queue is full,
      //               otherwise returns false.

    void initializeQueue();
      //Function to initialize the queue to an empty state.
      //Postcondition: The queue is empty.

    Type front() const;
      //Function to return the first element of the queue.
      //Precondition: The queue exists and is not empty.
      //Postcondition: If the queue is empty, the program
      //               terminates; otherwise, the first
      //               element of the queue is returned.
    Type back() const;
      //Function to return the last element of the queue.
      //Precondition: The queue exists and is not empty.
      //Postcondition: If the queue is empty, the program
      //               terminates; otherwise, the last
      //               element of the queue is returned.

    void addQueue(const Type& queueElement);
      //Function to add queueElement to the queue.
      //Precondition: The queue exists and is not full.
      //Postcondition: The queue is changed and queueElement
      //               is added to the queue.

    void deleteQueue();
      //Function to remove the first element of the queue.
      //Precondition: The queue exists and is not empty.
      //Postcondition: The queue is changed and the first
      //               element is removed from the queue.

    queueType(int queueSize = 100);
      //Constructor

    queueType(const queueType<Type>& otherQueue);
      //Copy constructor

    ~queueType();
      //Destructor

private:
    int maxQueueSize;   //variable to store the maximum queue size
    int count;          //variable to store the number of
                        //elements in the queue
    int queueFront;     //variable to point to the first
                        //element of the queue
    int queueRear;      //variable to point to the last
                        //element of the queue
    Type *list;         //pointer to the array that holds
                        //the queue elements
};
```

We leave the UML class diagram of the `class` queueType as an exercise for you. (See Exercise 30 at the end of this chapter.)

Next, we consider the implementation of the queue operations.

EMPTY QUEUE AND FULL QUEUE

As discussed earlier, the queue is empty if count == 0, and the queue is full if count == maxQueueSize. So the functions to implement these operations are:

```
template <class Type>
bool queueType<Type>::isEmptyQueue() const
{
    return (count == 0);
} //end isEmptyQueue

template <class Type>
bool queueType<Type>::isFullQueue() const
{
    return (count == maxQueueSize);
} //end isFullQueue
```

INITIALIZE QUEUE

This operation initializes a queue to an empty state. The first element is added at the first array position. Therefore, we initialize queueFront to 0, queueRear to maxQueueSize – 1, and count to 0 (see Figure 17–35).

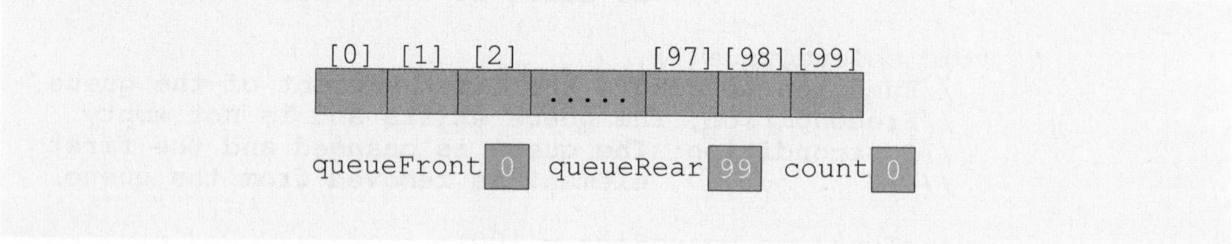

FIGURE 17-35 Empty queue

The definition of the function initializeQueue is:

```
template <class Type>
void queueType<Type>::initializeQueue()
{
    queueFront = 0;
    queueRear = maxQueueSize - 1;
    count = 0;
} //end initializeQueue
```

FRONT

This operation returns the first element of the queue. If the queue is nonempty, the element of the queue indicated by the index queueFront is returned; otherwise, the program terminates.

```
template <class Type>
Type queueType<Type>::front() const
{
    assert(!isEmptyQueue());
    return list[queueFront];
} //end front
```

BACK

This operation returns the last element of the queue. If the queue is nonempty, the element of the queue indicated by the index queueRear is returned; otherwise, the program terminates.

```
template <class Type>
Type queueType<Type>::back() const
{
    assert(!isEmptyQueue());
    return list[queueRear];
} //end back
```

addQueue

Next, we implement the addQueue operation. Because queueRear points to the last element of the queue, to add a new element to the queue, we first advance queueRear to the next array position and then add the new element to the array position indicated by queueRear. We also increment count by 1. So the function addQueue is:

```
template <class Type>
void queueType<Type>::addQueue(const Type& newElement)
{
    if (!isFullQueue())
    {
        queueRear = (queueRear + 1) % maxQueueSize; //use the
                             //mod operator to advance queueRear
                             //because the array is circular

        count++;
        list[queueRear] = newElement;

    }
    else
        cout << "Cannot add to a full queue." << endl;
} //end addQueue
```

deleteQueue

To implement the deleteQueue operation, we access the index queueFront. Because queueFront points to the array position containing the first element of the queue, in order to remove the first queue element, we decrement count by 1 and advance queueFront to the next queue element. So the function deleteQueue is:

```
template <class Type>
void queueType<Type>::deleteQueue()
{
    if (!isEmptyQueue())
    {
        count--;
        queueFront = (queueFront + 1) % maxQueueSize; //use the
                            //mod operator to advance queueFront
                            //because the array is circular

    }
    else
        cout << "Cannot remove from an empty queue." << endl;
} //end deleteQueue
```

CONSTRUCTORS AND DESTRUCTORS

To complete the implementation of the queue operations, we next consider the implementation of the constructor and the destructor. The constructor gets the maxQueueSize from the user, sets the variable maxQueueSize to the value specified by the user, and creates an array of size maxQueueSize. If the user does not specify the queue size, the constructor uses the default value, which is 100, to create an array of size 100. The constructor also initializes queueFront and queueRear to indicate that the queue is empty. The definition of the function to implement the constructor is:

```
template <class Type>
queueType<Type>::queueType(int queueSize)
{
    if (queueSize <= 0)
    {
        cout << "Size of the array to hold the queue must "
             << "be positive." << endl;
        cout << "Creating an array of size 100." << endl;

        maxQueueSize = 100;
    }
    else
        maxQueueSize = queueSize;       //set maxQueueSize to
                                        //queueSize

    queueFront = 0;                     //initialize queueFront
    queueRear = maxQueueSize - 1;       //initialize queueRear
    count = 0;
    list = new Type[maxQueueSize];      //create the array to
                                        //hold the queue elements
} //end constructor
```

The array to store the queue elements is created dynamically. Therefore, when the queue object goes out of scope, the destructor simply deallocates the memory occupied by the array that stores the queue elements. The definition of the function to implement the destructor is:

```
template <class Type>
queueType<Type>::~queueType()
{
    delete [] list;
}
```

The implementation of the copy constructor and overloading the assignment operator are left as exercises for you. (The definitions of these functions are similar to those discussed for linked lists and stacks.)

Linked Implementation of Queues

Because the size of the array to store the queue elements is fixed, only a finite number of queue elements can be stored in the array. Also, the array implementation of the queue requires the array to be treated in a special way together with the values of the indices queueFront and queueRear. The linked implementation of a queue simplifies many of the special cases of the array implementation and, because the memory to store a queue element is allocated dynamically, the queue is never full. This section discusses the linked implementation of a queue.

Because elements are added at one end and removed from the other end, we need to know the front of the queue and the rear of the queue. Thus, we need two pointers, **queueFront** and **queueRear**, to maintain the queue. The following class implements the functions of the abstract **class** queueADT:

```
//Definition of the node
template <class Type>
struct nodeType
{
    Type info;
    nodeType<Type> *link;
};

template <class Type>
class linkedQueueType: public queueADT<Type>
{
public:
    const linkedQueueType<Type>& operator=
                    (const linkedQueueType<Type>&);
        //Overload the assignment operator.

    bool isEmptyQueue() const;
        //Function to determine whether the queue is empty.
        //Postcondition: Returns true if the queue is empty,
        //               otherwise returns false.

    bool isFullQueue() const;
        //Function to determine whether the queue is full.
        //Postcondition: Returns true if the queue is full,
        //               otherwise returns false.
```

```
void initializeQueue();
  //Function to initialize the queue to an empty state.
  //Postcondition: queueFront = NULL; queueRear = NULL

Type front() const;
  //Function to return the first element of the queue.
  //Precondition: The queue exists and is not empty.
  //Postcondition: If the queue is empty, the program
  //               terminates; otherwise, the first
  //               element of the queue is returned.

Type back() const;
  //Function to return the last element of the queue.
  //Precondition: The queue exists and is not empty.
  //Postcondition: If the queue is empty, the program
  //               terminates; otherwise, the last
  //               element of the queue is returned.

void addQueue(const Type& queueElement);
  //Function to add queueElement to the queue.
  //Precondition: The queue exists and is not full.
  //Postcondition: The queue is changed and queueElement
  //               is added to the queue.

void deleteQueue();
  //Function  to remove the first element of the queue.
  //Precondition: The queue exists and is not empty.
  //Postcondition: The queue is changed and the first
  //               element is removed from the queue.

linkedQueueType();
  //Default constructor

linkedQueueType(const linkedQueueType<Type>& otherQueue);
  //Copy constructor

~linkedQueueType();
  //Destructor

private:
    nodeType<Type> *queueFront; //pointer to the front of
                                //the queue
    nodeType<Type> *queueRear;  //pointer to the rear of
                                //the queue
};
```

The UML class diagram of the class linkedQueueType is left as an exercise for you. (See Exercise 31 at the end of this chapter.)

Next, we write the definitions of the functions of the class linkedQueueType.

EMPTY AND FULL QUEUE

The queue is empty if queueFront is NULL. Memory to store the queue elements is allocated dynamically. Therefore, the queue is never full, so the function to implement the isFullQueue operation returns the value **false**. (The queue is full only if we run out of memory.)

```cpp
template <class Type>
bool linkedQueueType<Type>::isEmptyQueue() const
{
    return (queueFront == NULL);
} //end

template <class Type>
bool linkedQueueType<Type>::isFullQueue() const
{
    return false;
} //end isFullQueue
```

Note that in reality, in the linked implementation of queues, the function isFullQueue does not apply because, logically, the queue is never full. However, you must provide its definition because it is included as an abstract function in the parent **class** queueADT.

INITIALIZE QUEUE

The operation initializeQueue initializes the queue to an empty state. The queue is empty if there are no elements in the queue. Note that the constructor initializes the queue when the queue object is declared. So this operation must remove all of the elements, if any, from the queue. Therefore, this operation traverses the list containing the queue starting at the first node, and it deallocates the memory occupied by the queue elements. The definition of this function is:

```cpp
template <class Type>
void linkedQueueType<Type>::initializeQueue()
{
    nodeType<Type> *temp;

    while (queueFront!= NULL)   //while there are elements left
                                //in the queue
    {
        temp = queueFront;      //set temp to point to the
                                //current node
        queueFront = queueFront->link;   //advance first to
                                         //the next node
        delete temp;        //deallocate memory occupied by temp
    }

    queueRear = NULL;   //set rear to NULL
} //end initializeQueue
```

addQueue, front, back, AND deleteQueue OPERATIONS

The addQueue operation adds a new element at the end of the queue. To implement this operation, we access the pointer queueRear.

If the queue is nonempty, the operation `front` returns the first element of the queue, and so the element of the queue indicated by the pointer `queueFront` is returned. If the queue is empty, the function `front` terminates the program.

If the queue is nonempty, the operation `back` returns the last element of the queue, so the element of the queue indicated by the pointer `queueRear` is returned. If the queue is empty, the function `back` terminates the program. Similarly, if the queue is nonempty, the operation `deleteQueue` removes the first element of the queue, so we access the pointer `queueFront`.

The definitions of the functions to implement these operations are:

```
template <class Type>
void linkedQueueType<Type>::addQueue(const Type& newElement)
{
    nodeType<Type> *newNode;

    newNode = new nodeType<Type>;    //create the node

    newNode->info = newElement; //store the info
    newNode->link = NULL;   //initialize the link field to NULL

    if (queueFront == NULL) //if initially the queue is empty
    {
        queueFront = newNode;
        queueRear = newNode;
    }
    else           //add newNode at the end
    {
        queueRear->link = newNode;
        queueRear = queueRear->link;
    }
}//end addQueue

template <class Type>
Type linkedQueueType<Type>::front() const
{
    assert(queueFront != NULL);
    return queueFront->info;
} //end front

template <class Type>
Type linkedQueueType<Type>::back() const
{
    assert(queueRear!= NULL);
    return queueRear->info;
} //end back
```

```
template <class Type>
void linkedQueueType<Type>::deleteQueue()
{
    nodeType<Type> *temp;

    if (!isEmptyQueue())
    {
        temp = queueFront;   //make temp point to the
                             //first node
        queueFront = queueFront->link; //advance queueFront

        delete temp;      //delete the first node

        if (queueFront == NULL) //if after deletion the
                                //queue is empty
            queueRear = NULL;    //set queueRear to NULL
    }
    else
        cout << "Cannot remove from an empty queue" << endl;
}//end deleteQueue
```

The definition of the default constructor is:

```
template<class Type>
linkedQueueType<Type>::linkedQueueType()
{
    queueFront = NULL; //set front to null
    queueRear = NULL;   //set rear to null
} //end default constructor
```

When the queue object goes out of scope, the destructor destroys the queue; that is, it deallocates the memory occupied by the elements of the queue. The definition of the function to implement the destructor is similar to the definition of the function initializeQueue. Also, the functions to implement the copy constructor and overload the assignment operators are similar to the corresponding functions for stacks. Implementing these operations is left as an exercise for you.

EXAMPLE 17-5

The following program tests various operations on a queue. It uses the class linkedQueueType to implement a queue.

```
//Test Program linked queue

#include <iostream>
#include "linkedQueue.h"

using namespace std;
int main()
```

```
{
    linkedQueueType<int> queue;
    int x, y;

    queue.initializeQueue();
    x = 4;
    y = 5;
    queue.addQueue(x);
    queue.addQueue(y);
    x = queue.front();
    queue.deleteQueue();
    queue.addQueue(x + 5);
    queue.addQueue(16);
    queue.addQueue(x);
    queue.addQueue(y - 3);

    cout << "Queue Elements: ";

    while (!queue.isEmptyQueue())
    {
        cout << queue.front() << " ";
        queue.deleteQueue();
    }

    cout << endl;

    return 0;
}
```

Sample Run:

```
Queue Elements: 5 9 16 4 2
```

Queue Derived from the `class` `unorderedLinkedListType`

From the definitions of the functions to implement the queue operations, it is clear that the linked implementation of a queue is similar to the implementation of a linked list created in a forward manner (see Chapter 16). The `addQueue` operation is similar to the operation `insertFirst`. Likewise, the operations `initializeQueue` and `initializeList` and `isEmptyQueue` and `isEmptyList` are similar. The `deleteQueue` operation can be implemented as before. The pointer `queueFront` is the same as the pointer `first`, and the pointer `queueRear` is the same as the pointer `last`. This correspondence suggests that we can derive the class to implement the queue from the `class` `linkedListType` (see Chapter 16). Note that the `class` `linkedListType` is an abstract class and does not implement all of the operations. However, the `class` `unorderedLinkedListType` is derived from the `class` `linkedListType` and provides the definitions of the abstract functions of the `class` `linkedListType`. Therefore, we can derive the `class` `linkedQueueType` from the `class` `unorderedLinkedListType`.

We leave it as an exercise for you to write the definition of the **class** `linkedQueueType` that is derived from the **class** `unorderedLinkedListType`. See Programming Exercise 17 at the end of this chapter.

Application of Queues: Simulation

A technique in which one system models the behavior of another system is called simulation. For example, physical simulators include wind tunnels used to experiment with the design of car bodies and flight simulators used to train airline pilots. Simulation techniques are used when it is too expensive or dangerous to experiment with real systems. You can also design computer models to study the behavior of real systems. (We will describe some real systems modeled by computers shortly.)

Simulating the behavior of an expensive or dangerous experiment using a computer model is usually less expensive than using the real system and is a good way to gain insight without putting human life in danger. Moreover, computer simulations are particularly useful for complex systems when it is difficult to construct a mathematical model. For such systems, computer models can retain descriptive accuracy. In computer simulations, the steps of a program are used to model the behavior of a real system. Let us consider one such problem.

The manager of a local movie theater is hearing complaints from customers about the length of time they have to wait in line to buy tickets. The theater currently has only one cashier. Another theater is preparing to open in the neighborhood, and the manager is afraid of losing customers. The manager wants to hire enough cashiers so that a customer does not have to wait too long to buy a ticket, but does not want to hire extra cashiers on a trial basis and potentially waste time and money. One thing that the manager would like to know is the average time a customer has to wait for service. The manager wants someone to write a program to simulate the behavior of the theater.

In computer simulation, the objects being studied are usually represented as data. For the theater problem, some of the objects are the customers and the cashier. The cashier serves the customers, and we want to determine a customer's average waiting time. Actions are implemented by writing algorithms, which in a programming language are implemented with the help of functions. Thus, functions are used to implement the actions of the objects. In C++, we can combine the data and the operations on that data into a single unit with the help of classes. Thus, objects can be represented as classes. The member variables of the class describe the properties of the objects, and the function members describe the actions on that data. This change in simulation results can also occur if we change the values of the data or modify the definitions of the functions (that is, modify the algorithms implementing the actions). The main goal of a computer simulation is to either generate results showing the performance of an existing system or predict the performance of a proposed system.

In the theater problem, when the cashier is serving a customer, the other customers must wait. Because customers are served on a first come, first served basis and queues are an effective way to implement a First In First Out system, queues are important data structures for use in computer simulations. This section examines computer simulations in which queues are the basic data structure. These simulations model the behavior of systems, called **queuing systems**, in which queues of objects are waiting to be served by various servers. In other words, a queuing system consists of servers and queues of objects waiting to be served. We deal with a variety of queuing systems on a daily basis. For example, a grocery store and a banking system are both queuing systems. Furthermore, when you send a print request to a networked printer that is shared by many people, your print request goes in a queue. Print requests that arrived before your print request are usually completed before yours. Thus, the printer acts as the server when a queue of documents is waiting to be printed.

Designing a Queuing System

In this section, we describe a queuing system that can be used in a variety of applications, such as a bank, grocery store, movie theater, printer, or a mainframe environment in which several people are trying to use the same processors to execute their programs. To describe a queuing system, we use the term **server** for the object that provides the service. For example, in a bank, a teller is a server; in a grocery store or movie theater, a cashier is a server. We will call the object receiving the service the **customer**, and the service time—the time it takes to serve a customer—the **transaction time**.

Because a queuing system consists of servers and a queue of waiting objects, we will model a system that consists of a list of servers and a waiting queue holding the customers to be served. The customer at the front of the queue waits for the next available server. When a server becomes free, the customer at the front of the queue moves to the free server to be served.

When the first customer arrives, all servers are free and the customer moves to the first server. When the next customer arrives, if a server is available, the customer immediately moves to the available server; otherwise, the customer waits in the queue. To model a queuing system, we need to know the number of servers, the expected arrival time of a customer, the time between the arrivals of customers, and the number of events affecting the system.

Let us again consider the movie theater system. The performance of the system depends on how many servers are available, how long it takes to serve a customer, and how often a customer arrives. If it takes too long to serve a customer and customers arrive frequently, then more servers are needed. This system can be modeled as a time-driven simulation. In a **time-driven simulation**, the clock is implemented as a counter, and the passage of, say, one minute can be implemented by incrementing the counter by 1. The simulation is run for a fixed amount of time. If the simulation needs to be run for 100 minutes, the counter starts at 1 and goes up to 100, which can be implemented by using a loop.

For the simulation described in this section, we want to determine the average wait time for a customer. To calculate the average wait time for a customer, we need to add the waiting time of each customer and then divide the sum by the number of customers who have arrived. When a customer arrives, he or she goes to the end of the queue and the customer's waiting time begins. If the queue is empty and a server is free, the customer is served immediately, so this customer's waiting time is zero. On the other hand, if a customer arrives and either the queue is nonempty or all of the servers are busy, the customer must wait for the next available server and, therefore, this customer's waiting time begins. We can keep track of the customer's waiting time by using a timer for each customer. When a customer arrives, the timer is set to 0, which is incremented after each time unit.

Suppose that, on average, it takes five minutes for a server to serve a customer. When a server becomes free and the waiting customer's queue is nonempty, the customer at the front of the queue proceeds to begin the transaction. Thus, we must keep track of the time a customer is with a server. When the customer arrives at a server, the transaction time is set to five and is decremented after each time unit. When the transaction time becomes zero, the server is marked free. Hence, the two objects needed to implement a time-driven computer simulation of a queuing system are the customer and the server.

Next, before designing the main algorithm to implement the simulation, we design classes to implement each of the two objects: *customer* and *server*.

Customer

Every customer has a customer number, arrival time, waiting time, transaction time, and departure time. If we know the arrival time, waiting time, and transaction time, we can determine the departure time by adding these three times. Let us call the class to implement the customer object `customerType`. It follows that the `class customerType` has four member variables: the `customerNumber`, `arrivalTime`, `waitingTime`, and `transactionTime`, each of the data type `int`. The basic operations that must be performed on an object of type `customerType` are as follows: set the customer's number, arrival time, and waiting time; increment the waiting time by one time unit; return the waiting time; return the arrival time; return the transaction time; and return the customer number. The following `class`, `customerType`, implements the customer as an ADT:

```
class customerType
{
public:
    customerType(int cN = 0, int arrvTime = 0, int wTime = 0,
                 int tTime = 0);
      //Constructor to initialize the instance variables
      //according to the parameters.
      //If no value is specified in the object declaration,
      //the default values are assigned.
      //Postcondition: customerNumber = cN;
      //               arrivalTime = arrvTime;
      //               waitingTime = wTime;
      //               transactionTime = tTime;
```

```
    void setCustomerInfo(int customerN = 0, int inTime = 0,
                         int wTime = 0, int tTime = 0);
      //Function to initialize the instance variables.
      //Instance variables are set according to the parameters.
      //Postconditon: customerNumber = customerN;
      //                 arrivalTime = arrvTime;
      //                 waitingTime = wTime;
      //                 transactionTime = tTime;

    int getWaitingTime() const;
      //Function to return the waiting time of a customer.
      //Postcondition: The value of waitingTime is returned.

    void setWaitingTime(int time);
      //Function to set the waiting time of a customer.
      //Postcondition: waitingTime = time;

    void incrementWaitingTime();
      //Function to increment the waiting time by one time unit.
      //Postcondition: waitingTime++;

    int getArrivalTime() const;
      //Function to return the arrival time of a customer.
      //Postcondition: The value of arrivalTime is returned.

    int getTransactionTime() const;
      //Function to return the transaction time of a customer.
      //Postcondition: The value of transactionTime is returned.

    int getCustomerNumber() const;
      //Function to return the customer number.
      //Postcondition: The value of customerNumber is returned.

private:
    int customerNumber;
    int arrivalTime;
    int waitingTime;
    int transactionTime;
};
```

Figure 17-36 shows the UML class diagram of the class customerType.

```
                        customerType

-customerNumber: int
-arrivalTime: int
-waitingTime: int
-transactionTime: int

+setCustomerInfo(int = 0, int = 0, int = 0,
                 int = 0): void
+getWaitingTime() const: int
+setWaitingTime(int): void
+incrementWaitingTime(): void
+getArrivalTime() const: int
+getTransactionTime() const: int
+getCustomerNumber() const: int
+customerType(int = 0, int = 0, int = 0,
             int = 0)
```

FIGURE 17-36 UML class diagram of the **class** customerType

The definitions of the member functions of the **class** customerType follow easily from their descriptions. Next, we give the definitions of the member functions of the **class** customerType.

The function setCustomerInfo uses the values of the parameters to initialize customerNumber, arrivalTime, waitingTime, and transactionTime. The definition of setCustomerInfo is:

```
void customerType::setCustomerInfo(int customerN, int arrvTime,
                                   int wTime, int tTime)
{
    customerNumber = customerN;
    arrivalTime = arrvTime;
    waitingTime = wTime;
    transactionTime = tTime;
}
```

The definition of the constructor is similar to the definition of the function setCustomerInfo. It uses the values of the parameters to initialize customerNumber, arrivalTime, waitingTime, and transactionTime. To make debugging easier, we use the function setCustomerInfo to write the definition of the constructor, which is given next, as follows:

```
customerType::customerType(int customerN, int arrvTime,
                          int wTime, int tTime)
{
    setCustomerInfo(customerN, arrvTime, wTime, tTime);
}
```

The function getWaitingTime returns the current waiting time. The definition of the function getWaitingTime is:

```
int customerType::getWaitingTime() const
{
    return waitingTime;
}
```

The function incrementWaitingTime increments the value of waitingTime. Its definition is:

```
void customerType::incrementWaitingTime()
{
    waitingTime++;
}
```

The definitions of the functions setWaitingTime, getArrivalTime, getTransactionTime, and getCustomerNumber are left as an exercise for you.

Server

At any given time unit, the server is either busy serving a customer or is free. We use a string variable to set the status of the server. Every server has a timer and, because the program might need to know which customer is served by which server, the server also stores the information of the customer being served. Thus, three member variables are associated with a server: the status, the transactionTime, and the currentCustomer. Some of the basic operations that must be performed on a server are as follows: check whether the server is free; set the server as free; set the server as busy; set the transaction time (that is, how long it takes to serve the customer); return the remaining transaction time (to determine whether the server should be set to free); if the server is busy after each time unit, decrement the transaction time by one time unit; and so on. The following class, serverType, implements the server as an ADT:

```
class serverType
{
public:
    serverType();
      //Default constructor
      //Sets the values of the instance variables to their default
      //values.
      //Postcondition: currentCustomer is initialized by its
      //               default constructor; status = "free"; and
      //               the transaction time is initialized to 0.
```

```cpp
bool isFree() const;
    //Function to determine if the server is free.
    //Postcondition: Returns true if the server is free,
    //               otherwise returns false.

void setBusy();
    //Function to set the status of the server to busy.
    //Postcondition: status = "busy";

void setFree();
    //Function to set the status of the server to "free".
    //Postcondition: status = "free";

void setTransactionTime(int t);
    //Function to set the transaction time according to the
    //parameter t.
    //Postcondition: transactionTime = t;

void setTransactionTime();
    //Function to set the transaction time according to
    //the transaction time of the current customer.
    //Postcondition:
    //   transactionTime = currentCustomer.transactionTime;

int getRemainingTransactionTime() const;
    //Function to return the remaining transaction time.
    //Postcondition: The value of transactionTime is returned.

void decreaseTransactionTime();
    //Function to decrease the transactionTime by one unit.
    //Postcondition: transactionTime--;

void setCurrentCustomer(customerType cCustomer);
    //Function to set the info of the current customer
    //according to the parameter cCustomer.
    //Postcondition: currentCustomer = cCustomer;

int getCurrentCustomerNumber() const;
    //Function to return the customer number of the current
    //customer.
    //Postcondition: The value of customerNumber of the
    //               current customer is returned.

int getCurrentCustomerArrivalTime() const;
    //Function to return the arrival time of the current
    //customer.
    //Postcondition: The value of arrivalTime of the current
    //               customer is returned.

int getCurrentCustomerWaitingTime() const;
    //Function to return the current waiting time of the
    //current customer.
```

```
//Postcondition: The value of transactionTime is
//                returned.

int getCurrentCustomerTransactionTime() const;
   //Function to return the transaction time of the
   //current customer.
   //Postcondition: The value of transactionTime of the
   //               current customer is returned.

private:
    customerType currentCustomer;
    string status;
    int transactionTime;
};
```

Figure 17-37 shows the UML class diagram of the **class** serverType.

serverType
-currentCustomer: customerType
-status: string
-transactionTime: int
+isFree() const: bool
+setBusy(): void
+setFree(): void
+setTransactionTime(int): void
+setTransactionTime(): void
+getRemainingTransactionTime() const: int
+decreaseTransactionTime(): void
+setCurrentCustomer(customerType): void
+getCurrentCustomerNumber() const: int
+getCurrentCustomerArrivalTime() const: int
+getCurrentCustomerWaitingTime() const: int
+getCurrentCustomerTransactionTime() const: int
+serverType()

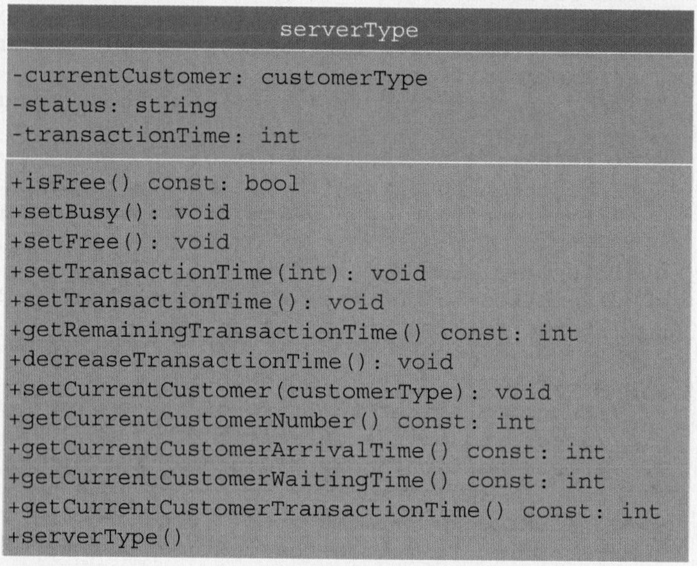

FIGURE 17-37 UML class diagram of the **class** serverType

The definitions of some of the member functions of the **class** serverType are:

```
serverType::serverType()
{
    status = "free";
    transactionTime = 0;
}
```

```
bool serverType::isFree() const
{
    return (status == "free");
}

void serverType::setBusy()
{
    status = "busy";
}

void serverType::setFree()
{
    status = "free";
}

void serverType::setTransactionTime(int t)
{
    transactionTime = t;
}

void serverType::setTransactionTime()
{
    int time;

    time = currentCustomer.getTransactionTime();

    transactionTime = time;
}

void serverType::decreaseTransactionTime()
{
    transactionTime--;
}
```

We leave the definitions of the functions getRemainingTransactionTime, setCurrentCustomer, getCurrentCustomerNumber, getCurrentCustomerArrivalTime, getCurrentCustomerWaitingTime, and getCurrentCustomerTransactionTime as an exercise for you.

Because we are designing a simulation program that can be used in a variety of applications, we need to design two more classes: one to create and process a list of servers and one to create and process a queue of waiting customers. The next two sections describe each of these classes.

Server List

A server list is a set of servers. At any given time, a server is either free or busy. For the customer at the front of the queue, we need to find a server in the list that is free. If all of the servers are busy, then the customer must wait until one of the servers becomes free. Thus, the class that implements a list of servers has two member variables: one to store the number of servers and one to maintain a list of servers. Using dynamic arrays, depending on the number of servers specified by the user, a list of servers is created during program execution. Some of the operations that must be performed on a server list are as follows: return the server number of a free server; when a customer gets ready to do business and a server is available, set the server to busy; when the simulation ends, some of the servers might still be busy, so return the number of busy servers; after each time unit, reduce the `transactionTime` of each busy server by one time unit; and if the `transactionTime` of a server becomes zero, set the server to free. The following `class`, `serverListType`, implements the list of servers as an ADT:

```
class serverListType
{
public:
    serverListType(int num = 1);
      //Constructor to initialize a list of servers
      //Postcondition: numOfServers = num
      //               A list of servers, specified by num,
      //               is created and each server is
      //               initialized to "free".

    ~serverListType();
      //Destructor
      //Postcondition: The list of servers is destroyed.

    int getFreeServerID() const;
      //Function to search the list of servers.
      //Postcondition: If a free server is found, returns
      //               its ID; otherwise, returns -1.

    int getNumberOfBusyServers() const;
      //Function to return the number of busy servers.
      //Postcondition: The number of busy servers is returned.

    void setServerBusy(int serverID, customerType cCustomer,
                       int tTime);
      //Function to set a server as busy.
      //Postcondition: The server specified by serverID is set
      //               to "busy", to serve the customer
      //               specified by cCustomer, and the
      //               transaction time is set according to the
      //               parameter tTime.

    void setServerBusy(int serverID, customerType cCustomer);
      //Function to set a server as busy.
      //Postcondition: The server specified by serverID is set
      //               to "busy", to serve the customer
      //               specified by cCustomer.

    void updateServers(ostream& outFile);
      //Function to update the status of a server.
      //Postcondition: The transaction time of each busy
```

```
//                    server is decremented by one unit. If
//                    the transaction time of a busy server
//                    is reduced to zero, the server is set
//                    to "free". Moreover, if the actual
//                    parameter corresponding to outFile is
//                    cout, a message indicating which customer
//                    has been served is printed on the screen,
//                    together with the customer's departing
//                    time. Otherwise, the output is sent to
//                    a file specified by the user.
private:
    int numOfServers;
    serverType *servers;
};
```

Figure 17-38 shows the UML class diagram of the **class** serverListType.

serverListType

-numOfServers: int
-*servers: serverType

+getFreeServerID() const: int
+getNumberOfBusyServers() const: int
+setServerBusy(int, customerType, int): void
+setServerBusy(int, customerType): void
+updateServers(ostream&): void
+serverListType(int = 1)
+~serverListType()

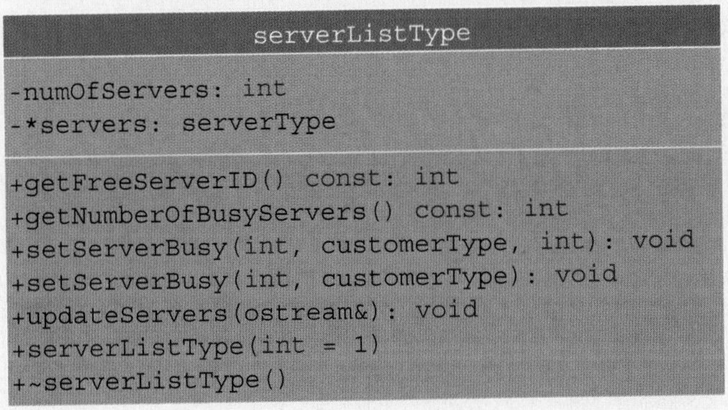

FIGURE 17-38 UML class diagram of the **class** serverListType

Following are the definitions of the member functions of the **class** serverListType. The definitions of the constructor and destructor are straightforward.

```
serverListType::serverListType(int num)
{
    numOfServers = num;
    servers = new serverType[num];
}

serverListType::~serverListType()
{
    delete [] servers;
}
```

The function getFreeServerID searches the list of servers. If a free server is found, it returns the server's ID; otherwise, the value -1 is returned, which indicates that all of the servers are busy. The definition of this function is:

```
int serverListType::getFreeServerID() const
{
    int serverID = -1;

    int i;

    for (i = 0; i < numOfServers; i++)
        if (servers[i].isFree())
        {
            serverID = i;
            break;
        }

    return serverID;
}
```

The function getNumberOfBusyServers searches the list of servers and determines and returns the number of busy servers. The definition of this function is:

```
int serverListType::getNumberOfBusyServers() const
{
    int busyServers = 0;

    int i;

    for (i = 0; i < numOfServers; i++)
        if (!servers[i].isFree())
            busyServers++;

    return busyServers;
}
```

The function setServerBusy sets a server to busy. This function is overloaded. The serverID of the server that is set to busy is passed as a parameter to this function. One function sets the server's transaction time according to the parameter tTime; the other function sets it by using the transaction time stored in the object cCustomer. The transaction time is later needed to determine the average wait time. The definitions of these functions are:

```
void serverListType::setServerBusy(int serverID,
                                   customerType cCustomer,
                                   int tTime)
{
    servers[serverID].setBusy();
    servers[serverID].setTransactionTime(tTime);
    servers[serverID].setCurrentCustomer(cCustomer);
}
```

```
void serverListType::setServerBusy(int serverID,
                                   customerType cCustomer)
{
    int time;

    time = cCustomer.getTransactionTime();

    servers[serverID].setBusy();
    servers[serverID].setTransactionTime(time);
    servers[serverID].setCurrentCustomer(cCustomer);
}
```

The definition of the function updateServers is quite straightforward. Starting at the first server, it searches the list of servers for busy servers. When a busy server is found, its transactionTime is decremented by 1. If the transactionTime reduces to zero, the server is set to free. If the transactionTime of a busy server reduces to zero, then the transaction of the customer being served by the server is complete. If the actual parameter corresponding to outFile is cout, a message indicating which customer has been served is printed on the screen, together with the customer's departing time. Otherwise, the output is sent to a file specified by the user. The definition of this function is as follows:

```
void serverListType::updateServers(ostream& outFile)
{
    int i;

    for (i = 0; i < numOfServers; i++)
        if (!servers[i].isFree())
        {
            servers[i].decreaseTransactionTime();

            if (servers[i].getRemainingTransactionTime() == 0)
            {
                outFile << "From server number " << (i + 1)
                        << " customer number "
                        << servers[i].getCurrentCustomerNumber()
                        << "\n    departed at time unit "
                        << servers[i].
                              getCurrentCustomerArrivalTime()
                           + servers[i].
                              getCurrentCustomerWaitingTime()
                           + servers[i].
                              getCurrentCustomerTransactionTime()
                        << endl;
                servers[i].setFree();
            }
        }
}
```

Waiting Customers' Queue

When a customer arrives, he or she goes to the end of the queue. When a server becomes available, the customer at the front of the queue leaves to conduct the transaction. After each time unit, the waiting time of each customer in the queue is incremented by 1. The ADT `queueType` designed in this chapter has all the operations needed to implement a queue, except the operation of incrementing the waiting time of each customer in the queue by one time unit. We will derive a `class`, `waitingCustomerQueueType`, from the `class` `queueType` and add the additional operations to implement the customer queue. The definition of the `class` `waitingCustomerQueueType` is as follows:

```cpp
class waitingCustomerQueueType: public queueType<customerType>
{
public:
    waitingCustomerQueueType(int size = 100);
    //Constructor
    //Postcondition: The queue is initialized according to
    //               the parameter size. The value of size
    //               is passed to the constructor of queueType.

    void updateWaitingQueue();
    //Function to increment the waiting time of each
    //customer in the queue by one time unit.
};
```

NOTE   Notice that the `class` `waitingCustomerQueueType` is derived from the `class` `queueType`, which implements the queue in an array. You can also derive it from the `class` `linkedQueueType`, which implements the queue in a linked list. We leave the details as an exercise for you.

The definitions of the member functions are given next. The definition of the constructor is as follows:

```cpp
waitingCustomerQueueType::waitingCustomerQueueType(int size)
                          :queueType<customerType>(size)
{
}
```

The function `updateWaitingQueue` increments the waiting time of each customer in the queue by one time unit. The `class` `waitingCustomerQueueType` is derived from the `class` `queueType`. Because the member variables of `queueType` are `private`, the function `updateWaitingQueue` cannot directly access the elements of the queue. The only way to access the elements of the queue is to use the `deleteQueue` operation. After incrementing the waiting time, the element can be put back into the queue by using the `addQueue` operation.

The `addQueue` operation inserts the element at the end of the queue. If we perform the `deleteQueue` operation followed by the `addQueue` operation for each element of the queue, then eventually the front element again becomes the front element. Given that each `deleteQueue` operation is followed by an `addQueue` operation, how do we determine that all of the elements of the queue have been processed? We cannot use the `isEmptyQueue` or `isFullQueue` operations on the queue, because the queue will never be empty or full.

One solution to this problem is to create a temporary queue. Every element of the original queue is removed, processed, and inserted into the temporary queue. When the original queue becomes empty, all of the elements in the queue are processed. We can then copy the elements from the temporary queue back into the original queue. However, this solution requires us to use extra memory space, which could be significant. Also, if the queue is large, extra computer time is needed to copy the elements from the temporary queue back into the original queue. Let us look into another solution.

In the second solution, before starting to update the elements of the queue, we can insert a dummy customer with a wait time of, say, -1. During the update process, when we arrive at the customer with the wait time of -1, we can stop the update process without processing the customer with the wait time of -1. If we do not process the customer with the wait time of -1, this customer is removed from the queue and, after processing all of the elements of the queue, the queue will contain no extra elements. This solution does not require us to create a temporary queue, so we do not need extra computer time to copy the elements back into the original queue. We will use this solution to update the queue. Therefore, the definition of the function `updateWaitingQueue` is:

```
void waitingCustomerQueueType::updateWaitingQueue()
{
    customerType cust;

    cust.setWaitingTime(-1);
    int wTime = 0;

    addQueue(cust);

    while (wTime != -1)
    {
        cust = front();
        deleteQueue();

        wTime = cust.getWaitingTime();
        if (wTime == -1)
            break;
        cust.incrementWaitingTime();
        addQueue(cust);
    }
}
```

Main Program

To run the simulation, we first need to get the following information:

- The number of time units the simulation should run. Assume that each time unit is one minute.
- The number of servers.
- The amount of time it takes to serve a customer—that is, the transaction time.
- The approximate time between customer arrivals.

These pieces of information are called simulation parameters. By changing the values of these parameters, we can observe the changes in the performance of the system. We can write a function, setSimulationParameters, to prompt the user to specify these values. The definition of this function is:

```
void setSimulationParameters(int& sTime, int& numOfServers,
                             int& transTime,
                             int& tBetweenCArrival)
{
    cout << "Enter the simulation time: ";
    cin >> sTime;
    cout << endl;

    cout << "Enter the number of servers: ";
    cin >> numOfServers;
    cout << endl;

    cout << "Enter the transaction time: ";
    cin >> transTime;
    cout << endl;

    cout << "Enter the time between customer arrivals: ";
    cin >> tBetweenCArrival;
    cout << endl;
}
```

When a server becomes free and the customer queue is nonempty, we can move the customer at the front of the queue to the free server to be served. Moreover, when a customer starts the transaction, the waiting time ends. The waiting time of the customer is added to the total waiting time. The general algorithm to start the transaction (supposing that serverID denotes the ID of the free server) is:

1. Remove the customer from the front of the queue.

   ```
   customer = customerQueue.front();
   customerQueue.deleteQueue();
   ```

2. Update the total wait time by adding the current customer's wait time to the previous total wait time.

   ```
   totalWait = totalWait + customer.getWaitingTime();
   ```

3. Set the free server to begin the transaction.

```
serverList.setServerBusy(serverID, customer, transTime);
```

To run the simulation, we need to know the number of customers arriving at a given time unit and how long it takes to serve the customer. We use the Poisson distribution from statistics, which says that the probability of y events occurring at a given time is given by the formula:

$$P(y) = \frac{\lambda^y e^{-\lambda}}{y!}, y = 0, 1, 2, \ldots,$$

in which λ is the expected value that y events occur at that time. Suppose that, on average, a customer arrives every four minutes. During this four-minute period, the customer can arrive at any one of the four minutes. Assuming an equal likelihood of each of the four minutes, the expected value that a customer arrives in each of the four minutes is, therefore, 1 / 4 = .25. Next, we need to determine whether or not the customer actually arrives at a given minute.

Now, $P(0) = e^{-\lambda}$ is the probability that no event occurs at a given time. One of the basic assumptions of the Poisson distribution is that the probability of more than one outcome occurring in a short time interval is negligible. For simplicity, we assume that only one customer arrives at a given time unit. Thus, we use $e^{-\lambda}$ as the cutoff point to determine whether a customer arrives at a given time unit. Suppose that, on average, a customer arrives every four minutes. Then, $\lambda = 0.25$. We can use an algorithm to generate a number between 0 and 1. If the value of the number generated is $> e^{-0.25}$, we can assume that the customer arrived at a particular time unit. For example, suppose that $rNum$ is a random number such that $0 \leq rNum \leq 1$. If $rNum > e^{-0.25}$, the customer arrived at the given time unit.

We now describe the function runSimulation to implement the simulation. Suppose that we run the simulation for 100 time units and customers arrive at time units 93, 96, and 100. The average transaction time is five minutes—that is, five time units. For simplicity, assume that we have only one server and that the server becomes free at time unit 97, and that all customers arriving before time unit 93 have been served. When the server becomes free at time unit 97, the customer arriving at time unit 93 starts the transaction. Because the transaction of the customer arriving at time unit 93 starts at time unit 97 and it takes five minutes to complete a transaction, when the simulation loop ends, the customer arriving at time unit 93 is still at the server. Moreover, customers arriving at time units 96 and 100 are in the queue. For simplicity, we assume that when the simulation loop ends, the customers at the servers are considered served. The general algorithm for this function is:

1. Declare and initialize the variables, such as the simulation parameters, customer number, clock, total and average waiting times, number of customers arrived, number of customers served, number of customers left in the waiting queue, number of customers left with the servers, waitingCustomersQueue, and a list of servers.

2. The main loop is:

```
for (clock = 1; clock <= simulationTime; clock++)
{
```

2.1. Update the server list to decrement the transaction time of each busy server by one time unit.

2.2. If the customer's queue is nonempty, increment the waiting time of each customer by one time unit.

2.3. If a customer arrives, increment the number of customers by 1 and add the new customer to the queue.

2.4. If a server is free and the customer's queue is nonempty, remove a customer from the front of the queue and send the customer to the free server.

```
}
```

3. Print the appropriate results. Your results must include the number of customers left in the queue, the number of customers still with servers, the number of customers arrived, and the number of customers who actually completed a transaction.

Once you have designed the function runSimulation, the definition of the function main is simple and straightforward because the function main calls only the function runSimulation.

When we tested our version of the simulation program, we generated the following results. (The program was executed two times.) We assumed that the average transaction time is five minutes and that, on average, a customer arrives every four minutes, and we used a random number generator to generate a number between 0 and 1 to decide whether a customer arrived at a given time unit.

Sample Runs:

Sample Run 1:

```
Customer number 1 arrived at time unit 4
Customer number 2 arrived at time unit 8
From server number 1 customer number 1
      departed at time unit 9
Customer number 3 arrived at time unit 9
Customer number 4 arrived at time unit 12
From server number 1 customer number 2
      departed at time unit 14
From server number 1 customer number 3
      departed at time unit 19
Customer number 5 arrived at time unit 21
From server number 1 customer number 4
      departed at time unit 24
From server number 1 customer number 5
      departed at time unit 29
```

Customer number 6 arrived at time unit 37
Customer number 7 arrived at time unit 38
Customer number 8 arrived at time unit 41
From server number 1 customer number 6
        departed at time unit 42
Customer number 9 arrived at time unit 43
Customer number 10 arrived at time unit 44
From server number 1 customer number 7
        departed at time unit 47
Customer number 11 arrived at time unit 49
Customer number 12 arrived at time unit 51
From server number 1 customer number 8
        departed at time unit 52
Customer number 13 arrived at time unit 52
Customer number 14 arrived at time unit 53
Customer number 15 arrived at time unit 54
From server number 1 customer number 9
        departed at time unit 57
Customer number 16 arrived at time unit 59
From server number 1 customer number 10
        departed at time unit 62
Customer number 17 arrived at time unit 66
From server number 1 customer number 11
        departed at time unit 67
Customer number 18 arrived at time unit 71
From server number 1 customer number 12
        departed at time unit 72
From server number 1 customer number 13
        departed at time unit 77
Customer number 19 arrived at time unit 78
From server number 1 customer number 14
        departed at time unit 82
From server number 1 customer number 15
        departed at time unit 87
Customer number 20 arrived at time unit 90
From server number 1 customer number 16
        departed at time unit 92
Customer number 21 arrived at time unit 92
From server number 1 customer number 17
        departed at time unit 97

The simulation ran for 100 time units
Number of servers: 1
Average transaction time: 5
Average arrival time difference between customers: 4
Total waiting time: 269
Number of customers that completed a transaction: 17
Number of customers left in the servers: 1
The number of customers left in queue: 3
Average waiting time: 12.81
************* END SIMULATION *************

Sample Run 2:
Customer number 1 arrived at time unit 4
Customer number 2 arrived at time unit 8
From server number 1 customer number 1
        departed at time unit 9

Customer number 3 arrived at time unit 9
Customer number 4 arrived at time unit 12
From server number 2 customer number 2
        departed at time unit 13
From server number 1 customer number 3
        departed at time unit 14
From server number 2 customer number 4
        departed at time unit 18
Customer number 5 arrived at time unit 21
From server number 1 customer number 5
        departed at time unit 26
Customer number 6 arrived at time unit 37
Customer number 7 arrived at time unit 38
Customer number 8 arrived at time unit 41
From server number 1 customer number 6
        departed at time unit 42
From server number 2 customer number 7
        departed at time unit 43
Customer number 9 arrived at time unit 43
Customer number 10 arrived at time unit 44
From server number 1 customer number 8
        departed at time unit 47
From server number 2 customer number 9
        departed at time unit 48
Customer number 11 arrived at time unit 49
Customer number 12 arrived at time unit 51
From server number 1 customer number 10
        departed at time unit 52
Customer number 13 arrived at time unit 52
Customer number 14 arrived at time unit 53
From server number 2 customer number 11
        departed at time unit 54
Customer number 15 arrived at time unit 54
From server number 1 customer number 12
        departed at time unit 57
From server number 2 customer number 13
        departed at time unit 59
Customer number 16 arrived at time unit 59
From server number 1 customer number 14
        departed at time unit 62
From server number 2 customer number 15
        departed at time unit 64
Customer number 17 arrived at time unit 66
From server number 1 customer number 16
        departed at time unit 67
From server number 2 customer number 17
        departed at time unit 71
Customer number 18 arrived at time unit 71
From server number 1 customer number 18
        departed at time unit 76
Customer number 19 arrived at time unit 78
From server number 1 customer number 19
        departed at time unit 83
Customer number 20 arrived at time unit 90
Customer number 21 arrived at time unit 92
From server number 1 customer number 20
        departed at time unit 95

From server number 2 customer number 21
      departed at time unit 97

The simulation ran for 100 time units
Number of servers: 2
Average transaction time: 5
Average arrival time difference between customers: 4
Total waiting time: 20
Number of customers that completed a transaction: 21
Number of customers left in the servers: 0
The number of customers left in queue: 0
Average waiting time: 0.95
************** END SIMULATION *************

QUICK REVIEW

1. A stack is a data structure in which the items are added and deleted from one end only.

2. A stack is a Last In First Out (LIFO) data structure.

3. The basic operations on a stack are as follows: push an item onto the stack, pop an item from the stack, retrieve the top element of the stack, initialize the stack, check whether the stack is empty, and check whether the stack is full.

4. A stack can be implemented as an array or a linked list.

5. The middle elements of a stack should not be accessed directly.

6. Stacks are restricted versions of arrays and linked lists.

7. Postfix notation does not require the use of parentheses to enforce operator precedence.

8. In postfix notation, the operators are written after the operands.

9. Postfix expressions are evaluated according to the following rules:

   a. Scan the expression from left to right.

   b. If an operator is found, back up to get the required number of operands, evaluate the operator, and continue.

10. A queue is a data structure in which the items are added at one end and removed from the other end.

11. A queue is a First In First Out (FIFO) data structure.

12. The basic operations on a queue are as follows: add an item to the queue, remove an item from the queue, retrieve the first or last element of the queue, initialize the queue, check whether the queue is empty, and check whether the queue is full.

13. A queue can be implemented as an array or a linked list.

14. The middle elements of a queue should not be accessed directly.

15. Queues are restricted versions of arrays and linked lists.

EXERCISES

1. Describe the two basic operations on a stack.

2. Suppose that stack is an object of type stackType<int>. What is the difference between stack.top and stack.top - 1?

3. Suppose that stack is an object of type stackType<double> and the value of stack.top is 5. What is the index of the top element of the stack?

4. Suppose that stack is an object of type stackType<string> and the value of stack.top - 1 is 2. How many elements are in the stack?

5. Consider the following statements:

```
stackType<int> stack;
int num1, num2;
```

Show what is output by the following segment of code:

```
stack.push(12);
stack.push(5);
num1 = stack.top() + 3;
stack.push(num1 + 5);
num2 = stack.top();
stack.push(num1 + num2);
num2 = stack.top();
stack.pop();
stack.push(15);
num1 = stack.top();
stack.pop();

while (!stack.isEmptyStack())
{
    cout << stack.top() << " ";
    stack.pop();
}
cout << endl;
cout << "num1 = " << num1 << endl;
cout << "num2 = " << num2 << endl;
```

6. Consider the following statements:

```
stackType<int> stack(50);
int num;
```

Suppose that the input is:

31 47 86 39 62 71 15 63

Show what is output by the following segment of code:

```
cin >> num;

while (cin)
{
    if (!stack.isFullStack())
    {
        if (num % 2 == 0 || num % 3 == 0)
            stack.push(num);
        else if (!stack.isEmptyStack())
        {
            cout << stack.top() << " ";
            stack.pop();
        }
        else
            stack.push(num + 3);
    }
    cin >> num;
}
cout << endl;

cout << "Stack Elements: ";

while (!stack.isEmptyStack())
{
    cout << " " << stack.top();
    stack.pop();
}
cout << endl;
```

7. Evaluate the following postfix expressions:

   a. 17 5 3 - * 6 + =

   b. 14 2 * 8 + 6 / 5 + =

   c. 15 16 3 10 2 + + - + 8 / =

   d. 1 8 12 - - 9 + 25 5 / * =

8. Convert the following infix expressions to postfix notations:

   a. x * (y + z) - (w + t)

   b. (x + y) / (z - w) * t

   c. ((x - y) + (z - w) / t) * u

   d. x - y / (z + w) * t / u + (v - s)

9. Write the equivalent infix expressions for the following postfix expressions:

   a. x y + z * w -

   b. x y * z / w +

   c. x y z + * w -

10. What is the output of the following program?

```cpp
#include <iostream>
#include <string>
#include "myStack.h"

using namespace std;

template <class type>
void mystery(stackType<type>& s1, stackType<type>& s2,
             stackType<type>& s3);

int main()
{
    stackType<string> stack1;
    stackType<string> stack2;
    stackType<string> newStack;

    string fNames[] = { "Chelsea", "Kirk", "David", "Stephanie",
                        "Bianca", "Katie", "Holly"};
    string lNames[] = { "Jackson", "McCarthy", "Miller", "Pratt",
                        "Hollman", "Smith", "Klien"};

    for (int i = 0; i < 7; i++)
    {
        stack1.push(fNames[i]);
        stack2.push(lNames[i]);
    }

    mystery(stack1, stack2, newStack);

    while (!newStack.isEmptyStack())
    {
        cout << newStack.top() << endl;
        newStack.pop();
    }
}

template <class type>
void mystery(stackType<type>& s1, stackType<type>& s2,
             stackType<type>& s3)
{
    while (!s1.isEmptyStack() && !s2.isEmptyStack())
    {
        s3.push(s1.top() + " " + s2.top());
        s1.pop();
        s2.pop();
    }
}
```

11. What is the output of the following program?

```cpp
#include <iostream>
#include <cmath>
#include "myStack.h"

using namespace std;

void mystery(stackType<int>& s, stackType<double>& t);

int main()
{
    int list[] = {1, 2, 3, 4, 5};

    stackType<int> s1;
    stackType<double> s2;

    for (int i = 0; i < 5; i++)
        s1.push(list[i]);

    mystery(s1, s2);

    while (!s2.isEmptyStack())
    {
        cout << s2.top() << " ";
        s2.pop();
    }
    cout << endl;
}

void mystery(stackType<int>& s, stackType<double>& t)
{
    double x = 1.0;

    while (!s.isEmptyStack())
    {
        t.push(pow(s.top(), x));
        s.pop();
        x = x + 1;
    }
}
```

12. Explain why, in the linked implementation of a stack, it is not necessary to implement the operation to determine whether the stack is full.

13. Suppose that stack is an object of type linkedStackType<int>. What is the difference between the statements stack.top(); and stack.pop();?

14. Write the definition of the function template printListReverse that uses a stack to print a linked list in reverse order. Assume that this function is a member of the class linkedListType, designed in Chapter 16.

15. Write the definition of the method `second` that takes as a parameter a stack object and returns the second element of the stack. The original stack remains unchanged.

16. Consider the following statements:

```
queueType<int> queue;
int num;
```

Show what is output by the following segment of code:

```
num = 7;
queue.addQueue(6);
queue.addQueue(num);
num = queue.front();
queue.deleteQueue();
queue.addQueue(num + 5);
queue.addQueue(14);
queue.addQueue(num - 2);
queue.addQueue(25);
queue.deleteQueue();

cout << "Queue elements: ";
while (!queue.isEmptyQueue())
{
    cout << queue.front() << " ";
    queue.deleteQueue();
}
cout << endl;
```

17. Consider the following statements:

```
linkedStackType<int> stack;
linkedQueueType<int> queue;
int num;
```

Suppose the input is:

```
48 35 72 88 92 11 10 15 44 52 67 36
```

Show what is written by the following segment of code:

```
stack.push(0);
queue.addQueue(0);
cin >> num;

while (cin)
{
    switch (num % 3)
    {
    case 0:
        stack.push(num);
        break;
    case 1:
        queue.addQueue(num);
        break;
```

```
          case 2:
              if (!stack.isEmptyStack())
              {
                  cout << stack.top() << " ";
                  stack.pop();
              }
              else if (!queue.isEmptyQueue())
              {
                  cout << queue.front() << " ";
                  queue.deleteQueue();
              }
              else
                  cout << "Stack and queue are empty." << endl;
              break;
         } //end switch

         cin >> num;
    } //end while

    cout << endl;

    cout << "stack: ";
    while (!stack.isEmptyStack())
    {
        cout << stack.top() << " ";
        stack.pop();
    }

    cout << endl;

    cout << "queue: ";
    while (!queue.isEmptyQueue())
    {
        cout << queue.front() << " ";
        queue.deleteQueue();
    }
    cout << endl;
```

18. What does the following function do?

```
    void mystery(queueType<int>& q)
    {
        stackType<int> s;

        while (!q.isEmptyQueue())
        {
            s.push(q.front());
            q.deleteQueue();
        }
```

```
    while (!s.isEmptyStack())
    {
        q.addQueue(2 * s.top());
        s.pop();
    }
}
```

19. Suppose that queue is a queueType object and the size of the array implementing queue is 100. Also, suppose that the value of queueFront is 50 and the value of queueRear is 99.

   a. What are the values of queueFront and queueRear after adding an element to queue?

   b. What are the values of queueFront and queueRear after removing an element from queue?

20. Suppose that queue is a queueType object and the size of the array implementing queue is 100. Also, suppose that the value of queueFront is 99 and the value of queueRear is 25.

   a. What are the values of queueFront and queueRear after adding an element to queue?

   b. What are the values of queueFront and queueRear after removing an element from queue?

21. Suppose that queue is a queueType object and the size of the array implementing queue is 100. Also, suppose that the value of queueFront is 25 and the value of queueRear is 75.

   a. What are the values of queueFront and queueRear after adding an element to queue?

   b. What are the values of queueFront and queueRear after removing an element from queue?

22. Suppose that queue is a queueType object and the size of the array implementing queue is 100. Also, suppose that the value of queueFront is 99 and the value of queueRear is 99.

   a. What are the values of queueFront and queueRear after adding an element to queue?

   b. What are the values of queueFront and queueRear after removing an element from queue?

23. Suppose that queue is implemented as an array with the special reserved slot, as described in this chapter. Also, suppose that the size of the array implementing queue is 100. If the value of queueFront is 50, what is the position of the first queue element?

24. Suppose that queue is implemented as an array with the special reserved slot, as described in this chapter. Suppose that the size of the array implementing queue is 100. Also, suppose that the value of queueFront is 74 and the value of queueRear is 99.

   a. What are the values of queueFront and queueRear after adding an element to queue?

   b. What are the values of queueFront and queueRear after removing an element from queue? Also, what is the position of the removed queue element?

25. Write a function template, reverseStack, that takes as a parameter a stack object and uses a queue object to reverse the elements of the stack.

26. Write a function template, reverseQueue, that takes as a parameter a queue object and uses a stack object to reverse the elements of the queue.

27. Add the operation queueCount to the **class** queueType (the array implementation of queues), which returns the number of elements in the queue. Write the definition of the function template to implement this operation.

28. Draw the UML class diagram of the **class** linkedStackType.

29. Draw the UML class diagram of the **class** queueADT.

30. Draw the UML class diagram of the **class** queueType.

31. Draw the UML class diagram of the **class** linkedQueueType.

PROGRAMMING EXERCISES

1. Two stacks of the same type are the same if they have the same number of elements and their elements at the corresponding positions are the same. Overload the relational operator == for the **class** stackType that returns **true** if two stacks of the same type are the same; it returns **false** otherwise. Also, write the definition of the function template to overload this operator.

2. Repeat Programming Exercise 1 for the **class** linkedStackType.

3. a. Add the following operation to the **class** stackType:

   ```
   void  reverseStack(stackType<Type> &otherStack);
   ```

   This operation copies the elements of a stack in reverse order onto another stack.

   Consider the following statements:

   ```
   stackType<int> stack1;
   stackType<int> stack2;
   ```

   The statement:

   ```
   stack1.reverseStack(stack2);
   ```

copies the elements of stack1 onto stack2 in reverse order. That is, the top element of stack1 is the bottom element of stack2, and so on. The old contents of stack2 are destroyed, and stack1 is unchanged.

b.   Write the definition of the function **template** to implement the operation reverseStack.

4.   Repeat Programming Exercises 3a and 3b for the **class** linkedStackType.

5.   Write a program that takes as input an arithmetic expression. The program outputs whether the expression contains matching grouping symbols. For example, the arithmetic expressions {25 + (3 − 6) * 8} and 7 + 8 * 2 contain matching grouping symbols. However, the expression 5 + { (13 + 7) / 8 − 2 * 9 does not contain matching grouping symbols.

6.   Write a program that uses a stack to print the prime factors of a positive integer in descending order.

7.   The Programming Example, Converting a Number from Binary to Decimal, in Chapter 15, uses recursion to convert a binary number into an equivalent decimal number. Write a program that uses a stack to convert a binary number into an equivalent decimal number.

8.   The Programming Example, Converting a Number from Decimal to Binary, in Chapter 15, contains a program that uses recursion to convert a decimal number into an equivalent binary number. Write a program that uses a stack to convert a decimal number into an equivalent binary number.

9.   Write a program that reads a string consisting of a positive integer or a positive decimal number and converts the number to the numeric format. If the string consists of a decimal number, the program must use a stack to convert the decimal number to the numeric format.

10. **(Infix to Postfix)** Write a program that converts an infix expression into an equivalent postfix expression.

The rules to convert an infix expression into an equivalent postfix expression are as follows:

Suppose infx represents the infix expression and pfx represents the postfix expression. The rules to convert infx into pfx are as follows:

a.   Initialize pfx to an empty expression and also initialize the stack.

b.   Get the next symbol, sym, from infx.

b.1.   If sym is an operand, append sym to pfx.

b.2.   If sym is (, push sym into the stack.

b.3.   If sym is), pop and append all of the symbols from the stack until the most recent left parentheses. Pop and discard the left parentheses.

b.4. If `sym` is an operator:

b.4.1. Pop and append all of the operators from the stack to `pfx` that are above the most recent left parentheses and have precedence greater than or equal to `sym`.

b.4.2. Push `sym` onto the stack.

c. After processing `infx`, some operators might be left in the stack. Pop and append to `pfx` everything from the stack.

In this program, you will consider the following (binary) arithmetic operators: +, -, *, and /. You may assume that the expressions you will process are error free.

Design a class that stores the infix and postfix strings. The class must include the following operations:

- **getInfix**: Stores the infix expression.
- **showInfix**: Outputs the infix expression.
- **showPostfix**: Outputs the postfix expression.

Some other operations that you might need are:

- **convertToPostfix**: Converts the infix expression into a postfix expression. The resulting postfix expression is stored in `pfx`.
- **precedence**: Determines the precedence between two operators. If the first operator is of higher or equal precedence than the second operator, it returns the value `true`; otherwise, it returns the value `false`.

Include the constructors and destructors for automatic initialization and dynamic memory deallocation.

Test your program on the following expressions:

a. A + B - C;

b. (A + B) * C;

c. (A + B) * (C - D);

d. A + ((B + C) * (E - F) - G) / (H - I);

e. A + B * (C + D) - E / F * G + H;

For each expression, your answer must be in the following form:

```
Infix Expression: A + B - C;
Postfix Expression: A B + C -
```

11. Write the definitions of the functions to overload the assignment operator and copy constructor for the **class** `queueType`. Also, write a program to test these operations.

12. Write the definitions of the functions to overload the assignment operator and copy constructor for the **class** `linkedQueueType`. Also, write a program to test these operations.

13. This chapter describes the array implementation of queues that use a special array slot, called the reserved slot, to distinguish between an empty and a full queue. Write the definition of the class and the definitions of the function members of this queue design. Also, write a test program to test various operations on a queue.

14. Write the definition of the function `moveNthFront` that takes as a parameter a positive integer, *n*. The function moves the *n*th element of the queue to the front. The order of the remaining elements remains unchanged. For example, suppose:

    queue = {5, 11, 34, 67, 43, 55} and *n* = 3.

    After a call to the function `moveNthFront`:

    queue = {34, 5, 11, 67, 43, 55}.

    Add this function to the **class** `queueType`. Also, write a program to test your method.

15. Write a program that reads a line of text, changes each uppercase letter to lowercase, and places each letter both in a queue and onto a stack. The program should then verify whether the line of text is a palindrome (a set of letters or numbers that is the same whether read forward or backward).

16. The implementation of a queue in an array, as given in this chapter, uses the variable count to determine whether the queue is empty or full. You can also use the variable count to return the number of elements in the queue. On the other hand, **class** `linkedQueueType` does not use such a variable to keep track of the number of elements in the queue. Redefine the **class** `linkedQueueType` by adding the variable count to keep track of the number of elements in the queue. Modify the definitions of the functions `addQueue` and `deleteQueue` as necessary. Add the function `queueCount` to return the number of elements in the queue. Also, write a program to test various operations of the class you defined.

17. Write the definition of the **class** `linkedQueueType`, which is derived from the **class** `unorderedLinkedList`, as explained in this chapter. Also, write a program to test various operations of this class.

18. a. Write the definitions of the functions `setWaitingTime`, `getArrivalTime`, `getTransactionTime`, and `getCustomerNumber` of the **class** `customerType` defined in the section Application of Queues: Simulation.

    b. Write the definitions of the functions `getRemainingTransactionTime`, `setCurrentCustomer`, `getCurrentCustomerNumber`, `getCurrentCustomerArrivalTime`, `getCurrentCustomerWaitingTime`, and `getCurrentCustomerTransactionTime` of the **class** `serverType` defined in the section Application of Queues: Simulation.

    c. Write the definition of the function `runSimulation` to complete the design of the computer simulation program (see the section Application of Queues: Simulation). Test run your program for a variety of data. Moreover, use a random number generator to decide whether a customer arrived at a given time unit.

CHAPTER

18

SEARCHING AND SORTING ALGORITHMS

IN THIS CHAPTER, YOU WILL:

- Learn the various search algorithms
- Explore how to implement the sequential and binary search algorithms
- Discover how the sequential and binary search algorithms perform
- Become aware of the lower bound on comparison-based search algorithms
- Learn the various sorting algorithms
- Explore how to implement the bubble, selection, insertion, quick, and merge sorting algorithms
- Discover how the sorting algorithms discussed in this chapter perform

Chapters 12 and 13 described how to organize data into computer memory using an array and how to perform basic operations on that data. Chapter 16 described how to organize data using linked lists. The most important operation that can be performed on a list is the search algorithm. Using the search algorithm, you can do the following:

- Determine whether a particular item is in the list.
- If the data is specially organized (e.g., sorted), find the location in the list where a new item can be inserted.
- Find the location of an item to be deleted.

The search algorithm's performance, therefore, is crucial. If the search is slow, it takes a large amount of computer time to accomplish your task; if the search is fast, you can accomplish your task quickly.

In the first part of this chapter, we describe the search algorithms: sequential search and binary search. Certain search algorithms work only on sorted data. Therefore, the second half of this chapter discusses various sorting algorithms.

Searching and Sorting Algorithms

The searching and sorting algorithms that we describe are generic. Because searching and sorting require comparisons of data, the algorithms should work on the type of data that provides appropriate functions to compare data items. Now data can be organized with the help of an array or a linked list. You can create an array of data items, or you can use the `class` `unorderedLinkedList` to organize data. The algorithms that we describe should work on either organization. Consequently, we will write the function templates to implement a particular algorithm. All algorithms described in this chapter, with the exception of the merge sort algorithms, are for array-based lists. Because of storage issues and some other overheads, merge sort works better for linked lists. Therefore, after describing the merge sort algorithm, we will add it as a function to the `class` `unorderedLinkedList`. We will also show how to use the searching and sorting algorithms on objects of the `class` `unorderedArrayListType`. Moreover, we will place all of the array-based searching and sorting functions in the header file `searchSortAlgorithms.h`. Therefore, if you need to use a particular searching and/or sorting function designed in this chapter, your program can include this header file and use that function.

Search Algorithms

Chapters 12, 13, and 16 described how to implement the sequential search algorithm. This chapter discusses other search algorithms and analyzes them. Analysis of the algorithms enables programmers to decide which algorithm to use for a specific application. Before exploring these algorithms, let us make the following observations.

Associated with each item in a data set is a special member that uniquely identifies the item in the data set. For example, if you have a data set consisting of student records, then the student ID uniquely identifies each student in a particular school. This unique member of the item is called the **key** of the item. The keys of the items in the data set are used in such operations as searching, sorting, inserting, and deleting. For instance, when we search the data set for a particular item, we compare the key of the item for which we are searching with the keys of the items in the data set.

When analyzing searching and sorting algorithms, the key comparisons refer to comparing the key of the search item with the key of an item in the list. The number of key comparisons refers to the number of times the key of the search item (in algorithms such as searching and sorting) is compared with the keys of the items in the list.

Sequential Search

The sequential search (also called a linear search) on array-based lists was described in Chapters 12 and 13, and the sequential search on linked lists was covered in Chapter 16. The sequential search works the same for both array-based and linked lists. The search always starts at the first element in the list and continues until either the item is found in the list or the entire list is searched.

Because we are interested in the performance of the sequential search (that is, the analysis of this type of search), for easy reference and the sake of completeness, we provide the sequential search algorithm for array-based lists (as described in Chapters 12 and 13). If the search item is found, its index (that is, its location in the array) is returned. If the search is unsuccessful, −1 is returned. Note that the following sequential search does not require the list elements to be in any particular order.

```cpp
template <class elemType>
int seqSearch(const elemType list[ ], int length,
              const elemType& item)
{
    int loc;
    bool found = false;

    loc = 0;

    while (loc < length && !found)
        if (list[loc] == item)
            found = true;
        else
            loc++;

    if (found)
        return loc;
    else
        return -1;
} //end seqSearch
```

NOTE   The sequential search algorithm, as given here, uses an iterative control structure (the `while` loop) to compare the search item with the list elements. You can also write a recursive algorithm to implement the sequential search algorithm. (See Programming Exercise 1 at the end of this chapter.)

SEQUENTIAL SEARCH ANALYSIS

This section analyzes the performance of the sequential search algorithm in both the worst case and the average case.

The statements before and after the loop are executed only once and hence require very little computer time. The statements in the `while` loop are the ones that are repeated several times. For each iteration of the loop, the search item is compared with an element in the list, and a few other statements are executed, including some other comparisons. Clearly, the loop terminates as soon as the search item is found in the list. Therefore, execution of the other statements in the loop is directly related to the outcome of the key comparison. Also, different programmers might implement the same algorithm differently, although the number of key comparisons would typically be the same. The speed of a computer can also easily affect the time an algorithm takes to perform, but it, of course, does not affect the number of key comparisons required.

Therefore, when analyzing a search algorithm, we count the number of key comparisons because this number gives us the most useful information. Furthermore, the criteria for counting the number of key comparisons can be applied equally well to other search algorithms.

Suppose that L is a list of length n. We want to determine the number of key comparisons made by the sequential search when the list L is searched for a given item.

If the search item is not in the list, we then compare the search item with every element in the list, making n comparisons. This is an unsuccessful case.

Suppose that the search item is in the list. Then, the number of key comparisons depends on where in the list the search item is located. If the search item is the first element of L, we make only one key comparison. This is the best case. On the other hand, if the search item is the last element in the list, the algorithm makes n comparisons. This is the worst case. The best and worst cases are not likely to occur every time we apply the sequential search on L, so it would be more helpful if we could determine the average behavior of the algorithm. That is, we need to determine the average number of key comparisons the sequential search algorithm makes in the successful case.

To determine the average number of comparisons in the successful case of the sequential search algorithm:

1. Consider all possible cases.
2. Find the number of comparisons for each case.
3. Add the number of comparisons and divide by the number of cases.

If the search item, called the **target**, is the first element in the list, one comparison is required. If the target is the second element in the list, two comparisons are required. Similarly, if the target is the kth element in the list, k comparisons are required. We assume that the target can be any element in the list; that is, all list elements are equally likely to be the target. Suppose that there are n elements in the list. The following expression gives the average number of comparisons:

$$\frac{1 + 2 + \cdots + n}{n}.$$

It is known that:

$$1 + 2 + \cdots + n = \frac{n(n + 1)}{2}.$$

Therefore, the following expression gives the average number of comparisons made by the sequential search in the successful case:

$$\frac{1 + 2 + \cdots + n}{n} = \frac{1}{n}\frac{n(n + 1)}{2} = \frac{n + 1}{2}.$$

This expression shows that, on average, a successful sequential search searches half of the list. It thus follows that if the list size is 1,000,000, on average, the sequential search makes 500,000 comparisons. As a result, the sequential search is not efficient for large lists.

Binary Search

As you can see, the sequential search is not efficient for large lists because, on average, it searches half the list. We, therefore, describe another search algorithm called the **binary search**, which is very fast. However, a binary search can be performed only on sorted lists. We, therefore, assume that the list is sorted. Later in this chapter, we will describe several sorting algorithms.

The binary search algorithm uses the "divide and conquer" technique to search the list. First, the search item is compared with the middle element of the list. If the search item is less than the middle element of the list, we restrict the search to the first half of the list; otherwise, we search the second half of the list.

Consider the sorted list of `length = 12` in Figure 18-1.

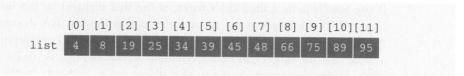

FIGURE 18-1 List of length 12

Suppose that we want to determine whether 75 is in the list. Initially, the entire list is the search list (see Figure 18-2).

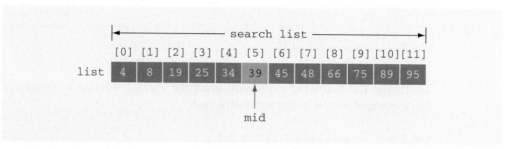

FIGURE 18-2 Search list, list[0]...list[11]

First, we compare 75 with the middle element in this list, list[5] (which is 39). Because 75 ≠ list[5] and 75 > list[5], we then restrict our search to the list list[6]...list[11], as shown in Figure 18-3.

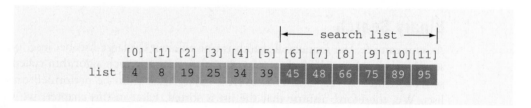

FIGURE 18-3 Search list, list[6]...list[11]

This process is now repeated on the list list[6]...list[11], which is a list of length = 6.

Because we need to determine the middle element of the list frequently, the binary search algorithm is typically implemented for array-based lists. To determine the middle element of the list, we add the starting index, first, and the ending index, last, of the search list and then divide by 2 to calculate its index. That is:

$$\text{mid} = \frac{\text{first} + \text{last}}{2}.$$

Initially, `first` = 0 and `last` = `length` − 1 (this is because an array index in C++ starts at 0, and `length` denotes the number of elements in the list).

The following C++ function implements the binary search algorithm. If the item is found in the list, its location is returned; if the search item is not in the list, −1 is returned.

```cpp
template <class elemType>
int binarySearch(const elemType list[], int length,
                 const elemType& item)
{
    int first = 0;
    int last = length - 1;
    int mid;

    bool found = false;

    while (first <= last && !found)
    {
        mid = (first + last) / 2;

        if (list[mid] == item)
            found = true;
        else if (list[mid] > item)
            last = mid - 1;
        else
            first = mid + 1;
    }

    if (found)
        return mid;
    else
        return -1;
} //end binarySearch
```

In the binary search algorithm, each time through the loop, we make two key comparisons. The only exception is in the successful case; the last time through the loop, only one key comparison is made.

NOTE The binary search algorithm, as given in this chapter, uses an iterative control structure (the `while` loop) to compare the search item with the list elements. You can also write a recursive algorithm to implement the binary search algorithm. (See Programming Exercise 2 at the end of this chapter.)

Example 18-1 further illustrates how the binary search algorithm works.

EXAMPLE 18-1

Consider the list given in Figure 18-4.

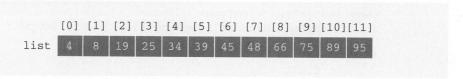

FIGURE 18-4 Sorted list for a binary search

The size of this list is 12; that is, the length is 12. Suppose that we are searching for item 89. Table 18-1 shows the values of `first`, `last`, and `mid` each time through the loop. It also shows the number of times the item is compared with an element in the list each time through the loop.

TABLE 18-1 Values of `first`, `last`, and `mid` and the Number of Comparisons for Search Item 89

Iteration	first	last	mid	list[mid]	Number of comparisons
1	0	11	5	39	2
2	6	11	8	66	2
3	9	11	10	89	1 (found is true)

The item is found at `location 10`, and the total number of comparisons is 5.

Next, let us search the list for item 34. Table 18-2 shows the values of `first`, `last`, and `mid` each time through the loop. It also shows the number of times the item is compared with an element in the list each time through the loop.

TABLE 18-2 Values of `first`, `last`, and `mid` and the Number of Comparisons for Search Item 34

Iteration	first	last	mid	list[mid]	Number of comparisons
1	0	11	5	39	2
2	0	4	2	19	2
3	3	4	3	25	2
4	4	4	4	34	1 (found is true)

The item is found at `location 4`, and the total number of comparisons is 7.

Let us now search for item 22, as shown in Table 18-3.

TABLE 18-3 Values of `first`, `last`, and `mid` and the Number of Comparisons for Search Item 22

Iteration	first	last	mid	list[mid]	Number of comparisons
1	0	11	5	39	2
2	0	4	2	19	2
3	3	4	3	25	2
4	3	2	the loop stops (because `first > last`)		

This is an unsuccessful search. The total number of comparisons is 6.

Example 18-2 illustrates how to use the binary search algorithm in a program.

EXAMPLE 18-2

```
#include <iostream>
#include "searchSortAlgorithms.h"

using namespace std;

int main()
```

```
{
    int intList[] = {2, 16, 34, 45, 53,
                     56, 69, 70, 75, 96};          //Line 1

    int pos;                                       //Line 2

    pos = binarySearch(intList, 10, 45);           //Line 3

    if (pos != -1)                                 //Line 4
        cout << "Line 5: " << 45
             << " found at position "
             << pos << endl;                       //Line 5
    else                                           //Line 6
        cout << "Line 7: " << 45
             << " is not in intList " << endl;     //Line 7
    return 0;
}
```

Sample Run:

```
Line 5: 45 found at position 3
```

The preceding program works as follows. The statement in Line 1 creates the array `intList`. (Note that the array `intList` is sorted.) The statement in Line 2 declares `pos` to be an `int` variable. The statement in Line 3 uses the binary search algorithm to determine whether 45 is in `intList`. Note that the array `intList`, its lengths, and the search item, which is 45, are passed as parameters to the function `binarySearch`. The statements in Lines 4 to 7 output the result of the search, which is successful.

Performance of Binary Search

Suppose that L is a sorted list of size 1024 and we want to determine if an item x is in L. From the binary search algorithm, it follows that every iteration of the `while` loop cuts the size of the search list by half. (For example, see Figures 18-2 and 18-3.) Because $1024 = 2^{10}$, the `while` loop will have, at most, 11 iterations to determine whether x is in L. Because every iteration of the `while` loop makes two item (key) comparisons, that is, x is compared twice with the elements of L, the binary search will make, at most, 22 comparisons to determine whether x is in L. On the other hand, recall that a sequential search on average will make 512 comparisons to determine whether x is in L.

To better understand how fast binary search is compared to sequential search, suppose that L is of size 1048576. Because $1048576 = 2^{20}$, it follows that the `while` loop in a binary search will have, at most, 21 iterations to determine whether an element is in L. Every iteration of the `while` loop makes two key (that is, item) comparisons. Therefore, to determine whether an element is in L, a binary search makes, at most, 42 item comparisons.

Note that $40 = 2 * 20 = 2 * \log_2 2^{20} = 2 * \log_2(1048576)$.

In general, suppose that L is a sorted list of size n. Moreover, suppose that n is a power of 2, that is, $n = 2^m$, for some nonnegative integer m. After each iteration of the `while` loop, about half of the elements are left to search, that is, the search sublist for the next iteration is half the size of the current sublist. For example, after the *first* iteration, the search sublist size is about $n/2 = 2^{m-1}$. It is easy to see that the maximum number of the iteration of the `while` loop is about $m + 1$. Also, $m = \log_2 n$. Each iteration makes two key comparisons. Thus, the maximum number of comparisons to determine whether an element x is in L is $2(m + 1) = 2(\log_2 n + 1) = 2\log_2 n + 2$.

In the case of a successful search, it can be shown that for a list of length n, on average, a binary search makes $2\log_2 n - 3$ key comparisons. In the case of an unsuccessful search, it can be shown that for a list of length n, a binary search makes approximately $2\log_2 n$ key comparisons.

Binary Search Algorithm and the `class` `orderedArrayListType`

The `class` `orderedArrayListType`, designed in Chapter 13, does not contain the binary search algorithm. Now that you know how to implement the binary search algorithm, you can learn how to use it in the `class` `orderedArrayListType`.

To use the binary search algorithm within the `class` `orderedArrayListType`, we add the function `binSearch` to this class and call the functions `binarySearch` with the appropriate parameters.

```
#include "arrayListType.h"
#include "searchSortAlgorithms.h"

template <class elemType>
class orderedArrayListType: public arrayListType<elemType>
{
public:
    void insertAt(int location, const elemType& insertItem);
    void insertEnd(const elemType& insertItem);
    void replaceAt(int location, const elemType& repItem);
    int seqSearch(const elemType& searchItem) const;
    void insert(const elemType& insertItem);
    void remove(const elemType& removeItem);

    int binSearch(const elemType& removeItem);

    orderedArrayListType(int size = 100);
        //Constructor
};
```

The definition of the member function `binSearch` is:

```
template <class elemType>
int orderedArrayListType<elemType>::
                binSearch(const elemType& item) const
```

```
{
    return binarySearch(list, length, item);
}
```

Asymptotic Notation: Big-O Notation

Just as a problem is analyzed before writing the algorithm and the computer program, after an algorithm is designed, it should also be analyzed. Usually, there are various ways to design a particular algorithm. Certain algorithms take very little computer time to execute, while others take a considerable amount of time. Consider the following examples.

EXAMPLE 18-3

Consider the following algorithm (assume that all variables are properly declared):

```
cout << "Enter the first number: ";       //Line 1
cin >> num1;                              //Line 2
cout << endl;                            //Line 3

cout << "Enter the second number: ";      //Line 4
cin >> num2;                             //Line 5
cout << endl;                            //Line 6


if (num1 >= num2)                        //Line 7
    max = num1;                          //Line 8
else                                     //Line 9
    max = num2;                          //Line 10

cout << "The maximum number is: " << max << endl;  //Line 11
```

Lines 1 to 6 each have one operation, << or >>. Line 7 has one operation, >=. Either Line 8 or Line 9 executes; each has one operation. There are three operations, <<, in Line 11. Therefore, the total number of operations executed in the preceding code is $6 + 1 + 1 + 3 = 11$. In this algorithm, the number of operations executed is fixed.

EXAMPLE 18-4

Consider the following algorithm (assume that all variables are properly declared):

```
cout << "Enter positive integers ending with -1"
     << endl;                            //Line 1

count = 0;                               //Line 2
sum = 0;                                 //Line 3

cin >> num;                              //Line 4
```

```
while (num != -1)                                     //Line 5
{                                                     //Line 6
    sum = sum + num;                                  //Line 7
    count++;                                          //Line 8
    cin >> num;
}

cout << "The sum of the numbers is: " << sum
        << endl;                                      //Line 9

if (count != 0)                                       //Line 10
    average = sum / count;                            //Line 11
else                                                  //Line 12
    average = 0;                                      //Line 13

cout << "The average is: " << average << endl;        //Line 14
```

This algorithm has five operations (Lines 1 through 4) before the `while` loop. Similarly, there are nine or eight operations after the `while` loop, depending on whether Line 11 or Line 13 executes.

Line 5 has one operation, and there are four operations within the `while` loop (Lines 6 through 8). Thus, Lines 5 through 8 have five operations. If the `while` loop executes 10 times, these five operations execute 10 times, plus one extra operation is executed at Line 5 to terminate the loop. Therefore, the number of operations executed from Lines 5 through 8 is 51.

If the `while` loop executes 10 times, the total number of operations executed is:

$5 \times 10 + 1 + 5 + 9$ or $5 \times 10 + 1 + 5 + 8$.

That is:

$5 \times 10 + 15$ or $5 \times 10 + 14$.

We can generalize it to the case when the `while` loop executes n times. If the `while` loop executes n times, the number of operations executed is:

$5n + 15$ or $5n + 14$.

In these expressions, for very large values of n, the term $5n$ becomes the dominating term, and the terms 15 and 14 become negligible.

Usually, in an algorithm, certain operations are dominant. For example, in the algorithm in Example 18-4, to add numbers, the dominant operation is in Line 6. Similarly, in a search algorithm, because the search item is compared with the items in the list, the dominant operations would be comparison, that is, the relational operation. Therefore, in the case of a search algorithm, we count the number of comparisons.

Suppose that an algorithm performs $f(n)$ basic operations to accomplish a task, in which n is the size of the problem. Suppose that you want to determine whether an item is in a list and that the size of the list is n. To determine whether the item is in the list, there are various algorithms. However, the basic method is to compare the item with the items in the list. Therefore, the performance of the algorithm depends on the number of comparisons.

Thus, in the case of a search, n is the size of the list and $f(n)$ becomes the count function; that is, $f(n)$ gives the number of comparisons done by the search algorithm. Suppose that on a particular computer, it takes c units of computer time to execute one operation. Thus, the computer time it would take to execute $f(n)$ operations is $cf(n)$. Clearly, the constant c depends on the speed of the computer and, therefore, varies from computer to computer. However, $f(n)$, the number of basic operations, is the same on each computer. If we know how the function $f(n)$ grows as the size of the problem grows, we can determine the efficiency of the algorithm. Consider Table 18-4.

TABLE 18-4 Growth Rate of Various Functions

n	$\log_2 n$	$n\log_2 n$	n^2	2^n
1	0	0	1	2
2	1	2	2	4
4	2	8	16	16
8	3	24	64	256
16	4	64	256	65536
32	5	160	1024	4294967296

Table 18-4 shows how certain functions grow as the parameter n (the problem size) grows. Suppose that the problem size is doubled. From Table 18-4, it follows that if the number of basic operations is a function of $f(n) = n^2$, the number of basic operations is quadrupled. If the number of basic operations is a function of $f(n) = 2^n$, then the number of basic operations is squared. However, if the number of operations is a function of $f(n) = \log_2 n$, the change in the number of basic operations is insignificant.

Suppose that a computer can execute 1 billion steps per second. Table 18-5 shows the time that the computer takes to execute $f(n)$ steps.

TABLE 18-5   Time for $f(n)$ Instructions on a Computer That Executes 1 Billion Instructions per Second

n	$f(n) = n$	$f(n) = \log_2 n$	$f(n) = n\log_2 n$	$f(n) = n^2$	$f(n) = 2^n$
10	0.01μs	0.003μs	0.033μs	0.1μs	1μs
20	0.02μs	0.004μs	0.086μs	0.4μs	1ms
30	0.03μs	0.005μs	0.147μs	0.9μs	1s
40	0.04μs	0.005μs	0.213μs	1.6μs	18.3min
50	0.05μs	0.006μs	0.282μs	2.5μs	13 days
100	0.10μs	0.007μs	0.664μs	10μs	4×10^{13} years
1000	1.00μs	0.010μs	9.966μs	1ms	
10000	10μs	0.013μs	130μs	100ms	
100000	0.10ms	0.017μs	1.67ms	10s	
1000000	1 ms	0.020μs	19.93ms	16.7m	
10000000	0.01s	0.023μs	0.23s	1.16 days	
100000000	0.10s	0.027μs	2.66s	115.7 days	

In Table 18-5, $1\mu s = 10^{-6}$ seconds and $1ms = 10^{-3}$ seconds.

Figure 18-5 shows the growth rate of functions in Table 18-5.

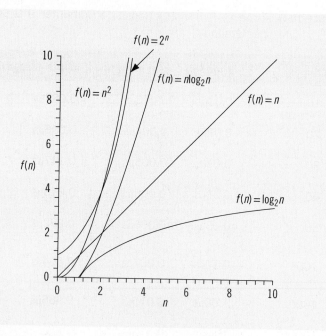

FIGURE 18-5 Growth rate of various functions

The remainder of this section develops a notation that shows how a function $f(n)$ grows as n increases without bound. That is, we develop a notation that is useful in describing the behavior of the algorithm, which gives us the most useful information about the algorithm. First, we define the term "asymptotic."

Let f be a function of n. By the term **asymptotic**, we mean the study of the function f as n becomes larger and larger without bound.

Consider the functions $g(n) = n^2$ and $f(n) = n^2 + 4n + 20$. Clearly, the function g does not contain any linear term; that is, the coefficient of n in g is zero. Consider Table 18-6.

TABLE 18-6 Growth Rate of n^2 and $n^2 + 4n + 20$

n	$g(n) = n^2$	$f(n) = n^2 + 4n + 20$
10	100	160
50	2500	2720
100	10000	10420
1000	1000000	1004020
10000	100000000	100040020

Clearly, as n becomes larger and larger, the term $4n + 20$ in $f(n)$ becomes insignificant, and the term n^2 becomes the dominant term. For large values of n, we can predict the behavior of $f(n)$ by looking at the behavior of $g(n)$. In the algorithm analysis, if the complexity of a function can be described by the complexity of a quadratic function without the linear term, we say that the function is of $O(n^2)$, called Big-O of n^2.

Let f and g be real-valued functions. Assume that f and g are nonnegative; that is, for all real numbers n, $f(n) \geq 0$ and $g(n) \geq 0$.

Definition: We say that $f(n)$ is **Big-O** of $g(n)$, written $f(n) = O(g(n))$, if there exist positive constants c and n_0 such that:

$f(n) \leq cg(n)$ for all $n \geq n_0$.

EXAMPLE 18-5

Let $f(n) = a$, wherein a is a nonnegative real number and $n \geq 0$. Note that f is a constant function.

Now:

$f(n) = a \leq a \cdot 1$ for all $n \geq a$.

Let $c = a$, $n_0 = a$, and $g(n) = 1$. Then, $f(n) \leq cg(n)$ for all $n \geq n_0$. It now follows that $f(n) = O(g(n)) = O(1)$.

From Example 18-5, it follows that if f is a nonnegative constant function, then f is $O(1)$.

EXAMPLE 18-6

Let $f(n) = 2n + 5$, $n \geq 0$. Note that:

$f(n) = 2n + 5 \leq 2n + n = 3n$ for all $n \geq 5$.

Let $c = 3$, $n_0 = 5$, and $g(n) = n$. Then, $f(n) \leq cg(n)$ for all $n \geq 5$. It now follows that $f(n) = O(g(n)) = O(n)$.

EXAMPLE 18-7

Let $f(n) = n^2 + 3n + 2$, $g(n) = n^2$, $n \geq 0$. Note that:

$3n + 2 \leq n^2$ for all $n \geq 4$.

This implies that:

$f(n) = n^2 + 3n + 2 \leq n^2 + n^2 \leq 2n^2 = 2g(n)$ for all $n \geq 4$.

Let $c = 2$ and $n_0 = 4$. Then, $f(n) \leq cg(n)$ for all $n \geq 4$. It now follows that $f(n) = O(g(n)) = O(n^2)$.

In general, we can prove the following theorem. We state the theorem without proof.

Theorem: Let $f(n)$ be a nonnegative real-valued function such that:

$f(n) = a_m n^m + a_{m-1} n^{m-1} + \cdots + a_1 n + a_0,$

in which a_is are real numbers, $a_m \neq 0$, $n \geq 0$, and m is a nonnegative integer. Then:

$f(n) = O(n^m)$.

In Example 18-8, we use the preceding theorem to establish the Big-O of certain functions.

EXAMPLE 18-8

In the following, $f(n)$ is a nonnegative real-valued function.

Function	Big-O
$f(n) = an + b$, in which a and b are real numbers and a is nonzero	$f(n) = O(n)$
$f(n) = n^2 + 5n + 1$	$f(n) = O(n^2)$
$f(n) = 4n^6 + 3n^3 + 1$	$f(n) = O(n^6)$
$f(n) = 10n^7 + 23$	$f(n) = O(n^7)$
$f(n) = 6n^{15}$	$f(n) = O(n^{15})$

EXAMPLE 18-9

Suppose that $f(n) = 2\log_2 n + a$, in which a is a real number. It can be shown that $f(n) = O(\log_2 n)$.

EXAMPLE 18-10

Consider the following code, in which m and n are `int` variables and their values are nonnegative.

```
for (int i = 0; i < m; i++)          //Line 1
    for (int j = 0; j < n; j++)      //Line 2
        cout << i * j << endl;       //Line 3
```

This code contains nested `for` loops. The outer `for` loop, at Line 1, executes m times. For each iteration of the outer loop, the inner loop at Line 2 executes n times. For each iteration of the inner loop, the output statement in Line 3 executes. It follows that the total number of iterations of the nested `for` loop is mn. So the number of times the statement in Line 3 executes is mn. It follows that this algorithm is $O(mn)$. Note that if $m = n$, then this algorithm is $O(n^2)$.

Table 18-7 shows some common Big-O functions that appear in the algorithm analysis. Let $f(n) = O(g(n))$, wherein n is the problem size.

TABLE 18-7 Some Big-O Functions That Appear in Algorithm Analysis

Function $g(n)$	Growth rate of $f(n)$
$g(n) = 1$	The growth rate is constant, so it does not depend on n, the size of the problem.
$g(n) = \log_2 n$	The growth rate is a function of $\log_2 n$. Because a logarithm function grows slowly, the growth rate of the function f is also slow.
$g(n) = n$	The growth rate is linear. The growth rate of f is directly proportional to the size of the problem.
$g(n) = n\log_2 n$	The growth rate is faster than the linear algorithm.
$g(n) = n^2$	The growth rate of such functions increases rapidly with the size of the problem. The growth rate is quadrupled when the problem size is doubled.
$g(n) = 2^n$	The growth rate is exponential. The growth rate is squared when the problem size is doubled.

NOTE It can be shown that:

$$O(1) \leq O(\log_2 n) \leq O(n) \leq O(n\log_2 n) \leq O(n^2) \leq O(2^n).$$

Using the notations developed in this section, we can conclude that the algorithm in Example 18-3 is of order $O(1)$, and the algorithm in Example 18-4 is of $O(n)$. Table 18-8 summarizes the algorithm analysis of the search algorithms discussed earlier.

TABLE 18-8 Number of Comparisons for a List of Length n

Algorithm	Successful Search	Unsuccessful Search
Sequential search	$\dfrac{n+1}{2} = \dfrac{1}{2}n + \dfrac{1}{2} = O(n)$	$n = O(n)$
Binary search	$2\log_2 n - 3 = O(\log_2 n)$	$2\log_2 n = O(\log_2 n)$

Lower Bound on Comparison-Based Search Algorithms

Sequential and binary search algorithms search the list by comparing the target element with the list elements. For this reason, these algorithms are called **comparison-based search algorithms**. Earlier sections of this chapter showed that a sequential search is of the order n, and a binary search is of the order $\log_2 n$, where n is the size of the list. The obvious question is: Can we devise a search algorithm that has an order less than $\log_2 n$? Before we answer this question, first we obtain the lower bound on the number of comparisons for the comparison-based search algorithms.

Theorem: Let L be a list of size $n > 1$. Suppose that the elements of L are sorted. If $SRH(n)$ denotes the minimum number of comparisons needed, in the worst case, by using a comparison-based algorithm to recognize whether an element x is in L, then $SRH(n) \geq \log_2(n + 1)$.

Corollary: The binary search algorithm is an optimal worst-case algorithm for solving search problems by the comparison method.

From these results, it follows that if we want to design a search algorithm that is of an order less than $\log_2 n$, then it cannot be comparison based.

Sorting Algorithms

There are several sorting algorithms in the literature. In this chapter, we discuss some of the commonly used sorting algorithms. To compare their performance, we also provide some analysis of these algorithms. These sorting algorithms can be applied to either array-based lists or linked lists. We will specify whether the algorithm being developed is for array-based lists or linked lists.

Sorting a List: Bubble Sort

Many sorting algorithms are available in the literature. This section describes using the sorting algorithm called the **bubble sort** to sort a list.

Suppose list[0...n - 1] is a list of n elements, indexed 0 to n - 1. We want to rearrange, that is, sort, the elements of list in increasing order. The bubble sort algorithm works as follows.

In a series of n - 1 iterations, the successive elements list[index] and list[index + 1] of the list are compared. If list[index] is greater than list[index + 1], then the elements list[index] and list[index + 1] are swapped.

It follows that the smaller elements move toward the top, and the larger elements move toward the bottom.

In the first iteration, we consider the list[0...n - 1]. As you will see after the first iteration, the largest element of the list is moved to the last position, which is position n - 1, in the list. In the second iteration, we consider the list[0...n - 2]. After the second iteration, the second largest element in the list is moved to the position n - 2, which is second to the last position in the list. In the third iteration, we consider the list[0...n - 3], and so on. As you will see, after each iteration, the size of the unsorted portion of the list shrinks.

Consider the list[0...4] of five elements, as shown in Figure 18-6.

	list
list[0]	10
list[1]	7
list[2]	19
list[3]	5
list[4]	16

FIGURE 18-6 List of five elements

Iteration 1: Sort list[0...4]. Figure 18-7 shows how the elements of list get rearranged in the first iteration.

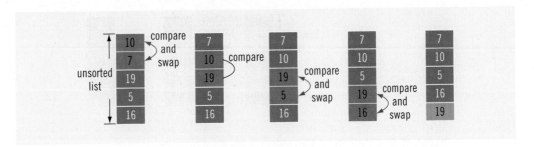

FIGURE 18-7 Elements of list during the first iteration

Notice that in the first diagram of Figure 18-7, list[0] > list[1]. Therefore, list[0] and list[1] are swapped. In the second diagram, list[1] and list[2] are compared. Because list[1] < list[2], they do not get swapped. The third diagram of Figure 18-7 compares list[2] with list[3]; because list[2] > list[3], list[2] is swapped with list[3]. Then, in the fourth diagram, we compare list[3] with list[4]. Because list[3] > list[4], list[3] and list[4] are swapped.

After the first iteration, the largest element is at the last position. Therefore, in the next iteration, we consider the list[0...3].

Iteration 2: Sort list[0...3]. Figure 18-8 shows how the elements of list get rearranged in the second iteration.

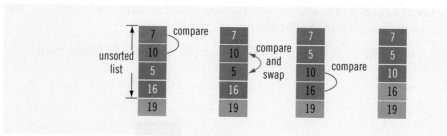

FIGURE 18-8 Elements of list during the second iteration

The elements are compared and swapped as in the first iteration. Here, only the list elements list[0] through list[3] are considered. After the second iteration, the last two elements are in the right place. Therefore, in the next iteration, we consider list[0...2].

Iteration 3: Sort list[0...2]. Figure 18-9 shows how the elements of list get rearranged in the third iteration.

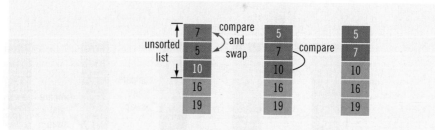

FIGURE 18-9 Elements of list during the third iteration

After the third iteration, the last three elements are in the right place. Therefore, in the next iteration, we consider list[0...1].

Iteration 4: Sort list[0...1]. Figure 18-10 shows how the elements of list get rearranged in the fourth iteration.

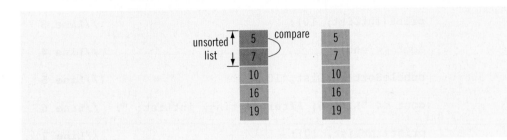

FIGURE 18-10 Elements of list during the fourth iteration

After the fourth iteration, list is sorted.

The following C++ function implements the bubble sort algorithm:

```cpp
template <class elemType>
void bubbleSort(elemType list[], int length)
{
    for (int iteration = 1; iteration < length; iteration++)
    {
        for (int index = 0; index < length - iteration;
                             index++)
        {
            if (list[index] > list[index + 1])
            {
                elemType temp = list[index];
                list[index] = list[index + 1];
                list[index + 1] = temp;
            }
        }
    }
} //end bubbleSort
```

Example 18-11 illustrates how to use the bubble sort algorithm in a program.

EXAMPLE 18-11 (BUBBLE SORT)

```cpp
#include <iostream>
#include "searchSortAlgorithms.h"

using namespace std;

template <class elemType>
void print(elemType list[], int length);
```

```
int main()
{
    int intList[] = {2, 56, 34, 25, 73,
                    46, 89, 10, 5, 16};          //Line 1

    cout << "Line 2: Before sorting, intList: "; //Line 2

    print(intList, 10);                          //Line 3

    cout << endl;                                //Line 4

    bubbleSort(intList, 10);                     //Line 5

    cout << "Line 6: After sorting, intList: ";  //Line 6

    print(intList, 10);                          //Line 7

    return 0;
}

template <class elemType>
void print(elemType list[], int length)
{
    for (int i = 0; i < length; i++)
        cout << list[i] << " ";

    cout << endl;
}
```

Sample Run:

```
Line 2: Before sorting, intList: 2 56 34 25 73 46 89 10 5 16

Line 6: After sorting, intList: 2 5 10 16 25 34 46 56 73 89
```

The statement in Line 1 declares and initializes `intList` to be an array of 10 components of type `int`. The statement in Line 3 outputs the values of the array `intList` before sorting this array. The statement in Line 5 uses the function `bubbleSort` to sort `list`. Notice that both `intList` and its length (the number of elements) are passed as parameters to the function `bubbleSort`. The statement in Line 7 outputs the sorted `intList`.

Analysis: Bubble Sort

In the case of search algorithms, our only concern was with the number of key (item) comparisons. A sorting algorithm makes key comparisons and also moves the data. Therefore, in analyzing the sorting algorithm, we look at the number of key comparisons as well as the number of data movements.

Suppose a list L of length n is to be sorted using bubble sort. Consider the function **bubbleSort** as given in this chapter. This function contains nested **for** loops. Because L is of length n, the outer loop executes $n-1$ times. For each iteration of the outer loop, the inner loop executes a certain number of times. Let us consider the first iteration of the outer loop. During the first iteration of the outer loop, the number of iterations of the inner loop is $n-1$. So there are $n-1$ comparisons. Similarly, during the second iteration of the outer loop, the number of iterations of the inner loop is $n-2$, and so on. Thus, the total number of comparisons is:

$$(n-1) + (n-2) + \cdots + 2 + 1 = \frac{n(n-1)}{2} = \frac{1}{2}n^2 - \frac{1}{2}n = O(n^2).$$

In the worst case, the body of the **if** statement always executes. So in the worst case, the number of assignments is:

$$3\frac{n(n-1)}{2} = \frac{3}{2}n^2 - \frac{3}{2}n = O(n^2).$$

If the list is already sorted, which is the best case, the number of assignments is 0. It can be shown that, on average, bubble sort makes about $\frac{n(n-1)}{4}$ item assignments. However, the number of comparisons for the bubble sort, as given in this chapter, is always $\frac{n(n-1)}{2}$.

Therefore, to sort a list of size 1000, bubble sort makes about 500,000 key comparisons and about 250,000 item assignments. The next section presents the selection sort algorithm that reduces the number of item assignments.

 NOTE Exercise 7 at the end of this chapter gives a version of the bubble sort algorithm in which the number of comparisons in the best case is $O(n)$.

Bubble Sort Algorithm and the `class` `unorderedArrayListType`

The **class** **unorderedArrayListType**, designed in Chapter 13, does not contain any sorting algorithm. Now that you know how to implement the bubble sort algorithm, you can learn how to use it in the **class** **unorderedArrayListType**.

To use the binary search algorithm within the **class** **unorderedArrayListType**, we add the function **sort** to this class and call the functions **bubbleSort** with the appropriate parameters. (Note that we have also added the function to use the binary search algorithm.)

```
template <class elemType>
class unorderedArrayListType: public arrayListType<elemType>
```

```
{
public:
    void insertAt(int location, const elemType& insertItem);
    void insertEnd(const elemType& insertItem);
    void replaceAt(int location, const elemType& repItem);
    int seqSearch(const elemType& searchItem) const;
    void remove(const elemType& removeItem);

    void sort();
    int binSearch(const elemType& item) const;

    unorderedArrayListType(int size = 100);
      //Constructor
};
```

The definitions of the member functions `binSearch` and `sort` are:

```
template <class elemType>
int unorderedArrayListType<elemType>::
                    binSearch(const elemType& item) const
{
    return binarySearch(list, length, item);
}

template <class elemType>
void unorderedArrayListType<elemType>::sort()
{
    selectionSort(list, length);
}
```

We leave it as an exercise for you to write a program to test the member functions `sort` and `binSearch`.

Selection Sort: Array-Based Lists

Chapter 9 described the selection sort algorithm for array-based lists. However, the selection sort algorithm given in Chapter 9 works only for arrays of type `int`. In this section, using templates we give a generic selection sort algorithm. Note that the algorithm given here is slightly different than the one given in Chapter 8.

Suppose that `list` is the array to be sorted and `length` denotes the length, that is, the number of elements in `list`. As described in Chapter 8, a selection sort involves the following steps:

   a.   Find the location of the smallest element.

   b.   Move the smallest element to the beginning of the unsorted list.

Given the starting index, `first`, and the ending index, `last`, of the list, the following C++ function returns the index of the smallest element in `list[first]`... `list[last]`.

```
template <class elemType>
int minLocation(elemType list[], int first, int last)
{
    int loc, minIndex;

    minIndex = first;
    for (loc = first + 1; loc <= last; loc++)
        if (list[loc] < list[minIndex])
            minIndex = loc;

    return minIndex;
} //end minLocation
```

Given the locations in the list of the elements to be swapped, the following C++ function, swap, swaps those elements:

```
template <class elemType>
void swap(elemType list[], int first, int second)
{
    elemType temp;

    temp = list[first];
    list[first] = list[second];
    list[second] = temp;
} //end swap
```

We can now complete the definition of the function selectionSort:

```
template <class elemType>
void selectionSort(elemType list[], int length)
{
    int loc, minIndex;

    for (loc = 0; loc < length; loc++)
    {
        minIndex = minLocation(list, loc, length - 1);
        swap(list, loc, minIndex);
    }
} //end selectionSort
```

We leave it as an exercise for you to write a program to test the selection sort algorithm. (See Programming Exercise 6 at the end of this chapter.)

NOTE
1. A selection sort can also be implemented by selecting the largest element in the unsorted portion of the list and moving it to the bottom of the list. You can easily implement this form of selection sort by altering the if statement in the function minLocation and passing the appropriate parameters to both the corresponding function and the function swap (when these functions are called in the function selectionSort).

2. A selection sort can also be applied to linked lists. The general algorithm is the same, and the details are left as an exercise for you. See Programming Exercise 7 at the end of this chapter.

Analysis: Selection Sort

Suppose that a list L of length n is to be sorted using the selection sort algorithm. The function swap does three item assignments and is executed $n - 1$ times. Hence, the number of item assignments is $3(n - 1) = O(n)$.

The key comparisons are made by the function minLocation. For a list of length k, the function minLocation makes $k - 1$ key comparisons. Also, the function minLocation is executed $n - 1$ times (by the function selectionSort). The first time, the function minLocation finds the index of the smallest key item in the entire list and, therefore, makes $n - 1$ comparisons. The second time, the function minLocation finds the index of the smallest element in the sublist of length $n - 1$ and so makes $n - 2$ comparisons, and so on. Hence, the number of key comparisons is as follows:

$$(n - 1) + (n - 2) + \cdots + 2 + 1 = \frac{n(n - 1)}{2}$$
$$= \frac{1}{2}n^2 - \frac{1}{2}n$$
$$= \frac{1}{2}n^2 + O(n)$$
$$= O(n^2).$$

It thus follows that if $n = 1000$, the number of key comparisons the selection sort algorithm makes is:

$$\frac{1}{2}(1000)^2 - \frac{1}{2}(1000) = 499500 \approx 500000.$$

Note that the selection sort algorithm does not depend on the initial arrangement of the data. The number of comparisons is always $O(n^2)$ and the number of assignments is $O(n)$. In general, this algorithm is good only for small lists because $O(n^2)$ grows rapidly as n grows. However, if data movement is expensive and the number of comparisons is not, then this algorithm could be a better choice over other algorithms.

Insertion Sort: Array-Based Lists

The previous section described and analyzed the selection sort algorithm. It was shown that if $n = 1000$, the number of key comparisons is approximately 500,000, which is quite high. This section describes the sorting algorithm called the **insertion sort**, which tries to improve—that is, reduce—the number of key comparisons.

The insertion sort algorithm sorts the list by moving each element to its proper place in the sorted portion of the list. Consider the list given in Figure 18-11.

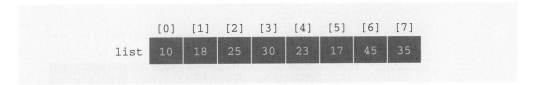

FIGURE 18-11 `list`

The length of the list is 8. In this list, the elements `list[0]`, `list[1]`, `list[2]`, and `list[3]` are in order. That is, `list[0]...list[3]` is sorted (see Figure 18-12).

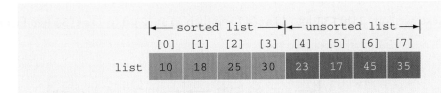

FIGURE 18-12 Sorted and unsorted portion of `list`

Next, we consider the element `list[4]`, the first element of the unsorted list. Because `list[4] < list[3]`, we need to move the element `list[4]` to its proper location. It thus follows that element `list[4]` should be moved to `list[2]` (see Figure 18-13).

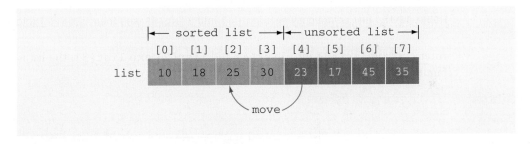

FIGURE 18-13 Move `list[4]` into `list[2]`

To move `list[4]` into `list[2]`, first we copy `list[4]` into `temp`, a temporary memory space (see Figure 18-14).

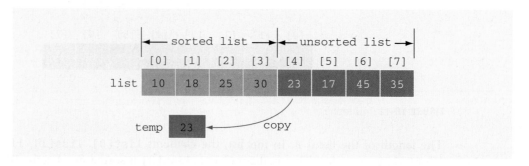

FIGURE 18-14 Copy list[4] into temp

Next, we copy list[3] into list[4] and then list[2] into list[3] (see Figure 18-15).

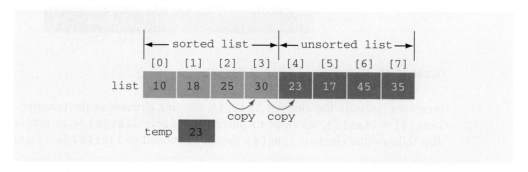

FIGURE 18-15 List before copying list[3] into list[4] and then list[2] into list[3]

After copying list[3] into list[4] and list[2] into list[3], the list is as shown in Figure 18-16.

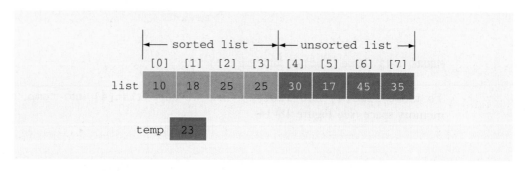

FIGURE 18-16 List after copying list[3] into list[4] and then list[2] into list[3]

We now copy `temp` into `list[2]`. Figure 18-17 shows the resulting list.

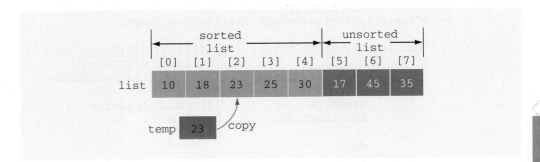

FIGURE 18-17 List after copying `temp` into `list[2]`

Now `list[0]...list[4]` is sorted, and `list[5]...list[7]` is unsorted. We repeat this process on the resulting list by moving the first element of the unsorted list into the sorted list in the proper place.

From this discussion, we see that during the sorting phase, the array containing the list is divided into two sublists: *sorted* and *unsorted*. Elements in the sorted sublist are in order; elements in the unsorted sublist are to be moved one at a time to their proper places in the sorted sublist. We use an index—say, `firstOutOfOrder`—to point to the first element in the unsorted sublist; that is, `firstOutOfOrder` gives the index of the first element in the unsorted portion of the array. Initially, `firstOutOfOrder` is initialized to `1`.

This discussion translates into the following pseudocode algorithm:

```
for (firstOutOfOrder = 1; firstOutOfOrder < length; firstOutOfOrder++)
  if (list[firstOutOfOrder] is less than list[firstOutOfOrder - 1])
  {
      copy list[firstOutOfOrder] into temp

      initialize location to firstOutOfOrder

      do
      {
          a. copy list[location - 1] into list[location]
          b. decrement location by 1 to consider the next element
             of the sorted portion of the array
      }
      while (location > 0 && the list element at location - 1 is
                            greater than temp)
  }
copy temp into list[location]
```

The following C++ function implements the previous algorithm:

```cpp
template <class elemType>
void insertionSort(elemType list[], int length)
{
    for (int firstOutOfOrder = 1; firstOutOfOrder < length;
                                  firstOutOfOrder++)
        if (list[firstOutOfOrder] < list[firstOutOfOrder - 1])
        {
            elemType temp = list[firstOutOfOrder];
            int location = firstOutOfOrder;

            do
            {
                list[location] = list[location - 1];
                location--;
            }
            while (location > 0 && list[location - 1] > temp);

            list[location] = temp;
        }
} //end insertionSort
```

We leave it as an exercise for you to write a program to test the insertion sort algorithm. (See Programming Exercise 8 at the end of this chapter.)

 NOTE An insertion sort can also be applied to linked lists. The general algorithm is the same, and the details are left as an exercise for you. See Programming Exercise 9 at the end of this chapter.

Analysis: Insertion Sort

Let L be a list of length n. Suppose L is to be sorted using insertion sort. The `for` loop executes $n - 1$ times. In the best case, when the list is already sorted, for each iteration of the `for` loop, the `if` statement evaluates to `false`, so there are $n - 1$ key comparisons. Thus, in the best case, the number of key comparisons is $n - 1 = O(n)$. Let us consider the worst case. In this case, for each iteration of the `for` loop, the `if` statement evaluates to `true`. Moreover, in the worst case, for each iteration of the `for` loop, the `do...while` loop executes `firstOutOfOrder - 1` times. It follows that in the worst case, the number of key comparisons is:

$$1 + 2 + \cdots + (n - 1) = n(n - 1)/2 = O(n^2).$$

It can be shown that the average number of key comparisons and the average number of item assignments in an insertion sort algorithm are:

$$\frac{1}{4}n^2 + O(n) = O(n^2).$$

Table 18-9 summarizes the behavior of the bubble sort, selection sort, and insertion sort algorithms.

TABLE 18-9 Average Case Behavior of the Bubble Sort, Selection Sort, and Insertion Sort Algorithms for a List of Length n

Algorithm	Number of Comparisons	Number of Swaps
Bubble sort	$\dfrac{n(n-1)}{2} = O(n^2)$	$\dfrac{n(n-1)}{4} = O(n^2)$
Selection sort	$\dfrac{n(n-1)}{2} = O(n^2)$	$3(n-1) = O(n)$
Insertion sort	$\dfrac{1}{4}n^2 + O(n) = O(n^2)$	$\dfrac{1}{4}n^2 + O(n) = O(n^2)$

Lower Bound on Comparison-Based Sort Algorithms

In the previous sections, we discussed the selection and insertion sort algorithms and noted that the average-case behavior of these algorithms is $O(n^2)$. Both of these algorithms are comparison based; that is, the lists are sorted by comparing their respective keys. Before discussing any additional sorting algorithms, let us discuss the best-case scenario for comparison-based sorting algorithms.

We can trace the execution of a comparison-based algorithm by using a graph called a **comparison tree**. Let L be a list of n distinct elements, wherein $n > 0$. For any j and k, wherein $1 \leq j \leq n$ and $1 \leq k \leq n$, either $L[j] < L[k]$ or $L[j] > L[k]$. Because each comparison of the keys has two outcomes, the comparison tree is a **binary tree**. While drawing this figure, we draw each comparison as a circle called a **node**. The node is labeled as $j{:}k$, representing the comparison of $L[j]$ with $L[k]$. If $L[j] < L[k]$, follow the left branch; otherwise, follow the right branch. Figure 18-18 shows the comparison tree for a list of length 3. (In Figure 18-18, the rectangle, called a **leaf**, represents the final ordering of the nodes.)

18

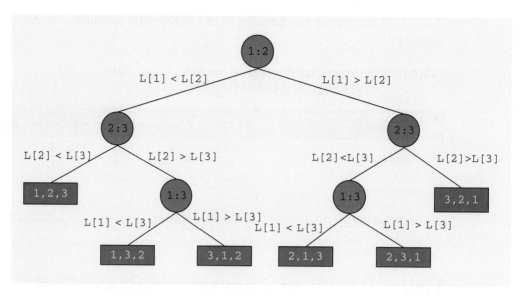

FIGURE 18-18 Comparison tree for sorting three items

We call the top node in the figure the **root** node. The straight line that connects the two nodes is called a **branch**. A sequence of branches from a node, x, to another node, y, is called a **path** from x to y.

Associated with each path from the root to a leaf is a unique permutation of the elements of L. This uniqueness follows because the sort algorithm only moves the data and makes comparisons. Furthermore, the data movement on any path from the root to a leaf is the same regardless of the initial inputs. For a list of n elements, $n > 0$, there are $n!$ different permutations. Any one of these $n!$ permutations might be the correct ordering of L. Thus, the comparison tree must have at least $n!$ leaves.

Now let us consider the worst case for all comparison-based sorting algorithms. We state the following result without proof.

Theorem: Let L be a list of n distinct elements. Any sorting algorithm that sorts L by comparison of the keys only, in its worst case, makes at least $O(n\log_2 n)$ key comparisons.

As analyzed in the previous sections, both the selection and insertion sort algorithms are of the order $O(n^2)$. The remainder of this chapter discusses sorting algorithms that, on average, are of the order $O(n\log_2 n)$.

Quick Sort: Array-Based Lists

In the previous section, we noted that the lower bound on comparison-based algorithms is $O(n\log_2 n)$. The sorting algorithms bubble sort, selection sort, and insertion sort, discussed earlier in this chapter, are of the order $O(n^2)$. In this and the next two sections, we discuss sorting algorithms that are of the order $O(n\log_2 n)$. The first algorithm is the quick sort algorithm.

The quick sort algorithm uses the divide-and-conquer technique to sort a list. The list is partitioned into two sublists, which are then sorted and combined into one list in such a way so that the combined list is sorted. Thus, the general algorithm is:

```
if (the list size is greater than 1)
{
    a. Partition the list into two sublists, say lowerSublist and
       upperSublist.
    b. Quick sort lowerSublist.
    c. Quick sort upperSublist.
    d. Combine the sorted lowerSublist and sorted upperSublist.
}
```

After partitioning the list into two sublists called `lowerSublist` and `upperSublist`, the sublists are sorted using the quick sort algorithm. In other words, we use *recursion* to implement the quick sort algorithm.

The quick sort algorithm described here is for array-based lists. The algorithm for linked lists can be developed in a similar manner and is left as an exercise for you.

In the quick sort algorithm, the list is partitioned in such way that combining the sorted `lowerSublist` and `upperSublist` is trivial. Therefore, in a quick sort, all of the sorting work is done in partitioning the list. Because all of the sorting work occurs during the partitioning of the list, we first describe the partition procedure in detail.

To partition the list into two sublists, first we choose an element of the list called **pivot**. The pivot is used to divide the list into two sublists: `lowerSublist` and `upperSublist`. The elements in `lowerSublist` are smaller than `pivot`, and the elements in `upperSublist` are greater than or equal to `pivot`. For example, consider the list in Figure 18-19.

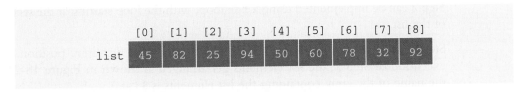

FIGURE 18-19 `list` before the partition

There are several ways to determine `pivot`. However, `pivot` is chosen so that, it is hoped, `lowerSublist` and `upperSublist` are of nearly equal size. For illustration purposes, let us choose the middle element of the list as `pivot`. The partition procedure that we describe partitions this list using `pivot` as the middle element, in our case 50, as shown in Figure 18-20.

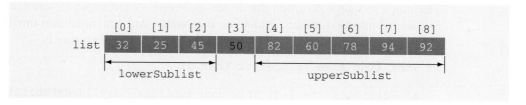

FIGURE 18-20 `list` after the partition

From Figure 18-20, it follows that after partitioning `list` into `lowerSublist` and `upperSublist`, `pivot` is in the right place. Thus, after sorting `lowerSublist` and `upperSublist`, combining the two sorted sublists is trivial.

The partition algorithm is as follows (we assume that `pivot` is chosen as the middle element of the list).

1. Determine `pivot`, and swap `pivot` with the first element of the list.

   Suppose that the index `smallIndex` points to the last element less than `pivot`. The index `smallIndex` is initialized to the first element of the list.

2. For the remaining elements in the list (starting at the second element):

   If the current element is less than `pivot`,

   a. Increment `smallIndex`.
   b. Swap the current element with the array element pointed to by `smallIndex`.

3. Swap the first element, that is, `pivot`, with the array element pointed to by `smallIndex`.

Step 2 can be implemented using a **for** loop, with the loop starting at the second element of the list.

Step 1 determines the `pivot` and moves `pivot` to the first array position. During the execution of Step 2, the list elements get arranged as shown in Figure 18-21. (Suppose the name of the array containing the list elements is `list`.)

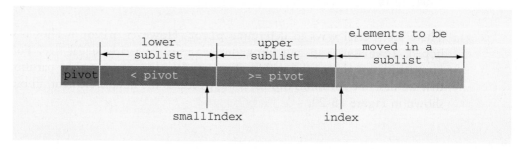

FIGURE 18-21 List during the execution of Step 2

As shown in Figure 18-21, `pivot` is in the first array position. Elements in the lower sublist are less than `pivot`; elements in the upper sublist are greater than or equal to `pivot`. The variable `smallIndex` contains the index of the last element of the lower sublist; the variable `index` contains the index of the next element that needs to be moved, either in the lower sublist or in the upper sublist. As explained in Step 2, if the next element of the list (that is, `list[index]`) is less than `pivot`, we advance `smallIndex` to the next array position and swap `list[index]` with `list[smallIndex]`. Next, we illustrate Step 2.

Suppose that the list is as given in Figure 18-22.

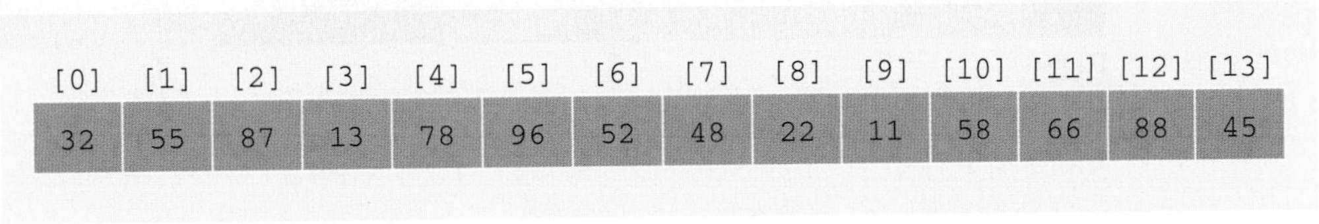

[0] [1] [2] [3] [4] [5] [6] [7] [8] [9] [10] [11] [12] [13]
32 55 87 13 78 96 52 48 22 11 58 66 88 45

FIGURE 18-22 List before sorting

Step 1 requires us to determine the `pivot` and swap it with the first array element. For the list in Figure 18-22, the middle element is at the position `(0 + 13) / 2 = 6`. That is, `pivot` is at position `6`. Therefore, after swapping `pivot` with the first array element, the list is as shown in Figure 18-23. (Notice that in Figure 18-23, `52` is swapped with `32`.)

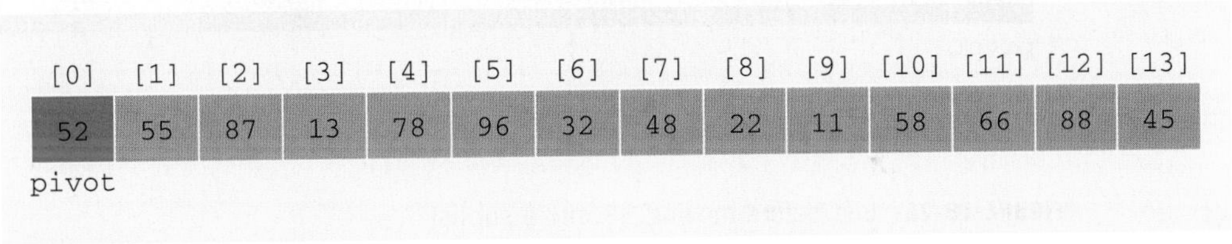

[0] [1] [2] [3] [4] [5] [6] [7] [8] [9] [10] [11] [12] [13]
52 55 87 13 78 96 32 48 22 11 58 66 88 45
pivot

FIGURE 18-23 List after moving `pivot` to the first array position

Suppose that after executing Step 2 a few times, the list is as shown in Figure 18-24.

lower
sublist
upper
sublist
52 13 32 48 22 96 87 55 78 11 58 66 88 45
pivot
smallIndex
index

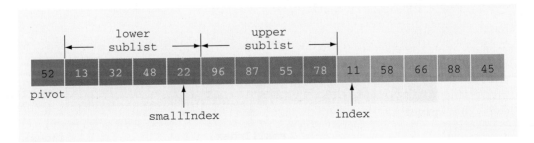

FIGURE 18-24 List after a few iterations of Step 2

As shown in Figure 18-24, the next element of the list that needs to be moved into a sublist is indicated by index. Because list[index] < pivot, we need to move the element list[index] into the lower sublist. To do so, we first advance smallIndex to the next array position and then swap list[smallIndex] with list[index]. The resulting list is as shown in Figure 18-25. (Notice that 11 is swapped with 96.)

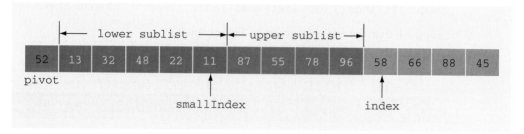

FIGURE 18-25 List after moving 11 into the lower sublist

Now consider the list in Figure 18-26.

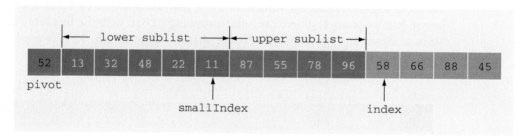

FIGURE 18-26 List before moving 58 into a sublist

For the list in Figure 18-26, list[index] is 58, which is greater than pivot. Therefore, list[index] is to be moved into the upper sublist. This is accomplished by leaving 58 at its position and increasing the size of the upper sublist by one, to the next array position. After moving 58 into the upper sublist, the list is as shown in Figure 18-27.

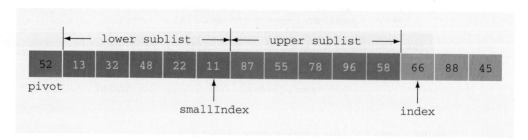

FIGURE 18-27 List after moving 58 into the upper sublist

After moving the elements that are less than `pivot` into the lower sublist and elements that are greater than `pivot` into the upper sublist (that is, after completely executing Step 2), the resulting list is as shown in Figure 18-28.

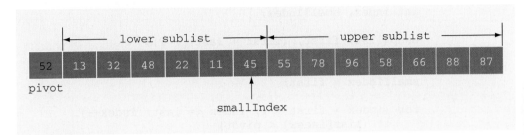

FIGURE 18-28 List elements after arranging into the lower sublist and upper sublist

Next, we execute Step 3 and move `52`, `pivot`, to the proper position in the list. This is accomplished by swapping `52` with `45`. The resulting list is as shown in Figure 18-29.

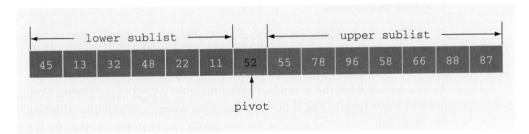

FIGURE 18-29 List after swapping `52` with `45`

As shown in Figure 18-29, Steps 1, 2, and 3 in the preceding algorithm partition the list into two sublists. The elements less than `pivot` are in the lower sublist; the elements greater than or equal to `pivot` are in the upper sublist.

To partition the list into the lower and upper sublists, we need to keep track of only the last element of the lower sublist and the next element of the list that needs to be moved into either the lower sublist or the upper sublist. In fact, the upper sublist is between the two indices `smallIndex` and `index`.

We now write the function, `partition`, to implement the preceding partition algorithm. After rearranging the elements of the list, the function `partition` returns the location of `pivot` so that we can determine the starting and ending locations of the sublists. The definition of the function `partition` is:

```
template <class elemType>
int partition(elemType list[], int first, int last)
{
    elemType pivot;

    int index, smallIndex;

    swap(list, first, (first + last) / 2);

    pivot = list[first];
    smallIndex = first;

    for (index = first + 1; index <= last; index++)
        if (list[index] < pivot)
        {
            smallIndex++;
            swap(list, smallIndex, index);
        }

    swap(list, first, smallIndex);

    return smallIndex;
} //end partition
```

Note that the formal parameters `first` and `last` specify the starting and ending indices, respectively, of the sublist of the `list` to be partitioned. If `first = 0` and `last = length – 1`, the entire list is partitioned.

As you can see from the definition of the function `partition`, certain elements of the list need to be swapped. The following function, `swap`, accomplishes this task. (Notice that this `swap` function is the same as the one given earlier in this chapter for the selection sort algorithm.)

```
template <class elemType>
void swap(elemType list[], int first, int second)
{
    elemType temp;

    temp = list[first];
    list[first] = list[second];
    list[second] = temp;
} //end swap
```

Once the list is partitioned into `lowerSublist` and `upperSublist`, we again apply the quick sort function to sort the two sublists. Because both sublists are sorted using the same quick sort algorithm, the easiest way to implement this algorithm is to use recursion. Therefore, this section gives the recursive version of the quick sort algorithm. As explained previously, after rearranging the elements of the list, the function `partition` returns the index of `pivot` so that the starting and ending indices of the sublists can be determined.

Given the starting and ending indices of a list, the following function, `recQuickSort`, implements the recursive version of the quick sort algorithm:

```
template <class elemType>
void recQuickSort(elemType list[], int first, int last)
{
    int pivotLocation;

    if (first < last)
    {
        pivotLocation = partition(list, first, last);
        recQuickSort(list, first, pivotLocation - 1);
        recQuickSort(list, pivotLocation + 1, last);
    }
} //end recQuickSort
```

Finally, we write the quick sort function, `quickSort`, that calls the function `recQuickSort` on the original list:

```
template <class elemType>
void quickSort(elemType list[], int length)
{
    recQuickSort(list, 0, length - 1);
} //end quickSort
```

We leave it as an exercise for you to write a program to test the quick sort algorithm. See Programming Exercise 10 at the end of this chapter.

Analysis: Quick Sort

The general analysis of the quick sort algorithm is beyond the scope of this book. However, let us determine the number of comparisons in the worst case. Suppose that L is a list of n elements, $n \geq 0$. In a quick sort, all of the sorting work is done by the function `partition`. From the definition of the function `partition`, it follows that to partition a list of length k, the function `partition` makes $k - 1$ key comparisons. Also, in the worst case, after partition, one sublist is of length $k - 1$, and the other sublist is of length 0.

It follows that in the worst case, the first call of the function `partition` makes $n - 1$ key comparisons. In the second call, the function `partition` partitions a list of length $n - 1$, so it makes $n - 2$ key comparisons, and so on. We can now conclude that to sort a list of length n, in the worst case, the total number of key comparisons made by a quick sort is:

$$(n - 1) + (n - 2) + \cdots + 2 + 1 = n(n - 1)/2 = O(n^2).$$

Table 18-10 summarizes the behavior of the quick sort algorithm for a list of length n.

TABLE 18-10 Analysis of the Quick Sort Algorithm for a List of Length n

	Number of Comparisons	Number of Swaps
Average case	$(1.39)n\log_2 n + O(n) = O(n\log_2 n)$	$(0.69)n\log_2 n + O(n) = O(n\log_2 n)$
Worst case	$\dfrac{n^2}{2} - \dfrac{n}{2} = O(n^2)$	$\dfrac{n^2}{2} + \dfrac{3n}{2} - 2 = O(n^2)$

Merge Sort: Linked List-Based Lists

In the previous section, we described the quick sort algorithm and stated that the average-case behavior of a quick sort is $O(n\log_2 n)$. However, the worst-case behavior of a quick sort is $O(n^2)$. This section describes the sorting algorithm whose behavior is always $O(n\log_2 n)$.

Like the quick sort algorithm, the merge sort algorithm uses the divide-and-conquer technique to sort a list. A merge sort algorithm also partitions the list into two sublists, sorts the sublists, and then combines the sorted sublists into one sorted list. This section describes the merge sort algorithm for linked list-based lists. We leave it for you to develop the merge sort algorithm for array-based lists, which can be done by using the techniques described for linked lists.

The merge sort and the quick sort algorithms differ in how they partition the list. As discussed earlier, a quick sort first selects an element in the list, called `pivot`, and then partitions the list so that the elements in one sublist are less than `pivot` and the elements in the other sublist are greater than or equal to `pivot`. By contrast, a merge sort divides the list into two sublists of nearly equal size. For example, consider the list whose elements are as follows:

```
list: 35  28  18  45  62  48  30  38
```

The merge sort algorithm partitions this list into two sublists as follows:

```
first sublist: 35  28  18  45
second sublist: 62  48  30  38
```

The two sublists are sorted using the same algorithm (that is, a merge sort) used on the original list. Suppose that we have sorted the two sublists. That is, suppose that the lists are now as follows:

```
first sublist: 18  28  35  45
second sublist: 30  38  48  62
```

Next, the merge sort algorithm combines, that is, merges, the two sorted sublists into one sorted list.

Figure 18-30 further illustrates the merge sort process.

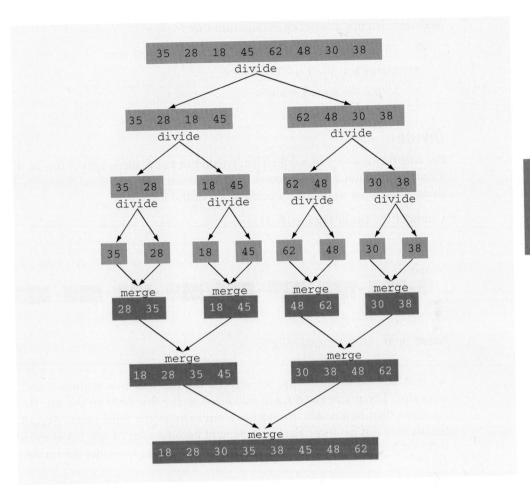

FIGURE 18-30 Merge sort algorithm

From Figure 18-30, it is clear that in the merge sort algorithm, most of the sorting work is done in merging the sorted sublists.

The general algorithm for the merge sort is as follows:

```
if the list is of a size greater than 1
{
    a. Divide the list into two sublists.
    b. Merge sort the first sublist.
    c. Merge sort the second sublist.
    d. Merge the first sublist and the second sublist.
}
```

As remarked previously, after dividing the list into two sublists—the first sublist and the second sublist—the two sublists are sorted using the merge sort algorithm. In other words, we use recursion to implement the merge sort algorithm.

We next describe the necessary algorithm to:

- Divide the list into two sublists of nearly equal size.
- Merge sort both sublists.
- Merge the sorted sublists.

Divide

Because data is stored in a linked list, we do not know the length of the list. Furthermore, a linked list is not a random access data structure. Therefore, to divide the list into two sublists, we need to find the middle node of the list.

Consider the list in Figure 18-31.

FIGURE 18-31 Unsorted linked list

To find the middle of the list, we traverse the list with two pointers—say, `middle` and `current`. The pointer `middle` is initialized to the first node of the list. Because this list has more than two nodes, we initialize `current` to the third node. (Recall that we sort the list only if it has more than one element because a list of size 1 is already sorted. Also, if the list has only two nodes, we set `current` to NULL.) Consider the list shown in Figure 18-32.

FIGURE 18-32 `middle` and `current` before traversing the list

Every time we advance `middle` by one node, we advance `current` by one node. After advancing `current` by one node, if `current` is not NULL, we again advance `current` by one node. That is, for the most part, every time `middle` advances by one node, `current` advances by two nodes. Eventually, `current` becomes NULL and `middle` points to the last node of the first sublist. For example, for the list in Figure 18-32, when `current` becomes NULL, `middle` points to the node with `info 25` (see Figure 18-33).

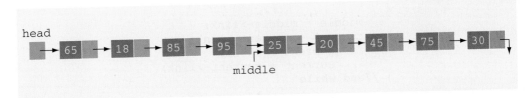

FIGURE 18-33 `middle` after traversing the list

It is now easy to divide the list into two sublists. First, using the link of `middle`, we assign a pointer to the node following `middle`. Then, we set the link of `middle` to NULL. Figure 18-34 shows the resulting sublists.

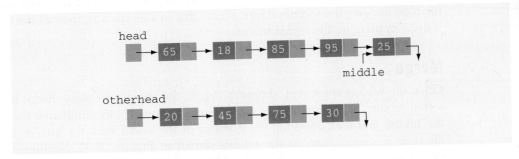

FIGURE 18-34 List after dividing it into two lists

This discussion translates into the following C++ function, `divideList`:

```cpp
template <class Type>
void unorderedLinkedList<Type>::
            divideList(nodeType<Type>* first1,
                       nodeType<Type>* &first2)
{
    nodeType<Type>* middle;
    nodeType<Type>* current;

    if (first1 == NULL)     //list is empty
        first2 = NULL;
    else if (first1->link == NULL)  //list has only one node
        first2 = NULL;
    else
    {
        middle = first1;
        current = first1->link;

        if (current != NULL)    //list has more than two nodes
            current = current->link;
        while (current != NULL)
```

```
        {
            middle = middle->link;
            current = current->link;
            if (current != NULL)
                current = current->link;
        } //end while

        first2 = middle->link;  //first2 points to the first
                                //node of the second sublist
        middle->link = NULL;    //set the link of the last node
                                //of the first sublist to NULL
    } //end else
} //end divideList
```

Now that we know how to divide a list into two sublists of nearly equal size, next we focus on merging the sorted sublists. Recall that in a merge sort, most of the sorting work is done in merging the sorted sublists.

Merge

Once the sublists are sorted, the next step in the merge sort algorithm is to merge the sorted sublists. Sorted sublists are merged into a sorted list by comparing the elements of the sublists and then adjusting the pointers of the nodes with the smaller `info`. Let us illustrate this procedure on the sublists shown in Figure 18-35. Suppose that `first1` points to the first node of the first sublist, and `first2` points to the first node of the second sublist.

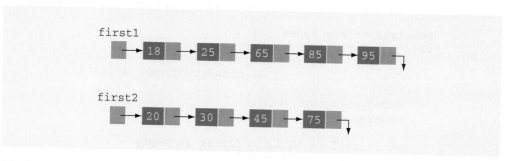

FIGURE 18-35 Sublists before merging

We first compare the `info` of the first node of each sublist to determine the first node of the merged list. We set `newHead` to point to the first node of the merged list. We also use the pointer `lastMerged` to keep track of the last node of the merged list. The pointer of the first node of the sublist with the smaller node then advances to the next node of that sublist. Figure 18-36 shows the sublist of Figure 18-35 after setting `newHead` and `lastMerged` and advancing `first1`.

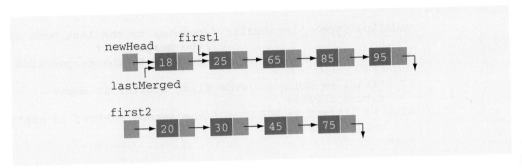

FIGURE 18-36 Sublists after setting `newHead` and `lastMerged` and advancing `first1`

In Figure 18-36, `first1` points to the first node of the first sublist that is yet to be merged with the second sublist. So, we again compare the nodes pointed to by `first1` and `first2`, and adjust the link of the smaller node and the last node of the merged list so as to move the smaller node to the end of the merged list. For the sublists shown in Figure 18-36, after adjusting the necessary links, we have Figure 18-37.

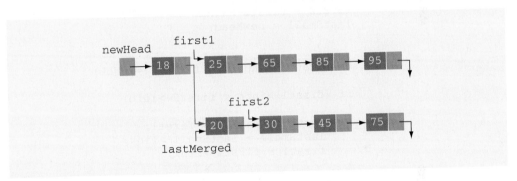

FIGURE 18-37 Merged list after putting the node with `info` 20 at the end of the merged list

We continue this process for the remaining elements of both sublists. Every time we move a node to the merged list, we advance either `first1` or `first2` to the next node. Eventually, either `first1` or `first2` becomes NULL. If `first1` becomes NULL, the first sublist is exhausted first, so we attach the remaining nodes of the second sublist at the end of the partially merged list. If `first2` becomes NULL, the second sublist is exhausted first, so we attach the remaining nodes of the first sublist at the end of the partially merged list.

Following this discussion, we can now write the C++ function `mergeList` to merge the two sorted sublists. The pointers of the first nodes of the sublists are passed as parameters to the function `mergeList`.

```
template <class Type>
nodeType<Type>* unorderedLinkedList<Type>::
                mergeList(nodeType<Type>* first1,
                          nodeType<Type>* first2)
```

```
{
    nodeType<Type> *lastSmall;  //pointer to the last node of
                                //the merged list
    nodeType<Type> *newHead;    //pointer to the merged list

    if (first1 == NULL)    //the first sublist is empty
        return first2;
    else if (first2 == NULL)    //the second sublist is empty
        return first1;
    else
    {
        if (first1->info < first2->info) //compare the
                                         //first nodes
        {
            newHead = first1;
            first1 = first1->link;
            lastSmall = newHead;
        }
        else
        {
            newHead = first2;
            first2 = first2->link;
            lastSmall = newHead;
        }

        while (first1 != NULL && first2 != NULL)
        {
            if (first1->info < first2->info)
            {
                lastSmall->link = first1;
                lastSmall = lastSmall->link;
                first1 = first1->link;
            }
            else
            {
                lastSmall->link = first2;
                lastSmall = lastSmall->link;
                first2 = first2->link;
            }
        } //end while

        if (first1 == NULL) //first sublist is exhausted first
            lastSmall->link = first2;
        else                //second sublist is exhausted first
            lastSmall->link = first1;

        return newHead;
    }
}//end mergeList
```

Finally, we write the recursive merge sort function, recMergeSort, which uses the divideList and mergeList functions to sort a list. The pointer of the first node of the list to be sorted is passed as a parameter to the function recMergeSort.

```
template <class Type>
void unorderedLinkedList<Type>::recMergeSort(
                                    nodeType<Type>* &head)
{
    nodeType<Type> *otherHead;

    if (head != NULL)     //if the list is not empty
        if (head->link != NULL)   //if the list has more than
                                  //one node
        {
            divideList(head, otherHead);
            recMergeSort(head);
            recMergeSort(otherHead);
            head = mergeList(head, otherHead);
        }
} //end recMergeSort
```

We can now give the definition of the function mergeSort, which should be included as a public member of the class unorderedLinkedList. (Note that the functions divideList, merge, and recMergeSort can be included as private members of the class unorderedLinkedList because these functions are used only to implement the function mergeSort.) The function mergeSort calls the function recMergeSort and passes first to this function. It also sets last to point to the last node of the list. The definition of the function mergeSort is:

```
template <class Type>
void unorderedLinkedList<Type>::mergeSort()
{
    recMergeSort(first);

    if (first == NULL)
        last = NULL;
    else
    {
        last = first;
        while (last->link != NULL)
            last = last->link;
    }
} //end mergeSort
```

We leave it as an exercise for you to write a program to test the merge sort algorithm. See Programming Exercise 13 at the end of this chapter.

Analysis: Merge Sort

Suppose that L is a list of n elements, in which $n > 0$. Suppose that n is a power of 2, that is, $n = 2^m$ for some nonnegative integer m, so that we can divide the list into two sublists, each of size:

$$\frac{n}{2} = \frac{2^m}{2} = 2^{m-1}.$$

Moreover, each sublist can also be divided into two sublists of the same size. Each call to the function recMergeSort makes two recursive calls to the function recMergeSort, and each call divides the sublist into two sublists of the same size. Suppose that $m = 3$, that is, $n = 2^3 = 8$. So, the length of the original list is 8. The first call to the function recMergeSort divides the original list into two sublists, each of size 4. The first call then makes two recursive calls to the function recMergeSort. Each of these recursive calls divides each sublist, of size 4, into two sublists, each of size 2. We now have four sublists, each of size 2. The next set of recursive calls divides each sublist, of size 2, into sublists of size 1. So, we now have eight sublists, each of size 1. It follows that the exponent 3 in 2^3 indicates the level of the recursion (see Figure 18-38).

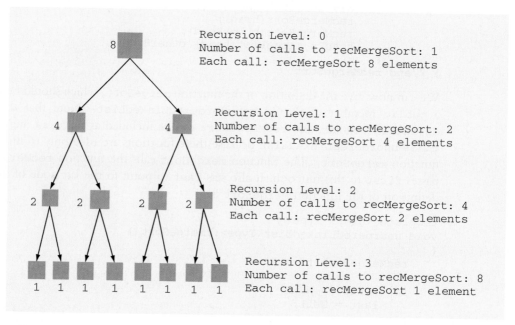

FIGURE 18-38   Levels of recursion to recMergeSort for a list of length 8

Let us consider the general case when $n = 2^m$. Note that the number of recursion levels is m. Also, note that to merge a sorted list of size s with a sorted list of size t, the maximum number of comparisons is $s + t - 1$.

Consider the function mergeList, which merges two sorted lists into a sorted list. Note that this is where the actual work (comparisons and assignments) is done. The initial call to the function recMergeSort, at level 0, produces two sublists, each of the size $n/2$. To merge these two lists, after they are sorted, the maximum number of comparisons is:

$$\frac{n}{2} + \frac{n}{2} - 1 = n - 1 = O(n).$$

At level 1, we merge two sets of sorted lists, in which each sublist is of the size $n/4$. To merge two sorted sublists, each of the size $n/4$, we need, at most:

$$\frac{n}{4} + \frac{n}{4} - 1 = \frac{n}{2} - 1$$

comparisons. Thus, at level 1 of the recursion, the number of comparisons is $2(n / 2 - 1) = n - 2 = O(n)$. In general, at level k of the recursion, there are a total of 2^k calls to the function `mergeList`. Each of these calls merges two sublists, each of the size $n / 2^{k+1}$, which requires a maximum of $n / 2^k - 1$ comparisons. Thus, at level k of the recursion, the maximum number of comparisons is:

$$2^k \left(\frac{n}{2^k} - 1 \right) = n - 2^k = O(n).$$

It now follows that the maximum number of comparisons at each level of the recursion is $O(n)$. Because the number of levels of the recursion is m, the maximum number of comparisons made by the merge sort algorithms is $O(nm)$. Now $n = 2^m$ implies that $m = \log_2 n$. Hence, the maximum number of comparisons made by the merge sort algorithm is $O(n \log_2 n)$.

If $W(n)$ denotes the number of key comparisons in the worst case to sort L, then $W(n) = O(n \log_2 n)$.

Let $A(n)$ denote the number of key comparisons in the average case. In the average case, during merge, one of the sublists will exhaust before the other list. From this, it follows that, on average, when merging two sorted sublists of combined size n, the number of comparisons will be less than $n - 1$. On average, it can be shown that the number of comparisons for merge sort is given by the following equation: If n is a power of 2, $A(n) = n \log_2 n - 1.25n = O(n \log_2 n)$. This is also a good approximation when n is not a power of 2.

NOTE We can also obtain an analysis of the merge sort algorithm by constructing and solving certain equations as follows. As noted before, in merge sort, all of the comparisons are made in the procedure `mergeList`, which merges two sorted sublists. If one sublist is of size s and the other sublist is of size t, then merging these lists would require, at most, $s + t - 1$ comparisons in the worst case. Hence:

$$W(n) = W(s) + W(t) + s + t - 1.$$

Note that $s = n / 2$ and $t = n / 2$. Suppose that $n = 2^m$. Then, $s = 2^{m-1}$ and $t = 2^{m-1}$. It follows that $s + t = n$. Hence:

$$W(n) = W(n/2) + W(n/2) + n - 1 = 2W(n/2) + n - 1, n > 0.$$

Also:

$$W(1) = 0.$$

It is known that when n is a power of 2, $W(n)$ is given by the following equation:

$$W(n) = n \log_2 n - (n - 1) = O(n \log_2 n).$$

NOTE **(Heap Sort)** This chapter also discusses the heap sort algorithm. This algorithm and its related exercises are available at the Web site, *www.course.com/malik/cpp,* accompanying this book.

PROGRAMMING EXAMPLE: Election Results

Watch
the Video

The presidential election for the student council of your local university is about to be held. The chair of the election committee wants to computerize the voting and has asked you to write a program to analyze the data and report the winner.

The university has four major divisions, and each division has several departments. For the election, the four divisions are labeled as region 1, region 2, region 3, and region 4. Each department in each division handles its own voting and reports the votes received by each candidate to the election committee. The voting is reported in the following form:

```
firstName lastName regionNumber numberOfVotes
```

The election committee wants the output in the following tabular form:

```
--------------------Election Results--------------------
```

Candidate Name	Region1	Region2	Votes Region3	Region4	Total
------------------	-------	-------	-------	-------	------
Sheila Bower	23	70	133	267	493
Danny Dillion	25	71	156	97	349
Lisa Fisher	110	158	0	0	268
Greg Goldy	75	34	134	0	243
Peter Lamba	285	56	0	46	387
Mickey Miller	112	141	156	67	476

```
Winner: Sheila Bower, Votes Received: 493

Total votes polled: 2216
```

The names of the candidates must be in alphabetical order in the output.

For this program, we assume that six candidates are seeking the student council's president post. This program can be enhanced to handle any number of candidates.

The data are provided in two files. One file, `candData.txt`, consists of the names of the candidates seeking the president's post. The names of the candidates in this file are in no particular order. In the second file, `voteData.txt`, each line consists of the voting results in the following form:

```
firstName lastName regionNumber numberOfVotes
```

Each line in the file `voteData.txt` consists of the candidate's name, the region number, and the number of votes received by the candidate in that region. There is one entry per line. For example, the input file containing the voting data looks like the following:

```
Greg Goldy 2 34
Mickey Miller 1 56
Lisa Fisher 2 56
Peter Lamba 1 78
Danny Dillion 4 29
Sheila Bower 4 78
    .
    .
    .
```

The first line indicates that `Greg Goldy` received 34 votes from region 2.

Input Two files: One containing the candidates' names and the other containing the voting data, as described previously.

Output The election results in a tabular form, as described previously, and the winner's name.

PROBLEM
ANALYSIS
AND
ALGORITHM
DESIGN

From the output, it is clear that the program must organize the voting data by region and calculate the total votes received by each candidate and polled for the election overall. Furthermore, the names of the candidates must appear in alphabetical order.

The main component of this program is a candidate. Therefore, first we will design the `class candidateType` to implement a candidate object. Moreover, in this program, we use an array of `candidateType` object to implement the list of candidates.

Every candidate has a name and receives votes. Because there are four regions, we can use an array of four components. In Example 10-10 (Chapter 10), we designed the `class personType` to implement the name of a person. Recall that an object of type `personType` can store the first name and the last name. Now that we have discussed operator overloading, we redesign the `class personType` and define the relational operators so that the names of two people can be compared. We will also overload the assignment operator for easy assignment and use the stream extraction and insertion operators for input/output. Because every candidate is a person, we will derive the `class candidateType` from the `class personType`.

personType The `class personType` implements the first name and last name of a person. Therefore, the `class personType` has two member variables: `firstName` to store the first name and `lastName` to store the last name. We declare these as protected so that the definition of the `class personType` can be easily extended to accommodate the requirements of a specific application needed to implement a person's name. The definition of the `class personType` is given next.

```
//**********************************************************
// Author: D.S. Malik
//
// class personType
// This class specifies the members to implement a person's
// name. It overloads the stream insertion and extraction
// operators and relational operators for comparison.
//**********************************************************

#include <string>

using namespace std;

class personType
{
    friend istream& operator>>(istream&, personType&);
    friend ostream& operator<<(ostream&, const personType&);

public:
    void setName(string first, string last);
      //Function to set firstName and lastName according
      //to the parameters.
      //Postcondition: firstName = first; lastName = last

    string getFirstName() const;
      //Function to return the first name.
      //Postcondition: The value of firstName is returned.

    string getLastName() const;
      //Function to return the last name.
      //Postcondition: The value of lastName is returned.

    personType(string first = "", string last = "");
      //Constructor
      //Sets firstName and lastName according to the
      //parameters. The default values of the parameters are
      //empty strings.
      //Postcondition: firstName = first; lastName = last

        //overload the relational operators
    bool operator==(const personType& right) const;
    bool operator!=(const personType& right) const;
    bool operator<=(const personType& right) const;
    bool operator<(const personType& right) const;
    bool operator>=(const personType& right) const;
    bool operator>(const personType& right) const;

protected:
    string firstName; //variable to store the first name
    string lastName;  //variable to store the last name
};
```

We now give the definitions of the functions to implement the various operations of the class personType.

The definitions of the member functions setName, getFirstName, getLastName, and the constructors are the same as those given in Chapter 10. We, therefore, consider the definitions of the functions to overload the relational and stream operators.

The names of two people are the same if their first and last names are the same. Therefore, the definition of the function to overload the equality operator is:

```
bool personType::operator==(const personType& right) const
{
    return (firstName == right.firstName
            && lastName == right.lastName);
}
```

The names of two people are different if either their first or last names are different. Therefore, the definition of the function to overload the not equal to operator is:

```
bool personType::operator!=(const personType& right) const
{
    return (firstName != right.firstName
         || lastName != right.lastName);
}
```

Similarly, the definitions of the functions to overload the remaining relational operators are:

```
bool personType::operator<=(const personType& right) const
{
    return (lastName <= right.lastName ||
            (lastName == right.lastName &&
             firstName <= right.firstName));
}

bool personType::operator<(const personType& right) const
{
    return (lastName < right.lastName ||
            (lastName == right.lastName &&
             firstName < right.firstName));
}

bool personType::operator>=(const personType& right) const
{
    return (lastName >= right.lastName ||
            (lastName == right.lastName &&
             firstName >= right.firstName));
}
```

18

```
bool personType::operator>(const personType& right) const
{
    return (lastName > right.lastName ||
            (lastName == right.lastName &&
             firstName > right.firstName));
}
```

The definitions of the functions to overload the stream extraction and insertion operators are given next.

```
istream& operator>>(istream& isObject, personType& pName)
{
    isObject >> pName.firstName >> pName.lastName;

    return isObject;
}
```

```
ostream& operator<<(ostream& osObject, const personType& pName)
{
    osObject << pName.firstName << " " << pName.lastName;

    return osObject;
}
```

Candidate   As remarked previously, the main component of this program is candidate. Every candidate has a name and can receive votes. Because there are four regions, we can use an array of four components to store the votes received.

There are six candidates. Therefore, we declare a list of six candidates of type `candidateType`. This chapter extended the `class unorderedArrayListType` by illustrating how to include the searching and sorting algorithms developed in this chapter. We will use this class to maintain the list of candidates. This list of candidates will be sorted and searched. Therefore, we must define (that is, overload) the assignment and relational operators for the `class candidateType` because these operators are used by the searching and sorting algorithms.

Data in the file containing the candidates' data consists of only the names of the candidates. Therefore, in addition to overloading the assignment operator so that the value of one object can be assigned to another object, we also overload the assignment operator for the `class candidateType` so that only the name (of the `personType`) of the candidate can be assigned to a candidate object. That is, we overload the assignment operator twice: once for objects of type `candidateType` and once for objects of types `candidateType` and `personType`.

```
//**************************************************************
// Author: D.S. Malik
//
// class candidateType
// This class specifies the members to implement the properties
```

```
// of a candidate. It overloads the assignment operator
// and relational operators for comparison.
//*************************************************************

#include <string>
#include "personType.h"

const int NO_OF_REGIONS = 4;

class candidateType: public personType
{
public:
    const candidateType& operator=(const candidateType&);
        //Overload the assignment operator for objects of the
        //type candidateType.

    const candidateType& operator=(const personType&);
        //Overload the assignment operator for objects so that
        //the value of an object of type personType can be
        //assigned to an object of type candidateType.

    void updateVotesByRegion(int region, int votes);
        //Function to update the votes of a candidate for a
        //particular region.
        //Postcondition: Votes for the region specified by
        //               the parameter are updated by adding
        //               the votes specified by the parameter
        //               votes.

    void setVotes(int region, int votes);
        //Function to set the votes of a candidate for a
        //particular region.
        //Postcondition: Votes for the region specified by
        //               the parameter region are set to the votes
        //               specified by the parameter votes.

    void calculateTotalVotes();
        //Function to calculate the total votes received by a
        //candidate.
        //Postcondition: The votes in each region are added
        //               and assigned to totalVotes.

    int getTotalVotes() const;
        //Function to return the total votes received by a
        //candidate.
        //Postcondition: The value of totalVotes is returned.

    void printData() const;
        //Function to output the candidate's name, the votes
        //received in each region, and the total votes received.
```

18

```
candidateType();
   //Default constructor.
   //Postcondition: Candidate's name is initialized to
   //               blanks, the number of votes in each
   //               region, and the total votes are
   //               initialized to 0.

      //Overload the relational operators.
   bool operator==(const candidateType& right) const;
   bool operator!=(const candidateType& right) const;
   bool operator<=(const candidateType& right) const;
   bool operator<(const candidateType& right) const;
   bool operator>=(const candidateType& right) const;
   bool operator>(const candidateType& right) const;

private:
   int votesByRegion[NO_OF_REGIONS];   //array to store the
                                       //votes received in
                                       //each region

   int totalVotes; //variable to store the total votes
};
```

Figure 18-39 shows the UML diagram of the **class** candidateType.

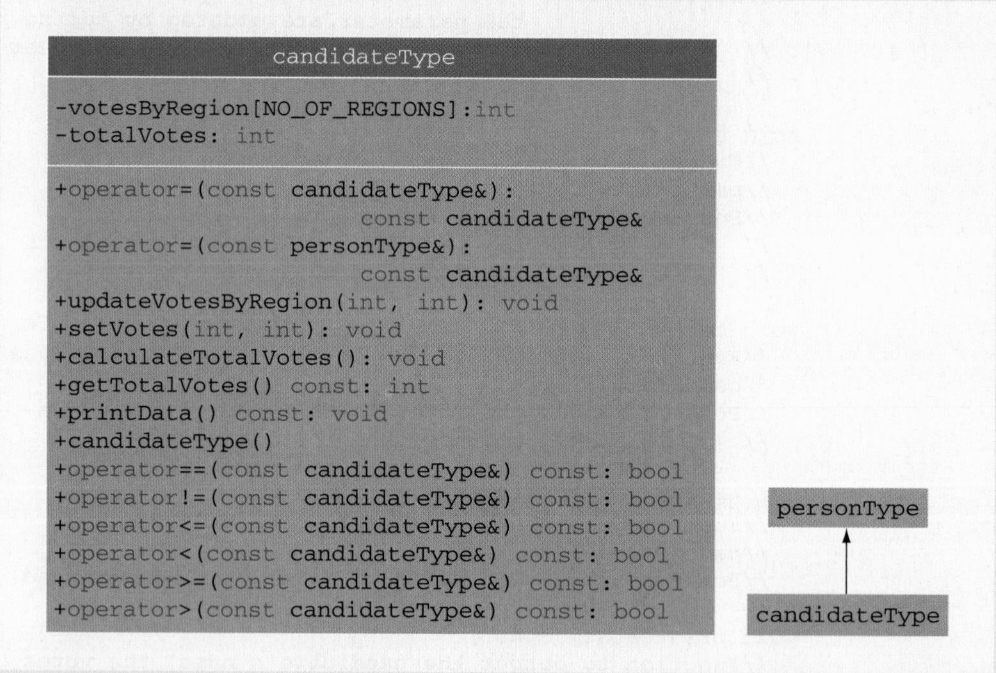

```
                    candidateType

-votesByRegion[NO_OF_REGIONS]:int
-totalVotes: int

+operator=(const candidateType&):
                    const candidateType&
+operator=(const personType&):
                    const candidateType&
+updateVotesByRegion(int, int): void
+setVotes(int, int): void
+calculateTotalVotes(): void
+getTotalVotes() const: int
+printData() const: void
+candidateType()
+operator==(const candidateType&) const: bool
+operator!=(const candidateType&) const: bool
+operator<=(const candidateType&) const: bool
+operator<(const candidateType&) const: bool
+operator>=(const candidateType&) const: bool
+operator>(const candidateType&) const: bool
```

```
personType

    ↑

candidateType
```

FIGURE 18-39 UML class diagram of **class** candidateType

The definitions of the functions of the `class candidateType` are given next.

To set the votes of a particular region, the region number and the number of votes are passed as parameters to the function `setVotes`. Because an array index starts at 0, region 1 corresponds to the array component at position 0, and so on. Therefore, to set the value of the correct array component, 1 is subtracted from the region. The definition of the function `setVotes` is:

```
void candidateType::setVotes(int region, int votes)
{
    votesByRegion[region - 1] = votes;
}
```

To update the votes for a particular region, the region number and the number of votes for that region are passed as parameters. The votes are then added to the region's previous value. The definition of the function `updateVotesByRegion` is:

```
void candidateType::updateVotesByRegion(int region, int votes)
{
    votesByRegion[region - 1] = votesByRegion[region - 1]
                                + votes;
}
```

The definitions of the functions `calculateTotalVotes`, `getTotalVotes`, `printData`, and the default constructor are quite straightforward and are given next.

```
void candidateType::calculateTotalVotes()
{
    int i;

    totalVotes = 0;

    for (i = 0; i < NO_OF_REGIONS; i++)
        totalVotes += votesByRegion[i];
}

int candidateType::getTotalVotes() const
{
    return totalVotes;
}

void candidateType::printData() const
{
    cout << left
        << setw(8) << firstName << " "
        << setw(8) << lastName << " ";

    cout << right;
    for (int i = 0; i < NO_OF_REGIONS; i++)
        cout << setw(8) << votesByRegion[i] << " ";
    cout << setw(7) << totalVotes << endl;
}
```

```cpp
candidateType::candidateType()
{
    for (int i = 0; i < NO_OF_REGIONS; i++)
        votesByRegion[i] = 0;

    totalVotes = 0;
}
```

To overload the relational operators for the class candidateType, the names of the candidates are compared. For example, two candidates are the same if they have the same name. The definitions of these functions are similar to the definitions of the functions to overload the relational operators for the class personType and are given next.

```cpp
bool candidateType::operator==(const candidateType& right) const
{
    return (firstName == right.firstName
            && lastName == right.lastName);
}
bool candidateType::operator!=(const candidateType& right) const
{
    return (firstName != right.firstName
        || lastName != right.lastName);
}

bool candidateType::operator<=(const candidateType& right) const
{
    return (lastName <= right.lastName ||
            (lastName == right.lastName &&
             firstName <= right.firstName));
}

bool candidateType::operator<(const candidateType& right) const
{
    return (lastName < right.lastName ||
            (lastName == right.lastName &&
             firstName < right.firstName));
}

bool candidateType::operator>=(const candidateType& right) const
{
    return (lastName >= right.lastName ||
            (lastName == right.lastName &&
             firstName >= right.firstName));
}

bool candidateType::operator>(const candidateType& right) const
{
    return (lastName > right.lastName ||
            (lastName == right.lastName &&
             firstName > right.firstName));
}
```

```
const candidateType& candidateType::operator=
                                (const candidateType& right)
{
    if (this != &right)   // avoid self-assignment
    {
        firstName = right.firstName;
        lastName = right.lastName;

        for (int i = 0; i < NO_OF_REGIONS; i++)
            votesByRegion[i] = right.votesByRegion[i];

        totalVotes = right.totalVotes;
    }

    return *this;
}

const candidateType& candidateType::operator=
                                (const personType& right)
{
    firstName = right.getFirstName();
    lastName = right.getLastName();

    return *this;
}
```

MAIN PROGRAM Now that the **class** candidateType has been designed and implemented, we focus on designing the main program.

Because there are six candidates, we create a list, candidateList, containing six components of type candidateType. The first thing that the program should do is read each candidate's name from the file candData.txt into the list candidateList. Then, we sort candidateList.

The next step is to process the voting data from the file voteData.txt, which holds the voting data. After processing the voting data, the program should calculate the total votes received by each candidate and print the data, as shown previously. Thus, the general algorithm is:

1. Read each candidate's name into candidateList.
2. Sort candidateList.
3. Process the voting data.
4. Calculate the total votes received by each candidate.
5. Print the results.

The following statement creates the object candidateList.

```
unorderedArrayListType<candidateType> candidateList(NO_OF_CANDIDATES);
```

Figure 18-40 shows the object candidateList. Every component of the array list is an object of type candidateType.

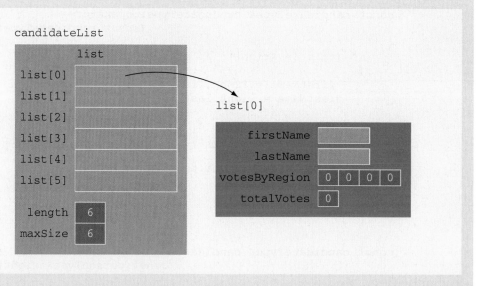

FIGURE 18-40 candidateList

In Figure 18-40, the array **votesByRegion** and the variable **totalVotes** are initialized to 0 by the default constructor of the **class candidateType**. To save space, whenever needed, we will draw the object **candidateList**, as shown in Figure 18-41.

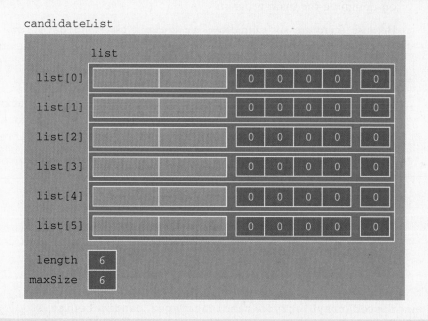

FIGURE 18-41 candidateList

fillNames The first thing that the program must do is read the candidates' names into candidateList. Therefore, we write a function to accomplish this task. The file candData.txt is opened in the function main. The names of the input file and candidateList are, therefore, passed as parameters to the function fillNames. Because the member variable list of the object candidateList is protected, it cannot be accessed directly. We, therefore, create an object temp of type candidateType to store the candidates' names and use the function insertEnd (of list) to store each candidate's name in the object candidateList. The definition of the function fillNames follows:

```
void fillNames(ifstream& inFile,
               unorderedArrayListType<candidateType>& cList)
{
    string firstN;
    string lastN;
    int i;
    candidateType temp;

    for (i = 0; i < NO_OF_CANDIDATES; i++)
    {
        inFile >> firstN >> lastN;
        temp.setName(firstN, lastN);
        cList.insertEnd(temp);
    }
}
```

Figure 18-42 shows the object candidateList after a call to the function fillNames.

1
8

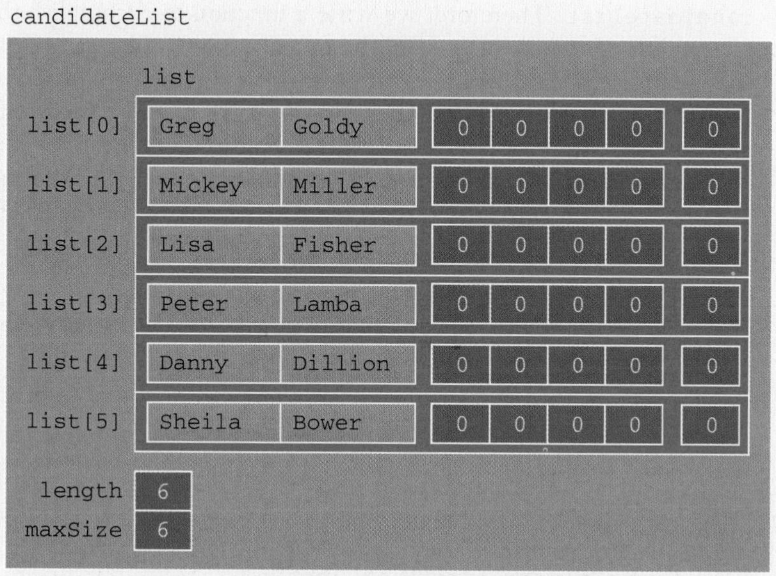

candidateList

	list						
list[0]	Greg	Goldy	0	0	0	0	0
list[1]	Mickey	Miller	0	0	0	0	0
list[2]	Lisa	Fisher	0	0	0	0	0
list[3]	Peter	Lamba	0	0	0	0	0
list[4]	Danny	Dillion	0	0	0	0	0
list[5]	Sheila	Bower	0	0	0	0	0

length	6
maxSize	6

FIGURE 18-42 Object candidateList after a call to the function fillNames

Sort Names   After reading the candidates' names, we next sort the array list of the object
candidateList using any of the (array-based) sorting algorithms discussed in this
chapter. Because candidateList is an object of type unorderedArrayListType,
we use the member function sort to sort candidateList. (For illustration purposes,
we use selection sort in the function sort. In fact, you can use any array-based sorting
algorithm discussed in this chapter.) The following statement accomplishes this task:

candidateList.sort();

After this statement executes, candidateList is as shown in Figure 18-43.

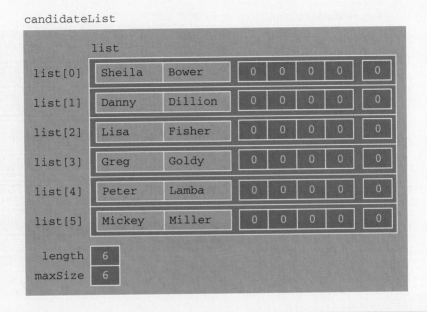

candidateList

list							
list[0]	Sheila	Bower	0	0	0	0	0
list[1]	Danny	Dillion	0	0	0	0	0
list[2]	Lisa	Fisher	0	0	0	0	0
list[3]	Greg	Goldy	0	0	0	0	0
list[4]	Peter	Lamba	0	0	0	0	0
list[5]	Mickey	Miller	0	0	0	0	0
length	6						
maxSize	6						

FIGURE 18-43 Object `candidateList` after the statement `candidateList.sort();` executes

Process Voting Data

Processing the voting data is quite straightforward. Each entry in the file `voteData.txt` is of the form:

`firstName lastName regionNumber numberOfVotes`

After reading an entry from the file `voteData.txt`, we locate the row in the array `list` (of the object `candidateList`) corresponding to the specific candidate and update the entry specified by `regionNumber`.

The component `votesByRegion` is a `private` member of each component of the array `list`. Moreover, `list` is a `private` member of `candidateList`. The only way we can update the votes of a candidate is to make a copy of that candidate's record into a temporary object, update the object, and then copy the temporary object back into `list` by replacing the old value with the new value of the temporary object. We can use the member function `retrieveAt` to make a copy of the candidate whose votes need to be updated. After updating the temporary object, we can use the member function `replaceAt` to copy the temporary object back into the list. Suppose the next entry read is:

`Lisa Fisher 2 35`

This entry says that `Lisa Fisher` received 35 votes from region 2. Suppose that before processing this entry, `candidateList` is as shown in Figure 18-44.

candidateList

list							
list[0]	Sheila	Bower	0	0	50	0	0
list[1]	Danny	Dillion	10	0	56	0	0
list[2]	Lisa	Fisher	76	13	0	0	0
list[3]	Greg	Goldy	0	45	0	0	0
list[4]	Peter	Lamba	80	0	0	0	0
list[5]	Mickey	Miller	100	0	0	20	0

length 6
maxSize 6

FIGURE 18-44 Object `candidateList` before processing entry Lisa Fisher 2 35

We make a copy of the row corresponding to **Lisa Fisher** (see Figure 18-45).

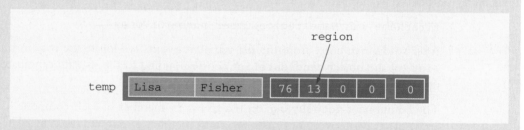

region

temp | Lisa | Fisher | 76 | 13 | 0 | 0 | 0

FIGURE 18-45 Object `temp`

Next, the following statement updates the voting data for region 2. (Here, **region** = 2 and **votes** = 35.)

```
temp.updateVotesByRegion(region, votes);
```

After this statement executes, the object **temp** is as shown in Figure 18-46.

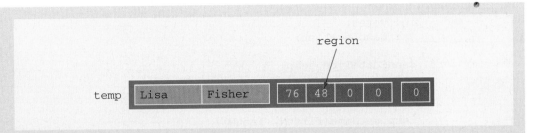

FIGURE 18-46 Object `temp` after `temp.updateVotesByRegion(region,votes);` executes

Now we copy the object `temp` into `list` (see Figure 18-47).

candidateList

	list						
list[0]	Sheila	Bower	0	0	50	0	0
list[1]	Danny	Dillion	10	0	56	0	0
list[2]	Lisa	Fisher	76	48	0	0	0
list[3]	Greg	Goldy	0	45	0	0	0
list[4]	Peter	Lamba	80	0	0	0	0
list[5]	Mickey	Miller	100	0	0	20	0

length 6
maxSize 6

FIGURE 18-47 `candidateList` after copying `temp`

Because the member `list` of `candidateList` is sorted, we can use the binary search algorithm to find the row position in `list` corresponding to the candidate whose votes need to be updated. Essentially, the definition of the function `processVotes` is:

```
void processVotes(ifstream& inFile,
                  unorderedArrayListType<candidateType>& cList)
{
    string firstN;
    string lastN;
    int region;
```

```
    int votes;
    int candLocation;

    candidateType temp;

    inFile >> firstN >> lastN >> region >> votes;

    temp.setName(firstN, lastN);
    temp.setVotes(region, votes);

    while (inFile)
    {
        candLocation = cList.binSearch(temp);

        if (candLocation != -1)
        {
            cList.retrieveAt(candLocation, temp);
            temp.updateVotesByRegion(region, votes);
            cList.replaceAt(candLocation, temp);
        }

        inFile >> firstN >> lastN >> region >> votes;

        temp.setName(firstN, lastN);
        temp.setVotes(region, votes);
    }
}
```

Add Votes After processing the voting data, the next step is to find the total votes received by each candidate. This is done by adding the votes received in each region.

Now votesByRegion is a `private` member of candidateType, and list is a `protected` member of candidateList. Therefore, to add the votes for each candidate, we use the function retrieveAt to make a temporary copy of each candidate's data, add the votes in the temporary object, and then copy the temporary object back into candidateList. The following function does this:

```
void addVotes(unorderedArrayListType<candidateType>& cList)
{
    int i;

    candidateType temp;

    for (i = 0; i < NO_OF_CANDIDATES; i++)
    {
        cList.retrieveAt(i, temp);
        temp.calculateTotalVotes();
        cList.replaceAt(i, temp);
    }
}
```

Figure 18-48 shows `candidateList` after adding the votes for each candidate—that is, after a call to the function `addVotes`.

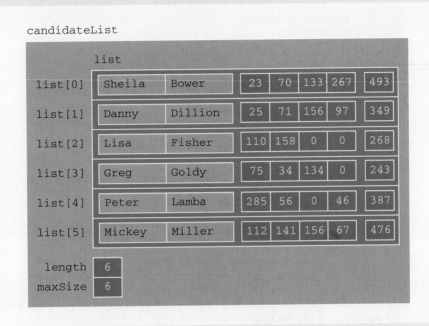

candidateList

	list						
list[0]	Sheila	Bower	23	70	133	267	493
list[1]	Danny	Dillion	25	71	156	97	349
list[2]	Lisa	Fisher	110	158	0	0	268
list[3]	Greg	Goldy	75	34	134	0	243
list[4]	Peter	Lamba	285	56	0	46	387
list[5]	Mickey	Miller	112	141	156	67	476

length 6
maxSize 6

FIGURE 18-48 `candidateList` after a call to the function `addVotes`

Print Heading and Print Results

To complete the program, we include a function to `print` the heading, which outputs the first four lines of the output. The following function accomplishes this task:

```cpp
void printHeading()
{
    cout << "          ---------------------Election Results---------"
         << "-----------" << endl << endl;
    cout << "                                        Votes" << endl;
    cout << "  Candidate Name      Region1  Region2  Region3  "
         << "Region4    Total"<<endl;
    cout << "-------------------- -------  -------  "
         << "-------  -------  ------" << endl;
}
```

We now describe the function `printResults`, which prints the results. Suppose that the variable `sumVotes` holds the total votes polled for the election, the variable `largestVotes` holds the largest number of votes received by a candidate, and the variable `winLoc` holds the index of the winning candidate in the array list. Further suppose that `temp` is an object of type `candidateType`. The algorithm for this function is:

1. Initialize `sumVotes`, `largestVotes`, and `winLoc` to zero.
2. For each candidate:
   a. Retrieve the candidate's data into `temp`.
   b. Print the candidate's name and relevant data.
   c. Retrieve the total votes received by the candidate and update `sumVotes`.
   d.
   ```
   if (largestVotes < temp.getTotalVotes())
   {
       largestVotes = temp.getTotalVotes();
       winLoc = i;
   }
   ```
3. Output the final lines of output.

We leave the definition of the function `printResults` as an exercise. (See Programming Exercise 18.)

PROGRAM LISTING (MAIN PROGRAM)

```cpp
//************************************************************
// Author: D.S. Malik
//
// This program processes voting data for the student council
// president's post. It outputs each candidate's name and the
// votes they received. The name of the winner is also printed.
//************************************************************

#include <iostream>
#include <string>
#include <fstream>
#include "candidateType.h"
#include "unorderedArrayListType.h"

using namespace std;

const int NO_OF_CANDIDATES = 6;

void fillNames(ifstream& inFile,
            unorderedArrayListType<candidateType>& cList);
void processVotes(ifstream& inFile,
            unorderedArrayListType<candidateType>& cList);
void addVotes(unorderedArrayListType<candidateType>& cList);

void printHeading();
void printResults
        (const unorderedArrayListType<candidateType>& cList);
```

```
int main()
{
    unorderedArrayListType<candidateType>
                        candidateList(NO_OF_CANDIDATES);
    candidateType temp;

    ifstream inFile;

    inFile.open("candData.txt");
    if (!inFile)
    {
        cout << "Input file (candData.txt) does not exist. "
             << "Program terminates!!" << endl;
        return 1;
    }

    fillNames(inFile, candidateList);

    candidateList.sort();

    inFile.close();
    inFile.clear();

    inFile.open("voteData.txt");
    if (!inFile)
    {
        cout << "Input file (voteData.txt) does not exist. "
             << "Program terminates!!" << endl;
        return 1;
    }

    processVotes(inFile, candidateList);

    addVotes(candidateList);

    printHeading();
    printResults(candidateList);

    return 0;
}

//Place the definitions of the functions fillNames,
//addVotes, processVotes, and printHeading here. Also, write and place
//the definition of the function printResults here.
```

Sample Run: After you have written the definitions of the functions of the class candidateType and of the function printResults and then run your program, it should produce the following output. (See Programming Exercise 18.)

18

```
--------------------Election Results--------------------
```

Candidate Name	Region1	Region2	Votes Region3	Region4	Total
Sheila Bower	23	70	133	267	493
Danny Dillion	25	71	156	97	349
Lisa Fisher	110	158	0	0	268
Greg Goldy	75	34	134	0	243
Peter Lamba	285	56	0	46	387
Mickey Miller	112	141	156	67	476

```
Winner: Sheila Bower, Votes Received: 493

Total votes polled: 2216
```

Input Files candData.txt

```
Greg Goldy
Mickey Miller
Lisa Fisher
Peter Lamba
Danny Dillion
Sheila Bower
```

voteData.txt

```
Greg Goldy 2 34
Mickey Miller 1 56
Lisa Fisher 2 56
Peter Lamba 1 78
Danny Dillion 4 29
Sheila Bower 4 78
Mickey Miller 2 63
Lisa Fisher 1 23
Peter Lamba 2 56
Danny Dillion 1 25
Sheila Bower 2 70
Peter Lamba 4 23
Danny Dillion 4 12
Greg Goldy 3 134
Sheila Bower 4 100
Mickey Miller 3 67
Lisa Fisher 2 67
Danny Dillion 3 67
Sheila Bower 1 23
Mickey Miller 1 56
Lisa Fisher 2 35
Sheila Bower 3 78
Peter Lamba 1 27
Danny Dillion 2 34
```

Greg Goldy 1 75
Peter Lamba 4 23
Sheila Bower 3 55
Mickey Miller 4 67
Peter Lamba 1 23
Danny Dillion 3 89
Mickey Miller 3 89
Peter Lamba 1 67
Danny Dillion 2 37
Sheila Bower 4 89
Mickey Miller 2 78
Lisa Fisher 1 87
Peter Lamba 1 90
Danny Dillion 4 56

QUICK REVIEW

1. The sequential search algorithm searches the list for a given item, starting with the first element in the list. It continues to compare the search item with the elements in the list until either the item is found or no more elements are left in the list with which it can be compared.

2. On average, the sequential search algorithm searches half of the list.

3. For a list of length n, in a successful search, on average, the sequential search makes $\dfrac{n+1}{2} = O(n)$ comparisons.

4. A sequential search is not efficient for large lists.

5. A binary search is much faster than a sequential search.

6. A binary search requires the list elements to be in order, that is, sorted.

7. To search for an item in a list of length 1024, a binary search requires no more than 11 iterations of the loop, and so no more than 22 comparisons.

8. For a list of length n, in a successful search, on average, the binary search makes $2\log_2 n - 3$ key comparisons.

9. Let f be a function of n. By the term asymptotic, we mean the study of the function f as n becomes larger and larger without bound.

10. Let f and g be real-valued functions. Assume that f and g are nonnegative, that is, for all real numbers n, $f(n) \geq 0$ and $g(n) \geq 0$. We say that $f(n)$ is Big-O of $g(n)$, written $f(n) = O(g(n))$, if there exist positive constants c and n_0 such that $f(n) \leq cg(n)$ for all $n \geq n_0$.

11. Let $f(n)$ be a nonnegative, real-valued function such that $f(n) = a_m n^m + a_{m-1} n^{m-1} + \cdots + a_1 n + a_0$, wherein a_is are real numbers, $a_m \neq 0$, $n \geq 0$, and m is a nonnegative integer. Then, $f(n) = O(n^m)$.

12. Let L be a list of size $n > 1$. Suppose that the elements of L are sorted. If $SRH(n)$ is the minimum number of comparisons needed, in the worst case, by using a comparison-based algorithm to recognize whether an element x is in L, then $SRH(n) \geq \log_2(n + 1)$.

13. The binary search algorithm is the optimal worst-case algorithm for solving search problems by using the comparison method.

14. To construct a search algorithm of the order less than $\log_2 n$, it cannot be comparison based.

15. For a list of length n, on average, the bubble sort algorithm makes $\dfrac{n(n-1)}{2}$ key comparisons and about $\dfrac{n(n-1)}{4}$ item assignments.

16. The selection sort algorithm sorts a list by finding the smallest (or equivalently largest) element in the list and then moving it to the beginning (or end) of the list.

17. For a list of length n, in which $n > 0$, the selection sort algorithm makes $\dfrac{1}{2}n^2 - \dfrac{1}{2}n$ key comparisons and $3(n-1)$ item assignments.

18. For a list of length n, in which $n > 0$, on average, the insertion sort algorithm makes $\dfrac{1}{4}n^2 + O(n)$ key comparisons and $\dfrac{1}{4}n^2 + O(n)$ item assignments.

19. Let L be a list of n distinct elements. Any sorting algorithm that sorts L by comparison of the keys only, in its worst case, makes at least $O(n\log_2 n)$ key comparisons.

20. Both the quick sort and merge sort algorithms sort a list by partitioning it.

21. To partition a list, the quick sort algorithm first selects an item from the list called `pivot`. The algorithm then rearranges the elements so that the elements in one of the sublists are less than `pivot` and the elements in the other sublist are greater than or equal to `pivot`.

22. In a quick sort, the sorting work is done in partitioning the list.

23. On average, the number of key comparisons in a quick sort is $O(n\log_2 n)$. In the worst case, the number of key comparisons in a quick sort is $O(n^2)$.

24. The merge sort algorithm partitions the list by dividing it in the middle.

25. In a merge sort, the sorting work is done in merging the list.

26. The number of key comparisons in a merge sort is $O(n\log_2 n)$.

EXERCISES

1. Mark the following statements as true or false.

   a. A sequential search of a list assumes that the list is in ascending order.

   b. A binary search of a list assumes that the list is sorted.

c. A binary search is faster on ordered lists and slower on unordered lists.

d. A binary search is faster on large lists, but a sequential search is faster on small lists.

2. Consider the following list:

35, 82, 45, 12, 56, 67, 92, 77

Using the sequential search as described in this chapter, how many comparisons are required to find whether the following items are in the list? (Recall that by comparisons we mean item comparisons, not index comparisons.)

a. 12   b. 92   c. 65   d. 35

3. a. Write a version of the sequential search algorithm that can be used to search a sorted list.

b. Consider the following list:

8, 12, 15, 27, 35, 48, 65, 77, 86, 94, 120

Using a sequential search on ordered lists, which you designed in (a), how many comparisons are required to determine whether the following items are in the list? (Recall that comparisons mean item comparisons, not index comparisons.)

i. 65   ii. 8   iii. 80   iv. 125

4. Consider the following list:

5, 12, 25, 32, 38, 46, 58, 62, 85, 90, 97, 105, 110

Using the binary search as described in this chapter, how many comparisons are required to find whether the following items are in the list? Show the values of `first`, `last`, and `middle` and the number of comparisons after each iteration of the loop.

a. 32   b. 20   c. 105   d. 60

5. Suppose that L is a sorted list of 4096 elements. What is the maximum number of comparisons made by the binary search algorithm, given in this chapter, to determine if an item is in L?

6. Sort the following list using the bubble sort algorithm as discussed in this chapter. Show the list after each iteration of the outer `for` loop.

38, 60, 43, 5, 70, 58, 15, 10

7. a. The number of comparisons in the best case of a bubble sort algorithm, as given in this chapter, is $O(n^2)$. Show that the following version of the bubble sort algorithm reduces the number of comparisons in the best case of the bubble sort algorithm to $O(n)$.

```
//list - list to be sorted
//elemType - type of the list elements
//length - length of the list

bool isSorted = false;

for (int iteration = 1; (iteration < length) && !isSorted;
                        iteration++)
{
    isSorted = true;   //assume that the sublist is sorted

    for (int index = 0; index < length - iteration; index++)
    {
        if (list[index] > list[index + 1])
        {
            elemType temp = list[index];
            list[index] = list[index + 1];
            list[index + 1] = temp;
            isSorted = false;
        }
    }
}
```

b. Using the algorithm given in part (a), find the number of iterations that are needed to sort the following list:

65, 14, 52, 43, 75, 25, 80, 90, 95

8. Sort the following list using the bubble sort algorithm as discussed in this chapter. Show the list after each iteration of the outer `for` loop.

46, 58, 16, 25, 83, 98, 8, 70, 5, 62

9. Assume the following list of keys:

8, 28, 31, 20, 55, 46

The first three keys are in order. To move 20 to its proper position using the insertion sort algorithm as described in this chapter, exactly how many key comparisons are executed?

10. Assume the following list of keys:

12, 38, 45, 50, 55, 5, 30

The first five keys are in order. To move 5 to its proper position using the insertion sort algorithm as described in this chapter, exactly how many key comparisons are executed?

11. Assume the following list of keys:

25, 32, 20, 15, 45, 4, 18, 91, 62, 88, 66

This list is to be sorted using the insertion sort algorithm as described in this chapter for array-based lists. Show the resulting list after seven passes of the sorting phase—that is, after seven iterations of the `for` loop.

12. Recall the insertion sort algorithm (contiguous version) as discussed in this chapter. Assume the following list of keys:

    30, 20, 35, 27, 96, 82, 56, 60, 48, 75, 5, 80

    Exactly how many key comparisons are executed to sort this list using the insertion sort algorithm?

13. Both the merge sort and quick sort algorithms sort a list by partitioning it. Explain how the merge sort algorithm differs from the quick sort algorithm in partitioning the list.

14. Assume the following list of keys:

    36, 55, 89, 95, 65, 75, 13, 62, 86, 9, 23, 74, 2, 100, 98

    This list is to be sorted using the quick sort algorithm as discussed in this chapter. Use `pivot` as the `middle` element of the list.

    a. Give the resulting list after one call to the function `partition`.

    b. What is the size of the list that the function `partition` partitioned?

    c. What are the sizes of the two sublists created by the function `partition`?

15. Suppose that the list of keys is as given in Exercise 14 and that this list is to be sorted using the quick sort algorithm as discussed in this chapter. Use `pivot` as the `middle` element of the list.

    a. Give the resulting list after two calls to the function `partition`.

    b. What is the size of the list that the function `partition` partitioned?

    c. What are the sizes of the two sublists created by the function `partition`?

16. Suppose that the list of keys is as given in Exercise 14. Use the quick sort algorithm, as discussed in this chapter, to determine the number of times the function `partition` is called to completely sort the list.

17. Assume the following list of keys:

    48, 30, 66, 50, 9, 95, 80, 15, 25, 18, 94, 55, 3, 22, 62

    This list is to be sorted using the quick sort algorithm as discussed in this chapter. Use `pivot` as the median of the `first`, `last`, and `middle` elements of the list.

    a. What is the `pivot`?

    b. Give the resulting list after one call to the function `partition`.

    c. What is the size of the list that the function `partition` partitioned?

    d. What are the sizes of the two sublists created by the function `partition`?

18. Suppose that the list of keys is as given in Exercise 17 and that this list is to be sorted using the quick sort algorithm as discussed in this chapter. Use `pivot` as the median of the `first`, `last`, and `middle` elements of the list.

    a. What is the pivot during the second call of the function `partitioned`?

    b. Give the resulting list after two calls to the function `partition`.

c. What is the size of the list that the function `partition` partitioned?

d. What are the sizes of the two sublists created by the function `partition`?

19. Suppose that the list of keys is as given in Exercise 17. Use the quick sort algorithm, as discussed in this chapter, to determine the number of times the function `partition` is called to completely sort the list.

20. Suppose that L is a list of 10,000 elements. Find the average number of comparisons made by bubble sort, selection sort, and insertion sort to sort L.

21. Suppose that L is a list of 10,000 elements. Find the average number of comparisons made by quick sort and merge sort to sort L.

22. Suppose that the elements of a list are in descending order and they need to be put in ascending order. Write a C++ function that takes as input an array of items in descending order and the number of elements in the array. The function rearranges the element of the array in ascending order. Your function must not incorporate any sorting algorithms, that is, no item comparisons should take place.

PROGRAMMING EXERCISES

1. **(Recursive sequential search)** The sequential search algorithm given in this chapter is nonrecursive. Write and implement a recursive version of the sequential search algorithm.

2. **(Recursive binary search)** The binary search algorithm given in this chapter is nonrecursive. Write and implement a recursive version of the binary search algorithm. Also, write a program to test your algorithm.

3. Write a program to test the function you designed in Exercise 3.

4. Write a program to find the number of comparisons using `binarySearch` and the sequential search algorithm as follows:

Suppose `list` is an array of 1000 elements.

a. Use a random number generator to fill `list`.

b. Use any sorting algorithm to sort `list`.

c. Search `list` for some items as follows:

i. Use the binary search algorithm to search the list. (You may need to modify the algorithm given in this chapter to count the number of comparisons.)

ii. Use the binary search algorithm to search the list, switching to a sequential search when the size of the search list reduces to less than 15. (Use the sequential search algorithm for a sorted list.)

d. Print the number of comparisons for Steps c(i) and c(ii). If the item is found in the list, then print its position.

5. **(Modified Bubble Sort)** Write a complete C++ function template to implement the modified bubble sort algorithm given in Exercise 7 of this chapter. Call this function `modifiedBubbleSort`. Also, write a program to test your function.

6. Write a program to test the selection sort algorithm for array-based lists as given in this chapter.

7. Write and test a version of the selection sort algorithm for linked lists.

8. Write a program to test the insertion sort algorithm for array-based lists as given in this chapter.

9. Write and test a version of the insertion sort algorithm for linked lists.

10. Write a program to test the quick sort algorithm for array-based lists as given in this chapter.

11. **(C. A. R. Hoare)** Let L be a list of size n. The quick sort algorithm can be used to find the kth smallest item in L, wherein $0 \leq k \leq n - 1$, without completely sorting L. Write and implement a C++ function, `kThSmallestItem`, that uses a version of the quick sort algorithm to determine the kth smallest item in L without completely sorting L.

12. Sort an array of 10,000 elements using the quick sort algorithm as follows:

    a. Sort the array using `pivot` as the `middle` element of the array.

    b. Sort the array using `pivot` as the median of the `first`, `last`, and `middle` elements of the array.

    c. Sort the array using `pivot` as the `middle` element of the array. However, when the size of any sublist reduces to less than 20, sort the sublist using an insertion sort.

    d. Sort the array using `pivot` as the median of the `first`, `last`, and `middle` elements of the array. When the size of any sublist reduces to less than 20, sort the sublist using an insertion sort.

    e. Calculate and print the CPU time for each of the preceding four steps.

    To find the current CPU time, declare a variable, say, `x`, of type `clock_t`. The statement `x = clock();` stores the current CPU time in `x`. You can check the CPU time before and after a particular phase of a program. Then, to find the CPU time for that particular phase of the program, subtract the before time from the after time. Moreover, you must include the header file `ctime` to use the data type `clock_t` and the function clock. Use a random number generator to initially fill the array.

13. Write a program to test the merge sort algorithm for linked lists as given in this chapter.

14. Write and test a version of the merge sort algorithm for array-based lists.

15. Write a program that creates three identical arrays, `list1`, `list2`, and `list3`, of 5000 elements. The program then sorts `list1` using bubble sort, `list2` using selection sort, and `list3` using insertion sort and outputs the number of comparisons and item assignments made by each sorting algorithm.

16. Write a program that creates three identical lists, `list1`, `list2`, and `list3`, of 5000 elements. The program then sorts `list1` using quick sort, `list2` using insertion sort, and `list3` using merge sort and outputs the number of comparisons and item assignments made by quick sort and insertion sort and the number of comparisons made by merge sort.

17. Write a program to test the function you designed in Exercise 22.

18. Write the definitions of the function `printResults` of the Election Results programming example. Also, write a program to produce the output shown in the sample run of this programming example.

19. In the Election Results programming example, the `class candidateType` contains a function `calculateTotalVotes`, which calculates the total number of votes received by a candidate. After processing the voting data, this function calculates the total number of votes for a candidate. The function `updateVotesByRegion` (of the `class candidateType`) updates only the number of votes for a particular region. Modify the definition of this function so that it also updates the total number of votes received by the candidate. By doing so, the function `addVotes` in the main program is no longer needed. Modify and run your program with the modified definition of the function `updateVotesByRegion`.

20. In the Election Results programming example, the object `candidateList` of type `unorderedArrayListType` is declared to process the voting data. The operations of inserting a candidate's data and updating and retrieving the votes were somewhat complicated. The member variable `list` is a `protected` member of `candidateList`, and each component of `list` is a private member. To update the candidates' votes, copy each candidate's data from `candidateList` into a temporary object of type `candidateType`, update the temporary object, and then replace the candidate's data with the temporary object. In this exercise, you are to modify the Election Results programming example to simplify the accessing of a candidate's data. Derive the `class candidateListType` from the `class unorderedArrayListType` as follows:

```
class candidateListType:
            public unorderedArrayListType<candidateType>
    {
public:
    candidateListType(int size = 0);
      //constructor
    void processVotes(string fName, string lName, int region,
                int votes);
```

```
        //Function to update the number of votes for
        //a particular candidate for a particular region.
        //The name of the candidate, the region number, and
        //the number of votes are passed as parameters.
    void addVotes();
        //Function to find the total number of votes
        //received by each candidate.
    void printResult();
        //Function to output the voting data.
};
```

Because the class candidateListType is derived from the class unorderedArrayListType, and list is a protected member of the class unorderedArrayListType (inherited from the class arrayListType), list can be directly accessed by a member of the class candidateListType.

Write the definitions of the member functions of the class candidateListType. Rewrite and run your program using the class candidateListType.

18

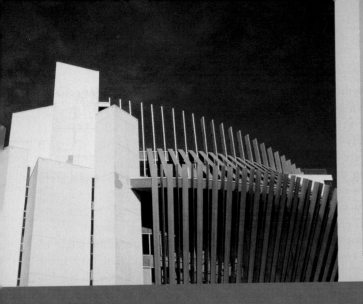

BINARY TREES

IN THIS CHAPTER, YOU WILL:

· Learn about binary trees

· Explore various binary tree traversal algorithms

· Learn how to organize data in a binary search tree

· Learn how to insert and delete items in a binary search tree

· Explore nonrecursive binary tree traversal algorithms

When data is being organized, a programmer's highest priority is to organize it in such a way that item insertion, deletion, and lookups (searches) are fast. You have already seen how to store and process data in an array. Because an array is a random-access data structure, if the data is properly organized (say, sorted), then we can use a search algorithm, such as a binary search, to effectively find and retrieve an item from the list. However, we know that storing data in an array has its limitations. For example, item insertion (especially if the array is sorted) and item deletion can be very time consuming, especially if the list size is very large, because each of these operations requires data movement. To speed up item insertion and deletion, we used linked lists. Item insertion and deletion in a linked list do not require any data movement; we simply adjust some of the links in the list. However, one of the drawbacks of linked lists is that they must be processed sequentially. That is, to insert or delete an item, or simply to search the list for a particular item, we must begin our search at the first node in the list. As you know, a sequential search is good only for very small lists because the average search length of a sequential search is half the size of the list.

Binary Trees

This chapter discusses how to organize data dynamically so that item insertion, deletion, and lookups are more efficient.

We first introduce some definitions to facilitate our discussion.

Definition: A **binary tree**, T, is either empty or such that:

   i. T has a special node called the **root** node;

  ii. T has two sets of nodes, L_T and R_T, called the **left subtree** and **right subtree** of T, respectively; and

 iii. L_T and R_T are binary trees.

Suppose that T is a binary tree with the root node A. Let L_A denote the left subtree of A and R_A denote the right subtree of A. Now L_A and R_A are binary trees. Suppose that B is the root node of L_A and C is the root node of R_A. B is called the **left child** of A; C is called the **right child** of A. Moreover, A is called the **parent** of B and C.

A binary tree can be shown pictorially. In the diagram of a binary tree, each node of the binary tree is represented as a circle, and the circle is labeled by the node. The root node of the binary tree is drawn at the top. The left child of the root node (if any) is drawn below and to the left of the root node. Similarly, the right child of the root node (if any) is drawn below and to the right of the root node. Children are connected to the parent by an arrow from the parent to the child. An arrow is usually called a **directed edge** or a **directed branch** (or simply a **branch**) (see Figure 19-1). Because the root node, B, of L_A is already drawn, we apply the same (recursive) procedure to draw the remaining parts of L_A. R_A is drawn similarly. If a node has no left child, for example, we draw an arrow from the node to the left, ending with three stacked lines. That is, three lines at the end of an arrow indicate that the subtree is empty.

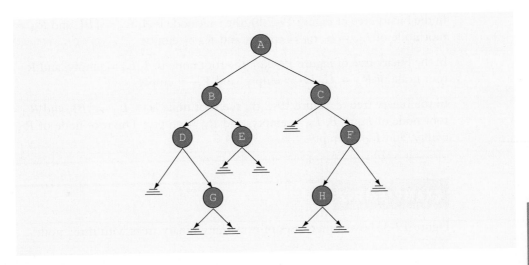

FIGURE 19-1 Binary tree

In Figure 19-1, the root node of this binary tree is A. The left subtree of the root node, which we denote by L_A, is the set $L_A = \{B, D, E, G\}$, and the right subtree of the root node, which we denote by R_A, is the set $R_A = \{C, F, H\}$. The root node of the left subtree of A—that is, the root node of L_A—is node B. The root node of R_A is C, and so on. Clearly, L_A and R_A are binary trees. Because three lines at the end of an arrow mean that the subtree is empty, it follows that the left subtree of D is empty. Also, note that for node F, the left child is H and node F has no right child.

Example 19-1 shows nonempty binary trees.

EXAMPLE 19-1

Figure 19-2 shows binary trees with one, two, or three nodes.

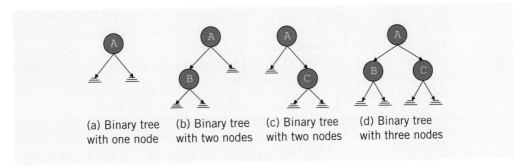

(a) Binary tree with one node   (b) Binary tree with two nodes   (c) Binary tree with two nodes   (d) Binary tree with three nodes

FIGURE 19-2 Binary tree with one, two, or three nodes

In the binary tree of Figure 19-2(a), the root node is A, L_A = empty, and R_A = empty.

In the binary tree of Figure 19-2(b), the root node is A, $L_A = \{B\}$, and $R_A =$ empty. The root node of $L_A = B$, $L_B =$ empty, and $R_B =$ empty.

In the binary tree of Figure 19-2(c), the root node is A, $L_A =$ empty, and $R_A = \{C\}$. The root node of $R_A = C$, $L_C =$ empty, and $R_C =$ empty.

In the binary tree of Figure 19-2(d), the root node is A, $L_A = \{B\}$, and $R_A = \{C\}$. The root node of $L_A = B$, $L_B =$ empty, and $R_B =$ empty. The root node of $R_A = C$, $L_C =$ empty, and $R_C =$ empty.

EXAMPLE 19-2

Figure 19-3 shows other cases of nonempty binary trees with three nodes.

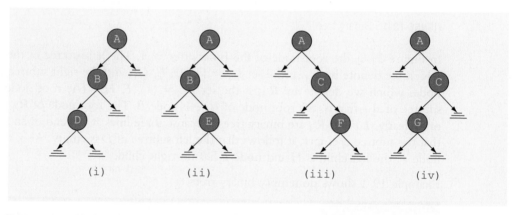

(i)   (ii)   (iii)   (iv)

FIGURE 19-3   Various binary trees with three nodes

As you can see from the preceding examples, every node in a binary tree has, at most, two children. Thus, every node, other than storing its own information, must keep track of its left subtree and right subtree. This implies that every node has two pointers, say, `lLink` and `rLink`. The pointer `lLink` points to the root node of the left subtree of the node; the pointer `rLink` points to the root node of the right subtree of the node.

The following `struct` defines the node of a binary tree:

```
template <class elemType>
struct nodeType
{
    elemType info;
    nodeType<elemType> *lLink;
    nodeType<elemType> *rLink;
};
```

From the definition of the node, it is clear that for each node:

1. The data is stored in `info`.
2. A pointer to the left child is stored in `lLink`.
3. A pointer to the right child is stored in `rLink`.

Furthermore, a pointer to the root node of the binary tree is stored outside of the binary tree in a pointer variable, usually called the **root**, of type `nodeType`. Thus, in general, a binary tree looks like the diagram in Figure 19-4.

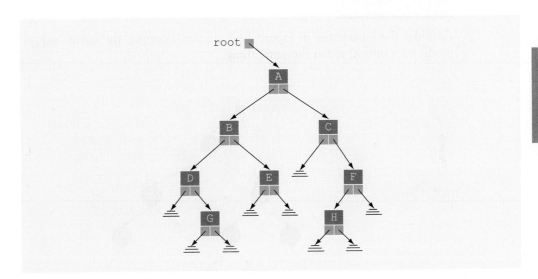

FIGURE 19-4 Binary tree

For simplicity, we will continue to draw binary trees as before. That is, we will use circles to represent nodes and left and right arrows to represent links. As before, three lines at the end of an arrow mean that the subtree is empty.

Before we leave this section, let us define a few terms.

A node in a binary tree is called a **leaf** if it has no left and right children. Let U and V be two nodes in the binary tree T. U is called the **parent** of V if there is a branch from U to V. A **path** from a node X to a node Y in a binary tree is a sequence of nodes X_0, X_1, ..., X_n such that:

i. $X = X_0$, $X_n = Y$
ii. X_{i-1} is the parent of X_i for all $i = 1, 2, ..., n$. That is, there is a branch from X_0 to X_1, X_1 to X_2, ..., X_{i-1} to X_i, ..., X_{n-1} to X_n.

If X_0, X_1, ..., X_n is a path from node X to node Y, sometimes we denote it by $X = X_0 - X_1 - \cdots - X_{n-1} - X_n = Y$ or simply $X - X_1 - \cdots - X_{n-1} - Y$.

Because the branches only go from a parent to its children, from the previous discussion it is clear that in a binary tree, there is a unique path from the root to every node in the binary tree.

Definition: The **length** of a path in a binary tree is the number of branches on that path.

Definition: The **level** of a node in a binary tree is the number of branches on the path from the root to the node.

Clearly, the level of the root node of a binary tree is 0, and the level of the children of the root node is 1.

Definition: The **height** of a binary tree is the number of nodes on the longest path from the root to a leaf.

EXAMPLE 19-3

Consider the binary tree of Figure 19-5. In this example, the terms such as node A and (node with info A) mean the same thing.

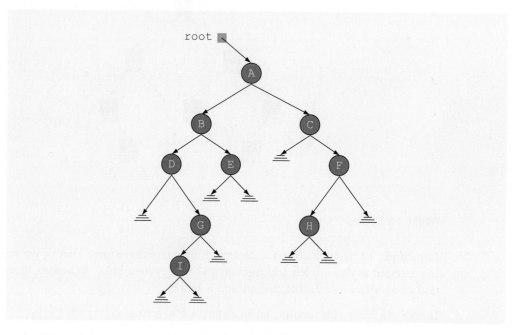

FIGURE 19-5 Binary tree

In this binary tree, the nodes I, E, and H have no left and right children. So, the nodes I, E, and H are leaves.

There is a branch from node A to node B. So, node A is the parent of node B. Similarly, node A is the parent of node C, node B is the parent of nodes D and E, node C is the parent of node F, node D is the parent of node G, and so on.

A–B–D–G is a path from node A to node G. Because there are three branches on this path, the length of this path is 3. Similarly, B–D–G–I is a path from node B to node I.

There are three leaves in this binary tree, which are I, E, and H. Also, the paths from root to these leaves are: A–B–D–G–I, A–B–E, and A–C–F–H. Clearly, the longest path from root to a leaf is A-B-D-G-I. The number of nodes on this path is 5. Hence, the height of the binary tree is 5.

Suppose that a pointer, p, to the root node of a binary tree is given. We next describe a C++ function, height, to find the height of the binary tree. The pointer to the root node is passed as a parameter to the function height.

If the binary tree is empty, then the height is 0. Suppose that the binary tree is nonempty. To find the height of the binary tree, we first find the height of the left subtree and the height of the right subtree. We then take the maximum of these two heights and add 1 to find the height of the binary tree. To find the height of the left (right) subtree, we apply the same procedure because the left (right) subtree is a binary tree. Therefore, the general algorithm to find the height of a binary tree is as follows. Suppose height (p) denotes the height of the binary tree with root p.

```
if (p is NULL)
    height(p) = 0
else
    height(p) = 1 + max(height(p->lLink), height(p->rLink))
```

Clearly, this is a recursive algorithm. The following function implements this algorithm:

```
template <class elemType>
int height(nodeType<elemType> *p)
{
    if (p == NULL)
        return 0;
    else
        return 1 + max(height(p->lLink), height(p->rLink));
}
```

The definition of the function height uses the function max to determine the larger of two integers. The function max can be easily implemented.

Similarly, we can implement algorithms to find the number of nodes and number of leaves in a binary tree.

Copy Tree

One useful operation on binary trees is to make an identical copy of a binary tree. A binary tree is a dynamic data structure; that is, memory for the nodes of a binary tree is allocated and deallocated during program execution. Therefore, if we use just the value of the pointer of the root node to make a copy of a binary tree, we get a shallow copy of the data. To make an identical copy of a binary tree, we need to create as many nodes as there are in the binary tree to be copied. Moreover, in the copied tree, these nodes must appear in the same order as they are in the original binary tree.

Given a pointer to the root node of a binary tree, we next describe a function that makes a copy of a given binary tree. This function is also quite useful in implementing the copy constructor and overloading the assignment operator, as described later in this chapter (see "Implementing Binary Trees").

```
template <class elemType>
void copyTree(nodeType<elemType>* &copiedTreeRoot,
              nodeType<elemType>* otherTreeRoot)
{
    if (otherTreeRoot == NULL)
        copiedTreeRoot = NULL;
    else
    {
        copiedTreeRoot = new nodeType<elemType>;
        copiedTreeRoot->info = otherTreeRoot->info;
        copyTree(copiedTreeRoot->lLink, otherTreeRoot->lLink);
        copyTree(copiedTreeRoot->rLink, otherTreeRoot->rLink);
    }
} //end copyTree
```

We will use the function `copyTree` when we overload the assignment operator and implement the copy constructor.

Binary Tree Traversal

The item insertion, deletion, and lookup operations require that the binary tree be traversed. Thus, the most common operation performed on a binary tree is to traverse the binary tree, or visit each node of the binary tree. As you can see from the diagram of a binary tree, the traversal must start at the root node because there is a pointer to the root node of the binary tree. For each node, we have two choices:

- Visit the node first.
- Visit the subtrees first.

These choices lead to three commonly used traversals of a binary tree:

- Inorder traversal
- Preorder traversal
- Postorder traversal

INORDER TRAVERSAL

In an inorder traversal, the binary tree is traversed as follows:

1. Traverse the left subtree.
2. Visit the node.
3. Traverse the right subtree.

PREORDER TRAVERSAL

In a preorder traversal, the binary tree is traversed as follows:

1. Visit the node.
2. Traverse the left subtree.
3. Traverse the right subtree.

POSTORDER TRAVERSAL

In a postorder traversal, the binary tree is traversed as follows:

1. Traverse the left subtree.
2. Traverse the right subtree.
3. Visit the node.

Clearly, each of these traversal algorithms is recursive.

The listing of the nodes produced by the inorder traversal of a binary tree is called the **inorder sequence**. The listing of the nodes produced by the preorder traversal is called the **preorder sequence**, and the listing of the nodes produced by the postorder traversal is called the **postorder sequence**.

EXAMPLE 19-4

Consider the binary tree in Figure 19-6. Let T be a binary tree. Suppose that T is nonempty and the root node of T is A. Then inorder(T) or inorder(A) denotes the listing of nodes of T in the inorder sequence and root(T) denotes the root node of T. For simplicity, we assume that visiting a node means to output the data stored in the node. In the section "Binary Tree Traversal and Functions as Parameters," we will explain how to modify the binary tree traversal algorithms so that by using a function, the user can specify the action to be performed on a node when the node is visited.

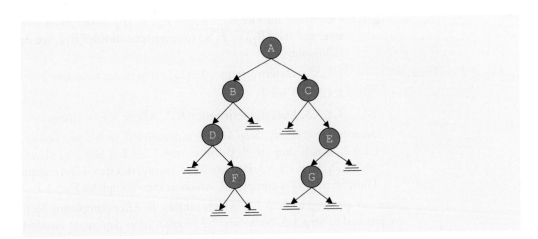

FIGURE 19-6 Binary tree for an inorder traversal

Let T denote the binary tree in Figure 19-6. Then, root(T) = A. Therefore, we start the traversal at A. That is, determine inorder(A). Because the binary tree is nonempty, to determine inorder(A), we do the following:

1. Determine inorder(L_A), where L_A is the left subtree of A. Note that $L_A = \{B, D, F\}$.

2. Visit A.

3. Determine inorder(R_A), where R_A is the right subtree of A. Note that $R_A = \{C, E, G\}$.

Now we cannot do Step 2 until we have finished Step 1.

1. inorder(L_A): Now L_A is a binary tree, and root(L_A) $= B$. So to determine inorder(L_A), we do the following:

   1.1. Determine inorder(L_B), where $L_B = \{D, F\}$.

   1.2. Visit B.

   1.3. Determine inorder(R_B), where $R_B =$ empty.

   As before, first we complete Step 1.1 before proceeding to Step 1.2.

   1.1. inorder(L_B): Now L_B is a binary tree, and root(L_B) $= D$. So to determine inorder(L_B), we do the following:

   1.1.1. Determine inorder(L_D), where $L_D =$ empty.

   1.1.2. Visit D.

   1.1.3. Determine inorder(R_D), where $R_D = \{F\}$.
   Because $L_D =$ empty, Step 1.1.1 is completed, so we proceed to Step 1.1.2, which outputs D. Because Step 1.1.2 is also completed, we proceed to Step 1.1.3.

   1.1.3. Determine inorder(R_D), where $R_D = \{F\}$. Now R_D is a binary tree, and root(R_D) $= F$. So to determine inorder(R_D), we do the following:

   1.1.3.1. Determine inorder(L_F), where $L_F =$ empty.

   1.1.3.2. Visit F.

   1.1.3.3. Determine inorder(R_F), where $R_F =$ empty.
   Because $L_F =$ empty, Step 1.1.3.1 is completed, so we proceed to Step 1.1.3.2, which outputs F. Because Step 1.1.3.2 is also completed, we proceed to Step 1.1.3.3. Because $R_F =$ empty, this step is also completed. Thus, Step 1.1.3 is completed, which in turn completes Step 1.1.

   Next, we proceed to Step 1.2, which outputs B. After completing Step 1.2, we proceed to Step 1.3. Now Step 1.3 requires us to determine inorder(R_B). However, $R_B =$ empty, so Step 1.3 is completed, which in turn completes Step 1.

2. Next, we proceed to Step 2, which outputs A. At this point we have completed inorder(L_A) and visited A.

3. Now, we proceed to Step 3, that is, determine inorder(R_A), where $R_A = \{C, E, G\}$. Now R_A is a nonempty binary tree and root(R_A) = C, so to determine inorder(R_A), we need to do the following:

3.1. Determine inorder(L_C), where L_C = empty.

3.2. Visit C.

3.3. Determine inorder(R_C), where $R_C = \{E, G\}$.

Now L_C = empty, so Step 3.1 is completed. Next, in Step 3.2, we output C, which completes this step. After completing Step 3.2, we proceed to Step 3.3.

3.3. Determine inorder(R_C), where $R_C = \{E, G\}$. Now R_C is a nonempty binary tree with root(R_C) = E. Thus, inorder(R_C) requires us to complete the following steps:

3.3.1. Determine inorder(L_E), where $L_E = \{G\}$.

3.3.2. Visit E.

3.3.3. Determine inorder(R_E), where R_E = empty.

To complete Step 3.3.1, we must determine inorder(L_E), where $L_E = \{G\}$. Now L_E is a binary tree with root(L_E) = $\{G\}$. Therefore, to determine inorder(L_E), we must complete the following steps:

3.3.1.1. Determine inorder(L_G), where L_G = empty.

3.3.1.2. Visit G.

3.3.1.3. Determine inorder(R_G), where R_G = empty.

Now L_G = empty, so Step 3.3.1.1 is completed. Next Step 3.3.1.2 outputs G, which completes this step. Because R_G = empty, Step 3.3.1.3 is also completed. This in turn completes Step 3.3.1.

After completing Step 3.3.1, to complete Step 3.3.2, we output E. Next because R_E = empty, Step 3.3.3 is also completed, which in turn completes Step 3.3.

Because Step 3.3 is completed, Step 3 is also completed, that is we have determined inorder(R_A). It now follows that:

inorder(A) = DFBACGE

In a similar manner, the preorder and postorder traversals output the nodes in the following order:

preorder(A) = ABDFCEF

postorder(A) = FDBGECA

As you can see from the walk-through of the inorder traversal, after visiting the left subtree of a node, we must come back to the node itself. The links are only in one direction; that is, the parent node points to the left and right children, but there is no pointer from each child to the parent. Therefore, before going to a child, we must somehow save a pointer to the parent node. A convenient way to do this is to write a recursive inorder function because in a recursive call, after completing a particular call, the control goes back to the caller. (Later, we will discuss how to write nonrecursive traversal functions.) The recursive definition of the function to implement the inorder traversal algorithms is:

```cpp
template <class elemType>
void inorder(nodeType<elemType> *p) const
{
    if (p != NULL)
    {
        inorder(p->lLink);
        cout << p->info << " ";
        inorder(p->rLink);
    }
}
```

To do the inorder traversal of a binary tree, the root node of the binary tree is passed as a parameter to the function inorder. For example, if root points to the root node of the binary tree, a call to the function inorder is:

```cpp
inorder(root);
```

Similarly, we can write the functions to implement the preorder and postorder traversals. The definitions of these functions are given next.

```cpp
template <class elemType>
void preorder(nodeType<elemType> *p) const
{
    if (p != NULL)
    {
        cout << p->info << " ";
        preorder(p->lLink);
        preorder(p->rLink);
    }
}
```

```cpp
template <class elemType>
void postorder(nodeType<elemType> *p) const
{
    if (p != NULL)
    {
        postorder(p->lLink);
        postorder(p->rLink);
        cout << p->info << " ";
    }
}
```

 NOTE This section described the binary tree traversal algorithms inorder, preorder, and postorder. If you want to make a copy of a binary tree while preserving the structure of the binary tree, you can use preorder traversal. To delete all of the nodes of a binary tree, you can use the postorder traversal. Later in this chapter, we will discuss binary search trees. The inorder traversal of a binary search tree visits the nodes in sorted order.

NOTE In addition to the inorder, preorder, and postorder traversals, a binary tree can also be traversed **level-by-level**, also known as **breadth-first traversal**. In Chapter 20, we discuss graphs. A binary tree is also a graph. We discuss how to implement breadth-first traversal algorithms for graphs. You can modify that algorithm to do a breadth-first traversal of binary trees.

Implementing Binary Trees

The preceding sections described various operations that can be performed on a binary tree, as well as the functions to implement these operations. This section describes binary trees as an abstract data type (ADT). Before designing the class to implement a binary tree as an ADT, let us list the various operations that are typically performed on a binary tree.

1. Determine whether the binary tree is empty.
2. Search the binary tree for a particular item.
3. Insert an item in the binary tree.
4. Delete an item from the binary tree.
5. Find the height of the binary tree.
6. Find the number of nodes in the binary tree.
7. Find the number of leaves in the binary tree.
8. Traverse the binary tree.
9. Copy the binary tree.

The item search, insertion, and deletion operations all require the binary tree to be traversed. However, because the nodes of a binary tree are in no particular order, these algorithms are not very efficient on arbitrary binary trees. That is, no criteria exist to guide the search on these binary trees, as we will see in the next section. Therefore, we will discuss these algorithms when we discuss special binary trees.

The following class defines binary trees as an ADT. The definition of the node is the same as before. However, for the sake of completeness and easy reference, we give the definition of the node followed by the definition of the class.

```
    //Definition of the Node
template <class elemType>
struct nodeType
{
    elemType info;
    nodeType<elemType> *lLink;
    nodeType<elemType> *rLink;
};
```

```cpp
    //Definition of the class
template <class elemType>
class binaryTreeType
{
public:
    const binaryTreeType<elemType>& operator=
                  (const binaryTreeType<elemType>&);
      //Overload the assignment operator.

    bool isEmpty() const;
      //Function to determine whether the binary tree is empty.
      //Postcondition: Returns true if the binary tree is empty;
      //               otherwise, returns false.

    void inorderTraversal() const;
      //Function to do an inorder traversal of the binary tree.
      //Postcondition: Nodes are printed in inorder sequence.

    void preorderTraversal() const;
      //Function to do a preorder traversal of the binary tree.
      //Postcondition: Nodes are printed in preorder sequence.

    void postorderTraversal() const;
      //Function to do a postorder traversal of the binary tree.
      //Postcondition: Nodes are printed in postorder sequence.

    int treeHeight() const;
      //Function to determine the height of a binary tree.
      //Postcondition: Returns the height of the binary tree.

    int treeNodeCount() const;
      //Function to determine the number of nodes in a
      //binary tree.
      //Postcondition: Returns the number of nodes in the
      //               binary tree.

    int treeLeavesCount() const;
      //Function to determine the number of leaves in a
      //binary tree.
      //Postcondition: Returns the number of leaves in the
      //               binary tree.

    void destroyTree();
      //Function to destroy the binary tree.
      //Postcondition: Memory space occupied by each node
      //               is deallocated.
      //               root = NULL;

    virtual bool search(const elemType& searchItem) const = 0;
      //Function to determine if searchItem is in the binary
      //tree.
      //Postcondition: Returns true if searchItem is found in
      //               the binary tree; otherwise, returns
      //               false.
```

```
    virtual void insert(const elemType& insertItem) = 0;
      //Function to insert insertItem in the binary tree.
      //Postcondition: If there is no node in the binary tree
      //               that has the same info as insertItem, a
      //               node with the info insertItem is created
      //               and inserted in the binary search tree.

    virtual void deleteNode(const elemType& deleteItem) = 0;
      //Function to delete deleteItem from the binary tree.
      //Postcondition: If a node with the same info as
      //               deleteItem is found, it is deleted from
      //               the binary tree.
      //               If the binary tree is empty or
      //               deleteItem is not in the binary tree,
      //               an appropriate message is printed.

    binaryTreeType(const binaryTreeType<elemType>& otherTree);
      //Copy constructor

    binaryTreeType();
      //Default constructor

    ~binaryTreeType();
      //Destructor

protected:
    nodeType<elemType>  *root;

private:
    void copyTree(nodeType<elemType>* &copiedTreeRoot,
                  nodeType<elemType>* otherTreeRoot);
      //Makes a copy of the binary tree to which
      //otherTreeRoot points.
      //Postcondition: The pointer copiedTreeRoot points to
      //               the root of the copied binary tree.

    void destroy(nodeType<elemType>* &p);
      //Function to destroy the binary tree to which p points.
      //Postcondition: Memory space occupied by each node, in
      //               the binary tree to which p points, is
      //               deallocated.
      //               p = NULL;

    void inorder(nodeType<elemType> *p) const;
      //Function to do an inorder traversal of the binary
      //tree to which p points.
      //Postcondition: Nodes of the binary tree, to which p
      //               points, are printed in inorder sequence.

    void preorder(nodeType<elemType> *p) const;
      //Function to do a preorder traversal of the binary
      //tree to which p points.
      //Postcondition: Nodes of the binary tree, to which p
      //               points, are printed in preorder
      //               sequence.
```

1
9

```
void postorder(nodeType<elemType> *p) const;
  //Function to do a postorder traversal of the binary
  //tree to which p points.
  //Postcondition: Nodes of the binary tree, to which p
  //               points, are printed in postorder
  //               sequence.

int height(nodeType<elemType> *p) const;
  //Function to determine the height of the binary tree
  //to which p points.
  //Postcondition: Height of the binary tree to which
  //               p points is returned.

int max(int x, int y) const;
  //Function to determine the larger of x and y.
  //Postcondition: Returns the larger of x and y.

int nodeCount(nodeType<elemType> *p) const;
  //Function to determine the number of nodes in
  //the binary tree to which p points.
  //Postcondition: The number of nodes in the binary
  //               tree to which p points is returned.
int leavesCount(nodeType<elemType> *p) const;
  //Function to determine the number of leaves in
  //the binary tree to which p points.
  //Postcondition: The number of leaves in the binary
  //               tree to which p points is returned.
};
```

We leave the UML class diagram of the `class binaryTreeType` as an exercise for you. See Exercise 31 at the end of this chapter.

The functions `search`, `insert`, and `deleteNode` are declared as abstract in the definition of the `class binaryTreeType`. This is because, in this section, we are discussing arbitrary binary trees. Implementing these operations for arbitrary binary trees is inefficient, if not impossible, as we will discuss in the section "Binary Search Trees." Because the `class binaryTreeType` contains abstract functions, this `class` is an abstract class. So, you cannot create objects of this `class`. In the section "Binary Search Tree," we will derive a class from the `class binaryTreeType` and provide the definitions of these functions.

Note that the definition of the `class binaryTreeType` contains the statement to overload the assignment operator, copy constructor, and destructor. This is because the `class binaryTreeType` contains pointer member variables. Recall that for classes with pointer member variables, we must explicitly overload the assignment operator, include the copy constructor, and include the destructor.

The definition of the `class binaryTreeType` contains several member functions that are **private** members of the class. These functions are used to implement the **public** member functions of the `class`. For example, to do an inorder traversal, the function `inorderTraversal` calls the function `inorder` and passes the pointer `root` as a parameter to this function. Moreover, the pointer `root` is declared as a **protected** member so that we can later derive special binary trees.

Next, we give the definitions of the nonabstract member functions of the `class` `binaryTreeType`.

The binary tree is empty if `root` is NULL. So the definition of the function `isEmpty` is:

```
template <class elemType>
bool binaryTreeType<elemType>::isEmpty() const
{
    return (root == NULL);
}
```

The default constructor initializes the binary tree to an empty state; that is, it sets the pointer `root` to NULL. Therefore, the definition of the default constructor is:

```
template <class elemType>
binaryTreeType<elemType>::binaryTreeType()
{
    root = NULL;
}
```

The definitions of the other functions are:

```
template <class elemType>
void binaryTreeType<elemType>::inorderTraversal() const
{
    inorder(root);
}

template <class elemType>
void binaryTreeType<elemType>::preorderTraversal() const
{
    preorder(root);
}

template <class elemType>
void binaryTreeType<elemType>::postorderTraversal() const
{
    postorder(root);
}

template <class elemType>
int binaryTreeType<elemType>::treeHeight() const
{
    return height(root);
}

template <class elemType>
int binaryTreeType<elemType>::treeNodeCount() const
{
    return nodeCount(root);
}
```

19

```cpp
template <class elemType>
int binaryTreeType<elemType>::treeLeavesCount() const
{
    return leavesCount(root);
}


template <class elemType>
void binaryTreeType<elemType>::inorder
                                  (nodeType<elemType> *p) const
{
    if (p != NULL)
    {
        inorder(p->lLink);
        cout << p->info << " ";
        inorder(p->rLink);
    }
}

template <class elemType>
void binaryTreeType<elemType>::preorder
                                  (nodeType<elemType> *p) const
{
    if (p != NULL)
    {
        cout << p->info << " ";
        preorder(p->lLink);
        preorder(p->rLink);
    }
}

template <class elemType>
void binaryTreeType<elemType>::postorder
                                  (nodeType<elemType> *p) const
{
    if (p != NULL)
    {
        postorder(p->lLink);
        postorder(p->rLink);
        cout << p->info << " ";
    }
}

template<class elemType>
int binaryTreeType<elemType>::height
                                  (nodeType<elemType> *p) const
{
    if (p == NULL)
        return 0;
    else
        return 1 + max(height(p->lLink), height(p->rLink));
}
```

```
template <class elemType>
int binaryTreeType<elemType>::max(int x, int y) const
{
    if (x >= y)
        return x;
    else
        return y;
}
```

The definitions of the functions `nodeCount` and `leavesCount` are left as exercises for you. See Programming Exercises 1 and 2 at the end of this chapter.

Next, we give the definitions of the functions `copyTree`, `destroy`, `destroyTree`; the copy constructor; and the destructor. We also overload the assignment operator.

The definition of the function `copyTree` is the same as before; here, this function is a member of the `class binaryTreeType`.

```
template <class elemType>
void binaryTreeType<elemType>::copyTree
                    (nodeType<elemType>* &copiedTreeRoot,
                     nodeType<elemType>* otherTreeRoot)
{
    if (otherTreeRoot == NULL)
        copiedTreeRoot = NULL;
    else
    {
        copiedTreeRoot = new nodeType<elemType>;
        copiedTreeRoot->info = otherTreeRoot->info;
        copyTree(copiedTreeRoot->lLink, otherTreeRoot->lLink);
        copyTree(copiedTreeRoot->rLink, otherTreeRoot->rLink);
    }
} //end copyTree
```

To destroy a binary tree, for each node, first we destroy its left subtree, then its right subtree, and then the node itself. We must use the operator `delete` to deallocate the memory occupied by the node. The definition of the function `destroy` is:

```
template <class elemType>
void binaryTreeType<elemType>::destroy(nodeType<elemType>* &p)
{
    if (p != NULL)
    {
        destroy(p->lLink);
        destroy(p->rLink);
        delete p;
        p = NULL;
    }
}
```

To implement the function `destroyTree`, we use the function `destroy` and pass the root node of the binary tree to the function `destroy`. The definition of the function `destroyTree` is:

```
template <class elemType>
void binaryTreeType<elemType>::destroyTree()
{
    destroy(root);
}
```

Recall that when a class object is passed by value, the copy constructor copies the value of the actual parameters into the formal parameters. Because the **class** binaryTreeType has pointer member variables and a pointer is used to create dynamic memory, we must provide the definition of the copy constructor to avoid the shallow copying of data. The definition of the copy constructor, given next, uses the function copyTree to make an identical copy of the binary tree that is passed as a parameter.

```
    //copy constructor
template <class elemType>
binaryTreeType<elemType>::binaryTreeType
                (const binaryTreeType<elemType>& otherTree)
{
    if (otherTree.root == NULL) //otherTree is empty
        root = NULL;
    else
        copyTree(root, otherTree.root);
}
```

The definition of the destructor is quite straightforward. When the object of type binaryTreeType goes out of scope, the destructor deallocates the memory occupied by the nodes of the binary tree. The definition of the destructor uses the function destroy to accomplish this task.

```
    //Destructor
template <class elemType>
binaryTreeType<elemType>::~binaryTreeType()
{
    destroy(root);
}
```

Next, we discuss the definition of the function to overload the assignment operator. To assign the value of one binary tree to another binary tree, we make an identical copy of the binary tree to be assigned by using the function copyTree. The definition of the function to overload the assignment operator is:

```
    //Overload the assignment operator
template <class elemType>
const binaryTreeType<elemType>& binaryTreeType<elemType>::
        operator=(const binaryTreeType<elemType>& otherTree)
{
    if (this != &otherTree) //avoid self-copy
    {
        if (root != NULL)      //if the binary tree is not empty,
                               //destroy the binary tree
            destroy(root);
```

```
        if (otherTree.root == NULL) //otherTree is empty
            root = NULL;
        else
            copyTree(root, otherTree.root);
    }//end else

    return *this;
}
```

Binary Search Trees

Now that you know the basic operations on a binary tree, this section discusses a special type of binary tree called the binary search tree.

Consider the binary tree in Figure 19-7.

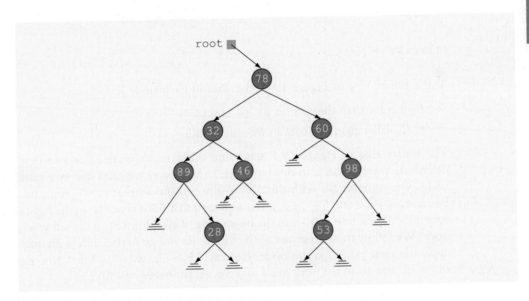

FIGURE 19-7 Arbitrary binary tree

Suppose that we want to determine whether 53 is in the binary tree. To do so, we can use any of the previous traversal algorithms to visit each node and compare the search item with the data stored in the node. However, this could require us to traverse a large part of the binary tree, so the search will be slow. The reason that we need to visit each node in the binary tree until either the item is found or we have traversed the entire binary tree is that no criteria exist to guide our search. This case is like an arbitrary linked list, in which we must start our search at the first node and continue looking at each node until either the item is found or the entire list is searched.

On the other hand, consider the binary tree in Figure 19-8.

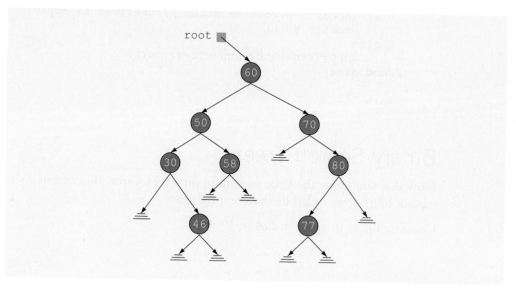

FIGURE 19-8 Binary search tree

In the binary tree in Figure 19-8, the data in each node is:

- Larger than the data in its left child
- Smaller than the data in its right child

The binary tree in Figure 19-8 has some order to its nodes. Suppose that we want to determine whether 58 is in this binary tree. As before, we must start our search at the root node. We compare 58 with the data in the root node; that is, we compare 58 with 60. Because 58 ≠ 60 and 58 < 60, it is guaranteed that 58 will not be in the right subtree of the root node. Therefore, if 58 is in the binary tree, then it must be in the left subtree of the root node. We follow the left pointer of the root node and go to the node with info 50. We now apply the same criteria at this node. Because 58 > 50, we must follow the right pointer of this node and go to the node with info 58. At this node, we find 58.

This example shows that every time we move down to a child, we eliminate one of the subtrees of the node from our search. If the binary tree is nicely constructed, then the search is very similar to the binary search on arrays.

The binary tree given in Figure 19-8 is a special type of binary tree called a binary search tree. (In the following definition, by the term key of the node, we mean the key of the data item that uniquely identifies the item.)

Definition: A **binary search tree**, T, is either empty or:

   i. T has a special node called the **root** node;

   ii. T has two sets of nodes, L_T and R_T, called the left subtree and right subtree of T, respectively;

iii. The key in the root node is larger than every key in the left subtree and smaller than every key in the right subtree; and

iv. L_T and R_T are binary search trees.

The following operations are typically performed on a binary search tree.

1. Determine whether the binary search tree is empty.

2. Search the binary search tree for a particular item.

3. Insert an item in the binary search tree.

4. Delete an item from the binary search tree.

5. Find the height of the binary search tree.

6. Find the number of nodes in the binary search tree.

7. Find the number of leaves in the binary search tree.

8. Traverse the binary search tree.

9. Copy the binary search tree.

Clearly, every binary search tree is a binary tree. The height of a binary search tree is determined in the same way as the height of a binary tree. Similarly, the operations to find the number of nodes, to find the number of leaves, and to do inorder, preorder, and postorder traversals of a binary search tree are the same as those for a binary tree. Therefore, we can inherit all of these operations from the binary tree. That is, we can extend the definition of the binary tree by using the principle of inheritance and hence define the binary search tree.

The following class defines a binary search tree as an ADT by extending the definition of the binary tree:

```
template <class elemType>
class bSearchTreeType: public binaryTreeType<elemType>
{
public:
    bool search(const elemType& searchItem) const;
    //Function to determine if searchItem is in the binary
    //search tree.
    //Postcondition: Returns true if searchItem is found in
    //               the binary search tree; otherwise,
    //               returns false.

    void insert(const elemType& insertItem);
    //Function to insert insertItem in the binary search tree.
    //Postcondition: If there is no node in the binary search
    //               tree that has the same info as
    //               insertItem, a node with the info
    //               insertItem is created and inserted in the
    //               binary search tree.
```

```
      void deleteNode(const elemType& deleteItem);
        //Function to delete deleteItem from the binary search tree.
        //Postcondition: If a node with the same info as deleteItem
        //               is found, it is deleted from the binary
        //               search tree.
        //               If the binary tree is empty or deleteItem
        //               is not in the binary tree, an appropriate
        //               message is printed.

    private:
      void deleteFromTree(nodeType<elemType>* &p);
        //Function to delete the node to which p points is
        //deleted from the binary search tree.
        //Postcondition: The node to which p points is deleted
        //               from the binary search tree.
    };
```

We leave it as an exercise for you to draw the UML class diagram of the `class bSearchTreeType` and the inheritance hierarchy. See Exercise 32 at the end of this chapter.

Next, we describe each of these operations.

SEARCH

The function `search` searches the binary search tree for a given item. If the item is found in the binary search tree, it returns `true`; otherwise, it returns `false`. Because the pointer `root` points to the root node of the binary search tree, we must begin our search at the root node. Furthermore, because `root` must always point to the root node, we need a pointer—say, `current`—to traverse the binary search tree. The pointer `current` is initialized to `root`.

If the binary search tree is nonempty, we first compare the search item with the info in the root node. If they are the same, we stop the search and return `true`. Otherwise, if the search item is smaller than the info in the node, we follow `lLink` to go to the left subtree; otherwise, we follow `rLink` to go to the right subtree. We repeat this process for the next node. If the search item is in the binary search tree, our search ends at the node containing the search item; otherwise, the search ends at an empty subtree. Thus, the general algorithm is:

```
if root is NULL
    Cannot search an empty tree, returns false.
else
{
    current = root;
    while (current is not NULL and not found)
      if (current->info is the same as the search item)
        set found to true;
      else
        if (current->info is greater than the search item)
          follow the lLink of current
        else
          follow the rLink of current
}
```

This pseudocode algorithm translates into the following C++ function:

```cpp
template <class elemType>
bool bSearchTreeType<elemType>::search
                    (const elemType& searchItem) const
{
    nodeType<elemType> *current;
    bool found = false;

    if (root == NULL)
        cout << "Cannot search an empty tree." << endl;
    else
    {
        current = root;

        while (current != NULL && !found)
        {
            if (current->info == searchItem)
                found = true;
            else if (current->info > searchItem)
                current = current->lLink;
            else
                current = current->rLink;
        }//end while
    }//end else

    return found;
}//end search
```

INSERT

After inserting an item in a binary search tree, the resulting binary tree must be a binary search tree. To insert a new item, first we search the binary search tree and find the place where the new item is to be inserted. The search algorithm is similar to the search algorithm of the function search. Here, we traverse the binary search tree with two pointers—a pointer, say, current, to check the current node and a pointer, say, trailCurrent, pointing to the parent of current. Because duplicate items are not allowed, our search must end at an empty subtree. We can then use the pointer trailCurrent to insert the new item at the proper place. The item to be inserted, insertItem, is passed as a parameter to the function insert. The general algorithm is:

a. Create a new node and copy insertItem into the new node. Also set lLink and rLink of the new node to NULL.

b. if the root is NULL, the tree is empty, so make root point to the new node.
   else
   {
   ```
       current = root;
       while (current is not NULL)      //search the binary tree
   ```

```
                {
                        trailCurrent = current;
                        if (current->info is the same as the insertItem)
                            Error: Cannot insert duplicate
                            exit
                        else
                            if (current->info > insertItem)
                                Follow lLink of current
                            else
                                Follow rLink of current
                }

            //insert the new node in the binary tree

            if (trailCurrent->info > insertItem)
                make the new node the left child of trailCurrent
            else
                make the new node the right child of trailCurrent
        }
```

This pseudocode algorithm translates into the following C++ function:

```
template <class elemType>
void bSearchTreeType<elemType>::insert
                (const elemType& insertItem)
{
    nodeType<elemType> *current; //pointer to traverse the tree
    nodeType<elemType> *trailCurrent; //pointer behind current
    nodeType<elemType> *newNode;   //pointer to create the node

    newNode = new nodeType<elemType>;
    newNode->info = insertItem;
    newNode->lLink = NULL;
    newNode->rLink = NULL;

    if (root == NULL)
        root = newNode;
    else
    {
        current = root;

        while (current != NULL)
        {
            trailCurrent = current;

            if (current->info == insertItem)
            {
                cout << "The item to be inserted is already ";
                cout << "in the tree -- duplicates are not "
                    << "allowed." << endl;
                return;
            }
            else if (current->info > insertItem)
                current = current->lLink;
            else
                current = current->rLink;
        }//end while
```

```
        if (trailCurrent->info > insertItem)
            trailCurrent->lLink = newNode;
        else
            trailCurrent->rLink = newNode;
    }
}//end insert
```

DELETE

As before, first we search the binary search tree to find the node to be deleted. To help you better understand the delete operation, before describing the function to delete an item from the binary search tree, let us consider the binary search tree in Figure 19-9.

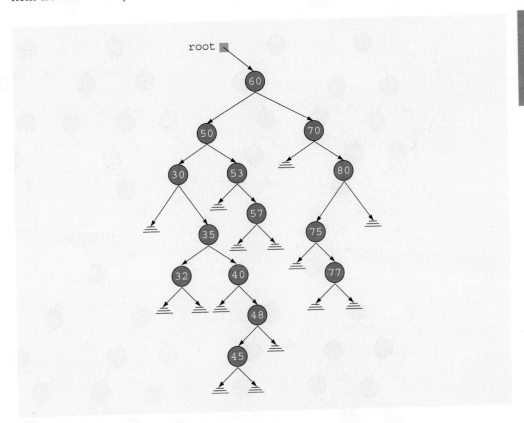

FIGURE 19-9 Binary search tree before deleting a node

After deleting the desired item (if it exists in the binary search tree), the resulting tree must be a binary search tree. The delete operation has four cases, as follows:

Case 1: The node to be deleted has no left and right subtrees; that is, the node to be deleted is a leaf. For example, the node with info 45 is a leaf.

Case 2: The node to be deleted has no left subtree; that is, the left subtree is empty, but it has a nonempty right subtree. For example, the left subtree of node with info 40 is empty, and its right subtree is nonempty.

Case 3: The node to be deleted has no right subtree; that is, the right subtree is empty, but it has a nonempty left subtree. For example, the left subtree of node with info 80 is empty, and its right subtree is nonempty.

Case 4: The node to be deleted has nonempty left and right subtrees. For example, the left and the right subtrees of node with info 50 are nonempty.

Figure 19-10 illustrates these four cases.

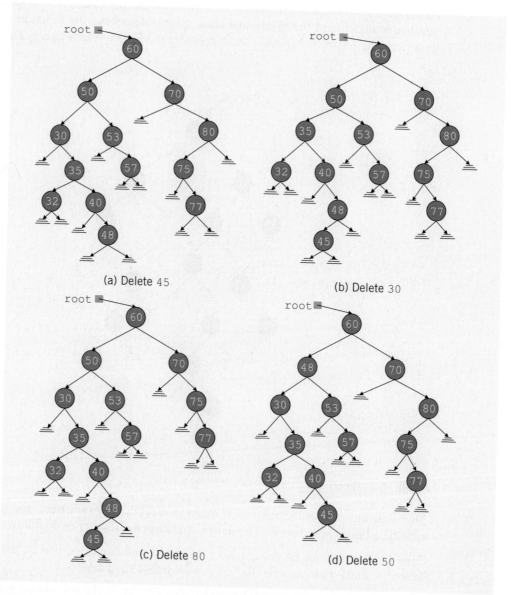

(a) Delete 45

(b) Delete 30

(c) Delete 80

(d) Delete 50

FIGURE 19-10 Binary trees of Figure 19-9 after deleting various items

Case 1: Suppose that we want to delete 45 from the binary search tree in Figure 19-9. We search the binary tree and arrive at the node containing 45. Because this node is a leaf and is the left child of its parent, we can simply set the lLink of the parent node to NULL and deallocate the memory occupied by this node. After deleting this node, Figure 19-10(a) shows the resulting binary search tree.

Case 2: Suppose that we want to delete 30 from the binary search tree in Figure 19-9. In this case, the node to be deleted has no left subtree. Because 30 is the left child of its parent node, we make the lLink of the parent node point to the right child of 30 and then deallocate the memory occupied by 30. Figure 19-10(b) shows the resulting binary tree.

Case 3: Suppose that we want to delete 80 from the binary search tree of Figure 19-9. The node containing 80 has no right child and is the right child of its parent. Thus, we make the rLink of the parent of 80—that is, 70—point to the left child of 80. Figure 19-10(c) shows the resulting binary tree.

Case 4: Suppose that we want to delete 50 from the binary search tree in Figure 19-9. The node with info 50 has a nonempty left subtree and a nonempty right subtree. Here, we first reduce this case to either case 2 or case 3 as follows. To be specific, suppose that we reduce it to case 3—that is, the node to be deleted has no right subtree. For this case, we find the immediate predecessor of 50 in this binary tree, which is 48. This is done by first going to the left child of 50 and then locating the rightmost node of the left subtree of 50. To do so, we follow the rLink of the nodes. Because the binary search tree is finite, we eventually arrive at a node that has no right subtree. Next, we swap the info in the node to be deleted with the info of its immediate predecessor. In this case, we swap 48 with 50. This reduces to the case wherein the node to be deleted has no right subtree. We now apply case 3 to delete the node. (*Note:* Because we will delete the immediate predecessor from the binary tree, we, in fact, copy only the info of the immediate predecessor into the node to be deleted.) After deleting 50 from the binary search tree in Figure 19-9, the resulting binary tree is as shown in Figure 19-10(d).

In each case, we clearly see that the resulting binary tree is again a binary search tree. From this discussion, it follows that to delete an item from the binary search tree, we must do the following:

1. Find the node containing the item (if any) to be deleted.

2. Delete the node.

We accomplish the second step by a separate function, which we will call deleteFromTree. Given a pointer to the node to be deleted, this function deletes the node by taking into account the previous four cases.

From the preceding examples, it is clear that whenever we delete a node from the binary tree, we adjust one of the pointers of the parent node. Because the adjustment has to be made in the parent node, we must call the function deleteFromTree by using an appropriate pointer of the parent node. For example, suppose that the node to be deleted is 35, which is the right child of its parent node. Suppose that trailCurrent points to the node containing 30, the parent node of 35. A call to the function deleteFromTree is:

```
deleteFromTree(trailCurrent->rLink);
```

Of course, if the node to be deleted is the root node, then the call to the function deleteFromTree is:

```
deleteFromTree(root);
```

We now define the C++ function deleteFromTree.

```cpp
template <class elemType>
void bSearchTreeType<elemType>::deleteFromTree
                              (nodeType<elemType>* &p)
{
    nodeType<elemType> *current; //pointer to traverse the tree
    nodeType<elemType> *trailCurrent;  //pointer behind current
    nodeType<elemType> *temp;       //pointer to delete the node

    if (p == NULL)
        cout << "Error: The node to be deleted is NULL."
             << endl;
    else if (p->lLink == NULL && p->rLink == NULL)
    {
        temp = p;
        p = NULL;
        delete temp;
    }
    else if (p->lLink == NULL)
    {
        temp = p;
        p = temp->rLink;
        delete temp;
    }
    else if (p->rLink == NULL)
    {
        temp = p;
        p = temp->lLink;
        delete temp;
    }
    else
    {
        current = p->lLink;
        trailCurrent = NULL;

        while (current->rLink != NULL)
        {
            trailCurrent = current;
            current = current->rLink;
        }//end while

        p->info = current->info;

        if (trailCurrent == NULL) //current did not move;
                            //current == p->lLink; adjust p
            p->lLink = current->lLink;
```

```
        else
            trailCurrent->rLink = current->lLink;

        delete current;
    }//end else
} //end deleteFromTree
```

Next, we describe the function `deleteNode`. The function `deleteNode` first searches the binary search tree to find the node containing the item to be deleted. The item to be deleted, `deleteItem`, is passed as a parameter to the function. If the node containing `deleteItem` is found in the binary search tree, the function `deleteNode` calls the function `deletefromTree` to delete the node. The definition of the function `deleteNode` is given next.

```
template <class elemType>
void bSearchTreeType<elemType>::deleteNode
                            (const elemType& deleteItem)
{
    nodeType<elemType> *current; //pointer to traverse the tree
    nodeType<elemType> *trailCurrent; //pointer behind current
    bool found = false;

    if (root == NULL)
        cout << "Cannot delete from an empty tree."
            << endl;
    else
    {
        current = root;
        trailCurrent = root;

        while (current != NULL && !found)
        {
            if (current->info == deleteItem)
                found = true;
            else
            {
                trailCurrent = current;

                if (current->info > deleteItem)
                    current = current->lLink;
                else
                    current = current->rLink;
            }
        }//end while

        if (current == NULL)
            cout << "The item to be deleted is not in the tree."
                << endl;
        else if (found)
        {
            if (current == root)
                deleteFromTree(root);
```

```
            else if (trailCurrent->info > deleteItem)
                deleteFromTree(trailCurrent->lLink);
            else
                deleteFromTree(trailCurrent->rLink);
    }
    else
        cout << "The item to be deleted is not in the tree."
            << endl;
}
} //end deleteNode
```

Binary Search Tree: Analysis

Let T be a binary search tree with n nodes, in which $n > 0$. Suppose that we want to determine whether an item, x, is in T. The performance of the search algorithm depends on the shape of T. Let us first consider the worst case. In the worst case, T is linear. That is, the T is one of the forms shown in Figure 19-11.

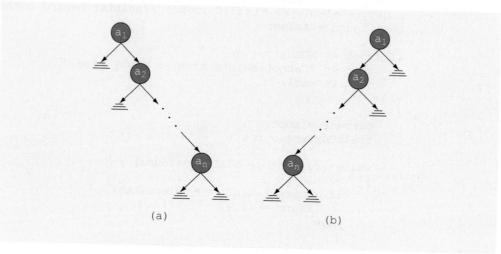

(a)
(b)

FIGURE 19-11 Linear binary search trees

Because T is linear, the performance of the search algorithm on T is the same as its performance on a linear list. Therefore, in the successful case, on average, the search algorithm makes $\frac{n+1}{2} = O(n)$ key comparisons. In the unsuccessful case, it makes n comparisons.

Let us now consider the average-case behavior. In the successful case, the search would end at a node. Because there are n items, there are $n!$ possible orderings of the keys. We assume that all $n!$ orderings of the keys are possible. Let $S(n)$ denote the number of comparisons in the average successful case, and let $U(n)$ denote the number of comparisons in the average unsuccessful case.

The number of comparisons required to determine whether x is in T is one more than the number of comparisons required to insert x in T. Furthermore, the number of comparisons required to insert x in T is the same as the number of comparisons made in the unsuccessful search, reflecting that x is not in T. From this, it follows that:

$$S(n) = 1 + \frac{U(0) + U(1) + \ldots + U(n-1)}{n} \qquad (19\text{-}1)$$

It is also known that:

$$S(n) = \left(1 + \frac{1}{n}\right)U(n) - 3 \qquad (19\text{-}2)$$

Solving equations (19-1) and (19-2), it can be shown that:

$$U(n) \approx 2.77\log_2 n = O(\log_2 n)$$

and:

$$S(n) \approx 2.77\log_2 n = O(\log_2 n)$$

We can now formulate the following result.

Theorem: Let T be a binary search tree with n nodes, in which $n > 0$. The average number of nodes visited in a search of T is approximately $1.39\log_2 n = O(\log_2 n)$, and the number of key comparisons is approximately $2.77\log_2 n = O(\log_2 n)$.

Nonrecursive Binary Tree Traversal Algorithms

The previous sections described how to do the following:

- Traverse a binary tree using the inorder, preorder, and postorder methods.
- Construct a binary tree.
- Insert an item in the binary tree.
- Delete an item from the binary tree.

The traversal algorithms—inorder, preorder, and postorder—discussed earlier are recursive. Because traversing a binary tree is a fundamental operation, this section discusses the nonrecursive inorder, preorder, and postorder traversal algorithms.

Nonrecursive Inorder Traversal

In the inorder traversal of a binary tree, for each node, the left subtree is visited first, then the node, and then the right subtree. It follows that in an inorder traversal, the first node visited is the leftmost node of the binary tree. For example, in the binary tree in Figure 19-12, the leftmost node is the node with info 28.

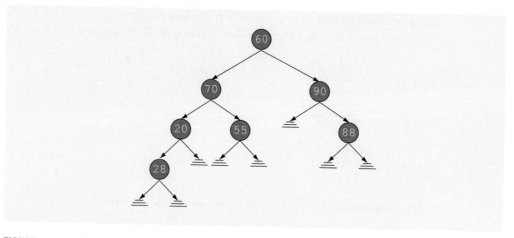

FIGURE 19-12 Binary tree; the leftmost node is 28

To get to the leftmost node of the binary tree, we start by traversing the binary tree at the root node and then follow the left link of each node until the left link of a node becomes null. From this point, we back up to the parent node, visit the node, and then move to the right node. Because links go in only one direction, to get back to a node, we must save a pointer to the node before moving to the child node. Moreover, the nodes must be backtracked in the order they were traversed. It follows that while backtracking, the nodes must be visited in a last-in first-out manner. This can be done by using a stack. We, therefore, save a pointer to a node in a stack. The general algorithm is as follows:

1. `current = root; //start traversing the binary tree at the root node`

2. ```
   while (current is not NULL or stack is nonempty)
        if (current is not NULL)
        {
            push current onto stack;
            current = current->lLink;
        }
        else
        {
            current = stack.top();
            pop stack;
            visit current;              //visit the node
            current = current->rLink;   //move to the right child
        }
   ```

The following function implements the nonrecursive inorder traversal of a binary tree:

```
template <class elemType>
void binaryTreeType<elemType>::nonRecursiveInTraversal() const
{
    stackType<nodeType<elemType>*> stack;
    nodeType<elemType> *current;
    current = root;
```
```

```
    while ((current != NULL) || (!stack.isEmptyStack()))
        if (current != NULL)
        {
            stack.push(current);
            current = current->lLink;
        }
        else
        {
            current = stack.top();
            stack.pop();
            cout << current->info << " ";
            current = current->rLink;
        }

    cout << endl;
} //end nonRecursiveInTraversal
```

Nonrecursive Preorder Traversal

In a preorder traversal of a binary tree, for each node, first the node is visited, then the left subtree is visited, and then the right subtree is visited. As in the case of an inorder traversal, after visiting a node and before moving to the left subtree, we must save a pointer to the node so that after visiting the left subtree, we can visit the right subtree. The general algorithm is as follows:

```
1.  current = root;   //start the traversal at the root node

2.  while (current is not NULL or stack is nonempty)
    if (current is not NULL)
    {
        visit current node;
        push current onto stack;
        current = current->lLink;
    }
    else
    {
        current = stack.top();
        pop stack;
        current = current->rLink; //move to the right child
    }
```

The following function implements the nonrecursive preorder traversal algorithm:

```
template <class elemType>
void binaryTreeType<elemType>::nonRecursivePreTraversal() const
{
    stackType<nodeType<elemType>*> stack;
    nodeType<elemType> *current;

    current = root;
```

```
    while ((current != NULL) || (!stack.isEmptyStack()))
        if (current != NULL)
        {
            cout << current->info << " ";
            stack.push(current);
            current = current->lLink;
        }
        else
        {
            current = stack.top();
            stack.pop();
            current = current->rLink;
        }

    cout << endl;
} //end nonRecursivePreTraversal
```

Nonrecursive Postorder Traversal

In a postorder traversal of a binary tree, for each node, first the left subtree is visited, then the right subtree is visited, and then the node is visited. As in the case of an inorder traversal, in a postorder traversal, the first node visited is the leftmost node of the binary tree. Because—for each node—the left and right subtrees are visited before visiting the node, we must indicate to the node whether the left and right subtrees have been visited. After visiting the left subtree of a node and before visiting the node, we must visit its right subtree. Therefore, after returning from a left subtree, we must tell the node that the right subtree needs to be visited, and after visiting the right subtree, we must tell the node that it can now be visited. To do this, other than saving a pointer to the node (to get back to the right subtree and to the node itself), we also save an integer value of 1 before moving to the left subtree and an integer value of 2 before moving to the right subtree. Whenever the stack is popped, the integer value associated with that pointer is popped as well. This integer value tells whether the left and right subtrees of a node have been visited.

The general algorithm is:

1. `current = root; //start the traversal at the root node`

2. `v = 0;`

3. `if current is NULL`
      `The binary tree is empty`

4. `if current is not NULL`

    a. `push current onto stack;`

    b. `push 1 onto stack;`

    c. `current = current->lLink;`

    d. `while (stack is not empty)`
          `if (current is not NULL and v is 0)`

```
      {
          push current and 1 onto stack;
          current = current->lLink;
      }
      else
      {
          assign the top element of stack to current and v;
          pop stack;
          if (v == 1)
          {
              push current and 2 onto stack;
              current = current->rLink;
              v = 0;
          }
          else
              visit current;
      }
```

We will use two (parallel) stacks: one to save a pointer to a node and another to save the integer value (1 or 2) associated with this pointer. We leave it as an exercise for you to write the definition of a C++ function to implement the preceding postorder traversal algorithm. See Programming Exercise 6 at the end of this chapter.

Binary Tree Traversal and Functions as Parameters

Suppose that you have stored employee data in a binary search tree, and at the end of the year pay increases or bonuses are to be awarded to each employee. This task requires that each node in the binary search tree be visited and that the salary of each employee be updated. The preceding sections discussed various ways to traverse a binary tree. However, in these traversal algorithms—inorder, preorder, and postorder—whenever we visited a node, for simplicity and for illustration purposes, we output only the data contained in each node. How do we use a traversal algorithm to visit each node and update the data in each node? One way to do so is to first create another binary search tree in which the data in each node is the updated data of the original binary search tree and then destroy the old binary search tree. This would require extra computer time and perhaps extra memory and, therefore, is not efficient. Another solution is to write separate traversal algorithms to update the data. This solution requires you to frequently modify the definition of the class implementing the binary search tree. However, if the user can write an appropriate function to update the data of each employee and then pass the function as a parameter to the traversal algorithms, we can considerably enhance the program's flexibility. This section describes how to pass functions as parameters to other functions.

In C++, a function name without any parentheses is considered a pointer to the function. To specify a function as a formal parameter to another function, we specify the function type, followed by the function name as a pointer, followed by the parameter types of the function. For example, consider the following statements:

```
void fParamFunc1(void (*visit) (int));          //Line 1
void fParamFunc2(void (*visit) (elemType&));     //Line 2
```

The statement in Line 1 declares fParamFunc1 to be a function that takes as a parameter any **void** function that has one value parameter of type **int**. The statement in Line 2 declares fParamFunc2 to be a function that takes as a parameter any **void** function that has one reference parameter of type elemType.

We can now rewrite, say, the inorder traversal function of the **class** binaryTreeType. Alternately, we can overload the existing inorder traversal functions. To further illustrate function overloading, we will overload the inorder traversal functions. Therefore, we include the following statements in the definition of the **class** binaryTreeType:

```
void inorderTraversal(void (*visit) (elemType&)) const;
   //Function to do an inorder traversal of the binary tree.
   //The parameter visit, which is a function, specifies
   //the action to be taken at each node.
   //Postcondition: The action specified by the function
   //               visit is applied to each node of the
   //               binary tree.

void inorder(nodeType<elemType> *p,
             void (*visit) (elemType&)) const;
   //Function to do an inorder traversal of the binary tree
   //starting at the node specified by the parameter p.
   //The parameter visit, which is a function, specifies the
   //action to be taken at each node.
   //Postcondition: The action specified by the function visit
   //               is applied to each node of the binary tree
   //               to which p points.
```

The definitions of these functions are as follows:

```
template <class elemType>
void binaryTreeType<elemType>::inorderTraversal
                         (void (*visit) (elemType& item)) const
{
    inorder(root, *visit);
}

template <class elemType>
void binaryTreeType<elemType>::inorder(nodeType<elemType>* p,
                      void (*visit) (elemType& item)) const
{
    if (p != NULL)
    {
        inorder(p->lLink, *visit);
        (*visit)(p->info);
        inorder(p->rLink, *visit);
    }
}
```

The statement:

```
(*visit)(p->info);
```

in the definition of the function inorder makes a call to the function with one reference parameter of type elemType pointed to by the pointer visit.

Example 19-5 further illustrates how functions are passed as parameters to other functions.

EXAMPLE 19-5

This example shows how to pass a user-defined function as a parameter to the binary tree traversal algorithms. For illustration purposes, we show how to use only the inorder traversal function.

The following program uses the class bSearchTreeType, which is derived from the class binaryTreeType, to build the binary tree. The traversal functions are included in the class binaryTreeType, which are then inherited by the class bSearchTreeType.

```cpp
#include <iostream>
#include "binarySearchTree.h"

using namespace std;

void print(int& x);
void update(int& x);

int main()
{
    bSearchTreeType<int> treeRoot;              //Line 1

    int num;                                     //Line 2

    cout << "Line 3: Enter numbers ending "
         << "with -999." << endl;                //Line 3
    cin >> num;                                  //Line 4

    while (num != -999)                          //Line 5
    {
        treeRoot.insert(num);                    //Line 6
        cin >> num;                              //Line 7
    }

    cout << endl
         << "Line 8: Tree nodes in inorder: ";   //Line 8
    treeRoot.inorderTraversal(print);            //Line 9
    cout << endl << "Line 10: Tree Height: "
         << treeRoot.treeHeight()
         << endl << endl;                        //Line 10

    cout << "Line 11: ******* Update Nodes "
         << "*******" << endl;                   //Line 11
    treeRoot.inorderTraversal(update);           //Line 12

    cout << "Line 13: Tree nodes in inorder "
         << "after the update: " << endl
         << "             ";                     //Line 13
    treeRoot.inorderTraversal(print);            //Line 14
```

```
    cout << endl << "Line 15: Tree Height: "
        << treeRoot.treeHeight() << endl;          //Line 15

    return 0;                                       //Line 16
}

void print(int& x)                                  //Line 17
{
    cout << x << " ";                               //Line 18
}

void update(int& x)                                 //Line 19
{
    x = 2 * x;                                      //Line 20
}
```

Sample Run: In this sample run, the user input is shaded.

```
Line 3: Enter numbers ending with -999.
56 87 23 65 34 45 12 90 66 -999


Line 8: Tree nodes in inorder: 12 23 34 45 56 65 66 87 90
Line 10: Tree Height: 4


Line 11: ******* Update Nodes *******
Line 13: Tree nodes in inorder after the update:
        24 46 68 90 112 130 132 174 180
Line 15: Tree Height: 4
```

This program works as follows. The statement in Line 1 declares `treeRoot` to be a binary search tree object, in which the data in each node is of type `int`. The statements in Lines 4 through 7 build the binary search tree. The statement in Line 9 uses the member function `inorderTraversal` of `treeRoot` to traverse the binary search tree `treeRoot`. The parameter to the function `inorderTraversal`, in Line 9, is the function `print` (defined at Line 17). Because the function `print` outputs the value of its argument, the statement in Line 9 outputs the data of the nodes of the binary search tree `treeRoot`. The statement in Line 10 outputs the height of the binary search tree.

The statement in Line 12 uses the member function `inorderTraversal` to traverse the binary search tree `treeRoot`. In Line 12, the actual parameter of the function `inorderTraversal` is the function `update` (defined at Line 19). The function `update` doubles the value of its argument. Therefore, the statement in Line 12 updates the data of each node of the binary search tree by doubling the value. The statements in Lines 14 and 15 output the nodes and the height of the binary search tree.

NOTE   **(AVL trees)** This chapter also discusses AVL trees. The necessary material is in the file AVL Trees.pdf. This file is on the Web site, *www.course.com/malik/cpp*, accompanying this book.

PROGRAMMING EXAMPLE: DVD Store (Revisited)

Watch the Video

In Chapter 16, we designed a program to help a DVD store automate its DVD rental process. That program used an (unordered) linked list to keep track of the DVD inventory in the store. Because the search algorithm on a linked list is sequential and the list is fairly large, the search could be time consuming. In this chapter, you learned how to organize data into a binary tree. If the binary tree is nicely constructed (that is, it is not linear), then the search algorithm can be improved considerably. Moreover, in general, item insertion and deletion in a binary search tree are faster than in a linked list. We will, therefore, redesign the DVD store program so that the DVD inventory can be maintained in a binary tree. As in Chapter 16, we leave the design of the customer list in a binary tree as exercises for you.

DVD Object

In Chapter 16, a linked list was used to maintain a list of DVDs in the store. Because the linked list was unordered, to see whether a particular DVD was in stock, the sequential search algorithm used the equality operator for comparison. However, in the case of a binary tree, we need other relational operators for the search, insertion, and deletion operations. We will, therefore, overload all of the relational operators. Other than this difference, the `class` dvdType is the same as before. However, we give its definition for the sake of completeness.

```cpp
//************************************************************
// Author: D.S. Malik
//
// class dvdType
// This class specifies the members to implement a DVD. It
// overloads the stream insertion operator and relational
// operators.
//************************************************************

class dvdType
{
    friend ostream& operator<< (ostream&, const dvdType&);

public:
    void setDVDInfo(string title, string star1,
                    string star2, string producer,
                    string director, string productionCo,
                    int setInStock);
    //Function to set the details of a DVD.
    //The member variables are set according to the
    //parameters.
    //Postcondition: dvdTitle = title; movieStar1 = star1;
    //               movieStar2 = star2;
    //               movieProducer = producer;
    //               movieDirector = director;
    //               movieProductionCo = productionCo;
    //               copiesInStock = setInStock;
```

19

```
int getNoOfCopiesInStock() const;
  //Function to check the number of copies in stock.
  //Postcondition: The value of copiesInStock is returned.

void checkOut();
  //Function to rent a DVD.
  //The number of copies in stock is decremented by one.
  //Postcondition: copiesInStock--;

void checkIn();
  //Function to check in a DVD.
  //The number of copies in stock is incremented by one.
  //Postcondition: copiesInStock++;

void printTitle() const;
  //Function to print the title of a movie.

void printInfo() const;
  //Function to print the details of a DVD.
  //Postcondition: The title of the movie, stars, director,
  //               and so on are output on the screen.

bool checkTitle(string title);
  //Function to check whether the title is the same as the
  //title of the DVD.
  //Postcondition: Returns the value true if the title is
  //               the same as the title of the DVD, and
  //               false otherwise.

void updateInStock(int num);
  //Function to increment the number of copies in stock by
  //adding the value of the parameter num.
  //Postcondition: copiesInStock = copiesInStock + num;

void setCopiesInStock(int num);
  //Function to set the number of copies in stock.
  //Postcondition: copiesInStock = num;

string getTitle() const;
  //Function to return the title of the DVD.
  //Postcondition: The title of the DVD is returned.

dvdType(string title = "", string star1 = "",
        string star2 = "", string producer = "",
        string director = "", string productionCo = "",
        int setInStock = 0);
  //Constructor
  //The member variables are set according to the incoming
  //parameters. If no values are specified, the default
  //values are assigned.
```

```
    //Postcondition: dvdTitle = title; movieStar1 = star1;
    //                movieStar2 = star2;
    //                movieProducer = producer;
    //                movieDirector = director;
    //                movieProductionCo = productionCo;
    //                copiesInStock = setInStock;

        //Overload relational operators
    bool operator==(const dvdType&) const;
    bool operator!=(const dvdType&) const;
    bool operator<(const dvdType&) const;
    bool operator<=(const dvdType&) const;
    bool operator>(const dvdType&) const;
    bool operator>=(const dvdType&) const;

private:
    string dvdTitle;        //variable to store the name
                            //of the movie
    string movieStar1;      //variable to store the name
                            //of the star
    string movieStar2;      //variable to store the name
                            //of the star
    string movieProducer;   //variable to store the name
                            //of the producer
    string movieDirector;   //variable to store the name
                            //of the director
    string movieProductionCo; //variable to store the name
                              //of the production company
    int copiesInStock;      //variable to store the number of
                            //copies in stock
};
```

The definitions of the member functions of the class dvdType are the same as in Chapter 16. Because here we are overloading all of the relational operators, we give only the definitions of these member functions.

```
    //Overload the relational operators
bool dvdType::operator==(const dvdType& right) const
{
    return (dvdTitle == right.dvdTitle);
}

bool dvdType::operator!=(const dvdType& right) const
{
    return (dvdTitle != right.dvdTitle);
}

bool dvdType::operator<(const dvdType& right) const
{
    return (dvdTitle < right.dvdTitle);
}
```

```
bool dvdType::operator<=(const dvdType& right) const
{
    return (dvdTitle <= right.dvdTitle);
}

bool dvdType::operator>(const dvdType& right) const
{
    return (dvdTitle > right.dvdTitle);
}

bool dvdType::operator>=(const dvdType& right) const
{
    return (dvdTitle >= right.dvdTitle);
}
```

DVD List The DVD list is maintained in a binary search tree. Therefore, we derive the `class` `dvdBinaryTree` from the `class bSearchTreeType`. The definition of the `class dvdBinaryTree` is as follows:

```
//**************************************************************
// Author: D.S. Malik
//
// class dvdBinaryTree
// This class extends the class bSearchTreeType to create
// a DVD list.
//**************************************************************

class dvdBinaryTree: public bSearchTreeType<dvdType>
{
public:
    bool dvdSearch(string title);
    //Function to search the list to see whether a
    //particular title, specified by the parameter title,
    //is in the store.
    //Postcondition: Returns true if the title is found,
    //               and false otherwise.

    bool isDVDAvailable(string title);
    //Function to determine whether a copy of a particular
    //DVD is in the store.
    //Postcondition: Returns true if at least one copy of
    //               the DVD specified by title is in the
    //               store, and false otherwise.

    void dvdCheckIn(string title);
    //Function to check in a DVD returned by a customer.
    //Postcondition: copiesInStock is incremented by one.

    void dvdCheckOut(string title);
    //Function to check out a DVD, that is, rent a DVD.
    //Postcondition: copiesInStock is decremented by one.
```

```
    bool dvdCheckTitle(string title) const;
      //Function to determine whether a particular DVD is in
      //the store.
      //Postcondition: Returns true if the DVD's title is
      //               the same as title, and false otherwise.

    void dvdUpdateInStock(string title, int num);
      //Function to update the number of copies of a DVD
      //by adding the value of the parameter num. The
      //parameter title specifies the name of the DVD for
      //which the number of copies is to be updated.
      //Postcondition: copiesInStock = copiesInStock + num;

    void dvdSetCopiesInStock(string title, int num);
      //Function to reset the number of copies of a DVD.
      //The parameter title specifies the name of the DVD
      //for which the number of copies is to be reset, and
      //the parameter num specifies the number of copies.
      //Postcondition: copiesInStock = num;

    void dvdPrintTitle() const;
      //Function to print the titles of all the DVDs in
      //the store.

private:
    void searchDVDList(string title, bool& found,
                        nodeType<dvdType>* &current) const;
      //This function searches the DVD list for a
      //particular DVD, specified by the parameter title.
      //If the DVD is found, the parameter found is set to
      //true, otherwise false; the parameter current points
      //to the node containing the DVD.

    void inorderTitle(nodeType<dvdType> *p)  const;
      //This function prints the titles of all the DVDs
      //in stock.
};
```

The definitions of the member functions isDVDAvailable, dvdCheckIn,
dvdCheckOut, dvdCheckTitle, dvdUpdateInStock,
dvdSetCopiesInStock, and dvdSearch of the class dvdBinaryTree are
similar to the definitions of these functions given in Chapter 16. The only difference
is that, here, these are members of the class dvdBinaryTree. You can find the
complete definitions of these functions on the Web site that accompanies this book.
Next, we discuss the definitions of the remaining functions of the
class dvdBinaryTree.

The function searchDVDList uses a search algorithm similar to the search
algorithm for a binary search tree given earlier in this chapter. It returns true if the
search item is found in the list. It also returns a pointer to the node containing the
search item. The definition of this function is as follows:

```
void dvdBinaryTree::searchDVDList(string title,
                              bool& found,
                              nodeType<dvdType>* &current) const
{
    found = false;

    dvdType temp;

    temp.setDVDInfo(title, "", "", "", "", "", 0);

    if (root == NULL)  //tree is empty
        cout << "Cannot search an empty list. " << endl;
    else
    {
        current = root; //set current point to the root node
                        //of the binary tree
        found = false;  //set found to false

        while (current != NULL && !found) //search the tree
            if (current->info == temp)      //item is found
                found = true;
            else if (current->info > temp)
                current = current->lLink;
            else
                current = current->rLink;
    } //end else
} //end searchDVDList
```

Given a pointer to the root node of the binary tree containing the DVDs, the function `inorderTitle` uses the inorder traversal algorithm to print the titles of the DVDs. Notice that this function outputs only the DVD titles. The definition of this function is as follows:

```
void dvdBinaryTree::inorderTitle
                            (nodeType<dvdType> *p) const
{
    if (p != NULL)
    {
        inorderTitle(p->lLink);
        p->info.printTitle();
        inorderTitle(p->rLink);
    }
}
```

The function `dvdPrintTitle` uses the function `inorderTitle` to print the titles of all DVDs in the store. The definition of this function is:

```
void dvdBinaryTree::dvdPrintTitle() const
{
    inorderTitle(root);
}
```

MAIN
PROGRAM

The main program is the same as before. Here, we give only the listing of this program. We assume that the name of the header file containing the definition of the class dvdBinaryTree is dvdBinaryTree.h, and so on.

```cpp
//***********************************************************
// Author: D.S. Malik
//
// This program uses the classes dvdType and dvdBinaryTree
// to create a list of DVDs for a DVD store. It performs
// basic operations such as check in and check out DVDs.
//***********************************************************

#include <iostream>
#include <fstream>
#include <string>
#include "binarySearchTree.h"
#include "dvdType.h"
#include "dvdBinaryTree.h"

using namespace std;

void createDVDList(ifstream& infile,
                   dvdBinaryTree& dvdList);
void displayMenu();

int main()
{
    dvdBinaryTree  dvdList;
    int choice;
    string title;

    ifstream infile;

    infile.open("dvdDat.txt");
    if (!infile)
    {
        cout << "The input file does not exist. "
             << "Program terminates!!"<< endl;
        return 1;
    }

    createDVDList(infile, dvdList);
    infile.close();

    displayMenu();                  //show the menu
    cout << "Enter your choice: ";
    cin >> choice;                  //get the request
    cin.ignore(100, '\n');          //ignore the remaining
                                    //characters in the line

    cout << endl;

    while (choice != 9)
```

```cpp
{
    switch (choice)
    {
    case 1:
        cout << "Enter the title: ";
        getline(cin, title);
        cout << endl;

        if (dvdList.dvdSearch(title))
            cout << "The store carries " << title << endl;
        else
            cout << "The store does not carry " << title
                 << endl;
        break;

    case 2:
        cout << "Enter the title: ";
        getline(cin, title);
        cout << endl;

        if (dvdList.dvdSearch(title))
        {
            if (dvdList.isDVDAvailable(title))
            {
                dvdList.dvdCheckOut(title);
                cout << "Enjoy your movie: " << title
                     << endl;
            }
            else
                cout << "Currently " << title
                     << " is out of stock." << endl;
        }
        else
            cout << "The store does not carry " << title
                 << endl;
        break;

    case 3:
        cout << "Enter the title: ";
        getline(cin, title);
        cout << endl;

        if (dvdList.dvdSearch(title))
        {
            dvdList.dvdCheckIn(title);
            cout << "Thanks for returning " << title
                 << endl;
        }
        else
            cout << "The store does not carry " << title
                 << endl;
        break;
```

```cpp
        case 4:
            cout << "Enter the title: ";
            getline(cin, title);
            cout << endl;

            if (dvdList.dvdSearch(title))
            {
                if (dvdList.isDVDAvailable(title))
                    cout << title << " is currently in "
                         << "stock." << endl;
                else
                    cout << title << " is currently out "
                         << "of stock." << endl;
            }
            else
                cout << "The store does not carry " << title
                     << endl;
            break;

        case 5:
            dvdList.dvdPrintTitle();
            break;

        case 6:
            dvdList.inorderTraversal();
            break;

        default: cout << "Invalid selection." << endl;
        } //end switch

        displayMenu();               //display the menu
        cout << "Enter your choice: ";
        cin >> choice;               //get the next request
        cin.ignore(100, '\n');       //ignore the remaining
                                     //characters in the line

        cout << endl;
    } //end while

    return 0;
}

void createDVDList(ifstream& infile,
                   dvdBinaryTree& dvdList)
{
    string title;
    string star1;
    string star2;
    string producer;
    string director;
    string productionCo;
    int inStock;
```

```
        dvdType newDVD;

        getline(infile, title);

        while (infile)
        {
            getline(infile, star1);
            getline(infile, star2);
            getline(infile, producer);
            getline(infile, director);
            getline(infile, productionCo);
            infile >> inStock;
            infile.ignore(100, '\n');
            newDVD.setDVDInfo(title, star1, star2, producer,
                              director, productionCo, inStock);
            dvdList.insert(newDVD);

            getline(infile, title);
        } //end while
    } //end createDVDList

    void displayMenu()
    {
        cout << "Select one of the following:" << endl;
        cout << "1: To check whether the store carries a "
             << "particular DVD." << endl;
        cout << "2: To check out a DVD." << endl;
        cout << "3: To check in a DVD." << endl;
        cout << "4: To check whether a particular DVD is "
             << "in stock." << endl;
        cout << "5: To print only the titles of all the DVDs."
             << endl;
        cout << "6: To print a list of all the DVDs." << endl;
        cout << "9: To exit" << endl;
    }
```

QUICK REVIEW

1. A binary tree is either empty or it has a special node called the root node. If the tree is nonempty, the root node has two sets of nodes, called the left and right subtrees, such that the left and right subtrees are also binary trees.

2. The node of a binary tree has two links in it.

3. A node in the binary tree is called a leaf if it has no left and right children.

4. A node U is called the parent of a node V if there is a branch from U to V.

5. A path from a node X to a node Y in a binary tree is a sequence of nodes $X_0, X_1, \ldots, X_n$ such that (a) $X = X_0$, $X_n = Y$, and (b) X_{i-1} is the parent of X_i for all $i = 1, 2, \ldots, n$. That is, there is a branch from X_0 to X_1, X_1 to X_2, $\ldots$, X_{i-1} to X_i, $\ldots$, X_{n-1} to X_n.

6. The length of a path in a binary tree is the number of branches on that path.

7. The level of a node in a binary tree is the number of branches on the path from the root to the node.

8. The level of the root node of a binary tree is 0, and the level of the children of the root node is 1.

9. The height of a binary tree is the number of nodes on the longest path from the root to a leaf.

10. In an inorder traversal, the binary tree is traversed as follows:

   a. Traverse the left subtree.
   b. Visit the node.
   c. Traverse the right subtree.

11. In a preorder traversal, the binary tree is traversed as follows:

   a. Visit the node.
   b. Traverse the left subtree.
   c. Traverse the right subtree.

12. In a postorder traversal, the binary tree is traversed as follows:

   a. Traverse the left subtree.
   b. Traverse the right subtree.
   c. Visit the node.

13. A binary search tree T is either empty or:

   i. T has a special node called the *root* node;
   ii. T has two sets of nodes, L_T and R_T, called the left subtree and the right subtree of T, respectively;
   iii. The key in the root node is larger than every key in the left subtree and smaller than every key in the right subtree; and
   iv. L_T and R_T are binary search trees.

14. To delete a node from a binary search tree that has both left and right nonempty subtrees, first its immediate predecessor is located, then the predecessor's info is copied into the node, and finally the predecessor is deleted.

EXERCISES

1. Mark the following statements as true or false.

   a. A binary tree must be nonempty.

   b. The level of the root node is 0.

   c. If a tree has only one node, the height of this tree is 0 because the number of levels is 0.

   d. The inorder traversal of a binary tree always outputs the data in ascending order.

2. There are 14 different binary trees with four nodes. Draw all of them.

   The binary tree of Figure 19-13, is to be used for Exercises 3 through 18.

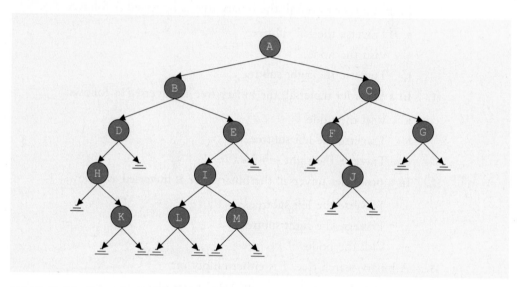

FIGURE 19-13 Figure for Exercises 3 to 18

3. Find L_A, the node in the left subtree of A.
4. Find R_A, the node in the right subtree of A.
5. Find L_B, the node in the left subtree of B.
6. Find R_B, the node in the right subtree of B.
7. Find L_E, the node in the left subtree of E.
8. Find the height of the tree with root A.
9. Find the height of the tree with root D.
10. Find the level of the node H.
11. Find the level of the node F.
12. Find the number of leaves in the binary tree with root A.

13. Find the number of leaves in the binary tree with root *C*.

14. List the leaves in the binary tree with root *E*.

15. List the nodes in the path from node *A* to node *L*.

16. List the nodes of this binary tree in an inorder sequence.

17. List the nodes of this binary tree in a preorder sequence.

18. List the nodes of this binary tree in a postorder sequence.

The binary tree of Figure 19-14 is to be used for Exercises 19 through 23. (*Note:* These exercises are independent of each other.)

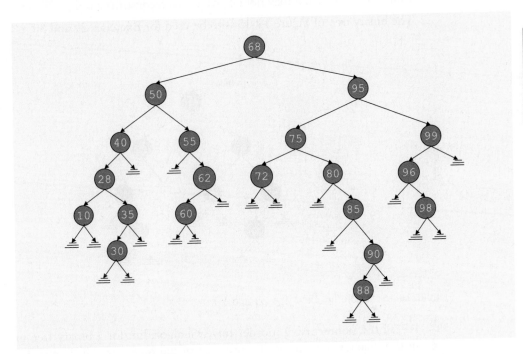

FIGURE 19-14 Figure for Exercises 19 to 23

19. List the path from the node with info 68 to the node with info 90.

20. A node with info 58 is to be inserted in the tree. List the nodes that are visited by the function `insert` to insert 58. Redraw the tree after inserting 58.

21. Delete node 60 and redraw the binary tree.

22. Delete nodes 50 and 95 in that order. Redraw the binary tree after each deletion.

23. Delete node 75 and redraw the binary tree.

24. Insert 28, 25, 26, 42, 47, 30, 45, 29, 5 into an initially empty binary search tree. Draw the final binary search tree.

25. Prove that a binary tree with *n* nodes has exactly *n* + 1 empty subtree (NULL pointers).

26. Suppose that you are given two sequences of elements corresponding to the inorder sequence and the preorder sequence. Prove that it is possible to reconstruct a unique binary tree.

27. The following lists the nodes in a binary tree in two different orders:

    ```
    preorder:    ABCDEFGHIJKLM
    inorder:     CEDFBAHJIKGML
    ```

    Draw the binary tree.

28. Given the nodes of a binary tree in the preorder sequence and the postorder sequence, show that it may not be possible to reconstruct a unique binary tree.

    The binary tree of Figure 19-15 is to be used for Exercises 29 and 30.

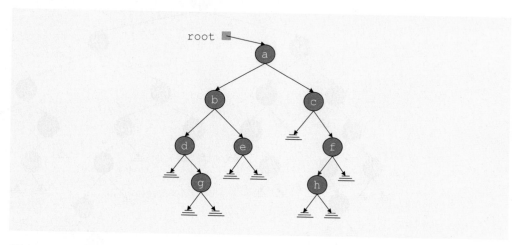

FIGURE 19-15 Figure for Exercises 29 and 30

29. Recall the nonrecursive inorder traversal algorithm for a binary tree given in this chapter. Do an inorder traversal of the binary tree in Figure 19-15. Show the stack contents after each push and pop operation.

30. Recall the nonrecursive preorder traversal algorithm for a binary tree given in this chapter. Do a preorder traversal of the binary tree in Figure 19-15. Show the stack contents after each push and pop operation.

31. Draw the UML class diagram of the **class** binaryTreeType.

32. Draw the UML class diagram of the **class** bSearchTreeType. Also, show the inheritance hierarchy.

PROGRAMMING EXERCISES

1. Write the definition of the function, nodeCount, that returns the number of nodes in the binary tree. Add this function to the **class** binaryTreeType and create a program to test this function.

2. Write the definition of the function, `leavesCount`, that takes as a parameter a pointer to the root node of a binary tree and returns the number of leaves in a binary tree. Add this function to the **class** `binaryTreeType` and create a program to test this function.

3. Write a function, `swapSubtrees`, that swaps all of the left and right subtrees of a binary tree. Add this function to the **class** `binaryTreeType` and create a program to test this function.

4. Write a function, `singleParent`, that returns the number of nodes in a binary tree that have only one child. Add this function to the **class** `binaryTreeType` and create a program to test this function. (*Note*: First create a binary search tree.)

5. Write a program to test various operations on a binary search tree.

6. a. Write the definition of the function to implement the nonrecursive postorder traversal algorithm.

   b. Write a program to test the nonrecursive inorder, preorder, and postorder traversal algorithms. (*Note*: First create a binary search tree.)

7. Write a version of the preorder traversal algorithm in which a user-defined function can be passed as a parameter to specify the visiting criteria at a node. Also, write a program to test your function.

8. Write a version of the postorder traversal algorithm in which a user-defined function can be passed as a parameter to specify the visiting criteria at a node. Also, write a program to test your function.

9. Write a function that inserts the nodes of a binary tree into an ordered linked list. Also write a program to test your function.

10. Write a program to do the following:

    a. Build a binary search tree, T_1.

    b. Do a postorder traversal of T_1 and, while doing the postorder traversal, insert the nodes into a second binary search tree T_2.

    c. Do a preorder traversal of T_2 and, while doing the preorder traversal, insert the node into a third binary search tree T_3.

    d. Do an inorder traversal of T_3.

    e. Output the heights and the number of leafs in each of the three binary search trees.

11. (**DVD Store Program**) In Programming Exercise 14 in Chapter 16, you were asked to design and implement a class to maintain customer data in a linked list. Because the search on a linked list is sequential and, therefore, can be time consuming, design and implement the **class** `customerBTreeType` so that this customer data can be stored in a binary search tree. The **class** `customerBTreeType` must be derived from the **class** `bSearchTreeType`, as designed in this chapter. (To output the number of DVDs rented by a customer, write the definition of the function `nodeCount`, as in Programming Exercise 1, of the **class** `binaryTreeType`.)

12. (**DVD Store Program**) Using classes to implement the DVD data, DVD list data, customer data, and customer list data, as designed in this chapter and in Programming Exercise 11, design and complete the program to put the DVD store into operation. (To output the number of DVDs rented by a customer, write the definition of the function nodeCount, as in Programming Exercise 1, of the class binaryTreeType.)

GRAPHS

IN THIS CHAPTER, YOU WILL:

· Learn about graphs

· Become familiar with the basic terminology of graph theory

· Discover how to represent graphs in computer memory

· Explore graphs as ADTs

· Examine and implement various graph traversal algorithms

· Learn how to implement the shortest path algorithm

· Examine and implement the minimal spanning tree algorithm

In previous chapters, you learned various ways to represent and manipulate data. This chapter discusses how to implement and manipulate graphs, which have numerous applications in computer science.

Introduction

In 1736, the following problem was posed. In the town of Königsberg (now called Kaliningrad), the river Pregel (Pregolya) flows around the island Kneiphof and then divides into two branches (see Figure 20-1).

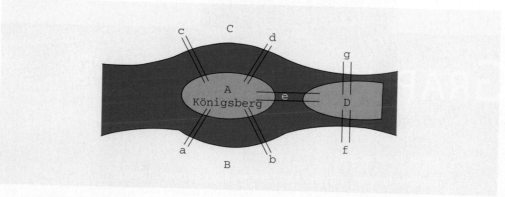

FIGURE 20-1   Königsberg bridge problem

The river has four land areas (*A*, *B*, *C*, *D*), as shown in the figure. These land areas are connected using seven bridges, as shown in Figure 20-1. The bridges are labeled *a*, *b*, *c*, *d*, *e*, *f*, and *g*. The Königsberg bridge problem is as follows: Starting at one land area, is it possible to walk across all of the bridges exactly once and return to the starting land area? In 1736, Euler represented the Königsberg bridge problem as a graph, as shown in Figure 20-2, and answered the question in the negative. This marked (as recorded) the birth of graph theory.

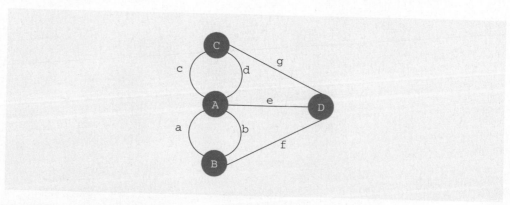

FIGURE 20-2   Graph representation of Königsberg bridge problem

NOTE
A solution of the Königsberg bridge problem is given in the book *Discrete Mathematics: Theory and Applications (Revised Edition)* listed in Appendix H.

Over the past 200 years, graph theory has been applied to a variety of applications. Graphs are used to model electrical circuits, chemical compounds, highway maps, and so on. They are also used in the analysis of electrical circuits, finding the shortest route, project planning, linguistics, genetics, social science, and so forth. In this chapter, you will learn about graphs and their applications in computer science.

Graph Definitions and Notations

To facilitate and simplify our discussion, we borrow a few definitions and terminology from set theory. Let X be a set. If a is an element of X, then we write $a \in X$. (The symbol "$\in$" means "belongs to.") A set Y is called a **subset** of X if every element of Y is also an element of X. If Y is a subset of X, we write $Y \subseteq X$. (The symbol "$\subseteq$" means "is a subset of.") The **intersection** of sets A and B, written $A \cap B$, is the set of all of the elements that are in A and B; that is, $A \cap B = \{x \mid x \in A \text{ and } x \in B\}$. (The symbol "$\cap$" means "intersection.") The **union** of sets A and B, written $A \cup B$, is the set of all of the elements that are in A or in B; that is, $A \cup B = \{x \mid x \in A \text{ or } x \in B\}$. (The symbol "$\cup$" means "union." Moreover, note that $x \in A \cup B$ means x is in A or x is in B or x is in both A and B. Also, the symbol "$\mid$" is read as "such that.")

For sets A and B, the set $A \times B$ is the set of all of the ordered pairs of elements of A and B; that is, $A \times B = \{(a, b) \mid a \in A, b \in B\}$.

A **graph** G is a pair, $G = (V, E)$, in which V is a finite nonempty set, called the set of **vertices** of G, and $E \subseteq V \times V$. That is, the elements of E are the pair of elements of V. E is called the set of **edges**.

Let $V(G)$ denote the set of vertices and $E(G)$ denote the set of edges of a graph G. If the elements of $E(G)$ are ordered pairs, G is called a **directed graph** or **digraph**; otherwise, G is called an **undirected graph**. In an undirected graph, the pairs (u, v) and (v, u) represent the same edge. If (u, v) is an edge in a directed graph, then sometimes the vertex u is called the **origin** of the edge, and the vertex v is called the **destination**.

Let G be a graph. A graph H is called a **subgraph** of G if $V(H) \subseteq V(G)$ and $E(H) \subseteq E(G)$; that is, every vertex of H is a vertex of G, and every edge in H is an edge in G.

NOTE To learn more about sets and graph terminology, the interested reader is referred to the book *Discrete Mathematics: Theory and Applications (Revised Edition)*, listed in Appendix H.

A graph can be shown pictorially. The vertices are drawn as circles, and a label inside of the circle represents the vertex. In an undirected graph, the edges are drawn using lines. In a directed graph, the edges are drawn using arrows. Moreover, in a directed graph, the tail of a pictorial directed edge is the origin, and the head is the destination.

EXAMPLE 20-1

Figure 20-3 shows some examples of undirected graphs.

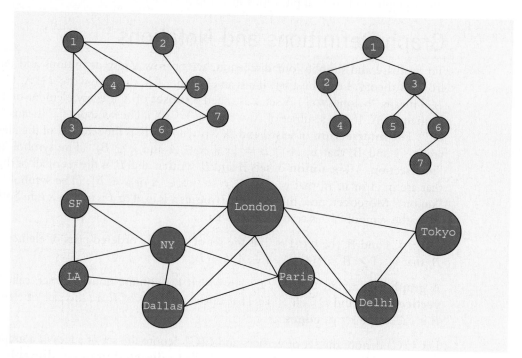

FIGURE 20-3 Various undirected graphs

EXAMPLE 20-2

Figure 20-4 shows some examples of directed graphs.

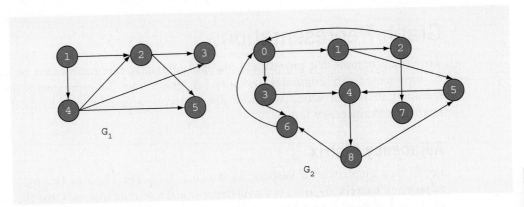

FIGURE 20-4   Various directed graphs

For the graphs of Figure 20-4, we have

$V(G_1) = \{1, 2, 3, 4, 5\}$ $E(G_1) = \{(1, 2), (1, 4), (2, 3), (2, 5), (4, 2), (4, 3), (4, 5)\}$

$V(G_2) = \{0, 1, 2, 3, 4, 5, 6, 7, 8\}$ $E(G_2) = \{(0, 1), (0, 3), (1, 2), (1, 5), (2, 0), (2, 7), (3, 4),$
$(3, 6), (4, 8),(5, 4), (6, 0), (8, 5), (8, 6),\}$

Let G be an undirected graph. Let u and v be two vertices in G. Then, u and v are called **adjacent** if there is an edge from one to the other; that is, $(u, v) \in E(G)$. Let $e = (u, v)$ be an edge in G. We then say that edge e is **incident** on the vertices u and v. An edge incident on a single vertex is called a **loop**. If two edges, e_1 and e_2, are associated with the same pair of vertices, then e_1 and e_2 are called **parallel edges**. A graph is called a **simple graph** if it has no loops and no parallel edges. There is a **path** from u to v if there is a sequence of vertices $u_1, u_2, \ldots, u_n$ such that $u = u_1$, $u_n = v$, and (u_i, u_{i+1}) is an edge for all $i = 1, 2, \ldots, n - 1$. Vertices u and v are called **connected** if there is a path from u to v. A **simple path** is a path in which all of the vertices, except possibly the first and last vertices, are distinct. A **cycle** in G is a simple path in which the first and last vertices are the same. G is called **connected** if there is a path from any vertex to any other vertex. A maximal subset of connected vertices is called a **component** of G.

Let G be a directed graph, and let u and v be two vertices in G. If there is an edge from u to v, that is, $(u, v) \in E(G)$, then we say that u is **adjacent to** v and v is **adjacent from** u. The definitions of the paths and cycles in G are similar to those for undirected graphs. G is called **strongly connected** if any two vertices in G are connected.

Consider the directed graphs of Figure 20-4. In G_1, 1-4-2-5 is a path from vertex 1 to vertex 5. There are no cycles in G_1. In G_2, 0-3-4-8-5 is a path from vertex 0 to vertex 5; 6-0-1-2-7 is a path from vertex 6 to vertex 7; 0-1-2-0 is a cycle; 3-4-8-6-0-3 is a cycle; and 0-1-5-4-8-6-0 is a cycle.

Graph Representation

To write programs that process and manipulate graphs, the graphs must be stored—that is, represented—in computer memory. A graph can be represented (in computer memory) in several ways. We now discuss two commonly used methods: adjacency matrices and adjacency lists.

Adjacency Matrix

Let G be a graph with n vertices, in which $n > 0$. Let $V(G) = \{v_1, v_2, \ldots, v_n\}$. The **adjacency matrix** A_G of G is a two-dimensional $n \times n$ matrix such that the (i, j)th entry of A_G is 1 if there is an edge from v_i to v_j; otherwise, the (i, j)th entry is zero. That is:

$$A_G(i,j) = \begin{cases} 1 & \text{if } (v_i, v_j) \in E(G) \\ 0 & \text{otherwise} \end{cases}$$

In an undirected graph, if $(v_i, v_j) \in E(G)$, then $(v_j, v_i) \in E(G)$, so $A_G(i, j) = 1 = A_G(j, i)$. It follows that the adjacency matrix of an undirected graph is symmetric.

EXAMPLE 20-3

Consider the directed graphs of Figure 20-4. The adjacency matrices of the directed graphs G_1 and G_2 are as follows:

$$A_{G_1} = \begin{bmatrix} 0 & 1 & 0 & 1 & 0 \\ 0 & 0 & 1 & 0 & 1 \\ 0 & 0 & 0 & 0 & 0 \\ 0 & 1 & 1 & 0 & 1 \\ 0 & 0 & 0 & 0 & 0 \end{bmatrix} \quad \text{and} \quad A_{G_2} = \begin{matrix} 0 \\ 1 \\ 2 \\ 3 \\ 4 \\ 5 \\ 6 \\ 7 \\ 8 \end{matrix} \begin{bmatrix} 0 & 1 & 0 & 1 & 0 & 0 & 0 & 0 & 0 \\ 0 & 0 & 1 & 0 & 0 & 1 & 0 & 0 & 0 \\ 1 & 0 & 0 & 0 & 0 & 0 & 0 & 1 & 0 \\ 0 & 0 & 0 & 0 & 1 & 0 & 1 & 0 & 0 \\ 0 & 0 & 0 & 0 & 0 & 0 & 0 & 0 & 1 \\ 0 & 0 & 0 & 0 & 1 & 0 & 0 & 0 & 0 \\ 1 & 0 & 0 & 0 & 0 & 0 & 0 & 0 & 0 \\ 0 & 0 & 0 & 0 & 0 & 0 & 0 & 0 & 0 \\ 0 & 0 & 0 & 0 & 0 & 1 & 1 & 0 & 0 \end{bmatrix}$$

Adjacency Lists

Let G be a graph with n vertices, in which $n > 0$. Let $V(G) = \{v_1, v_2, \ldots, v_n\}$. In the adjacency list representation, corresponding to each vertex, v, there is a linked list such that each node of the linked list contains the vertex, u, such that $(v, u) \in E(G)$. Because there are n nodes, we use an array, A, of size n, such that $A[i]$ is a reference variable pointing to the first node of the linked list containing the vertices to which v_i is adjacent. Clearly, each node has two components, say **vertex** and **link**. The component **vertex** contains the index of the vertex adjacent to vertex i.

EXAMPLE 20-4

Consider the directed graphs of Figure 20-4. Figure 20-5 shows the adjacency list of the directed graphs G_1 and G_2.

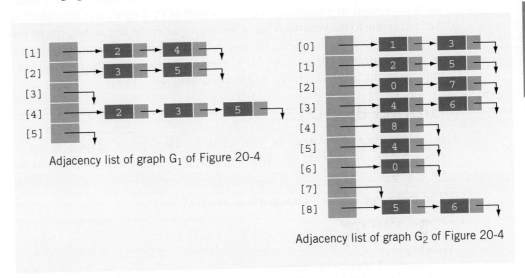

Adjacency list of graph G_1 of Figure 20-4

Adjacency list of graph G_2 of Figure 20-4

FIGURE 20-5   Adjacency list of graphs of Figure 20-4

Operations on Graphs

Now that you know how to represent graphs in computer memory, the next obvious step is to learn the basic operations on a graph. The operations commonly performed on a graph are as follows:

1. Create the graph. That is, store the graph in computer memory using a particular graph representation.

2. Clear the graph. This operation makes the graph empty.

3. Determine whether the graph is empty.

4. Traverse the graph.

5. Print the graph.

We will add more operations on a graph when we discuss a specific application or a particular graph later in this chapter.

How a graph is represented in computer memory depends on the specific application. For illustration purposes, we use the adjacency list (linked list) representation of graphs. Therefore, for each vertex, *v*, the vertices adjacent to *v* (in a directed graph, also called the **immediate successors**) are stored in the linked list associated with *v*.

To manage the data in a linked list, we use the `class` `unorderedLinkedList`, discussed in Chapter 16.

The labeling of the vertices of a graph depends on a specific application. If you are dealing with the graph of cities, you could label the vertices by the names of the cities. However, to write algorithms to manipulate a graph as well as to simplify the algorithm, there must be some ordering to the vertices. That is, we must specify the first vertex, the second vertex, and so on. Therefore, for simplicity, throughout this chapter, we assume that the *n* vertices of the graphs are numbered $0, 1, \ldots, n - 1$. Moreover, it follows that the class that we will design to implement the graph algorithm will *not* be a template.

Graphs as ADTs

In this section, we describe the class to implement graphs as an abstract data type (ADT) and provide the definitions of the functions to implement the operations on a graph.

The following class defines a graph as an ADT:

```
class graphType
{
public:
    bool isEmpty() const;
      //Function to determine whether the graph is empty.
      //Postcondition: Returns true if the graph is empty;
      //               otherwise, returns false.

    void createGraph();
      //Function to create a graph.
      //Postcondition: The graph is created using the
      //               adjacency list representation.

    void clearGraph();
      //Function to clear graph.
      //Postcondition: The memory occupied by each vertex
      //               is deallocated.

    void printGraph() const;
      //Function to print graph.
      //Postcondition: The graph is printed.
```

```
    void depthFirstTraversal();
      //Function to perform the depth first traversal of
      //the entire graph.
      //Postcondition: The vertices of the graph are printed
      //               using depth first traversal algorithm.

    void dftAtVertex(int vertex);
      //Function to perform the depth first traversal of
      //the graph at a node specified by the parameter vertex.
      //Postcondition: Starting at vertex, the vertices are
      //               printed using depth first traversal
      //               algorithm.

    void breadthFirstTraversal();
      //Function to perform the breadth first traversal of
      //the entire graph.
      //Postcondition: The vertices of the graph are printed
      //               using breadth first traversal algorithm.

    graphType(int size = 0);
      //Constructor
      //Postcondition: gSize = 0; maxSize = size;
      //               graph is an array of pointers to linked
      //               lists.

    ~graphType();
      //Destructor
      //The storage occupied by the vertices is deallocated.

protected:
    int maxSize;      //maximum number of vertices
    int gSize;        //current number of vertices
    unorderedLinkedList<int> *graph; //array to create
                                     //adjacency lists


private:
    void dft(int v, bool visited[]);
      //Function to perform the depth first traversal of
      //the graph at a node specified by the parameter vertex.
      //This function is used by the public member functions
      //depthFirstTraversal and dftAtVertex.
      //Postcondition: Starting at vertex, the vertices are
      //               printed using depth first traversal
      //               algorithm.
};
```

We leave the UML class diagram of the class graphType as an exercise.

The definitions of the functions of the class graphType are discussed next.

A graph is empty if the number of vertices is zero—that is, if gSize is 0. Therefore, the definition of the function isEmpty is:

```
bool graphType::isEmpty() const
{
    return (gSize == 0);
}
```

The definition of the function `createGraph` depends on how the data is input into the program. For illustration purposes, we assume that the data to the program is input from a file. The user is prompted for the input file. The data in the file appears in the following form:

```
5
0 2 4 ... -999
1 3 6 8 ... -999
...
```

The first line of input specifies the number of vertices in the graph. The first entry in the remaining lines specifies the vertex, and all of the remaining entries in the line (except the last) specify the vertices that are adjacent to the vertex. Each line ends with the number -999.

Using these conventions, the definition of the function `createGraph` is:

```
void graphType::createGraph()
{
    ifstream infile;
    char fileName[50];

    int index;
    int vertex;
    int adjacentVertex;

    if (gSize != 0)   //if the graph is not empty, make it empty
        clearGraph();

    cout << "Enter input file name: ";
    cin >> fileName;
    cout << endl;

    infile.open(fileName);

    if (!infile)
    {
        cout << "Cannot open input file." << endl;
        return;
    }

    infile >> gSize;    //get the number of vertices

    for (index = 0; index < gSize; index++)
    {
        infile >> vertex;
        infile >> adjacentVertex;
```

```
        while (adjacentVertex != -999)
        {
            graph[vertex].insertLast(adjacentVertex);
            infile >> adjacentVertex;
        } //end while
    } // end for

    infile.close();
} //end createGraph
```

The function `clearGraph` empties the graph by deallocating the storage occupied by each linked list and then setting the number of vertices to zero.

```
void graphType::clearGraph()
{
    int index;

    for (index = 0; index < gSize; index++)
        graph[index].destroyList();

    gSize = 0;
} //end clearGraph
```

The definition of the function `printGraph` is given next.

```
void graphType::printGraph() const
{
    int index;

    for (index = 0; index < gSize; index++)
    {
        cout << index << " ";
        graph[index].print();
        cout << endl;
    }

    cout << endl;
} //end printGraph
```

The definitions of the constructor and the destructor are:

```
    //Constructor
graphType::graphType(int size)
{
    maxSize = size;
    gSize = 0;
    graph = new unorderedLinkedList<int>[size];
}

    //Destructor
graphType::~graphType()
{
    clearGraph();
}
```

Graph Traversals

Processing a graph requires the ability to traverse the graph. This section discusses the graph traversal algorithms.

Traversing a graph is similar to traversing a binary tree, except that traversing a graph is a bit more complicated. Recall that a binary tree has no cycles. Also, starting at the root node, we can traverse the entire tree. On the other hand, a graph might have cycles, and we might not be able to traverse the entire graph from a single vertex (for example, if the graph is not connected). Therefore, we must keep track of the vertices that have been visited. We must also traverse the graph from each vertex (that has not been visited) of the graph. This ensures that the entire graph is traversed.

The two most common graph traversal algorithms are the **depth first traversal** and **breadth first traversal**, which are described next. For simplicity, we assume that when a vertex is visited, its index is output. Moreover, each vertex is visited only once. We use the `bool` array `visited` to keep track of the visited vertices.

Depth First Traversal

The **depth first traversal** is similar to the preorder traversal of a binary tree. The general algorithm is:

```
for each vertex, v, in the graph
    if v is not visited
        start the depth first traversal at v
```

Consider the graph G of Figure 20-6.

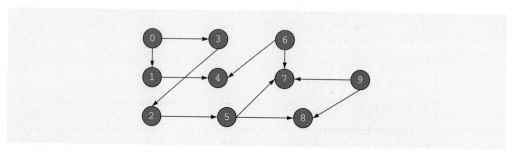

FIGURE 20-6   Directed graph G

A depth first ordering of the vertices of the graph G in Figure 20-6 is

0, 1, 4, 3, 2, 5, 7, 8, 6, 9

For the graph of Figure 20-6, the depth first search starts at the vertex 0. After visiting all of the vertices that can be reached starting at the vertex 0, the depth first search starts at the next vertex that is not visited. There is a path from the vertex 0 to every other vertex except the vertices 6 and 9. Therefore, when the depth first search starts at the vertex 0, all of the vertices except 6 and 9 are visited before these vertices. After completing the depth first search that started at the vertex 0, the depth first search starts at the vertex 6 and then at the vertex 9. Note that there is no path from the vertex 6 to the vertex 9. Therefore, after completing the depth first search that started at the vertex 6, the depth first search starts at the vertex 9.

The general algorithm to do a depth first traversal *at a given node*, v, is:

1. Mark node v as visited

2. Visit the node

3. `for` each vertex u adjacent to v
   `if` u is not visited
   start the depth first traversal at u

Clearly, this is a recursive algorithm. We use a recursive function, `dft`, to implement this algorithm. The vertex at which the depth first traversal is to be started, and the `bool` array `visited`, are passed as parameters to this function:

```
void graphType::dft(int v, bool visited[])
{
    visited[v] = true;
    cout << " " << v << " ";   //visit the vertex

    linkedListIterator<int> graphIt;

        //for each vertex adjacent to v
    for (graphIt = graph[v].begin(); graphIt != graph[v].end();
                                     ++graphIt)
    {
        int w = *graphIt;
        if (!visited[w])
            dft(w, visited);
    } //end while
} //end dft
```

In the preceding code, note that the statement:

```
linkedListIterator<int> graphIt;
```

declares `graphIt` to be an iterator. In the `for` loop, we use it to traverse a linked list (adjacency list) to which the pointer `graph[v]` points. Next, let us look at the statement:

```
int w = *graphIt;
```

The expression `*graphIt` returns the label of the vertex, adjacent to the vertex v, to which `graphIt` points.

Next, we give the definition of the function `depthFirstTraversal` to implement the depth first traversal of the graph:

```
void graphType::depthFirstTraversal()
{
    bool *visited; //pointer to create the array to keep
                   //track of the visited vertices
    visited = new bool[gSize];

    int index;

    for (index = 0; index < gSize; index++)
        visited[index] = false;

        //For each vertex that is not visited, do a depth
        //first traverssal
    for (index = 0; index < gSize; index++)
        if (!visited[index])
            dft(index,visited);
    delete [] visited;
} //end depthFirstTraversal
```

The function `depthFirstTraversal` performs a depth first traversal of the entire graph. The definition of the function `dftAtVertex`, which performs a depth first traversal at a given vertex, is as follows:

```
void graphType::dftAtVertex(int vertex)
{
    bool *visited;

    visited = new bool[gSize];

    for (int index = 0; index < gSize; index++)
        visited[index] = false;

    dft(vertex, visited);

    delete [] visited;
} // end dftAtVertex
```

Breadth First Traversal

The **breadth first traversal** of a graph is similar to traversing a binary tree level by level (the nodes at each level are visited from left to right). All of the nodes at any level, *i*, are visited before visiting the nodes at level $i + 1$.

A breadth first ordering of the vertices of the graph G (Figure 20-6) is:

0, 1, 3, 4, 2, 5, 7, 8, 6, 9

For the graph *G*, we start the breadth traversal at vertex 0. After visiting the vertex 0, next we visit the vertices that are directly connected to it and are not visited, which are

1 and 3. Next, we visit the vertices that are directly connected to 1 and are not visited, which is 4. After this, we visit the vertices that are directly connected to 3 and are not visited, which in this instance is the single vertex 2. After this, we visit the vertices that are directly connected to 2 and are not visited, and so on.

As in the case of the depth first traversal, because it might not be possible to traverse the entire graph from a single vertex, the breadth first traversal also traverses the graph from each vertex that is not visited. Starting at the first vertex, the graph is traversed as much as possible; we then go to the next vertex that has not been visited. To implement the breadth first search algorithm, we use a queue. The general algorithm is:

a.   **for** each vertex **v** in the graph
       if v is not visited
           add **v** to the **queue** **//start the breadth first search at v**

b.   Mark **v** as **visited**

c.   **while** the **queue** is not empty

   c.1.   Remove vertex **u** from the **queue**

   c.2.   Retrieve the vertices adjacent to **u**

   c.3.   **for** each vertex **w** that is adjacent to **u**

       if w is not visited

       c.3.1.   Add **w** to the **queue**

       c.3.2.   Mark **w** as **visited**

The following C++ function, `breadthFirstTraversal`, implements this algorithm:

```
void graphType::breadthFirstTraversal()
{
    linkedQueueType<int> queue;

    bool *visited;
    visited = new bool[gSize];

    for (int ind = 0; ind < gSize; ind++)
        visited[ind] = false; //initialize the array
                              //visited to false

    linkedListIterator<int> graphIt;

    for (int index = 0; index < gSize; index++)
        if (!visited[index])
        {
            queue.addQueue(index);
            visited[index] = true;
            cout << " " << index << " ";
```

```
        while (!queue.isEmptyQueue())
        {
            int u = queue.front();
            queue.deleteQueue();

            for (graphIt = graph[u].begin();
                 graphIt != graph[u].end(); ++graphIt)
            {
                int w = *graphIt;
                if (!visited[w])
                {
                    queue.addQueue(w);
                    visited[w] = true;
                    cout << " " << w << " ";
                }
            }
        } //end while
    }

    delete [] visited;
} //end breadthFirstTraversal
```

As we continue to discuss graph algorithms, we will be writing C++ functions to implement specific algorithms, so we will derive (using inheritance) new classes from the `class graphType`.

Shortest Path Algorithm

**Watch
the Video**

The graph theory has many applications. For example, we can use graphs to show how different chemicals are related or to show airline routes. They can also be used to show the highway structure of a city, state, or country. The edges connecting two vertices can be assigned a nonnegative real number, called the **weight of the edge**. If the graph represents a highway structure, the weight can represent the distance between two places or the travel time from one place to another. Such graphs are called **weighted graphs**.

Let G be a weighted graph. Let u and v be two vertices in G, and let P be a path in G from u to v. The **weight of the path** P is the sum of the weights of all the edges on the path P, which is also called the **weight** of v from u via P.

Let G be a weighted graph representing a highway structure. Suppose that the weight of an edge represents the travel time. For example, to plan monthly business trips, a sales-person wants to find the **shortest path** (that is, the path with the smallest weight) from her or his city to every other city in the graph. Many such problems exist in which we want to find the shortest path from a given vertex, called the **source**, to every other vertex in the graph.

This section describes the **shortest path algorithm**, also called a **greedy algorithm**, developed by Dijkstra.

Let G be a graph with n vertices, in which $n > 0$. Let $V(G) = \{v_1, v_2, \ldots, v_n\}$. Let W be a two-dimensional $n \times n$ matrix such that:

$$W(i,j) = \begin{cases} w_{ij} & \text{if } (v_i, v_j) \text{ is an edge in } G \text{ and } w_{ij} \text{ is the weight of the edge } (v_i, v_j) \\ \infty & \text{if there is no edge from } v_i \text{ to } v_j \end{cases}$$

The input to the program is the graph and the weight matrix associated with the graph. To make inputting the data easier, we extend the definition of the **class** `graphType` (using inheritance) and add the function `createWeightedGraph` to create the graph and the weight matrix associated with the graph. Let us call this **class** `weightedGraphType`. The functions to implement the shortest path algorithm will also be added to this class.

```
class weightedGraphType: public graphType
{
public:
    void createWeightedGraph();
        //Function to create the graph and the weight matrix.
        //Postcondition: The graph using adjacency lists and
        //               its weight matrix is created.

    void shortestPath(int vertex);
        //Function to determine the weight of a shortest path
        //from vertex, that is, source, to every other vertex
        //in the graph.
        //Postcondition: The weight of the shortest path from
        //               vertex to every other vertex in the
        //               graph is determined.

    void printShortestDistance(int vertex);
        //Function to print the shortest weight from vertex
        //to the other vertex in the graph.
        //Postcondition: The weight of the shortest path from
        //               vertex to every other vertex in the
        //               graph is printed.

    weightedGraphType(int size = 0);
        //Constructor
        //Postcondition: gSize = 0; maxSize = size;
        //               graph is an array of pointers to linked
        //               lists.
        //               weights is a two-dimensional array to
        //               store the weights of the edges.
        //               smallestWeight is an array to store the
        //               smallest weight from source to vertices.

    ~weightedGraphType();
        //Destructor
        //The storage occupied by the vertices and the arrays
        //weights and smallestWeight is deallocated.
```

```
protected:
    double **weights;     //pointer to create weight matrix
    double *smallestWeight; //pointer to create the array to
                          //store the smallest weight from
                          //source to vertices
};
```

We leave the UML class diagram of the **class** weightedGraphType and the inheritance hierarchy as an exercise. The definition of the function createWeightedGraph is also left as an exercise for you. Next, we describe the shortest path algorithm.

Shortest Path

Given a vertex, say, vertex (that is, a source), this section describes the shortest path algorithm.

The general algorithm is:

1. Initialize the array smallestWeight so that:

    smallestWeight[u] = weights[vertex, u]

2. Set smallestWeight[vertex] = 0.

3. Find the vertex, v, that is closest to the vertex for which the shortest path has not been determined.

4. Mark v as the (next) vertex for which the smallest weight is found.

5. For each vertex w in G, such that the shortest path from vertex to w has not been determined and an edge (v, w) exists, if the weight of the path to w via v is smaller than its current weight, update the weight of w to the weight of v + the weight of the edge (v, w).

Because there are n vertices, Steps 3 through 5 are repeated $n - 1$ times.

Example 20-5 illustrates the shortest path algorithm. (We use the **bool** array weightFound to keep track of the vertices for which the smallest weight from the source vertex has been found. If the smallest weight for a vertex, from the source, has been found, then this vertex's corresponding entry in the array weightFound is set to **true**; otherwise, the corresponding entry is **false**.)

EXAMPLE 20-5

Let G be the graph shown in Figure 20-7.

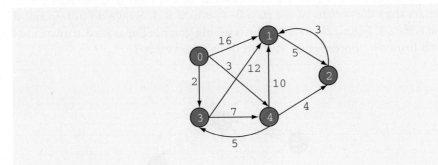

FIGURE 20-7 Weighted graph *G*

Suppose that the source vertex of G is 0. The graph shows the weight of each edge. After Steps 1 and 2 execute, the resulting graph is as shown in Figure 20-8.

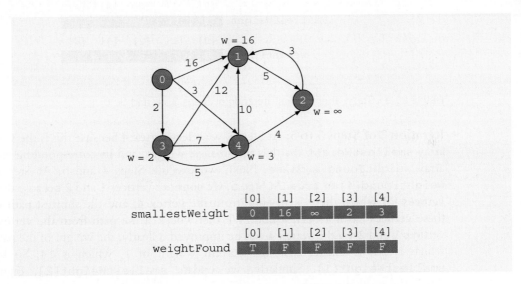

	[0]	[1]	[2]	[3]	[4]
smallestWeight	0	16	∞	2	3

	[0]	[1]	[2]	[3]	[4]
weightFound	T	F	F	F	F

FIGURE 20-8 Graph after Steps 1 and 2 execute

Iteration 1 of Steps 3 to 5: At Step 3, we select a vertex that is closest to the vertex 0 and for which the shortest path has not been found. We do this by finding a vertex in the array `smallestWeight` that has the smallest weight and a corresponding entry in the array `weightFound` of **false**. Therefore, in this iteration, we select the vertex 3. At Step 4, we mark `weightFound[3]` as **true**. Next, at Step 5, we consider vertices

1 and 4 because these are the vertices for which there is an edge from the vertex 3, and the shortest part from 0 to these vertices has not been found. We then check if the path from the vertex 0 to the vertices 1 and 4 via the vertex 3 can be improved. The weight of the path 0-3-1 from 0 to 1 is less than the weight of the path 0-1. So we update smallestWeight[1] to 14. The weight of the path 0-3-4, which is 2 + 7 = 9, is greater than the weight of the path 0-4, which is 3. So we do not update the weight of the vertex 4. Figure 20-9 shows the resulting graph. (The dotted arrow shows the shortest path from the source—that is, from 0—to the vertex.)

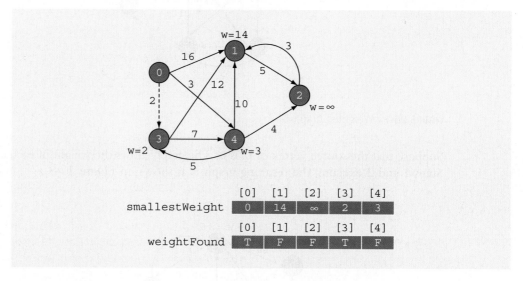

	[0]	[1]	[2]	[3]	[4]
smallestWeight	0	14	∞	2	3

	[0]	[1]	[2]	[3]	[4]
weightFound	T	F	F	T	F

FIGURE 20-9 Graph after the first iteration of Steps 3, 4, and 5

Iteration 2 of Steps 3 to 5: At Step 3, we select vertex 4 because this is the vertex in the array smallestWeight that has the smallest weight, and its corresponding entry in the array weightFound is false. Next, we execute Steps 4 and 5. At Step 4, we set weightFound[4] to true. At Step 5, we consider vertices 1 and 2 because these are the vertices for which there is an edge from the vertex 4, and the shortest path from 0 to these vertices has not been found. We then check if the path from the vertex 0 to the vertices 1 and 2 via the vertex 4 can be improved. Clearly, the weight of the path 0-4-1, which is 13, is smaller than the current weight of 1, which is 14. So we update smallestWeight[1]. Similarly, we update smallestWeight[2]. Figure 20-10 shows the resulting graph.

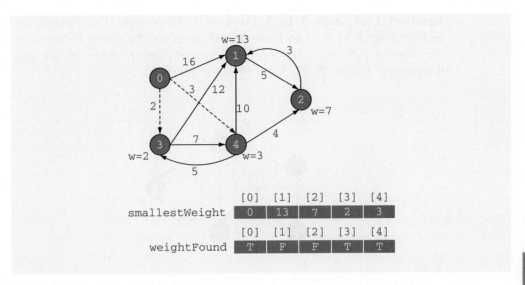

FIGURE 20-10   Graph after the second iteration of Steps 3, 4, and 5

Iteration 3 of Steps 3 to 5: At Step 3, the vertex selected is 2. At Step 4, we set `weightFound[2]` to `true`. Next, at Step 5, we consider the vertex 1 because this is the vertex for which there is an edge from the vertex 2, and the shortest part from 0 to this vertex has not been found. We then check if the path from the vertex 0 to the vertex 1 via the vertex 2 can be improved. Clearly, the weight of the path 0–4–2–1, which is 10, from 0 to 1 is smaller than the current weight of 1 (which is 13). So we update `smallestWeight[1]`. Figure 20-11 shows the resulting graph.

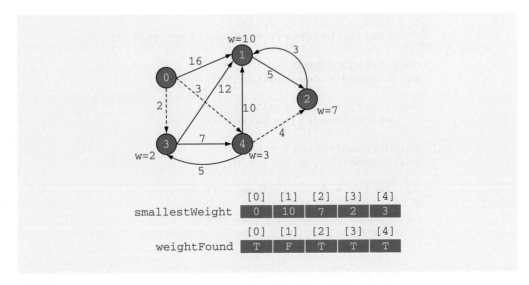

FIGURE 20-11   Graph after the third iteration of Steps 3, 4, and 5

Iteration 4 of Steps 3 to 5: At Step 3, the vertex 1 is selected, and at Step 4, `weightFound[1]` is set to `true`. In this iteration, the action of Step 5 is null because the shortest path from the vertex 0 to every other vertex in the graph has been determined. Figure 20-12 shows the final graph.

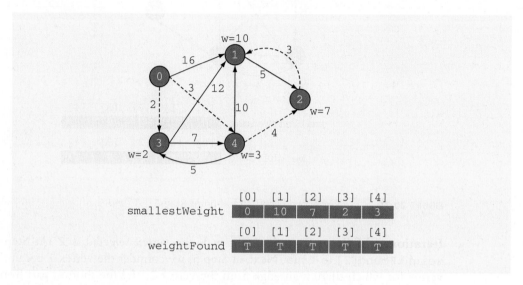

	[0]	[1]	[2]	[3]	[4]
smallestWeight	0	10	7	2	3

	[0]	[1]	[2]	[3]	[4]
weightFound	T	T	T	T	T

FIGURE 20-12   Graph after the fourth iteration of Steps 3, 4, and 5

The following C++ function, `shortestPath`, implements the previous algorithm:

```cpp
void weightedGraphType::shortestPath(int vertex)
{
    for (int j = 0; j < gSize; j++)
        smallestWeight[j] = weights[vertex][j];

    bool *weightFound;
    weightFound = new bool[gSize];

    for (int j = 0; j < gSize; j++)
        weightFound[j] = false;

    weightFound[vertex] = true;
    smallestWeight[vertex] = 0;

    for (int i = 0; i < gSize - 1; i++)
    {
        double minWeight = DBL_MAX;
        int v;
```

```
        for (int j = 0; j < gSize; j++)
            if (!weightFound[j])
                if (smallestWeight[j] < minWeight)
                {
                    v = j;
                    minWeight = smallestWeight[v];
                }

        weightFound[v] = true;

        for (int j = 0; j < gSize; j++)
            if (!weightFound[j])
                if (minWeight + weights[v][j] < smallestWeight[j])
                    smallestWeight[j] = minWeight + weights[v][j];
    } //end for
} //end shortestPath
```

Note that the function shortestPath records only the weight of the shortest path from the source to a vertex. We leave it for you to modify this function so that the shortest path from the source to a vertex is also recorded. Moreover, this function used the named constant DBL_MAX, which is defined in the header file cfloat.

The definitions of the function printShortestDistance and the constructor and destructor are:

```
void weightedGraphType::printShortestDistance(int vertex)
{
    cout << "Source Vertex: " << vertex << endl;
    cout << "Shortest Distance from Source to each Vertex."
         << endl;
    cout << "Vertex  Shortest_Distance" << endl;

    for (int j = 0; j < gSize; j++)
        cout << setw(4) << j << setw(12) << smallestWeight[j]
             << endl;
    cout << endl;
} //end printShortestDistance

    //Constructor
weightedGraphType::weightedGraphType(int size)
                :graphType(size)
{
    weights = new double*[size];

    for (int i = 0; i < size; i++)
        weights[i] = new double[size];

    smallestWeight = new double[size];
}
```

```
    //Destructor
weightedGraphType::~weightedGraphType()
{
    for (int i = 0; i < gSize; i++)
        delete [] weights[i];

    delete [] weights;
    delete smallestWeight;
}
```

Minimal Spanning Tree

Consider the graph of Figure 20-13, which represents the airline connections of a company between seven cities. The number on each edge represents some cost factor of maintaining the connection between the cities.

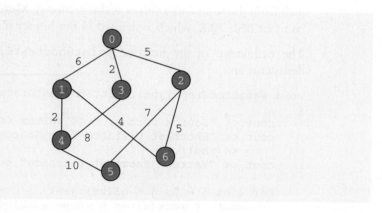

FIGURE 20-13 Airline connections between cities and the cost factor of maintaining the connections

Due to financial hardship, the company needs to shut down the maximum number of connections and still be able to fly from one city to another (the flights need not be direct). The graphs of Figure 20-14(a), (b), and (c) show three different solutions.

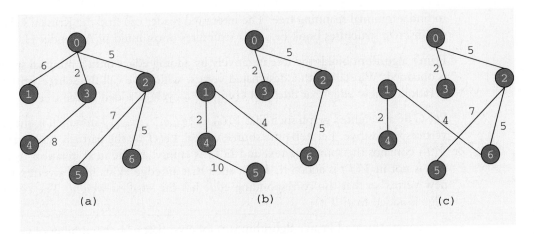

FIGURE 20-14 Possible solutions to the graph of Figure 20-13

The total cost factor of maintaining the remaining connections in Figure 20-14(a) is **33**, in Figure 20-14(b) it is **28**, and in Figure 20-14(c) it is **25**. Out of these three solutions, obviously, the desired solution is the one shown by the graph of Figure 20-14(c) because it gives the lowest cost factor. The graphs of Figure 20-14 are called spanning trees of the graph of Figure 20-13.

Let us note the following from the graphs of Figure 20-14. Each of the graphs is a subgraph of the graph of Figure 20-13, and there is a unique path from a node to any other node. Such graphs are called trees. There are many other situations in which, given a weighted graph, we need to determine a graph with the smallest weight, such as in Figure 20-14. In this section, we give an algorithm to determine such graphs. However, first we introduce some terminology.

A **(free) tree** T is a simple graph such that if u and v are two vertices in T, then there is a unique path from u to v. A tree in which a particular vertex is designated as a root is called a **rooted tree**. If a weight is assigned to the edges in T, T is called a **weighted tree**. If T is a weighted tree, the **weight** of T, denoted by $W(T)$, is the sum of the weights of all of the edges in T.

A tree T is called a **spanning tree** of graph G if T is a subgraph of G such that $V(T) = V(G)$; that is, all of the vertices of G are in T.

Suppose that G denotes the graph of Figure 20-13. Then, the graphs of Figure 20-14 show three spanning trees of G. Let us note the following theorem.

Theorem: A graph G has a spanning tree if and only if G is connected.

From this theorem, it follows that in order to determine a spanning tree of a graph, the graph must be connected.

Let G be a weighted graph. A **minimal spanning tree** of G is a spanning tree with the minimum weight.

Prim's algorithm and Kruskal's algorithm are two well-known algorithms that can be used to find the minimal spanning tree of a graph. This section discusses Prim's algorithm to find a minimal spanning tree. The interested reader can find the Kruskal's algorithm in the discrete structures book or a data structures book listed in Appendix H.

Prim's algorithm builds the tree iteratively by adding edges until a minimal spanning tree is obtained. We start with a designated vertex, which we call the source vertex. At each iteration, a new edge that does not complete a cycle is added to the tree.

Let G be a weighted graph such that $V(G) = \{v_0, v_1, \ldots, v_{n-1}\}$, in which n, the number of vertices, is positive. Let v_0 be the source vertex. Let T be the partially built tree. Initially, $V(T)$ contains the source vertex, and $E(T)$ is empty. At the next iteration, a new vertex that is not in $V(T)$ is added to $V(T)$, such that an edge exists from a vertex in T to the new vertex so that the corresponding edge has the smallest weight. The corresponding edge is added to $E(T)$.

The general form of Prim's algorithm is as follows. (Let n be the number of vertices in G.)

1. Set V(T) = {source}

2. Set E(T) = empty

3. `for i = 1 to n`

    3.1. `minWeight = infinity;`

    3.2. `for j = 1 to n`
```
        if v_j is in V(T)
          for k = 1 to n
            if v_k is not in T and weight[v_j, v_k] < minWeight
            {
                endVertex = v_k;
                edge = (v_j, v_k);
                minWeight = weight[v_j, v_k];
            }
```

    3.3. `V(T) = V(T) ∪ {endVertex};`

    3.4. `E(T) = E(T) ∪ {edge};`

Let us illustrate Prim's algorithm using the graph G of Figure 20-15 (which is same as the graph of Figure 20-13).

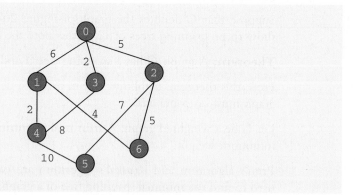

FIGURE 20-15 Weighted graph G

Let N denote the set of vertices of G that are not in T. Suppose that the source vertex is 0. After Steps 1 and 2 execute, $V(T)$, $E(T)$, and N are as shown in Figure 20-16(a).

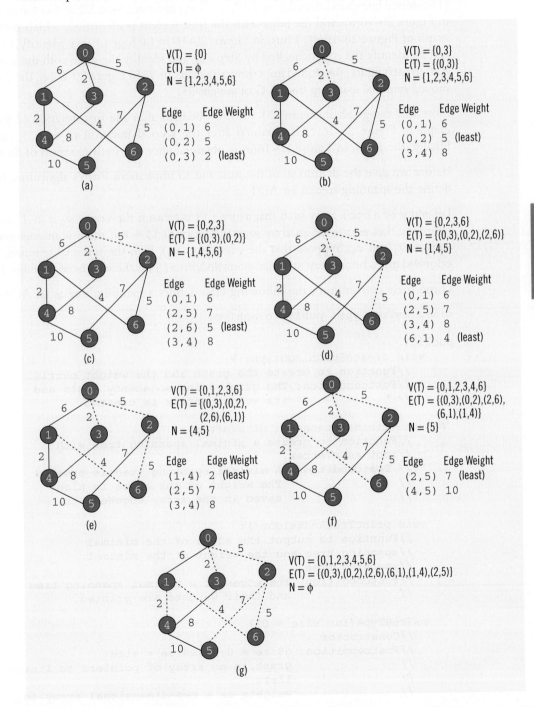

FIGURE 20-16 Prim's algorithm to find a minimal spanning tree

In Figure 20-16(a), Step 3.2 checks the edges shown in this figure; and the edge with the least weight is identified. Figure 20-16(b), shows the resulting graph, $V(T)$, $E(T)$, and N. (The dotted line shows the edge in T.) At the next iteration, Step 3.2 checks the edges shown in Figure 20-16(b); and the edge with the least weight is identified, which results in the graph of Figure 20-16(c). Thus, in Figure 20-16 in each graph, we identify $V(T)$, $E(T)$, and N; identify the edges checked by Step 3.2; and identify the edge with the least weight. Also in each figure, the dotted lines show the edges in T. In Figure 20-16(g), the dotted lines show a minimal spanning tree of G of weight 25.

Note that the graph in Figure 20-16(b) is obtained after the first iteration of Step 3, the graph in Figure 20-16(c) is obtained after the second iteration of Step 3, and so on. Finally, the graph in Figure 20-16(g) is obtained after the sixth iteration of Step 3.

Before we give the definition of the function to implement Prim's algorithm, let us first define the spanning tree as an ADT.

Let `mstv` be a `bool` array such that `mstv [j]` is `true` if the vertex v_i is in T, and `false` otherwise. Let `edges` be an array such that `edges[j]` = `k` if there is an edge connecting vertices v_j and v_k. Suppose that the edge (v_i, v_j) is in the minimal spanning tree. Let `edgeWeights` be an array such that `edgeWeights[j]` is the weight of the edge (v_i, v_j).

Using these conventions, the following class defines a spanning tree as an ADT:

```
class msTreeType: public graphType
{
public:
    void createSpanningGraph();
      //Function to create the graph and the weight matrix.
      //Postcondition: The graph using adjacency lists and
      //               its weight matrix is created.

    void minimalSpanning(int sVertex);
      //Function to create a minimal spanning tree with
      //root as sVertex.
      // Postcondition: A minimal spanning tree is created.
      //                The weight of the edges is also
      //                saved in the array edgeWeights.

    void printTreeAndWeight();
      //Function to output the edges of the minimal
      //spanning tree and the weight of the minimal
      //spanning tree.
      //Postcondition: The edges of a minimal spanning tree
      //               and their weights are printed.

    msTreeType(int size = 0);
      //Constructor
      //Postcondition: gSize = 0; maxSize = size;
      //               graph is an array of pointers to linked
      //               lists.
      //               weights is a two-dimensional array to
```

```
//              store the weights of the edges.
//              edges is an array to store the edges
//              of a minimal spanning tree.
//              edgeWeight is an array to store the
//              weights of the edges of a minimal
//              spanning tree.

    ~msTreeType();
    //Destructor
    //The storage occupied by the vertices and the arrays
    //weights, edges, and edgeWeights is deallocated.

protected:
    int source;
    double **weights;
    int *edges;
    double *edgeWeights;
};
```

We leave the UML class diagram of the **class** msTreeType and the inheritance hierarchy as an exercise. The definition of the function createSpanningGraph is also left as an exercise for you. This function creates the graph and the weight matrix associated with the graph.

The following C++ function, minimalSpanning, implements Prim's algorithm, as described previously:

```
void msTreeType::minimalSpanning(int sVertex)
{
    int startVertex, endVertex;
    double minWeight;

    source = sVertex;

    bool *mstv;
    mstv = new bool[gSize];

    for (int j = 0; j < gSize; j++)
    {
        mstv[j] = false;
        edges[j] = source;
        edgeWeights[j] = weights[source][j];
    }

    mstv[source] = true;
    edgeWeights[source] = 0;

    for (int i = 0; i < gSize - 1; i++)
    {
        minWeight = DBL_MAX;

        for (int j = 0; j < gSize; j++)
            if (mstv[j])
                for (int k = 0; k < gSize; k++)
                    if (!mstv[k] && weights[j][k] < minWeight)
```

```
                          {
                              endVertex = k;
                              startVertex = j;
                              minWeight = weights[j][k];
                          }

                  mstv[endVertex] = true;
                  edges[endVertex] = startVertex;
                  edgeWeights[endVertex] = minWeight;
          } //end for
   } //end minimalSpanning
```

The definition of the function `minimalSpanning` contains three nested `for` loops. Therefore, in the worst case, Prim's algorithm given in this section is of the order $O(n^3)$. It is possible to design Prim's algorithm so that it is of the order $O(n^2)$. Programming Exercise 5 at the end of this chapter asks you to do this.

The definition of the function `printTreeAndWeight` is:

```
void msTreeType::printTreeAndWeight()
{
    double treeWeight = 0;

    cout << "Source Vertex: " << source << endl;
    cout << "Edges    Weight" << endl;

    for (int j = 0; j < gSize; j++)
    {
        if (edges[j] != j)
        {
            treeWeight = treeWeight + edgeWeights[j];
            cout << "("<<edges[j] << ", " << j << ")        "
                 << edgeWeights[j] << endl;
        }
    }

    cout << endl;
    cout << "Minimal Spanning Tree Weight: "
         << treeWeight << endl;
} //end printTreeAndWeight
```

The definitions of the constructor and the destructor are as follows:

```
msTreeType::msTreeType(int size)
           :graphType(size)
{
    weights = new double*[size];

    for (int i = 0; i < size; i++)
        weights[i] = new double[size];

    edges  = new int[size];

    edgeWeights = new double[size];
}
```

```
//Destructor
msTreeType::~msTreeType()
{
    for (int i = 0; i < gSize; i++)
        delete [] weights[i];

    delete [] weights;
    delete [] edges;
    delete edgeWeights;
}
```

NOTE (**Topological Ordering**) This chapter also discusses topological ordering. The necessary material is in the file TopologicalOrder.pdf. This file is on the Web site, *www.course.com/malik/cpp*, accompanying this book.

QUICK REVIEW

1. A graph G is a pair, $G = (V, E)$, in which V is a finite nonempty set, called the set of vertices of G, and $E \subseteq V \times V$, called the set of edges.

2. In an undirected graph $G = (V, E)$, the elements of E are unordered pairs.

3. In a directed graph $G = (V, E)$, the elements of E are ordered pairs.

4. Let G be a graph. A graph H is called a subgraph of G if every vertex of H is a vertex of G and every edge in H is an edge in G.

5. Two vertices u and v in an undirected graph are called adjacent if there is an edge from one to the other.

6. Let $e = (u, v)$ be an edge in an undirected graph G. The edge e is said to be incident on the vertices u and v.

7. An edge incident on a single vertex is called a loop.

8. In an undirected graph, if two edges e_1 and e_2 are associated with the same pair of vertices, then e_1 and e_2 are called parallel edges.

9. A graph is called a simple graph if it has no loops and no parallel edges.

10. A path from a vertex u to a vertex v is a sequence of vertices $u_1, u_2, \ldots, u_n$ such that $u = u_1$, $u_n = v$, and (u_i, u_{i+1}) is an edge for all $i = 1, 2, \ldots, n - 1$.

11. The vertices u and v are called connected if there is a path from u to v.

12. A simple path is a path in which all of the vertices, except possibly the first and last vertices, are distinct.

13. A cycle in G is a simple path in which the first and last vertices are the same.

14. An undirected graph G is called connected if there is a path from any vertex to any other vertex.

15. A maximal subset of connected vertices is called a component of G.

16. Suppose that u and v are vertices in a directed graph G. If there is an edge from u to v, that is, $(u, v) \in E$, we say that u is adjacent to v and v is adjacent from u.

17. A directed graph G is called strongly connected if any two vertices in G are connected.

18. Let G be a graph with n vertices, in which $n > 0$. Let $V(G) = \{v_1, v_2, \ldots, v_n\}$. The adjacency matrix A_G is a two-dimensional $n \times n$ matrix such that the (i, j)th entry of A_G is 1 if there is an edge from v_i to v_j; otherwise, the (i, j)th entry is zero.

19. In an adjacency list representation, corresponding to each vertex v is a linked list such that each node of the linked list contains the vertex u, and $(v, u) \in E(G)$.

20. The depth first traversal of a graph is similar to the preorder traversal of a binary tree.

21. The breadth first traversal of a graph is similar to the level-by-level traversal of a binary tree.

22. The shortest path algorithm gives the shortest distance for a given node to every other node in the graph.

23. In a weighted graph, every edge has a nonnegative weight.

24. The weight of the path P is the sum of the weights of all of the edges on the path P, which is also called the weight of v from u via P.

25. A (free) tree T is a simple graph such that if u and v are two vertices in T, there is a unique path from u to v.

26. A tree in which a particular vertex is designated as a root is called a rooted tree.

27. Suppose T is a tree. If a weight is assigned to the edges in T, T is called a weighted tree.

28. If T is a weighted tree, the weight of T, denoted by $W(T)$, is the sum of the weights of all the edges in T.

29. A tree T is called a spanning tree of graph G if T is a subgraph of G such that $V(T) = V(G)$, that is, if all of the vertices of G are in T.

EXERCISES

Use the graphs in Figure 20-17 for Exercises 1 through 8.

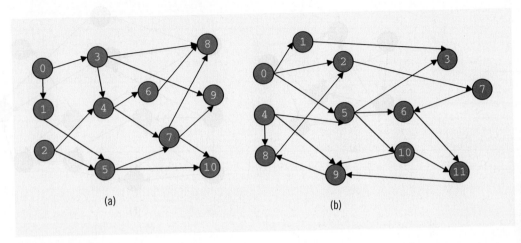

(a)   (b)

FIGURE 20-17   Graphs for Exercises 1 to 8

1. In Figure 20-17(a), find a path from vertex 0 to vertex 10.

2. In Figure 20-17(a), find a path from vertex 1 to vertex 10 via vertex 7.

3. In Figure 20-17(a), determine if the graph is simple. Also, determine if there is a cycle in this graph.

4. In Figure 20-17(a), determine if the vertices 1 and 9 are connected. If these vertices are connected, find a path from vertex 1 to vertex 9.

5. In Figure 20-17(b), determine if the vertices 2 and 4 are connected. If these vertices are connected, find a path from vertex 2 to vertex 4.

6. In Figure 20-17(b), determine if the vertices 0 and 9 are connected. If these vertices are connected, find a path from vertex 0 to vertex 9.

7. In Figure 20-17(b), find a path, if any, from vertex 0 to vertex 11 that has 4 edges.

8. In Figure 20-17(b), determine if the graph is simple. Also, determine if there is a cycle in this graph.

Use the graphs in Figure 20-18 for Exercises 9 through 14.

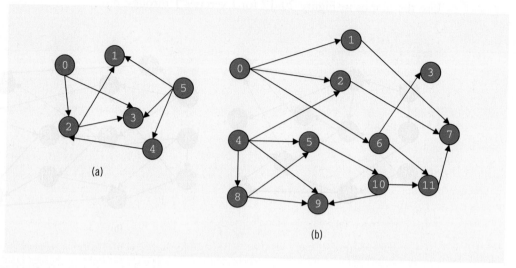

FIGURE 20-18 Graphs for Exercises 9 through 14

9. Find the adjacency matrix of the graph in Figure 20-18(a).
10. Draw the adjacency list of the graph in Figure 20-18(a).
11. List the nodes of the graph, in Figure 20-18(a), in a depth first traversal.
12. List the nodes of the graph, in Figure 20-18(a), in a breadth first traversal.
13. List the nodes of the graph, in Figure 20-18(b), in a breadth first traversal.
14. List the nodes of the graph, in Figure 20-18(b), in a depth first traversal.
15. Find the weight matrix of the graph in Figure 20-19.

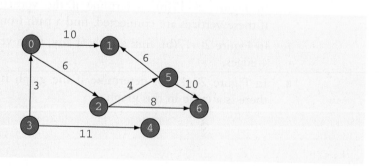

FIGURE 20-19 Graph for Exercise 15

16. Consider the graph in Figure 20-20. Find the shortest distance from node 0 to every other node in the graph.

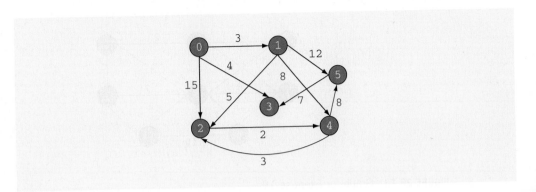

2
0

FIGURE 20-20 Graph for Exercise 16

17. Find a spanning tree in the graph in Figure 20-21.

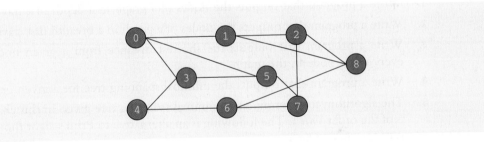

FIGURE 20-21 Graph for Exercise 17

18. Find a spanning tree in the graph in Figure 20-22.

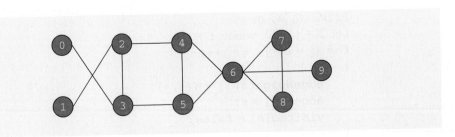

FIGURE 20-22 Graph for Exercise 18

19. Find the minimal spanning tree for the graph in Figure 20-23, using the algorithm given in this chapter.

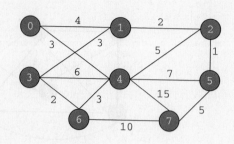

FIGURE 20-23   Graph for Exercise 19

PROGRAMMING EXERCISES

1. Write a program that outputs the nodes of a graph in a depth first traversal.
2. Write a program that outputs the nodes of a graph in a breadth first traversal.
3. Write a program that outputs the shortest distance from a given node to every other node in the graph.
4. Write a program that outputs the minimal spanning tree for a given graph.
5. The algorithm to determine the minimal spanning tree given in this chapter is of the order $O(n^3)$. The following is an alternative to Prim's algorithm that is of the order $O(n^2)$.

> **Input:**   A connected weighted graph $G = (V, E)$ of n vertices, numbered $0, 1, \ldots, n - 1$; starting with vertex s, with a weight matrix of W.
>
> **Output:**   The minimal spanning tree.

```
Prim2 (G, W, n, s)
Let T = (V, E), where E = φ.
for (j = 0; j < n; j++)
{
    edgeWeights[j] = W(s,j);
    edges[j] = s;
    visited[s] = false;
}
edgeWeights[s] = 0;
visited[s] = true;
while (not all nodes are visited)
```

```
{
    Choose the node that is not visited and has the smallest weight, and call it k.
    visited[k] = true;
    E = E ∪ {(k, edges[k])}
    V = V ∪ {k}
    for each node j that is not visited
        if (W(k,j) < edgeWeights[j])
        {
            edgeWeights[j] = W(k,j);
            edges[j] = k;
        }
}
return T;
```

Write a definition of the function `Prim2` to implement this algorithm, and also add this function to the `class msTreeType`. Furthermore, write a program to test this version of Prim's algorithm.

CHAPTER 21

STANDARD TEMPLATE LIBRARY (STL)

IN THIS CHAPTER, YOU WILL:

- Learn about the Standard Template Library (STL)

- Become familiar with the three basic components of the STL: containers, iterators, and algorithms

- Explore how various containers are used to manipulate data in a program

- Learn how iterators are used

- Learn about various generic algorithms

Chapter 13 introduced and examined templates in detail. With the help of class templates, we developed (and used) a generic code to process lists. For example, we used the **class listType** to process a list of integers and a list of strings. In Chapters 16 and 17, we studied the three most important data structures: linked lists, stacks, and queues. In these chapters, using class templates, we developed generic code to process linked lists. In addition, using the second principle of object-oriented programming (OOP), we developed generic code to process ordered lists. Furthermore, in Chapter 17, we used class templates to develop generic code to implement stacks and queues. Along the way, you saw that a template is a powerful tool that promotes code reuse.

ANSI/ISO Standard C++ is equipped with a Standard Template Library (STL). Among other things, the STL provides class templates to process lists (contiguous or linked), stacks, and queues. This chapter discusses many important features of the STL and shows how to use the tools provided by the STL in a program.

Components of the STL

The main objective of a program is to manipulate data and generate results. Achieving this goal requires the ability to store data into computer memory, access a particular piece of data, and write algorithms to manipulate the data.

For example, if all data items are of the same type and we have some idea of the number of data items, we could use an array to store the data. We can then use an index to access a particular component of the array. Using a loop and the array index, we can step through the elements of the array. Algorithms, such as those for initializing the array, sorting, and searching, are used to manipulate the data stored in an array. On the other hand, if we do not want to be concerned about the size of the data, we can use a linked list to process it. If the data needs to be processed in a Last In First Out (LIFO) manner, we can use a stack. Similarly, if the data needs to be processed in a First In First Out (FIFO) manner, we can use a queue.

The STL is equipped with these features to effectively manipulate data. More formally, the STL has three main components:

- Containers
- Iterators
- Algorithms

Containers and iterators are class templates. Iterators are used to step through the elements of a container. Algorithms are used to manipulate data. The following sections discuss each of these components in detail.

Container Types

Containers are used to manage objects of a given type. The STL containers are classified into three categories, as follows:

- Sequence containers (also called sequential containers)
- Associative containers
- Container adapters

Sequence Containers

Every object in a sequence container has a specific position. The three predefined sequence containers are:

- vector
- deque
- list

Before discussing container types in general, let us first briefly describe the sequence container vector. We do so because vector containers are similar to arrays and thus can be processed like arrays. Also, with the help of vector containers, we can describe several properties that are common to all containers. In fact, all containers use the same names for the common operations. Of course, there are operations that are specific to a container, which will be discussed when describing a specific container.

Sequence Container: vector

A vector container stores and manages its objects in a dynamic array. Because an array is a random access data structure, the elements of a vector can be accessed randomly. Item insertion in the middle or beginning of an array is time consuming, especially if the array is large. However, inserting an item at the end is quite fast.

The name of the class that implements the vector container is vector. (Recall that containers are class templates.) The name of the header file containing the class vector is vector. Thus, to use a vector container in a program, the program must include the following statement:

```
#include <vector>
```

Furthermore, to define an object of type vector, we must specify the type of the object because the class vector is a class template. For example, the statement:

```
vector<int> intList;
```

declares intList to be a vector and the component type to be int. Similarly, the statement:

```
vector<string> stringList;
```

declares stringList to be a vector container and the component type to be string.

DECLARING VECTOR OBJECTS

The **class** vector contains several constructors, including the default constructor. Therefore, a vector container can be declared and initialized several ways. Table 21-1 describes how a vector container of a specific type can be declared and initialized.

TABLE 21-1 Various Ways to Declare and Initialize a Vector Container

Statement	Effect
vector<elemType> vecList;	Creates the empty vector container vecList. (The default constructor is invoked.)
vector<elemType> vecList(otherVecList);	Creates the vector container vecList and initializes vecList to the elements of the vector otherVecList. vecList and otherVecList are of the same type.
vector<elemType> vecList(size);	Creates the vector container vecList of size size. vecList is initialized using the default constructor.
vector<elemType> vecList(n, elm);	Creates the vector container vecList of size n. vecList is initialized using n copies of the element elm.
vector<elemType> vecList(beg, end);	Creates the vector container vecList. vecList is initialized to the elements in the range [beg, end), that is, all the elements in the range beg...end-1. Both beg and end are pointers, called iterators in STL terminology. (Later in this chapter, we explain how iterators are used.)

Now that we know how to declare a vector sequence container, let us discuss how to manipulate the data stored in a vector container. In order to manipulate the data in a vector container, we must know the following basic operations:

- Item insertion
- Item deletion
- Stepping through the elements of a vector container

The elements in a vector container can be accessed directly by using the operations given in Table 21–2. The name of the function is shown in bold.

TABLE 21-2 Operations to Access the Elements of a Vector Container

Expression	Description
vecList.**at**(index)	Returns the element at the position specified by index.
vecList[index]	Returns the element at the position specified by index.
vecList.**front**()	Returns the first element. (Does not check whether the container is empty.)
vecList.**back**()	Returns the last element. (Does not check whether the container is empty.)

From Table 21–2, it follows that the elements in a vector can be processed just as they can in an array. See Example 21–1. (Recall that in C++, arrays start at location 0. Similarly, the first element in a vector container is at location 0.)

EXAMPLE 21-1

Consider the following statement, which declares intList to be a vector container of size 5 with an element type of int:

```
vector<int> intList(5);
```

You can use a loop, such as the following, to store elements into intList:

```
for (int j = 0; j < 5; j++)
    intList[j] = j;
```

Similarly, you can use a **for** loop to output the elements of intList.

The **class** vector also contains member functions that can be used to find the number of elements currently in the container, the maximum number of elements that can be inserted into a container, and so on. Table 21-3 describes some of these operations. The name of the function is shown in bold. (Suppose that vecCont is a vector container.)

TABLE 21-3 Operations to Determine the Size of a Vector Container

Expression	Description
vecCont.**capacity**()	Returns the maximum number of elements that can be inserted into the container vecCont without reallocation.
vecCont.**empty**()	Returns true if the container vecCont is empty, false otherwise.
vecCont.**size**()	Returns the number of elements currently in the container vecCont.
vecCont.**max_size**()	Returns the maximum number of elements that can be inserted into the container vecCont.

The **class** vector also contains member functions that can be used to manipulate the data, as well as insert and delete items, in a vector container. Suppose that vecList is a container of type vector. Item insertion and deletion in vecList are accomplished using the operations given in Table 21-4. These operations are implemented as member functions of the **class** vector and are shown in bold. Table 21-4 also shows how these operations are used.

TABLE 21-4 Various Operations on a Vector Container

Statement	Effect
vecList.**clear**()	Deletes all of the elements from the container.
vecList.**erase**(position)	Deletes the element at the position specified by position.
vecList.**erase**(beg, end)	Deletes all of the elements starting at beg until end-1.
vecList.**insert**(position, elem)	A copy of elem is inserted at the position specified by position. The position of the new element is returned.
vecList.**insert**(position, n, elem)	n copies of elem are inserted at the position specified by position.
vecList.**insert**(position, beg, end)	A copy of the elements, starting at beg until end-1, is inserted into vecList at the position specified by position.
vecList.**push_back**(elem)	A copy of elem is inserted into vecList at the end.
vecList.**pop_back**()	Deletes the last element.
vecList.**resize**(num)	Changes the number of elements to num. If size() increases, the default constructor creates the new elements.
vecList.**resize**(num, elem)	Changes the number of elements to num. If size() increases, the new elements are copies of elem.

NOTE   In Table 21-4, the identifiers position, beg, and end in STL terminology are called iterators. An iterator is just like a pointer. In general, iterators are used to step through the elements of a container. In other words, with the help of an iterator, we can walk through the elements of a container and process them one at a time. Because iterators are an integral part of the STL, they are discussed in the section "Iterators" located later in this chapter.

Example 21-1 used a `for` loop and the array subscripting operator, [], to access the elements of `intList`. We declare `intList` to be a vector object of size 5. Does this mean that we can store only five elements in `intList`? The answer is no. We can, in fact, add more elements to `intList`. However, because when we declared `intList` we specified the size to be 5, in order to add elements past position 4, we use the function `push_back`. Furthermore, if we initially declare a vector object and do not specify its size, then to add elements to the vector object, we use the function `push_back`. Example 21-2 explains how to use the function `push_back`.

EXAMPLE 21-2

The following statement declares `intList` to be a vector object of size 0:

```
vector<int> intList;
```

To add elements to `intList`, we can use the function push_back as follows:

```
intList.push_back(34);
intList.push_back(55);
```

After these statements execute, the size of `intList` is 2 and:

```
intList = {34, 55}
```

In Example 21-2, because `intList` is declared to be of size 0, we use the function `push_back` to add elements to `intList`. However, we can also use the `resize` function to increase the size of `intList` and then use the array subscripting operator. For example, suppose that `intList` is declared as in Example 21-2. Then, the following statement sets the size of `intList` to 10:

```
intList.resize(10);
```

Similarly, the following statement increases the size of `intList` by 10:

```
intList.resize(intList.size() + 10);
```

However, at times, the push_back function is more convenient because it does not need to know the size of the vector; it simply adds the elements at the end.

Next, we describe how to declare an iterator in a vector container.

DECLARING AN ITERATOR TO A VECTOR CONTAINER

The **class** vector contains a **typedef** iterator, which is declared as a **public** member. An iterator to a vector container is declared using the **typedef** iterator. For example, the statement:

```
vector<int>::iterator intVecIter;
```

declares `intVecIter` to be an iterator in a vector container of type `int`.

Because `iterator` is a **typedef** defined inside the **class** vector, we must use the container name (which is `vector`), the container element type, and the scope resolution operator to use the **typedef** `iterator`.

The expression:

```
++intVecIter
```

advances the iterator `intVecIter` to the next element in the container, and the expression:

```
*intVecIter
```

returns the element at the current iterator position.

Note that these operations are the same as the operations on pointers, discussed in Chapter 12. Recall that when used as a unary operator, `*` is called the dereferencing operator.

We now discuss how to use an iterator in a vector container to manipulate the data stored in the vector container.

Suppose that we have the following statements:

```
vector<int> intList;                    //Line 1
vector<int>::iterator intVecIter;       //Line 2
```

The statement in Line 1 declares `intList` to be a vector container, and the element type is `int`. The statement in Line 2 declares `intVecIter` to be an iterator in a vector container whose element type is `int`.

CONTAINERS AND THE FUNCTIONS `begin` AND `end`

Every container has the member functions **begin** and **end**. The function `begin` returns the position of the first element in the container; the function `end` returns the position of one past the last element in the container. Also, these functions have no parameters.

After the following statement executes:

```
intVecIter = intList.begin();
```

the iterator `intVecIter` points to the first element in the container `intList`.

The following **for** loop outputs the elements of `intList` to the standard output device.

```
for (intVecIter = intList.begin(); intVecIter != intList.end();
                            ++intVecIter)
    cout << *intVecIter << " ";
```

Example 21-3 shows how the function `insert` works with vector objects.

EXAMPLE 21-3

Consider the following statements:

```
int intArray[7] = {1, 3, 5, 7, 9, 11, 13};      //Line 1
vector<int> vecList(intArray, intArray + 7);    //Line 2
vector<int>::iterator intVecIter;               //Line 3
```

The statement in Line 2 declares and initializes the vector container vecList. Now consider the following statements:

```
intVecIter = vecList.begin();                   //Line 4
++intVecIter;                                    //Line 5
vecList.insert(intVecIter, 22);                 //Line 6
```

The statement in Line 4 initializes the iterator intVecIter to the first element of vecList; the statement in Line 5 advances intVecIter to the second element of vecList. The statement in Line 6 inserts 22 at the position specified by intVecIter. After the statement in Line 6 executes, vecList = {1, 22, 3, 5, 7, 9, 11, 13}. Notice that the size of the container also increases.

The following example illustrates how to use a vector container in a program and how to process the elements in a vector container.

EXAMPLE 21-4

```
#include <iostream>
#include <vector>

using namespace std;

int main()
{
    vector<int> intList;                        //Line 1
    int i;                                      //Line 2

    intList.push_back(13);                      //Line 3
    intList.push_back(75);                      //Line 4
    intList.push_back(28);                      //Line 5
    intList.push_back(35);                      //Line 6

    cout << "Line 7: List elements: ";          //Line 7
    for (i = 0; i < 4; i++)                      //Line 8
        cout << intList[i] << " ";              //Line 9
    cout << endl;                               //Line 10

    for (i = 0; i < 4; i++)                      //Line 11
        intList[i] *= 2;                        //Line 12
```

```
cout << "Line 13: List elements: ";          //Line 13
for (i = 0; i < 4; i++)                       //Line 14
    cout << intList[i] << " ";                //Line 15
cout << endl;                                 //Line 16

vector<int>::iterator listIt;                 //Line 17

cout << "Line 18: List elements: ";          //Line 18
for (listIt = intList.begin();
        listIt != intList.end(); ++listIt)    //Line 19
    cout << *listIt << " ";                   //Line 20
cout << endl;                                 //Line 21

listIt = intList.begin();                     //Line 22
++listIt;                                      //Line 23
++listIt;                                      //Line 24

    //Insert 88 at the position specified
    //by listIt
intList.insert(listIt, 88);                   //Line 25

cout << "Line 25: List elements: ";          //Line 26
for (listIt = intList.begin();
        listIt != intList.end(); ++listIt)    //Line 27
    cout << *listIt << " ";                   //Line 28
cout << endl;                                 //Line 29

    return 0;
}
```

Sample Run:

```
Line 7: List elements: 13 75 28 35
Line 13: List elements: 26 150 56 70
Line 18: List elements: 26 150 56 70
Line 25: List elements: 26 150 88 56 70
```

The statement in Line 1 declares a vector container (or vector for short), intList, of type int. The statement in Line 2 declares i to be an int variable. The statements in Lines 3 through 6 use the operation push_back to insert four numbers—13, 75, 28, and 35—into intList. The statements in Lines 8 and 9 use the for loop and the array subscripting operator, [], to output the elements of intList. In the output, see the line marked Line 7, which contains the output of Lines 7 through 10. The statements in Lines 11 and 12 use a for loop to double the value of each element of intList; the statements in Lines 14 and 15 output the elements of intList. In the output, see the line marked Line 13, which contains the output of Lines 13 through 16.

The statement in Line 17 declares listIt to be a vector iterator that processes any vector container whose elements are of type int. Using the iterator listIt, the statements in Lines 19 and 20 output the elements of intList. After the statement in Line 22 executes, listIt points to the first element of intList. The statements in Lines 23 and 24 advance listIt twice; after these statements execute, listIt points to the third element of `intList`. The statement in Line 25 inserts 88 into `intList` at the position specified by the iterator `listIt`. Because `listIt` points to the component at position 2 (the third element of `intList`), 88 is inserted at position 2 in `intList`; that is, 88 becomes the third element of `intList`. The statements in Lines 27 and 28 output the modified `intList`.

Member Functions Common to All Containers

The previous section discussed vector containers. This section discusses operations that are common to all containers. For example, every container class has the default constructor, several constructors with parameters, the destructor, a function to insert an element into a container, and so on.

Recall that a class encapsulates data and operations on that data into a single unit. Because every container is a class, several operations are directly defined for a container and are provided as part of the definition of the class. Also, recall that the operations to manipulate the data are implemented with the help of functions and are called member functions of the class. Table 21-5 describes the member functions that are common to all containers; that is, these functions are included as members of the class template implementing the container.

Suppose `ct`, `ct1`, and `ct2` are containers of the same type. In Table 21-5, the name of the function is shown in bold. This table also shows how a function is called.

TABLE 21-5 Operations Common to All Containers

Member function	Description
Default constructor	Initializes the object to an empty state.
Constructor with parameters	In addition to the default constructor, every container has constructors with parameters. We will describe these constructors when we discuss a specific container.
Copy constructor	Executes when an object is passed as a parameter by value and when an object is declared and initialized using another object of the same type.
Destructor	Executes when the object goes out of scope.
`ct.empty()`	Returns `true` if container `ct` is empty, `false` otherwise.
`ct.size()`	Returns the number of elements currently in container `ct`.

TABLE 21-5 Operations Common to All Containers (continued)

Member function	Description
ct.**max_size**()	Returns the maximum number of elements that can be inserted in container ct.
ct1.**swap**(ct2)	Swaps the elements of containers ct1 and ct2.
ct.**begin**()	Returns an iterator to the first element into container ct.
ct.**end**()	Returns an iterator to the position after the last element into container ct.
ct.**rbegin**()	Reverse begin. Returns a pointer to the last element into container ct. This function is used to process the elements of ct in reverse.
ct.**rend**()	Reverse end. Returns a pointer to the position before the first element into container ct.
ct.**insert**(position,elem)	Inserts elem into container ct at the position specified by position. Note that here, position is an iterator.
ct.**erase**(beg, end)	Deletes all of the elements between beg...end-1 from container ct. Both beg and end are iterators.
ct.**clear**()	Deletes all of the elements from the container. After a call to this function, container ct is empty.
Operator functions	
ct1 = ct2;	Copies the elements of ct2 into ct1. After this operation, the elements in both containers are the same.
ct1 == ct2	Returns true if containers ct1 and ct2 are equal, false otherwise.
ct1 != ct2	Returns true if containers ct1 and ct2 are not equal, false otherwise.

2
1

NOTE Because these operations are common to all containers, when discussing a specific container, to save space, these operations will not be listed again.

Member Functions Common to Sequence Containers

The previous section described the member functions that are common to all containers. In addition to these member functions, Table 21-6 describes the member functions that are common to all sequence containers, that is, containers of type `vector`, `deque`, and `list`. The name of the function is shown in bold. (Suppose that `seqCont` is a sequence container.)

TABLE 21-6 Member Functions Common to All Sequence Containers

Expression	Description
seqCont.**insert**(position, elem)	A copy of `elem` is inserted at the position specified by the iterator `position`. The position of the new element is returned.
seqCont.**insert**(position, n, elem)	n copies of `elem` are inserted at the position specified by the iterator `position`.
seqCont.**insert**(position, beg, end)	A copy of the elements, starting at `beg` until `end-1`, is inserted into `seqCont` at the position specified by the iterator `position`. Also, `beg` and `end` are iterators.
seqCont.**push_back**(elem)	A copy of `elem` is inserted into `seqCont` at the end.
seqCont.**pop_back**()	Deletes the last element.
seqCont.**erase**(position)	Deletes the element at the position specified by the iterator `position`.
seqCont.**erase**(beg, end)	Deletes all of the elements starting at `beg` until `end-1`. Both `beg` and `end` are iterators.
seqCont.**clear**()	Deletes all of the elements from the container.
seqCont.**resize**(num)	Changes the number of elements to num. If `size()` grows, the new elements are created by their default constructor.
seqCont.**resize**(num, elem)	Changes the number of elements to num. If `size()` grows, the new elements are copies of `elem`.

The copy Algorithm

Example 21-4 used a for loop to output the elements of a vector container. The STL provides a convenient way to output the elements of a container with the help of the function copy. The function copy is provided as a part of the generic algorithm and can be used with any container type. Because we frequently need to output the elements of a container, before continuing with our discussion of containers, let us describe this function.

The function copy does more than output the elements of a container. In general, it allows us to copy the elements from one place to another. For example, to output the elements of a vector or to copy the elements of a vector into another vector, we can use the function copy. The prototype of the function template copy is:

```
template <class inputIterator, class outputIterator>
outputIterator copy(inputIterator first1, inputIterator last,
                    outputIterator first2);
```

The parameter first1 specifies the position from which to begin copying the elements; the parameter last specifies the end position. The parameter first2 specifies where to copy the elements. Therefore, the parameters first1 and last specify the source; parameter first2 specifies the destination.

Note that the elements within the range first1...last-1 are copied.

The definition of the function template copy is contained in the header file algorithm. Thus, to use the function copy, the program must include the statement:

```
#include <algorithm>
```

The function copy works as follows. Consider the following statement:

```
int intArray[] = {5, 6, 8, 3, 40, 36, 98, 29, 75};
```

This statement creates an array intArray of nine components. Here, intArray[0] = 5, intArray[1] = 6, and so on.

The statement:

```
vector<int> vecList(9);
```

creates an empty container of nine components of type vector and the element type int.

Recall that the array name, intArray, is actually a pointer and contains the base address of the array. Therefore, intArray points to the first component of the array, intArray + 1 points to the second component of the array, and so on.

Now consider the statement:

```
copy(intArray, intArray + 9, vecList.begin());
```

This statement copies the elements starting at the location intArray, which is the first component of the array intArray, until intArray + 9 - 1 (that is, intArray + 8), which is the last element of the array `intArray`, into the container `vecList`. (Note that here, `first1` is `intArray`, `last` is `intArray + 9`, and `first2` is `vecList.begin()`.) After the previous statement executes:

```
vecList = {5, 6, 8, 3, 40, 36, 98, 29, 75}
```

Next, consider the statement:

```
copy(intArray + 1, intArray + 9, intArray);
```

Here, `first1` is `intArray + 1`; that is, `first1` points to the location of the second element of the array `intArray`, and `last` is `intArray + 9`. Also, `first2` is `intArray`; that is, `first2` points to the location of the first element of the array `intArray`. Therefore, the second array element is copied into the first array component, the third array element into the second array component, and so on. After the preceding statement executes:

```
intArray = {6, 8, 3, 40, 36, 98, 29, 75, 75}
```

Clearly, the elements of the array `intArray` are shifted to the left by one position.

Now consider the statement:

```
copy(vecList.rbegin() + 2, vecList.rend(), vecList.rbegin());
```

Recall that the function `rbegin` (reverse begin) returns a pointer to the last element into a container; it is used to process the elements of a container in reverse. Therefore, `vecList.rbegin() + 2` returns a pointer to the third-to-last element into the container `vecList`. Similarly, the function `rend` (reverse end) returns a pointer to the first element into a container. The previous statement shifts the elements of the container `vecList` to the right by two positions. After the previous statement executes, the container `vecList` is:

```
vecList = {5, 6, 5, 6, 8, 3, 40, 36, 98}
```

Example 21-5 shows the effect of the preceding statements using a C++ program. Before discussing Example 21-5, let us describe a special type of iterators called **ostream iterators**. These iterators work well with the function `copy` to copy the elements of a container to an output device.

THE `ostream` ITERATOR AND THE FUNCTION `copy`

One way to output the contents of a container is to use a `for` loop, the function `begin` to initialize the `for` loop control variable, and the function `end` to set the limit. Alternatively, the function `copy` can be used to output the elements of a container. In this case, an iterator of type `ostream` specifies the destination. (`ostream` iterators are discussed in detail later in this chapter.) When we create an iterator of type `ostream`, we also specify the type of element that the iterator will output.

The following statement illustrates how to create an `ostream` iterator of type **int**:

```
ostream_iterator<int> screen(cout, " ");        //Line A
```

This statement creates `screen` to be an `ostream` iterator with the element type `int`. The iterator `screen` has two arguments: the object `cout` and a space. Thus, the iterator `screen` is initialized using the object `cout`. When this iterator outputs elements, they are separated by a space.

The statement:

```
copy(intArray, intArray + 9, screen);
```

outputs the elements of `intArray` on the screen.

Similarly, the statement:

```
copy(vecList.begin(), vecList.end(), screen);
```

outputs the elements of the container `vecList` on the screen.

We will frequently use the function `copy` to output the elements of a container by using an `ostream` iterator. Also, until we discuss `ostream` iterators in detail, we will use statements similar to Line A to create an `ostream` iterator.

Of course, we can directly specify an `ostream` iterator in the function `copy`. For example, the statement (shown previously):

```
copy(vecList.begin(), vecList.end(), screen);
```

is equivalent to the statement:

```
copy(vecList.begin(), vecList.end(),
            ostream_iterator<int>(cout, " "));
```

Finally, the statement:

```
copy(vecList.begin(), vecList.end(),
            ostream_iterator<int>(cout, ", "));
```

outputs the elements of `vecList` with a comma and space between them.

Example 21-5 shows how to use the function `copy` and an ostream iterator in a program.

EXAMPLE 21-5

```cpp
#include <algorithm>
#include <vector>
#include <iterator>
#include <iostream>

using namespace std;

int main()
{
    int intArray[] = {5, 6, 8, 3, 40,
                      36, 98, 29, 75};        //Line 1
```

2
1

```
    vector<int> vecList(9);                                  //Line 2

    ostream_iterator<int> screen(cout, " ");                 //Line 3

    cout << "Line 4: intArray: ";                            //Line 4
    copy(intArray, intArray + 9, screen);                    //Line 5
    cout << endl;                                            //Line 6

    copy(intArray, intArray + 9, vecList.begin());           //Line 7

    cout << "Line 8: vecList: ";                             //Line 8
    copy(vecList.begin(), vecList.end(), screen);            //Line 9
    cout << endl;                                            //Line 10

    copy(intArray + 1, intArray + 9, intArray);              //Line 11

    cout << "Line 12: After shifting the elements "
         << "one position to the left, " << endl
         << "           intArray: ";                         //Line 12

    copy(intArray, intArray + 9, screen);                    //Line 13

    cout << endl;                                            //Line 14

    copy(vecList.rbegin() + 2, vecList.rend(),
                          vecList.rbegin());                 //Line 15
    cout << "Line 16: After shifting the elements "
         << "down by two positions, "<< endl
         << "           vecList: ";                          //Line 16

    copy(vecList.begin(), vecList.end(), screen);            //Line 17

    cout << endl;                                            //Line 18

    return 0;
}
```

Sample Run:

```
Line 4: intArray: 5 6 8 3 40 36 98 29 75
Line 8: vecList: 5 6 8 3 40 36 98 29 75
Line 12: After shifting the elements one position to the left,
        intArray: 6 8 3 40 36 98 29 75 75
Line 16: After shifting the elements down by two positions,
        vecList: 5 6 5 6 8 3 40 36 98
```

Sequence Container: deque

This section describes the **deque** sequence containers. The term deque stands for double-ended queue. Deque containers are implemented as dynamic arrays in such a way that the elements can be inserted at both ends. Thus, a deque can expand in either direction. Elements can also be inserted in the middle. Inserting elements in the beginning or at the end is fast; inserting elements in the middle, however, is time consuming because the elements in the queue need to be shifted.

The name of the class defining the deque containers is deque. The definition of the class deque, and the functions to implement the various operations on a deque object, are also contained in the header file deque. Therefore, to use a deque container in a program, the program must include the following statement:

```
#include <deque>
```

The class deque contains several constructors. Thus, a deque object can be initialized in various ways when it is declared, as described in Table 21-7.

TABLE 21-7 Various Ways to Declare a deque Object

Statement	Description
deque<elementType> deq;	Creates an empty deque container deq. (The default constructor is invoked.)
deque<elementType> deq(otherDeq);	Creates the deque container deq and initializes it to the elements of otherDeq; deq and otherDeq are of the same type.
deque<elementType> deq(size);	Creates the deque container deq of size size. deq is initialized using the default constructor.
deque<elementType> deq(n, elm);	Creates the deque container deq of size n. deq is initialized using n copies of the element elm.
deque<elementType> deq(beg, end);	Creates the deque container deq. deq is initialized to the elements in the range [beg, end), that is, all elements in the range beg...end-1. Both beg and end are iterators.

In addition to the operations that are common to all sequence containers (Table 21-6), Table 21-8 describes the operations that can be used to manipulate the elements of a deque container. The name of the function implementing the operations is shown in bold. Each statement also shows how to use a particular function. Suppose that deq is a deque container.

TABLE 21-8 Various Operations that Can Be Performed on a deque Object

Expression	Description
deq.**assign**(n,elem)	Assigns n copies of elem.
deq.**assign**(beg, end)	Assigns all of the elements in the range beg...end-1.
deq.**push_front**(elem)	Inserts elem at the beginning of deq.
deq.**pop_front**()	Removes the first element from deq.
deq.**at**(index)	Returns the element at the position specified by index.
deq[index]	Returns the element at the position specified by index.
deq.**front**()	Returns the first element. (Does not check whether the container is empty.)
deq.**back**()	Returns the last element. (Does not check whether the container is empty.)

Example 21-6 illustrates how to use a deque container in a program.

EXAMPLE 21-6

```
//deque Example
#include <iostream>
#include <deque>
#include <algorithm>
#include <iterator>

using namespace std;
```

```cpp
int main()
{
    deque<int> intDeq;                                     //Line 1
    ostream_iterator<int> screen(cout, " ");               //Line 2

    intDeq.push_back(13);                                  //Line 3
    intDeq.push_back(75);                                  //Line 4
    intDeq.push_back(28);                                  //Line 5
    intDeq.push_back(35);                                  //Line 6

    cout << "Line 7: intDeq: ";                            //Line 7
    copy(intDeq.begin(), intDeq.end(), screen);            //Line 8
    cout << endl;                                          //Line 9

    intDeq.push_front(0);                                  //Line 10
    intDeq.push_back(100);                                 //Line 11

    cout << "Line 12: After adding two more "
         << "elements, one at the front " << endl
         << "            and one at the back, intDeq: "; //Line 12
    copy(intDeq.begin(), intDeq.end(), screen);            //Line 13
    cout << endl;                                          //Line 14

    intDeq.pop_front();                                    //Line 15
    intDeq.pop_front();                                    //Line 16

    cout << "Line 17: After removing the first "
         << "two elements, " << endl
         << "            intDeq: ";                        //Line 17
    copy(intDeq.begin(), intDeq.end(), screen);            //Line 18
    cout << endl;                                          //Line 19

    intDeq.pop_back();                                     //Line 20
    intDeq.pop_back();                                     //Line 21

    cout << "Line 22: After removing the last "
         << "two elements, " << endl
         << "            intDeq = ";                       //Line 22
    copy(intDeq.begin(), intDeq.end(), screen);            //Line 23
    cout << endl;                                          //Line 24

    deque<int>::iterator  deqIt;                           //Line 25

    deqIt = intDeq.begin();                                //Line 26
    ++deqIt;                        //deqIt points to the
                                    //second element       //Line 27

    intDeq.insert(deqIt, 444);      //Insert 444 at the
                                    //location deqIt        //Line 28
```

2
1

```
    cout << "Line 29: After inserting 444, "
         << "intDeq:  ";                                    //Line 29
    copy(intDeq.begin(), intDeq.end(), screen);            //Line 30
    cout << endl;                                           //Line 31

    intDeq.assign(2, 45);                                   //Line 32

    cout << "Line 33: After assigning two "
         << "copies of 45, intDeq: ";                       //Line 33
    copy(intDeq.begin(), intDeq.end(), screen);            //Line 34
    cout << endl;                                           //Line 35

    intDeq.push_front(-10);                                 //Line 36
    intDeq.push_back(-999);                                 //Line 37

    cout << "Line 38: After inserting two "
         << "elements, one at the front " << endl
         << "              and one at the back, intDeq: ";  //Line 38
    copy(intDeq.begin(), intDeq.end(), screen);            //Line 39
    cout << endl;                                           //Line 40

    return 0;
}
```

Sample Run:

```
Line 7: intDeq: 13 75 28 35
Line 12: After adding two more elements, one at the front
         and one at the back, intDeq: 0 13 75 28 35 100
Line 17: After removing the first two elements,
         intDeq: 75 28 35 100
Line 22: After removing the last two elements,
         intDeq = 75 28
Line 29: After inserting 444, intDeq:  75 444 28
Line 33: After assigning two copies of 45, intDeq: 45 45
Line 38: After inserting two elements, one at the front
         and one at the back, intDeq: -10 45 45 -999
```

The statement in Line 1 declares a deque container intDeq of type int; that is, all of the elements of intDeq are of type int. The statement in Line 2 declares screen to be an ostream iterator initialized to the standard output device. The statements in Lines 3 through 6 use the push_back operation to insert four numbers—13, 75, 28, and 35—into intDeq. The statement in Line 8 outputs the elements of intDeq. In the output, see the line marked Line 7, which contains the output of the statements in Lines 7 through 9.

The statement in Line 10 inserts 0 at the beginning of intDeq; the statement in Line 11 inserts 100 at the end of intDeq. The statement in Line 13 outputs the modified intDeq.

The statements in Lines 15 and 16 use the function pop_front to remove the first two elements of intDeq; the statement in Line 18 outputs the modified intDeq. The statements in Lines 20 and 21 use the function `pop_back` to remove the last two elements of `intDeq`, and the statement in Line 23 outputs the modified `intDeq`.

The statement in Line 25 declares `deqIt` to be a `deque` iterator that processes all `deque` containers whose elements are of type `int`. After the statement in Line 26 executes, `deqIt` points to the first element of `intDeq`. The statement in Line 27 advances `deqIt` to the next element of `intDeq`. The statement in Line 28 inserts `444` into `intDeq` at the position specified by `deqIt`. The statement in Line 30 outputs `intDeq`.

The statement in Line 32 assigns two copies of `45` to `intDeq`. After the statement in Line 32 executes, the old elements of `intDeq` are removed and `intDeq` now contains only two copies of `45`. The output of the statement in Line 34 illustrates this. In the output, see the line marked Line 33, which contains the output of the statements in Lines 33 through 35 of the program.

The meaning of the remaining statements is self-explanatory.

Sequence Container: `list`

This section describes the sequence container **list**. List containers are implemented as doubly linked lists. Thus, every element in a list points to both its immediate predecessor and its immediate successor (except the first and last elements). Recall that a linked list is not a random access data structure, such as an array. Therefore, to access, say, the fifth element in the list, we must first traverse the first four elements.

The name of the class containing the definition of the `class list` is `list`. The definition of the `class list`, and the definitions of the functions to implement the various operations on a list, are contained in the header file `list`. Therefore, to use `list` in a program, the program must include the following statement:

```
#include <list>
```

Like other container classes, the `class list` contains several constructors. Thus, a `list` object can be initialized in several ways when it is declared, as described in Table 21-9.

TABLE 21-9 Various Ways to Declare a `list` Object

Statement	Description
`list<elementType> listCont;`	Creates the empty `list` container `listCont`. (The default constructor is invoked.)
`list<elementType> listCont(otherList);`	Creates the `list` container `listCont` and initializes it to the elements of `otherList`. `listCont` and `otherList` are of the same type.
`list<elementType> listCont(size);`	Creates the `list` container `listCont` of size `size`. `listCont` is initialized using the default constructor.
`list<elementType> listCont(n, elm);`	Creates the `list` container `listCont` of size n. `listCont` is initialized using n copies of the element `elm`.
`list<elementType> listCont(beg, end);`	Creates the `list` container `listCont`. `listCont` is initialized to the elements in the range `[beg, end)`, that is, all of the elements in the range `beg...end-1`. Both beg and end are iterators.

Table 21-5 described the operations that are common to all containers. Table 21-6 described the operations that are common to all sequence containers. In addition to these common operations, Table 21-10 describes the operations that are specific to a `list` container. The name of the function implementing the operation is shown in bold.

In Table 21-10, `listCont` is a container of type `list`.

TABLE 21-10 Various Operations Specific to a `list` Container

Expression	Description
listCont.**assign**(n, elem)	Assigns n copies of elem.
listCont.**assign**(beg, end)	Assigns all of the elements in the range beg...end-1. Both beg and end are iterators.
listCont.**push_front**(elem)	Inserts elem at the beginning of listCont.
listCont.**pop_front**()	Removes the first element from listCont.
listCont.**front**()	Returns the first element. (Does not check whether the container is empty.)
listCont.**back**()	Returns the last element. (Does not check whether the container is empty.)
listCont.**remove**(elem)	Removes all of the elements that are equal to elem.
listCont.**remove_if**(oper)	Removes all of the elements for which oper is true.
listCont.**unique**()	If the consecutive elements in listCont have the same value, removes the duplicates.
listCont.**unique**(oper)	If the consecutive elements in listCont have the same value, removes the duplicates, for which oper is true.

2
1

TABLE 21-10 Various Operations Specific to a `list` Container (continued)

Expression	Description
listCont1.**splice**(pos, listCont2)	All of the elements of listCont2 are moved to listCont1 before the position specified by the iterator pos. After this operation, listCont2 is empty.
listCont1.**splice**(pos, listCont2, pos2)	All of the elements starting at pos2 of listCont2 are moved to listCont1 before the position specified by the iterator pos.
listCont1.**splice**(pos, listCont2, beg, end)	All of the elements in the range beg...end−1 of listCont2 are moved to listCont1 before the position specified by the iterator pos. Both beg and end are iterators.
listCont.**sort**()	The elements of listCont are sorted. The sort criteria is <.
listCont.**sort**(oper)	The elements of listCont are sorted. The sort criteria is specified by oper.
listCont1.**merge**(listCont2)	Suppose that the elements of listCont1 and listCont2 are sorted. This operation moves all of the elements of listCont2 into listCont1. After this operation, the elements in listCont1 are sorted. Moreover, after this operation, listCont2 is empty.

TABLE 21-10 Various Operations Specific to a `list` Container (continued)

Expression	Description
`listCont1.merge(listCont2, oper)`	Suppose that the elements of `listCont1` and `listCont2` are sorted according to the sort criteria `oper`. This operation moves all of the elements of `listCont2` into `listCont1`. After this operation, the elements in `listCont1` are sorted according to the sort criteria `oper`.
`listCont.reverse()`	The elements of `listCont` are reversed.

Example 21-7 illustrates how to use the various operations on a list container.

EXAMPLE 21-7

```
//List Container Example

#include <iostream>
#include <list>
#include <iterator>
#include <algorithm>

using namespace std;

int main()
{
    list<int> intList1, intList2, intList3, intList4;    //Line 1

    ostream_iterator<int> screen(cout, " ");             //Line 2

    intList1.push_back(23);                              //Line 3
    intList1.push_back(58);                              //Line 4
    intList1.push_back(58);                              //Line 5
    intList1.push_back(58);                              //Line 6
    intList1.push_back(36);                              //Line 7
    intList1.push_back(15);                              //Line 8
    intList1.push_back(93);                              //Line 9
    intList1.push_back(98);                              //Line 10
    intList1.push_back(58);                              //Line 11
```

2
1

```
    cout << "Line 12: intList1: ";                          //Line 12
    copy(intList1.begin(), intList1.end(), screen);         //Line 13
    cout << endl;                                           //Line 14

    intList2 = intList1;                                    //Line 15

    cout << "Line 16: intList2: ";                          //Line 16
    copy(intList2.begin(), intList2.end(), screen);         //Line 17
    cout << endl;                                           //Line 18

    intList1.unique();                                      //Line 19

    cout << "Line 20: After removing the consecutive "
         << "duplicates," << endl
         << "            intList1: ";                       //Line 20
    copy(intList1.begin(), intList1.end(), screen);         //Line 21
    cout << endl;                                           //Line 22

    intList2.sort();                                        //Line 23

    cout << "Line 24: After sorting, intList2: ";           //Line 24
    copy(intList2.begin(), intList2.end(), screen);         //Line 25
    cout << endl;                                           //Line 26

    intList3.push_back(13);                                 //Line 27
    intList3.push_back(23);                                 //Line 28
    intList3.push_back(25);                                 //Line 29
    intList3.push_back(136);                                //Line 30
    intList3.push_back(198);                                //Line 31

    cout << "Line 32: intList3: ";                          //Line 32
    copy(intList3.begin(), intList3.end(), screen);         //Line 33
    cout << endl;                                           //Line 34

    intList4.push_back(-2);                                 //Line 35
    intList4.push_back(-7);                                 //Line 36
    intList4.push_back(-8);                                 //Line 37

    cout << "Line 38: intList4: ";                          //Line 38
    copy(intList4.begin(), intList4.end(), screen);         //Line 39
    cout << endl;                                           //Line 40

    intList3.splice(intList3.begin(), intList4);            //Line 41

    cout << "Line 42: After moving the elements of "
         << "intList4 into intList3," << endl
         << "            intList3: ";                       //Line 42
    copy(intList3.begin(), intList3.end(), screen);         //Line 43
    cout << endl;                                           //Line 44

    intList3.sort();                                        //Line 45
```

```
    cout << "Line 46: After sorting, intList3: ";        //Line 46
    copy(intList3.begin(), intList3.end(), screen);      //Line 47
    cout << endl;                                        //Line 48

    intList2.merge(intList3);                            //Line 49

    cout << "Line 50: After merging intList2 and "
         << "intList3, intList2: " << endl
         << "            ";                               //Line 50
    copy(intList2.begin(), intList2.end(), screen);      //Line 51
    cout << endl;                                        //Line 52

    intList2.unique();                                   //Line 53

    cout << "Line 54: After removing the consecutive "
         << "duplicates, intList2: " << endl
         << "            ";                               //Line 54
    copy(intList2.begin(), intList2.end(), screen);      //Line 55
    cout << endl;                                        //Line 56

    return 0;
}
```

Sample Run:

```
Line 12: intList1: 23 58 58 58 36 15 93 98 58
Line 16: intList2: 23 58 58 58 36 15 93 98 58
Line 20: After removing the consecutive duplicates,
         intList1: 23 58 36 15 93 98 58
Line 24: After sorting, intList2: 15 23 36 58 58 58 58 93 98
Line 32: intList3: 13 23 25 136 198
Line 38: intList4: -2 -7 -8
Line 42: After moving the elements of intList4 into intList3,
         intList3: -2 -7 -8 13 23 25 136 198
Line 46: After sorting, intList3: -8 -7 -2 13 23 25 136 198
Line 50: After merging intList2 and intList3, intList2:
         -8 -7 -2 13 15 23 23 25 36 58 58 58 58 93 98 136 198
Line 54: After removing the consecutive duplicates, intList2:
         -8 -7 -2 13 15 23 25 36 58 93 98 136 198
```

For the most part, the output of the preceding program is straightforward. The statements in Lines 3 through 11 insert the element numbers 23, 58, 58, 58, 36, 15, 93, 98, and 58 (in that order) into intList1. The statement in Line 15 copies the elements of intList1 into intList2. After this statement executes, intList1 and intList2 are identical. The statement in Line 19 removes any consecutive occurrences of the same elements. For example, the number 58 appears consecutively three times. The operation unique removes two occurrences of 58. Note that this operation has no effect on the 58 that appears at the end of intList1.

The statement in Line 23 sorts intList2. The statements in Lines 27 through 31 insert 13, 23, 25, 136, and 198 into intList3. Similarly, the statements in Lines 35 through 37 insert -2, -7, and -8 into intList4. The statement in Line 41 uses the operation splice to move the elements of `intList4` to the beginning of `intList3`. After the `splice` operation, `intList4` is empty. The statement in Line 45 sorts `intList3`, and the statement in Line 49 merges `intList2` and `intList3` into `intList2`. After the `merge` operation, `intList3` is empty. The meanings of the remaining statements are similar.

Examples 21-5 through 21-7 further clarify that iterators are important to efficiently process the elements of a container. Before describing associative containers, let us discuss iterators in some detail.

Iterators

Iterators are similar to pointers. In general, an iterator points to the elements of a container (sequence or associative). Thus, with the help of iterators, we can successively access each element of a container.

The two most common operations on iterators are ++ (the increment operator) and * (the dereferencing operator). Suppose that `cntItr` is an iterator into a container. The statement:

`++cntItr;`

advances `cntItr` so that it points to the next element in the container. Similarly, the statement:

`*cntItr;`

gives access to the element of the container pointed to by `cntItr`.

Types of Iterators

There are five types of iterators:

- Input iterators
- Output iterators
- Forward iterators
- Bidirectional iterators
- Random access iterators

The following sections describe these iterators.

INPUT ITERATORS

Input iterators, with read access, step forward element by element; consequently, they return the values element by element. These iterators are provided for reading data from an input stream.

Suppose `inputIterator` is an input iterator. Table 21-11 describes the operations on `inputIterator`.

TABLE 21-11 Operations on an Input Iterator

Expression	Effect
`*inputIterator`	Gives access to the element to which `inputIterator` points.
`inputIterator->member`	Gives access to the member of the element.
`++inputIterator`	Moves forward, returns the new position (pre-increment).
`inputIterator++`	Moves forward, returns the old position (post-increment).
`inputIt1 == inputIt2`	Returns `true` if the two iterators are the same, and `false` otherwise.
`inputIt1 != inputIt2`	Returns `true` if the two iterators are not the same, and `false` otherwise.

2
1

OUTPUT ITERATORS

Output iterators, with write access, step forward element by element. These iterators are provided for writing data to an output stream. They are also used as inserters.

Suppose `outputIterator` is an output iterator. Table 21-12 describes the operations on `outputIterator`.

TABLE 21-12 Operations on an Output Iterator

Expression	Effect
`*outputIterator = value;`	Writes the value at the position specified by `outputIterator`.
`++outputIterator`	Moves forward, returns the new position (pre-increment).
`outputIterator++`	Moves forward, returns the old position (post-increment).

NOTE Output iterators cannot be used to iterate over a range twice. Thus, if we write data at the same position twice, there is no guarantee that the new value will replace the old value.

FORWARD ITERATORS

Forward iterators combine all of the functionality of input iterators and almost all of the functionality of output iterators. Suppose `forwardIterator` is a forward iterator. Table 21-13 describes the operations on `forwardIterator`.

TABLE 21-13 Operations on a Forward Iterator

Expression	Effect
`*forwardIterator`	Gives access to the element to which `forwardIterator` points.
`forwardIterator->member`	Gives access to the member of the element.
`++forwardIterator`	Moves forward, returns the new position (pre-increment).
`forwardIterator++`	Moves forward, returns the old position (post-increment).
`forwardIt1 == forwardIt2`	Returns `true` if the two iterators are the same, and `false` otherwise.
`forwardIt1 != forwardIt2`	Returns `true` if the two iterators are not the same, and `false` otherwise.
`forwardIt1 = forwardIt2`	Assignment

NOTE A forward iterator can refer to the same element in the same collection and process the same element more than once.

BIDIRECTIONAL ITERATORS

Bidirectional iterators are forward iterators that can also iterate backward over the elements. Suppose `biDirectionalIterator` is a bidirectional iterator. The operations defined for forward iterators (Table 21-13) are also applicable to bidirectional iterators. To step backward, the decrement operations are also defined for `biDirectionalIterator`. Table 21-14 shows additional operations on a bidirectional iterator.

TABLE 21-14 Additional Operations on a Bidirectional Iterator

Expression	Effect
`--biDirectionalIterator`	Moves backward, returns the new position (pre-decrement).
`biDirectionalIterator--`	Moves backward, returns the old position (post-decrement).

NOTE Bidirectional iterators can be used with containers of type `vector`, `deque`, `list`, `set`, `multiset`, `map`, and `multimap`.

RANDOM ACCESS ITERATORS

Random access iterators are bidirectional iterators that can randomly process the elements of a container. These iterators can be used with containers of types `vector`, `deque`, and `string`, as well as arrays. The operations defined for bidirectional iterators (for example, Tables 21-13 and 21-14) are also applicable to random access iterators. Table 21-15 describes the additional operations that are defined for random access iterators. Suppose `rAccessIterator` is a random access iterator.

TABLE 21-15 Additional Operations on a Random Access Iterator

Expression	Effect
`rAccessIterator[n]`	Accesses the nth element.
`rAccessIterator += n`	Moves `rAccessIterator` forward n elements if n >= 0 and backward if n < 0.
`rAccessIterator -= n`	Moves `rAccessIterator` backward n elements if n >= 0 and forward if n < 0.
`rAccessIterator + n`	Returns the iterator of the next nth element.
`n + rAccessIterator`	Returns the iterator of the next nth element.
`rAccessIterator - n`	Returns the iterator of the previous nth element.
`rAccessIt1 - rAccessIt2`	Returns the distance between the iterators `rAccessIt1` and `rAccessIt2`.

TABLE 21-15 Additional Operations on a Random Access Iterator (continued)

Expression	Effect
rAccessIt1 < rAccessIt2	Returns true if rAccessIt1 is before rAccessIt2, and false otherwise.
rAccessIt1 <= rAccessIt2	Returns true if rAccessIt1 is before or equal to rAccessIt2, and false otherwise.
rAccessIt1 > rAccessIt2	Returns true if rAccessIt1 is after rAccessIt2, and false otherwise.
rAccessIt1 >= rAccessIt2	Returns true if rAccessIt1 is after or equal to rAccessIt2, and false otherwise.

Figure 21-1 shows the iterator hierarchy.

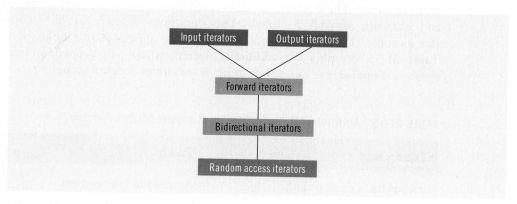

FIGURE 21-1 Iterator hierarchy

Now that you know the different types of iterators, next we describe how to declare an iterator into a container.

typedef ITERATOR

Every container (sequence or associative) contains a typedef iterator. Thus, an iterator into a container is declared using the typedef iterator. For example, the statement:

vector<int>::iterator intVecIter;

declares intVecIter to be an iterator into a vector container of type int.

Because iterator is a typedef defined inside a container (that is, a class) such as vector, we must use the appropriate container name, container element type, and the scope resolution operator to use the typedef iterator.

typedef CONST_ITERATOR

Because an iterator works like a pointer, with the help of an iterator into a container and the dereferencing operator, `*`, we can modify the elements of the container. However, if a container is declared as `const`, then we must prevent the iterator from modifying the elements of the container, especially accidentally. To handle this situation, every container contains another `typedef` const_iterator. For example, the statement:

```
vector<int>::const_iterator intConstVecIt;
```

declares `intConstVecIt` to be an iterator into a `vector` container whose elements are of type `int`. The iterator `intConstVecIt` is used to process the elements of those vector containers that are declared as constant vector containers of type `vector<int>`.

An iterator of type `const_iterator` is a read-only iterator.

typedef REVERSE_ITERATOR

Every container also contains the `typedef` reverse_iterator. An iterator of this type is used to iterate through the elements of a container in reverse.

typedef CONST_REVERSE_ITERATOR

An iterator of this type is a read-only iterator and is used to iterate through the elements of a container in reverse. It is required if the container is declared as `const`, and we need to iterate through the elements of the container in reverse.

In addition to the previous four `typedef`s, several other `typedef`s are common to all containers and are described in Table 21-16.

TABLE 21-16 Various `typedef`s Common to All Containers

typedef	Effect
difference_type	The type of result from subtracting two iterators referring to the same container.
pointer	A pointer to the type of elements stored in the container.
reference	A reference to the type of elements stored in the container.
const_reference	A constant reference to the type of elements stored in the container. A constant reference is read-only.
size_type	The type used to count the elements in a container. This type is also used to index through sequence containers, except `list` containers.
value_type	The type of container elements.

Stream Iterators

Another useful set of iterators is that of `stream` iterators—`istream` iterators and `ostream` iterators. This section describes both types of iterators.

istream_iterator

The `istream` iterator is used to input data into a program from an input stream. The `class` `istream_iterator` contains the definition of an input stream iterator. The general syntax to use an `istream` iterator is:

```
istream_iterator<Type> isIdentifier(istream&);
```

in which `Type` is either a built-in type or a user-defined class type, for which an input iterator is defined. The identifier `isIdentifier` is initialized using the constructor whose argument is either an `istream` class object, such as `cin`, or any publicly defined `istream` subtype, such as `ifstream`.

ostream_iterator

The `ostream` iterators are used to output data from a program into an output stream. These iterators were defined earlier in this chapter. We review them here for the sake of completeness.

The `class` `ostream_iterator` contains the definition of an output stream iterator. The general syntax to use an `ostream` iterator is:

```
ostream_iterator<Type> osIdentifier(ostream&);
```

or:

```
ostream_iterator<Type> osIdentifier(ostream&, char* deLimit);
```

in which `Type` is either a built-in type or a user-defined class type, for which an output iterator is defined. The identifier `osIdentifier` is initialized using the constructor whose argument is either an `ostream` class object, such as `cout`, or any publicly defined `ostream` subtype, such as `ofstream`. In the second form used to declare an `ostream` iterator, by using the second argument (`deLimit`) of the initializing constructor, we can specify a character separating the output.

Associative Containers

This section discusses associative containers. Elements in an associative container are automatically sorted according to some ordering criteria. The default ordering criterion is the relational operator < (less than). Users also have the option of specifying their own ordering criterion.

Because elements in an associative container are sorted automatically, when a new element is inserted into the container, it is inserted at the proper place. A convenient and fast way to implement this type of data structure is to use a binary search tree. This is, in fact, how associative containers are implemented. Thus, every element in the container has a parent node (except the root node) and, at most, two children. For each element, the key in the parent node is larger than the key in the left child and smaller than the key in the right child.

The predefined associative containers in the STL are:

- Sets
- Multisets
- Maps
- Multimaps

This book discusses only the associative containers `set` and `multiset`.

Associative Containers: `set` and `multiset`

As described earlier, both the containers `set` and `multiset` automatically sort their elements according to some sort criteria. The default sorting criterion is the relational operator < (less than); that is, the elements are arranged in ascending order. The user can also specify other sorting criteria. For user-defined data types, such as classes, the relational operators must be overloaded properly.

The only difference between the containers `set` and `multiset` is that the container `multiset` allows duplicates; the container `set` does not.

The name of the class defining the container `set` is `set`; the name of the class defining the container `multiset` is `multiset`. The name of the header file containing the definitions of the classes `set` and `multiset`, and the definitions of the functions to implement the various operations on these containers, is `set`. Thus, to use any of these containers, the program must include the following statement:

```
#include <set>
```

Declaring `set` or `multiset` Associative Containers

The classes `set` and `multiset` contain several constructors to declare and initialize containers of these types. This section discusses the various ways that these types of associative containers are declared and initialized. Table 21-17 describes how a `set`/`multiset` container of a specific type can be declared and initialized.

TABLE 21-17 Various Ways to Declare a Set/Multiset Container

Statement	Effect
`ctType<elmType> ct;`	Creates an empty set/multiset container, ct. The sort criterion is <.
`ctType<elmType, sortOp> ct;`	Creates an empty set/multiset container, ct. The sort criterion is specified by sortOp.
`ctType<elmType> ct(otherCt);`	Creates a set/multiset container, ct. The elements of otherCt are copied into ct. The sort criterion is <. Both ct and otherCt are of the same type.
`ctType<elmType, sortOp> ct(otherCt);`	Creates a set/multiset container, ct. The elements of otherCt are copied into ct. The sort criterion is specified by sortOp. Both ct and otherCt are of the same type. Note that the sort criteria of ct and otherCt must be the same.
`ctType<elmType> ct(beg, end);`	Creates a set/multiset container, ct. The elements starting at the position beg until the position end−1 are copied into ct. Both beg and end are iterators.
`ctType<elmType, sortOp> ct(beg, end);`	Creates a set/multiset container, ct. The elements starting at the position beg until the position end−1 are copied into ct. Both beg and end are iterators. The sort criterion is specified by sortOp.

If you want to use sort criteria other than the default, you must specify this option when the container is declared. For example, consider the following statements:

```
set<int> intSet;                                         //Line 1
set<int, greater<int> > otherIntSet;                    //Line 2
multiset<string> stringMultiSet;                        //Line 3
multiset<string, greater<string> > otherStringMultiSet; //Line 4
```

The statement in Line 1 declares intSet to be an empty set container, the element type is int, and the sort criterion is the default sort criterion. The statement in Line 2 declares otherIntSet to be an empty set container, the element type is int, and the sort criterion is greater-than. That is, the elements in the container otherIntSet will be arranged in descending order. The statements in Lines 3 and 4 have similar conventions.

The statements in Lines 2 and 4 illustrate how to specify the descending sorting criterion.

> **NOTE** In the statements in Lines 2 and 4, note the space between the two > symbols—that is, the space between greater<int> and >. If you are using an old compiler, then this space is important because >> is also a shift operator in C++. However, this restriction is removed in C++0X and the compiler that we used to write programs in this book has implemented it. Therefore, in C++0X, the statements in Lines 2 and 4 can be written as:
>
> ```
> set<int, greater<int>> otherIntSet;                     //Line 2
> multiset<string, greater<string>> otherStringMultiSet; //Line 4
> ```

Item Insertion and Deletion from set/multiset

Suppose that ct is either of type set or multiset. Table 21-18 describes the operations that can be used to insert or delete elements from a set. It also illustrates how to use these operations. The name of the function is shown in bold.

TABLE 21-18 Operations to Insert or Delete Elements from a Set

Expression	Effect
ct.**insert**(elem)	Inserts a copy of elem into ct. In the case of sets, it also returns whether the insert operation succeeded.
ct.**insert**(position, elem)	Inserts a copy of elem into ct. The position where elem is inserted is returned. The first parameter, position, hints where to begin the search for insert. The parameter position is an iterator.
ct.**insert**(beg, end);	Inserts a copy of all of the elements into ct starting at the position beg until end-1. Both beg and end are iterators.

TABLE 21-18 Operations to Insert or Delete Elements from a Set (continued)

Expression	Effect
ct.**erase**(elem);	Deletes all of the elements with the value elem. The number of deleted elements is returned.
ct.**erase**(position);	Deletes the element at the position specified by the iterator position. No value is returned.
ct.**erase**(beg, end);	Deletes all of the elements starting at the position beg until the position end−1. Both beg and end are iterators. No value is returned.
ct.**clear**();	Deletes all of the elements from the container ct. After this operation, the container ct is empty.

Example 21-8 shows the various operations on a set/multiset container.

EXAMPLE 21-8

```cpp
#include <iostream>
#include <set>
#include <string>
#include <iterator>
#include <algorithm>

using namespace std;

int main()
{
    set<int> intSet;                                    //Line 1
    set<int, greater<int> > intSetA;                    //Line 2

    set<int, greater<int> >::iterator intGtIt;          //Line 3

    ostream_iterator<int> screen(cout, " ");            //Line 4

    intSet.insert(16);                                  //Line 5
    intSet.insert(8);                                   //Line 6
    intSet.insert(20);                                  //Line 7
    intSet.insert(3);                                   //Line 8

    cout << "Line 9: intSet: ";                         //Line 9
    copy(intSet.begin(), intSet.end(), screen);         //Line 10
    cout << endl;                                       //Line 11

    intSetA.insert(36);                                 //Line 12
    intSetA.insert(84);                                 //Line 13
```

```
intSetA.insert(30);                                        //Line 14
intSetA.insert(39);                                        //Line 15
intSetA.insert(59);                                        //Line 16
intSetA.insert(238);                                       //Line 17
intSetA.insert(156);                                       //Line 18

cout << "Line 19: intSetA: ";                              //Line 19
copy(intSetA.begin(), intSetA.end(), screen);              //Line 20
cout << endl;                                              //Line 21

intSetA.erase(59);                                         //Line 22

cout << "Line 23: After removing 59, intSetA: ";           //Line 23
copy(intSetA.begin(), intSetA.end(), screen);              //Line 24
cout << endl;                                              //Line 25

intGtIt = intSetA.begin();                                 //Line 26
++intGtIt;                                                 //Line 27
++intGtIt;                                                 //Line 28
++intGtIt;                                                 //Line 29

intSetA.erase(intGtIt);                                    //Line 30

cout << "Line 31: After removing the fourth "
     << "element, " << endl
     << "          intSetA: ";                             //Line 31
copy(intSetA.begin(), intSetA.end(), screen);              //Line 32
cout << endl;                                              //Line 33


set<int, greater<int> >  intSetB(intSetA);                 //Line 34

cout << "Line 35: intSetB: ";                              //Line 35
copy(intSetB.begin(), intSetB.end(), screen);              //Line 36
cout << endl;                                              //Line 37

intSetB.clear();                                           //Line 38

cout << "Line 39: After removing all elements, "
     << endl << "            intSetB: ";                   //Line 39
copy(intSetB.begin(), intSetB.end(), screen);              //Line 40
cout << endl;                                              //Line 41

multiset<string, greater<string> > namesMultiSet;          //Line 42
multiset<string, greater<string> >::iterator iter;         //Line 43

ostream_iterator<string> pScreen(cout, " ");               //Line 44

namesMultiSet.insert("Donny");                             //Line 45
namesMultiSet.insert("Zippy");                             //Line 46
namesMultiSet.insert("Goofy");                             //Line 47
namesMultiSet.insert("Hungry");                            //Line 48
```

21

```
namesMultiSet.insert("Goofy");                          //Line 49
namesMultiSet.insert("Donny");                          //Line 50

cout << "Line 51: namesMultiSet: ";                     //Line 51
copy(namesMultiSet.begin(), namesMultiSet.end(),
     pScreen);                                          //Line 52
cout << endl;                                           //Line 53

return 0;
}
```

Sample Run:

```
Line 9: intSet: 3 8 16 20
Line 19: intSetA: 238 156 84 59 39 36 30
Line 23: After removing 59, intSetA: 238 156 84 39 36 30
Line 31: After removing the fourth element,
         intSetA: 238 156 84 36 30
Line 35: intSetB: 238 156 84 36 30
Line 39: After removing all the elements,
         intSetB:
Line 51: namesMultiSet: Zippy Hungry Goofy Goofy Donny Donny
```

The statement in Line 1 declares `intSet` to be a `set` container. The statement in Line 2 declares `intSetA` to be a set container whose elements are to be arranged in descending order. The statement in Line 3 declares `intGtIt` to be a `set` iterator. The iterator `intGtIt` can process the elements of any set container whose elements are of type `int` and are arranged in descending order. The statement in Line 4 declares `screen` to be an `ostream` iterator that outputs the elements of any container whose elements are of type `int`.

The statements in Lines 5 through 8 insert `16`, `8`, `20`, and `3` into `intSet`, and the statement in Line 10 outputs the elements of `intSet`. In the output, see the line marked Line 9; it contains the output of the statements in Lines 9 through 11.

The statements in Lines 12 through 18 insert `36`, `84`, `30`, `39`, `59`, `238`, and `156` into `intSetA`, and the statement in Line 20 outputs the elements of `intSetA`. In the output, see the line marked Line 19. It contains the output of the statements in Lines 19 through 21. Notice that the elements of `intSetA` appear in descending order.

The statement in Line 22 removes `59` from `intSetA`. After the statement in Line 26 executes, `intGtIt` points to the first element of `intSetA`. The statement in Line 27 advances `intGtIt` to the next element of `intSetA`. After the statement in Line 29 executes, `intGtIt` points to the fourth element of `intSetA`. The statement in Line 30 removes the element of `intSetA` pointed to by `intGtIt`. The meanings of the statements in Lines 34 through 41 are similar.

The statement in Line 42 declares `namesMultiSet` to be a container of type `multiset`. The elements in `namesMultiSet` are of type `string` and are arranged in descending order. The statement in Line 43 declares `iter` to be a `multiset` iterator.

The statements in Lines 45 through 50 insert `Donny`, `Zippy`, `Goofy`, `Hungry`, `Goofy`, and `Donny` into `namesMultiSet`. The statement in Line 52 outputs the elements of `namesMultiSet`.

Container Adapters

The previous sections discussed several types of containers. In addition to the containers that work in a general framework, the STL provides containers to accommodate special situations. These containers, called **container adapters**, are adapted standard STL containers to work in a specific environment. The three container adapters are:

- Stacks
- Queues
- Priority queues

Container adapters do not support any type of iterator. That is, iterators cannot be used with these types of containers. The next two sections describe two types of container adapters: stack and queue.

Stack

Chapter 17 discussed the data structure stack in detail. Because a stack is an important data structure, the STL provides a class to implement a stack in a program. The name of the class defining a stack is `stack`; the name of the header file containing the definition of the `class` `stack` is `stack`. Table 21-19 defines the various operations supported by the stack container class.

TABLE 21-19 Various Operations on a `stack` Object

Operation	Description
`size`	Returns the actual number of elements in the stack.
`empty`	Returns `true` if the stack is empty, `false` otherwise.
`push(item)`	Inserts a copy of `item` onto the stack.
`top`	Returns the top element of the stack, but does not remove the element from the stack. This operation is implemented as a value-returning function.
`pop`	Removes the top element of the stack.

In addition to the operations size, empty, push, top, and pop, the stack container class provides relational operators to compare two stacks. For example, the relational operator == can be used to determine whether two stacks are identical.

The program in Example 21-9 illustrates how to use the stack container class.

EXAMPLE 21-9

```cpp
#include <iostream>
#include <stack>

using namespace std;

int main()
{
    stack<int> intStack;                                //Line 1

    intStack.push(16);                                  //Line 2
    intStack.push(8);                                   //Line 3
    intStack.push(20);                                  //Line 4
    intStack.push(3);                                   //Line 5

    cout << "Line 6: The top element of intStack: "
         << intStack.top() << endl;                     //Line 6

    intStack.pop();                                     //Line 7

    cout << "Line 8: After the pop operation, "
         << "the top element of intStack: "
         << intStack.top() << endl;                     //Line 8

    cout << "Line 9: intStack elements: ";              //Line 9

    while (!intStack.empty())                           //Line 10
    {
        cout << intStack.top() << " ";                  //Line 11
        intStack.pop();                                 //Line 12
    }

    cout << endl;                                       //Line 13

    return 0;
}
```

Sample Run:

```
Line 6: The top element of intStack: 3
Line 8: After the pop operation, the top element of intStack: 20
Line 9: intStack elements: 20 8 16
```

The preceding output is self-explanatory. The details are left as an exercise for you.

Queue

Chapter 17 discussed the data structure queue in detail. Because a queue is an important data structure, the STL provides a class to implement queues in a program. The name of the class defining the queue is `queue`, and the name of the header file containing the definition of the `class` queue is `queue`. Table 21-20 defines the various operations supported by the queue container class.

TABLE 21-20 Various Operations on a `queue` Object

Operation	Description
size	Returns the actual number of elements in the queue.
empty	Returns `true` if the queue is empty, `false` otherwise.
push(item)	Inserts a copy of `item` into the queue.
front	Returns the next—that is, first—element in the queue, but does not remove the element from the queue. This operation is implemented as a value-returning function.
back	Returns the last element in the queue, but does not remove the element from the queue. This operation is implemented as a value-returning function.
pop	Removes the next element in the queue.

In addition to the operations `size`, `empty`, `push`, `front`, `back`, and `pop`, the queue container class provides relational operators to compare two stacks. For example, the relational operator `==` can be used to determine whether two stacks are identical.

The program in Example 21-10 illustrates how to use the queue container class.

EXAMPLE 21-10

```
#include <iostream>
#include <queue>

using namespace std;

int main()
{
    queue<int> intQueue;                        //Line 1

    intQueue.push(26);                          //Line 2
    intQueue.push(18);                          //Line 3
```

```
intQueue.push(50);                                    //Line 4
intQueue.push(33);                                    //Line 5

cout << "Line 6: The front element of intQueue: "
     << intQueue.front() << endl;                     //Line 6

cout << "Line 7: The last element of intQueue: "
     << intQueue.back() << endl;                      //Line 7

intQueue.pop();                                       //Line 8

cout << "Line 9: After the pop operation, "
     << "the front element of intQueue: "
     << intQueue.front() << endl;                     //Line 9

cout << "Line 10: intQueue elements: ";               //Line 10

while (!intQueue.empty())                             //Line 11
{
    cout << intQueue.front() << " ";                 //Line 12
    intQueue.pop();                                   //Line 13
}

cout << endl;                                         //Line 14

    return 0;
}
```

Sample Run:

```
Line 6: The front element of intQueue: 26
Line 7: The last element of intQueue: 33
Line 9: After the pop operation, the front element of intQueue: 18
Line 10: intQueue elements: 18 50 33
```

The preceding output is self-explanatory. The details are left as an exercise for you.

Containers, Associated Header Files, and Iterator Support

The previous sections discussed various types of containers. Recall that every container is a class. The definition of the class implementing a specific container is contained in the header file. Table 21-21 describes the container, its associated header file, and the type of iterator supported by the container.

TABLE 21-21 Containers, Their Associated Header Files, and the Type of Iterator Supported by Each Container

Sequence containers	Associated header file	Type of iterator support
vector	<vector>	Random access
deque	<deque>	Random access
list	<list>	Bidirectional
Associative containers	**Associated header file**	**Type of iterator support**
map	<map>	Bidirectional
multimap	<map>	Bidirectional
set	<set>	Bidirectional
multiset	<set>	Bidirectional
Adapters	**Associated header file**	**Type of iterator support**
stack	<stack>	No iterator support
queue	<queue>	No iterator support
priority queue	<queue>	No iterator support

Algorithms

Several operations can be defined for a container. Some of the operations are very specific to a container and, therefore, are provided as part of the container definition (that is, as member functions of the class implementing the container). However, several operations—such as **find**, **sort**, and **merge**—are common to all containers. These operations are provided as generic algorithms and can be applied to all containers, as well as the built-in array type. The algorithms are bound to a particular container through an iterator pair.

The generic algorithms are contained in the header file **algorithm**. This section describes several of these algorithms and shows how to use them in a program. Because algorithms are implemented with the help of functions, in this section, the terms *function* and *algorithm* mean the same thing.

STL Algorithm Classification

In earlier sections, you applied various operations on a sequence container, such as `clear`, `sort`, `merge`, and so on. However, those algorithms were tied to a specific container in terms of the members of a specific class. All of those algorithms and a few others are also available in more general forms, called **generic algorithms**, and can be applied in a variety of situations. This section discusses some of these generic algorithms.

The STL contains algorithms that look only at the elements in a container and that move the elements of a container. It also has algorithms that can perform specific calculations, such as finding the sum of the elements of a numeric container. In addition, the STL contains algorithms for basic set theory operations, such as set union and intersection. You have already encountered some of the generic algorithms, such as the `copy` algorithm. This algorithm copies the elements from a given range of elements to another place, such as another container or the screen. The algorithms in the STL can be classified into the following categories:

- Nonmodifying algorithms
- Modifying algorithms
- Numeric algorithms
- Heap algorithms

The next four sections describe these algorithms. Most of the generic algorithms are contained in the header file `algorithm`. Certain algorithms, such as the numeric algorithms, are contained in the header file `numeric`.

NONMODIFYING ALGORITHMS

Nonmodifying algorithms do not modify the elements of the container; they merely investigate the elements. Table 21-22 lists the nonmodifying algorithms.

TABLE 21-22 Nonmodifying Algorithms

adjacent_find	find_end	max
binary_search	find_first_of	max_element
count	find_if	min
count_if	for_each	min_element
equal	includes	search
equal_range	lower_bound	search_n
find	mismatch	upper_bound

MODIFYING ALGORITHMS

Modifying algorithms, as the name implies, modify the elements of the container by rearranging, removing, or changing the values of the elements. Table 21-23 lists the modifying algorithms.

TABLE 21-23 Modifying Algorithms

copy	prev_permutation	rotate_copy
copy_backward	random_shuffle	set_difference
fill	remove	set_intersection
fill_n	remove_copy	set_symmetric_difference
generate	remove_copy_if	set_union
generate_n	remove_if	sort
inplace_merge	replace	stable_partition
iter_swap	replace_copy	stable_sort
merge	replace_copy_if	swap
next_permutation	replace_if	swap_ranges
nth_element	reverse	transform
partial_sort	reverse_copy	unique
partial_sort_copy	rotate	unique_copy
partition		

Modifying algorithms that change the order of the elements, not their values, are also called mutating algorithms. For example, next_permutation, partition, prev_permutation, random_shuffle, reverse, reverse_copy, rotate, rotate_copy, and stable_partition are mutating algorithms.

NUMERIC ALGORITHMS

Numeric algorithms are designed to perform numeric calculations on the elements of a container. Table 21-24 lists these algorithms.

TABLE 21-24 Numeric Algorithms

accumulate	inner_product
adjacent_difference	partial_sum

HEAP ALGORITHMS

A special type of sorting algorithm, called the heap sort algorithm, is used to sort the data stored in an array. In the heap sort algorithm, the array containing the data is viewed as a binary tree. Thus, a heap is a form of binary tree represented as an array. In a heap, the first element is the largest element, and the element at the ith position (if it exists) is larger than the elements at positions $2i$ and $2i + 1$ (if they exist). In the heap sort algorithm, first the array containing the data is converted into a heap, and then the array is sorted using a special type of sorting algorithm. Table 21-25 lists the basic algorithms required by the heap sort algorithm.

TABLE 21-25 Heap Algorithms

make_heap	push_heap
pop_heap	sort_heap

Most of the STL algorithms are explained later in this chapter. For the most part, the function prototypes of these algorithms are given along with a brief explanation of what each algorithm does. You will then learn how to use these algorithms with the help of a C++ program. The STL algorithms are very powerful and accomplish amazing results. Furthermore, they have been made general, in the sense that other than using the natural operations to manipulate containers, they allow the user to specify the manipulating criteria. For example, the natural sorting order is ascending, but the user can specify criteria to sort the container in descending order. Thus, every algorithm is typically implemented with the help of overloaded functions. Before starting to describe these algorithms, we discuss **function objects**, which allow the user to specify the manipulating criteria.

Function Objects

To make the generic algorithms flexible, the STL usually provides two forms of an algorithm using the mechanism of function overloading. The first form of an algorithm uses the natural operation to accomplish this goal. In the second form, the user can specify criteria based on which algorithm processes the elements. For example, the algorithm `adjacent_find` searches the container and returns the position of the first two elements that are equal. In the second form of this algorithm, we can specify criteria (say, less than) to look for the first two elements, such that the second element is less than the first element.

These criteria are passed as a function object. More formally, a **function object** contains a function that can be treated as a function using the function call operator, (). In fact, a function object is a class template that overloads the function call operator, `operator()`.

In addition to allowing you to create your own function objects, the STL provides arithmetic, relational, and logical function objects, which are described in Table 21-26. The STL's function objects are contained in the header file `functional`.

TABLE 21-26 Arithmetic STL Function Objects

Function object name	Description
plus<Type>	plus<int> addNum; int sum = addNum(12, 35); The value of sum is 47.
minus<Type>	minus<int> subtractNum; int difference = subtractNum(56, 35); The value of difference is 21.
multiplies<Type>	multiplies<int> multiplyNum; int product = multiplyNum(6, 3); The value of product is 18.
divides<Type>	divides<int> divideNum; int quotient = divideNum(16, 3); The value of quotient is 5.
modulus<Type>	modulus<int> remainder; int rem = remainder(16, 7); The value of rem is 2.
negate<Type>	negate<int> num; int opposite = num(-25); The value of opposite is 25.

Example 21-11 shows how to use the STL's function objects.

EXAMPLE 21-11

```
#include <iostream>
#include <string>
#include <algorithm>
#include <numeric>
#include <iterator>
#include <vector>
#include <functional>
```

```cpp
using namespace std;

int funcAdd(plus<int>, int, int);

int main()
{
    plus<int> addNum;                                   //Line 1
    int num = addNum(34, 56);                           //Line 2

    cout << "Line 3: num = " << num << endl;            //Line 3

    plus<string> joinString;                            //Line 4

    string str1 = "Hello ";                             //Line 5
    string str2 = "There";                              //Line 6

    string str = joinString(str1, str2);                //Line 7

    cout << "Line 8: str = " << str << endl;            //Line 8

    cout << "Line 9: Sum of 34 and 26 = "
         << funcAdd(addNum, 34, 26) << endl;            //Line 9


    int list[8] = {1, 2, 3, 4, 5, 6, 7, 8};             //Line 10

    vector<int>  intList(list, list + 8);               //Line 11
    ostream_iterator<int> screenOut(cout, " ");         //Line 12

    cout << "Line 13: intList: ";                       //Line 13
    copy(intList.begin(), intList.end(), screenOut);    //Line 14
    cout << endl;                                       //Line 15

        //accumulate function
    int sum = accumulate(intList.begin(),
                        intList.end(), 0);              //Line 16

    cout << "Line 17: Sum of the elements of "
         << "intList = " << sum << endl;                //Line 17

    int product = accumulate(intList.begin(),
                            intList.end(),
                            1, multiplies<int>());       //Line 18

    cout << "Line 19: Product of the elements of "
         << "intList = " << product << endl;            //Line 19

    return 0;
}
```

```
int funcAdd(plus<int> sum, int x, int y)
{
    return sum(x, y);
}
```

Sample Run:

```
Line 3: num = 90
Line 8: str = Hello There
Line 9: Sum of 34 and 26 = 60
Line 13: intList: 1 2 3 4 5 6 7 8
Line 17: Sum of the elements of intList = 36
Line 19: Product of the elements of intList = 40320
```

Table 21-27 describes the relational STL function objects.

TABLE 21-27 Relational STL Function Objects

Function object name	Description
equal_to<Type>	Returns true if the two arguments are equal, and false otherwise. For example, equal_to<int> compare; bool isEqual = compare(5, 5); The value of isEqual is true.
not_equal_to<Type>	Returns true if the two arguments are not equal, and false otherwise. For example, not_equal_to<int> compare; bool isNotEqual = compare(5, 6); The value of isNotEqual is true.
greater<Type>	Returns true if the first argument is greater than the second argument, and false otherwise. For example, greater<int> compare; bool isGreater = compare(8, 5); The value of isGreater is true.
greater_equal<Type>	Returns true if the first argument is greater than or equal to the second argument, and false otherwise. For example, greater_equal<int> compare; bool isGreaterEqual = compare(8, 5); The value of isGreaterEqual is true.

2
1

TABLE 21-27 Relational STL Function Objects (continued)

Function object name	Description
less<Type>	Returns true if the first argument is less than the second argument, and false otherwise. For example, less<int> compare; bool isLess = compare(3, 5);. The value of isLess is true.
less_equal<Type>	Returns true if the first argument is less than or equal to the second argument, and false otherwise. For example, less_equal<int> compare; bool isLessEqual = compare(8, 15);. The value of isLessEqual is true.

The STL relational function objects can also be applied to containers, as shown next. The STL algorithm `adjacent_find` searches a container and returns the position in the container where the two elements are equal. This algorithm has a second form that allows the user to specify the comparison criteria. For example, consider the following vector, `vecList`:

```
vecList = {2, 3, 4, 5, 1, 7, 8, 9};
```

The elements of `vecList` are supposed to be in ascending order. To see if the elements are out of order, we can use the algorithm `adjacent_find` as follows:

```
intItr = adjacent_find(vecList.begin(), vecList.end(),
                       greater<int>());
```

in which `intItr` is an iterator of the `vector` type. The function `adjacent_find` starts at the position `vecList.begin()`—that is, at the first element of `vecList`—and looks for the first set of consecutive elements such that the first element is greater than the second. The function returns a pointer to element 5, which is stored in `intItr`.

The program in Example 21-12 further illustrates how to use the relational function objects.

EXAMPLE 21-12

This example shows how the relational STL function objects work.

```
#include <iostream>
#include <string>
#include <algorithm>
#include <iterator>
#include <vector>
#include <functional>
```

```cpp
using namespace std;

int main()
{
    equal_to<int> compare;                            //Line 1
    bool isEqual = compare(6, 6);                     //Line 2

    cout << "Line 3: isEqual = " << isEqual << endl;  //Line 3

    greater<string> greaterStr;                       //Line 4

    string str1 = "Hello";                            //Line 5
    string str2 = "There";                            //Line 6

    if (greaterStr(str1, str2))                       //Line 7
        cout << "Line 8: \"" << str1 << "\" is "
             << "greater than \"" << str2 << "\""
             << endl;                                 //Line 8
    else                                              //Line 9
        cout << "Line 10: \"" << str1 << "\" is "
             << "not greater than \"" << str2
             << "\"" << endl;                         //Line 10

    int temp[8] = {2, 3, 4, 5, 1, 7, 8, 9};           //Line 11

    vector<int> vecList(temp, temp + 8);              //Line 12
    vector<int>::iterator intItr1, intItr2;           //Line 13
    ostream_iterator<int> screen(cout, " ");          //Line 14

    cout << "Line 15: vecList: ";                     //Line 15
    copy(vecList.begin(), vecList.end(), screen);     //Line 16
    cout << endl;                                     //Line 17

    intItr1 = adjacent_find(vecList.begin(),
                            vecList.end(),
                            greater<int>());           //Line 18
    intItr2 = intItr1 + 1;                             //Line 19

    cout << "Line 20: In vecList, the first set of "
         << "out-of-order elements is: " << *intItr1
         << " " << *intItr2 << endl;                  //Line 20
    cout << "Line 21: In vecList, the first out-of-"
         << "order element is at position "
         << vecList.end() - intItr2 << endl;          //Line 21

    return 0;
}
```

21

Sample Run:

```
Line  3: isEqual = 1
Line 10: "Hello" is not greater than "There"
Line 15: vecList: 2 3 4 5 1 7 8 9
Line 20: In vecList, the first set of out-of-order elements is: 5 1
Line 21: In vecList, the first out-of-order element is at position 4
```

Table 21-28 describes the logical STL function objects.

TABLE 21-28   Logical STL Function Objects

Function object name	Effect
logical_not<Type>	Returns true if its operand evaluates to false; otherwise, it returns false. This is a unary function object.
logical_and<Type>	Returns true if both of its operands evaluate to true; otherwise, it returns false. This is a binary function object.
logical_or<Type>	Returns true if at least one of its operands evaluates to true; otherwise, it returns false. This is a binary function object.

PREDICATES

Predicates are special types of function objects that return Boolean values. There are two types of predicates: unary and binary. Unary predicates check a specific property for a single argument; binary predicates check a specific property for a pair—that is, two arguments. Predicates are typically used to specify searching or sorting criteria. In the STL, a predicate must always return the same result for the same value. Therefore, the functions that modify their internal states *cannot* be considered predicates.

Insert Iterator

Consider the following statements:

```
int list[5] = {1, 3, 6, 9, 12}; //Line 1
vector<int> vList;               //Line 2
```

The statement in Line 1 declares and initializes list to be an array of five components. The statement in Line 2 declares vList to be a vector. Because no size is specified for vList, no memory space is reserved for the elements of vList. Now suppose that we want to copy the elements of list into vList. The statement:

```
copy(list, list + 8, vList.begin());
```

will not work because no memory space is allocated for the elements of vList, and the copy function uses the assignment operator to copy the elements from the source to the destination. One solution to this problem is to use a `for` loop to step through the elements of list and use the function push_back of vList to copy the elements of list. However, there is a better solution, which is convenient and applicable whenever no memory space is allocated at the destination. The STL provides three iterators, called **insert iterators**, to insert the elements at the destination: back_inserter, front_inserter, and inserter.

- **back_inserter**: This inserter uses the push_back operation of the container in place of the assignment operator. The argument to this iterator is the container itself. For example, for the preceding problem, we can copy the elements of list into vList by using back_inserter as follows:

  ```
  copy(list, list + 5, back_inserter(vList));
  ```

- **front_inserter**: This inserter uses the push_front operation of the container in place of the assignment operator. The argument to this iterator is the container itself. Because the vector class does not support the push_front operation, this iterator *cannot* be used for the vector container.

- **inserter**: This inserter uses the container's insert operation in place of the assignment operator. There are two arguments to this iterator: the first argument is the container itself; the second argument is an iterator to the container specifying the position at which the insertion should begin.

The program in Example 21-13 illustrates the effect of inserters on a container.

EXAMPLE 21-13

```
//Inserters

#include <iostream>
#include <algorithm>
#include <iterator>
#include <vector>
#include <list>

using namespace std;

int main()
{
    int temp[8] = {1, 2, 3, 4, 5, 6, 7, 8};        //Line 1

    vector<int> vecList1;                          //Line 2
    vector<int> vecList2;                          //Line 3

    ostream_iterator<int> screenOut(cout, " ");    //Line 4

    copy(temp, temp + 8, back_inserter(vecList1)); //Line 5
```

```
cout << "Line 6: vecList1: ";                        //Line 6
copy(vecList1.begin(), vecList1.end(),
     screenOut);                                     //Line 7
cout << endl;                                        //Line 8

copy(vecList1.begin(), vecList1.end(),
     inserter(vecList2, vecList2.begin()));          //Line 9

cout << "Line 10: vecList2: ";                       //Line 10
copy(vecList2.begin(), vecList2.end(),
                    screenOut);                      //Line 11
cout << endl;                                        //Line 12

list<int> tempList;                                  //Line 13

copy(vecList2.begin(), vecList2.end(),
     front_inserter(tempList));                      //Line 14

cout << "Line 15: tempList: ";                       //Line 15
copy(tempList.begin(), tempList.end(),
                    screenOut);                      //Line 16
cout << endl;                                        //Line 17

return 0;
}
```

Sample Run:

```
Line 6: vecList1: 1 2 3 4 5 6 7 8
Line 10: vecList2: 1 2 3 4 5 6 7 8
Line 15: tempList: 8 7 6 5 4 3 2 1
```

STL Algorithms

The following sections describe most of the STL algorithms. For each algorithm, we give the function prototypes, a brief description of what the algorithm does, and a program showing how to use it. In the function prototypes, the parameter types indicate for which type of container the algorithm is applicable. For example, if a parameter is of type `randomAccessIterator`, then the algorithm is applicable only on random access type containers, such as vectors. Throughout, we use abbreviations such as `outputItr` to mean output iterator, `inputItr` to mean input iterator, `forwardItr` to mean forward iterator, and so on.

The Functions `fill` and `fill_n`

The function `fill` is used to fill a container with elements; the function `fill_n` is used to fill in the next n elements. The element that is used as a filling element is passed as a parameter to these functions. Both of these functions are defined in the header file `algorithm`. The prototypes of these functions are:

```
template <class forwardItr, class Type>
void fill(forwardItr first, forwardItr last, const Type& value);

template <class forwardItr, class size, class Type>
void fill_n(forwardItr first, size n, const Type& value);
```

The first two parameters of the function `fill` are forward iterators specifying the starting and ending positions of the container; the third parameter is the filling element. The first parameter of the function `fill_n` is a forward iterator that specifies the starting position of the container, the second parameter specifies the number of elements to be filled, and the third parameter specifies the filling element. The program in Example 21-14 illustrates how to use these functions.

EXAMPLE 21-14

```cpp
//STL functions fill and fill_n

#include <iostream>
#include <algorithm>
#include <iterator>
#include <vector>

using namespace std;

int main()
{
    vector<int>  vecList(8);                             //Line 1
    ostream_iterator<int> screen(cout, " ");             //Line 2

    fill(vecList.begin(), vecList.end(), 2);             //Line 3

    cout << "Line 4: After filling vecList "
         << "with 2s: ";                                 //Line 4
    copy(vecList.begin(), vecList.end(), screen);        //Line 5
    cout << endl;                                        //Line 6

    fill_n(vecList.begin(), 3, 5);                       //Line 7

    cout << "Line 8: After filling the first three "
         << "elements with 5s: "
         << endl << "         ";                         //Line 8
    copy(vecList.begin(), vecList.end(), screen);        //Line 9
    cout << endl;                                        //Line 10

    return 0;
}
```

Sample Run:

```
Line 4: After filling vecList with 2s: 2 2 2 2 2 2 2 2
Line 8: After filling first three elements with 5s:
         5 5 5 2 2 2 2 2
```

The statements in Lines 1 and 2 declare `vecList` to be a sequence container of size 8 and `screen` to be an `ostream` iterator initialized to `cout` with the delimit character space. The statement in Line 3 uses the function `fill` to fill `vecList` with 2; that is, all eight elements of `vecList` are set to 2. Recall that `vecList.begin()` returns an iterator to the first element of `vecList`, and `vecList.end()` returns an iterator to one past the last element of `vecList`. The statement in Line 5 outputs the elements of `vecList` using the `copy` function. The statement in Line 7 uses the function `fill_n` to store 5 in the elements of `vecList`. The first parameter of `fill_n` is `vecList.begin()`, which specifies the starting position to begin copying. The second parameter of `fill_n` is 3, which specifies the number of elements to be filled. The third parameter, 5, specifies the filling character. Therefore, 5 is copied into the first three elements of `vecList`. The statement in Line 9 outputs the elements of `vecList`.

The Functions `generate` and `generate_n`

The functions `generate` and `generate_n` are used to generate elements and fill a sequence. These functions are defined in the header file `algorithm`. The prototypes of these functions are:

```
template <class forwardItr, class function>
void generate(forwardItr first, forwardItr last, function gen);

template <class forwardItr, class size, class function>
void generate_n(forwardItr first, size n, function gen);
```

The function `generate` fills a sequence in the range `first...last-1`, with successive calls to the function `gen()`. The function `generate_n` fills a sequence in the range `first...first+n-1`—that is, starting at position `first`, with n successive calls to the function `gen()`. Note that `gen` can also be a pointer to a function. Moreover, if `gen` is a function, it must be a value-returning function without parameters. The program in Example 21-15 illustrates how to use these functions.

EXAMPLE 21-15

```
//STL Functions generate and generate_n

#include <iostream>
#include <algorithm>
#include <iterator>
#include <vector>

using namespace std;

int nextNum();
```

```
int main()
{
    vector<int>  vecList(8);                                  //Line 1

    ostream_iterator<int> screen(cout, " ");                 //Line 2

    generate(vecList.begin(), vecList.end(), nextNum); //Line 3

    cout << "Line 4: vecList after filling with "
         << "numbers: ";                                      //Line 4

    copy(vecList.begin(), vecList.end(), screen);            //Line 5
    cout << endl;                                             //Line 6

    generate_n(vecList.begin(), 3, nextNum);                 //Line 7

    cout << "Line 8: vecList after filling the "
         << "first three elements " << endl
         << "            with the next number: ";             //Line 8

    copy(vecList.begin(), vecList.end(), screen);            //Line 9
    cout << endl;                                            //Line 10

    return 0;
}

int nextNum()
{
    static int n = 1;

    return n++;
}
```

Sample Run:

```
Line 4: vecList after filling with numbers: 1 2 3 4 5 6 7 8
Line 8: vecList after filling the first three elements
            with the next number: 9 10 11 4 5 6 7 8
```

This program contains a value-returning function, nextNum, which contains a `static` variable n initialized to 1. A call to this function returns the current value of n and then increments the value of n. Therefore, the first call of nextNum returns 1, the second call returns 2, and so on.

The statements in Lines 1 and 2 declare vecList to be a sequence container of size 8 and screen to be an ostream iterator initialized to cout with the delimit character space. The statement in Line 3 uses the function generate to fill vecList by successively calling the function nextNum. Notice that after the statement in Line 3 executes, the value of the `static` variable n of nextNum is 9. The statement in Line 5 outputs the elements of vecList. The statement in Line 7 calls the function generate_n to fill the first three elements of vecList by calling the function nextNum three times. The starting position is vecList.begin(), which is the first element of vecList, and the number of elements to be filled is 3, given by the second parameter of generate_n (see Line 7). The statement in Line 9 outputs the elements of vecList.

The Functions find, find_if, find_end, and find_first_of

The functions find, find_if, find_end, and find_first_of are used to find the elements in a given range. These functions are defined in the header file algorithm. The prototypes of the functions find and find_if are:

```
template <class inputItr, class size, class Type>
inputItr find(inputItr first, inputItr last,
              const Type& searchValue);

template <class inputItr, class unaryPredicate>
inputItr find_if(inputItr first, inputItr last, unaryPredicate op);
```

The function find searches the range of elements first...last-1 for the element searchValue. If searchValue is found in the range, the function returns the position in the range where searchValue is found; otherwise, it returns last. The function find_if searches the range of elements first...last-1 for the element for which op(rangeElement) is true. If an element satisfying op(rangeElement) is true is found, it returns the position in the given range where such an element is found; otherwise, it returns last.

The program in Example 21-16 illustrates how to use the functions find and find_if.

EXAMPLE 21-16

```
//STL Functions find and find_if

#include <iostream>
#include <cctype>
#include <algorithm>
#include <iterator>
#include <vector>

using namespace std;

int main()
{
    char cList[10] = {'a', 'i', 'C', 'd', 'e',
                      'f', 'o', 'H', 'u', 'j'};        //Line 1

    vector<char> charList(cList, cList + 10);          //Line 2
```

```
    ostream_iterator<char> screen(cout, " ");          //Line 3

    cout << "Line 4: Character list: ";                //Line 4
    copy(charList.begin(), charList.end(), screen);     //Line 5
    cout << endl;                                       //Line 6

    vector<char>::iterator position;                    //Line 7

        //find
    position = find(charList.begin(),
                charList.end(), 'd');                    //Line 8

    if (position != charList.end())                     //Line 9
        cout << "Line 10: The element is found at "
            << "position "
            << (position - charList.begin())            //Line 10
            << endl;                                     //Line 11
    else
        cout << "Line 12: The element is not in "
            << "the list." << endl;                     //Line 12

        //find_if
    position = find_if(charList.begin(),
                charList.end(), isupper);                //Line 13

    if (position != charList.end())                     //Line 14
        cout << "Line 15: The first uppercase "
            << "letter is found at position "
            << (position - charList.begin())            //Line 15
            << endl;                                     //Line 16
    else
        cout << "Line 17: The element is not in "
            << "the list." << endl;                     //Line 17

    return 0;
}
```

Sample Run:

```
Line 4: Character list: a i C d e f o H u j
Line 10: The element is found at position 3
Line 15: The first uppercase letter is found at position 2
```

The statement in Line 1 creates and initializes a character array, cList, of 10 components. The statement in Line 2 creates the vector container charList and initializes it
using the character array cList. The statement in Line 3 creates an ostream iterator.
The statement in Line 5 outputs charList. (In the output, the line marked Line 4
contains the output of Lines 4 through 6 of the program.) The statement in Line 7
declares the iterator position of type vector<char>. The statement in Line 8
searches charList for the first occurrence of 'd' and returns an iterator, which is
stored in position. The statements in Lines 9 through 12 output the result of the
search. Because 'd' is the fourth character in charList, its position is 3. (In the output,

see the line marked Line 10.) The statement in Line 13 uses the function `find_if` to find the first uppercase character in `charList`. Note that the function `isupper` from the header file `cctype` is passed as the third parameter to the function `find_if` (see Line 13). The statements in Lines 14 through 17 output the result of the search. The first uppercase character in `charList` is `'C'`, which is the third element of `charList`; its position is 2. (In the output, see the line marked Line 15.)

Next, we describe the functions `find_end` and `find_first_of`. Both of these functions have two forms. The prototypes of the function `find_end` are:

```
template <class forwardItr1, class forwardItr2>
forwardItr1 find_end(forwardItr1 first1, forwardItr1 last1,
                     forwardItr2 first2, forwardItr2 last2);

template <class forwardItr1, class forwardItr2,
          class binaryPredicate>
forwardItr1 find_end(forwardItr1 first1, forwardItr1 last1,
                     forwardItr2 first2, forwardItr2 last2,
                     binaryPredicate op);
```

Both forms of the function `find_end` search the range `first1...last1-1` for the last occurrence as a subrange of the range `first2...last2-1`. If the search is successful, the function returns the position in `first1..last1-1` where the match occurs; otherwise, it returns `last1`. That is, the function `find_end` returns the position of the last element in the range `first1...last1-1` where the range `first2...last2-1` is a subrange of `first1...last1-1`. In the first form, the elements are compared for equality; in the second form, the comparison `op(elementFirstRange, elementSecondRange)` must be `true`.

The prototypes of the function `find_first_of` are:

```
template <class forwardItr1, class forwardItr2>
forwardItr1 find_first_of(forwardItr1 first1, forwardItr1 last1,
                          forwardItr2 first2, forwardItr2 last2);

template <class forwardItr1, class forwardItr2,
          class binaryPredicate>
forwardItr1 find_first_of(forwardItr1 first1, forwardItr1 last1,
                          forwardItr2 first2, forwardItr2 last2,
                          binaryPredicate op);
```

The first form returns the position, within the range `first1...last1-1`, of the first element of `first2...last2-1` that is also in the range `first1...last1-1`. The second form returns the position, within the range `first1...last1-1`, of the first element of `first2...last2-1` for which `op(elemRange1, elemRange2)` is `true`. If no match is found, both forms return `last1-1`.

The program in Example 21-17 illustrates how to use the functions `find_end` and `find_first_of`.

EXAMPLE 21-17

```cpp
//STL Functions find_end and find_first_of

#include <iostream>
#include <algorithm>
#include <iterator>

using namespace std;

int main()
{
    int list1[10] = {12, 34, 56, 21, 34,
                     78, 34, 56, 12, 25};      //Line 1
                                               //Line 2
    int list2[2] = {34, 56};                   //Line 3
    int list3[3] = {56, 21, 35};               //Line 4
    int list4[5] = {33, 48, 21, 34, 73};

                                               //Line 5
    int* location;

    ostream_iterator<int> screenOut(cout, " ");  //Line 6

    cout << "Line 7: list1: ";                 //Line 7
    copy(list1, list1 + 10, screenOut);        //Line 8
    cout << endl;                              //Line 9

    cout << "Line 10: list2: ";                //Line 10
    copy(list2, list2 + 2, screenOut);         //Line 11
    cout << endl;                              //Line 12

        //find_end
    location = find_end(list1, list1+10,
                    list2, list2 + 2);         //Line 13

                                               //Line 14
    if (location != list1 + 10)
        cout << "Line 15: list2 is found in list 1. "
             << "The last occurrence of \n        "
             << "list2 in list 1 is at position "
             << (location - list1) << endl;    //Line 15
                                               //Line 16
    else
        cout << "Line 17: list2 is not in list1."
             << endl;                          //Line 17

    cout << "Line 18: list3: ";                //Line 18
    copy(list3, list3 + 3, screenOut);         //Line 19
    cout << endl;                              //Line 20

    location = find_end(list1, list1 + 10,
                    list3, list3 + 3);         //Line 21
```

```
       if (location != list1 + 10)                          //Line 22
           cout << "Line 23: list3 is found in list 1. "
               << "The last occurrence of list3 in "
               << endl << "list 1 is at position "
               << (location - list1) << endl;               //Line 23
       else                                                 //Line 24
           cout << "Line 25: list3 is not in list1."
               << endl;                                     //Line 25

       //find_first_of
       cout << "Line 26: list4: ";                          //Line 26
       copy(list4, list4 + 5, screenOut);                   //Line 27
       cout << endl;                                        //Line 28

       location = find_first_of(list1, list1 + 10,
                               list4, list4 + 5);           //Line 29

       if (location != list1 + 10)                          //Line 30
           cout << "Line 31: The first element "
               << *location << " of list4 is found in "
               << endl << "          list 1 at position "
               << (location - list1) << endl;               //Line 31
       else                                                 //Line 32
           cout << "Line 33: No element of list4 is "
               << "in list1." << endl;                      //Line 33

       return 0;
   }
```

Sample Run:

```
Line 7: list1: 12 34 56 21 34 78 34 56 12 25
Line 10: list2: 34 56
Line 15: list2 is found in list 1. The last occurrence of
         list2 in list 1 is at position 6
Line 18: list3: 56 21 35
Line 25: list3 is not in list1.
Line 26: list4: 33 48 21 34 73
Line 31: The first element 34 of list4 is found in
         list 1 at position 1
```

The statements in Lines 1 through 4 create and initialize the int arrays list1, list2, list3, and list4. The statements in Lines 5 and 6 declare an int pointer and an ostream iterator, respectively. The statements in Lines 8 and 11 output the values of list1 and list2. (In the output, see the lines marked Line 7 and Line 10.) The statement in Line 13 uses the function find_end to find the last occurrence of list2, as a subsequence, within list1. The last occurrence of list2 in list1 starts at position 6 (that is, at the seventh element). The statements in Lines 14 through 17 output the result of the search. (In the output, see Line 15.) The statement in Line 19 outputs list3. The statement in Line 21 uses the function find_end to find the last occurrence of list3, as a subsequence, within list1. Because list3 does not appear as a subsequence in list1, it is an unsuccessful search.

The statement in Line 27 outputs `list4`. The statement in Line 29 uses the function `find_first_of` to find the position in `list1` where the first element of `list4` is also an element of `list1`. The first element of `list4`, which is also an element of `list1`, is 33. Its position in `list1` is 1, the second element of `list1`. The statements in Lines 30 through 33 output the result of the search. (In the output, see Line 31.)

The Functions `remove`, `remove_if`, `remove_copy`, and `remove_copy_if`

The function `remove` is used to remove certain elements from a sequence, and the function `remove_if` is used to remove elements from a sequence by using some criteria. The function `remove_copy` copies the elements of a sequence into another sequence by excluding certain elements of the first sequence. Similarly, the function `remove_copy_if` copies the elements of a sequence into another sequence by excluding certain elements, using some criteria, of the first sequence. These functions are defined in the header file `algorithm`.

The prototypes of the functions `remove` and `remove_if` are:

```
template <class forwardItr, class Type>
forwardItr remove(forwardItr first, forwardItr last,
                  const Type& value);

template <class forwardItr, class unaryPredicate>
forwardItr remove_if(forwardItr first, forwardItr last,
                     unaryPredicate op);
```

The function `remove` removes each occurrence of a given element in the range `first...last-1`. The element to be removed is passed as the third parameter to this function. The function `remove_if` removes those elements, in the range `first...last-1`, for which the `op(element)` is `true`. Both of these functions return `forwardItr`, which points to the position after the last element of the new range of elements. These functions do not modify the size of the container; in fact, the elements are moved to the beginning of the container. For example, if the sequence is {3, 7, 2, 5, 7, 9} and the element to be removed is 7, then after removing 7, the resulting sequence is {3, 2, 5, 9, 9, 9}. The function returns a pointer to element 9 (which is after 5).

The program in Example 21-18 further illustrates the importance of this returned `forwardItr`. (See Lines 8, 10, 12, and 14.)

Let us now look at the prototypes of the functions `remove_copy` and `remove_copy_if`.

```
template <class inputItr, class outputItr, class Type>
outputItr remove_copy(inputItr first1, inputItr last1,
                      outputItr destFirst, const Type& value);
```

```
template <class inputItr, class outputItr, class unaryPredicate>
outputItr remove_copy_if(inputItr first1, inputItr last1,
                         outputItr destFirst,
                         unaryPredicate op);
```

The function `remove_copy` copies all of the elements in the range `first1...last1-1`, except the elements specified by value, into the sequence starting at the position `destFirst`. Similarly, the function `remove_copy_if` copies all of the elements in the range `first1...last1-1`, except the elements for which `op(element)` is `true`, into the sequence starting at the position `destFirst`. Both of these functions return an `outputItr`, which points to the position after the last element copied.

The program in Example 21-18 shows how to use the functions `remove`, `remove_if`, `remove_copy`, and `remove_copy_if`.

EXAMPLE 21-18

```cpp
//STL Functions remove, remove_if, remove_copy, and
//                  remove_copy_if

#include <iostream>
#include <cctype>
#include <algorithm>
#include <iterator>
#include <vector>

using namespace std;

bool lessThanEqualTo50(int num);

int main()
{
    char cList[10] = {'A', 'a', 'A', 'B', 'A',
                      'c', 'D', 'e', 'F', 'A'};        //Line 1

    vector<char> charList(cList, cList + 10);          //Line 2
    vector<char>::iterator lastElem, newLastElem;      //Line 3

    ostream_iterator<char> screen(cout, " ");          //Line 4

    cout << "Line 6: Character list: ";                //Line 5
    copy(charList.begin(), charList.end(), screen);    //Line 6
    cout << endl;                                      //Line 7

        //remove
    lastElem = remove(charList.begin(),
                      charList.end(), 'A');            //Line 8

    cout << "Line 9: Character list after "
         << "removing A: ";                            //Line 9
```

```
    copy(charList.begin(), lastElem, screen);          //Line 10
    cout << endl;                                       //Line 11

        //remove_if
    newLastElem = remove_if(charList.begin(),
                        lastElem, isupper);             //Line 12
    cout << "Line 13: Character list after "
        << "removing the uppercase " << endl
        << "          letters: ";                       //Line 13
    copy(charList.begin(), newLastElem, screen);        //Line 14
    cout << endl;                                       //Line 15

    int list[10] = {12, 34, 56, 21, 34,
                    78, 34, 55, 12, 25};                //Line 16

    vector<int>  intList(list, list + 10);              //Line 17
    vector<int>::iterator endElement;                   //Line 18

    ostream_iterator<int> screenOut(cout, " ");         //Line 19

    cout << "Line 20: intList: ";                       //Line 20
    copy(intList.begin(), intList.end(), screenOut);    //Line 21
    cout << endl;                                        //Line 22

    vector<int> temp1(10);                              //Line 23

        //remove_copy
    endElement = remove_copy(intList.begin(),
                        intList.end(),
                        temp1.begin(), 34);             //Line 24

    cout << "Line 25: temp1 list after copying "
        << "all the elements of intList "
        << endl << "          except 34: ";             //Line 25
    copy(temp1.begin(), endElement, screenOut);         //Line 26
    cout << endl;                                       //Line 27

    vector<int> temp2(10, 0);                           //Line 28

        //remove_copy_if
    remove_copy_if(intList.begin(), intList.end(),
            temp2.begin(), lessThanEqualTo50);          //Line 29

    cout << "Line 30: temp2 after copying all the "
        << "elements of intList except " << endl
        << "          numbers less than 50: ";          //Line 30
    copy(temp2.begin(), temp2.end(), screenOut);        //Line 31
    cout << endl;                                       //Line 32

    return 0;
}
```

```
bool lessThanEqualTo50 (int num)
{
    return (num <= 50);
}
```

Sample Run:

```
Line 6: Character list: A a a A B A c D e F A
Line 9: Character list after removing A: a B c D e F
Line 13: Character list after removing the uppercase
         letters: a c e
Line 20: intList: 12 34 56 21 34 78 34 55 12 25
Line 25: temp1 list after copying all the elements of intList
         except 34: 12 56 21 78 55 12 25
Line 30: temp2 after copying all the elements of intList except
         numbers less than 50: 56 78 55 0 0 0 0 0 0 0
```

The statement in Line 2 creates a vector list, charList, of type char and initializes charList using the array cList created in Line 1. The statement in Line 3 declares two vector iterators: lastElem and newLastElem. The statement in Line 4 declares an ostream iterator, screen. The statement in Line 6 outputs the value of charList. The statement in Line 8 uses the function remove to remove all occurrences of 'A' from charList. The function returns a pointer to one past the last element of the new range, which is stored in lastElem. The statement in Line 10 outputs the elements in the new range. (Note that the statement in Line 10 outputs the elements in the range charList.begin()...lastElem-1.) The statement in Line 12 uses the function remove_if to remove the uppercase letters from the list charList and stores the pointer returned by the function remove_if in newLastElem. The statement in Line 14 outputs the elements in the new range.

The statement in Line 17 creates a vector, intList, of type int and initializes intList using the array list, created in Line 16. The statement in Line 21 outputs the elements of intList. The statement in Line 24 copies all of the elements, except the occurrences of 34, of intList into temp1. The list intList is not modified. The statement in Line 26 outputs the elements of temp1. The statement in Line 28 creates a vector, temp2, of type int of 10 components and initializes all of the elements of temp2 to 0. The statement in Line 29 uses the function remove_copy_if to copy those elements of intList that are greater than 50. The statement in Line 31 outputs the elements of temp2.

The Functions replace, replace_if, replace_copy, and replace_copy_if

The function replace is used to replace all occurrences, within a given range, of a given element with a new value. The function replace_if is used to replace the values of the elements, within a given range, satisfying certain criteria with a new value. The prototypes of these functions are:

```
template <class forwardItr, class Type >
void replace(forwardItr first, forwardItr last,
             const Type& oldValue, const Type& newValue);

template <class forwardItr, class unaryPredicate, class Type>
void replace_if(forwardItr first, forwardItr last,
                unaryPredicate op, const Type& newValue);
```

The function `replace` replaces all of the elements in the range `first...last-1` whose values are equal to `oldValue` with the value specified by `newValue`. The function `replace_if` replaces all of the elements in the range `first...last-1`, for which `op(element)` is `true`, with the value specified by `newValue`.

The function `replace_copy` is a combination of `replace` and `copy`. Similarly, the function `replace_copy_if` is a combination of `replace_if` and `copy`. Let us first look at the prototypes of the functions `replace_copy` and `replace_copy_if`.

```
template <class forwardItr, class outputItr, class Type>
outputItr replace_copy(forwardItr first, forwardItr last,
                       outputItr destFirst,
                       const Type& oldValue,
                       const Type& newValue);

template <class forwardItr, class outputItr,
          class unaryPredicate, class Type>
outputItr replace_copy_if(forwardItr first, forwardItr last,
                          outputItr destFirst,
                          unaryPredicate op,
                          const Type& newValue);
```

The function `replace_copy` copies all of the elements in the range `first...last-1` into the container starting at `destFirst`. If the value of an element in this range is equal to `oldValue`, it is replaced by `newValue`. The function `replace_copy_if` copies all of the elements in the range `first...last-1` into the container starting at `destFirst`. If, for any element in this range, `op(element)` is `true`, at the destination, its value is replaced by `newValue`. Both of these functions return an `outputItr` (a pointer) positioned one past the last element copied at the destination.

The program in Example 21-19 shows how to use the functions `replace`, `replace_if`, `replace_copy`, and `replace_copy_if`.

EXAMPLE 21-19

```
//STL Functions replace, replace_if, replace_copy, and
//                replace_copy_if

#include <iostream>
#include <cctype>
#include <algorithm>
#include <iterator>
#include <vector>
```

```cpp
using namespace std;

bool lessThanEqualTo50(int num);

int main()
{
    char cList[10] = {'A', 'a', 'A', 'B', 'A',
                      'c', 'D', 'e', 'F', 'A'};       //Line 1

    vector<char>  charList(cList, cList + 10);        //Line 2

    ostream_iterator<char> screen(cout, " ");         //Line 3

    cout << "Line 4: Character list: ";               //Line 4
    copy(charList.begin(), charList.end(), screen);   //Line 5
    cout << endl;                                     //Line 6

        //replace
    replace(charList.begin(), charList.end(),
            'A', 'Z');                                //Line 7

    cout << "Line 8: Character list after replacing "
         << "A with Z: " << endl
         << "          ";                             //Line 8
    copy(charList.begin(), charList.end(), screen);   //Line 9
    cout << endl;                                     //Line 10

        //replace_if
    replace_if(charList.begin(), charList.end(),
               isupper, '*');                         //Line 11
    cout << "Line 12: Character list after "
         << "replacing the uppercase  " << endl
         << "             letters with *: ";          //Line 12
    copy(charList.begin(), charList.end(), screen);   //Line 13
    cout << endl;                                     //Line 14

    int list[10] = {12, 34, 56, 21, 34,
                    78, 34, 55, 12, 25};              //Line 15

    vector<int>  intList(list, list + 10);            //Line 16

    ostream_iterator<int> screenOut(cout, " ");       //Line 17

    cout << "Line 18: intList: ";                     //Line 18
    copy(intList.begin(), intList.end(), screenOut);  //Line 19
    cout << endl;                                     //Line 20

    vector<int> temp1(10);                            //Line 21

        //replace_copy
    replace_copy(intList.begin(), intList.end(),
                 temp1.begin(), 34, 0);               //Line 22
```

```
        cout << "Line 23: temp1 list after copying "
            << "intList and " << endl
            << "             replacing 34 with 0: ";      //Line 23
        copy(temp1.begin(), temp1.end(), screenOut);     //Line 24
        cout << endl;                                     //Line 25

        vector<int> temp2(10);                            //Line 26

            //replace_copy_if
        replace_copy_if(intList.begin(), intList.end(),
                temp2.begin(), lessThanEqualTo50, 50);   //Line 27

        cout << "Line 28: temp2 after copying intList "
            << "and replacing any " << endl
            << "             numbers less than 50 "
              << "with 50: " << endl << "           ";    //Line 28
        copy(temp2.begin(), temp2.end(), screenOut);     //Line 29
        cout << endl;                                     //Line 30

        return 0;
}

bool lessThanEqualTo50(int num)
{
        return (num <= 50);
}
```

Sample Run:

```
Line 4: Character list: A a A B A c D e F A
Line 8: Character list after replacing A with Z:
        Z a Z B Z c D e F Z
Line 12: Character list after replacing the uppercase
         letters with *: * a * * * c * e * *
Line 18: intList: 12 34 56 21 34 78 34 55 12 25
Line 23: temp1 list after copying intList and
         replacing 34 with 0: 12 0 56 21 0 78 0 55 12 25
Line 28: temp2 after copying intList and replacing any
         numbers less than 50 with 50:
         50 50 56 50 50 78 50 55 50 50
```

The statement in Line 2 creates a vector list, charList, of type **char** and initializes charList using the array cList created in Line 1. The statement in Line 3 declares an ostream iterator, screen. The statement in Line 5 outputs the value of charList. The statement in Line 7 uses the function replace to replace all occurrences of 'A' with 'Z' in charList. The statement in Line 9 outputs the elements of charList. In the output, the line marked Line 8 contains the outputs of Lines 8 through 10. The statement in Line 11 uses the function replace_if to replace the uppercase letters with '*' in the list charList. The statement in Line 13 outputs the elements of charList. In the output, the line marked Line 12 contains the output of Lines 12 through 14.

The statement in Line 16 creates a vector, `intList`, of type `int` and initializes `intList` using the array `list`, created in Line 15. The statement in Line 19 outputs the elements of `intList`. The statement in Line 21 declares a vector `temp1` of type `int`. The statement in Line 22 copies all of the elements of `intList` and replaces 34 with 0. The list `intList` is not modified. The statement in Line 24 outputs the elements of `temp1`. The statement in Line 26 creates a vector, `temp2`, of type `int`, of 10 components. The statement in Line 27 uses the function `replace_copy_if` to copy the elements of `intList` and replaces all of the elements less than 50 with 50. The statement in Line 29 outputs the elements of `temp2`. In the output, the line marked Line 28 contains the output of Lines 28 through 30.

The Functions `swap`, `iter_swap`, and `swap_ranges`

The functions `swap`, `iter_swap`, and `swap_ranges` are used to swap elements. These functions are defined in the header file `algorithm`. The prototypes of these functions are:

```
template <class Type>
void swap(Type& object1, Type& object2);

template <class forwardItr1, class forwardItr2>
void iter_swap(forwardItr1 first, forwardItr2 second);

template <class forwardItr1, class forwardItr2>
forwardItr2 swap_ranges(forwardItr1 first1, forwardItr1 last1,
                        forwardItr2 first2);
```

The function `swap` swaps the values of `object1` and `object2`. The function `iter_swap` swaps the values to which the iterators `first` and `second` point.

The function `swap_ranges` swaps the elements of the range `first1...last1-1` with the consecutive elements starting at position `first2`. It returns the iterator of the second range positioned one past the last element swapped. The program in Example 21-20 illustrates how to use these functions.

EXAMPLE 21-20

```
//STL functions swap, iter_swap, and swap_ranges

#include <iostream>
#include <algorithm>
#include <vector>
#include <iterator>

using namespace std;
```

```cpp
int main()
{
    char cList[10] = {'A', 'B', 'C', 'D', 'F',
                      'G', 'H', 'I', 'J', 'K'};          //Line 1

    vector<char> charList(cList, cList + 10);            //Line 2
    vector<char>::iterator  charItr;                     //Line 3

    ostream_iterator<char> screen(cout, " ");            //Line 4

    cout << "Line 5: Character list: ";                  //Line 5
    copy(charList.begin(), charList.end(), screen);      //Line 6
    cout << endl;                                        //Line 7

    swap(charList[0], charList[1]);                      //Line 8

    cout << "Line 9: Character list after swapping "
         << "the first and second  " << endl
         << "           elements: ";                     //Line 9
    copy(charList.begin(), charList.end(), screen);      //Line 10
    cout << endl;                                        //Line 11

    iter_swap(charList.begin() + 2,
              charList.begin() + 3);                     //Line 12

    cout << "Line 13: Character list after swapping "
         << "the third and fourth " << endl
         << "           elements: ";                     //Line 13

    copy(charList.begin(), charList.end(), screen);      //Line 14
    cout << endl;                                        //Line 15

    charItr = charList.begin() + 4;                      //Line 16
    iter_swap(charItr, charItr + 1);                     //Line 17

    cout << "Line 18: Character list after swapping "
         << "the fifth and sixth " << endl
         << "           elements: ";                     //Line 18
    copy(charList.begin(), charList.end(), screen);      //Line 19
    cout << endl;                                        //Line 20

    int list[10] = {1, 2, 3, 4, 5, 6, 7, 8, 9, 10};      //Line 21

    vector<int> intList(list, list + 10);                //Line 22

    ostream_iterator<int> screenOut(cout, " ");          //Line 23

    cout << "Line 24: intList: ";                        //Line 24
    copy(intList.begin(), intList.end(), screenOut);     //Line 25
    cout << endl;                                        //Line 26
```

```
                //swap_ranges
        swap_ranges(intList.begin(), intList.begin() + 4,
                    intList.begin() + 5);                      //Line 27

        cout << "Line 28: intList after swapping the first "
             << "four elements " << endl
             << "         with four elements starting at "
             << "the sixth element " << endl
             << "         of intList: ";                       //Line 28
        copy(intList.begin(), intList.end(), screenOut);      //Line 29
        cout << endl;                                          //Line 30

        swap_ranges(list, list + 10, intList.begin());        //Line 31

        cout << "Line 32: list and intList after "
             << "swapping their elements " << endl;            //Line 32
        cout << "Line 33: list: ";                            //Line 33
        copy(list, list+10, screenOut);                       //Line 34
        cout << endl;                                          //Line 35
        cout << "List 36: intList: ";                         //Line 36
        copy(intList.begin(), intList.end(), screenOut);      //Line 37
        cout << endl;                                          //Line 38

        return 0;
}
```

Sample Run:

```
Line 5: Character list: A B C D F G H I J K
Line 9: Character list after swapping the first and second
        elements: B A C D F G H I J K
Line 13: Character list after swapping the third and fourth
        elements: B A D C F G H I J K
Line 18: Character list after swapping the fifth and sixth
        elements: B A D C G F H I J K
Line 24: intList: 1 2 3 4 5 6 7 8 9 10
Line 28: intList after swapping the first four elements
        with four elements starting at the sixth element
        of intList: 6 7 8 9 5 1 2 3 4 10
Line 32: list and intList after swapping their elements
Line 33: list: 6 7 8 9 5 1 2 3 4 10
List 36: intList: 1 2 3 4 5 6 7 8 9 10
```

The statement in Line 2 creates the vector charList and initializes it using the array cList declared in Line 1. The statement in Line 6 outputs the values of charList. The statement in Line 8 swaps the first and second elements of charList. The statement in Line 12, using the function iter_swap, swaps the third and fourth elements of charList. (Recall that the position of the first element in charList is 0.) After the statement in Line 16 executes, charItr points to the fifth element of charList. The statement in Line 17 uses the iterator charItr to swap the fifth and sixth elements of charList. The statement in Line 19 outputs the values of the elements of charList.

(In the output, the line marked Line 18 contains the output of Lines 18 through 20 of the program.)

The statement in Line 22 creates the vector `intList` and initializes it using the array declared in Line 21. The statement in Line 25 outputs the values of the elements of `intList`. The statement in Line 27 uses the function `swap_ranges` to swap the first four elements of `intList` with the four elements of `intList`, starting at the sixth element of `intList`. The statement in Line 29 outputs the elements of `intList`. (In the output, the line marked Line 28 contains the output of Lines 28 through 30 of the program.)

The statement in Line 31 swaps the elements of the array `list` with the elements of the vector `intList`. The statement in Line 34 outputs the elements of the array `list`, and the statement in Line 37 outputs `intList`.

The Functions `search`, `search_n`, `sort`, and `binary_search`

Watch the Video

The functions `search`, `search_n`, `sort`, and `binary_search` are used to search and sort elements. These functions are defined in the header file `algorithm`.

The prototypes of the function `search` are:

```
template <class forwardItr1, class forwardItr2>
forwardItr1 search(forwardItr1 first1, forwardItr1 last1,
                   forwardItr2 first2, forwardItr2 last2);

template <class forwardItr1, class forwardItr2,
          class binaryPredicate>
forwardItr1 search(forwardItr1 first1, forwardItr1 last1,
                   forwardItr2 first2, forwardItr2 last2,
                   binaryPredicate op);
```

Given two ranges of elements, `first1...last1-1` and `first2...last2-1`, the function `search` searches the first element in the range `first1...last1-1` where the range `first2...last2-1` occurs as a subrange of `first1...last1-1`. The first form makes the equality comparison between the elements of the two ranges. For the second form, the comparison `op(elemFirstRange, elemSecondRange)` must be `true`. If a match is found, the function returns the position in the range `first1...last1-1` where the match occurs; otherwise, the function returns `last1`.

The prototypes of the function `search_n` are:

```
template <class forwardItr, class size, class Type>
forwardItr search_n(forwardItr first, forwardItr last,
                    size count, const Type& value);
```

```
template <class forwardItr, class size, class Type,
          class binaryPredicate>
forwardItr search_n(forwardItr first, forwardItr last,
                    size count, const Type& value,
                    binaryPredicate op);
```

Given a range of elements `first...last-1`, the function `search_n` searches `count` consecutive occurrences of `value`. The first form returns the position in the range `first...last-1` where a subsequence of `count` consecutive elements has values equal to `value`. The second form returns the position in the range `first...last-1` where a subsequence of `count` consecutive elements exists for which `op(elemRange, value)` is `true`. If no match is found, both forms return `last`.

The prototypes of the function `sort` are:

```
template <class randomAccessItr>
void sort(randomAccessItr first, randomAccessItr last);
```

```
template <class randomAccessItr, class compare>
void sort(randomAccessItr first, randomAccessItr last,
          compare op);
```

The first form of the `sort` function reorders the elements in the range `first...last-1` in ascending order. The second form reorders the elements according to the criteria specified by `op`.

The prototypes of the function `binary_search` are:

```
template <class forwardItr, class Type>
bool binary_search(forwardItr first, forwardItr last,
                   const Type& searchValue);
```

```
template <class forwardItr, class Type, class compare>
bool binary_search(forwardItr first, forwardItr last,
                   const Type& searchValue, compare op);
```

The first form returns `true` if `searchValue` is found in the range `first...last-1`, and `false` otherwise. The second form uses a function object, `op`, that specifies the search criteria.

Example 21-21 illustrates how to use these searching and sorting functions.

EXAMPLE 21-21

```
//STL Functions search, search_n, sort, and binary_search

#include <iostream>
#include <algorithm>
#include <iterator>
#include <vector>
```

```
using namespace std;

int main()
{
    int intList[15] = {12, 34, 56, 34, 34,
                       78, 38, 43, 12, 25,
                       34, 56, 62, 5, 49};          //Line 1

    vector<int>  vecList(intList, intList + 15);    //Line 2
    int list[2] = {34, 56};                         //Line 3

    vector<int>::iterator location;                 //Line 4

    ostream_iterator<int> screenOut(cout, " ");     //Line 5

    cout << "Line 6: vecList: ";                    //Line 6
    copy(vecList.begin(), vecList.end(), screenOut); //Line 7
    cout << endl;                                   //Line 8

    cout << "Line 9: list: ";                       //Line 9
    copy(list, list + 2, screenOut);                //Line 10
    cout << endl;                                   //Line 11

        //search
    location = search(vecList.begin(), vecList.end(),
                      list, list + 2);              //Line 12

    if (location != vecList.end())                  //Line 13
        cout << "Line 14: list found in vecList. "
             << "The first occurrence of " << endl
             << "          list in vecList is at "
             << "the position "
             << (location - vecList.begin()) << endl; //Line 14
    else                                            //Line 15
        cout << "Line 16: list is not in vecList."
             << endl;                               //Line 16

        //search_n
    location = search_n(vecList.begin(),
                      vecList.end(), 2, 34);        //Line 17

    if (location != vecList.end())                  //Line 18
        cout << "Line 19: two consecutive "
             << "occurrences of 34 found in " << endl
             << "          vecList at the position "
             << (location - vecList.begin()) << endl; //Line 19
    else                                            //Line 20
        cout << "Line 21: vecList does not contain "
             << "two consecutive occurrences of 34."
             << endl;                               //Line 21

        //sort
    sort(vecList.begin(), vecList.end());           //Line 22
```

```
        cout << "Line 23: vecList after sorting:"
            << endl << "         ";                    //Line 23
        copy(vecList.begin(), vecList.end(), screenOut);  //Line 24
        cout << endl;                                  //Line 25

            //binary_search
        bool found;                                    //Line 26

        found = binary_search(vecList.begin(),
                              vecList.end(), 78);      //Line 27

        if (found)                                     //Line 28
            cout << "Line 29: 78 found in vecList."
                << endl;                               //Line 29
        else                                           //Line 30
            cout << "Line 31: 78 not in vecList."
                << endl;                               //Line 31

        return 0;
}
```

Sample Run:

```
Line 6: vecList: 12 34 56 34 34 78 38 43 12 25 34 56 62 5 49
Line 9: list: 34 56
Line 14: list found in vecList. The first occurrence of
        list in vecList is at the position 1
Line 19: two consecutive occurrences of 34 found in
        vecList at the position 3
Line 23: vecList after sorting:
        5 12 12 25 34 34 34 34 38 43 49 56 56 62 78
Line 29: 78 found in vecList.
```

The statement in Line 2 creates a vector, vecList, and initializes it using the array intList created in Line 1. The statement in Line 3 creates an array, list, of two components and initializes list. The statement in Line 7 outputs vecList. The statement in Line 12 uses the function search and searches vecList to find the position (of the first occurrence) in vecList where list occurs as a subsequence. The statements in Lines 13 through 16 output the result of the search; see the line marked Line 14 in the output.

The statement in Line 17 uses the function search_n to find the position in vecList where two consecutive instances of 34 occur. The statements in Lines 18 through 21 output the result of the search.

The statement in Line 22 uses the function sort to sort vecList. The statement in Line 24 outputs vecList. In the output, the line marked Line 23 contains the output of the statements in Lines 23 through 25.

The statement in Line 27 uses the function binary_search to search vecList. The statements in Lines 28 through 31 output the search result.

The Functions `adjacent_find`, `merge`, and `inplace_merge`

The algorithm `adjacent_find` is used to find the first occurrence of consecutive elements that meet certain criteria. The prototypes of the functions implementing this algorithm are:

```
template <class forwardItr>
forwardItr adjacent_find(forwardItr first, forwardItr last);

template <class forwardItr, class binaryPredicate>
forwardItr adjacent_find(forwardItr first, forwardItr last,
                         binaryPredicate op);
```

The first form of `adjacent_find` uses the equality criteria; that is, it looks for the first consecutive occurrences of the same element. In the second form, the algorithm returns an iterator to the element in the range `first...last-1` for which `op(elem, nextElem)` is `true`, in which `elem` is an element in the range `first...last-1` and `nextElem` is an element in this range next to `elem`. If no matching elements are found, both algorithms return `last`.

The algorithm `merge` merges the sorted lists. The result is a sorted list. Both lists must be sorted according to the same criteria. For example, both lists should be in either ascending or descending order. The prototypes of the functions to implement the merge algorithms are:

```
template <class inputItr1, class inputItr2, class outputItr>
outputItr merge(inputItr1 first1, inputItr1 last1,
                inputItr2 first2, inputItr2 last2,
                outputItr destFirst);

template <class inputItr1, class inputItr2,
          class outputItr, class binaryPredicate>
outputItr merge(inputItr1 first1, inputItr1 last1,
                inputItr2 first2, inputItr2 last2,
                outputItr destFirst, binaryPredicate op);
```

Both forms of the algorithm `merge` merge the elements of the sorted ranges `first1...last1-1` and `first2...last2-1`. The destination range, beginning with the iterator `destFirst`, contains the merged elements. The first form uses the less-than operator, `<`, for ordering the elements. The second form uses the binary predicate `op` to order the elements; that is, `op(elemRange1, elemRange2)` must be `true`. Both forms return the position after the last copied element in the destination range. Moreover, the source ranges are not modified, and the destination range should not overlap with the source ranges.

The algorithm `inplace_merge` is used to combine the sorted consecutive sequences. The prototypes of the functions implementing this algorithm are:

```
template <class biDirectionalItr>
void inplace_merge(biDirectionalItr first,
                   biDirectionalItr middle,
                   biDirectionalItr last);

template <class biDirectionalItr, class binaryPredicate>
void inplace_merge(biDirectionalItr first,
                   biDirectionalItr middle,
                   biDirectionalItr last,
                   binaryPredicate op);
```

Both forms merge the sorted consecutive sequences `first...middle-1` and `middle...last-1`. The merged elements overwrite the two ranges beginning at `first`. The first form uses the less-than criterion to merge the two consecutive sequences. The second form uses the binary predicate `op` to merge the sequences; that is, for the elements of the two sequences, `op(elemSeq1, elemSeq2)` must be `true`. For example, suppose that:

```
vecList = {1, 3, 5, 7, 9, 2, 4, 6, 8}
```

in which `vecList` is a vector container. Further suppose that `vecItr` is a vector iterator pointing to element 2. Then, after the execution of the statement:

```
inplace_merge(vecList.begin(), vecItr, vecList.end());
```

the elements in `vecList` are in the following order:

```
vecList = {1, 2, 3, 4, 5, 6, 7, 8, 9}
```

The program in Example 21-22 illustrates how these algorithms work.

EXAMPLE 21-22

```
//STL Functions adjacent_find, merge, and inplace_merge

#include <iostream>
#include <functional>
#include <algorithm>
#include <iterator>
#include <vector>
#include <list>

using namespace std;

int main()
{
    int list1[10] = {1, 3, 5, 7, 9, 0, 2, 4, 6, 8};    //Line 1
    int list2[10] = {0, 1, 1, 2, 3, 4, 4, 5, 6, 6};    //Line 2

    int list3[5] = {0, 2, 4, 6, 8};                    //Line 3
    int list4[5] = {1, 3, 5, 7, 9};                    //Line 4
```

```cpp
    list<int> intList(list2, list2 + 10);              //Line 5
    list<int>::iterator listItr;                       //Line 6

    vector<int> vecList(list1, list1 + 10);            //Line 7
    vector<int>::iterator     intItr;                  //Line 8

    ostream_iterator<int> screen(cout, " ");           //Line 9

    cout << "Line 10: intList : ";                     //Line 10
    copy(intList.begin(), intList.end(), screen);      //Line 11
    cout << endl;                                      //Line 12

        //adjacent_find
    listItr = adjacent_find(intList.begin(),
                        intList.end());                //Line 13

    if (listItr != intList.end())                      //Line 14
        cout << "Line 15: Adjacent equal "
             << "elements are found " << endl
             << "            The first set of "
             << "adjacent equal elements: "
             << *listItr << endl;                      //Line 15
    else                                               //Line 16
        cout << "Line 17: No adjacent equal "
             << "element found" << endl;               //Line 17

    intList.clear();                                   //Line 18

        //merge
    merge(list3, list3 + 5, list4, list4 + 5,
         back_inserter(intList));                      //Line 19

    cout << "Line 20: intList after merging list3 "
         << "and " << "list4:\n"
         << "          ";                              //Line 20
    copy(intList.begin(), intList.end(), screen);      //Line 21
    cout << endl;                                      //Line 22

        //adjacent_find; second form
    intItr = adjacent_find(vecList.begin(),
                        vecList.end(),
                        greater<int>());               //Line 23

    cout << "Line 24: Last element of first "
         << "sorted sublist: " << *intItr << endl;     //Line 24
    intItr++;                                          //Line 25
    cout << "Line 26: First element of second "
         << "sorted sublist: " << *intItr << endl;     //List 26

    cout << "Line 27: vecList before "
         << "inplace_merge: ";                         //Line 27
    copy(vecList.begin(), vecList.end(), screen);      //Line 28
    cout << endl;                                      //Line 29
```

2
1

```
                //inplace_merge
        inplace_merge(vecList.begin(), intItr,
                    vecList.end());                          //Line 30

        cout << "Line 31: vecList after inplace_merge: "; //Line 31
        copy(vecList.begin(), vecList.end(), screen);      //Line 32
        cout << endl;                                      //Line 33

        return 0;
}
```

Sample Run:

```
Line 10: intList : 0 1 1 2 3 4 4 5 6 6
Line 15: Adjacent equal elements are found
         The first set of adjacent equal elements: 1
Line 20: intList after merging list3 and list4:
         0 1 2 3 4 5 6 7 8 9
Line 24: Last element of first sorted sublist: 9
Line 26: First element of second sorted sublist: 0
Line 27: vecList before inplace_merge: 1 3 5 7 9 0 2 4 6 8
Line 31: vecList after inplace_merge: 0 1 2 3 4 5 6 7 8 9
```

The statement in Line 5 creates an `intList` of type `list<int>` and initializes `intList` using `list2`. Thus, `intList` is a linked list. The statement in Line 7 creates the vector `vecList` of type `int` and initializes it using `list1`. The statement in Line 11 outputs `intList`. The statement in Line 13 uses the function `adjacent_find` to find the position of the (first set of) consecutive identical elements. The function returns a pointer to the first set of consecutive elements, which is stored in `listItr`. The statements in Lines 14 through 17 output those consecutive identical elements, if any are found. Notice that the statement in Line 15 outputs `* listItr`—the contents of the memory space to which `listItr` is pointing.

The statement in Line 18 clears `intList` by deleting all of the elements of `intList`. The statement in Line 19 uses the function `merge` to merge `list3` and `list4`. The third parameter of the function `merge`, in Line 19, is a call to `back_inserter`, which places the merged list into `intList`. After the statement in Line 19 executes, `intList` contains the merged list. The statement in Line 21 outputs `intList`. In the output, see the line marked Line 20, which contains the output of the statements in Lines 20 through 22.

Notice that `vecList` is {1, 3, 5, 7, 9, 0, 2, 4, 6, 8}, which contains two sorted subsequences. The statement in Line 23 uses the second form of the function `adjacent_find` to find the starting position of the second subsequence. Notice that the third parameter of the function `adjacent_find` is the binary predicate `greater`, which returns the position in `vecList` where the first element is greater than the second element. The returned position is stored in the iterator `intItr`, which now points to element 9. The statement in Line 25 advances `intItr` to point to element 0, which is the first element of the second subsequence. The statement in Line 30 uses the function inplace_merge and the iterator intItr to merge the sorted subsequences of vecList. Notice that vecList contains the resulting sequence. In the output, the line marked Line 27 contains the output of the statements in Lines 27 through 29; the line marked Line 31 contains the output of the statements in Lines 31 through 33.

The Functions reverse, reverse_copy, rotate, and rotate_copy

The algorithm **reverse** reverses the order of the elements in a given range. The prototype of the function to implement the algorithm **reverse** is:

```
template <class biDirectionalItr>
void reverse(biDirectionalItr first, biDirectionalItr last);
```

The elements in the range first...last-1 are reversed. For example, if vecList = {1, 2, 5, 3, 4}, then the elements in reverse order are vecList = {4, 3, 5, 2, 1}.

The algorithm **reverse_copy** reverses the elements of a given range while copying into a destination range. The source is not modified. The prototype of the function implementing the algorithm **reverse_copy** is:

```
template <class biDirectionalItr, class outputItr>
outputItr reverse_copy(biDirectionalItr first,
                       biDirectionalItr last,
                       outputItr destFirst);
```

The elements in the range first...last-1 are copied in the reverse order at the destination, beginning with destFirst. The function also returns the position one past the last element copied at the destination.

The algorithm rotate rotates the elements of a given range. Its prototype is:

```
template <class forwardItr>
void rotate(forwardItr first, forwardItr newFirst,
            forwardItr last);
```

The elements in the range first...newFirst-1 are moved to the end of the range. The element specified by newFirst becomes the first element of the range. For example, suppose that:

vecList = {3, 5, 4, 0, 7, 8, 2, 5}

and the iterator vecItr points to 0. Then, after the statement:

rotate(vecList.begin(), vecItr, vecList.end());

executes, vecList is as follows:

vecList = {0, 7, 8, 2, 5, 3, 5, 4}

The algorithm rotate_copy is a combination of rotate and copy. That is, the elements of the source are copied at the destination in a rotated order. The source is not modified. The prototype of the function implementing this algorithm is:

```
template <class forwardItr, class outputItr>
outputItr rotate_copy(forwardItr first, forwardItr middle,
                      forwardItr last,
                      outputItr destFirst);
```

The elements in the range first...last-1 are copied into the destination range beginning with destFirst in the rotated order, so that the element specified by middle in the range first...last-1 becomes the first element of the destination. The function also returns the position one past the last element copied at the destination.

The algorithms reverse, reverse_copy, rotate, and rotate_copy are contained in the header file algorithm. The program in Example 21-23 illustrates how to use these algorithms.

EXAMPLE 21-23

```
//STL Functions: reverse, reverse_copy, rotate, and rotate_copy

#include <iostream>
#include <algorithm>
#include <iterator>
#include <list>

using namespace std;

int main()
{
    int temp[10] = {1, 3, 5, 7, 9, 0, 2, 4, 6, 8};         //Line 1

    list<int> intList(temp, temp + 10);                    //Line 2
    list<int> resultList;                                  //List 3
    list<int>::iterator listItr;                           //Line 4

    ostream_iterator<int> screen(cout, " ");               //Line 5

    cout << "Line 6: intList: ";                           //Line 6
    copy(intList.begin(), intList.end(), screen);          //Line 7
    cout << endl;                                           //Line 8

        //reverse
    reverse(intList.begin(), intList.end());               //Line 9

    cout << "Line 10: intList after reversal: ";           //Line 10
    copy(intList.begin(), intList.end(), screen);          //Line 11
    cout << endl;                                           //Line 12
```

```
    //reverse_copy
reverse_copy(intList.begin(), intList.end(),
             back_inserter(resultList));                    //Line 13

cout << "Line 14: resultList: ";                            //Line 14
copy(resultList.begin(), resultList.end(),
     screen);                                               //Line 15
cout << endl;                                               //Line 16

listItr = intList.begin();                                  //Line 17
listItr++;                                                  //Line 18
listItr++;                                                  //Line 19

cout << "Line 20: intList before rotating: ";               //Line 20
copy(intList.begin(), intList.end(), screen);               //Line 21
cout << endl;                                               //Line 22

    //rotate
rotate(intList.begin(), listItr, intList.end());            //Line 23

cout << "Line 24: intList after rotating: ";                //Line 24
copy(intList.begin(), intList.end(), screen);               //Line 25
cout << endl;                                               //Line 26

    //rotate_copy
resultList.clear();                                         //Line 27

rotate_copy(intList.begin(), listItr,
            intList.end(),
            back_inserter(resultList));                     //Line 28

cout << "Line 29: intList after rotating and "
     << "copying:\n"
     << "            ";                                     //Line 29
copy(intList.begin(), intList.end(), screen);               //Line 30
cout << endl;                                               //Line 31

cout << "Line 32: resultList after rotating "
     << "and copying:\n"
     << "            ";                                     //Line 32
copy(resultList.begin(), resultList.end(),
     screen);                                               //Line 33
cout << endl;                                               //Line 34

resultList.clear();                                         //Line 35

rotate_copy(intList.begin(),
            find(intList.begin(), intList.end(), 6),
            intList.end(),
            back_inserter(resultList));                     //Line 36
```

2
1

```
cout << "Line 37: resultList after rotating and "
     << "copying:\n"
     << "              ";                              //Line 37
copy(resultList.begin(), resultList.end(), screen);   //Line 38
cout << endl;                                          //Line 39

    return 0;
}
```

Sample Run:

```
Line 6: intList: 1 3 5 7 9 0 2 4 6 8
Line 10: intList after reversal: 8 6 4 2 0 9 7 5 3 1
Line 14: resultList: 1 3 5 7 9 0 2 4 6 8
Line 20: intList before rotating: 8 6 4 2 0 9 7 5 3 1
Line 24: intList after rotating: 4 2 0 9 7 5 3 1 8 6
Line 29: intList after rotating and copying:
         4 2 0 9 7 5 3 1 8 6
Line 32: resultList after rotating and copying:
         0 9 7 5 3 1 8 6 4 2
Line 37: resultList after rotating and copying:
         6 4 2 0 9 7 5 3 1 8
```

The Functions `count`, `count_if`, `max`, `max_element`, `min`, `min_element`, and `random_shuffle`

The algorithm `count` counts the occurrences of a given value in a given range. The prototype of the function implementing this algorithm is:

```
template <class inputItr, class type>
iterator_traits<inputItr>:: difference_type
     count(inputItr first, inputItr last, const Type& value);
```

The function `count` returns the number of times the value specified by the parameter `value` occurs in the range `first...last-1`.

The algorithm `count_if` counts the occurrences of a given value in a given range, satisfying a certain criterion. The prototype of the function implementing this algorithm is:

```
template <class inputItr, class unaryPredicate>
iterator_traits<inputItr>::difference_type
    count_if(inputItr first, inputItr last, unaryPredicate op);
```

The function `count_if` returns the number of elements in the range `first...last-1` for which `op(elemRange)` is `true`.

The algorithm `max` is used to determine the maximum of two values. It has two forms, as shown by the following prototypes:

```
template <class Type>
const Type& max(const Type& aVal, const Type& bVal);

template <class Type, class compare>
const Type& max(const Type& aVal, const Type& bVal, compare comp);
```

In the first form, the greater-than operator associated with `Type` is used. The second form uses the comparison operation specified by `comp`.

The algorithm `max_element` is used to determine the largest element in a given range. This algorithm has two forms, as shown by the following prototypes:

```
template <class forwardItr>
forwardItr max_element(forwardItr first, forwardItr last);

template <class forwardItr, class compare>
forwardItr max_element(forwardItr first, forwardItr last,
                       compare comp);
```

The first form uses the greater-than operator associated with the data type of the elements in the range `first...last-1`. In the second form, the comparison operation specified by `comp` is used. Both forms return an iterator to the element containing the largest value in the range `first...last-1`.

The algorithm `min` is used to determine the minimum of two values. It has two forms, as shown by the following prototypes:

```
template <class Type>
const Type& min(const Type& aVal, const Type& bVal);

template <class Type, class compare>
const Type& min(const Type& aVal, const Type& bVal, compare comp);
```

In the first form, the less-than operator associated with `Type` is used. In the second form, the comparison operation specified by `comp` is used.

The algorithm `min_element` is used to determine the smallest element in a given range. This algorithm has two forms, as shown by the following prototypes:

```
template <class forwardItr>
forwardItr min_element(forwardItr first, forwardItr last);

template <class forwardItr, class compare>
forwardItr min_element(forwardItr first, forwardItr last,
                       compare comp);
```

The first form uses the less-than operator associated with the data type of the elements in the range `first...last-1`. The second form uses the comparison operation specified by `comp`. Both forms return an iterator to the element containing the smallest value in the range `first...last-1`.

The algorithm `random_shuffle` is used to randomly order the elements in a given range. There are two forms of this algorithm, as shown by the following prototypes:

```
template <class randomAccessItr>
void random_shuffle(randomAccessItr first,
                    randomAccessItr last);

template <class randomAccessItr, class randomAccessGenerator>
void random_shuffle(randomAccessItr first,
                    randomAccessItr last,
                    randomAccessGenerator rand);
```

The first form reorders the elements in the range `first...last-1` using a uniform distribution random number generator. The second form reorders the elements in the range `first...last-1` using a random number-generating function object or a pointer to a function.

Example 21-24 illustrates how to use these functions.

EXAMPLE 21-24

```cpp
//STL Functions count, count_if, min_element,
//                max_element, random_shuffle

#include <iostream>
#include <cctype>
#include <algorithm>
#include <iterator>
#include <vector>

using namespace std;

void doubleNum(int num);

int main()
{
    char cList[10] = {'Z', 'a', 'Z', 'B', 'Z',
                      'c', 'D', 'e', 'F', 'Z'};        //Line 1

    vector<char>  charList(cList, cList + 10);          //Line 2

    ostream_iterator<char> screen(cout, " ");           //Line 3

    cout << "Line 4: charList: ";                       //Line 4
    copy(charList.begin(), charList.end(), screen);     //Line 5
    cout << endl;                                       //Line 6

        //count
    int noOfZs = count(charList.begin(),
                    charList.end(), 'Z');               //Line 7
```

```
        cout << "Line 8: Number of Zs in charList = "          //Line 8
             << noOfZs << endl;

            //count_if
        int noOfUpper = count_if(charList.begin(),
                                 charList.end(), isupper);      //Line 9

        cout << "Line 10: Number of uppercase letters "         //Line 10
             << "in charList = " << noOfUpper << endl;

        int list[10] = {12, 34, 56, 21, 34,                     //Line 11
                        78, 34, 55, 12, 25};

        ostream_iterator<int> screenOut(cout, " ");             //Line 12

        cout << "Line 13: list: ";                              //Line 13
        copy(list, list + 10, screenOut);                       //Line 14
        cout << endl;                                           //Line 15

            //max_element
        int *maxLoc = max_element(list, list + 10);             //Line 16

        cout << "Line 17: Largest element in list = "           //Line 17
             << *maxLoc << endl;

            //min_element
        int *minLoc = min_element(list, list + 10);             //Line 18

        cout << "Line 19: Smallest element in list = "          //Line 19
             << *minLoc << endl;

            //random_shuffle
        random_shuffle(list, list + 10);                        //Line 20

        cout << "Line 21: list after random shuffle:\n"         //Line 21
             << "        ";                                     //Line 22
        copy(list, list + 10, screenOut);                       //Line 23
        cout << endl;

        return 0;
}

void doubleNum(int num)
{
        cout << 2 * num << " ";
}
```

Sample Run:

```
Line 4: charList: Z a Z B Z c D e F Z
Line 8: Number of Zs in charList = 4
Line 10: Number of uppercase letters in charList = 7
Line 13: list: 12 34 56 21 34 78 34 55 12 25
```

```
Line 17: Largest element in list = 78
Line 19: Smallest element in list = 12
Line 21: list after random shuffle:
         12 34 25 56 12 78 55 21 34 34
```

The preceding output is self-explanatory. The details are left as an exercise for you.

The Functions `for_each` and `transform`

The algorithm `for_each` is used to access and process each element in a given range by applying a function, which is passed as a parameter. The prototype of the function implementing this algorithm is:

```
template <class inputItr, class function>
function for_each(inputItr first, inputItr last, function func);
```

The function specified by the parameter `func` is applied to each element in the range `first...last-1`. The function `func` can modify the element. The returned value of the function `for_each` is usually ignored.

The algorithm `transform` has two forms. The prototypes of the functions implementing this algorithm are:

```
template <class inputItr, class outputItr,
          class unaryOperation>
outputItr transform(inputItr first, inputItr last,
                    outputItr destFirst,
                    unaryOperation op);
```

```
template <class inputItr1, class inputItr2,
          class outputItr, class binaryOperation>
outputItr transform(inputItr1 first1, inputItr1 last,
                    inputItr2 first2,
                    outputItr destFirst,
                    binaryOperation bOp);
```

The first form of the function `transform` has four parameters. This function creates a sequence of elements at the destination, beginning with `destFirst`, by applying the unary operation `op` to each element in the range `first1...last-1`. This function returns the position one past the last element copied at the destination.

The second form of the function `transform` has five parameters. This function creates a sequence of elements by applying the binary operation `bOp`—that is, `bOp(elemRange1, elemRange2)`—to the corresponding elements in the range `first1...last1-1` and the range beginning with `first2`. The resulting sequence is placed at the destination beginning with `destFirst`. The function returns the position one element past the last element copied at the destination.

Example 21-25 illustrates how to use these functions.

EXAMPLE 21-25

```cpp
//STL Functions for_each and transform

#include <iostream>
#include <cctype>
#include <algorithm>
#include <iterator>
#include <vector>

using namespace std;

void doubleNum(int& num);

int main()
{
    char cList[5] = {'a', 'b', 'c', 'd', 'e'};          //Line 1

    vector<char>  charList(cList, cList + 5);            //Line 2

    ostream_iterator<char> screen(cout, " ");           //Line 3

    cout << "Line 4: cList: ";                          //Line 4
    copy(charList.begin(), charList.end(), screen);     //Line 5
    cout << endl;                                        //Line 6

        //transform
    transform(charList.begin(), charList.end(),
            charList.begin(), toupper);                 //Line 7

    cout << "Line 8: cList after changing all "
        << "lowercase letters to \n"
        << "          uppercase: ";                     //Line 8
    copy(charList.begin(), charList.end(), screen);     //Line 9
    cout << endl;                                        //Line 10

    int list[7] = {2, 8, 5, 1, 7, 11, 3};              //Line 11

    ostream_iterator<int> screenOut(cout, " ");        //Line 12

    cout << "Line 13: list: ";                         //Line 13
    copy(list, list + 7, screenOut);                   //Line 14
    cout << endl;                                        //Line 15

    cout << "Line 16: The effect of for_each "
        << "function:\n             ";                  //Line 16

        //for_each
    for_each(list, list + 7, doubleNum);               //Line 17
    cout << endl;                                        //Line 18
```

```
        cout << "Line 19: list after a call to "
             << "for_each function:\n            ";        //Line 19
        copy(list, list + 7, screenOut);                   //Line 20
        cout << endl;                                      //Line 21

        return 0;
}

void doubleNum(int& num)
{
        num = 2 * num;

        cout << num << " ";
}
```

Sample Run:

```
Line 4: cList: a b c d e
Line 8: cList after changing all lowercase letters to
        uppercase: A B C D E
Line 13: list: 2 8 5 1 7 11 3
Line 16: The effect of for_each function:
         4 16 10 2 14 22 6
Line 19: list after a call to for_each function:
         4 16 10 2 14 22 6
```

The statement in Line 7 uses the function `transform` to change every lowercase letter of `charList` into its uppercase counterpart. The statement in Line 9 outputs the elements of `charList`. In the output, the line marked Line 8 contains the output of the statements in Lines 8 through 10 in the program. Notice that the fourth parameter of the function `transform` (in Line 7) is the function `toupper` from the header file `cctype`.

The statement in Line 17 calls the function `for_each` to process each element in the list using the function `doubleNum`. The function `doubleNum` has a reference parameter, `num`, of type `int`. Moreover, this function doubles the value of `num` and then outputs the value of `num`. Because `num` is a reference parameter, the value of the actual parameter is changed. In the output, the line marked Line 16 contains the output produced by the `cout` statement in the function `doubleNum`, which is passed as the third parameter of the function `for_each` (see Line 17). The statement in Line 20 outputs the values of the elements of `list`. In the output, Line 19 contains the output of the statements in Lines 19 through 20.

The Functions `includes`, `set_intersection`, `set_union`, `set_difference`, and `set_symmetric_difference`

This section describes the set theory operations `includes` (subset), `set_intersection`, `set_union`, `set_difference`, and `set_symmetric_difference`. All of these algorithms assume that the elements within each given range are already sorted.

The algorithm `includes` determines whether the elements in one range appear in another range. This function has two forms, as shown by the following prototypes:

```
template <class inputItr1, class inputItr2>
bool includes(inputItr1 first1, inputItr1 last1,
              inputItr2 first2, inputItr2 last2);

template <class inputItr1, class inputItr2,
          class binaryPredicate>
bool includes(inputItr1 first1, inputItr1 last1,
              inputItr2 first2, inputItr2 last2,
              binaryPredicate op);
```

Both forms of the function `includes` assume that the elements in the ranges `first1...last1-1` and `first2...last2-1` are sorted according to the same sorting criterion. The function returns `true` if all of the elements in the range `first2...last2-1` are also in `first1...last1-1`. In other words, the function returns `true` if `first1...last1-1` contains all of the elements in the range `first2...last2-1`. The first form assumes that the elements in both ranges are in ascending order. The second form uses the operation `op` to determine the ordering of the elements.

Example 21-26 illustrates how the function `includes` works.

EXAMPLE 21-26

```cpp
//STL function includes
//This function assumes that the elements in the given ranges
//are ordered according to some sorting criteria

#include <iostream>
#include <algorithm>
#include <iterator>

using namespace std;

int main()
{
    char setA[5] = {'A', 'B', 'C', 'D', 'E'};           //Line 1
    char setB[10] = {'A', 'B', 'C', 'D', 'E',
                     'F', 'I', 'J', 'K', 'L'};           //Line 2
    char setC[5] = {'A', 'E', 'I', 'O', 'U'};            //Line 3

    ostream_iterator<char> screen(cout, " ");            //Line 4
    cout << "Line 5: setA: ";                            //Line 5
```

```
    copy(setA, setA + 5, screen);                       //Line 6
    cout << endl;                                        //Line 7

    cout << "Line 8: setB: ";                            //Line 8
    copy(setB, setB + 10, screen);                       //Line 9
    cout << endl;                                        //Line 10

    cout << "Line 11: setC: ";                           //Line 11
    copy(setC, setC + 5, screen);                        //Line 12
    cout << endl;                                        //Line 13

    if (includes(setB, setB + 10, setA, setA + 5))  //Line 14
        cout << "Line 15: setA is a subset of "
             << "setB." << endl;                         //Line 15
    else                                                 //Line 16
        cout << "Line 17: setA is not a subset "
             << "of setB." << endl;                      //Line 17

    if (includes(setB, setB + 10, setC, setC + 5))  //Line 18
        cout << "Line 19: setC is a subset of "
             << "setB." << endl;                         //Line 19
    else                                                 //Line 20
        cout << "Line 21: setC is not a subset "
             << "of setB." << endl;                      //Line 21

    return 0;
}
```

Sample Run:

```
Line 5: setA: A B C D E
Line 8: setB: A B C D E F I J K L
Line 11: setC: A E I O U
Line 15: setA is a subset of setB
Line 21: setC is not a subset of setB
```

The preceding output is self-explanatory. The details are left as an exercise for you.

The algorithm set_intersection is used to find the elements that are common to two ranges of elements. This algorithm has two forms, as shown by the following prototypes:

```
template <class inputItr1, class inputItr2,
          class outputItr>
outputItr set_intersection(inputItr1 first1, inputItr1 last1,
                           inputItr2 first2, inputItr2 last2,
                           outputItr destFirst);
```

```
template <class inputItr1, class inputItr2,
          class outputItr, class binaryPredicate>
outputItr set_intersection(inputItr1 first1, inputItr1 last1,
                           inputItr2 first2, inputItr2 last2,
                           outputItr destFirst,
                           binaryPredicate op);
```

Both forms create a sequence of sorted elements that are common to two sorted ranges, first1...last1-1 and first2...last2-1. The created sequence is placed in the container beginning with destFirst. Both forms return an iterator positioned one past the last element copied at the destination range. The first form assumes that the elements are in ascending order; the second form assumes that both ranges are sorted using the operation specified by op. The elements in the source ranges are not modified.

Suppose that:

```
setA[5] = {2, 4, 5, 7, 8};
setB[7] = {1, 2, 3, 4, 5, 6, 7};
setC[5] = {2, 5, 8, 8, 15};
setD[6] = {1, 4, 4, 6, 7, 12};
setE[7] = {2, 3, 4, 4, 5, 6, 10};
```

Then:

```
AintersectB = {2, 4, 5, 7}
AintersectC = {2, 5, 8}
DintersectE = {4, 4, 6}
```

Notice that because 8 appears only once in setA, 8 appears only once in AintersectC, even though 8 appears twice in setC. However, because 4 appears twice in both setD and setE, 4 also appears twice in DintersectE.

The algorithm set_union is used to find the elements that are contained in two ranges of elements. This algorithm has two forms, as shown by the following prototypes:

```
template <class inputItr1, class inputItr2,
          class outputItr>
outputItr set_union(inputItr1 first1, inputItr1 last1,
                    inputItr2 first2, inputItr2 last2,
                    outputItr destFirst);
```

```
template <class inputItr1, class inputItr2,
          class outputItr, class binaryPredicate>
outputItr set_union(inputItr1 first1, inputItr1 last1,
                    inputItr2 first2, inputItr2 last2,
                    outputItr result,
                    binaryPredicate op);
```

Both forms create a sequence of sorted elements that appear in either two sorted ranges, first1...last1-1 or first2...last2-1. The created sequence is placed in the container beginning with destFirst. Both forms return an iterator positioned one past the last element copied at the destination range. The first form assumes that the elements are in ascending order. The second form assumes that both ranges are sorted using the operation specified by op. The elements in the source ranges are not modified.

Suppose that you have setA, setB, setC, setD, and setE as defined previously. Then:

```
AunionB = {1, 2, 3, 4, 5, 6, 7, 8}
AunionC = {2, 4, 5, 7, 8, 8, 15}
BunionD = {1, 2, 3, 4, 4, 5, 6, 7, 12}
DunionE = {1, 2, 3, 4, 4, 5, 6, 7, 10, 12}
```

Notice that because 8 appears twice in setC, it appears twice in AunionC. Because 4 appears twice in setD and setE, 4 appears twice in DunionE.

Example 21-27 illustrates how the functions set_union and set_intersection work.

EXAMPLE 21-27

```cpp
//STL set theory functions set_union and set_intersection
//These functions assume that the elements in the given ranges
//are ordered according to some sorting criteria.

#include <iostream>
#include <algorithm>
#include <iterator>

using namespace std;

int main()
{
    int setA[5] = {2, 4, 5, 7, 8};                    //Line 1
    int setB[7] = {1, 2, 3, 4, 5, 6, 7};              //Line 2
    int setC[5] = {2, 5, 8, 8, 15};                   //Line 3
    int setD[6] = {1, 4, 4, 6, 7, 12};                //Line 4

    int AunionB[10];                                  //Line 5
    int AunionC[10];                                  //Line 6
    int BunionD[15];                                  //Line 7
    int AintersectB[10];                              //Line 8
    int AintersectC[10];                              //Line 9

    int *lastElem;                                    //Line 10

    ostream_iterator<int> screen(cout, " ");          //Line 11

    cout << "Line 12: setA = ";                       //Line 12
    copy(setA, setA + 5, screen);                     //Line 13
    cout << endl;                                     //Line 14

    cout << "Line 15: setB = ";                       //Line 15
    copy(setB, setB + 7, screen);                     //Line 16
    cout << endl;                                     //Line 17
```

```
    cout << "Line 18: setC = ";                        //Line 18
    copy(setC, setC + 5, screen);                      //Line 19
    cout << endl;                                       //Line 20

    cout << "Line 21: setD = ";                        //Line 21
    copy(setD, setD + 6, screen);                      //Line 22
    cout << endl;                                       //Line 23

    lastElem = set_union(setA, setA + 5,
                         setB, setB + 7,
                         AunionB);                      //Line 24

    cout << "Line 25: Set AunionB: ";                  //Line 25
    copy(AunionB, lastElem, screen);                   //Line 26
    cout << endl;                                       //Line 27

    lastElem = set_union(setA, setA + 5,
                         setC, setC + 5,
                         AunionC);                      //Line 28

    cout << "Line 29: Set AunionC: ";                  //Line 29
    copy(AunionC, lastElem, screen);                   //Line 30
    cout << endl;                                       //Line 31

    lastElem = set_union(setB, setB + 7,
                         setD, setD + 6,
                         BunionD);                      //Line 32

    cout << "Line 33: Set BunionD: ";                  //Line 33
    copy(BunionD, lastElem, screen);                   //Line 34
    cout << endl;                                       //Line 35

    lastElem = set_intersection(setA, setA + 5,
                                setB, setB + 7,
                                AintersectB);           //Line 36

    cout << "Line 37: Set AintersectB: ";              //Line 37
    copy(AintersectB, lastElem, screen);               //Line 38
    cout << endl;                                       //Line 39

    lastElem = set_intersection(setA, setA + 5,
                                setC, setC + 5,
                                AintersectC);           //Line 40

    cout << "Line 41: Set AintersectC: ";              //Line 41
    copy(AintersectC, lastElem, screen);               //Line 42
    cout << endl;                                       //Line 43

    return 0;
}
```

Sample Run:

```
Line 12: setA = 2 4 5 7 8
Line 15: setB = 1 2 3 4 5 6 7
Line 18: setC = 2 5 8 8 15
Line 21: setD = 1 4 4 6 7 12
Line 25: Set AunionB: 1 2 3 4 5 6 7 8
Line 29: Set AunionC: 2 4 5 7 8 8 15
Line 33: Set BunionD: 1 2 3 4 4 5 6 7 12
Line 37: Set AintersectB: 2 4 5 7
Line 41: Set AintersectC: 2 5 8
```

The preceding output is self-explanatory. The details are left as an exercise for you.

The algorithm `set_difference` is used to find the elements in one range of elements that do not appear in another range of elements. This algorithm has two forms, as shown by the following prototypes:

```
template <class inputItr1, class inputItr2,
          class outputItr>
outputItr set_difference(inputItr1 first1, inputItr1 last1,
                         inputItr2 first2, inputItr2 last2,
                         outputItr destFirst);

template <class inputItr1, class inputItr2,
          class outputItr, class binaryPredicate>
outputItr set_difference(inputItr1 first1, inputItr1 last1,
                         inputItr2 first2, inputItr2 last2,
                         outputItr destFirst,
                         binaryPredicate op);
```

Both forms create a sequence of sorted elements that are in the sorted range `first1...last1-1` but not in the sorted range `first2...last2-1`. The created sequence is placed in the container beginning with `destFirst`. Both forms return an iterator positioned one past the last element copied at the destination range. The first form assumes that the elements are in ascending order. The second form assumes that both ranges are sorted using the operation specified by `op`. The elements in the source ranges are not modified.

Suppose that:

```
setA = {2, 4, 5, 7, 8}
setC = {1, 5, 6, 8, 15}
setD = {2, 5, 5, 6, 9}
setE = {1, 5, 7, 9, 12}
```

Then:

```
AdifferenceC = {2, 4, 7}
DdifferenceE = {2, 5, 6}
```

Because 5 appears twice in `setD` but only once in `setE`, 5 appears once in `DdifferenceE`.

The algorithm `set_symmetric_difference` has two forms, as shown by the following prototypes:

```
template <class inputItr1, class inputItr2,
          class outputItr>
outputItr set_symmetric_difference(inputItr1 first1,
                                   inputItr1 last1,
                                   inputItr2 first2,
                                   inputItr2 last2,
                                   outputItr destFirst);


template <class inputItr1, class inputItr2,
          class outputItr, class binaryPredicate>
outputItr set_symmetric_difference(inputItr1 first1,
                                   inputItr1 last1,
                                   inputItr2 first2,
                                   inputItr2 last2,
                                   outputItr destFirst,
                                   binaryPredicate op);
```

Both forms create a sequence of sorted elements that are in the sorted range `first1...last1-1` but not in `first2...last2-1`, or elements that are in the sorted range `first2...last2-1` but not in `first1...last1-1`. In other words, the sequence of elements created by `set_symmetric_difference` contains the elements that are in `range1_difference_range2` union `range2_difference_range1`. The created sequence is placed in the container beginning with `destFirst`. Both forms return an iterator positioned one past the last element copied at the destination range. The first form assumes that the elements are in ascending order. The second form assumes that both ranges are sorted using the operation specified by `op`. The elements in the source ranges are not modified. It can be shown that the sequence created by `set_symmetric_difference` contains elements that are in `range1_union_range2` but not in `range1_intersection_range2`.

Suppose that:

```
setB = {3, 4, 5, 6, 7, 8, 10}
setC = {1, 5, 6, 8, 15}
setD = {2, 5, 5, 6, 9}
```

Notice that `BdifferenceC = {3, 4, 7, 10}` and `CdifferenceB = {1, 15}`. Therefore:

`BsymDiffC = {1, 3, 4, 7, 10, 15}`

Now `DdifferenceC = {2, 5, 9}` and `CdifferenceD = {1, 8, 15}`. Therefore:

`DsymDiffC = {1, 2, 5, 8, 9, 15}`

Example 21-28 illustrates how the functions `set_difference` and `set_symmetric_difference` work.

EXAMPLE 21-28

```
//STL set theory functions: set_difference and
//                           set_symmetric_difference.
//These functions assume that the elements in the given
//ranges are ordered according to some sorting criteria.

#include <iostream>
#include <algorithm>
#include <iterator>

using namespace std;

int main()
{
    int setA[5] = {2, 4, 5, 7, 8};                      //Line 1
    int setB[7] = {3, 4, 5, 6, 7, 8, 10};               //Line 2
    int setC[5] = {1, 5, 6, 8, 15};                     //Line 3

    int AdifferenceC[5];                                //Line 4
    int BsymDiffC[10];                                  //Line 5

    int *lastElem;                                      //Line 6

    ostream_iterator<int> screen(cout, " ");            //Line 7

    cout << "Line 8: setA = ";                          //Line 8
    copy(setA, setA + 5, screen);                       //Line 9
    cout << endl;                                       //Line 10

    cout << "Line 11: setB = ";                         //Line 11
    copy(setB, setB + 7, screen);                       //Line 12
    cout << endl;                                       //Line 13

    cout << "Line 14: setC = ";                         //Line 14
    copy(setC, setC + 5, screen);                       //Line 15
    cout << endl;                                       //Line 16


    lastElem = set_difference(setA, setA + 5,
                              setC, setC + 5,
                              AdifferenceC);            //Line 17

    cout << "Line 18: AdifferenceC: ";                  //Line 18
    copy(AdifferenceC, lastElem, screen);               //Line 19
    cout << endl;                                       //Line 20

    lastElem = set_symmetric_difference(setB, setB + 7,
                                setC, setC + 5,
                                BsymDiffC);             //Line 21
```

```
    cout << "Line 22: BsymDiffC: ";          //Line 22
    copy(BsymDiffC, lastElem, screen);       //Line 23
    cout << endl;                            //Line 24

    return 0;
}
```

Sample Run:

```
Line 8: setA = 2 4 5 7 8
Line 11: setB = 3 4 5 6 7 8 10
Line 14: setC = 1 5 6 8 15
Line 18: AdifferenceC: 2 4 7
Line 22: BsymDiffC: 1 3 4 7 10 15
```

The preceding output is self-explanatory. The details are left as an exercise for you.

The Functions `accumulate`, `adjacent_difference`, `inner_product`, and `partial_sum`

The algorithms `accumulate`, `adjacent_difference`, `inner_product`, and `partial_sum` are numerical functions and thus manipulate numeric data. Each of these functions has two forms. The first form uses the natural operation to manipulate the data. For example, the algorithm `accumulate` finds the sum of all of the elements in a given range. In the second form, we can specify the operation to be applied to the elements of the range. For example, rather than add the elements of a given range, we can specify the multiplication operation to the algorithm `accumulate` to multiply the elements of the range. Next, we give the prototype of each of these algorithms followed by a brief explanation. The algorithms are contained in the header file `numeric`.

```
template<class inputItr, class Type>
Type accumulate(inputItr first, inputItr last, Type init);

template<class inputItr, class Type, class binaryOperation>
Type accumulate(inputItr first, inputItr last,
                Type init, binaryOperation op);
```

The first form of the algorithm `accumulate` adds all of the elements to an initial value specified by the parameter `init` in the range `first...last-1`. For example, if the value of `init` is 0, the algorithm returns the sum of all of the elements. In the second form, we can specify a binary operation, such as multiplication, to be applied to the elements of the range. For example, if the value of `init` is 1 and the binary operation is multiplication, the algorithm returns the products of the elements of the range.

Next, we describe the algorithm `adjacent_difference`. Its prototypes are:

```
template <class inputItr, class outputItr>
outputItr adjacent_difference(inputItr first, inputItr last,
                              outputItr destFirst);
```

```
template <class inputItr, class outputItr,
          class binaryOperation>
outputItr adjacent_difference(inputItr first, inputItr last,
                              outputItr destFirst,
                              binaryOperation op);
```

The first form creates a sequence of elements in which the first element is the same as the first element in the range `first...last-1`, and all other elements are the differences of the current and previous elements. For example, if the range of elements is:

`{2, 5, 6, 8, 3, 7}`

then the sequence created by the function `adjacent_difference` is:

`{2, 3, 1, 2, -5, 4}`

The first element is the same as the first element in the original range. The second element is equal to the second element in the original range minus the first element in the original range. Similarly, the third element is equal to the third element in the original range minus the second element in the original range, and so on.

In the second form of `adjacent_difference`, the binary operation `op` is applied to the elements in the range. The resulting sequence is copied at the destination specified by `destFirst`. For example, if the sequence is {2, 5, 6, 8, 3, 7} and the operation is multiplication, the resulting sequence is {2, 10, 30, 48, 24, 21}.

Both forms return an iterator positioned one past the last element copied at the destination.

The algorithm `inner_product` is used to manipulate the elements of two ranges. The prototypes of this algorithm are:

```
template <class inputItr1, class inputItr2, class Type>
Type inner_product(inputItr1 first1, inputItr1 last1,
                   inputItr2 first2, Type init);
```

```
template <class inputItr1, class inputItr2, class Type
          class binaryOperation1, class binaryOperation2>
Type inner_product(inputItr1 first1, inputItr1 last1,
                   inputItr2 first2, Type init,
                   binaryOperation1 op1, binaryOperation2 op2);
```

The first form multiplies the corresponding elements in the range `first1...last-1` and the range of elements starting with `first2`. The products of the elements are then added to the value specified by the parameter `init`. To be specific, suppose that `elem1` ranges over the first range and `elem2` ranges over the second range starting with `first2`. The first form computes:

`init = init + elem1 * elem2`

for all of the corresponding elements. For example, suppose that the two ranges are {2, 4, 7, 8} and {1, 4, 6, 9} and that `init` is 0. The function computes and returns:

`0 + 2 * 1 + 4 * 4 + 7 * 6 + 8 * 9 = 132`

In the second form, the default addition can be replaced by the operation specified by op1, and the default multiplication can be replaced by the operation specified by op2. This form, in fact, computes:

```
init = init op1 (elem1 op2 elem2);
```

The algorithm `partial_sum` has two forms, as shown by the following prototypes:

```
template <class inputItr, class outputItr>
outputItr partial_sum(inputItr first, inputItr last,
                      outputItr destFirst);

template <class inputItr, class outputItr,
          class binaryOperation>
outputItr partial_sum(inputItr first, inputItr last,
                      outputItr destFirst, binaryOperation op);
```

The first form creates a sequence of elements in which each element is the sum of all of the previous elements in the range `first...last-1` up to the position of the element. For example, the first element of the new sequence is the same as the first element in the range `first...last-1`, the second element is the sum of the first two elements in the range `first...last-1`, the third element of the new sequence is the sum of the first three elements in the range `first...last-1`, and so on. For example, for the sequence of elements:

```
{1, 3, 4, 6}
```

the function `partial_sum` generates the following sequence:

```
{1, 4, 8, 14}
```

In the second form, the default addition can be replaced by the operation specified by op. For example, if the sequence is:

```
{1, 3, 4, 6}
```

and the operation is multiplication, the function `partial_sum` generates the following sequence:

```
{1, 3, 12, 72}
```

The created sequence is copied at the destination specified by `destFirst` and returns an iterator positioned one past the last copied element at the destination.

Example 21-29 illustrates how the functions of this section work.

EXAMPLE 21-29

```cpp
//Numeric algorithms: accumulate, adjacent_difference,
//                     inner_product, and partial_sum

#include <iostream>
#include <algorithm>
#include <numeric>
#include <iterator>
#include <vector>
#include <functional>

using namespace std;

void print(vector<int> vList);

int main()
{
    int list[8] = {1, 2, 3, 4, 5, 6, 7, 8};           //Line 1

    vector<int> vecList(list, list + 8);              //Line 2
    vector<int>    newVList(8);                        //Line 3

    cout << "Line 4: vecList: ";                      //Line 4
    print(vecList);                                   //Line 5

        //accumulate function
    int sum = accumulate(vecList.begin(),
                         vecList.end(), 0);            //Line 6

    cout << "Line 7: Sum of the elements of "
         << "vecList = " << sum << endl;               //Line 7

    int product = accumulate(vecList.begin(),
                            vecList.end(),
                            1, multiplies<int>());      //Line 8

    cout << "Line 9: Product of the elements of "
         << "vecList = " << product << endl;           //Line 9

        //adjacent_difference function
    adjacent_difference(vecList.begin(),
                        vecList.end(),
                        newVList.begin());             //Line 10

    cout << "Line 11: newVList: ";                    //Line 11
    print(newVList);                                  //Line 12

    adjacent_difference(vecList.begin(), vecList.end(),
                        newVList.begin(),
                        multiplies<int>());            //Line 13
```

```cpp
    cout << "Line 14: newVList: ";                    //Line 14
    print(newVList);                                  //Line 15

        //inner_product function
    sum = inner_product(vecList.begin(), vecList.end(),
                    newVList.begin(), 0);              //Line 16

    cout << "Line 17: Inner product of vecList "
        << "and newVList: " << sum << endl;           //Line 17

    sum = inner_product(vecList.begin(), vecList.end(),
                    newVList.begin(), 0,
                    plus<int>(), minus<int>());        //Line 18

    cout << "Line 19: Inner product of vecList and "
        << "newVList, using - for *: "
        << sum << endl;                               //Line 19

        //partial_sum function
    partial_sum(vecList.begin(), vecList.end(),
            newVList.begin());                        //Line 20

    cout << "Line 21: newVList with partial sum : ";  //Line 21
    print(newVList);                                  //Line 22

        //partial_sum: the default + is replaced by *
    partial_sum(vecList.begin(), vecList.end(),
            newVList.begin(), multiplies<int>());     //Line 23

    cout << "Line 24: newVList with partial "
        << "multiplication: " << endl
        << "             ";                           //Line 24
    print(newVList);                                  //Line 25

    return 0;
}

void print(vector<int>  vList)
{
    ostream_iterator<int> screenOut(cout, " ");       //Line 26

    copy(vList.begin(), vList.end(), screenOut);      //Line 27
    cout << endl;                                     //Line 28
}
```

Sample Run:

```
Line 4: vecList: 1 2 3 4 5 6 7 8
Line 7: Sum of the elements of vecList = 36
Line 9: Product of the elements of vecList = 40320
Line 11: newVList: 1 1 1 1 1 1 1 1
Line 14: newVList: 1 2 6 12 20 30 42 56
```

```
Line 17: Inner product of vecList and newVList: 1093
Line 19: Inner product of vecList and newVList, using - for *: -133
Line 21: newVList with partial sum: 1 3 6 10 15 21 28 36
Line 24: newVList with partial multiplication:
         1 2 6 24 120 720 5040 40320
```

The preceding output is self-explanatory. The details are left as an exercise for you.

QUICK REVIEW

1. The three main components of the STL are containers, iterators, and algorithms.

2. STL containers are class templates.

3. Iterators are used to step through the elements of a container.

4. Algorithms are used to manipulate the elements in a container.

5. The main categories of containers are sequence containers, associative containers, and container adapters.

6. The three predefined sequence containers are `vector`, `deque`, and `list`.

7. A vector container stores and manages its objects in a dynamic array.

8. Because an array is a random access data structure, elements of a vector can be accessed randomly.

9. The name of the class that implements the vector container is `vector`.

10. Item insertion in a vector container is accomplished by using the operations `insert` and `push_back`.

11. Item deletion in a vector container is accomplished by using the operations `pop_back`, `erase`, and `clear`.

12. An iterator to a vector container is declared using the `typedef` iterator, which is declared as a `public` member of the `class` `vector`.

13. Member functions common to all containers are the default constructor, constructors with parameters, the copy constructor, the destructor, `empty`, `size`, `max_size`, `swap`, `begin`, `end`, `rbegin`, `rend`, `insert`, `erase`, `clear`, and the relational operator functions.

14. The member function `begin` returns an iterator to the first element into the container.

15. The member function `end` returns an iterator to one past the last element into the container.

16. In addition to the member functions listed in item 13 above, the other member functions common to all sequence containers are `insert`, `push_back`, `pop_back`, `erase`, `clear`, and `resize`.

17. The `copy` algorithm is used to copy the elements in a given range to another place.

18. The function `copy`, using an `ostream` iterator, can also be used to output the elements of a container.

19. When we create an iterator of type `ostream`, we also specify the type of element that the iterator will output.

20. Deque containers are implemented as dynamic arrays in such a way that the elements can be inserted at both ends of the array.

21. A `deque` can expand in either direction.

22. The name of the class containing the definition of the **class** `deque` is `deque`.

23. In addition to the operations that are common to all containers, other operations that can be used to manipulate the elements of a `deque` are `assign`, `push_front`, `pop_front`, `at`, the array subscripting operator `[]`, `front`, and `back`.

24. List containers are implemented as doubly linked lists. Thus, every element in the list points to its immediate predecessor and its immediate successor (except the first and last elements).

25. The name of the class containing the definition of the **class** `list` is `list`.

26. In addition to the operations that are common to sequence containers, other operations that can be used to manipulate the elements in a list container are `assign`, `push_front`, `pop_front`, `front`, `back`, `remove`, `remove_if`, `unique`, `splice`, `sort`, `merge`, and `reverse`.

27. The five categories of iterators are input, output, forward, bidirectional, and random access iterator.

28. Input iterators are used to input data from an input stream.

29. Output iterators are used to output data to an output stream.

30. A forward iterator can refer to the same element in the same collection and process the same element more than once.

31. Bidirectional iterators are forward iterators that can also iterate backward over the elements.

32. Bidirectional iterators can be used with containers of type `list`, `set`, `multiset`, `multimap`, `map`, and `multimap`.

33. Random access iterators are bidirectional iterators that can randomly process the elements of a container.

34. Random access iterators can be used with containers of type `vector`, `dequeue`, and `string`, as well as arrays.

2
1

35. Elements in an associative container are automatically sorted according to some various ordering criteria. The default ordering criterion is the relational operator less-than, <.

36. The predefined associative containers in the STL are `set`, `multiset`, `map`, and `multimap`.

37. Containers of the type `set` do not allow duplicates.

38. Containers of the type `multiset` allow duplicates.

39. The name of the class defining the container `set` is `set`.

40. The name of the class defining the container `multiset` is `multiset`.

41. The name of the header file containing the definition of the `class`es `set` and `multiset`, and the definitions of the functions to implement the various operations on these containers, is `set`.

42. The operations `insert`, `erase`, and `clear` can be used to insert or delete elements from sets.

43. Most of the generic algorithms are contained in the header file `algorithm`.

44. The main categories of STL algorithms are nonmodifying, modifying, numeric, and heap.

45. Nonmodifying algorithms do not modify the elements of the container.

46. Modifying algorithms modify the elements of the container by rearranging, removing, and/or changing the values of the elements.

47. Modifying algorithms that change the order of the elements, not their values, are also called mutating algorithms.

48. Numeric algorithms are designed to perform numeric calculations on the elements of a container.

49. A function object is a class template that overloads the function call operator, `operator()`.

50. The predefined arithmetic function objects are `plus`, `minus`, `multiplies`, `divides`, `modulus`, and `negate`.

51. The predefined relational function objects are `equal_to`, `not_equal_to`, `greater`, `greater_equal`, `less`, and `less_equal`.

52. The predefined logical function objects are `logical_not`, `logical_and`, and `logical_or`.

53. Predicates are special types of function objects that return Boolean values.

54. Unary predicates check a specific property for a single argument; binary predicates check a specific property for a pair—that is, two arguments.

55. Predicates are typically used to specify a searching or sorting criteria.

56. In the STL, a predicate must always return the same result for the same value.

57. The functions that modify their internal states cannot be considered predicates.

58. The STL provides three iterators—`back_inserter`, `front_inserter`, and `inserter`—called insert iterators to insert the elements at the destination.

59. The `back_inserter` uses the `push_back` operation of the container in place of the assignment operator.

60. The `front_inserter` uses the `push_front` operation of the container in place of the assignment operator.

61. Because the vector class does not support the `push_front` operation, this iterator cannot be used for the vector container.

62. The `inserter` iterator uses the container's `insert` operation in place of the assignment operator.

63. The function `fill` is used to fill a container with elements, and the function `fill_n` is used to fill in the next n elements.

64. The functions `generate` and `generate_n` are used to generate elements and fill a sequence.

65. The functions `find`, `find_if`, `find_end`, and `find_first_of` are used to find the elements in a given range.

66. The function `remove` is used to remove certain elements from a sequence.

67. The function `remove_if` is used to remove elements from a sequence using a specified criterion.

68. The function `remove_copy` copies the elements in a sequence into another sequence by excluding certain elements from the first sequence.

69. The function `remove_copy_if` copies the elements in a sequence into another sequence by excluding certain elements, using a specified criterion, from the first sequence.

70. The functions `swap`, `iter_swap`, and `swap_ranges` are used to swap elements.

71. The functions `search`, `search_n`, `sort`, and `binary_search` are used to search elements.

72. The function `adjacent_find` is used to find the first occurrence of consecutive elements satisfying a certain criterion.

73. The algorithm `merge` merges two sorted lists.

74. The algorithm `inplace_merge` is used to combine two sorted, consecutive sequences.

75. The algorithm `reverse` reverses the order of the elements in a given range.

76. The algorithm `reverse_copy` reverses the elements in a given range while copying into a destination range. The source is not modified.

77. The algorithm `rotate` rotates the elements in a given range.

78. The algorithm `rotate_copy` copies the elements of the source at the destination in a rotated order.

79. The algorithm `count` counts the occurrences of a given value in a given range.

80. The algorithm `count_if` counts the occurrences of a given value in a given range, satisfying a certain criterion.

81. The algorithm `max` is used to determine the maximum of two values.

82. The algorithm `max_element` is used to determine the largest element in a given range.

83. The algorithm `min` is used to determine the minimum of two values.

84. The algorithm `min_element` is used to determine the smallest element in a given range.

85. The algorithm `random_shuffle` is used to randomly order the elements in a given range.

86. The algorithm `for_each` is used to access and process each element in a given range by applying a function, which is passed as a parameter.

87. The function `transform` creates a sequence of elements by applying certain operations to each element in a given range.

88. The algorithm `includes` determines whether the elements of one range appear in another range.

89. The algorithm `set_intersection` is used to find the elements that are common to two ranges of elements.

90. The algorithm `set_union` is used to find the elements that are contained in two ranges of elements.

91. The algorithm `set_difference` is used to find the elements in one range of elements that do not appear in another range of elements.

92. Given two ranges of elements, the algorithm `set_symmetric_difference` determines the elements that are in the first range but not the second range or the elements that are in the second range but not the first range.

93. The algorithms `accumulate`, `adjacent_difference`, `inner_product`, and `partial_sum` are numerical functions and manipulate numeric data.

EXERCISES

1. What are the three main components of the STL?

2. What is the difference between an STL container and an STL iterator?

3. What is the difference between an STL container and an STL algorithm?

4. What is the difference between a set and a multiset?

5. What is an STL function object?

6. Suppose that `vecList` is a `vector` container and:

   ```
   vecList = { 13, 56, 17, 28, 77, 36, 88, 10, 20, 25}
   ```

   Show `vecList` after the following statement executes:

   ```
   copy(vecList.begin() + 3, vecList.end(), vecList.begin() + 1);
   ```

7. Suppose that `vecList` is a `vector` container and:

   `vecList = { 35, 67, 87, 10, 92, 11, 17, 82, 5, 15, 17, 25}`

   Show `vecList` after the following statement executes:

   `copy(vecList.rbegin() + 2, vecList.rend(), vecList.rbegin());`

8. Suppose that `intList` is a `list` container and:

   `intList = { 7, 12, 12, 7, 38, 27, 12, 38, 38, 70, 45}`

   Show `intList` after the following statement executes:

   `intList.unique();`

9. Suppose that `intList1`, `intList2`, and `intList3` are `list` containers and:

   `intList1 = { 13, 15, 16, 18, 90, 30, 11, 88, 26}`
   `intList2 = { 7, 8, 19, 90, 15}`
   `intList3 = { 12, 12, 14, 20, 20, 13, 13, 13}`

   a. Show `intList1` after the following statement executes:

      `intList1.splice(intList1.begin(), intList2);`

   b. Show `intList1` after the following statements execute. (Note that this part is independent of part a.)

      `intList1.splice(intList1.begin(), intList3);`
      `intList1.unique();`

10. What is a predicate?

11. What is the difference between a `back_inserter` and a `front_inserter`?

12. Suppose that you have the following statements:

    ```
    int numList[] = { 7, 6, 9, 1, 2, 3, 4};
    vector<int> intVec;
    list<int> intList;
    ```

    a. What are the contents of `intVec` after the following statement executes?

       `copy(numList, numList + 7, back_inserter(intVec));`

    b. What are the contents of `intList` after the following statement executes?

       `copy(numList, numList + 7, front_inserter(intList));`

13. Suppose that you have the following statements:

    ```
    vector<int> vec;
    vector<int>::iterator intItr;
    ```

    Suppose that `vec = { 10, 9, 8, 7, 6, 5, 5, 8, 2}`. What is the output of the following statements?

    ```
    intItr = adjacent_find(vec.begin(), vec.end(), less_equal<int>());
    cout << *intItr << endl;
    ```

14. Suppose that you have the following statements:

```
char list[10] = {'A', 'B', 'C', 'D', 'E', 'F', '*', '%', '$', '&'};
ostream_iterator<char> screen(cout, " ");
vector<char> charVec(list, list + 10);
swap_ranges(charVec.begin(), charVec.begin() + 3,
            charVec.begin() + 6);
```

What is the output of the following statement?

```
copy(charVec.begin(), charVec.end(), screen);
```

15. Suppose that you have the following statements:

```
char list[10] = {'A', 'B', 'C', '*', 'E', '%', 'F', '$', 'H', '8'};
vector<char>  charVec(list, list + 10);
ostream_iterator<char> screen(cout, " ");
transform(charVec.begin(), charVec.end(),
          charVec.begin(), tolower);
```

What is the output of the following statement?

```
copy(charVec.begin(), charVec.end(), screen);
```

16. Suppose that charList is a vector container and:

```
charList = {' ', 'A', '\t', 'B', '\n', 'c', '*',
            '9', '\r', 'h', '8'}
```

Further suppose that:

```
lastElem = remove_if(charList.begin(), charList.end(), isspace);
ostream_iterator<char> screen(cout, " ");
```

in which lastElem is a vector iterator into a vector container of type char. What is the output of the following statement?

```
copy(charList.begin(), lastElem, screen);
```

17. Suppose that intList is a vector container and:

```
numList[] = {18, 24, 24, 5, 11, 56, 27, 24, 11, 2, 24, 18,
             78, 30, 24, 35, 48, 18, 11, 36, 11};
```

Furthermore, suppose that:

```
vector<int>::iterator lastElem = intList.end();
ostream_iterator<int> screen(cout, " ");
int tempList[] = {11, 18, 24};
```

What is the output of the following statement?

```
for (int i = 0; i < 3; i++)
    lastElem = remove_copy(intList.begin(), lastElem,
                           intList.begin(), tempList[i]);

copy(intList.begin(), lastElem, screen);

cout << endl;
```

18. Suppose that `intList` is a **vector** container and:

```
intList = { 3, 5, 7, 9, 11, 13, 15}
```

What is the value of `result` after the following statement executes?

```
result = accumulate(intList.begin(), intList.end(), 2);
```

19. Suppose that `intList` is a **vector** container and:

```
intList = { 3, 3, 3, 3}
```

What is the value of `result` after the following statement executes?

```
result = accumulate(intList.begin(), intList.end(),
                    729, divides<int>());
```

20. Suppose that `setA`, `setB`, `setC`, and `setD` are defined as follows:

```
int setA[] = { 1, 3, 4, 6, 7, 9, 10, 12};
int setB[] = { 2, 5, 7, 8, 10, 12, 15};
int setC[] = { 2, 6, 7, 7, 11};
int setD[] = { 3, 5, 5, 11, 15, 18};
```

Further suppose that you have the following declarations:

```
int AunionB[12];
int AunionC[11];
int BunionD[11];
int AintersectB[3];
int AintersectC[2];
```

What is stored in `AunionB`, `AunionC`, `BunionD`, `AintersectB`, and `AintersectC` after the following statements execute?

```
set_union(setA, setA + 8, setB, setB + 7, AunionB);
set_union(setA, setA + 8, setC, setC + 5, AunionC);
set_union(setB, setB + 7, setD, setD + 6, BunionD);
set_intersection(setA, setA + 8, setB, setB + 7, AintersectB);
set_intersection(setA, setA + 8, setC, setC + 5, AintersectC);
```

PROGRAMMING EXERCISES

1. Redo the Election Results programming example of Chapter 18 so that it uses the STL **class** `list` to process candidates data.

2. Redo the DVD Store programming example of Chapter 16 so that it uses the STL **class** `list` to process a list of DVDs.

3. Redo Programming Exercise 14 of Chapter 16 so that it uses the STL **class** `list` to process the list of DVDs rented by the customer and the list of store members.

4. Redo Programming Exercise 15 of Chapter 16 so that it uses the STL **class** `list` to process the list of DVDs owned by the store, the list of DVDs rented by each customer, and the list of store members.

5. Redo the Postfix Expression Calculator program of Chapter 17 so that it uses the STL **class** `stack` to evaluate the postfix expressions.

6. Redo Programming Exercise 10 of Chapter 17 so that it uses the STL class stack to convert the infix expressions to postfix expressions.

7. Redo the simulation program of Chapter 17 so that it uses the STL class queue to maintain the list of waiting customers.

8. Write a program to play the Card Guessing Game. Your program must give the user the following choices:

   a. Guess only the face value of the card.

   b. Guess only the suit of the card.

   c. Guess both the face value and suit of the card.

   Before the start of the game, create a deck of cards. Before each guess, use the function random_shuffle to randomly shuffle the deck.

APPENDIX A
RESERVED WORDS

and	and_eq	asm	auto
bitand	bitor	bool	break
case	catch	char	class
compl	const	const_cast	continue
default	delete	do	double
dynamic_cast	else	enum	explicit
export	extern	false	float
for	friend	goto	if
include	inline	int	long
mutable	namespace	new	not
not_eq	operator	or	or_eq
private	protected	public	register
reinterpret_cast	return	short	signed
sizeof	static	static_cast	struct
switch	template	this	throw
true	try	typedef	typeid
typename	union	unsigned	using
virtual	void	volatile	wchar_t
while	xor	xor_eq	

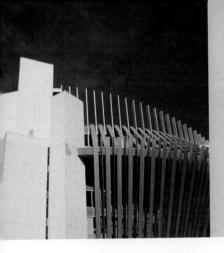

The following table shows the precedence (highest to lowest) and associativity of the operators in C++.

Operator	Associativity
:: (binary scope resolution)	Left to right
:: (unary scope resolution)	Right to left
()	Left to right
[ ] -> .	Left to right
++ -- (as postfix operators)	Right to left
typeid dynamic_cast	Right to left
static_cast const_cast	Right to left
reinterpret_cast	Right to left
++ -- (as prefix operators) ! + (unary) - (unary)	Right to left
~ & (address of) * (dereference)	Right to left
new delete sizeof	Right to left
->* -- .*	Left to right
* / %	Left to right
+ -	Left to right
<< >>	Left to right
< <= > >=	Left to right
== !=	Left to right
&	Left to right
^	Left to right

Operator	Associativity
`|`	Left to right
`&&`	Left to right
`||`	Left to right
`?:`	Right to left
`=` `+=` `-=` `*=` `/=` `%=`	Right to left
`<<=` `>>=` `&=` `|=` `^=`	Right to left
`throw`	Right to left
`,` (the sequencing operator)	Left to right

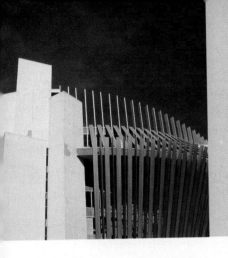

CHARACTER SETS

ASCII (American Standard Code for Information Interchange)

The following table shows the ASCII character set.

ASCII										
	0	1	2	3	4	5	6	7	8	9
0	nul	soh	stx	etx	eot	enq	ack	bel	bs	ht
1	lf	vt	ff	cr	so	si	dle	dc1	dc2	dc3
2	dc4	nak	syn	etb	can	em	sub	esc	fs	gs
3	rs	us	<u>b</u>	!	"	#	$	%	&	'
4	(	)	*	+	,	-	.	/	0	1
5	2	3	4	5	6	7	8	9	:	;
6	<	=	>	?	@	A	B	C	D	E
7	F	G	H	I	J	K	L	M	N	O
8	P	Q	R	S	T	U	V	W	X	Y
9	Z	[	\	]	^	_	`	a	b	c
10	d	e	f	g	h	i	j	k	l	m
11	n	o	p	q	r	s	t	u	v	w
12	x	y	z	{	|	}	~	del		

The numbers 0-12 in the first column specify the left digit(s), and the numbers 0-9 in the second row specify the right digit of each character in the ASCII data set. For example, the character in the row marked 6 (the number in the first column) and the column marked 5 (the number in the second row) is A. Therefore, the character at position 65 (which is the 66th character) is A. Moreover, the character $\underline{b}$ at position 32 represents the space character.

The first 32 characters, that is, the characters at positions 00-31 and at position 127 are nonprintable characters. The following table shows the abbreviations and meanings of these characters.

nul	null character	ff	form feed	can	cancel
soh	start of header	cr	carriage return	em	end of medium
stx	start of text	so	shift out	sub	substitute
etx	end of text	si	shift in	esc	escape
eot	end of transmission	dle	data link escape	fs	file separator
enq	enquiry	dc1	device control 1	gs	group separator
ack	acknowledge	dc2	device control 2	rs	record separator
bel	bell	dc3	device control 3	us	unit separator
bs	back space	dc4	device control 4	$\underline{b}$	space
ht	horizontal tab	nak	negative acknowledge	del	delete
lf	line feed	syn	synchronous idle		
vt	vertical tab	etb	end of transmitted block		

EBCDIC (Extended Binary Coded Decimal Interchange Code)

The following table shows some of the characters in the EBCDIC character set.

EBCDIC									
	0	1	2	3	4	5	6	7	8	9
6					$\underline{b}$					
7							.	<	(	+	|
8	&									
9	!	$	*	)	;	¬	-	/		
10								,	%	_

EBCDIC	0	1	2	3	4	5	6	7	8	9
11	>	?								
12		`	:	#	@	'	=	"		a
13	b	c	d	e	f	g	h	i		
14						j	k	l	m	n
15	o	p	q	r						
16		~	s	t	u	v	w	x	y	z
17										
18	[	]								
19				A	B	C	D	E	F	G
20	H	I								J
21	K	L	M	N	O	P	Q	R		
22							S	T	U	V
23	W	X	Y	Z						
24	0	1	2	3	4	5	6	7	8	9

The numbers 6–24 in the first column specify the left digit(s), and the numbers 0–9 in the second row specify the right digits of the characters in the EBCDIC data set. For example, the character in the row marked 19 (the number in the first column) and the column marked 3 (the number in the second row) is A. Therefore, the character at position 193 (which is the 194th character) is A. Moreover, the character b at position 64 represents the space character. The preceding table does not show all the characters in the EBCDIC character set. In fact, the characters at positions 00–63 and 250–255 are nonprintable control characters.

The following table lists the operators that can be overloaded.

Operators that can be overloaded							
+	–	*	/	%	^	&	|
!	&&	||	=	==	<	<=	>
>=	!=	+=	-=	*=	/=	%=	^=
|=	&=	<<	>>	>>=	<<=	++	--
->*	,	->	[]	()	~	new	delete

The following table lists the operators that cannot be overloaded.

Operators that cannot be overloaded				
.	.*	::	?:	sizeof

Binary (Base 2) Representation of a Nonnegative Integer

Converting a Base 10 Number to a Binary Number (Base 2)

Chapter 1 remarked that A is the 66th character in the ASCII character set, but its position is 65 because the position of the first character is 0. Furthermore, the binary number 1000001 is the binary representation of 65. The number system that we use daily is called the **decimal number system** or **base 10 system**. The number system that the computer uses is called the **binary number system** or **base 2 system**. In this section, we describe how to find the binary representation of a nonnegative integer and vice versa.

Consider 65. Note that:

$$65 = 1 \times 2^6 + 0 \times 2^5 + 0 \times 2^4 + 0 \times 2^3 + 0 \times 2^2 + 0 \times 2^1 + 1 \times 2^0$$

Similarly:

$$711 = 1 \times 2^9 + 0 \times 2^8 + 1 \times 2^7 + 1 \times 2^6 + 0 \times 2^5 + 0 \times 2^4 + 0 \times 2^3 + 1 \times 2^2 + 1 \times 2^1 + 1 \times 2^0$$

In general, if m is a nonnegative integer, then m can be written as:

$$m = a_k \times 2^k + a_{k-1} \times 2^{k-1} + a_{k-2} \times 2^{k-2} + \cdots + a_1 \times 2^1 + a_0 \times 2^0,$$

for some nonnegative integer k, and where $a_i = 0$ or 1, for each $i = 0, 1, 2, \ldots, k$. The binary number $a_k a_{k-1} a_{k-2} \ldots a_1 a_0$ is called the **binary** or **base 2 representation** of m. In this case, we usually write:

$$m_{10} = (a_k a_{k-1} a_{k-2} \cdots a_1 a_0)_2$$

and say that m to the base 10 is $a_k a_{k-1} a_{k-2} \ldots a_1 a_0$ to the base 2.

For example, for the integer 65, $k = 6$, $a_6 = 1$, $a_5 = 0$, $a_4 = 0$, $a_3 = 0$, $a_2 = 0$, $a_1 = 0$, and $a_0 = 1$. Thus, $a_6 a_5 a_4 a_3 a_2 a_1 a_0 = 1000001$, so the binary representation of 65 is 1000001, that is:

$$65_{10} = (1000001)_2.$$

If no confusion arises, then we write $(1000001)_2$ as 1000001_2.

Similarly, for the number 711, $k = 9$, $a_9 = 1$, $a_8 = 0$, $a_7 = 1$, $a_6 = 1$, $a_5 = 0$, $a_4 = 0$, $a_3 = 0$, $a_2 = 1$, $a_1 = 1$, and $a_0 = 1$. Thus:

$$711_{10} = 1011000111_2.$$

It follows that to find the binary representation of a nonnegative, we need to find the coefficients, which are 0 or 1, of various powers of 2. However, there is an easy algorithm, described next, that can be used to find the binary representation of a nonnegative integer. First, note that:

$$0_{10} = 0_2, 1_{10} = 1_2, 2_{10} = 10_2, 3_{10} = 11_2, 4_{10} = 100_2, 5_{10} = 101_2, 6_{10} = 110_2,$$
and $7_{10} = 111_2.$

Let us consider the integer 65. Note that $65 / 2 = 32$ and $65 \% 2 = 1$, where % is the mod operator. Next, $32 / 2 = 16$, and $32 \% 2 = 0$, and so on. It can be shown that $a_0 = 65 \% 2 = 1$, $a_1 = 32 \% 2 = 0$, and so on. We can show this continuous division and obtaining the remainder with the help of Figure E-1.

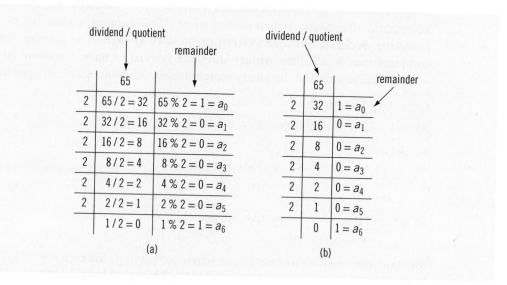

FIGURE E-1 Determining the binary representation of 65

Notice that in Figure E-1(a), starting at the second row, the second column contains the quotient when the number in the previous row is divided by 2 and the third column contains the remainder of that division. For example, in the second row, $65 / 2 = 32$, and $65 \% 2 = 1$. In the third row, $32 / 2 = 16$ and $32 \% 2 = 0$, and so on. For each row, the number in the second column is divided by 2, the quotient is written in the next row, below the current row, and the remainder is written in the third column. When using a figure, such as E-1, to find the binary representation of a nonnegative integer, typically, we show only the quotients and remainders as in Figure E-1(b). You can write the binary representation of the number starting with the last remainder in the third column, followed by the second to last remainder, and so on. Thus:

$65_{10} = 1000001_2$.

Next, consider the number 711. Figure E-2 shows the quotients and the remainders.

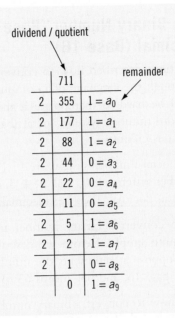

FIGURE E-2 Determining the binary representation of 711

From Figure E-2, it follows that:

$711_{10} = 1011000111_2$.

Converting a Binary Number (Base 2) to Base 10

To convert a number from base 2 to base 10, we first find the weight of each bit in the binary number. The weight of each bit in the binary number is assigned from right to left. The weight of the rightmost bit is 0. The weight of the bit immediately to the left of the rightmost bit is 1, the weight of the bit immediately to the left of it is 2, and so on. Consider the binary number 1001101. The weight of each bit is as follows:

```
weight  6  5  4  3  2  1  0
        1  0  0  1  1  0  1
```

We use the weight of each bit to find the equivalent decimal number. For each bit, we multiply the bit by 2 to the power of its weight and then we add all of the numbers. For the above binary number, the equivalent decimal number is:

$$1 \times 2^6 + 0 \times 2^5 + 0 \times 2^4 + 1 \times 2^3 + 1 \times 2^2 + 0 \times 2^1 + 1 \times 2^0$$

$$= 64 + 0 + 0 + 8 + 4 + 0 + 1$$

$$= 77.$$

Converting a Binary Number (Base 2) to Octal (Base 8) and Hexadecimal (Base 16)

The previous sections described how to convert a binary number to a decimal number (base 2). Even though the language of a computer is binary, if the binary number is too long, then it will be hard to manipulate it manually. To effectively deal with binary numbers, two more number systems, octal (base 8) and hexadecimal (base 16), are of interest to computer scientists.

The digits in the octal number system are 0, 1, 2, 3, 4, 5, 6, and 7. The digits in the hexadecimal number system are 0, 1, 2, 3, 4, 5, 6, 7, 8, 9, A, B, C, D, E, and F. So A in hexadecimal is 10 in decimal, B in hexadecimal is 11 in decimal, and so on.

The algorithm to convert a binary number into an equivalent number in octal (or hexadecimal) is quite simple. Before we describe the method to do so, let us review some notations. Suppose a_b represents the number a to the base b. For example, $2A0_{16}$ means 2A0 to the base 16, and 63_8 means 63 to the base 8.

First we describe how to convert a binary number into an equivalent octal number and vice versa. Table E–1 describes the first eight octal numbers.

TABLE E-1 Binary representation of first eight octal numbers

Binary	Octal	Binary	Octal
000	0	100	4
001	1	101	5
010	2	110	6
011	3	111	7

Consider the binary number 1101100010101. To find the equivalent octal number, starting from right to left we consider three digits at a time and write their octal representation. Note that the binary number 1101100010101 has only 13 digits. So when we consider three digits at a time, at the end we will be left with only one digit. In this case, we just add two 0s to the left of the binary number; the equivalent binary number is 001101100010101. Thus,

$$1101100010101_2 = 001101100010101_2$$

$$= 001\ 101\ 100\ 010\ 101$$

$$= 15425_8 \text{ because } 001_2 = 1_8,\ 101_2 = 5_8,\ 100_2 = 4_8,\ 010_2 = 2_8,$$
$$\text{and } 101_2 = 5_8$$

Thus, $1101100010101_2 = 15425_8$.

To convert an octal number into an equivalent binary number, using Table E-1, write the binary representation of each octal digit in the number. For example,

$$3761_8 = 011\ 111\ 110\ 001_2$$

$$= 011111110001_2$$

$$= 11111110001_2$$

Thus, $3761_8 = 11111110001_2$.

Next we discuss how to convert a binary number into an equivalent hexadecimal number and vice versa. The method to do so is similar to converting a number from binary to octal and vice versa, except that here we work with four binary digits. Table E-2 gives the binary representation of the first 16 hexadecimal numbers.

TABLE E-2 Binary representation of first 16 hexadecimal numbers

Binary	Hexadecimal	Binary	Hexadecimal
0000	0	1000	8
0001	1	1001	9
0010	2	1010	A
0011	3	1011	B
0100	4	1100	C
0101	5	1101	D
0110	6	1110	E
0111	7	1111	F

Consider the binary number 1111101010001010101_2. Now,

$$1111101010001010101_2 = 111\ 1101\ 0100\ 0101\ 0101_2$$

$$= 0111\ 1101\ 0100\ 0101\ 0101_2,\text{ add one zero to the left}$$

$$= 7D455_{16}$$

Hence, $1111101010001010101_2 = 7D455_{16}$.

Next, to convert a hexadecimal number into an equivalent binary number, write the four-digit binary representation of each hexadecimal digit into that number. For example,

$$A7F32_{16} = 1010\ 0111\ 1111\ 0011\ 0010_2$$

$$= 10100111111100110010_2$$

Thus, $A7F32_{16} = 10100111111100110010_2$.

More on File Input/Output

In Chapter 3, you learned how to read data from and write data to a file. This section expands on the concepts introduced in that chapter.

Binary Files

In Chapter 3, you learned how to make a program read data from and write data to a file. However, the files that the programs have used until now are called text files. Data in a text file is stored in the character format. For example, consider the number 45. If 45 is stored in a file, then it is stored as a sequence of two characters—the character '4' followed by the character '5'. The eight-bit machine representation of '4' is 00000100 and the eight-bit machine representation of '5' is 00000101. Therefore, in a text file, 45 is stored as 0000010000000101. When this number is read by a C++ program, it must first be converted to its binary format. Suppose that the integers are represented as 16-bit binary numbers. The 16-bit binary representation of 45 is then 0000000000101101. Similarly, when a program stores the number 45 in a text file, it first must be converted to its text format. It thus follows that reading data from and writing data to a text file is not efficient, because the data must be converted from the text to the binary format and vice versa.

On the other hand, when data is stored in a file in the binary format, reading and writing data is faster because no time is lost in converting the data from one format to another format. Such files are called binary files. More formally, **binary files** are files in which data is stored in the binary format. Data in a text file is also called **formatted data**, and in a binary file it is called **raw data**.

C++ allows a programmer to create binary files. This section explains how to create binary files and also how to read data from binary files.

To create a binary file, the file must be opened in the binary mode. Suppose `outFile` is an `ofstream` variable (object). Consider the following statement:

```
outFile.open("employee.dat", ios::binary);
```

This statement opens the file `employee.dat`. Data in this file will be written in its binary format. Therefore, the file opening mode `ios::binary` specifies that the file is opened in the binary mode.

Next, you use the stream function `write` to write data to the file `employee.dat`. The syntax to use the function `write` is:

```
fileVariableName.write(reinterpret_cast<const char *> (buffer),
                       sizeof(buffer));
```

where `fileVariableName` is the object used to open the output file, and the first argument `buffer` specifies the starting address of the location in memory where the data is stored. The expression `sizeof(buffer)` specifies the size of the data, in bytes, to be written.

For example, suppose `num` is an `int` variable. The following statement writes the value of `num` in the binary format to the file associated with `outFile`:

```
outFile.write(reinterpret_cast<const char *> (&num),
              sizeof(num));
```

Similarly, suppose `empSalary` is an array of, say, 100 components and the component type is `double`. The following statement writes the entire array to the file associated with `outFile`:

```
outFile.write(reinterpret_cast<const char *> (empSalary),
              sizeof(empSalary));
```

Next, let us discuss how to read data from a binary file. The operation of reading data from a binary file is similar to writing data to a binary file. First, the binary file must be opened. For example, suppose `inFile` is an `ifstream` variable, and a program has already created the binary file `employee.dat`. The following statement opens this file:

```
inFile.open("employee.dat");
```

or:

```
inFile.open("employee.dat", ios::binary);
```

To read data in the binary format, the stream function `read` is used. The syntax to use the function `read` is:

```
fileVariableName.read(reinterpret_cast<char *> (buffer),
                      sizeof(buffer));
```

The first argument `buffer` specifies the starting address of the location in memory where the data is to be stored. The expression `sizeof(buffer)` specifies the size of the data, in bytes, to be read.

The program in the following example further explains how to create binary files and read data from a binary file.

EXAMPLE E-1

```cpp
//Creating and reading binary files

#include <iostream>
#include <fstream>

using namespace std;

struct studentType
{
    char firstName[15];
    char lastName[15];
    int ID;
};

int main()
{
        //create and initialize an array of students' IDs
    int studentIDs[5] = {111111, 222222, 333333,
                    444444, 555555};                    //Line 1

        //declare and initialize the struct newStudent
    studentType newStudent = {"John", "Wilson",
                        777777};                        //Line 2

    ofstream outFile;                                   //Line 3

        //open the output file as a binary file
    outFile.open("ids.dat", ios::binary);               //Line 4

        //write the array in the binary format
    outFile.write(reinterpret_cast<const char *> (studentIDs),
            sizeof(studentIDs));                        //Line 5
        //write the newStudent data in the binary format
    outFile.write(reinterpret_cast<const char *> (&newStudent),
            sizeof(newStudent));                        //Line 6

    outFile.close();   //close the file                 //Line 7

    ifstream inFile;                                    //Line 8
    int arrayID[5];                                     //Line 9
    studentType student;                                //Line 10
```

```
        //open the input file
    inFile.open("ids.dat");                              //Line 11

    if (!inFile)                                          //Line 12
    {
        cout << "The input file does not exist. "
             << "The program terminates!!!!" << endl;     //Line 13
        return 1;                                         //Line 14
    }

        //input the data into the array arrayID
    inFile.read(reinterpret_cast<char *> (arrayID),
                sizeof(arrayID));                         //Line 15
        //output the data of the array arrayID
    for (int i = 0; i < 5; i++)                           //Line 16
        cout << arrayID[i] << " ";                        //Line 17
    cout << endl;                                         //Line 18

        //read the student's data
    inFile.read(reinterpret_cast<char *> (&student),
                sizeof(student));                         //Line 19

        //output studentData
    cout << student.ID << " " << student.firstName
         << " " << student.lastName << endl;              //Line 20

    inFile.close();      //close the file                 //Line 21

    return 0;                                             //Line 22
}
```

Sample Run:

```
111111 222222 333333 444444 555555
777777 John Wilson
```

The output of the preceding program is self-explanatory. The details are left as an exercise for you.

 NOTE In the program in Example E-1, the statement in Line 2 declares the `struct` variable `newStudent` and also initializes it. Because `newStudent` has three components and we want to initialize all the components, three values are specified in braces separated by commas. In other words, `struct` variables can also be initialized when they are declared.

The program in the following example further explains how to create binary files and then read the data from the binary files.

EXAMPLE E-2

```cpp
//Creating and reading a binary file consisting of
//bank customers' data

#include <iostream>
#include <fstream>
#include <iomanip>

using namespace std;

struct customerType
{
    char firstName[15];
    char lastName[15];
    int ID;
    double balance;
};

int main()
{
    customerType cust;                                    //Line 1
    ifstream inFile;                                      //Line 2
    ofstream outFile;                                     //Line 3

    inFile.open("customerData.txt");                      //Line 4

    if (!inFile)                                          //Line 5
    {
        cout << "The input file does not exist. "
             << "The program terminates!!!!" << endl;     //Line 6
        return 1;                                         //Line 7
    }

    outFile.open("customer.dat", ios::binary);            //Line 8

    inFile >> cust.ID >> cust.firstName >> cust.lastName
           >> cust.balance;                               //Line 9

    while (inFile)                                         //Line 10
    {
        outFile.write(reinterpret_cast<const char *> (&cust),
                      sizeof(cust));                       //Line 11
        inFile >> cust.ID >> cust.firstName >> cust.lastName
               >> cust.balance;                            //Line 12
    }

    inFile.close();                                        //Line 13
    inFile.clear();                                        //Line 14
    outFile.close();                                       //Line 15
```

```
    inFile.open("customer.dat", ios::binary);              //Line 16

    if (!inFile)                                            //Line 17
    {
        cout << "The input file does not exist. "
             << "The program terminates!!!!" << endl;       //Line 18
        return 1;                                           //Line 19
    }

    cout << left << setw(8) << "ID"
         << setw(16) << "First Name"
         << setw(16) << "Last Name"
         << setw(10) << " Balance" << endl;                 //Line 20
    cout << fixed << showpoint << setprecision(2);          //Line 21

        //read and output the data from the binary
        //file customer.dat
    inFile.read(reinterpret_cast<char *> (&cust),
            sizeof(cust));                                  //Line 22
    while (inFile)                                          //Line 23
    {
        cout << left << setw(8) << cust.ID
             << setw(16) << cust.firstName
             << setw(16) << cust.lastName
             << right << setw(10) << cust.balance
             << endl;                                       //Line 24
        inFile.read(reinterpret_cast<char *> (&cust),
                sizeof(cust));                              //Line 25
    }

    inFile.close();        //close the file                 //Line 26

    return 0;                                               //Line 27
}
```

Sample Run:

```
ID        First Name      Last Name       Balance
77234     Ashley          White             4563.50
12345     Brad            Smith           128923.45
87123     Lisa            Johnson           2345.93
81234     Sheila          Robinson           674.00
11111     Rita            Gupta            14863.50
23422     Ajay            Kumar            72682.90
22222     Jose            Ramey            25345.35
54234     Sheila          Duffy            65222.00
55555     Tommy           Pitts              892.85
23452     Salma           Quade             2812.90
32657     Jennifer        Ackerman          9823.89
82722     Steve           Sharma           78932.00
```

Random File Access

In Chapter 3 and the preceding section, you learned how to read data from and write data to a file. More specifically, you used `ifstream` objects to read data from a file and `ofstream` objects to write data to a file. However, the files were read and/or written sequentially. Reading data from a file sequentially does not work very well for a variety of applications. For example, consider a program that processes customers' data in a bank. Typically, there are thousands or even millions of customers in a bank. Suppose we want to access a customer's data from the file that contains such data, say, for an account update. If the data is accessed sequentially, starting from the first position and read until the desired customer's data is found, this process might be extremely time consuming. Similarly, in an airline's reservation system to access a passenger's reservation information sequentially, this might also be very time consuming. In such cases, the data retrieval must be efficient. A convenient way to do this is to be able to read the data randomly from a file, that is, randomly access any record in the file.

In the preceding section, you learned how to use the stream function `read` to read a specific number of bytes, and the function `write` to write a specific number of bytes.

The stream function `seekg` is used to move the read position to any byte in the file. The general syntax to use the function `seekg` is:

```
fileVariableName.seekg(offset, position);
```

The stream function `seekp` is used to move the write position to any byte in the file. The general syntax to use the function `seekp` is:

```
fileVariableName.seekp(offset, position);
```

The `offset` specifies the number of bytes the reading/writing positions are to be moved, and `position` specifies where to begin the offset. The offset can be calculated from the beginning of the file, end of the file, or the current position in the file. Moreover, `offset` is a long integer representation of an offset. Table E-3 shows the values that can be used for `position`.

TABLE E-3 Values of `position`

position	Description
ios::beg	The offset is calculated from the beginning of the file.
ios::cur	The offset is calculated from the current position of the reading marker in the file.
ios::end	The offset is calculated from the end of the file.

EXAMPLE E-3

Suppose you have the following line of text stored in a file, say, `digitsAndLetters.txt`:

0123456789ABCDEFGHIJKLMNOPQRSTUVWXYZ

Also, suppose that `inFile` is an `ifstream` object and the file `digitsAndLetters.txt` has been opened using the object `inFile`. One byte is used to store each character of this line of text. Moreover, the position of the first character is 0.

Statement	Explanation
`inFile.seekp(10L, ios::beg);`	Sets the reading position of `inFile` to the 11th byte (character), which is at position 10. That is, it sets the reading position just after the digit 9 or just before the letter A.
`inFile.seekp(5L, ios::cur);`	Moves the reading position of `inFile` five bytes to the right of its current position.
`inFile.seekp(-6L, ios::end);`	Sets the reading position of `inFile` to the sixth byte (character) from the end. That is, it sets the reading position just before the letter U.

The program in the following example further explains how the functions `seekg` and `seekp` work.

EXAMPLE E-4

```cpp
#include <iostream>
#include <fstream>

using namespace std;

int main()
{
    char ch;                                        //Line 1
    ifstream inFile;                                //Line 2

    inFile.open("digitsAndAlphabet.txt");           //Line 3

    if (!inFile)                                     //Line 4
    {
        cout << "The input file does not exist. "
             << "The program terminates!!!!" << endl;   //Line 5
        return 1;                                       //Line 6
    }
```

```
    inFile.get(ch);                                          //Line 7
    cout << "Line 8: The first byte: " << ch << endl; //Line 8

        //position the reading marker six bytes to the
        //right of its current position
    inFile.seekg(6L, ios::cur);                              //Line 9
    inFile.get(ch);   //read the character                  //Line 10
    cout << "Line 11: Current byte read: " << ch
         << endl;                                            //Line 11

        //position the reading marker seven bytes
        //from the beginning
    inFile.seekg(7L, ios::beg);                              //Line 12
    inFile.get(ch);   //read the character                  //Line 13
    cout << "Line 14: Seventh byte from the beginning: "
         << ch << endl;                                      //Line 14

        //position the reading marker 26 bytes
        //from the end
    inFile.seekg(-26L, ios::end);                            //Line 15
    inFile.get(ch);   //read the character                  //Line 16
    cout << "Line 17: Byte 26 from the end: " << ch
         << endl;                                            //Line 17

    return 0;                                                //Line 18
}
```

Sample Run:

```
Line 8: The first byte: 0
Line 11: Current byte read: 7
Line 14: Seventh byte from the beginning: 7
Line 17: Byte 26 from the end: A
```

The input file contains the following line of text:

0123456789ABCDEFGHIJKLMNOPQRSTUVWXYZ

The following program illustrates how the function seekg works with structs.

EXAMPLE E-5

Suppose customerType is a struct defined as follows:

```
struct customerType
{
    char firstName[15];
    char lastName[15];
    int ID;
    double balance;
};
```

The program in Example E-2 created the binary file `customer.dat` consisting of certain customers' data. You can use the function `seekg` to move the reading position of this file to any record. Suppose `inFile` is an `ifstream` object used to open the binary file `customer.dat`.

The following statement calculates the size of a `customerType` `struct` and stores it in the variable `custSize`:

```
long custSize = sizeof(cust);
```

We can use the value of the variable `custSize` to move the reading position to a specific record in the file. For example, consider the following statement:

```
inFile.seekg(6 * custSize, ios::beg);
```

This statement moves the reading position just after the sixth customer's record, that is, just before the seventh customer's record.

The following program further illustrates how the function `seekg` works with `struct`s.

EXAMPLE E-6

```cpp
//Reading a file randomly

#include <iostream>
#include <fstream>
#include <iomanip>

using namespace std;

struct customerType
{
    char firstName[15];
    char lastName[15];
    int ID;
    double balance;
};

void printCustData(const customerType& customer);

int main()
{
    customerType cust;                              //Line 1
    ifstream inFile;                                //Line 2

    long custSize = sizeof(cust);                   //Line 3

    inFile.open("customer.dat", ios::binary);       //Line 4
    if (!inFile)                                    //Line 5
```

```
    {
        cout << "The input file does not exist. "
            << "The program terminates!!!!" << endl;  //Line 6
        return 1;                                       //Line 7
    }

    cout << fixed << showpoint << setprecision(2);      //Line 8

        //randomly read the records and output them
    inFile.seekg(6 * custSize, ios::beg);               //Line 9
    inFile.read(reinterpret_cast<char *> (&cust),
            sizeof(cust));                              //Line 10
    cout << "Seventh customer's data: " << endl;        //Line 11
    printCustData(cust);                                //Line 12

    inFile.seekg(8 * custSize, ios::beg);               //Line 13
    inFile.read(reinterpret_cast<char *> (&cust),
            sizeof(cust));                              //Line 14
    cout << "Ninth customer's data: " << endl;          //Line 15
    printCustData(cust);

    inFile.seekg(-8 * custSize, ios::end);              //Line 16
    inFile.read(reinterpret_cast<char *> (&cust),
            sizeof(cust));                              //Line 17
    cout << "Eighth (from the end) customer's data: "
        << endl;                                        //Line 18
    printCustData(cust);                                //Line 19

    inFile.close();       //close the file              //Line 20

    return 0;                                           //Line 21
}

void printCustData(const customerType& customer)
{
    cout << "  ID: " << customer.ID <<endl
        << "  First Name: " << customer.firstName <<endl
        << "  Last Name: " << customer.lastName <<endl
        << "  Account Balance: $" << customer.balance
        << endl;
}
```

Sample Run:

```
Seventh customer's data:
  ID: 22222
  First Name: Jose
  Last Name: Ramey
  Account Balance: $25345.35
Ninth customer's data:
  ID: 55555
  First Name: Tommy
  Last Name: Pitts
```

```
   Account Balance: $892.85
Eighth (from the end) customer's data:
   ID: 11111
   First Name: Rita
   Last Name: Gupta
   Account Balance: $14863.50
```

The program in Example E-6 illustrates how the function `seekg` works. Using the function `seekg`, the reading position in a file can be moved to any location in the file. Similarly, the function `seekp` can be used to move the write position in a file to any location. Furthermore, these functions can be used to create a binary file in which the data is organized according to the values of either a variable or a particular component of a `struct`. For example, suppose there are at most, say, 100 students in a class. Each student has a unique ID in the range 1 to 100. Using the students' IDs, we can create a random access binary file in such a way that in the file, a student's data is written at the location specified by its ID. This is like treating the file as an array. The advantage is that, once the file is created, a student's data from the file can be read, directly, using the student's ID. Another advantage is that in the file, the data is sorted according to the IDs.

Here, we are assuming that the student IDs are in the range 1 to 100. However, if you use, say, a three-, four-, or five-digit number as a student ID and there are only a few students in the class, the data in the file could be scattered. In other words, a lot of space could be used just to store only a few students' data. In such cases, more advanced techniques are used to organize the data so that it can be accessed efficiently.

The program in Example E-7 illustrates how to use the students' IDs to organize the data in a binary file. The program also shows how to output the file.

EXAMPLE E-7

```cpp
//Creating and reading a random access file.

#include <iostream>
#include <fstream>
#include <iomanip>

using namespace std;

struct studentType
{
    char firstName[15];
    char lastName[15];
    int ID;
    double GPA;
};

void printStudentData(const studentType& student);
```

```cpp
int main()
{
    studentType st;                                    //Line 1
    ifstream inFile;                                   //Line 2
    ofstream outFile;                                  //Line 3

    long studentSize = sizeof(st);                     //Line 4

        //open the input file, which is a text file
    inFile.open("studentData.txt");                    //Line 5

    if (!inFile)                                        //Line 6
    {
        cout << "The input file does not exist. "
            << "The program terminates!!!!" << endl; //Line 7
        return 1;                                      //Line 8
    }

        //open a binary output file
    outFile.open("student.dat", ios::binary);          //Line 9

    inFile >> st.ID >> st.firstName
          >> st.lastName >> st.GPA;                    //Line 10

    while (inFile)                                      //Line 11
    {
        outFile.seekp((st.ID - 1) * studentSize,
                      ios::beg);                        //Line 12
        outFile.write(reinterpret_cast<const char *> (&st),
                      sizeof(st));                      //Line 13
        inFile >> st.ID >> st.firstName
              >> st.lastName >> st.GPA;                 //Line 14
    };

    inFile.close();                                    //Line 15
    inFile.clear();                                    //Line 16
    outFile.close();                                   //Line 17

    cout << left << setw(3) << "ID"
        << setw(16) << "First Name"
        << setw(16) << "Last Name"
        << setw(12) << "Current GPA" << endl;          //Line 18
    cout << fixed << showpoint << setprecision(2);      //Line 19

        //open the input file, which is a binary file
    inFile.open("student.dat", ios::binary);           //Line 20

    if (!inFile)                                        //Line 21
    {
        cout << "The input file does not exist. "
            << "The program terminates!!!!" << endl; //Line 22
        return 1;                                      //Line 23
    }
```

```
        //read the data at location 0 in the file
    inFile.read(reinterpret_cast<char *> (&st),
            sizeof(st));                              //Line 24
    while (inFile)                                    //Line 25
    {
        if (st.ID != 0)                               //Line 26
            printStudentData(st);                     //Line 27

            //read the data at the current reading position
        inFile.read(reinterpret_cast<char *> (&st),
                sizeof(st));                          //Line 28
    };

    return 0;                                         //Line 29
}

void printStudentData(const studentType& student)
{
    cout << left << setw(3) << student.ID
         << setw(16) << student.firstName
         << setw(16) << student.lastName
         << right << setw(10)<< student.GPA
         << endl;
}
```

Sample Run:

ID	First Name	Last Name	Current GPA
2	Sheila	Duffy	4.00
10	Ajay	Kumar	3.60
12	Ashley	White	3.90
16	Tommy	Pitts	2.40
23	Rita	Gupta	3.40
34	Brad	Smith	3.50
36	Salma	Quade	3.90
41	Steve	Sharma	3.50
45	Sheila	Robinson	2.50
56	Lisa	Johnson	2.90
67	Jose	Ramey	3.80
75	Jennifer	Ackerman	4.00

The data in the file studentData.txt is as follows:

```
12 Ashley White 3.9
34 Brad Smith 3.5
56 Lisa Johnson 2.9
45 Sheila Robinson 2.5
23 Rita Gupta 3.4
10 Ajay Kumar 3.6
67 Jose Ramey 3.8
2 Sheila Duffy 4.0
16 Tommy Pitts 2.4
```

```
36 Salma Quade 3.9
75 Jennifer Ackerman 4.0
41 Steve Sharma 3.5
```

Naming Conventions of Header Files in ANSI/ISO Standard C++ and Standard C++

The programs in this book are written using ANSI/ISO Standard C++. As indicated in Chapter 1, there are two versions of C++—ANSI/ISO Standard C++ and Standard C++. For the most part, these two standards are the same. The header files in Standard C++ have the extension .h, while the header files in ANSI/ISO Standard C++ have no extension. Moreover, the names of certain header files, such as math.h, in ANSI/ISO Standard C++ start with the letter c. The language C++ evolved from C. Therefore, certain header files—such as math.h, stdlib.h, and string.h—were brought from C into C++. The header files—such as iostream.h, iomanip.h, and fstream.h—were specially designed for C++. Recall that when a header file is included in a program, the global identifiers of the header file also become the global identifiers of the program. In ANSI/ISO Standard C++, to take advantage of the namespace mechanism, all of the header files were modified so that the identifiers are declared within a namespace. Recall that the name of this namespace is std.

In ANSI/ISO Standard C++, the extension .h of the header files that were specially designed for C++ was dropped. For the header files that were brought from C into C++, the extension .h was dropped and the names of these header files start with the letter c. Following are the names of the most commonly used header files in Standard C++ and ANSI/ISO Standard C++:

Standard C++ Header File Name	ANSI/ISO Standard C++ Header File Name
assert.h	cassert
ctype.h	cctype
float.h	cfloat
fstream.h	fstream
iomanip.h	iomanip
iostream.h	iostream
limits.h	climits
math.h	cmath
stdlib.h	cstdlib
string.h	cstring

To include a header file, say, `iostream`, the following statement is required:

`#include <iostream>`

Furthermore, to use identifiers, such as `cin`, `cout`, `endl`, and so on, the program should use either the statement:

`using namespace std;`

or the prefix `std::` before the identifier.

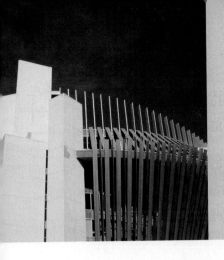

The C++ standard library contains many predefined functions, named constants, and specialized data types. This appendix discusses some of the most widely used library routines (and several named constants). For additional explanation and information on functions, named constants, and so on, check your system documentation. The names of the Standard C++ header files are shown in parentheses.

Header File cassert (assert.h)

The following table describes the function `assert`. Its specification is contained in the header file `cassert` (`assert.h`).

`assert(expression)`	`expression` is any `int` expression; `expression` is usually a logical expression	• If the value of `expression` is nonzero (`true`), the program continues to execute. • If the value of `expression` is 0 (`false`), execution of the program terminates immediately. The expression, the name of the file containing the source code, and the line number in the source code are displayed.

NOTE To disable all of the `assert` statements, place the preprocessor directive `#define` NDEBUG before the directive `#include <cassert>`.

Header File cctype (ctype.h)

The following table shows various functions from the header file cctype (ctype.h).

Function Name and Parameters	Parameter(s) Types	Function Return Value
isalnum(ch)	ch is a char value	Function returns an int value as follows: • If ch is a letter or a digit character, that is ('A'-'Z', 'a'-'z', '0'-'9'), it returns a nonzero value (true) • 0 (false), otherwise
iscntrl(ch)	ch is a char value	Function returns an int value as follows: • If ch is a control character (in ASCII, a character value 0–31 or 127), it returns a nonzero value (true) • 0 (false), otherwise
isdigit(ch)	ch is a char value	Function returns an int value as follows: • If ch is a digit ('0'-'9'), it returns a nonzero value (true) • 0 (false), otherwise
islower(ch)	ch is a char value	Function returns an int value as follows: • If ch is lowercase ('a'-'z'), it returns a nonzero value (true) • 0 (false), otherwise
isprint(ch)	ch is a char value	Function returns an int value as follows: • If ch is a printable character, including blank (in ASCII, ' ' through '~'), it returns a nonzero value (true) • 0 (false), otherwise
ispunct(ch)	ch is a char value	Function returns an int value as follows: • If ch is a punctuation character, it returns a nonzero value (true) • 0 (false), otherwise
isspace(ch)	ch is a char value	Function returns an int value as follows: • If ch is a whitespace character (blank, newline, tab, carriage return, form feed), it returns a nonzero value (true) • 0 (false), otherwise

Function Name and Parameters	Parameter(s) Types	Function Return Value
isupper(ch)	ch is a char value	Function returns an int value as follows: • If ch is an uppercase letter ('A'-'Z'), it returns a nonzero value (true) • 0 (false), otherwise
tolower(ch)	ch is a char value	Function returns an int value as follows: • If ch is an uppercase letter, it returns the ASCII value of the lowercase equivalent of ch • ASCII value of ch, otherwise
toupper(ch)	ch is a char value	Function returns an int value as follows: • If ch is a lowercase letter, it returns the ASCII value of the uppercase equivalent of ch • ASCII value of ch, otherwise

Header File cfloat (float.h)

In Chapter 2, we listed the largest and smallest values belonging to the floating-point data types. We also remarked that these values are system dependent. These largest and smallest values are stored in named constants. The header file cfloat contains many such named constants. The following table lists some of these constants.

Named Constant	Description
FLT_DIG	Approximate number of significant digits in a float value
FLT_MAX	Maximum positive float value
FLT_MIN	Minimum positive float value
DBL_DIG	Approximate number of significant digits in a double value
DBL_MAX	Maximum positive double value
DBL_MIN	Minimum positive double value
LDBL_DIG	Approximate number of significant digits in a long double value
LDBL_MAX	Maximum positive long double value
LDBL_MIN	Minimum positive long double value

A program similar to the following can print the values of these named constants on your system:

```cpp
#include <iostream>
#include <cfloat>

using namespace std;

int main()
{
    cout << "Approximate number of significant digits "
         << "in a float value " << FLT_DIG << endl;
    cout << "Maximum positive float value " << FLT_MAX
         << endl;
    cout << "Minimum positive float value " << FLT_MIN
         << endl;
    cout << "Approximate number of significant digits "
         << "in a double value " << DBL_DIG << endl;
    cout << "Maximum positive double value " << DBL_MAX
         << endl;
    cout << "Minimum positive double value " << DBL_MIN
         << endl;
    cout << "Approximate number of significant digits "
         << "in a long double value " << LDBL_DIG << endl;
    cout << "Maximum positive long double value " << LDBL_MAX
         << endl;
    cout << "Minimum positive long double value " << LDBL_MIN
         << endl;

    return 0;
}
```

Header File `climits` (`limits.h`)

In Chapter 2, we listed the largest and smallest values belonging to the integral data types. We also remarked that these values are system dependent. These largest and smallest values are stored in named constants. The header file `climits` contains many such named constants. The following table lists some of these constants.

Named Constant	Description
CHAR_BIT	Number of bits in a byte
CHAR_MAX	Maximum `char` value
CHAR_MIN	Minimum `char` value
SHRT_MAX	Maximum `short` value
SHRT_MIN	Minimum `short` value

Named Constant	Description
INT_MAX	Maximum int value
INT_MIN	Minimum int value
LONG_MAX	Maximum long value
LONG_MIN	Minimum long value
LLONG_MAX	Maximum long long value
LLONG_MIN	Minimum long long value
UCHAR_MAX	Maximum unsigned char value
USHRT_MAX	Maximum unsigned short value
UINT_MAX	Maximum unsigned int value
ULONG_MAX	Maximum unsigned long value

A program similar to the following can print the values of these named constants on your system:

```
#include <iostream>
#include <climits>

using namespace std;

int main()
{
    cout << "Number of bits in a byte " << CHAR_BIT << endl;
    cout << "Maximum char value " << CHAR_MAX << endl;
    cout << "Minimum char value " << CHAR_MIN << endl;
    cout << "Maximum short value " << SHRT_MAX << endl;
    cout << "Minimum short value " << SHRT_MIN << endl;
    cout << "Maximum int value " << INT_MAX << endl;
    cout << "Minimum int value " << INT_MIN << endl;
    cout << "Maximum long value " << LONG_MAX << endl;
    cout << "Minimum long value " << LONG_MIN << endl;
    cout << "Maximum long long value " << LLONG_MAX << endl;
    cout << "Minimum long long value " << LLONG_MIN << endl;
    cout << "Maximum unsigned char value " << UCHAR_MAX
        << endl;
    cout << "Maximum unsigned short value " << USHRT_MAX
        << endl;
    cout << "Maximum unsigned int value " << UINT_MAX << endl;
    cout << "Maximum unsigned long value " << ULONG_MAX
        << endl;

    return 0;
}
```

Header File cmath (math.h)

The following table shows various math functions.

Function Name and Parameters	Parameter(s) Type	Function Return Value
acos(x)	x is a floating-point expression, $-1.0 \leq x \leq 1.0$	Arc cosine of x, a value between 0.0 and π
asin(x)	x is a floating-point expression, $-1.0 \leq x \leq 1.0$	Arc sine of x, a value between $-\pi/2$ and $\pi/2$
atan(x)	x is a floating-point expression	Arc tan of x, a value between $-\pi/2$ and $\pi/2$
ceil(x)	x is a floating-point expression	The smallest whole number $\geq$ x, ("ceiling" of x)
cos(x)	x is a floating-point expression, x is measured in radians	Trigonometric cosine of the angle
cosh(x)	x is a floating-point expression	Hyperbolic cosine of x
exp(x)	x is a floating-point expression	The value e raised to the power of x; (e = 2.718...)
fabs(x)	x is a floating-point expression	Absolute value of x
floor(x)	x is a floating-point expression	The largest whole number $\leq$ x; ("floor" of x)
log(x)	x is a floating-point expression, in which x > 0.0	Natural logarithm (base e) of x
log10(x)	x is a floating-point expression, in which x > 0.0	Common logarithm (base 10) of x
pow(x,y)	x and y are floating-point expressions. If x = 0.0, y must be positive; if $x \leq 0.0$, y must be a whole number.	x raised to the power of y
sin(x)	x is a floating-point expression; x is measured in radians	Trigonometric sine of the angle
sinh(x)	x is a floating-point expression	Hyperbolic sine of x

Function Name and Parameters	Parameter(s) Type	Function Return Value
sqrt(x)	x is a floating-point expression, in which $x \geq 0.0$	Square root of x
tan(x)	x is a floating-point expression; x is measured in radians	Trigonometric tangent of the angle
tanh(x)	x is a floating-point expression	Hyperbolic tangent of x

Header File cstddef (stddef.h)

Among others, this header file contains the definition of the following symbolic constant:

NULL: The system-dependent null pointer (usually 0)

Header File cstring (string.h)

The following table shows various string functions.

Function Name and Parameters	Parameter(s) Type	Function Return Value
strcat(destStr, srcStr)	destStr and srcStr are null-terminated char arrays; destStr must be large enough to hold the result	The base address of destStr is returned; srcStr, including the null character, is concatenated to the end of destStr
strcmp(str1, str2)	str1 and str2 are null-terminated char arrays	The returned value is as follows: • An int value < 0 if str1 < str2 • An int value 0 if str1 = str2 • An int value > 0 if str1 > str2

Function Name and Parameters	Parameter(s) Type	Function Return Value
strcpy(destStr, srcStr)	destStr and srcStr are null-terminated **char** arrays	The base address of destStr is returned; srcStr is copied into destStr
strlen(str)	str is a null-terminated **char** array	An integer value ≥ 0 specifying the length of the str (excluding the '\0') is returned

HEADER FILE string

This header file—not to be confused with the header file cstring—supplies a programmer-defined data type named string. Associated with the string type are a data type string::size_type and a named constant string::npos. These are defined as follows:

string::size_type	An unsigned integer type
string::npos	The maximum value of type string::size_type

The type **string** contains several functions for string manipulation. In addition to the string functions listed in Table 7-1, the following table describes additional string functions. In this table, we assume that strVar is a string variable and str is a string variable, a string constant, or a character array. The name of the function is shown in bold.

Expression	Effect
getline(istreamVar, strVar);	istreamVar is an input stream variable (of type istream or ifstream). Characters until the newline character are input from istreamVar and stored in strVar. (The newline character is read but not stored into strVar.) The value returned by this function is usually ignored.
strVar.**append**(str, n)	The first n characters of the character array str are appended to strVar.
strVar.**c_str**()	The base address of a null-terminated C-string corresponding to the characters in strVar.

Expression	Effect
strVar.**capacity**()	Returns the size of the storage allocated for strVar.
strVar.**erase**(pos);	pos is a parameter of type string::size_type. Removes all of the characters from strVar starting at index pos.
strVar.**resize**(n, ch);	Changes the size of storage allocation for strVar to n. If n is less than the current storage size of strVar, the storage size of the string is truncated to n. If n is greater than the current storage size, the string is expanded to size n and the additional space is filled with copies of the character specified by the char variable ch.

A program similar to the following prints the memory size of the built-in data types on your system. (The output of the program shows the size of the built-in data type on which this program was run.)

```cpp
#include <iostream>

using namespace std;

int main()
{
    cout << "Size of char = " << sizeof(char) << endl;
    cout << "Size of int = " << sizeof(int) << endl;
    cout << "Size of short = " << sizeof(short) << endl;
    cout << "Size of unsigned int = " << sizeof(unsigned int) << endl;
    cout << "Size of long = " << sizeof(long) << endl;
    cout << "Size of long long = " << sizeof(long long) << endl;
    cout << "Size of bool = " << sizeof(bool) << endl;
    cout << "Size of float = " << sizeof(float) << endl;
    cout << "Size of double = " << sizeof(double) << endl;
    cout << "Size of long double = " << sizeof(long double) << endl;
    cout << "Size of unsigned short = "
         << sizeof(unsigned short) << endl;
    cout << "Size of unsigned long = "
         << sizeof(unsigned long) << endl;

    return 0;
}
```

Sample Run:

```
Size of char = 1
Size of int = 4
Size of short = 2
Size of unsigned int = 4
Size of long = 4
Size of long long = 8
Size of bool = 1
Size of float = 4
Size of double = 8
Size of long double = 8
Size of unsigned short = 2
Size of unsigned long = 4
```

Random Number Generator

To generate a random number, you can use the C++ function `rand`. To use the function `rand`, the program must include the header file `cstdlib`. The header file `cstdlib` also contains the constant RAND_MAX. Typically, the value of RAND_MAX is 32767. To find the exact value of RAND_MAX, check your system's documentation. The function `rand` generates an integer between 0 and RAND_MAX. The following program illustrates how to use the function `rand`. It also prints the value of RAND_MAX:

```cpp
#include <iostream>
#include <cstdlib>
#include <iomanip>

using namespace std;

int main()
{
    cout << fixed << showpoint << setprecision(5);
      cout << "The value of RAND_MAX: " << RAND_MAX << endl;
    cout << "A random number: " << rand() << endl;
    cout << "A random number between 0 and 9: "
         << rand() % 10 << endl;
    cout << "A random number between 0 and 1: "
         << static_cast<double> (rand())
             / static_cast<double>(RAND_MAX)
         << endl;

    return 0;
}
```

Sample Run:

```
The value of RAND_MAX: 32767
A random number: 41
A random number between 0 and 9: 7
A random number between 0 and 1: 0.19330
```

1. G. Booch, *Object-Oriented Analysis and Design*, 2nd ed., Addison-Wesley, 1995.
2. E. Horowitz, S. Sahni, and S. Rajasekaran, *Computer Algorithms C++*, Computer Science Press, 1997.
3. N.M. Josuttis, *The C++ Standard Library: A Tutorial and Reference*, Addison-Wesley, Reading, MA, 1999.
4. D.E. Knuth, *The Art of Computer Programming, Volume 1: Fundamental Algorithms*, 3rd ed., Addison-Wesley, Reading, MA, 1997.
5. D.E. Knuth, *The Art of Computer Programming, Volume 2: Seminumerical Algorithms*, 3rd ed., Addison-Wesley, Reading, MA, 1998.
6. D.E. Knuth, *The Art of Computer Programming, Volume 3: Searching and Sorting*, 2nd ed., Addison-Wesley, Reading, MA, 1998.
7. S.B. Lippman and J. Lajoie, *C++ Primer*, 3rd ed., Addison-Wesley, Reading, MA, 1998.
8. D.S. Malik and M.K. Sen, *Discrete Mathematics: Theory and Applications (Revised Edition)*, Cengage Learning Asia, Singapore, 2010.
9. E.M. Reingold and W.J. Hensen, *Data Structures in Pascal*, Little Brown and Company, Boston, MA, 1986.
10. R. Sedgewick, *Algorithms in C*, 3rd ed., Addison-Wesley, Reading, MA, Parts 1-4, 1998; Part 5, 2002.
11. B. Stroustrup, *The Design and Evolution of C++*, Addison-Wesley, Reading, MA, 1994.

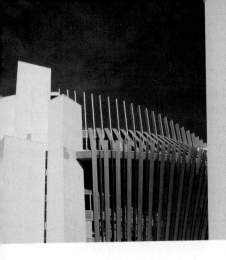

ANSWERS TO ODD-NUMBERED EXERCISES

Chapter 1

1. a. false; b. false; c. true; d. false; e. false; f; false; g. false; h. true; i. true; j. false; k. true; l. false

3. Central processing unit (CPU), main memory (MM), and input/output devices.

5. An operating system monitors the overall activity of the computer and provides services. Some of these services include memory management, input/output activities, and storage management.

7. In machine language, the programs are written using the binary codes, whereas in high-level language, the programs are closer to the natural language. For execution, a high-level language program is translated into machine language, whereas a machine language need not be translated into any other language.

9. Because the computer cannot directly execute instructions written in a high-level language, a compiler is needed to translate a program written in high-level language into machine code.

11. Every computer directly understands its own machine language. Therefore, for the computer to execute a program written in a high-level language, the high-level language program must be translated into the computer's machine language.

13. In linking, an object program is combined with other programs in the library used in the program to create the executable code.

15. To find the weighted average of the four test scores, first you need to know each test score and its weight. Next, you multiply each test score with its weight and then add these numbers to get the average. Therefore:

    1. Get `testScore1, weightTestScore1`

    2. Get `testScore2, weightTestScore2`

    3. Get `testScore3, weightTestScore3`

    4. Get `testScore4, weightTestScore4`

    5. ```
       weightedAverage = testScore1 * weightTestScore1 +
                         testScore2 * weightTestScore2 +
                         testScore3 * weightTestScore3 +
                         testScore4 * weightTestScore4;
       ```
       ```

17. To find the price per square inch, first we need to find the area of the pizza. Then we divide the price of the pizza by the area of the pizza. Let `radius` denote the radius, `area` denote the area of the circle, and `price` denote the price of the pizza. Also, let `pricePerSquareInch` denote the price per square inch.

   a.   Get `radius`

   b.   `area = π * radius * radius`

   c.   Get `price`

   d.   `pricePerSquareInch = price / area`

19. To calculate the area of a triangle using the given formula, we need to know the lengths of the sides—a, b, and c—of the triangle. Next, we calculate `s` using the formula:

   `s = (1/2)(a + b + c)`

and then calculate the area using the formula:

   `area = sqrt(s(s-a)(s-b)(s-c))`

where `sqrt` denotes the square root.

The algorithm, therefore, is:

   a.   Get a, b, c

   b.   `s = (1/2)(a + b + c)`

   c.   `area = sqrt(s(s-a)(s-b)(s-c))`

The information needed to calculate the area of the triangle is the lengths of the sides of the triangle.

21. Suppose that `numOfPages` denotes the number of pages to be faxed, and `billingAmount` denotes the total charges for the pages faxed. To calculate the total charges, you need to know the number of pages faxed.

If `numOfPages` is less than or equal to 10, the billing amount is service charges + (`numOfPages` × 0.20); otherwise, billing amount is service charges + 10 × 0.20 + (`numOfPages` − 10) × 0.10. That is,

   You can now write the algorithm as follows:

   a.   Get `numOfPages`.

   b.   Calculate billing amount using the formula:

```
if (numOfPages is less than or equal to 10)

    billingAmount = 3.00 + (numOfPages × 0.20);

otherwise

    billingAmount = 3.00 + 10 × 0.20 + (numOfPages - 10) × 0.10;
```

23. Suppose `averageTestScore` denotes the average test score, `highestScore` denotes the highest test score, `testScore` denotes a test score, `sum` denotes the sum of all of the test scores, `count` denotes the number of students in class, and `studentName` denotes the name of a student.

    a. First, you design an algorithm to find the average test score. To find the average test score, first you need to count the number of students in the class and add the test score of each student. You then divide the sum by count to find the average test score. The algorithm to find the average test score is as follows:

        i. Set `sum` and `count` to 0.

        ii. Repeat the following for each student in class.

            1. Get `testScore`

            2. Increment `count` and update the value of `sum` by adding the current test score to `sum`.

        iii. Use the following formula to find the average test score:

```
if (count is 0)
    averageTestScore = 0;
otherwise
    averageTestScore = sum / count;
```

    b. The following algorithm determines and prints the names of all of the students whose test score is below the average test score.

Repeat the following for each student in class:

        i. Get `studentName` and `testScore`

        ii. `if (testScore is less than averageTestScore)`
            `print studentName`

    c. The following algorithm determines the highest test score.

        i. Get first student's test score and call it `highestTestScore`.

        ii. Repeat the following for each of the remaining students in class:

            1. Get `testScore`

            2. `if (testScore is greater than highestTestScore)`
                `highestTestScore = testScore;`

    d. To print the names of all of the students whose test score is the same as the highest test score, compare the test score of each student with the highest test score, and if they are equal, print the name. The following algorithm accomplishes this. Repeat the following for each student in class:

        i. Get `studentName` and `testScore`

        ii. `if (testScore is equal to highestTestScore)`
            `print studentName`

You can use the solutions of the subproblems obtained in parts a through d to design the main algorithm as follows:

1. Use the algorithm in part a to find the average test score.
2. Use the algorithm in part b to print the names of all of the students whose score is below the average test score.
3. Use the algorithm in part c to find the highest test score.
4. Use the algorithm in part d to print the names of all of the students whose test score is the same as the highest test score.

Chapter 2

1. a. false; b. false; c. false; d. true; e. true; f. false; g. true; h. true; i. false; j. true; k. false
3. b, d, e
5. The identifiers `firstName` and `FirstName` are not the same. C++ is case sensitive. The first letter of `firstName` is lowercase `f`, whereas the first character of `FirstName` is uppercase `F`. So these identifiers are different.
7. a. 3
    b. Not possible. Both of the operands of the operator `%` must be integers. Because the second operand, `w`, is a floating-point value, the expression is invalid.
    c. Not possible. Both of the operands of the operator `%` must be integers. Because the first operand, which is `y + w`, is a floating-point value, the expression is invalid.
    d. `38.5`
    e. `1`
    f. `2`
    g. `2`
    h. `420.0`
9. 7
11. a and c are valid.
13. a. `32 * a + b`
    b. `'8'`
    c. `"Julie Nelson"`
    d. `(b * b - 4 * a * c) / (2 * a)`
    e. `(a + b) / c * (e * f) - g * h`
    f. `(-b + (b * b - 4 * a * c)) / (2 * a)`
15. `x = 28`
    `y = 35`
    `z = 1`
    `w = 22.00`
    `t = 6.5`
17. a. `0.50`; b. `24.50`; c. `37.6`; d. `8.3`; e. `10`; f. `38.75`

19. a and c are correct.

21. a. ```
    int num1;
    int num2;
    ```

    b. `cout << "Enter two numbers separated by spaces." << endl;`

    c. `cin >> num1 >> num2;`

    d. ```
    cout << "num1 = " << num1 << "num2 = " << num2
         << "2 * num1 - num2 = " << 2 * num1 - num2 << endl;
    ```

23. A correct answer is:
```cpp
#include <iostream>

using namespace std;

const char STAR = '*';
const int PRIME = 71;

int main()
{
   int count, sum;
   double x;

   int newNum;     //declare newNum

   count = 1;
   sum = count + PRIME;
   x = 25.67;      // x = 25.67;
   newNum = count * 1 + 2; //newNum = count * ONE + 2;
   sum = sum + count;    //sum + count = sum;
   x = x + sum * count; // x = x + sum * COUNT;
   cout << " count = " << count << ", sum = " << sum
        << ", PRIME = " << PRIME << endl;
   return 0;
}
```

25. An identifier must be declared before it can be used.

27. a. `x *= 2;`

    b. `x += y - 2;`

    c. `sum += num;`

    d. `z *= x + 2;`

    e. `y /= x + 5;`

29.
```
                          a    b    c
a = (b++) + 3;            9    7    und
c = 2 * a + (++b);        9    8    26
b = 2 * (++c) - (a++);    10   45   27
```

31. (The user input is shaded.)

```
a = 25
Enter two integers : 20 15

The numbers you entered are 20 and 15
z = 45.5
Your grade is A
The value of a = 65
```

33.
```cpp
#include <iostream>
#include <string>

using namespace std;

const double X = 13.45;
const int Y = 34;
const char BLANK = ' ';

int main()
{
    string firstName, lastName;
    int num;
    double salary;

    cout << "Enter first name: ";
    cin >> firstName;
    cout << endl;

    cout << "Enter last name: ";
    cin >> lastName;
    cout << endl;

    cout << "Enter a positive integer less than 70: ";
    cin >> num;
    cout << endl;

    salary = num * X;

    cout << "Name: " << firstName << BLANK << lastName << endl;
    cout << "Wages: $" << salary << endl;
    cout << "X = " << X << endl;
    cout << "X + Y = " << X + Y << endl;

    return 0;
}
```

Chapter 3

1. a. true; b. true; c. false; d. false; e. true; f. true

3. a. $x = 37$, $y = 86$, $z = 0.56$

   b. $x = 37$, $y = 32$, $z = 86.56$

   c. Input failure: $z = 37.0$, $x = 86$, trying to read the . (period) into y.

5. Input failure: Trying to read A into y, which is an `int` variable. $x = 46$, $y = 18$, and $z = $ 'A'. The values of y and z are unchanged.

7. iomanip

9. cmath

11. To use the function `putback`, the program must include the header file `iomanip`. To use the function `peek`, the program must include the header file `iostream`.

13. `getline(cin, name);`

15. a. name = " Lance Grant", age = 23

    b. name = " ", age = 23

17.
```
#include <iostream>
#include <fstream>

using namespace std;

int main()
{
    int num1, num2;
    ifstream infile;
    ostream outfile;

    infile.open("input.dat");
    outfile.open("output.dat");

    infile >> num1 >> num2;
    outfile << "Sum = " << num1 + num2 << endl;

    infile.close();
    outfile.close();

    return 0;
}
```

19. fstream

21. a. Same as before.

    b. The file contains the output produced by the program.

    c. The file contains the output produced by the program. The old contents are erased.

    d. The program would prepare the file and store the output in the file.

23. a. `outfile.open("travel.dat ");`

    b. `outfile >> fixed >> showpoint >> setprecision(2);`

    c. `outfile >> day >> " " >> distance >> " " >> speed >> endl;`

    d. `travelTime = distance / speed;`
       `outfile >> travelTime;`

    e. fstream and iomanip.

Chapter 4

1. a. false; b. false; c. false; d. true; e. false; f. false; g. false; h. false; i. false; j. true

3. a. true; b. false; c. true; d. true; e. false

5. a. `x = y: 0`

    b. `x != z: 1`

    c. `y == z - 3: 1`

    d. `!(z > w) : 0`

    e. `x + y < z: 0`

7. a. `%%`

    b. `10 2 * 5`

    c. `A`

    d. `C--`

    e. `Sam Tom`

        `Tom Sam`

    f. `-6`

        `**`

9. a. `R&`

    b. `1 2 3 4`

        `$$`

    c. `Jack Accounting`

        `John Business`

11. `The value of found is: 1`

13. Omit the semicolon after `else`. The correct statement is:
    ```
    if (score >= 60)
        cout << "You pass." << endl;
    else
        cout << "You fail." << endl;
    ```

15. The correct code is:

    ```
    if (0 < numOfItemsBought && numOfItemsBought < 5)
        shippingCharges = 5.00 * numOfItemsBought;
    else if (5 <= numOfItemsBought && numOfItemsBought < 10)
        shippingCharges = 2.00 * numOfItemsBought;
    else
        shippingCharges = 0.0;
    ```

17. `3 1`

19. ```
    if (sale > 20000)
        bonus = 0.10
    else if (sale > 10000 && sale <= 20000)
        bonus = 0.05;
    else
        bonus = 0.0;
    ```

21. a. The output is: `Discount = 10%`. The semicolon at the end of the `if` statement terminates the `if` statement. So the `cout` statement is not part of the `if` statement. The `cout` statement will execute regardless of whether the expression in the `if` statement evaluates to `true` or `false`.
    ```

b. The output is: `Discount = 10%`. The semicolon at the end of the `if` statement terminates the `if` statement. So the `cout` statement is not part of the `if` statement. The `cout` statement will execute regardless of whether the expression in the `if` statement evaluates to `true` or `false`.

23. a. `(x >= y) ? z = x - y : z = y - x;`

    b. `(hours >= 40.0) ? wages = 40 * 7.50 + 1.5 * 7.5 * (hours - 40)` `: wages = hours * 7.50;`

    c. `(score >= 60) ? str = "Pass" : str = "Fail";`

25. a. `40.00`

    b. `40.00`

    c. `55.00`

27. a. `16`   b. `3`   c. `18`   d. `23`

29. a. `3`   b. `-20`   c. `3`   d. `5`

31.
```
#include <iostream>

using namespace std;
const int SECRET = 5;

int main()
{
    int x, y, w, z;

    z = 9;

    if (z > 10)
    {
        x = 12;
        y = 5;
        w = x + y + SECRET;
    }
    else
    {
        x = 12;
        y = 4;
        w = x + y + SECRET;
    }

    cout << "w = " << w << endl;

    return 0;
}
```

33.
```
switch (classStanding)
{
case 'f':
    dues = 150.00;
    break;
```

```
case 's':
    if (gpa >= 3.75)
        dues = 75.00;
    else
        dues = 120.00;
        break;
case 'j':
    if (gpa >= 3.75)
        dues = 50.00;
    else
        dues = 100.00;
    break;
case 'n':
    if (gpa >= 3.75)
        dues = 25.00;
    else
        dues = 75.00;
    break;
default:
    cout << "Invalid class standing code." << endl;
}
```

Chapter 5

1. a. false; b. true; c. false; d. true; e. true; f. true; g. true; h. false

3. 181.00

5. if ch > 'Z' or ch < 'A'

7. Sum = 94

9. Sum = 37

11. a. 29

    b. 2 8

    c. 8 13 21 34

    d. The value of num1 + num2 becomes larger than the largest int value and the value of temp overflows its memory space. Some of the values output by the program are: 4 7 11 18 29 47 76 123 199 322 521 843 1364 2207 3571 5778 9349 15127 24476 39603 64079 103682 167761 271443 439204 710647 1149851 1860498 3010349 4870847 7881196 12752043 20633239 33385282 54018521 87403803 141422324 228826127 370248451 599074578 969323029 1568397607

13. Replace the while loop statement with the following:

    while (response == 'Y' || response == 'y')

    Replace the cout statement:

    ```
    cout << num1 << " + " << num2 << " = " << (num1 - num2)
        << endl;
    ```

with the following:

```
cout << num1 << " + " << num2 << " = " << (num1 + num2)
     << endl;
```

15. 4 3 2 1

17. 0 3 8 15 24

19. Loop control variable: j

The initialization statement: j = 1;

Loop condition: j <= 10;

Update statement: j++

The statement that updates the value of s: s = s + j * (j - 1);

21. -1 1 3 5 7 6

23. a. *

b. infinite loop

c. infinite loop

d. ****

e. ******

f. ***

25. The relationship between x and y is: $3^y = x$.

Output: x = 19683, y = 10

27.
```
0 - 24
25 - 49
50 - 74
75 - 99
100 - 124
125 - 149
150 - 174
175 - 200
```

29. a. both

b. do ... while

c. while

d. while

31. In a pretest loop, the loop condition is evaluated before executing the body of the loop. In a posttest loop, the loop condition is evaluated after executing the body of the loop. A posttest loop executes at least once, whereas a pretest loop may not execute at all.

33.
```
int num;
do
{
    cout << "Enter a number less than 20 or greater than 75: ";
    cin >> num;
}
while (20 <= num && num <= 75);
```

35.
```
int i = 0, value = 0;
do
{
    if (i % 2 == 0 && i <= 10)
        value = value + i * i;
    else if (i % 2 == 0 && i > 10)
        value = value + i;
    else
        value = value - i;
    i = i + 1;
}
while (i <= 20);

cout << "value = " << value << endl;
```

The Output is: Value = 200

37.
```
cin >> number;
while (number != -1)
{
    total = total + number;
    cin >> number;
}
cout << endl;
cout << total << endl;
```

39. a.
```
number = 1;
while (number <= 10)
{
    cout << setw(3) << number;
    number++;
}
```

b.
```
number = 1;
do
{
    cout << setw(3) << number;
    number++;
}
while (number <= 10);
```

41. a. 29

b. 2 8

c. 8 13 21 34

d. 28 43 71 114

43. −1 0 3 8 15 24

45. 12 11 9 7 6 4 2 1

Chapter 6

1. a. false; b. true; c. true; d. true; e. false; f. true; g. false; h. true; i. false; j. true; k. false; l. false; m. false; n. true

3. a. `12` b. `23.45` c. `7.8` d. `23.04` e. `32.00`
   f. `7.0` g. `2.7` h. `6.0` i. `36.00` j. `19.00`

5. (ii) and (iii)

7. a, b, c, d, e are valid. In f, the second argument in the function call is missing. In g and h, the function call requires one more argument.

9. a. 2; `int`

   b. 3; `double`

   c. 4; `char`

   d. 2; `string`

   e. The function `func1` requires 2 actual parameters. The type and the order of these parameters is: `int, double`

   f. `cout << func1(3, 8.5) << endl;`.

   g. `cout << join("John", "Project Manager") << endl;`

   h. `cout << static_cast<char>(static_cast<int>`
      `(three(4, 3, 'A', 17.6)) + 1) << endl;`

11. ```
    bool isUppercaseLetter(char ch)
    {
        if (isupper(ch))
            return true;
        else
            return false;
    }
    ```

13. a. (i) 45 (ii) 30

    b. The function computes $(k - 1) * k * m / 2$, where m and n are the arguments of the function and $k = \text{abs}(n)$.

15. a. 385

    b. This function computes 1+4+9+16+25+36+49+64+81+100

17. ```
    double funcEx17(double x, double y, double z)
    {
        return x * pow(y, z);
    }
    ```

19. a. In a void function, a return statement is used without any value such as `return;`.

    b. In a void function, a return statement is used to exit the function early.

21. a. A variable declared in the heading of a function definition is called a formal parameter. A variable or expression used in a function call is called an actual parameter.

    b. A value parameter receives a copy of the actual parameter's data. A reference parameter receives the address of the actual parameter.

    c. A variable declared within a function or block is called a local variable. A variable declared outside of every function definition is called a global variable.

23.
```
void funcThreeTimes (double x)
{
  cout << fixed << showpoint << setprecision (2);
  cout << 3 * x << endl;
}
```

25.
```
void initialize (int& x, double& y, string& str)
{
    x = 0;
    y = 0;
    str = "";
}
```

27.
```
5, 10, 15
20, 10, 15
25, 30, 15
45, 30, 60
```

29.
```
#include <iostream>

using namespace std;

int secret (int, int);

void func (int x, int& y);

int main ()
{
     int num1, num2;

1    num1 = 6;

2        cout << "Enter a positive integer: ";
3        cin >> num2;
4        cout << endl;
8        cout << secret (num1, num2) << endl;
9        num2 = num2 - num1;
10       cout << num1 << " " << num2 << endl;
15       func (num2, num1);
16       cout << num1 << " " << num2 << endl;

17       return 0;
     }
```

```
    int secret(int a, int b)
    {
         int d;

  5      d = a + b;
  6      b = a * d;

  7      return b;
    }

    void func (int x, int& y)
    {
         int val1, val2;

 11      val1 = x + y;
 12      val2 = x * y;
 13      y = val1 + val2;
 14      cout << val1 << " " << val2 << endl;
    }
```

If the input is 10, the output is:

```
96
6 4
10 24
34 4
```

31.
```
void traceMe (double& x, double y, double& z)
{
    if (x != 0)
        z = sqrt (y) / x;
    else
    {
        cout << "Enter a nonzero number: ";
        cin >> x;
        cout << endl;
        z = floor (pow (y, x));
    }
}
```

33. 10 20
    5 20

35. 11, 3
    16, 2
    19, 3
    24, 2

37. a, b, c, and e are correct.

Chapter 7

1. a. true; b. false; c. true; d. false; e. false; f. true; g. true; h. true; i. false; j. false; k. false

3. Only a and c are valid.

5.
```
courseType readIn()
{
    string course;

    cin >> course;

    if (course == "Algebra")
        class = ALGEBRA;
    else if (course == "Beginning Spanish")
        class = BEGINNING_SPANISH;
    else if (course == "Astronomy")
        class == ASTRONOMY;
    else if (course == "General Chemistry")
        class = GENERAL_CHEMISTRY;
    else if (course == "Physics")
        class = PHYSICS;
    else if (course == "Logic")
        class = LOGIC;
    else
        cout << "Invalid course" << endl;

    return course;
}
```

7. Because there is no name for an anonymous type, you cannot pass an anonymous type as a parameter to a function and a function cannot return an anonymous type value. Also, values used in one anonymous type can be used in another anonymous type, but variables of those types are treated differently.

9. The statement in Line 2 should be:

```
using namespace std;                              //Line 2
```

11. The statement in Line 2 should be:

```
using namespace std;                              //Line 2
```

13. Either include the statement:

```
using namespace aaa;
```

before the function `main` or refer to the identifiers `x` and `y` in `main` as `aaa::x` and `aaa::y`, respectively.

15. a. Heelo Thlre
    b. Giamond Dold
    c. Ca+ J+va

17. Summer or Fall Trip to Hawaii
    Trip to Hawaii in Summer or Fall
    29
    8
    7
    Fall Trip to Hawaii
    Summer or Fall Trip to ******
    C++ Programming
    15
    J+$ Programming

Chapter 8

1. a. true; b. true; c. false; d. false; e. true; f. false; g. false; h. false; i. true; j. false; k. false; l. false

3. a. This declaration is correct.
   b. The statement should be: `int age[80];`.
   c. This declaration is correct.
   d. The statement should be: `int list[100];`.
   e. The statement should be: `double salaries[50];`.
   f. The const declaration should be: `const double LENGTH = 30;`.
   g. This declaration is correct.

5. 0 to 63

7. 2.00 3.00 6.00 11.00 18.00
   27.00 12.00 22.00 11.00 18.00

9. 2 3 5 8 13 21 34 55 144 343

11. `int myList[10];`

    ```
    for (int i = 0; i < 10; i++)
        myList[i] = [i];
    ```

13. If array index is less than 0 or greater than `arraySize − 1`, we say that the array index is out of bounds. C++ does not check for array indices within bound.

15. a. `double heights[10] = { 5.2, 6.3, 5.8, 4.9, 5.2, 5.7, 6.7, 7.1, 5.10, 6.0};`
       or
       `double heights[] = { 5.2, 6.3, 5.8, 4.9, 5.2, 5.7, 6.7, 7.1, 5.10, 6.0};`
    b. `int weights[7] = { 120, 125, 137, 140, 150, 180, 210};`
       or
       `int weights[] = { 120, 125, 137, 140, 150, 180, 210};`
    c. `char specialSymbols[] = { '$ ', '# ', '% ', '@ ', '& ', '! ', '^ '};`
    d. `string seasons[4] = { "fall", "winter", "spring", "summer"};`
       or
       `string seasons[] = { "fall", "winter", "spring", "summer"};`

17. list[0] = 6, list[1] = 10, list[2] = 14, list[3] = 18, list[4] = 22, list[5] = 0, list[6] = 0.

19. 16 32 44 56 68 37 20

21.   a. Correct.
      b. Correct.
      c. Incorrect. The size of score is 50, so the call should be tryMe(score, 50);.
      d. Correct.
      e. Incorrect. The array gpa is of type double, whereas the parameter x of tryMe is of type int. So there will be a mismatch data type error.

23.   1 25000.00 750.00

      2 36500.00 1095.00

      3 85000.00 2550.00

      4 62500.00 1875.00

      5 97000.00 2910.00

25.   List elements: 11 16 21 26 30

27.   1 3.50 10.70 235.31

      2 7.20 6.50 294.05

      3 10.50 12.00 791.68

      4 9.80 10.50 646.54

      5 6.50 8.00 326.73

29.   No.

31.   List before the first iteration: 36, 55, 17, 35, 63, 85, 12, 48, 3, 66
      List after the first iteration: 3, 55, 17, 35, 63, 85, 12, 48, 36, 66
      List after the second iteration: 3, 12, 17, 35, 63, 85, 55, 48, 36, 66
      List after the third iteration: 3, 12, 17, 35, 63, 85, 55, 48, 36, 66
      List after the fourth iteration: 3, 12, 17, 35, 63, 85, 55, 48, 36, 66
      List after the fifth iteration: 3, 12, 17, 35, 36, 85, 55, 48, 63, 66
      List after the sixth iteration: 3, 12, 17, 35, 36, 48, 55, 85, 63, 66
      List after the seventh iteration: 3, 12, 17, 35, 36, 48, 55, 85, 63, 66
      List after the eighth iteration: 3, 12, 17, 35, 36, 48, 55, 63, 85, 66
      List after the ninth iteration: 3, 12, 17, 35, 36, 48, 55, 63, 66, 85

33.   a. Invalid; the assignment operator is not defined for C-strings.
      b. Invalid; the relational operators are not defined for C-strings.
      c. Invalid; the assignment operator is not defined for C-strings.
      d. Valid

35.   a. strcpy(str1, "Sunny Day");
      b. length = strlen(str1);
      c. strcpy(str2, name);

    d. `if (strcmp(str1, str2) <= 0)`
           `cout << str1 << endl;`
      `else`
           `cout << str2 << endl;`

37. `int temp[3][4] = {{ 6, 8, 12, 9},`
                    `{7, 5, 10, 6},`
                    `{4, 13, 16, 20}};`

39. a. 30; b. 5; c. 6; d. row; e. column

41. a. beta is initialized to 0.

    b. `First row of beta: 0 1 2`
       `Second row of beta: 1 2 3`
       `Third row of beta: 2 3 4`

    c. `First row of beta: 0 0 0`
       `Second row of beta: 0 1 2`
       `Third row of beta: 0 2 4`

    d. `First row of beta: 0 2 0`
       `Second row of beta: 2 0 2`
       `Third row of beta: 0 2 0`

Chapter 9

1. a. false; b. false; c. true; d. true; e. true; f. true; g. false

3. `carType newCar;`

   `newCar.manufacturer = "GMT";`
   `newCar.model = " Cyclone";`
   `newCar.modelType = "sedan";`
   `newCar.color = "blue"`
   `newCar.numOfDoors = 4;`
   `newCar.cityMilesPerGallon = 28;`
   `newCar.highwayMilesPerGallon = 32;`
   `newCar.yearBuilt = 2006;`
   `newCar.price = 25000.00;`

5. `fruitType fruit;`

   `fruit.name = "banana";`
   `fruit.color = "yellow";`
   `fruit.fat = 1;`
   `fruit.sugar = 15;`
   `fruit.carbohydrate = 22;`

7. `student.name.first = "Linda";`
   `student.name.last = "Brown";`
   `student.gpa = 3.78;`
   `student.course.name: "Calculus";`
   `student.course.callNum = 23827;`
   `student.course.credits = 4;`
   `student.course.grade = 'A';`

9. a. Invalid; the member `name` of `newEmployee` is a **struct**. Specify the member names to store the value `"John Smith"`. For example:

```
newEmployee.name.first = "John";
newEmployee.name.last = "Smith";
```

b. Invalid; the member `name` of `newEmployee` is a **struct**. There are no aggregate output operations on a **struct**. A correct statement is:

```
cout << newEmployee.name.first << " "
     << newEmployee.name.last << endl;
```

c. Valid

d. Valid

e. Invalid; `employees` is an array. There are no aggregate assignment operations on arrays.

11. `partsType inventory [100];`

13.
```
void getData (partsType& pType)
{
    for (int j = 0; j < length; j++)
    {
        cin >> pType.partName;
        cin >> pType.partNum;
        cin >> pType.price;
        cin >> pType.quantitiesInStock;
    }
}


for (int j = 0; j < 100; j++)
    getData (inventory [i]);
```

Chapter 10

1. a. false; b. false; c. true; d. false; e. false

3. The type of the function `print` is missing. The statement in Line 5 should be:

```
void print () const;                        //Line 5
```

5. The semicolon after `public` should be a colon, there is a missing semicolon after `}`, and a constructor has no type. The statements in Lines 3, 8, and 13 should be:

```
public:                                 //Line 3

discover(string, int, int);     //Line 8

};                                      //Line 13
```

7. a.
```
void bagType::set(string s, double a, double b, double c, double d)
{
    style = s;
    l = a;
    w = b;
    h = c;
    price = d;
}
```

   b.
```
void bagType::print() const
{
    cout << "Bag Type: " << style << ", length = " << l
         << ", width = " << w << ", height = " << h
         << ", price = $ " << price << endl;
}
```

   c.
```
bagType::bagType()
{
    style = "";
    l = 0.0;
    w = 0.0;
    h = 0.0;
    price = 0.0;
}
```

   d. `newBag.print();`

   e. `bagType tempBag("backPack", 15, 8, 20, 49.99);`

9. The functions `print`, `updatePay`, and `getNumOfServiceYears` are accessors; functions `setData` and `updatePay` are mutators.

11. a. 14

    b. 3

    c. The `class` temporary has only one constructor. Because this is a constructor with default parameters, it can be used to initialize an object without specifying any parameters. For example, the following statement creates the object `newObject` and its instance variables are initialized to `" "`, 0, and 0, respectively.
    `temporary newObject;`

13. The statement in Line 1 creates `object1` and initializes the instance variables of this object to `" "`, 0, 0, that is, `object1.description = " ";`, `object1.first = 0.0;`, and `object1.second = 0.0;`. The statement in Line 2 creates `object2` and initializes the instance variables of this object as follows: `object2.description = "rectangle";`, `object2.first = 3.0;`, and `object2.second = 5.0;`. The statement in Line 3 creates `object3` and initializes the instance variables of this object as follows: `object3.description = "circle";`, `object3.first = 6.5;`, and `object3.second = 0.0;`. The statement in Line 4 creates `object4` and

initializes the instance variables of this object as follows: `object4.description = "cylinder";`, `object4.first = 6.0;`, and `object4.second = 3.5;`.

15. There are two built-in operations for class objects: Member access (.) and assignment (=).

17. a.
```cpp
int testClass::sum()
{
     return x + y;
}

void testClass::print() const
{
     cout << "x = " << x << ", y = " << y << endl;
}

testClass::testClass()
{
     x = 0;
     y = 0;
}

testClass::testClass(int a, int b)
{
     x = a;
     y = b;
}
```

b. One possible solution. (We assume that the name of the header file containing the definition of the **class** `testClass` is `Exercise17Ch10.h`.)

```cpp
#include <iostream>
#include "Exercise17Ch10.h"

int main()
{
     testClass one;
     testClass two(4, 5);

     one.print();
     two.print();

     return 0;
}
```

19. a. `personType student("Buddy", "Arora");`

   b. `student.print();`

   c. `student.setName("Susan", "Gilbert");`

21. A constructor is a member of a class, and it executes automatically when a class object is instantiated and a call to the constructor is specified in the object declaration. A constructor is included in a class so that the objects are properly initialized when they are declared.

23. A destructor is a member of a class, and if it is included in a class, it executes automatically when a class object goes out of scope. Its main purpose is to deallocate the dynamic memory created by an object.

25. a. `myClass::count = 0;`

b. `myClass.incrementCount();`

c. `myClass.printCount();`

d. `int myClass::count = 0;`

```
void myClass::setX(int a)
{
    x = a;
}

void myClass::printX() const
{
    cout << x;
}

void myClass::printCount()
{
    cout << count;
}

void myClass::incrementCount()
{
    count++;
}

myClass::myClass(int a)
{
    x = a;
}
```

e. `myClass myObject1(5);`

f. `myClass myObject2(7);`

g. The statements in Lines 1 and 2 are valid.

The statement in Line 3 should be: `myClass::printCount();`.

The statement in Line 4 is invalid because the member function `printX` is not a `static` member of the class, and so cannot be called by using the name of class.

The statement in Line 5 is invalid because `count` is a `private static` member variable of the class.

h. 5
2
2
3
14
3
3

Chapter 11

1. a. true; b. true; c. true

3. Some of the member variables that can be added to the `class employeeType` are: department, salary, employeeCategory (such as supervisor and president), and employeeID. Some of the member functions are: setInfo, setSalary, getSalary, setDepartment, getDepartment, setCategory, getCategory, setID, and getID.

```cpp
class employeeType: public personType
{
public:
    void setInfo(string, string, string, double, string, string);
    void setSalary(double);
    void setDepartment(string);
    void setCategory(string);
    void setID(string);
    double getSalary() const;
    string getDepartment(string) const;
    string getCategory() const;
    string getID() const;

private:
    string department;
    double salary;
    string employeeCategory;
    string employeeID;
};
```

5. a. The base class is `atom` and the derived class is `molecules`.

   b. This is a private inheritance.

7. Private members of the object `newCylinder` are `xCoordinate`, `yCoordinate`, `radius`, and `height`.

9. Missing : in the first statement. The first statement should be:

```cpp
class derivedFromTemp: public temp
```

Also missing ; after }. It should be

```cpp
};
```

11. a. `void print() const;`

    b. `void set(int, int, int);`
       `void get(int&, int&, int&);`

13. First a constructor of `class one` will execute, then a constructor of `class two` will execute, and finally a constructor of `class three` will execute.

15. a. Invalid. `z` is an instance variable of the derived class, it cannot be accessed by the members of the `class` smart.

  b. Invalid. `secret` is a private member of the `class` smart. It cannot be accessed directly outside of the class. Also `z` is a private member of the `class` superSmart. It cannot be accessed directly outside of the class.

  c. Valid

  d. Invalid. `smart` is the name of a class, not an object of this class. It cannot be used to call its member function `print`.

  e. Invalid. `superSmart` is the name of a class. It cannot be used to access its members.

17. In a `private` inheritance, the `public` members of the base class are `private` members of the derived class. They can be accessed by the member functions (and `friend` functions) of the derived class. The `protected` members of the base class are `private` members of the derived class. They can be accessed by the member functions (and `friend` functions) of the derived class. The `private` members of the base class are hidden in the derived class. They cannot be directly accessed in the derived class. They can be accessed by the member functions (and `friend` functions) of the derived class through the `public` or `protected` members of the base class.

19. In a `public` inheritance, the `public` members of the base class are `public` members of the derived class. They can be directly accessed in the derived class. The `protected` members of the base class are `protected` members of the derived class. They can be directly accessed by the member functions (and `friend` functions) of the derived class. The `private` members of the base class are hidden in the derived class. They cannot be directly accessed in the derived class. They can be accessed by the member functions (and `friend` functions) of the derived class through the `public` or `protected` members of the base class.

21. The `protected` members of a base class can be directly accessed by the member functions of the derived class, but they cannot be directly accessed in a program that uses that class. The `public` members of a class can be directly accessed by the member functions of any derived class as well as in a program that uses that class.

23. The members setX, print, y, and setY are `protected` members in `class` third. The `private` member x of `class` first is hidden in `class` third, and it can be accessed in `class` third only through the `protected` and `public` members of `class` first.

25. Because the `memberAccessSpecifier` is not specified, it is a private inheritance. Therefore, all of the members of the `class` first become `private` members in `class` fifth.

27. a.
```
void two::setData(int a, int b, int c)
{
    one::setData(a, b);
    z = c;
}
```
b.
```
void two::print() const
{
    one::print();
    cout << z << endl;
}
```

Chapter 12

1. a. false; b. false; c. false; d. true; e. true; f. true; g. false; h. false

3. The operator * is used to declare a pointer variable and to access the memory space to which a pointer variable points.

5. *numPtr gives the address of the memory location to which numPtr points, while &numPtr gives the address of numPtr.

7.
```
numPtr = &num;
(*numPtr)++;
```

9. 47 47 73

11. 70 170

13. 90.00 86.00 88.00

15. In Line 6, the operator delete deallocates the memory space to which nextPtr points. So the expression *nextPtr, in Line 9, does not have a valid value.

17. 12 8 7 25 16 24 36

19. numPtr = 1058 and gpaPtr = 2024

21. The operator delete deallocates the memory space to which a pointer points.

23. a. `num = new int[10];`

    b.
```
for (int j = 0; j < 10; j++)
    cin >> num[j];
```

    c. `delete [] num;`

25. In a shallow copy of data, two or more pointers point to the same memory space. In a deep copy of data, each pointer has its own copy of the data.

27.
```
myList: 3 4 6 9 13
yourList: 7 8 10 13 17 10 6 3 1 0
```

29. The copy constructor makes a copy of the actual variable.

31. Classes with pointer data members should include the destructor, overload the assignment operator, and explicitly provide the copy constructor by including it in the class definition and providing its definition.

33. ClassA x: 4

    ClassA x: 6
    ClassB y: 10

35. Yes.

37. a. Because `employeeType` is an abstract class, you cannot instantiate an object of this class. Therefore, this statement is illegal.

    b. This statement is legal.

    c. This statement is legal.

Chapter 13

1. a. false; b. true; c. true; d. false; e. false; f. true; g. false; h. true; i. false; j. true; k. false

3. A `friend` function is a nonmember of a class, whereas a member function is a member of a class.

5. Because the left operand of `<<` is a stream object, which is not of the type `mystery`.

7. When the class has pointer data members.

9. a. `friend strange operator+(const strange&, const strange&);`

   b. `friend bool operator==(const strange&, const strange&);`

   c. `friend strange operator++(strange&, int);`

11. In Line 4, the return type of the function `operator*` should be `temp`. The correct statement is:

    `temp operator*(const temp& obj);`   `//Line 4`

13. In Line 3, the return type of the function `operator<` should be `bool`. The correct statement is:

    `friend bool operator<(const mystery& a,`
    `                      const mystery& b);`   `//Line 3`

15. In Lines 3 and 11, the return type of the function `operator+` should be `discover`. Also since `operator+` is a friend function of the class, the name of the class and the scope resolution operator in the heading of the function, in Line 11, are not needed. The correct statements are:

    `friend discover operator+(const discover&,`
    `                          const discover&);`   `//Line 3`

    `discover operator+(const discover& a,`
    `                   const discover& b)`   `//Line 11`

17. A reference to an object of the `class istream`.

19. Suppose that a class, say `temp`, overloads the pre- and postincrement operator ++, and `tempObj` is an object of the **class** `temp`. Then, the statement `++tempObj;` is compiled as `tempObj.operator++();`, and the statement `tempObj++;` is compiled as `tempObj.operator++(0);`. The dummy parameter distinguishes between the pre- and postincrement operator functions. Similar conventions for the pre- and postincrement operators.

21. None.

23. One.

25. The answer to this question is available at the Web site accompanying this book.

27. Error in Line 4. A template instantiation can be for only a built-in type or a user-defined type. The word "**type**" between the angular brackets must be replaced either with a built-in type or a user-defined type.

29. a. 12 b. Sunny Day

31.
```
template <class Type>
void swap(Type &x, Type &y)
{
    Type temp;
    temp = x;
    x = y;
    y = temp;
}
```

Chapter 14

1. a. false; b. true; c. true; d. false

3. The program will terminate with an error message.

5. If an exception is thrown in a `try` block, the remaining statements in that `try` block are ignored. The program searches the `catch` blocks in the order that they appear after the `try` block and looks for an appropriate exception handler. If the type of thrown exception matches the parameter type in one of the `catch` blocks, the code of that `catch` block executes, and the remaining `catch` blocks after this `catch` block are ignored.

7. The `catch` block has no associated `try` block, that is, the `catch` block does not follow any `try` block. Also, the `try` block has no associated `catch` block, that is, there is no `catch` block that follows the `try` block. The `cout` statement just before the `catch` block disassociates the `catch` block from the `try` block. The correct code is:

```
double radius;

try
{
    cout << "Enter the radius: ";
    cin >> radius;
    cout << endl;
```

```
        if (radius < 0.0)
            throw radius;

        cout << "Area: " << 3.1416 * radius * radius << endl;
    }
catch (double x)
    {
        cout << "Negative radius: " << x << endl;
    }
```

9. a. Leaving the try block.

    b. Current balance: 975
                Balance must be greater than 1000.00

    c. Current balance: -2000
                Balance must be greater than 1000.00

11. a. Entering the try block.
        Exception: Lower limit violation.
        After the catch block

    b. Entering the try block.
        Exception: 0
        After the catch block

    c. Entering the try block.
        Exiting the try block.
        After the catch block

    d. Entering the try block.
        Exception: 0
        After the catch block

13. A throw statement.

15. (Assume that the definition of the class tornadoException is in the header file
    tornadoException.h.)

```
#include <iostream>
#include "tornadoException.h"

using namespace std;

int main()
{
    int miles;

    try
    {
        cout << "Enter the miles: ";
        cin >> miles;
        cout << endl;

        if (miles < 5)
            throw tornadoException();
        else
            throw tornadoException(miles);
```

```
        }
        catch (tornadoException tE)
        {
            cout << tE.what() << endl;
        }

        return 0;
    }
```

17. A function specifies the exceptions it throws in its heading using the `throw` clause.

Chapter 15

1. a. true; b. true; c. false; d. false; e. false

3. The case in which the solution is defined in terms of smaller versions of itself.

5. A function that calls another function and eventually results in the original function call is said to be indirectly recursive.

7. a. The statements in Lines 2 and 3.
   b. The statements in Lines 4 and 5.
   c. Any nonpositive integer.
   d. It is a valid call. The value of `mystery(0)` is 0.
   e. It is an invalid call. It will result in infinite recursion.
   f. It is a valid call. The value of `mystery(-3)` is 6.

9. a. 8 5 2   b. 7   c. 6 3   d. -85

11. a. It does not produce any output.
    b. 5 6 7 8 9
    c. It does not produce any output.
    d. It does not produce any output.

13. a. 2; b. 3; c. 5; d. 21

15.

$$multiply(m, n) = \begin{cases} 0 & \text{if } n = 0 \\ m & \text{if } n = 1 \\ m + multiply(m, n - 1) & \text{otherwise} \end{cases}$$

The base cases are when $n = 0$ or $n = 1$. The general case is specified by the option otherwise.

Chapter 16

1. a. false; b. false; c. false; d. false

3. NULL

5. Before deletion, the link field of the third node stores the address of the fourth node. After deletion, the link field of the third node will store the address of the next node, which is the old fifth node. If there was no fifth node, then after deletion, the link field will store the value NULL. Therefore, after deleting the fourth node, the link field of the third node is changed. So a pointer to the third node is needed.

7. a. false; b. true; c. true; d. true; e. true

9. a. `current->link->info = 52;`

   b. `current = temp->link;`

   c. `trail = current->link;`

   d. `temp->link->link->link->info = 36;`

   e. ```
while (current->info != 10)
      current = current->link;
```

11. a. ```
while (current != NULL)
      current = current->link;
```

   b. ```
temp = new nodeType;
temp->info = 68;
temp->link = last;
trail->link = temp;
```

   c. ```
delete last;
trail->link = NULL;
last = trail;
```

   d. ```
trail = temp->link;
temp->link = trail->link;
delete trail;
```

13. After the execution of the statement in Line 5, `trail` is NULL, so `trail->info` does not exist. This code will result in a run-time error.

15. 33 62 28

17. ```
nodeType head, p, q;

head = new nodeType;
head->info = 72;
head->link = NULL;
p = new nodeType;
p->info = 43;
p->link = head;
head = p;
p = head->link;
q = new nodeType;
q->info = 8;
q->link = NULL;
p->link = q;
q = new nodeType;
```

```
        q->info = 12;
        q->link = p;
        head->link = q;

        p = head;
        while (p != NULL)
        {
            cout << p->info << " ";
            p = p->link;
        }
        cout << endl;
```

The output of this code is: 43 12 72 8

19. `Item to be deleted is not in the list.`
     `93 66 38 55 18 35`

21. The answer to this question is available at the Web site accompanying this book.

23. The answer to this question is available at the Web site accompanying this book.

Chapter 17

1. The two basic operations on a stack are push, to add an element to a stack, and pop, to remove an element from a stack.

3. 4

5. `13 5 12`
    `num1 = 15`
    `num2 = 21`

7. a. 40
    b. 11
    c. 2
    d. 70

9. a. (x + y) * z - w
    b. x * y / z + w
    c. x * (y + z) - w

11. 1 16 27 16 5

13. If the stack is nonempty, the statement `stack.top();` returns the top element of the stack, and the statement `stack.pop();` removes the top element of the stack.

15.
```
template <class elemType>
elemType second(stackType<elemType> stack)
{
    elemType temp1, temp2;

    if (stack.isEmptyStack())
```

```
        {
            cout << "Stack is empty." << endl;
            exit(0); //terminate the program
        }

        temp1 = stack.top();
        stack.pop();

        if (stack.isEmptyStack())
        {
            cout << "Stack has only one element." << endl;
            exit(0); //terminate the program
        }

        temp2 = stack.top();
        stack.push(temp1);

        return temp2;
    }
```

17. 48 72 0 15
     stack: 36
     queue: 0 88 10 52 67

19. a. queueFront = 50; queueRear = 0.

     b. queueFront = 51; queueRear = 99.

21. a. queueFront = 25; queueRear = 76.

     b. queueFront = 26; queueRear = 75.

23. 51

25.
```
template <class Type>
void reverseStack(stackType<Type> &s)
{
    linkedQueueType<Type> q;
    Type elem;

    while (!s.isEmptyStack())
    {
        elem = s.top();
        s.pop();
        q.addQueue(elem);
    }

    while (!q.isEmptyQueue())
    {
        elem = q.front();
        q.deleteQueue();
        s.push(elem);
    }
}
```

27.
```
template <class Type>
int queueType<Type>::queueCount()
{
    return count;
}
```

29. The answer to this question is available at the Web site accompanying this book.

31. The answer to this question is available at the Web site accompanying this book.

Chapter 18

1. a. false; b. true; c. false; d. false

3. a.

```
template <class elemType>
int seqOrdSearch(const elemType list[], int length,
                 const elemType& item)
{
    int loc;
    bool found = false;

    for (loc = 0; loc < length; loc++)
        if (list[loc] >= item)
        {
            found = true;
            break;
        }

    if (found)
        if (list[loc] == item)
            return loc;
        else
            return -1;
    else
        return -1;
} //end seqOrdSearch
```

b. i. 8 ii. 2 iii. 10 iv. 11

5. 26

7. a.

Suppose that the list is of length n. Then length = n. Consider the first iteration of the outer for loop, that is, when the value of iteration = 1. Now the inner loop executes $n - 1$. Before the execution of the inner for loop, the variable isSorted is set to true, assuming that the list is sorted. If the list is already sorted, then the expression list[index] > list[index + 1] in the if statement always evaluates to false, so the body of the if statement never executes. Because the inner loop executes $n - 1$ times, there are $n - 1$ comparisons. In the second iteration of the outer loop, because the variable isSorted is true, the loop condition, (iteration < length) && !isSorted, evaluates to `false`, so the outer `for` loop terminates. It follows that, if the list is already sorted, the outer `for` loop executes only once. Hence, the total number of comparisons is $n - 1 = O(n)$.

    b. 30

9. 3

11. 4, 15, 18, 20, 25, 32, 45, 91, 62, 88, 66

13. In quick sort, the list is partitioned according to an element, called pivot, of the list. After partitioning, elements in the first sublist are smaller than the pivot and in the second sublist are larger than the pivot. The merge sort partitions the list by dividing it into two sublists of nearly equal size by breaking the list in the middle.

15.   a. 9, 2, 13, 36, 55, 23, 62, 95, 86, 65, 75, 74, 89, 100, 98

     b. 6

     c. 2 and 3

17.   a. 48

     b. 22, 30, 9, 15, 25, 18, 3, 48, 66, 95, 94, 55, 80, 50, 62

     c. 15

     d. 7 and 7

19. The function `partition` is called 9 times and the number of comparisons to sort the list is 37.

21. Quick sort: $10000 \times \log_2(10000) = 132878$; merge sort: 132878.

Chapter 19

1. a. false; b. true; c. false; d. false

3. $L_A = \{B, D, E, H, I, K, L, M\}$.

5. $L_B = \{D, H, K\}$.

7. $L_E = \{I, L, M\}$.

9. 3

11. 2

13. 2

15. A, B, E, I, and L

17. $A, B, D, H, K, E, I, L, M, C, F, J, G$

19. 68–95–75–80–85–90

21. Binary search tree after deleting 60.

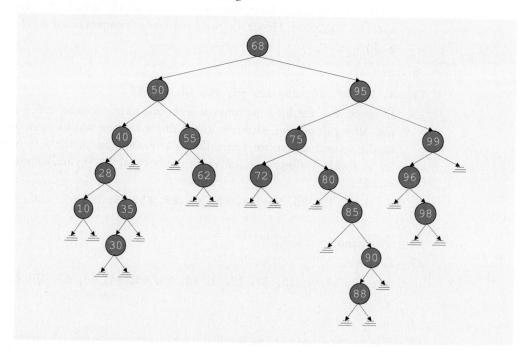

23. Delete node 75 and redraw the binary tree.

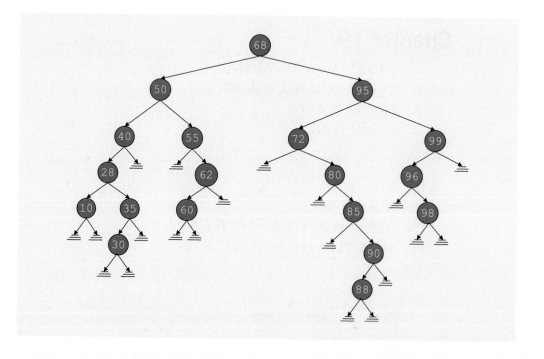

25. Each node has two pointers. Thus, there are $2n$ pointers in all the nodes of the binary tree. The pointer pointing to the root node is an external pointer. Each of the remaining $n-1$ nodes has one pointer pointing to it, which is a pointer from the parent node. The remaining pointers in all the nodes, which is $2n-(n-1)=n+1$, are NULL. This implies that the binary tree has $n+1$ empty subtrees.

27.

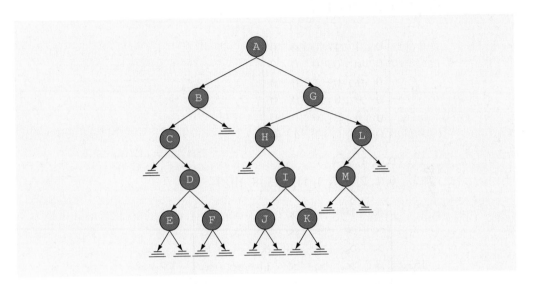

29.

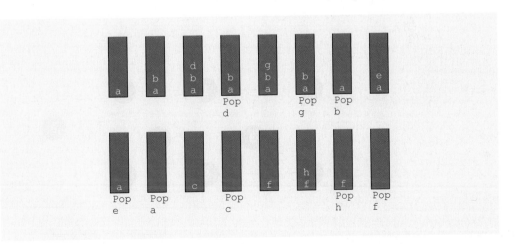

31. The answer to this question is available at the Web site accompanying this book.

Chapter 20

1. 0-3-4-7-10

3. This graph is simple.

5. Vertices 2 and 4 are not connected. So there is no path from vertex 2 to vertex 4.

7. 0-2-6-10-11

9.
$$\begin{bmatrix} 0 & 1 & 1 & 0 & 0 & 0 \\ 0 & 0 & 0 & 0 & 0 & 0 \\ 0 & 1 & 0 & 1 & 0 & 0 \\ 0 & 0 & 0 & 0 & 0 & 0 \\ 0 & 0 & 2 & 0 & 0 & 0 \\ 0 & 1 & 0 & 1 & 1 & 0 \end{bmatrix}$$

11. 0, 2, 1, 3, 4, 5

13. 0, 1, 2, 6, 7, 3, 11, 4, 5, 8, 10, 9

15.
$$\begin{bmatrix} \infty & 10 & 6 & \infty & \infty & \infty & \infty \\ \infty & \infty & \infty & \infty & \infty & \infty & \infty \\ \infty & \infty & \infty & \infty & \infty & 4 & 8 \\ 3 & \infty & \infty & \infty & 11 & \infty & \infty \\ \infty & \infty & \infty & \infty & \infty & \infty & \infty \\ \infty & 6 & \infty & \infty & \infty & \infty & 10 \\ \infty & \infty & \infty & \infty & \infty & \infty & \infty \end{bmatrix}$$

17.

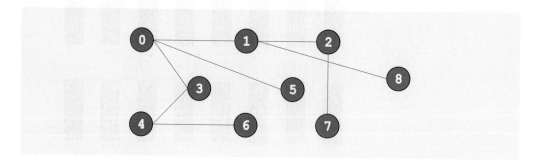

19.

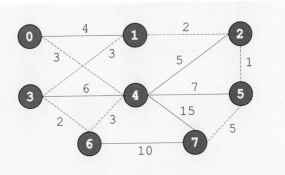

```
Source Vertex: 0
Edges      Weight
(3, 1)       3
(1, 2)       2
(6, 3)       2
(0, 4)       3
(2, 5)       1
(4, 6)       3
(5, 7)       5

A minimal spanning tree weight: 19
```

Chapter 21

1. The three main components of the STL are: containers, iterators, and algorithms.

3. A container is used to store data, while an algorithm is used to manipulate the data stored in a container.

5. An STL function object contains a function that can be treated as a function using the function call operator.

7. `vecList = {35, 67, 35, 67, 87, 10, 92, 11, 17, 82, 5, 15}`

9. a. `intList1 = {7, 8, 19, 90, 15, 13, 15, 16, 18, 90, 30, 11, 88, 26}`

   b. `intList1 = {12, 14, 20, 13, 15, 16, 18, 90, 30, 11, 88, 26}`

11. A `back_inserter` uses the `push_back` operation of the container, while a `front_inserter` uses the `push_front` operation of the container to add elements to the container. Furthermore, a `front_inserter` cannot be used for the vector container.

13. 5
15. a b c * e % f $ h 8
17. 5 56 27 2 78 30 35 48 36
19. 9

INDEX

Note: Page numbers in boldface indicate key terms.